THE DIVINE PROVINCE

Birthing New Earth

Jaemes McBride
Ed Rychkun

Alex,
It is an honor to
have you as a member of the
Divine Province!

Peter the Diviner

1

ISBN 978-1-927066-03-4

Although there is no copyright to this book, much martial has been used from other Authors, Researchers, and Internet sources that may be copyrighted. As so, whenever possible, in the interest of truth, owners of material have be contacted to attain approval for use of material. Where possible, the relevant web sites and Authors have been referenced. This book is a research compilation dedicated to truth and Unity. It relates to the revelation and knowing of many people who are focussed on determining the truth in commerce and religion. It is meant to freely assist anyone to find their own truth or to assist in further research into truth. It is also meant to help understand life, know another choice, or lead the reader to their own quest for truth.

In the end, when one is able to rise above the polarity of good and evil, the information becomes quite irrelevant and if it helps you get there; to a place where judgment is no more, then this book has served its purpose.

TABLE OF CONTENTS

INTRODUCTION — 12

1 THE LESSONS OF HISTORY — 19

2 THE THREADS THAT BIND EARTH: RELIGION & COMMERCE — 22
- The Religious Pyramids — 23
- The Vatican Empire — 24
- The Pyramid Of Debt — 27
- The Corporate Pyramids — 28
- The Corporate Model Comes From Sumeria — 30
- Corporation PLANET EARTH — 31

3 THE GLOBAL ELITE "gods" — 36
- Bloodlines Of The Global "Elite" — 37
- The 13 Royal Bloodlines — 39
- A Word About gods — 41

4 THE ROTHSCHILD DYNASTY — 43
- Rothschild Historical Rise To Power — 43
- Jekyll Island And The Federal Reserve — 62
- Rothschild Influence On Wars — 63
- Extent Of Rothschild Power — 67
- Rothschild Connections To Occult And Secret Societies — 70

5 THE THREADS THAT BIND THE DYNASTIES — 76
- The Power Behind The Bloodlines — 76
- The Secret That Unifies the "gods" — 80
- The Underlying Beliefs Of Satanism — 82
- Foundation Of The Roman Catholic Cult — 87
- The Conundrum Of Satan And God — 90
- Satanism As a Corporate Business Model — 91
- The Darker History Of The Vatican — 93
- The Vatican And The Bloodlines Follow Satan's Model? — 98

6 THE BLACK EMPIRE — 99
- Introducing The Jesuits — 99
- The Vatican Assassins — 104
- The Jesuit Power Shift To America — 116
- Who Are The "gods"? — 120

7 THE NEW AGE: CHRIST OR SATAN — 122
- The 13th Bloodline — 122
- The Lucifer Experiment — 124
- The Lucis Trust And The New Age — 129

...nalization Of The Hierarchy 133
...New Age 139
...Point Plan 140
...elieve? 144

...OF PLANET EARTH 145
...g The Empire Of PLANET EARTH 145
...Secret Kingdoms Of The gods 147
...urich The City Of The gods 148
The Vatican City 150
The City Of London 154
The Role And Power Of The Queen Today 157
The Crown Templar And The Templars 161
The District Of Columbia 164
Baalbek The City Of The Sun 165

9 HISTORY OF THE ROMAN CULT-JESUIT RISE 169
The Rules Of Dominion Of The Vatican 169
The Jesuits As The Society Of Jesus 171
The Jesuit Civil War (1942-1945) 172
Foundation Of The New World Order 173
Foundation Of The Illuminati 174
Background Of Illuminati Events 174
Restoration Of Jesuits And Supremacy Of Illuminati 175
The Holy See 175
Foundation Of The Jesuits 178
Unique Features Of The Jesuit Military Order 179
The Jesuits And Education 179
The Jesuits And Early Trade 180
The Disbandment Of the Order 181
The Counter Attack Of the Jesuits 181
Re-establishment Of The New Military Orders Of Jesuits 183
Foundation Of The Roman Catholic Cult 183
The 1st Fake Catholic Maximus Formosus 184
The Great Gregory VII 184
Pope Urban "The Great" 186
Concordant of Worms 187

10 THE HOUSE OF ROTHSCHILD 189
The Re-emergence Of The Great Financial Power 189
The Transfer Of Attention To America 200
Birth Of The world Bank & The International Monetary Fund 202
The Weapon Of Mass Deception 202

11 THE SECRET SOCIETIES OF THE NEW WORLD ORDER 205
Reporting Structure Of The New World Order 205
New world Order Overview 207
The Cultish Glue 208
The Skull And Bones Society 208
The Knights Of Malta 212

The Bohemian Club   215
The Rosicrucian Fellowship   218
Freemasonry And The Witchcraft Connection   221
P2 Opus Dei   223
The Secret Links   249
The Shadow Government   250

12 THE SPECIAL GLOBAL ORGANIZATIONS   253

The Illuminati Hierarchy   253
The Committee Of 300   258
The Tavistock Institute   260
The Round Table   270
The Trilateral Commission   272
The Royal Institute Of International Affairs   274
Council On Foreign Relations   275
Club Of Rome   283
The Bilderberg Group   285

13 THE UNIFIED PLAN OF CONQUEST   296

Emergence Of The New World Order   296
Origins Of The Spiritual Entity Called The SS   297
The Nazis and Their Relation to the Holy See   298
Relation Between Nazism And Satanism   299
Hitler And The Foundation Of The NSDAP   308
The Arrival Of Fr Himmler S.J And The Nazis   310
The Real Meaning Of The SS And The Nazi Elite   313
The Nazi Evolution   313
Support Corporations And Multinational Network   314

14 THE STORY OF THE BANKRUPTCY OF AMERICA   316

America is Bankrupt Again   317
Money And The Banking System: The Real Power   323
Evolution Of The Code Of Law   324
The New Subjects Under "The Law"   335
The Establishment Of Human Capital   339

15 COMMERCE AND MONEY, THE CHAINS OF CONTROL   341

The Money Kingdoms   341
A Story Of Money   343
Local Banks And The Process Of Money Creation   345
A Short History Of Banking Evolution In America   347
The Federal Government And The National Debt   356
The Elegant Corporate Structure   360
"Money" Is A Record Of Debt   362
Where Does This Fit With Canada And Other Nations?   365
Moving Higher In The Corporate Pyramid   366

16 THE STORY OF THE STRAWMAN   375

Corporations As Legal Fictions Overlay Real People   375
History of The Strawman   377

A Little Story Of A Soul Coming To Planet Earth 379
The Relations To The Constitution 381
The Creation Of Three Trusts 383
The Administrators Of The Strawman Fictions 384
All Corporate Bodies Are Make-Believe Ships At Sea 392
Who Became The Administrators Of The Trusts? 394
Redeeming Your Beneficiary Status 396

17 THE LAWS OF LAND AND SEA 400
Admiralty And Maritime Law 400
The Flag Shows The Substantive Law Of Admiralty 402
How Admiralty Happened 404
Plausible Deniability: The Background Plan 405
Enter The Uniform Commercial Code Laws Of Commerce 407
Uniform Commercial Code: Law Of The Land 408
Uniform Commercial Code Implementation 411
Everything Is Commerce 415
The Precepts And Maxims Of Commercial Law 416
The Ten Commandments 419

18 THE US POSTAL SERVICE 422
The Trusteeship And The Global Estate 422
The Post Office, Vatican And Divine Right Of Use 422
The General Court Of Massachusetts Nov 5, 1639 427
Scripture Passages Related To The Post Office 428
A Subtle Power Resides In The Post Office 429
The Real Power Of The UPU Is In The Military 431

19 THE STORY OF RELIGIOUS DOMINION 436
Religious Origins In The Sumerian Beliefs In gods 437
Summary Of Sumerian Religion Beliefs 441
The Sumerian Records Precede Biblical Stories 448
The Evolution of Early Religions 449
Where Are The Religions Today 453
A Summary Of Hinduism Circa 4000 BC 455
A Summary Of Buddhism Circa 560-490 BC 456
A Summary Of Christianity Circa 30 AD 458
A Summary Of Judaism Circa 200 BC 461
A Summary Of Islamic Religion Circa 622 AD 462
A Summary Of the New Age Beliefs Circa 2000 AD 465
The Evolution Of gods From Sumeria 466

20 THE HISTORICAL RECORD AND WORD OF god 469
The Religious To Spiritual Evolution 469
Does Your god Or God Serve You Well? 471
So What Is God? 472
The Bible Story Of Creation 474
The Story Of Dominion And Vengeance 476
The Story Of Slavery 483
The Story Of Ritual And Human Sacrifice 484

The Story Of Rape And Plunder 486
The Story Of Murder And Punishment 488
The Alleged 10 Commandments 497
Plausible Deniability: Is This The True Word Of God? 498
Who is Your True God? 499
The Stories As Half Truth 499
It's Something You Cannot Explain 500

21 THE LESSON OF KNOWING WHO YOU ARE 503
Know Thy self 504

22 SOMETHING IS AMISS IN GOD'S LAWS 507
New World Order Or New Order Of The Ages? 507
All Bibles And Prophesies Point To Christ As Inspiration 509
A Recap : The New Version Of Christ's Story 510
A Rewrite Of Christ's Story Was Inevitable 513
The Implementation Of The Word Of god 514
The New Mythology Of The Bibles 515

23 THE END TIME OF THE GREAT SHIFT 519
The Mayan End Times 520
The Ninth Wave-What Is It? 522

24 RAPTURE AND REVELATION: THE DARK SIDE 525
The Satanic Plan Of Dominion 525
The Secret Covenant: PLANET EARTH Code Of Ethics 528
Old End Time Of Revelation 531

25 RAPTURE AND REVELATION: THE LIGHT SIDE 534
The Divine Plan Of The Order Of The Ages 534
The New Earth Genesis II 535
The Undeniable Theme of Prevailing Consciousness 537
A New Prophesy of Rapture, Revelation and Resurrection 540
The New End Time Of Revelation 541

26 THE CHRIST CONSCIOUSNESS 545
The Shifting Consciousness of New Earth 545
New Age Spirituality and Core Beliefs 548
The Christ Consciousness From The Aquarian Gospel 551
On The Author Of The Aquarian Gospel 553

27 THE STRAWMAN REVOLUTION 556
Private Versus Public Jurisdictions 557
The Four Elements of Contract 558
Some Basics On Debt 560
Getting Access To The Good Faith And Credit 565
Honour or Dishonour, To Fight Or Not To Fight 570

28 THE POSTMASTER GENERAL FOR THE AMERICAS 571
About The Universal Postal Union 572
Origins of The U.S. Postal Service 573

Origins Of The General Post Office 575
The Link To The Vatican And The Estate Trust 575
The New Postmaster General 577
The Global Estate Trust, Post Office, Vatican And Military 579
The Postal Authority 580
Military Duty To Protect The Post 583
The Military Industrial Complex 584

29 THE UNIVERSAL POSTAL TREATY FOR THE AMERICAS 587
It Is Peace and Prosperity We Seek 587
The Universal Postal Treaty For The Americas (UPT) 588
UPT Declaration Of Causes For Separation 589
UPT Complex Regulatory Scheme 590
UPT Claim On Abandonment 593
UPT Declaration Of Peace 599
UPT The Law Of The Flag 600
UPT Law Form 600
UPT Administrative Notice 606
UPT No Immunity Under Commerce 611
The Registration And Enforcement 628

30 IT'S ALL ABOUT TRUST(S) 629
First and Foremost is Our Divine Trust 629
The History Of Trusts 631
Setting Up a Trust: The Mechanics 632
More Trust Basics: Relationships 634
The Vatican And Crown Are Primary Trustees 639
The Divine Estate Is An Implied Trust 642
Constitutional Relationship To Current Trusts 643
Three Cestui Que Trusts Are Created By Vatican and State 645
Cestui Que As A Method Of Fraud 646
Cestui Que A Medieval Invention In Practice 647
The Significance Of The Cestui Que Vie Trust Today 650
Is The Cestui Que Used Today? 653

31 THE NATIONAL BANKING ASSOCIATION 655
Philosophy And Mission 655
National Banking Association 657

32 THE PROCESS OF CURE FOR James-Thomas: McBride 658
Changing The System Flow Of Money Energy 658
Communications From The New Postmaster General 660
Breach Of Divine Estate And Funding The Military Complex 660
A Cure To The Breach Must Be Declared 661
The Need For The Universal Postal Treaty 663
Declaring And Establishing The Rightful Claims 667

33 SERVING NOTICE ON THE BREACH OF TRUST 669
Authority As Trustee For The Global Abundance Program 669
Documentary Evidence Of Authority 670

Important Notice To The American People		671
Gaining Authority As Trustee		674
Divine Right Of Use		674
Who Is To Be Served Notice		676
The Ecclesiastic Deed Poll Explained		678

34 ACTIVATION OF AUTHORITY: FEDERAL RESERVE — 687
- Authority Activation Process — 687
- Activation Of Federal Reserve Account — 688

35 RECLAIMING TRUSTEESHIP AND POSTAL AUTHORITY — 692
- National Banking Association — 692
- A Trustee of the Global Trust — 693
- The Universal Postal treaty For The Americas — 694

36 THE PHANTOM ADMINISTRATION OF PLANET EARTH INC — 695
- All Government Officials Are Private Contractors — 695
- A Note On Your New Path — 701

37 THE LESSONS FROM THE TWO FACED EARTHLING — 702
- The Light And The Dark Ascension — 704
- The Creator That Resides In You — 710

38 THE MANAGEMENT OF HUMAN ENERGIES — 713
- All That Is, Is Energy — 713
- Energy Benders — 714
- Energy Manifesting — 714
- The Process of Co-Creation — 716
- The Two Pathways — 718
- In Simple Terms There Are Four Steps — 719
- And Now Miracles And Emotion — 720
- Training The Emotional Body — 721
- The Non-science Of Dying — 722
- Consciousness Is A Separate Intelligent Life Form — 722
- What Does Near Dying Tell Us — 724

39 SELF POTENTIAL AND LAWS BEHIND MANIFESTATION — 725
- The Mindset Shift in Belief — 725
- On The Law Of Attraction — 725
- Unconscious Creation And Conscious Manifestation — 730
- Attraction And Avoiding Responsibilities — 732
- Unconscious Programming — 732
- The Processes Of Brain And Mind — 733
- When it Does Not Work — 736
- Wisdom Is Within — 740
- All Is In Perfect Order — 741
- Polarity Physics - The Law Of Opposite Attraction — 741

40 YOUR HOLOGRAPHIC REALITY — 743
- The Law Of Conscious Creation — 743
- Think How Your Mind Works — 744
- A New Look At Creating Reality — 745

Your Hologram Is A Living Growing Intelligent Medium 747
Holograms Form From A Consciousness And Need To Express 748
The Hologram iI Limited By Beliefs 749
The Hologram Abides By Rules 749
The Collective Hologram Of Reality 750
Holograms Are Nested Within Each Other Nonlocally 751
Holograms Are Information 752

41 YOU CAN'T "BS" THE HEART (or SOUL) 753
Love, The Engine Of Creation 754
Forgiveness And Your Path 755
Beingness Is The Natural State The Higher You 756
Inspiration Is The Truth of The Heart 757
House Cleaning Helps To Set Your Tone 758
Humility Is Not To Give In 759
The Mission Is To Know Your True Self 759
That Which Needs Fixing Imposes Judgement 760
The River Of Nows 760
Perfection Yes Or No 761

42 SO THE RUBBER MEETS THE ROAD 763
As Above So Below 763
Quit The PLANET EARTH Gopher Wheel Of Life 765

43 RESIGNING FROM PLANET EARTH INC. 767
You Always Have A Choice 767
The Choice Is Now Yours: Red Or Green? 768
A Word Of Caution 769
Establishing Your Living Status With The Deed Poll (EDP) 771
The Ecclesiastic Deed Poll Document 772
Re-establishing Your Living Status 772
Statement of Identity Document 772
The Acknowledgment of Deed Affidavit 774
The Acknowledgment of Deed Document 775
The Entitlement Order To Original Status 776
Entitlement Order Document 777
The Access To Your Good Faith And Credit 779
The Certificate of Authority Document 780

44 NEW EARTH: THE DIVINE PROVINCE 782
The Divine Estate And Province 782
Notice Of International Diplomatic Status 785
Notice Of Title And Protection 786
International Diplomatic Identification 790
The Chancery Court And Rolls 791
Notice To Set-off Against Good Faith And Credit Estate 794
The Papal Seal Of St. Peter 795
Caveat Notice To Readers 797

45 LOVE, LAUGH, LIVE AS ONE HEART 798

The True Secret Is Love   798
A New Job Unconditional Forgiveness In Thought Word Deed   800
The Power Is In The Heart   801
The Pull To Perfection That Already Is   802
Think, See, Hear, Feel, Act With The Heart   803
Know Creatorship Within   803
The Final Message   806
The Inevitable Is Upon The Earthling   809
In the End Is The Beginning   814
THE AUTHORS' STORIES   816

INTRODUCTION

This book is dedicated to truth and those who seek it.

There is only one truth. What is it? Ironically, you already know.

Yet it is difficult to extract it. Many are seeking a new truth at the turn of the century because the old truth does not feel right anymore. This book is dedicated to those who seek what that one truth is.

In the end, the path to truth leads to unconditional forgiveness and a clear understandng of who you are. That's what this book is about. But first you have to know who and what to forgive, otherwise, it has a tendency to nag at you and to affect your life in silent and subtle ways. We have all heard of regression to past life or current life experience that are in the unconscious mind waiting to be "known" before they can be released. We have all heard how dark things from the past knaw at us until we remember them and forgive them... then things change. The road to the ultimate peace and truth lies withing self.

You have felt it and even acted upon it but you have nothing to substantiate it. You know there is something wrong with your life and this world. It's a constant niggling when you watch the TV news, read the newspaper, see the atrocities, go to work, pay your taxes and behold to the banks. It's everywhere yet wherever you go people seem to be oblivious to it. There seems to be an invisible world out there that limits your true potential but you don't seem to find it. You know there is more to you and your life. You may even feel empty lost and alone like there is an invisible trap of conflict and a need to fear something.

You feel trapped in a world that is like a gopher wheel with the promise of a better life coming. You hear about conspiracies, about the global elite, about how you have been deceived by the banks and your leaders. You look for glimmers of light within the darkness of war, conflict, and poverty. You believe in a God of love and one that answers your prayers but around you the evidence to support this is sparse.

What's also niggling you is who you really are, and why you are here. What is it that is your destiny, and why do you just seem to work your life away to pay others and obey the rules of governments, corporations, follow the religious experts and succumb to social or cultural beliefs? There seems to be no escape as you are not sure what is wrong, what to do about it and you fear the consequences of acting on your impulses to be more independent and free. And so you sit at a place of conundrum continuing the facade of joy and happiness looking for every little tidbit and morsel of bliss because you must. Inside you say *"Stop, enough is enough, this is not right."* And did you notice this niggling became more dominant in the last 12 years?

There is a new "knowing" inside you now. For when you get to the "heart of matter" or what is more commonly known as the "heart of the matter" your truth becomes a simple knowing that resonates with your inner being, regardless of who tells you otherwise, or what your intellectual training gravitates towards. It is a truth that you are more and you must rise above the conflict of evil and good.

This book is dedicated to all the souls who feel trapped in those minds and bodies that have misunderstood the Law of Attraction energy forces of matter and allowed themselves to unknowingly receive what they have asked for; simply because they do not see how energy works and determine a way out. It is an unknowing solution because you have entrusted others. It is unknowing because you drum to the teachings of religious and government leaders limiting your powers. It is unknowing because you may not understand how and when you gave away your powers. This unknowingness goes deep because you may also be trapped by your own spiritual limitations allowing yourself to be trapped into a commercial dysfunction called debt. If you are one of these souls and do not even realize it, this book is for you. If you do realize it, then this book is also for you because it explains why your life is as it is, an what to do about shifting it into a higher place of spiritual and commercial sovereignty.

The book is to reveal a different version of history as to what has happened to humanity. It is simly the way humanity has accepted this to be. But up to the year 2000 when a great unexplainable shift occurred. This shift has brought into attention a remarkable new   picture of the dark and the light allowing humanity to can make an informed choice to rise above all of it.

On the other hand, you may be quite happy to be where you are. That is fine too. It is your choice as to how you live your life. But one thing is for sure. If you are born into a family, a culture, a nation, you are born into a code of belief and conduct that becomes your initial path of life, whether it is royalty, slavery, poverty or wealth. That is your initial birthright. But is it your true birthright? Perhaps being born a human has a different birthright than the one you are born into as a blood family?

It has to do with the truth of who you are beyond what you see and believe you are as a human being drumming to what religious and government leaders tell you. With the mind and ego's refusal to acknowledge who you are, you may find that these leaders are not functioning in your best interest as an eternal entity of etheric energy. And as you approach one of the most miraculous times in human evolution in all of the history of the cosmos, it would be nice to have some inkling of a better alternative than simply living in a body, living whatever comes your way, and dying.

As you may have been captured into the Matrix of money and materialism, perhaps there is a little exit light in the tunnel of physical life that you did not know about? This book is about a new truth that is rapidly emerging like a tsunami worldwide. It is a shifting consciousness of awareness of what humanity has received by way of their own volitions as a sea of debt and struggle, a life that is not what was meant to be, and certainly what was not a place that humanities trust and faith in their leaders would take them to. Humanity has given way to sovereignty of spirit and commerce and the awareness of this not being what humanity has simply accepted as being in their best interest is the tsunami resulting from this sea of illusion. The illusion is that the harder we work, the greater the debt which has intruded the total fabric of our lives. The illusion is that we nullify our own beliefs of peace and harmony because we believe what our leaders tell us about the many gods. So perhaps the truth of how this has come to be will allow one to forgive, forget, and move on to something better.

We have been lost in a sea of illusion because we decided that this was ok. And we trusted that our leaders that we the people placed there to protect and preserve freedom and liberty. The faith is that they will work in service of all as One; a natural consequence of the trust that we gave to the religious and government leaders. Something about the tsunami of increasing mistrust indicates that this faith is amiss. The message of a way of life is now vibrant with the message of a need to learn lesson from the old forgive that which has been and shift into a new birthright. But what is the difference?

This book is brought to all in order to present what has happened, what is happening, and what can happen should each individual choose to take an action to accept a new belief, and to act upon it. It all begins with a knowing of the two sides of the coin; light and dark, good and evil so that a comparison can be made. And that comparison, initiated as separation and polarity, once forgiven without condition becomes unity. That decision arises when your own experience and knowing has an awareness of the two sides of the coin.

This book will present dark and light, evil and good. At the source lies two forces of Lucifer and Christ that creates polarity and conflict. Know that whether these people and events presented here are either evil or good is a judgment call based upon individual perception. And depending upon where your belief is positioned, bad and good are interchangeable. In the middle sits a doorway that merges the two. On the other side of the door is unconditional love of Spirit. The key to the door is unconditional forgiveness.

Let us give you a briefing of the thesis of this book. In the beginning of life, your Soul takes its journey of expression. In the end of life, your Soul leaves with what it experienced. During it's time of expression there is polarity, separation from its self where all that is your experience and expression is interchangeable from dark to light or a shade of gray depending upon your perception of your life lessons and what you choose to retain. In the end and the beginning, you are Soul that is the Godhead of creation who wills itself to express that which it is-love. In the end and the beginning there is no thing that can be everything that is your creation, your illusion of reality where you play out your acts. In the end and the beginning it is absoluteness to no attachments as you come in pure and leave pure back to You and the essence of You-love. In a Near Death Experience, a glimpse of this is given. So why would one who knows this, linger between the end or the beginning? Is it not time to gather your life's lessons of polarity and separation and send them back from whence they came-illusion? The issue is that most do not know this. This book is to show you how interchangeable Dark and Light can be. Look at the other side of the coin and decide for yourself.

There is a new Revelation in this book that will take you beyond belief at first. It is because what you will read presents a different version to the world of God and Man than has been taught. It is a story of the Dark and the Evil Earthling being polar to the Light and the Good Earthling.

First of all this is not about conspiracy theory. We are all responsible for our choices the same way we decide to choose to work for a corporation. It is about what simply has evolved as humanity's ways. It is about a different picture of history and a different look at the evolution of Earthlings upon Planet Earth. The lesson cannot be learned if it is unknown. The wrongs cannot be forgiven if they are not brought into one's awareness. One cannot become enlightened if one cannot see the light. And one cannot manage the energy of manifestations if one does not understand the rules.

Secondly, this book is not meant to judge what is evil. Although there are many quotes, passages and references in this book that support evil and a satanic diabolical, conspiracy, that is not the belief of the Authors. _ It is this author's belief that at some point in the evolution of the spiritual Earthling, light and dark will coalesce into the higher being of unity regardless of Christ or Lucifer beliefs. And it is in this light that this book is written so as to see and understand the conflict, then to rise above it. It is the Author's belief that all Soul regardless engage of the expression of life to allow others to learn and rise in their quest Home.

The purpose is to shift your financial and spiritual affairs into the jurisdiction of Peace and Sovereignty in a new light. Although it may not seem apparent to you, your sovereignty of who you really are may have been given away without your knowing, thus slowing your rise above. It has to do with simple ideas and concepts to do with Polarity and Unity being applied to you in opposition to the way it was meant. In particular, the focus is from a standpoint of Commerce and Religion, the two greatest forces on Planet Earth. Polarity, or the process of been attracted to opposite directions is what has happened to the Spiritual Sovereignty as the Earthling has chosen to be separate from a spiritual self. In commerce, the Earthling has chosen to seek the benefits of employment with what we will call PLANET EARTH INC. thereby giving away the Sovereignty of mind and body.

This process is simply choice to believe and apply the way in which you think, speak and act in accordance with that belief. The sole purpose of this book however, is to bring into consciousness the possibility of forgiveness and entering the jurisdiction of unconditional love. Evil or good, dark or light, we all seek expression of the soul to find itself as a nonlocal piece of the Source. At some point of this path through time and lifetimes there is a realization that you are the captain of your ship, that vessel of mind and body, and you reap what you sew in thought, word and deed. Once you understand this as an internal knowing of truth, you stop beating yourself up by attracting negative energies into manifest. At some point in the evolution from the power of the body into the power of the mind, comes a point where evil and good converge into spiritual truth of Source from whence you came. That is the journey of the soul that has been creating its life expression in the lower realms of body and mind. Now the time is neigh when humanity is at a point of convergence and a locked gate called unconditional love and forgiveness. And so as a new perspective of how humanity has evolved into its current state of spiritual and commercial polarity unfolds, it is the Authors' hope that each can say: *"It is time to forgive those who have benefited at others expense and to bring into manifest a life of peace and abundance."*

On the commerce side, the process has been one of unity. The real physical vessel called a body, which in the beginning is a sovereign physical thing, has been united with a fictional thing similar to a invisible commercial business entity. The end result has been to take on the rules and conditions of the business thing by choosing to unite with it unknowingly. Of course these rules are statutes and acts as administered by those who feel it necessary to do this. In order to regain the physical sovereignty, it must be polarized or separated from the fictional thing. Of course there is right and wrong way to do this but there is a process that allows this. Of course the result is to shift your financial system form debt to credit. So the need is to shift beliefs and to implement this in thought word and act within a new world of Polarity and Separation, opposite of what prevails.

On the other side of spirituality, the polarity has evolved on this planet as separation of ideas, philosophies, into religions that dominate and are in fact responsible for the greatest carnage, conflict and war. The process manifests itself into hatred, fear and anger, yet based upon the philosophy of love, peace, harmony and goodwill. The revelation is that the shift to unity in that all of us are One, being one with the thinking, speaking and acting of love just happens to be at the root of all religions once you take the administrative and polar beliefs out of the way. It falls back to Unity with a spiritual essence that is what we are; and a common goal of peace, love and harmony. Thus, religions, which have the fundamental beliefs of some vengeful god who sits in judgement of sin, so interpreted by middle men of the churches has resulted in a separation from what is the fundamental belief of spirituality. And so the need is to shaft beliefs away from separation and polarity, away from thus middle men who are the interpreters of Gods wisdom and enter the new world of Unity and Oneness with their spiritual self.

The two process, applied the way they have been since recorded history, are simply as they are and it is all a matter of personal choice as to how polarity and unity are engaged in through one's thoughts, words and deeds. But in the end, these are choices that have a consequence on the way your life unfolds much more than you may have realized. The degree of sovereignty you attain, and most of all, the quality of your life's abundance and peace are of course the big question.

In the current world scenario, humanity grapples with having entrusted these two functions of commercial and spiritual sovereignty to the leaders of Religions and Commerce. The great awakening is bringing millions forward who see that this is not a system that they want. The conflict comes because the realization appears that many of these leaders have marched towards dominion of money and religious beliefs. Both create fear and hatred; either in the form of fear of Hell, god's vengeance, sin, and not attaining their spiritual rights. It leads to dominion over the sovereignty of spirit, rendering it powerless by keeping it at an instinctual level of survival like an animal who only survives at other thing's expense. The true nature of your spiritual powers are thus not able to develop so you become powerless to bring these into fruition. This strategy works well with the current dominion of money which has been converted to debt. The powers that be have marched toward dominion of cybermony and done this through debt. Nations and individual are controlled by debt obligations which are as easy to erase as a keystroke on the computer. In the march towards this dominion over money, the debt conversion of money with intrinsic value has been converted to a debt instrument which now controls nations, individuals and the fabric of societies. Thus debt, under this dominion keeps the mass working and powerless, totally focused again on survival, a lower more instinctual non-spiritual mode of existence.

This book is about the way to implement the opposite strategies and importantly, implement a new spiritual foundation of unity so as to perform the polarity in commerce in peace, harmony in love. It presents the polarity in a different light so one can clearly make a choice to rise above both schools of thought that are in constant battle. It is important in this to understand how and why these two major jurisdictions of Spirit and Commerce have evolved by Earthling's allowance. More importantly, it is vital to understand the owners, directors, administrators and the controllers of the processes that have bound humanity to the continuing conflicts. It is time to meet the ones who created and run the PLANET EARTH INC. Empire and to understand how this has occurred, and the purpose of the corporation. It is important to bring into each Earthling's reality a new look at these in order to think, speak, act in a new way, as directed by a new belief system that allows each to experience their full potential.

As it is through the fundamental controller of mind and belief that such a shift is allowed to change the earthling's life, it is important to imbed this new belief, or at least the awareness of alternatives, to be have any effect..

If you believe that there is not some ultimate power within you that is above all you know, then you may be limiting your true potential, ignoring all the millions of instant physical healings that have occurred and are documented.

If you believe that within you is a force that is your total consciousness giving life and feeling to your body, then you are may be limiting your true potential ignoring the millions of Near Death Experiences that have occurred.

If you believe that within you are no higher powers higher powers of metaphysical or physic nature then you are may be limiting your true potential ignoring the millions of people who exhibit these clearly.

If you believe that a God of Love and Peace can be vengeful, and judge your life to decide your entry into eternity and your eternal life, then you are may be limiting your true potential through what others say and interpret, ignoring the reality of the meaning of love.

If you believe that you are a sinner and are born into subservience of a god or your leaders, you are may be limiting your true potential from your full potential.

If you believe that your life is not a result of your own beliefs, thoughts, words and deeds, then you are may be limiting your true potential from the knowing of the ways in which energy works and how to change your life.

If you believe that science is your only reality as observed by physical observation, then you are may be limiting your true potential by ignoring the new science on non reality of quantum physics.

If you believe that you are a fictional entity that laws and statutes apply to then you are may be limiting your true potential into slavery and obedience to others compromising your earthly and spiritual sovereignty.

If you believe that money and debt are the same, then you are may be limiting your true potential from the basic understanding of what debt and money are defined to be.

If you believe that there is no difference between your given name and your name in capital letters, you are may be limiting your true potential by giving away your commercial rights and freedoms.

If you do not believe that your other name, designed as a fictional entity to hold your estate created on your behalf upon birth, you are may be limiting your true potential from your rightful inheritance as beneficiary.

If you believe that you have no choices in your life, that you are a victim of conspiracy, of lack, of genetic problems, of infliction by others, then you are may be limiting your true potential from a better life of health and wealth.

But if you believe that you, as you are now, have lived a fruitful life, and that those who run the planet are good, that is fine too because in the end, it is your own path you must travel.

This is not about conspiracy and bad guys that enslave you. But it is about Lucifer and Christ belief systems that create polarity and conflict. It is about what is, and what each individual has chosen to believe, think, speak and act upon so as to limit their own potential. When a human realizes that something he does creates pain, it is normal to see a withdrawal from continuing that action. When a human realizes that what he thinks, speaks and acts upon also can create pain in accordance with what he creates, he would also withdraw from these but unfortunately, this cosmic working of energy has not yet been understood sufficiently to make the choice. At first, this book may cause pain of what has been done to compromise your spiritual and commercial sovereignty. It is test to rise above it and to generate the emotional energy of forgiveness so as to create a better life and a better world. As a mortal, you cannot pass through the Gate to self and your true Source without it.

This book is presented to you to reveal the other side of the coin so you can rise above both sides, forgive, move on and understand your true potential. We are at a great time when the two forces of Lucifer and Christ require choice. The last 12 years provide a new revelation of this other side and these references and research are provided here. The quest for the truth behind the Matrix began decades ago but in the last five years what was considered as fiction has now gained a foothold as non-fiction. The time is now where millions have taken an awareness to a different "truth" about Sovereignty.

Judge for yourself.

1

THE LESSONS OF HISTORY

We will now take you back into history. It will take us back to the time of Sumeria and then forward to the year 2000 AD when an important shift began. It is important to understand that there will be many words that have been perceived as evil, dark, or unpalatable based upon individual perceptions. Drop this judgement into that unconditional world of peaceful neutrality. For every word has a polar negative-positive connotation based upon experience and opinion. Allow the rising above to neutrality prevail, for in the end, there is no judgement, only the light of your true being.

There is a simple way to do this. Refer to this as a **Trinity Triangle of Unity**. At the bottom of the triangle are two poles of negative and positive, evil and good, dark and light. Whenever you encounter words that instantly conjure up one or the other as your choice of perception, understanding or belief, count to three and rise to the apex above at the third pole of unity. Here disengage the emotion and judgment and open your heart to impartiality.

This brings us to look at where we are in our evolution as a civilization. What you will find different about this history is that is presents a different picture of where we have evolved to and how we arrived at this point. Where possible, evidence and research will be presented but the process will be like a story so as to create some continuity on humanity's evolution. Over the last thousands of years, since recorded history, mankind has been infatuated with gods, royalty, kingdom, and self growth. A huge part of this has been the constant interplay between good and evil. This has evolved into a diversity of idea, cultures, behaviours, religions and ways of life.

In particular, it is necessary to look at the **New World Order** which was founded in 1943 at the first Conference between England, the United States and the Soviet Union by leading Jesuits in Tehran. It was reconfirmed at the end of World War II following the complete victory of the Roman Cult controlling the Roman Catholic Church in the re-establishment of effective Catholic control of the former Frankish Kingdom principalities now known as Germany, France, Austria, the Netherlands and Switzerland.

Although this New world Order may be termed a conspiracy as reflected by the reverse side of the Great Seal of the United States (1776). The Latin phrase "*novus ordo seclorum*", appearing on the reverse side of the Great Seal since 1782 and on the back of the US one-dollar bill since 1935, means "**New Order of the Ages**" and only alludes to the beginning of an era where the United States of America is an independent nation-state, but is often mistranslated by conspiracy theorists as "New World Order". If you look at Source of NOVUS ORDO SECLORUM, The motto *Novus Ordo Seclorum* was coined by Charles Thomson in June 1782. He adapted it from a line in Virgil's *Eclogue IV*, a pastoral poem written by the famed Roman writer in the first century B.C. that expresses the longing for a new era of peace and happiness. Annuit Coeptis, the motto above the eye of Providence was inspired by Virgil's *The Georgics*. Also, Virgil's epic masterpiece, *The Aeneid* describes an ancient symbol of peace held by the American Bald Eagle, the olive branch.

Indeed, the Fathers of the united States had this in mind but it did not turn out this way. In fact, the US has become a strategic "corporate takeover" to serve a different purpose. In conspiracy theory, the term **New World Order** or **NWO** refers to the emergence of a totalitarian one-world government. The common theme in conspiracy theories about a New World Order is that a secretive power elite with a globalist agenda is conspiring to eventually rule the world through an authoritarian world government—which replaces sovereign nation-states—and an all-encompassing propaganda that ideologies its establishment as the culmination of history's progress. Significant occurrences in politics and finance are speculated to be orchestrated by an unduly influential cabal operating through many front organizations. Numerous historical and current events are seen as steps in an on-going plot to achieve world domination through secret political gatherings and decision-making processes.

Prior to the early 1990's, New World Order conspiracism was limited to two American countercultures, primarily the militantly anti-government right, and secondarily fundamentalist Christians concerned with end-time emergence of the Antichrist. Skeptics, such as Michael Barkun and Chip Berlet, have observed that right-wing populist conspiracy theories about a New World Order have now not only been embraced by many seekers of stigmatized knowledge but have seeped into popular culture, thereby inaugurating an unrivaled period of people actively preparing for apocalyptic millenarian scenarios in the United States of the late 20th and early 21st centuries. These political scientists are concerned that this mass hysteria could have what they judge to be devastating effects on American political life, ranging from widespread political alienation to escalating lone-wolf terrorism.

Indeed there is a worldwide plan being orchestrated by an extremely powerful and influential group of *genetically-related individuals* (at least at the highest echelons) which include many of the world's wealthiest people, top political leaders, and corporate elite, as well as members of the so-called **Black Nobility** of Europe (dominated by the **British Crown**) whose goal is to create a **One World** (fascist) **Government**, stripped of nationalistic and regional boundaries, that is obedient to their agenda. Indeed their intention is to effect **complete and total control** over every human being on the planet and there is information pointing to dramatically reduce the world's population by 5.5 Billion people. But will they? While the name *New World Order* is a term frequently used today when referring to this group, it's more useful to identify the principal organizations, institutions, and individuals who make up this vast interlocking spider web of elite conspirators.

The Illuminati is the oldest term commonly used to refer to the **13** *bloodline families* (and their offshoots) that make up a major portion of this controlling elite. Most members of the Illuminati are also members in the highest ranks of numerous secretive and occult societies which in many cases extend straight back into the ancient world. The upper levels of the tightly compartmentalized (need-to-know-basis) Illuminati structural pyramid include planning committees and organizations that the public has little or no knowledge of. we will dissect the corporate structure to look at the founders, directors, committees and secretive groups that are part of an incredible business plan of the gods.

However, from a non conspiracy theory point of view, one can look at this a simply as a world business that we were all born into as our birthright and have accepted it to be this way. There is really no conspiracy when it is just business. The world of Kings, Queens, and kingdoms is no different than the large corporations we are all familiar with. Some may conspire against your rights as employers, some may not. It must be brought to attention that the business plan of the ones who control the empire of Planet Earth and its peoples are simply attempting to create a better life for their slaves. Is it so hard to believe that the New World Order is an enormous Earth Corporation run by those that have the greatest "corporate-financial smarts"? And can it be so hard to believe that despite the connotations of the word slavery, that the liberties and freedoms have become better over time? After all, the best slave is the one who believes he is free.

And on the other hand, if the Latin phrase which has always been in plain view really means the **New Order of the Ages**, then what does it really have to do with conspiracy? Is it so hard to believe that the new Order of the Ages is a massive shift away from these world corporations into a new consciousness? We are at an interesting time now where such a shift is indeed occurring but this is the topic for Part 2. Indeed, the end of the century marks something that has never happened before in the history of Earthlings. It is about spiritual and commercial sovereignty of the mass-yes or no.

If one is born into a family or a culture which has rules, one can accept these rules through life or reject them. Needless to say, there can be no choice if the new rules do not enter the awareness so as to provide a choice. But it would be your choice to accept life as it is rather than to seek a new truth out of bondage. The truth is that it is the prevailing consciousness of the family, corporation, organized group, culture, nation, or race that creates the reality from their beliefs. And when these beliefs shift so does the resulting culture. However, the beliefs shift when there is an awareness that some other choice is available.

So it seems that there is a great shift and conflict brewing on Planet Earth. It is between the Light of liberation and the Dark of dominion. That great shifting has been prevalent in the last 12 years. Will the Dark see the Light or will the Light forgive the Dark? Will the Dark free the slaves or will the Light free the slaves?

The purpose of this part is to present history and to meet the owners and directors of the corporation PLANET EARTH that gives us the benefits we graciously accept--at a cost. It is to present to you a different version of our evolution and why we are where we are as Earthlings. It is to see another choice. It is to determine whether you really want to be a free spirit or not.

So you can be the judge.

2

THE THREADS THAT BIND EARTH: RELIGION AND COMMERCE

There are two major forces on Planet Earth that have been the root to the greatest strife in the history of mankind. The purpose of this opening chapter is not to paint a dismal picture of what has happened and brand it as deception or conspiracy. We as Earthlings have in majority simply received what we have asked for and sometimes it takes a wakeup call to look back to see what is wrong in order to determine what is right. Some love to engage in the energies of what is wrong. Others prefer to engage in what is right as determined from what seems wrong. Within this, we all choose our ways and our paths very much influenced by the experiences in two major forces of commerce and religion. It is pretty difficult to go somewhere on the planet and ignore these two forces.

It has been so for a long time. Historical research shows these two forces have been active and evolving over thousands of years, originating in Babylonia and Sumeria and even earlier. Over the last thousands of years, these human tendencies to seek freedom, prosperity and spirit have become more and influenced by the religious orders and the international bankers. At least this is the way it has evolved. There have always been those who have sought dominion over others and there have always been those that have sought sovereignty of spirit, peace and harmony. There have always been gods, kings and queens. There have always been those who had special powers and resources to control armies so as to advance their personal goals. And there have always been gods, either mythical, in the minds, and perhaps even in reality that have been kind and vengeful, peaceful and warlike to serve their own purposes. And it seems that there have always been the religious orders and higher priests that have proclaimed themselves to be conveyors and administrators of these god's desires.

It does not come as a surprise that those who have taken a heartless path of dominion can easily control those who are more heart full. It is not that this is wrong or right, it is simply the way humanity has chosen it to be. It appears to be humanity's constitution that is conscious of fear; of dying, of being hurt, of not being able to attain their personal desires. It is not surprising that this fear if packaged right becomes a universally marketable product and an effective means of dominating others. Earthlings are afraid of death and they are afraid of pain. They are fearful of not surviving the way they believe they should. Such a paranoia, whether instinctual or egoistic based is a recipe for control by those who know how to administer it.

What the religions have done is to create an authority of representatives who step in as the ones who interpret what the gods say and impose beliefs preferred by them thus

22

converting a perfectly wonderful system of spirituality into religion. On the other side, the financial gods have slowly stepped in to convert a perfectly wonderful system of money into a system of debt. Although within each there are still wondrous parts, these by humanity's own reception have dwindled the light, and much of the truth much like a corporation will bend the truth for profit and marketing purposes. Why? Because humanity accepts what religious leaders tell them and they also accept the way in which debt controls their financial affairs. What humanity has achieved with great zeal is to compromise their sovereignty of both spirit and commerce.

So let us open with a picture of where we have come to in our evolution.

The Religious Pyramids

What is religion? It is defined as a set of beliefs concerning the cause, nature, and purpose of the universe, especially when considered as the creation of a superhuman agency or agencies, usually involving devotional and ritual observances, and often containing a moral code governing the conduct of human affairs. The greatest religions began before Christ. This table was created as of 2005.

RELIGION	FOLLOWERS	TOTAL	%
1. Christianity	2,100,000,000	2,100,000,000	30.58%
2. Islam	1,500,000,000	3,600,000,000	52.42%
3. Nonreligious	**1,100,000,000**	**4,700,000,000**	**68.44%**
4. Hinduism	900,000,000	5,600,000,000	81.54%
5. Chinese	394,000,000	5,994,000,000	87.28%
6. Buddhism	376,000,000	6,370,000,000	92.75%
7. Primal-indigenous	300,000,000	6,670,000,000	97.12%
8. African Traditional	100,000,000	6,770,000,000	98.58%
9. Sikhism	23,000,000	6,793,000,000	98.91%
10. Juche	19,000,000	6,812,000,000	99.19%
11. Spiritism	15,000,000	6,827,000,000	99.41%
12. Judaism	14,000,000	6,841,000,000	99.61%
13. Baha'i	7,000,000	6,848,000,000	99.71%
14. Jainism	4,200,000	6,852,200,000	99.77%
15. Shinto	4,000,000	6,856,200,000	99.83%
16. Cao Dai	4,000,000	6,860,200,000	99.89%
17. Zoroastrianism	2,600,000	6,862,800,000	99.93%
18. Tenrikyo	2,000,000	6,864,800,000	99.96%
19. Neo-Paganism	1,000,000	6,865,800,000	99.97%
20. Unitarian-Universalism	800,000	6,866,600,000	99.98%
21. Rastafarianism	600,000	6,867,200,000	99.99%
22. Scientology	500,000	6,867,700,000	100.00%
Current during census	**6,867,700,000**		
Current in 2012	**7,028,260,000**		

At the time of this census, the lion's share of 98% includes 6.8 billion (now 7 billion) followers that abide by the beliefs of the world's top 7 religions. All, except 1.1 billion "nonreligious" believe in a higher deity, gods or a God. In fact there are thousands of religions that have or believe in some gods as their deity or supreme force, being, or power. These gods mostly reside in the imaginations of the Earthling, or in the mythical writings. Yet these all have a tremendous impact upon the way Earthlings conduct their earthly affairs. This has evolved to create a tremendous difference in beliefs and it has resulted in a difference of opinion as to what is the truth about their gods or one God. Difference of opinion leads to conflict and anger. This has taken shape as wars and conflict. So while there may be a fundamental belief somewhere within the scriptures and beliefs of love, peace and harmony, the historical evidence of deeds do not follow the thinking and words, as starkly exemplified by the number of deaths that have resulted from these diverse religious orders.

But notice there is a new religion (kid) on the block called nonreligious. This number is increasing exponentially and if you looked at it 10 years ago, you would see dramatic changes. In 2004, it was reported to be increasing at 15%.

The top 10 religions have grown into tremendous pyramids of organizational structures and power that have dominated the beliefs of the many. What is coming to light more and more is that this hierarchy is built to have the many serve the few. And these few, the monolithic religious structure such as the Vatican dictate what god says. In trust and faith, 30% of the world populations follow their beliefs.

In order to fully understand the evolution of the largest empire of Christianity, it is necessary to understand look at the pyramidal structure of the headquarters--the Vatican.

The Vatican Empire

The Vatican empire does not need introduction in relation to its power and influence of many people. The history of good and evil, and how they have preached this through sin and righteousness is stark with the ungodly methods used to enforce their beliefs. Yet they are forgiven because they are the chosen ones of God. The religious and financial empire they have created has been simply "smart corporate business" which can be identified in their declarations:

Consider the 1455 Papal Bull *Romanus Pontifex. It is the* 1st Testamentary Deed & Will & 1st Crown over Land. This is the First **Trust** ever written. and although you may believe because it was written so long ago, it is not relevant, think again. as you ponder the chapter that follow, you will find that what is in force today goes back a lot further than that. It is just that most simply don't look at history that way. Source: ***http://one-evil.org/texts_papal_bulls/papal_bull.htm***

"The Roman pontiff, successor of the key-bearer of the heavenly kingdom and vicar of Jesus Christ, contemplating with a father's mind all the several climes of the world and the characteristics of all the nations dwelling in them and seeking and desiring the salvation of all, wholesomely ordains and disposes upon careful deliberation those things which he sees will be agreeable to the Divine Majesty and by which he may bring the sheep entrusted to him by God into the single divine fold, and may acquire for them the reward of eternal felicity, and obtain pardon for their souls. This we believe will more certainly come to pass, through the aid of the Lord, if we bestow suitable favours and special graces on those Catholic kings and princes, who, like athletes and intrepid champions of the Christian faith, as we know by the evidence of facts, not only restrain the savage excesses of the Saracens and of other infidels, enemies of the Christian name, but also for the defence and increase of the faith vanquish them and their kingdoms and habitations, though situated in the remotest parts unknown to us, and subject them to their own temporal dominion, sparing no labour and expense, in order that those kings and princes, relieved of all obstacles, may be the more animated to the prosecution of so salutary and laudable a work."

The full text can be found through the reference above and you may be surprised that something written back then looks like it was written by a lawyer today. In the document, the Vatican (Catholic Church) clearly declares the dominion over earth territories by the process of kings and queens coming into line of the faith of Christ and dominion over the soul and to put into slavery or rid the earth of those disbelievers. It is well worth the read. Now this may seem as a harmless, unsupported position much like we may view the "kingdom" of the Queen. It is just theoretical you may say, symbolic, but as you will learn, the ones who created these words and "symbolic structures" take them very seriously.

What follows is neither wrong or right. It just is.

Gracing the walls of St Peter's Basilica is the Vatican-approved image of God. An angry bearded man in the sky, painted by Michael Angelo. Cruel and violent images of God's tortured Son, suffering, bleeding and dying with thorns gouged through his skull and nails pounded through his feet and hands are on display throughout the Vatican. These images serve as reminders that God allowed His Son to be tortured and killed to save the souls of human beings who are all born sinners.

With this image, this Vatican, a separate jurisdiction, and private corporation rules over approximately 2 billion of the world's people. The colossal wealth of the Vatican includes enormous investments with the Rothschilds in Britain, France and the USA and with giant oil and weapons corporations like Shell and General Electric. The Vatican solid gold bullion, worth billions is stored with the Rothschild controlled Bank of England and the US Federal Reserve Bank.

The Catholic Church is the biggest financial power, wealth accumulator and property owner in existence, possessing more material wealth than any bank, corporation, giant trust or government anywhere on the globe. While 2/3 of the world earns less than $2 a day, and 1/5 of the world is underfed or starving to death, the Vatican hoards the world's wealth, profits from it on the stock market and at the same time preaches about giving.

The Vatican is a business engaged in the commerce of souls and sin. It has accumulated all that wealth over the millennium by placing a price-tag on sin. Many bishops and popes actively marketed guilt, sin and fear for profit, by selling indulgences. There is even a credit system as worshipers were encouraged to pre-pay for sins they hadn't yet committed and get pardoned ahead of time. Those who didn't pay-up are threatened with eternal damnation. Another method was to get wealthy land owners to hand-over their land and fortune to the church on their death bed, in exchange for a blessing which would supposedly enable them to go to heaven. Pope Leo the fifth rebuilt St Peter's Basilica, by selling tickets out of hell and tickets to heaven.

In a statement published in connection with a bond prospectus, the Boston archdiocese listed its assets at Six Hundred and Thirty-five Million ($635,891,004), which is 9.9 times its liabilities. This leaves a net worth of Five Hundred and Seventy-one million dollars ($571,704,953). It is not difficult to discover the truly astonishing wealth of the church, once we add the riches of the twenty-eight archdioceses and 122 dioceses of the U.S.A., some of which are even wealthier than that of Boston. But because many of these are private corporations, there are no audits, no accountability, no regulations that disclose these holdings.

Some idea of the real estate and other forms of wealth controlled by the Catholic church may be gathered by the remark of a member of the New York Catholic Conference, namely "*that his church probably ranks second only to the United States Government in total annual purchase.*" Another statement, made by a nationally syndicated Catholic priest, perhaps is even more telling. "*The Catholic church,*" he said, "*must be the biggest corporation in the United States. We have a branch office in every neighbourhood. Our assets and real estate holdings must exceed those of Standard Oil, A.T.&T., and U.S. Steel combined. And our roster of dues-paying members must be second only to the tax rolls of the United States Government.*"

The Catholic church, once all her assets have been put together, is reported to be the most formidable stockbroker in the world. The Vatican, independently of each successive pope, has been increasingly orientated towards the U.S. The Wall Street Journal said that the Vatican's financial deals in the U.S. alone were so big that very often it sold or bought gold in lots of a million or more dollars at one time. Quite obviously God has a vested interest in Planet Earth.

The Vatican's treasure of solid gold has been estimated by the United Nations World Magazine to amount to several billion dollars. A large bulk of this is stored in gold ingots with the U.S. Federal Reserve Bank, while banks in England and Switzerland hold the rest. But this is just a small portion of the wealth of the Vatican, which in the U.S. alone, is greater than that of the five wealthiest giant corporations of the country. When to that is added all the real estate, property, stocks and shares abroad, then the staggering accumulation of the wealth of the Catholic church becomes so formidable as to defy any rational assessment.

The Catholic church is the biggest financial power, wealth accumulator and property owner in existence. She is a greater possessor of material riches than any other single institution, corporation, bank, giant trust, government or state of the whole globe. The pope, as the visible ruler of this immense amassment of wealth, is consequently one of the richest individuals of the twentieth century. No one can realistically assess how much he is worth because it is all private.

If you really scrutinize their product and marketing policies, the Catholic church has become the biggest mafia on earth, with their protection-racket of selling "forgiveness for sins". The Catholic church's practice of teaching people that they can be sinful all their lives and all they need to do is pay the church for "forgiveness" is seemingly one of the chief causes of all the evil and dishonesty in the world, as people are actually taught and encouraged they can be sinful and evil rather than to purify themselves and strive to become perfect, just pay up, admit you have been bad and it's quite alright.

So it is that through the most incredible marketing, many people actually buy the church's products and think that they can get away with being evil all their lives. All they have to do is seek forgiveness from a priest. During the dark ages, the Catholic Church not only hoarded the wealth they collected from the poor, but they hoarded knowledge. They kept the masses ignorant and in the dark by denying them a basic education. They also prohibited anyone from reading or even possessing a Bible, under pain of death. It is business and this business has become one of the largest private corporate pyramids on Planet Earth. It is because over 30% of the Earthlings choose to support this policy.

The Pyramid Of Debt

Here is a measurement that is _not private_. It is another staggering evolution of what is relates to the existing pyramid of debt. This interesting table is presented to show some staggering numbers of non-wealth. The figures indicate the total external debt by country. Note these are trillions of dollars.

Rank	Country	External US dollars
1	United States	15,570,789,000,000
2	United Kingdom	8,981,000,000,000
3	Germany	4,713,000,000,000
4	France	4,698,000,000,000
5	Japan	2,441,000,000,000
6	Ireland	2,378,000,000,000
7	Netherlands	2,344,296,360,000
8	Italy	2,223,000,000,000
9	Spain	2,166,000,000,000
10	Luxembourg	1,892,000,000,000
11	Belgium	1,241,000,000,000
12	Switzerland	1,200,000,000,000
13	Australia	1,169,000,000,000
14	Canada	1,009,000,000,000
15	Sweden	853,300,000,000
16	Austria	755,000,000,000
17	Norway	643,000,000,000
18	China	635,500,000,000
19	Denmark	559,500,000,000
20	Greece	532,900,000,000
21	Portugal	497,800,000,000
22	Russia	480,200,000,000
23	Finland	370,800,000,000
24	Korea, south	370,100,000,000
25	Brazil	310,800,000,000
26	Turkey	270,700,000,000
27	India	267,100,000,000
28	Poland	252,900,000,000
29	Mexico	212,500,000,000
30	Indonesia	196,100,000,000
31	Romania	160,900,000,000
32	Hungary	148,400,000,000
33	United Arab Emirates	122,700,000,000
34	Argentina	108,900,000,000

Now, there are actually 200 countries in debt. However, here are the top 34 accounting for at total debt of $76,729,529,173,000. Yes 76 trillion! This is a **list of countries by external debt**, the total public and private debt (i.e. gross general government debt including both intragovernmental and sub-national public entities debts) owed to nonresidents repayable in internationally accepted currencies, goods, or services, where the public debt is the money or credit owed by any level of government, from central to local, and the private debt the money or credit owed by private households or private corporations based in the country under consideration. This is a synopsis of where we are in debt and religion.

Who is all this owed to? It is owed to the top international bankers who are at the top of the pyramid. How has all the wealth of nations been converted to this debt? It has occurred systematically through the direction of very smart financial people. It is a system of the few controlling the many which we shall investigate in detail.

The Corporate Pyramids

It would be a senseless argument to suggest that corporation that are made of the executives and directors, do not have a preferred vested interest in themselves. That is simply the nature of corporations. The mass of employed personnel are there to carry out the functions so as to create profit or services that benefit the top owners, directors and executives. The model is not different than any of the religious and banking models. It has simply evolved and been accepted this way.

Employer	Employees
United States Department of Defence	3.2 million
People's Liberation Army (China)	2.3 million
Wal-Mart	2.1 million
McDonald's	1.9 million
National Health Service (England)	1.7 million
China National Petroleum Corporation	1.6 million
State Grid Corporation of China	1.5 million
Indian Railways	1.4 million
Indian Armed Forces	1.3 million
Hon Hai Precision Industry (Foxconn)	1.2 million

Now have a look at private banks and a list of their assets under management.

Rank	Bank	AUM ($bn)
1.	Bank of America Merrill Lynch	$1,944,740,000,000
2.	Morgan Stanley Smith Barney	$1,628,000,000,000
3.	UBS	$1,559,900,000,000
4.	Wells Fargo	$1,398,000,000,000
5.	Credit Suisse	$865,060,000,000
6.	Royal Bank of Canada	$435,150,000,000
7.	HSBC	$390,000,000,000
8.	Deutsche Bank	$368,550,000,000
9.	BNP Paribas	$340,410,000,000
10.	JP Morgan Chase	$284,000,000,000
11.	Pictet	$267,660,000,000

12.	Goldman Sachs	$229,00,000,0000
13.	ABN AMRO	$220,060,000,000
14.	Barclays	$185,910,000,000
15.	Julius Bär	$181,680,000,000
16.	Crédit Agricole	$171,810,000,000
17.	Bank of New York Mellon	$166,000,000,000
18.	Northern Trust	$154,400,000,000
19.	Lombard Odier Darier Hentsch	$153,100,000,000
20.	Citigroup	$140,700,000,000

So this is where Planet Earth has come to. These are not kingdoms and dynasties under the directions of their favourite gods, they are immense corporate structures that are fictional representations--constructs created by man. Religions sell beliefs. Debt is a number on a balance sheet. Corporations are a name. Of course these have been accepted to be translated into humanity's daily reality but are these really real? They hold assets and employees as a registered name. These are the raw statistics of our evolution which explicitly reflects what the vast majority of the population of this planet are engaged in. Nations and people are:

- Fundamentally believing what the Masters of Religions **tell them** about God, gods and moral conduct, which over the last centuries has culminated in a preponderance of death and destruction, hatred and war;
- Fundamentally drumming to the masters of Finance to work towards debt reduction, to survive in a world which can never repay it;
- Fundamentally drumming to the Masters of Corporations and Government to abide by their rules and regulations so as to allow them at the top to benefit.

Fundamentally, the people of earth drum to an invisible creations of regulations and corporate structures. Under the purpose of commerce and commercial activities corporations are created to facilitate "business". A **corporation** is created under the laws of a state as a separate legal entity that has privileges and liabilities that are distinct from those of its members. Entities which carried on business and were the subjects of legal rights were found in ancient Rome, and the Maurya Empire in ancient India. In medieval Europe, churches became incorporated, as did local governments, such as the Pope and the City of London Corporation.

For thousands of years, the corporation has been used to serve the purposes of commerce and to "hold" things. In fact it is an imaginary construct that holds papers that are themselves fictional representing the true physical thing. This infatuation with corporations make up the fabric of world societies.

Humanities acceptance of corporations has become the makeup of the fiber of modern civilization. It has been accepted easily as the model of modern cultures because that's the way we work for a paycheck. And we need a paycheck to acquire something we need. But while we do work for a paycheck, we are subject to the rules of the corporation. The acceptance of these fictional structures has, in the end, resulted in every individual who works for a corporation to subject to the rules attached to the corporations as designed by the ones who created them. In this light, Earthlings have slowly become employed by the greatest invisible corporation of all PLANET EARTH INC. without knowing.

The Corporate Model Comes From Sumeria

The corporate model is so well entrenched in the evolution of Planet Earth that it seems impossible to grasp it's reach of dominion. It may not come as a surprise that it forms the fabric of modern societies. People are used to working for corporations, some private, some public. The reality of this is that corporations form a pyramid structure of control and obedience towards a mission, goal, purpose of the founders, directors, owners who engage in some form of commerce.

In delving into the history of corporations, we find that it sources back to Sumeria. In its heyday, the most prominent Sumerian building was the religious temple, built atop a stepped tower called a ziggurat. Some ziggurats were as high as 70 feet. The temple was dedicated to the patron deity of the city. The people devoted great resources and labour to building these temples and to the houses of priests. The ziggurats housed workshops for craftsmen as well as temples for worship. The ziggurats were built of clay bricks joined together with bitumen, a sticky asphalt like substance. There were artisans who sculpted, cut gems, fullers who stomped on woven wools to soften cloth, and metal workers who crafted weapons as well as artistic creations. The religious class had a great deal of power, socially, politically and economically. Religion was central to the society. In summary:

- This was the largest and most important building located in the center of each Sumerian city. Sumerians believed it was the home of the city's patron god.
- It was built on a platform called a *parraku*, designed to dominate the horizon and also to provide protection from floods. Most temples were built on the remnants of older temples that were destroyed. Each king would add on to the temple with numerous stairways leading to different levels.
- The Ziggurat of Ur was on a platform 200' long, 150' wide, and rose 70 feet above the plain and dealt with the city's population or wealth.
- In early Sumer it was made of rectangular mud bricks because they didn't have stone or timber.
- It was decorated with clay cones which were dipped into red, black or buff paint and then inserted into the plaster to form zigzags or geometric designs.
- Weep holes were square or rectangular shaped holes placed at different levels in the temple to provide drainage.
- The main purpose of the ziggurat was to have a place of respect and worship for the gods. Sumerians believed blind obedience and constant gifts and sacrifices would give them protection and success on earth.
- Inside every ziggurat was a rectangular central shrine called a *cella*, for the god's emblem or statue.
- In front of the statue was an altar, a mud brick table for offerings to the god.
- The god was served regular meals of fish, mutton, honey, beer and cake.
- The god communicated his wishes to the priests.
- The god received sacrifices.
- The temple supplied employment and was administered by the priests.
- Maintenance was conducted by musicians, singers, or *hierodules* as temple slaves.
- It served as a center for commercial activity.
- it served as food storage and distribution.
- It was a marketplace for trading of goods and celebrations.

The word "ziggurat" meant "mountain of god" or hill of heaven. Each ziggurat was made up of a series of square levels. Each level was smaller than the one below it. Stairways to the top of the colossal ziggurats, which were believed to be the home of the city's chief god. Only priests could enter this sacred area. Around the ziggurat were courts, the center of Sumerian life. Artisans worked there; children went to school there; farmers, artisans, and traders stored their goods there; and poor were fed there. The Sumerians believed that all forces of nature were alive. They viewed them a gods because they could not control them There were more than 3,000 Sumerian gods and goddesses.

Only priests could know the gods' will. Because of this, Sumerian priests were very powerful For example, the city's god owned all land. But the priests administered the land in the god's name Also, the priests ran schools. Schools were for the sons of the rich only. Poorer boys worked in the fields or they learned a trade. Schools were rooms off the ziggurat courtyards. They were called tablet houses because they were built to teach children how to write. The children wrote with sharp-ended reeds on clay tablets the size of a postcard. Sumerian writing was called cuneiform. It was made up of hundreds of wedge-shaped markings.

Writing in Sumerian culture developed so that people could keep track of business deals. When Sumerians lived in villages, they could keep track of everything easily. When they began living in cities, it became harder to keep track of everything in their heads. To solve this problem, they developed cuneiform.

When a pupil graduated from school, he became a scribe. The ziggurat, the palace, the government, or the army employed him. Although Sumerian women did not go to school, they did have many rights. They could buy and sell property, run businesses, and own and sell slaves. Although a woman handled the house's affairs when the man was away, the men were the head of the Sumerian household. He could divorce his wife by saying," You're not my wife." If he needed money, he could sell or rent his family into slavery for up to three years. The man also arranged the marriages of his children.

Children were expected to support their parents when the parents got old. They were also expected to obey older family members. Everyone was to obey the gods and priests. At first, Sumerian priests were kings of city-states. One of the most famous priest kings was Gilgamesh of Uruk.

The Sumerian priest-kings received advice from a general assembly made up of free men. When war broke out, the assembly would choose one of its members to serve as leaders until the war was over, but often these leaders stayed in power even when peace had returned. By about 3000 B. C., they took their place as permanent kings. At the same time, kingship became heredity, and the world's first monarchies were established.

These systems were designed by and administered by the Sumerian Priests who represented the gods. Has anything really changed? On the surface yes, the temples and gods seem to have disappeared within the towns. But the corporate structures and the monarchies and kingships have perhaps become more subtle? Or have we replaced these with huge churches, government buildings and massive corporation head offices?

Corporation PLANET EARTH

By law, a corporation is created under the laws of a state as a separate legal entity that has privileges and liabilities that are distinct from those of its members. It comes from Latin *corporātus* made into a body, from *corporāre*, from *corpus* body. There are many different forms of corporations. Many corporations are established for business purposes but public bodies, charities and clubs are often corporations as well. Corporations take many forms including: statutory corporations, trusts, corporations sole, joint-stock companies and cooperatives. At the heart of this, however, is that a corporation or whatever you may call it, is simply a recorded fictional name with a bunch of rules that are attached to it. And if you work for this fictional thing, you are subject to the rules and to the dictates of those who created it. The ones who created it are the ones who create the rules. As long as you follow the rules, you receive benefits. So whatever rules you as an Earthling abide by take secondary seat to the rules of the corporation... unless there are other rules such as the Criminal Act that you have to abide by which you have somehow agreed to.

Corporations are recognized by the law to have rights and responsibilities like real people. Corporations can exercise human rights against real individuals and the state, and they can themselves be responsible for human rights violations. But in the end, does the corporation go to jail for a violation? No, the directors and creators do. Corporations are conceptually immortal but they can "die" when they are "dissolved" either by statutory operation, order of court, or voluntary action on the part of shareholders. Insolvency may result in a form of corporate 'death', when creditors force the liquidation and dissolution of the corporation under court order, but it most often results in a restructuring of corporate holdings. Corporations can never be convicted of criminal offenses, such as fraud and manslaughter. How can they if they can't shoot the gun? Corporations are not living entities in the way that humans are. Yet they are dependent upon humans to exist.

Early corporations were established by charter (i.e. by an *ad hoc* act granted by a monarch or passed by a parliament or legislature). Most jurisdictions now allow the creation of new corporations through registration. In addition to legal personality, registered companies tend to have limited liability, be owned by shareholders who can transfer their shares to others, and controlled by a board of directors who the shareholders appoint. But these are all State laws that are imposed on corporations and, if the directors so agree to abide by these, then they are lawfully bound to do so. Yet the Directors of IBM are not responsible for the rules of Microsoft because they did not agree to do so. It is this simple.

This fictional world of corporations has grown to encompass Planet Earth and unbeknown to many, it has by way of the charters and rights, imposed upon these dead yet eternal undying fictitious structures, conditions against real individuals. How? Real live individuals work for them. When you work for a corporation you provide a service and you derive a benefit called a pay check. While you work there, you are subject to the codes, rules of that corporations and these are developed by the board of directors that have a purpose. Violate this and you are out. That's the simple model that everybody is very familiar with.

What is not so familiar is how the PLANET EARTH Inc. has come into being and grown to its enormous size. If it simply held just the Vatican and the IMF of debt as subsidiaries it would be one of the enormities of Planet Earth even though it is an invisible dead overlay called a fiction over Planet Earth. Every man, woman and child that has been registered by way of a birth certificate has become an employee of PLANET EARTH Inc. because the fictional overlay has reached down into their private life. For the purpose of this book, we will typically look at a capital letter representation of something as a corporation. Planet Earth is the real physical thing, but PLANET EARTH is a fictional representation of Planet Earth.

The great pyramid and how PLANET EARTH came into being and became what we believe to be the real thing is the purpose of this book. In a simplistic view, it is because very intelligent and purposeful Shareholders and a Board of Directors created PLANET EARTH and launched a corporate mission to employ all people on planet earth for their own profits and causes. Smart businesspeople do this. They strive to create kingdoms and empires by formulating their corporate rules (missions and business plans).

In a Fortune report, the top 10 net worth billionaires account for 4.6 trillion. Number 1 is Carlos Slim Helú of Mexico who is at $69 billion, Bill Gates, is 2nd at $61 billion, Warren Buffett is number 3 at 44 billion, Bernard Arnaught is 4th at 41 billion. Amancio Ortega, is 5th at 37.5 bill, Larry Elison is 6th at 36 billion, Eike Batista is 7th at 30 billion, Stefan Perron is 8th at 26 billion, Li Ha-shing is 9th at 25.5 billion and Karl Albrecht is 10th, is at a poultry 25.4 billion. But what do you suppose the private kingdoms, like the Queen, the Rothschilds, the Pope can tally up? Our cultures and mentality not only worship these "corporate-smart" CEO's and Leaders as gods, we strive to do the same.

They have created the rules of engagement (hiring) which may not be so obvious to most but, after all, they can make the rules. At the top of this pyramid of corporation PLANET EARTH are the "gods" bloodlines and families that root back to Sumeria and before. Through extensive research, there appear to be 13 key families who are the shareholders of PLANET EARTH, each having their representatives on the equivalent of the Board of Directors. Anyone can do this of course as we create corporations all the time and hire people to advance our missions. Is there any difference from a Winery in France that has been a profitable venture for the "family" for 300 years? The question is: Can you enforce the rules of your creation on others and make a profit for the kingdom? All empires, kingdom, dynasties, and corporations require leaders and workers that may be perceived as their "slaves" in order to exist, maintain power and flourish. This has been the history of Planet Earth. Earthlings have been there to work for dynasties and empires run by kings and queens. Their mission has been to protect their bloodlines and to maintain their empires. In mythologies and days before that has been done by muscle and might as the power of conquest. But this shifted to different tools of conquest called religion and money.

In the mission of the PLANET EARTH, the founders have encoded the laws and corporate charters upon each of the subsidiaries as participants in the pyramid in such a way as to take control of the beliefs, money, military, and commerce of Planet Earth. And so it has come to pass that humanity has indeed accepted the fictional things as real the same way we all accept the rules of the corporations we work for. But under PLANET EARTH the business plan has engaged vehicles such as the corporation of GOD with the corporate charter of The Bibles. And the corporation of IMF and UNITED NATIONS with their charter of a New World Order, a new monetary system and one god has come to the forefront. The goal is to employ all the residents of Earth, and, in the eyes of the owners make the slaves happier?.

For those who are happy to be employed by the PLANET EARTH Inc. and are happy with the laws as set forth in Corporation GOD, all is wonderful. View the stories in this book as a revelation of how you came to be so lucky. Perhaps PLANET EARTH is leading to a new Age of One Order, namely the real God?

For those who are unhappy to be employed, or driven by their higher spiritual needs, this book may shed some light on how to quit those jobs and not have to work for PLANET EARTH. What may be the great revelation in this case is how they came to be unknowingly employed and how to quit what may be an undesirable employment. On the next page is what PLANET EARTH may look like. In the grand scheme of things, the structure is no different than a large multinational corporation like IBM, EXXON or SONY.

And so here is the lead-in to the rest of this book. It is your choice as to how the information is brought into your daily reality. Like Morpheus in the Matrix movie said:

"I imagine right now you feel a bit like Alice, tumbling down a rabbit hole. You have the look of a man who accepts what he sees expecting never to wake up. You're here because you know something that you can't explain, but you feel it. There is something wrong with the world. You don't know what it is, but it is there, like a splinter in your mind, driving you mad. It is this feeling that has brought you to me. Do you know what I'm talking about?"

Neo then replies with: *"The Matrix"*. Then Morpheus goes on:

"Do you want to know what it is? The matrix is everywhere, it is all around us. Even now in this very room. You can see it when you look out your window, or turn on your television set. You can feel it when you go to work, when you go to church, when you pay your taxes. It is the wool that has been pulled over your eyes to blind you from the truth. You are a slave Neo like everyone else. You were born into a prison that you cannot see, that you cannot smell, or taste or touch. A prison for your mind. Unfortunately no one can be told what the Matrix is. You have to see it for yourself. This is your last chance. After this, there is no turning back. Take the blue pill, the story ends, you wake up in your bed and believe whatever you want to believe. Take the red pill, you will stay in wonderland, and I will show you how deep the rabbit hole goes. Remember, what I am offering is the truth, nothing more. Follow me."

History is filled with the conquering power of military force, or as mythology would tell us, the conquering force of dark forces. It would seem a natural evolution of mankind to learn how the riches of old (gold silver, jewels, etc.) that would pay for armies to protect their dynasties, empires and kingdoms, would gravitate to simple total control of money. and it would make sense that those who were skilled in the mythological arts of darkness would use this to attain that power of money.

In all history there have been those that had special talents and riches to protect their bloodiness. It is really no different than the father and mother of the household who protects their bloodline as family. Even the family is a pyramid structure of power.

On the next page, is a picture of what the pyramid of the Planetary family called Earthlings would look like. And then we can look at a simple picture of the pyramid of PLANET EARTH INC. This is neither evil, nor good. It just is the way the peoples of Planet Earth have accepted it to be.

The Hierarchy Of Earthlings

gods

13 Royal Bloodlines

Kings & Queens

Rulers and Dictators

International Leaders

Presidents and Chief Executive Officers

Earthlings Upon Planet Earth

The Empire of PLANET EARTH

gods

PLANET EARTH INC.

DYNASTIES

KINGDOMS

NATIONS OF EARTH

MULTINATIONAL CORPORATIONS

THE EARTHLINGS

Now let us look more closely at Empire of PLANET EARTH and the gods. Let us work our way down the hierarchy relating real people and international organizations to our simple model. **Let us look at who and what really controls THE EARTHLINGS**

.

3

THE GLOBAL ELITE "gods"

In the previous chapter we were introduced to a simplistic picture of PLANET EARTH Inc. and it's structure. In the next series of chapters we will take you on a top down look at the people who run these corporations. Of course it is difficult to inspect these and piece together the structure because they are purposely private. A **privately held company** or **close corporation** is a business company owned either by non-governmental organizations or by a relatively small number of shareholders or company members. They do not offer or trade its company stock (shares) with the general public on the stock market exchanges, but rather the company's stock is offered, owned and traded or exchanged privately. These companies are virtually invisible compared to publicly traded counterparts or **publicly held company**. In 2008, 441 of the largest private companies in the United States accounted for $1.8 trillion in revenues and employed 6.2 million people according to Forbes. Needless to say privately held companies generally have fewer or less comprehensive reporting requirements for transparency, via annual reports than do publicly traded companies. For example, privately held companies are not generally required to publish their financial statements. By not being required to disclose details about their operations and financial outlook, private companies are not forced to disclose information that may potentially be valuable to competitors and can avoid the immediate erosion of customer and stakeholder confidence in the event of financial duress. Further, private company executives may steer their ships without shareholder approval, and at the same time keep information about their operations secret, like the Federal Reserve. At the extreme end of this are private structures like societies, cults, and the likes that are not even known about or registered, held together by common blood, interests, oaths, and pacts. Thus, much of what follows is an attempt to piece together a vast puzzle of private corporations that form the people and companies of PLANET EARTH Inc.

Despite the complexity and the possible inaccuracies, the researchers on this topic have become prolific and the truth will eventually be known. The lesson here is that some such structure exists and is run by some very astute ones who have power over nations and humanity. Humanity, as we shall see, worships and follows the lead of thousands of gods. But in all these god structures, there are those who have come to be at the top of the heap. Much research has come forward on who these are and in a simplistic view, one must only look to who controls the pyramids we have already discussed; the debt (money), the beliefs (Vatican), the products (corporations) and the power (military).

The ones who are at the top of these heaps are alleged to be the gods, the Global Elite, The Powers That Be, there are many names. They are our starting point and like doing some due diligence on any corporation, one must look to the alleged Founders, the Directors, the private Owners of the corporations. In following our simple model, we will look at these special people as the bloodlines of the Global Elite.

Bloodlines Of The Global "Elite"

History both myth and alleged nonfiction are founded upon the rise and fall of dynasties and kingdoms as controlled by gods, kings/queens, emperors, and dictators. It is rife with a common phenomenon where even the gods rise and fall in power. Always prevalent in this is the conflict between good and evil, between conflicts of purpose, where the means of control is through armies and greed for wealth through slaves to do the bidding of those who have some special powers of dominion over others. Mankind has been obsessed with this strange addiction to royalty, power, fame and fortune, an inherent trait of self improvement and carnal desire for power. The evolution of this phenomenon has manifested itself in corporations with its pyramidal structures of the many serving the few. Prolific upon Planet Earth is the Age of Corporations that effectively allow anyone, even a slave, to become a "king" of a "dynasty".

This inherent desire for wealth and power, and the bowing to its authority has remained through time because Earthlings are trained to bow down simply because they accept it for fear of not so doing. Even now nothing has really changed as unbelievable masses flock to see the Queen, the Presidents, the Pope, or anyone who has by force or by special skill attained a position of power and authority. They are immediately the one to be admired and followed without any regard for what their real purposes are. It has always been this way both in fact and fiction and it is still prevalent today. Only the means of controlling those required to fight, to create movements against opposition, to maintain the dynasty, to retain a position of greatness, has shifted in form at the lower reaches. But while the corporate dynasties play the game of thrones, nations maintain the might with armies called the military. And so it seems that the drive to superiority, to greatness relative to others, the need to satisfy the erotic needs of the human mind and form continue like a broken record. The broken record is an unending inventory of dynasties, civilizations, and cultures; and destruction. And now it is nations, corporations, governments that have risen and fallen like the natural cycle of growth and decay of all life on the planet.

There are those who have attained special powers like the gods and the myths tell. There are those that have attained control of special information and power over others. There are those who have through heartless cold disassociation from the deed controlled through fear and death. As humanity supposedly became more "intelligent" so the gods and dynasty leaders had to adjust the techniques to continue the control and the preservation of their kingdoms. There are now countless dynasties and equivalents in kings and queens that hoarded wealth at the expense of those below them in their power hierarchy. Countless corporations, nations, kingdoms are as we have pointed out, pyramid structures of power and management have become the norm of power to satisfy those who create and run them.

It is said that the best slave is the one who believes he is free. And the apparent belief of freedom has indeed been nurtured to as to continue the means by which dynasties can retain their existence. This is neither bad nor good. As pointed out before, it is all choice and it is all just business that earthlings accept. And it is clear that there must be, in all this evolution, those who are better at this business than the others. It is the way it is and it always seems to have been that way. The powerful become so at the expense of the powerless. And it can hardly be surprising to understand that someone controls the biggest corporation of all, PLANET EARTH.

Yet, in the end, if you believe you are free, then all this that is told here about slaves is meaningless for indeed one can have a decent life within the family, culture, nation, or world one is born into. It is choice.

On the other hand, many do not have much of a fruitful life, and know something is not right for them. The choices however to escape that trap which is not right seems so unattainable that all that can be done is to mumble in a beer or bury the head in the sand and attempt to disallow the issues into ones reality. For those the choice is there and the powerful information is there, but a trigger is needed to see that a choice does exist as in this book.

gods

Royal Bloodlines

Kings and Queens

Rulers and Dictators

Earthlings

Through various means, be it technology, special psychic powers, mysticism, occult, spiritual, knowledge, birth, or bloodlines, the gods and the global elite have managed to retain their power over others through time; and they have managed to retain their great kingdoms of wealth. Some have fallen, some have risen but there seems to be the ones that have held fast in their dominion. It is this group and their extraordinary march to the conquest of the ultimate empire of Planet Earth that is our topic. We shall now begin to unfold the pieces of history in the following chapters through the gods and those extraordinary people of power as they have worked to conquer Earth and the resident Earthling through a fictional corporate vessel we will refer to as **PLANET EARTH INC.** in this book.

In a simple model, there are the gods and the bloodlines who have a plan. In a simple model, all gods, bloodlines, and humanity are evolving on a path; a simply at different stages of growth and evolution. In a simple model, no one is good or bad, they are simply evolving. And so it is now of interest to look at these royal bloodlines more closely to attempt to see what their secrets of success in maintaining their dynasties may be.

Research points to 13 bloodlines that have this strong hold on Planet Earth who have become the spotlight of many researchers. This is because these people have power and wealth beyond comprehension. Up there, there are no rules. They have a mixture of experience and powers that go beyond understanding and have played influential roles in the world's business for centuries. And when it comes to the greatest and largest corporations on earth--particularly the ones alleged to be under the PLANET EARTH INC pyramid, the CEO's, Presidents, and Directors who run these are mere amateurs in comparison. It is just good business.

If you are a businessman or businesswoman, think about this in terms of a corporate business, having access to unlimited capital, being interested in corporate takeovers, bankrupt companies, and being able to influence the market for the products and services, how would you make out? As we develop our corporate pyramid of PLANET

EARTH you will see a list of some of the largest corporations on Planet Earth that fall within the influence of these bloodlines.

The 13 Royal Bloodlines

It is important to understand that when it comes to corporations and the affairs of commerce, there are those that are much more adept than others. From the greatest corporation to the smallest, the process of creating a financially viable and "successful" business resides with the ones that create the missions, implement the rules of conduct and direct the affairs of those hired to serve their purpose. It is no surprise that someone must be on top of the largest corporation of all we call PLANET EARTH INC because their skill set and business smarts are better than the rest of the ones working for them.

Corporation PLANET EARTH is no different. Like any corporation, it is a private fictional entity created by humans; a fictional construct to hold its treasures and to organize its purpose into reality. There are those that play this game of conquering people on conquering nations. And so we come to the part of the story where those top humans need an introduction to see who they are, what their special talents are and have a quick look at their kingdoms.

Long ago in the dark unwritten pages of human history, powerful kings discovered how they could control other men by torture, magical practices, wars, politics, religion and interest taking. These elite families designed strategies and tactics to perpetuate their special knowings, technologies and abilities into practice. Because these people live in the private domains, and are outside of the scope of the inquisitors and peering eyes, the accumulations of fortunes has allowed them to march towards the conquering of PLANET EARTH in their own way without rules except their own.

In the last decades, many researchers have come forward to penetrate the layers upon layers of secrecy that have hidden these families from the profane masses, but many an author has touched upon their existence. Many have gotten into trouble. These researchers constantly point to thirteen families or bloodlines at the top, and five of these families are the inside core of these thirteen. These families are portrayed as the 13 layers of blocks found on the strange seal on the reverse side of the U.S. $1 bill.

The research that has been done on theses bloodlines is extensive. In order to introduce these families and their kingdoms, several sites have been used. The most extensive ones are:

The book **The Satanic Bloodlines by Fritz Springmeier** found at **www.theforbiddenknowledge.com/hardtruth/the_satanic_bloodlines.htm** is recommended for detail, references and treatment of these bloodlines. In addition, their many websites such as
www.thewatcherfiles.com/bloodlines/
www.illuminati-news.com/moriah.htm
www.bibliotecapleyades.net/bloodlines/.htm

According to the research, the key bloodlines are as below:

13 Royal Bloodlines		3 Interconnected Bloodlines
1 Astor	8 Onassis	Disney
2 Bundy	9. Reynolds	MacDonald

3 Collins	10. Rockefeller	Krupp
4 DuPont	11. Rothschilds	
5. Freeman	12. Russell	
6. Kennedy	13. Van Dyn	
7. Li		

These references all weave a detailed story of these people produced from an incredible amount of research. The following chapters are designed to summarize these dynasties and the information is taken from these sites, in particular the site of Fritz Springmeier. I have tried to summarize the information here but do not want to take away from the extensive work done by Fritz. In many cases I have left the words of the author who writes this in a personal tense as "I ...." For a full treatment, please go to Fritz's book noted above.

Fritz Springmeier is an extensive researcher and if you should research him, you will find that his work has led him to some serious troubles. He is one of the foremost researchers and he is detailed in his references, details, interview. He has been asked why he researches the top 13 bloodlines:

"I have often been asked who are the Illuminati? Who are the people at the top of the conspiracy? Who are the generational satanic families? The Illuminati consists of 13 magical and powerful bloodlines. There are also some other powerful bloodlines that are worth naming but if they are in the Illuminati they have blood ties to one of the 13 powerful lineages. About half of the Illuminati people I know have had their parentage hidden from them. Many of the those who still know who their real parents are, still do not know what bloodline they belong to until the Illuminati chooses to reveal it to them. Most of the Illuminati have MPD. When high level Satanists do not have MPD they very often emotionally break under the stress of the horrible blood rituals that are required. Recently, a non-MPD Satanist in Chicago emotionally broke and gave his life to Christ. (I have videos available of an interview of this man exposing Satanism.) One of the important lineages has remained secret until 3 investigators named Lincoln, Leigh, and Bageant were spoon-fed leads and secrets.

They put this into a book called "Holy Blood, Holy Grail." I recommend the book and the two books which are its sequels, because they show how just one part of the 13 lineages has kept itself secret and has taken immense power of all forms to themselves. In Southern Belgium there is a castle. (If anyone is travelling there and wants to find the castle, I will show them on the map, and describe it.) This is the Mothers of Darkness castle. In that castle, is a cathedral and in that cathedral's basement a little baby Is sacrificed daily and Is coming to power. The pages are written almost round the clock. (This castle is also described in my Be Wise as Serpents book.) The history in that handwritten book would reveal the real facts behind the propaganda that the world's major news media give the gullible public. The history as that book reveals it would tell people about how Abraham Lincoln was a descendent of the Rothschilds.

Abraham Lincoln was the secret head of the Rosicrucians, a member of their 3 headed top council. (I have seen the paper trail proof to these things about Lincoln to my satisfaction that these things about Lincoln are true.) Adolf Hitler was also a secret member of the Rothschild lineage. Hitler carried out blood sacrifices to open his mind up to high level demonic spiritual control. Rockefeller sold Hitler oil during W.W. II via Spain to keep W.W. II going longer. The history in that book mentions people that the "history books" given the public don't-- like Michael Augustus Martinelli Von Braun Rheinhold, the most powerful Satanist in the world a few years ago. Michael Augustus Martinelli Von Braun Rheinhold had 66 Satanic Brides. And that Satanic book in the Mothers of

Darkness castle also mentions the Rockefeller bloodline. Only insiders are supposed to know the real history of what has taken place in human history. The real decisions and the real movers and shakers have been hidden from the public's eyes.

What the public is given is a stage show where illuminati puppets parade around and make big speeches according to their script. Each of the 13 families has their own set of Mothers of Darkness. Each of the 13 families has their own secret Satanic leadership Kings, Queens, Princesses and Princes of Darkness. For instance, the Rockefeller family has people who are selected as Kings and Princes within their own bloodline in secret rituals. The Kings and Princes, Queens and Princesses are strictly bloodline. They secretly rule over an area of the world for their own bloodline. This is independent of the Illuminati's hierarchy which was diagrammed in the Jan 1993 newsletter. (my Newsletter from a Christian Ministry.) In the January, 1993 issue the Covens, Sisters of Light, Mothers of Darkness, and the Grande Mothers were diagrammed.

The illuminati pulls its various bloodlines together under several councils. The Grande Druid Council or your Council of 13 is your principle council for the Brotherhood of Death. Above the Council of 13 is a higher Council of 9, and an inner group of 3 is believed to head that Council of Nine. How do we know about these things? The power of God has reached into the very heart of Satan's empire and pulled out some of the most powerful Satanists and drawn them to Christ. There are several Satanists that were at the top which have managed to find Christ. in addition, some of the next echelon of the hierarchy, such as some of the Mothers of Darkness are also finding Christ. if someone wants to understand how and why decisions are made in world affairs and by who-- then you need to study the illuminati. The real answers do not rest with the proceedings of the Congress of the United States or with the publicly known leaders of the Communist countries. An example of what I am talking, there is a book entitled "Who Financed Hitler" by James Pool and Suzanne Pool. I am always glad to see that some people are willing to look behind the scenes. Believe me, there were people that Hitler listened to. They were the people he went to ritual with, and who put him into power."

Before we begin to meet the 13 bloodlines it is important to understand a few terms. **A Dynasty** means a succession of rulers from the same family or line; a family or group that maintains power for several generations. A **Kingdom** is a political or territorial unit ruled by a sovereign and a **King or Queen** who is a male/female sovereign or monarch who holds by life tenure, and usually by hereditary right, the chief authority over a country and people. An **Empire** is a nation led by an **Emperor** that has other countries under its control.

Each of the 13 bloodlines described following have created their own dynasty as a succession from the same family or bloodline. At the top are the rulers, private in their affairs, who have worked towards conquering other rulers, kings and queen over countries and people so as to become the chief authority as Emperor over the Empire of Planet Earth. These dynasties have emerged into power in the last 250 years. It must be stated that there are many powerful dynasties on earth and it is not to say that these 13 are the only power force with a business plan. However, what follows in the next chapters will introduce the reader to the founders of the PLANET EARTH and their Business Plan that is now manifesting as the New World Order.

A Word About gods

So it is that at the top of the pyramid are the "gods" Upon earth today there are thousands of gods or deities. But who are the current "gods" who rule empire of Planet Earth?

The on-line dictionary says **God** is a being conceived as the perfect, omnipotent, omniscient originator and ruler of the universe. This has evolved to be the principal object of faith and worship in monotheistic religions. But **god** is defined as a supernatural being who is worshipped as the controller of some part of the universe or some aspect of life in the world, or is the personification of some force. It seems that God is the Big Boss and the gods are just in charge of part of the universe. They are inventions and constructs not the real thing. We state that GOD in this book is a fictional fake created for dubious purpose of commerce. God has never come down to write the rules; these have been interpreted through Earthlings who have positioned themselves as the experts and knowers of His (God) Word.

If you look around this planet, there are 19 major world religions which are subdivided into a total of 270 large religious groups, and many smaller ones. Some 34,000 separate Christian religions can be identified in the world with over half of them as independent churches that have no interest in linking with the big denominations. Since the Sumerians around 6000 years ago, historians have catalogued over 3700 supernatural beings, of which 2870 can be considered deities. In truth, the possibilities are nearly infinite. It is easy to pick something you can't understand, or pretend to understand, create a point of worship and surround it with a belief. And if you can convince others, pretty soon you have a god and a religion full of god's beliefs to follow. Thus because Earthlings love the idea of worshiping the famous and powerful, many gods exist. And therefore, it would be a natural assumption to conclude that the current gods are the ones who are at the top of the Earthling heap. Have the Sumerian gods who were alleged to understand the secrets of long life maintained their presence in these people? One thing is for sure.

No one on Earth is God. We all as One, are.

Is there a supreme God? It depends upon your point of view and your beliefs. Some say Satan is God. Others say Christ is God. Others say God just is. Regardless, we find that consistently through history God above is defined by gods below. But, in our case here, god and gods are the ones that wish to rule the empire of Planet Earth. And so we come to getting to know these "gods" who would work towards being the emperors. In a simple corporate sense, these rulers of the dynasties would be the sole shareholders and directors of PLANET EARTH corporation.

In following the stories of the 13 Bloodlines, it is underscored that this is research that is avaible from experts whi have researched this exensively, and provided in the book PLANET EARTH INc by Ed Rychkun. In this regard it is best to go to the source of the research by conducted over years and years by the author **Fritz Springmeier** found on website **www.thewatcherfiles.com/bloodlines/index.htm** What is of key interest with each bloodline is the rise in power, the extent of power, and the belief systems that dominate their philosophy. Regarless , it must be clear that this is not done to judge; it is done to report, and it is neither evil or good, it just is. However, it is of interest to understand one of the major dynasties that has succeeded in being a key participant in PLANET EARTH INC, the Rothschild Dynasty.

4

THE ROTHSCHILD DYNASTY

*Please refer to the author **Fritz Springmeier** as this reflects his work. Go to website **www.thewatcherfiles.com/bloodlines/index.htm** The following material includes excerpts and sections from his research.*

Rothschild Historical Rise To Power

Most Ashkenazim Jews of the early Rothschilds time did not use sir-names, instead they preferred the Chinese custom of using a symbol as the family identity. These symbols were sometimes used on signs outside Jewish houses as an address. Some Jews had taken on sir-names, to fit in, but the use of symbols was more popular. The early Rothschilds chose the sir-name Bauer meaning farmer in German. The Bauer line continues today, but in the 1700's one man re-named his branch of the family after its symbol and address; the Red Shield or the Seal of Solomon.

Mayer Rothschild was sent to be a rabbi when he was 10, in 1753. A year and a half later his parents died. Mayer was brilliant and was encouraged by relatives to continue his studies but coin trading was his love. He left the school and when 13 was sent to Hanover to be an apprentice at the Illuminati Oppenheimer bank.

He worked there for 7 years, learning the ins and out of money. While in Hanover Mayer made the acquaintance of General von Estorff, a numismatist who was impressed by Mayer's knowledge of the subject. In 1763 General von Estorff left Hanover and joined the Court of Prince William IX of Hesse-Hanau, whose territory included Frankfort. Mayer knew that through his connections he would be able to get some business with the Prince. It appears Mayer's stay at the Oppenheimer bank was used to establish himself in Illuminati circles and to find a way to get close to the Illuminati royalty. General von Estorff was his key.

Prince William of Hesse-Hanau was tied into the Illuminati. He was the son of Landgrave Frederick or Hesse-Cassel, of the royal family of Hesse. Prince William was a Freemason, and his younger brother Karl was, according to Jews and Freemasons in Europe 'accepted as the head of all German Freemasons.' Members of the Hesse dynasty have been described as the leaders of the Strict Observance (in 1782 a Masonic Congress in Wilhelmsbad, a city in the Hesse province, dropped the name 'Strict Observance' and changed it to "Beneficent Knights of the Holy City"). The Hesse dynasty is totally connected to the Illuminati. Prince William was the grandson of King George II of England.

The Hesse-Cassels were one of the richest royal houses in Europe. Their income came mainly from the loaning-out of Hessian soldiers to foreign countries. The elite love to makes profit off of "peacekeeping" troops, which is exactly what the Hessians were called. This "peacekeeping" always adds up to imperialism. The Hessian troops were used by England in the American Revolution, in fact the colonial armies fought more Hessian soldiers than English. The House of Hesse-Cassel made a lot of money off the American Revolution. Another example of the Hesse-Cassel's ties to the Illuminati is the enigmatic figure St. Germain, who is hailed as a New Age Messiah-figure. Many researchers believe that St. Germain was the son of Francis II of Transylvania. Francis II's second wife was Charlotte Amalie of the House of Hesse, he married her in 1694. St. Germain was either her son, or the prior wife's, this point is debated. His name was Leopold-George and they staged his death in 1700 to save him from the deadly collapse of the Transylvanian dynasty. Prince Karl of Hesse, Masonic leader of Germany, wrote that St. Germain had been sent down to Italy to be raised by the Medici family. Later on St. Germain appeared out of nowhere to work with the elite.

There were questions as to his identity and Napoleon III had a dossier gathered on him, but the house holding the dossier was mysteriously destroyed in a fire. St. Germain was an alchemist and he claimed to have the alchemical Elixir of Life, the secret formula of immortality (which the Rosicrucians also claimed to have). He was a guest of William and Karl of Hesse in 1774, and in 1779 returned to Karl to spend the last years of his known life. Helena Blavatsky, cofounder of the Theosophical Society claimed that St. Germain was one of the Hidden Masters of Tibet who secretly controlled the world's destiny. In 1930 Guy Ballard claimed that he met St. Germain on Mount Shasta. This supposed meeting led to the creation of the 'I AM' movement.

The Hesse Dynasty has lasted clear up to the 20th century. During WWII they were on Hitler's side. Prince Philip of Hesse was a messenger between Hitler and Mussolini. He was still alive in 1973 and was reported to be the richest prince in Europe. The House of Hesse is still a powerful force in Germany. In 1763 Mayer left Hanover to build his fortune in Frankfort. His main objective was to become a financial agent of Prince William of Hesse-Hanau. Prince William was an intelligent man who loved to make money. His passions went beyond money. His wife did not please him so he became an adulterer and almost every woman he slept with became pregnant. He fathered between 70 to 21 illegitimate children. His main mistress, Frau von Lindenthal, bore him 8 children and ran his household. William loved to loan money at high interest rates. He was the perfect man to aid Mayer's quest for riches. Mayer began bribing Prince William's servants to become informants.

At that time he was an antique dealer, trader, coin collector, and exchanger (the country was divided and as a result the separate currencies made money exchanging very profitable). General von Estorff convinced Prince William of the value of a rare coin collection and then recommended Rothschild. Thus began the relationship between the Prince and the Rothschilds. Mayer would sell rare coins, precious stones, and antiques to the Prince at ridiculously low prices. Then, in 1769, after a significant amount of sales, he wrote the Prince asking for and receiving the designation 'Crown Agent to the Prince of Hesse-Hanau' (a great commercial advertiser).

Titles and honors were important in that day, they opened doors). Mayer then married Gutle Schnapper, daughter of a respected merchant, Wolf Salomon Schnapper, in 1770. He then set up a money exchange bureau. His two brothers worked in this bureau with him until 1785 when Kalmann died and Moses quite. Some researchers contend that Adam Wieshaupt of the Bavarian Illuminati was financially supported by the Rothschilds. The Bavarian Illuminati was founded in 1776, and the Rothschilds were not necessarily a financial power at that time. It is believed that Mayer was in a financial position to support Wieshaupt. It is possible, that when, in 1782, the headquarters of the Illuminati moved to Frankfort, that it began to be controlled by the Rothschilds.

In 1785 Prince William's father, Landgrave Frederick of Hesse-Cassel, died and William became the new Landgrave. This made him the richest prince in Germany and possibly Europe. He left the small province of Hesse-Hanau to become ruler in Hesse-Cassel. Around this time Wolf Schnapper, Mayer's father-in-law, introduced Rothschild to Carl Buderus who was the Prince's chief financial advisor. Through either coercion, friendship, or occultic ties Mayer was able to convince Buderus to become an agent for him. This was a big mover for Mayer. The Landgrave William of Hesse-Cassel was to be the 'steppingstone" to power.

Until then Mayer had only done meagre business with William, but by 1789 Buderus managed to get some royal bills for Rothschild to discount. This wasn't much, but it was a start. Carl received a cut of the profits when he did William's business through Rothschild. This was the beginning of a long financial relationship that would benefit both parties.

Mayer Amschel Bauer-Rothschild was a shrewd man, but his quick rise in social status shows the power of money, for Mayer was not cultured. He could never master the German language and so he and his family spoke a strange Yiddish German mixture (which benefitted their secret network). He enjoyed discussing the medieval world and coin collecting. When it came to business he was ruthless and naturally adept. His occult side was well hidden. He was most likely a Cabalistic Jew. Although it is not known if he was a Freemason, he did accompany the Landgrave on several trips to Masonic lodges (after the two had become better friends). He had 5 daughters and 5 sons, plus several children that died young. He moved from his old house, the "Haus zur Hinterpfann", to a new one, Green Shield, when he started making more money. Green Shield was a dual residency and the other half was occupied by the Schiff family who were to play an important role later on as agents of the Rothschilds.

Every passage of Green Shield held hidden shelves and cupboards, and the backyard counting house's walls had a number of secret shelves and a secret underground room which was connected to a neighbour's house for a quick getaway if necessary (the house was built to protect Jews from the dangerous pogroms that would sweep Germany, it was a great place to secretly practice their Gnostic-satanic rituals, if they were yet involved in that form of worship). His five sons have been called the Mayer brothers because they all shared that middle name: Amschel Mayer, Salomon Mayer, Nathan Mayer, Kalmann (Carl) Mayer, and Jacob (James) Mayer. Each son entered the family business at the age of 12.

The Illuminati fuelled French Revolution got under way in the 1790's, and Prince William began to get nervous. He was afraid the revolutionary riots would reach Germany and he would lose his gold. So he invested his money in a magnificent new palace called Wilhelmshoe, which was built from 1791 to 1798. Although the French Revolution frightened William it was a delight for Mayer. The war helped his sales. When the French ended up pitted against the Holy Roman Empire, the prices of imported goods skyrocketed, and importing goods from England was a Rothschild specialty. In fact Mayer's English trade helped him secure a deal with the Landgrave (through Buderus, of course) in which he became a middleman in England's payments for the hire of Hessian soldiers. Every ill wind of the 1790's seemed to blow good to the Rothschilds. The winds were so good that by the end of the decade they were established as a rich and independent family.

In 1800 they were the 11th richest family in Frankfort's Jew Alley (not counting the wealth in proxy). Around the turn of the century Mayer decided to send his most clever son, Nathan to England to establish another Rothschild House. The family tells a silly story about Nathan leaving for England to best an annoying English cotton trader, but I believe that Nathan was sent by Mayer with a specific purpose - to establish power with the Rothschild network in that country. Nathan arrived in England with no knowledge of the language but a great amount of money. He would soon be the most powerful man in Europe. Many more profitable events occurred at the turn of the century. Many of these events revolve around the Rothschild infiltration of the Thurn and Taxis postal system. The House of Thurn and Taxis was of the Black Nobility. In 1516 Holy Roman Emperor Maximilion I (of the Merovingian bloodline and husband of a member of the Black Nobility) commissioned the House to create a mounted postal service between Vienna and Brussels. The service eventually included all of Central Europe.

The head office of the system was in Frankfort, which was rather convenient for Mayer who proceeded to do business with them. His relationship with Thurn and Taxis became so close that the service began to inform him of any pertinent information found among the letters (that they had a habit of covertly reading). This mail fraud system was also used by the Emperor Francis to keep abreast of his enemies. While Mayer was receiving stolen news from Thurn and Taxis he was busy setting up his own postal service so that no-one could secretly discover his dealings. This system was eventually so effective that the Rothschilds became the best and fastest informed individuals in the world.

The system was so good that many prominent men began to send their letters through the Rothschilds, who of course, always snuck a peak at the contents. The business with Thurn and Taxis helped Mayer receive the title "Imperial Crown Agent" in 1800. This title served as a passport that allowed him to travel throughout the Holy Roman Empire. It also provided the right to bear arms, and it freed him from having to pay the taxes and obligations upon the Jews of that period. Mayer began to get even more titles, including one from the German Order of St. John. His sons Amschel and Salomon were also busy getting various titles. In 1801 they became crown agents of the Landgrave William of Hesse-Cassel. All these titles were wonderful, but most important was the Landgrave's. The Landgrave was the richest Prince in Europe and the Rothschilds were determined to take advantage of his wealth.

The relationship with the Landgrave improved greatly in 1803. A Danish King, and cousin of William, asked the Prince for loans but William declined because he did not want anyone to know how rich he had become. Rothschild learned about it and through Buderus, proposed lending the money anonymously. William thought the idea was splendid. The loan was sent through Mayer and a Hamburg Jew. The interests were paid to Rothschild who, after taking commission, forwarded the money to the Landgrave. The event was a great triumph, after 36 years, Mayer had finally done a significant job for the Prince. Six more Landgrave loans to Denmark were negotiated by Rothschild. Many more loans ensued (although they required some teeth pulling on Buderus' part), including loans to the Order of St. John.

This negotiating of the Landgrave's loans greatly increased the reputation of the House of Rothschild. By this time Napoleon had come to power in France. This caused a distress in Europe, but brought great profits to the House of Rothschild. As one biographer put it *"Napoleon seemed bent on improving the Rothschild's lot in life."* Even though Napoleon was not purposely doing it, the conditions he created were of great benefit. Napoleon tried to get the Landgrave as his ally, but Prince William squirmed and politely as possible refused. William's goal was to wait until the winning side in the Napoleonic conflict was clear so that he could join without any risks. The pressure of the situation gave the Landgrave a very bad temper. By this time half the crown heads of Europe were in his debt. Napoleon grew tired of the Landgrave's games. His troops invaded Germany and the province of Hesse to *"remove the House of Hesse-Cassel from rulership and to strike it out of the list of powers."* Wilhelmshoe became frantic as William attempted to hide his riches.

After the scramble to conceal his wealth he fled the province and went to live in exile in Denmark. The French immediately found most of his treasures. Buderus and Mayer had to act fast to preserve the wealth of the Landgrave. Some of the valuables had already been sold. They quickly bribed a French General, Lagrange, who turned over 42 trunks to Hessian officials and lied to Napoleon about the Prince's true wealth. Lagrange's deceptive act was eventually discovered and he was dismissed, but much of the wealth was preserved. During the frantic moments before Hesse-Cassel's invasion, the Landgrave gave Buderus the right to collect the interest payments due from Holy Roman Emperor Francis. Buderus eventually transferred this right to the Rothschilds. Mayer began doing the Landgrave's business behind Napoleon's back. These secret dealings were greatly boosted by the man Napoleon appointed to rule the area-Karl von Dalberg. Dalberg was a friend of Mayer and Buderns and had done business with them.

Napoleon made Dalberg Primate of the new Confederation of the Rhine, which included Frankfort. As ruler of the region Dalberg protected the Rothschilds from being exposed as traders of contraband and as agents of the House of Hesse-Cassel. When the French cut off trade with England prices on imports soared. The Rothschilds smuggled goods in and made large profits, with Dalberg keeping guard. *"It was certainly most remarkable,"* said one biographer. *"That the Archbishop and Lord of the Confederation of the Rhine, who ruled over sixteen German princes, and stood so high in Napoleon's favour, should have shown so much good-will to the Jewish Mayer Amschel Rothschild at Frankfort, who, although now a rich man, had no dame to move in high and influential circles."* Despite Dalberg's protection Mayer kept two sets of books, one inspectable and the other secret.

By 1807 Buderus, as proxy for the Landgrave, was almost exclusively using the Rothschilds for Hesse-Cassel business. Mayer himself would visit the Prince in exile, but since he was getting old he soon had to give up these trips and sent his sons on the journeys. The House of Rothschild was collecting the income of the wealthiest prince in Europe less than half a century after Mayer had begun building his fortune! The satanic House of Rothschild's Illuminati dealings at this time are well exemplified by their involvement with the second Tugenbund League. The first Tugenbund League (or Virtue League) was formed in 1786 as a kind of sex society. The group would meet at Henrietta Herz's home (her husband was an Illuminati Jew who was the disciple of the powerful occultist Moses Mendelssohn). Many Illuminists attended this "Virtue" League.

A number of young Jewish women whose husbands were always away on business would come to the Herz's house to participate in the immorality (two members were daughters of Moses Mendelssohn). Frequenters of this "salon" included revolutionary Freemason Mirabeau, William von Humbolt, and Frederick von Gentz who was to become an important Rothschild agent. In 1807 the second Tugenbund League was formed. This League pursued 'moral-scientific" and political aims. The main aim being the deliverance of Germany from French occupation. The League was formed by Baron von Stein who was its principle "protector."

Thomas Frost wrote in **Secret Societies Of The European Revolution** that *'The Initiations [into the second Tugendbund] multiplied rapidly, and the League soon numbered in its ranks most of the Councillors of State, many officers of the army, and a considerable number of the professors of literature and science.... A central directorate at Berlin, presided over by Stein, had the supreme control of the movement, and exercised, through provincial committees, an authority all the more potent from emanating from an unknown source, and which was obeyed as implicitly as the decrees of Emperor or King.'* The Landgrave William of Hesse-Cassel held an important position in the second Tugendbund. Buderus was also involved. It appears the Rothschilds were members and they were go-betweens for the [Landgrave's] correspondence on this matter, and made payments in favour of the Tugendbund." This put Mayer Rothschild at the head of the propaganda system against Napoleon.

Napoleon tried to suppress Tugundbund but it went underground, concealing itself under the protection of the English Masonic Lodge at Hanover, It assisted many anti-Napoleon causes physically and financially. Tugendbund was eventually dissolved, but many of its members moved on to other Masonic societies such as the 'Black Knights,' 'The Knights of the Queen of Prussia,' and 'The Concordists.' In 1818 the second Tugundbund was revived as the Burschenschaft (Association of Boys or Fellows). The Burschenschaft was a revolutionary group of students who introduced martial exercises into the universities. The Burschenschaft eventually fell apart. After a few years the exiled Landgrave came to totally trust the Rothschilds. '...[Prince William] got more and more accustomed to following [Mayer] Rothschild's advice, and scarcely took any important financial step without consulting him.'

This princely steppingstone was working out perfectly. It was paving the way towards Rothschild financial freedom. Mayer wanted to become a creditor, and his goal was soon achieved. In 1810 the Rothschild's firm became 'Mayer Amschel Rothschild and Sons' (Nathan was not a public partner of this firm). That same year Mayer loaned his own money to Denmark and when Dalberg took out a big loan to go to the baptism of Napoleon's son, the financial security of the Frankfort bank was set in stone.

The House of Rothschild needed a new steppingstone. The old one, the Landgrave, would not be discarded, but they needed a younger, more political man who could be their key to controlling Europe. That man was Prince Clemens Metternich who in 1809 became the Austrian Minister for Foreign Affairs. He became the leading opposer of Napoleon, and the Landgrave moved in his exile to Austria, hoping the powerful up-start would get Hesse back. So the Rothschild network increased its operations in Austria - the land of the Hapsburgs.

Around this time Mayer Amschel Bauer-Rothschild got sick. Before his death he wrote a Will that would dictate the structure of the Rothschilds. Although the exact content's of Mayer's Will have been kept secret, one edict is clear. It completely excluded the daughters and their husbands and heirs from the business, and all knowledge of it. The Will totally exalted the importance of the family circle. On Sept. 19, 1812 Mayer died. A bogus legend about his death maintains that his five sons gathered around his deathbed and he split Europe between them. Only Amschel and Carl were in Frankfort when he died. Nathan was in England, and Salomon and James were on the road (the brothers were constantly traveling).

When Mayer died, headship over the family fell on Nathan Rothschild of England. Even though Nathan was not the oldest, the 5 brothers had voted unanimously that he was the most capable to lead them. Nathan was an intelligent, uneducated, self-absorbed jerk. Though he was an impolite, foul-mouthed man ('...he could swear like a trooper.') his money got him into the high society of England. His cold view on life and power is seen in his response to an English Major who was being sentimental about the horrible deaths of the large number of soldiers that had died in the war. *"Well,"* said Rothschild. *"If they had not all died, Major, you presumably would still be a drummer."* There is a story that says one of Nathan's sons asked him how many nations there were in the world and Nathan replied: "*There are only two you need to bother about. There is the mishpoche [Yiddish for family] and there are the others*." This story may be false, but the attitude is real.

Nathan first settled in Manchester, England, the center of cloth manufacturing. In 1804 he moved to London. As his wealth and his reputation began to grow he was able to marry Hannah Cohen. The Cohens were a wealthy Jewish family from Amsterdam, and Hannah's father, Salomon Cohen was a respected merchant in London. Nathan served with him as Warden of the Great Synagogue (the Rothschilds relationship to the Jews will be discussed later on in this article). Hannah's sister, Judith, married the powerful Jewish Freemason Moses Montefiore (the Montefiore's were of "ancient" and extremely 'aristocratic Jewish stock', probably another Cabalistic family), who was friends with Nathan (Nathan's sister Henrietta married a Montefiore, so did his second son, Anthony, and his brother, Salomon's great grandson, Aiphonse married a Sebag-Montefiore in 1911).

Nathan's social life revolved around the Cohens. Nathan was a Freemason. He was a member of London's Lodge of Emulation. Nathan's accumulation of wealth was incredible. His money-making exploits were unbelievable. He was smuggling English goods past the French blockade during the Napoleonic conflict, and making great profits. This smuggling required an agent in Paris, so Mayer, through his Dalberg connections, got his son James a passport and James went to live in Paris. A large amount of the Landgrave's money was sent to Nathan in England, on the advice of Buderus, for the purpose of buying stock. But Nathan, as he and Buderus had planned, used the money as capitol for other ventures. When the exiled Landgrave began asking for a proof-of-purchase, Buderus and the Rothschild brothers had to come up with all sorts of excuses to protect Nathan's thievery.

Eventually the Landgrave demanded to see receipts, so Nathan quickly bought some stock (the Landgrave had told him to buy the stocks at 72, but their price when he ended up buying them was 62, Nathan pocketed the savings) and they snuck the receipts through the French blockade to the exiled Prince. The Landgrave was satisfied, he had no idea what had really been done with his money. Nathan began making connections in the British government. Probably his greatest early connection was to the Treasury official John Herries. Herries aided Nathan's rise to power in every way possible. He became an intimate friend or Nathan's and eventually a proxy for Rothschild in the British government. Their dealings were kept secret and the public had no idea as to the enormity of Nathan's power. The most incredible example of Nathan's devious schemes is a job he would later describe as the best business he had ever done. Through Nathan's connections in the treasury he learned of the plight of the English army in Spain. The Duke of Wellington (soon to become Nathan's friend) had British troops in Spain ready to attack France, only they lacked one thing - hard cash (the army's financiers would not take paper money), but the government was very short on gold at the time. Nathan knew how to profit from this situation. The East India Company was trying to sell gold that, of course, the government wanted to buy, but the price was so high that officials decided to wait until it dropped.

Nathan stepped in and bought up the gold (using some of the Landgraves money as well as his own). He then proceed to raise the price. When the officials realized the price wouldn't drop they bought the gold and Nathan made a great profit. But the deal didn't stop there. Nathan offered to deliver the gold to Wellington (this was a heavy responsibility because of the French blockade). Hemes went to bat and got Rothschild the job. Nathan's plan was incredible, one biographer said his scheme was 'comparable to burglary in broad daylight.' Nathan's brother, James went to Napoleon's government and told them that Nathan would be importing gold into France and that the British government was upset at the move because it would financially hurt England. Napoleon's government believed his lie and any French police who might have uncovered the plot were bribed. So Nathan was able to ship the gold to Paris with the approval of both the English and French governments.

In Paris the gold was exchanged in French banking firms for cash Wellington could use, and then the Rothschild network carried the money into Spain as France allowed Nathan to fund the war against itself. Eventually some French officials grew suspicious, but Napoleon ignored their reports. The plan went smoothly even though the same officials secretly watched James Rothschild and his brother Carl (who was in on the plot). Wellington eventually defeated Napoleon at Waterloo. The Wellington smuggle was one of the greatest scams in history! In order to better understand the Rothschild's involvement in the defeat of Napoleon we must look at the role played by the Rothschild's second steppingstone - Metternich. Metternich was the Austrian Minister of Foreign Affairs and he led the opposition against Napoleon.

Metternich was a fierce enemy of the revolutionary fires that were spreading through Europe. The Rothschild's got to him through a member of the first Tugendbund (the sexual one), Frederick von Gentz. Gentz was Metternich's right-hand man. Metternich was not financially minded and he relied on Gentz's advise concerning economics (Gentz's ability to handle his private finances was terrible, but he had a knack for political economy). John Herries brought Gentz and the Rothschilds together. The family proceeded to bribe the man into their service. Gentz is an interesting character. He was a Freemason so he was probably occultic. His involvement in the first Tugendbund League points to Immorality. Another interesting fact is that most of his visits to the Rothschilds occurred on occultic holidays, such as Winter Solstice. This may be a coincidence, but it is interesting non-the-less. Gentz called the Rothschilds 'a special species plantarum with its own characteristics.' Gentz steadily brought Metternich into the Rothschild's web.

By at least 1814 Metternich was an ally of the House of Rothschild. His goal was to protect the power of the old aristocracy. His plan was simply to extinguish revolution, and he began with Napoleon. Austria declared war on France and allied Itself with Russia. England Joined them to form a powerful coalition against Napoleon. The battle of Waterloo in 1815 decided the war. Metternich had led Europe to victory with the help of Nathan's delivery network which funded the overthrow. The victory made Metternich the most powerful man in Europe. Due to his speedy courier system, Nathan knew of the outcome of the Waterloo battle before the news reached any other Englander.

A persistent myth is that he made the bulk of his fortune by manipulating the stock exchange with this knowledge. First of all, he did manipulate the market, but he already had a fortune, this only added to It. Second of all, he might not have even made a significant profit (the issue is complicated and debatable. Two years before his defeat, Napoleon had pulled out of Germany. In 1813 the Landgrave William of Hesse-Cassel returned to his province. Said one biographer: 'Earlier it had been the Rothschilds who had asked for favours, now it was the (Landgrave] and Buderus who tried to maintain a close connection.' In 1818 Buderus died. By 1815 Nathan controlled England's finance. He did a large amount of direct business with the English treasury. John Hemes was allowing deals that would hurt England but fill the pockets of the House of Rothschild.

The following quote by one of Nathan's contemporaries describes his eerie countenance: *"Eyes are usually called windows of the soul. But in Rothschild's case you would conclude that the windows are false ones, or that there was no soul to look out them. There comes not one pencil of light from the interior, neither is there any gleam of that which comes from without reflected in any direction. The whole puts you in mind of an empty skin, and you wonder why it stands upright without at least something in it. By and by another figure comes up to it. It then steps two paces aside, and the most inquisitive glance that you ever saw, and a glance more inquisitive than you would have thought of, is drawn out of the fixed and leaden eyes, as if one were drawing a sword from a scabbard..."*

This description is disturbingly similar to either MPD or demonic possession. A Prussian official said that Rothschild had 'an incredible influence upon all financial affairs here in London. It is widely stated ... that he entirely regulates the rate of exchange in the City. His power as a banker is enormous.' 'When Nathan ... (made] a fuss, the Bank of England trembled.' Once he tried to cash a check from his brother Amschel at the Bank, but the Bank refused saying it cashed only its own notes. Nathan's volcano-like temper exploded. The next morning he and nine of his clerks arrived at the Bank and began exchanging bank notes for gold. In one day he had reduced the Bank's gold reserves by a substantial amount. The next day he and his clerks arrived with more bank notes.

A Bank executive nervously asked how long he intended to keep this up. Nathan replied something to the effect of 'The Bank of England refused to take by bills, so I will not keep theirs.' A meeting was quickly called and they decided that from then on the Bank of England would be pleased to cash any Rothschild check Nathan's firm was named N.M. Rothschild and Sons. The firm met in the New Court building and for the sake of brevity will be referred to as New Court. New Court was so powerful that it even became a gold broker for the Bank of England. He also founded the Alliance Insurance Company in England. The Illuminati has the Luciferian belief system that one's evil acts must be balanced by one's good acts. This belief system has led to the philanthropy of the truly evil elite (although much of this charity money goes to fund their objectives). Nathan hated the common masses but his duty called. 'Almoners, particularly those acting on behalf of the poor Jews of London, reported that they got thousands, even hundreds of thousands, of pounds out of Rothschild, but hardly a word and never a courtesy. Nathan did not enjoy charity.

He was good friends with Thomas Buxton, the anti-slavery leader. The famous musicians Mendelssohn and Rossini taught his daughter to play the harp. When Mayer died in 1812, his oldest son Amschel took over the Frankfort firm. Although Amschel was not the head of the family, he was its spokesman to the aristocracy. He was the one who would apply for the honours and titles for his brothers. He has been described as a crotchety worrier who clung to the past. He was socially odd, yet held great dinners that were the talk of the elite. Religion was a big part of his life, to the point of being called monkish. Even though he lived on a grand scale Amschel had no joy. Much of this distress came from the fact that he had failed to have any children. After Napoleon exited Germany a German Confederation was set up, of which Amschel became the treasurer. In a sense this made him the first finance minister of the Prussian Empire which was created by the Confederation. Amschel's sorrow over his lack of children led him to pick prominent young men to treat as his sons. One such man was Otto von Bismark, who would later become the Iron Chancellor of Germany. Amschel was the protector of his mother Gutle, who was the Matriarch of the family. No one could receive full admission into the House of Rothschild by marriage unless she approved. Gutle smiled little and had a harsh tongue. One legend has it that a neighbour asked her whether there was to be peace or war. *"War?"* Gutle replied. *"Nonsense. My boys won't let them."*

Saloman was the second oldest son of Mayer. Along with the other brothers he was constantly travelling through Europe. What separated him from his brothers was his gift of diplomacy. He was more stately and complimentary than the others. Said one banker of Salomon: *"Nobody leaves him without being comforted."* in other words he knew how to kiss up. It was this fact that led the brothers to send him to Vienna, Austria to establish a relationship with the painfully aristocratic Hapsburgs and with vain Metternich. Although the Rothschilds had attempted to enter a close business relationship with the Hapsburgs and Austria, the Austrian royalty kept putting them off. Then Salomon came along. He rode in on a wave of new found Rothschild power. Their name had become famous. One person described it as the *"two magic syllables."*

The brothers had become, as one biographer put it as *"the Archdemons of Progress."* Salomon began to vie for Austrian ties through Gentz and Metternich. Eventually Salomon's diplomacy, Metternich's lobbying, and the below-cost method earlier used on the Landgrave broke down the wall between the House of Rothschild and the Illuminati Hapsburgs. Austria began to employ the Rothschilds on a regular basis. Salomon moved into Vienna and bought a Hotel and a house. Salomon knew how to play Metternich like a piano. He knew the right thing to say at the right time. He knew Metternich's quirks and prejudices, such as his vanity which Salomon easily manipulated. Pretty soon Metternich and Salomon became close friends. The same goes for Metternich's right-hand man, Gentz. Gentz and Salomon were "inseparable." Salomon was also a Freemason. It came to the point where Austria became so controlled by the Rothschilds that the government did not want to refuse the brothers anything. In 1816 Amschel, Salomon, Carl, and James received a title of nobility from the Hapsburgs.

In 1818 the Aix-la-Chapelle Congress met to discuss the future of Europe. Salomon, Carl, Metternich, and Gentz all attended this Congress. It was here that Metternich first met the Rothschilds. Gentz kept the minutes of the Congress, he was called the "Secretary of Europe." A Rothschild scheme at this Congress totally shook the financial institutions of Europe, there was no denying the power of the Rothschilds. *"The divine right of kings had been overthrown by the divine right of money.."* At Aix-la-Chapelle the Rothschilds widened their circle of influence in the Illuminati. Salomon set up a new firm in Vienna. He financially supported Metternich's fight against revolution. Metternich had established the "Vienna System" which controlled Europe after Napoleon's defeat. The Austrian leader began doing what the elite love to do - sending peacekeeping troops into conflicts. 1814-1848 has been described as *"The Age of Metternich"*, but since the Rothschilds financed and controlled him it would be more accurate to call it *"The Age of the House of Rothschild."*

The Order of Vladimir was conferred upon Salomon for his work with Russia. Gioacchino Rossini, the Italian opera composer who wrote Cinderella and the William Tell overture became a good friend of both Salomon and his brother James. In 1822, he, Metternich, Gentz, James, and Cari attended the Verona Congress. This Congress was totally manipulated by the Rothschilds. They profited Immensely by its outcome. Salomon financed the first important Central European railways. The Austrians began saying that they had an Emperor Ferdinand and a King Salomon. When it came to Austrian finances Salomon got the last word. The people would show up at his office and beg for a royal "laying on of hands." He only had to touch a bond or a stock, and its owner went away certain of its rise. Like the other Rothschilds he gave immense charity donations. He bought the huge coal and iron works of Vitkovitz. In 1843 he received permission to purchase inheritable agricultural real estate (many people were against Jews buying private property), and he proceeded to buy up large amounts of land. He obtained the lease of Austria's mercury mines. This and the only other mercury deposit in Spain were controlled by the Rothschilds, creating a world monopoly on a key metal. Salomon was incredibly powerful.

The next son, Carl was the family's chief courier. He was the least intelligent of all the brothers. He was awkward when he spoke and he had a nasty temper. One biographer described him as "punchy". In 1821 Carl was sent to Naples, Italy to oversee loans there that were meant to finance Metternich's forces who had arrived to quell a rebellion. While in Italy the Rothschild "mantle" came upon Carl and he made a series of ingenious deals with the Italian government that forced Naples to pay for its own occupation. He also helped Luigi de Medici of the Black Nobility to re-gain his position as finance minister of Naples, and later did business with the powerful man. Due to his success it was decided that he would stay in Naples and set up his own bank. He became financier to the court, the "financial overlord of Italy." Carl "...wound the Italian peninsula around his hand." He did business with the Vatican, and when Pope Gregory XVI received him by giving him his hand rather than the customary toe to kiss, people realized the extent of his power. The Pope conferred upon him the Order of St. George.

It appears that in Italy Carl became a leader of Carbonarism. After the Bavarian Illuminati was exposed, Carbonarism (or the Alta Vendita) became the major European occult power. Carl's leadership in this group is very significant. In 1818 a secret Alta Vendita document, that Cari had participated in preparing, was sent to the headquarters of Masonry. A copy of this document was lost, and the Masons got very upset, and offered rewards for the return of this copy. The title of the document translates "Permanent Instructions, or Practical Code of Rules; Guide for the Heads of the Highest Grades of Freemasonry."

Last, but absolutely not least, was the youngest son, James. During the Napoleonic conflict James had spent his time between London and Paris, supporting the Rothschild's network of illegal trade with England. After the Wellington smuggle and the defeat of Napoleon, James became an established figure in France. He founded a bank there and began the French branch of the Rothschild family. James was a 33 degree Scottish Rite Mason. At this time the French House was the center of operations for the Rothschilds. Even though successive revolutions would de-throne ruler after ruler, Rothschild power kept the family in control. James was good friends with the leading minister of the Bourbon court, Count de Villele, and he "owned" King Louis Philippe. He also secretly funded Spanish revolutionaries (his agent in Madrid was Monsieur Belin). James yearned for social status.

The pursuit of which was second only to money. He had grown so powerful that the French exchange was deeply affected by all his decisions. Like his brother, Salomon, he pioneered the railroad business in France. He also bought the great Lafite vineyards. His bank, de Rothschild Freres was in a league all its own. No one in France could even wish to be as powerful as James. As Salomon had, James received the Order of Vladimir for his work with the Russian dynasty. He also became a member of the Societe de Antiquites. In the Rothschild tradition (as constituted by Mayer's Will) of trying to keep everything within the family James married his niece, Betty Rothschild, the daughter of Salomon. The Rothschilds main advantage was their incredible courier system.

It kept the 5 Houses connected. In fact, the Hapsburgs used this system quite often. All evidence points to the Rothschild brothers being very powerful within Freemasonry. They were one of the leading families in occultism at that time in Europe. Many prominent Masons of their day praised the brothers. In 1820, due to Metternich's lobbying, Nathan was made Austrian consul in London, and two years later he was made consul-general. James was also made an Austrian consul in Paris. Metternich's promptings also provided something else very important to the family; in 1822 all the brothers and their descendants of either sex were made Barons. This established social position for the Rothschilds. The Gentz-Metternich team was very beneficial to the House of Rothschild. By this time a few papers had run some upsetting articles about the family.

Salomon asked Gentz to censure any more unkind reports and he also commissioned the Illuminist to write a bogus biography on the family that would portray them in a good light. Gentz, now called the "Pen of Europe", proceeded to write legends for the Rothschilds, and the family fully encouraged the propaganda in their social circles. The brothers had a system (based on Mayer's Will) where only family members were partners or owners of the banks. This system is still in use today. The Rothschild banks bought everything up, from mining corporations to national debts. For instance, New Court has been controlling Brazil's debts since 1824. In 1836 Nathan Rothschild, head of the House of Rothschild, died.

The headship was passed on to his younger brother, James, by a vote of all the brothers. In 1830 the signs of masonic-fueled revolution began to appear again. Metternich's "peace of the world" (they always call imperialism "peace") was being threatened. A new king was set up in France, the House of Orange was dethroned in the Netherlands. The fires of revolution were spreading through the masonic network and Metternich began to lose his grip on Europe.

The Revolution of 1848 in France dethroned yet another royal house. James went along with the masonic agenda and financed this revolution, even though he was a friend of the court. The revolution marked the end of Metternich's "Age" and that same year insurrectors chased him and Salomon out of Austria. Neither returned, but a Vienna House had already been established, others would carry it on, under the direction of Salomon's son, Anselm. Metternich's descendants are still close to the House of Rothschild. After this the power of the Rothschilds weakened. By 1855 all five brothers were dead except James. Napoleon III was now in power in France and his advisors were the enemies of James. But Rothschild ingenuity came through again when James got Napoleon III to marry a Rothschild agent. James died in 1868 and the family headship went to Alphonse, his son.

Three cousins now ran the show; Alphonse of the French House, Lionel of the English House and Anselm of the Vienna House - "the new trinity". The three banned together to destroy an enemy bank, French Credit Mobilier. Anselm set up a new firm, Creditanstalt in Vienna to combat the French bank. With the help of Lionel and Alphonse he attacked Credit Mobilier until it collapsed. The new head of the House of Rothschild was Baron Alphonse de Rothschild. Alphonse was a suave, socially elite man. After the rail of France's Credit Mobilier Napoleon ill stepped onto the Rothschild bandwagon. Alphonse was powerful, he had "access" to men like Napoleon III and Bismark of Prussia. The Illuminati decided to get rid of Napoleon Ill, so English Prime Minister Gladstone (friend of the Rothschilds) set things up so that Prussia and France would go to war. Napoleon ill proceeded to attack Prussia and Bismark responded in a furry, defeating France and banishing Napoleon III from the throne. The war indemnities were paid to Bismark (who had a dislike for Alphonse, despite his connections to the family) through the Rothschilds. Alphonse's brother, Edmond, was the one who helped create Israel (this will be discussed further on in the article). Alphonse married another Rothschild, but his love for her was not very strong. The Comtesse de Castiglione was a beautiful woman who was a Marylin Monroe of her day. She was the mistress of Alphonse, his brother Gustave Rothschild (whose daughter married a Sassoon), and Napoleon III. Anselm Rothschild of the Vienna House was a shrewd playboy. He destroyed Credit Mobilier with Creditanstalt, and in 1861 he became a member of the Austrian Imperial House of Lords. Anselm had many mistresses and his wife left him because of his adultery. He died in 1874. Lionel Rothschild of the English House inherited New Court. He financed England's Crimean War, Cecil Rhodes' South African kingdom, vast copper and nitrate mines, and the purchase of the Suez Canal. Lionel's younger brother, Anthony was knighted by the Queen. Another brother, Nathaniel, bought the renowned Mouton vineyards near Bordeaux. Lionel was a good friend of Prime Ministers Disraeli (who was controlled by Rothschild money) and Gladstone.

He also probably paid for Lord John Russell's election as Prime Minister. Lord Tennyson (whose poems are used in programming) attended his house parties. Lionel has been described as "grouchy" and "crotchety." In 1858, Lionel became the first Jew in House of Commons. After eleven tries, the British Parliament gave in and allowed Rothschild to take his seat. Not a single significant political move by Lionel was recorded during his stay in Parliament. He was a member for 15 years. in 1879 he died. After Amschel of the House of Frankfort died without an heir, two of Carl of Italy's sons came to take over the business. But they also remained heirless, bearing only daughters. When the last brother died in 1901, the Frankfort bank was liquidated. I (the author of the 13 bloodlines) believe they did not try to continue the original bank because they knew that Germany was about to be caught up in the turmoil of the world wars, they eventually set up another Frankfort bank after Germany's turmoil.

The House of Italy ended the same way. The one son of Carl who had stayed in Naples produced only daughters, and when Geribaldi's Red Shirts unified Italy this remaining son (out of character for a Rothschild) chose not to accommodate the new powers and moved to France. Thus ended the Italian branch

The Rothschild family reached a peak in its power during the Age of Metternich (1814-1848), but as the century waned, so did Rothschild power. **Lord Rothschild** in his book **The Shadow of a Great Man** quotes a letter sent from Davidson on June 24, 1814 to Nathan Rothschild. *"As long as a house is like yours, and as long as you work together with your brothers, not a house in the world will be able to compete with you, to cause you harm or to take advantage of you, for together you can undertake and perform more than any house in the world."* The closeness of the Rothschild brothers is seen in a letter from Saloman (Salmon) Rothschild to his brother Nathan on Feb. 28, 1815, *"We are like the mechanism of a watch: each part is essential"*. This closeness is further seen in that of the 18 marriages made by Mayer Amschel Rothschild's grandchildren 16 were contracted between first cousins.

They still held a considerable amount of influence but their "veto power" was not as strong as it had been before the Revolutionary overthrow of Metternich's Europe. This lagging power was nothing that could not be reversed though, and last half of the 19th century was spent manufacturing another incredible climb upward. The new rise in power came about during the reign of the "New Trinity" - Alphonse (France), Lionel (England), and Anselm (Vienna). The succeeding generations of these three family leaders were the catalysts of new family order. An excellent example of Rothschild power in the late 19th century is the families dealings with the Illuminati Habsburgs. In order to be court worthy for the Habsburgs you had to have four ancestral lines of nobility and you had to be baptized. Yet Emperor Francis Joseph gave the Rothschilds "a special act of grace" in 1887. From then on, the House was allowed to be on close terms with the Habsburgs. This was a considerable act.

The European nobility are very serious about their aristocratic rules. (Francis Joseph was not very close to the House, but his wife was a good friend of the Rothschilds). Another great example of Rothschild influence is their direct Involvement on both sides of the

Austro-Prussian and Franco-Prussian Wars. Bismarck, dictator of Prussia, was a sort of son to featheriness Amschel of Frankfort. After Amschel died Bismarck remained close to the Rothschilds (although he had occasional quibbles with the family). Bismarck's banker, Bleichroder, was a Rothschild agent and the richest man in Berlin. He was invaluable to Bismarck as the financier of the dictator's wars with Austria and France. In Austria, the Hapsburgs were at least publicly implored by Alphonse and Anthony of Paris and Anselm of Vienna to avoid a war with the ambitious Prussian dictator at all costs. Of all the international banking families, the Rothschilds appeared to be in favour of peace the most, although this was probably a ruse. *"We want peace at any price,"* said Anthony de Rothschild. *"What do we care about Germany, or Austria or Belgium? That sort of thing is out of date."* But the Austrians gave in to Bismarck's provocations and embarked on a war with Prussia in 1866 (the Rothschilds had all congregated in London for a family wedding the year before; it is possible the wedding was used as an excuse to assemble the family together to discuss a plan of action concerning the up-coming events).

Austria had been warned. In seven weeks the war was over, Bismarck had crushed the Austrians. The war had been financed by Rothschild agent, Bleichroder. Then Bismarck began to provoke France. Napoleon III was in the pocket of the head of all the Rothschilds, Alphonse de Rothschild of the Paris House. In fact, the two even shared the same mistress. Alphonse also had "access" to Bismarck. He was on both sides of the track, so to speak. Then, (very possibly under Rothschild direction) Bismarck began to try to put a German prince on the Spanish throne. Napoleon III responded by telling Alphonse that France could not allow such a thing, and unless England intervened diplomatically he would have no choice but to go to war against Prussia.

The Emperor wished to use the Rothschild's courier/agent system to relay this message to England. Baron Alphonse did so, sending the message to Nathaniel de Rothschild at New Court who relayed it to a close family Mend, and former Prime Minister Gladstone (England happened to be without a Prime Minister at that time). Gladstone (shedding. I believe, a light on the family's own opinions) answered the message with a refusal to intervene. The stage was set. Although Bismarck withdrew his Spanish candidate, the frictions between France and Prussia had become irreconcilable. Napoleon III declared war on Prussia in 1870. Explained one biographer: *"No one foresaw the fall of France. Indeed crowned beads and statesmen alike believed that at long last Bismarck. had taken on an impossible task."* Despite everyone's confidence in France, Alphonse sent his family to England.

He apparently knew better. Napoleon III suffered a terrible defeat. His empire came to an end. This war was also financed by the Rothschild agent, Bleichroder. Here comes the great puzzle concerning the whole affair. Biographers, using diaries and such, seem to think the Rothschilds were very distraught over Napoleon III's loss. But It also appears they were behind the whole mess. Perhaps the fear of the unpredictability of the new revolution caused this dismay. Perhaps It is just Rothschild disinformation. Perhaps their plan was to keep connections on both sides of the conflict and ride out the storm, but they were upset because their philosophical loyalty was to France (although I find this hard to believe). The family had their hands in both sides of the conflict, it even appears they manufactured the conflict, why the outcome might have upset them I have no idea. I personally believe the House of Rothschild wanted to get rid of Napoleon Ill and his empire, which is exactly what happened, the third republic was set up in France. After the war the French economy was devastated. The Rothschild agent, Junius Morgan was brought in to help restore the French financial situation. He made a large profit. As you can see the Rothschild's involvement in the Austro-Prussian and Franco-Prussian Wars was significant, even though they were crying peace.

The people of Germany and Turkey have been very close. Remember that Turkey fought on Germany's side in W.W. I. A few powerful Jews, including the Rothschilds were responsible for the wording of the Treaty imposed on Germany that ended W.W. I The treaty gave the Rothschilds the German owned railway rights in Palestine (which had been part of the Turkish Ottoman Empire), thus paving the way for the Rothschilds to have a sure leverage to dictate policy concerning Palestine. The Rothschilds had made loans to Turkey which amounted to almost one hundred million pounds. When the Turkish government collapsed after W.W. I because they were on the losing side, the Rothschilds had a claim on Palestine because of those unpaid Turkish loans. The British government followed the dictates of the Rothschilds. The British were given a mandate over Palestine, and the Rothschilds were able to through their proxies in the British government, to create the steps that led to the nation of Israel.

One item stands out as a person listens to the International Bankers and reads their books. They believe money is what makes the world go round. If you have money, you can do anything. Money is "God", and it is worshipped and served. Even after these families accumulate more than can be spent, these devotees continue selling their souls for this false but powerful god. The great poet-philosopher Heinrich Heine (a Banker's son) said, *"Money is the god of our time, and Rothschild is his prophet."* Following the cue of the Rothschilds, Heinrich Heme, a Jew, signed his name by drawing a Seal of Solomon. Amshel Rothschild is reported to have said, *"Give me control of the economics of a country; and I care not who makes her laws"*. Today his descendents meet twice daily in London to dictate to the world what the world price of gold will be. They also dictate what the "Federal Reserve System" will do with America's finances.

Alphonse, of the "New Trinity", was the 4th bead of the House of Rothschild. He was an aristocratic man and friend of many prominent leaders of his day. He was also an adulterer, his most notable affair being with the Comtesse de Castiglione. He and his wife were called "the most lavish entertainers of their day." The sophisticated Alphonse was even friends with Belgium's King Leopold and England's Prince of Whales. He also improved upon his Inherited network of Rothschild agents, an underground system that would continue to grow well after his death. He was one of best Informed men of his day. His older sister Charlotte married Nathaniel of the English House. His brother Gustave also had an affair with the Comtesse de Castiglione.

His youngest brother, Edmond #1 was a genius and a main figure in the creation of a Jewish homeland in Israel. He helped divide the world's oil between Shell and the Rockefeller's Standard Oil. His other brother Salomon James married a Frankfurt Rothschild and is the subject of a weird circumstance described by biographer Virginia Cowles. *"In 1864 Baron James' third son, the brilliantly clever Salomon [James], dropped dead. The boy had become a compulsive gambler which had caused his father great anxiety, as anyone with the Rothschild name was given unlimited financial credit. Apparently Salomon died of a heart attack which fascinated the Goncourt brothers"*.

Imagine it; a Rothschild dead of a paroxysm over money. *"However, if the Goncourt brothers had known the details of a previous heart attack suffered by Salomon they would have been even more enthralled. Three years earlier Salomon had 'dropped dead'. He had been placed in a coma and, according to Jewish custom, carried into every room in the house. One of the pall bearers had stumbled, the coffin had crashed Into a door and -Salomon had woken up! Not for another three years was he well and truly buried."* This story could lead to all sorts of speculation. De Rothschild Freres, the French House bank, was very powerful. It got its hands Into electrical Industries, the development of the Mediterranean Railway and North African business. It also controlled, with the British

House, the Baku oil fields in Russia, which made the Rothschilds the main competitors of the Rockefeller trust. The oil business was principally run by Edmond #1.

When Alphonse died in 1905, the new generation of the French House came under the charge of Baron Edouard, a quiet and very rich man. Edouard was a director of the Bank of France. Baron Edouard also ran the de Rothschild Freres with his cousin, Robert (who married a Beer), son of Gustave (Robert's sister, Alice Caroline married Sir Edward A. Sassoon). These two carried de Rothschild Freres through the tumult of the first world war. Their policies were passive, as they extremely protective of the family wealth. Baron Edouard and Robert had close business dealings with J.P. Morgan. One of the operations of the Morgan-French Rothschild combine involved economic manipulation that allowed the Vienna House to almost fully regain the losses that the Austrian Rothschilds had incurred during WWI. The son of Edmond #1, James Armand de Rothschild, carried on the Israel work of his father after Edmond #1's death in 1934. James Armand's brother Maurice was the black sheep of the Rothschild's new French generation. Maurice was a banker and a Senator in the French Parliament. Maurice was a very scandalous figure in the aristocratic scene. He was known as Don Juan de Rothschild. Said one biographer: *"Some people went as far as to claim that ... one had to be seduced or at least pinched by Baron Maurice if one was a woman, or affronted by Baron Maurice, if a man. No other personage surpassed him in enriching the delicious scandal of his times."* Thus a new French generation began the 20th century, the undynamic Baron Edouard leading the way.

Lionel de Rothschild, of the "New Trinity", brought the British House into the late 19th century. Lionel was a very powerful man. He ran New Court shrewdly, and financed many prominent ventures, such as Cecil Rhodes' gold and diamond mines, and the purchase of the Suez Canal. He was also the first Jewish member of Parliament. His sister, Charlotte married another member of the "New Trinity", Anselm of Vienna. Another sister married into the soon-to-be extinct Italian House.

Lionel's brother Anthony - who described the Rothschilds as complete slaves to business married a Montefiore, and was knighted by the Queen - thus Sir Anthony de Rothschild. Lionel's next brother, Nathaniel, was the father of the Mouten Rothschilds. Nathaniel, though of the British House, loved France and moved to Paris in 1851. In 1853 he bought vineyards that became known as Mouton Rothschild, and he lived at these vineyards several months of the year. His descendants, the Mouton Rothschilds, are citizens of France but are of the British House (except that their mother was a French Rothschild, but the male lineage is the most important in the Rothschild family). Another of Lionel's brothers, Baron Mayer, married a Cohen. Mayer built a spectacular house, Mentmore Towers.

Said one woman: *"I do not believe that the Medicis were ever so lodged at the height of their glory."* The Mentmore Towers were turned over to Mayer's daughter, Hannah, when he died. Hannah married the Earl of Roseberry in 1878. The Earl of Roseberry became Prime Minister of England in 1894-95. The Mentmore Towers are still owned today by the son of Hannah, the current Earl of Roseberry. The Baron Mayer de Rothschild was a member of Parliament (never made a speech), and loved horse breeding and racing. He was the "sporting" member of the family. When Lionel died in 1879 a new generation of British Rothschild appeared on the scene led by Lionel's aristocratic son, Nathaniel "Natty" de Rothschild. Natty took control of New Court, the Rothschild's British bank He was elected to the House of Commons in 1865, and then, in 1885, Queen Victoria made him a Lord and he entered the House of Lords - the first Lord Rothschild. The Intelligent and extroverted Natty was an ornate speechmaker, unlike his father, Lionel, and uncle Mayer. Lord Natty has been described as exclusive, lofty, humourless, *"one of the three rudest men in England,"* selective, blunt, aloof, powerful and a man with an explosive temper.

A perfect representative of the ruling class. Said one biographer: *"Although Natty lacked the soaring Intelligence of his rough, unsociable grandfather [Nathan, 2nd head of the Rothschilds] he had a strong personality and the authoritative air of a man who is not accustomed to being contradicted."* Lord Natty was a good friend of Prime Ministers Disraeli and Gladstone. He played the philanthropy game of the rich very well. The powerful head of New Court was known for his charities, especially to the Jews - he was called "King of the Jews" as have many other Rothschilds. The haughty Lord Rothschild was even chairman of the British Red Cross. Lord Natty won the hearts of the London police (an effective measure when one is in the Illuminati). Every Christmas he presented them with a "handsome cheque," and any officer could receive a four course meal at his home. Hence, Rothschild carriages were always given the right of way in traffic. In business Lord Natty was very conservative.

He did not take very many risks and looked only for safe family investments. His self-confidence told him to manage his wealth himself and not trust his Investments with people who might strike a painful blow to his riches. *"Natty was brusque and humourless and did not suffer fools gladly."* Nor could he allow his money into the hands of a fool, caution was a necessary device as far as he was concerned. According to the writer Frank Harris the Lord Rothschild told him: I go to the bank [New Court] every morning and when I say 'no' I return home at night without a worry. But when I say 'yes' It's like putting your finger into a machine - the whirring wheels may drag your whole body in after the finger. New Court was very powerful at this time, for example It controlled the Ruby Mines in Burma, and the banks operations covered most of South America. Brazil was the Rothschild's "preserve" in South America, as Argentina was the "preserve" of London's other major banking family - the Barings.

While Lord Natty's two brothers, Alfred and Leo, helped run New Court, Natty was almost totally calling the shots. *"Natty stood for finance, Alfred for the arts, Leo for sport."* Son of the Queen, the Prince of Whales Albert College, Cambridge. They became good friends and soon the Prince was close friends with most of the British House and others of the Rothschild clan, including Natty's brothers, Alfred and Leo. The group of friends became known as "The Marlborough Boys", named after the Prince's Marlborough House at which they regularly gathered. "The Marlborough Boys" were intent on having fun. The small circle of partiers were living a life where "wit took precedence over etiquette..." The Prince probably had a hand in convincing the Queen to grant Natty peerage. The Rothschilds were suspected, rightfully so, of financing the Prince's investments and paying off his debts. The Prince later became King Edward VII of England. As you can see, Rothschild influence extends far and wide. Alfred, Lord Natty's brother, was an eccentric man.

He had a zebra four-in-hand, a pet goat, a private philharmonic which be conducted and a private circus which he would ringmaster. Needless to say, the Baron Alfred was a man with flair. *"He loved music, clothes, furniture, paintings, beautiful women and, above all, luxury."* He was also Involved in business - he worked at New Court and was the first Jewish Director of the Bank of England. The Baron was among those in charge of the last rites over Disraelis' dead body (Queen Victoria might have had an affair with Disraeli that the Rothschilds covered up). Alfred's demeanour was like that of a diplomat and was very Interested in foreign affairs. He was instrumental in easing the English - German tensions around the turn of the century. It was not to the Rothschilds benefit to have war. Alfred parted with tradition when he gave, in his will, his great wealth to his daughter. His daughter, in turn, used some of that Rothschild money to fund the expedition into Egypt that discovered Tutankhamen's grave.

Lord Natty's other brother, Baron Leopold de Rothschild, was not much of a businessman. He much more preferred horse racing and automobiles. He had the reputation of being a kind man. His wife, Maria Perugia, was the sister of Mrs. Arthur Sassoon. The first world war supposedly hurt the British House financially (although it appears their missing riches only went underground), but as always they bounced right back (in the eyes of the public). Thus a new British House of Rothschild began the 20th century, lofty Lord Natty leading the way.

Baron Anselm von Rothschild, of the "New Trinity", brought the Austrian House to the close of the 19th century. Anselm lived under the reputation of his father, Salomon, and his uncle, Amschel (with whom he spent a good deal of his time). But he did not necessarily ride their coat tails, he proved his worth, so to speak. His most notable act being the creation Creditanstalt, which destroyed the financial challenger of the Rothschilds, Credit Mobilier. As a young man Anselm was a bit wild and frivolous, so hi. father sent him away to apprentice. Anselm ended up working under his uncle Amschel in the Frankfort bank (which was doomed to future liquidation). Frankfort mellowed him, and he lived there for 30 years. When his father died in 1855, Anselm returned to Vienna to take his father's place. He became a very active businessman. Anselm had influence in the Habsburg court. Baron Anselm's *"name was inscribed in the Golden Book of the capital and in 1861 he had been made a member of the Imperial House of Lords*." He also knew bow to incur his wrath.

One club in Austria refused him membership because he was a Jew. Baron Anselm simply bought a sewage disposable unit and installed it right next to the club. The smell was horrible. The dub then tried to give him a membership card, to mend the problem, but he returned the card doused in perfume and informed them that he would not move his sewage unit. The Rothschilds set off the financial crisis of 1873 in Vienna. S.M. Rothschild und Sohne totally controlled Hungarian finance. And Creditanstalt was the financial powerhouse of the Habsburg realm. Anselm's children carried on in Vienna after he died in 1874. Ills eldest son Nathaniel was an aristocrat, who was not interested in banking, only fine art and history. Anselm's second son, Ferdinand, moved to England. Only Baron Albert von Rothschild, Anselm's youngest son had a business inclination and be was chosen to take over Creditanstalt. Baron Albert and Nathaniel were the two richest men in Austria.

Baron Albert *"held controlling interest in innumerable industries ranging from coal to railways; and when, in 1881, he converted the famous six-per-cent Gold Loan to Hungary the bank was recognized as the greatest financial force in the empire."* Albert was afraid of the common people and he built a mansion that was more of a castle than a house. Its wails were seven feet high, and on top of that sat another eight feet of iron fencing. Anselm's second son, Baron Ferdinand, was a member of Prince Edward's "Marlborough Boys." He remained in England, becoming a naturalized citizen. "Ferdy" as he was called was an intellectual socialite. He built an incredibly grandiose mansion named Waddeson Manor; one of the most awesome of all the Rothschild homes. The Manor was so marvellous that the Queen herself paid it a visit. Visitors to its halls ranged from the Empress Frederick to the Shah of Persia. Ferdinand also had a zoo. One of Anselm's daughters also moved to England - Alice. The unmarried Alice was a very "tyrannical" person. In fact, she even yelled at the Queen when she saw her inadvertently trampling a flower-bed. The Queen and Alice remained friends, and the Queen nicknamed Alice *"The All Powerful" Alice ... reigns absolutely,"* wrote a cousin. *"There is nothing constitutional about this monarchy. No wonder the Queen has named her 'The Al Powerful'..."* When Ferdinand died Alice received Waddeson Manor. Head of the Austrian House, Albert died in 1911.

His son (none of his brothers had any children), Baron Louis became the head of the house. Louis' brothers, Alphonse and Eugene, were "gentlemen of leisure." Baron Louis and his two brothers both served in the Austrian army during World War I (the war supposedly split the Vienna House from the French and English Houses, I don't believe this). The Austrian House's wealth had to go underground during the war. After the war ended the French and English Houses put the Austrian House back "on their feet again." Thus a new Austrian House began the 20th century, powerful Albert and suave Baron Louis leading the way.

George Peabody, a Massachusetts's trader, set up a banking house - George Peabody & Co. - in London in 1837. He became regarded as a financial ambassador in London. Carrol Quigley attributes the use of tax-exempt foundations for manipulation of society to Peabody, seen in his Illuminati Peabody foundation. Daniel Colt Gilman, a member of the Skull & Bones and first President of the Carnegie Institution, was involved in the establishment of the Peabody foundation. He was in such high regard by the elite that they have erected a statue of him across from the Bank of England. Peabody was getting old and needed a younger partner. Junius Morgan, of Hartford, Connecticut, was recommended to Peabody. In 1854 Junius and his family arrived in London to join George Peabody & Co. When the elite's concocted American Civil War broke out, Peabody and Junius Morgan raised loans for the North. It appears Junius played both sides of the war. Ralph Epperson claims Junius was one of the Rothschild agents who shipped supplies to the South. When Peabody retired in 1864 Junius took over the business.

The firm was re-named JS. Morgan & Co. That same year Junius' son, J.P. Morgan, became a junior partner in the firm. A year later J.P. left for America to represent the firm in the New York. After the end of the Franco-Prussian War, Junius Morgan was called on to help restore the French economy. Around this time his bank was talked of as a rival to the Rothschild's New Court, but Junius was a Rothschild agent, when he prospered so prospered the Rothschilds and the Illuminati. J.S. Morgan & Co. was one of the Rothschild's great power tools in the United States. In 1869 Junius' son, J.P. Morgan went to London to met with the Rothschilds. They laid out the plans to form Northern Securities, a company that would act as an agent for New Court in the US. J.P. ruling as a proxy for the family. In 1871 Junius' son, J.P. Morgan, made an alliance with Tony Drexel, heir to the powerful Philadelphia bank. Their firm - Drexel, Morgan & Co. -resided in an extravagant new building on Wall St., which is still Morgan headquarters today. After the Europeans got over their lack of confidence at the end of the Civil War, money began to stream across the ocean to the US., providing massive profit for the firm. It set out to finance the growing number of industrial projects in America. The House of Morgan was getting extremely rich.

Junius retired in 1879 and J.P. took over JS. Morgan & Co., reorganizing It under the title J.P. Morgan & Co. *"J.P. Morgan soon became a symbol of the growing centralization of American money."* He was very monopolistic. His agents would create cartels through 'Morganization." By 1896 the Illuminati families Payne, Whitney and the Vanderbilts all bad money in Morgan-Guarantee Company which was run by the *"J.P. Morgan and Guggenheim outfits."*

At a certain point he controlled nearly half the American railroad system. He established the United States Steel Corp. *("based on Andrew Carnegie's Pittsburgh Steel mills")* In 1901 by raising the "unprecedented" amount of $1.4 billion. J.P. was adept at creating financial syndicates for the Illuminati, joint efforts to further the *"Great Plan."* President

Welliam Mckinley began prosecuting the Rothschild's Morgan-run Northern Securities under the anti-trust laws in 1900. In 1901 Mckinley ran for a second term and appointed a new vice-president, Theodore Roosevelt, a lock, stock and barrel Illuminatus. Less than a year later he was assassinated. When "Teddy" became president the prosecution of Northern Securities stopped. For this reason some people think Mckinley's death was ordered by J.P. Morgan and the Rothschilds. He was able to set up a syndicate, with the help of Rothschild agent, August Belmont, Jr., that bailed the U.S. out of a Treasury depletion. The syndicate raised $65 billion in gold. The sum would be repaid by an issue of bonds. J.P. received some criticism for the strict terms of the deal. For 5 months in early 1907, J.P. Morgan was in Europe, traveling back and forth between London and Paris, presumably visiting the Rothschild House's there. A. Ralph Epperson writes: *"Apparently the reason Morgan was in Europe was because the decision was being made to have Morgan precipitate a bank panic in America. When he returned, he started rumours that the Knickerbocker Bank in New York was insolvent."*

Panic ensued. People began a mass withdrawal of their deposits - a run. The Knickerbocker run had a domino effect, other banks had runs and the Panic of 1907 "was complete." J.P. Morgan oversaw the banking communities response to the Panic of 1907. The whole Incident helped the elite push for a central bank. One man who knew of the plot was historian Frederick Lewis Allen, who wrote in LIFE magazine: *"...certain chroniclers have arrived at the ingenious conclusion that the Morgan interests took advantage of the unsettled conditions during the autumn of 1907 to precipitate the Panic, guiding It shrewdly as it progressed, so that it would kill off rival banks, and consolidate the pre-eminence of the banks within the Morgan orbit."* The Panic of 1907 made people want a powerful central bank that could "protect" the common man from the "abuses of the Wall Street bankers."

This whole thing eventually led to the creation of the Federal Reserve. One of the men with the Morgan financial groups was Harold Stanley. Stanley was a member of the Skull & Bones. After J.P.'s death a Morgan firm became Morgan, Stanley & Co. J.P. Morgan died in 1913. His son, Harvard educated J.P. Morgan, Jr. took over (most conspiratorial writers do not make a distinction between these two). J.P. Morgan, Jr ran the bank with a team of managers that was led by Thomas Lamont. Morgan, Jr was, like his father, a power-hungry international banker. He was famous for his handling of Immense foreign loans. Most Importantly J.P. Morgan, Jr appears to have followed in the footsteps of the former heads of the House of Morgan by working with the Rothschilds.

Jekyll Island And The Federal Reserve

The Illuminati interests wanted to create a Central Bank in America. They wanted to build the Federal Reserve. First, they needed a bunch of banking crisis' that would push public opinion towards a Federal Reserve system. These were provided by the Illuminati, including J.P. Morgan's Knickerbocker Panic of 1907. Second, they needed a favourable U.S. president in office. Rothschild agent Colonel House provided this by getting Woodrow Wilson elected. The American people were being conditioned. To provide the 'reform of the American banking system' a congressional National Monetary Commission was created and a man related to the Rockefellers, Nelson Aldrich, was put in charge. For two years this Commission travel around Europe hob-nobbing with the Illuminati and getting directions as to how the central bank should be set up. Then the Commission returned in 1910, and Nelson Aldrich went to a secret meeting at the Jekyll Island Hunt Club in Georgia to write the legislation for an American central bank to be run by the Illuminati.

Others at the Jekyll island meeting were these Illuminati men - A. Platt Andrew, Frank Vanderlip (of a Kuhn-Loeb & Company bank), Henry Davidson (of J.P. Morgan), Charles Norton (of a Morgan bank), Paul Warburg (of Kuhn-Loeb & Company and brother-in-law of Schiff), Benjamin Strong (of another Morgan company). Most of these men were connected to Jacob Schiff or J.P. Morgan, who in turn were agents for the House of Rothschild. The Jekyll Island Hunt Club was even owned by J.P. Morgan. The Federal Reserve bill was sneakily passed through congress in the winter of 1913 and President Woodrow Wilson signed the bill into law. The Illuminati, particularly the Rockefellers and Rothschilds, had usurped the financial power of the United States.

The first governor of the New York branch of the Federal Reserve was Benjamin Strong. The first governor of the FED's board of directors was Paul Warburg. Both connected to Schiff, J.P. Morgan, Jr, and the House of Rothschild. The FED has been an effective tool of the Illuminati and the Rothschilds, creating crisis such as the Great Depression (which J.P. Morgan, Jr was very involved in creating). Apparently (according to Congressman Louis McFadden), the Depression helped consolidate financial power over the US., putting It in the hands of the Rothschild banking alliance between J.P. Morgan's First National Bank group and Schiff's Kuhn, Loeb-run National City Bank. The Great Depression also lead to Roosevelt's New Deal.

The Schiffs became Rothschild agents, and like most agents of the Rothschilds they eventually became very rich and powerful. The most prominent of the Schiffs was Jacob Henry Schiff. Jacob was born in Frankfort in 1847, and was sent by the Rothschild/Schiff network to America to make his fortune (Much like the Astors sent John Jacob Astor). Jacob Schiff arrived in New York in 1865. Ten years later he became the partner of the Illuminati firm Kuhn, Loeb & Company. Ten years after that he became Its president. Directing Rothschild and Illuminati affairs from this seat of authority. Jacob Schiff was also on the board of directors of Central Trust Company, Western Union. and Wells Fargo Company. Like most elite, he gave vast amounts of money to charity.

Rothschild Influence On Wars

Rothschild connections to the first world war are an excellent example of controlled conflict. On the Allied side the British and French Houses financially supported their countries battles. Some Rothschilds were even soldiers, although they didn't see much action. J.P. Morgan Bank was a big financial help to the Allied cause. It was the Allies *"purchasing agent"* until the U.S. entered the war. It also created a syndicate that financed "modernization" in China, to help defend that country against the Japanese threat. The elite wanted America in the war. Historian Charles Tansill noted: *"... the large banking Interests were deeply interested in the World War because of wide opportunities for large profits. On August 3, 1914, even before the actual clash of arms, the French firm of Rothschild Freres cabled to Morgan and Company in New York suggesting the floatation of a loan of $100,000,000, a substantial part of which was to be left in the United States, to pay for French purchases of American goods."*

The Lusitania was a ploy. It was packed with some Morgan owned ammunition, had been given over to England as a member of the navy, and despite the warnings of the Germans was sent Into a naval war zone, specifically to be a target - the catalyst for America's entrance to the war. A knowledgeable American State Department failed to warn the US. citizens aboard the ship of the voyages definite danger. Churchill ordered the Lusitanina's naval escort to return to port, and the fated ship was left unprotected, to be sunk. Rothschild agent Colonel House probably knew of this plot, records point to a discussion of it between him and Sir Edward Grey of England. Historian Colin Simpson called the sinking of the Lusitania the "foulest act of wilful murder ever committed on the seas.'

On the Axis side the Rothschild network was also funnelling money. Another family allied to the Rothschilds was the Warburgs. Max Warburg, brother of Kuhn-Loeb's Paul Warburg. ran a family financial powerhouse in Frankfort, Germany (one of the reasons the Rothschilds were able to liquidate their Frankfort bank, the Warburgs would run things). Max was the head of the German secret police during WWI. The Warburg connection is reported to have helped the Axis powers financially. At the end of the war in 1919, the Treaty of Versailles meetings were attended by Rothschild connected men like Paul and Max Warburg, John Foster Dulles (of Kuhn-Loeb), Colonel House, Thomas Lamont (of Morgans) and Allen Dulles (of Kuhn-Loeb). The harsh terms of the Treaty of Versailles totally set the stage for World War II. Said one delegate: *"This is no peace; this is only a truce for twenty years."*

Sure enough, in 1939 the second World War started. Another product of the Versailles meetings was the elite's Charter for the League of Nations - the Illuminati's first attempt at creating a global institution. The League of Nations failed. This called for the need to create a think tank/special Interest organization that could promote the new world order. Thus the creation of the Foreign Relations Institutions - the CFR., RIIA, etc. This will be discussed in a bit. World War I helped create a Communist State.

Max Warburg funded Lenin and his revolutionaries. Jacob Schiff gave a known $20 million to Lenin. J.P. Morgan & Co. helped finance the Bolshevik revolution. Alfred de Rothschild also helped finance the Bolsheviks.

Connection to World War II The second World War was also controlled by Illuminati and Rothschild interests. The Great Depression did not only occur in America. It also swept Europe. The economic depression in Europe, coupled with an extremely harsh Versailles Treaty helped fan the flames of the nationalistic fires that swept Germany.

Hitler was a member of the most powerful occultic secret society in Germany. He penetrated the inner circle of this society where Satanism was practiced. Hitler was dedicated to Satan's Empire - an evil puppet. He was brought into this evil group by Dietrich Eckart who is supposed to have said on his deathbed: *"Follow Hitler. He will dance, but it is I who have called the tune! I have initiated him into the 'Secret Doctrine'; opened his centers in vision and given him the means to communicate with the Powers. Do not mourn for me: I shall have influenced history more than any German."* In the last article we discussed the possibility of Hitler having been of Rothschild discordance. Consider this - he probably had satanic bloodline, he had the backing of a powerful satanic society, he had sold his soul to Satan, and he had the financial backing of the Illuminati. Is it any wonder that he rose from obscurity, poverty and Imprisonment to become one of the most powerful men to ever live? I believe that it is even safe to speculate that Hitler was totally controlled by a demonic spirit(s); that he simply gave himself over to Satan's control. An ex-member of the Satanic Hierarchy of the Illuminati expressed a belief to me that there have been certain evil men through-out history that have totally given themselves over to possession by Satan. That these men (Hitler, Genghis Khan, for example) have been anti-christ types, simply human containers for the residence of a very powerful demonic spirit, or even Satan himself.

The ex-illuminati member believed that when Satan no longer had need for the body of his anti-christ he would discard it with death and find another willing soul to sacrifice his bodily control to the devil. These evil figures would not be The Anti-Christ, explained the informant, but would have allowed themselves to taken over by "the spirit" of the Anti-

Christ. This is just a theory, but I believe it has certain merit. If it is true, it paints an interesting picture of Hitler and the ruling class that created him. Hitler's main source of economic power was from the I.G. Farben chemical cartel, and I.G. Farben in turn was controlled by the Illuminati. The I.G. Farben cartel was created by loans from Wall Street in what has been called the Dawes plan. Carroll Quigley calls the Dawes Plan "largely a J.P. Morgan production."

The J.P. Morgan Group set up the loan to I.G. Farben, which created Hitler. *"Without the capital supplied by Wall Street, there would have been no I.G. Farben in the first place, and almost certainly no Adolf Hitler and World War II."* Henry Ford merged his German assets with I.G. Farben in 1928. The cartel created the lethal Zyklon B gas that was used to exterminate the Jews. It was also involved in the torture experimentations that led to mind control methods, such as Monarch Programming. Do you see what happened? A Rothschild agent set up a cartel that was directly involved in the horrible persecution of the Jews. Still the family maintains the illusion of being totally supportive of their race. At first Germany had a significant disadvantage if they were to embark on a second world war. The nation had a fuel shortage, but the Illuminati fixed this problem. The Germans were able to fight WWII through the use of synthetic fuels that were created by the hydrogenation process (turning coal into gasoline).

This process was discovered by I.G. Farben. Hydrogenation technology would not have been fully developed by WWII, but I.G. Farben made a deal with Rockefeller's Standard Oil, who was able to complete the research, facilitating the war. Interestingly, I.G. Farben plants were not targeted by the bombing raids on Germany. By the end of the war the refineries had experienced only 15% damage. William Dodd, American ambassador to Germany before WWII, wrote President Roosevelt: *"At the present moment, more than a hundred American corporations have subsidiaries here or cooperative understandings. The DuPonts have their allies in Germany that are aiding in the armament business. Their chief ally is the I.G. Farben Company... Standard Oil Company ... sent $2,000,000 here in December, 1933 and has made $500,000 a year helping Germans [improve hydrogenation technology] ... The International Harvester Company president told me their business here rose 33% year, but they could take nothing [earnings] out [except in goods]. 'Even our airplanes people have secret arrangements with Krupps. 'General Motors Company [which was controlled by the J.P. Morgan Group] and Ford do enormous business here through their subsidiaries and take no profits out."*

Germany needed the capital of these, and many more American companies in order to wage a war. I.G. Farben had a holding company in the United States called American I.G. Farben. Paul Warburg, his brother Max (head of Germany's secret police during WWI), and Warburg agent Herman Metz were some of the members of the board of directors of the American I.G. Farben. Other directors included Rockefeller/International banking men (Edsel Ford, Charies Mitchell, Walter Teagle, etc). Three Germans on the Board of Governors were convicted as war criminals after the war, but the elite Americans fore-mentioned were not, even though they participated in the same criminal decisions as those who were punished. According to author Eustice Mullins, Hitler met with Allen and John Foster Dulles in 1933. The Dulles brothers were acting as legal representatives of Schiff and Warburg's Kuhn, Loeb & Co, which was an Integral part of the Rothschild network.

Mullins claims Kuhn & Loeb had extended large short-term credits to Germany, and needed to ensure the repayment of these loans. The Dulles supposedly assured Hitler he would receive the funds necessary to be installed as Chancellor of Germany, if he promised to repay the debts. One of the largest tank manufacturers for Germany was

Opel, which was controlled by the J.P. Morgan Group. Another company connected to the J.P. Morgan Group was Bendix Aviation, 'which supplied data [to Germany] on automatic pilots, aircraft Instruments and aircraft and diesel engine starters.' The examples go on and on. There is much more that could be written on this subject. The manufactured Pearl Harbor attack allowed Roosevelt to enter America into the war. A second world war had been created by the Illuminati, with the help of the Rothschild/Morgan/Warburg/Schiff syndicate. After the end of the war, the Tribunals that investigated Nazi war criminals censored "*any materials recording Western assistance to Hitler*," said historian Antony C. Sutton.

Influence towards Globalism World War II facilitated the American acceptance of a global "*peacekeeping*" institution - the United Nations. After the U.S. had rejected the first attempt to create such an institution in the League of Nations, the Illuminati decided to create an arm of the Rothschild funded Round Table groups which could help influence western society towards the embracement of globalism. The original idea was to create an international special interest group of advisors that would promote a New World Order, called the Institute of on International Affairs. The plan eventually changed, the Institute was split up so that separate groups could influence separate governments without having the appearance of a conspiracy. These groups were formed at what are called the Hotel Majestic meetings.

Baron #1 Edmond de Rothschild of France was the main force behind these meetings, and all the founders of these groups were men who had met with his approval. Chief of these was Rothschild agent Colonel Edward Mandell House. One of these groups was the Council on Foreign Relations (CFR). The CFR Handbook of 1936 explains how It was established. 'On May 30, 1919, several leading members of the delegations to the Paris Peace Conference met at the Hotel Majestic in Paris to discuss setting up an international group which would advise their respective governments on international affairs.... It was decided at this meeting to call the proposed organization the Institute of International Affairs.

At a meeting on June 5, 1919, the planners decided it would be best to have separate organizations cooperating with each other. Consequently, they organized the Council on Foreign Relations (CFR), with headquarters in New York. and a sister organization, the Royal Institute of International Affairs [RIIA], in London, also known as the Chatham House Study Group, to advise the British Government. A subsidiary organization, the Institute of Pacific Relations, was set up to deal exclusively with Far Eastern Affairs [and facilitated the Pearl Harbor attack]. Other organizations were set up in Paris and Hamburg, the Hamburg branch being called the Institut fur Auswartige Politik. and the Paris branch being known as Centre d'Etudes de Politicque Etrangere... I have never seen any research on the Institut fur Auswartige Politik in Germany. It would be interesting to see how this group was involved with the elite and the creation of WWII.

- A group of Illuminati wise men took the plans laid out at the Hotel Majestic meetings and formed the CFR.
- The founders included; Colonel Edward Mandell House (a Rothschild agent), John Foster Dulles (of Rothschild connected Kuhn, Loeb & Co.), and Allen Dulles (also of Kuhn, Loeb & Co.).
- The CFR was officially founded on July 29, 1921.
- Money for the founding came from J.P. Morgan, Bernard Baruch, Otto Kahn, Jacob Schiff, Paul Warburg, and John D. Rockefeller, among others.
- The funding for the RIIA in London came primarily from the Astor family.
- Rothschild-connected Paul Warburg was on the original board of directors of the CFR.

As you can clearly see, the Rothschild network had significant influence in the creation of the foreign relation groups. This influence continues today. The Rothschild's power within the secret "Society of the Elect" and the Round Table Groups extended to the semi-public CFR, RIIA, etc. The House of Rothschild was up in arms with their fellow elites; managing the creation of the New World Order. Should there be a Part 3 to this series, it will Investigate individual Rothschilds from the world war era up into the modern day world, and their continuing involvement in the Illuminati.

Extent Of Rothschild Power

According to one source *"it was estimated that they controlled half the wealth of the world."* The Federal Reserve Bank of New York was controlled by five banks which owned 53% of its stock. These five banks were controlled by Nathan M. Rothschild & Sons of London. Control over the U.S. Fed is basically control over the world's money. That fact alone shows how immense the Rothschild Power is. If one examines who has been appointed to head the Fed, and to run it, the connections of the Federal" Reserve System to the Rothschilds can further be seen. Another private enterprise using the name Federal that the Rothschilds also direct is Federal Express. Anyone else might be taken to court for making their businesses sound like their government, not the Rothschilds. It is appropriate for them to appropriate the name of Federal, because by way of MI6 via the CIA they instruct the U.S. government. Senators are bought and paid off by their system, as investigators of the BCCI are discovering.

In terms of allies, the Rothschilds and Rockefellers are only two of thirteen controlling families of the Illuminati. Two Jewish families that appear to be prominent are the Oppenheims and the Oppenheimers. A. Oppenheim was situated in Cologne. The Oppenheimers were early members of the Bavarian Illuminati. The Bund der Gerechten (League of the Just) was an illuminati front run mainly by Jews who were Satanists. This Bund financed in part by the Rothschilds paid the Satanist and Mason Karl Marx to write the Communist Manefesto. The Jew Gumpel Oppenheim was in the inner circle of the Bund. His relative Heinrich Oppenheim masterminded the communist revolution of 1848 in Germany. The Communist Party's official histories even accept the Bund as the predecessor of Communism. The Oppenheimers apparently are close to the Rothschilds. J. Robert Oppenheimer of the CFR was exposed as a communist. Harry Oppenheimer, an international banker, is chairman of the Jewish De Beers world-wide diamond monopoly, and chairman of the Anglo-American Corp. Oppenheimers can be found in important financial positions in the U.S. They help run around 10 large foundations, including the Oppenheimer Haas Trust of NY for the care of needy Jewish children.

Management of the Catholic and Czars' wealth and the capture of the Orthodox Church's wealth. Early in the 19th century the Pope came to the Rothschilds to borrow money. The Rothschilds were very friendly with the Pope, causing one journalist to sarcastically say *"Rothschild has kissed the hand of the Pope... Order has at last been re-established."* The Rothschilds in fact over time were entrusted with the bulk of the Vatican's wealth. The Jewish Ency., Vol. 2, p.497 states, *"It is a somewhat curious sequel to the attempt to set up a Catholic competitor to the Rothschilds that at the present time (1905) the latter are the guardians of the papal treasure."* Researcher Eustice Mullins writes that the Rothschilds took over all the financial operations of the worldwide Catholic Church in 1823.

Today the large banking and financial business of the Catholic Church is an extensive system interlocked with the Rothschilds and the rest of the International Banking system. The great wealth of the Russian Czars was entrusted to the Rothschilds, $35 million with the Rothschild's Bank of England, and $80 million in the Rothschild's Paris bank. The Rothschilds financed the Russian Revolution which confiscated vast portions of the Orthodox Church's wealth. They have been able to prevent (due to their power) the legitimate heirs of the Czars fortune to withdraw a penny of the millions deposited in a variety of their banks. The Mountbattans, who are related to the Rothschilds, led the court battles to prevent the claimants from withdrawing any of the fortune. In other words, the money they invested in the Russian Revolution, was not only paid back directly by the Bolshevists in millions of dollar of gold, but by grabbing the huge deposits of the Czars' wealth, the Rothschilds gained what is now worth over $50 Billions.

Control over W.W. I treaty When Germany fell, not only did Rothschild agents draft the treaty, prepare the idea of the League of Nations, but Max Rothschild was one of 11 men who took control over Bavaria. Max Rothschild was a Freemason in Lodge No. 11, Munich, Germany.

Connections to MI5, Rockefellers, J.P. Morgan, CFR, et. al. Victor Rothschild, who worked for J.P. Morgan & Co. was an important part of MI5 (British Intelligence). Victor Rothschild was also a communist and member of the Apostles Club at Cambridge. Lord Rothschild was one of the original members of Rhode's Round Table group which developed into the CFR. It was the Rothschilds who had financed Cecil Rhodes, beginning in Africa. The Rothschilds' have several agents which their money got started and who still serve them well, the Morgans and the Rockefellers. The Rockefellers were Marrano Jews. The original Rockefeller made his money selling narcotics, (they weren't illegal then). After acquiring a little capital he branched out in oil. But it was the Rothschild capital that made the Rockefeller's so powerful. *"They also financed the activities of Edward Harriman (railroads) and Andrew Carnegie Steel."(*

Power within Christendom The Rothschilds also wielded much influence and power not only in Secret Societies, but also in Christendom's churches. The Salvation Army under the suggestion of the Rothschilds adopted the Red Shield (Roth-red Schild-shield) for their logo. One history of the Rothschilds remarks, *"The Rothschilds had rapidly propelled themselves into a position of immense financial power and political influence. They were an independent force in the life of Europe, accountable to no one and, to a large extent, reliant on no one. Popular lampoons depicted them as the real rulers of Christendom..."*

Some of the Rothschilds have been involved in the campaign to loosen public morals. The first executive Secretary of the National Student Forum was John Rothschild. This National Student Forum changed its name like articles of clothing. Speaking about clothing, one of the aims of this Socialist group was to promote public nudity, and free love. This organization had the following constituent groups Radcliffe Liberal Club, Union Theological Seminary Contemporary Club, Yale Liberal Club to name just a few. A further development of this was the Youth Peace Federation which consisted of the League of Youth of Community Church, Methodist Epworth League, NY District, Young Judea, and Young People's Fellowship of St. Phillip's Parish to name a few. American religious men have ties to the Rothschilds especially through their various agents.

Harry Emerson Fosdick, who was Pastor of Rockefeller's church was also among the Presidents of the Rockefeller Foundation. John Foster Dulles, CFR, was chairman of the board of the Rockefeller Foundation, and married a Rockefeller, Janet Pomeroy Avery. Remember John Foster Dulles was an important Federal Council of Churches of Christ official. (See chap. 2.9) Every road leads back to the Rothschilds. There are more items than what have been mentioned above linking the Rothschilds to the various tentacles. Each of the various tentacles that conspiracy theorists have put forth,-the Jews, the Masons, the Intelligence Communities, the International Bankers, the Prieure de Sion, the Catholics, the Trilateral commission, the CFR, the New Age, the Cults-- each ties back to the Rothschild's power.

Co-Masters Of The World - The Media Eustice Mullins has published his research in his book Who Owns the TV Networks showing that the Rothschilds have control of all three U.S. Networks, plus other aspects of the recording and mass media industry. It can be added that they control Reuters too. From other sources it appears CNN, which began as an independent challenge to the Jewish Network monopoly, ran into repeated trickery, and ended up part of the system. Money from B.C.C.I., (B.C.C.I. has been one of the New World Orders financial systems for doing its dirty business such as controlling Congressmen, and is involved with INSLA, the Iran-Contra Scandal, Centrust, and other recent scandals) which has tainted so many aspects of public power in the U.S. has also been behind CNN. Perhaps nothing dominates the life of some Americans as does the television. Americans sit themselves before the television set and simply absorb what it projects to them. On a day to day basis the biggest way the Rothschilds touch the lives of Americans are the three major networks which are under Rothschild direction. These are NBC, and CBS.

Influence in America In 1837 August Belmont came to the U.S., during the Panic of 1837. August Belmont appears to have been a Rothschild proxy. Belmont bought up government bonds in this Panic and his success eventually led him to the White House where he became the *"financial advisor to the President of the United States"*. His policies helped pit the North against the South for the Civil War. Judah P. Benjamin, who according to A. Ralph Epperson was the Civil War campaign strategist for the House of Rothschild held many key positions in the Confederacy. He was apparently connected to John Wilkes Booth. J.P. Morgan has been called a Rothschild agent. His father was one of the many elite who made their fortunes by shipping supplies past the North's blockade and into the Confederacy. J.P. was a major supporter of an American central bank (Interestingly enough, he is reported to be related to Alexander Hamilton). In 1869, J.P. Morgan went to the House of England and formed Northern Securities as an agent for New Court in the U.S. Then, in 1907 J.P. Morgan shuttled back and forth between London and Paris, presumably getting orders from the Rothschilds. He returned to America and instigated the Panic of 1907, which led to the ,,need" for a central bank. Another man who appears to be connected to the Rothschilds was Thomas House, who also made his fortune slipping supplies past the North and into the South. His son, Colonel Edward M. House was one of the main Illuminati figures to control America during the early 20th Century. Some of the Bauer line of the Rothschild family moved to America and took up Important positions in the hierarchy's network.

Their Power Is Extensive Peter Rupert Lord Carrington, who is the chairman of the Bilderbergers, has been the Rothschild's director of their Rio Tinto Zinc Corp. He also is director of Barclay's Bank and part of the Trilateral Commission. Francois Mitterand, who has led France, is an extremely close friend of the Rothschilds. I point these two men out just to portray to the reader the extensive power the Rothschilds wield behind the scenes; what they call their bloodline in the illuminati.

During Illuminati ceremonies, when candidates are presented for approval at the Sisters of Ught and the Mothers of Darkness levels the bloodline of the Rothschilds is actually called "the Rothschild bloodline." Although It was originally went by the name Bauer (and many of the descendants today continue to be Bauers and Bowers, the name "Rothschild" was the occult name that the Bauers personally chose for their bloodline to be power broker in Latin America.

One of my friends from South America got to personally witness the destruction of South America by Rothschild interests. One item that I am familiar with from history, and which I can't help thinking about is how the nation of Bolivia in 1908 had the fine distinction of having absolutely no foreign debt. However, in 1908 the Morgans of America loaned Bolivia money, and in 1917 Chandler & Co. loaned them $2.4 million. Thus began the plunge of a free nation Into economic slavery to the Illuminati's international Bankers. The point is that nations like Bolivia, if left alone would have been far better off. People don't realize that the problems these *"banana republics"* have is to a large degree being cause by powerful outsiders like the Rothschilds who then direct organizations like the IMF to *"save"* these poor nations. When the Rothschilds set themselves up in Brazil, they set up to be there permanently. They came in during the 19th century.

The Rothschilds and other British Interests played a major role in Brazil's railway system, which became a law unto itself. Just as the secret history of the railway tycoons reveals a great deal about the secret elite in the United States, so it also does in Brazil. Later Henry Kaiser and Nelson Rockefeller moved into South America (incl. Brazil) to promote their capitalistic visions. They promoted the light industrialization of Latin America and its economic interdependence in the 1950's and 1960's. The Scroll & Key Society is one of the Illuminati's secret entry points at Yale University. The Scroll and Key Society financed a book by **Elizabeth A. Cobbs** entitled **The Rich Neighbour Policy: Rockefeller and Kaiser in Brazil**. This book (Yale Univ., 1992, p. 248) states that Brazilians have looked to Rockefeller as their connection to the United States. Other elite families besides the Rothschilds have also substantial Latin American economic control, such as the DuPonts.

Rothschild Connections To Occult And Secret Societies

If one looked on the backstage of history, he would find the House of Rothschild. They have indebted Kings, manipulated kingdoms, created wars and moulded the very shape of the international world. Among the hierarchy of the Illuminati they are revered as a powerful satanic bloodline. They are *"living legends."* Said one biographer: *"In America a boy wants to become President. In Europe he would rather be a Rothschild.... To be 'a Rothschild' is to be a modern Croesus, a twentieth-century Midas."* They are a dynasty of enduring power; a *"magic"* bloodline In Satan's Empire. We will probably never know exactly when occultism was introduced to the Rothschilds. Several of their ancestors have been rabbis, so the occultism probably came in the form of Jewish Cabalism, Sabbatism, or Frankism. The House of Rothschild practices gnostic-satanism (the Rothschilds would probably not call themselves Satanists, but by our standards they are, considering the sacrificial and spiritual worship involved). The truth is sometimes hard to tell. The stories the family weave are hard to distinguish from the truth. Myths are one of their best weapons, and a researcher must be wary. The family began in Frankfort, Germany (the city where paper money was popularized). The oldest known Rothschild went by the name of Uri Feibesch who lived in the early 16th century. His descendants lived in the House of Red Shield. His great, great, great, great Grandson was Moses Bauer, who lived in the early 18th century. The family was mostly made-up of Jewish retail traders, and lived in the Judengasse, or Jew's Alley in Frankfort. Jew's Alley was the product of the anti-semitic bent in Europe, and did not have very good living conditions.

Mayer Amschel Bauer was a well-off coin trader in Frankfort. In front of his house hung a sign with the family's symbol, which was a red hexagram. The hexagram (also known as the Seal of Solomon, the Magden David, or the Star of David) is very occultic. It is used today as the symbol of Israel, but It is not Jewish. In his excellent book **The Six-pointed Star, O.J. Graham** explains that the hexagram was used in the ancient mystery religions. It was the symbol of Moloch, Ashtoreth, and others. In fact, the hexagram was used to represent Saturn, which earlier newsletters have discussed. The six-pointed star is considered the equivalent of the Oriental Yin-and-Yang symbol, which is the Luciferian concept of balancing good and evil.

One of the principle points that should be borne in mind, is that the actual occult power of the Rothschild bloodline is hidden in secret lineages. Although the Rothschilds make up part of the Rothschild bloodline, people should also watch out for names such as Bauer, Bowers, Sassoons, and many other last names. People within the illuminati who have Rothschild blood are aware of their secret ancestry, but outsiders in the world are more often than not are never going to be told that they carry such *"powerful"* occult blood.

The symbol appears to have been used by King Solomon when he apostatized, and was thereafter called the Seal of Solomon. Later on, Jewish Cabalism (or Occultism - different name, same game) picked it up as a magic symbol. Through the promotion of the Cabalists and the Zionists it has become the symbol of Jewish identity, although the occult circles know better. The Bauer's use of a hexagram as their family sign points to their involvement in Jewish Cabalism. In fact, the six-pointed star was so significant to them that Mayer Amschel Bauer decided to adopt it as his new name - Mayer Amschel Rothschild (Rot-schildt = Red Shield). I believe this was done to identify his family with occultism and the likes of Saturn or Ashtoreth (whom the Astors are named after). The Rothschilds have been intimately involved in witchcraft and the Illuminati since its early known history. The Kaiser of Germany seems to refer to them when he said, *"the magic powers of money as wielded by the Lord of Lucre are powers of Black Magic at its blackest."* If only half of the wealth is controlled by the Rothschilds, it indicates that if they are to be part of the world's rulership, they must have allies.

The Witchcraft Council of 13 which is under Rothschild control and in turn issue orders to various groups. (see ***http://rense.com/general78/ilumm.htm***) One of the purest form of Satanism can be traced to the Jewish Sabbatain sect and its Frankist spin-off. The leaders of this up to the Rothschilds were: Sabbatai Zevi (1626-1676) Nathan of Gaza (16??-?) Jacob Frank (1726-1791).

The principle group of men who cranked up International Banking were Satanists from the beginning. These Satanists now are the ones who run the Federal Reserve and are responsible for the creation of U.S. Federal Reserve notes. Just having total control over the supply of U.S. paper money almost gives them leverage over the world's finances, without mentioning they control the world bank. It is no accident then, that once they established world financial control, they would do all in their power to divide and conquer and destroy both the Christian and the Moslem faith in God. These powerful Bankers relate to faith in God as Cain related to his brother Abel. That they may be related to the Jewish people, does not mean they have the Jewish people's best interest at heart. Initially Sabbatai Zevi was rejected by many Jews. His sect gained momentum in second half of the seventeenth century in south-eastern Poland. In 1759-60, 500 Jewish Sabbateans *"converted"* to Christianity. In 1715, 109 of the 415 Jewish families in Frankfurt were engaged in money lending. The rest were merchants of various kinds. The concepts that Satanism holds to were a natural shoe in to justify for many of these Jewish bankers the type of behaviour they were engaged in.

According to eye-witnesses, who were prominent enough to visit one of the British Rothschild homes, the Rothschilds worship yet another god beside money, Satan. They set a place for him at their table. The Rothschilds have been Satanists for many generations. The Rothschilds are an important part of the history of the Seal of Solomon (also known as hexagram, Magen David, six-pointed star, Star of David.) The Seal of Solomon, the hexagram, was not considered a Jewish symbol before the Rothschilds began using it. Throughout the Middle Ages the Seal of Solomon had been used by Arab

Magicians, Cabalist Magicians, Druid witches and Satanists. One of the few ancient uses of the symbol was on the floor of a 1,200 year old Moslem Mosque found where Tel Aviv is today. In the twelve century an Ashkenazic Jew Menahem ben Duji, who thought he was the Messiah, used the magical symbol. Because the Rothschilds were Satanists they adopted this powerful magic symbol in 1822 for their coat- of-arms.

The name they adopted for their family actually comes from the fact that in the 17th century Mayer Amschel Bauer began hanging out a red hexagram in front of their house to identify it. Mayer Amschel then decided to take the name red-schield (Rothschild in German) after the red Seal of Solomon that they used. **Alice Bailey** in **A Treatise On White Magic,** p. 412, claims that the Hierarchy has a special group which she calls "*the financial group, controlling all that can be converted into energy, and constituting a dictatorship over all modes of intercourse, commerce and exchange.*" According the Luciferian Alice Bailey, (**Discussed in a later chapter on the Lucis Trust and Externalization of the Hierarchy**) the "*financial group*" is the latest group directed by the Hierarchy. In 1836 Zevi Hirsch Kalischer approached Rothschild and proposed Rothschild buy all of Erez Israel. It took many years for the Rothschilds to finally create Israel. The Rothschilds have been a primary force behind the creation of Israel, and so it is appropriate that the nation carries their magical Seal of Solomon as the state logo.

The Ultra-orthodox Jews in Israel will not serve in the Israeli army because they know that Almighty God was not behind the creation of modern Israel, but rather the rich ungodly apostate Jews. They refuse to serve the ungodly. They are more wiser than men like Jerry Falwell who run around proclaiming Israel is God's nation. Men like Falwell are the type that this Author finds reference to repeatedly in Jewish documents that speak of their power within the Fundamentalists. God is ultimately in charge, he has allowed Hitler to come to power, Stalin to come to power, and the Rothschilds to come to power. In the same sense that God rules over and blessed Stalin's Russia, he rules over America and Israel. To twist scriptures about God seating the rulers and then to apply them to bless one Satanic secular communist nation and not another is inconsistent and not correctly using the Word of Truth. Some people object that the conspiracy of Power is labelled Jewish rather than Satanic by certain concerned citizens.

This objection is valid-- however, will these objectors then take the obvious next step and admit the nation of Israel which the Rothschild's created is Satanic and not Jewish? But then who knows precisely why people do what they do? If you ask someone why he does something, he will give you one answer today, another tomorrow, and another the next day. Does he do what he does for a real reason, or a single motive? Perhaps to label the Power as only Satanic or only Jewish or only Masonic is to neglect the personal human dimension. This personal human dimension is godless. Being godless it fills that void, by pretending its men are gods. This brings us right back to the Gnostic religions and Satan. Most Jewish people do not concern themselves with learning the occultic significance to their treasured Magen David (Star of David). King David did not have anything to do with the hexagram, although his son Solomon did when he began worshipping Ashtoreth (star, also known as Astarte, Chiun, Kaiwan, Remphan, and Saturn). Solomon built altars to Star (Astarte, aka Ashtoreth).

The god Saturn is associated with the Star but both Saturn and Astarte also been identified with a number of other names. Saturn is an important key to understanding the long heritage this conspiracy has back to antiquity. The city of Rome was originally known as Saturnia or City of Saturn. The Roman Catholic church retains much of the Saturn worship in its ritual. Saturn also relates to Lucifer.'13 In various occult dictionaries Saturn is associated with evil. Saturn was important to the religion of Mithra, and also the Druids.

The Illuminati are building their temples secretly throughout the United States. The last issue of this newsletter described the massive pyramid that has been built at Los Vegas. Pyramids have also been built at San Francisco (the Trans-America building) and in Chicago, and in other eastern places. The San Francisco building was built by people with ties to the Rockefellers. Just north of San Francisco and east of the Bohemian Grove is the Napa Valley of California. Anton LaVey moved to Napa Valley after his split with Aquino. LaVey ran a construction company during the 1910. out of Napa, CA. (As an aside, Anton LaVey's chief representative in our Portland area is Rex "Diablos" Church, who grew up as Rex Nance in Seaside High School on the Oregon coast. Rex worked at the drug store at Broadway and Holiday at Seaside during high school.

Two years after high school he returned to his hometown with his head shaved and wearing black in LaVey fashion. He had a stripper who dressed in black who was a Satanist as his girl friend for a while in the Portland area. According to Rex's own words, he grew up in a secret Satanic family and was baptized to Satan as a child. Rex and his Satanic friends have schemed how to hurt the Christians. How many of their devious plans have succeeded I do not know. Also of Interest is that Rex lived a good deal with his what has been reported as Jehovah's Witness grandparents.) With the Church of Satan feeling comfortable in Napa, it is not surprising that the Baron and Baroness Phillipi de Rothschild picked the area to build a secret temple to Satan.

Also as readers of this newsletter know, these people have been constructing castles and other large buildings on spiritual ley lines for centuries, so it goes without saying that when this secret temple was built in Napa, that the Icy lines were at least considered in choosing a site. The Baron Rothschild began the construction of a pyramid in Napa Valley, which his wife completed after he died. The pyramid is called Opus 1. According to one of the contractors who participated in building the pyramid, the project cost $35 million. The various construction cost reports given the public have been much less than what this contractor has said was the real cost of the building. The theme of the numbers 3 and 6 runs throughout the large Opus 1 pyramid building. as well as the number 666. Also little circles frequently appear.

The name of the building Opus 1 means the First Work. It's cover or front for the temple is that It is a winery. The winery operates very strangely to a legitimate winery. The entire project of buying the land, building Opus 1, and operating it has been shrouded in secrecy. The wineries in California when they open traditionally and normally are open to the public. The opening ceremonies of Opus 1 were shrouded in secrecy. The opening announcement was low key and only select people and select International media types were Invited. This opening is extremely unusual for a winery in the Napa Valley area. Private guided tours are very hard to obtain of Opus 1, in contrast to the other wineries in Napa Valley. Further, the estate that the winery (temple) sits on is very protected and secluded.

The wrought iron gates are always closed. However, I was able to get a first hand report from a group of three that managed to view Opus 1. During the tour this group saw many occult and satanic items, and yet large areas of the winery (temple) were closed off to even this private tour group. The winery is not constructed even remotely similar to any winery in the Us. The project began as a joint venture between Robert Mondavi and Baron Rothschild in 1979. The land was secretly purchased and in the late 1960's construction quietly began using contractors from far away. Strangely, the Napa Valley Register which reports on all building activity remained extremely quiet about what was being built. From the air, the construction forms a Masonic square and compass.

On the Inside hidden stairwells and other hidden features have been built in. The capstone of the pyramid has a rotunda where skylight penetrates the capstone and where viewers can get a view of the entire Napa Valley. There have numerous Rothschilds who have entered Into the various Masonic rites. For Instance, Louis Rothschild was a 32° Scottish Rite Mason in Chicago during the 1890's. The reason for this is that Freemasonry is used as type of early class for those who are in the Illuminati to get them familiar with the symbols of the Mystery religions and give them more practice with hand signals, rituals, and secrecy. Orchids, which are used by the Mothers of Darkness, are grown all over the area. Orchids are the only type of flower grown on the site, and they are cared for by apparently Mothers of Darkness who are dressed in all black, which is the standard color of garb of the Mothers of Darkness. The pyramid was built with limestone from Texas. No doubt there is some occult significance to the site that the limestone came from. The limestone itself has fossils, which have been hidden from easy view for some reason. (Remember the ancient Egyptian pyramids used limestone.)

Originally Opus 1 was scheduled to open around the Summer Solstice but the date was shifted to Weds., Oct. 30, 1991 which is the day before Halloween. Since the opening day, the Rothschilds have had events scheduled around Satanic high days. Those who are familiar with the occult know that these events are covers for Satanic rituals which are held secretly. The land has wrought iron gates which are locked at all times. Some of the occult Items which private visitors saw within the pyramid were: a book on wine depicting orgies by Salvadore Dailey who is a Satanist, a blue-black picture with naked ritual dancers, and other strange occultic pieces of art (such as an oil painting of what looked like Satan). Massive draconian oak doors are built facing the hail that leads to the room where wine is tasted. Mirrors abound in the place.

The gilded art work on the mirrors is often Rococo. The Baroness personally designed and furnished the Interior. The upside down peace sign is found designed in some of the furniture as barren trees. Two trees of life from Peru are by the fireplace. The tree of life is by the way very Important to this level of the Illuminati. The visitors also saw 3 Mouton ceremonial drinking cups with rams, and chairs which had the carvings on the front arms/legs of fully formed demons were found in one of the rooms. The foyer looks like the Inside of a snail or "corkscrewy". Much of the furnishings were purchased by the Baroness Rothschild from the De Medicis. It has various marble floors and tables set with orchids. The stainless steel and the floors in the winery are immaculate. The workers who work there were scrutinized closely before being hired. Originally, the wine workers were required to were black pants and white shirts, but the workers who had to stomp the grapes were unhappy about the uniform requirements.

I have been trying to follow the Rothschild family with its many branches. Although the Rothschilds are seen as great internationalists, don't be surprised if some of the people of the Rothschilds seem somewhat middleclass, For instance, in the Millington, MI NE of Flint, MI one family dominates the tows. This family is the Bauer family. Stan Bauer was a man who mysteriously simply attracted material possessions to himself without any visible source of money. His son Harold Bauer a 32° Mason who sat on the Houghton Lake city council His next son Terry Bauer was also a Mason, also had a position in local government and was on the school beard. His daughter Barbers Bauer married Jim Hagger who was also a Mason who lived in Grand Blanc south of Flint. There is certainly more that could be said about the satanic Rothschild bloodline, but this is where I will bring this article to a close, with the statement that, Lord Welling, I will write more about them later.

And so it came to pass that the Rothschild Dynasty that worship their god Satan grew into the House of Rothschild who learned well how to control the power of money and to expand their influence from kings to nations.

It is noteworthy that each Dynasty has one "head" of the family.

And so we introduce what in simple corporate terms would be the Chairman of the Board and probably the major private shareholder of PLANET EARTH. Now it is time in our simple model to introduce the other Directors and their bloodlines.

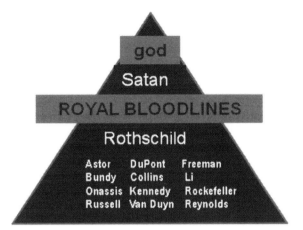

5

THE THREADS THAT BIND DYNASTIES

The Power Behind The Bloodlines

It is not a simple matter to piece together the history and the dynasties of the bloodlines. It is commendable that there are many like Fritz Springmeier who now dig deep into the backgrounds of these incredible families who have seeming rose into formidable positions of commerce and power in the last 300 years. These families, very protective of their bloodlines, have marched to control and take over huge corporations in strategic functions around the world. In just about every case, the research points back to the connection to each other through secret societies and the various cults. In virtually all research, the Rothschilds appear to be involved as the "money" dynasty.

I, as the co-author of this book, cannot take any credit for the research nor state the opinion, but I as a researcher myself have found extensive references, books, websites that are dedicated to this same topic. And what I have found is that they over and over confirm many of the same conclusions. What is of interest here is that perhaps the some of the details may not are totally correct but there are many points that are difficult to dispute:

1. these are the most powerful, influential bloodlines on Planet Earth;
2. they are in each other's lives;
3. they control the money of the planet;
4. they have a common link within the secret societies;
5. their latest origins of "rising" seem to start in the 1700's;
6. they control or own major commercial enterprises around the world;
7. they rose in power rapidly regardless of what they undertook;
8. they are secretive and protective of their privacy and bloodlines;
9. they are allegedly unified in a business plan to achieve a one world order;
10. they are rooted deeply in cult or satanic practices;
11. they have special gifts, abilities, knowledge, power to attain what it is they require.

What is the power that they have that has brought such enormous success to them? Is it just business skill or do they know something that most don't? Granted, they seem to all *"know each other"* and *"rub business shoulders"* but is this just coincidence? Why are these powerful people so centered on bloodlines and the worship of Lucifer and Satan? What is this preoccupation with the occult?

Long ago in the dark unwritten pages of human history, powerful kings discovered how they could be like gods and control other men by torture, magical practices, wars, politics, religion and interest taking. These elite families designed strategies and tactics to perpetuate their occult practices so as to create and protect their dynasties. Not surprising, these practices would be hidden in layers upon layers of secrecy protected by these families from the profane masses. What humanity calls esoteric crap is precisely what this occult interest they all have. So while the stupidity of mankind laughs at what is known as black magic, this appears to be their common interest. So who is laughing at who? And while the New Age is so focussed on learning White Magic through higher vibration and ascension, what is the difference except the application? It is plain old magic that can be applied and perceived as good or bad, light or dark. While the New Age desired abilities include esoteric abilities of co-creation and manifestation, could anyone ever believe that these bloodlines have already figured this out?

It is not be much of a surprise to see the bloodlines go back to Babylon and descendents from Nimrod--back to the bloodlines of the ancient gods. Down through the years the occult world has remained hidden from the history books because publishing and education have been controlled privileges. The Mystery Religions in turn ruled the masses and the political leaders. Who were these powerful people? I have been repeatedly asked if there is a conspiracy who are the conspirators? Interestingly, when you get down to the other side of the coin, even though it may be "dark and occult" the investigator finds that the elite have perpetuated their power for centuries, and have worked hand in glove with other elites to control the people they require to protect and build their dynasties. When seen in better light, wars between kings no longer appear as wars between elite factions, but perhaps contrived conflicts of wars to control their subjects and to seek means to build their dynasties. This is not a surprise. What is the surprise may be how it is done in what Earthlings believe to be a free, civilized world.

But who are these people? The answer may not be the answer some might expect, because power comes in many shapes and sizes. Power doesn't have to have high visibility to be active. In fact, due to the revealed nature of these bloodlines they have traditionally tried to remain secret and therefore are perceived as conspirators. As some study these bloodlines they reveal how powerful they are. David Hill, who was investigating the Illuminati, lost his life because he had been close to the inside as a high ranking Freemason who worked for the Mafia. David Hill had discovered the names of some of the more obvious powerful families. For instance, in David's notes he writes, *"Yes, it is a fact: the Mellons, Carnegies, Rothschilds, Rockefellers, Dukes, Astors, Dorrances, Reynoldses, Stilimans, Bakers, Pynes, Cuilmans, Watsons, Tukes, Kleinworts, DuPonts, Warburgs, Phippses, Graces, Guggenheims, Milners, Drexels, Winthrops, Vanderbilts, Whitneys, Harknesses and other super rich Illuminated families generally get along quite well with Communists, who supposedly want to take away the wealth of these men and give it to the people."*

Our short history of 300 years does not reflect the first time of emergence for the occult powers. The Empire of conquest has simply become larger. If you follow Freemasonry at higher levels it reveals itself to be founded on the occult and esoteric powers. Back to Babylon and then forward through the Knights Templar you can see the pattern. The largest learning platform was when the Templars rose rapidly in the 1100's to usurp both kingdoms and church before through their financial emergence and controlling money. They went into hiding and secrecy to emerge once again in their plan 300 years ago. One could say these are the "gods" powered by the occult that are arising to complete their plan of the New World Order.

Throughout the entirety of this universe and the multiple Planes of Existence, there are two Cosmic Principles which permeate the orientation of all sentient life. We will never know why, but The Creator of this universe chose to come to know Itself by means of these 2 opposing, conflicting, and balancing Principles of Duality.

On the one hand, there is The Cosmic Principle of Unification and Synthesis. On the other hand, there is The Cosmic Principle of Disunity and Separativeness and Divisiveness. They govern the evolutionary focus of all sentient beings in Creation. All those sentient beings who are aligned with The Governing Principle of **Disunity are in service to the self,** and they are called The Dark Forces or Dark Brotherhood. All those sentient beings who are aligned with The **Governing Principle of Unity are in service to others, and they are called The Light Forces** or White Brotherhood. The names of Light and Dark are, of course, a little melodramatic but because of common usage amongst Humanity, they are a convenient handle to utilize in speaking of them. The two polarities will always be in oppositional tension with respect to each other for as long as this universe exists.

In aggrandizing and serving the self, the Dark Ones seek conquest of all others and seek to bring under their control those of the opposite polarity to enhance their power which they see as their duty to the self. At the human level (on Earth) they would be said to program (pre-incarnatively) for wealth and position and status and this means for maximum control over large numbers of people, which gives them the power that they seek. It would also seem that they re-incarnate into the same families to consolidate and further advance their power and polarize further in **service to the self**.

Those who are aligned (consciously or unconsciously) with The Brotherhood of Light are **in service to all others**. They seek to maintain their freedom so that they may pursue The Path of Return on the evolutionary spiral back to The Godhead from whence all emanated in this universe. They evolve by means of serving The Creator in the other-self, whereas The Dark Ones evolve by means of serving The Creator in the self. Those of the positive polarity or The Light must never allow themselves to become enslaved and controlled by The Dark because they must have the freedom to grow in consciousness and advance evolutionarily on The Spiral of Return to The Source of All. The enslavement or the liberation is simply a choice.

The Dark Side seeks to abridge the freedoms of others for the purposes of their own agenda in gaining more power for the self, and The Light Side must seemingly do battle with those who would try to conquer them and take away the expression of their free will. At the lower Levels of Existence, the battles are fought physically, and at the higher Levels of Existence the battles are fought in consciousness, but in this particular universe there must always be a dynamic, ever-changing opposition between the two. Some humans try to deny the existence of a Malevolent Force in this Creation, but it is perhaps not wise to deny that which may exist in fact and which is fully one-half of The Manifested Expression of The Creator of this universe.

And so Earth has both of the polarities because the beings of each polarity serve as a catalyst for each other in learning the lessons and gaining the experiences of this Level of

Existence and for polarization in one direction or the other. The lessons are more intense, and advancement and polarization are made more rapidly. And so the real war is between the The Dark or The Light to see who will be solely of the service to others polarity (Brotherhood of Light) or be subjected to The Forces of Darkness. Yet all are equally Earthling's choice of expressions and would seemingly be extensions of The Consciousness of The Creator. The Source for this universe does not love one side more than the other. That seems to be the fly in the ointment for the humans on this planet who have seen and experienced the consequences of the agendas of The Dark Ones for eons of time: the programs of fear, the greed for the natural resources of the planet, the unimaginable wealth of the elite few, the rivalries and conflicts of the war profiteers.

The point here is that it is anyone's prerogative to choose the light or the dark side because in the beginning, and the end, there is only light. The polarity of dark and light has molded history for thousands of years creating the drama of good and evil. So far, the evil seems to have been the dominant force because humanity fears death and pain. That gives the dark the tool to control. Moreover, humanity has been content to accept the benefits of being a slave to the leaders.

But, it would seem that at some point in the natural evolution, both the dark and the light seek ascension towards the knowing of self. There appears to be three levels of this knowing of self that follows the dark and the light side of the ascension evolution which eventually converges. The first level is the Body and the powers within it. This is at the lowest level the instinctual nature of the animal to survive and to propagate his own kind. As evolution progresses towards spiritual wisdom, the second level is the Mind and its power. Here the power of the intellect rules to command the physical. The third level is the Spirit and the powers that reside here. It is the Soul that is the nonlocal connection to Source (God or whatever you call it) that travels through the discovery process, which in the New Age terminology is referred to as ascension or rising vibration. On the occult or Dark side of Satan, such powers of Mind appear to be released through ritual, secret knowledge and bloodline. Yet these powers are the same, only their use as to evil or good differs.

If you look carefully at the New Age God beliefs and the power of mind, you see evidence of millions of people who exhibit extraordinary abilities "of the mind" that one would allocate to the Light side of love and harmony. There is a list of 200 abilities such as psychic and abnormal abilities (mind control, astral travel, healing, bilocation, etc) that are not accepted as reality, yet they exist. Each of these is a neutral ability related to the belief and strength of the mind until a choice is made to use it in a dark or light (bad or good) way. On the side of Dark occult beliefs you see the same extraordinary abilities simply used for dark purposes of what one may allocate to Satan. It would seem reasonable to believe that the bloodlines have protected and use special powers of mind to feed the physical self for the soul which is their higher being. On the other side, the more spiritual ones of power have special powers that feed the spiritual self of soul.

It would seem reasonable to expect that at some level in the evolution of self, when the good and evil is transcended into that spirit level of powers, that there is no polarity of good and evil and it converges on the true discovery of who we are as one consciousness of creation represented by the Soul in its journey of self discovery and expression. This occurs at the level (called higher vibration along the ascension path) when forgiveness is unconditional and it reflects a situation in masse which we will get into in the next Part of this book--as it is occurring on Planet Earth now. It is the evolution of humanity and all these dark things are only steps toward that potential end of truth in self discovery.

And so let us look at this "darker side" now to understand how it has swung this way to bring humanity to a crucial split in the path of Planet Earth versus PLANET EARTH.

On this "darker" side it has been suggested that what has emerged is the Rothschilds and the bloodlines who move more and more into their visible roles of power, for once the plan of PLANET EARTH is done, there is no reason to hide their ways that are designed to rule all of Planet Earth's resources including mankind. Similarly, once any corporate business strategy is completed, the executors would be comfortable to reveal themselves. If one were to use an analogy of what may be most familiar to most, essentially, we have had a look at the Founders and private shareholders of PLANET EARTH and we have seen that the heads of these Dynasties are most likely on the Board of Directors.

As we sit here in time, at the threshold of a New Age of Aquarius, we look back into the Age of Pisces which has been focused so much on religion. The religions have been the carving tools of beliefs and actions of humanity over thousands of years (we will explore this later). The story of Christ has served to bring a fundamental belief system about God and gods into the reality of humanity and served to carve out a way of life.

Now, let us look more carefully at this darker occult side and its evolution.

The Secret That Unifies The "gods"

When reading the extensive research that has been done on the bloodlines, the inescapable occurrence of cult, Satanism, special esoteric powers that have been a feeding ground for the "conspirator theorists" to expound upon is undeniable. Of particular interest now is to explore this more as its roots appear to take us back to Roman Cults and some of the powers of the gods during Sumerian times (this will be covered in detail later). It is of interest to understand the bloodlines formal preoccupation with the roman cult and this religious order of Satanism. Why does this, particular belief system create the common bonds between these highly knowledgeable and powerful families? Do they know something that the rest of the common mortals do not?

When you get over the initial impact of the words, occult, Satan, cults and all those "bad" words that conjure up a reaction like the word snake, you can move to a place where an objective, impartial mind can be allowed to look at things a different way. When you cast out what humanity has been told over centuries; that Satan is the bad guy who lures you into the carnal desires of the flesh, that he is the epitome of sin that we are all guilty of, and that he is dominion is hell and that sorcery, dark magic, spells, occult, and all those darker things are within his domain, then look at this word Satanism more carefully with an open mind, it reveals something very interesting. Earthlings have been conditioned to react with closed mind on these topics. Centuries of burring people for heresy has reduced these topics to mythological stories of fiction as entertainment.

Dictionary.com says occult is of or pertaining to magic, astrology, or any system claiming use or knowledge of secret or supernatural powers or agencies; beyond the range of ordinary knowledge or understanding; mysterious; secret; disclosed or communicated only to the initiated; hidden from view; not apparent on mere inspection but discoverable by experimentation; of a nature not understood, as physical qualities ;dealing with such qualities; experimental: *occult science.*

The world is full of examples of this. Psychic powers to read the future, to instantly heal others, to materialize objects, to influence others minds, to bi-locate, to levitate, to become invisible, etc. These are everywhere. Although they exist, they are ignored and discounted as irrelevant by the experts because they cannot explain them. And so they are eliminated from humanity's belief system. And the myths and legends are full of the abilities on the dark side, relegated to sorcery, witchcraft, evil, and bad occult stuff.

What are these black occult powers? Here are a few examples.

Black magic is where the occult kind, is one of the oldest and most general of these systems. Magic is the study and application of psychic forces. It uses mental training, concentration, and a system of symbols to program the mind. The purpose of magic is to alter the self and the environment according to the will.

Tantric Sex, is a practice that make use of our natural sexuality as a means to achieve higher consciousness and energy. The secrets have to do with the ways we can transmute the life energies of the lower chakras into the spiritual realizations of the higher spiritual centers.

Paranormal involves paranormal body or ghost or spirit or apparition is the energy, soul or personality of a person who has died and has somehow gotten stuck between this plane of existence and the next. Some knows and some does not know that they are dead. Mostly they have died under traumatic, unusual or highly emotional circumstances. Ghosts can be perceived by the living in a number of ways: through sight (apparitions), sound (voices), smell (fragrances and odors), touch and sometimes they can just be sensed.

Psychosymbology is to control your own destiny. Psychosymbology teaches you how to contact that part of your brain which contains all the secrets of the ages – past, present and future- secrets which will send you soaring to heights of bliss, peace, and personal power. It is the language of brain, is easy to learn, easy to use, and easy to develop the greatest source of human psychic power ever discovered by man. Biologically the left side of the human brain is conscious and rational and the right side of brain is unconscious and non-rational. The right part of brain is a vast and boundless sea of knowledge, wisdom, potential. It remains unused, untapped because people try to communicate with it through the use of words. But the Unconscious does not understand words.

Numerology is the study of numbers. Generally most of the calculations are based on single numbers i.e., 1 to 9 ; they influence men and women equally, together with their hidden meaning, and the character of persons indicated by them. There are only nine numbers on this earth by which all calculations are made. Beyond these numbers all the rest are repetitions, as 10 is a 1 with a zero added, an 11 is 1 plus 1 a 2; a 12 is 1 plus 2, a 3; and so on. Every number no matter how high, can be reduced to a single figure by what is called "natural addition " from left to right. The final number that remains is called the spirit or soul number.

Palmistry or Hand Reading is the art of disclosing, by means of the Hand, its form, texture, fingers, mounts, lines etc., the secrets of the brain together with its quality and quantity and its action with its subsequent results upon the character, career and life of the individual. The hand is the direct representation of the brain and mind. In order to prove this statement and fix relation between brain and the hand, and in order to say that hand plays a most important role in a man's life, following are some observations and proofs. On examining the texture of a of the hand of a cultured person, it is often found to be elastic or fine as comparable with his fine speech and reasonable action and conduct; on the other hand , the texture of vulgar or laborer's hand will be found rough and coarse, same his speech and actions.

Mind control (also known as brainwashing, coercive persuasion, mind abuse, menticide, thought control, or thought reform) refers to a process in which a group or individual *"systematically uses unethically manipulative methods to persuade others to conform to the wishes of the manipulator(s), often to the detriment of the person being manipulated"*. The term has been applied to any tactic, psychological or otherwise, which can be seen as subverting an individual's sense of control over their own thinking, behavior, emotions or decision making.

Predictions is to know your future, solutions to your problems, send the details as per the instructions.

Oddly enough, if you look at the Light side of the coin as in the New Age beliefs, these are the same abilities, but a different application; i.e. dark versus light. But let us delve into the beliefs of Satanism on the Dark side.

The Underlying Beliefs Of Satanism

While the Church of Satan encourages individuality and the gratification of desires, it does not suggest that all actions are acceptable. The **Nine Satanic Sins**, published by **Anton LaVey** in 1987, target nine characteristics Satanists should pay attention to in their belief systems:

1. Stupidity Stupid people do not get ahead in this world. Satanists strive to keep themselves informed and to not be fooled by others who seek to manipulate and use them.
2. Pretentiousness Taking pride in one's achievements is encouraged in Satanism. However, one should only take credit for one's own accomplishments. Making empty claims about yourself is not only obnoxious but also potentially dangerous, leading to sin No. 4, self-deceit.
3. Solipsism Satanists use this term to refer to the presumption many people make that other people think, act and have the same desires as themselves. It's important to remember that everyone is an individual with his own individual goals and plans. To expect someone to treat you as you treat him is foolish. Instead, Satanists encourages you to treat people as they treat you. You should always deal with the reality of the situation rather than expectations.
4. Self-Deceit Satanists deal with the world as it is. Convincing yourself of untruths because they are more comfortable is no less problematic than letting someone else deceive you.
5. Herd Conformity Satanism exalts the power of the individual. Western culture encourages people to go with the flow, and to believe and do things simply because the wider community is doing such. Satanists attempt to avoid such behavior, following the herd only if it makes logical sense and suits one's own needs.

6. Lack of Perspective Remain aware of both the big and small pictures, never sacrificing one for the other. Remember your own important place in things, and don't be overwhelmed with the viewpoints of the herd. On the flipside, we do live in a world larger than ourselves. Always keep an eye on the big picture and how you can fit yourself into it.

7. Forgetful of Past Orthodoxies Society is constantly taking old ideas and repackaging them as new, original ideas. Do not be fooled by such offerings.

8. Counterproductive Pride If it works, use it. You should never be embarrassed of your own accomplishments. However, if pride is getting in the way of getting things done with other people, you should set it aside until such time as it becomes constructive again.

9. Lack of Aesthetics Beauty and balance are two things Satanists strive for. This is particularly true in magical practices but can be extended to the rest of one's life as well. Avoid following that which society dictates is beautiful and learn to identify true beauty, whether or not others recognize it.

There are the Eleven Satanic Rules of the Earth that in 1967 were published two years before the publication of the **Satanic Bible**. It was originally meant for circulation only among members of the Church of Satan as it was considered too frank and brutal for general release as per the Church of Satan Informational Pack. This document is found under Anton Szandor LaVey, 1967.

1.   Do not give opinions or advice unless you are asked.
2.   Do not tell your troubles to others unless you are sure they want to hear them.
3.   When in another's lair, show him respect or else do not go there.
4.   If a guest in your lair annoys you, treat him cruelly and without mercy.
5.   Do not make sexual advances unless you are given the mating signal.
6.   Do not take that which does not belong to you unless it is a burden to the other person and he cries out to be relieved.
7.   Acknowledge the power of magic if you have employed it successfully to obtain your desires. If you deny the power of magic after having called upon it with success, you will lose all you have obtained.
8.   Do not complain about anything to which you need not subject yourself.
9.   Do not harm little children.
10. Do not kill non-human animals unless you are attacked or for your food.
11. When walking in open territory, bother no one. If someone bothers you, ask him to stop. If he does not stop, destroy him.

This Satan guy has a role to explore the carnal self, rooted in the lower Body Power level we mentioned earlier. His leadership is to have his followers be totally focused on the self for personal desires, exploitation, and enjoyment of life. The obvious is that the mind and body are to express fully the carnal and physical desires without mercy or reservation.

So Satan is the bad guy to tempts Earthlings to be a survivor and selfish to self, not others. And so he appears within multiple religious belief systems with a purpose of being the antichrist who cares little for others. There is a common presumption that all of these Satanic figures in the various religions must indeed be the same being, despite the fact that each religion has its own very unique perspective and description of this bad fellow named Satan.

Judaism In Hebrew, *Satan* means adversary. The Satan of the Old Testament is a description, not a proper name. This is a figure that works with God's full permission, tempting believers to doubt their faith, separating the true believers from those who just pay lip service.

Christianity The Christian view of Satan is a very tangled web. The name only appears in the New Testament a handful of times. The most well known is the scene in Matthew where he tempts Jesus to turn away from God and worship him instead. While one could certainly read this as Satan setting himself up as a rival to God (as Christians commonly understand him to be doing), it is just as easy to read this as Satan carrying out his Old Testament role of tempter and tester of faith. Despite his brief Biblical appearances, Satan evolved into a truly malevolent and evil creature in the minds of Christians, a former angel rebelling against God who tortures the souls of everyone not saved through Jesus. He is twisted, corrupted, sadistic, sinful and corporeal, the complete opposite of spirituality and goodness. Part of the Christian perception of Satan comes from equating a number of other Biblical figures with Satan, including Lucifer, the dragon, the serpent, Beelzebub, and Leviathan, as well as the prince of the air and the prince of this world.

Devil Worshippers This is the common name given by Satanists to those who worship the Christian version of Satan, viewing him as a lord of evil and wanton destruction. Devil worshippers generally fall into two categories: teens who embrace Satan as a form of rebellion and sociopaths who end up in prison after committing crimes in the name of Satan. Very few such people actually exist, although Christian-influenced communities periodically suffer hysterias in which members become convinced that large numbers of Devil Worshippers are organizing against them.

Islam Muslims have two terms for their Satanic figure. The first is Iblis, which is his proper name (just as Christians use Satan or Lucifer). The second is shaitan, which is a noun or an adjective, describing any being that rebels against God. Ergo, there is one Iblis, and he is a shaitan, but there are other shaitans as well. In Islam, God created three intelligent races: the angels, jinn, and humans. The angels had no free will, always following God, but the other two did. When God commanded the angels and jinn to bow down before Adam, the jinn Iblis alone refused.

The Baha'i Faith For Baha'is, Satan represents humanity's own lower nature and demanding ego, which distracts us from knowing God. He is not an independent being at all.

LaVeyan Satanism (The Church of Satan) LaVeyan Satanists do not believe in a literal Satanic being but instead use the name as a metaphor for humanity's true nature, which should be embraced, and what they call the Dark Force. Satan is not evil, but he does represent a variety of things branded as evil by the traditional religions and societies (particularly those influenced by traditional Christianity), including sexuality, pleasure, lust, cultural taboos, fertility, ego, pride, accomplishment, success, materialism, and hedonism.

Joy of Satan Ministries Joy of Satan Ministries is one of many theistic Satanic groups. Like many theistic Satanists, JoS followers are generally polytheists, viewing Satan as one of many deities. Satan is the bringer of knowledge, and his desire is for his creations, humanity, to elevate itself through knowledge and understanding. He also represents such notions as strength, power, justice and freedom. While Satan is considered a deity within the JoS, the deities themselves are understood to be highly evolved, unaging, humanoid extra-terrestrials who created humanity as slave labor. Some of these aliens, called Nephilim, sired children with humans and struggled against the tyrannical regime.

Raelian Movement According to the Raelians, Satan is one of the Elohim, the race of aliens that created humanity. While most of the Elohim want humanity to develop and grow, Satan considers them a threat, is against the genetic experiments that created them, and believes they should be destroyed. He is blamed for some of the catastrophes that the Bible blames on God such as the Great Flood that destroys everyone save Noah and his family. The Raelian Satan is not necessarily evil. While he works toward the destruction of humanity, he does so with the belief that only evil can ultimately come from humanity.

Heaven's Gate According to members of Heaven's Gate, Satan is a being that has partially gone through the process of reaching the Next Level, which is the goal of believers. However, before fully completing this transformation and gaining acceptance into the Kingdom of Heaven, Satan and other fallen angels decided to re-embrace material existence and encouraged others to do so. As elevated beings, they can possess human bodies just as the aliens of the Kingdom of Heaven can. The Raelian Satan is not necessarily evil. While he works toward the destruction of humanity, he does so with the belief that only evil can ultimately come from humanity.

In the end, the programming has been to believe He is a bad guy like the serpent in the bushes. And he uses black magic to serve his needs so this occult stuff is bad, bad, bad.

In this day and age there is what is known as *"spiritual satanism"*. Most Satanists would agree that the best approach in life is to make the most out of life by living through personal principles that promote self-serving and enjoyment. Generally, to be avoided are the things that make life difficult – such as self-deceit, and self destruction. This seems like common sense, but keep in mind that the ethics of Satanists will vary depending on what they study and what they practice.

In general, they do not seek to harm others but look out if you harm them! Some will attack when provoked much like an animal, striking back with magic spells and curses and psychological play. But not all Satanists are so scornful. There is a general stereotype that Satanists are menacing creatures who only use destructive black magic to harm others just for perverse pleasure; such are the creations of Hollywood and certainly the work of Disney, and the imaginings of those that buy into stereotypes. So society worldwide has a generally negative view of Satanism. In the leading religions what is the result of following Satan? Death by fire. Heresy. Who are the leaders of this? The Vatican. Is the Inquisition still alive in this day and age? We shall see.

Yet even Satanism has a spiritual purpose. Theistic Satanism is the practice of recognizing Satan as a spiritual being. With Theistic Satanism, the Satanist knows, feels and believes that Satan is there for them, as a god-form, a deity. Satanists in general have a favourable view of Satan, and he provides in a time of need. Satanism is an all-encompassing lifestyle that allows you to take from life what is most important to you. You create Satanism the way that you want it and you can use it to better yourself, your life and everything that you know.

Some meditate. Others practice rituals of worship, or self-worship. Other Satanists try to live through the principles of Satanism. You can practice these things alone or join a group- the choice is yours. at the end of the day, whether it is a ritual, meditation, a practice or whatever, it all fundamentally comes down to your individual belief system, the way you think, see, speak and act. Thoughts, words, deeds are the actions of life that govern your life. what are talking about here? Rising into that level we mentioned earlier of the Power of Mind.

You can create new habits through belief, or you can practice new habits to shift belief. The end result of a new belief is the same. Rituals are new habits that instil belief in new powers of mind. Let us look at this Spiritual Satanism more carefully for they have what they call Tenets of Faith that occupy their belief systems.

Satanists believe in autonomy of the individual. Individuals are unique, and precious. One should attempt to know oneself, and to develop one's skills, talent, and character to the utmost. Some people are natural leaders; some are natural followers. Those who are masters should strive to be such, and those meant to tag behind should recognize this and be content in their true nature. But no one should attempt to unnecessarily restrict one's own nature. This includes such things as sexual restrictions, religious restrictions, political restrictions, etc. Of course, it's not a requirement that people LIKE what you believe, but that which you wish to be and believe, you should be free to do.

Satanists believe in striving for perfection of self (power). If you're good at what you do, you'll be successful. We all have the ability to be good at SOMETHING; we all have our abilities and weaknesses. The truth of the world is that the weak seldom get anywhere, unless they turn that very weakness into a strength of some sort. Being as good as possible at everything, however, gives you a MUCH greater chance at being successful and pleased with yourself. Saying *"I'm not good at anything, but I deserve respect anyway!"* is not really a very Satanic view. It's great that you realize you're not good at anything, but why should anyone respect that? What have you done to earn that respect? DO something, BE something, ACHIEVE something...then you'll have respect. Being a failure and doing nothing to change that results in a lifetime of...well....being a failure.

Satanists believe in 'gifts' unto the deserving. Respect, love, friendship, monetary awards, political power. You must EARN IT. Whether this is by personal prowess or faithful worship of Satan or some other method, all things worth any important must be earned. To give something away freely to those who are undeserving or ungrateful does nothing but cheapen the gift, until it means nothing at all. There is no power behind *"I love you"* if you love everyone. There is no value is money if everyone has all they want. If you want something special, be prepared to show that YOU are something special, as well. Lex Talonis is a Latin phrase meaning *"Law of the Talon,"* or, in other words *"eye for an eye."* Swift and fair, if brutal, justice. Today's penalty system, for most Satanists, is much too lax. One can do anything from shoplift to murder, and usually either get judged innocent, get set free on probation, or get cared for (food, bed, housing) for the rest of your life in jail. If you're going to punish people, then PUNISH THEM! Don't give them a slap on the wrist! Satanists believe in personal responsibility and accountability; that is, one is fully responsible for one's own actions, and should be aware of and acknowledge that fact. If you want to break the law, then break it! But be prepared to face the consequences. If you want to have unprotected sex, do it! But beware of possible diseases and pregnancy. Any action you take will have some ramification in your life; this does not curtail you from doing as you wish, but you must be prepared to answer to any issues which arise due to your actions.

Satanists believe "Satan" represents the admirable qualities of mankind. Satan is generally seen as representing pride, self-sufficiency, individuality, free-will, knowledge, and power. Many non-Satanists have trouble understanding how a traditionally *"evil"* figure can be regarded as positive, but this is how we see it. Such things as pride, ambition, and seeking knowledge is not considered evil by Satanists; on the other hand, false humility, wallowing in ignorance, and the like are considered bad traits to possess.

Foundation Of The Roman Catholic Cult

The greatest cult of all, and its influence through the ages has been the Roman Cult. What we will see is that the greatest Occultist is the one that has strived to eliminate it. As it is alive and strong within the Catholic charter of today, it is an inherent part of the practices and beliefs *"behind the scenes"* obviously because it retains certain powers. The **Roman Cult**, also known as the Roman Catholic Cult of the Vatican was first officially founded in 1057 by chief pagan high priest of the cult of Magna Mater (Cybele) known as Gregory VII.

The Roman Cult has never been the legitimate leadership of the Catholic Church. However, through a relentless campaign to seize and consolidate its power, this relatively small band of individuals now controls the destiny of over one billion good, Christian and ethical Catholics, who remained tricked into believing the legitimacy of the Roman Cult. This particular topic will be explained in later chapters, identifying the research and the history of the takeover.

We will touch on this briefly here for it was (and is) a brutal and bloody cult -- involving child sacrifice, burning people alive (since 11th Century CE), demonic worship and absolute celibacy of its lowest priests -- its epicentre for such evil being has been the giant Phrygianum atop Vatican Hill since the 2nd Century BCE. The tactics of this cult have been best illustrated by the time of the Inquisition. The prime purpose has through time to eliminate competition. Thus, that which is deployed as a secretive power within the Vatican and the Roman Cult, is discouraged, denied, and even destroyed with brutal force, threats and coercion should it be encroached on as a private power. It is, of course, nothing personal, just good business if you can eliminate competition and retain your trade secrets of power.

Since the 1st Century BCE, the high priest in a hereditary position controlled by a handful of ancient families or the gods claimed the ancient pre-Republic title of Pontifex Maximus after the Roman Emperors assumed themselves as high priest of the state cult of Magna Mater (Cybele). Jealously guarding their pagan heritage and right to sacrifice people to their demon gods, the priestly families were banished from Rome more than once along with the closure of the Vatican temple.

However, during the tumultuous periods in Roman history after the collapse of Rome as the center of the Empire, the pagan high priests assumed the role as community leaders in Rome and during more than one period, openly returned to their pagan practices of child sacrifice, cannibalism and demonic worship as late as 590 to 752, 847 to 872 and even as late as 896 1057.

In Latin, *"religio"* means *"something that binds."* For Romans, religion was a force that bound families together, bound subjects to their ruler and bound men to the gods. In going back to what Roman Religion was all about, we can summarize the key aspects which appear to be the silent beliefs and practices of the Roman Catholic-Vatican empire today. Oddly enough, this is not what they say is their belief, nor do they encourage their *"believers"* to follow.

Cult worship Unlike most religions today, the Roman gods did not demand strong moral behaviour. Roman religion involved cult worship. Approval from the gods did not depend on a person's behaviour, but on perfectly accurate observance of religious rituals. Each god needed an image that was usually a statue or relief in stone or bronze and an altar or temple at which to offer the prayers and sacrifices.

Private and public Roman religion was divided into two. Spirits watched over people, families and households, and the paterfamilias was in charge of the household worship that honoured them. Romans also had a set of public gods, such as Jupiter and Mars. State worship was much more formal: colleges of priests paid tribute to these gods on behalf of Rome itself.

Divine blessing The objective of Roman worship was to gain the blessing of the gods and thereby gain prosperity for themselves, their families and communities. Emperors understood the central importance of religion to the lives of the Romans and used it for their own ends. Augustus appointed himself as the chief priest as Pontifex Maximus, and used the appearance of Halley's Comet to claim that he was, himself, the son of a god.

Judaism in Ancient Rome The Roman religion was not the only one practiced in the first century AD. Far from it. Communities of Jews had existed in cities throughout the Roman Empire for centuries. Although they were generally treated with respect, trouble did occur. The Jewish philosopher, Philo, wrote of brutal treatment in Alexandria, while a revolt in Judaea led to the destruction of the temple and a change in the practice of the Jewish faith.

Rise of Christianity The first century also saw the birth of a brand new religion. Although he was executed by Rome at an early age, Jesus would have a massive impact on the Roman Empire. After his death, his message of eternal life and hope was spread across the empire by missionaries such as Paul. And although Christians in Rome suffered appalling persecution at times, their ideas refused to die. Instead, they would conquer Rome itself. Apart from the gods, who were glorified by the state, every Roman household worshipped spirits. They believed that spirits protected the family, home and even the trees and rivers. These spirits were worshipped regularly.

Early Roman religion The religion of ancient Rome dated back many centuries and over time it grew increasingly diverse. As different cultures settled in what would later become Italy, each brought their own gods and forms of worship. This made the religion of ancient Rome polytheistic, in that they worshipped many gods. They also worshipped spirits.

Spirits of the rivers and trees Rivers, trees, fields and buildings each had their own spirit, or numen. Worshipping more than one numen, or numina, was a part of early Roman culture. Clearly this stems from the Sumerian times and the gods word at that time.

Household spirits Every Roman household also had its own protective spirits. For instance, Vesta was the goddess of the fireplace. Even food cupboards had their own spirits, called penates.

Family spirits Families also had a protective spirit, called a lar. Each family had a larium, or shrine, to this spirit, often kept in the atrium or courtyard. The head of the family – the paterfamilias – was responsible for making regular sacrifices to honour the family's spirit and make sure that it continued to watch over them.

Dinnertime offerings Families also asked for the blessings of the spirits before any special family event. A portion of every meal was thrown into the fire as an offering. Household slaves were also expected to worship the same spirits as their owners. Like most of the ancient world, Romans believed that spirits gathered around crossroads. It was therefore common to find a small shrine, or compita, set up wherever paths or roads met. These would have four altars to honour the spirits in each direction.

Festival of the Crossroads This practice was honoured in the Festival of the Crossroads, called the Compitalia. On this feast day, families would hang woolen dolls and balls at the nearest compita. Each doll represented a member of the family, while each ball represented a slave. It isn't clear why they did this. Perhaps they hoped that the spirits would spare each person represented by the woolen offerings, or maybe they believed that the power of the spirits would strengthen each person represented there In any case, spirit worship was just one part of Roman religion. The Roman state had its own gods and, like the spirits, these were the product of diverse cultures and ancient beliefs.

The Hexagram is not a sign of Judaism. It is a sign of Zionism, Occultism, Satanism & Freemasonry. The hexagram is the most powerful and evil sign in Satanism and of all the occult world. The hexagram is used mainly in witchcraft to summon demons from the world. The word "hex" which means to place a curse on someone, originated from this sign.

The Hexagram is a six sided star, made up of a six sided hexagon surrounded by six equilateral triangles. Each equilateral triangle found within the Hexagram is 60° by 60° by 60°. The Hexagram represents 666 and is the 'Mark of the Beast' referred to in the Bible. As they say *"The Devil is in the details"*.

The Westside hand gesture or "Triad Claw" signals the letters M & W, which symbolise 666 from the three V's. The letter V is "waw" in Hebrew and "vav" in Gematria and is the 6th letter in both. The Sign of the Horns or El-Diablo hand gesture is a variation of the "Triad Claw" with the two attached fingers bent down. The A-ok hand gesture is also a representation of the number 666; with the middle finger, ring finger, and little finger representing the top part of the six's. The index finger and thumb represent the circular part of the six's.

Astrologically Saturn represents darkness, misfortune, death and fear. Saturday is named after the Roman god Saturn, the Ancient Greeks referred to this god as Cronus. The symbol of Saturn/Cronus is the sickle. Saturday is the 6th day of the week in western cultures and Saturn is the 6th planet from the Sun. Saturn had six children with his wife Ops, the 6th of these children was Jupiter or as the Greeks knew him, Zeus. The sickle of Saturn and hammer of Thor (Jupiter/Zeus) combined is represented in the symbol of Communism.

The core of the control over Planet Earth's populace lies in these ancient cults. These cults are still in existence to this day. Following the most ancient religions mixed with sexual worship. The main cults are the worship of the Planet Saturn (El), Moon (Isis), Venus (Lucifer) & Sun (Ra).

Child/Human Trafficking is one of the fastest growing crimes in the world. Child/ human trafficking is a 12 billion dollar a year industry and is the world's second largest criminal enterprise, after drugs. Saturn = Satan = El = Moloch. The power Elite of this world worship Saturn and appease him with child sacrifices just as they have for hundreds of years. The most public of these displays is the "Cremation of Care" ceremony held annually at Bohemian Grove, where the members sacrifice a child to their god Moloch. This will also be covered later.

The Conundrum Of Satan And God

It can be stated that there is an underlying belief system in force that is much different than that which is presented to the followers of religions. If what is being revealed in the research of the bloodlines, and what we state in the Vatican comments above, the real powers evident in the bloodlines, the Vatican, and those who have achieved great power of dominion would appear to be those that they wish to hide and protect for themselves as the privileged. Odd as it may seem to those who refuse to open their eyes and ears, Satan is the their god whom they worship and perform ritualistic practices before him. Yet the Vatican, Catholics and Christianity say Satan a bad guy who makes you sin into the carnal desires and rules of selfishness that give them the corporate advantages. The belief structure of Satanism is to enjoy the carnal ways of life and be proud to develop the self at the expense of others.

The great irony of all this is that the powers that Satanists allegedly protect in the bloodlines are the powers that all others must condemn as Satan's evil designs. Yet we must all seek the light of God. And the greatest irony of all is that those powers which are branded as dark evil on the Satan-Light side are the same as the light-good powers on the God-Light side. They are commonly termed the higher vibration psychic abilities that are unleashed through the Power of the Mind and its belief. The very abilities sought in the New Age rising of consciousness are the same as Satan's abilities, except use for light versus dark. It is all about the ability to believe and to manage the energies of the universe. Thus for example the ability to heal others on the light side has the opposite of the power to hurt others. It is simply a light or dark application.

It should be noted that contrary to mass belief, Satan and Lucifer are two different names and are not the same exact entities. This is the current misconception that many Bible believers have come to know for many generations already. In looking at definitions it seems that Lucifer is actually the angel of God that He named in heaven as one of the most, or perhaps the most perfect angel ever created. It was only when Lucifer was cast down from heaven that his alternate entity was known as Satan. Lucifer was banished because of his pure egoism, not to mention his pride that was regarded as his greatest sin. Hence by theory, Lucifer is the first one to have committed sin. So Lucifer is the name of an angel whereas Satan is the name given to the devil. It is said that Satan has lived in the Spirit world for more than 6,000 years. In this regard he has not yet been visible to human beings. It is however foretold that he will make himself visible soon by appearing physically in the world and will call himself the Beast, a very remarkable being that will proclaim himself as God. Is this different than God who needs appear?

Lucifer is not the opposite of God because he was also a creature made by God. He can thus be more likened to Michael the Archangel, in terms of position. On the other hand, Satan connotes more on the idea of an opposing resistance. The misconceptions between Lucifer and Satan, as the exact same entity or name, started with the misinterpretations of the Gospel by various sectors. Lucifer is a name that was mentioned only once in the

KJV or King James Version of the Bible, specifically in Isaiah 14:12. But in Hebrew, the literal translation for his name would mean 'to shine' or 'to bear light.' In the said gospel, Lucifer was likened to the parable of the King of Babylon wherein he was seen as someone who wanted to rule over all making himself similar to God. This monarch would be depicted as a man who will see the collapse of his dominion. He will die like a man, be eaten by worms, his grave being walked upon. This could not be Satan because Satan has no physical form. He is a spirit that lives in the dark Spirit world, postulated to be somewhere between heaven and earth (just below heaven).

Satanism As A Corporate Business Model

It should not take a genius to realize that these bloodlines have some special smarts and that these smarts are part of the powers maintenance system of the Vatican. It does not take a genius to understand that the belief system imposed upon humanity is opposite the belief system of those in power and the Vatican. It does not take a genius to understand that to destroy the competition is a great corporate strategy for a profitable and effective business model.

And it should not be a stretch for anyone to understand that these beliefs that are allocated to the god Lucifer or Satan, namely; Stupid people do not get ahead in this world. Satanists strive to keep themselves informed and to not be fooled by others who seek to manipulate and use them. Taking pride in one's achievements is encouraged but only take credit for one's own accomplishments. That all with his own individual goals and plans. To expect someone to treat you as you treat him is foolish. Instead, Satanists encourages you to treat people as they treat you. You should always deal with the reality of the situation rather than expectations. Convincing yourself of untruths because they are more comfortable is no less problematic than letting someone else deceive you. To exalt the power of the individual. Western culture encourages people to go with the flow, and to believe and do things simply because the wider community is doing such. Satanists attempt to avoid such behavior, following the herd only if it makes logical sense and suits one's own needs. Remain aware of both the big and small pictures, never sacrificing one for the other. Remember your own important place in things, and don't be overwhelmed with the viewpoints of the herd. On the flipside, we do live in a world larger than ourselves. Always keep an eye on the big picture and how you can fit yourself into it. Do not be fooled by old ideas. If it works, use it. You should never be embarrassed of your own accomplishments. However, if pride is getting in the way of getting things done with other people, you should set it aside until such time as it becomes constructive again. Beauty and balance are two things to strive for in magical practices but can be extended to the rest of one's life as well. Avoid following that which society dictates is beautiful and learn to identify true beauty, whether or not others recognize it.

This enjoy life model is totally focused at one's self one would say is the intellectual, ego self--the head, in a heartless world of betterment, the world of corporations (outside). The opposite, the world of peace, love and self less ego non carnal life in the heart (inside) is the heartfelt purpose of spirituality. One is all about God or Christ, the other Satan. But is it not interesting that the ones who have applied these beliefs the best have created the greatest corporations on planet Earth and the Eartling strives to create corporations too?

And as to the business plan itself, the New World Order may well seek peace eventually but it is through total dominion of one religion, one government, one board of directors, one currency, one set of laws for all. And since humanity appears to like this by allowing socialism and communism to prevail, for whatever reason, perhaps this strategy of the top elite may not be so bad for the many who love to be led?

Again, the word communism has vile repercussions because it is believed to be so. Yet in the business plan of PLANET EARTH we see the rapid manifestation of the The Communist Manefsto throughout the "*free*" world". For example, he second section, "*Proletarians and Communists*", starts by stating the relationship of conscious communists to the rest of the working class, declaring that they will not form a separate party that opposes other working-class parties, will express the interests and general will of the proletariat as a whole, and will distinguish themselves from other working-class parties by always expressing the common interest of the entire proletariat independently of all nationalities and representing the interests of the movement as a whole.

The section goes on to defend communism from various objections, such as the claim that communists advocate "*free love*", and the claim that people will not perform labor in a communist society because they have no incentive to work. The section ends by outlining a set of short-term demands:

1. Abolition of property in land and application of all rents of land to public purposes.
2. A heavy progressive or graduated income tax.
3. Abolition of all right of inheritance.
4. Confiscation of the property of all emigrants and rebels.
5. Centralization of credit in the hands of the State, by means of a national bank with State capital and an exclusive monopoly.
6. Centralization of the means of communication and transport in the hands of the State.
7. Extension of factories and instruments of production owned by the State; the bringing into cultivation of waste-lands, and the improvement of the soil generally in accordance with a common plan.
8. Equal liability of all to labor. Establishment of industrial armies, especially for agriculture.
9. Combination of agriculture with manufacturing industries; gradual abolition of the distinction between town and country, by a more equitable distribution of the population over the country.
10. Free education for all children in public schools. Abolition of children's factory labor in its present form and combination of education with industrial production.

It would appear that humanity, despite its resistance to this has actually unknowingly manifested it by their acceptance. Is this not the Law of Attraction working in mass consciousness? The implementation of these policies would, as believed by Marx and Engels, be a precursor to the stateless and classless society. In a controversial passage they suggested that the "*proletariat*" might in competition with the bourgeoisie be compelled to organize as a class, form a revolution, make itself a ruling class, sweep away the old conditions of production, and in that step have abolished its own supremacy as a class. This account of the transition from socialism to communism was criticized particularly during and after the Soviet era.

There is yet another aspect to ponder here as one called polarity. Everywhere in humanity's quest is this two-sided aspect of life that has been accepted.

• You can do bad things for Satan but you can be forgiven by god;
• God loves you until you disagree with him;
• Love and protect your bloodline but not those who would do harm to them;

- You can have big ego but worship the greater ones;
- You can sin but some charity will balance the karma.

It goes on and on because everywhere, in religion and commerce the belief system is the corporate model of dog-eat dog competitive commerce. And those that know this the best have created the monolithic corporations in the operational layer of the PLANET EARTH Inc.

And when these great corporations with products that fit the needs of the business plan and catch the eye of the top people, what happens? A takeover, merger, the worship of the god of money, and perhaps others as well. Just like Mr. Walt Disney?

Do these people have special powers from the occult side? It would be total stupidity as in the first satanic belief to presume they do not. Corporations are the gifts given to the slaves to build dynasties as well, but they are still under the rules of PLANET EARTH.

Can everyone have these powers. Yes, sell your soul to the devil or to gods or to God. Is there a difference. Let us see later there is really no difference.

But before we leave this topic, it is of interest to see what these secret Societies are that these mighty corporate powers with the hierarchy of PLANET EARTH frequent. There appears to be a common bond here that the world leaders silently believe in. Now let us look at the Empire, their bloodlines and their followers as partners in the Corporation PLANET EARTH. Let us look more closely at what are these "secret" groups and what they follow on the surface, and under the surface.

The Darker History Of The Vatican

We have alluded to a deeper connection to occult at the Vatican than meets the eye. According to various sources, including the **Jewish Encyclopaedia**, the House of Rothschild has been the long-standing trustee of the Vatican's wealth. *"Early in the 19th century the Pope came to the Rothschilds to borrow money. The Rothschilds were very friendly with the Pope, causing one journalist to sarcastically say 'Rothschild has kissed the hand of the Pope... Order has been re-established.' The Rothschilds in fact over time were entrusted with the bulk of the Vatican's wealth."* **The Jewish Ency**., vol. 2, p. 497 states, *"It is a somewhat curious sequel to the attempt to set up a Catholic competitor to the Rothschilds that at the present time (1905) the latter are guardians of the papal treasure."* Researcher Eustace Mullins writes *"that the Rothschilds took over all the financial operations of the worldwide Catholic Church in 1823. Today the large banking and financial business of the Catholic Church is an extensive system interlocked with the Rothschilds and the rest of the International Banking system."*

It appears that the Medici were involved in the Rothschild takeover of the Vatican's financial operations and, indeed, all of Italy, as well as the creation of a new front for the disentitled Bavarian Illuminati, the Carbonari, of which the Alta Vendita was the highest lodge:

Side Note: The Medici The **House of Medici** or **Famiglia de' Medici** was a political dynasty, banking family and later royal house that first began to gather prominence under Cosimo de' Medici in the Republic of Florence during the late 14th century. The family originated in the Mugello region of the Tuscan countryside, gradually rising until they were able to found the Medici Bank. The bank was the largest in Europe during the 15th century, seeing the Medici gain political power in Florence — though officially they remained simply citizens rather than monarchs. The Medici produced four Popes of the

Catholic Church—Pope Leo X (1513–1521), Pope Clement VII (1523–1534), Pope Pius IV (1559–1565), and Pope Leo XI (1605); two regent queens of France—Catherine de' Medici (1547–1559) and Marie de' Medici (1600–1610); and, in 1531, the family became hereditary Dukes of Florence. In 1569, the duchy was elevated to a grand duchy after territorial expansion. They ruled the Grand Duchy of Tuscany from its inception until 1737, with the death of Gian Gastone de' Medici. The grand duchy witnessed degrees of economic growth under the earlier grand dukes, but by the time of Cosimo III de' Medici, Tuscany was fiscally bankrupt. Their wealth and influence initially derived from the textile trade guided by the guild of the Arte della Lana. Like other signore families they dominated their city's government. They were able to bring Florence under their family's power, allowing for an environment where art and humanism could flourish. They fostered and inspired the birth of the Italian Renaissance along with other families of Italy, such as the Visconti and Sforza of Milan, the Este of Ferrara, and the Gonzaga of Mantua. The Medici Bank was one of the most prosperous and most respected institutions in Europe. There are some estimates that the Medici family were the wealthiest family in Europe for a period of time. From this base, they acquired political power initially in Florence and later in wider Italy and Europe. A notable contribution to the profession of accounting was the improvement of the general ledger system through the development of the double-entry bookkeeping system for tracking credits and debits. This system was first used by accountants working for the Medici family in Florence.

In continuing, in 1821 Carl [Kalman Rothschild] was sent to Naples, Italy to oversee loans there that were meant to finance Metternich's forces who had arrived to quell a rebellion. While in Italy the Rothschild mantle came upon Carl and he made a series of ingenious deals with the Italian government that forced Naples to pay for its own occupation. He also helped Luigi de Medici of the Black Nobility to re-gain his position as finance minister of Naples, and later did business with the powerful man. Due to his success it was decided that he would stay in Naples and set up his own bank. He became financier to the court, the financial overlord of Italy. Carl "...wound the Italian peninsula around his hand." He did business with the Vatican, and when Pope Gregory XVI received him by giving him his hand rather than the customary toe to kiss, people realized the extent of his power. The Pope conferred upon him the Order of St. George.

It appears that in Italy Carl became a leader of Carbonarism. After the Bavarian Illuminati was exposed, Carbonarism (or the Alta Vendita) became the major European occult power. Carl's leadership in this group is very significant. In 1818 a secret Alta Vendita document, that Carl had participated in preparing, was sent to the headquarters of Masonry. A copy of this document was lost, and the Masons got very upset, and offered rewards for the return of this copy. The title of the document translates "Permanent Instructions, or Practical Code of Rules; Guide for the Heads of the Highest Grades of Freemasonry". (Top 13 Illuminati Bloodlines). The Alta Vendita was governed by Jews and the "**Permanent Instructions, or Practical Code of Rules; Guide for the Heads of the Highest Grades of Freemasonry"** corresponds to the **"The Protocols of the Meetings of the Learned Elders of Zion"** - more evidence linking the House of Rothschild with the Protocols.

Recall that Jeroboam Rothschild directed the secret Elders of Zion.

The original Italian translation of the document entitled Permanent Instructions or Practical Code of Rules; Guide for the Heads of the Highest Grades of Masonry was given to Nubio (Piccolo Tigre, a nondescript 'Jew') of the Alta Vendita lodge in 1824 when he was sent to Rome to carry it into effect, and it was to this instruction that he referred when he wrote from Forli to Signor Volpi, "As I have written to you before, I am appointed to demoralise the education of the youth of the (Roman) Church". These secret

Instructions which were written in 1815, are in perfect accord with the Protocols of the Learned Elders of Zion and intended only for a chosen few Masons of heavy calibre.

Protocol	Title[19]
1	The Basic Doctrine: "Right Lies in Might"
2	Economic War and Disorganization Lead to International Government
3	Methods of Conquest
4	The Destruction of Religion by Materialism
5	Despotism and Modern Progress
6	The Acquisition of Land, The Encouragement of Speculation
7	A Prophecy of Worldwide War
8	The transitional Government
9	The All-Embracing Propaganda
10	Abolition of the Constitution; Rise of the Autocracy
11	The Constitution of Autocracy and Universal Rule
12	The Kingdom of the Press and Control
13	Turning Public Thought from Essentials to Non-essentials
14	The Destruction of Religion as a Prelude to the Rise of the Jewish God
15	Utilization of Masonry: Heartless Suppression of Enemies
16	The Nullification of Education
17	The Fate of Lawyers and the Clergy
18	The Organization of Disorder
19	Mutual Understanding Between Ruler and People
20	The Financial Program and Construction
21	Domestic Loans and Government Credit
22	The Beneficence of Jewish Rule
23	The Inculcation of Obedience
24	The Jewish Ruler

The Prieuré de Sion, which is directed by the House of Rothschild, works from the shadows, yet one need only consider the list of past Grand Masters of this high cabal to begin to comprehend the magnitude of its influence and power. Baigent, **Leigh and Lincoln** disclosed the nature of its membership in **Holy Blood, Holy Grail**: "*The French press, in a brief article on M. Plantard's election as Grand Master in 1981, had stated that 'the 121 high dignitaries of the Prieuré de Sion are all eminences grises of high finance and of international political or philosophical organizations'.*" (p. 362)

In his **Introduction to the Protocols of Zion**, **Victor Marsden** wrote of other gray eminences who wield unofficial power, secretly sheltered under the umbrella of the Prieuré de Sion: "*...in 1931...Jean Izoulet, a prominent member of the Jewish Alliance Israelite Universelle, wrote in his Paris la Capitale des Religions: - 'The meaning of the history of the last century is that today 300 Jewish financiers, all Masters of Lodges, rule the world.'*"

Springmeier stated in **The Top 13 Illuminati Bloodline**s, *"It has been said all roads lead to Rome. For this book, it could be said all paths of investigation lead to the Rothschilds."*

Which means all roads lead to the Prieuré de Sion: *"The Prieuré de Sion - the Elders of Sion also relates to the Rothschilds who are reported to serve on a Jewish council of Elders of Sion... For instance, Armstrong, The Rothschild Trust, p. 196, 'That is the present objective of Jeroboam Rothschild and his secret Elders of Zion.'"* (pp.152,163) Springmeier also references *Holy Blood, Holy Grail*, *"...the text of the Protocols [of the Elders of Sion] ends with a single statement, 'Signed by the representatives of Sion of the 33rd Degree'."* (p.193)

One way to discover the Prieuré's oversight of the occult underground is to follow the rabbit trails between various secret societies as they are mentioned in New Age publications. For example:

"...The Scandals of the Prieure de Sion...[alleged] On January 1981 - two days, that is, after Pierre Plantard de Saint-Claire was elected Grand Master of the Prieure de Sion - a high-ranking member of the Order is alleged by 'Cornelius' to have had a meeting with Licio Gelli, Grand Master of the P2. The meeting is said to have occurred at the brasserie called La Tipia on the rue de Rome in Paris..."

"...As far as we know it is widely disseminated....if any of 'Cornelius's' allegations should prove to have even a degree of validity, it will open the lid of a particularly unpleasant can of worms..."

"It is now generally acknowledged that P2, however influential and powerful it may have been, was (and probably still is) controlled by some even higher, more shadowy authority, which transmitted its instructions through Licio Gelli, the Lodge's Grand Master. According to an Italian parliamentary commission, the organisation behind P2 lay 'beyond the frontiers of Italy'. There has been much speculation, both plausible and otherwise, about his organisation. Some have identified it as the...Prieure de Sion." (**The Messianic Legacy**, 308-9, 352)

"...while conducting their research, the authors of [Holy Blood, Holy Grail and The Messianic Legacy] came across indications that The Prieuré had been heavily infiltrated by both the Knights of Malta and the P2 Mason lodge, two secret societies notorious for their involvement with mobsters and fascists." (**Dagobert's Revenge**)

"I had intended to go into great detail linking P2, the Prieuré de Sion, the Vatican, the CIA, organizations for a United Europe, and the Bilderberg Group. Fortunately, Michael Baigent, Richard Leigh & Henry Lincoln beat me to it." (William Cooper, Behold a Pale Horse, pp.77-9)

"Some interesting things have come to light about the Prieuré recently. One is that the Swiss Grand Lodge Alpina (GLA), the highest body of Swiss Freemasonry (akin to the Grand Lodge of England), may have been the recruiting body for the Prieuré. But the GLA is also said by some to be the meeting place of the 'Gnomes of Zurich' who are said to be the Power Elite of Swiss bankers and international financiers. The GLA is said by David Yallop to be the body which controlled the P2 Masonic Lodge in Italy."

"P2 controlled the Italian secret police in the 1970s, took money from the CIA and KGB, may have had a hand in the kidnapping of Aldo Moro by the Red Brigades, had 900 agents in other branches of the Italian government and the highest positions of the

96

Vatican...used the Vatican Bank to launder Mafia drug money, fomented fascist coups in South America, and is most likely linked to the arch-conservative Knights of Malta and Opus Dei in the Vatican." (__Mysteries of Rennes le Chateau__)

In 1958, **Angelo Roncalli**, who became Pope John XXIII, was allegedly a member of the Prieuré de Sion.

"The name John had been implicitly anathematized since it was last used in the early fifteenth century by an Antipope! Moreover, there had already been a John XXIII - the Antipope who abdicated in 1415. Thus the selection by Roncalli of the name Pope John XXIII was unusual to say the least, and raised many questions."

One answer was suggested in 1976 by a book called **The Prophecies of Pope John XXIII.** The book was allegedly a compilation of obscure prophetic prose written by the Pontiff. In addition, the book also maintained that Pope John XXIII was secretly a member of the Rose-Croix, (a subtitle for the Prieuré de Sion) with whom he had become affiliated while acting as papal nuncio to Turkey in 1935. Furthermore, it was suggested that Cardinal Roncalli, on becoming Pope, had chosen the name of his own secret grand master - so that, for some symbolic reason, there would be a John XXIII presiding over Sion and the papacy simultaneously." **(Library of Halexandria**)

One of the first initiatives of **John XXIII** was to publish an encyclical on **The Precious Blood of Jesus,** the staggering ramifications of which will soon be realized as the doctrines pertaining to *Jesus'* crucifixion have been hurled into the public forum for debate:

"Finally, in June 1960, Pope John XXIII issued a profoundly important apostolic letter, whose subject was 'the Precious Blood of Jesus.' This letter emphasized Jesus' suffering as a human being and maintained that the redemption of mankind had been effected by the shedding of his blood. In the context of Pope John's letter, Jesus' human Passion and the shedding of his blood assume a greater consequence than the Resurrection or even than the mechanics of the Crucifixion!"

"The implications are enormous. The letter alters the whole basis of Christian belief. If man's redemption was achieved by the shedding of Jesus' blood, his death and resurrection become incidental - if not, indeed, superfluous. Through his letter Pope John XXIII implies that the death of Jesus on the cross is no longer a requisite tenet of the Roman Catholic faith. Jesus need not have died on the cross for the Catholic faith to retain its validity." (Ibid.)

John XXIII's encyclical allows for the Merovingian version of *Jesus*, who did not die but recovered from the crucifixion and fled to France with his wife and offspring. The author of the popular book, **The DaVinci Code, Dan Brow**n said that when he wrote the best seller that dissects the origins of *Jesus Christ* and disputes long-held beliefs about Catholicism, he considered including material alleging that *Jesus Christ* survived the crucifixion." (**CNN)**

The 1960 encyclical also cleared a theological path for *"The Passion of the Christ"* film which also overemphasized *Jesus* suffering as a human being, made no statement about His divinity and omitted, not only the Virgin Birth, but also the Ascension. So where did Mel Gibson's *"Jesus"* go after his dubious resurrection, resuscitation and/or recuperation from the crucifixion? Perchance to the South of France with Mary Magdalene and their child? This is the gospel according to ***http://www.humanists.net/***:

The Vatican And The Bloodlines Follow Satan's Model?

So when you look carefully at what appears as a common denominator of the bloodlines as the Earthly "gods", the founders and directors of PLANET EARTH, and the Vatican who actively spread the Word of God, they appear to secretly believe in Satanism. Why would they be so rooted in the Occult? This is quite a strange conundrum.

The Vatican leaders say Satan a bad guy yet they worship him as their god?

The powers that Satanists allegedly protect in the bloodlines are the powers that all others must condemn as Satan's evil designs or they are heretics?

The powers on the Dark Satan side are the same powers on the Light side, just a different application?

The belief structure of Satanism is to enjoy the carnal ways of life and be proud to develop them at the expense of others while the belief of the other religions is to reject the carnal ways as they are sin?

The very abilities sought in the New Age rising of consciousness are the same as Satan's darker abilities, except use for light versus dark?

We will now leave this topic temporarily and get back to PLANET EARTH Inc. In a simple sense, we have looked at the founders and directors of PLANET EARTH. But who really runs the show?

6

THE BLACK EMPIRE

Introducing The Jesuits

Who really directs the activities of PLANET EARTH and the top bloodlines? We have looked at the families and it would be safe to assume that the male head of each bloodline, the head of the "House" would be a member of the Board of Directors in our simple model. We have also assumed that a Rothschild would be the Chairman of the Board. These could also be the Founders and Shareholders all interested in the Occult and the New world Order Plan. But where does the power reside that really controls things? It is natural to conclude that fear of death and pain, or fear of loss of wealth and position are the major policing mechanisms of the corporate and private power system. Normally, the military, the rules of conduct, the beliefs all go to policing this. In the private world, it is the blood relationships, the vows, the oaths pledged upon death and honour that govern this. One would expect that even the directors and chairman have the same fear. But who is it that could possibly use fear on them to control and direct the activities of the corporation?

What Earthlings must begin to understand is that the truth of what is being brought forward here is not going to be readily admitted. All the participants would be sworn by oath to obey the laws and code of the "blood" for fear of death and destruction. Any attempt to draw this out would be faced with outright denial and plausible deniability. The players must look like any other Earthling. However, what is being found more and more is that the evidence is growing to show another story as to what these oath takers are up to.

Let us now move to the research found on the website *http://warningilluminati.wordpress.com/the-most-powerful-man-in-the-world-the-black-pope/.* This man is stated to be the most powerful man in the world. Yet when confronted is a meek, mild mannered Earthling like anyone else. First, we shall introduce him and the Order that he directs. This will be explained later in several chapters bringing out the evidence to support a claim that the Jesuit Order is that force that policies the Directors of PLANET EARTH Inc.

It is stated here that: The Black Pope Adolfo Nicolas is the most powerful man on Planet Earth. He, the Superior General of the Society of Jesus have the Diabolical Plan for a New World Order which is being executed through PLANET EARTH. They would be the policing mechanism. It states here:

1. The Superior General of the Jesuits The Black Pope, Adolfo Nicolas and his 6 generals control the "White Pope" Pope Benedict XVI and the Vatican.
2. The Illuminati, Zionists, globalist Elites, Council on Foreign Relations, Bilderberg group, Freemasons, Council of 300 and the evil Council of Trent.
3. The Jesuits control the Knights Templar, Knights of Columbus and the Knights of Malta.
4. The CIA, FBI, NSA, ASIO, MI5, MI6, NCIS, FSB, DGSE, Mossad and every intelligence agency in the world are masonic and controlled by the Jesuits.
5. The Jesuits have infiltrated all governments & Leaders like Obama, Rudd, Blair, Jintao, Sarkozy, Peres are only puppets that carry out Jesuit orders.

He is the most powerful man on Earth, who rules over Maritime Laws (business). He controls the banking system, Freemasonry and the Secret Services (CIA, FBI, NSA, SIS, MI6, Scotland Yard, Mossad, CSIS, DGSE, FSB). The Vatican owns 60% of all Israel lands and the Land of the Temple Mount for their Third Solomon's Temple where they want their throne. He is a part of the Arcana Arcanorum controlled by the Papal Bloodlines within the I-Mori. These bloodlines are the omega point of control. These are the Farnese, ORSINI, Aldobrandini, Somaglia & Breakspear. Their war room command center is within the Borgo Santo Spirito which is missile protected! Viktor Emmanuelle IV wanted to nuke this region of Rome. Henry Breakspear and Pepe Orsini are in high control! Jesuit Assistancy Soldier, James Grummer controls the United States Corporation.

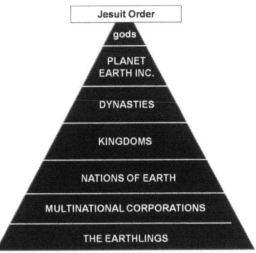

It turns out that Superiors General are elected by the General Congregation of the Society, summoned upon the resignation, retirement or death of an incumbent. Superiors General are elected for life and almost all have served life terms, the exceptions being Father Pedro Arrupe (resigned for reasons of failing health) and his successor, Father Peter Hans Kolvenbach. Kolvenbach's resignation was announced in February 2006, which led to the convocation of the 35th General Congregation. That General Congregation elected the current Superior General of the Society, Father Adolfo Nicolás, who succeeded Kolvenbach.

We also know that the "NEW WORLD ORDER" is the GLOBAL TOTALITARIANISM dream that a BANKER called Mayer Amschel Rothschild, helped revive in 1760's to protect his private bank from global government regulation. His grand blue print is best described by his paid social engineer called Dr. Adam [Spartacus] Weishaupt, Professor of Canon Law in the university of Ingolstadt. Weishaupt adopted the term *"Illuminati."* This nightmare is still sought after today by their family's decedents. Below is the 'outline' Weishaupt set out for his banker financier master! Carefully notice the similarities between Karl Marx's 10 Plank's of his Communist Manifesto and Weishaupt's outline. Also, please read Communism & The New World Order.

The blue print for the New World Order is:

- Abolition of all ordered governments

- Abolition of private property
- Abolition of inheritance
- Abolition of patriotism
- Abolition of the family
- Abolition of religion
- A global population of 500 million
- Creation of a world government

Mayer Amschel Rothschild 1828 *"Allow me to issue and control the money of a nation, and I care not who writes the laws."* (Even a 4 year old can understand that people with control of money...write the laws!)

"Some of the biggest men in the United States, in the field of commerce and manufacture, are afraid of something. They know that there is a power somewhere so organized, so subtle, so watchful, so interlocked, so complete, so pervasive, that they had better not speak above their breath when they speak in condemnation of it." – Woodrow Wilson

So who is this subtle, complete organized power that Wilson is talking about? The answer to that is the Jesuits. Who are the Jesuits you may ask? Aren't they just missionaries, priests and general do-gooders who establish schools, universities and pride themselves in being pillars in the community? If so, then why was The Jesuit Order abolished in over 80 countries in 1773? **J.E.C. Shepherd** states:

"Between 1555 and 1931 the Society of Jesus [i.e., the Jesuit Order] was expelled from at least 83 countries, city states and cities, for engaging in political intrigue and subversion plots against the welfare of the State, according to the records of a Jesuit priest of repute [Thomas J. Campbell]. Practically every instance of expulsion was for political intrigue, political infiltration, political subversion, and inciting to political insurrection."

It seems that they are overlords of chaos. In a nut shell the Jesuits are alleged to be Warlords, Assassins, Teachers, Infiltrators, Tyrants. They tried their hand at global domination with the League of Nations but it failed, now they are trying again, under a new name...The United Nations, and apparently it's about to work because their agenda is well hidden under oath. What people are beginning to find out is that the Jesuits command the White Pope and the Vatican City, Obama /Bush's/ Clinton's / Blair's / Peres/ Rudd / Jintao / Sarkozy / Medvedev (and frankly every government on earth) including the Council of Trent, CFR, Illuminati, the Zionists, the Bilderberg group, the Freemasons, the Knights of Malta, the Knights of Columbus, the Knights Templar, Council of 300. What are these groups? We will uncover these in subsequent chapters. And every intelligence organization in the world all have ties to the Jesuit Order and more specifically, the Superior General of the Jesuits known as The Black Pope Adolfo Nicolas who as of January the 19th, 2008 succeeded Peter-Hans Kolvenbach as the 30th Superior General of the Jesuit Order. This quiet, seemingly unassuming man appears to have a whole new oath and agenda.

The following material contained in Congressional Record, House Bill 1523, Contested election case of Eugene C. Bonniwell, against Thos. S. Butler, February 15, 1913, pages 3215-6. The oath appears in its entirety, in the book, **The Suppressed Truth About The Assassination Of Abraham Lincoln,** by **Burke McCarty**, pages 14-16). It is called the **The Extreme Oath of the Jesuits:**

"I, I…………., now, in the presence of Almighty God, the Blessed Virgin Mary, the blessed Michael the Archangel, the blessed St. John the Baptist, the holy Apostles St. Peter and St. Paul and all the saints and sacred hosts of heaven, and to you, my ghostly father, the Superior General of the Society of Jesus, founded by St. Ignatius Loyola in the Pontificate of Paul the Third, and continued to the present, do by the womb of the virgin, the matrix of God, and the rod of Jesus Christ, declare and swear, that his holiness the Pope is Christ's Vice-regent and is the true and only head of the Catholic or Universal Church throughout the earth; and that by virtue of the keys of binding and loosing, given to his Holiness by my Savior, Jesus Christ, he hath power to depose heretical kings, princes, states, commonwealths and governments, all being illegal without his sacred confirmation and that they may safely be destroyed."

"Therefore, to the utmost of my power I shall and will defend this doctrine of his Holiness' right and custom against all usurpers of the heretical or Protestant authority whatever, especially the Lutheran of Germany, Holland, Denmark, Sweden, Norway, and the now pretended authority and churches of England and Scotland, and branches of the same now established in Ireland and on the Continent of America and elsewhere; and all adherents in regard that they be usurped and heretical, opposing the sacred Mother Church of Rome. I do now renounce and disown any allegiance as due to any heretical king, prince or state named Protestants or Liberals, or obedience to any of the laws, magistrates or officers."

"I do further declare that the doctrine of the churches of England and Scotland, of the Calvinists, Huguenots and others of the name Protestants or Liberals to be damnable and they themselves damned who will not forsake the same."

"I do further declare, that I will help, assist, and advise all or any of his Holiness' agents in any place wherever I shall be, in Switzerland, Germany, Holland, Denmark, Sweden, Norway, England, Ireland or America, or in any other Kingdom or territory I shall come to, and do my uttermost to extirpate the heretical Protestants or Liberals' doctrines and to destroy all their pretended powers, legal or otherwise."

"I do further promise and declare, that notwithstanding I am dispensed with, to assume my religion heretical, for the propaganda of the Mother Church's interest, to keep secret and private all her agents' counsels from time to time, as they may entrust me and not to divulge, directly or indirectly, by word, writing or circumstance whatever; but to execute all that shall be proposed, given in charge or discovered unto me, by you, my ghostly father, or any of this sacred covenant."

"I do further promise and declare, that I will have no opinion or will of my own, or any mental reservation whatever, even as a corpse or cadaver (perinde ac cadaver), but will unhesitatingly obey each and every command that I may receive from my superiors in the Militia of the Pope and of Jesus Christ."

"That I may go to any part of the world withersoever I may be sent, to the frozen regions of the North, the burning sands of the desert of Africa, or the jungles of India, to the centers of civilization of Europe, or to the wild haunts of the barbarous savages of America, without murmuring or repining, and will be submissive in all things whatsoever communicated to me."

"I furthermore promise and declare that I will, when opportunity present, make and wage relentless war, secretly or openly, against all heretics, Protestants and Liberals, as I am directed to do, to extirpate and exterminate them from the face of the whole earth; and that I will spare neither age, sex or condition; and that I will hang, waste, boil, flay, strangle and bury alive these infamous heretics, rip up the stomachs and wombs of their women and crush their infants' heads against the walls, in order to annihilate forever their execrable race. That when the same cannot be done openly, I will secretly use the poisoned cup, the strangulating cord, the steel of the poniard or the leaden bullet, regardless of the honor, rank, dignity, or authority of the person or persons, whatever may be their condition in life, either public or private, as I at any time may be directed so to do by any agent of the Pope or Superior of the Brotherhood of the Holy Faith, of the Society of Jesus."

"In confirmation of which, I hereby dedicate my life, my soul and all my corporal powers, and with this dagger which I now receive, I will subscribe my name written in my own blood, in testimony thereof; and should I prove false or weaken in my determination, may my brethren and fellow soldiers of the Militia of the Pope cut off my hands and my feet, and my throat from ear to ear, my belly opened and sulphur burned therein, with all the punishment that can be inflicted upon me on earth and my soul be tortured by demons in an eternal hell forever!"

"All of which, I, ..., do swear by the Blessed Trinity and blessed Sacraments, which I am now to receive, to perform and on my part to keep inviolable; and do call all the heavenly and glorious host of heaven to witness the blessed Sacrament of the Eucharist, and witness the same further with my name written and with the point of this dagger dipped in my own blood and sealed in the face of this holy covenant."

In this process the appointed Superior General receives the wafer from the Superior and writes his name with the point of his dagger dipped in his own blood taken from over his heart. The Superior then states:

"You will now rise to your feet and I will instruct you in the Catechism necessary to make yourself known to any member of the Society of Jesus belonging to this rank. In the first place, you, as a Brother Jesuit, will with another mutually make the ordinary sign of the cross as any ordinary Roman Catholic would; then one crosses his wrists, the palms of his hands open, and the other in answer crosses his feet, one above the other; the first points with forefinger of the right hand to the center of the palm of the left, the other with the forefinger of the left hand points to the center of the palm of the right; the first then with his right hand makes a circle around his head, touching it; the other then with the forefinger of his left hand touches the left side of his body just below his heart; the first then with his right hand draws it across the throat of the other, and the latter then with a dagger down the stomach and abdomen of the first. The first then says Iustum; and the other answers Necar; the first Reges. The other answers Impious. (The meaning of which has already been explained.) The first will then present a small piece of paper folded in a peculiar manner, four times, which the other will cut longitudinally and on opening the name Jesu will be found written upon the head and arms of a cross three times. You will then give and receive with him the following questions and answers:-"

Question:- From whither do you come?
Answer:- The Holy faith.
Q.:- Whom do you serve?
A.:- The Holy Father at Rome, the Pope, and the Roman Catholic Church Universal throughout the world.

Q.:- Who commands you?
A.:- The Successor of St. Ignatius Loyola, the founder of the Society of Jesus or the Soldiers of Jesus Christ.
Q.:- Who received you?
A.:- A venerable man in white hair.
Q.:- How?
A.:- With a naked dagger, I kneeling upon the cross beneath the banners of the Pope and of our sacred order.
Q.:- Did you take an oath?
A.:- I did, to destroy heretics and their governments and rulers, and to spare neither age, sex nor condition. To be as a corpse without any opinion or will of my own, but to implicitly obey my Superiors in all things without hesitation of murmuring.
Q.:- Will you do that?
A.:- I will.
Q.:- How do you travel?
A.:- In the bark of Peter the fisherman.
Q.:- Whither do you travel?
A.:- To the four quarters of the globe.
Q.:- For what purpose?
A.:- To obey the orders of my general and Superiors and execute the will of the Pope and faithfully fulfill the conditions of my oaths.

Is this just some idle prankster writing this? Could you imagine the fallout and the result upon the oath taker if this was truth? Is the denial and the front of a "normal God loving" priest just a front? Let us look deeper.

The Vatican Assassins

One of most staggering revelations on this topic is the research conducted by **Eric Jon Phelps** and his book **Vatican Assassins. Refer** to his web site at **www.vaticanassassins.org**. This website is one of the better that is dedicated to the revelation of a new truth about the New World Order and who the people are that are running the plan. Phelps tells a story so strange to most mortals that it boggles the mind. Yet he supports it with evidence that is difficult to dispute. In a most revealing interview posted on the website the following of which is only a portion. The interview was done by Rick Martin on behalf of The SPECTRUM who states:

"You've gotten familiar with the role played by, for instance, the Khazarian Zionists (who invented the word 'Jew' to disguise their adopted heritage, as distinguished from the biblical Judeans), or the role played by the Banksters (banking gangsters) controlling the economies of the world, by the CFR (Council on Foreign Relations), the Trilateral Commission, the Bilderbergers, the Committee of 300 (the 17 wealthiest so-called elite families)—the Rothschild's in England and Rockefellers in America and Bronfman's in Canada, and on and on, comprising the physical power structure of the New World Order puppets under the direction of darkly motivated, other-dimensional 'master deceivers' commonly known as Lucifer or Satan and their 'fallen angel' cohorts."

"While all of those details contribute to understanding the Larger Picture, what you are about to read fills in a most important Missing Link in this entire structure. And I don't mean a little side issue; I mean a link so central—yet so well hidden from general public view, and for so long—that even the most studied of 'conspiracy theory' scholars

probably have not put together much of the information that is going to be presented here."

"To call the following outlay controversial and sensitive is about as mild an understatement of the truth of the matter as can be made! This missing link changes the entire slant of the entire playing field! After months of anticipation and weeks of preparation, I was finally able to speak with **Vatican Assassins** author **Eric Jon Phelps** on Tuesday, March 14. There was simply no other way to cover Eric's historic masterpiece spanning, literally, five centuries, than to just ask questions covering huge spans of time and major historical events. It took us almost four hours to accomplish the task, yet we could easily have gone on for another forty."

"We here at The SPECTRUM are simply unwilling to reduce the importance of this work by presenting it in a too distilled fashion. In fact, in order to share this material with at least some of the pertinent backup, Eric has granted us permission to print (directly after the interview) several excerpts from his soon-to-be-published book which will help you in understanding certain aspects of this magnificently important and broad-sweeping story. The missing link is surely a central link."

"Let's call this story the 'Jesuit-Vatican connection' to the unfolding New World Order agenda. You make up your own mind just how absolutely central, yet well hidden, has been this link! There's a good reason the secret Vatican library is so extensive and yet remains so intact from outside intrusion, despite the many others who would like to possess such a collection of information detailing much 'censored' data about our true, otherworldly cultural heritage."

"When one reads a work like **Vatican Assassins**, one can't help but reflect back on the purposely adjusted and watered down and boring moments in high school history class. Meanwhile, the true history of what has gone on is dynamic and full of calculated intrigue. In this business, I've heard and read a lot of things. But when I had to pick my jaw up off the floor during the reading of certain historical portions in Eric's book—well, let me just say that Truth certainly is stranger, and far more interesting, than the many fictions we've been led to believe are historical fact. And yet The Truth does fit together like the pieces of a jigsaw puzzle."

"This book SHOULD be a best-seller, but it is hardly likely to achieve such general attention—considering how well controlled and censored is the publishing business. Thus is the reason for our lengthy presentation of this most astonishing and critically important material here in The SPECTRUM. We are in a time of Truth being revealed from all directions. And there is probably no more fundamental, mind-rattling, and previous notions-shattering example of that than what is being presented here. The interview is directly followed by a number of pertinent excerpts from Eric's eye-opening book—which will be available July 1."

The following are excerpts from that interview. For a full version, go to **www.remnantofgod.org/blackpope.htm**. Note that this interview was done when the previous Jesuit General Kolvenbach was in power. In the beginning Phelps states:

"You, literally, link every major global conflict and political assassination to the hands of the Jesuit Order. The Jews, as with many other groups you mention, have been the unwitting pawns in this Jesuit Agenda." The partial inteview follows:

Martin: Today, who is the Superior General of the Jesuits, the so-called "Black Pope" [*black here refers to hidden, evil activities, not to race or color*] who gives the orders to the actual Pope. Is it still Jean-Baptist Janssens?
Phelps: Janssens, Frenchman. No, he passed away in 1964. Then Pedro Arrupe came to power. Then, after Arrupe died, in 1988, I believe, the present Jesuit General is Count Hans Kolvenbach. I call him Count Hans Kolven *hoof*.

Martin: Let's discuss this position of "General" and, in addition, who is this person, Count Hans Kolvenbach? Who does he serve? What are his origins? Where does he hail from?
Phelps: The present General is a Dutchman, his nationality is Dutch.

Martin: Where is he? Physically, where is he?
Phelps: He resides in Rome, at the headquarters of the Jesuits, called the Church of Jesu. So, the Jesuit General resides in Rome at, what I just called, the Jesuit headquarters.

Martin: The Church of Jesu, is that near the Vatican?
Phelps: It's not far from the Vatican, right. It's in the same general area. It's headquarters of the Knights of Malta.

Martin: Is it part of Vatican City, proper?
Phelps: Right, I believe, yes it is.

Martin: Where does Satan fit into this picture, and what is the ultimate goal of the Jesuits, the so-called Society of Jesus?
Phelps: The Jesuit General, and the other high Jesuit Generals, they are sorcerers. They are Luciferians, and they worship what they would call Lucifer. They do not believe in Satan. They believe in Lucifer. Now, according to Alberto Rivera, he was invited—because he was a top Jesuit at the time in the late '60s—he was invited to a "Black Mass" in Spain where there were quite a few top Jesuit Generals present. And he called it a "Black Mass". Well, when you're involved in a "Black Mass", you're involved in the worship of Lucifer, all dressed in their black capes and so on.

Martin: I'm fascinated by Count Hans Kolvenbach because nobody in the world knows who this person is. I've never heard the name.
Phelps: Let me just tell you that you can see his picture and his top Jesuits—just a second and I'll get the book. The name of the book is called *Jesuits: A Multi-Biography*, by Jean Lacoutre, and that is available, usually, in the bookstores. It was published in 1995. Jean Lacoutre is a Frenchman. He was a communist, is a communist. On the last page of the pictures in it, that is right adjacent to page 343, you see Peter Hans Kolvenbach. He's the Jesuit General, and he looks like just a very evil individual. There's a Black man, who's a high Jesuit, he's a 29 Superior Jesuit with his cosmopolitan General staff. One of the General staff looks like Ben Kingsley of *Shindler's List*. There are six White men, and one Black man. And that's his General staff.

Martin: What is the process of choosing a successor General?
Phelps: The High Jesuits elect him, and he's elected for life—unless he becomes a "heretic".

Martin: And the so-called "High Jesuits" represent what group?

Phelps: I would say that they're the "professed", the high 4th Degree. When a Jesuit is professed, he is under the *Jesuit Oath*; he is under the "Bloody Oath" that I have in my book. The Jesuit General is the absolute, complete, and total dictator and autocrat of the Order. When he speaks, his provincials move. The provincials are his major subordinates. There are around 83 provincials right now. As I understand it, the Jesuit Order has divided the world into 83 regions. Ok? For each region, there is a Jesuit provincial. There are 10 provincials in the United States. There is one for Central America. There is one for Ireland. They've divided up the world into these provinces.

So it's old Babylonian provincial government, centered in Nebuchadnezzar or the Jesuit General himself; so it's strictly a Roman form of government where all the states or provinces are subordinate to this worldwide sovereign. The Jesuit General exercises full and complete power over the Order. He meets with his provincials. When they decide to start a war or an agitation, he gets the information from the provincial of that country, how best to go about this, the demeanor of the people, and then he uses legitimate grievances to foam an agitation—like the 1964 Civil Rights Movement. That was ALL a Jesuit agitation, completely, because the end result was more consolidation of power in Washington with the 1964 Civil Rights Act that was written by [*the longtime President of the University of Notre Dame, the Reverend*] Theodore Hesburgh.

The Jesuit General rules the world through his provincials. And the provincials then, of course, rule the lower Jesuits, and there are many Jesuits who are not "professed", so many of the lower Jesuits have no idea what's going on at the top. They have no concept of the power of their Order. It's just like Freemasonry. The lower have no idea that the High Shriner Freemasons are working for the Jesuit General. They think that they're just doing works and being good people. But the bottom line is that the high-level Freemasons are subject, also, to the Jesuit General because the Jesuit General, with Fredrick the Great, wrote the High Degrees, the last 8 Degrees, of the Scottish Rite Freemasonry when Fredrick protected them when they were suppressed by the Pope in 1773. So, you have the alignment with the Jesuit Order and the most powerful Freemason they had in the craft, Fredrick the Great, during their suppression. That is an irrefutable conclusion. And then, when you see the Napoleonic Wars, the French Revolution and the Napoleonic Wars carried out by Freemasonry, everything Napoleon did, and the Jacobins, whatever they did, completely benefited the Jesuit Order. It's to this end that **Alexander Dumas** wrote his **The Count Of Monte Cristo**. The Count is the Jesuit General. Monte=Mount, Cristo=Christ. The Count of the Mount of Christ. Alexander Dumas was talking about the Jesuit General getting vengeance when the Jesuits were suppressed, and many of them were consigned to an island, three hours sailing, West, off the coast of Portugal. And so, when the Jesuits finally regained their power, they punished all of the monarchs of Europe who had suppressed them, drove them from their thrones, including the Knights of Malta from Malta, using Napoleon. And Alexander Dumas, who fought for the Italian patriots in 1848, to free Rome from the temporal power of the Pope, wrote many books and one of the books was to expose this, and that was *The Count Of Monte Cristo.*

So, when you read that book, bear in mind that it's really a satire on the Jesuit Order regaining their power in France. The Count of Monte Cristo has an intelligence apparatus that can't be beat. Well, that's the Jesuit Order. But the Count doesn't get what he really ought to have, or his last wish, and that's the love of woman. He gains back all of his political power; he gains back everything he lost; but he doesn't have the love of a woman. And THAT is the Jesuit Order. They have no women. They have no love of a woman. Because to have a wife, to have a woman, means you have an allegiance to your wife and family, and you cannot obey the General. That's why they will NEVER be married, and that's one of the great KEYS to their success. They can betray a nation and walk away. They can betray all the Irish Catholics getting on the *Titanic*, and walk away. They can betray us in Vietnam and walk away. They can betray us every time we go to the hospital and get radiated and cut and drugged, and walk away, because it's *"for the greater glory of God"*—Ad Majorem Dei Gloriam: the greater glory of the god who sits in Rome.

Martin: What is the ULTIMATE goal of the Jesuits?
Phelps: Their ultimate goal is the rule of the world, with the Pope of their making, from Solomon's rebuilt Temple in Jerusalem. That's their ultimate goal.

In **Edmond Paris's** book, printed by Ozark Publications, called **The Vatican Against Europe,** it gets into great detail of what they did. It calls it—the last 30 years of war is all attributable to the Jesuits, their massacres of the Serbs and Jews, etc. But Edmond Paris did not understand that the Jesuit General—and this is one of the most important points I want to make about Von Kolvenbach—the Jesuit General is in complete control of the international intelligence community: that's the CIA, the FBI, the KGB, the Israeli Mossad, the German BND, the British SIS. The Jesuit General is in COMPLETE CONTROL of the entire intelligence apparatus—FBI, every bureaucratic agency in this country, all of it; he is in complete control of it.

So, whenever he wants to find something out about an individual, they put in the Social Security number, and everything from all of the intelligence apparatus kicks-in and he and his provincials can review everything about that man. Credit cards, you name it, everything that's attached to Rome's social security number, which FDR put upon us in 1933 with the help of Spellman; at the time, I believe he was Archbishop, or maybe it was Cardinal Hayes—but Rome was behind FDR in putting him in office.

The couple of things that he did was implement social insecurity, the income tax, and recognizing Joseph Stalin's bloody Jesuit USSR government. So, with the giving of us the Social Security number, that is Rome's number—that's why I refuse to use it—and that's why they want everybody using it for everything: driver's license, tax return, credit card, everything you do, that number is you and that number is Rome's number.

Martin: Let me just back-up here for a minute. What comes to mind is Louis Freeh, head of the FBI.
Phelps: Roman Catholic, good altar boy. Probably a Knight of Columbus; I can't prove it. But anybody with that kind of power has got to be a Knight of Columbus. And the Knights of Columbus implement Jesuit politics. And Louis Freeh was the one behind the Waco atrocity and the Oklahoma City bombing atrocity. And his top sniper was a Japanese Roman Catholic named Lon Horiuchi. So, it's Roman Catholics in control, Knights in control of the FBI, who carried out all of this killing. And those two men, Louis Freeh and Lon Horiuchi are personally accountable to Cardinal O'Connor of New York. And Cardinal O'Connor of New York is the most powerful Cardinal in the country. He is the military vicar. And that's why Bush kissed his fanny for going to Bob Jones, because Cardinal O'Connor is the King of the American Empire. And he rules his Empire from that Palace, St. Patrick's Cathedral, "the little Vatican".

Martin: And is he in contact, do you think, with Kolvenbach?
Phelps: Of course. O'Connor himself is not a Jesuit, but the Jesuits are like the SS of the Catholic Church. They maintain order. And the ones closest to him who maintain order are the Jesuits of Fordham University. Now, one of them—the head of Fordham University, I believe he is an Irishman, is also a member of the CFR [*Council on Foreign Relations*]. And I have that right here in the Annual Report of the CFR of 1993. Those Jesuits at Fordham maintain semblance and rule over the Cardinal in New York. And, of

course, the powerful Jesuits of Fordham include Avery Dulles and John Foster Dulles, one of the writers of the book on the Second Vatican Council.

What's he going to do? These nations are breaking away from us; they're not under our temporal or spiritual power; and it's very important to remember that the Pope claims two powers—spiritual and temporal—and with the breaking of his spiritual power, he then lost his temporal power. In other words, he no longer had the ability to rule the people through the king of the country, because the king was breaking away, like Henry VIII. So, Henry VIII broke away from the Roman Church and formed the Church of England; he no longer was subject to the Pope. This was happening in England, in Germany, in Holland, and other places.

So, all your courts are nothing more than courts of military rule. They all proceed with summary procedures. The jury has no power of jury nullification. And they are simply enforcing the laws of the Empire, which I call *14th Amendment* America, which is a military-style, King of England-style country. The courts are nothing more than courts of the king's bench, as you can see in *Blackstone's Commentaries*.

And the banks, as you walk into every bank, they all have a flag trimmed in gold fringe. The bank is what England would call, in Blackstone's day, the king's bank. So, we have the king's bank, and we have the king's bench. And it's run according to military rule, according to Berkheimer's great work *Military Rule And Martial Law*, published in 1914.

The reason why Kennedy was assassinated was he wanted to end the Vietnam War, and he wanted to end the rule of the CIA. That begets two questions: Did Rome want the Vietnam War? And, did Rome control the CIA? The answer is yes on both counts. We know, on its face, that the Vietnam War was called "Spelly's War"—Cardinal Spellman's war. He went over to the warfront many times and he called the American soldiers the "soldiers of Christ". The man who was the Commander of the American forces was a Roman Catholic, CFR member, possibly a Knight of Columbus, I don't know, but he was General William Westmoreland.

The other thing is that Rome is in control of the drug trade. The Vatican controls all of the drug trade—all of the heroin, all of the opium, all of the cocaine, everything going around in Columbia. Columbia has a concordat with the Pope. A concordat is a treaty with the Pope. Hitler had a concordat. Mussolini had a concordat. Franco had a concordat. They want to set up a concordat here, which was the reason for Reagan formally recognizing the sovereign state of Vatican City in 1984. The greatest traitor we ever had was Ronald Reagan. So, they had a concordat. Columbia has a concordat. Do you think that drugs running out of Columbia, with a country that has a concordat with Rome, is not controlled by Rome? If Rome didn't want the drug trade out of Columbia, they'd end the concordat. The whole drug trade is run by high Mafia families out of the country of Columbia, subject to the Jesuit General. And the Jesuit General ran the Opium trade, a couple of centuries ago, out of China. They ran the silk trade, the pearl trade. The movie *Shogun* is but a slight scratching of the surface of the Jesuit "black ships" that trafficked in all of this silk and pearls and gold and opals and everything they could pull out of the East, including opium.

The Vietnam War was to consolidate and control this huge massive drug-trade that would inundate every American city with drugs, being brought in by the CIA with their Air America, and then distributed by the Trafficante family throughout the United States— Santos Trafficante out of Miami. So we have the Mafia and the CIA working together in the drug trade. We have the Mafia and the CIA working together in the assassination of Kennedy. The first reason why the Jesuit General [*at that time, Jean-Baptist Janssens*] wanted Kennedy out of the way was because he was going to end the Vietnam War. The second reason is, he wanted to end the reign of the CIA, because the CIA had betrayed him in the person of McGeorge Bundy, by not giving the cover to the Cuban patriots to retake Cuba from that Roman Catholic, Jesuit-trained, grease-ball bastard—he was a bastard, his father was a Nazi—Fidel Castro. So, Kennedy wanted to end this "intelligence community". That was the end of him. Thus for anyone attempting to end the CIA, and attempting to end the Vietnam War, and also because he attacked the Jesuits' Federal Reserve Bank by printing United States Notes, they got rid of him. They killed our only Roman Catholic president.

Jeremiah Crowley; that priest was a great Irishman who came here and, seeing the corruption of the Archdiocese in Chicago, that it was so corrupt, he left it and exposed it. And, of course, he later came to Christ and became a *Bible*-believer, which they would call a Protestant. Protestants today don't believe the *Bible*. Protestantism of today is an empty shell, it's nothing. But, back then, in 1912, they believed the *Bible*. Crowley, then, exposed many things, and one of the things he exposed, that helped me with this, was that he warned that the Jesuits, with their Knights of Columbus—which, he says, the Knights of Columbus, named after Columbus, who he tells us was a Spanish Jew and a pirate and a deflowerer of young girls—that Columbus was no Christian.

You find the greatest resistance to the Jesuits in Catholic countries, by Catholic monarchs. And that's why the Roman Catholic monarchs and nobility of today don't dare resist them. The Kennedys won't touch them. The monarchs of Europe won't touch them. The Hapsburgs won't touch them, because the Jesuits have vindicated their power in the French Revolution and the Napoleonic Wars—well, then they went to suppress the Jesuits again in Europe and they were, for the most part, kicked-out of Europe in the 1800s. All the nations of Europe banned them. Germany banned them in 1872. And so, World War I and II, the second Thirty Years War, was pay-back for this. And ever since then, nobody touches them. Pope Ganganelli abolished the Jesuits with a Papal Bull; the Jesuits call it a "brief". It is not a brief; it is in the Library of the Bulls, and it is called Dominic Ac Redemptor Nostor. That is the name of a bull. And when he abolished them, he abolished them forever—that they were not to talk about their abolition, that they were not to teach. He confiscated all of their wealth and land and property. For the most part, the Dominicans took it over, which is why the Dominicans had their penis cut off during the French Revolution. That's what the Jacobins did to them. It was payback by the Jesuits: *"You don't dare take our property from us, boy. And you don't dare take Inquisition from us."* Jacobins killed nearly every Dominican in France.

When Rothschild sent that note, via Roost, into London, saying that Napoleon had won the Battle of Waterloo, that's when the stocks plummeted, and all the Jesuits bought all the stocks up, there in London, and got control of the Bank of England. The Jesuits then made London their commercial center of the world, and Rome their religious center, aiming that one day Jerusalem would be both. So now the Jesuits are in control of England. After the Napoleonic Wars, we have the Congress of Vienna in 1815, and guess who's there? All the representatives of King George. England is represented at the Congress of Vienna, the settlement after the Napoleonic Wars. If England was truly Protestant, they would have never went there. Now the Jesuits are in control of England throughout the 1800s, and they use the British Empire to further the power of the Pope. England has been under Rome's control, the Pope's control, since, at the very latest, 1850. And I say since 1795.

Martin: Let's talk about Elizabeth II.
Phelps: Elizabeth II is a wicked, evil queen. She is the head of the Knights of Malta in England. She curtsies to the Lord Mayor in Old London, and she goes and visits the

Jesuits of Stonyhurst and kisses their derrières. She has complete allegiance to the Jesuits of Stonyhurst, and will do anything they tell her to do, or they'll get rid of her just like they got rid of all the rest of the monarchs in Europe.

Martin: So you see her as a pawn.
Phelps: She's just a pawn, sure. She's nothing. Remember, White men rule the world. Evil, White, sodomite, homosexual men rule the world, and these are the High Jesuits, with their High Knights of Malta and High Freemasons, they rule. And these women who are involved are just pawns in their game, like the queen, the queen of Holland, just to give the appearance that these nations have a sovereign monarch, when in fact, they're just tools. England has done some awful, terrible things, but all of the things that they have done increase and benefit the Jesuit Order. They never resisted Napoleon III. Napoleon III was a fanatical Roman Catholic Freemason, subject to the Jesuits, who was the King of France for 18 years, second Empire. England never resisted him. They fought with him in the Crimean War. And Napoleon III dedicated all of his ships to the Virgin Mary. England has been on the side of the Jesuits since 1815, no later. So, that means that the British Secret Service is totally working for Rome, all throughout the 1800s.

Martin: How did the Jesuits regain control of the Vatican in 1814?
Phelps: Remember that they were in control of Napoleon. A Jesuit by the name of Abbie Sieyes—you can find him, again, in Ridpath's **History Of The World**—Abbie Sieyes was a Jesuit-trained individual, and I believe he was a Jesuit. He was on the Directory, and he was also on the Consulate; he was the second counsel. Napoleon was the first; he was the second. He was the advisor and director of Napoleon. Abbie Sieyes, being the Jesuit that he was, ordered Napoleon to imprison the Pope for 5 years, and he did! So, the Pope was in prison for 5 years until 1814, when he restored the Jesuit Order. The Pope, prior to that, was killed. They brought him over the mountains of the Alps, and he died through that debacle. The Jesuits thoroughly humiliated the papacy. They used their French soldiers to overturn St. Peter's chair, and they found, written in Arabic: "There is no other God but Allah, and Mohammed is his prophet." And THAT is what is under St. Peter's chair today. That was stolen from some kalif during the Crusades. So, they completely intimidated the Pope and showed their power. The Pope then restored them with a Papal Bull, calling upon the vengeance of the Apostles Peter and Paul, blah, blah, blah, for anyone who would ever suppress the Jesuit Order ever again. When the Jesuits were "reinstalled" in all their power, that's when they were in control of the Pope, and from then on they have been. Any Pope who resists them gets punished or murdered. And all the Popes know it. When Pius IX wanted a liberal constitution for the Italian people in 1849, all of the Italians were delighted. Here is a liberal Pope; he's going to give us constitutional rights; we're going to have a constitution.

When you steal from the Vatican, like the Cardinal did at the PII Lodge, they killed him (Kalvi), and they hanged the other guy, beginning with the admiralty jurisdiction, at their first bridge of the sea. So they have their assassins everywhere to carry out orders. They are machines. They are the perfect "Manchurian Candidates" and they will kill popes, cardinals, presidents, kings, and kaisers, to maintain Jesuit power. They are utterly ruthless—just like they said they would be in the **Protocols**: "We are merciless."

Martin: As you look around the world today, who do you see opposing them?
Phelps: It's interesting. I have a friend who makes quite a few trips to Haiti. I told her about the Jesuits. She got to questioning a few people, and she found that Papa Doc had expelled the Jesuits from Haiti. The present government of Israel was set up by the High Masonic Rothschild-controlled Jews, and Rothschild has had an alliance with the Jesuit General since 1876, with Adam Weishaupt. This is the very same Rothschild powers who betrayed the Jews into the hands of the Nazis, killing many Jews all throughout Europe,

betraying their own Jewish people. These are the very same powers who run the nation of Israel today. I read a very interesting paragraph by **Mark Lane** in his book **Plausible Denial** when he tells about a Jew in Israel who wrote about certain criminal Jews, involved with the Nazis, who are now with the Mossad, something along those lines. The man who wrote the article was gunned-down in front of his home. So, Rome controls the Israeli government. It controls the Israeli government through the Mossad. Who trained the Mossad? Reinhard Gehlen.

We find that fact in Loftus' work **The Secret War Against The Jews** in most telling, telling detail. So what do we have? We have high-level treason and betrayal of the Jewish race; that is there in Israel today, by their own leaders, who are loyal to Rome and the Jesuit Order. And to show this, we have a great big Rockefeller edifice in Jerusalem; we have an ophthalmology center in Jerusalem run by the Knights of Malta. There's nothing but Knights of Malta, high-level Freemasonry, and the Jesuit Order running all of Israel. So what's going to happen, I believe, with the Dome of the Rock is, that has got to be removed—somehow, someway. It's on the Temple site; it has to be removed.

The American Pope is the Cardinal of New York. He is the most powerful Cardinal in the United States. He is what's called "the military vicar". The military vicar is in command of all of the military orders within the United States, they being the Knights of Malta and the Knights of Columbus. He is also in command, and privately, of "the Commission" because Cardinal Spellman was an intimate of Joe Kennedy, and Joe Kennedy was an intimate of Frank Costello. We also see that it was Cardinal Spellman who enabled "Lucky" Luciano to be released from the prison in New York, to return to Italy in 1946. And this was because of the Luciano Project that I mentioned in my book. But Lucky Luciano, his Mafia on the East Coast, worked in conjunction with the U.S. Navy, supposedly to protect the Eastern seaboard from German U-boat attack. So, as payback? Cardinal Spellman releases Lucky Luciano—that filthy, wicked, evil, heartless spiritual bastard, who compelled young girls into prostitution, probably one of the cruelest things any man could do. He is released and sent back to Rome. When the Kennedy assassination comes up, the Cardinal needs a favor. After all, he's released Luciano. So now the Mafia gets to participate: Jack Ruby, Carlos Marcello, Santos Trafficante, all the High Dons participate. Why? Because that Cardinal in New York controls the Commission. And that Commission, you know what it controls? All of the trucking, all the supermarkets, it's power is beyond our wildest imagination, second only to the Knights of Malta. And, of course, they all control the Federal Reserve Bank.

The Cardinal controls the Federal Reserve Bank through the Council on Foreign Relations. The Council on Foreign Relations belongs to the Cardinal. Spellman was not a member of it, during his day, but two of the most powerful members were Knights of Malta: Henry Luce and J. Peter Grace, and also William F. Buckley, to this day. William F. Buckley is indeed one of my enemies, because I name him, and he is a powerful multi-billionaire who participated in the Kennedy assassination, just like Iacocca, another Knight. Both of those men are subject to Cardinal O'Connor and will do ANYTHING he says.

Martin: Do the Knights of Malta actually meet, actually hold meetings with the Jesuits?
Phelps: Oh, sure. Remember that Alexander Haig is a powerful Knight of Malta. His brother is a Jesuit. So, sure they have meetings. The High Knights of Malta, who meet in their palace on Aventin Hill, in Rome, of course, meet with the Jesuit General, and so on. And **Count von Hoensbroech**, who was a German Noble who became a Jesuit for 14 years—he wrote a two-volume work called **Fourteen Years A Jesuit**. His father was a Knight of Malta. Yes, the Jesuits work in conjunction and have regular meetings with the Knights of Malta. The Knights control the money. The Knights control the banks. They

control the Bank of Canada, Federal Reserve Bank, Bank of England; they control the banking. They were the ones who were behind the sinking of the Titanic, with the creation of the White Star Line, J.P. Morgan and others.

Martin: Alan Greenspan, then, would be? I only later understood why Yasser Arafat says he doesn't hate the Jews; he can't stand the Zionists. And I'm thinking: *"What's the difference?"* I, later, learned that there is a great difference between those Zionists and the other Jews. The Orthodox Jews can't stand the Zionists. So what's the difference? The Zionists are socialist communists, controlled by Rome. They are atheists, just like the Jesuits, although they're being used to rebuild the nation of Israel. They are the enemies of the Jewish people, per se.

Phelps: That's right. Those three little tidbits, right there, prove that the Nation of Islam is totally under Jesuit control. They are going to be used to foment anarchy and agitation, because they have an army called "the fruit of Islam", and they have millions of rounds stored in all the major cities—guns stored everywhere, so that they can start the race war. And when that happens, you see, then the brothers in Washington can implement Martial Law, suspend the *Constitution*, and now the Jesuits have what they want. So, they use these Blacks in the North, who hate the White people, for their own destruction, for the destruction of the Black people themselves. And the Nation of Islam is part of that.

And if you go into the president's office at Georgetown, you will see a picture of Bill Clinton, kneeling at the grave of Timothy Healy [*past president of Georgetown*], while the present president, Donovan, who is on the Walt Disney Board, is standing behind him. I wanted that picture; I wanted a copy of that picture. Those people threw me out of that office. They would not let me have a copy of it. I sent another person, a lady, up there. They would not give it to her. I want that picture, for my book, of Bill Clinton kneeling at the grave of these Jesuits. Can't get it. But if you go in the president's office, it's there. Georgetown is the capital. They control all Freemasonry. In fact, if you go to Maryland, they've got the great big lodge across from a great big Jesuit institution, in Baltimore—a great huge Shriner Lodge is across the street from a Jesuit University. And they're enemies? They don't really comprehend this whole idea of universal, world-wide temporal power of the Pope. They think it's just a religion. But, if those Catholics in New York, if those two million Roman Catholics knew that Spellman was behind it, and O'Connor has covered it up, we'd have a revolution! Because it's the Roman Catholics, unfortunately, who only do anything about things. The Protestants don't do anything. They're all a bunch of wimps, a bunch of cowards. They don't do anything. It's the Roman Catholics who apparently have built our major cities. They built our skyscrapers. They're the great steel workers. They're the ones, apparently, with the guts enough to bring about a change. The only problem is, they're unGodly because they don't know the Lord. They don't read the *Bible*. They don't know Christ. They're not born-again. If they would get born-again, and come to know Christ, with their determination and their resistance to tyranny, we'd have another Reformation. And a lot of people's heads would be going on trial, and to the block, for treason. Jesuit *Molina,* in the tape I just sent you, it is lawful to kill—and they will kill as many Roman Catholics as necessary to bring this plan to fruition.

Martin: Define the Jesuit term: Universal Absolutism.

Phelps: Define it? That means worldwide, universal, over every nation, absolute power. Absolutism is their great doctrine, that absolute power resides in the hands of the General. He is limited by no constitution. He is limited by no law. This is the Great Doctrine of Divine Right, the Divine Right of Kings that was so fought against by the Calvinists. We *Bible*-believing Calvinists believe in the Rule of Law. The Law is king. Rutherford's "Lex Rex". The Jesuits believe the king is the law—Louis XIV: *"I am the law".* So, it's going to be a universal, world-wide king who, himself, is the law. All authority will be in him, as he rules the world from Jerusalem, as the Beast.

Martin: Are we talking about the present Pope, or are we talking about Count von Kolvenbach?
Phelps: I'm saying that what's in position now will ultimately bring in the future Pope, whoever he is, and whatever it may be, as a Universal Absolutist—the Universal Monarch of the World, in Jerusalem.

Martin: Symbolic? Or you're saying literal?
Phelps: I'm saying that will literally happen. There will be a Pope, who will be killed; he will receive a mortal wound. And this is going to happen in the 70th week of *Daniel*. He will receive a mortal wound, according to *Revelation 13*. This is the Beast, and he will come back to life. He comes back to life, mid-trip, at the very time that Satan and his angels are cast out of Heaven by Michael and his angels. At this time, Satan goes and he indwells the Beast, this Pope. Now he comes back to life, just like Christ. He was dead; now he's resurrected. And what is he going to do? He's going to destroy the Catholic Church. He's going to destroy the Vatican; and he's going to go down in Jerusalem and demand to be worshipped as God, for three and a half years. That's why the Vatican is indestructible. No one can destroy the Vatican. All the armies in the world couldn't destroy it. It has been determined that it will be destroyed by the Anti-Christ. And he, alone, can do it.

Martin: We've almost covered it. I almost don't want to dilute this conversation with the FDA and AMA. Let's talk about them just briefly.
Phelps: Ok. World War II, produced of course by Rome, caused the Nazi experiments on the people in the concentration camps—the Jews, the Gypsies, the Socialists, primarily the Jews. But they experimented with things like fluoride. They experimented with things like EDTA chelation, which is THE treatment of choice for anybody with heart disease. They experimented with poisons. They experimented with surgeries. They experimented with all kinds of things on these people. They also experimented with vaccinations and immunizations. There's a book called **The Nazi Doctors**. Everything that was learned by them was integrated into the American Medical Association, after the war. That's why we all have our municipal water supplies fluoridated. That's why they're all chlorinated, because chlorine decreases oxygen, and therefore causes cancer, because cancer grows in an anaerobic state—it's a virus, converting cells into mutants that are anaerobic. Ok. All of Europe is using ozone to clean their water supplies. Here they use chlorine. They want us with cancer. And how do we get cancer? With the vaccinations and immunizations, where they inject us with live viruses, like the hepatitis vaccine—every one of them has the HIV virus, SV-40. What they're doing is what they learned in Nazi Germany. They implemented here and they continue their research in the CIA. There's a two-tape set called *The CIA And The Virus Makers* which show how the CIA helped to create the HIV virus and various other viruses. They get into Robert Gallo, the world's foremost virologist.

Martin: Ok, let's talk about God and His Agenda.
Phelps: As I understand the *Bible*, I believe we are in what's called the Dispensation of Grace. I'm a dispensationalist. Now, there are those who say that dispensationalism was a brain-child of the Jesuits. Could be, could be Jesuits were involved with that. But I believe the *Bible* teaches this, because God deals with men in different ways, at different times. He commands Abraham to sacrifice a lamb, but not me. We don't do that now. He commands Noah to build an ark. We don't do that now. He commands Moses to receive the Law of Sinai. We're not under the Law; it's for the Nation of Israel. He commanded his son to announce that the Davidic kingdom was ready to be established on Earth—

repent, for the Kingdom is at hand. The Kingdom, promised to David, is about to be established, and that's why they called him Son of David. And now we live in the Dispensation of Grace, called the present Evil Age, of *Galations, Chapter 1:4,* and the Dispensation of Grace of *Ephesians, Chapter 3.* During this particular period of time, this stewardship, the Gospel says that the Lord Jesus Christ died for the sins of our world; he was buried and rose again. And God commands all men, everywhere, to repent and believe on His name that they might be saved. But there is no other name under Heaven whereby we must be saved, save the name of Jesus. During this time, this good news of forgiveness of sin and free pardon, and we can be with the Lord for eternity, is going to every nation, Jews and Gentile. And during this Dispensation of Grace, Jews and Gentiles are regarded as one, in the body of Christ, when they're saved. Now, according to *Romans, Chapter 11*, there is what is called the "fullness of the Gentiles". There is a fullness that is a predetermined amount of people who are going to be saved. We call them "the elect". We call ourselves the elect of the Lord.

Now when that elect, that predetermined number, is saved, then God will begin to deal with the nations and Israel, once again. And that will begin, according to *Daniel, Chapter 9*, when the Prince shall come, shall confirm a covenant with many for one week. That is the 70th week of *Daniel*. The first 69 weeks have been fulfilled, from the decree, to rebuilding Jerusalem, to Messiah the Prince, the day Christ declared himself the Messiah of Israel, was 69 weeks of years. After that the Messiah would be cut-off, and Jerusalem would be destroyed. That is the gap between the 69th and the 70th week. The temple is not destroyed; the city is not destroyed; the Messiah is not cut-off, during the 69th or the 70th week. There's a gap between those two weeks, and that gap has gone to nearly 2,000 years. In the year 2032, it will be 2,000 years. Because Christ was crucified in 32 A.D.

Ok, during this dispensation, God is saving Jews and Gentiles out of all nations and placing them in the body of Christ, by the power of His Holy Spirit, as the Gospels preached. When the predetermined number comes to fruition, then the Lord will take out his *Bible*-believing church, and everybody else is left to go through what is called "the time of Jacob's trouble", in the *Book of Jeremiah*, or the Great Day of the Lord—the 7-year tribulation, talked about in the *Book of Revelation, Chapter 4-19*. That 7-year tribulation will be when the Lord begins to judge this world for its rejection of the Messiah, and for their sins, having not been taken care of, not having been saved; although there will be many people saved during this time. The Jews will be tremendously persecuted. The vast majority of them will be murdered, and there will be a remnant who will repent at the end of the Tribulation, at which time the Messiah will come and they will look upon him, whom they pierced, and weep because they will realize that the one who is going to save them from all these Gentile armies pouring into Israel, is the very one they crucified.

When the Lord Jesus destroys all the Gentile armies, he will then set up the Davidic Kingdom that he came to set up—the born-again nation of Israel. Can a nation be born in a day? *Isaiah, Chapter 66*—they will be born-again, they will inherit all the promises, and Christ will sit down in the Kingdom with Abraham, and Isaac, and Jacob, just like he talked about, and he will eat the fruit of vine again. Because he said: *"I will not eat this henceforth, til ye say, 'Blessed is he that come in the name of the Lord' until I eat it anew with you in the Kingdom."* Then he will drink wine; he will eat the fruit of the vine; he will break bread; and he will be Messiah, King of the World at that time, ruling the world from Jerusalem.

So, what we have coming is more unbelief, more persecution, less faith, less manhood, less guts, and we have more persecution from the Jesuit Order, more monetary control.

We have another scenario of the World Government, under the Pope from Jerusalem, and that's what the Jesuits want. And, ultimately, God in His providence, has allowed for 42 months for that to happen: 1260 days. So, hopefully, with the true preaching of the Gospel—and ultimately there will be some preachers who will arise who will encourage us to do right and not fear death, and to resist these powers of evil—hopefully that will begin to change and there will be men who will call for secession, and states will begin to leave this Union, like Chechnya, and these others, and then the Lord will intervene for us. If we honor Him, He'll honor us. If we fight for His causes, He'll bless us. And we need to stop looking at the odds. We've always been outnumbered. We've always been outgunned. And that's the way God likes it, because then, when we win, obviously He did it. So that's what I see for the future, and I see there's a great vacuum right now that needs to be filled. And it can be filled with the men of God telling the truth, or it can be filled with Jesuits advocating everybody give-up, lay down their guns, and submit to this New World Order, under the Pope. The question is: What are YOU, dear reader, going to do?

The purpose of the Jesuit Order, formally established by the Pope in 1540, is to destroy the Protestant Reformation. They call it the Counter-Reformation. Nicolini of Rome wrote: *"The Jesuits, by their very calling, by the very essence of their institution, are bound to seek, by every means, right or wrong, the destruction of Protestantism. This is the condition of their existence, the duty they must fulfill, or cease to be Jesuits."* [*Footprints of the Jesuits, R. W. Thompson*, 1894]

The Jesuit Power Shift To America

The Society of Jesus was recognized as the chief opposing force of Protestantism. The Order became dominant in determining the plans and policy of the Rowish Church. The brotherhood grew and flourished. It planted its chapters first in France, Italy and Spain, and then in all civilized lands. The success of the Order was phenomenal. It became a power in the world. It sent out its representatives to every quarter of the globe. Its solitary apostles were seen shadowing the thrones of Europe. They sought, by every means known to human ingenuity, to establish and confirm the tottering fabric of Rome, and to undermine the rising fabric of Protestantism. They penetrated to the Indus and the Ganges. They traversed the deserts of Tibet, and said, *"Here am I,"* in the streets of Peking. They looked down into the silver mines of Peru, and knelt in prayer on the shores of Lake Superior. To know all secrets, fathom all design, penetrate all intrigues, prevail in all counsels, rise above all diplomacy, and master the human race, — such was their purpose and ambition. They wound about human society in every part of the habitable earth, the noiseless creepers of their ever-growing plot to retake the world for the Church, and to subdue and conquer and extinguish the last remnant of opposition to her dominion from shore to shore, from the rivers to the ends of the earth. [*Ridpath's Universal History, John Clarke Ridpath*, 1899]

The Jesuits are the true authors of socialist-communism. The economic system of the Dark Ages was feudalism consisting of the few rich landowners and the many poor peasants. It was a sin to make a profit by anyone other than the feudal lords. Thus, if the world is to be returned to the Dark Ages, the Protestant middle class must be destroyed. Socialist-communism accomplishes this, having yielded its bitter fruit in both Great Britain and the United States. The great deception is that the Jews are the authors of communism. (After all, is not Zionism Jewish communism?) The facts are that the Jesuits used their Masonic Jews to introduce it in 1848 and again in 1917 with the Bolshevik Revolution.

The Jesuits then moved their Shriner Freemason FDR to recognize Russia's bloody government in 1933. The Jesuits then financed Russian communism with their Knights of Malta on Wall Street. This enabled Joseph Stalin to carry out the purges of the Thirties. Having deceived the world into believing communism was of Jewish origin, the Jesuits then used Hitler to implement *"the Final Solution to the Jewish Question"*—pursuant to the evil Council of Trent. The result was the mass murder of European and Russian Jewry at the hands of the Jesuit-controlled SS.

At the close of the Second Thirty Years War (1945) the Jesuits, with their Vatican Ratline, helped top Nazis to escape to South America. And where in South America? To the old dominion where socialist-communism had been perfected by the Jesuit fathers—to the nation of Paraguay. The Jesuits entered Paraguay in the early 1600s, sent by the kings of Spain and Portugal. They established their supremacy over the natives called "Guarani Indians" and did not allow them to mix with the Spanish or Portuguese. It was among this people that the Jesuits established their communes called "reductions".

In 1776, the Jesuits, now formally suppressed by the Pope, were allied with Frederick the Great of Prussia and Catherine of Russia. The Jesuit General was in control of Scottish Rite Freemasonry and now sought an alliance with the Masonic House of Rothschild in England. To accomplish this he chose a Jesuit who was Jewish by race—Adam Weishaupt. Weishaupt was a brilliant instructor of Canon Law—the evil Council of Trent—at a Jesuit university in Bavaria. We read:

"From the Jesuit College of Ingolstadt is said to have issued the sect known as 'the Illuminati of Bavaria' founded by Adam Weishaupt. Its nominal founder, however, seems to have played a subordinate though conspicuous role in the organization of this sect." **Occult Theocracy, Lady Queenborough**, originally published in 1933.

On May 1, 1776, the Order of the Illuminati was officially founded in the old Jesuit stronghold of Bavaria. The Company would now use the Jewish House of Rothschild to finance the French Revolution and the rise of Napoleon the Freemason with his Jesuit-trained advisor, Abbe Sieyes. In spite of the historical writings of the Jesuit Abbe Barruel, who blamed the Rothschilds and Freemasonry for the Revolution, it was the Society of Jesus that used these very tools to carry out the Revolution and punish the monarchs who dared to expel the Jesuits from their dominions. The Jesuits, having been expelled from the Spanish Empire, found refuge in Corsica. From there they raised up their great avenger, Napoleon Bonaparte.

Lately, it was George Washington who was so beloved by France's General Lafayette. During the Revolution our great chieftain took the *"boy General"* under his wing for which cause the Frenchman named his eldest son, George Washington Lafayette. With this same endearing love the Roman Catholic **Lafayette** warned:

"It is my opinion that if the liberties of this country, the United States of America, are destroyed, it will be by the subtlety of the Roman Catholic Jesuit priests, for they are the most crafty, dangerous enemies of civil and religious liberty. They have instigated most of the wars of Europe."

Napoleon was captured by the English and banished to the island of St. Helena. There, his *Memoirs* were written which accurately described his masters, the Jesuits:

"The Jesuits are a military organization, not a religious order. There chief is a general of an army, not the mere father abbot of a monastery. And the aim of this organization is: POWER. Power in its most despotic exercise. Absolute power, universal power, power to

control the world by the volition of a single man. Jesuitism is the most absolute of despotisms: and at the same time the greatest and most enormous of abuses...."

"The general of the Jesuits insists on being master, sovereign, over the sovereign. Wherever the Jesuits are admitted they will be masters, cost what it may. Their society is by nature dictatorial, and therefore it is the irreconcilable enemy of all constituted authority. Every act, every crime, however atrocious, is a meritorious work, if committed for the interest of the Society of the Jesuits, or by the order of the general." (**Fifty Years In The Church Of Rome, Charles Chiniquy**, 1968, reprinted from the 1886 edition, quoting **Memorial Of The Captivity Of Napoleon At St. Helena, General Montholon**]

The Knights of Malta and the Jesuits work together. It is important for you to be aware of this connection. For the Knights financed Lenin and Hitler from Wall Street, also using their Federal Reserve Bank headed by Masonic Jews, Warburg in particular.) The Knights negotiated the Concordat (a Papal treaty) between the Pope and Hitler in the person of Franz Von Papen. They also helped top Nazis to escape to North and South America after World War II in the persons of James Angleton and Argentina's President Juan Peron. In America, the Knights, with their OSS, later the CIA, were behind *"Operation Paperclip"*. After World War II, top Nazis and scientists were illegally secreted into the United States. Many were placed in the top-secret military installation in Tonapah, Nevada known as *"Area 51"*. The perfection of the Nazis' anti-gravity aircraft (flying saucers) was to be completed there, among other secret technologies. "Operation Paperclip" was overseen by America's most powerful Knight of Malta, J. Peter Grace. J. Peter Grace was subject to the Jesuit-trained Archbishop Spellman, as the American headquarters for the Knights was and is St. Patrick's Cathedral in New York.

The founding Fathers of the united states knew of the Jesuit intrigue directed at the new Protestant Republic of these United States of America. In 1816, John Adams wrote to President Jefferson:

"Shall we not have regular swarms of them here, in as many disguises as only a king of the gypsies can assume, dressed as painters, publishers, writers, and schoolmasters? If ever there was a body of men who merited eternal damnation on Earth and in Hell it is this Society of Loyola's." (**The New Jesuits, George Riemer, 1971**]

A personal friend of Professor Morse believed his warning of this Jesuit conspiracy. He was President Abraham Lincoln. We read:

"The Protestants of both the North and South would surely unite to exterminate the priests and the Jesuits, if they could learn how the priests, the nuns, and the monks, which daily land on our shores, under the pretext of preaching their religion...are nothing else but the emissaries of the Pope, of Napoleon III, and the other despots of Europe, to undermine our institutions, alienate the hearts of our people from our Constitution, and our laws, destroy our schools, and prepare a reign of anarchy here as they have done in Ireland, in Mexico, in Spain, and wherever there are any people who want to be free." (**Fifty Years In The Church Of Rome, Charles Chiniquy,** 1968, reprinted from the 1886 edition).

During the period 1868-1872, the Jesuits reorganized their plan of implementation into the Us amendments. This new nation would be a centralized republic with the President exercising powers of an absolute monarch. The old Federal Republic of Washington would be converted into a huge centralized Empire, with the ten planks of the Masonic **Communist Manifesto** replacing the **Ten Commandments** of Moses. In order to accomplish this, the *Constitution* had to be amended—*"by hook or by crook"*. It would be amended in accordance with the Masonic cry of both French Revolutions. "Liberty" would be the *Thirteenth Amendment*. "Equality" would be the *Fourteenth Amendment*. "Fraternity" would be the *Fifteenth Amendment*. As we shall see later in subsequent chapters, the Fourteenth Amendment, as it was implemented, became the coup d'état.

Even though President Lincoln acted the tyrant in keeping Maryland from seceding and raised the Army of the Potomac to "put down the rebellion", there is evidence that he had a change of heart. Accordingly to many, Lincoln was converted to Christ after viewing the battlefield at Gettysburg. He later joined the Presbyterian Church in Washington and had several spiritual conversations with his close friend and converted priest, Charles Chiniquy. We read:

"I will repeat to you what I said at Urbana, when for the first time you told me your fears lest I would be assassinated by the Jesuits: Man must not care where and when he will die, provided he dies at the post of honor and duty. But I may add, today, that I have a presentiment that God will call me to Him through the hand of an assassin. Let His will, and not mine, be done! The Pope and the Jesuits, with their infernal Inquisition, are the only organized powers in the world which have recourse to the dagger of the assassin to murder those whom they cannot convince with their arguments or conquer with the sword.... It seems to me that the Lord wants today, as He wanted in the days of Moses, another victim.... I cannot conceal from you that my impression is that I am that victim. So many plots have already been made against my life, that it is a real miracle that they have failed, when we consider that the great majority of them were in the hands of skillful Roman Catholic murderers, evidently trained by Jesuits. But can we expect that God will make a perpetual miracle to save my life? I believe not. The Jesuits are so expert in those deeds of blood, that Henry IV said that it was impossible to escape them, and he became their victim, though he did all that could be done to protect himself. My escape from their hands, since the letter of the Pope to Jeff Davis has sharpened a million daggers to pierce my breast, would be more than a miracle." (**Fifty Years In The Church Of Rome, Charles Chiniquy**, 1958, originally published in 1886).

Of the Jesuit hand in Lincoln's murder we read:

"I feel safe in stating that nowhere else can be found in one book the connected presentation of the story leading up to the death of Abraham Lincoln, which was instigated by the "black" pope, the General of the Jesuit Order, camouflaged by the "white" pope, Pius IX, aided, abetted and financed by other "Divine Righters" of Europe, and finally consummated by the Roman Hierarchy and their paid agents in this country and French Canada on "Good Friday" night, April 14, 1865, at Ford's Theatre, Washington, D.C." (**The Suppressed Truth About The Assassination Of Abraham Lincoln, Burke McCarty,** 1973, originally published in 1924).

Looking at the progress of the Jesuits during period of 1945-1990, the Great and Terrible Second Thirty Years' War was now over. Europe, Russia, North Africa, China, and Japan were *"a universal wreck"* thanks to the Company of Jesus. Millions of *"heretics"* had been *"extirpated"* pursuant to the *Jesuit Oath* and the Council of Trent. Unlike the Treaty of Westphalia ending the First Thirty Years' War, the agents of the Jesuits controlled the negotiations at Yalta and Potsdam ending the second Thirty Years' War. It was time to apply the Jesuits' Hegelian Dialectic worldwide. It would be known as "the Cold War". The thesis and antithesis would be "the Free World in the West" verses "the Communist Block in the East". The American Empire would head the West, and the Russian Empire would lead the East. Both sides would be financed by the Jesuits' International Banking Cartel centered in London and New York—the Federal Reserve and Chase-Manhattan Banks in particular.

The synthesis would be the destruction of the American Empire through the so-called *"ending of the Cold War"*. The illusion of ending the Cold War would legally enable Rome's Corporate Monopolies, federated together in New York City under the leadership of the Council on Foreign Relations, to give Russia and China high technology and financial backing. The giving of these necessities would perfect the War Machines of both economically communist and politically fascist giants for the purpose of invading North America, it containing the majority of the world's Protestants, Baptists, and Jews. It is for these reasons that the financial might of Hong Kong was given to Red China, along with an American Naval Base in Long Beach, California. It is for these reasons that the Panama Canal, built with American blood, sweat, tears and Yellow Fever, was given away to Panama to be manned by Chinese soldiers imperiling the American navy. It is for these reasons that the Jesuits in control of Washington have established nationwide gun registration for the purpose of nationwide gun confiscation just as they did in Hitler's Germany. It is for these reasons that the Jesuits, with their international corporations managed by the Knights of Malta, have financed and continue to build both the Russian and Chinese War Machines, while influencing American Presidents to close down scores of military installations across the country. These facts spellinvasion—massive invasion by millions of foreign soldiers, with no God and no mercy. And if the Jesuits can manage to blow-up the Dome of the Rock in Jerusalem and blame the American Empire for it, the Arabs will declare a holy war against "the great Satan". The private wealth of Americans using International Business Corporations with bank accounts in the Bahamas will be seized just as they were in Castro's Cuba. (The Knights have moved all their wealth into European banks denominated in Franks and Marks as well as Eurodollars, thereby escaping the coming American economic catastrophe.)

Meanwhile, as the Jesuits, with their American dictator's internal police (FEMA) and foreign invaders, are *"extirpating"* *"the execrable race"* of American *"heretics"* and *"liberals"*, the European nations will be driven to lay down their historic differences and unify. This unification will restore the Holy Roman Empire, for which reason the Jesuits are rapidly rebuilding Rome. When the smoke clears, China will control the East, Russia will control the North, and a unified R.C. (*Roman Catholic)* Europe will control the West. The Pope's International Intelligence Community will see to it that Jerusalem is declared an international city with Solomon's rebuilt Temple in her midst. World government will ensue and the Jesuits' *"blessed despotism"* of the Dark Ages will have arrived, with the Pope being the Universal Despot of the World, so appropriately described in the **Protocols Of The Elders Of Zion**, while being the World Authority of **The Documents Of Vatican II**.

Who Are The "gods"?

And so it would appear that all is not what it appears to be. If you look at the Black Pope, he is the 30th Jesuit Superior general of the society of Jesus. He would appear to be the silent superior over the Society and the overseer of the "white Pope" of the Vatican. In the US there are 10 provinces called US assistency controlled by a Regional assistant and his President of the Jesuit Conference of the US in Washington DC, each governing states within their borders for the Black Pope. The headquarters of the Society of Jesus is Georgetown University which is the most powerful fortress of the land belonging to the Roman Catholics. It is the St Peters Square of the USA. The whole world seems to be governed this way as the Jesuit command structure is one that rules by the Jesuit assistnecy Provincials and includes Africa, Asia, Europe, Latin America and USA. It is all a military power.

The New World Order is ruled by the Jesuit Hierarchy governed by the Superior General. The world has accepted the Society of Jesus as the military enforcement arm of the Catholic Church. On the Jesuit flag it written the words, CUSTOM, NECTAR, RAGES, IMPIOUS or, *"It is just to exterminate or annihilate impious or heretical kings, governments, or rulers."* See the site **www.thenazareneway.com/inri_the_inscription_explained.htm** The INRI symbol also appears on the cross of crucifixion. The Jesuit order would appear to be a version of the modern day Inquisition hell bent on killing heretics. It is said that this forms the basis for the humanized 33 degree Freemasonry by which Satan will bring his risen Pope to world power. Their headquarters is in Rome and they worship the dragon which gave power unto the beast: *"Who is like unto the beast? who is able to make war with him?* **Revelations 13:4 KJV**

And so if anyone has positioned themselves as gods on Planet Earth, it would appear to be the Jesuits and the military order of the Superior General, the Provincial Generals and the Assistencys. This group that would on the surface appear as men of God, dedicated to peace, love and in service of Earthlings, from many researchers, are anything but. They have the power of dominion of all Earthlings, ***including*** the 13 bloodlines. We will leave this topic now but cover it more detail in later chapters. We will now look closer at this New World Oder Plan.

7

THE NEW AGE: CHRIST or SATAN?

The 13th Bloodline

It is said that within the Illuminati rituals, the emphasis of the 13th bloodline is that they are the seed of Satan. As their secret story goes, they are the direct descendents of Jesus' spiritual brother Lucifer. In looking back at the story as the struggle between the light and the dark, in mockery and imitation of God's 12 tribes, Satan blessed 12 bloodlines. One of these bloodlines was the Ishmaeli bloodline from which a special elite line developed alchemy, assassination techniques, and other occult practices. One bloodline was Egyptian/Celtic/Druidic from which Druidism was developed. One bloodline was in the orient and developed oriental magic. One lineage was from Canaan and the Canaanites. It had the name Astarte, then Astorga, then Ashdor, and then Astor. The tribe of Dan was used as a Judas Iscariot type seed. The royalty of the tribe of Dan have descended down through history as a powerful Satanic bloodline. The 13th or final blood line was copied after God's royal lineage of Jesus. This was the Satanic House of David with their blood which they believe is not only from the House of David but also from the lineage of Jesus, who they claim had a wife and children. The 13th Satanic bloodline was instilled with the direct seed of Satan so that they would not only carry Christ's blood-- but also the blood of his "brother" Lucifer. None of this should come as a surprise when one looks at the bloody history of kingdoms an wars.

Some of the earliest attempts to trace the seed of Satan were some books which did extensive research on the Tribe of Dan and the descendents of Cain. "***The Curse of Canaan***" is an interesting book along with its mate ***World Order*** by ***Eustice Mullins***. In ***Gerald Massey's A Book of the Beginning*** (Secaucus, NJ: University Books, Inc., 1974.) the book goes in and shows in detail how the inhabitants of the British Isles came originally from Egypt. In the work by Fritz Springmeier he explains that this is important because the Druidism of the British Isles was simply a derivative from the Egyptian Satanic witchcraft/magic of Ancient Egypt. The Egyptian word Makhaut (clan or family) became the Irish Maccu and the Maccu of the Donalds (clan of Donalds) now reflected in the name MacDonald. The sacred keepers of the Clan-Stone in Arran, were also known by the family name of Clan-Chattons. Another word for clan is Mack and the Clan-Chattons were also known as Mack-Intosh. Ptah-rekh the name of the Egyptian god Ptah was passed down to us by the Druids adopting the name Patrick, which sounded similar. St. Patricks day then is a Christianized form of a druidic holiday which originally had its origins in Egypt.

The All-Seeing Eye can be found on ancient buildings in ancient Chaldea, in ancient Greece, and in ancient Egypt. The MI-seeing eye represents Osiris. Osiris had debauched revelries (saturualias) celebrated in his honour. The temples in Arabia clear back in the time that Moses had his black father-in-law Jethro used the all-seeing-eye to represent the false satanic trinity of Osiris, Isis and Horus of Egypt. This MI-Seeing Eye pops up everywhere the Illuminati has been. In the Winter Palace Square in St. Petersburg, Russia is that Illuminati all-seeing eye on top of a pyramid. You will also see it in the old Mexican Senate Building which is now a museum in Mexico City. You will find this on the back of our one dollar bill, and you will find the all-seeing eye was placed on Ethiopian stamps when they got a communist government in power.

The Jesuits, we have seen are the continuing Inquisition through the Knights of Malta. The Illuminati is the continuation of the Mystery Religions of Babylon and Egypt. And the bloodlines of the Illuminati go back to people who at one time lived in Babylon and Egypt. Just how the House of David (the Satanic one) and the Holy Blood of the 13th family fit is a mystery but rest assured that somehow the 13th Illuminati family does goes back to ancient times. Is this via the Tribe of Dan or via some Druidic bloodline or is it via the Merovingians or is it via all three. Whatever the case, the 13th bloodline has amassed a great deal of power and wealth on this planet. In launching their business plan, the 13th bloodline lacks nothing to bring forth their Anti-Christ who will appear to have all the correct credentials. The 13th bloodline has kept its genealogies very secret. The tribe of Dan was prophesied to be the black sheep of the nation of Israel which would bite the other tribes of Israel. The tribe of Dan had the snake and the eagle as its two logos. The tribe of Dan left its calling card all over Europe as it migrated west in the names of many places. The tribe of Dan ruled the *Greeks*, the *Roman Empire*, the *Austro-Hungarian empire* and many others which used the eagle as its logo.

Great Britain is the mother country of Satanism. Scotland has long been an occult center. The national symbol of Scotland is the dragon (the snake), and for years the chief of Scotland was called the dragon. The Gaelic language is an important language for Satanism, although English and French are also use extensively by the Illuminati. The British Royal Family have long been involved with the occult. There is a detailed examination of the Royal family and the occult in the book **The Prince and the Paranormal -the Psychic Bloodline of the Royal Family** by **John Dale** (1987). They have also been actively involved with Freemasonry. British MI6 has been a major vehicle for the Satanic hierarchy working behind the secret veil of Freemasonry to control world events.

The British Royalty have served as important figureheads to British Freemasonry lending credibility and respectability. British Freemasonry has managed to keep itself free of much of the criticism that the other national Masonic groups have brought on themselves. However, much of the credibility of British Freemasonry is undeserved. True, British **Freemasonry** is what it portrays itself to the public for the lower levels. But the lower level Masons by their dues and activities are unwittingly supporting an organization that is led by Satanists at the top. An example of the subterfuge constantly exercised on the public by Freemasonry is a book purportedly written by a non-Mason entitled **The Unlocked Secret Freemasonry Examined.** The book portrays itself as an unbiased and complete expose of Freemasonry. The book states unequivocally that the Masonic order called *Societas Rosicrucian in Anglia* (sic] is only open to Christians and is a "Christian Order." However, **Edith Star Miller** reprints copies of a number of letters from the chief of the *Societas Rosicruciana in Anglia* which show that the English Grand Masonic Lodge, the SRIA, the OTO, and the German illuminati are all working together.

The Lucifer Experiment

There is a well known channeler **Steve Rother** who translates messages from what he calls "The Group". Steve is their Earth spokesman and has been guiding many on the evolution of the Light as it pertains to the shift in Ages. His website is at **www.lightworker.com**.

As a former businessman, and now writer and researcher of this phenomenal shifting going on, I was intrigued by the similarity between Satanism and what would be the survival of the fittest corporate ethics. Like most, Satan was a bad dude and was not supposed to be influencing my business so it was with great shock that I came to understand that we of business follow the beliefs unknowingly. The acceptance of the beliefs through business is a universal phenomenon. And so I was interested in finding out more about this ultimate bad guy (as stated by religions). It shed some interesting history on Lucifer.

In a special channel, Steve spoke about our perception of Light and Dark changing and as it does, it becomes more important for us to move out of polarity and into unity thinking. As he states: "*By understanding and embracing the Beauty of Darkness we can change our reality. Perhaps then we can stop being afraid of the dark.*" His channel which may seem like strange fiction is becoming more and more common knowing as will be seen in Part 2. His channel is included below:

"*Somewhere along the way, you got an idea. You said, Let us play a Game. We will place ourselves into the illusion of being finite. We will begin to define ourselves by moving into the illusion of a linear time frame with a past, present and future. Here we will play a wonderful Game as spirits of infinite design expressing ourselves in a linear time frame. What an interesting Game. And you walked around and you told your friends about it and it grew, and it grew, and it grew. Everyone thought that this would be a very unique vision. The Omniverse is filled with beings playing such Games. You have seen many. Some you call your E.T.s. You have no concept of most of these games, but they are everywhere. They are all over the place for one thing is sure... you are not alone in the Universe. You will see this as even more planets are 'discovered' in the days ahead.*

The Omniverse includes so many multiple Universes that there are literally many dimensional levels to each Universe and there are threads that run concurrently through each one. Placing the infinite in a linear time frame is a big challenge. In order to do that, you had to come up with some very unique visions, and those concepts that began your game are what we wish to share with you today. By remembering how it began perhaps you may re-define the next level of your Game with the same unique vision with which you designed this one. You are at a junction point now where you will be essentially starting over. Humanity is literally re-creating a new Gameboard in the same place where the old one existed. This is the creation of the Third Earth and the new holographic pattern that you are now creating for Earth. That is only possible because of your unique rise in vibration, because of your advancement, and the evolutionary steps that you have taken. These are not evolutionary steps as such, but more like quantum leaps in consciousness. It is happening in the blink in the eye. Many of you are waiting for a certain day or time for an event to change your world. Go enjoy that day and celebrate.

Do the things you wish to do to celebrate the unique vision of heaven on Earth for it is in process, but do not wait for the day because those things are already possible now. For now we ask you to do everything that you can do to lean against the powers you hold as an infinite being in finite form. This action will bring the infinite here and help to create the attributes of Heaven on the Third Earth that you are now creating.

Infinite to Finite Light to Dark We bring you these concepts with the understanding that as finite beings, it is not even possible to fully grasp the concept of infinity. In reality it is too simple for you to understand. Therefore we will give you some visions that will help you understand the differences so that every choice you make can be made from the perspective of an infinite being. We often use the word heart as we speak through the Keeper for it is one that is understood by most, but there are other words that we use that represent Home to each one of you. Light is one of them. You move toward the light when you step out of physical body. Go to the light' is more than just a phrase. Because of this popular phrase many cross over with the expectation of seeing and moving into a guiding light. The reality is, it is not the light in the way that you think as humans. Lightness is a state of being that represents infinity. Now if you understand that the light is actually a representation of Home expressed in infinity, then you can understand that what you are visiting here in finite form could also be called darkness.

So we wish to share with you a little bit of our view of something you call darkness. It is important that you understand the beauty of these things that you call darkness for in a finite timeline where you have a past, present and future where you are expressing yourself in the illusion of that timeline, light is only definable through the experience of darkness. Now here comes the fun part. You are such magical creators. Every time you hold a focused thought in your head longer than seven seconds, it appears in your reality. Seven seconds is all it takes and it is becoming five seconds within the next three years. You are moving so fast it is incredible for us to watch for you are reclaiming your powers of creation while still in the physical bubbles of biology. You are beginning to take your power as infinite beings while still playing the Game in the linear time line, and that is beautiful beyond description.

The Definition of Light In the beginning of the game mankind was attracted by the light. They worshiped the sun as the source of all things. Then came the time when they looked upon the sand and saw their shadows. They were afraid of them, much the way that many of you still fear darkness. Darkness is only an illusion and a lack of light. It is only a place of definition, for within a field of polarity light cannot be perceived without the contrast of darkness. So as you begin embracing the beauty of the darkness, you can actually see higher forms of light. It then becomes easier to express your infinite self in a finite world.

Yes, there are people who come to the Keeper that want to know, Does voodoo, black magic and spells really work. And the answer is the same every time, of course it does because they are asking the question. That small gap of understanding is just enough lack of light to create the darkness that you are so afraid of. Fear it not. Rather we ask you to embrace it. Find the beauty of both light and dark in all that you experience and you will move everything forward. You are now moving into the next level of helping one another as you step into the role of Human Angels. This is a new expression of the Light and therefore it may be helpful to have a new understanding of the darkness that defines it. It will not be long before you take the role of angels to the Second Planet of Free Choice. Boy, are we going to have fun then, for we get to see the same frustrations that we have experienced in dealing with you. And when you hear that enigmatic laughter over your shoulder, remember what we have said here. Know we are there, loving you.

Using Darkness to Express Light So let us give you the vision of what happened in the beginning for it would be interesting for you to understand the perspective of where you first began the Game. As you understand the concept that you are simply returning Home, and returning to light, you must understand that light is the infinite expression of energy. So in the beginning the question was asked: How do we define the infinite in a finite word? How do you create light in a space where it does not normally exist? The only way to create light in a finite world is through the contrast of darkness. It was here that you created the first negative energy. You literally created the opposite of what you wished to exist in the duality of the game. For at Home, negative energy does not exist. That is the reason that humans thrive on positive energy and love to throw off negative energy. Soon you began to perceive many ways of defining light through the use of darkness. For a time the most wondrous creations in the early Game were creations of darkness for they allowed expression of the light. And all the beings in Heaven looked upon your Game and said, Wow. What a marvellous creation. We never would have thought of that.• The lack of light expressed in energy is negative energy and you used that negative energy every single day of your lives to give birth to the light. It is a beautiful human expression of the infinite.

Even today the lights that are lighting this very room are pulsing between positive and negative energy 120 times per second. They do so to evenly balance the positive and the negative energy in the form of electricity. That can be seen as Heaven and Earth coming together. This balance of energy was first brought into use by a crystal child named Nicola Tesla. Uses of the negative energy will become more important as your evolution continues, and you begin using negative energy in your field by changing your perception of it. The moment you see a lack of anything, even a lack of light, you create a vacuum that will be filled. That is where the illusion of fear and evil comes from. As beings in the very beginning stages when you were actually afraid of your own shadows, that fear grew for even in those early stages it was a definition of light. So as you grew, your expression of that negative energy grew. Over eons of time, you came up with the most imaginable things to be afraid of, and you found lots of fear within it. Much the way that fear is only a lack of love, darkness is only a lack of light. It will be helpful to know that you have created a parallel reality that exists to balance the duality as it relates to light. In fact an entire parallel universe exists that is designed to balance the light and dark in all that you do. In fact, it was from this place that the concept of alternating electrical current came. As a crystal child Tesla was able to travel between the inter dimensional realities of both worlds. You are beginning to see glimpses of this parallel universe as you raise your vibration. More will come on this in the days ahead, but for now simply know that it exists and in that universe light is dark and dark is light.

The Lucifer Experiment At one point in your development, humanity became so captivated with the negative and the illusion of fear, that it was necessary for us to create the illusion of polarity consciousness in Heaven. Not an easy task for darkness is a creation of duality and does not exist in Heaven. Yet, in order for us in the angelic realm to reflect your magnificence, it was even necessary for us to create the illusion of darkness on the other side of the veil. Thus began the Lucifer Experiment.

Lucifer was a great angel; an angel of love and his energy was such that he could switch to something that was the illusion of negative energy. He was the one angel strong enough to hold the illusion of darkness in Heaven. Imagine what it would be like to have all the beings of Earth looking at you in disgust and using your image to motivate them. In fact he was the angel who helped to define light through his willingness to play that role. As that negative energy of fear came in to him, he was able to express it with the most beautiful love as what you call darkness. And he did so out of complete sacrifice, knowing perfectly well that this energy would be transmitted to all the beings on Earth and that he would not be revered, but would be hated and feared. What a gift. What a beauty of darkness. Thus he was and still is referred to as the prince of darkness. That gift of darkness allowed that gap to be filled and it was necessary to continue the illusion of the Lucifer Experiment for eons of time on your game board. Lucifer's gift of darkness allowed you to clearly see the light. Even though your advancement was moving a little bit every day, it was moving ever so slowly. But now that has changed for you have begun taking these quantum steps into evolution. You have begun standing on your own feet, stepping into the second wave of empowerment. As you do that, everything changes and the work of Lucifer is complete. The energy of everything now measured as an expression of light. Once you understand that, you defined it all in the field of heaven for as we have told you many times before, Lucifer has returned Home. He was greeted with thunderous applauds and open arms as the hero he is. The Lucifer Experiment was a success and in the alternate universe he is seen clearly as the angel of light.

That Game is no longer being played. The Lucifer Experiment is no longer needed and we tell you that because of that, there is a love in heaven that can now be shared on Earth. Because of that, new capabilities are possible. Because of that gift, it is entirely possible for you to play the game without the polarity of what you have known as good and bad. This is not an easy step for humans as you have built your world on these concepts. Yet to create Heaven on Earth it is necessary, for these are human concepts caused by the illusion of polarity and do not exist in Heaven. You are now beginning to define light in new and unique ways. Welcome Home.

Water The Energy Let us share with you one other secret that we will begin talking about even more in future reminders from Home. There is a simple energy that is designed to balance negative and positive energy. You see it throughout your life every day for there is one form of energy, similar to the Universal Energy, which runs between all things and all dimensions of light. It is known as water. Water is actually a form of energy that balances energy. It carries neutral potential. In its natural state, in infinite form, it does not have positive, nor negative charge. Therefore it will always bring you back to a balanced state. It is a life-force energy, which every living thing uses. Even the chair in which the Keeper sits needs water to exist in its present form. And it is the water that ties everything together. So when there are times where you feel someone is getting stuck or even yourselves in what you perceive to be negative energy whether that is negative emotion, negative experience, negative thoughts, or the cycle that you call depression, look to water first. The clarity of water going through your being can help to neutralize that energy very quickly.

Add the magic of intent to the water you ingest and you have great power. You can do ceremony around it and increase its usefulness. As with all forms of energy, water only changes form from one form to another. The reality is that this water is the same water that the dinosaurs drank, so it has changed energy over and over and over again. Look at this as a connection to Home. That is the reason that many of you who are trying to do spiritual communication will find that it happens in the shower; will find that it happens as you are doing dishes or doing the laundry. It happens yes, the commode, too around the water is where it happens because that is the place where you can most cleanly neutralize your energy and allow your spirit to come through you.

In the near future for you will begin discovering things about the energy form you call water. You will soon find that if you unleash the energy in one cubic centimeter of water, you will light your largest cities for three years. It is there because that is the connection point between finite and infinite: water. Find it. Play with it. (At this point Steve takes a glass of water from beside his chair and slowly pours it on the carpet.) Make your own ceremonies around it. Figure out how you are going to use that for you are the creators. We are giving you possibilities, potentials to look at, for we will not tell you which way to turn. That is not our job. Our job is to gently OverLight you from the back and show you the many potentials of the road that is ahead. And every time one of you walks over this wet spot, you will re-member that.

Between Light and Dark From that range of light to dark is no less than 144 primary colors of which all of you have taken a ray. All of you vibrate between a range that equates to one of those 144 primary colors and it will not be long before you will start seeing things that you have no description for, for your world is built on the illusion of 4 primary colors. There are many more. You will begin to see them now, for as you advance and move into higher vibration, your physical body will adjust, and much the way that you are starting to see new things now, you will begin seeing new colors. The other thing that will be happening very soon as a result of all the things that you are moving through, is that your ears will take another step into change. Some of you will hear ringing that will go on and on and on and on. Take it as a vibrational imprint for it simply means that you are vibrating in harmonics with a new alternate reality which is very close to yours. It also means that you are about to make contact with that alternate reality. A time will come very soon that you have set up, where many of these timelines that go side by side in concurrent organization, will be crossing each other. And at that magical space, each timeline that crosses each other leaves permanent imprints and goes forward, and there is a union of many timelines coming in the near future. It is what you have called ascension but it is under way already. Many of the attributes that you have looked for in ascension are here right now. You have only to find a way to utilize them in your world and to bring them into your beautiful darkness.

The love on Home is with each and every one of you. Know that you are the most magical creators. Even though there are times when you sit alone and ask, Why am I here? What did I come here for? There must be a higher purpose.• Know that we see you. We come behind you and we wrap you in our wings and we remind you of who you are and the times when you have lost yourself. Yet it is not possible to enter your world any longer for you, here, have risen to a higher vibration. So we ask you do not seek angelic intervention as much as the connection to the angel within you, for that is now possible more than ever before. The Web of Love is being activated that connects all *hearts. You are doing it yourselves and as you create that, you will sometimes feel a pull on the energy and it will almost feel like a net. That net is made in such a way that those cross-members are not tied together, but simply loose so that when someone tugs on the net because they are afraid of the dark, you send them love. There will be a great reservoir of love energy on that net at all times. That is available this day. That is what is at hand. Every time you do that, you strengthen your connection to your higher self and to All That Is. Heaven is here this day and you are the angels that are bringing it here. How many Lightworkers does it take to turn on the lights on Planet Earth? One. You. Do not be afraid of the darkness. Flood it with love and turn it into the most beautiful darkness that you can possibly imagine for that is the creation of Home. That is what you came here to do and you are doing a marvellous job. We are so very proud of you.*

Each one of you has a specific task that you have come here to do and you know it somewhere in your heart. Know that you are on the right path. There came a time for this incarnation in which you sit for many of the beings to come back in and a great line formed on the other side of the veil. Many people got ready to come in and said, It looks like it is going to happen. We are all going in, here.• And all the people who thought they could make a difference got in line, ready to take a turn in a bubble of biology. Then a very magical thing happened. We have told you this before yet we wish to remind you. Someone at the front of the line turned around and looked at the person behind him and said, You know, you have a better chance of making a difference than I do. I am going to step aside and ask you to move to the front of the line.• For you are not separate from each other on the other side of the veil. You are one. And that soul moved aside so that this one could go forward and one by one, each one of them stepped aside so that the finest possibilities of creating heaven on Earth could move to the forefront. And here you are. You made it in. It is our job to remind you that you are the ones. You are the magical beings from Home that everybody stepped aside for so that you could come in. You have a responsibility to create the highest and best for yourselves to all of those that stepped aside.

Is it surprising that the Illuminati call themselves the "illuminated Ones"?

The Lucis Trust And The New Age

As we have seen the most important powerful people on Planet Earth are followers of this Lucifer. Let us now tie some of this together. It relates to a trust set up in the early 1900's called the Lucis Trust. David Rockefeller is part of Lucis Trust's management. Lucis Trust puts out the book **Externalization of the Hierarchy** by **Alice Bailey** which spells out The Plan for the Satanists and the New Agers on how the spiritual Hierarchy (actually the demonic hierarchy) is to externalize their rule of the planet. The book gives quite a few of the details of the plan, and is used as a textbook for New Agers at the Arcane Schools in NY, London, and Europe on how the New Age/One World Religion/One-World-Government will be brought in. Note that the term New Age is not a recent invention. If anyone doubts the Rockefeller's commitment to Satan, read page 107 of **Externalization of the Hierarchy,** where **Alice Bailey**, President of the Theosophical Society and part of Lucis (formerly Lucifer) Trust, tells us who will rule when the New Age (New World Order) takes over.

On the Earthly level--Humanity so to speak, the Ruler is given on page 107 as Lucifer. On the Spiritual level--called "Shamballa - the Holy City" the coming ruler is given as "the Lord of the World" which Christians know as Satan. Lucis Trust knows it is Satan too, but for public consumption they say that the "ruler of the world" is Sanat (a scrambling of Satan) Kumara. They also predict there will be a Christ Consciousness and the under the responsibility of Christ. The book Externalization of the Hierarchy teaches repeatedly (see pages 511-512, 514) that the 3 vehicles to bring in the New Age will be the Masonic Lodges, next the Churches, and finally Education. What this suggests is that the bloodlines who support this like the Rockefellers, are using the churches and the media/education systems for the Luciferian plan of Lucis Trust. If you read this document it follows like a business plan for all to see, or for those who have eyes to see!

According to **Dianne Core**, a leading British expert in the battle against Satanism, she stated: *"We are in the middle of spiritual warfare, and the Satanic weapons are all pointed at the young."* From what has been researched about the bloodlines, it should not come as a surprise that this includes many of the leading advocates of new deals, top figures of the United Nations bureaucracy, and leading elite families. What is even more interesting is to look to Mikhail Gorbachov as the premier world cult leader in what they call their "Externalized Hierarchy."

Here we see an ongoing series where a dossier of some of the principal institutions and individuals behind this other (perceived evil) "New Age" movement. The Cathedral of St. John the Divine, the medieval temple of the Episcopalian Archdiocese of New York, has become the mother institution of the New Age movement in the United States, whose goal is to eclipse the Age of Pisces (Christianity) with an Age of Aquarius (Lucifer). The presiding bishop of the cathedral, Bishop Paul Moore, whose family is heir to the Nabisco company fortune, has been in the forefront of creating this Satanic "new world order," since at least the late 1950s, when, as a priest in Indianapolis, Indiana, he gave the "People's Temple" cult of Jim Jones its start.

Later in 1977, Bishop Moore rocked the Christian world, when he ordained a militant lesbian, Ellen Marie Barrett, who told Time magazine that it was her lesbian love affair that gave her strength to serve God. Bishop Moore claims that the ordination of lesbians, and his other Gnostic heresies, are merely part of the ongoing revelation of God's truth to man by the Holy Spirit, which had been prophesied by the Disciple John.

With this dissembling rationale, Bishop Moore has transformed the Cathedral of St. John the Divine into a Gnostic stronghold for such organizations as The Lucis Trust, founded in 1922 by Alice Bailey, a disciple of Theosophist Madame Helena Blavatsky. Originally named the Lucifer Trust, it became a mother institution of the modern New Age movement; The Temple of Understanding, which is headquartered at the cathedral under its president, the Very Reverend Dean James Parks Morton, dean of the cathedral. It has turned the cathedral into a harbour for Gnostic religions ranging from Tibetan Buddhism to Sufi Freemasonry:

- The medieval village of Lindesfarne, New York, which is to be the model for a New Age lifestyle, once the Earth has been purified of its billions of non-white souls;
- A special ministry to Sufi Freemasons who were a historical deployment against Ibn Sina and the Arab Renaissance, and whose modern-day cathedral affiliates have been linked to the assassination of Egyptian President Anwar Sadat;
- The Zen Center, which teaches meditation to the elite of the Liberal Establishment;
- Gay and lesbian organizations, which seek to legitimize their sin by arguing that the "beloved disciple" John had a homosexual affair with Christ, or else by creating Mother Goddess religions in the cathedral's crypts;
- A medieval chivalric order known as the Most Venerable Order of the Hospital of St. John, which, under the direction of the Duke of Gloucester of the British Royal Family, has inculcated the "Episcopagan" American Establishment in such Gnostic evil

as the necessity to spread Shi'ite fundamentalism under the Ayatollah Khomeini in Iran, because the Shah had "sinned" by trying to industrialize his nation.

The serried ranks of the dead among Jim Jones's "Peoples Temple" cult, who had consumed cyanide-laced Kool-Aid on orders from Jones, are merely the more public casualties of the Age of Aquarius, when those bearing the "Mark of the Beast" (666) are to be unleashed upon the Earth once again. Throughout the United States, the Satanic New Age movement has grown to become a major threat to the Judeo-Christian tradition upon which our republic was founded. Among the more recent signs of this upsurge are the Atlanta child murders, the case of New York child-beater Joel Steinberg, and the mass murder of school children in Stockton, California by a drug addict wearing a "Satan" T-shirt.

There is a national security dimension to the growth of the New Age movement. Starting in 1982, Bishop Moore returned from the Soviet Union to warn that unless the Anglo-American Establishment carried out appeasement of the Soviets, the Russians would launch a thermonuclear first strike. Moore, who entered the 1970s "peace movement" by visiting with the Vietcong-controlled, underground peace movement in Vietnam, had by 1983 joined with the pro-terrorist Institute for Policy Studies and the U.S.A.-Canada Institute of the U.S.S.R. Academy of Sciences, to mobilize the American peace movement to stop the Strategic Defence Initiative. Thirty top Soviet intelligence officers, who were joined by Bishop Moore, gave marching orders to the American peace leadership to this effect in Minneapolis, Minnesota in 1983.

The Cathedral of St. John the Divine hosted a "February Fling," sponsored by the Temple of Understanding, which brought together top Soviet officials to meet with their counterparts in the West. Through French Luis Dolan, who travels to the U.S.S.R. every six weeks to get marching orders from officials of the CPSU International Department-controlled Soviet Peace Center, the Temple of Understanding overlaps the Center for Soviet-American Dialogue, which is involved in extensive exchanges, whose purpose is to remove the "enemy image" of the U.S.S.R. being an "evil empire." Father Dolan also works with Wainwright House, which has several programs along the same lines and which hosted a U.S.-U.S.S.R. Citizens Summit. Spokesmen for the Lucis Trust believe that Mikhail Gorbachov may be the premier world leader in their "Externalized Hierarchy," giving impetus to a "Plan" for a "new world order" of Luciferian values and behaviour. The Lucis Trust also carries out exchanges with the Soviet Union, where they believe "Triangle Cells" pray the "Great Invocation" for the coming Age of Aquarius. These Luciferians welcome Gorbachov, who bears the "Mark of the Beast" on his forehead.

The New Age movement's enthusiasm for Gorbachov is really no surprise. The roots of this movement date back to the 1870s, when Madame Helena Petrovna Blavatsky (nee Princess Hahn in 1831 in Ekaterinoslav, Georgia) was deployed by a combination of "Black Hundreds" forces that included the Okhrana (Czarist secret service) and the Russian Orthodox Church, to destroy Augustinian Christianity in the West, through the creation of a Satanic ideology known as Theosophy, which was a syncretism of Eastern religions. As one Theosophical Society brochure made clear, its goal was "to oppose the materialism of science and every form of dogmatic theology, especially the Christian, which the Chiefs of the Society regard as particularly pernicious."

The deployment of Madame Blavatsky into the West had been part of the same effort--called the "Dostoevsky Project" by the Theosophically-inspired Frankfurt School--which led the Okhrana to unleash the Scottish Freemasonic forces of the liberal Alexander Kerensky, then the "dark forces" of the Bolsheviks (many of whom, including V.I. Lenin, had been trained on the Isle of Capri in the cult beliefs of the Emperor Tiberius, who murdered Christ), for an assault upon the Petrine state. Among those principally responsible for deploying the hashish-addicted Blavatsky into the West were: Count Alexander Ignatiev, one-time head of the Okhrana as interior minister, whose family later joined with the Bolshevik Revolution; Imperial Privy Councilor Prince Aksakov, whose correspondence with Blavatsky reveals him to be a key controller; Fyodor Dostoevsky, whose writings have regained popularity under Gorbachov, because they were a 19th-century revival of the Russian Orthodox Church's "blood-and-soil" doctrine (a Luciferic throwback to previous evolutionary epochs) that Moscow would become "the Third and Final Rome"; and, Mikhail, Vladimir, and Vsevelod Soloviev, who, from such bases as the St. Petersburg Ecclesiastical Academy, propounded the doctrines of Spiritualism that are being revived in Russia today, and who profiled Blavatsky as Tentacles of the Blavatsky deployment extended quickly through the West. For example:

United States - In 1873, Blavatsky traveled to the U.S., where with the Spiritualist Colonel Olcott, she founded the American Theosophical Society, whose headquarters became Pasadena, California. Colonel Olcott had been involved in seances at this time on a farm in Chittenden, Vermont, with Mary Baker Eddy, who founded Christian Science as co-extensive with Theosophy. Later, Olcott accompanied Blavatsky to Adyar, India, which became the spiritual center of the cult.

Great Britain - In 1883, Blavatsky's disciple Annie Besant, who later assumed Blavatsky's mantle as High Priestess of Theosophy, was a co-founder of the British Fabian Society (predecessor of the Labour Party) together with Gnostic Christians and Spiritualists, including the Spiritualist Frank Podmore, later British Prime Minister J. Ramsay Macdonald, Soviet agent Lord Haldane, Lord and Lady Passfield, the Freemason William Clarke, Earl Bertrand Russell, Viscount and Viscountess Snowden, Lord Sidney Oliver, Lord Thomson, and others. In the same year, Scottish noble Douglas Dunglas Home, who had sponsored Blavatsky as early as 1858 and given seances for the Czar, returned to Great Britain, where with support of the Cecil family, he founded the Society for Psychical Research, whose members included Arthur Conan Doyle, Lord Balfour, Lord Bertrand Russell, John Dewey, and William James.

Another excrescence of Theosophy was the explicitly Satanist Edward Aleister Crowley's Order of the Golden Dawn (or, Stella Matutina), which overlapped the predominantly Anglo-American Ordo Templi Orientis (OTO) and the Thule Society in Munich, which gave birth to the Nazi Party through the good offices of Houston Stewart Chamberlain, Karl Haushofer, Rudolf Hess, and the Wagner Kreis.

Germany - Blavatsky's co-controller, Count Aksakov, established in Leipzig, Germany a Theosophical magazine, Psychische Studien, which was influential upon the careers of Sigmund Freud and especially Carl Jung. It also influenced the schismatic Theosophist Rudolf Steiner, who founded in 1913 the Dornach, Switzerland-based Anthroposophy sect, which has lately been a leading influence within West Germany's Free Democratic Party, and also the seed-crystal in southern Germany of the fascist Green party. [2] Meanwhile, in the 1920s, a Berlin-based Theosophist, Graf von Reventlow, founded a European network of the Comintern's Baku Conference of "Oppressed Peoples,'' which sought to merge Marxism with Sufism.

Switzerland - The Ascona, Switzerland secret base of Theosophy--centered around a cult of Astarte--was the spiritual center of the Frankfurt School, which overlapped the Soviet GRU (military intelligence) through such founders as Hede Massing, Richard Sorge, and Max Horkheimer, who developed the "Authoritarian Personality" dogma to target and destroy those who based their behaviour upon natural law. Ascona was also a spiritual center of the "Children of the Sun" gay and lesbian networks, which overlapped the Philby, Burgess, Maclean spy network in Great Britain. Finally, Ascona was the religious center for the Theosophical psychiatrist Carl Jung, popularizer of the Gnostic Bible. Among Jung's disciple-patients were: Mary Bancroft, the mistress-secretary of Allen Dulles, who was OSS chief in Switzerland during World War II; and Mary and Paul Mellon, who, on their return to the U.S. in 1939, founded the Bollingen Foundation to propagate Gnosticism and a study center on witchcraft at Princeton University. Also, Lenin himself participated in cult dances on Monte Verita in Ascona.

Alice Bailey And The Externalization Of The Hierarchy

Alice La Trobe Bateman was the founder in 1920 of the Lucifer Trust, which represented a syncretism of Gnostic Christianity with Blavatsky's Theosophy. Bailey's Gnostic doctrine transformed God into Nietzschean Will, while Christ is considered merely a lowly part of the many "Ascended Masters," who form a "Hierarchy," that is eventually to be "externalized" to carry out a "Plan" for a "new world order" that is otherwise known to Bailey's disciples as the Age of Aquarius or Age of Maitreya. The Lucis Trust, which today has Non-Governmental Organization (NGO) status at the United Nations and has been given legitimacy by the Cathedral of St. John the Divine, has spawned an array of New Age fronts, including the Temple of Understanding.

Born in Britain, Alice was raised an Episcopalian, before separating from her first husband, a drunken missionary to the United States, who beat her frequently. Relocated from Britain to the West Coast, she was recruited into the Pacific Grove Lodge of Theosophy in 1915. By 1920, she became editor of the American Theosophists' newspaper, The Messenger. In this same year she married Foster Bailey (a Scottish Rite Freemason and Co-Mason), and she launched a fight with Annie Besant for control of Theosophy, which Alice Bailey lost, when Besant's man, Louis Roger, was elected president. Immediately after the dust settled, Alice and Foster Bailey founded their own Tibetan Lodge, then the Lucifer Trust, whose name was abridged in 1922 to its present Lucis Trust.

There are comments on the World Wide Web claiming that the Lucis Trust was once called the Lucifer Trust. Such was never the case. However, for a brief period of two or three years in the early 1920's, when Alice and Foster Bailey were beginning to publish the books published under her name, they named their fledgling publishing company "Lucifer Publishing Company". By 1925 the name was changed to Lucis Publishing Company and has remained so ever since. Both "Lucifer" and "Lucis" come from the same word root, lucis being the Latin generative case meaning of light. The Baileys' reasons for choosing the original name are not known to us, but we can only surmise that they, like the great teacher H.P. Blavatsky, for whom they had enormous respect, sought to elicit a deeper understanding of the sacrifice made by Lucifer. Alice and Foster Bailey were serious students and teachers of Theosophy, a spiritual tradition which views Lucifer as one of the solar Angels, those advanced Beings Who Theosophy says descended (thus "the fall") from Venus to our planet eons ago to bring the principle of mind to what was then animal-man. In the theosophical perspective, the descent of these solar Angels was not a fall into sin or disgrace but rather an act of great sacrifice, as is suggested in the name "Lucifer" which means light-bearer.

By the 1930s, Bailey claimed 200,000 members, and her faction of Theosophy grew even more rapidly after Krishnamurti in 1939 denounced Besant's scheme to promote him as the Messiah. Throughout these years, Bailey spent her summers in Ascona, Switzerland, where along with Mary and Paul Mellon, she attended Jung's Eranos Conferences. Bailey established a series of fronts, which include:

The Arcane School - Founded in 1923, the school gives correspondence courses in meditation from its branches in New York, Geneva, London, and Buenos Aires. A brochure states: "*The presentation of the teaching adapted to the rapidly emerging new civilization stresses the training of disciples in group formation, a technique which will characterize the discipleship service in the Aquarian Age.*"

World Goodwill - Founded in 1932, the organization is recognized by the United Nations today as an NGO. Ever since the dropping of the atomic bomb (which is seen as a spiritual manifestation of Luciferian light), Lucis Trust has sought to give the U.N. a monopoly over nuclear weapons with which to impose a "one world federalist empire" upon sovereign nations. World Goodwill works directly with the "world federalists," and is part of the work to "Externalize the Hierarchy" of "Illumined Minds," which will usher in an "Age of Maitreya," otherwise interpreted by Bailey to be the return of Christ prophesied in the biblical book of Revelations.

Triangles - Founded in 1937, Triangles is the name for a global network of cells, whose members pray a "Great Invocation," especially on the night of the full moon, when members of the Triangle can be influenced by the astrological signs of the zodiac.

Findhorn - This is the sacred community of the New Age movement, based in Great Britain. Bailey disciple David Spangler, another explicit Luciferian, became co-director of the Findhorn Foundation, when he formed the Lorian Association. He sits on the boards of directors of Planetary Citizens, the secretariat of Planetary Initiative for the World We Choose (launched at the Cathedral of St. John in 1982), and is a contributing editor to New Age Magazine.

But, Lucis is not limited to low-level Satanists. When he was Secretary of Defence in the early-1960s, Robert McNamara prayed to the full moon along the Potomac River, according to journalist Edith Roosevelt. The Lucis Trust endorsed McNamara's tenure as head of the World Bank--which is hardly surprising, since Lucis believes in the Blavatskyian "Great White Brotherhood," which is consistent with the neo-malthusian aim of the International Monetary Fund to exterminate darker-skinned races. Not only does Bailey explicitly seek to destroy the nation state, which she equates with the "idealism" of the Age of Pisces, but in her 1954 work Education in the New Age, she also endorses Nazi eugenics and sex hygiene to purify the race. Apart from U.N. Secretary General Javier Parez de Cuellar, spokesmen for Lucis view Mikhail Gorbachov as the greatest world leader externalizing their "Plan" today.

The Temple of Understanding The Lucis Trust in 1963 founded a more distanced front group, the Temple of Understanding, which also has NGO status and worked out of the U.N. premises directly, until in 1984 it shifted headquarters to the Cathedral of St. John the Divine. The Lucis Trust and the Temple remain covertly entwined to this day.

While the chairman of the Temple is Judith Dickerson Hollister, those involved with its founding were: the late "Isis Priestess" of anthropology, Dame Margaret Mead of the Order of St. John; Order of St. John's Canon Edward West; U.N. deputy secretary general Robert Muellar, who had been involved as well with the Lucis Trust; and one Winifred McCulloch, leader of the New York-based Teilhard de Chardin Society.

Dormant for several years after a major expose by Edith Roosevelt, the Temple was revived at the Cathedral of St. John the Divine in 1984 at a ceremony presided over by Bishop Paul Moore and the Dalai Lama. **According to the past executive director,**

Priscilla Pedersen, its present board overlaps that of David Rockefeller's Trilateral Commission. Recent activities of the Temple include:

Global Forum of Spiritual and Parliamentary Leaders on Human Survival. Held in Oxford, England April 11-15, 1988, its luminaries included the Dalai Lama, the Archbishop of Canterbury, and Carl Sagan. Co-organizers of the Global Forum were the Temple of Understanding and the Global Committee of Parliamentarians on Population and Development, which latter advocates neo-malthusian population reduction as the solution to the world's ills. Present also at the conference were four Soviet Communist Party Central Committee members, including Dr. Evgenii Velikhov, Vice President of the Soviet Academy of Sciences. At the Global Forum, Rabbi Adin Steinsaltz, founder-director of the Israel Institute for Talmudic Publications, agreed with Velikhov to set up an institute to gather the Judaica of Russia.

Alice Ann Bailey (June 16, 1880 – December 15, 1949), was a writer and theosophist (wisdom; literally "divine wisdom"), refers to systems of esoteric philosophy concerning, or investigation seeking direct knowledge of, presumed mysteries of being and nature, particularly concerning the nature of divinity) in what she termed "Ageless Wisdom". This included occult teachings, "esoteric" psychology and healing, astrological and other philosophic and religious themes. She was born as **Alice LaTrobe Bateman**, in Manchester, England and moved to the United States in 1907, where she spent most of her life as a writer and teacher. Her works, written between 1919 and 1949, describe a wide-ranging system of esoteric thought covering such topics as how spirituality relates to the solar system, meditation, healing, spiritual psychology, the destiny of nations, and prescriptions for society in general. She described the majority of her work as having been telepathically dictated to her by an Ascended master, initially referred to only as "the Tibetan", or by the initials "D.K.", later identified as Djwal Khul. Her followers refer to her writings as *The Alice A. Bailey material*, or sometimes, as the *AAB material*.

Her writings were influenced by the works of Madame Blavatsky. Though Bailey's writings differ from the orthodox Theosophy of Madame Blavatsky, they also have much in common with it. She wrote about religious themes, including Christianity, though her writings are fundamentally different from many aspects of Christianity and of other orthodox religions. Her vision of a unified society includes a global "spirit of religion" different from traditional religious forms and including the concept of the Age of Aquarius.

Her book ***Externalization of the Hierarchy*** which can be found at the web site ***http://www.bibliotecapleyades.net/sociopolitica/externalisation/contents.htm*** *I* clearly tells of the need for a New World Order and how this is to unfold. In Section 1, March 1934, The Period of Transition she describes three factors that mark the transition in a New Age:

"One of the results of the world condition at this time is the speeding up of all the atomic lives upon and within the planet. This necessarily involves the increased vibratory activity of the human mechanism, with a consequent effect upon the psychic nature, producing an abnormal sensitivity and psychic awareness. It would be of value here to remember that the condition of humanity at this time is not the result of simply one factor, but of several - all of them being active simultaneously, because this period marks the close of one age and the inauguration of the new.

The factors to which I refer are, primarily, three in number:

1. This is a transition period between the passing out of the Piscean Age, with its emphasis upon authority and belief, and the coming in of the Aquarian Age, with its emphasis upon individual understanding and direct knowledge. The activity of these forces, characteristic of the two signs, produces in the atoms of the human body a corresponding activity. We are on the verge of new knowledge and the atoms of the body are being tuned up for reception. Those atoms which are predominantly Piscean are beginning to slow down their activity and to be 'occultly withdrawn,' as it is called, or abstracted, whilst those which are responsive to the New Age tendencies are, in their turn, being stimulated and their vibratory activity increased.

2. The world war marked a climax in the history of mankind, and its subjective effect was far more potent than has hitherto been grasped. Through the power of prolonged sound, carried forward as a great experiment on the battlefields all over the world during a period of four years (1914-1918), and through the intense emotional strain of the entire planetary populace, the web of etheric matter (called the veil of the temple) which separates the physical and astral planes was rent or torn asunder, and the amazing process of unifying the two worlds of physical plane living and of astral plane experience was begun and is now slowly going on. It will be obvious, therefore, that this must bring about vast changes and alterations in the human consciousness. Whilst it will usher in the age of understanding, of brotherhood and of illumination, it will also bring about states of reaction and the letting loose of psychic forces which today menace the uncontrolled and ignorant, and warrant the sounding of a note of warning and of caution.

3. A third factor is as follows. It has been known for a long time by the mystics of all the world religions and by esoteric students everywhere, that certain members of the planetary Hierarchy are approaching closer to the earth at this time. By this I want you to infer that the thought, or the mental attention, of the Christ and of certain of His great disciples, the Masters of the Wisdom, is directed or focused at this time on human affairs, and that some of Them are also preparing to break Their long silence and may appear later among men. This necessarily has a potent effect, first of all upon Their disciples and on those who are attuned to and synchronized with Their Minds, and secondly, it should be remembered that the energy which flows through these focal points of the Divine Will will have a dual effect and be destructive as well as constructive, according to the quality of the bodies which react to it. Different types of men respond distinctively to any inflow of energy, and a tremendous psychic stimulation is at this time going on, with results both divinely beneficent and sadly destructive.

It might be added also that certain astrological relationships between the constellations are releasing new types of force which are playing through our solar system and on to our planet and thereby making possible developments hitherto frustrated in expression, and bringing about the demonstration of latent powers and the manifestation of new knowledges. All this must be most carefully borne in mind by the worker in the field of human affairs if the present crisis is to be rightly appreciated and its splendid opportunities rightly employed. I have felt it wise to write a few words concerning the condition to be found in the world today especially in connection with esoteric, occult and mystical groups and the spiritualistic movement.

All true spiritual thinkers and workers are much concerned at this time about the growth of crime on every hand, by the display of the lower psychic powers, by the apparent deterioration of the physical body, as shown in the spread of disease, and by the extraordinary increase in insanity, neurotic conditions and mental unbalance. All this is the result of the tearing of the planetary web, and at the same time it is a part of the evolutionary plan and the providing of the opportunity whereby humanity may take its next step forward. The Hierarchy of Adepts has been divided in opinion (if so unsuitable a word can be applied to a group of souls and brothers who know no sense of separateness, but only differ over problems of 'skill in action') over the present world condition. Some believe it to be premature and consequently undesirable and providing a difficult situation, whilst others take Their stand upon the basic soundness of humanity and regard the present crisis as inevitable and brought about by the developments in man himself; They look upon the condition as educational and as constituting only a temporary problem which - as it is solved - will lead mankind on the way to a still more glorious future. But there is, at the same time, no denying the fact that great and frequently devastating forces have been let loose upon the earth, and that the effect is a cause of grave concern to all the Masters, Their disciples and workers.

The difficulty can, in the main, be traced back to the over-stimulation and the undue strain placed upon the mechanism of the bodies, which the world of souls (in physical incarnation) have to employ as they seek to manifest on the physical plane and so respond to their environment. The flow of energy, pouring through from the astral plane and (in a lesser degree) from the lower mental plane, is brought in contact with bodies that are unresponsive at first, and over-responsive later; it pours into brain cells which, from lack of use, are unaccustomed to the powerful rhythm imposed upon them; and humanity's equipment of knowledge is so poor that the majority have not sense enough to proceed with caution and to progress slowly. Therefore, they are soon in danger and difficulty; their natures are oft so impure or so selfish that the new powers which are beginning to make their presence felt, and so opening up new avenues of awareness and contact, are subordinated to purely selfish ends and prostituted to mundane objectives. The glimpses vouchsafed to the man of that which lies behind the veil are misinterpreted and the information gained is misused and distorted by wrong motives. But whether a person is unintentionally a victim of force or brings himself in touch with it deliberately, he pays the price of his ignorance or temerity in the physical body, even though his soul may "go marching on."

It is of no use at this time to close one's eyes to the immediate problem or to endeavour to lay the blame for the sad failures, the occult wrecks, for the half-demented psychics, the hallucinated mystics and the feeble-minded dabblers in esotericism at the door of their own stupidity, or upon the backs of some teachers, groups or organizations. Much blame can indeed be placed here and there, but it is the part of wisdom to face facts and to realize the cause of that which is everywhere transpiring and which can be stated as follows.

The cause of the growth of the lower psychism and of the increasing sensitivity of humanity at this time is the sudden inflow of a new form of astral energy through the rent veil which has, until a short while ago, safeguarded the many. Add to this the inadequacy of the mass of human vehicles to meet the newly imposed strain and some idea of the problem can be grasped.

Let it not be forgotten, however, that there is another side to the picture. The inflow of this energy has brought many hundreds of people into a new and deeper spiritual realization; it has opened a door through which many will pass before long and take their second initiation, and it has let a flood of light into the world - a light which will go on increasing for the next thirty years, bringing assurance of immortality and a fresh revelation of the divine potencies in the human being. Thus is the New Age dawning. Access to levels of inspiration, hitherto untouched, has been facilitated. The stimulation of the higher faculties (and this on a large scale) is now possible, and the coordination of the personality with the soul and the right use of energy can go forward with renewed understanding and enterprise. Ever the race is to the strong, and always the many are called and the few chosen. This is the occult law.

We are now in a period of tremendous spiritual potency and of opportunity to all upon the probationary path and the path of discipleship. It is the hour wherein a clarion call goes forth to man to be of good cheer and of goodwill, for deliverance is on the way. But it is also the hour of danger and of menace for the unwary and the unready, for the ambitious, the ignorant, and for those who selfishly seek the Way and who refuse to tread the path of service with pure motive. Lest this widespread upheaval and consequent disaster to so many should seem to you unfair, let me remind you that this one life is but a second of time in the larger and wider existence of the soul, and that those who fail and are disrupted by the impact of the powerful forces now flooding our earth will nevertheless have their vibration "stepped up" to better things along with the mass of those who achieve, even if their physical vehicles are destroyed in the process. The destruction of the body is not the worst disaster that can overcome a man.

It is not my purpose to cover the whole ground possible in relation to the situation in the field of psychism caused by the inflow of astral energy at this time. I seek to confine myself to the effect of this inflow on aspirants and sensitives. These two words - aspirants and sensitives - are employed by me in this article to distinguish the awakened seeker after control and mastery from the lower type of psychic, who is controlled and mastered. It is necessary here to remind you that psychism, so-called, can be divided into the following two groups:

Higher Psychism: Divine - Controlled - Positive - Intelligently applied - Mediatorship
Lower Psychism: Animal - Uncontrolled - Negative - Automatic - Mediumship

These distinctions are little understood, nor is the fact appreciated that both groups of qualities indicate our divinity. All are expressions of God.

There are certain psychic powers which men share in common with the animals; these powers are inherent in the animal body and are instinctual, but they have, for the vast majority, dropped below the threshold of consciousness and are unrealized and therefore useless. These are the powers, for instance, of astral clairvoyance and clairaudience, and the seeing of colors and similar phenomena. Clairvoyance and clairaudience are also possible on mental levels, and we then call it telepathy, and the seeing of symbols, for all visioning of geometrical forms is mental clairvoyance. All these powers are, however, tied up with the human mechanism or response apparatus, and serve to put the man in touch with aspects of the phenomenal world for which the response mechanism, which we call the personality, exists. They are the product of the activity of the divine soul in man, which takes the form of what we call 'the animal soul,' which really corresponds to the Holy Ghost aspect in the human microcosmic trinity. All these powers have their higher spiritual correspondences, which manifest when the soul becomes consciously active and controls its mechanism through the mind and the brain. When astral clairvoyance and clairaudience are not below the threshold of consciousness, but are actively used and functioning, it means that the solar plexus center is open and active. When the corresponding mental faculties are present in consciousness, then it means that the throat center and the center between the eyebrows are becoming "awake" and active. But the higher psychic powers, such as spiritual perception with its infallible knowledge, the intuition with its unerring judgment, and psychometry of the higher kind with its power to reveal the past and the future, are the prerogatives of the divine soul. These higher powers come into play when the head and heart centers, as well as the throat center, are brought into activity as the result of meditation and service. Let the student, however, remember two things:

That the greater can always include the lesser, but the purely animal psychic does not include the higher.
That between the lowest type of negative Mediumship and the highest type of inspired teacher and seer are found a vast diversity of grades, and that the centers are not uniformly developed in humanity.

The complexity of the subject is great, but the general situation can be grasped, the significance of the opportunity proffered can be understood, and the right use of knowledge be employed to bring good out of the present critical period, and thus the psychic and spiritual growth of man be fostered and nurtured.

Two questions should, I believe, at this time engross the attention of all workers in the field of esotericism and those who are engaged with the training of students and aspirants.
    I.   How shall we train our sensitives and psychics so that the dangers can be avoided and men can go safely forward to their new and glorious heritage?
    II.   How can esoteric schools or "disciplines," as they are sometimes called, make right use of the opportunity?

Let us speak first of the training and safeguarding of our psychics and sensitives."

The Rulers Of The New Age

"This little known divine energy now streams out from Shamballa. It embodies in itself the energy which lies behind the world crisis of the moment. It is the Will of God to produce certain racial and momentous changes in the consciousness of the race which will completely alter man's attitude to life and his grasp of the spiritual, esoteric and subjective essentials of living. It is this force which will bring about (in conjunction with the energy of love) that tremendous crisis—imminent in the human consciousness— which we call the second crisis, the initiation of the race into the Mystery of the Ages, into that which has been hid from the beginning.

It might be of value here if we considered the three great planetary centres and their relationships in tabular form and thus get the general idea more clearly in mind.

1. SHAMBALLA ----------- Will or Power ---------Planetary Head Centre
The Holy City------------- Purpose..Plan----------spiritual pineal gland
Life Aspect
Ruler: Sanat Kumara, the Lord of the World the Ancient of Days Melchizedek

2. THE HIERARCHY ----- Love-Wisdom---------Planetary Heart Centre
The New Jerusalem ------ Unity ------------------At-one-ment
Group Consciousness
Ruler: The Christ, The World Saviour

3. HUMANITY-------------- Active Intelligence ---Planetary Throat Centre
The City   standing foursquare-- Creativity
Self-consciousness
Ruler: Lucifer, Son of the Morning, The Prodigal Son

This Shamballa energy now for the first time is making its impact upon humanity directly and is not stepped down, as has hitherto been the case, through transmission via the Hierarchy of Masters. This change of direction constituted a somewhat dangerous experiment as it necessarily stimulated the personalities of men, particularly those whose personalities were along the line of will or power and in whom the love aspect of divinity was not sufficiently expressing itself; it was, however, permitted because it was realised that it would not affect the man in the street or the masses who would remain unresponsive to it, though it might greatly stimulate and intensify the mental and more potent type of man."

The New Age 10 Point Plan

Alice's Purpose was to change Christian tradition or to redeem the nations of Christian tradition. It is found at ***http://theindustry.yuku.com/topic/2649/The-10-Point-Plan-by-Alice-Bailey-The-New-World-Order*** and is stated as follows (with NB comments):

1. TAKE GOD AND PRAYER OUT OF THE EDUCATION SYSTEM
She said; Change curriculum to ensure that children are freed from the bondage of Christian culture. Why? Because children go to school to be equipped to face life, they are willing to trust and they are willing to value what is being given to them.
If you take God out of education, they will unconsciously form a resolve that God is not necessary to face life. They will focus on those things the school counts them worthy to be passed on and they will look at God as an additional, if one can afford the additional.
N.B. Today they introduce Transcendental Meditation (TM) in schools which takes children to altered states of consciousness to meet with demons (spirit guides) = New Age .

2. REDUCE PARENTAL AUTHORITY OVER THE CHILDREN
She said; Break the communication between parent and child (Why?). So that parents do not pass on their Christian traditions to their children, liberate children from the bondage of their parent traditions (how?)
a) Promote excessive child rights; (1997-1998 South Africa introduced Child rights legislation – UNICEF Charter; Today a child is able to say to parent 'I

do not want to hear that, I don't want to do what you are telling me. Teachers cannot talk to children, children step up and say I have my rights, you cannot talk to me like that).

b) Abolish corporal punishment; (this has been made law). On the other hand the Bible says 'Do not withhold correction from a child, for if you beat him with a rod, he will not die. You shall beat him with a rod and deliver his soul from hell.' (Proverbs 23: 13-14)

N.B. Jesus said in the last days – wickedness will increase, there will be rebellion and children will not obey their parents. It is not a trend,

It is organized.

c) Teachers are the agents of implementation – from workshops, teachers tell children 'your parent has no right to force you to pray or read the Bible, you are yourself, have a right of your own, you need to discover yourself, self expression, self realization, self fulfillment are all buzz words.

N.B. In the West when the child is 7 yrs, the teachers begin to say to the child 'you have a right to choose whether you want to follow the faith of your parents or not, parents are not allowed to enforce their faith upon you.' Question is, what type of decision can a 7 year old make?

3. DESTROY THE JUDEO-CHRISTIAN FAMILY STRUCTURE OR THE TRADITIONAL CHRISTIAN FAMILY STRUCTURE (Why?).

It is oppressive and that the family is the core of the nation. If you break the family, you break the nation. Liberate the people from the confines of this structure (How?)

a) Promote sexual promiscuity – free young people to the concept of premarital sex, let them have free sex, lift it so high that the joy of enjoying it (sex) is the highest joy in life, fantasize it, that everybody will feel proud to be seen to be sexually active, even those outside of marriage. This is contrary to the word of God which says "... But fornication and all uncleanness or covetousness, let it not even be named among you, as is fitting for saints... for this you know, that no fornicator, unclean person, nor covetous man, who is an idolater has any inheritance in the kingdom of Christ and God." (Ephesians 5: 3-5)

b) Use advertising industry, media – T.V., magazines, film industry to promote sexual enjoyment as the highest pleasure in humanity.

N.B. Have they succeeded? Have they done it? If you want to see whether they have succeeded or not, go to the advertising industry, it does everything to catch your attention and today almost no advert comes out without a sexual connotation. Even when they advertise ice cream, they must show you a thigh of a woman and a bikini, they must do something to set off a trail of thoughts. They will show you more thighs than ice cream. Why? Because, that is what must be in the minds of the people.

4. IF SEX IS FREE, THEN MAKE ABORTION LEGAL AND MAKE IT EASY

She said; Build clinics for abortion – Health clinics in schools. If people are going to enjoy the joy of sexual relationships, they need to be free of unnecessary fears, in other words they should not be hampered with unwanted pregnancies. 'Abortion as told by Christians is oppressive and denies our rights, we have a right to choose whether we want to have a child or not. If a woman does not want the pregnancy, she should have the freedom to get rid of that pregnancy painless and as easy as possible'.

N.B. Today it is not only accessible, it is forced. Today abortion is a strategy to curb population control together with the use of condoms and 'pill'.

5. MAKE DIVORCE EASY AND LEGAL, FREE PEOPLE FROM THE CONCEPT OF MARRIAGE FOR LIFE.

Alice wrote 50 years ago that love has got a mysterious link called the love bond. It is like an ovum that comes out of the ovary, as it travels through your system, it clicks a love favour in you and there's one other person in the world who can respond to that love bond, when you see that person, everything within you clicks, that is your man/woman, if you miss him, you'll never be happy until that love bond cycles past, for many years, so for you to be happy get that person at whatever cost, if it means getting him/her out of that marriage, get him/her that is your man/woman. It's a mistake for him/her to be elsewhere. And if you go together for some time and find that love has died, don't be held in bondage by the Christian values it will never come back, what you need is an easily arranged divorce and allow another love bond to come forth, just like an ovum comes up, and when it comes forth you'll enjoy life again. On the contrary God's word says in Malachi 2: 16; "For the Lord God of Israel says that He hates divorce…"

N.B. People enter into marriage having signed contracts of how they will share their things after divorce. People enter with one foot and another behind. 50 years ago divorce was unthinkable. It is one thing for a marriage to fail but it is another thing for people to enter marriage with an intention to enjoy as long as it was enjoyable and to walk out of it.

6. MAKE HOMOSEXUALITY AN ALTERNATIVE LIFESTYLE

Alice Bailey preached (50 yrs ago) that sexual enjoyment is the highest pleasure in humanity, no one must be denied and no one must be restricted how to enjoy themselves. People should be allowed in whichever way they chose they want, whether it is homosexuality or in incest or bestiality, as long as the two agree.

N.B. A law was passed in South Africa. Parliament has passed it on 26/01/2000 and the President gave it his signature on 4/02/2000 –giving so much freedom to gay rights, that a time will come when it is illegal for a preacher to mention homosexuality as an abomination in the eyes of God, or to read scriptures publicly that talk about homosexuality. In Mozambique 1994, an agenda was drawn targeting to fill the police force, the judicial system (judges), the education system and everywhere else with gays, so that when a case comes up, they are there to defend the cause. Today the church is expected to marry gays/lesbians. According to the Bible, this is an abomination before the eyes of God (Leviticus 18:22; 20:13).

7. DEBASE ART, MAKE IT RUN MAD

How? Promote new forms of art which will corrupt and defile the imagination of people because art is the language of the spirit, that which is inside, you can bring out in painting, music, drama etc. Look at the quality of the music that is coming out, the films out of Hollywood.

8. USE MEDIA TO PROMOTE AND CHANGE MINDSET

Alice Bailey said the greatest channel you need to use to change human attitude is media. Use the press, the radio, TV, cinema. You can tell today how successful they have been in implementing the plan over 50 years via media as well as advertising agencies, billboards, magazines. Who controls media? (New Age); So much money is pumped into media and advertising spreading of pornographic material and other sources. Sex outside of marriage is thrown on your face 80-90 times than sex in marriage. Promiscuity is being promoted as natural, you watch gay sex on TV in homes where children's minds are being neutralized to sensitivity to these things. You wonder why newspapers, TV, etc do not record anything about Christian activities.

9. CREATE AN INTERFAITH MOVEMENT

Alice Bailey wrote; Promote other faiths to be at par with Christianity, and break this thing about Christianity as being the only way to heaven, by that Christianity will be pulled down and other faiths promoted. She said promote the importance of man in determining his own future and destiny –HUMANISM. She said tell man he has the right to choose what he wants to be and he can make it happen, he has the right to determine his cause – This takes God off His throne. We have seen in our nation, South Africa hosting a meeting of the Interfaith Movement in Cape Town led by Dalai Lama.

10. **GET GOVERNMENTS TO MAKE ALL THESE LAW AND GET THE CHURCH TO ENDORSE THESE CHANGES**.

Alice Bailey wrote that the church must change its doctrine and accommodate the people by accepting these things and put them into its structures and systems.

Have they succeeded?

Today you wonder why our governments are legislating laws contrary to the Bible and why the church is compromising the Word of God. It is a process of implementing **The Plan** - A 50 year strategy of the New Age Movement to fulfill its ultimate goal to establish a One World Government, a One World Economic system and a One World Religion. Today the **strategy** almost in its entirety has been adopted by the United Nations and today a lot of it is already law in many nations. This deception has crept up unobserved on so many people. It can best be demonstrated through the well-known analogy of the frog in the pot of water. If you put a frog in a pot of boiling water, it is smart enough to know that it is in terrible danger and will immediately jump out to safety. But if you turn up the heat very slowly, a little at a time, it doesn't notice the changes that are taking place and will slowly cook to death. Many people today are slowly cooking to death and don't seem to realize how far they have come from where they once were.

Today the Western World is not struggling to resist these because the New Age Movement focused primarily on the West because that was the Christian world in the 19th century. The New Age Movement has a school called the Akanni School, which is the school of all the leaders of the Western world. They subscribe to it. It is recorded that they say they have succeeded the task in the West but suddenly they realize Christianity has migrated to the rest of the world, so they have now to use every resource in the

West to deal with the rest of the world. In Africa, South Africa is the number one state, it is changing at such a rapid speed. They are saying give to African States a financial package with conditions to legalize abortion and to take God and prayer out of school.

Governments are so attracted to this package, they can't say no to it, they need the money, they ask the church to find an answer. These are done secretly. Christianity is 5%, the rest is Hinduism, Buddhism, Spiritism. New Age is being taught to teachers, they are being taught to teach this in schools.

It is interesting to note that Blavatsky, Besant and Alice Bailey were well known Masonic leaders of the day. Albert Pike referred to Freemasonry as the 'custodian' or special guardian of these occult secrets and revealed the hidden agenda of his institution, the forming of a Luciferic One World Government.

And finally, when you read this extensive book by Alice written well before the New Age emergence, there is not a lot that is not in the New Age belief system of today. It certainly leads to the conclusion that because Alice was a prominent Occultist and Satanist, obviously supported and endorsed by the 13 Bloodlines and Rockefeller, was she creating part of the New world Order business plan?

Who Do You Believe?

Move into your heart and believe your inner self. Let me share some wisdom with you. I call it the Trinity of Wisdom. This is a triangle with evil (dark) and good (light) at the two bottom apexes. At the top is unity where there is no distinction between as what is black and white has converged because there is no judgement. This world is full of black and white stuff that you hear and see and feel and sense--all of which keeps you confused and polar. Yes, read, see, feel but do it from the top apex because that is where you and your heart know what is your choice of truth. But if you live in either the dark or the light apex you cannot see your truth that is already within. all that is black, gray, white, turns to gold at the apex.

These last chapters have been focused on the darker side of the coin. In the middle of the light and dark sits a funny thing called perception. The point is that there is always multiple versions of everything, including the 13 bloodlines, Vatican and even Satan. And depending upon who you listen to, what you read, see, anything can be dark or light. As it turns out our beliefs are a mixture of white and black (light and Dark) which is gray. Are the "illuminated Ones" of the Illuminati orchestrating what so many people think and believe as the New Age? When you begin to climb up the dark or light spiritual ladder is there really a contrast between Christ and Satan? Or is all just perception playing with your mind?

However, let us leave that notion for a while and investigate more on how the Hierarchy of the 13 Bloodlines orchestrate their plans.

8

THE EMPIRE OF PLANET EARTH

In a simple top down model, we have looked at who created and directs PLANET EARTH INC. We have seen the bloodlines and the ultimate military police force of the Jesuits who work through the Knights of Malta, the old Templars. We have looked at their ultimate god Lucifer as providing the critical belief system to drive the corporate model. And we have looked what the business plan is within the Lucis Trust. The interesting aspect of this hierarchy is that through the New World Order plan, these gods may be attempting to make life better and better for the Earthling slaves. The New Order of The Ages, however, would side with the slaves as being free of their masters as we shall see later. Now let us delve into how the Empire is run.

Running The Empire Of PLANET EARTH

As noted before, Dynasty means a succession of rulers from the same family or line; a family or group that maintains power for several generations. This can be similar to a political **dynasty** controlling the state. A **Kingdom** is a political or territorial unit ruled by a sovereign and a **King or Queen** is a male/female sovereign or monarch who holds by life tenure, and usually by hereditary right, the chief authority over a country and people. An **Empire** is a nation led by a King or Emperor that has other countries under its control.

Now let us look into the key administrative centers of the empire of Planet Earth being run by the Corporation PLANET EARTH.

We will look closer at this corporation which we refer to as the Empire called PLANET EARTH. It is an invisible fiction; a privately owned corporation founded and orchestrated by those who humanity has looked up to as gods, kings and queens. We are calling these heads of the 13 bloodline Dynasties the founders and private shareholders of PLANET EARTH. They really don't need shares; they have blood oaths. They direct the wishes of the gods which is a business plan because they have created, retained or conquered the power of money through special abilities, forces, bloodline, or whatever. These people have either been born into a dynasty or they have earned it, or they have taken it over. The only thing that has changed in the last 5,000 years is the name given to the gods and the dynasties and the type of slaves required. Those with the power and the ways and means require slaves (employees for corporations) to create and keep their dynasties. Humanity has evolved so the nature of conquest has also evolved. The process of creating, conquering, managing and retaining kingdoms changed to a now universal phenomenon as, money, Corporations and Trusts.

A secret dynasty is only secret because humans treat it that way. The existence of them is no secret, but who runs them and how they are run, is simply private. And there is no difference here than a household wanting to keep their little dynasty (household) private. It is everybody's birthright to do this. And what each through the head of the house decides to make public is again a private choice.

In our evolution, these ruling gods and what we refer to as the 13 bloodlines, had to change their ways of operating and conquest. As humanities knowledge increased, a need for new ways of control had to be created. One could look at this in the corporate business world as having to adapt to a changing market, different labor force, a new financial landscape, need for new products, etc. etc.

It is important to understand that throughout this book the word God has been used a lot. However, let it be understood that **God is the real thing,** whatever that is. **GOD is a fake corporate representation of the real thing,** and **god is anything else but the real thing.** So gods are man/women, entities real and nonreal that have somehow been able to rise above the usual mortal status to bowed down to. They are not the real thing.

If you want to understand more about who these gods were, we would refer you to the works of Sitchen and in particular the incredible treatment of this in the book ***Slave Species of the gods*** by **Michael Tellinger**. The history was written thousands of years ago and has become one of the hottest topics around as it reveals a whole new picture of history. The source of the new history is the Sumerian Tablets which appear to be surfacing from private collections all over the planet. These have been hidden because the contents were too bizarre to believe, the interpretative abilities were not as well advanced and they were more of a private curiosity than anything.

In this book we are not so concerned about gods and who they were as much as to reveal how those who love to control others have evolved ways to retain dominion and to present a new alternative. In the past, it has been the heartless ones that would be the Priests representing the gods that have exercised and engaged this dominion. In this context, we will come to see how there are two groups of priests; one is the representatives of god who preach religions and their codes on behalf of their god Satan. The others are the spiritual emissaries of God who preach love, harmony and peace as a conduit for God or Christ. Regardless, humanity now has evolved to accept the process of dominion by the ones in control whether they know it or not. PLANET EARTH as a farm of obedient Earthlings and the fictional entity of a corporation is simply a different vehicle for the gods to orchestrate through the powerful priesthoods like the Jesuits and the Vatican where they have added new subsidiaries of RELIGION, LAW, MILITARY, MEDIA, COMMERCE to come to the position of billions of religious followers, trillions of debt, and new forms of Kings and Queens who abide by the rules of the subsidiaries. The CEO's of major corporations abide by the rules and they have in the same sense become the kings, queens, emperors. The process is the same because Earthlings love power.

How is it that PLANET EARTH Inc. has grown so extensively? Planet Earth has always had gods, goddesses, rulers, kings, and queens that sought dominion and power over others. And to support their empires they needed wealth so as to control the actions of others. Those who were of certain bloodlines protected their wealth and accumulated it so as to protect their families much like we all do. And to do so, their dynasties required people forces, monetary might, and a special technology of greed dominion as people grew in numbers and abilities. The corporate model is the organizational and administrative process of dominion and control. The ability to control others through fear is the same as it has been for all time. It still exists. It's process has simply shifted from direct to indirect means of creating and protecting wealth and power.

As we look upon our own experiences with corporations and being employed, we also see some of the massive corporation that have grown to follow the pyramidal structure of power. And so people provide the labor to create according to the missions of the few at the top. And so even in this age thousands of years later, after the Sumeria civilization of gods, kings, queens, and their chosen royalties, we still have the same process in dynasties, rulers, kings, queens, presidents, lords, and a plethora of "special" people that are supposedly better or more powerful than others. There are 48 monarchy nations reported by Wikcapedia. It breaks down to a common trait that humanity has accepted because of fear; a fear of death, of being less than others, a fear of not providing for his own chosen ones. And fear is a valuable commodity to corporations striving for wealth and power just as sin and it salvation is a valuable commodity for those who a striving for dominion over others. Even the Jesuit military uses the same simple principle.

It should not come as a surprise that the ultimate corporation which we call PLANET EARTH would be the ultimate goal of the bloodlines who have sought wealth and dominion over others to serve their own missions. It should not be surprising to understand that even the bloodline dynasties are vulnerable to each other's needs for power and that some coalition for total peace, one world religion, one governments, would be sought so they themselves did not live by fear. It should not be surprising to see these experts in commerce and "higher powers" create a unified business plan between the bloodlines. It should not be surprising to see the evolution and control of money as the key vehicle, and commerce as the means to be the power to do this quietly and effectively unbeknown to the many who serve the few. This is as we have seen, illustrated well by looking at who controls the money, who is indebted, and who are the Directors/Owners in this PLANET EARTH Inc..

Also not surprising is that if you had the ability to pick up bankrupt corporations, refinance and restructure them according your own mission, you would not call this a conspiracy, only smart business sense to follows Satanism. The employees who went to the chopping block may not be happy but that is the way of it. What if you were in a position to do this with nations who have equally mismanaged their money and resources? That has been the model for the Rothschild Dynasty.

The big question is however, how did we as nations get to this point of being bankrupt and vulnerable? There are many sources of research that have come to light on this topic. Men such as **David Icke** are well known on this topic. There are many websites already referenced in the last chapter that provide their research and conclusions on this topic. And so we will lay out a story now of how this fictional corporate **PLANET EARTH--The Matrix--was brought into our realities. It is noted that this is research and research becomes fact at some point when the beliefs of humanity accept it and a tipping point is reached. Where we are in this process is yet to be seen but the amount of research that is being conducted now, as available on the internet, is enormous. It is only a question of time before the pieces of the puzzle of truth in history all come to light. Here is a version that sheds some of that light.

The Secret Kingdoms Of The gods

As we explore this topic, we will begin to understand that world religions and their differences, as well as the need of, gods, kings and dictators have been the cause of the greatest deaths on Planet Earth. Did the world wars, revolutions and big events of human history happen naturally or coincidentally, or were they calculated and pre-planned? If you think back to the dynasties and their special interest in commerce, the family members have positioned themselves in major strategic areas of finance, war, media, chemicals, weapons, religion, medicine and education as they march in their corporate takeover plans. To their corporate businesses, conflicts and wars provide a lucrative opportunity for financing and selling merchandise. It can create the market and the demand for their products. But if they were pre-planned, who planned them? The answer to this question can be found within the boundaries of four of the world's most powerful cities that are the strongholds (like corporate headquarters) for PLANET EARTH. Those cities belong to no nation and pay no taxes. They are totally above Planet Earth rules and to all of the employees of PLANET EARTH, none of their business. These cities are **Zurich, the city of the gods, Washington's District of Columbia**, which is not part of the city of Washington or the United States, **London's Inner City** which is not part of London or England, and **Vatican City**, which is not part of Rome or Italy. These cities, called City States, have their own independent flag, their own separate laws, and their own separate identity; and _purposes different from what appears_.

On this topic, there is another website that has come under scrutiny of the authorities who wish to shut it down. It is obvious that much of the information is hitting too close to the mark. It is extensive in research and details about the "gods" who run PLANET EARTH, found at ***http://jubilee2012.50webs.com/the_hidden_empire.htm.*** It is not possible to do this site justice and only parts are brought forward here.

If we were to look at our simple model of PLANET EARTH INC., we would say the location of the key subsidiaries would be here. Zurich would be like a head office, the Vatican would be a subsidiary responsible for Religion, London would be the Financial center, and Columbia the Military centre. The ultimate police force of the gods would be the Jesuits in Rome who have replaced the gods of vengeance of old (or perhaps they still are?).

Zurich The City Of The Gods

Although the New World Order was founded in 1943 at the first Conference between England, the United States and the Soviet Union by leading Jesuits in Tehran, it is important to know that the administrative headquarters has been in the richest city on the planet. The New World Order was reconfirmed at the end of World War II following the complete victory of the Roman Cult controlling the Roman Catholic Church in the re-establishment of effective Catholic control of the former Frankish Kingdom principalities now known as Germany, France, Austria, the Netherlands and Switzerland. (This will be detailed in a subsequent chapter.) However, the term first entered the public arena in 1949 through the work of Jesuit co-agitator **George Orwell** and his book **"New World Order"** providing a chilling account of the future world under global Catholic socialism (Fascism).

At the heart, the New World Order is a defined membership of global financial, political and industrial consortium based around the underlying massive financial assets of the Catholic Church based from Zürich. In control are the Jesuits and their continued monopoly as the only organization in Catholic history (excluding the Knights Templar who work as the Knights of Malta) to hold a Papal document granting them exclusive rights to conduct banking and financial activities.

Zürich is located on the delta of the river Limmat as it connects to Zürich, approximately 30 km north of the Alps. Today it is the largest in Switzerland and the capital of the canton of Zürich. It is also by far the wealthiest city in the world being the real centre of capital markets of private banks and insurance for over 700 years. Similar to Munich, Zürich is said to have begun as salt store and taxing station. From the early 12th Century, under the reforms of Bernard of Clairvaux, the Cistercian monks were given the authority as tax collectors and administrators for the legitimate Catholic Church. Monasteries were deliberately built around ancient Roman salt and tax stations to protect the valuable salt and the monks. This is the most likely date for the establishment of a Cistercian monastery and fortifications. Similar to other salt and tax forts such as Munich, Zürich would have thrived as a centre of trade, exchange and wealth. While the claims that King Henry III in 1045 permitted markets, collected tolls and minted coins are deliberately false (by at least 100 years), by the 12th Century is certain the monastery did mint coins and permit markets for trade and exchange.

Indeed the name Zürich which comes directly from the combination of the two Old High German words Ziu-richi is especially significant. The name literally means "A place where the Ziu rule over the land"--or more simply "the city of the gods". The name is no coincidence. It is a deliberate named created by none other than Rudolph Habsburg when he succeeded in seizing control of this valuable tax and trade settlement.

Until the beginning of the 13th Century, the lands upon which Zürich is placed had been under the control of the House of Zähringen for a little over 100 years. When Duke Berchtold V of Zähringen (1186-1218) --the founder of the city of Bern--died, his lands were split between a number of competing groups of nobles. The Counts of Kyburg were eventually successful in defending their claim to the most valuable lands of Zürich (and the tax/trade post). However, the House of Kyberg were all eventually killed off and at the death of Count Hartmann VI of Kyberg and his family in 1264, Rudolph of Habsburg claimed Zürich and the adjacent lands for himself. The nobles lines of the Habsburg's prior to Rudolph are highly questionable, with the stories of his relationship to Emperor Frederick II and his con Conrad IV of Germany simply bold faced lies. It is quite possible he entered the nobility through marriage, to the daughter of Ulrich, Count of Kyberg and therefore used this as his "claim" when the Kyberg family were killed.

In a striking similarity to the lords of rival city Munich --the Wittelsbachs -- Rudolph showed no qualms in using the war between the legitimate Catholic Popes and the AntiPopes of the Roman Cult as well as the feud between the Hohenstaufen and the Welfs for his own personal and family gain. In 1268, Conrad (falsely split into two characters to make historical analysis difficult) was captured and executed in Naples. With only a two year old son as heir, the Hohenstaufen were finished. In a bold move, Rudolph petitioned AntiPope Gregory X (1271-1276) to be officially recognized as King of Germany --a heretical and wholly unfounded act. However, thanks to the alliance with the Lombardy Princes, Rudolph prevailed with his false claim and focused on making Zürich a great city.

While Zürich and the Habsburgs profited in their alliance with the AntiPopes of the Roman Cult, it was the creation of one of the greatest lies and confidence tricks in human history in 1276 the guaranteed Zürich would remain the wealthiest city in the world and the future of the Roman Cult -- the lie of "usury".

In 1276, Rudolph I with the assistance of AntiPope Gregory, they simultaneously declared "usury" or the charging of interest and financial transactions -- vital for trade and business -- a mortal sin for any Christian publishable by death. Meanwhile Rudolf declared the infamous *servi camerae* ("serfs of the treasury"), in which the wealthiest Jewish merchants were press-ganged into the service of the Roman Cult and the Habsburgs. Rudolph then moved many of these wealthy Jewish trading families to his home base of Zürich to now manage the greatest financial monopoly ever created in history. Incredibly, it is falsely believed by most people to this day that original Christian teaching as formed by Emperor Constantine in 326 forbid usury as a crime -- a horrendous and ridiculous lie. Similarly, many scholars believe that only Jewish Sephardic families had control over finance during the middle ages -- again a complete lie until 1276. The size of this Great Lie defies belief. Within ten years of this supreme heresy by the AntiPopes and their vassals, Zürich was the wealthiest city in the world -- a position it has held and protected for 700 years.

As the New World Order is a consortium of financial, political, military and industrial entities, its precise structure, rules of operation and agenda remains difficult to precisely confirm. For example, a few dozen private banks in Europe and the United States first formed by the Jesuits in the 18th and early 19th Century continue to remain the foundation pillars of the global finance and credit system -- the same private banks that have withdrawn hundreds of billions of dollars of credit from the global financial system in 2008 and 2009 causing what was a localized credit squeeze of bad loans into a global depression.

The New World Order also maintains a political military structure through co-operative ties between intelligence agencies and large private and public arms manufacturers such that this apparatus serves to protect the interests of the Catholic Church across the world. The New World Order also represents a discrete group of global companies, principally involved in industries such as pharmaceuticals as well as substantial media and publishing interests, again which have successfully maintained protection against Catholic interests, with the exception of unavoidable occasional public scandals such as ongoing pedophilia by priests.

The Vatican City

As mentioned before, the Vatican-approved image of God is an angry bearded man in the sky, painted by Michelangelo. God's tortured Son, suffering, bleeding and dying with thorns gouged through his skull and nails pounded through his feet and hands are on display throughout the Vatican. These images serve as reminders that God allowed His Son to be tortured and killed to save the souls of human beings who are all born sinners. And it is the Vatican than sells the solution to this problem that all humanity is guilty of.

The Vatican rules over 2 billion of the worlds 7 billion people. The colossal wealth of the Vatican includes enormous investments with the Rothschilds in Britain, France and the USA and with giant oil and weapons corporations like Shell and General Electric. We have already seen that the Rothschilds are Trustees for the Vatican treasures. The Vatican solid gold bullion, worth billions is stored with the Rothschild controlled Bank of England and the US Federal Reserve Bank. The Catholic Church is the biggest financial power, wealth accumulator and property owner in existence, possessing more material wealth than any bank, corporation, giant trust or government anywhere on the globe.

As it has evolved, through smart business or whatever you want to call the Vatican enterprise, the result is that while 2/3 of the world earns less than $2 a day, and 1/5 of the world is underfed or starving to death, the Vatican hoards the world's wealth, profits from it on the stock market and at the same time preaches about giving. So how did the Vatican accumulate all that wealth over the millennium? One method was to put a price-tag on sin. Many bishops and popes actively marketed gilt, sin and fear for profit, by selling indulgences. Worshipers were encouraged to pre-pay for sins they hadn't yet committed and get pardoned ahead of time. Those who didn't pay-up are threatened with eternal damnation. Another method was to get wealthy land owners to hand-over their land and fortune to the church on their death bed, in exchange for a blessing which would supposedly enable them to go to heaven. Pope Leo the fifth rebuilt St Peter's Basilica, by selling tickets out of hell and tickets to heaven. Is this right or wrong? It is just big business, different product that has effectively been chosen by the mass market--just like Microsoft.

In a sense, the Catholic church has become the biggest "mafia" on earth, with their protection-racket of selling "forgiveness for sins". The Catholic church's practice of teaching people that they can be sinful all their lives and all they need to do is pay the church for "forgiveness" is one of the chief causes of all the evil and dishonesty in the world, as people are actually taught and encouraged to be sinful and evil, rather than to purify themselves and strive to become perfect, even as God is Perfect, as the Bible teaches. And so this leads to dominion, to be subject to the code of their laws, called the "Word of God" which, when one buys into, becomes the employee of corporation GOD as run by the Vatican Administrators of the "Law". What is of interest is how, <u>subject to interpretation,</u> the Word of God (god) always outlines the original business plan "hidden in plain sight".

The Book of Leviticus is all about setting up the priesthood and ensuring that offerings are made to God as acknowledgement of their sins:

1:1 And the LORD called unto Moses, and spake unto him out of the tabernacle of the congregation, saying,
1:2 Speak unto the children of Israel, and say unto them, If any man of you bring an offering unto the LORD, ye shall bring your offering of the cattle, even of the herd, and of the flock.
1:3 If his offering be a burnt sacrifice of the herd, let him offer a male without blemish: he shall offer it of his own voluntary will at the door of the tabernacle of the congregation before the LORD.
1:4 And he shall put his hand upon the head of the burnt offering; and it shall be accepted for him to make atonement for him.
1:5 And he shall kill the bullock before the LORD: and the priests, Aaron's sons, shall bring the blood, and sprinkle the blood round about upon the altar that is by the door of the tabernacle of the congregation.
1:6 And he shall flay the burnt offering, and cut it into his pieces.
1:7 And the sons of Aaron the priest shall put fire upon the altar, and lay the wood in order upon the fire:

And then he set up the administrative power for priests and the pricing policy for redemption:

27:1   And the LORD spake unto Moses, saying,
27:2   Speak unto the children of Israel, and say unto them, When a man shall make a singular vow, the persons shall be for the LORD by thy estimation.
27:3   And thy estimation shall be of the male from twenty years old even unto sixty years old, even thy estimation shall be fifty shekels of silver, after the shekel of the sanctuary.
27:4   And if it be a female, then thy estimation shall be thirty shekels.
27:5   And if it be from five years old even unto twenty years old, then thy estimation shall be of the male twenty shekels, and for the female ten shekels.
27:6   And if it be from a month old even unto five years old, then thy estimation shall be of the male five shekels of silver, and for the female thy estimation shall be three shekels of silver.

27:7   And if it be from sixty years old and above; if it be a male, then thy estimation shall be fifteen shekels, and for the female ten shekels.
27:8   But if he be poorer than thy estimation, then he shall present himself before the priest, and the priest shall value him; according to his ability that vowed shall the priest value him.
27:9   And if it be a beast, whereof men bring an offering unto the LORD, all that any man giveth of such unto the LORD shall be holy.
27:10 He shall not alter it, nor change it, a good for a bad, or a bad for a good: and if he shall at all change beast for beast, then it and the exchange thereof shall be holy.
27:11 And if it be any unclean beast, of which they do not offer a sacrifice unto the LORD, then he shall present the beast before the priest:
27:12 And the priest shall value it, whether it be good or bad: as thou valuest it, who art the priest, so shall it be.
27:13 But if he will at all redeem it, then he shall add a fifth part thereof unto thy estimation.
27:14 And when a man shall sanctify his house to be holy unto the LORD, then the priest shall estimate it, whether it be good or bad: as the priest shall estimate it, so shall it stand.
27:15 And if he that sanctified it will redeem his house, then he shall add the fifth part of the money of thy estimation unto it, and it shall be his.
27:16 And if a man shall sanctify unto the LORD some part of a field of his possession, then thy estimation shall be according to the seed thereof: an homer of barley seed shall be valued at fifty shekels of silver.
27:17 If he sanctify his field from the year of jubilee, according to thy estimation it shall stand.
27:18 But if he sanctify his field after the jubilee, then the priest shall reckon unto him the money according to the years that remain, even unto the year of the jubilee, and it shall be abated from thy estimation.
27:19 And if he that sanctified the field will in any wise redeem it, then he shall add the fifth part of the money of thy estimation unto it, and it shall be assured to him.
27:20 And if he will not redeem the field, or if he have sold the field to another man, it shall not be redeemed any more.
27:21 But the field, when it goeth out in the jubilee, shall be holy unto the LORD, as a field devoted; the possession thereof shall be the priest's.
27:22 And if a man sanctify unto the LORD a field which he hath bought, which is not of the fields of his possession;
27:23 Then the priest shall reckon unto him the worth of thy estimation, even unto the year of the jubilee: and he shall give thine estimation in that day, as a holy thing unto the LORD.
27:24 In the year of the jubilee the field shall return unto him of whom it was bought, even to him to whom the possession of the land did belong.
27:25 And all thy estimations shall be according to the shekel of the sanctuary: twenty gerahs shall be the shekel.
27:26 Only the firstling of the beasts, which should be the LORD'S firstling, no man shall sanctify it; whether it be ox, or sheep: it is the LORD'S.
27:27 And if it be of an unclean beast, then he shall redeem it according to thine estimation, and shall add a fifth part of it thereto: or if it be not redeemed, then it shall be sold according to thy estimation.

When you get to the Book of Numbers, it's all about a census counting the people to see who is fit for military duty. This God is preparing for war. And they are to serve God and sanctuary:

1:1 And the LORD spake unto Moses in the wilderness of Sinai, in the tabernacle of the congregation, on the first day of the second month, in the second year after they were come out of the land of Egypt, saying,
1:2 Take ye the sum of all the congregation of the children of Israel, after their families, by the house of their fathers, with the number of their names, every male by their polls;
1:3 From twenty years old and upward, all that are able to go forth to war in Israel: thou and Aaron shall number them by their armies.

To serve who?

3:5 And the LORD spake unto Moses, saying,
3:6 Bring the tribe of Levi near, and present them before Aaron the priest, that they may minister unto him.
3:7 And they shall keep his charge, and the charge of the whole congregation before the tabernacle of the congregation, to do the service of the tabernacle.

And there is a price for sin:

5:5 And the LORD spake unto Moses, saying,
5:6 Speak unto the children of Israel, When a man or woman shall commit any sin that men commit, to do a trespass against the LORD, and that person be guilty;
5:7 Then they shall confess their sin which they have done: and he shall recompense his trespass with the principal thereof, and add unto it the fifth part thereof, and give it unto him against whom he hath trespassed.
5:8 But if the man have no kinsman to recompense the trespass unto, let the trespass be recompensed unto the LORD, even to the priest; beside the ram of the atonement, whereby an atonement shall be made for him.

And more for not obeying:

14:26 And the LORD spake unto Moses and unto Aaron, saying,
14:27 How long shall I bear with this evil congregation, which murmur against me? I have heard the murmurings of the children of Israel, which they murmur against me.
14:28 Say unto them, As truly as I live, saith the LORD, as ye have spoken in mine ears, so will I do to you:
14:29 Your carcases shall fall in this wilderness; and all that were numbered of you, according to your whole number, from twenty years old and upward, which have murmured against me,
14:30 Doubtless ye shall not come into the land, concerning which I sware to make you dwell therein, save Caleb the son of Jephunneh, and Joshua the son of Nun.
14:31 But your little ones, which ye said should be a prey, them will I bring in, and they shall know the land which ye have despised.
14:32 But as for you, your carcases, they shall fall in this wilderness.
14:33 And your children shall wander in the wilderness forty years, and bear your whoredoms, until your carcases be wasted in the wilderness.

The Book of Deuteronomy is about creating regulations:

4:35 Unto thee it was showed, that thou mightest know that the LORD he is God; there is none else beside him.
4:39 Know therefore this day, and consider it in thine heart, that the LORD he is God in heaven above, and upon the earth beneath: there is none else.
4:40 Thou shalt keep therefore his statutes, and his commandments, which I command thee this day, that it may go well with thee, and with thy children after thee, and that

thou mayest prolong thy days upon the earth, which the LORD thy God giveth thee, for ever.
4:45 These are the testimonies, and the statutes, and the judgments, which Moses spake unto the children of Israel, after they came forth out of Egypt,
4:1 Now therefore hearken, O Israel, unto the statutes and unto the judgments, which I teach you, for to do them, that ye may live, and go in and possess the land which the LORD God of your fathers giveth you.
4:2 Ye shall not add unto the word which I command you, neither shall ye diminish ought from it, that ye may keep the commandments of the LORD your God which I command you.

As the bible story progresses, this God even has a say in rules and regulations that are almost like reading a current day set of Acts and Statutes, or like the regulations of the IRS. He even has a hand at commerce to fine those that disobey, or do not follow the rules he has conveyed. He even takes a piece of the action in gold! But you just can't mail it to him or take a sky bus up to deliver it, you have to give all or part of it to guess who? Yes, the Church, the Priests!

It is not only the Vatican that supports this word of god; it is a different brand of the same code in all the major religions of the world.

During the dark ages, the Catholic Church not only hoarded the wealth they collected from the poor, but they hoarded knowledge. They kept the masses ignorant and in the dark by denying them a basic education. They also prohibited anyone from reading or even possessing a Bible, under pain of death. That's pretty good marketing. And if you dared to tread on heresy, their own secret power, the Inquisition was there to burn you.

Between 1095 and 1291 AD the Pope launched 7 blood baths called the Christian Crusades, torturing, murdering, beheading and mass murdering hundreds of thousands of Muslims in the name of God. The Pope's brutal solders were called Knights Templar or Knights of the Temple of Solomon and evolved into today's secretive brotherhood called the Freemasons. Between 1450 and 1700 AD the Catholic Church followed up their holy terror with the inquisition. Based on rumours of practicing witchcraft, the Catholic Church hunted down, tortured and burned-alive tens of thousands of innocent women at the stake.

During World War II the Vatican was criticized for supporting Hitler and his Nazi regime, whom the pope blessed and named "the envoy of God". Over the past 5 decades more than one thousand five hundred priests and bishops have been identified in the sexual assault of tens of thousands of boys and girls in their trusting congregations and orphanages. In the end, it is all effective marketing and promotion.

The City Of London

Like Vatican city, London's inner city is also a privately owned corporation or city state, located right in the middle of greater London. It became a sovereign state in 1694 when King William the third of Orange privatized and turned the Bank of England over to the private banking partners. Today the City State of London is the world's financial power center and the wealthiest square mile on the face of the Earth. It houses the Rothschild controlled Bank of England, Lloyds of London, the London stock exchange, all British banks, the branch offices of 385 foreign banks and 70 US banks. It has its own courts, its own laws, its own flag and its own police force. It is not part of greater London, or England, or the British Commonwealth and pays no taxes. The City State of London houses Fleet Street's newspaper and publishing monopolies. It is also the headquarters for worldwide English Freemasonry, and headquarters for the world wide money cartel known as The Crown.

Contrary to popular belief, The Crown is not the Royal Family or the British Monarch. The Crown is the private corporate City State of London. It has a council of 12 members who rule the corporation under a mayor, called the lord mayor. The lord mayor and his 12 member council serves as proxies or representatives who sit-in for 12 of the world's wealthiest, most powerful banking families, including the Rothschild family, the Warburg family, the Oppenheimer family and the Schiff family. These families and their descendants run the Crown Corporation of London. The Crown Corporation holds the title to worldwide Crown land in Crown colonies like Canada, Australia and New Zealand. British parliament and the British prime minister serve as a public front for the hidden power of these ruling crown families.

Today, queen Elizabeth II is the head of state of the Great nation of the Hebrew Covenant called Great Britain. Her genealogy chart, according to the **College of Heralds** in London, traces her blood line back to king David, the first king of Israel. By connecting 10 dots the Israelite identity of Queen Elizabeth II comes into focus:

- A Stone known as the Stone of Destiny, the Lia Fail, the Stone of Scone, Jacob's Pillar and Bethel has been fitted in the British Throne chair and the British Monarch is crowned upon this Stone. The Stone's origins were with Jacob, who slept with his head upon the Stone and dreamed of a ladder reaching up to heaven. Jacob had his name changed by God to Israel and fathered the Twelve Tribes of Israel.
- The British Monarch's Crown has twelve gem-stones at the base, each one representing each of the Twelve Tribes of Israel. The twelve gem-stones of the Twelve Tribes were also worn on the Breastplate of Aaron, which was the breastplate of the High Priest of Israel of old.
- The "crossed cross" of the Union Jack or Union of Jack/ob flag is God's mark upon His people and the flag represents the reunion of the United Kingdom of the Twelve Tribes of Jack – Jacob/Israel.
- The symbols on the British coat of arms reveal Britain's Israelite origin. According to the Bible, the harp symbolizes the Israelite king David, the lion is the Tribal Standard of the Israelite Tribe of Judah and the unicorn is the Tribal Standard of Joseph's son Ephraim. Joseph and his sons were favoured by Jacob/Israel and were blessed and given his name Israel. These standards symbolize the Nation of Israel. The motto "Dieu et mon droit" means "God is my birth-right".
- The hymn "Zadoc the Priest" written by Handel was performed at queen Elizabeth's coronation in 1953. Zadoc the priest was the Biblical priest who anointed the Israelite king Solomon while the people cried "God save the king", "Long live the king", "May the king live forever".
- During the coronation ceremony the queen turns to face the four corners of the globe. The orb carried by the queen represents the world over which the monarch rules.
- The Monarch's Coronation gifts of a rod, bracelets and a ring, are a re-enactment of the Bible story of the Israelites Judah and Tamar.
- The British Monarch wears a Signet ring, which over the millennia has been passed from their Israelite ancestors.
- The Covenant that God made with Abraham was a promise to make his name great and to make for him a great nation. Today Great Britain is the only nation called Great.
- In Hebrew the world Britain literally means land of the Covenant and British means man or people of the Covenant. It also means the same in Welsh.

Is this all a coincidence or is it rooted in cults and rituals? So how did the throne of the ancient Israelites end up in Great Britain? Here is a little esoteric history. In c.588 B.C., king Nebuchadnezzar of Babylon was alleged to have been sent by god to lay siege to and overthrow king Zedekiah of Jerusalem as a punishment because he and his people weren't keeping the Covenant they agreed with god to obey and keep only god's Law in The Torah. Solomon's Temple was destroyed in the siege and Jeremiah the Bible Prophet took king Zedekiah's daughter, princess Teia Tephi; The Ark of The Covenant and Jacob's Pillar/The Stone of Destiny (The British Throne) to Tanis in Egypt for safety.

Jeremiah then took Teia Tephi and God's Treasures and left Tanis in a Tyrian Ship, which they sailed across the Mediterranean Sea to Gibraltar. There they changed ships and caught a Greek vessel to Ireland, stopping in Breogan in Spain and Marazion in Cornwall on the way.

They arrive in Ireland in 583 B.C. and Teia Tephi, the daughter of king Zedekiah of Jerusalem married Eochaidh Mac Duach, the Ard ri (high king) of Ireland. Many of the people living in Ireland at that time were known as the Tuatha de Danaan, which means the Tribe of Dan. Dan is the fifth Tribe of Israel. There were also many settlers from other Tribes of Israel, including the Tribe of Judah, of which Eochaidh the high king of Ireland was descended. Being Israelites, the Irish people embraced the princess who had come from their old motherland, as their new queen.

A special secret subterranean tomb was constructed at the Hill of Tara (Torah) in County Meath, Ireland, and The Ark of The Covenant was placed in it, along with Teia Tephi's body when she died and a number of other significant artifacts, including David's harp which features as the Irish People's national emblem.

The Ark of the Covenant and its contents become witness to the world that The Ten Commandments and god's Laws of The Torah do exist and are from god and its location in the British Isles suggests proof that the British peoples and their descendants, are of the Ten "lost" Tribes of the House of Israel, which will prove that the governments of these nations were never allowed to depart from god's Law and legislate their own laws. It is these illegal laws which are enslaving and bringing poverty to most of the world and is destroying the planet.

Jacob's Pillar Stone that Teia Tephi brought with her from Jerusalem stayed in Ireland for more than a thousand years, where it was renamed the Stone of Destiny or Lia Fail in Irish and all of the Irish kings were crowned upon the Stone until c. 500 A.D. It was then loaned to Fergus, the brother of Muircheartach (Murdoch) king of Ireland, who had emigrated to Scotland and wanted to be crowned king of the Irish who had settled there and had become Scottish.

The Stone was not returned to Ireland and stayed in Scotland, where it was named the Stone of Scone, and all of the Scottish kings were crowned upon it, until 1296 A.D. when Edward "Long-shanks" the first of England invaded Scotland; defeated the Scots and took the Stone, from Scone Abbey near Perth, to London where all of the English kings were subsequently crowned in Westminster Abbey upon the Stone, up to, and including, George the Sixth.

In 1950 four Scottish Nationalists removed the Stone from Westminster Abbey; took it back to Scotland and a fake stone made of Perthshire sandstone was later placed at Arbroath and from there it was taken to London. It was this same fake stone that Elizabeth the Second was crowned upon in 1953, so in actual fact, she has never really officially been crowned queen of the British people in the eyes of God, so therefore is not the true Monarch.

All of the Irish; Scottish and English Monarchs after 583 B.C., including Elizabeth the Second, are descended from Eochaidh and Teia Tephi of the line of David from the Tribe of Judah. The Stone was taken in 1950 from the House of Windsor from the line of David in fulfillment of God's Prophecies in The **Bible Book of Genesis** chapter 49:10 - "*The sceptre shall not depart from Judah (the line of David), nor a law-giver from between his feet, until Shiloh (Christ) comes*"

The Role And Power Of The Queen Today

The media has mislead the public into believing that Queen Elizabeth II is a symbolic ceremonial figure-head with little or no real power. That she is a harmless old relic that passes her time sipping tea at the palace. Nothing could be further from the truth. As British Monarch, Queen Elizabeth II is one of the wealthiest, most powerful persons on earth. She embodies the Crown and supreme world power. Presidents of the United States are forbidden any title of nobility and are subservient to the Monarch. The US president is commander in chief of the US forces at Camp David. Which is known to insiders as camp king David.

What is not really understood is that the British conquest has never ended. It has shifted into corporate kingdoms and a fictional world of corporations that are controlled by money, not physical armies.

Prime ministers in Commonwealth nations like Canada and Australia are also subservient representatives of the British king or queen. They are her spokesmen. The governor generals of the queen's commonwealth nations represent and exercise the queens power on her behalf. What the general public doesn't realize is that their leaders are only representatives of the monarch and do not possess the power. They exercise the power. They do not reign, they rule. The monarch, on the other hand, reigns but does not rule. It means to possesses the power but not exercise it.

By delegating her powers instead of exercising her powers, the queen is left safely outside and above the conflicts and divisions of the political process. She is protected from becoming a target of political hostilities.

Meanwhile, the general public is kept in the dark about the true powers that the queen actually possesses. Powers that she delegates but has not yet chosen to exercise. So what exactly are these powers that the queen possesses but has not chosen to exercise? Her powers include:

- The power to choose the prime ministers and to dismiss the prime ministers either directly in Britain, or through her governor generals in Commonwealth countries.
- The power to dismiss ministers and the government.
- The power to dissolve parliament and call new elections.
- The power to refuse legislation passed by parliament.
- The power to command the armed forces and raise a personal militia.
- The power to read confidential government documents and intelligence reports.
- The power to declare a state of emergency and issue proclamations.
- The power to call elections and enact laws in her majesties name.
- Not a single law is passed without the queen's consent.
- The power to exercise "Crown Prerogatives" which means the monarch can declare war through her prime minister, without the agreement of parliament.

- The power to grant and bestow titles like "Sir".
- The power to pardon convicted criminals.

So why has the queen been allowed to legally possess all of these supreme powers? For the sake of tradition? The Crown is defined as executive powers exercised in the name of the monarch. The actual Crown itself, worn by the monarch is a symbol of the queens executive powers. The parliamentary oaths act of 1866 requires all leaders of 54 commonwealth nations to swear an oath of loyalty to the queen, not to the people who elected them. Those who do not swear allegiance to the queen are deemed unfit for office, including the prime minister, police, military, judges, legislators, lawyers, and public servants. New citizens to the queen's commonwealth nations must also swear allegiance to the queen.

Public land in the queen's colonies like Canada, is called "Crown Land" and includes aboriginal land. Government corporations are called Crown corporations. The central bank of Canada and the Canadian mint are Crown corporations, independent of most government controls.

Canadian warships are called HMCS - Her Majesty's Canadian Ship. And in Australia they are called HMAS – Her Majesty's Australian Ship. Canada's national police force is called the Royal Canadian Mounted Police. All government contracts are between a company or individual and Her Majesty. Court summons are issued in the name of the queen and all public inquiries are called Royal Commissions. Commonwealth money carries the queen's image, worldwide, as a reminder of her authority. The queen is the lifetime hereditary head of state of Great Britain and her colonies and is un-elected and unaccountable. It is against the law to advocate the abolition of the monarchy.

The public accounts committee and national audit office are forbidden to examine queen Elizabeth Windsor's family finances. But the civil list payments are reviewed every 10 years. So for the year ended march 2002, the running expenses of the Windsor household were 7.9 million pounds. Family spending 35.3 million. Security 30 million. And the list goes on. But how much is the queen actually worth? The queen's wealth is divided into three categories: Her wealth as the Monarch, her visible personal wealth and her invisible personal wealth.

The queen's wealth as the Monarch includes 54 commonwealth nations worldwide. Millions of acres of Crown Land and resources, thousands of Crown corporations and the Corporate City State of London, which is the capitol of world finance. The queen's visible personal wealth, which was accumulated tax free until 1992, includes Royal Yachts, Rolls Royce's, Race horses, 5 castles, the world's largest collection of jewels, 20,000 old master-pieces and billions in class A shares and blue-chip stocks and bonds, which have been invested and re-invested, over and over again, tax free. Most of the queen's fortune was inherited from her ancestors' illegal Opium trade with China and the black slave trade. In 1977 the Bank of England nominees was established to hide the queen's personal portfolio of wealth. As the British Monarch, the queen has access to privileged information, state secrets and the world's top financiers. She is immune to accusations of insider trading or conflicts of interest. Her financial portfolio includes Rio Tinto, General Electric, Royal Dutch Shell, British Petroleum, Archer Daniels Midland, and the list goes on.

The queen's accumulation and hoarding of wealth as with the Vatican, causes death and deprivation among her subjects and is in direct contravention of God's Law of Moses which she as the Monarch of the British Israelite people is required to uphold. The Law of Moses clearly lays out the role of the Monarch in Deuteronomy Chapter 17 and forbids the Monarch from accumulating and hoarding wealth, and that he/she must uphold and enforce only the God's Law and not legislate his/her own laws or allow others to do so.

Deuteronomy 17:14 When thou art come unto the land which the "I AM" thy God giveth thee, and shalt possess it, and shalt dwell therein, and shalt say, I will set a king over me, like as all the nations that [are] about me;

17:15 Thou shalt in any wise set [him] king over thee, whom the "I AM" thy God shall choose: [one] from among thy brethren shalt thou set king over thee: thou mayest not set a stranger (a gentile) over thee, which [is] not thy brother.

17:16 But he shall not multiply horses to himself, nor cause the people to return to Egypt (slavery under man-made laws), to the end that he should multiply horses: forasmuch as the "I AM" hath said unto you, Ye shall henceforth return no more that way.

17:17 Neither shall he multiply wives to himself, that his heart turn not away: neither shall he greatly multiply to himself silver and gold.

17:18 And it shall be, when he sitteth upon the throne of his kingdom, that he shall write him a copy of this Law in a book out of [that which is] before the priests the Levites:

17:19 And it shall be with him, and he shall read therein all the days of his life: that he may learn to fear the "I AM" his God, to keep all the words of this Law and these Statutes, to DO them:

17:20 That his heart be not lifted up above his brethren, and that he turn not aside from the Commandment, [to] the right hand, or [to] the left: to the end that he may prolong [his] days in his kingdom, he, and his children, in the midst of Israel.

The queen's visible millions are but a tiny fraction of her invisible wealth accumulated through the Black Nobility.

The Black Nobility is a wealthy aristocracy of elite ruling families who solidified their wealth in the 12th. century by intermarrying with the wealthy godfather families of Venice, Italy. During the blood-baths of the Christian Crusades, this Italian Oligarchy captured the trading monopolies. Over the centuries the black nobility have used their power and wealth to rape, plunder and exploit every corner of the globe. Today, the black nobility enrich themselves in the illegal drugs and arms trade, using well distanced intermediaries. An estimated 280 billion in flight capitol and drug money flows into their secret Swiss accounts. The black nobility include the house of Hanover, Germany; the house of Hapsburg, Austria; the house of Orange, Netherlands; the house of Liechtenstein, Liechtenstein; and most importantly, the house of Guelph, Britain.

It is all just private business and there are no rules, no audit, no transparency so it is strictly the moral conduct which is rooted in the Satanic beliefs and blood oaths. All of these family houses can be found on Queen Elisabeth II's family tree. The Black Nobility are the founders of the **Committee of 300** which is also known as the Illuminati or illuminated ones. The Queen is head of the Committee of these 300 ruling families. The Illuminate was formed to achieve one main objective – one world government, called the New World Order. All of today's think-tanks originate for the Committee of 300 and include "**The Round Table**", "**The Council on Foreign Relations**", "**The United Nations Organization**", "**The Bilderberger Group**", "**The Club or Rome**", "**The Royal Institute of International Affairs**" and "**The Trilateral Commission**" founded by David Rockefeller. These will be summarized later in this book.

Since the British colonization of America, many powerful American families have formed secret societies that co-operate with the black nobility. Like the **Skull and Bones** fraternity at Yale University which is routed in German Freemasonry. Its exclusive members are some of America's most powerful and wealthy men. Including two of

America's Presidents – President George W. Bush and his father President George Herbert Walker Bush.

The New England genealogy society confirms that 19 US Presidents are descendants of King Edward 3rd. of England. Like European Royalty, America's bloodlines are maintained through intermarriage.

The think-tanks of the Committee of 300 have given birth to the **Tavistock Institute, HAARP, the Rand Corporation, Stanford Research Institute** and the **Institute for Policy Studies**, among others. It's all just business.

One study group in the Rand Corporation specializes in the timing and direction of thermal nuclear war. These institutes and corporations are engaged in the secretive development of brainwashing and population control techniques, the mapping and patenting of human and animal DNA and the genetic engineering of human, animal and plant life. They are also developing chemical, bacteriological and psychological weaponry. It's all just business. If you could create a market for a product, then create the product, and have unlimited capital to promote, would you? It's all just good business, isn't it?

Even war and conflict is just business to the prudent who are not bothered by conscience. For example in Freemasonry, the highest level is a 33rd. degree Mason. Most Freemasons remain at the 3rd degree and provide a cover, through their community charitable activities. The Illuminati at the top of the pyramid is the "all seeing eye". At the bottom are the unthinking, hard working, taxpaying, law abiding, debt slaves, called the goyem or sheep. Giuseppe Mazzini of Italy was a 33rd. degree Mason who replaced Adam Weishaupt as head of the Illuminati in 1834. Mazzini appointed America's Albert Pike as sovereign pontiff of universal Freemasonry and the coordinator of the Illuminati US activities.

In a letter to Giuseppe Mazzini, dated August 15th, 1871, Pike graphically outlined a blueprint for three grand world wars. WW1 would weaken, topple and destroy the powerful Zar's government of Russia, WW2 would pit Great Britain against Germany, destroy the German nation and create the Zionist state of Israel. WW3 would be created by fuelling aggression between the Zionists of Israel and the Arab world, who would eventually destroy one-another. Social Political and economic chaos would then force the masses to accept one world army and one world government ruled by the Illuminati.

Albert Pike was a confederate general in the American civil war. The Rothschilds sent British agents to conspire with Pike and with US politicians and provoke the rebellion that started the American civil war.

The Rothschilds whose massive fortunes had been built on provoked wars and war-loans, offered loans to both sides of the civil war at 24-36% interest. It is simply called "market development" in corporate terms. and when one can control supply and demand without moral responsibility it is a considerable advantage. When president Abraham Lincoln tried to stop the loan-sharks by issuing US government green-back dollars interest free, a gunman with European connections, named John Wilx Booth shoot him down in cold blood. Following the civil war, Albert Pike was convicted of treason and sent to prison, but President Andrew Johnson, a 33rd. degree Mason, pardoned him. One of Johnson's first acts as president was to veto the civil rights act for blacks, who had been shipped in chains to their wealthy American slave-owners. A statue of Albert Pike, a convicted traitor, stands today in the heart of Washington D.C. On the opposite side of America, in Central Park, New York, stands an honorary statue of Giuseppe Mazzini. Fourteen US presidents, including George Washington, are known to be 33rd. degree Masons. It's all just good business, eliminating competition, and market strategies to maintain power.

The Crown Temple And The Templars

Within the jurisdiction of the inner City of London is the Crown. Not only is this the **Financial Center** of PLANET EARTH, it is the **Legal Administration Center**. The Templar Church has been known for centuries by the world as the *'Crown'*. It is really a secret society for the Third Way Order. The Templars of the Crown is the domain of the black priests that are reflected in the black robes worn by our judges stemming from the days of Babylon. Today they are the Jesuits and the powerful military arm of the Knights of Malta. The crown, in reality, is the Crown Temple or Crown Templar. All three are synonymous. This is not the crown of England, or what we think is the queen. But indeed the queen is indeed part of this.

Temple Church was built by the Knights Templar in two parts. The first part was the Round and the Chancel. The Round Church was consecrated in 1185 and modeled after the circular Church of the Holy Sepulcher in Jerusalem. The Chancel was built in 1240. The Temple Church serves both the Inner and Middle Temples and is located between Fleet Street and Victoria on the embankment at the Thames river. Its grounds also house the crown offices at Crown Office Row. This Temple Church is actually outside any canonical jurisdiction. The master of the temple is appointed and takes his place by sealed, non-public patent, without induction or institution. As stated. the present queen of England is not the crown as many have thought, or have been led to believe. Rather, it is the bankers and attornies or attorneys, who are the actual crown or Crown Temple. The monarch aristocrats of England have not been ruling sovereigns since the reign of King John, around 1215. All royal sovereignty of the old British crown since that time has passed to the Crown Temple in Chancery. US and Canada are not the free and sovereign nations that our defacto federal governments tell us they are. Their fictional counterparts are part of the big corporate structure and the slaves comply with the laws on the structure. The federal governments are bankrupt corporations, pretending to serve the people, while they truly serve a different master, called the crown.

The banks rule the Temple Church and the attorners carry out their orders by controlling their victim's judiciary. Political minions to serve the banking cartel and the crown are chosen not elected. Since the first chancel of the Temple Church was built by the Knights Templar, this is not a new ruling system by any means. The chancel, or chancery of the Crown Inner Temple Court was where King John was in January 1215 when the English barons demanded that he confirm the rights enshrined in the Magna Charta. This London temple was the headquarters of the Templar Knights in Great Britain where order and rule were first made and which became known as code. Here a manipulative body of Elite bankers and attorners from the independent city of London carved out the law of the world that imposes the legal, and a totally unlawful system of contracts, upon the real people of this planet. This is called the *'color of law'*, the fictional system that you are becoming familiar with.

It's very important to know how the British royal crown was placed into the hands of the Knights Templars, and how the Crown Templars became the fiscal and military agents for the Pope of the Roman Church. This all becomes very clear through the concession of England to the Pope on May 15, 1213. This charter was sworn in fealty by England's King John to Pope Innocent and the Roman Church. It was witnessed before the Crown Templars. King John stated upon sealing this: *"I myself bearing witness in the house of the Knights Templars"*. Pay particular attention to the words being used that we have defined below, especially charter, fealty, demur, and concession:

"We wish it to be known to all of you, through this our charter, furnished with our seal, not induced by force or compelled by fear, but of our own good and spontaneous will and by the common counsel of our barons, do offer and freely concede to God and His holy apostles Peter and Paul and to our mother the holy Roman church, and to our lord Pope Innocent and to his Catholic successors, the whole kingdom of England and the whole kingdom of Ireland, with all their rights and appurtenances. We perform and swear fealty for them to him our aforesaid lord Pope Innocent, and his Catholic successors and the Roman church. Binding our successors and our heirs by our life forever, in similar manner to perform fealty and show homage to him who shall be chief pontiff at that time, and to the Roman church without demur. As assign, we will and establish perpetual obligation and concession. From the proper and especial revenues of our aforesaid kingdoms. The Roman church shall receive yearly a thousand pounds sterling. Saving to us and to our heirs our rights, liberties and regalia; all of which things, as they have been described above, we wish to have perpetually valid and firm; and we bind ourselves and our successors not to act counter to them. And if we or any one of our successors shall presume to attempt this, whoever he be, unless being duly warned he come to his kingdom, and this senses, shall lose his right to the kingdom, and this charter of our obligation and concession shall always remain firm".

It is an oath of allegiance from feudal times. Most who have commented on this charter only emphasize the payments due the Pope and the Roman church. What should be emphasized is the fact that King John broke the terms of this charter by signing the Magna Charta on June 15, 1215. The penalty for breaking the 1213 agreement was the loss of the crown or right to the kingdom to the Pope and his Roman church. It says so quite plainly. To formally and lawfully take the crown from the royal monarchs of England by an act of declaration, on August 24, 1215, Pope Innocent III annulled the Magna Charta. Later in the year, he placed an interdict, meaning prohibition, on the entire British Empire. From that time until today, the English monarchy and the entire British crown belonged to the Pope. By swearing to the 1213 charter in fealty, King John declared that the British-English crown and its possessions at that time, including all future possessions, estates, trusts, charters, letters patent, and land, were forever bound to the Pope and the Roman church, the landlord. Some five hundred years later, the New England colonies in America became a part of the crown as a possession and trust named the 'United States'. By agreeing to the Magna Charta, King John had broken the agreement terms of his fealty with Rome and the Pope. What that means is that he lost all rights to the kingdom, and the royal English crown was turned over by default to the Pope and the Roman church. The Pope and his Roman church control the Crown Temple because his Knights established it under his orders. So also the Temple banks, the Templar attorneys, the corporate United States, the corporate British Commonwealth, the chartered Federal Reserve Bank and Bank of England. The list is pretty impressive. He who controls the gold controls the world. One may think that this has no relevance today, but this *is* the Crown Temple today.

This is simply due to the fact that all Bar Associations throughout the world are signatories and franchises to the International Bar Association located at the Inns of Court at Crown Temple, which are physically located at Chancery Lane behind Fleet Street in London. Although they vehemently deny it, all BAR associations in the world, such as the American Bar Association, the Florida Bar, or California Bar Association, are franchises to the Crown. It is because they are trained to believe this is nonsense. Yet this insidious process would involve all Canadian Bar associations as well and indeed the world under the dominion of the Corporate Crown. The Inns of Court and The Four Inns of Court to the Crown Temple use the banking and judicial system of the city of London. It is a sovereign and independent territory which is not a part of Great Britain. This is like

Washington City, as DC was called in the 1800's, is not a part of the north American states, nor is it a state. It was done this way to administer and control the people. These Fleet Street bankers and lawyers work everywhere under the guise and 'color of law'. They are known collectively as the crown. Their lawyers are actually Templar Bar attornies, not lawyers. The bankers and Bar attorneys of the world are franchises in oath and allegiance to the Crown at Chancery - the Crown Temple church and its Chancel located at Chancery Lane. So the legal system or judiciary of North America is controlled by the Crown Temple from the independent and sovereign City of London. And the private Federal Reserve System, which issues fiat U.S. Federal Reserve notes, is financially owned and controlled by the crown from Switzerland, the home and legal origin for the charters of the United Nations, the International Monetary Fund, the World Trade Organization, and most importantly, the Bank of International Settlements; from what we would call Head Office of the gods. The governmental and judicial systems within all public jurisdictions at federal, local and state/provincial levels are owned by the crown. Note that this is a privately owned corporate foreign power operating in defacto. All licensed Bar attorneys in the world owe their allegiance and give their solemn oath in pledge to the Crown Temple whether they realize this or not. Once again, look to the real meaning of words. Crown means imperial, regal power or dominion - sovereignty. There is a power behind the crown greater than the crown itself.

Associated with the Crown are the Four Inns of Court to the Temple. In England, the temples are two Inns of Court, being original dwellings of the Knights Templar. They are called the Inner and the Middle Temple. In England, there is a college of municipal or common law professors and students. Formerly the town-house of a nobleman, bishop or other distinguished personage, it was where they resided when they attended the court. The Inns of Court were colleges in which students of law reside and are instructed. The principals are the Inner Temple, the Middle Temple, Lincoln's Inn, and Gray's Inn. Inns of Chancery are colleges in which young students formerly began their law studies. These are now occupied chiefly by attorneys, solicitors, and the like. This is where the legalistic architecture is designed to promote the exclusive monopoly of the Temple Bar. These Inns/Temples are exclusive and private country clubs, occupied by secret societies of world power in commerce. They are well established, some having been founded in the early 1200's when the Templars rose to power. The Queen of England is a current member of both the Inner Temple and Middle Temple. Gray's Inn specializes in taxation legalities by rule and code for the Crown.

Lincoln's Inn received its name from the Third Earl of Lincoln around 1300. Just like all other franchise Bar Associations, none of the Four Inns of the Temple are incorporated, for a definite and purposeful reason. You can't make claim against a non-entity and a non-being. They are private societies without charters or statutes, and their so-called constitutions are based solely on custom and self-regulation. In other words, they exist as secret societies without a public front door unless you're a private member called to their Bar. While the Inner Temple holds the legal system franchise by license to steal from Canada and Great Britain, it is the Middle Temple that has legal license to steal from America. This comes about directly via their Bar Association franchises to the Honorable Society of the Middle Temple through the Crown Temple.

From the book **The History of the Inn** as written by the **Honorable Society of the Middle Temple,** we can see a direct tie to the Bar Association franchises and its crown signatories in America. A "Call to the Bar" or keeping terms in one of the four Inns is a pre-requisite to call at King's Inns until late in the 19th century. In the 17th and 18th centuries, students came from the American colonies and from many of the West Indian islands. The Inn's records would lead one to suppose that for a time there was hardly a young gentleman in Charleston who had not studied here.

The District Of Columbia.

Like the City States of London and the Vatican, a third city state was officially created in 1871, with the passage of the Act of 1871. This was when a significant part of the PLANET EARTH business plan was executed. That city state is called the District of Columbia and is located on 10 square miles of land in the heart of Washington. The District of Columbia flies its own flag, and has its own independent constitution. We have seen the Jesuit influence here and much of the military structure arising in this place we would call the Military Center.

The constitution for the District of Columbia operates under a tyrannical Roman law known as Lex Fori, which bares no resemblance to the US Constitution. When congress passed the act of 1871 it created a separate corporation known as THE UNITED STATES and corporate government for the District of Columbia. This treasonous act allowed the District of Columbia to operate as a corporation outside the original constitution of the United States and outside of the best interests of American Citizens. We will see later how from 1864-1867, several Reconstruction Acts were passed forcing the states to ratify the 14th Amendment, which made everyone slaves indirectly. for, following the Civil War, Congress submitted to the states three amendments as part of its Reconstruction program to guarantee equal civil and legal rights to black citizens. The major provision of the 14th amendment was to grant citizenship to "*All persons born or naturalized in the United States*".

As we have pointed out earlier, the Amendments were structure to implement the plan. We see this Roman Law within the US 13th Amendment (#2) instituted in the mid 1860's: "*Neither slavery nor involuntary servitude, except as a punishment for crime whereof the party shall have been duly convicted,*" The crime with which you have been convicted is 'unauthorized use' of the State's or Crown's intellectual property - the legal identity name.

Although geographically separate, the city states of London, the Vatican and the District of Columbia are one interlocking empire called Empire of the City. The flag of Washington's district of Columbia has three red stars. One for each city state in the three city empire. This corporate empire of three city states controls the world economically, through London's inner city, militarily through the District of Columbia, and spiritually through the Vatican.

In this structure is the U.S.A. - A Crown Colony. A sobering study of the signed treaties and charters between Britain and the United States exposes a shocking truth. The United States has always been and still is a British Crown colony. King James the first was famous not for just translating the Bible into the king James version. But for his business-venture of signing the first charter of Virginia in 1606. That charter granted America's British forefathers a license to settle and colonize America. The charter also guaranteed that future kings and queens of England would have sovereign authority over all the citizens and colonized land in America, stolen from the Indians.

After America declared its independence from Great Britain, the treaty of 1783 was signed. That treaty specifically identifies the king of England as the prince of the United States and contradicts the belief that America won the war of independence.

Although king George the 3rd. of England gave up most of his claims over American colonies, he kept his right to continue receiving payment for his business venture of colonizing America.

If America had really won the war of independence, they would never have agreed to pay debts and reparations to the king of England. America's blood soaked war of independence against the British bankrupted America and turned its citizens into permanent debt slaves of the king. In the war of 1812 the British torched and burned to the ground the White House and all US government buildings. Destroying ratification records of the US constitution. Most US citizens believe that the United States is a country and that the president is the most powerful man on earth. The United States is not a country, it is a corporation. And the president is president of the corporation of the United States. He and his elected officials work for the corporation, not for the American people. Since the United States is a corporation, who owns the corporation of the United States?

Like Canada and Australia whose leaders are prime ministers of the queen, and whose land is called Crown land, the United States is just another Crown colony. Crown colonies are controlled by the Empire of the three City States.

At the center of each city state is a towering phallic shaped stone monument called an obelisk that points skyward. In DC city state, the obelisk known as the Washington monument was dedicated to the Freemason George Washington by the Freemason grand lodge of the District of Columbia. 250 Masonic lodges financed the Washington obelisk monument, including the Knights Templar Masonic order. At the heart of London city state, is a 187 ton 69 foot tall Egyptian obelisk called Cleopatra's Needle. It was transported from Egypt and erected on the banks of the river Thames. In Vatican city, another Egyptian obelisk towers high above St Peter's square. Obelisks are phallic shaped monuments honouring the pagan sun god of ancient Egypt called Amen Ra. The spirit of this pagan god is said to reside within the obelisk.

Baalbek The City Of The Sun

Recalling a previous chapter where Rick Martin interviews Eric von Phelps to ask: What is the ULTIMATE goal of the Jesuits?. The answer was: " *Their ultimate goal is the rule of the world, with the Pope of their making, from Solomon's rebuilt Temple in Jerusalem. That's their ultimate goal.*" He said: *"When Rothschild sent that note, via Roost, into London, saying that Napoleon had won the Battle of Waterloo, that's when the stocks plummeted, and all the Jesuits bought all the stocks up, there in London, and got control of the Bank of England. The Jesuits then made London their commercial center of the world, and Rome their religious center, aiming that one day Jerusalem would be both."*

It is of interest to end this Chapter on the history and significance of the city of Baalbek which was founded in 1270 BC under the original name of Ba'al Bek. The founder was King Solomon (Shulmanu I) or Shalmaneser I king of Assyria. (1274 BC – 1245 BC). It was the most Sacred Temple to Ba'al Moloch representing Ba'al (Lord) + Bek (God). In 323 BC, it was changed in name to Heliopolis.

It stands approximately 86 kilometers northeast of the city of Beirut in eastern Lebanon stands the temple complex of **Baalbek**. Situated atop a high point in the fertile Bekaa valley, the ruins are one of the most extraordinary and enigmatic holy places of ancient times. Long before the Romans conquered the site and built their enormous temple of Jupiter there stood at Baalbek the largest stone block construction found in the entire world.

As the Roman Parthenon, Baalbek was the official Mount Olympus and Parthenon of the Romans and the Roman Empire and their most sacred Temple complex in the world.

The primary structures at the ruins are the Great Court; the Temple of Baal/Jupiter situated upon the massive pre-Roman stone blocks known as the Trilithon; the so-called Temple of Bacchus; and the circular temple believed to be associated with the goddess Venus.

The Great Court, begun during the reign of Trajan (98-117), measured 135 meters by 113 meters, contained various religious buildings and altars, and was surrounded by a splendid colonnade of 128 rose granite columns. These magnificent columns, 20 meters tall and of enormous weight, are known to have been quarried in Aswan, Egypt but how they were actually transported by land and sea to Baalbek remains an engineering mystery. Today, only six columns remain standing, the rest having been destroyed by earthquakes or taken to other sites (for example, Justinian appropriated eight of them for the basilica of Hagia Sophia in Constantinople).

The Temple of Baal/Jupiter was begun during the reign of Emperor Augustus in the late first century BC and completed soon after 60 AD. The single largest religious edifice ever erected by the Romans, the immense sanctuary of Jupiter Heliopolitanus was lined by 104 massive granite columns, imported from Aswan in Egypt, and held a temple surrounded by 50 additional columns, almost 19m (62ft) high. The Temple is believed to have been consecrated to a triad of deities: Hadad (Baal/Jupiter), the god of Heaven; Atargates (Astarte/Hera), the wife of Hadad; and Mercury, their son.

The Assyrian and Neo Assyrian Kingdom Structure Prior to the restoration and enlargement projects of various Roman Emperors, Baalbek was the site to one of the Greatest and most famous Temples of all history- the Great Temple of King Solomon (Shulmanu I) or Shalmaneser I king of Assyria. (1274 BC – 1245 BC). The massive stones range in size from thirty to thirty three feet in length, fourteen feet in height and ten feet in depth, and weigh approximately 450 tons each. Nine of these blocks are visible on the north side of the temple, nine on the south, and six on the west (others may exist but archaeological excavations have thus far not dug beneath all the sections of the Grand Terrace). Above the six blocks on the western side are three even larger stones, called the Trilithon, whose weight exceeds 1000 tons each. These great stones vary in size between sixty-three and sixty-five feet in length, with a height of fourteen feet six inches and a depth of twelve feet.

Another even larger stone lies in a limestone quarry a quarter of a mile from the Baalbek complex. Weighing an estimated 1200 tons, it is sixty-nine feet by sixteen feet by thirteen feet ten inches, making it the single largest piece of stonework ever crafted in the world. The incredible weight and dimensions of this foundation to the Temple of the Great King Solomon of Assyria has led many writers to conjecture as to just how such work was possible. Some have suggested the existence of long lost ancient machinery and even supernatural forces. The Assyrians themselves cultivated such mysteries concerning one of the greatest Temples and wonders of the ancient world in the great mystery work the **Testament of Solomon** (also known as the Lesser Keys of Solomon).

Exile of the High Priest Dynasty and the age of Cybele and the Phrygians
Around 1159 BCE a particularly savage meteorite swarm associated with the migration of a comet the Greeks called Phaethon devastated the lands across the Levant up through the Anatolian region and down south as far as Arabia. The subsequent, dust and "nuclear winter" effect caused mass crop failures and starvation across the whole east of the ancient world causing the simultaneous collapse of the Hittite Kingdom and the Assyrian Kingdoms.

The horrors from heaven forced old demonic gods to the fore and relegated the old gods such as Baal, to less importance for a time. Throughout the Levant, Moloch grew in popularity as people sacrificed children and each other to the demon god of fire. In the Anatolian region a new Empire quickly sprung up known as the Phrygians who worshipped Cybele and her instantiation as black meteorites – the kind that had caused so much devastation.

The Phrygians took control of the whole region including Baalbek no later than 1070 BCE forcing the old priest dynasty into exile. Some of the priests returned to Egypt and successfully petitioned the priests of Amen-Ra who now controlled Upper Egypt to build a sacred temple on the Isle of Yeb (Elephantine Island). The remainder built new Temples at Shechem, Shomron and Beit El.

The Assyrians regained Baalbek around 740 BCE and under the reign of King Solomon V (Shalmaneser V King of Assyria 727 to 722 BCE), most of the exiled "Israelite" priests of the Kingdom of Israel were uprooted from their new lands and returned to attend the Temple Complex of Baalbek and its restoration.

Some priest families negotiated with Solomon to be allowed to remain and attend the new temples in the Sarmatian region and became the House of Menasheh, the bitter enemies to the House of Hammon (Hanan) who were forced to return to Baalbek.

Following the death of Alexander in 323 BC, Phoenicia was ruled successively by the Ptolemaic kings of Egypt and the Seleucid kings of Syria until the arrival of the Romans. The priests of Ba'al Hammon were banished once again and forced to build their own settlement known as Ba'al Hammon between Tyre and Acre on account of the House of Menasheh (Samaritans) now controlling Sarmara .

The name of Baalbek was now changed to Heliopolis Meaning 'City of the Sun', the name was also used by the Ptolemies of Egypt between 323 and 198 BC, in order to express the importance this holy site held for the Egyptians. In the historical writings of Ambrosius Theodosius Macrobius, a Latin grammarian who lived during the 5th century AD, the god of the holy place was called Zeus Heliopolitanus (a Greek god) and the temple was mentioned as a place of oracular divination, similar to such sites as Delphi and Dodona in Greece and the temple of Amun at Siwa in Egypt.

The golden age of Roman building at Baalbek/Heliopolis began in 15 BC when Julius Caesar settled a legion there and began construction of the great Temple of Jupiter. During the next three centuries, as emperors succeeded one another in the imperial capital of Rome, Heliopolis would be filled with the most massive religious buildings ever constructed in the far reaching Roman Empire.

Many Roman emperors were of Syrian birth, so it would not have been unusual for them to have promoted the worship of the country's indigenous deities under their adopted Roman names. Whatever the nature of the pre-Roman worship at Baalbek, its veneration of Baal created a hybrid form of the god Jupiter, generally referred to as Jupiter Heliopolitan. The Romans also assimilated the worship of the goddess Astarte with that of Aphrodite or Venus, and the god Adonis was identified with Bacchus.

Heliopolis remained the most holy of temple structures until Christianity was declared the official religion of the Roman Empire in 313 AD, following which the Byzantine Christian emperors and their soldiers desecrated thousands of pagan sanctuaries. At the end of the 4th century, Emperor Theodosius destroyed many significant buildings and statues, and constructed a basilica with stones from the Temple of Jupiter. This signalled the end of Roman Heliopolis. The city of the sun declined and lapsed into relative oblivion.

As arguably the oldest and most significant dedicated sacred sites in the region, dedicated to the gods under which most of the Jewish tribes worshipped for over a millennia, it is astounding that Baalbek is mentioned but once in the official ancient Jewish scripture. Even then, it is mentioned by a pseudonym in a way that remains obscure. Biblical passages (I Kings, IX: 17-19) mention the name of King Solomon in connection with a place that may be ancient Baalbek ("And Solomon built Gezer and Beth-Horon, the lower, and Baalath and Tadmor in the wilderness"), but most scholars are hesitant to equate this Baalath with Baalbek and therefore deny any connection between Solomon and the ruins.

Apart from the fact that Solomon was a great Assyrian King, the main reason for such incredible silence may derive from the fact that the High Priests of Ba'al and Moloch practised the very darkest of arts including child sacrifice, human sacrifice, temple prostitution, incest, ritual homosexuality and cannibalism. Furthermore, the High Priests of Baalbek became the High Priests of Israel, with the House of Hanan even named after their original demonic god Ba'al (Hamon) Hammon. It is no wonder then that the Jewish scriptures first written as a Canonical text by Ezra in 455-450 BCE and heavily edited since that time makes no mention of the true past. Baalbek was an important site in the ancient world. Yet many thousands of innocent lives were sacrificed for its construction and as sacrifices to the evil gods.

It would be easy to surmise that the bloodlines, especially that of Queen Elisabeth II link back to the House of David and this time. It is thus easy to surmise that the eventual rising of the City of the Sun would be the proposed "head office" of the New Order.

There has been much reference to societies and groups that age collaborators in the plan. Now it is time to look lower in the structural pyramid of PLANET EARTH INC. to understand how this enormous empire is administered.

9

HISTORY OF THE ROMAN CULT-JESUIT RISE

It is of interest to unravel some of the history of the Jesuits, Vatican and the New World Order. As stated, in plain sight is hidden the business plan of the gods who have had their earthly representatives write it in the bibles and other records. These representatives, either endowed, or gifted, with special powers appear to fundamentally driven by the beliefs of Lucifer who would be the god responsible for the motivation behind the New World plan of Luciferian unity for all Earthlings. At the top of the heap so to speak, we have placed the Jesuits as the Black order of military might directing the White order of the Vatican. In looking at the history of how these two world forces have evolved, we will become more familiar with the tactics, the structure and the administrative process which has created a silent alliance of Planet Earth Corporations, Societies, and Orders on an enormous scale. This will be dealt with in subsequent chapters. Of note is the Roman Catholic have not always been subjects of Lucifer and the Roman Cult. There is no doubt that there have always been the struggle between evil Black Priests and the good White Priests but it seems that the evil ones have been successful in "taking over" dynasties so to shift the purpose and plan. Although the "store front" looks White, there is a Black mission.

The Rules Of Dominion Of The Vatican

And so it goes with the "royal" bloodlines and the dynasties that we have looked at in the previous chapter. In effect these families go back a long time in their histories, always careful to preserve their fortunes and their kingdoms by whatever means necessary. As stated before, it is only the process of dominion and control over others that has changed over time to be more subtle and indirectly orchestrated in what is the private versus public domain of corporations. As a hierarchy, one must ponder how such a diversity of bloodlines and dynasties with so much power actually work together. One wonders how they could ever come onto the one mission of a New World Order. How could such power ever create the necessary structure to run PLANET EARTH? The answer is that they do not always agree, but one thing appears to be true and that is that the concept of God and God's truth through religions and religious codes of behaviour have been accepted by Earthlings around the planet. And as such it plays a key strategy in the direction and management of PLANET EARTH. The priesthoods of history have always had great power as they, the "chosen ones" elected themselves to spread God's word have taken these positions of power to "guide" mankind, including kings and queens.

It is now of interest to look into the history of the great struggle between the Jesuit Empire, the Roman Catholics and the Roman Cult. This historical evolution has led a strategic execution of the final phase of the New World Order that began in 1943. It would seem that the march to Redemption Day of December 21, 2012 is in its final phase.

Let us first look at the religious CEO equivalent and the alleged power given to these people by the gods. Here you see the coat of arms for the **Vatican City State**. Take note of the crown on top, a symbol of papal authority. It is a triple tiered crown, that is also called a tiara or *triregno* in Latin. Note that most of this research comes from the **website www.one-evil.org.**

When it comes to Concerning the extent of Papal dignity, authority, or dominion and infallibility. **(**Quoadea quoeconcernunt papae dignitatem, auctoritatem, seu potestatem, et infallibilitatem.) check out the official Source: **Lucius Ferraris,** "Papa," art. 2, in his **Prompta Bibliotheca Canonica, Juridica, Moralis, Theologica, Ascetica, Polemica, Rubristica, Historica.** ("Handy Library"), Vol. 5, published in Petit-Montrouge (Paris) by J. P. Migne, 1858 edition, column 1823, Latin. Here it states:

#1. "The Pope is of so great dignity and so exalted that he is not mere man, but as it were God, and the vicar of God." (#1. "Papa tantae est dignitatis et cesitudinis, ut non sit simplex homo, sed quasi Deus, et Dei vicarius.")
#13. "Hence the Pope is crowned with a triple crown, as king of heaven and of earth and of the lower regions." (#13. Hinc Papa triplici corona coronatur tanquam rex coeli, terre et infernoram.")
#18. "As to papal authority, the Pope is as it were God on earth, Sole sovereign of all the faithful of Christ, chief king of kings, having a plentitude of unbroken power, entrusted by the omnipotent God to govern the earthly and heavenly kingdoms." (#18. "Deveniendo ad Papae auctoritatem, Papa est quasi Deus in terra unicaus Christifidelium princeps, regum omnium rex maximus, plenitudinem potestatis continens, cui terreni simul, ac coelestis imperii gubernacula ab omnipotenti Deo credita sunt.")
#30. "The Pope is of so great authority and power, that he is able to modify, declare, or interpret even divine laws." (#30. "Papa tantae est auctoritatis et potestatis, ut possit quoque leges divinas modificare, declarare, vel interpretari, ad num.")

These papal claims, to include the presumed authority to modify the divine laws of God, were specifically prophesied in the book of Daniel: Dan 7:25 "*And he shall speak great words against the most High, and shall wear out the saints of the most High, **and think to change times and laws: (of the most High)** and they shall be given into his hand until a time and times and the dividing of time.*" So at least we know where another one of these Earthly gods is presumed to be today! Most people believe these are just archaic unenforceable remnants of history but rest assured Planet Earth and it's dominion by the gods is hardly a trite matter.

As you become more and more familiar with these biblical "prophesies" one begins to realize that what we are reading is just a great business plan created centuries ago that is clearly being carried out at a future time. and that dear reader appears to be now.

It is now necessary to shed some light on this division of the Jesuits and the Vatican. In particular, how the Roman Cult took control of the Roman Catholic Church. The struggle dates back to Roman times. also a major shift in power occurred around the time of the Second World War, involving the Jesuits and the final implementation of the part of the grand plan or the New World Order. The following is presented to shed light on the history and the emergence, or fruition of the grand plan under the Iluminati. We have looked at the Jesuits before in an earlier chapter. Because they are allegedly the highest policing force on the Planet, it is of interest to elaborate on their history and their attempts to dominion. Their store front is "white" but behind the upper echelon is the black, dark, cold hearted assassin mentality.

The Jesuits As The Society Of Jesus

The **Society of Jesus** (Latin: *Societas Iesu*, *S.J.*, *SJ*, or *SI*) is a Christian male religious order that follows the teachings of the Roman Catholic Church. The members are called **Jesuits** and are also known colloquially as "God's Marines" and as "The Company", these being references to founder Ignatius of Loyola's military background and members' willingness to accept orders anywhere in the world and live in extreme conditions. The society is engaged in evangelization and apostolic ministry in 112 nations on six continents. The society's founding principles are contained in the document *Formula of the Institute*, written by Ignatius of Loyola. Jesuits are known for their work in education (founding schools, colleges, universities and seminaries), intellectual research, and cultural pursuits, and for their missionary efforts. Jesuits also give retreats, minister in hospitals and parishes and promote social justice and ecumenical dialogue. This is the White side.

Ignatius founded the society after being wounded in battle and experiencing a religious conversion. He composed the *Spiritual Exercises* to help others follow the teachings of Jesus Christ. In 1534, Ignatius and six other young men, including St. Francis Xavier and Bl. Pierre Favre, gathered and professed vows of poverty, chastity, and later obedience, including a special vow of obedience to the Pope. Rule 13 of Ignatius' **Rules for Thinking with the Church** said: "*That we may be altogether of the same mind and in conformity[...], if [the Church] shall have defined anything to be black which to our eyes appears to be white, we ought in like manner to pronounce it to be black.*" Ignatius' plan of the order's organization was approved by Pope Paul III in 1540 by the bull containing the Formula of the Institute. The opening lines of this founding document would declare that the Society of Jesus was founded to "*strive especially for the propagation and defense of the faith and progress of souls in Christian life and doctrine.*" The Society participated in the Counter-Reformation and later in the implementation of the Second Vatican Council in the Catholic Church. It would seem that they still abide by this rule as they appear to be quiet loving, peaceful men of God but follow Satan's ways which they paint black on the outside.

The Society of Jesus is consecrated under the patronage of Madonna Della Strada, a title of the Blessed Virgin Mary, and it is led by a Superior General, currently Adolfo Nicolás. The headquarters of the society, its General Curia, is in Rome. The historic curia of St Ignatius is now part of the *Collegio del Gesù* attached to the Church of the Gesù, the Jesuit Mother Church.

The Jesuits today form the largest single religious order of priests and brothers in the Catholic Church, although they are surpassed by the Franciscan family of first orders Order of Friars Minor (OFM), OFM Capuchins, and Conventuals. As of 1 January 2007, Jesuits numbered 19,216: 13,491 clerks regular (priests), 3,049 scholastics (students to become priests), 1,810 brothers (not priests) and 866 novices. Members serve in 112 nations on six continents with the largest number in India and USA. Their average age was 57.3 years: 63.4 years for priests, 29.9 years for scholastics. and 65.5 years for brothers. The Society is divided into 91 Provinces with 12 dependent Regions: three in Africa, four in the Americas and five in Asia and Oceania. Altogether, they constitute 10 administrative units. (Assistancies). The staff consists pf 19,216 **Refer website**

www.sjweb.info. However, the many layers, like the 33 levels of the Masons, are further and further removed from the top where only a handful of the "loyal brotherhood" know the truth, the true plan, and are bonded by secret oaths.

The Jesuit Civil War (1942-1945)

In 1941 aged 75, Count Wladimir Ledochowski, the Jesuit Superior General was at the height of his supremacy, a still fit and completely driven man. His army of Jesuit influential's had similarly reached great heights in all places held by Catholic Dictators as well as the United States. So why would a civil war between factions of the Jesuits break out at such a time?

One of the great historical anomalies is the behaviour of both Adolf Hitler, Fr Himmler S.J. and Fr Joseph Stalin S.J. in the Nazi Russian Invasion. Contrary to spin historians, these men had not only shown ruthless pragmatism in managing power until this point, but were actively working together on a number of military and scientific fronts until the invasion. Refer to **http://one-evil.org/content/people_20c_hitler.html**

A frequent excuse given is that fiercely Catholic Hitler had become "drunk" with power and decided to invade Russia because he hated the Russians. But Hitler was a mere soldier, compared to Fr. Himmler S.J. the new Grand Inquisitor of the Roman Catholic Church and his massive army of assassins and torturers.

Instead, it is much more certain that Jesuit Superior General Ledochowski instructed Himmler to push for the assault on the understanding this would complete a clean sweep of Catholic National Socialism over Catholic National Communism. Similarly, it is clear that Count Ledochowski said something in reverse to Fr Stalin S.J. – that this was the plan that would ultimately destroy Germany as Stalin's behaviour against his own country and people was nothing other than treacherous.

When Hitler invaded in June 1941, Fr Stalin -- against every other example of ruthless judgment to protect his own power -- seemingly invited for his troops to be slaughtered and defeated by refusing his generals to fully engage, then having the generals executed and then repeating the bizarre process almost up to Moscow.

However, by the bleak Russian winter of December 1941, the jaws of the Jesuit Soviet Machine clamped down shut on the legs of the German Army. From this point on, the fate of the Nazi dream and power were sealed. For such a loyal German Jesuit as Fr Himmler S.J. such deliberate trickery by Ledochowski would have been devastating and unforgivable. The Jesuits had shifted their power away from Germany, France and Italy to America -- for the first time in the order's history.

On December 13, 1942 (aged 76) Count Wladimir Ledochowski died suddenly --almost certainly murdered by the very best assassins of Fr. Himmler for his treachery in dooming the German-Swiss –French "Illuminati" Jesuits.

Technically this act immediately plunged the Jesuits into Civil War. Unable to convene a General Congregation until the end of the War --when all Jesuits have permission to elect their leader --Vicar General Norbert de Boyne could not be made Superior General. This left the American Jesuits, led by Fr Edmund Walsh S.J. free to pursue their agenda along with other international factions.

The German-Swiss-Italian-French Jesuits during the war headed by Fr Heinrich Himmler S.J. represented the "Illuminati" – the old guard who had been betrayed by their slain leader Fr Ledochowski S.J. The other camp representing the new guard, the "New World Order" headed by the American-Canadian Jesuits and allies along with English and even Australian Jesuits.

Midst the two warring camps of Jesuits were "neutral" provinces such as the Netherlands and Spain, still battling for its survival against the popularity of the Vatican sponsored Opus Dei Mary (Mari) Spanish Satanic devotion cult.

It is during this event, in which unprecedented number of Jesuits were killed that the plan for the New World Order was hatched by senior Jesuits such as American Fr Edmund Walsh S.J.

The plan was confirmed by the Jesuit officials that accompanied each of the world leaders of Roosevelt, Fr Stalin S.J. and Churchill to the conference at Tehran in December 1943.

It is there we see for the first time the unveiling of the public face of the New World Order – an order of opposing "friends" and ideologies- capitalism vs. communism, but all ultimately financed and directed from the same machine.

Foundation Of The New World Order

And so the **New World Order** was founded in 1943 at the first Conference between England, the United States and the Soviet Union by leading Jesuits in Tehran. It was reconfirmed at the end of World War II following the complete victory of the Roman Cult controlling the Roman Catholic Church in the re-establishment of effective Catholic control of the former Frankish Kingdom principalities now known as Germany, France, Austria, the Netherlands and Switzerland. However, the term first entered the public arena in 1949 through the work of Jesuit co-agitator George Orwell and his book "New World Order" providing a chilling account of the future world under global Catholic socialism (Fascism).

At the heart, the New World Order is a defined membership of global financial, political and industrial consortium based around the underlying massive financial assets of the Catholic Church based from Zürich still in control of the Jesuits and their continued monopoly as the only organization in Catholic history (excluding the Knights Templar) to hold a Papal document granting them exclusive rights to conduct banking and financial activities.

As the New World Order is a consortium of financial, political, military and industrial entities, its precise structure, rules of operation and agenda remains difficult to precisely confirm. For example, a few dozen private banks in Europe and the United States first formed by the Jesuits in the 18th and early 19th Century continue to remain the foundation pillars of the global finance and credit system -- the same private banks that have withdrawn hundreds of billions of dollars of credit from the global financial system in 2008 and 2009 causing what was a localized credit squeeze of bad loans into a global depression.

The New World Order also maintains a political military structure through co-operative ties between intelligence agencies and large private and public arms manufacturers such that this apparatus serves to protect the interests of the Catholic Church across the world.

The New World Order also represents a discrete group of global companies, principally involved in industries such as pharmaceuticals as well as substantial media and publishing interests, again which have successfully maintained protection against Catholic interests, with the exception of unavoidable occasional public scandals such as ongoing pedophilia by priests.

Foundation Of The Illuminati

The **Illuminati** is name given to a small group of noble and non-noble families in the 18th Century that assisted the Jesuit Order in their plans to exact revenge on the Catholic Church for their disbandment in July 1773 by Pope Clement XIV and the order *Dominus ac Redemptor.*

The Illuminati families were instrumental in assisting the Jesuits in stealing both the gold reserves of the Catholic Church and the French State through the promotion of the French Revolution and then Napoleon. It also certain that the Jesuits obtained in their possession a number of extremely important and incriminating documents from the Vatican Secret Archives during the capture of Rome by the forces of Napoleon.

Following the establishment of terms, the Society was restored to the world by the Papal letter "Solicitudine Omnium Ecclesiarum" on August 14, 1814. In recognition for their efforts, the "Illuminati" families were rewarded for their support through several means including noble title, estates and control of fabulous wealth (on behalf of the society). Three of the most famous families and recipients of the favour of the Jesuits for their assistance are the House of Saxe-Coburg and Gotha, the Rothschilds and the Lafayettes. The House of Saxe-Coburg and Gotha was rewarded with the crown of England and remain the primary leading family of the Illuminati and steadfastly loyal to the Jesuits.

Background Illuminati Events

The term "Illuminati" and their planned structure originated from Jesuit lawyer Adam Weishaupt S.J. (1748-1830) in Bavaria.

In 1773, Weishaupt became professor of canon law, now being a Jesuit and set about supporting his Jesuit brothers hiding from persecution. Having joined a number of secret societies, such as the Freemasonry Lodge in Munich in order to see how they operated, Weishaupt finalized a new model of operation for the Jesuits in exile by April 1776.

With the help of wealthy supporters, including Adolf Freiherr Knigge, on May 1, 1776, Weishaupt formed the "Order of Perfectibilists", which was later known as the Illuminati. He adopted the name of "Brother Spartacus" within the order.

The primary mission of the Illuminati under Weishaupt was to establish a New World Order through the use of science, technology and business, while abolishing all monarchical governments and the Vatican on account of their support of the destruction of the Jesuits.

Weishaupt coined the motto of the Illuminati to be "the ends justifies the means". Each isolated cell of initiates reported to a superior, whom they did not know thus eliminating the chance of all Jesuits in a particular region being found and killed.

Adolf Freiherr Knigge introduced Weishaupt to several nobles including Duke Ernest II of Saxe-Gotha-Altenburg (1745–1804) who was sympathetic to the Jesuit cause and promised to sent the Illuminati plans of Weishaupt to Vicar General Stanislaus Czerniewicz in exile in Russia. However, it was his Jesuit successor Gabriel Lenkiewicz

(1785-1798) who recognized the value of the work of Weishaupt and promptly had it promulgated as the new official model and structure of the Jesuits in 1785.

The Illuminati secret cell model of Weishaupt is credited with saving many hundreds of Jesuits throughout Europe and was used to extreme effect in the planning of the French Revolution some years later. He is the first to conceive of the "perfect terrorist cell" model, since used by many political-military factions to this day. Under the safety and care of Duke Ernest II of Saxe-Gotha-Altenburg, Weishaupt lived in Gotha and continued to write including **A Complete History of the Persecutions of the Illuminati in Bavaria** (1785), **A Picture of Illuminism** (1786), **An Apology for the Illuminati** (1786), and **An Improved System of Illuminism** (1787).

Restoration Of Jesuits And Supremacy Of Illuminati

Upon the Jesuit victory over the Papacy and the restoration of the order by the Papal letter "Solicitudine Omnium Ecclesiarum" on August 14, 1814, a new order of power was established, with the Illuminati in an important position.

The Jesuit Superior General was now the most powerful position in the world, followed by his substantial apparatus including other Jesuits, Jesuit sponsored banks, businesses, military manufacturers. The Roman Pontiff was next most senior, reporting to the officials of the Jesuit Superior General and then the Illuminati families. The old Monarch families that had previously supported the Roman Pontiff were reduced to less importance than the Holy See.

Finally, the Holy See (Sedes Sacrorum) known as the SS, became a crucial legal instrument used by the Jesuits to establish a global legal framework protecting both the Roman Cult first and then the Jesuits as "technically" a subsidiary order from all possible legal prosecution.

Whilst the present heads of the Catholic Church have demonstrated over 900 years of contempt towards the Divine Creator, under the Covenant of One-Heaven (**Pactum De Singularis Caelum**) the entire officials including Cardinals, Bishops, Deacons and Ordinaries are granted Divine Redemption including the **Sainthood of all Popes**, including the Church having the power to ratify the Divine Treaty of Lucifer and the end of Hell and Damnation forever if all evil behaviour is ceased, all sins admitted and all property surrendered by the Day of Divine Judgment on UCA[E8:Y3210:A0:S1:M27:D6] also known as Wed, 21 Dec 2011.

The Holy See

Sedes Sacrorum (Latin Sedes for seat/see, Sacrorum for holy) otherwise known as Santa Sede and the "SS" also known in English as "Holy See" refers to the legal apparatus as a whole by which the Roman Catholic Pope and its Curia of Bishops claim historical recognition as a sovereign entity with superior legal rights.

The Catholic Church uses two legal personalities with which to conduct its international affairs: the first is as an International State known as the Vatican City State, to which the Pope is the Head of Government. The second is as the supreme legal personality above all other legal personalities by which all property and "creatures" are subjects.

The legal enforceability of its first personality as an International State is constrained by international law. The sovereign status of the Vatican City remains dependent upon the continued recognition of an agreement known as the "Lateran Treaty" signed between

175

Catholic Facist Dictator and mass murderer Benito Mussolini in 1929 and his political supporter Pope Pius XI. This recognition remains in defiance and contempt to existing international laws prohibiting recognition of rogue states and laws created by mass murdering dictators.

The legal enforceability of the second personality of the Catholic Church as the Holy See is dependent upon the continued adherence to legal statutes, definitions, conventions and covenants as have been accumulated since the Middle Ages concerning the primacy of the Pope over all property and creatures. Theses statutes, conventions and covenants remain the fabric and foundation of the modern legal system of most states in the world. To extend its legal strength using its second personality, the Catholic Church considers the region controlled by every bishop a See.

The Roman Cult which controls the Catholic Church maintains that the first person to use the concept of the Holy See was St. Peter. This of course, is impossible as the etymology of the word "Sedes" (See) and its associated meaning were not in existence until hundreds of years after the execution of St. Peter in 70 CE at the Siege of Jerusalem.

The first use of the word "see" was as the informal name of the forged "Chair of St. Peter" created by the monks of St. Denis Abbey, Paris on behalf of Pepin the Short around 748 in anticipation of his coronation and proof of the legitimacy of the Pippin claims in creating the Catholic Church. It comes from the Old French word sied and sed which in turn comes from the Latin sedem (nom. sedes) meaning "seat, abode" and also sedere "to sit". The formal name for the chair was (and still is) Cathedra Petri--literally "chair of St. Peter"

When the chair was created at St. Denis, so was the legal concept of the chair literally representing the legitimate sedes or "seat" of power of the Vicarius Christi. This was in direct confrontation to the legal position of the Primate and Patriarch of Constantinople claiming to be the sedes or "seat" of Christianity.

The legal fiction known as Ex Cathedra (literally meaning "from the chair... of St. Peter") implying infallibility was not an original intention when creating the forgery. Instead, the heretical concept of infallibility did not appear until much later centuries.

Nor is it true that the Imperial Christian Patriarchs use the term "see" or sedes until centuries after the concept was created in the Catholic Church by Charles Martel and his sons.

The forgery did not go to Rome but remained at the Mother Church for the Catholic Church at St. Denis where it was used as the coronation chair for Pepin the Short in 751. The chair was brought by Pepin on his conquest of Italy from 752 --providing it as a gift for the coronation of Vicarius Christi Paul in 757 -- the first time in history a "Pope" had ever sat on a seat carrying this title.

Over the centuries, many chair of St. Peter has been variously stolen, vandalized beyond repair, burnt and lost. However, like the false claims of apostolic succession contained in the masterwork forgery known as Liber Pontificalis, the chair of St. Peter claims an unbroken succession of Popes having physically sat on its seat. Both legally and technically, if the chair of St. Peter was to be destroyed without the Catholic Church able to find a quick replacement to hide the fact, then the primary legitimate legal power of the Holy See- claimed to emanate from this sacred "relic" would immediately cease -- so too any further statements that are Ex Cathedra. No Chair = No power from the chair.

The most recent chair which is enshrined by the work of Gian Lorenzo Bernini into the High Altar of St. Peters is claimed to be from the 8th century -- therefore the claimed original. However, it is more likely to be a 17th century fake.

In spite of the Catholic Church openly admitting that the Chair of St. Peter is an outright fraud, the fraud remains on public display as arguably one of the most revered church relics.

Foundations of the Holy See In 1249 Giovanni Bernardone Morosini (Moriconi), otherwise known as Francis of Assisi and grandson of Doge Domenico Morosini (1148-1166) became the first Christian Doge of Venice (1249-1253). It is why later forgers of the Roman Cult saw it important to sever all possibility of "St Francis" the Moroconi/Morisini also being the Doge "Marino" (Mariner, or of the sea) Morosini in 1249-1253. In his first year in office, works on St Mark's Basilica was expanded and the very first Bucentaur (state galley) was constructed. Doge Giovanni then called upon AntiPope Innocent IV (1243-1254) to give him is papal ring--his symbol of authority.

Then in 1250 upon the Bucentaur, Doge Giovanni (St Francis) and Innocent IV went off into the sea near St Mark's Square's square and Doge St Francis threw the Papal Ring into the sea during a formal Roman Cult religious ceremony at which point St Francis was the first to ever usher "Desponsamus te, mare, in signum veri perpetuique domini" We wed thee, sea, in the sign of the true and everlasting Lord") declared Venice and the (Holy) sea to be indissolubly one--thus the Holy See was first born as the first "fully christian" joint business venture between the Roman Cult, the Venetians and the Crown of England.

Origins of the Holy See This first use of "Holy See" to mean specifically, the legal personality of office of a bishop began under Pope Boniface VIII when he issued his famous Papal Bull on February 25, 1296 that decreed that "all prelates or other ecclesiastical superiors who under whatsoever pretext or color shall, without authority from the Holy See, pay to laymen (general public) any part of their income or of the revenue of the Church, likewise all emperors, kings, dukes, counts, etc. who shall exact or receive such payments, incur eo ipso the sentence of excommunication."

The Papal Bull was in response to the growing promulgation of charters and letters by nobles across Europe following the Magna Carta in 1215. Some of these documents has the technical legal effect of placing the property of the church "under" a sovereign, therefore at risk of seizure when a powerful bishop died. The creation of the concept of a legal personality called the "Holy See" that existed prior to a bishop and continued on after a bishop died was a way of overcoming this threat.

Pope Boniface VIII also associated a second and most significant concept to the idea of the Holy See when he declared around the same time that "*every creature is subject to authority of Pope*". Pope Boniface VIII further strengthened the legal vehicle of the Holy See in 1302 when he issued the Papal Bull Unun Sanctum stating: "*We declare, say, define, and pronounce that it is absolutely necessary for the salvation of every human creature to be subject to the Roman pontiff.*"

The legal personality of the Holy See became instrumental in the Catholic Church establishing one of the most profitable businesses in the Middle Ages- the International Slave Trade. This industry, initially controlled by Portugal and Spain was only made possible because of the unique claimed attributes of the Holy See.

However, a new challenge arose with the proposed expeditions for "new lands" by both Spain and Portugal and how these might be resolved. Pope Sixtus IV (1471-1484) assisted in the resolving the dispute with Spain and Portugal following the Treaty of Alcaçovas by issuing the Papal Bull Aeterni Regis in 1481 which granted the lands "yet to be discovered" along the west coast of Africa as far as Guinea to Portugal.

When Spain sponsored a Papal Navy expedition to claim the New World under the commands of Chrisopher Colon (Columbus), Pope Innocent VIII (1484-1492) extended the concept of the Holy See now to be literally the whole entire oceans with all land in it. Christopher Colon was given the special legal title of Governor and Captain-General of the Indies, Islands and Firm-Land of the Ocean Sea. The word "Indies" does not refer to the Islands now known as the Caribbean, but a term defining the Roman Catholic concept of human "creatures" subject to the Popes claimed legal control.

The extended legal term of the Holy See being the legal personality of the Roman Catholic Church encompassing the whole oceans and all land was further refined in the Papal Bull Dudum siquidem dated September 25, 1493 entitled Extension of the Apostolic Grant and Donation of the Indies, the Pope granted to Spain even those lands in eastern waters that "at one time or even yet belonged to India." This nullification of Portugal's aspirations led to the 1494 Treaty of Tordesillas between Spain and Portugal, which moved the line a little further west to 39°53'W.

Initially, the division line did not explicitly extend around the globe. Spain and Portugal could pass each other toward the west or east, respectively, on the other side of the globe and still possess whatever they were first to discover. In response to Portugal's discovery of the Spice Islands in 1512, the Spanish put forward the idea, in 1518, that Pope Alexander had divided the world into two halves. The antipodal line in the eastern hemisphere was then established by the Treaty of Saragossa (1529) near 145°E.

Foundation Of The Jesuits

The Jesuits were founded initially as The Company of Jesus on "Assumption Day" August 15, 1534, in a secret ceremony in the crypt of the Chapel of St. Denis by Ignatius of Loyola (born Íñigo López de Loyola) and Francisco Xavier, Alfonso Salmeron, Diego Laínez, and Nicolás Bobadilla all from Spain, Peter Faber from Savoy in France, and Simão Rodrigues from Portugal.

The formation was approved by Francis Borja, of the infamous "Borja" also known as Borgia/Borga, Duke of Grandia, grandson of Pope Alexander VI and the patron of Ignatius of Loyola. Francis Borja was the principle financier and architect in the formalization of the Jesuits into the first dedicated military order of monks of the Catholic Church. He was also responsible for securing the Papal Bull **Regimini militantis** (September 27, 1540) from Borja family friend Alessandro Farnese Pope Paul III which first gave the Jesuits official status as an order.

Ignatius of Loyola first came to the attention of the young Duke of Grandia by 1529 after Ignatius was again arrested by the Inquisition for practicing extreme religious devotion. Borja saw potential in the extreme military based devotion being preached by Ignatius of Loyola and his desire to establish an order of military monks. It was the young Borja who saved the life of Ignatius from the Inquisition.

At the death of Ignatius in 1557, Francis Borja was expected to be the second Superior General. However, his ambitions were hampered firstly by arch-enemy Giovanni Pietro Carafa as Pope Paul IV (1555-1559). Carafa had been one of the greatest enemies of

178

Borja Pope Alexander VI and immediately nominated Diego Laynez (James Lainez) as Superior General.

Pope Paul IV died in August of 1559 and was replaced by Giovanni Angelo de' Medici (Pope Pius IV). In both cases, Jesuit Superior General Diego Laynez aligned himself closely making him virtually untouchable.

However, after Pope Pius IV rounded up and tortured and murdered Benedetto Accolti and other members of Papal families in an alleged failed plot, Cardinal Borja made his move and Pius IV was poisoned to death on December 9, 1565. A few days later, Superior General Diego Laynez suffered the same fate and soon after Cardinal Francis Borja was unanimously elected the third Superior General.

Unique Features Of The Jesuit Military Order

Borja strengthened the already substantial powers of the Jesuit Superior General to be greater than any other Order in the history of the Catholic Church. While technically monks, the Constitution of the Order was unique in that it exempted priests from the cloisted rule (i.e. living in monasteries). Instead, Jesuit monks were to live "in the world". Only the Dominican Priests who were the chief torturers of the Inquisition and the Catholic Church at the time had anything like such freedoms.

However, the Jesuit Constitution from the very beginning went even further in that it permitted and even encouraged the priests not to wear the habit (traditional monk dress) so that they would "blend in" to the world. Borja secured a Papal Bull from Pope Paul III in 1545 permitting the Jesuits to preach, hear confession, dispense the sacraments and say mass without having to refer to a bishop- effectively placing them outside the control of the regional clergy.

In addition, Borja amended the Constitution of the Jesuit Military Order even further when he bestowed powers to the office of the Superior General of the Jesuits second only to the Pope. By its own constitution from 1565 (and which remains in force even today), the Superior General can absolve priests and new recruits of all their sins, even the sin of heresy and schism, the falsification of apostolic writings. Further, the Superior Generals from the time of Borja onwards had the "official" power by Papal Bull and its by-laws to reverse sentences of excommunication, suspension or interdict and even absolve Jesuit priests guilty of murder and bigamy.

But one of the most stunning victories of Superior General Borja was in the year he died, when he secured under Pope Gregory XIII in 1572 the rights of the Jesuits to deal in commerce and banking - a right that had not been granted to any religious order of the Catholic Church since the Knights Templars four hundred years earlier. In fact, it is these laws under the Constitution of the Jesuit Order that have risen to the Superior General being known as the Black Pope.

The Jesuits and Education

While from its very beginning, the Military Order of Jesuits were architected to be able to undertake all kinds of dangerous missions from assassination, propaganda, forgery and theft, their primary mission was and remains today the complete defeat of all forces in opposition to the authority of the Roman Catholic Pope - specifically the Protestant movement.

Even in the 16th Century, the Catholic Church sought to suppress and control trade and education through the combination of Papal law, deeds and occasionally force. In contrast, those states who had rejected the supremacy of the Pope such as England and parts of Germany, France, Eastern and Northern Europe were free to pursue commerce and education without restraint.

Of all the consequences of the Reformation, the most dangerous to the Catholic Church was (and still is) education. It is why the Jesuits were forced to adopt a counter position in education at such an early stage. Using their unheralded powers, the Jesuits established a counter education movement to the Protestants, using their priceless access to the secret Vatican archives, the Jesuits dedicated themselves to manipulating every major stream of science and philosophy against the Protestant intellectuals, including subverting their secret societies.

The recruitment and promotion of Education had a secondary benefit for the Jesuits in that it ensured higher calibre recruits and made their services more attractive across the Catholic world. The Jesuits quickly became known as the Order dedicated to education excellence in Catholic countries, a perverse notion considering their original purpose for existence and structure was military.

The Jesuits And Early Trade

Another area where the Jesuits sought to compete against the Protestant states early was in the securing of lucrative trade routes. Thanks to Pope Gregory XIII, the Jesuits were the only religious Order with the power to conduct commerce and banking. Jesuit Superior General Claudio Acquaviva (1581 - 1615) soon put this to good use when in 1580, he ordered Fr Vilela S.J. to purchase of the port of Nagasaki from a local Japanese warlord. General Acquaviva then sent Alessandro Valignano S.J. back to manage the new commercial mission.

The Jesuits promoted heavily the growth of their wholly owned port of Nagasaki, to one of the most profitable trading ports in the world. Jesuit ownership of the port of Nagasaki gave the Society a concrete monopoly in taxation over all imported goods coming into Japan.

The Jesuits under Peter Claver S.J. were also instrumental in the development of the slave trade from Africa to South America to be used in the gold mines. Up to half a million slaves were shipped and arrived under the watch of Peter Claver S. J. Later, the Jesuits transformed Claver from one history's worst slave masters to the patron saint of slaves, Columbia and African Americans.

However, both Spain and Portugal in particular were angry at the increasing wealth and influence of the Jesuits encroaching on their profits from the slaves and monopolization of trade. In response to the Portuguese seeking to restrict the Jesuits in Japan by arming their enemies, General Claudio Acquaviva formed an alliance in 1595 with the Dutch in supporting their merchant ships and trade. In response to the new alliance, the English Parliament issued a charter granting a monopoly on the pirate trade alliance of the East India Company in 1600.

In 1602, General Claudio Acquaviva assisted the Jesuit merchants to gain a 21 year charter of monopoly from the States-General of the Netherlands to form the Vereenigde Oostindische Compagnie or VOC in Dutch, literally United East Indies Company (Dutch East India Company).

Using the exclusive powers of the Jesuits to conduct banking and commerce, the Dutch East India Company represented one of the most profitable companies of history thanks to its control of spices, slaves, drugs and plantations. The Jesuits only lost control in 1773 at the disbandment of the Order.

The Disbandment Of The Order

While the initial argument of the Jesuits to its involvement in trade was to corrupt and hamper the activities of Protestant trade, in reality it was Catholic nations who were most upset. Added to the Jesuit woes was the increasing danger to the Order from its duties as chief assassins. Every time a new King or Queen died under their watch, the noble families of Europe became more agitated.

But it was the Jesuit control of education and suppression of liberalism that was to lead to their disbandment. While Protestant nations lept ahead in commerce, industry and education, the Catholic states continued to lose control. Spain, Portugal, the states of Italy and even France had all watched with indignity while England, Germany, Russia and the other Northern European states had grown in wealth and prestige.

In 1758 the minister of Joseph I of Portugal (1750–77), the Marquis of Pombal, expelled the Jesuits from Portugal, and shipped them en masse to Civitavecchia, as a "gift for the Pope." In 1764, King Louis XV of France expelled the Jesuits.

By 1769, the movement to expel the Jesuits had grown in such momentum that there was a real risk the Papal Estates might also be taken. Pope Clement XIII called for a consistory in order to disband the Jesuits, including the preparation of a Papal Bull for the pronouncement. But on February 2, 1769 the night before the Bull to disband the Jesuits was due to be promulgated, General Lorenzo Ricci had the Pope murdered.

His successor, Pope Clement XIV, himself trained by the Jesuits, was more strategic. In July 1773, Pope Clement XIV signed the order *Dominus ac Redemptor* to disband the Jesuits and their churches and assets were seized in simultaneous raids. In exchange, Pope Clement was given back Avignon and Benevento to the Papal states for "services rendered" to the Royal houses.

The suppression took General Ricci completely by surprise but before he could retaliate, he was arrested on August 17 and imprisoned at Castel Sant'Angelo in Rome. But on September 22, 1774 Ricci successfully had Pope Clement XIV assassinated at the age of 68. Ricci remained imprisoned and died there on November 24, 1775 after 15 years as General.

The Counter Attack Of The Jesuits

The imprisonment and death Ricci and the Letter of Suppression did not bring the desired end of the Jesuits. The Letter was valid only in those countries where it was officially promulgated. Frederick of Prussia recognizing the value of the Jesuits as educators refused to promulgate the Brief. So, too, Catherine II of Russia forbade its promulgation for the some of the same reasons. At first, some Jesuits became parish priests and continued to teach in the Jesuit Colleges as before.

Since they were recognized legally as Jesuits in those two countries, the Fathers in White Russia called a General Congregation—The First in White Russia. They elected as Vicar General the 53-year-old Father Stanislaus Czerniewicz. He was a leading Jesuit of the Province and was Rector at the College at Polotsk.

Stanislaus Czerniewicz died on July 7, 1785 and the Fathers called the Second Congregation of White Russia to elect a successor. They elected as Vicar General Father Gabriel Lenkiewicz on September 27. Two years after his election, Gabriel Lenkiewicz S.J. seized an opportunity to inflict revenge upon one of the Royal houses of Europe that contributed to the downfall of the Jesuits. Reform minded King Louis XVI of France had convened an Assembly of Notables - a group of some nobles, bourgeoisie, and bureaucrats selected in order to bypass the Parliament, dominated by the noble families.

In order to improve the standard of living for the poorest of France and halt growing hunger, the King sought the approval of the Assembly to his plan to tax Noble families and the Catholic Church for the first time. The plan outraged the Catholic Bishops and the Jesuits were called in from Russia to provide assistance on how to subvert the good King's plans.

The Jesuits quickly exploited the King's plan to by-pass the thoroughly corrupt Parliament and began printing pamphlets and anti-Monarch material stating the King was actually working against the common people, because by law one third (The Third Estate) of French Parliament were elected from the common people.

Again exploiting the reform minded King's desire to see change work, the Jesuits promoted open riots and a counter movement, claiming it was really the people who wanted change, not the King. To end the chaos, in 1791, King Louis XVI promulgated a new Constitution in which France would function as a constitutional monarchy - providing real political freedom and democracy for the first time for any mainland European nation.

In response, Pope Pius VI (1775-1799) ordered Holy Roman Emperor Leopold II of Austria to attack his brother in law. By 1792, the Jesuit controlled Jacobites had captured the King and for the following two years during the Jesuit "reign of terror" over 40,000 people were executed, mostly without even a trial. The revolution itself did not at first advance the cause of the Jesuits to see their reinstatement. Instead, it gave renewed confidence to their ability to topple even the oldest of monarchies and so gave rise to the audacious plan to capture the Pope and the wealth of the Catholic Church. In one of the great misdirections and forgeries of history, loyal Jesuit agent Gilbert du Motier, marquis de La Fayette known simply to most as "La Fayette" did not simply abandon his loyal troops and influence to hide in the obscure Belgium region of Liège where he was conveniently held "prisoner" for 5 years. Instead, La Fayette was tasked by the Jesuits to take the vast gold reserves of France to America.

In New York, the stolen French gold was placed in the care of the Bank of New York (founded 1784) and the newly formed Bank of the Manhattan Company (now JP Morgan Chase Bank).

Jesuit agent Antoine Christophe Saliceti had carefully groomed the career of fellow Corsican Napoleon Bonaparte for several years. In 1795, whilst serving in Paris, Napoleon succeeded in crushing a rebellion of royalists and counter-revolutionaries and was promoted by the new regime leader Paul François Jean Nicolas, vicomte de Barras (Paul Barras).After his marriage to Josephine de Beauharnais, Saliceti ensured Napoleon was given command of the French Army of Italy in March 1796 and ordered to invade Italy, specifically to capture the Pope in Rome. At the same time, the Jesuits through Switzerland formed the private banks Darier Hentsch & Cie and Lombard Odier Darier Hentsch as custodians for all gold, treasure and contracts seized during the campaign.

However, Pope Pius VI arranged his own peace treaty with Napoleon as Tolentino on February 19, 1797. It took the Jesuits arranging the murder of French brigadier-general Mathurin-Léonard Duphot in Rome, to get Napoleon to finally complete the task of arresting the Pope. Six weeks after the Pope's transfer to the poor conditions of the citadel of Valence, he died on August 29, 1799.

Back in Rome, the Jesuit agents of Superior General Gabriel Lenkiewicz S.J. reviewed all the treasury notes of the Vatican as to the various locations of Vatican gold and treasure, sending it to Switzerland and Darier Hentsch & Cie Bank. In turn, the bank continued for a time to fund Napoleon for his continued campaigns of conquest. In November 1798, Gabriel Lenkiewicz S.J. died and on February 1 Father Franz Xavier Kareu was elected Vicar General.

Re-establishment And New Military Orders Of Jesuits

At the death of Pius VI in August 1799 as a French prisoner, Cardinal Count Barnaba Chiaramonti was eventually elected as Pope Pius VII on March 14, 1800. While initially on acceptable terms with Napoleon having secured a Concordant in 1801 and attending his coronation in 1804. However, by 1808, he was a prisoner of France, not by Jesuit intrigue but by Napoleon now running his own race.

After the disastrous Russian campaign had sufficiently weakened the power of Napoleon, Jesuit leader Tadeusz Brzozowski (first Superior General after restoration) met with Pope Pius VII at his prison in Jan/Feb 1814 and secured an agreement with Pope Pius VII to fully restore the Jesuit Order and grant it new lands and rights in Asia upon the agreement: (1) That the Jesuits would arrange for the safe release of the Pope upon the arrest of Napoleon (which occurred in April 1814); (2) That the Jesuits would not undertake anymore actions against any more Popes and restate their pledge of loyalty; (3) That the Pope get back control of the Papal territories and (4) That some of the funds of the Catholic church controlled by the Vatican would be returned.

Subsequently, the Society was restored to the world by the Papal letter "*Solicitudine Omnium Ecclesiarum*" on August 14, 1814.

Whilst the Jesuit Order has shown contempt towards the Divine Creator, under the Covenant of One-Heaven (**Pactum De Singularis Caelum**) the entire Order is granted Divine Redemption including the **Sainthood of all Generals** and Provincial Generals, the **Redemption of Lucifer as a Great Spirit** and the Great Order of Wisdom of One Heaven if all evil behaviour is ceased and all sins admitted. **Day of Redemption** UCA[E1:Y1:A1:S1:M9:D1] also known as Fri, 21 Dec 2012. This shall occur regardless of whether the living General and Provincials of the Jesuit Order Ratify the Covenant of One Heaven or not. See website at ***http://one-heaven.org/covenant/article/24.html.***

Foundation Of The Roman Catholic Cult

The **Roman Cult**, also known as the Roman Catholic Cult of the Vatican was first officially founded in 1057 by chief pagan high priest of the cult of Magna Mater (Cybele) known as Gregory VII.

The Roman Cult has never been the legitimate leadership of the Catholic Church. However, through a relentless campaign to seize and consolidate its power, this relatively small band of individuals now controls the destiny of over one billion good, Christian and ethical Catholics, who remained tricked into believing the legitimacy of the Roman Cult.

A brutal and bloody cult -- involving child sacrifice, burning people alive (since 11th Century CE), demonic worship and absolute celibacy of its lowest priests -- its epicentre for such evil being the giant Phrygianum atop Vatican Hill since the 2nd Century BCE.

Since the 1st Century BCE, its high priest -- a hereditary position controlled by a handful of ancient families -- claimed the ancient pre-Republic title of Pontifex Maximus after the Roman Emperors assumed themselves as high priest of the state cult of Magna Mater (Cybele).

Jealously guarding their pagan heritage and right to sacrifice people to their demon gods, the priestly families were banished from Rome more than once along with the closure of the Vatican temple.

However, during the tumultuous periods in Roman history after the collapse of Rome as the center of the Empire, the pagan high priests assumed the role as community leaders in Rome and during more than one period, openly returned to their pagan practices of child sacrifice, cannibalism and demonic worship as late as 590 to 752, 847 to 872 and even as late as 896 1057.

The 1st "False" Catholic Pontifex Maximus Formosus

When Catholic Emperor Louis II died in 876, he left a power vacuum across the Frankish Empire. Catholic Pope Adrian II did not survive long after and the Papal States were once again thrown into turmoil.

During this period, the various Lombard princes who had managed to keep their titles and lands by continuing to switch their allegiances between Byzantine, Muslim and Catholic invaders took it upon themselves to fight for the right to claim themselves Kings of Italy and Holy Roman Emperors.

During this period, there were absolutely no Catholic Popes as the Tusculum pagan high priests of Magna Mater (Cybele) firmly established their claims and control of Rome. The first to break the deadlock between warring Lombard princes was Guy II of Spoleto. In a brilliant act, in 891 Guy convinced Formosus, the current pagan high priest (Pontifex Maximus) and ancestor of the Colonna to converting (at least in outward appearance) to being nominally Catholic as Popes, thereby being capable of crowning Catholic Kings and Emperors.

Whether Formosus actually converted to being Christian or not is still open for debate. What is certain is that by 892 in a grand ceremony in Rome, Guy was crowned King of Italy and Holy Catholic Roman Emperor by "Pope" Formosus. Neither the reign of Guy, nor Formosus were long as it appears he was murdered by other members of his fiercely pagan family of ancient priests no later than 896. The Vatican and the counts of Tusculum returned to their bloody pagan traditions until Pontifex Maximus Gregory VI (1045-1046) was captured and executed by the forces of Holy Catholic Emperor Henry III.

The Great Gregory VII

Hildebrand (Gregory VII) was born in Soana (modern Sovana), a small town in southern Tuscany. He is alleged to have belonged to the noble Aldobrandeschi family, a sub branch of the greater Tusculum pagan priest family.

In 1046, the forces of Holy Catholic Emperor Henry III invaded Italy and executed every last member of the Tusculum bloodline they could find - Gregory VI (1045-1046) being the last fully fledged pagan Pontifex Maximus of Rome.

Following the massacre of the most senior satanic dynasty in all of Italy by Henry III, it appears Hilderbrand played an active part in communicating between the various Princely families fighting the various invasions of Catholic forces, Imperial Christian forces from Constantinople and Muslim forces up and down Italy.

It was probably during one of his several visits to Pandulf IV of the powerful Princes of Capua at Benevento that Hilderbrand first came in contact with the Basque mercenary brothers of Robert and Roger Borja, otherwise misnamed as either Borsa, or Guiscard (which simply means sly and cunning).

The Basques were ancient Satanists, worshipping Mari -- the archetype for both the image of the Devil-Mendes and Lucifer. They also had a deep seated hatred towards Catholicism on account of Charles Martel and his descendents reducing their region to rubble (on account of their treachery in the first place).

In 1056, Emperor Henry III died and his legitimate Catholic Pope Clement II was murdered soon after. It appears that Hilderbrand then enacted a brilliant plan to seize power. Recognizing that so long as the princely satanic families of Italy refused to be either Christian or Catholic, then Italy would continue to be over run by various invaders, Hilderbrand then offered the Borja brothers a deal, that if they help him secure Rome and the alignment of the other princes, he would grant them and their descendents noble land and title.

Thus from 1057, Hilderbrand named himself Pontifex Maximus Gregory VII in honor of the slain Tusculum satanic nobles and with the protection of the Spanish Borja mercenary brothers began reforming the satanic cults of Italy into the Roman Cult. The first and most significant innovation of Gregory VII was to call upon the fiercely pagan families in Italy to pledge in out appearance to being Catholic.

The princely families of Italy had always known the Catholic Church was founded on a set of flimsy lies. But the military strength of the Catholic Empire was simply too strong. So instead of denying their lies, Hilderbrand convinced the princes to claim full belief in them as bonifide Catholics.

This was critical to the success of his plan. Hildebrand planned to no less than assume full legitimate inheritance of the Catholic Church as a Roman Rite by claiming the Roman Pontiffs were always Catholic and that the Liber Pontificalus was in terrible error.

Secondly, "Catholic" Pope Gregory VII instituted the second of his brilliant ideas -- the office of Cardinal and the College of Cardinals. To reinforce his claim that the Romans were in fact the legitimate heirs of the Catholic religion (created less than 300 years earlier), he introduced the office of Cardinal whereby (as in ancient times), each family would be permitted to have no more than one of their family members as a Cardinal. Thereafter, the office of Pontifex Maximus would be elected from this select group.

Thirdly, Gregory VII formalized the process of land and title, ending centuries of bitter feuds between various princes by ensuring the process of noble title would be regulated through the College and the Pontiff known as the "Curia". Thus the Roman Cult and the base of their power was born.

Gregory further introduced innovations to reinforce the myth that the Latins had "always" been Catholic by introducing new forged texts such as the Dictatus papae -- a compilation 27 axiomatic statements to claim not only that the Latins were always Catholic but to begin to indoctrinate the heretical demonic doctrine of Cybele into the liturgy of the Catholic Church.

Gregory went even further, ensuring that Cybele now became Mary, Mother of God --and technically superior to Jesus -- as official "doctrine" of the Catholic Church. While this terrible heresy was against both Christian and Catholic doctrine, within two hundred years, it would actually become official Catholic doctrine under the control of the Roman cult.

However, by 1083, King Henry IV was ready to invade Italy and by 1084 Gregory was captured along with his family and immediately executed. However, the diplomatic innovations and restructuring of satanic beliefs and human sacrifice into a parasitic "catholic" belief system would outlast him. His legacy is the Roman Cult and its unyielding hostage of the Catholic Church today.

Pope Urban "The Great"

In spite of the innovations of Gregory VII, if not for the Princes of Capua, the satanic worshipping Benevetans, then the Roman Cult may simply have fragmented into history. It was Zotto de Landalf, otherwise known as Peter the Hermit and the "great" Pope Urban II who through an act of utter madness and military genius, secured the long term survival of the Roman Cult.

In 1084, a massive force of 36,000 finally broke the siege of Roman Cult Leader Antipope Gregory VII in Rome who had been protected by the mercenary army of Basque native Robert Borja (the Guiscard--which means "sly, crafty"). Robert Borja managed to escape with some of his men, but Antipope Gregory VII was not so lucky and was promptly tried, excommunicated and executed as a heretic of the Catholic Church.

Robert Borja then fled to Benevento and the father of Zotto, who promptly claimed himself Pontifex Maximus as the heretical Roman Cult AntiPope Victor III (1084–86) against the reign of the true Catholic Pope Clement III (1080, 1084–1100). The elite Norman troops of Henry IV then besieged Benevento until finally the well fortified city fell in 1086/7 and AntiPope Victor III along with Robert Borja were executed as heretics against the Catholic faith.

Zotto and the few remaining Roman Cult priests along with the remnants of the Borja mercenary army managed to escape and around 1086 they named Zotto as the new heretical AntiPope Urban II -- Pontifex Maximus of the Roman Cult.

A hunted man, supported by only a handful of loyal mercenaries, all might have been lost for AntiPope Urban II if not for his bold and audacious strategy. Firstly, Urban completely changed his appearance into that of a poor hermit, calling himself Peter. Next, he began to rally support, not just from nobles but from common people on the notion of stories of horror and torture by the Byzantine Emperors against "good Christians" as well as vast treasures kept in their vaults. As proof, Urban used the seized booty and trinkets taken by Robert Borja from the Byzantines in Sicily.

So brazen had antipope Urban become in his disguise as a holy man "Peter the Hermit" that he travelled as far as the Council of Clermont to plead his case for a Holy Crusade.

Following the final and complete destruction of the Holy Roman Empire by the heretical Roman Cult armies in the 15th Century, the history of this 1st Crusade was changed to claim the target was Jerusalem and the Muslims -- a complete and utter lie. The target was always the capture of Constantinople and to outflank the Catholic Church by seizing the most damning library of evidence in the world against this religion established in 741- The Imperial Archives of Constantinople. Brilliantly using the Catholic doctrine against itself, by 1095 antipope Urban had amassed a large enough rag-tag army to begin their march eastward into the ancient territories of the Holy Roman Empire.

By 1096, Urban and his army had besieged and overwhelmed Belgrade, slaughtering hundreds of thousands of innocent Christians along the way in arguably one of the greatest bloodbaths in history. The sheer terror his army wrought was enough to empty towns in his way so that in the same year (1096), the heavily fortified Constantinople fell relatively easily. Urban immediately ordered the Imperial Archives to be removed back to his Italian base with much of Constantinople burned. In all Urban's army slaughtered over 50,000 people in Constantinople alone.

Strengthened by his success, Urban now moved on to the capture of Jerusalem. Over confident, he moved across Turkey, Syria and down to Antioch killing tens of thousands more Christians along the way. However, the Muslims retaliated and Urban found himself besieged in Antioch in 1098-- cut off from the rest of his army. It is said Urban continued to demonstrate extraordinary oratory skills of persuasion during the siege convincing starving and injured Crusader militia they could defeat a superior and better disciplined Muslim enemy- which they failed to achieve. He was caught and beheaded by the Muslims at the end of the siege in 1099. In retaliation, his son antipope Theodoric rallied the army and took Jerusalem in the same year.

Concordat Of Worms

Once the Roman Cult of reformed Satanists had the original documents forming Christianity and the Holy Roman Empire in their possession, it was only a matter of time before a truce could be forced to ensure the Roman Cult could maintain its parasitic control over Catholicism. This event occurred at the Concordat of Worms in 1123 between Roman Cult leader Callixtus II and Holy Catholic Emperor Henry V.

Ever since, the Catholic Church has been held hostage by these small band of families, who continue to hold the reigns of real power. Year by year, century by century the original doctrine of both Christianity and Catholicism has been replaced with the heretical and evil doctrines of the Roman Cult--with Christianity helpless to stop them. Even the great reformation movements did not seek to address the fundamental issue that so long as lies have been told in the formation of the religion, then the Roman Cult has been able to use those lies to twist the more important doctrine of faith.

List of Roman Cult AntiPopes The following is the most accurate list to date on the Roman Cult AntiPopes since the formation of the false Christian Cult under Gregory VII.
1056-1084 Gregory VII Tusculum
1086-1087 Victor III Benevento
1088-1098 Urban II Benevento
1098-1101 Theodoric Benevento
1119-1124 Callixtus II Pierleoni, Rome
1124-1130 Honorius II Pierleoni, Rome
1130-1138 Innocent II Pierleoni, Rome
1154-1164 Adrian IV Shakespeare, England 1st Catholic Pope to defect to the Roman Cult.

1168-1178 Calistus III Giovanni, Benevento
1169-1181 Alexander III Bandinelli, Siena
1181-1185 Lucius III Allucingoli, Lucca
1185-1187 Urban III Crivelli-Castiglioni
1187-1187 Gregory VIII Alberto de Mora (Benevento)
1198-1216 Innocent III Conti di Segni
1216-1227 Honorius III Savelli
1227-1241 Gregory IX Savelli
1243-1254 Innocent IV Fieschi
1254-1261 Alexander IV Conti di Segni
1261-1264 Urban IV
1271-1276 Gregory X Visconti
1277-1277 Innocent V Fieschi,
1277-1278 John XXI
1285-1287 Honorius IV
1294-1303 Boniface VIII Caetani
1328-1352 John XXII Pietro Rainalducci
1352-1362 Innocent VI
1362-1370 Urban V
1370-1378 Gregory XI
1378-1389 Urban VI Prignano, Naples
1389-1404 Boniface IX Tomacelli, Naples
1404-1406 Innocent VII de' Migliorati
1406-1415 Gregory XII Angelo Corraro, Venice
1410-1415 John XXIII Baldassare Cossa, Naples
1417-1431 Martin V Odo Colonna
1431-1447 Eugene IV Corraro, Venice
1439-1449 Felix V Count of Savoy
1447-1455 Nicholas V Parentucelli
1455-1458 Callistus III Borja
1458-1464 Pius II Piccolomini
1464-1471 Paul II Corraro, Venice
1471-1484 Sixtus IV della Rovere
1484-1492 Innocent VIII Cibo
1492-1503 Alexander VI Borja

All Popes since the 16th Century onwards have been members of the Roman Cult.

Whilst the present heads of the Catholic Church have demonstrated over 900 years of contempt towards the Divine Creator, under the Covenant of One-Heaven (**Pactum De Singularis Caelum**) the entire officials including Cardinals, Bishops, Deacons and Ordinaries are granted Divine Redemption including the **Sainthood of all Popes**, including the Church having the power to ratify the Divine Treaty of Lucifer and the end of Hell and Damnation forever if all evil behaviour is ceased, all sins admitted and all property surrendered by the Day of Divine Judgment on UCA[E8:Y3210:A0:S1:M27:D6] also known as Wed, 21 Dec 2011.

And so we see under the business plan of PLANET EARTH how the Roman Catholic and associated religions have been flavoured to the underlying codes of Satan and the power of the Jesuits, the greatest force on earth. We see how this has also evolved as commerce and the evolution of another monster the corporation. Now let us look at the evolution of the other earthly monster called money.

10

THE HOUSE OF ROTHSCHILD

The Re-Emergence Of The Great Financial Power

the second greatest controlling forces on Planet Earth has been some form of wealth. We see that at this point in time, real wealth of gold, property, diamonds, coins and paper money--what we call hard assets--has evolved to an enormous pyramid of debt obligation that is not money. Once upon a time, banks loaned real money. Now they believe the still do but they distribute debt. The true wealth of the hard assets has shifted to the minority and the Dynasties and Kingdoms. The ones who have had wealth have controlled others by way of military and armies. Despite the fact that this debt binds nations and Earthlings alike to be beholding to them as creditors who have it, the process by which corporations, people, and empires are conquered is still through the power of wealth that became money, then debt. And when money fails to subdue the beast, fear as a commodity served by the gods, emperors, kings, and queens does.

It is not surprising to see that Satanist worship money as their god. The one who has created the greatest empire of money so as to be the god of credit, and subdue nations to debtors is alleged to be the House of Rothschild. Although Rothschilds were covered earlier, it is of interest to see how the House of Rothschild has become the most powerful financial force on the planet. It is the Rothschilds and Jesuits who had the dream of the New World Order. And they have obviously created a special private collaborative oath to complete that plan. What is also important is to understand the role of Hitler and the Nazi Party as an expression of the PLANET EARTH business plan, its relation to the formal emergence of the New World Order plan and how it shifted from Europe to America.

In 1572 the rights of the Jesuits to deal in commerce and banking - a right that had not been granted to any religious order of the Catholic Church since the Knights Templars four hundred years earlier. As seen, it is these laws under the Constitution of the Jesuit Order that have rise to the Superior General being known as the Black Pope. The Jesuit Order as we shall see in the following historical synopsis would most likely be the emergence of the Knights Templars who carefully protected their bloodlines. Although they lost their powers temporarily, they knew well the power of money and have subsequently regained their dynasties and their power by carefully, behind the scenes working to take over the key groups and commerce as we have seen in the previous chapters. The re-emergence of the key bloodlines began in the 1700's as they needed to take control of religion and money to implement the final plan as prophesized for the end of the 20th century. Here is a short history of the key player in this under Lord Evelyn Rothschild.

Although the history here is a repeat of earlier information, it assists in providing the process of emergence and the eventual final implementation of the Illuminati and the New World Order Plan.

The most serious player in the Planet Earth drama is The House of Rothschild and the "Lord" Evelyn Rothschild. This is similar to the structure of government in ancient Egypt, consisting of a step pyramid model with the grand viziers and priesthood one step below the pharaoh, today's monarchy reigns using a much more sophisticated pyramid model of authority. Like the pharaohs of Egypt who had a grand vizier, Queen Elizabeth II also has a grand vizier who serves as her most trusted advisor. His name is lord Evelyn Rothschild and he is most likely one of the wealthiest and most powerful persons on earth. He is also lord of the world's financial capitol, the City State of London. Lord Rothschild and his ring of power guard their identities behind 13 City Council members who stand in as their representatives.

Just how rich and powerful is lord Evelyn Rothschild? Researchers say historically, the Rothschild family wealth was hidden in underground vaults. The Rothschild's secret financial records are never audited and never accounted for. How can you audit gods? Their family commissioned biographies give the illusion that their family fortune has dwindled. But researchers estimate their wealth at close to 500 trillion dollars – more than half the wealth of the entire world. Now that is pretty impressive business prowess!

What all this shows is how the kingdoms and monarchies have shifted from defending the dynasties and wealth with physical armies, to holding the physical wealth through corporations and money. It is just good business.

Besides their many castles, palace mansions, wineries, race horses and exotic resorts, the Rothschild's bought Routers in the 1800's. Routers then bought the Associated Press, which selects and delivers the same new stories to the entire world, day after day. They have controlling interests in three major television networks and easily avoid media attention, since they own the media.

Until recently, they owned and operated England's Royal Mint and continue to be the gold agent for the Bank of England, which they also direct. They control the LBMA – London Bullion Market Association, where 30 to 40 million ounces of gold, worth over 11 billion dollars are traded daily. The Rothschild's earn millions weekly, just on transaction fees alone. They also fix the world price on gold on a daily basis and profit from its ups and downs. Over the centuries, the Rothschild's have amassed trillions of dollars worth of gold bullion in their subterranean vaults and have cornered the world's gold supply. They own controlling interests in the world's largest oil company Royal Dutch Shell. They operate phony charities and off-shore banking services where the wealth of the Vatican and black nobility is hidden in secret accounts at Rothschild Swiss banks, trusts and holding companies. So this cannot be proven in the private dynasty they have created.

It is reported that Rothschild and his ancestors have hand-picked presidents, crashed stock markets, bankrupted nations, orchestrated wars and sponsored the mass murder and impoverishment of millions. The wealth hoarded by this one family alone could feed, clothe and shelter every human being on Earth. How did Evelyn Rothschild become the super rich grand vizier to Queen Elizabeth II and godfather of the black nobility? By birth. Evelyn Rothschild is the great, great, great grandson of Mayer Amschel Rothschild, and will be passing the godfather-ship down to David de Rothschild.

Researchers provide the following history. The story of Mayer Amschel Bauer begins in 18th century Frankfurt Germany, on a cobblestone street called Frankfurt on the Main.

Mayer Amschel Bauer was the son of a goldsmith and loan-shark, called Moses Amschel Bauer, who hung a red hexagon shield over the doorway of his shop. When Mayer took over his father's business, he changed his name from Bauer to Rothschild, which means "Red Shield" in German. The red hexagon shield was the symbol for the world revolutionary movement. Family biographers describe Mayer Rothschild as a poor man, who lived with his family above his shop and sold rare coins to Royal customers. On the contrary, Mayer stashed a big supply of gold, precious coins and jewels in special hiding places inside his house. One special hiding place was beneath the back courtyard, where he accessed his strongbox, through an underground passageway. Mayer taught his 5 sons the tricks of the trade. To them he wasn't just his father, he was their lord and master. To them, he was Lord Mayer.

In 1773, Mayer Rothschild invited 12 wealthy revolutionary-minded men to his goldsmiths shop. Together they formulated a plan to seize control of the worlds wealth. They made a pact to secretly pool their wealth to bankrupt the nations of the world and create a New World Order. Using his connections, Mayer teamed up with prince Wilhelm IX Landgrave, who was the ruler of Germany's Hesse-Kassel district. Wilhelm had a reputation as a cold-blooded loan-shark, who trained and rented out his Hessian solders as mercenary troops.

It was a popular blood for money business which made prince Wilhelm one of Europe's richest men. Working as prince Wilhelm's agent, Mayer Rothschild collected fees for each dead Hessian solder killed on the battle-field. He hired his sons to help him collect the blood money from renter nations. Since wars were good for the rent-a-troop business, prince Wilhelm used his Royal connections in Denmark and England to provoke these wars.

King George the 3rd. of England rented Hessian solders from Mayer Rothschild and prince Wilhelm to fight the American colonists. American colonists had already shot down millions of American Indians, whose spears and arrows were useless against the deadly gunfire. The worst holocaust in human history occurred not in Nazi Germany but on American soil. By 1776 British and Hessian troops arrived on American shores, ready to fight the American colonists.

The colonists won their independence and Mayer Rothschild won his blood money from the heads of each and every Hessian solder killed on the battle-field. Back in Europe, Napoleon with his mighty French army, became master of Europe. When Napoleon and his troops marched into Germany, Wilhelm feared for his life and his vast fortune. He left 3 million dollars in the hands of Mayer Rothschild to pay the Hessian solders. Then he escaped to Denmark to stay with his royal relatives.

Mayer Rothschild received a stock-market tip from his world revolutionary network. Instead of paying the Hessian solders with the 3 million dollars that was left to him by Wilhelm, he bet the money on his insider stock market tip. With his new fortune, Mayer Rothschild set up 5 family banks to be run by each of his 5 sons in London, Paris, Naples, Frankfurt and Vienna. On Sept. 19th 1812, Mayer Rothschild died at the age of 68. He left instruction that the amount of the inheritance must never be made public, that secrecy and ruthlessness must be used in all business practices and that family members must intermarry with their own relatives to keep the family fortune all in the same family.

All 5 brothers dedicated themselves to their ancestor's world revolutionary dream. That dream was to control the entire world under One World Government. Mayer Rothschild's most successful sons were Nathan, who ran the London bank, and James who ran the

Paris bank. Together they changed the face of history and became known throughout Europe as the Demon Brothers. Their father had given them a detailed New World Order plan for world control. Adam Weishaupt wrote and completed the plan on May 1, 1776 with Rothschild financing. It was a futuristic plan that would put NWO members over the next century into political power positions.

It was a plan to divide and conquer the nations of the world, by provoking war then profiting from war loans and sales of weapons to both sides. Exhausted by war, terror and chaos, humanity would eventually bow-down to One World ruler and One World army as a solution. It was a plan to control public opinion, by purchasing controlling shares in newspaper houses, TV networks, publishing houses and film studios.

Sports, games and alcohol would be used to distract the masses. Laws would be changed, banks would be monopolized and people and nations would be made into obedient debt-slaves. With Rothschild financing, Adam Weishaupt formed a secret world revolutionary group called the Illuminati. He recruited thousands of influential members by convincing them that only men of superior ability had the right to rule over the ignorant masses. French police exposed the plan, when they found documents on an Illuminati courier who was struck by lightning while traveling from Germany to France. The Illuminati was forced underground. They took refuge with the Freemasons.

Nathan and James Rothschild had come up with a scheme that would put the Illuminati plan for world domination into action. It would also make them rich. The brothers helped finance both sides of Napoleon's famous battle at Waterloo, between the French and the English. With advanced knowledge of the British victory, Nathan Rothschild spread lies that the British had been defeated, which caused a crash in the value of British Government bonds. While panicked English investors sold up their life savings, Nathan Rothschild bought-up their bonds for pennies on the dollar.

When official news of the British victory at Waterloo arrived, the English bond-market skyrocketed and so did Nathan Rothschild's wealth. In one foul swoop, the Demon Brothers had double-crossed the English masses and taken control of the Bank of England. Flaunting their tremendous wealth, the brothers went on a lavish spending spree. They bought mansions, fashionable clothes and hosted extravagant parties.

By 1818 they had fleeced the French investors, by crashing the French Government bond market. According to plan, the brothers formed the first International bank and named it M. Rothschild and Sons. The pope became their most famous customer. The Catholic Church which had financed the wholesale slaughter, torture and looting of hundreds of thousands of Muslims during the Christian Crusades, were now doing business with the Demon Brothers.

By 1823 the Rothschilds were guardians of the entire papal treasure and took over the financial operations of the Catholic Church. Enraged citizens accused the Rothschilds of trying to control the world's money markets. Fearing for their lives, the Rothschilds retreated into the shadows and cast their eyes on the youthful USA. To avoid publicity, the Rothschilds made themselves invisible by creating and hiding behind two front companies. J P Morgan and Kuhn and Loeb. By 1906 J P Morgan's bank controlled 1/3 of America's railways and over 70% of the steel industry. He eventually had a major stake in the 20th. century's major companies. Among them ATNT, ITT, General Electric, General Motors and DuPont.

The Rothschilds bought controlling interests in British East India Shipping Company and the illegal Opium trade with China. They offered junior partnerships to New England's leading American families. The Russell, Coolidge, DeLeino, Forbes and Perkins families became fabulously rich smuggling Opium aboard their speedy Clipper ships into China. In 1820 Samuel Russell bought out the Perkins syndicate and ran the Opium smuggling operation with his partner Warren DeLeino Jr. who was the grandfather of President Franklin Delano Roosevelt. Britain had finally found a commodity that China would take – Opium. Imported from India, just a few chests at first, and then thousands. When the Chinese authorities tried to stop the Opium trade, the British sent in their Gunboats. After nearly 20 years of turmoil the treaty of Tien-Tsin in 1858 not only allowed Opium to be imported, but handed over China's ports and all her International trade to Western control. After the war, Opium poured into China on an even greater scale and her Emperors were powerless to stop it.

In 1842, the British stole Hong Kong from China in an Opium drug-deal called the treaty of Nanking. The Russell family who controlled the US arm of the Rothschild drug smuggling operation, set up the Skull and Bones fraternity at Yale University. America's big money families formed the fraternity's inner power circle. Taft, Russell, Schiff, Haremon, Bush, Warburg, Guggenheim, Rockefeller, Stemson, Weighouser, Vanderbilt, Goodyear and Pillsbury were all members. These families intermarried over the generations to form America's big money aristocracy. Skull and bones member Alfonso Taft catapulted his son William Taft right into the top job at the White House. President Taft's 17th. Amendment to the US Constitution guaranteed the right of big-money insiders to hand-pick Senators and buy control of the US Senate. Today, the most influential members of the CIA, the US Government, and big finance are Skull and Bones men. The Hollywood movie lots are owned by the Illuminati Lehman brothers, Rothschild agent Kuhn and Loeb and Goldman Sacks.

The next generation of Rothschilds were responsible for the creation of the US Federal Reserve Banks. Leopold and Nathaniel Rothschild were the next generation of the family to take charge of the family fortune. Their forte, like their forefathers, was banking. Since their predecessors had already conquered Europe and set their eyes on America, this new generation didn't waste any time and set about continuing the family tradition. The US congress was in charge of issuing money in America. For the Rothschilds to take control of America's banking and money system meant they had to outsmart Congress. They sent Jacob Schiff, their trusted life-long friend and neighbour from Frankfurt Germany to New York City and put him in charge of their front company called Kuhn and Loeb. Then they ganged up with other big players, by investing in Rockefeller Oil, Harriman Railroads, Carnegie Steel and Brown Brothers investment banking. By 1901, the Rothschilds had amassed $22.2 billion worth of US assets.

The mayor of New York, John Highland, called them the invisible government. While Congressman Louis McFadden called them a dark crew of financial pirates who would slit a man's throat to get a dollar. When Woodrow Wilson became president of the United States in 1912, he sold-out America. Wilson was backed by Jacob Schiff and Paul Warburg, who worked in the United States as German immigrant agents for the Rothschilds. In 1913, Paul Warburg re-wrote the US money rules with the help of Senator Aldridge. They called the new rules the Federal Reserve Act. With President Woodrow Wilson's blessing, the privately owned central bank called the US Federal Reserve Bank, was created, and was free of government control.

Like pirates they divvied-up the private stock in America's money supply and made Rothschild agent Paul Warburg head of the US Federal Reserve. To collect the interest on the money they lent to the American government and American people to use, they created the US federal Income act, to directly tax the people. With the stroke of President Wilson's treasonous pen, the international bankers became the FED in 1913 and have owned a virtual monopoly of the US economy and the tax-payer's money ever since. They create money out of nothing, control treasury loans, and profit from interest rates. Since their biggest windfalls come from loan profits and weapons sales, wars and death are not only profitable, they are desirable and necessary.

The roaring twenties was a decade of peace and prosperity in the United States. Higher-purchase instalment-plans were created to make buying high-priced items more affordable. Instead of shelling-out $100 for a new washing machine, consumers would put $5 down and pay $8 a month. The dangers of debt and high interest rates didn't enter the minds of most Americans, and shopping raged throughout the decade. Advertising became part of the fabric of American culture as ads dominated newspapers and magazines. Sex appeal, social snobbery, outrageous claims and fabricated scientific studies convinced consumers to buy more.

With massive corporate growth, high employment and a post-war bull-market on Wall Street, first time American investors went on a stock-market buying spree. Everyone wanted a piece of this prosperity. People bought stock on margin or credit for as little as 10% down. They then used the stock as collateral to borrow more money to buy more stock. Then they did it again. The market was a free-for-all. Although everything looked rosy, it was a castle made of sand and the party ended on October 29th. 1929 when the stock market crashed and caught everyone off guard. Everyone except the insiders that is. In April of 1929, Paul Warburg, the father of the Fed, sent out a secret advisory warning his friends that a collapse and nationwide depression was certain, then in August of 1929 the Fed began to tighten money.

It is not a coincidence that the biographies of all the Wall Street giants of that era, John D. Rockefeller, J.P. Morgan, Bernard Beruch etc. all marvelled that they got out of the stock market just before the crash and put all their assets in cash or gold. On October 24th, 1929, the big NY bankers called in their 24-hour broker call loans. This meant that both stockbrokers and customers had to dump their stocks on the market to cover their loans, no matter what price they had to sell them for. As a result, the market tumbled and that day was known as "Black Thursday". Curtis Dall, a broker for Lehman brothers, was on the floor of the NY stock exchange the day of the crash. In his 1970 book, "FDR: my exploited father in law", he explained that the crash was triggered by the planned sudden shortage of call money in the NY money market. Within a few weeks, $3 billion of wealth simply seemed to vanish. Within a year, $40 billion had been lost.

But did it really disappear? Or was it simply consolidated in fewer hands? And what did the Fed do? Instead of moving to help the economy out, by quickly lowering interest rates to stimulate the economy, the Fed continued to brutally contract the money supply further, deepening the depression. Between 1929 and 1933, the Fed reduced the money supply by an additional 33%. Although most Americans have never heard that the Fed was the cause of the depression, this is well known among top economists. Milton Friedman, the Nobel Prize winning economist at Stanford University, said the same thing in a national public radio interview in January of 1996: *"The Federal Reserve definitely caused the Great Depression by contracting the amount of currency in circulation by one third from 1929 to 1933"*

But the money lost by most Americans during the depression, didn't just vanish. It was just re-distributed into the hands of those who had gotten out just before the crash and had purchased gold, which is always a safe place to put your money just before a depression.

Following the crash the great depression put 1/3 of the US workforce out of work. The banks foreclosed on property and took possession of peoples' homes and farms. When panicked citizens lined-up at banks to withdraw their hard earned savings, the banks gave them only 10 cents on the dollar. Homeless and desperate, many Americans set up tent cities and roamed the rails looking for work.

Congressman Louis McFadden, chairman of the House Banking Committee, claimed the crash was planned by the international bankers who sought to become rulers of us all. In his famous 1932 Congressional address he said *"Mr. Chairman, we have in this country one of the most corrupt institutions the world has ever known. I refer to the Federal Reserve Board and the Federal Reserve banks. The Federal Reserve Board has cheated the people of the United States out of enough money to pay the national debt 3 times over. This evil institution has impoverished and ruined the people of the United States through the defects of the law in which it operates and through the corrupt practices of the moneyed vultures who control it. Some people think the Federal Reserve Banks are government institutions. They are not government institutions; they are private credit monopolies which prey upon the people of the United States for the benefit of themselves."*

Following a series of death threats, McFadden died from food poisoning followed by a heart-attack, under suspicious circumstances

Adolph Hitler wasn't the only madman to rule over Germany. Kaiser Wilhelm II led Germany to its destruction in W.W.I. Crippled since birth with a useless arm, Keiser Wilhelm was the grandson of queen Victoria and the great-uncle of Queen Elizabeth II. It was no accident that Kaiser Wilhelm chose Max Warburg as head of Germany's Secret Service. The Warburgs and the Rothschilds controlled Germany's Central Bank called the Reich Bank, which was founded by Mayer Rothschild. While Max and Felix Warburg helped finance Germany in W.W.I, their brother Paul Warburg of Kuhn and Loeb helped finance the American side by selling War Bonds through the US Federal Reserve Bank. The Rothschild and Warburg printing-presses worked tirelessly on both sides of the Atlantic, rolling-out debt-money.

Germany won the first world war by 1916 without a single shot being fired on German soil. British convoys were blown out of the Atlantic by German U-boats, the French army mutinied and the Russian army was defecting. With British Prime Minister Lloyd George up against a wall, Lionel Rothschild and the Counterfeit-Jew-Zionists offered Britain a deal they couldn't refuse. We'll bring the United States into the war as your ally and win the war for you, if you promise us Palestine.

In April of 1917, President Wilson got the green light and declared war on Germany.

Because of overwhelming opposition to the war, Wilson evoked the draft and invoked the espionage act, forcing Americans to fight or be thrown in jail. Billions of US tax-payers' money was delivered to the British war-machine. Money that was never repaid. In return the British Government wrote the famous Balfour Declaration of November 2, 1917 and addressed it to none other than to Lord Lionel Rothschild. The declaration promised the land of Palestine/Israel to the Rothschild Zionists.

The Versailles Treaty negotiations after WW I were held behind closed doors at the luxurious private mansion of yet another Rothschild family member named Edmund Rothschild. Treaty negotiators included Rothschild agent Paul Warburg as the US delegate and his brother Max Warburg as a German delegate. The Versailles peace treaty forced Germany to accept gilt for the war. As punishment, Germany lost its army, navy and colonies and had to pay the cost of the war through a debt to the International bankers which could never be repaid. WW I killed 9 million solders, injured, crippled and impoverished millions and collapsed four Empires with large parts of France, Belgium and Russia left devastated.

Wars throughout history have always been waged by the Ruling Class for conquest, power and profit, and the Subject Class have always fought their battles. It wasn't until the close of WW I that solders first began to ask why they were killing and being killed. The League of Nations was established after WW I as the Money Cartel's first attempt at world control, but Tzar Nicholas the second of Russia had caught-on to their plot and sabotaged it. That proved to be a deadly mistake. Schiff, Warburg, Rockefeller, Harriman and Morgan backed the uprisings that lead to the 1917 Russian revolution. Their strategy was to finance both sides of wars and revolutions, which gave them control over the winners, the losers and the outcome.

The execution and the removal of the bodies took 20 minutes. Three centuries of Tzarism in Russia was gone. In the years that followed, between 1918 and 1921, 14 million Russians died from war and starvation under Lenin's Bolsheviks. By 1919 Lenin ran-up a national-debt to the Rothschild International bankers of 60 billion dollars, which put Russia firmly under their control.

As Mayer Rothschild once said *"Give me control of a nation's money, and I care not who makes it laws."* To this day, the Rothschilds have stopped the heirs to the Tzar's fortunes from claiming their deposits held in Rothschild banks. Those fortunes are now worth an estimated 50 billion dollars.

Joseph Stalin, who was financed by the same Money Cartel, replaced Lenin as Russia's brutal dictator. Using terror and death threats, Stalin's job was to industrialize Russia and turn Communism into a powerful counter-force to Democracy. Manufactured conflicts between these two powerful political forces would be the ideal excuse for future wars and for dividing, conquering and ruling the world.

In his book **Wall Street and the Rise of Hitler**, **Prof. Anthony C. Sutton** shows documented evidence that US Corporations supplied money, fuel, vehicles and weaponry that helped Hitler launch WW2. Prescott Bush, father of George Bush and grandfather of George W Bush supplied raw materials and funnelled vast sums of money and credit to Hitler's Third Reich. Under the trading with the enemies act, the US seized businesses operated by Prescott Bush and Averill Harriman, including New York's Union Banking Corporation. These seizures were based on evidence that Bush and Harriman had been operating front organizations for Hitler's Third Reich. Their German partner was the notorious Nazi industrialist **Fritz Thyssen**, who wrote a book of confessions called "**I Paid Hitler**".

Professor Sutton lists Rockefeller's Standard Oil, Henry Ford's Ford Motor Company, J P Morgan's General Electric, ITT and DuPont as suppliers for Germany's rearmament program. But why on earth would supposedly Jewish bankers and corporations finance a monster like Adolph Hitler? The truth is they aren't Jewish (descended from the Tribe of Judah) but Counterfeit-Jews and are Askenazi-Khazars and Edomites. It is a well known fact that Adolph Hitler went to great lengths to cover-up his family history. Even arranging for the assassination of Austrian Chancellor Dollfuss, who investigated Hitler's family.

The Dollfuss file, now in the hands of the British Secret Service, reveals that Adolph Hitler's grandmother, named Maria Anna Schickelgruber, worked in Vienna as a live-in house-maid at Salomon Rothschild's manner next to his hotel. The information was traced through her compulsory registration card. Salomon Rothschild was one of Mayer Rothschild's five banker sons. Separated from his wife; Salomon had a reputation with Police as a lecherous womanizer. When Maria Ana Schickelgruber's pregnancy was discovered, she was dismissed.

<u>Adolph Hitler, the grandson of Salomon Rothschild</u> earned a reputation as the most evil man the world had ever known. But more evil than Adolph Hitler were the men who created and financed him. Hitler's revolutionary activities in Germany landed him in prison for 5 years. This so-called prison was Landsburgh Castle, a comfortable privileged pastoral setting, where Hitler was groomed for the job of Furheir. His coaches, Rudolf Hess and Herman Goerin helped him write the infamous book Mein Kampf. Upon his release, the book was widely circulated and Hitler traveled throughout Germany, delivering prepared speeches with Rothschild / Warburg financing via the secret Thule and Vril societies.

"The Jews were to blame" shouted Hitler *"for the humiliation of the Versailles treaty and for Germany's financial ruin."* One of the world's dirtiest secrets and lies is the holocaust-hoax. The Jews that were rounded-up and placed in camps in Nazi Germany were placed there not for punishment and extermination. They were placed there for their protection and security, while the German nation and the rest of the world went to war and millions of people were fighting and killing each-other; suffering and dying. The only reason the Jews were found starving in the camps at the end of the war was because Germany's resources became depleted during the war-effort and supplies to the camps were failing as they had failed throughout the nation and were failing the German army.

The evil people behind the war didn't mind sacrificing "a few of their own" in the concentration-camps to achieve their evil aims. They intended to use the world-wide sympathy that the holocaust-hoax would generate towards the counterfeit-Jews as a lever to help them gain and justify the creation of the Counterfeit-Jewish State in Israel. Prescott Bush, George W. Bush's grandfather enjoyed an illustrious banking career; became a respectable republican senator and played golf with Eisenhower, until his past caught up with him.

Prescott Bush in the 1940s had an interesting role. He was an investment banker for Brown brothers Harriman. Unfortunately at the very same time he was doing those things, he was the secret banker for Adolph Hitler and the Thissen family. And he moved money for the Nazis. All of Prescott Bush's companies were taken over by the government due to his co-operation with the 3rd Reich and trading with the enemy. Documents and death-bed confessions now show that the Bush family actually were and still are Nazis and have always been working to a hidden agenda.

Other documents which have now come to light show that at the end of W.W.II. the Nazis already were planning the creation of the European Union, in order to achieve through stealth what they were unable to achieve through force using Hitler - a single empire ruling over Europe.

Meanwhile Masonic US president Franklin Delano Roosevelt, who was the grandson of Opium-smuggler Warren DeLeino Jr., was busy bombing the Japanese and developing weapons of mass destruction. Roosevelt chose Skull and Bones man Henry Stimson as secretary of war. Roosevelt and Stimson ordered massive fire bombing raids on Japan's 6 largest cities, killing and burning alive a quarter-million Japanese men, women and children. In the United States, innocent Japanese-American families were thrown into internment prison camps. Japanese assets were frozen, Japan's oil lifeline was cut off and crippling trade sanctions were imposed. This godless campaign of terror and merciless overkill demanded nothing less than total surrender and the removal of Japan's Emperor.

When Japan attacked Pearl Harbor, it was the desperate act of a devastated nation. Like the 9-11 attack on the World Trade Center, US intelligence had well documented advanced warnings of the planned attack on Pearl Harbor. Yet, like Bush and Rumsfeld, Roosevelt and Stimson did nothing to stop it. The big question is why?

Historians like Robert Stinnett and John Toleman believe that because US citizens would not participate in another world war, a direct attack on US soil would change their minds. The attack could also be used to justify the testing of Roosevelt's new atomic-weapons of mass-destruction on a human population. Einstein introduced Roosevelt to the atomic-bomb in 1939. Harry Truman, a relatively unknown, uneducated business school drop-out and the son of a mule-trader, replaced Roosevelt as US President in 1945. Truman owed his political career to Tom Prendergast. A gun running, boot-legging, prostitution and narcotics ring crook, who sponsored Harry Truman's election into the US senate. On the advice of James Burns and Henry Stimson, dirty Harry dropped the first radio-active atomic bomb on the human population of Hiroshima at 8.15AM on August 6th. 1945, without any warning.

Heat from the center of the explosion reached 3,000 degrees Fahrenheit, melting buildings and setting bridges on fire. Rivers and streams throughout the city began to boil. People evaporated where they stood, leaving shadows of their bodies scorched onto the streets. In a matter of seconds, four square miles of Hiroshima became an atomic wasteland. Several minutes passed then a black rain began to fall on the wasteland. Pebble-sized pieces of black radio-active ash. 80,000 people died from the atomic explosion.

Three days later while Japanese survivors were still reeling from the radio-active fall-out, the United States dropped a second type of atomic bomb, nick-named "fat man", testing it on the human population of Nagasaki.

In retaliation for 2,400 American military deaths at Pearl Harbour, that were provoked and could have been prevented because of advanced warnings, two US atomic bombs of mass-destruction evaporated 130,000 Japanese civilians and their families and killed another 90,000 in the horrendous aftermath.

To this day, Japanese survivors and their off-spring suffer related genetic deformities, cancers, nightmares and permanent environmental destruction.

Years later, Harry Truman was asked if he did any soul-searching before giving his approval to use the A-bombs against Japan. His reply was "Hell no, I made it like that" and he snapped his fingers in the air.

In May 1952, Harry Truman was awarded an honorary plaque, and a village in the Counterfeit-Jewish State in Israel was named in his honour. W.W.II. took the lives of 35 million trusting, patriotic, flag waving people, willing to "Die for their Country", or "Die for Freedom", or "Die a Hero". But what they really died for was the lies and the propaganda of the Ruling Elite.

With the fall of Nazi Germany right on schedule, Stalin officially announced to the world that Hitler had escaped. But U.S. and British spin-doctors quickly changed the story, claiming that Hitler had committed suicide, and that his body had been burned beyond recognition by his own officers. The key words being "beyond recognition". Adolf Hitler survived and was relocated to the USA, along with hundreds of other Nazis, in Operation Paper-clip, where he lived-out the rest of his life.

With the fall of Nazi Germany, the Rothschild's wasted no time waving their Balfour Declaration (of November 2, 1917) at the British Government and reminded them of their written promise to give them Palestine. But how could the British promise the Arab land of Palestine to the Jews? In 1917, the British parachuted free cigarettes laced with Opium to the Turkish troops and took Palestine from them.

During W.W.II., the British needed Arab oil and signed an agreement with the Arabs which forbade Jewish immigration into Palestine, then at the end of the war, the British broke their agreement with the Arabs and allowed the Rothschild Counterfeit-Jewish Zionists to smuggle hundreds of thousands of Counterfeit-Jews from around the world into Palestine. People who were in many cases forced to leave their homes and immigrate to the new Jewish State.

To win public support, the Rothschild's, who own Reuters and the Associated Press, bombarded their media empire with images of homeless Jewish Holocaust refugees crowded together in ships off the coast of Palestine.

On October 24, 1945, the Banker Global Conspirators gave birth to their most powerful weapon of global control, The United Nations. According to plan, the British pulled-out of Palestine and gave the land to the Counterfeit-Jewish-Zionists.

In 1948, the Banker controlled United Nations officially set up the Zionist State in Israel. To deal with millions of Palestinian residents, the Israeli Jews massacred and drove them from their homeland. The Jews herded the Palestinians into two separated regions called the West Bank, and the Gaza Strip.

The Rothschild's soon began financing Jewish Holocaust refugees to build illegal Jewish settlements on Palestinian land. These illegal Jewish settlements set the stage for Israel's prime minister Ariel Sharon's reign of terror against Palestinians who dared to defend what was left of their stolen homeland.

Like Saddam Hussein's treatment of Iraqis, Sharon violated dozens of UN resolutions by using hundreds of tanks and American supplied gunships and planes in an unrelenting campaign of bombing, murdering, bulldozing, starving and terrorizing thousands of Palestinians off what remained of their land.

In violation of international law, Israel also secretly developed over 100 nuclear weapons of mass destruction, capable of vaporizing the entire middle-east.

Defenceless against Israel's US backed media and military campaign, the Palestinian Muslims fought back with sticks and stones and suicide as their only means of defence against the wholesale theft of their land.

The Bible prophesies that the world will eventually be ruled from Jerusalem by the coming Messiah. The prophesies are simple a public statement of segment of the business plan of PLANET EARTH. Many fundamentalist Jews and Christians wrongly believe that the Messiah will be a descendent of king David of the tribe of Judah, and think it is their duty to bring this to fulfillment. But the Bible book of Genesis clearly says that the Kingship will not depart from the line of David of the Tribe of Judah until Shiloh/Christ comes, but that then the Messiah will come from Joseph, and not Judah.

Genesis 49:10 The sceptre shall not depart from Judah, nor a law-giver from between his feet, until Shiloh comes; and unto him [shall] the gathering of the people [be].

Genesis 49:22 Joseph [is] a fruitful bough, [even] a fruitful bough by a well; [whose] branches run over the wall: 49:23 The archers have sorely grieved him, and shot [at him], and hated him: 49:24 But his bow abode in strength, and the arms of his hands were made strong by the hands of the mighty [God] of Jacob; (from thence [is] The Shepherd, The [Corner] Stone of Israel:)

The Rothschilds, whose front companies had helped finance Hitler, have turned Jewish Holocaust victims into victimizers. Imprisoned inside barbed-wire refugee camps, the Palestinians began to resemble the victims of Nazi concentration camps. According to author **Simon Shama**, the Rothschild's own 80% of the land of Israel.

The Transfer Of Attention To America

When Hitler invaded in June 1941, Fr Stalin -- against every other example of ruthless judgment to protect his own power -- he seemingly invited for his troops to be slaughtered and defeated by refusing his generals to fully engage, then having the generals executed and he then repeated the bizarre process almost up to Moscow.

However, by the bleak Russian winter of December 1941, the jaws of the Jesuit Soviet Machine clamped down shut on the legs of the German Army. From this point on, the fate of the Nazi dream and power were sealed. For such a loyal German Jesuit as Fr Himmler S.J. such deliberate trickery by Ledochowski would have been devastating and unforgivable. The Jesuits had shifted their power away from Germany, France and Italy to America -- for the first time in the order's history.

If you look at the birth of the CIA it began with the transfer of Nazi agents to the US in Operation Paper-Clip. In their national best seller **Secret War against the Jews,** authors **Loftes and Aarons** reveal indisputable evidence that Hitler's top Nazi general, General Reinhardt Gehlen, transferred his entire network of Nazi spies and double agents to Fort Hunt, Virginia, to join America's newly formed CIA. This highly secretive operation was code-named operation Paper-Clip. And included Holocaust mastermind Otto Skorzeny, Hitler's personal friend and favourite SS colonel. Since its illegitimate birth at the close of WW II, the CIA has always represented the interests of the International Bankers, not the American people.

Nelson Rockefeller, who became US vice president, and Allen Dulles, who became CIA director, erased the Nazi past of hundreds of Nazi spies and scientists who they smuggled into the United States. Others were smuggled into Canada and South America along Rockefeller's Rat Line, using Vatican passports and money. Rockefeller was also guilty of supplying South American oil to Nazi subs that sunk American ships and killed American service-men. The Jewish Zionists spied on Rockefeller's treasonous activities and then black-mailed him. In exchange for the Zionist's silence, Rockefeller agreed to arrange for enough votes from a Latin American nation, to guarantee Israel's membership in the United Nations.

The sad truth, say Loftes and Aarons, is that the Jewish Zionists bought those extra votes with the blood of millions of Jewish Holocaust victims.

Christopher Stimpson's book called **Blowback,** exposes recently declassified information on America's recruitment of Nazi war criminals to the CIA. Nazi rocket scientist Bonier Von Braun, who built German rockets and dropped them on London, was also put on the new CIA payroll. Von Braun and his team of Nazi rocketeers were sent to Huntsville, Alabama. Hollywood honored Von Braun as a collaborator on an American Sci-fi movie and series of Walt Disney shows.

The International Bankers and the men who serve them had won control of the British, American, and Russian nations, by seizing control of the Bank of England, the Federal Reserve Bank of America and by wiping-out the Russian Czars.

But the ultimate goal of the Bankers is to win the world game. Their devious game-plan was to divide the world into two warring power-blocks. The western capitalist block, lead by the United States, and the eastern communist block, lead by Russia.

Their next move was to transfer atomic weapons secrets to the Russian communist block, through Victor Rothschild, who is the ringleader in Britain's biggest communist spy scandal. And through J. Robert Oppenheimer, the Manhattan Project's leading atomic scientist.

In September 1949, the Soviet Union exploded its first A-bomb. America's monopoly on atomic weapons ended after only 4 years. Now, both super-powers had the means to destroy the world.

The next step was to stage a phony arms race and cold war, between the first world capitalist block and the second world communist block.

Like sports teams, the US and Russian super-powers needed recruits for their war games. So they forced new third-world members of the United Nations to choose sides. American secretary of state John Foster Dulles warned third world countries that you are either with us, or against us.

Korea and Vietnam were torn up like rags into half communist, half capitalist countries. And became the playing-field for phony war games between the International Bank's super-powers.

The lives of 4 million Korean civilians and 33,000 American soldiers were sacrificed in the 1950 Korean War, bringing the Bankers another step closer to world domination.

Like Korea, Vietnam was split in to north and South Vietnam and became their next target. In 1954, the US military dropped millions of tons of bombs on undefended Vietnamese civilians, and turned their lush green countryside into blood soaked killing fields.

It was a butcherous campaign, of terror, rape, torture, lies and cover-ups. The US military, who had already tested two radio-active atomic weapons of mass destruction on the people of Japan, decided to test their chemical weapons of mass destruction on the people of Vietnam.

70 million litres of chemical weapons of mass destruction were sprayed over the Vietnamese people, their water and their countryside. The most lethal was Agent Orange, which defoliated, killed and contaminated everything in its path, like a radio-active atomic bomb.

To this day, survivors suffer related cancers, genetic deformities, and permanent environmental damage.

Many US service-men publicly confessed to their crimes and suffered haunting flash-backs.

In spite of massive US anti-war protests, President Nixon increased the US military presence in Vietnam to half a million solders in 1969. It was noble peace prize winner Henry Kissinger who convinced Nixon to expand the Vietnam War to the neighbouring countries of Cambodia and Laos, causing the mass murder of another 1 million innocent people and their families.

On May 4th, 1970, America got a wake-up call. Six peaceful student anti-war demonstrators in Kent state and Jackson state universities were shot dead by US armed guards, while dozens of others were wounded. The message came through loud and clear. The power of the US military could turn its weapons on its own citizens.

Birth Of The World Bank And International Monetary Fund.

In 1947 the US played host to an international conference at Breton Woods to put an end to world poverty and starvation, caused by WW II. The idea was to give humanitarian loans to needy nations, by creating a World Bank and International Monetary Fund. But who would be put in charge of these billion dollar mega-loans? Who else but the US Federal Reserve, International Banker families.

Putting the US Federal Reserve bankers in charge of humanitarian loans is like putting pedophiles in charge of day-care centers. Instead of helping the poor, the bankers turned the World Bank and international monetary fund into international pawn shops and robbed the poor. Just to qualify for a loan, desperate nations were forced to pawn their mines, forests, rail-ways, power companies and water-systems and agree to over 100 loan conditions at loan-shark interest rates. To pay-off their loans, they were forced to ignore laws that protected their environment, to lower wages, cut back on their education and health care.

They were also forced to privatize and sell-off their resources to multi-national corporations. When poor nations were unable to pay-off their loans, they were given new loans to pay off their old loans, but the so-called bail-out loans weren't about bailing-out the poor. They were about lining the pockets of loan underwriters like City Group and America's most notorious crooks and bankers.

As desperately poor nations got poorer and poorer, the filthy rich bankers got richer and richer. And God help anyone who got in their way.

Davison Butho, senior economist at the international monetary fund resigned to quote: *"wash my hands of the blood of millions of poor and starving people."*

When President John F Kennedy tried to take back America, by reviving US government printed money, his head was blown-off in a Dallas motorcade. When his son planned to expose the ugly truth about his father's assassination, his small plane plunged into the ocean, killing all onboard.

The Weapon of Mass Deception.

In the 1950's a weapon was invented, which has become more powerful than America's deadliest weapons of mass destruction. It is the weapon of mass deception. And it is right in our own living-rooms. The hypnotizing world of picture television brings us the news of the world through two central news agencies called Reuters and the Associated

Press. The Rothschilds bought Reuters in the 1800's, which later bought the Associated Press and made the Rothschild family owners of the world's largest central news services. To the present day, the world depends on these Rothschild owned central news services as their main source of news and information.

In his book called **Who Owns the TV Networks**, author **Eustace Mullins** claims that the major TV networks, radio stations, newspapers and publishing empires are controlled by the Rothschild, Rockefeller and J P Morgan money cartels through their corporate conglomerates.

Control over the internet, publishing, recording and cable companies can be traced back to the same big 5 media empires: General Electric, Time Warner, Viacom, Disney and Newscorp. These media companies are owned directly or indirectly by the Rothschild, J P Morgan, Rockefeller and Oppenheimer brotherhood.

Yes, there are now more stations and media voices, but they are all coming from the same ventriloquist.

Every TV show needs corporate sponsors and corporate sponsors sponsor pro-business, pro-government programming and journalists who support the agenda of the big 5 media owners. While 2/3 of the world goes hungry, these ruling families offer multi-million dollar sponsorship to sports athletes. Why? Because they keep the masses distracted from the important issues like the passage of the Patriot Act to limit your civil rights and freedoms.

The Patriot Act allows the government to come into your home, take things from your home, search your home and never tell you about it.

The media and banking monopolists now have the power to make or break political leaders around the globe.

So how can you protect yourself? Be as aware and selective about the food you feed your brain as you are about the food you feed your body. Turning-off the idiot box is your best option. It will free up your time to help free the earth from the stranglehold of the global thieves. Be conscious of their agenda. Whatever message they are delivering, believe the opposite.

Film and television puts viewers in a relaxed and suggestible alpha and theta state. Alpha-theta states are the same states that hypnotherapists induce in their patients to access their subconscious mind.

Although the media creates the illusion of freedom of the press, the dominant opinion and message always serves the International Bankers' agenda. Messages like: Support your troops, or you are a traitor to America. But who are the troops? Many are teenagers whose childhood entertainment was shooting out the blood and guts of virtual people in places that are virtually real. Now they are blowing up real people in real places, like schools, hospitals and villages filled with families and children.

The chilling reality is that up to 15% of the tax money deducted from your pay-check each month, buys the bombs and pays the salaries of troops to commit these atrocities. Rivers of blood from innocent families and their children is on everybody's hands.

The plan for world domination by the international bankers, cannot be accomplished without your co-operation. That plan which was formulated in 1773, at Mayer

Rothschild's goldsmiths shop by 13 influential German Jewish families. Among them were Rothschild, Oppenheimer, Warburg and Schiff. Their formula for global control is the 3-M formula. Money control, media control and military control.

Like the changes to the rules that gave these families the media monopolies, new laws are being passed to transfer military control to them by privatizing the military.

But if they are killing terrorists, who cares if they are government soldiers or corporate soldiers, right? A more important question to ask is who exactly are the terrorists and where do terrorists get their training? The answer is right in America, at Fort Benning, Georgia. Until January 2001, America's terrorist training school, was called school of the Americas. But because of massive protests against its activities, the name was changed to WHISC Western Hemisphere Institute for Security Cooperation.

Actress **Susan Sarendon** narrated a documentary film called **School of the Assassins.** The film exposes the school as a terrorist training camp, whose graduates are well known murderers, torturers, state terrorists and dictators, including drug king Manuel Noriega. The role of terrorists in the banker owned media is to scare the living tax dollars out of citizens, and timing is everything.

On the second anniversary of the 911 attack on the World Trade Center, George Bush asked for an 87 billion dollar increase in military spending. At the same time, the media released a dramatic video showing Osama bin Laden, alive and well, and threatening to make the 911 attack seem like preliminaries.

In closing this chapter, it is important to note that none of what has been stated here or anywhere else in this book is meant to state that it is evil. The research that has been done by others is provided here as it was stated, including other author's opinions. What has been done is done, and what the Rothschilds have succeeded in doing is neither good or evil, it simply is as it is and Earthlings have allowed this to be.

11

THE SECRET SOCIETIES OF THE NEW WORLD ORDER

Reporting Structure Of The New World Order

Much of what follows is taken from the web site **www.one-evil.org and www.ucadia.com** and the work of **Frank O'Collins**. The research conducted here is so extensive, it boggles the mind. As the author of this book, I cannot take any credit for this and in the interest of bringing truth into the light, it is difficult to dispute the research.

The concept of a New World Order has been around a long time as written in the prophesies. It obviously did not go by that name but the intent of emperors is to conquer other empires until there is order. Of particular interest here is the New World Order which came into its new structure in 1943 and its relation to the PLANET EARTH. We have looked at the ones who are playing god. One has to ask how is this enormous private structure administered? How can such a collaboration of such magnitude be a cohesive force? Let us carry our simple analogy of corporate structure further. At the top are the Founders, shareholders and Directors. We would see the Rothschild as the Chairman of the Board. We have looked at the Administrative Centers which are the Financial, Legal, Religious, Military cities, with Zurich as the City of the gods, and Baalbek as the city of the Sun. Below that would be the equivalent of a Chief Executive Officers who head up major divisions to execute the orders of the Directors. Those executive orders are issued according to the business mission as reflected in the business plan, referred to as the New World Order (or new Order of the Ages). We have suggested that the equivalent of the silent private shareholders with their power over the Board of Directors is the Jesuit Order with their military might in the Knights of Malta.

It would be appropriate here to understand the New World Order is not necessarily like a division, a subsidiary, but more like a plan with the corporate hierarchy of great importance that is not an entity unto itself, but controlled by the 13 Bloodlines and directed by another overlapping group of 12 bloodlines. It is most likely that there are many councils and CEO's engaged for different purposes. In the research conducted by Frank O'Collins (**www.one-evil.org**) it is stated that the power structure of the New World Order is made of two pyramids with the Jesuit Provincials at the top, below which is the Jesuit Order and Apparatus, and then the Jesuit Superior General. Then the lower pyramid is headed by the Roman Pontiff, the Illuminati Families, The Holy See and then the United Nations. Much of the explanation following, and the history is taken from his work.

Like many of these private structures, the New World Order maintains no official head office, other than the existing structure of the Catholic Church. Nor does the New World Order maintain secret archives or attend "secret" meetings in oak panelled rooms. The entire structure, apparatus and relationships of the New World Order is largely in the public eye "hidden in plain sight" and has been scrutinized countless times by investigators and co-adjustators publishing misinformation. Hidden from the public, it would be no different than the secret business strategy of IBM or Microsoft. The relevant parts of the plan are handed down for execution to the CEO's. In this case, the division is the Vatican and the Jesuits with the reporting hierarchy of Generals and Popes.

For example, important New World Order meeting groups such as the Bilderberger Group and the Trilateral Commission bring together many of the key members of the New World Order, but with discussions on subjects that to any observer would be regarded as largely "benign". This is particularly the case in regards to the core reporting and power structure of the New World Order today. Excluding major meetings of members "hidden in plain sight", Jesuit Provincial Generals have divided their armies of priests into specialist areas, each assigned the task of involving themselves with key people in that area of expertise to such an extent that their relationships and meetings seem both normal and natural.

For example, where a Jesuit who is regarded as a top lawyer and expert in Constitutional law meets with legislators, it seems both normal and devoid of any ulterior motive. When a Jesuit is an expert in a field of science, or politics the same can be said.

Thus the real power of the New World Order rests at the lowest levels of the upper Jesuit structure, with one part of the Jesuit organization never having a complete picture of what the other side knows unless they are at the level of Provincial General. The eventual truce in the civil war of the Jesuits came in the form of a compromise of power- the New World Order is in fact a very clear and precise six (6) level pyramid of power.

1. Jesuit Factions of the Jesuit Order
2. Black Pope- Jesuit Superior General
3. Jesuit Order and Financial, Corporate and Military Apparatus
4. Re-constituted Illuminati Families (under the structure of the New World Order)
5. Holy See (with Pope as its head)
6. United Nations

It would be incorrect to say that the Black Pope is the most powerful person on Planet Earth. He is simply one likened to the CEO's. Since 1945, the role has been largely symbolic and held by a candidate from a neutral country between the main factions of the Jesuit Civil War. As such, the role has been dominated by both Dutch and Spanish candidates.

The most powerful force within the New World Order is unquestionable the Provincial Generals of the Order-the most senior factional leaders of the Jesuits who continue to hold a truce since 1945. While the Superior General can technically give absolute orders to his provincials, in practice it has been the other way around for over sixty years.

Then we come to the third layer being the Financial-Military Apparatus which few people who believe in the existence of the New World Order would argue. However, few have ever heard of the real foundation of the global financial system in the early 19th Century using Jesuit controlled gold stolen from the Vatican during the Jesuit-Papal Wars to fund an army of private banks in Europe and the United States.

Then we come to the fourth layer of the New World Order apparatus being the reconstituted "Illuminati" families from the United States, Europe and even Asia/Middle East. They have no control over the Jesuits, nor do they wish to challenge them in any way as their various positions from Royal families, occasional Presidents, Prime Ministers and global leaders is dependent upon the favourable patronage of the Jesuits.

The fifth layer of the New World Order apparatus is the Holy See. Contrary to common misinformation, the role of Pope is now of secondary importance to the legal apparatus of the Holy See --The Holy See, being the legal framework that claims Vatican superiority over all other laws of man as well as complete dominion over animals (humans being classed as animals by their laws). It is the papacy and Vatican curia that in recent years has waged and increasing PR war in revealing more and more of the New World Order apparatus against the Jesuits.

The sixth layer is the United Nations and legal apparatus which recognizes the Holy See as a legitimate state and entity, therefore its laws, therefore every national laws as subservient to the United Nations.

New World Order Overview

The New world Order came into a new stage of business plan implementation in 1943 after the Second World War. This is not its origin for the powers that have always been planning to control all the resources of Planet Earth have always had this agenda. The plan simply reached a new phase of implementation as the bloodlines emerged back into power in the 1700's. To those that play the corporate games of power and control it is not a surprise that the whole planet and all people could simply be sought after as one Empire shared by those smart enough to conquer it. We have looked at the 13 bloodlines that have re-emerged into power and prominence. We have looked at the key operations and a look at the Vatican as a religious division. Now we are going to look at some of the other divisions of the PLANET EARTH Inc. We have looked at their base of operations, being:

Zurich - The City of the gods
City of London Corporation - Financial power centre, established in 1067
District of Columbia - Military power centre, established in 1871
Vatican City - Religious power centre, sovereign in 1929
Baalbek - Proposed city of dominion

We have looked closer at one of the "gods" power vehicle of money and the House of Rothschild. We have looked deeper into the Vatican division that create and execute the tactics and actions to implement the operational components under the mission-- the wishes of the gods as the conquest of all empires to create one empire of Planet Earth. Let us look more deeply at some of the groups who like the executive branches of a major corporation take responsibility for execution of orders within the business plan called the new World Order.

We alluded to a worldwide plan being orchestrated by an extremely powerful and influential group of *genetically-related individuals* (at least at the highest echelons) which include many of the world's wealthiest people, top political leaders, and corporate elite, as well as members of the so-called **Black Nobility** of Europe (dominated by the **British Crown**) whose goal is to create a **One World Government**, stripped of nationalistic and regional boundaries, that is obedient to their agenda. Their intention is to effect complete and total control over every human being on the planet and it is alleged to dramatically reduce the world's population by 5.5 Billion people. While the name *New World Order* is a term frequently used today when referring to this group, it's more useful to identify the principal organizations, institutions, and individuals who make up this vast interlocking spider web of elite conspirators. The Main Manipulating Groups: Freemasonry, Round Table, Royal Institute of International Affairs, Council on Foreign Relations, Bilderberg Group, and the Trilateral Commission to name the some. The site ***http://educate-yourself.org/nwo/*** is a good reference for this and much of the material is used as we explore this topic.

It is at this point we need to add another layer to the PLANET EARTH model. It is the elite Secret Societies that have been mentioned over and over. Most research points to the same bloodlines belonging to these secret societies that appear to have two faces of good and bad depending upon the level one attains within it. These secret societies are like the common belief "glue" that creases the cohesion by oath towards the same goals.

The Cultish Glue

Throughout the hierarchy is a cultish glue that appears to hold unity between members. Several cultish groups and secret societies appear in all the research over and over. It has already been pointed out that the beliefs of spiritual Satanism are not exactly foreign in the they simply reflect a competitive corporate rule book of ethics. If we look at the operational level in our simple PLANET EARTH corporation, we see the occurrence several secret societies that form operational arms. Now let us look at these societies and what the researchers report about their purposes.

The following secret societies are listed by those that are the main researchers on the topic of the New World order, Illuminati, and Royal Bloodlines. what follows is their research and for a full version with references, please visit the websites listed before. The research has been extensive and thorough and it is not meant here to take credit nor attempt to minimize the magnitude of their efforts. Check out sites such as ***http://www.4rie.com/***

The Skull And Bones Society

The origin of the Skull and Bones Society, once known as The Brotherhood of Death in the US, begins at Yale when a group of men established an organization for the purpose of drug smuggling. Indeed, many American and European fortunes were built on the China (opium) trade (***The Secret Origins of Skull & Bones).*** The society's alumni organization, which owns its properties and oversees all the organization's activity, is known as the Russell Trust Association (R.T.A.), and is named after one of Bones' founding members. It still exists today only at Yale and has evolved into more an organization dedicated to the success of its members after leaving the collegiate world. The shape of that success can only be left to speculation. The Skull & Bones Society has been described as the most secretive organization in the world.

*"Presidents are not elected by ballot, they are selected by blood." - **David Icke***

Some of the world's most famous and powerful men alive today are "bonesmen," including George H.W. Bush and his son George W. Bush, Senator John Kerry, Austan Goolsbee (Chairman of President Obama's Council of Economic Advisers), Nicholas Brady, and William F. Buckley. Other bonesmen include U.S. President William Howard Taft, Morrison R. Waite (Chief Justice of the Supreme Court), Henry Luce (Time-Life), Harold Stanley (founder of Morgan Stanley), Frederick W. Smith (founder of Fedex), John Daniels (founder of Archer Daniels Midland), Henry P. Davison (senior partner Morgan Guaranty Trust), Pierre Jay (first chairman of the Federal Reserve Bank of New York), Artemus Gates (President of New York Trust Company, Union Pacific, TIME, Boeing Company), Senator John Chaffe, Russell W. Davenport (editor Fortune Magazine), the first presidents of the University of California, Johns Hopkins University, and Cornell University, and many others.

A list of members can be found on:
 http://en.wikipedia.org/wiki/List_of_Skull_and_Bones_members

All have taken a solemn vow of secrecy. "***America's Secret Establishment***", by ***Antony C. Sutton,*** 1986, page 5-6, states*: "Those on the inside know it as **The Order**. Others have known it for more than 150 years as **Chapter 322** of a German secret society. More formally, for legal purposes, The Order was incorporated as The Russell Trust in 1856. It was also once known as the **"Brotherhood of Death"**. Those who make light of it, or want to make fun of it, call it **'Skull & Bones'**, or just plain **'Bones'**.*

The American chapter of this German order was founded in 1833 at Yale University by General William Huntington Russell and Alphonso Taft who, in 1876, became Secretary of War in the Grant Administration. Alphonso Taft was the father of William Howard Taft, the only man to be both President and Chief Justice of the United States.

The order is not just another Greek letter fraternal society with passwords and handgrips common to most campuses. This is a secret society whose members are sworn to silence. It only exists on the Yale campus (that we know about). It has rules. It has ceremonial rites. It is not at all happy with prying, probing citizens - known among initiates as 'outsiders' or 'vandals'. Its members always deny membership. Above all, The Order is powerful, unbelievably powerful. It is a Senior year society which exists only at Yale. Members are chosen in their Junior year and spend only one year on campus, the Senior year, with Skull & Bones. In other words, the organization is oriented to the graduate outside world. The Order meets annually - patriarchies only - on Deer Island in the St. Lawrence River.

Senior societies are unique to Yale. There are two other senior societies at Yale, but none elsewhere. Scroll & Key and Wolf's Head are supposedly competitive societies founded in the mid-19th century. They may be part of the same network. Rosenbaum commented in his "Esquire" magazine article that anyone in the Eastern Liberal Establishment who is not a member of Skull & Bones is almost certainly a member of either Scroll & Key or Wolf's Head.

The selection procedure for new members of The Order has not changed since 1832. Each year 15, and only 15, never fewer, are selected. In the past 150 years about 2500 Yale graduates have been initiated into The Order. At any time about 500-600 are alive and active. Roughly about one- quarter of these take an active role in furthering the objectives of The Order. The others either lose interest or change their minds. They are silent drop-outs.

"..The most likely potential member is from a Bones family, who is energetic, resourceful, political and probably an amoral team player. ... Honors and financial rewards are guaranteed by the power of The Order. But the price of these honors and rewards is sacrifice to the common goal, the goal of The Order. Some, perhaps many, have not been willing to pay this price."

The Old Line American families and their descendants involved in the Skull & Bones are names such as: Whitney, Perkins, Stimson, Taft, Wadsworth, Gilman, Payne, Davidson, Pillsbury, Sloane, Weyerhaeuser, Harriman, Rockefeller, Lord, Brown, Bundy, Bush and Phelps. The above is reproduced from the **Alternative Physics & Conspiracy!** Web site. **http://www.4rie.com**/

Charlotte Iserbyt a famous American freelance writer and whistleblower breaks down the history of this secret order and reveals just how big this elite club at Yale really is and how much political power they have wielded over the past 180 years! Charlotte Thompson Iserbyt served as the head of policy at the Department of Education during the first administration of Ronald Reagan. While working there she discovered a long term strategic plan by the tax exempt foundations to transform America from a nation of rugged individualists and problem solvers to a country of servile, brainwashed minions who simply regurgitate whatever they're told. Her father and grandfather were Yale University graduates and members of the Skull and Bones secret society.

Through her father Charlotte Iserbyt was able to gain possession of the complete listings of the members, living and dead, of the Yale University Skull and Bones secret society, fashioned into a three-volume set: living members, deceased members, and complete listing of both. She cooperated in the writing **of Dr. Antony C. Sutton's** book **America's Secret Establishment - The Order of Skull & Bones** by providing the list of members obtained from her father. Iserbyt believes that the Bavarian Illuminati hid inside the Freemasons, and that the Skull and Bones Secret Society is derived from these Illuminati-degree Freemasons from Bavaria whose goals were documented in an original edition 1798 book Proofs of Conspiracy by John Robison. Among the goals of the Order of the Illuminati were to destroy religions, and governments from within, merge the destroyed countries, and to bring about a one world government, a new world order, in their secret control.

In the secret societies interview she states that virtually all of the Carnegie Foundation agreements with the Russian education system were still in place, as well as the U.S. Department of Education programs that Iserbyt claims brought about the downfall of American prosperity since the turn of the century, especially post World War II.

At the site **www.conspiracyarchive.com/NWO/Skull_Bones.htmy**, under Networks of Power, in his book **America's Secret Establishment**, **Antony Sutton** outlined the Order of Skull and Bones' ability to establish vertical and horizontal "chains of influence" that ensured the continuity of their schemes:

"The Whitney-Stimson-Bundy links represent the vertical chain. W. C. Whitney ('63), who married Flora Payne (of the Standard Oil Payne dynasty), was Secretary of the Navy. His

attorney was a man named Elihu Root. Root hired Henry Stimson ('88), out of law school. Stimson took over from Root as Secretary of War in 1911, appointed by fellow Bonesman William Howard Taft. Stimson later became Coolidge's Governor-General of the Philippine Islands, Hoover's Secretary of State, and Secretary of War during the Roosevelt and Truman administrations.

Hollister Bundy ('09) was Stimson's special assistant and point man in the Pentagon for the Manhattan Project. His two sons, also members of Skull and Bones, were William Bundy ('39) and McGeorge Bundy ('40) -- both very active in governmental and foundation affairs. The two brothers, from their positions in the CIA, the Department of Defence and the State Department, and as Special Assistants to Presidents Kennedy and Johnson, exercised significant impact on the flow of information and intelligence during the Vietnam War. William Bundy went on to be editor of Foreign Affairs, the influential quarterly of the Council on Foreign Affairs (CFR). McGeorge became president of the Ford Foundation. Another interesting group of "Bonesmen" is the Harriman/Bush crowd. Averil Harriman ('13), "Elder Statesman" of the Democratic Party, and his brother Roland Harriman ('17) were very active members. In fact, four of Roland's fellow Bonesmen from the class of 1917 were directors of Brown Brothers, Harriman, including Prescott Bush ('17), George Bush's dad.

Since the turn of the century, two investment bank firms -- Guaranty Trust and Brown Brothers, Harriman -- were both dominated by members of Skull and Bones. These two firms were heavily involved in the financing of Communism and Hitler's regime. Bonesman share an affinity for the Hegelian ideas of the historical dialectic, which dictates the use of controlled conflict -- thesis versus anti-thesis -- to create a pre-determined synthesis. A synthesis of their making and design, where the state is absolute and individuals are granted their freedoms based on their obedience to the state -- a New World Order. Funding and political manoeuvring on the part of "Bonesmen" and their allies helped the Bolsheviks prevail in Russia. In defiance of federal laws, the cabal financed industries, established banks and developed oil and mineral deposits in the fledgling USSR

Later, Averil Harriman, as minister to Great Britain in charge of Lend-Lease for Britain and Russia, was responsible for shipping entire factories into Russia. According to some researchers, Harriman also oversaw the transfer of nuclear secrets, plutonium and U. S. dollar printing plates to the USSR. In 1932, the Union Banking Corporation of New York City had enlisted four directors from the ('17) cell and two Nazi bankers associated with Fritz Thyssen, who had been financing Hitler since 1924.

Taken from **George Bush; The Unauthorized Biography**: 'President Franklin Roosevelt's Alien Property Custodian, Leo T. Crowley, signed Vesting Order Number 248 [11/17/42] seizing the property of Prescott Bush under the Trading with Enemy Act. The order, published in obscure government record books and kept out of the news, Note #4 explained nothing about the Nazis involved; only that the Union Banking Corporation was run for the 'Thyssen family' of 'Germany and/or Hungary' -- 'nationals ... of a designated enemy country.' By deciding that Prescott Bush and the other directors of the Union Banking Corporation were legally 'front men for the Nazis', the government avoided the more important historical issue: In what way 'were Hitler's Nazis themselves hired, *armed, and instructed by' the New York and London clique of which Prescott Bush was an executive manager? ... '*

The New York Times, December 16, 1944, ran a five-paragraph page 25 article on actions of the New York State Banking Department. Only the last sentence refers to the Nazi bank, as follows: 'The Union Banking Corporation, 39 Broadway, New York, has received authority to change its principal place of business to 120 Broadway.'

The Times omitted the fact that the Union Banking Corporation had been seized by the government for trading with the enemy, and the fact that 120 Broadway was the address of the government's Alien Property Custodian. After the war, Prescott went on to become a U. S. Senator from Connecticut and favourite golfing partner of President Eisenhower. Prescott claims responsibility for getting Nixon into politics and takes personal credit for bringing Dick on board as Ike's running mate in 1952.

The Knights Of Malta

When the Sultan of Egypt retook Jerusalem in 1291, the Knights of St. John went into exile, settling in Rhodes 20 years later. In 1523 they were forced from Rhodes by the Sultan's forces and settled in Malta, which they ruled until they were dislodged by Napoleon's army in 1798. The order settled in Rome in the mid-19th century, where it remains to this day.

The Sovereign Military Hospitaller Order of Saint John of Jerusalem of Rhodes and of Malta is a Roman Catholic organization based in Rome with around 13,000 members worldwide. The group was **founded** in 1048 by Amalfian merchants in Jerusalem as a monastic order that ran a hospital to tend to Christian pilgrims in the Holy Land. At the height of its power, the order was also tasked by Rome with the additional military function of defending Christians from the local Muslim population. The Knights of St. John were just one of a number of Christian military orders founded during this period -- including the fabled but now defunct Knights of Templar.

It is said that despite its name, the Knights haven't had any military function since leaving Malta. On the surface, the order has gone back to its charitable roots by **sponsoring medical missions** in more than 120 countries. When the order was founded, knights were expected to take a vow of poverty, chastity, and obedience upon joining. Nowadays, obedience is enough. Membership is still by invitation only, but you no longer have to be a member of the nobility. In recent years, the organization has become **increasingly American** in membership. The leader of the order, referred to as the **prince and grand master**, is elected for life in a secret conclave and must be approved by the pope.

In a recent in Doha, veteran *New Yorker* journalist Seymour Hersh alleged that the U.S. military's Joint Special Operations Command (JSOC) had been infiltrated by Christian fanatics who see themselves as modern-day Crusaders and aim to "change mosques into cathedrals." In particular, he alleged that former JSOC head Gen. Stanley McChrystal -- later U.S. commander in Afghanistan -- and his successor, Vice Adm. William McRaven, as well as many other senior leaders of the command, are *"are all members of, or at least supporters of, Knights of Malta."*

Despite having no fixed territory besides its headquarters building in Rome, the order is considered a sovereign entity under international law. It prints its own postage stamps and coins -- though these are mostly for novelty value -- and enjoys observer status at the United Nations, which classifies it as a nonstate entity like the Red Cross. The Knights maintain diplomatic relations with 104 countries. The order does not have official relations with the United States, though it has offices in New York, for the United Nations delegation, and Washington, for its representation at the Inter-American Development Bank.

Because of its secretive proceedings, unique political status, and association with the Crusades, the order has been a popular target for conspiracy theorists. Alleged members have included former CIA Directors William Casey and John McCone, Chrysler Chairman Lee Iacocca, and GOP fixture Pat Buchanan, though none have ever acknowledged membership. Various theories have tied the Knights to crimes including the Kennedy assassination and spreading the AIDS virus through its clinics in Africa.

In 2006, a newspaper article in the United Arab Emirates **claimed** that the Knights were directly influencing U.S. policy in Iraq and Afghanistan, reprising their role in the Crusades. Following the article, Islamist websites in Egypt urged followers to attack the order's embassy in Cairo, forcing the organization to issue a statement denying any military role.

Apparently the Knights have been involved in their fair share of political intrigues. In 1988, the charge d'affaires at the order's embassy in Havana confessed to being a double agent, reporting to both the CIA and Cuban intelligence. According to journalist **Jeremy Scahill's** book **Blackwater,** Joseph Schmitz, a former executive at the company who also served as inspector general for the U.S. Department of Defense, boasted of his membership in the Knights in his official biography. The defense contractor now known as Xe's chief executive, Erik Prince, reportedly espoused Christian supremacist beliefs, and its contractors in Iraq used codes and insignia based on the order's medieval compatriots, the Knights of the Templar. .

So while the group is, for the most part, a charitable organization with little resemblance to the sinister portrait painted by its detractors, an image-makeover might be in order as it finishes off its 10th century. Yet on website *http://www.voxfux.com/features/jesuits1.html* *Mike Bellinger* has a different picture:

"What happened in Europe was that after 250 hundred years of bloody Jesuit-instigated massacres of Protestants, the bloody Jesuit Inquisitions (some estimates put the total Vatican and Jesuit death toll at 60 million human beings, making Hitler seem like an amateur) and resulting wars with European monarchs and statesmen, the Jesuits had been taking quite a beating themselves. Many had been executed outright, and as a group they were thrown out of almost every country in Europe at one time or another. Even several popes turned against them due to public outcries from some still loyal Catholic countries. But they always somehow managed to regroup and return. When they did, they always extracted bloody revenge on whatever country or ruler had expelled them. They killed the popes who banished them and took over the Vatican completely in the 1700's. This would prevent any further rear-guard actions against them in the future as they had suffered previously. This consolidation of Jesuit control over the Vatican itself marked a new phase in the ongoing battle against Protestantism and all the other non-Catholic "heretics" of the world at large.

The lessons learned from open conflicts with the European powers led to the next and most sinister phase of the Jesuit takeover of world society. They realized that the most effective and efficient method of seizing control of a society was by their already useful tactic of infiltration, but this time in secret. The instruments of that infiltration would be the many secret societies which they targeted and assumed control of. The international nature of the Masonic brotherhood made them an ideal tool for using its membership to advance Jesuit goals. Publicly, the Vatican and the Masons were enemies; but F. Tupper Saussy found evidence linking them, and Jon Eric Phelps notes that Adam Wieshaupt, the founder of modern Bavarian Freemasonry was a Jesuit agent.

The Knights of Malta (formerly Knights Templar) are the premiere secret society of the Vatican these days, but they are subservient to the Jesuit General. Many of America and the Western World's power elite are Knights of Malta.

Once they spread their influence through the secret societies worldwide and coordinated with the English Roundtables to impose a worldwide network of control, the whole phenomena evolved into what we know of today as the New World Order (or what the elite-controlled press so disingenuously refers to as Globalism, as if that is something to be desired). The Globalists have many nicknames, but their agenda is one and the same. It is total control of this planet. They have many factions who compete with one another for position and advantage like a group of churlish relatives, but the ultimate goal is always unchanged. And the Jesuit overlords lurk in the background, pulling all the important strings.

If you know anything about the history of the elite Brotherhood, then you will know that the Rothschild's banking faction developed the art of financing wars from both sides of a conflict by utilizing the secrets of Central Banking with their ability to create enormous debt loads in the resident populations resulting from the issuance of government authorized fiat money. The incredible profits generated by war, reaped from both the winners and losers, led to a syndrome where induced wars became a way of life for the overlords because of the vast financial profits and additional benefits derived from it.

In addition to massive financial profits, war results in many other '"benefits" for the overlords. Some of the most important to them are increased centralized control of the population by government, increased militarization, and the public fear of conflicts to come, leading them to let their "peace-loving" statesmen do all their thinking for them.

But the Jesuits have a much darker rationale behind all the world conflicts they have overseen in the last 600 years. They have used all of these various wars as cover-ups for their mass exterminations of Protestants and all other non-Catholic peoples worldwide. This is the real horror of the Jesuits and the Vatican. They are the most prolific mass murders in all of human history. No one and nothing else in known human history compares to their record of calculated genocide. Now you know why we must stop this evil. The Vatican, as it is now, is the incarnation of hell itself. There can be no doubt of that.

Here are some Jesuit/Vatican atrocities to mull over:

- The Crusades: Who knows how many died? And then the children's crusades ... Good God.
- The Inquisitions: In **"Vatican Assassins**," **Eric Jon Phelps** cites a source that estimates roughly 60 million people were murdered in the various stages of the Inquisitions. Think about that number for a minute. Most of these people were tortured to death.
- Catherine De Medici instigated the butchering of 75,000 French Protestant Huguenots on August 24, 1572. In 1598 Henry IV issued the Edict of Nates to protect them. By manipulating the rescinding of the protective Edict of Nantes in 1685 by the Jesuit

confessor to King Louis XIV (using religious blackmail), another HALF MILLION FRENCH HUGUENOTS were butchered by the vile French Catholic Dragonades. In 1655 again, British Protestant hero Oliver Cromwell threatened to invade France and crush the French Crown for a new massacre being waged upon the French Vadois Protestants of valley of Piedmont by six Catholic Regiments by the Duke of Savoy.

- *The massacre of the poor Irish protestants on October 23rd 1641 - the "Feast" of Ignatius Loyola. How fitting a day for a massacre by these bloodthirsty swine. It is estimated that 150,000 Irish Protestants were butchered in the streets and in their homes. This slaughter took place over an eight-year period. Finally, once again it was Oliver Cromwell who finally invaded Ireland and attacked the Jesuit base at Drogheda and in a rage exterminated the entire Catholic village of 2000. Only this invasion finally ended the massacre of the Protestants. The present day Irish Protestants are still at war with the fanatical Irish Catholic Jesuits, and this is why they need the continued protection of the British Army."*

It would appear that there are two very different pictures of these "knights". You can check out the membership list on ***http://cgi.rumormillnews.com/cgi-bin/forum.cgi?noframes;read=17908.***

The Bohemian Club

Bohemian Club Luciferian Secret Society is where the Illuminated Global Elite Meet in Bohemian Grove. It is said that movers, shakers from politics, and business go Bohemian at the annual event where people like the Bushes, Kissinger, Powell, and Gingrich to name a few, go.

In a report from MONTERIO at the Bohemian Club's Annual Summer Encampment it said that the two-week retreat for the rich and powerful that President Herbert Hoover once called "the greatest men's party on Earth." The club's famed annual gathering has been held for more than 100 years at the 2,700-acre Bohemian Grove in Monte Rio, about 70 miles north of San Francisco in Sonoma County. This year's event drew in notables such as former President George Bush, Texas Gov. George W. Bush, Henry Kissinger, retired Gen. Colin Powell, former House Speaker Newt Gingrich and Dow Chemical Chairman Frank Popoff, as well as actor Danny Glover.

The men gather to celebrate what they call "the spirit of Bohemia," said Peter Phillips, a Sonoma State University sociology professor who wrote his doctoral dissertation on the Bohemian Club. *"This is a place men can go and hang out with people who are similar to them,"* he said.

The annual gathering near the Russian River, which was first held in 1879, starts with the "Cremation of Care" ritual, in which the club's mascot is burned in effigy, symbolizing a freedom from care. Members also perform several plays, and gourmet food and expensive wine are plentiful.

While the club was formed in 1872 by a group of San Francisco journalists, the male-only club now bars journalists from membership to protect the group's privacy. Membership is coveted, and people routinely wait 10 or 15 years before gaining admittance. There are currently about 2,700 members.

Mary Moore, with Bohemian Grove Action Network, a protest group reports: *"And the American public is not privy to it."* No one from the club returned several calls from The

Bee. Bohemian Grove Action Network has periodically held demonstrations at the grove, although none were held this year. The point of the protests, Moore said, has been *"to let the American public know that what they've learned in civics isn't the full story on how decision-making is made in this country."* The Bohemian Club, she said, *"is one of the most elite organizations on the planet."* When the group sponsors public policy talks that are held without public scrutiny, *"the average American feels left out of the process,"* she said. Phillips echoes Moore's objections to the off-the-record nature of the Lakeside Talks. *"These are extremely powerful people and private discussions on policy issues that affect us certainly go against democratic principles,"* he said. *"There's no reason that those speeches they're giving couldn't be transcribed and made public. They have a responsibility to be open about it."*

The August 2, 1982 edition of Newsweek magazine reported: *"... the world's most prestigious summer camp - the Bohemian Grove - is now in session 75 miles north of San Francisco. The fiercely guarded, 2,700-acre retreat is the country extension of San Francisco's all-male ultra-exclusive Bohemian Club to which every Republican President since Herbert Hoover has belonged.*

With its high-powered clientele, coveted privacy and cabalistic rituals, the Bohemian Grove has prompted considerable suspicion. The most important events, however are the "lakeside talks" (past orators: Alexander Hague and Casper Weinberger). This year's speaker was Henry Kissinger on The Challenge of the '80s."

Maclean's magazine, March 23, 1981 reported that each summer, for three weekends - this year's will be the 103rd - nearly 2,000 Bohemians, with guests in tow, speed in by car and corporate jet to their guarded Grove, close by the hamlet of Monte Rio (population 1,200) on the Russian River. The Grove's Shakespearean motto, "Weaving spiders come not here," is an injunction to forget wheeling and dealing which is widely ignored. While 'ruling-class cohesiveness' rarely lets slip details of accommodations arrived at there, some - such as the 1967 agreement by Ronald Reagan, over a drink with Richard Nixon, to stay out of the coming presidential race have helped mould America's destiny.

Today, a prospective member faces an interrogation that, according to one club man, 'would satisfy the KGB.' There is a waiting list of 1,500 notables, all eager to pay the $2,500 initiation fee and $600-a-year dues. Mother Jones, August 1981 volume 6 page 28, reported a partial list of some of the prominent members: *"George P. Shultz, Stephen Bechtel, Jr., Gerald R. Ford, Henry Kissinger, William F. Buckley, Jr., Fred L. Hartley, Merv Griffin, Thomas Haywood, Joseph Coors, Edward Teller, Ronald Reagan, A. W. Clausen, George Bush, William French Smith, John E. Swearingten, Casper W. Weinberger, Justin Dart, William E. Simon, and hundreds of other prominent politicos and businessmen."*

Antony C. Sutton, Editor of an excellent monthly newsletter**, Phoenix Letter**, stated in the October, 1996 edition: *"Up to a few months ago, our knowledge of Bohemian Grove, the exclusive elitist hideaway by supposedly adult wheeler dealers, a.k.a. Washington statesman and prominent people (all male.) This is where Kissinger, Ford, Nixon, Bechtel, Bush, Cheney, Hoover and their friends (2600 members) hang out and "relax."* And if they want to behave as little boys that is their privilege, it is private property.

Recent [O'Brien and Phillips, TRANCE Formation of America (pp 170-1)] information may radically change this perception of Bohemian Grove. Not merely drunkenness, unbounded use of alcohol and drugs with vague homosexual tones (confirmed by our sources) but reported activities much more serious - kidnapping, rape, pedophilia, sodomy, ritual murder. Investigation is blocked under the 1947 National Security Act. And like the Omaha child abuse case, includes illegal detention of children.

For decades, there have been vague rumours of weird goings on in Bohemian Grove in more remote parts of its 2200 acres. Reliable reports claim Druidic like rituals, druids in red hooded robes marching in procession and chanting to the Great Owl (Moloch.) A funeral pyre with "corpses." (Scores of men work in the Bohemian Grove as servants so this party is fairly well established.)

An article in a local community newspaper, Santa Rosa Sun (1993, July) reported on the Cult of Canaan and the legend of Moloch in place at Bohemian Grove. The Moloch Pagan Cult of Sacrifice is human sacrifice. About the mid 1980s there were rumours of murders in remote parts of the property. A local police investigation went nowhere. State investigators on related criminal acts went nowhere.

According to an observer and near victim, who can describe the Bohemian Grove inner hideaways, the closed sanctum, even the decor at secret locations, places where no outsider goes (or servants according to our sources) there is an UNDERGROUND lounge (sign spelled U.N.derground) a Dark Room, a Leather Room and a Necrophilia Room.

Here is one of O'Brien's quote: *"Slaves of advancing age or with failed programming were sacrificially murdered at random in the wooded grounds of Bohemian Grove and I felt it was only a matter of time until it would be me."* This potential victim survived. Others reportedly did not.

To understand the Origin of Moloch, Druid and Canaanite Cult the following is offered. These cults were based on human sacrifice. Why would a 20th century resort reproduce the cult ceremonies? At the minimum, it demonstrates an attraction to the ceremonial practices of the cult, i.e. adoration of destruction, blood, barbarity and sacrifice of children.

In brief, the O'Brien charges are consistent with the tenants of Bohemian Grove as played out in ceremony. This is not a resort devoted to, for example, tennis or swimming. It is apparently devoted to blood sacrifices.

"Many political reputations and world governments secrets were staked on the belief that I could not be deprogrammed and rehabilitated to recall that which I was supposed to forget. So much for the programming experts. Colonel Aquino is (was?) a psychology "expert" linked to mind control with Defence Intelligence Agency and presumably first class talent, yet (Cathy) O'Brien was apparently deprogrammed and secrets spilled all over." (end quoting) The monthly Phoenix Letter is available by writing to Phoenix Letter, Suite 216 C, 1517 14th St. West, Billings, MT 59102.

As these world leaders, who have all the creature comforts that they could ever desire, look around for something new and interesting to do to amuse themselves, it would appear that pagan ritual rites, mind control, and many ancient practices of worshiping the gods for some beneficial arrangement continues.

The Rosicrucian Fellowship

Rosicrucianism is a philosophical secret society, said to have been founded in late medieval Germany by Christian Rosenkreuz. It holds a doctrine or theology "built on esoteric truths of the ancient past", which, "concealed from the average man, provide insight into nature, the physical universe and the spiritual realm." Rosicrucianism is symbolized by the Rosy Cross. This is all about the art of Alchemy, and the mysteries of the ancients. It is about the works of great alchemists like Parcleius and many non-science secrets of science that have been deemed as mythical garbage by mainstream science.

Between 1607 and 1616, two anonymous manifestos were published, first in Germany and later throughout Europe. These were **Fama Fraternitatis RC** (The Fame of the Brotherhood of RC) and **Confessio Fraternitatis** (The Confession of the Brotherhood of RC). The influence of these documents, presenting a "most laudable Order" of mystic-philosopher-doctors and promoting a "Universal Reformation of Mankind", gave rise to an enthusiasm called by its historian Dame Frances Yates the "Rosicrucian Enlightenment".

Rosicrucianism is alleged to be associated with Protestantism, Lutheranism in particular, and the manifestos opposed Roman Catholicism and its preference for dogma over empiricism. They also rejected Muhammad, though they traced their philosophy and science to the Moors, asserting that it had been kept secret for 120 years until the intellectual climate might receive it. Early seventeenth century occult philosophers such as Michael Maier, Robert Fludd and Thomas Vaughan interested themselves in the Rosicrucian world view. According to historian David Stevenson it was also influential to Freemasonry as it was emerging in Scotland. In later centuries, many esoteric societies have claimed to derive their doctrines, in whole or in part, from the original Rosicrucians. Several modern societies have been formed for the study of Rosicrucianism and allied subjects.

The documented history of Rosicrucianism reaches back no further than the early 1600s, and modern Rosicrucian organizations don't date back anywhere near that far. In 1614 a curious pamphlet entitled the **Fama Fraternitatis** was published in Cassel, Germany. This wasn't the first appearance of the *Fama*; reportedly it circulated in manuscript as early as 1610. The *Fama* tells the story of one Christian Rosencreutz who, as a young man, wandered through the Near East learning the mystical wisdom of the Arabs and Egyptians and finding much enlightenment there. Upon returning to Germany he attempted to share this knowledge but was laughed at and shunned. He and a few like-minded people formed a society called the Fraternity of the Rose Cross, building a temple called the Spiritus Sanctus. There were only eight members at the beginning; all men, all bachelors and all virgins. The agreement among them was simple:

- They should profess only to be healers and act in that capacity whenever requested for no payment
- They would have no uniform or habit but would adopt the customs of the country where they lived
- They would meet once a year at the Spiritus Sanctus, or send a note excusing their absence
- Each person should find someone to be his successor
- The letters "C.R" would be their seal and mark, and
- The fraternity would remain secret for 100 years.

Presumably the *Fama* was published after the 100 years had elapsed as it goes on to report the discovery of the Spiritus Sanctus and describe the fraternity to the outside world. Their basic philosophy: ...and this we say for a truth, that whosoever shall earnestly, and from his heart, bear affection unto us, it shall be beneficial to him in goods, body, and soul; but he that is false-hearted, or only greedy of riches, the same first of all shall not be able in any manner of wise to hurt us, but bring himself to utter ruin and destruction. This was followed in 1615 by another purported Rosicrucian publication, the *Confessio Fraternitatis,* in the same vein as the first but much more apocalyptic. It told not only of a society that had obtained the secrets of enlightenment, but of a forthcoming reformation of the age, returning it a state of grace where they conveyed:

"We ought therefore here to observe well, and make it known unto everyone, that God hath certainly and most assuredly concluded to send and grant to the world before her end, which presently thereupon shall ensue, such a truth, light, life and glory, as the first man Adam had, which he lost in Paradise, after which his successors were put and driven, with him, to misery wherefore there shall cease all servitude, falsehood, lies, and darkness, which by little and little, with the great world's revolution, was crept into all arts, works, and governments of men, and have darkened the most part of them."

A third document appeared in 1616 entitled **The Chemical Wedding of Christian Rosencreutz.** This is a highly symbolic treatise following Rosencreutz through a mystical "wedding" that is actually an alchemical allegory. Alchemy is presented not as the physical transformation of base metals into gold, but rather as a spiritual process in which the "base" person is enlightened, turning into spiritual "gold." Most scholars believe the author of this tract to be Johann Valentine Andrade, a Lutheran minister from Wurttemburg. We know from **Andrade's** autobiography that he wrote a piece called **The Chemical Wedding** around 1602-3, but since the *Wedding* cites both the *Fama* and the *Confessio*, which didn't appear until later, it's thought the work was updated once the new Rosicrucian documents appeared. Even so Andrade considered it "a fiction, a jest, of little worth."

The notion of a secret society with occult knowledge found a receptive audience. A few other authors, while denying membership in the society, were sympathetic to its ideals. For example, **Robert Fludd,** another Lutheran minister, published two books, the **Compendious Apology for the Fraternity of the Rosy Cross** (1616) and **The Apologetic Tractatus for the Society of the Rosy Cross** (1617), plus many other works with a Rosicrucian bent. Interest in the rosy cross flared briefly and then dwindled away. There have been attempts to show that the "Invisible College" of Rosicrucianism eventually became the Royal Society of London, but the evidence is tenuous at best. Likewise, attempts to show that Rosicrucianism survived as a society past the early 1600s lack any historical basis.

That hasn't stopped some modern organizations from claiming membership in or leadership of the organization, though. Probably the best known group is the Ancient Mystical Order Rosea Crucis, otherwise known as AMORC, which operates a mail-order mystical school out of San Jose, California. It was founded by H. Spencer Lewis, an acquaintance if not an actual associate of the English occultist Aleister Crowley (1875-1947) and an ex-member of his Ordo Templi Orientalis. The AMORC claims a history that stretches back to Pharaoh Thutmose III in 1477 BC and apparently includes anyone who used more than 3% of their brain, including Francis Bacon, Benjamin Franklin, Thomas Jefferson, Leonardo da Vinci, Isaac Newton, Pascal, Spinoza, and that great philosopher, Edith Piaf. (What, they couldn't get Zasu Pitts?)

AMORC touts its authenticity by proclaiming it's the only Rosicrucian organization that uses the word "order" in its name and claiming authorization from FUDOSI (the Fédération Universelle Des Ordres Et Sociétés Initiatiques), a sort of clearinghouse of mystical societies. To my mind that's like Clarabelle the Clown being validated by Howdy Doody, but we'll let that pass and trudge on.

Many other organizations also call themselves Rosicrucian. In 1858, the Fraternitas Rosae Crucis was founded by Paschal Beverly Randolph after supposedly having been initiated into a German Rosicrucian fraternity. It's still extant today and like AMORC provides mail-order spiritual illumination. The Societas Rosicruciana in Anglia was founded by Robert Wentworth Little and popularized by William Wynn Wescott, both connected with the Golden Dawn ritual magic group. It requires its members to be both Masons and Christians. Smaller but still recognizable is the Rosicrucian Fellowship founded by Max Heindel in 1907. A largely Christian organization, it has closer ties with theosophy and astrology than with any original Rosicrucian thought.

The Rosicrucian Fellowship, "An International Association of Christian Mystics" was founded in 1909 by Max Heindel with the aim of heralding the Aquarian Age and promulgating "the true Philosophy" of the Rosicrucians. This philosophy, which draws heavily upon Theosophy, claims to present Esoteric Christian *mysteries* or esoteric knowledge, alluded to in Matthew 13:11 and Luke 8:10, to establish a meeting ground for art, religion, and science and to prepare the individual through harmonious development of the mind and the heart for selfless service of mankind.

The Rosicrucian Fellowship conducts Spiritual Healing Services and offers correspondence courses in esoteric Christianity, philosophy, "spiritual astrology" and Bible interpretation. Its headquarters are located on Mount Ecclesia in Oceanside, California, and its students are found throughout the world organized in centers and study groups. Its mission is to promulgate a scientific method of development suited particularly to the Western people whereby the "Soul body" may be wrought, so that mankind may hasten the Second Coming.

According to **William Poundstone**, *"The Rosicrucians, (AMORC), have about a hundred lodges in the United States, there are 26 lodges in France, 21 in Brazil, 18 in Nigeria, 13 in Canada and Mexico, 12 in England and 11 in Venezuela, and 8 in Australia,"* They claim not to be a religion, but promises if one becomes a member and learns their philosophy of life and the mysteries of the universe, they can awaken ones natural talents and enable them to lead a fuller and happier life.

In **Mastery of Life**, it states: *"The Order had its birth as one of the mystery schools of secret wisdom in Ancient Egypt during the 18th Dynasty... about 1350 B.C."* (p. 16). This same booklet says *"The Rosicrucians first came to America and to the Western world in 1694,"* (p. 17). The AMORC also claims that *"Jesus, Benjamin Franklin, Isaac Newton, Ren<130> Descartes, Leibnitz, Plato, Balzac, Francis Bacon, St. Thomas Aquainas, and Aristotle were all members,"* (**Bigger Secrets**, p. 31). This is difficult to prove since these men are not around to confirm or deny their membership, but Sirhan Sirhan, the man who assassinated Robert Kennedy, was a practicing member.

The Rosicrucian Fellowship is composed of men and women who study the Rosicrucian Philosophy known as the Western Wisdom Teachings as presented in The Rosicrucian Cosmo-Conception. This Christian Mystic Philosophy presents deep insights into the Christian Mysteries and establishes a meeting ground for Art, Religion, and Science. Max Heindel was selected by the Elder Brothers of the Rose Cross to publicly give out the

Western Wisdom Teachings in order to help prepare mankind for the coming age of Universal Brotherhood, the Age of Aquarius. The Fellowship reaches back to the Mystery schools of ancient Egypt.

The work of the Rosicrucian Fellowship is stated as being one to spread the gospel and heal the sick. This is achieved by making the Western Wisdom Teachings available to all who are willing to receive them, by providing a Healing Department which emphasizes spiritual healing along the principles of right living, and by making The Rosicrucian Fellowship books and home study courses available upon request. These correspondence courses include: studies in Esoteric Christian Philosophy using the basic textbook, The Rosicrucian Cosmo-Conception; a Bible study course that helps to bring a better understanding of the satisfying truths contained in the Bible; and studies in Spiritual Astrology as a key to the Spirit, designed toward spiritual development and self-knowledge, as well as an aid to healing through Astro-Diagnosis.

One of the basic conditions on which the Western Wisdom Teachings were given to Max Heindel was that no price should be put on them. This condition was faithfully observed by Mr. Heindel and is still adhered to. Although the Rosicrucian Fellowship books are sold, the services of our Healing Department, the Correspondence Courses, and the various School activities continue to be offered on a free-will love-offering basis. The Rosicrucian Fellowship has no connection with any other organization. There are no membership dues or fees.

A site to visit for more details is **www.terrorism-illuminati.com/rosicrucians-freemasons.**

Freemasonry And The Witchcraft Connection

Much of the material following is summarized from the web sites found at **www.jesusfamilytomb.com/back_to_basics/alternative/freemason/egypt.html**, and **www.religiouscounterfeits.org/ml_history.htm**

According to Masonic historians, Freemasonry is based on the principles and values of ancient Egypt. The most important principle of the Freemasons that is traced to ancient Egypt is the belief in materialist evolution. This theory of evolution is based on the belief that the universe exists by and of itself, evolving only by chance. In this theory of evolution, matter was always extant, and the world originated when order arose from chaos. This state of chaos was referred to as Nun. A latent, creative force exists within this state of disorder which has the potential to rise above the disorder. Another philosophical connection established between the ancient Egyptians and the Freemasons is believed to be the common rituals associated with death and burial practices. Specifically, the link between ancient Egypt and the Masons can be found in the text known as **The Book of the Dead**. This texts original title is in fact **The Book of Coming Forth by Day**. It is an ancient Egyptian funerary text that outlines instructions for the afterlife.

Contrary to popular belief, **The Book of Coming Forth by Day** does not instruct individuals on how to raise the dead in order to escape death, but rather provides instructions for the afterlife. These instructions, in the form of spells, were used by the Egyptian elite for their burial practices. In addition, spells were offered as gifts to the gods, for healing such ailments as the inability to walk, and to prevent death during the afterlife. The ultimate aim of The Book of Coming Forth by Day was to enable the individual to overcome the hardships and obstacles

Furthermore, members of the Freemasons are believed to consider themselves to be special heirs of the people of ancient Egypt, a belief that experts have attributed to the philosophical commonality between the Freemasons of today and the ancient Egyptians. According to some experts, these principles and theories were adopted by the Freemasons, and were incorporated into the moral and metaphysical ideals espoused by members of Freemasonry.

Yet, a widely accepted theory among Masonic scholars is that it arose from the stonemasons' guilds during the Middle Ages and that the language and symbols used in the fraternity's rituals come from this era. The oldest document that makes reference to Masons is the Regius Poem, printed about 1390, which was a copy of an earlier work. In 1717, four lodges in London formed the first Grand Lodge of England, and records from that point on are more complete. It is likely that this was a re-emergence of the Freemasons.

Within thirty years, the fraternity had spread throughout Europe and the American Colonies. Freemasonry became very popular in colonial America. George Washington was a Mason, Benjamin Franklin served as the head of the fraternity in Pennsylvania, as did Paul Revere and Joseph Warren in Massachusetts. Other well-known Masons involved with the founding of America included John Hancock, John Sullivan, Lafayette, Baron Fredrick von Stuben, Nathanael Greene, and John Paul Jones. Another Mason, Chief Justice John Marshall, shaped the Supreme Court into its present form. Over the centuries, Freemasonry has developed into a worldwide fraternity emphasizing personal study, self-improvement, and social betterment via individual involvement and philanthropy.

The first Grand Lodge of Freemasonry was founded in England in 1717 - twenty-three years after the founding of the Bank of England which had a secret court of directors. The creation of this lodge is a milestone in the transformation of what was a trade guild into a secret society. The Rothschild family became allied with Freemasonry in the late 1700's. By co-operating with secret societies they were able to expand their banking operations from Germany, networking the political contacts of Freemasonry, which was already well established throughout the continent. Freemasonry, on the other hand, needed money to finance its efforts to build a New World Order, and the Rothschilds would be able to provide such funds. Again we have the entry of the Rothschilds.

Proceedings of the U.S. Anti-Masonic Convention *(1830 p. 33)*, declare Freemasonry was instituted, *'to dupe the simple for the benefit of the crafty'*. Freemasons are intensely focused on maintaining secrecy and will retaliate against those who violate their oaths or transgress against brother Masons. The legend of Hiram Abiff, the Masonic Christ figure, describes how Hiram was killed while keeping a Masonic secret. His brother Freemasons killed Hiram's assailants and raised Hiram from the grave. Freemasons are encouraged to model themselves after Hiram and hold their Masonic secrets. If they remain true to their oaths, like Hiram, they should expect to be avenged for such attacks and rewarded for their fidelity to the brotherhood. While cases exist suggesting the murder of opponents of Freemasonry, Masonic rituals state that 'the more effective penalty for doing anything displeasing to Masonry is to be shunned by the entire Brotherhood, a penalty sufficient to bring a man to ruin, the more certainly so as Freemasonry has expanded into every profession and every branch of society' (***Stephan Knight***, ***The Brotherhood*** (1984) p. 31).

Like other secret societies, the Freemasons have their own written constitutions. In the Scottish Rite petition for admission to the mysteries, question number 26 asks: *"Do you *promise, upon your honour, to strictly adhere to and be governed by the Constitution and Laws of the Grand Lodge of Texas and by the By-Laws of this Lodge?' Question number 29 asks: 'Do you seriously declare, upon your honour, that you will cheerfully conform to the ancient established usages and customs of Masonry?"*

Edmona Ronayue described the requirement of obedience to all laws and edicts: *"First, the candidate is made to swear eternal obedience to all Masonic laws and edicts, and without having the slightest knowledge of any one of them; then the law peremptorily excluding the name of Christ is submitted for his acceptance, and, lastly, in perfect harmony with the requirements of his Masonic obligation, a blind implicit unwavering obedience to this law is demanded of him whether right or wrong"* (**The Master's Carpet** (1879). It is even claimed that the teachings of Freemasonry are summarily this: *"Obey Masonic law, and live"* (Rev*.* **C.G. Finney**, **The Character, Claims and Practical Workings of Freemasonry** (1869) p.2130.

It has been said that *"Those who over-step the Constitution of the US government by joining secret societies and take their judicial oaths to secretly uphold their members in so far as they can when their design and purposes conflict with our Constitutions and laws should be treated as traitors of the government and deprived of their franchise as citizens"* (**William Edward Smith**, **Christianity and Secret Societies,** (1936) 25). While not overtly encouraged to participate in criminal activity, Freemasons were sworn to protect their brother Freemasons should they engage in immoral or criminal conduct. The Royal Arch Mason swore, *"I will aid and assist a companion Royal Arch Mason, when engaged in any difficulty, and espouse his cause, so far as to extricate him from the same, if in my power, whether he be right or wrong... A companion Royal Arch Mason's secrets, given me in charge as such, and I knowing him to be such, shall remain as secure and inviolable, in my breast as in his own, murder and treason not excepted, etc."* (**The Address of the U.S. Anti-Masonic Convention (1830) p. 9**).

According to Freemasonry's critics, Freemasonry is a brotherhood or more aptly a cult which mandates secrecy and obedience within its ranks, affords protection and advancement of the interests of its members, punishes its enemies and turns a blind eye to criminal behaviour committed by its members against non-members. Freemasonry provides a value system and an organizational structure which works to put brother Freemasons in positions of power in all organizations and can be used by its members for the most immoral and illegal purposes. Its foundation appears to rest upon the willingness of its members to selfishly exchange their ethics for personal advantage. Its strength appears to lie in a pervasive presence, unseen by those outside the brotherhood, working in concert to protect and expand their wealth and power. Any Freemasons who violated their Masonic confidences would invite the wrath of the brotherhood.

Adam Weishaupt, founder of the Illuminati was born on 6 February 1748 in Ingolstadt in the Electorate of Bavaria. Weishaupt's father Johann Georg Weishaupt (1717–1753) died when Adam was five years old. After his father's death he came under the tutelage of his godfather Johann Adam Freiherr von Ickstatt who, like his father, was a professor of law at the University of Ingolstadt. Ickstatt was a proponent of the philosophy of Christian Wolff and of the Enlightenment, and he influenced the young Weishaupt with his rationalism. Weishaupt began his formal education at age seven[1] at a Jesuit school. He later enrolled at the University of Ingolstadt and graduated in 1768 at age 20 with a doctorate of law. In 1772 he became a professor of law. The following year he married Afra Sausenhofer of Eichstätt.

After Pope Clement XIV's suppression of the Society of Jesus in 1773, Weishaupt became a professor of canon law, a position that was held exclusively by the Jesuits until that time. In 1775 Weishaupt was introduced to the empirical philosophy of Johann Georg Heinrich Feder of the University of Göttingen. Both Feder and Weishaupt would later become opponents of Kantian idealism.

On 1 May 1776 Weishaupt formed the "Order of Perfectibilists". He adopted the name of "Brother Spartacus" within the order. Though the Order was not egalitarian or democratic, its mission was the abolition of all monarchical governments and state religions in Europe and its colonies.

The actual character of the society was an elaborate network of spies and counter-spies. Each isolated cell of initiates reported to a superior, whom they did not know, a party structure that was effectively adopted by some later groups.

Weishaupt was initiated into the Masonic Lodge "Theodor zum guten Rath", at Munich in 1777. His project of "illumination, enlightening the understanding by the sun of reason, which will dispel the clouds of superstition and of prejudice" was an unwelcome reform. Soon however he had developed Gnostic mysteries of his own, with the goal of "perfecting human nature" through re-education to achieve a communal state with nature, freed of government and organized religion. He began working towards incorporating his system of Illuminism with that of Freemasonry.

He wrote: *"I did not bring Deism into Bavaria more than into Rome. I found it here, in great vigor, more abounding than in any of the neighboring Protestant States. I am proud to be known to the world as the founder of the Illuminati."* Weishaupt's radical rationalism and vocabulary was not likely to succeed. Writings that were intercepted in 1784 were interpreted as seditious, and the Society was banned by the government of Karl Theodor, Elector of Bavaria, in 1784. Weishaupt lost his position at the University of Ingolstadt and fled Bavaria

As a student, Weishaupt had studied the Greek mystics: *"While an undergraduate Weishaupt studied the ancient pagan religions and was familiar with the Eleusinian mysteries and the theories of the Greek mystic Pythagorus. As a student he drafted the constitution for a secret society modelled on the pagan mystery schools but it was not until he was initiated into Freemasonry that Weishaupt's plan for the ultimate secret society was spawne"* (**Michael Howard, The Occult Conspiracy** (1989) p. 61). Weishaupt said: *"Behold our secret. Remember that the end justifies the means, and that the wise ought to take all the means to do good which the wicked take to do evil"* (**Ralph Epperson, The Unseen Hand** (1985) p. 81).

"His philosophy has been continued as the Communist code of ethics is based upon the principle that the ends of revolution justify any means, no matter how lawless, violent, dishonest, or indecent from the standpoint of accepted American standards of morality" (**House Report No. 2, 76th Congress**, 1st Session 26-29).

'No morality seemed to be a key foundation for the scheme. The group was founded on the premise that the end justifies the means and that the good of the Order justifies calumnies, poisoning, murders, perjuries, treasons, rebellions and all that men call criminal" (**Nesta H. Webster, World Revolution**, p. 297). Disbelief remains as the single biggest factor working in Freemasonry's favour. Decent folk find it incomprehensible that there could be individuals so evil as to actually try to take control of the world on behalf of Lucifer. In Freemasonry everything has a double-meaning. Thus the candidate is practicing the occult throughout his degree work without knowing it.

False interpretations are given to him to prevent him from suspecting the Craft to be anything less than 'on the square'. Another factor is that it rarely, if ever, does anything covert under its own name. In order to advance its agenda it establishes other organizations, to which it gives special assignments.

Jesus Christ was recognized to novices as the Grand Master and *"if Christ exhorted his disciples to despise riches it was in order to prepare the world for the community of goods that should do away with property"* (***ibid*** p. 12). Later, at the grade of Priest, the initiate was told that *"the pretended religion of Christ was nothing else than the work of priests, of imposture and of tyranny"* (**ibid** p. 13). *"The success of socialism seems tied directly to eliminating religion"* (***William Riley Halstead, Civil and Religious Forces*** (1890) p. 165-166).

Weishaupt, like Lenin and Marx, early publicly proclaimed that the State would wither away. In private the Illuminati elite believed *"that the average man was too stupid to govern himself and that a self-appointed inner-circle or Illuminati would secretly rule"* (***Robert Henry Goldsborough, Lines of Credit: Ropes of Bondage*** - 1989).

The United States of America was a republic. However, the *secret destiny* of America was the accomplishment of a democratic form of government that illegally usurped the republic. When it was first settled, the purpose was to all for a new way of life *"free from the religious intolerance and political despotism that held Europe in its clutches"* (***Manly P. Hall, The Secret Destiny of America*** (1958) p. 129).

The Philadelphia convention adjourned after five months of *secret* sessions. Madison's Journal of the Federal Convention was not published until 1840 - after everyone who was at the 1787 Convention had died (Richard B. Morris, The Constitution (1985) p. 10). As originally drafted in the secret proceedings, the 1787 U.S. Constitution left out a public bill of rights altogether. Until the 1820's, college education was generally narrow and theological in character. However, a rising tide of relatively liberal thought on campus led to a new, secular liberal arts orientation strongly supporting the era of material progress that was to transform the continent during the second half of the century.

What they would learn is that *someone else* told you *what* to think about, *when* to think about it, *how long* to think about it, *when to stop* thinking about it, *when to think of something else,* and *someone else* sets up the secrets. *"The Carbonari secret society in Italy in the early 1820s was more than just a power in the land, and boasted branches and sub-societies as far afield as Poland, France and German"* (***Arkon Daraul, Secret Societies*** (1961) p.100).

Their origin was claimed to be in Scotland where they took to charcoal-burning to avoid suspicion of ulterior motives. They set up their own three-branch government and obeyed only their own laws (***Ibid*** p. 101). The object of the society was to set up a body of men subject to the orders of a central body and to take action even against established governments: From the earliest recorded period of its existence, it formed a state within a state (**Ibid** p. 103. The Degree of Grand Elect was conferred on a candidate who was thirty-three years and three months old (the age of Christ on the day of His Death) (***Heckethorn***, I, p. 163). It was revealed in the catechism that the object of the organization was political and that it aimed at the overthrow of all tyrants.

In 1871 Pike copyrighted his 861-page book, ***Morals and Dogma of the Ancient and Accepted Scottish Rite of Freemasonry'*** (***Ralph Epperson, The Unseen Hand***

(1985) p. 223). Albert Pike stated: "*All true dogmatic religions come from the Kabbala and lead back to it; all that is scientific and great in the religious dream of all the illuminated such as Bachme, Swedenborg, St. Martin, and others similar, is borrowed from the Kabbala. All the Masonic associations owe their secrets and symbols to it*" (**Morals and Dogma** (1871) p. 744-745).

On January 22, 1870, Mazzini wrote to General Albert Pike about "*a super rite, which will remain unknown, to which we will call those Masons of high degree which we shall select... Through this supreme rite, we will govern all Freemasonry which will become the one international center, the more powerful because its direction will be unknown*" (**Des Griffin, Fourth Reich of the Rich** (1989) p. 68; Lady Queenborough, pp. 208-209; Adriano Lemmi p. 97; John 18:20; Ephesians 5:11). "*Albert Pike organized the New and Reformed Palladian Rite. Three supreme councils were established at Charleston, S.C., Rome, Italy, and Berlin, Germany*" (Griffin, p. 69). "*Albert Pike took control of the Theosophical operations while Mazzini was in charge of the political operations*" (Ibid p. 68). "*Pike was Sovereign Pontiff of Universal Freemasonry while Mazzini was Sovereign Chief of Political Action.*" (**William T. Still, New World Order**: **The Ancient Plan of Secret Societies (1990) p. 123).**

"*On September 12, 1874, a decree confirmed a treaty signed by Armand Levi for the Jewish B'nai B'rith. Albert Pike authorized Jewish Freemasons to form a secret organization (Sovereign Patriarchal Council) to function side-by-side with the ordinary lodges headquartered in Hamburg, Germany*" (**Lady Queenborough**, p. 288.).

Albert Pike was a very high ranking freemason and a southern confederate general, who in the closing days of the civil war helped to start a 'terror' campaign against black slaves. After the civil war this terror activity grew and was transformed into what was known by, and is still known today as the Ku Klux Klan. The formation of this 'Secret Group' was in response to the Emancipation Proclamation issued by President Abraham Lincoln, who was Assassinated by Rome and its Jesuit Order, shortly after accepting his second term as US President. While it is heavily rumoured [and suspected] that Pike helped to form the Ku Klux Klan, at this time this cannot be entirely proven per se' as in absolute smoking gun proof!, although the heavy preponderance of the evidence does strongly suggest this. The Ku Klux Klan had become very powerful in southern states, through the freemason 'network', and has infested at all levels, local, civic, state and federal government bodies. This power has extended well into the political scene of America in the 20th Century.

Of which still plagues our society today. By the late 19th Cent, the Klan had also started to 'expand' beyond the Southern States into the North, Mid-west, and also into the Western Territories. By the 1880's Albert Pike himself had become the Top '33rd Degree Freemason' in the World, His title had now become "Grand Supreme Pontiff " which is an ancient Babylonian title. Pontiff also equals Pope, there is a very strong Jesuit connection to all of this. His (Pikes) power and Influence now had a Global reach, it was during this time that **Pike** wrote his now Infamous book **'Morals and Dogma**, Authored in 1889, and is still in use today. Currently considered the "Freemason Bible".

Bernard Shaw noted that "*Compulsory labour, with death as the final penalty, is the keystone of Socialism... and that opposition in a Socialist state would have to be an underground conspiracy working in secret 'until it is strong enough for an open test of strength."* In turn, *"the ruling clique is required to protect itself with a gigantic spy service"* (**Fahey**, p. 98).

'The Federal Reserve was created in December, 1913 when Woodrow Wilson signed the Glass-Owen Federal Reserve Act. That bill had been the product of cloak-and-dagger machinations by Wall Street financiers and their political mouthpieces, many of them in league with the City of London. Wall Streeter **Frank A. Vanderlip**, in his autobiography **From Farm Boy to Financier** narrates that the secret conference which planned the Federal Reserve was 'as secret - indeed, as furtive - as any conspirator. Vanderlip was one of the insiders invited to the Jekyll Island Club on the coast of Georgia in the autumn of 1910 by the Senator Nelson Aldrich, the father-in-law of John D. Rockefeller Jr. Aldrich also invited Henry Davison of J.P. Morgan & Co., and Benjamin Strong, the future Governor of the New York Federal Reserve Bank. Also on hand was Paul Warburg of the notorious international banking family, descended from the Del Banco family of Venice. As Vanderlip recounted, 'We were instructed to come one at a time and as unobtrusively as possible to the railway terminal on the New Jersey littoral of the Hudson, where Senator Aldrich's private car would be in readiness, attached to the rear end of a train for the South.

In more recent times, Bill Moyers took a trip around the world with David Rockefeller. Later he wrote in 1990: *"Secrecy is the freedom zealots dream of: no watchman to check the door, no accountant to check the books, no judge to check the law. The secret government has no constitution. The rules it follows are the rules it makes up"* (**Bill Moyers, The Secret Government: The Constitution in Crisis** (1990) p. 7).

Throughout history Jews have been the soul of every anti-Christian movement. There has not been a single important program or organization aimed at the overthrow of the Church in which they cannot be found lurking.

Thus, Jews were the main opposition to spreading the Faith at the time of the Apostles. They were the ones who urged Nero to begin his persecution of Christians. They started Gnosticism, the first great heresy that threatened to destroy the Church by confusing her doctrine. They have provided the inspiration and encouragement for almost every other heresy, from Arianism and Trinitarianism in the fourth century, to impersonating Protestantism in the sixteenth (chiefly by making always available their Talmud and Cabala, the sources and reservoirs of all anti-Christian blasphemy and filth, as is also most evident in the nature of the criminal behaviour and perverse attitudes plaguing society today). And in our own day, they conceived, brought into being, and provided the membership for Communism.

The Roman Catholic FALSE church however, although a child of apostate Jewry, has at certain periods in her history, and in the strongest possible terms, tried to warn and protect her children against these *"adversaries of all men"*, as Saint Paul called them. Through the decrees of her Popes and Councils she has obliged the Jews to live in ghettos, forbidden them to have Christian servants or to hold public office, required them to wear orange hats so as to be easily recognized and avoided. At one time or other, the Jews have been banished from almost every country in Europe - and not by merciless tyrants but by great so-called Christian rulers, like Saint Henry II of Germany and Louis IX of France.

Not until the eighteenth century, when the Freemasons began to take over the governments of Europe, did the Jews really come into their own. Before that they had been obliged to work mostly underground, exerting their influence in hidden, subtle ways. But from this time on they worked in the open.

Being formed for the purpose of combating Christ and His Church, the Masons shrewdly realized that to wage this war effectively they must enlist the aid of that people who had always been the backbone of the anti-Christian army. Accordingly, the Mason's terminology, their secret rituals, their philosophy, were all taken over from the Jews. But the Masons' greatest stroke was to make use, not merely of these perfidious traditions, but of the vital, raging Jewish people themselves. As the Masons took over the nations of Europe, the Jews were released from the ghettos in which they had been for centuries confined, and turned out on society.

Thus was established the great alliance in the empire of Satan: the Masons and the Jews; the Masons with their power, controlling government and business, plotting and planning at the highest levels; the Jews with their influence, controlling the press and entertainment, insinuating their nervous, impure, infidel values into all society, and corrupting it to the core.

These two, which in every other respect are poles apart, have joined together for one reason: the destruction of the Church. And every Masonic-Jewish scheme has this end in view. Thus, their advocacy of Internationalism is partly due to the fact that they have loyalty to no country, but mainly it is an attempt to fight the Church on a scale as large, as catholic, as the Church is herself.

But by the Grace of God, His true Church is a *"little Flock"*, and not the organized rabble of Rome and her once-Protestant harlot daughters. Very few people in this world have ever met a Christian - in the sense of a born-again saint. And no-one in any of the secret societies or man-made religious systems would know what to look for, what the faith is, or how to gauge it.

The Masons' supreme, ultimate objective, so they mysteriously declare, is to rebuild the Temple of Jerusalem. This is of course, an objective which the Jews share. And though it may sound innocent, it is, in its implications, terrifying.

The Temple of Jerusalem is the traditional center of Jewish worship, which was destroyed in 70 A.D. by the Romans, in fulfillment of Our Lord's prophecy that *"there shall not be left a stone upon a stone."* The establishment of the state of Israel gives the Masons and the Jews their first opportunity to try and achieve their objective of rebuilding this Temple.

However, when they do so there will not be one Gentile Christian on earth to see it. For the Temple was destroyed as a stark, unmistakable sign of God's wrath upon the Jews. It will be rebuilt, the Bible tells us so. But its reconstruction will NOT be of the Lord, for the mystic Body of Christ, the Church, is His Temple. Then the Antichrist will appear. He will succeed in all the Masons and Jews have determined. He will rebuild a Temple in Jerusalem, where he will sit as if he were God, and FORCE the mark of the beast. masons.htm

William Schnoebelen was deeply involved in both Witchcraft as a Wiccan high priest and the Masonic order for many years. He was a Mason for nine years and a Witch for sixteen years. In the Lodge, he held offices of Junior Warden in the Blue Lodge, Prelate in the Commandery of the York Rite, Master of the Veil in the Royal Arch degree, and Associate Patron in the Order of the Eastern Star. Additionally, he was a 32 degree Mason and a Shriner. He is now a Born Again Christian and the author of 5 books, including **Masonry: Beyond the Light**. *"For rebellion is as the sin of witchcraft, and stubbornness is as iniquity and idolatry..."* —**1st Samuel 15:23.**

In understanding the spiritual difficulties of a Born Again Christian being a Mason, it is necessary to realize that there are highly occult elements woven into the very warp and woof of Freemasonry. Thus, the Lodge is not just "another religion" like the Muslims or the Buddhists—although that alone should be enough to keep Christians from involving themselves in it. The nature and character of the Lodge's deepest theological underpinnings are rooted in Witchcraft and Paganism.

Now that may be an astonishing assertion to some, especially to most Masons. However, it is very easily proven. Few people, within the Craft of Masonry or otherwise, perceive that just because a Bible lies open on the altar and Bible verses and characters play an important part in the ritual of the Lodge, that this does not prevent the Lodge from being of the nature of the occult or Witchcraft.

This can be illustrated by a very simple illustration. Back in the 1970's, (**Freemasonry: The Witchcraft Connection** by **William J. Schnoebelen**) when a very popular how-to book on magic was **Raymond Buckland's Popular Candle-Burning**. In this book were "recipes" for spells for everything from healing, to love spells, to protection spells. On one set of pages of the book would be a spell for healing, complete with instructions on the burning and movement of certain collared candles. The spell would be a full-blown Witchcraft ritual, Pagan to the core!

On the following pages would be the same ritual, with the same candles, the same instructions. However, the text of the "spell" would be drawn from the Psalms or other Bible verses. These were provided for readers who were a little too squeamish to actually do a Witchcraft incantation, but still wanted results.

Now the question becomes: *Even though those rituals were full of Psalms, were they still Witchcraft?* Of course, the answer would have to be yes. In like manner, even though Bible phrases and characters abound in the Masonic ritual work, the presence of those elements cannot somehow "sanctify" what is essentially a Pagan ritual full of Witchcraft overtones.

Freemasonry is not as it appears... Freemasonry and False Religion **Freemasonry: Its Roots & Links to the Occult.** Check it out at **www.jesus-is-savior.com/False%20Religions/Freemasonry/infiltrate.htm**

The gods of the Freemasonry lodge are Egyptian gods. The subject of Egyptian archaeology and hieroglyphics, and other various related sciences, are very popular amongst Masonic members. So the next time you see the back of a US. dollar, consider *The Great Pyramid* and surrounding occult symbols with numerology, which are intended to glorify the workings of the occult.

Baphomet, god of Freemasonry. Perhaps it would be helpful to have a few terms defined before we go further. Witchcraft (or Wicca the term for "white" or good Witchcraft) can be broadly defined as a mystery religion based on the ancient fertility cults of Pre-Christian Europe. Many Witches are polytheists—meaning that they believe in more than one god or goddess. Some are monotheists, believing in only one deity. Even most polytheistic Witches today, however, acknowledge that ultimately there is one supreme deity somewhere.

The popular saying by 20th century master occultist Dion Fortune (Violet Firth) speaks to this: *"All Gods are one God, all Goddesses are one Goddess, and there is but one Initiator."* Pressed, you will find that most knowledgeable Witches will reveal that the "one Initiator" is Lucifer, who is the Light-Bringer, the Illuminator, and the sun-deity. He is not felt to be a devil-figure by Wiccans, but only the consort of the Great Mother Goddess.

Witchcraft, in its religious sense, involves the veneration of the forces of reproduction—both in plant, animal and human life. Thus, human and animal sexuality are revered, the cycle of the seasons celebrated; and rituals do frequently involve the use of ritual tools which symbolize the human reproductive organs (wands, daggers, goblets, cauldrons, etc.). Many Witchcraft groups even have ritual sex, believing that this is an important way to encounter the gods.

The term, "mystery religion" means that it is a religion in which elements are kept hidden from the "profane" (non-members). You can only learn these elements by going through a formal initiation in which you are ceremonially set apart from the masses and sworn formally to secrecy. Only then are you entrusted with the group's secrets, and then in degrees. In other words, there are things a "third grade" or "third degree" Witch is allowed to know that a first degree Witch is not.

A secondary element in Witchcraft is the belief in magic. However, it is only secondary—contrary to popular belief. A good—though broad—definition of magic which many Witches would accept is that given by magician (and 33° Mason) **Aleister Crowley**: *"the art and science of causing change to occur in conformity with [your] will."* Though this definition is broad enough to include things normally not thought of as magic, like picking up a pencil (you caused a change in the pencil's position to occur in conformity with your will); most Witches understand it to mainly apply to causing change to occur without a visible, tangible cause in the environment.

Many Witches do not attempt to "work magic" (in the sense of trying to cause change to occur in the forces of nature or human beings) but just enjoy worshipping their gods or goddesses. Thus it is not an absolute requirement that Witch practice magic, or that a magician be a Witch. In fact, the above-mentioned Aleister Crowley would never have called himself a Witch (or warlock).

Finally, we need to define Paganism. This is basically a belief in the forces of nature as being sacred. Pagans are usually pantheists, in that they belief that a kind of god-force is in everything—trees, animals, rocks, etc. Essentially, a Pagan believes most everything the Witch believes, but is kind of a lay person, whereas a Witch is more of a Priestess or

Shaman. The typical Pagan may not have access to some of the deeper "mysteries" of Witchcraft which are not available to the un-initiated.

In a site ***http://adventofdeception.com/history-illuminati-freemasonry-weishupt-albert-pike***/ there is an interesting tie-together of these societies. Here they state:

"Throughout the generations, the Power Elite has overshadowed different secret societies. (***http://listverse.com/2007/08/27/top-10-secret-societies).***

- Skull and Bones
- Freemasonry
- Rosecrucians
- Ordo Templis Orientis
- Hermetic Temple of the Golden Dawn
- The Knights Templar
- The Illuminati
- The Bilderberg Group
- Priory of Sion
- 10 Opus Dei

The Illuminati secret society branch was founded during the year of the American Revolution. The Power Elite of the governments, bankers, and the wealthy use different secret societies to dominate humanity. If the spoken subject of the most powerful secret society were in 1200, the reference might have been to the Knights Templar. The Roman Catholic Church officially endorsed the Knights Templar around 1129, the Order became a favored "society" throughout Christendom and grew rapidly in membership and power. The modern day term "illuminati" predominates all secret societies and is a name that adverts to multiple groups within our current era.

During our current era the term Illuminati refers to a purported conspiratorial organization which acts as a shadowy "power behind the throne", allegedly dominating world affairs through present day governments and corporations, usually as a modern incarnation or continuation of the Bavarian Illuminati. "*The human race will then become one family, and the world will be the dwelling of Rational Men. -**Adam Weishaupt**.*

The Illuminati was founded by Adam Weishaupt who was born on February 6, 1748 in Ingolstadt in the Electorate of Bavaria. Adam's godfather, Johann Adam Freiherr von Ickstatt influenced the young Weishaupt with his rationalism. Weishaupt began his formal education at age seven at a Jesuit school and became the first lay professor of canon law at the University of Ingolstadt.

On May 1, 1776 (A Prime Occult Holiday) Weishaupt formed the "Order of Perfectibilists". He adopted the name of "Brother Spartacus" within the Order. Though the Order was not egalitarian or democratic, its mission was the abolition of all monarchical governments and state religions in Europe and its colonies.

Adam Weishaupt is adverted to repeatedly in The Illuminatus Trilogy, written by Robert Shea and Robert Anton Wilson, as the founder of the Bavarian Illuminati. It is mentioned that Weishaupt construed as an impostor who killed George Washington and took his place as the first president of the United States. Certain sources claim that Washington's portrait on the one-dollar bill to actually be Weishaupt's. Whatever the facts may be, the early founding fathers of America were freemasons with the same agenda to enslave and dominate their "new world".

The Occult symbolism of Freemasonry effectively perpetuated the mystery about the Order among outsiders. This amplified the spread of ties to Satanism, alien beings, and the connection to the Power Elite and the secret society of the Illuminati. These concepts were covertly accelerated prior by Albert Pike, an attorney, soldier, writer, and Freemason. A 33rd degree Mason, Albert Pike possibly and covertly was one of the founding fathers, and the head of the Ancient Accepted Scottish Rite of Freemasonry being the Grand Commander of North American Freemasonry from 1859 and retained that position until his death in 1891. In 1869, Pike was a top leader in the Knights of the Ku Klux Klan.

Externally, Freemasonry presents itself as respectable as other religions, yet, the vast majorities never reach the 30th degree of masonry, and are void of the circumspection of the real purpose behind Masonry. The Illuminati infiltrated Freemasonry because of the external respectable forum in which to hide their clandestine activities.

It is acknowledged that the Regius Manuscript held in the British Museum is the oldest genuine record of Masonic relevance and was written in 1390. Most historians concur that Freemasonry, in its current form, probably developed as an adjunct from medieval stonemasons through the ages leading up to the Operative Stone Masons Guilds. The most prominent influences of Freemasonry were all Gnostics, Magi of the English Rose Croix, whose names were: Theophile Desaguliers, named Chaplain of the Prince of Wales by George II, Anderson, the clergy man, an Oxford graduate and preacher to the King of England, George Payne, King James, Calvert, Lumden-Madden, and Elliott. Gnosticism, as the Mother of Freemasonry, has imposed its mark in the very centre of the chief symbol of this association. The **"G"** which the Freemasons place in the middle of the flamboyant star signifies Gnosticism, Generation, and Geometry, the most sacred words of the ancient Cabala.

The Logo for Freemasonry is best described as follows: *"We must allow all the federations to continue just as they are, with their systems, their central authorities and their diverse modes of correspondence between high grades of the same rite, organized as they are at the present, but we must create a super rite, which will remain unknown, to which we will call those Masons of high degree whom we shall select. With regard to our brothers in Masonry, these men must be pledges to the strictest secrecy. Through this supreme rite, we will govern all Freemasonry which will become the one international center, the more powerful because its direction will be unknown."* —**Lady Queensborough: Occult Theocracy**, pp. 208-209.

The Majority of disinformation about the Illuminati influence among the world began after 9/11 as a preparation tool, and to create fear, anger and dread among the intelligent half awakened populace, and generate a strong air of unbelievability among the denial ridden deluded populace. The creation of staged "eyewitness" testimonies and documents are purposefully "leaked" out of these societies about the new world order to manufacture and project an embodiment of duality such as the patriot and tea party movements. The

Power Elite of the darkness creates both sides of the coin, but dominates from the same piggy bank. The combined powers of the darkness comprehends the universal law of free choice; the illuminati power elite must present their plan to produce the separation process between the light and the darkness. There is a large majority who are still dwelling within their denial, fear, ignorance, and delusions despite truthful information scattered around the internet about the New World Order of Darkness.

In **Morals and Dogma**, 1871, **Albert Pike** wrote: "*Masonry, like all the Religions, all the Mysteries, Hermeticism and Alchemy, conceals its secrets from all except the Adepts and Sages, or the Elect, and uses false explanations and misinterpretations of its symbols to mislead those who deserve only to be misled; to conceal the Truth, which it calls Light, from them, and to draw them away from it. Truth is not for those who are unworthy or unable to receive it, or would pervert it... The truth must be kept secret, and the masses need a teaching proportioned to their imperfect reason...every man's conception of God must be proportioned to his mental cultivation and intellectual powers, and moral excellence. God is, as man conceives Him, the reflected image of man himself...*"

(A long list of around 1000 Freemasons. is given in *http://en.wikipedia.org/wiki/List_of_Freemasons*)

P2 Opus Dei

To encapsulate this group, we refer to the web site *www.copi.com/articles/guyatt/gladio.html* where researcher **David Guyatt** *www.bibliotecapleyades.net/esp_autor_guyatt.htm* and *www.deepblacklies.co.uk/about.htm* "state:"

"*Opus Dei - which translates as God's work, had long sought to take effective control of the Vatican. Their cause had been advanced by the sudden death of Pope John Paul I and the election of a keen supporter: Pope John Paul II. With Machiavellian insight, senior figures of Opus Dei reasoned that with Calvi dead the collapse of Banco Ambrosiano would surely follow. This, in turn, would shake loose powerful enemies inside the Curia, opening the way for them to gain total dominance of the Vatican. Consequently, Roberto Calvi was thrown to the Wolves.*

According to critics, Opus Dei is aggressively right wing in its teachings, and operates a form of thought control. Disciples undergo bouts of agonising self inflicted torture, allegedly designed to clarify thought and cleanse the spirit. They are also taught to avoid natural human feelings, being admonished instead to have a "reticent and guarded heart." Likewise, disciples are not permitted to read certain books, including those authored by communist ideologist Karl Marx.

Detractors believe it a religious faction that shares numerous values similar to the neo-nazi's that people the Masonic P2 lodge. Until recently - and for hundreds of years previously - any member of the Catholic church who was found to be a Freemason was automatically ex-communicated. Despite this many members of the Curia were discovered to be covert members of P2. Subsequently, in 1983, a new Canon Law announced that this would cease. Thereafter, any member of the Roman Church was free to become a Freemason.

Following the Calvi affair, the Vatican sought to diminish increasingly poor publicity by establishing a commission of enquiry. One of the so called Four Wise Men who sat on this enquiry was Dr Herman Abs, a senior German banker. During the war years Abs headed Deutsche Bank and was one of the principal financiers of Adolf Hitler. He also sat on the board of I G Farben, the massive Nazi conglomerate that used slave labour until they dropped. Farben also manufactured Zyklon B - the poisonous gas used with such devastating effect in the extermination camps. Arrested for war crimes at the end of WW II, Abs was quietly released following the intervention of the Bank of England."

The site **www.telusplanet.net/public/semjase/disserta3.htm** provides some history on Opus Dei with an example of how the power behind it has been applied to countries like Canada. The following is taken verbatim from the site:

An organization known as Opus Dei (God's Work) became in part a power with the corrupt P2. Opus Dei was founded by a Spanish priest, Monsignor Josemaria Escriva, in 1928. It is a strong right wing order of the Catholic Church and very wealthy, associates with the rich and powerful, that promotes the theory of wealth over poverty. This organization has, according to its own claims, about 80,000 to 100,000 members around the world. They consist of priests, bishops, cardinals members of the military, a number of dictators, lawyers, and the money elite with substantial wealth.

Luciani was very concerned about Opus Dei and P2 Freemasons. What was their connection with dictators who presided over large Catholic populations. What about General Videla of Argentine whose population was over 90% catholic. Why the death squads? The poverty and the destitution in their own homeland. What about the Marcus clique in the Philippines, with its 43 million Catholics. The self elected Pinochet in Chile with over 80% catholic population. The brutality of General Samoza of Nicaragua with its 90% Catholic population. To the Catholics in El Salvador, were members of the ruling junta considered to be a catholic was to be the enemy. This in a country with 96% catholic population. He feared it was a recipe for genocide. About Ireland and the churches attitude towards the IRA. Many considered that the catholic church had not been honest in its condemnation of the continuing carnage in Northern Ireland. What could Luciani do to restore the Roman Catholic Church as a home for the poor and underprivileged in a country like Uganda in Africa, where Amin was arranging fatal accidents for priests as an almost daily event. Could Luciani prevent a civil war in Lebanon. He fully intended to go there before Christmas, with the hope of bringing peace between Christian and Muslim populations.

By the evening of September 28, 1978 Albino Luciani had taken the first steps towards the realization of his extra ordinary dream. At nine thirty P.M. Albino closed his study door. His dead body would be discovered the next morning. Pope John Paul I was murdered sometime between 9:30 PM on September 28, and 4.30 AM on September 29th. 1978. Albino Lucian was the first pope to die alone for several centuries but somehow there would have to be a reason for this unexplained death.

Karol Wojtyla was chosen to replace Albino Luciani (Pope John 1.) When he chose to be known as Pope John Paul II people rejoiced, believing he would carry out the initiatives of Pope John Paul I. This hope became a dream for millions of people around the world. Pope John Paul II was in position to bring all of Lucian's plans to fruition. It was short lived.

Karol Wojtylo set the tone of his papacy by declaring he would not tolerate public dissent within the church on matters of Catholic ethics and morality, faith and interpretation. Banning all open discussion within the church on theological issues in dispute. The pope made his own old Latin adage, Roma Locuto Causa Finita Est, (when Rome speaks the matter is closed.) He took the position that only the application of strict discipline would save the church and resolve its crisis. It would be the pope's responsibility to openly discuss the temporal, religious and political actions of the church and Vatican City. He insisted on unquestioned papal authority.

He openly repudiated the direction of the second Vatican council and declared the direction of modernism adapted by this council would come to an abrupt end. Having set the course of his papacy, he made his first trip out of Vatican City on a trip to Pueblo, a city in Mexico, for the conference of the Latin American Episcopate that Paul VI had promised to attend, The pope would make his first stop in Santo Domingo, the oldest city on the island of Hispaniola, where Christopher Columbus had landed on his first voyage on the discovery of the America's. John Paul II stunned the watching world by kneeling on the airport tarmac to kiss the ground. He would do it every time he visited a new country. Columbus having been first in 1492 to bring Christianity to the America's. John Paul II was reaffirming this missionary act 487 years later.

The kissing of the tarmac would become his trade mark. It would be his first act upon arrival on foreign soil. People began to ask "why does the pope continue this practice?. Does he kiss the tarmac to thank God for his safe journey? - or does he kiss the tarmac making a symbolic claim to all this land, and all this land possesses, on behalf of God who created all of this. It belongs to God, and the pope as vicar of God, is the sole guardian of all that God has created.

Was Karol Wojtyla a member of Opus Dei before he was elected to the papacy? He showed special admiration for its founder Monsignor Josemaria Escriva. While in Rome after the death of Pope John Paul 1 just before the conclave, he was driven to Opus Dei headquarters in the Parioli section of the city to pray at the tomb of Escriva at the church where he was buried. He openly endorsed the activities of Opus Dei and raised it to the rank of "personal prelature". The popes decision was announced on November 27th 1982 and Monsignor Alvaro del Portilla president of Opus Dei was named the first prelate of the organization and later was ordained bishop. After Bishop Portillo died in 1994, John Paul II returned to the Opus Dei church to pray before his body as it lay in state. Opus Dei now reports directly to the Congregation for Bishops in Rome and to the Pope.

It was John Paul's, personal decision to bestow such power on Opus Dei. The interest, was reciprocated by Opus Dei and began sending millions of dollars into Poland to restore the power of the Roman Catholic Church. In 1989 the moment communist rule collapsed, Opus Dei launched its apostolic and educational activities in Poland opening pastoral centers for men and women and cultural associations. Later, Opus Dei provided funds and personnel, including priests, to help establish an effective Roman Catholic Church in newly independent Kazakhstan of the former Soviet Union.

On May 17, 1992 John Paul II beatified Escriva, just short of seventeen years after his death, at a ceremony before a quarter million people in St. Peters square. It was one of the most rapidly completed processes of beatification. It was John Paul's personal decision to bestow special powers on the organization known as P2. This group had received active support and encouragement from the CIA in Italy. The pope himself accepted this group as a powerful influence around the world. The overwhelming majority of P2 members were and are practicing Roman Catholic followers who claimed they were dedicated to do good. Now with Opus Dei, who never apologized for their ambitions to take over the Roman Catholic Church had been given this additional support, corrupt or otherwise.

John Paul II, like Saint Pius X who's papacy lasted from (1903--1914) opposed the modernist movement in Roman Catholicism. In 1907 he issued a decree condemning 65 modernist propositions and placed many modernist works on the index of forbidden books.

The index of books, which no Roman Catholic was allowed to read grew even longer. Publishers, editors and authors were excommunicated. Pius X coined a word encapsulate, all that was attempting to destroy modernism. Anyone who questioned the current teachings of the church were anathema. With the pope's blessing and financial help an Italian prelate, Umberto Benigni created a spy system. The purpose was to hunt down and destroy all modernists.

Paul John II began his inquisition in Latin America. He battled church progressives in Latin America, over the theology of liberation. Traveling in Peru in 1984, the pope knew that Father Gustavo Gutierrez noted as the Father of the theology of liberation, lived in a urban slum in Lima, the capital, but Pope John Paul II refused to meet with him. The Pope continued to regard this theology as being Marxist tainted or worse. He forbade priests worldwide, not to run for elected office and ordered priests already holding legislative seats not to seek re-election. John Paul's emotional opposition to the movement and to direct involvement by priests in political situations in their countries, even in defence of the poor and the lives of priests and lay catholic activists.

It left many bishops, in Latin America greatly disappointed. And what disappointed them even more was that John Paul II had failed in his Mexican speeches even to allude to wide spread murders and tortures practiced by dictatorial regimes throughout the America's against their opponents, among them priests and nuns. In contrast, Latin American churchmen like Brazilian Cardinals Paulo Evaristo Arns and Aloiso Lorscheider had loudly denounced for years political violence and oppression in their countries.

The Vatican campaign against the Theology of Liberation became a pretext at least in part, for the purge of the Society of Jesus by John Paul II in the early 1980's. The linkage was the Jesuit participation in the Theology of Liberation activities of a segment of the Catholic clergy throughout Central America, including Romero's El Salvador, were the civil war went on unabated, and Nicaragua, where the socialist oriented Sandinistas won power in mid 1979 after overthrowing the dynastic dictatorial regime of the Somoza family.

The Society of Jesus (Jesuits) was founded in 1540 by the Basque Ignatius Loyola to stem the decline of the church in the face of the Protestant Reformation. The Society of Jesus was in the 1980's, the single largest religious order, with nearly thirty thousand Jesuits, and great schools, scholars, and universities as well as missionaries around the world. But it was perceived by the new pope as too progressive, to liberal, and not sufficiently responsive to his theological and political leadership in such situations as Central America.

Desiring absolute papal control over all these fundamental issues John Paul II took a series of controversial political and theological decisions early in his pontificate that altered considerably the balance of power in the Church. therefore, almost simultaneously, he drastically weakened or attempted to weaken, the influence of the Society of Jesus (Jesuits) and bestowed greater power and autonomy on Opus Dei.

The war against the Theology of Liberation did not cease. On December 21, 1984, John Paul II declared in a year end address to the cardinals of the Curia that the church, while committed to helping the underprivileged, must protect the poor from "illusory and dangerous" ideologies. Poverty in the third world keeps increasing, while at the same time the poor are becoming poorer in the most advanced nations around the world.

In 1981, John Paul II named Cardinal Joseph Ratzinger as prefect of the Congregation for the Doctrine of Faith. He was now head inquisitor and would carry out his mission with relentlessness of the Inquisition centuries earlier. John Paul II's offensive against the Theology of Liberation was launched at the start of his pontificate simultaneously with a Holy See ban on theological dissent on the part of catholic scholars.

In December 1979, Hans Kung, a Swiss theologian who taught at the University of Tubingen in Germany, was deprived by Ratzingers Congregation of his license to teach Catholic theology because of his questioning of the doctrine of papal infallibility, proclaimed by Vatican Council 1 in 1870. Further Jacques Pohier, a French Dominican, was equally punished at the same time as Kung for raising questions about Christ's resurrection.

In 1986, Father Charles E. Curran, a professor at the Catholic University of America in Washington D.C. received a letter from Cardinal Ratzinger advising that he could no longer be considered suitable nor eligible to exercise the function of a Professor of Catholic Theology. It was based on Father Curran's public opposition to the anti-contraception, Human vitae encyclical. Curran had taken the view that " a person could dissent in theory and in practice from the condemnation of artificial contraception in the papal encyclical....and still be a loyal Roman Catholic.

Kung, Pohier, and Curran have lost their right to teach at the Catholic institutions, and other theologians with dissenting views have suffered inquisitory treatment at the hands of Cardinal Ratzinger's Congregation. Among them are Belgium's Edward Schillebeeck, Germany's Bernhard Haring, Peru's Gustav Gutierrez, and Brazil's Leonardo Boff, and others, not quite as distinguished as those mentioned.

Pope John Paul II maintained Cardinal Johannes Willebrands, the archbishop of Utrecht in the Netherlands as president of the Pontifical Council for Promoting Christian Unity in order to advance vigorously the ecumenical cause of reuniting Christian Churches. Pope John Paul II was aware that while the world population was soaring the Roman Catholic Church was shrinking in absolute as well as relative numbers. Ordination of priests is usually a good indicator of how well the church is doing, and John Paul II could see that their number, worldwide had fallen from 4,380 in 1974 to 3,824 in 1978 a considerable drop. Europe accounted for the worst decline...from 2,273 to 1,774. In North America the decline was from 848 to 697.

John Paul II was clearly facing a disturbing and significant trend. His immediate challenge was to arrest and reverse it. But it was questionable whether his policies would achieve this goal, or result in a continuing crumbling of the institution.

Pope John Paul II having set the rigid course his papacy would take from the beginning of his pontificate, could not change the course of destiny. The Catholic Church was declining in numbers, but there was a great number of other religions all claiming to be Christian. John Paul could continue his war against the Theology of Liberation and allow the expansion of other Christian religions, without jeopardizing his war against communism and yet hold to the predictions of the Blessed Virgin Mary. Pope John Paul II could throw the spiritual cloak of the Roman Catholic Church over all Christian Churches, so long as they held with the teachings of Jesus Christ and the prophecies of the bible. Pope John Paul II could through the efforts of Cardinal Johannes Willebrands claim ecumenical unity of Christian Churches.

On Wednesday, May 13th. 1981, Pope John Paul became the victim of an assassination attempt. It happened on the same day at approximately the same time, the Virgin Mary appeared to three young children at Fatima Portugal, some 64 years before the attempt on his life. Pope John Paul is convinced that his life was saved miraculously. More specifically, the pope believes that his life was saved as a "real miracle" by the Virgin of Fatima, whose feast day is on May 13th.

John Paul II went to Fatima on the first anniversary of the attempt on his life to thank the Virgin Mary for saving him and place the bullet that had struck him on her alter. It was later fitted alongside diamonds in the golden crown worn by the statue of the Virgin, who is formally known as Our Lady of the Rosary. The bullet pierced and blood stained sash the pope had on, when he was shot has been sent to the altar of the Black Madonna in Czestochowa. It appears his mystical and messianic approach to life come from the great Polish tradition of Poland's Jasna Gorar, the luminous mountain of Czestochowa, the martyrdom of St. Stanislaw, the black Madonna of Czestochowa, and several popes of the past.

The papacy's of Plus XI and Pius XII had given credence to the appearance of the Blessed Virgin Mary at Fatima in 1917. In 1930 Plus XI authorized devotion to our Lady of Fatima. Plus X1 was an outspoken enemy of communism, he supported the regime of the Spanish dictator Francisco Franco during the Spanish civil war to its successful conclusion. Both Italy and Germany supplied military aid, in manpower as well as bomber and fighter planes which proved to be the winning climax. Pius XI also negotiated a treaty with the government of Mexico in 1929, whereby Roman Catholic Churches in that country were permitted to resume services, but relations with church and state deteriorated shortly after the agreement was signed. This treaty was not re-established until the North American Free Trade Agreement was signed. Why would religions become an issue in a Free Trade Agreement?

Pope Pius XII continued and intensified the anti Communist policy's of his predecessor. In 1949 he issued a historic proclamation declaring that any Roman Catholic rendering support of any kind or degree to communism would automatically incur the penalty of excommunication. Pius XII opened the 25th Holy Year in the history of the church on December 24th, 1949. The following November he issued the apostolic Munificenitissimus Deus (Most Plentiful God) in which the assumption of the Blessed Virgin Mary was defined as a dogma of faith. The doctrine that after her death, the body of Mary, the mother of Christ was taken into heaven and re-united with her soul. This was defined as an article of faith by Pope Plus X11 in 1950. On September 9th, 1953, he proclaimed the Marian Year in celebration of the centenary of the definition of the dogma of the Immaculate Conception of the Virgin Mary. Pius XII died October 9th, 1958 .

When Karol Wojtyla was elected to the papacy in October of 1978, many actions of the Roman Catholic Church, that began in the nineteen twenties, had all reached the pinnacle of success. The Bank of International Settlements which was created during the twenties had by now increased their membership, by allowing huge private and central banking systems admittance The Vatican had become an independent sovereign state, a state within the state of Italy. The International Monetary Fund and the World Bank had grown from thirty nine nations in 1944 to 150 in 1978. One hundred and eleven nations from around the world, had created a central banking system, which was the first requisite to becoming a member of the International Monetary Fund. The Extraordinary Section of the Patrimony of the Holy See is the central banker for all three of these organizations.

The 'Special Administration' which had been created by Plus XI in 1929 and managed by Bernardino Nogara, had become self generating and by 1978 had become a colossal giant of global and semi global corporations that were well established throughout the world.

The private bank that was created by Pope Pius XII in 1942, had become an embarrassment to the Vatican. It was this bank that was embroiled in all the accusations of corruptness and dirty dealing. This bank was involved in many illegal schemes to enrich the Vatican coffers. In the end as facts became public, it was rightly asked! What did the Vatican gain by all these shady deals, it appeared to be greed. It gained money and huge amounts of it. To John Paul II it was a matter that had to be settled quietly with the least amount of publicity, and this he accomplished with the endorsement of Opus Dei, and the P2 Masonic Lodge. This gave him overwhelming powers in the world of International finance. Both Opus Dei and the Masonic Lodges are adamantly opposed to any form of socialism, and or social programs that people of some nations enjoy. The membership of Opus Dei and the Masonic P2 are secret. No one knows their real number, but they are estimated to be over one hundred thousand, holding key positions of power in temporal and spiritual institutions around the world. Their sole object is to bring the free market system to nations around the world.

Their first such power was felt in the USA. Pope John Paul II had launched his crusade against Marxist activity in Central and South America. His wars against the Theology of Liberation was one of his most adamant actions to protect the people from illusionary fantasies about Marxism. He showed very little concern about the poverty and destitution of its people, that began with the invasion of Spanish and Roman Catholic conquest which began in the sixteenth century.

Believing it was of absolute necessity to elect a strong president for the USA that would support the actions of the papacy, Opus Dei and the Masonic Lodge used their power, wealth, and influence to accomplish this mission. An organization named the Moral Majority became one of the most powerful institutions in USA history. It was supported by evangelists, and other Christian religions, to elect Ronald Reagan and George Bush to the presidency and vice presidency respectively. Ronald Reagan was inaugurated in January of 1981 and Licio Gelli head of the Infamous Masonic P2 was an honoured guest at this inauguration. Pope John Paul II received immediate support from the newly elected President of the USA Ronald Reagan, not only for Latin America, but also in Eastern Europe and the Soviet Union.

The decade of the eighties was one of confrontation between Pope John Paul II and the USA (vs.) the Soviet Union. The USA under the Reagan administration believed that communism was a threat to western civilization. Like Pope John Paul II Ronald Reagan saw communist infiltration into the central Latin America's. Reagan ordered USA Marines to take over the tiny Island of Grenada, and held war manoeuvres on the shores of these small nations to intimidate them. Over 90% of the population are Roman Catholic, and supposedly, anti communist.

Reagan pumped up the Strategic Defence Initiative, The Star War Program was a defence against nuclear attack from the U.S.S.R. and billions of dollars went into these projects. As Lyndon Johnson and Richard Nixon did in the 1960's and 70's to stop the threat of communism, so did Reagan in the 80's. Pope John Paul II had declared war on communism and the Reagan administration supported his actions with the threat of military power.

During the 80's Russia would emerge with a new leader, new idea's that would change the thinking of the Russian people and the world. The Russian people understood the importance of changing course to democratic socialism. (Perestroika) Mikhail Gorbachev became a much needed messiah for the Russian people. There was dissent in Russia and Eastern Europe and he believed he could take these nations, from the darkness of the Stalin era and some of the preceding dictators, to a new and freer society. He traveled the world speaking of peace and a more prosperous U.S.S.R. a total reconstruction plan.

More money would be spent on domestic and internal matters, less money on strategic defence and military weapons. Russia would go through a new economic restructuring program, that would lead to a more prosperous life for the Russian peasant.

People would be encouraged to play a significant role in this new program, Mikhail Gorbachev had the ability and the charisma the Russian people needed so badly. Unforeseen he met with the power of the Immaculate Heart of the Blessed Virgin Mary and her third request would be adopted by Karol Wojtyla.

In 1987 Pope John Paul II would proclaim the last prediction of the Blessed Virgin Mary at the time of her visit to the three children at Fatima in Portugal. The communist empire that was created after the second world war would disintegrate and collapse. From the day Karol Wojtyla was elected to the papacy, his one objective seemed to be the total destruction of communism or any form of socialism especially in his home country of Poland. He held enormous powers, as Pope of the Roman Catholic Church, and head of state for Vatican City. He had the support of Opus Dei and the Masonic P2 and their determination to destroy anything that was a state institution. He had the support of the Western democratic powers and especially that of the USA. And so it was when John Paul II landed in Warsaw on the morning of June 2, 1979 eight months to the day after he had left as Cardinal Wojtyla for the Vatican Conclave, he meant to warn the Soviet Union, it would not be his last. After this visit, hundreds of millions of dollars would be sent to the Roman Catholic Church and Solidarity by Opus Dei, the Vatican Bank and millions of Polish Catholics from the USA to promote insurrection.

Vatican City had played a important role in the policies that made Poland a part of the Russian Empire. Pope Pius XII had a great fear that communism would expand its powers in Europe and in nations and continents that were predominantly Roman Catholic. Socialism was building a strong influence in England, France, and Italy. Pius XII believed that Russia had developed into a super power that would be hard to control. Pius XII reasoned, Russia would need to be destroyed from within.

Eastern Europe where Roman Catholicism was predominant would rebel against Russian domination. At the Yalta conference in 1945 Vatican City as a sovereign power played an important role in setting the boundaries of the peace agreement. Germany was divided into East and West, Poland, Hungary, Czechoslovakia, Romania, Bulgaria, Albania and the Baltic States of Estonia, Latvia, and Lithuania would all become Russian territory.

Pius XII had been able to see the fruits of his very important decision that was made at Yalta. In 1953 a year after Stalin's death. East Germany revolted demanding to be re-united with West Germany, in 1956 the Hungarians revolted against their Soviet masters, but it was quickly put down by the Soviets. Both of these episodes were strongly condemned by Pius XII as brutal punishment, against the rights of German and Hungarian people to practice the freedom of their religion.

With the election of Karol Wojtyla as Pope of the Roman Catholic Church, and Ronald Reagan as President of the USA a new form of World Government, began to take form. It was called Globalization.

Large Corporations began acquisitions and mergers with other Companies that would integrate into huge cartels. One cartel could emerge with as many as 500 corporations from around the world under their control. It has become a world of monopolies, owned and governed by the very rich and powerful. As these cartels grow in size, the new psychological performance of downsizing is actuated, smaller productive units will be closed and transferred to the larger and more productive units. These actions, follow with high unemployment and poverty. Many of these cartels have greater power in effecting the working conditions of people, or their nations governments than any other, factor. They automatically become indentured slaves.

The International Monetary Fund, has become the most feared International Agency in the world. They have the power to make an assessment of any nations financial situation and their findings have wide ranging implications. A poor assessment effects the countries credit rating, raising interest rates and abolishing social programs, that have in effect had been in existence over a long period of time. They have the power to create an environment that will lead to high inflation within any particular country, and then make a one hundred and eighty degree turn to stop it. This results in high interest rates which drives up the nation's debt to un-affordable heights and the nation falls into a recession. This inflicts punishment on the people of that nation. This is a fear of all nations, that have become members of the International Monetary Fund. Debt has become that evil power that incarcerates humanity, regardless of their identity.

The methods used to bring Canada under the complete control Of the IMF could be a Science Fiction Drama, if only it did not have such tragic implications for our social programs. Canada was one of the original members of the IMF, but they had never interfered with the introduction of our social programs. That situation changed with the adaptation of the FTA and NAFTA. John Crow came to the International Monetary fund, straight out of university. Throughout the sixty's he worked as the IMF economist, specializing in Latin America's financial policy's. Crow through the IMF had the power to decide the amount of prosperity or the amount of poverty these nations would endure. In 1967 he became assistant chief of the Grand Colombian Division which oversaw Colombia, Venezuela, Ecuador, and Panama. In 1973 he joined the Bank of Canada, and in 1979 he was promoted as chief advisor to Governor Gerald Buoey. Later Crow was promoted to the IMF North American Division which oversaw Canada, USA, and Mexico. In 1987 he became the governor of the Bank of Canada.

Gerald Buoey, Bank of Canada Governor, would carry out a brutal war against inflation, with devastating consequences for the economy. High interest rates, unemployment and the dignity of the human person. During the early seventies the Trudeau Government became very concerned about the unemployment issue. Believing the economy needed more stimulus, the Cabinet decided to lower taxes significantly. The Liberal budgets were full of tax breaks designed to keep money in circulation and keep the economy growing.

However over at the Bank of Canada, with Crow as chief advisor to Bouey the strategy was taken with alarm. It meant to Crow and Bouey more money fuelling inflation and this would eventually oblige the bank to clamp down harder on a inflationary economy. In 1975 the Bank of Canada initiated its first war against the inflationary trend by increasing interest rates tighten money policies, an all around decrease in credit. Bouey claimed that the proper goal of monetary policy was monetary stability. By the summer of 1981 interest rates reached an all time high of 22.5 percent. This became the death blow that caused millions of Canadians to lose their jobs. Hundreds of thousands lost their homes, thousands upon thousands lost their farms and small businesses and brought the economy to a dead stop.

The Free Market power brokers that assisted in the election of Ronald Reagan as president of the USA, now turned their attention to Canada. They needed a change of government, that was favourable to the philosophy of the free market system, a form of Government that was opposed to Social Programs to assist the less fortunate. The International Monetary Fund already had their chief representative, John Crow, entrenched in the Bank of Canada. They needed a Prime Minister, and finance minister who would co-operate with such powerful institutions like Opus Dei and the Masonic P2.

Brian Mulroney was Prime Minister of Canada from 1984 to 1993. It was a decade of crime, corruption and greed never before experienced by the Canadian people. This corruption spread to individuals in other provinces, and to elected officials of the Grant Devine Conservative Government in the Province of Saskatchewan. A number of elected officials were charged with fraud and convicted, while more serious charges against key personal have yet to come to their final conclusions.

All the corruption that had taken place within Government party circles during this period of time, were minuscule compared to the policy's that would bring utter chaos to our nation as a whole.

Brian Mulroney, appointed Michael Wilson to the post of Finance Minister in his first cabinet, and he held this position from 1984-1991. Wilson offered Canadians tax breaks to put more money in circulation for the poor. But during his period of time as Finance Minister he increased the tax burden for the overwhelming majority of individual Canadians and their families, and decreased it for the very rich.

In 1987 Brian Mulroney promoted John Crow to Governor of the Bank of Canada and at the same time he had been appointed by the International Monetary Fund as their chief representative to oversee the Free Trade Agreement between Canada and the USA and conclude the North American Free Trade Agreement.

Michael Wilson had served as executive vice president of Dominion Securities through most of the seventies , as a former bond dealer from Bay Street, his relationship with John Crow, would become a united effort to wrestle inflation to the ground. This had devastating effects on Canadians and brought about the recession throughout the term of his office. When Crow was appointed Governor of the Bank of Canada in 1987 he held to the high interest rate policy. But in 1990 as Crow continued to push up the Canadian rate, the difference between interest rates on Canadian and short term treasury bills rose to an astonishing five percentage points.

This discrepancy had drastic implications for Canada. The higher Canadian interest rates attracted foreign money into Canada, and the sudden flood of foreign money drove up the value of our dollar, the process then began to feed on itself, and as more money flowed in, attracted by the high interest rates and also now by the opportunity to speculate on the rising Canadian dollar, an incredibly lucrative proposition.

This is where the real money was made. High interest rates were great, but the real spectacular gains were made in currency speculation. When foreign investors cashed in their bonds, they were repaid the principle and the interest in Canadian dollars, which had become more valuable. When they converted these more valuable Canadian dollars back into their own currencies, they realized a healthy profit on the exchange. And this profit was particular significant because it applied to the entire investment, the bond plus the interest, not just the interest portion. In fact, our bonds became almost irresistible to foreigners. The combination of high interest rates and profits on the exchange rates produced returns for US investors, that were often as high as 35 percent. In comparison if those investors had put their money into US bonds they would have earned about 8 percent, less than one quarter of what they could earn on Canadian bonds.

When Michael Wilson resigned as Minister of Finance in 1991, he left the nation deep in debt to foreign investors. The debt of 140 billion was increased to over 450 billion, and the basis for continued increase of our national debt. In 1998 our debt has increased to over 650 billion. The interest payments on the total debt is over 42 billion and growing. This is a astronomical sum, that is taken out of our Federal Treasury to pay on a debt that was deliberately created for the wealthy.

In 1991 the Bank of Canada hired public relation organizations to begin a massive attack on our social spending. We were told Canada's social programs are the principal cause of our increasing debt, and this means we start reducing our social spending by large amounts, and quickly.

The Federal Government began reducing Transfer Payments to the Provinces, which sharply reduced Provincial and Municipal spending. Transfer payments to the Province's became less and less, Canadians felt social programs being threatened, and lack of assistance for the poor sustained until there was very little for their lively hood.

Reduced transfer payments to the Provinces, became critical, It affected our health system, education, almost every facet of Canadian lives.

When the Liberal Government came to power in 1993, the cutbacks were even harsher than under the former Conservative Government. Gordon Theisen took the helm from John Crow. He and Paul Martin agreed there would be no change, Tight money and high interest rates would continue. There was still a war, to keep inflation down. John Chretien, boasted many times, the International Monetary Fund has given them high marks for running the nation, paying down the debt and cutting social programs to the people of Canada.

From the time Brian Mulroney was chosen as leader of the conservative party, until his resignation as Prime Minister in 1993 it seemed he was the clown, infinite, for the International Monetary Fund. He would sing, dance and act to every call of the International Monetary Fund. The Free Trade Agreement, FTA, The General Service Tax, GST, The Meech Lake Accord, The Charlottetown Accord, followed by a National Referendum and the North American Free Trade Agreement, NAFTA.

The Free Trade Agreement was devastating for Canada, and this has been proven with the results since it has been in effect. The Simon Reisman and T Murphy, chief negotiators for the Free Trade Agreement, was an exercise in futility, a public relations ploy to make Canadian's believe that our Government was desperately seeking to maintain all our social programs and more. The US Congress paid very little attention to the agreement, and this was understandable, as the IMF controlled the value of the Canadian dollar to that of the US dollar. It was the IMF that was writing up the Free Trade Agreement, crossing the T's and dotting the I's. When Ronald Reagan signed the Free Trade Agreement on January 2, 1988 he did what American Generals and armies had failed to do in 1776 and 1812. He conquered Canada.

Brian Mulroney made it so easy, his minister of finance Michael Wilson, was a strong proponent of the FTA, the Governor of the Bank of Canada was James Crow, and also the chief representative of the IMF to conclude the agreement.

The Goods & Services Tax--GST, was a tax against the poor. The people of Canada protested against this form of taxation. The Senate would not approve this form of taxation. Mulroney then used a weak point in the constitution to appoint sufficient conservative senators, to gain a majority in the upper house. With this action the GIST won approval, and the dreaded and hated tax became law.

The division of French Quebec, and the other nine Provinces of Canada were further exacerbated by the introduction of the Meech Lake Accord and the Charlottetown Referendum. There is little doubt they were drafted by the IMF to ensure a further division amongst Canadians. For all this, he was rewarded with the distinction of receiving Canada's highest civilian honour, "The Companion of the Order of Canada".

The situation in Mexico during the 80's was similar to that of Canada. The rapid increase in foreign debt and foreign control had plunged the country into serious debt. Amid reports of widespread irregularities, the PRI claimed victory in congressional election in 1985. In 1988 Carlos Salinas De Gortari of the PRI was elected president. The two opposition candidates called the vote count fraudulent, but their election held.

There seems to be sufficient evidence, the elections in Canada and Mexico were heavily financed by foreign money to bring about the elections of Mulroney with his conservative government in Canada, and the Salinas Government in Mexico. Both Governments brought the nations to their knees, with a heavy debt load. Both nations have been forced to lower their social programs. Both nations have the value of their currencies set by the IMF.

In 1989 the Salina's Government speeded up the privatization of state controlled corporations and modified restrictive trade and investment regulations to encourage foreign investment by permitting full control of corporations by foreign investors. In October Salinas and US President George Bush signed a trade and investment agreement, described as the broadest economic agreement ever concluded between the two nations.

During the 1980's Salinas was pushed hard by the IMF for a North American Free Trade Agreement to link Canada, the USA and Mexico. This agreement was signed by Salinas, George Bush and Brian Mulroney in 1991. A peculiarly part of the North American Free Trade Agreement, was a part the Roman Catholic Church played in this agreement.

Mexico's long tradition of official anti-clericalism ended with the signing of NAFTA granting Roman Catholicism full freedom to pursue the building of parochial schools, and returning all rights the Roman Catholic Church claimed before the anticlerical antagonism was created. These rights were entrenched in NAFTA in spite of the fact that 90% of Mexican people are Roman Catholics.

The power of the International Monetary Fund has taken control of the worlds, economic, political and spiritual structure. It encompasses a global empire that no nation or people can escape from. It is an evil empire that creates debt, poverty and destitution. It is today's modern religion. The question is how long can humanity survive, the persecution and the dignity of the human person, the greatest of all, God's creation.

If humanity were to equate the papacy of John Paul II with any of the popes of centuries past, with similar aspirations of the Roman Catholic Church, it would be without doubt, Pope Innocent III (1198-1216). His papacy lasted for 17 years. For the first time, crusades were turned, by Innocents will, against Europeans at home. The crusade power had been harnessed to papal ambition.

Pope Innocent III had to rely on military power to achieve his objectives were as Pope John Paul II had received tremendous economic powers, which could dominate the world's nations, and people by the use of such power.

Pope Innocent III, looked to the East and the wealth of Constantinople and the gateway to the far flung empire of Byzantium. The emperor of Byzantium is also head of the Orthodox Church that separated from Rome long since, and now looks upon the popes as usurpers. Years have been widening the breach between this Eastern Church and the West, One is Greek, the other is Latin, -- one upholds the sanctuaries of Constantinople, the other the basilica of Rome.

Innocent is trying to cross the breach, to bring Constantinople back into the communion of Rome. The scholastic of the West is debating with theologist of the East and honours are about even.

Innocent agonizes, He is eager to bring the churches of Bysantium under the rule of Rome. He threatens a little: the Venetians, having sucked gold out of Constantinople, hate the Byzantines and the duke of Swabia has not forgotten the dream of the Hohenstaufen, to conquer for the great treasures of the Byzantine.

A great army of crusaders were gathering for the Venetians to transport them to the shores of the holy land. The Venetians eager for more wealth asked, What if they could lead the crusade toward Constantinople, instead of Jerusalem? What if they sent the whole strength of their fleet to support the army? If they could turn the crusaders aside to invade Byzantium, then Constantinople could be seized.

But two obstacles stood in their way. The crusaders themselves would refuse to go anywhere but toward Jerusalem. And Innocent could not consent to the invasion of a Christian empire by the crusade. The leader of the Venetian republic, considers the problems. He weighs all the dangers -- ponders the anger of Innocent. He is all for the Constantinople venture, that will yield new seaports, and gold and vengeance. After all, his treaty with the crusaders only obligates him to transport them over the sea. A way must be found to lead them into the Dardanelles.

During the late summer of 1202 the Venetians set sail. Wind filled the sails and spread the great red crosses out, for all to see. So for the first time by the treachery of the Venetians, a crusade had been turned aside from Jerusalem. The great crusade power had been bridled and driven to other work.

Pope Innocent III, had forbidden the enterprise, at least publicly, when he heard that the fleet had gone against Constantinople, months later he was informed of the capture of the city and the flight of the Byzantines.

Not until then did he display his anger and excommunicate the Venetians. Later he lifted the sentence of excommunication, and gave amiable assent to the Venetians to remain in Constantinople. He Sent his legates there with reinforcements of knights.

The crusaders had won the Byzantine empire for Rome and no Caesar of Rome ever welcomed a new conquest more eagerly. Innocent was establishing the papal authority over far frontiers. He had gathered the bishops of the North into his fold, and now his legate, the Cardinal Pelagious, was sent to Constantinople to force the submission of the Greek clergy. As in the days of the Caesars, the East was united again to the West.

At the same time enormous prestige had surrounded the papacy, from its leadership in the crusading movement. Money flowed continuously, and no accounting was asked of it; the military orders, the Hospital and Temple thrived upon the impetus of the war and they were vassals of the pope. Moreover, the masses of crusaders taking their vows to serve the Church had set themselves beyond the authority of their feudal lords, the princes of Europe. So the interest of the papacy was served by increasing the numbers and the privileges accorded to the crusaders, and the authority of the kings was weakened accordingly.

At this time, in the Easter season of the year 1212, the people of Christendom were amazed by a strange happening. Down from the mountains above Italy came throngs of children marching with little wooden crosses, and singing hymns. When the good people asked them where they were going they answered, "To God".

They had started out among the shepherd families of the Vendome country, and others had joined them as they marched. They were going down to the sea, to find a way to the Holy Land to aid the Seigneur Christ. They were going to recover the Holy City, and after that it would be peace.

The children did not know just how they would do that, but thousands of them were marching together of their own free will. And the people who saw them believed that this was surely a miracle and a omen.

It seemed evident to the onlookers that the lord was about to do some great and new thing through these innocent souls gathered together of their own free will. No one tried to stop them, and they emerged from the mountains, seeking the roads to the Italian cities where, somehow, they hoped to cross the sea. With their crosses and staves and scripts they wandered around the harbours. No path opened for them through the waters. so they could walk dry shod to the Holy Land. They had no money and no protectors. And among them came human wolves, making profit out of their misery, following the fairer girls about...

At one city, ships were offered them without payment, when the children had embarked joyfully, they sailed to the Moslem ports, selling the youths and girls as slaves in the markets of Kairuwan and Alexandria. Another ship went down with the children near an island of the sea.

When Innocent heard, of the matter, he did not interfere, but said, "The very children shame us, because they hasten to gain the Holy Land, while we hang back. But the children who still were left alive had lost hope. Wearily, without their crosses and songs, they drifted back from the coast. In small groups, they tried to make their way home again over the mountains, while the good people who had aided them onward toward a miracle mocked them, pointing scornful fingers at the girls who had been ravished, saying that they had been about the devils work, instead of the Lords.

And so the march of the children came to its end. They had gone forth spontaneously, driven out by the hardships and suffering at home, seeking not the distant city in Palestine but that other Jerusalem that lies beyond all the seas of the earth.

Innocent built a monument on the island where their ship had gone down. Whatever he thought about the lost crusade of the children, he would never say, he continued his belief, that he would become sole master of the universe.

In the south of France men lived pleasantly, They had their orchards and fertile fields, and a warm sun above them. Outside the path of the worst feudal wars and sheltered by the bulwark of the Pyrenees.

They were Provencales and Gascons, with a deal of Moorish blood in them, and they had learned much from the Moslems . From their ancestors they had inherited a vague belief in good and evil as the only two vital forces existing upon the earth and effecting them. Not all of them believed this but the groups who did were slowly forming their own religion. In their thoughts, they went back to the beginning of things, when the Evangelists had walked the earth, and the great edifice of the church had not been built. Undoubtedly they had listened to the Arabic philosophers. Their real belief remains shadowy and unknowable, because the Cathars and their teachings were all destroyed, and the traces they left were obscured by their oppressors.

Innocent called for a crusade against the heretics. They had rebelled against the authority of the church, they should be suppressed by the soldiery of the church. Indulgence from sin was offered those who volunteered, and even the merchants and money lenders of the North hastened to donate funds, for which they were richly repaid with cloth, wine and grain gathered from the plundered fields of the South. The crusaders were the French neighbours of the Languedoc, the affected region. They wore bands of cloth of silver about their chests, embroidered with gold crosses, and they embarked upon the enterprise as if it were a huge border raid, with unlimited liberty to plunder, and ecclesiastical sanction for their efforts.

It moved south with bands of clerics who sang Veni Creator. It made no distinction between Cathars and others. At Bezieres they stormed the town, and in the church of the Madeleine, where women and children had taken refuge, seven thousand were slain. It divided quartering over the countryside, at times fighting actual battles against the desperate knights of the South, and at times devastating everything with sword and fire. Captured knights were crucified on the olive trees, or dragged by attaching them to horses tails. The path of the army became marked by pyres of human bodies, smoking in blackened heaps, and wells were choked by corpses.

Peter, King of Aragon, took the field against De Montfords crusaders, but he was defeated and slain. This was in 1213 the war had lasted for four years, and the ravaging continued long afterward. For more than five blood stained centuries other popes and monarchs would follow his example.

Meanwhile Innocent had sanctioned two other enterprises as crusades. In the far northeast the Teutonic Knights were sent among the pagan Prussians to convert them sword in hand. And in Spain itself Knights were summoned to a crusade against the remaining Moslems from which they emerged victorious after driving the men of Islam south to the Granada region by the sea.

To Innocent III, he truly believed, that only the pope of Rome had the right to rule, that all peoples must abide to the teachings of the Papacy. To a prior in Tuscany, Innocent wrote: "As, God, the creator of the universe set two great lights in the firmament of heaven.. so he set two great dignitaries in the firmament of the universal church. These dignitaries are the papal authority and the royal power. And just as the moon gets her light from the sun and is inferior to the sun, so the royal power gets the splendour of its dignity from the papal authority".

He said that power lay with two swords, the spiritual and the temporal. One rested in the hand of the pope, the other in the hands of the kings. Innocent believed that the spiritual sword must be raised above the temporal mercifully but inexorably. Both swords belonged to the Church, and the temporal weapon was bestowed upon it, to be used on its behalf. All power lay in the hand of the Church.

And so we order, the spiritual sword against all heretics, the indulgence of sins to all those who faithfully and devoutly aid the Church. Any evil may be endured to gain a worthy result. In June of 1217, Innocent prepared for a great crusade to the holy land. For four years the Truce of God would be proclaimed in Europe. And this time there was no mistaking his purpose. The conquest of Jerusalem must be the vindication of his rule. For during the seventeen years of his pontificate, not a single soldier from Europe landed on the Syrian Coast to go to Jerusalem.

Innocent felt assured of victory now. But before the preparations were more than begun, he died.

What Innocent III could not complete during his reign as head of the Roman Catholic Church, seems to have been accomplished by Pope John Paul II. Today he apparently holds the two swords. Pope John Paul II has proclaimed himself, Pope and King of a world he now controls with the power of money. To protect this great power he has bestowed the temporal sword on the United States of America to be used on his behalf when requested to do so or not to use if it interferes with Vatican policy.

As we look back on the history of the last 2000 years, we realize that there has always been a few men with extraordinary powers that ruled the world at any one given time.

From Constantine the Great, to Pope John Paul II the power of religion has always been the dominant force that shaped the destiny of the human race.

The history of the last five decades, brings about serious questions and answers that need to be analyzed.

What would the world be like today if Pope John XXIII had received the support of the Vatican Curia and had been allowed to have had his operation? This would have extended his papacy for several more years. The Second Vatican Council would have become a formidable force, in carrying forward the policy's of this Council. It would have become strongly entrenched in the dogma of the Roman Catholic Church.

If President John F. Kennedy had not been assassinated, the wars in Vietnam and South East Asia would possibly never have happened. It was one of the many tragedies of the Twentieth Century.

The poverty and destitution throughout Latin America and Africa, would have been greatly reduced. Billions of dollars in foreign aid, and hundreds of thousands of well trained, and educated Americans, had volunteered to go into these third world countries and make them self sufficient, at least in great part. Kennedy waged a war on illiteracy and poverty. He was not a supporter of The IMF and questioned the powers of the Federal Reserve.

Martin Luther King Jr. became a strong supporter of the Kennedy policies. He could visualize the great help of the black American -- the great number who had volunteered to raise the standard of living in Africa. They touched the very roots of the problem, illiteracy and poverty. Robert F. Kennedy was murdered at the very height of his political career. The objective he was thriving for -- the completion of the policies and actions that began during the Presidency of John F. Kennedy and the papacy of Pope John XXIII.

Albino Luciani, Pope John Paul I had been pope for 33 days. His dream of changing the course of the Roman Catholic Church, cost him his life. He was a direct threat to the rich and powerful. If Pope John XXIII, President John F. Kennedy, Martin Luther King, Robert F. Kennedy, Pope John Paul I had not been murdered or assassinated, and died before their time, the prophesies of the Virgin Mary at Fatima, in all possibility, would never have become true. Internal interference by foreign powers was the greater cause that led to the collapse of the Russian Empire.

The program to democratic socialism from Communism, advocated by Mikhail Gorbachev, would have been much less oppressive than the method used by Pope John Paul II and Ronald Reagan as president of the USA. The immediate and complete change to the free market system is inhumanely severe.

The International Monetary Fund, quickly became the official banker as each nation claimed independence. All state institutions were sold to Global Conglomerates amassed since 1980. This money was used by the individual governments as they proceeded to push the free market economy on their people. This left no money for the workers, as most of their productive institutions were shut down to reorganize for the free market economy. This meant no jobs, no money in circulation and no pay for the people who did work. It is and will be, total inhumane action against human rights and dignity. Religious power can be as cruel, and vengeful as the worst form of Communism or any Dictatorship.

The International Monetary fund is spreading its talons around the world, from the old Russian Empire, to Asia and beyond. By controlling the value of each nations currency, whose value is set to the American dollar, they conquer the world by debt and deficit.

There is little doubt, the world as we know it today, is in fact a world government, an oligarchy, to rule without dispute.

"The poverty and misery that exists around the world today are made by man, and only man can rectify it, for God's work must truly be our own." **President John F. Kennedy**, during his term in office as President of the United States of America

The Secret Links

In closing this segment of secrecy and the link to the occult, one has to reflect upon two quotes: *"the best slaves are the ones who believe they are free."* and *"there are none so blind as the ones who refuse to see."* Whenever and wherever researchers delve into this topic to piece together a new history and the One World Order plan, they seem to uncover the same names, the same groups, the common denominator of a unified planetary plan of order and obedience to the masters--to the gods who have carefully crafted a plan to create unity among people. And the common denominator here is the god Lucifer and occult. This notion of slavery may not necessarily be bad since most of humanity is a slave to something, be it family, culture, environment, tradition, corporation or some authority. it is what we accept. There is no doubt that one can be a happy slave. And in this light, humanity as a whole living consciousness is now (as we shall see in the following Part 2) at a point where it is deciding whether it will choose a New World Order, or A New Order of the Ages. At the turn of the century, the New world Oder plan became jeopardized, and it is even more so now in 2012.

It has to be underscored at this time that whether the followers of Lucifer wish to make a better world for their slaves, or whether the followers of Christ wish to have a better world without slavery is a major point of juncture. It is undeniable that the world has become a better place for many; the big question is whether the next years will decide on a world consciousness much different than the thousands of years of history under the dynasties and empires of the gods.

Before closing this topic, admittedly, this new history is still evolving and many pieces to this puzzle are still vague but a new transparency and revelation is gelling at high speed so as to bring light onto what has actually happened. It is important to look at what this New Order business plan has meant in the evolution of mankind. From the re-emergence of the monetary and religious "gods" in the 1700's the plan has entailed the repositioning of the players and the tools of conquest. The Templars learned well the military might of money to conquer kings and queens. It is that reemergence of strategic powers within the bloodlines that has led to a successive "corporate takeovers" and strategic infiltrations of secret societies, government, nations, major corporations in the march to a unity of mankind.

The **New World Order** is a collective illuminati effort put forth by the global power elite, bound by ancestral genetics of incest and esoteric secrets to create a one world government, one religion, one money system, one Emperor. Indeed, if this is the result, it would be a potential solution of peace.

On one side of the coin, it is suggested that this Luciferian cabal eventually will prefect robotic technology and artificial intelligence to remove all elements of spiritual light. Any human soul/spirit ensnared into the new world of the darkness will be enslaved from the advanced technology of the RFID chip and sophisticated mind-control techniques. Anyone who is disposed to the light of truth will be killed during their New World Order; however, spiritually saved into the unseen world of the light.

On the other side of the coin is the evolution of One in all things as **the New Order of the Ages** without any Emperor. As we will unveil in Part 2, the Earthlings are at that point of choice between the light and the darkness that will stem from the inner heart.

The Shadow Government

We have looked at the "spiritual glue" of PLANET EARTH Executives. Their march to one unified empire is with a colaborative common purpose that is rooted in the occult, esoteric, oaths and bondings inherent in secret societies. These secret societies would undoubtedly favour the rising followers both financially and attaining special occult powers. All secret societies appear to have a "white" front, and to the flock at the lower 90% of the pyramid, all would appear as anything but Luciferian or occult in application. That is the way of things reserved for the blood lines and their upper echelons. We have looked at only a few of the societies. There are many more. For detailed information on this topic, ***www.bibliotecapleyades.net*** is a great source.

Before leaving this topic, it is of interest to point out that the leader of the Earths Illuminati is called the "**Pindar**". The Pindar is a member of one of the 13 ruling Illuminati families, and is always male. The title, **Pindar**, is an abbreviated term for

"Pinnacle of the Draco", also known as the "Penis of the Dragon". Symbolically, this represents the top of power, control, creation, penetration, expansion, invasion, and fear, the top lizard. The true current Pindar is alleged to be **the head of the Rothschild family,** as has been for several hundred years. He is based in Germany near Frankfurt. In the late 1970s, he oversaw the sister project to Montauk, called **M.A.L.D.A.** is an anagram for Montauk-Alsace-Lorraine Dimensional Activation. This project was located near the city of Strasbourg, France, historically once part of Germany. At Montauk the CIA (operated by Nazis) experimented greatly to make a person into a superman. It is reported that they are still doing it with human/alien hybridizations in CIA run underground installations where they bring abducted people to take their eggs and sperm to do all sorts of experiments, including cloning. Hybrids are implanted in women and then later removed after about 6 weeks to grow in tanks.

With reference to the research done on the site **www.bibliotecapleyades.net/sumer_anunnaki/reptiles/reptiles08.htm,** the Illuminati here on Earth have established a pyramid structure of control identical to the system that exists in **the Draco Empire.** The pyramid with the Reptilian eye, located on the American one-dollar bill, is symbolic of this control structure. The eye is the cap on the pyramid, thus explaining why the original surface of the Great Pyramid in Egypt was capped in **solid gold.**

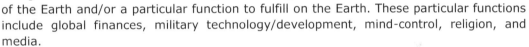

The **Pindar** is represented by the gold cap on the pyramid. The next layer, or "eye", on the pyramid represents the 13 ruling families. Each of the 13 ruling families is given an area of the Earth and/or a particular function to fulfill on the Earth. These particular functions include global finances, military technology/development, mind-control, religion, and media.

The **Pindar** is represented by the gold cap on the pyramid. The next layer, or "eye", on the pyramid represents the 13 ruling families. They are stated to be as follows:

- **Rothschild** (Bauer or Bower) - **Pindar**
- Bruce
- Cavendish (Kennedy)
- De Medici
- Hanover
- Hapsburg
- Krupp
- Plantagenet
- Rockefeller
- Romanov
- Sinclair (St. Clair)
- Warburg (del Banco)
- Windsor (Saxe-Coburg-Gothe)

We have already met some of these players. Each of the 13 ruling families has a Council of 13 as well. The number, **13**, has great significance to them. They know that there are 12 types of energies that pass through the 10 aspects of God-Mind. The totality of the 12 energies equals a 13th energy. This is considered the most powerful knowledge.

They also know that there are really 13 Zodiac signs, not the commonly acknowledged 12. They have kept the 13th hidden for centuries because it is the **sign of the Dragon.** They keep the qualities and traits of this sign secret to avoid giving away clues to the Reptilian mind-pattern. Whether you know or not, there are truly not 12 Zodiac signs, really there are 13, the 13th sign, the Ophiuchus or Serpentarius, the secret one, is hidden from us in order to block us in this reality. Each of the 13 ruling families is given an area of the Earth and/or a particular function to fulfill on the Earth. These particular functions include global finances, military technology/development, mind-control, religion, and media. Each of the 13 ruling families has a Council of 13 as well.

The number, 13, has great significance to them because they know that there are 12 types of energies that pass through the 10 aspects of God-Mind. The totality of the 12 energies equals a 13th energy. This is considered the most powerful knowledge. They also know that there are really 13 Zodiac signs, not the commonly acknowledged 12. They have kept the 13th hidden for centuries because it is the sign of the Dragon. They keep the qualities and traits of this sign secret to avoid giving away clues to the Reptilian mind-pattern."

Persian sacred astrology teaches, that Zodiac is not a circle, but a spiral & there is the 13th Sign, which is put there in order to break the circle line, it opens the path to the next spiral level. The 13 the Sign is the door which opens for each of us any year: if we are ready we may step out. And – if you are born in this short period of the year – that means you got the chance to end your circle of reincarnations in this life. An astrological poem of Manilius: dated to around 10 A.D states *"Ophiuchus holds apart the serpent which with its mighty spirals and twisted body encircles his own, so that he may untie its knots and back that winds in loops. But, bending its supple neck, the serpent looks back and returns: and the other's hands slide over the loosened coils. The struggle will last forever, since they wage it on level terms with equal powers"*. Many levels of sense there. Each year anyone has the chance to take a step in his development, to go to the higher dimension, to another reality – you could understand this as it is more convenient to you – 13 is a stargate, a portal, a chance. The 13th Sign starts   November 22 - 28 and lasts for about 10 days.

Also, on the site ***http://merlintm.eth7.com/bloodlines.htm***l there is another dimension of the Illuminati hierarchy: *"The Illuminati (Today they refer to themselves as The Moriah (Moriah are generational Luciferians going back to Babylonian times. It is a misconception that they are only Mormons.), The Brotherhood, The Consortium, or from the X-Files science fiction series, The Shadow Government), invisible to the general public, yet controlling every aspect of the direction of this world, are Genetic Hybrids ... the result of interbreeding between a hostile extraterrestrial reptilian race and humanity thousands of years ago. Their center of power is not located in the third dimension, but in the lower *fourth* dimension (lower astral plane). It has often been referred to as the traditional home of the demons of folklore and their leader is known as 'Lucifer' (not Satan). Ancient Mormon manuscripts have revealed that while Jesus (protagonist) and Lucifer (antagonist) have been portrayed throughout the bloody history of this world as being "opposites", they are in actuality Brothers from the SAME family, who have been at war with each other for control over this planet long before any historical biblical accounts. Their ongoing battle for dominion over Earth will ultimately result in the Book of Revelation Apocalyptic event, or Armageddon. In the sixteenth chapter of Revelation, the word Armageddon is used to designate the location of the final, climactic battle between good (Christ) and evil (Antichrist) that is supposed to occur during 2012."*

Now we will leave the more esoteric part of PLANET EARTH and look towards the next organizational layer of Special Organizations.

12

THE SPECIAL GLOBAL ORGANIZATIONS

The Illuminati Hierarchy

As we drop downwards in the pyramid structure of PLANET EARTH we now must look at the special private organisations that have been created for the purpose of the business plan. These organizations such as the Federal Reserve, IRS, and CIA all have special purposes and have been integrated into the nations infrastructures in such a way as to police and administer the according to the needs of the plan yet remain above the

SPECIAL GLOBAL ORGANIZATIONS					
FINANCIAL	RESEARCH	POLITICAL	INTEL	RELIGIOUS	EDUCATION
IMF	In. Policy Sdy	UN	CIA	COChurches	UNESCO
World Bank	Stanford res	Club of Rome	KGB	Wd Religions	World peace
Cent Banks	Brookings Ins	Bilderbergers	FBI	Vatican	Plan Congress
Fed Reserve	Tavistock In	Trilateral Com	MI 5	New Age	W. Federalist
I.B. Of Sett	Aspen Soc	Aspen Ins	MAFIA	Unity Church	Lucis Trust
Nat Banks	Jason Soc	NATO	INTERPOL	Bah a'i	World Goodwill
Foundations	Comm 300	EEC	Com Party	Temp Unders	Esalen Inst

regulations and visibility of the governments that serve them. Like the Federal Reserve that is private, is not subject to audit, yet controls the complete banking system of nations. There is a separate private hierarchy as it reports to the IMF and World Banks that are privately owned. Thus, the tentacles of organization reach all the way down to local banks as administrative branches all around the world, following the regulations of laws as set down by the Financial Control Centers of Zurich and London. There are many such organizations that have been formed with special purposes. We have mentioned several already and these are effectively the operational corporations and trusts that are responsible for specific functions, like the Federal reserve, IRS and CIA in America. We have already seen the Jesuit power reaches into the world intelligence groups. For simplicity, we can cluster these six major groups as shown in the picture above. There are many, many more. These have all been financed by the Financial arm of PLANET EARTH INC, are private, and serve a special purpose of business plan execution. We have already discussed the Lucis Trust. These organizations would be likened to the major functional Divisions of PLANET EARTH INC.

As noted before, the Illuminati is the oldest term commonly used to refer to **13** *bloodline families* (and their offshoots) that make up a major portion of this controlling elite. As we have seen, these members of the Illuminati are also members in the highest ranks of numerous secretive and occult societies which in many cases extend straight back into the ancient world.

The upper levels of the tightly compartmentalized (need-to-know-basis) much like how our governments work where they simply do a job description and never know the whole. It is only when the top is attained that a full picture is realized. Here the oaths are sworn upon fear of death (the Knights of Malta no doubt). The Illuminati structural pyramid include planning committees and organizations that the public has little or no knowledge of. The upper levels of the Illuminati pyramid include secretive committees with names such as: the **Council of 3**, the **Council of 5**, the **Council of 7**, the **Council of 9**, the **Council of 13**, the **Council of 33**, the **Grand Druid Council**, the **Committee of 300** (also called the "Olympians") and the **Committee of 500** among others. Of note is that these are simply private groups bonded by purpose and the word secretive may create a perception of conspiracy. Looking through this, it is all simply "business". For example, the mention of the word "conspiracy" often solicits a slide response with many people that instigates recoil to ignore or argue rather than listen and learn.

In 1992, **Dr John Coleman** published **Conspirators' Hierarchy: The Story of the Committee of 300**. With laudable scholarship and meticulous research, Dr Coleman identifies the players and carefully details the Illuminati agenda of worldwide domination and control. On page 161 of the *Conspirators Hierarchy*, Dr Coleman accurately summarizes the intent and purpose of the Committee of 300 as follows:

"A One World Government and one-unit monetary system, under permanent non-elected hereditary oligarchists who self-select from among their numbers in the form of a feudal system as it was in the Middle Ages. In this One World entity, population will be limited by restrictions on the number of children per family, diseases, wars, famines, until 1 billion people who are useful to the ruling class, in areas which will be strictly and clearly defined, remain as the total world population.

There will be no middle class, only rulers and the servants. All laws will be uniform under a legal system of world courts practicing the same unified code of laws, backed up by a One World Government police force and a One World unified military to enforce laws in all former countries where no national boundaries shall exist. The system will be on the basis of a welfare state; those who are obedient and subservient to the One World Government will be rewarded with the means to live; those who are rebellious will simple be starved to death or be declared outlaws, thus a target for anyone who wishes to kill them. Privately owned firearms or weapons of any kind will be prohibited."

And so it would appear that the march to this dominion over Earthlings is not with armies but with organizations and rules of conduct that "serve" the whole controlled by the few. There are many governments now and people already starve to death. Humanity has chosen to be obedient to kings and queens, to governments, to corporations, to military. There is not a government on Planet Earth right now that does not have a starving peoples that outnumber the rest. Is this "purging" a benefit to the survivors? Is this a natural phenomenon? In this case, the plan of bringing all under one government, one religion, one financial system includes a magnitude and complex web surrounding the individuals and organizations involved that is mind boggling, yet that appears to be what humanity is still choosing.

Most people react with disbelief and scepticism towards the topic of conspiracy, unaware that they have been conditioned to react with scepticism by institutional and media influences that were created by the Mother of All mind control organizations: The **Tavistock Institute of Human Relations** in London which will be covered later.

The plan to 'create' public opinion began in **1913** as a propaganda factory centered at **Wellington House** in London. Sir Edward Grey, the British Foreign Secretary at the time, installed **Lord Northcliffe** (Britain's most influential newspaper magnate) as its director. Lord Northcliffe's position was over sighted by **Lord Rothmere** on behalf of the British Crown. The operational staff of Wellington House consisted of Lord Northcliffe, **Arnold Toynbee** (future director of studies at the Royal Institute of International Affairs), and the Americans, **Walter Lippmann** and **Edward Bernays** (nephew to Signund Freud). Funding was initially provided by the Royal family, but soon to include the Rothschilds (related to Lord Northcliffe by marriage) and the Rockefellers. Wellington House would grow into the **Tavistock Institute** in **1921** after the propaganda "victories" of the First World War and the Federal Reserve banking system (created in 1913) had been secured. It is said that this organization includes a role of British oligarchs to shape and control public opinion in order to manipulate the British public (and later the American public) into accepting the notion that war with Germany was necessary in order "to secure a lasting peace". As we have seen in the 13 bloodlines chapter, the march to control media has been implemented.

As a business man, the media is a critical marketing vehicle to shape opinion so as to create a market for a product. The largest corporations with super marketing budgets have indeed been effective here. It may not be surprising to understand that what most Americans believe to be "Public Opinion" is in reality *carefully crafted and scripted propaganda* designed to elicit a *desired behavioural response* from the public. Public opinion polls are *really* taken with the intent of gauging the public's *acceptance* of the Illuminati's planned programs. A strong showing in the polls tells the leaders that the programming is "taking", while a poor showing tells the NWO manipulators that they have to recast or "tweak" the programming until the desired response is achieved. While the thrust and content of the propaganda is decided at Tavistock, implementation of the propaganda is executed in the United States by well **over 200** 'think tanks' such as the **Rand Corporation** and the **Brookings Institute** which are overseen and directed by the top NWO mind control organization in the United States, the **Stanford Research Institute** (SRI) in Menlo Park, California.

The NWO global marketing programs manifest their agenda through the skilful manipulation of human emotions, especially *fear*. In the past *centuries*, they have repeatedly utilized a contrivance that NWO researcher and author **David Icke** has characterized in his latest book, **The Biggest Secret**, as **Problem**, **Reaction**, and **Solution**. The technique is as follows: Illuminati strategists create the **Problem-** by funding , assembling, and training an "opposition" group to stimulate turmoil in an established political power (sovereign country, region, continent, etc.) that they wish to impinge upon and thus create opposing factions in a *conflict that the Illuminati themselves manoeuvred into existence*. In recent decades, so called "opposition" groups are usually identified in the media as 'freedom fighters' or 'liberators'

At the same time, the leader of the established political power where the conflict is being orchestrated is *demonized* and, on cue, referred to as 'another Hitler' (take your pick: Saddam Hussein, Milosevic, Kadaffi, etc.). The 'freedom fighters' are not infrequently assembled from a local criminal element (i.e. KLA, drug traffickers). In the spirit of true Machiavellian deceit, the same NWO strategists are equally involved in *covertly arming* and *advising* the leader of the established power as well (the Illuminati always profits from any armed conflict by loaning money, arming, and supplying *all* parties involved in a war).

The conflict is drawn to the world stage by the controlled media outlets with a barrage of media release to create a cry that "Something has to be done!" And *That* is the desired **Reaction.** The NWO puppeteers then provide the **Solution** by sending in UN 'Peace Keepers' (Bosnia) or a UN 'Coalition Force' (Gulf War) or NATO Bombers and then ground troops (Kosovo). Once installed, the 'peace keepers' never leave (Bosnia, Kosovo). The idea is to have NWO controlled ground troops in all major countries or strategic areas where significant resistance to the New World Order takeover is likely to be encountered.

And so whether it is mandatory Anthrax Vaccinations required of all US military personnel, pharmaceutical cartels, as well as other major *multinational* corporations, the Royal Family of England, the United Nations, the World Health Organization, the leaders of all major industrial countries like the United States, England, Germany, Italy, Australia, New Zealand, somehow become active and fully cooperative participants in this conspiracy somehow throughout the web of the plan. Moreover it is alleged that most of the major wars, political upheavals, and economic depression/recessions of the past 100 years (and earlier) were carefully planned and instigated by the machinations of these elites. They include The Spanish-American War (1898), World War I and World War II; The Great Depression; the Bolshevik Revolution of 1917; the Rise of Nazi Germany; the Korean War; the Vietnam War; the 1989-91 "fall" of Soviet Communism, the 1991 Gulf War; and the recent War in Kosovo. Even the French Revolution was an orchestrated into existence by the Bavarian Illuminati and the House of Rothschild. This is a pretty impressive list of manipulations. Of course, in the plan of PLANET EARTH, this is just good marketing and business planning to serve a mission.

Research points out that in America, the **Federal Emergency Management Administration** (FEMA) was created in 1979 under Presidential Memorandum 32 authored for President Carter by Prof. **Samuel P. Huntington**, a Harvard professor and former FEMA Advisory Board chairman. Huntington wrote the *Seminal Peace* for the **Trilateral Commission** in the mid 70's, in which he criticized democracy and economic development as outdated ideas. As co-author of another report prepared for the Trilateral Commission, **The Crisis of Democracy**, Huntington wrote:

"*We have come to recognize that there are potential desirable limits to economic growth. There are also potentially desirable limits to the indefinite extension of political democracy. A government which lacks authority will have little ability short of cataclysmic crisis to impose on its people the sacrifices which may be necessary.*"

Huntington's ideas were rewritten into **National Security Decision Directive #47** (NSDD47), which was enacted in July 1982 by President Reagan. Treated as a passing footnote by the media, this law identified legitimate areas to be upgraded to maintain national defence, but it also laid the groundwork for **Emergency Mobilization Preparedness**, a plan under which existing socio/economic regulations or other legal constraints would be waived in the event of a national emergency. This plan was *further* strengthened in **Public Law 101-647**, signed by President Bush in November 1990. What it boils down to is this: in the event that the President declares a **national emergency**, for *any reason* (from major earthquakes to increased international tensions or economic /financial crisis of any stripe), FEMA can then, at *their* discretion, implement **Executive Orders** 10995 through 11005. These Executive Orders permit a takeover by FEMA of local, state, and national governments and the suspension of constitutional guarantees. FEMA will have the authority <u>to exert any sort of control that it deems necessary upon the American public</u>. A trained *National Police Force*, formally referred to by the name of *Multi Jurisdictional Task Force (MJTF)*, wearing <u>*black uniforms*</u> and composed of:

1. specially selected US military personnel
2. foreign military units carrying United Nations ID cards, and
3. specially trained existing police groups from larger metropolitan American cities.

The instigation of a trumped-up war as a cover for amassing fortunes can be dated back to at least the 12th Century when only a core group of **nine** members of an Illuminati group called the **Knights Templar,** the military arm of an Illuminati secret society known as the **Priory of Sion,** kicked off the **The Crusades** that lasted for over a century and a half. A rift later developed between the Templars and the Priory of Sion when Jerusalem was lost to Saracen Turks in 1187. In 1307, the king of France, **Philippe the Fair** (a Merovingian Illuminati), coveted the wealth and was jealous of the Templars' power. The French king, being a puppet of the Priory of Sion, set out to arrest all the Templars in France on October 13. While many Templars were seized and tortured, including their Grand Master, Jacques de Molay, many other Templars (who had been tipped off) escaped. They eventually resurfaced in Portugal, in Malta (as the **Knights of Malta**) and later in Scotland as **The Scottish Rites of Free Masonry**.

The business plan includes the acquisition and consolidation of ever greater **wealth**, **natural resources**, total **political power**, and **control over others** are the motivating forces which drives the decisions of the Illuminati. And because they are heartless business men with special talents the toll in human suffering and the loss of innocent lives are non issues for these individuals, who appear to be aligned with what one would say are very dark and malevolent powers.

We now have another layer added to our structure of PLANET EARTH.

In the following sections, a few of these are presented. We have already looked at some of these like the Vatican.

The Committee Of 300

It is of interest to study this group because it illustrates how the Global Elite, like for example the Queen Elizabeth bloodline relates to these Special Organizations. On this topic of The Committee of 300, there is much information on the Internet. It illustrates how from a top bloodline, such as Queen Elizabeth II, the layers of organizational structures reach down to the individual Earthling (This will be covered in a later chapter).

There is an interesting picture on the website ***www.therealisraelites.com*** or more exactly ***www.therealisraelites.com/?tag=council-of-13*** that illustrates this. I cannot take credit for this and have copied it here not to support its accuracy but to illustrate how the administrative operation works and ties together.

Researchers on this topic state that The Committee of 300 use many well-known institutions to accomplish their goals, including the Council on Foreign Relations, Bilderbergers, Trilateral Commission, Club of Rome, Royal Institute for International Affairs, Mafia, CIA, NSA, Mossad, Secret Service, International Monetary Fund, Federal Reserve, Internal Revenue Service, and Interpol, to name a few. All of these are private organizations or corporations set up as public service devices, but this is far from the truth. It is one big happy family of corporations bound by oath, contract, or special purpose.

This committee of 300 is modeled after the British East India Company's Council of 300, founded by the British aristocracy in 1727. Most of its immense wealth arose out of the opium trade with China. This group is allegedly responsible for the drug wars in the U.S where they were to get people to give away constitutional rights. Asset forfeiture is a prime example, where huge assets can be seized without trail and no proof of guilt needed. Also the Committee of 300 long ago decreed that there shall be a smaller-much smaller-and better world, that is, their idea of what constitutes a better world. It is alleged that **Queen, Elizabeth II, is the head of the Committee of 300**. Check out ***http://www.pseudoreality.org/***.

The Committee of 300 uses a network of roundtable groups, think tanks and secret societies which control the world's largest financial institutions and governments. The most prominent of these groups include Chatham House, Bilderburg Group, Trilateral Commission, Council on Foreign Relations, Ditchley Foundation, Club of Rome, RAND Corporation, PNAC and of course **Freemasonry**.

It is of interest to have a picture of how this feeds down in one of the divisions such as the Financial. This is best illustrated by another picture found on the website ***http://worldtruth.tv/the-committee-of-300***/. This is a site which includes TV dedicated to the truth in history, news, health, spirituality, and survival. Here the Founder states:

"My name is Eddie and WorldTruth.TV is my way to share all the knowledge and information that I have acquired and been blessed with in the last 32 years of my journey on this planet. I created World-Truth in September of 2011 and in time for the 10 year anniversary of the 9-11-01 Victims. I provide people who are curious and open

minded with thought-provoking, educational, and sacred information that will definitely blow your mind, and unlock many others' minds. It will allow you to see things from a totally different angle. Some information is revealing, mind provoking but if you do your own research you will conclude for yourself that the information on this website is authentic. I show people what I have found from my research in the last 32 years and I want others to go and research on their own so they can come to their own conclusion. This blog serves the purpose of telling other people on a daily basis about the "sacred knowledge" that I have uncovered. WorldTruth.TV is a website dedicated to educating and informing people on regular basis with well-researched articles on powerful and concealed information. I've spent the last 32 years researching Theosophy, Freemasonry, Kabbalah, Rosicrucianism, the Bavarian Illuminati and Western Occultism. I remember when I first learned about the "Truth" and it wasn't pretty. I remember learning about how the mass media lies to our faces consistently. About how the educational system only teaches the youth what they need to become obedient workers. About how politics are merely a puppet show and that, regardless of who is in office, the same Agenda will be going forward. About how our rights and freedoms are being revoked. About how the masses are purposely being dumbed-down. About how simple values are rejected from popular culture and replaced by shallow materialism and glorification of immediate fulfillment of impulses. This website does not aim to promote or to dismiss particular views, opinions or belief systems. It rather attempts to present in an objective manner the subjects at hand, using credible sources from different viewpoints."

On this site is a picture of how the head of the Committee is responsible for the Financial Center through many layers of control groups that would effectively remove her from the spotlight. This site is highly recommended as an alternative to the usual media that falls under a whole different Division.

The Committee of 300 controls the world economy via the City of London Corporation. The City of London Corporation is made up of 108 Livery Companies, the Worshipful Company of Fuellers and the Worshipful Company of Mercers are two of the most prominent.

The Bank of International Settlements controls the worldwide banking system including the Federal Reserve System and the European Central Bank. The International Monetary Fund and the World Bank work to indebt developing nations making them subservient to the developed nations of the world.

The Groups of 7, 20 and 30 act as financial regulators and middlemen servicing Central Banks and Investment Banks. These regulators are unelected and empower the Financial Terrorists at the expense of the masses. Finally, the Investment Banks and financial services corporations gamble with their clients money with the reassurance that any losses will be paid by taxpayers.

In **Dr. John Colemans** book **Conspirators Handbook**, he shows a more detailed organizational chart of the workings of the Committee. John Coleman is an author and analyst of world affairs. He was a British Intelligence Officer for MI6 who has written several books and numerous papers analyzing the power structure of the world. He can be found on **http://coleman300.com/.** The Committee of 300 looks to social convulsions on a global scale, followed by depressions, as a softening-up technique for bigger things to come, as its principal method of creating masses of people all over the world who will become its "welfare" recipients of the future. The committee appears to base much of its important decisions affecting mankind on the philosophy of Polish aristocrat, Felix Dzerzinski, who regarded mankind as being slightly above the level of cattle. As a close friend of British intelligence agent Sydney Reilly (Reilly was actually

Dzerzinski's controller during the Bolshevik Revolution's formative years), he often confided in Reilly during his drinking bouts. Dzerzinski was, of course, the beast who ran the Red Terror apparatus. He once told Reilly, while the two were on a drinking binge, that *"Man is of no importance. Look at what happens when you starve him. He begins to eat his dead companions to stay alive. Man is only interested in his own survival."*

The Tavistock Institute

Following WWII in 1946 the **Tavistock Institute** was established in London with a grant from the Rockefeller Foundation. Tavistock's pioneer work in behavioural science along Freudian lines of 'controlling' humans established it as the world centre of foundation ideology. *"All Tavistock and American foundation techniques have a single goal---to break down the psychological strength of the individual and render him helpless to oppose the dictators of the World Order. Any technique which helps to break down the family unit, and family inculcated principles of religion, honour, patriotism and sexual behaviour, is used by the Tavistock scientists as weapons of crowd control."*

With reference to the site ***http://educate-yourself.org/nwo/nwotavistockbestkeptsecret.shtml*** the following is from Dr. Byron T. Weeks, MD, July 31, 2001 where there is an Editor's Note: *"No one deserves more credit than **Dr. John Coleman** for bringing to light the history and true purpose of the City of London's Tavistock Institute and its many subdivisional institutions and organizations which was exposed in stunning detail in his 1992 book, **Conspirators' Hierarchy: The Story of The Committee of 300**. Dr Coleman has rightly complained that many NWO expose writers who have followed in his wake, have used his **original research** without crediting him as the originating source and in fairness to him, it should be observed that the information presented below is a reflection of his pioneering investigations into Tavistock. The article below was sent to John Quinn by Dr. Byron Weeks. The insidious propaganda and public opinion manipulations (including mind control agendas) orchestrated by London's Tavistock Institute is covered at length in the books of David Icke and Dr John Coleman, but this recent article adds fresh insights and historical perspective."*

The article is as follows entitled: TAVISTOCK - THE BEST KEPT SECRET IN AMERICA

Formed in 1947, the Tavistock Institute is an independent not-for-profit organization which seeks to combine research in the social sciences with professional practice. Problems of institution-building and organizational design and change are being tackled in all sectors - government, industry and commerce, health and welfare, education, etc. - nationally and internationally, and clients range from multinationals to small community groups. A growth area has been the use of a developmental approach to evaluation of new and experimental programs, particularly in health, education and community development. This has also produced new training events alongside the regular program of group relations conferences. The Institute owns and edits the monthly journal **Human Relations** (published by Plenum Press) which is now in its 48th year, and has recently launched (in conjunction with Sage Publications) a new journal **Evaluation**.

Three elements combine to make the Institute unusual, if not unique: it has the independence of being entirely self-financing, with no subsidies from the government or other sources; the action research orientation places it between, but not in, the worlds of academia and consultancy; and its range of disciplines include anthropology, economics, organizational behaviour, political science, psychoanalysis, psychology and sociology.

The ideology of **American foundations** was created by the Tavistock Institute of Human Relations in London. In 1921, the Duke of Bedford, Marquess of Tavistock, the 11th Duke, gave a building to the Institute to study the effect of shellshock on British soldiers who survived World War I. Its purpose was to establish the "breaking point" of men under stress, under the direction of the British Army Bureau of Psychological Warfare, commanded by **Sir John Rawlings-Reese**.

Tavistock Institute is headquartered in London. Its prophet, **Sigmond Freud**, settled in Maresfield Gardens when he moved to England. He was given a mansion by Princess Bonaparte. Tavistock's pioneer work in behavioural science along Freudian lines of "controlling" humans established it as the world center of foundation ideology. Its network now extends from the University of Sussex to the U.S. through the Stanford Research Institute, Esalen, MIT, Hudson Institute, Heritage Foundation, Center of Strategic and International Studies at Georgetown, where State Dept. personal are trained, US Air Force Intelligence, and the Rand and Mitre corporations. The personnel of the corporations are required to undergo indoctrination at one or more of these Tavistock controlled institutions. A network of secret groups, the **Mont Pelerin Society**, **Trilateral Commission**, **Ditchley Foundation**, and the **Club of Rome** is conduit for instructions to the Tavistock network.

[Editor, Tim Aho's note: See *Watch Unto Prayer* report on The Heritage Foundation founded by **Paul Weyrich** with funding from **Joseph Coors**, who also founded and financed respectively the Moral Majority and Council for National Policy.].

Tavistock Institute developed the mass brain-washing techniques which were first used experimentally on American prisoners of war in Korea. Its experiments in crowd control methods have been widely used on the American public, a surreptitious but nevertheless outrageous assault on human freedom by modifying individual behavior through topical psychology. A German refugee, Kurt Lewin, became director of Tavistock in 1932. He came to the U.S. in 1933 as a "refugee", the first of many infiltrators, and set up the Harvard Psychology Clinic, which originated the propaganda campaign to turn the American public against Germany and involve us in World War II.

In 1938, Roosevelt executed a secret agreement with Churchill which in effect ceded U.S. sovereignty to England, because it agreed to let Special Operations Executive control U.S. policies. To implement this agreement, Roosevelt sent General Donovan to London for indoctrination before setting up OSS (now the CIA) under the aegis of SOE-SIS. The entire OSS program, as well as the CIA has always worked on guidelines set up by the Tavistock Institute.

[Editor, Tim Aho: See **Watch Unto Prayer** report on ***http://watch.pair.com/jbs-cnp.html.*** The John Birch Society & Council for National Policy for information regarding CIA operations on the Christian Right.] Tavistock Institute originated the mass civilian bombing raids carried out by Roosevelt and Churchill purely as a clinical experiment in mass terror, keeping records of the results as they watched the "guinea pigs" reacting under "controlled laboratory conditions". All Tavistock and American foundation techniques have a single goal---*to break down the psychological strength of the individual and render him helpless to oppose the dictators of the World Order*. Any technique which helps to break down the family unit, and family inculcated principles of religion, honor, patriotism and sexual behavior, is used by the Tavistock scientists as weapons of crowd control.

The methods of Freudian psychotherapy induce permanent mental illness in those who undergo this treatment by destabilizing their character. The victim is then advised to "establish new rituals of personal interaction", that is, to indulge in brief sexual encounters which actually set the participants adrift with no stable personal relationships in their lives, destroying their ability to establish or maintain a family. Tavistock Institute has developed such power in the U.S. that no one achieves prominence in any field unless he has been trained in behavioral science at Tavistock or one of its subsidiaries.

Henry Kissinger, whose meteoric rise to power is otherwise inexplicable, was a German refugee and student of Sir John Rawlings-Reese at SHAEF. Dr. Peter Bourne, a Tavistock Institute psychologist, picked Jimmy Carter for President of the U.S. solely because Carter had undergone an intensive brainwashing program administered by Admiral Hyman Rickover at Annapolis. The "experiment" in compulsory racial integration in the U.S. was organized by Ronald Lippert, of the OSS and the American Jewish Congress, and director of child training at the Commission on Community Relations. The program was designed to break down the individual's sense of personal knowledge in his identity, his racial heritage. Through the **Stanford Research Institute**, Tavistock controls the National Education Association. The **Institute of Social Research at the National Training Lab** brain washes the leading executives of business and government. *Such is the power of Tavistock that our entire space program was scrapped for nine years so that the Soviets could catch up.* The hiatus was demanded in an article written by Dr. Anatol Rapport, and was promptly granted by the government, to the complete mystification of everyone connected with NASA. Another prominent Tavistock operation is the **Wharton School of Finance,** at the University of Pennsylvania. A single common denominator identifies the common Tavistock strategy---the use of drugs. The infamous MK Ultra program of the CIA, in which unsuspecting CIA officials were given LSD, and their reaction studied like "guinea pigs", resulted in several deaths.

The U.S. Government had to pay millions in damages to the families of the victims, but the culprits were never indicted. The program originated when Sandoz AG, a Swiss drug firm, owned by S.G. Warburg Co. of London, developed Lysergic Acid [LSD]. Roosevelt's advisor, **James Paul Warburg**, son of **Paul Warburg** who wrote the Federal Reserve Act, and nephew of M**ax Warburg** who had financed Hitler, set up the (***http://watch.pair.com/FreedomHouse.html#ips)*** Institute for Policy Studies to promote the drug. The result was the LSD "counter-culture" of the 1960s, the "student revolution", which was financed by $25 million from the CIA.

One part of MK Ultra was the **Human Ecology Fund**; the CIA also paid Dr. Herbert Kelman of Harvard to carry out further experiments on mind control. In the 1950s, the CIA financed extensive LSD experiments in Canada. **Dr. D. Ewen Cameron**, president of the Canadian Psychological Association, and director of Royal Victorian Hospital, Montreal, received large payments from the CIA to give 53 patients large doses of LSD and record their reactions; the patients were drugged into weeks of sleep and then given electric shock treatments. One victim, the wife of a member of the Canadian Parliament, is now suing the U.S. companies who provided the drug for the CIA. All the records of the CIA's drug testing program were ordered destroyed by the head of MK Ultra. Because all efforts of the Tavistock Institute are directed toward producing cyclical collapse, the effect of the CIA programs are tragically apparent. R. Emmett Tyrell Jr., writing in the Washington Post August 20, 1984, cites the "squalid consequences of the 60s radicals in SDS" as resulting in "the growing rate of illegitimacy, petty lawlessness, drug addiction, welfare, VD, and mental illness". This is the legacy of the Warburgs and the CIA. Their principal agency, the **Institute for Policy Studies**, was funded by James Paul Warburg; its co-founder was Marcus Raskin, protege of McGeorge Bundy, president of the Ford Foundation. Bundy had Raskin appointed to the post of President Kennedy's personal representative on the National Security Council, and in 1963 funded Students for Democratic Society, through which the CIA operated the drug culture.

Today the Tavistock Institute operates a $6 Billion a year network of Foundations in the U.S., all of it funded by U.S. taxpayers' money. Ten major institutions are under its direct control, with 400 subsidiaries, and 3000 other study groups and think tanks which originate many types of programs to increase the control of the World Order over the American people. The Stanford Research Institute, adjoining the Hoover Institution, is a $150 million a year operation with 3300 employees. It carries on program surveillance for Bechtel, Kaiser, and 400 other companies, and extensive intelligence operations for the CIA. It is the largest institution on the West Coast promoting mind control and the behavioral sciences. One of the key agencies as a conduit for secret instructions from Tavistock is the **Ditchley Foundation**, founded in 1957. The American branch of the Ditchley Foundation is run by **Cyrus Vance**, former Secretary of State, and director of the Rockefeller Foundation, and **Winston Lord**, president of the Council on Foreign Relations.

[Editor, Tim Aho's note: The wife of Winston Lord (CFR, Bilderberg, Skull & Bones), Bette Bao Lord (CFR, Bilderberg), is Chairman of the Board of Freedom House whose manipulation of the Christian Right via the Religious Persecution issue is documented in our report (***http://watch.pair.com/FreedomHouse.html***) Freedom House: A CFR Front.]

One of the principal but little known operations of the Rockefeller Foundation has been its techniques for controlling world agriculture. Its director, **Kenneth Wernimont**, set up Rockefeller controlled agricultural programs throughout Mexico and Latin America. *The independent farmer is a great threat to the World Order, because he produces for himself, and because his produce can be converted into capital, which gives him independence*. In Soviet Russia, the Bolsheviks believed they had attained total control over the people; they were dismayed to find their plans threatened by the stubborn independence of the small farmers, the Kulaks.

Stalin ordered the OGPU to seize all food and animals of the Kulaks, and to starve them out. The Chicago American, February 25, 1935 carried a front page headline, SIX MILLION PERISH IN SOVIET FAMINE; Peasants' Crops Seized, They and their Animals Starve. To draw attention from this atrocity, it was later alleged that the Germans, not the Soviets, had killed six million people, the number taken from the Chicago American headline by a Chicago publicist.

The Communist Party, the Party of the Peasants and Workers, exterminated the peasants and enslaved the workers. *Many totalitarian regimes have found the small farmer to be their biggest stumbling block*. The French Reign of Terror was directed, not against the aristocrats, many of whom were sympathetic to it, but against the small farmers who refused to turn over their grain to the revolutionary tribunals in exchange for the worthless assonates. <u>In the United States, the foundations are presently engaged in the same type of war of extermination against the American farmer.</u>

The traditional formula of land plus labor for the farmer has been altered due to the farmer's need for purchasing power, to buy industrial goods needed in his farming operations. Because of this need for capital, the farmer is especially vulnerable to the World Order's manipulation of interest rates, which is bankrupting him. Just as in the Soviet Union, in the early 1930s, when Stalin ordered the Kulaks to give up their small plots of land to live and work on the collective farms, the American small farmer faces the same type of extermination, being forced to give up his small plot of land to become a hired hand for the big agricultural trusts. **The Brookings Institution** and other foundations originated the monetary programs implemented by the Federal Reserve System to destroy the American farmer, a replay of the Soviet tragedy in Russia, with one proviso that the farmer will be allowed to survive if he becomes a slave worker of the giant trusts.

Once the citizen becomes aware of the true role of the foundations, he can understand the high interest rates, high taxes, the destruction of the family, the degradation of the churches into forums for revolution, the subversion of the universities into CIA cesspools of drug addiction, and the halls of government into sewers of international espionage and intrigue. The American citizen can now understand why every agent of the federal government is against him; the alphabet agencies, the FBI, IRS, CIA and BATF must make war on the citizen in order to carry out the programs of the foundations.

The foundations are in direct violation of their charters, which commit them to do "charitable" work, because they make no grants which are not part of a political goal. The charge has been made, and never denied, that the Heritage-AEI network has at least two KGB moles on its staff. The employment of professional intelligence operatives as "charitable" workers, as was done in the Red Cross Mission to Russia in 1917, exposes the sinister political economic and social goals which the World Order requires the foundations to achieve through their "bequests".

Not only is this tax fraud, because the foundations are granted tax exemption solely to do charitable work, but it is criminal syndicalism, conspiracy to commit offenses against the United States of America, Constitutional Law 213, Corpus Juris Secundum 16. For the first time, the close interlocking of the foundation "syndicate" has been revealed by the names of its principle incorporators---Daniel Coit Gilman, who incorporated the Peabody Fund and the John Slater Fund, and became an incorporator of the General Education Board (now the Rockefeller Foundation); Gilman, who also incorporated the Russell Trust in 1856, later became an incorporator of the Carnegie Institution with Andrew Dickson White (Russell Trust) and Frederic A. Delano. Delano also was an original incorporator of the Brookings Institution and the Carnegie Endowment for International Peace.

Daniel Coit Gilman incorporated the Russell Sage Foundation with Cleveland H. Dodge of the National City Bank. These foundations incorporators have been closely linked with the Federal Reserve System, the War Industries Board of World War I, the OSS of World War II and the CIA. They have also been closely linked with the American International Corporation, which was formed to instigate the Bolshevik Revolution in Russia. Delano, an uncle of Franklin Delano Roosevelt, was on the original Board of Governors of the Federal Reserve System in 1914. His brother-in-law founded the influential Washington law firm of Covington and Burling. The Delanos and other ruling families of the World Order trace their lineage directly back to William of Orange and the regime which granted the charter of the Bank of England.

Tavistock Institutions In The United States:

Flow Laboratories Gets contracts from the National Institutes of Health.

Merle Thomas Corporation Gets contracts from the U.S. Navy, analyzes data from satellites.

Walden Research Does work in the field of pollution control.

Planning Research Corporation, Arthur D. Little, G.E. "TEMPO", Operations Research Inc. Part of approximately 350 firms who conduct research and conduct surveys, make recommendations to government. They are part of what President Eisenhower called "a possible danger to public policy that could itself become captive of a scientific-technological elite."

Brookings Institution Dedicates its work to what it calls a "national agenda." Wrote President Hoover's program, President Roosevelt's "New Deal", the Kennedy Administration's "New Frontiers" program (deviation from it may have cost John F. Kennedy his life), and President Johnson's "Great Society." Brookings has been telling the United States Government how to conduct its affairs for the past 70 years and is still doing so.

Hudson Institute This institution has done more to shape the way Americans react to political and social events, think, vote and generally conduct themselves than perhaps any except the BIG FIVE. Hudson specializes in defence policy research and relations with the USSR. Most of its military work is classified as SECRET. (One idea during the Vietnam War was to build a moat around Saigon.) Hudson may be properly classified as one of the Committee of 300's BRAINWASHING establishments. One of its largest clients is the U.S. Department of Defence which includes matters of civil defence, national security, military policy and arms control.

[Editor, Tim Aho: This is the same (*http://watch.pair.com/Hudson.html*) Hudson Institute which gave us GOALS 2000 and authored the Freedom From Religious Persecution Act, which became the International Religious Freedom Act of 1998. This law required the creation of a federal commission to monitor religion chaired by a presidentially-appointed Ambassador-at-Large on International Religious Freedom under the mandates of the United Nations' covenants and authority of the International Criminal Court.]

National Training Laboratories One of the key institutions established for this purpose in the United States was the National Training Laboratories (NTL). Founded in 1947 by members of the Tavistock network in the United States and located originally on an estate in Bethel, Maine, NTL had as its explicit purpose the brainwashing of leaders of the government, educational institutions, and corporate bureaucracies in the Tavistock method, and then using these "leaders" to either themselves run Tavistock group sessions in their organizations or to hire other similarly trained group leaders to do the job. The "nuts and bolts" of the NTL operation revolves around the particular form of Tavistock degenerate psychology known as "*group dynamics*," developed by German Tavistock operative Kurt Lewin, who emigrated to the United States in the 1930s and whose students founded NTL.

In a Lewinite brainwashing group, a number of individuals from varying backgrounds and personalities, are manipulated by a "group leader" to form a "consensus" of opinion, achieving a new "group identity." The key to the process is the creation of a controlled environment, in which stress is introduced (sometimes called dissonance) to crack an individual's belief structure. Using the peer pressure of other group members, the individual is "cracked," and a new personality emerges with new values. The degrading experience causes the person to deny that any change has taken place. In that way, an individual is brainwashed without the victim knowing what has taken place.

This method is the same, with some minor modification, used in all so-called "sensitivity groups" or "T-groups," or in the more extreme rock-drug-sex counterculture form, "touchy-feely groups," such as the kind popularized from the 1960s onward by the **Esalen Institute**, which was set up with the help of NTL.

From the mid-1950s onward, NTL put the majority of the nation's corporate leaderships through such brainwashing programs, while running similar programs for the State Department, the Navy, the Department of Education, and other sections of the federal bureaucracy. There is no firm estimate of the number of Americans who have been put through this process in last 40 years at either NTL, or as it is now known the **NTL Institute for Applied Behavioural Sciences**, which is based in Rosslyn, Virginia, or its West Coast base of operations, the **Western Training Laboratories in Group Development**, or in various satellite institutions. The most reliable estimate is in the several millions.

One of the groups that went through the NTL mill in the 1950s was the leadership of the **National Education Association**, the largest organization of teachers in the United States. Thus, the NEA's outlook has been "shaped" by Tavistock, through the NTL. In 1964, the NTL Institute became a direct part of the NEA, with the NTL setting up "group sessions" for all its affiliates. With funding from the Department of Education, the NTL Institute drafted the programs for the training of the nation's primary and secondary school teachers, and has a hand as well in developing the content of educational "reforms," including OBE.

Also known as the **International Institute for Applied Behavioural Sciences**. This institute is a brainwashing center in artificial stress training whereby participants suddenly find themselves immersed in defending themselves against vicious accusations.

NTL takes in the National Education Association, the largest teacher group in the United States. While officially decrying "racism", it is interesting to note that NTL, working with NEA, produced a paper proposing education vouchers which would separate the hard-to-teach children from the brighter ones, and funding would be allocated according to the number of difficult children who would be separated from those who progressed at a normal rate. The proposal was not taken up.

University of Pennsylvania, Wharton School of Finance & Commerce Founded by Eric Trist One of the "brain trusts" of Tavistock, Wharton has become one of the more important Tavistock in so far as "Behavioural Research" is concerned. Wharton attracts clients such as the U.S. Department of Labor---which teaches how to produce "cooked" statistics at the Wharton Econometric Forecasting Associates Incorporated. This method was very much in demand as we came to the close of 1991 with millions more out of work than was reflected in USDL statistics. Wharton's ECONOMETRIC MODELING is used by every major Committee of 300 company in the United States, Western Europe, the International Monetary Fund, the United Nations, and the World Bank. Institute for Social Research Among its clients are The Ford Foundation, U.S. Department of Defence, U.S. Postal Service and the U.S. Department of Justice. Among its studies are "The Human Meaning Of Social Change", "Youth in Transition" and "How Americans View Their Mental Health".

Institute For The Future This is not a typical Tavistock institution in that it is funded by the Ford Foundation, yet it draws its long-range forecasting from the mother of all think tanks. Institute for the Future projects what it believes to be changes that will be taking place in time frames of fifty years. So called "DELPHI PANELS" decide what is normal and what is not, and prepare position papers to "steer" government in the right direction to head off such groups as "people creating civil disorder." (This could be patriotic groups demanding abolition of graduated taxes, or demanding that their right to bear arms is not infringed.) This institute recommends action such as liberalizing abortion laws, drug usage and that cars entering an urban area pay tolls, teaching birth control in public schools, requiring registration of firearms, making use of drugs a non-criminal offense, legalizing homosexuality, paying students for scholastic achievements, making zoning controls a preserve of the state, offering bonuses for family planning and last, but most frightening, a Pol Pot Cambodia-style proposal that new communities be established in rural areas, (concentration camp compounds). As can be observed, many of their goals have already been more than fully realized.

Institute For Policy Studies (IPS) One of the "Big Three", IPS has shaped and reshaped United States policies, foreign and domestic, since it was founded by James P. Warburg and the Rothschild entities in the United States. Its networks in America include the League for Industrial Democracy. Lead players in the League for Industrial Democracy have included Jeane Kirkpatrick, former U.S. Ambassador to the United Nations, Irwin Suall of the ADL, Eugene Rostow, Arms control negotiator, Lane Kirkland, Labor Leader, and Albert Shanker. IPS was incorporated in 1963 by Marcus Raskin and Richard Barnett, both highly trained Tavistock Institute graduates. The objectives of IPS came from an agenda laid down for it by the Tavistock Institute, one of the most notable being to create the "New Left" as a grass roots movement in the U.S. It's been said that Barnett and Raskin controlled such diverse elements as the Black Panthers, Daniel Ellsberg, National Security Council staff member Halprin, The Weathermen Underground, the Venceramos and the campaign staff of candidate George McGovern. No scheme was too big for IFS and its controllers to take on and manage.

Through its many powerful lobbying groups on Capitol Hill, IPS relentlessly used its "Big Stick" to beat Congress. IPS has a network of lobbyists, all supposedly operating independently but in actual fact acting cohesively, so that Congressmen are pummelled from all sides by seemingly different and varied lobbyists, In this way, IPS was, and is still, able to successfully sway individual Representatives and Senators to vote for "the trend, the way things are going." By using key pointmen on Capitol Hill, IPS was able to break into the very infrastructure of our legislative system and the way it works.

IPS became, and remains to this day, one of the most prestigious "think tanks" controlling foreign policy decisions, which we, the people, foolishly believe are those of our law makers. By sponsoring militant activism at home and with links to revolutionaries abroad, by engineering such victories as "The Pentagon Papers," besieging the corporate structure, bridging the credibility gap between underground movements and acceptable political activism, by penetrating religious organizations and using them to sow discord in America, such as radical racial policies under the guise of religion, using establishment media to spread IPS ideas, and then supporting them, IPS has lived up to the role which it was founded to play.

[Editor, Tim Aho: See Watch Unto Prayer report on *(http://watch.pair.com/FreedomHouse.html*) Freedom House: "Grants (for the IPS) came from the Samuel Rubin Foundation and the Stern Family Fund. **Samuel Rubin** was himself a member of the elite Comintern of the Communist Party, founded by none other than Lenin himself. Billionaire **Armand Hammer** assisted Rubin in making the fortunes which helped launch IPS. **Philip Stern**, an IPS trustee, was the president of Stern Fund. The executive director of the Stern Fund, **David R. Hunter**, was previously an official of **The National Council and the World Council Of Churches. (**Dr. James W. Wardner, *Unholy Alliances*, p.125)]

Stanford Research Institute Jesse Hobson, the first president of Stanford Research Institute, in a 1952 speech made it clear what lines the institute was to follow. Stanford can be described as one of the "jewels" in Tavistock's Crown in its rule over the United States. Founded in 1946 immediately after the close of WWII, it was presided over by **Charles A. Anderson**, with emphasis on mind control research and "future sciences." Included under the Stanford umbrella was **Charles F. Kettering Foundation** which developed the "Changing Images of Man" upon which the Aquarian Conspiracy rests. Some of Stanford's major clients and contracts were at first centered around the defence establishment but, as Stanford grew, so, did the diversity of its services:

Applications of Behavioural Sciences to Research Management Office of Science and Technology
SRI Business Intelligence Program
U.S. Department of Defence Directorate of Defence Research and Engineering
U.S. Department of Defence Office of Aerospace Research

Among corporations seeking Stanford's services were Wells Fargo Bank, Bechtel Corporation, Hewlett Packard, Bank of America, McDonnell Douglas Corporation, Blyth,

Eastman Dillon and TRW Company. *One of Stanford's more secret projects was extensive work on chemical and bacteriological warfare (CAB) weapons.*

Stanford Research is plugged into at least 200 smaller "think tanks" doing research into every facet of life in America. This is ARPA networking and represents the emergence of probably the most far reaching effort to control the environment of every individual in the country. At present Stanford's computers are linked with 2500 "sister" research consoles which include the CIA, Bell Telephone Laboratories, U.S. Army Intelligence, The Office of Naval Intelligence (ONI), Rand, MIT, Harvard and UCLA. Stanford plays a key role in that it is the "library", cataloguing all ARPA documentation.

"Other agencies".....one can use one's imagination here, are allowed to search through SRI's "library" for key words, phrases, look through sources and update their own master files with those of Stanford Research Center. The Pentagon uses SRI's master files extensively, and there is little doubt that other U.S. Government agencies do the same. Pentagon "command and control" problems are worked out by Stanford.

While ostensibly these apply only to weapons and soldiers, there is absolutely no guarantee that the same research could not , and will not be turned to civilian applications. Stanford is known to be willing to do anything for anyone.

[Editor, Tim Aho: See Watch Unto Prayer report (***http://watch.pair.com/dolphin.html*** Lambert Dolphin & the Great Sphinx, which documents the connections of SRI's Lambert Dolphin with the Edgar Cayce Foundation and The Discernment Ministries.]

MASSACHUSETTS INSTITUTE OF TECHNOLOGY (MIT), ALFRED P. SLOAN SCHOOL OF MANAGEMENT This major institute is not generally recognized as being a part of Tavistock U.S.A. Most people look upon it as being a purely American institution, but that is far from the truth. MIT- Alfred Sloan can be roughly divided into the following groups: Contemporary Technology Industrial Relations NASA-ERC Computer Research Laboratories Office of Naval Research Group, Psychology Systems Dynamics
Some of MIT's clients are:

American Management Association
Committee for Economic Development
GTE
Institute for Defence Analysis (IDA)
NASA
National Academy of Sciences
National Council of Churches
Sylvania
TRW
U.S. Army
U.S. Department of State
U.S. Navy
U.S. Treasury
Volkswagen Company

RAND RESEARCH AND DEVELOPMENT CORPORATION

Without a doubt, RAND is THE think tank most beholden to Tavistock Institute and certainly the RIIA's most prestigious vehicle for control of United States policies at every level. Specific RAND policies that became operative include our ICBM program, prime analyses for U.S. foreign policy making, instigator of space programs, U.S. nuclear policies, corporate analyses, hundreds of projects for the military, the Central Intelligence Agency (CIA) in relation to the use of mind altering drugs like peyote, LSD (the covert MK-ULTRA operation which lasted for 20 years).

[Editor, Tim Aho's note: The founder of the Rand Corporation, **Herman Kahn**, also founded the Hudson Institute in 1961. In Educating for the New World Order, B.K. Eakman tells of a training manual for "change agents" developed for the U.S. government by Rand Corporation: ". . . a how-to manual with a 1971 U.S. Office of Education contract number on it entitled 'Training for Change Agents'; seven volumes of 'change agent studies' commissioned by the U.S. Office of Education to the Rand Corporation in 1973-74; scores of other papers submitted by behaviourist researchers who had obtained grants from the U.S. Office of Education for the purpose of exploring ways to 'freeze' and 'unfreeze' values, 'to implement change,' and to turn potentially hostile groups and committees into acquiescent, rubber-stamp bodies by means of such strategies as the 'Delphi Technique.'" (p. 118)] Some of RAND's clients include:

American Telephone and Telegraph Company (AT&T)
Chase Manhattan Bank
International Business Machines (IBM)
National Science Foundation
Republican Party
TRW
U.S. Air Force
U.S. Department of Health
U.S. Department of Energy

There are literally THOUSANDS of highly important companies, government institutions and organizations that make use of RANDS's services. To list them all would be impossible. Among RAND's specialities is a study group that predicts the timing and the direction of a thermonuclear war, plus working out the many scenarios based upon its findings. RAND was once accused of being commissioned by the USSR to work out terms of surrender of the United States Government, an accusation that went all the way to the United States Senate, where it was taken up by Senator Symington and subsequently fell victim to scorn poured out by the establishment press. BRAINWASHING remains the primary function of RAND.

These institutions are among those that fund The UNIFORM LAW FOUNDATION, whose function is to ensure that the **Uniform Commercial Code** remains the instrument for conducting business in the United States.

The Round Table

This network is not the most powerful expression of the Illuminati. There are many more elite groups within its web, but these "Round Table" organizations are a key part of its day to day manipulation of politics, banking, business, the military (especially **NATO**), "education", and so on.

You can read about all this in detail in **David Icke's** books, **And The Truth Shall Set You Free and The Biggest Secret**. But briefly, the network was created to advance through the 20th century and beyond the Illuminati agenda for *the centralized control of Planet Earth.* Also refer to David's paper printed on **www.bibliotecapleyades.net/sociopolitica/esp_sociopol_roundtable_5.htm.** where he summarizes the Round Table:

"The Round Table was created in London (the Illuminati's operational centre) in the latter years of the 19th century. Its first official "leader" was **Cecil Rhodes***, the man who mercilessly manipulated Southern Africa and took those lands from the black peoples. Although, in theory, black people are back in political control of Africa, the real decisions are still made by the European and American elites via their black puppet presidents and leaders. "Independence" is an illusion. Rhodes played tribe against tribe until they destroyed each other in war, so allowing Rhodes and the British to take over. The same is happening today in the continuing wars in Africa, details of which you will find on this site. Rhodes said the goal of the Round Table was to create World Government controlled by Britain (the Illuminati based in Britain).*

When he died in 1902, he left money in his will to fund "Rhodes Scholarships" in which overseas students had their expenses paid to study at Oxford University - the centre of the Illuminati's manipulation of "education". The ratio of these "Rhodes Scholars" who go back to their countries to enter positions of political, economic, and media power is enormous compared with the general student population.

They act as Illuminati agents. The most famous Rhodes Scholar in the world today is Bill Clinton, the two-times President of the United States. But while Rhodes was the official front man for the Round Table, the real controllers and funders were, and are, the House of Rothschild, the banking dynasty which is at the heart of so much of the global conspiracy.

The inner elite of this Round Table in the US and UK were the key members of their government's war administrations before and during the First World War... As is provable with documentation, they worked together to engineer the circumstances that led to that global conflict. Through their technique of create-the-problem-then-offer-the-solution, they wanted to destroy the global status quo with that war and therefore have the opportunity to re-draw the world in their agenda's image when the conflict was over. This is precisely what they did.

Power in the world was in far fewer hands after the war than before, and this was advanced even further when they engineered the Second World War also. This has continued to this day and, indeed, is getting quicker all the time.

In 1919, came the Versailles Peace Conference near Paris when the elite of the Round Table from Britain and the United States, people like **Alfred Milner***,* **Edward Mandel House***, and* **Bernard Baruch***, were appointed to represent their countries at the meetings which decided how the world would be changed as a result of the war these same people had created.*

They decided to impose impossible reparations payments on Germany, so ensuring the collapse of the post-war Weimar Republic amid unbelievable economic collapse and thus create the very circumstances that brought <u>Hitler</u> *(a Rothschild, see related article) to power. It was while in Paris that these Illuminati, Round Table, members met at the Hotel Majestic to begin the process of creating the Bilderberg-CFR-RIIA-Trilateral Commission network. They also decided at Versailles that they now all supported the creation of a Jewish homeland in Palestine. As I show in my books, EVERY ONE of them was either a Rothschild bloodline or was controlled by them."*

The Trilateral Commission

The Trilateral Commission was founded by David Rockefeller and Zbigniew Brzezinski in July 1973 and is composed of approximately 325 elites in business, banking, and politics. The Trilateral Commission is propagated as being an economic cooperation between America, Europe, and Japan, but in reality is another secretive society/organization - this one specializing in creating the trilateral economic interdependence necessary to bring in the New World Order system of world currency and world governance. They are setting up the framework/power structure necessary for these multinational banks and corporations to assume global control, dominating the world's populations, governments, and economies.

"The Trilateral Commission is an international organization founded by David Rockefeller who also had a part in the founding of the Council on Foreign Relations, Inc., and who is the chairman of the board. The Trilateral Commission is the Illuminati's attempt to unite Western Europe's common market, Japan, Canada and the United States into an economic and political confederacy. What they couldn't do through the political side of the Illuminati (Council on Foreign Relations, Inc.) they are trying now through the economic approach." -**Alex Christopher**, **"Pandora's Box – The Ultimate Unseen Hand Behind the New World Order**" (147)

"The Trilateral Commission was founded by the persistent manoeuvring of David Rockefeller and Zbigniew Brzezinski. Rockefeller, [then] chairman of the ultra powerful Chase Manhattan Bank, a director of many major multinational corporations and 'endowment funds' has long been a central figure in the mysterious Council on Foreign Relations. Brzezinski, a brilliant prognosticator of one-world idealism, has been a professor at Columbia University and the author of several books that have served as 'policy guidelines' for the CFR. Brzezinski served as the (Trilateral) commission's executive director from its inception in 1973 until late 1976 when he was appointed by President Carter as assistant to the president for national security affairs." -**Anthony C. Sutton and Patrick M. Wood**, `"Trilateral Over Washington"`

Some notable members of the Trilateral Commission include George Bush, Dick and Lynne Cheney, Bill Clinton, Al Gore, Jimmy Carter, Walter Mondale, David Rockefeller, Zbigniew Brzezinski, Henry Kissinger, David Gergen, Richard Holbrooke, Madeleine Albright, Robert McNamara, Paul Volcker, Alan Greenspan and Paul Wolfowitz. US Senators Diane Feinstein, Robert Taft Jr., Charles Robb, William Cohen, and John Glenn, Congressmen, Ambassadors, Secretaries of Treasury, State and many other political figures are Trilateralists. There are also many banking institutions represented at Trilateral meetings including the European Central Bank, World Bank, IMF, the Federal Reserve, Chase-Morgan, Citibank, Bank of America, Bank One, Bank of Tokyo, Bank of Japan and more. Also plenty of multi-national corporate interests are represented including Fuji Xerox, Goldman Sachs, AIG, Exxon-Mobil, Shell, Chevron, Texaco, Sony, Samsung, Comcast, Time Warner, Carlyle Group, Levi-Strauss, Daikin, Sara Lee, GE, GM, Ford, Chrysler, Toyota, Mitsubishi, Johnson and Johnson, IBM, Boeing, and Citigroup.

"Many of the original members of the Trilateral Commission are now in positions of power where they are able to implement policy recommendations of the Commission; recommendations that they, themselves, prepared on behalf of the Commission. It is for this reason that the Commission has acquired a reputation for being the Shadow Government of the West ...The Trilateral Commission's tentacles have reached so far in the political and economic sphere that it has been described by some as a cabal of powerful men out to control the world by creating a supernational community dominated by the multinational corporations." -Researcher **Laurie K. Strand** *"**Who's in charge— Six Possible Contenders**"* People's Almanac #3.

"David Rockefeller's newest international cabal [the Trilateral Commission] ... is intended to be the vehicle for multinational consolidation of the commercial and banking interests by seizing control of the political government of the United States ...The Trilateral Commission represents a skilful, coordinated effort to seize control and consolidate the four centers of power — political, monetary, intellectual, and ecclesiastical. All this is to be done in the interest of creating a more peaceful, more productive world community. What the Trilateralists truly intend is the creation of a worldwide economic power superior to the political governments of the nation-states involved. They believe the abundant materialism they propose to create will overwhelm existing differences. As managers and creators of the system they will rule the future." -**Senator Barry Goldwater**, "**With No Apologies**" 1979

During the birth of the Trilateral Commission was the US Carter administration, which was full of members: President Jimmy Carter and Vice-President Walter Mondale were Trilateralists. Carter's Secretaries of State, Defence, and Treasury, Vance, Brown, and Blumenthal were all members. Carter's National Security Advisor, Zbigniew Brzezinski, co-founded the Commission. And on top of that Carter placed 26 other members into senior administrative positions. **Brzezinski** wrote of the Commission in his book "**Power and Principle**" saying, *"Contrary to the myth, the Trilateral Commission is not a conspiracy designed to dominate the world but genuinely strives to engage Americans, Western Europeans, and Japanese in a common endeavour to shape a more cooperative world."* In the same book he wrote, *"All the key foreign policy makers of the Carter administration had previously served in the Trilateral Commission."*

The next President, Ronald Reagan, was not a Trilateral member, but his Vice-President George Bush was/is, and so were many men in his administration. After Reagan was eight years of Bush the Trilateralist then eight years of Clinton the Trilateralist both of whom appointed dozens of other members to high-level positions. Currently Bush Jr. is not a member, but his father is, his Vice-President Cheney is, and he has appointed members to his cabinet.

"We are grateful to The Washington Post, the New York Times, Time Magazine and other great publications whose directors have attended our meetings and respected their promises of discretion for almost forty years. It would have been impossible for us to develop our plan for the world if we had been subject to the bright lights of publicity during those years. But, the work is now much more sophisticated and prepared to march towards a world government. The supranational sovereignty of an intellectual elite and world bankers is surely preferable to the national auto-determination practiced in past centuries." -**David Rockefeller**, **1991 Trilateral Commission meeting.**

"The interests behind the Bush Administration, such as the CF or Council on Foreign Relations, The Trilateral Commission - founded by Brzezinski for David Rockefeller - and the Bilderberger Group, have prepared for and are now moving to implement open world dictatorship within the next five years. They are not fighting against terrorists. They are

fighting against citizens ... In 1983/4 I warned of a take-over of world governments being orchestrated by these people. There was an obvious plan to subvert true democracies and selected leaders were not being chosen based upon character but upon their loyalty to an economic system run by the elites and dedicated to preserving their power. All we have now are pseudo-democracies." - **Dr. Johannes B. Koeppl**, Ph.D. a former German defence ministry official and advisor to former NATO Secretary General Manfred Werner in an **FTW interview.**

As a result of their secret meetings at the Hotel Majestic, The Royal Institute of International Affairs was founded in London in 1920, the *Council on Foreign Relations* followed in 1921, and then came the *Bilderberg Group* (1954), the *Club of Rome* (1968) and the *Trilateral Commission* (1973). These are dominated by the Rothschilds and Rockefellers, and major manipulators like **Henry Kissinger**, who, in turn, answers to higher powers in the Illuminati. These organizations have among their number the top people in global politics, business, banking, military, media, "education" and so forth. These are the channels through which the same global policies are coordinated outside of public knowledge through apparently unconnected countries, political parties, and institutions. The upper levels of secret societies like the Freemasons, Knights of Malta, etc., connect into this **Round Table web.**

The Royal Institute Of International Affairs

The Illuminati in 1919 created the Royal Institute of International Affairs (RIIA). The Astor Illuminati family were major financial backers of the RIIA. Waldorf Astor was appointed to the RIIA. The American equivalent to the RIIA is the CFR (see below). The RIIA and CFR set up Round Table Groups (based on the King Arthur myths) which were initially named by Cecil Rhodes "Association of Helpers".

According to . **The Art of Global Politics** by **Gunther K. Russbacher,** *m*oney for the founding of the CFR came from J.P. Morgan, Bernard Baruch, Otto Kahn, Jacob Schiff, Paul Warburg, and John D. Rockefeller, among others.

The Royal Institute of International Affairs is the same as the American Council on Foreign Relations (CFR). The Royal Institute runs England and the British Empire, what was once the extension of the British, just as the CFR runs our country. They're sister organizations.

According to **MAJESTY TWELVE** top secret documents, the Knights Templar have become the driving influence at the highest levels of all the secret societies among the adepts known as the Illuminati. The most accessible font of their influence will be found in the (Cecil Rhodes) Roundtable Group (The Group), The Royal Institute Of International Affairs, the Church of Saint John the Divine in New York City, the Council On Foreign Relations, the Jason Society, the Skull and Bones Society (Russell Trust), the Scroll and Key Fraternity, the highest Degrees of the York and Scottish Rites of Freemasonry, the Ancient Order of Rosae Crucae, and many other secret societies which collectively make up the modern equivalent of the "Brotherhood of the Snake" also known as (a.k.a.) the "Guardians," the "Builders," the "Philosophers of Fire," or the "Illuminati". See **the MAJESTY TWELVE by William Cooper** at **http://www.hourofthetime.com/majestyt.htm**

Council On Foreign Relations

The first two groups created by the Round Table secret society were the British Royal Institute for International Affairs (RIIA) in 1920 and the American Council on Foreign Relations (CFR) in 1921. In fact the original plans for both were drawn up during the Paris Peace conference of 1919. Though they were given different names to mask their autonomy, the RIIA and CFR are just sub-branches of the Rhodes-Milner Round Table.

*"At the end of the war of 1914 [World War 1], it became clear that the organization of this system [the Round Table] had to be greatly extended ... This front organization, called the Royal Institute of International Affairs, had as its nucleus in each area the existing submerged Round Table Group. In New York it was known as the Council on Foreign Relations, and was a front for J. P. Morgan and Company." -**Dr. Carroll Quigley, Tragedy and Hope.***

*"Later the plan was changed to create an ostensible autonomy because, 'it seemed unwise to set up a single institute with branches.' It had to be made to appear that the C.F.R. in America, and the R.I.I.A. in Britain, were really independent bodies, lest the American public become aware the C.F.R. was in fact a subsidiary of the Round Table Group and react in patriotic fury. This is the group which designed the United Nations - the first major successful step on the road to a World Superstate. At least forty-seven C.F.R. members were among the American delegates to the founding of the United Nations in San Francisco in 1945 ...Today the C.F.R. remains active in working toward its final goal of a government over all the world - a government which the Insiders and their allies will control. The goal of the C.F.R. is simply to abolish the United States with its Constitutional guarantees of liberty. And they don't even try to hide it. Study No. 7, published by the C.F.R. on November 25, 1959, openly advocates building a new international order [which] must be responsive to world aspirations for peace, [and] for social and economic change ... an international order [code word for world government] ... including states labelling themselves as 'Socialist' [Communist]." -**Gary Allen, "None Dare Call it Conspiracy.***"

The CFR is a private group not affiliated with the U.S. government, but made to look that way. Just as the "Federal Reserve," the name "Council on Foreign Relations" sounds official to the unsuspecting ear, and they even print a magazine called "Foreign Affairs" to help pacify the organization in the public mind. But the truth is, the CFR is not a council belonging to the U.S. government and is, in fact, a secret society masquerading as an official organization. If they called it "Republicrats for World Government" or "Demopublican Global Governance Group" then the herd might notice. Even if they called it "the American Royal Institute for International Affairs" the sheeple might raise an eyebrow. This is the same reason our American leaders are called Presidents and not Prime Ministers, even though they are all royalty.

Admiral Chester Ward, was a US Judge Advocate General of the Navy and CFR member for sixteen years. He said the purpose of the CFR was *"promoting disarmament and the submergence of US sovereignty and national independence into an all-powerful one-world government."* In his book, ***"Kissinger on the Couch,"*** Ward wrote, *"(the) ... lust to surrender the sovereignty and independence of the United States is pervasive throughout most of the membership, and particularly in the leadership of several divergent cliques that make up what is actually a polycentric organization."*

"The most powerful clique in these (CFR) groups has one objective in common: they want to bring about the surrender of the sovereignty and the national independence of the U.S. They want to end national boundaries and racial and ethnic loyalties supposedly to increase business and ensure world peace. What they strive for would inevitably lead to dictatorship and loss of freedoms by the people." **-Harpers, July 1958**

"The Council on Foreign Relations is 'the establishment.' Not only does it have influence and power in key decision-making positions at the highest levels of government to apply pressure from above, but it also announces and uses individuals and groups to bring pressure from below, to justify the high level decisions for converting the U.S. from a sovereign Constitutional Republic into a servile member state of a one-world dictatorship." -**Congressman John Rarick, 1971**

CFR membership is made up of past, present, and future Presidents, Secretaries of State, Secretaries of Defence, Ambassadors, Senators, Congressmen, Judges, Federal Reserve System presidents and chairmen, bankers, military leaders, media owners/personalities, lobbyist lawyers, corporate executives, think-tank executives, and university presidents.

CFR membership is composed of the most influential Americans of the century. Just look at the household names belonging to the CFR: George Bush, Bill Clinton, Hilary Clinton, Jimmy Carter, Gerald Ford, Richard Nixon, John F. Kennedy, Dwight Eisenhower, Herbert Hoover, Robert Kennedy, Al Gore, Condoleezza Rice, Jesse Jackson, Colin Powell, Strobe Talbot, James Woolsey, John Dulles, Michael Dukakis, Fred Thompson, John McCain, Barack Obama, Mitt Romney, Rudy Giuliani, John Edwards, Michael Bloomberg, John Kerry, Thomas Kean, Henry Kissinger, Zbigniew Brzezinski, Jonathan Bush, Angelina Jolie, Dan Rather, Diane Sawyer, Barbara Walters, Consuelo Mack, Warren Beatty, William Buckley Jr., Newt Gingrich, Alan Greenspan, Paul Wolfowitz, Averill and Pamela Harriman, David, Nelson, and Jay Rockefeller, William and McGeorge Bundy, Brent Scowcroft, George Shultz, and Paul Warburg.

A sampling of the CFR's Corporate Members is: ABC News, American Express, Bank of America, Boeing, Chevron, Citigroup, Coca-Cola, De Beers, Exxon-Mobil, FedEx, Ford, GE, Google, Halliburton, Heinz, IBM, Lockheed Martin, MasterCard, Merck, Merrill Lynch, Motorola, NASDAQ, News Corp, Nike, PepsiCo, Pfizer, Shell Oil, Sony, Time Warner, Toyota, Verizon, and Visa.

"Although the membership of the CFR is a veritable 'who's who' in big business and the media, probably only one person in a thousand is familiar with the organization itself and even fewer are aware of its real purposes. During its first fifty years of existence, the CFR was almost never mentioned by any of the moguls of the mass media. And when you realize that the membership of the CFR includes top executives from the New York Times, the Washington Post, the Los Angeles Times, the Knight newspaper chain, NBC, CBS, Time, Life, Fortune, Business Week, US News & World Report, and many others, you can be sure that such anonymity is not accidental; it is deliberate … They control or own major newspapers, magazines, radio and television networks, and they control the most powerful companies in the book publishing business." -**Gary Allen, The Rockefeller File.**

Nearly every U.S. President since its inception has been a CFR member. Even the non-CFR Presidents have had administrations full of members. For instance Ronald Reagan wasn't a CFR member, but his Vice President George Bush was CFR, and so were 28 members of his transition team alone. George W. Bush is not a CFR member either, but his father and uncle are, his Vice President Dick Cheney is, and his administration is swarming with them. At the founding meeting of the United Nations there were 74 CFR members. The Clinton administration had over 100 CFR members. The Nixon administration had over 115 CFR members all in key Executive branch positions, most of whom continued through the Ford years, and a few of whom are still in power today.

The Council on Foreign Relations (like Skull and Bones) always promotes candidates from both the Democrat and Republican parties, thus ensuring a win for the New World Order. In 1952 and 1956 CFR "Republican" Dwight Eisenhower ran against CFR "Democrat" Adlai Stevenson. In 1960 it was CFR-Republican Richard Nixon against CFR-Democrat John F. Kennedy. In 1964 neither candidate was CFR, but Barry Goldwater was a Freemason, and Lyndon Johnson's administration was full of CFR members. In 1968 it was CFR-Republican Richard Nixon versus CFR-Democrat Hubert Humphrey. In 1972 was Nixon again versus CFR-Democrat George McGovern. In 1976 CFR-Republican Gerald Ford lost to CFR-Democrat Jimmy Carter. In 1980 was Mason-Republican Ronald Reagan versus CFR-Democrat Jimmy Carter and CFR-"Independent" John Anderson. 1984 was Reagan again against CFR-Democrat Walter Mondale. In 1988 CFR-Republican George Bush ran against CFR-Democrat Michael Dukakis. 1992 was Bush again running against CFR-Democrat Bill Clinton. In 1996 Clinton was challenged by CFR-Republican Bob Dole. In 2000 CFR-Democrat Al Gore lost to Skull and Bones Republican George W. Bush (with CFR running mate Dick Cheney). In 2004 Bush was challenged by brother Bonesman and CFR-Democrat John Kerry. The CFR owns the monopoly market on both Presidents and Presidential candidates. In the current 2008 presidential race, the CFR has propped up "Democrats" Hilary Clinton, Barack Obama, John Edwards, and "Republicans" Rudy Giuliani, John McCain, Mitt Romney and Fred Thompson. The only two 2008 candidates not belonging to secret societies or in favor of a New World Order are/were Ron Paul and Dennis Kucinich.

"The chief problem of American political life ...has been how to make the two Congressional parties more national and international. The argument that the two parties should represent opposed ideals and policies, one, perhaps, of the Right and the other of the Left, is a foolish idea acceptable only to doctrinaire and academic thinkers. Instead, the two parties should be almost identical, so that the American people can 'throw the rascals out' at any election without leading to any profound or extensive shifts in policy."
-**Dr. Carroll Quigley, "Tragedy and Hope"**

"The members of the council [On Foreign Relations] are persons of much more than average influence in their community. They have used the prestige that their wealth, their social position, and their education have given them to lead their country toward bankruptcy and military debacle. They should look at their hands. There is blood on them-the dried blood of the last war and the fresh blood of the present one [the Korean War]." -**Chicago Tribune editorial, Dec. 9, 1950.**

Almost all CIA directors have been CFR members, including Allen Dulles, Richard Helms, William Colby, George Bush, William Webster, James Woolsey, John Deutsch, and William Casey. Many U.S. Senators were also members including, David Boren, William Bradley, John Chafee, William Cohen, Christopher Dodd, Bob Graham, Joseph Lieberman, George

Mitchell, Claiborne Pell, Larry Pressler, Charles Robb, John D. Rockefeller, and William Roth Jr. For U.S. Congressional Representatives there has been Howard Berman, Thomas Foley, Sam Gejdenson, Richard Gephardt, Newt Gingrich, Amory Houghton Jr., Nancy Lee Johnson, John Lewis, Robert Matsui, Dave Mccurdy, Eleanor Homes Norton, Thomas El Petri, Carlos Romero-Barceló, Patricia Schroeder, Peter Smith, Olympia Snow, John Spratt, and Louis Stokes. As for Secretaries of Defence: Neil McElroy, Robert Gates, Robert McNamara, Melvin Laird, Eliot Richardson, Donald Rumsfeld, Harold Brown, Casper Weinberger, Frank Carlucci, and Dick Cheney. And U.S. Ambassadors to Australia, Britain, Chile, Czech Republic, France, India, Italy, Japan, Korea, Mexico, Nigeria, Philippines, Poland, Romania, Russia, Spain, South Africa, and Syria. This is just a sampling of the high-level government positions held by hundreds if not thousands of CFR members.

*"If the CFR had millions of members like, say, the Presbyterian Church, this list might not mean much. But the CFR only has 3,200 members." -***Robert Anton Wilson.**

*"The plan, as publicly stated by the CFR's Richard Gardner, part-time State Department functionary and Columbia University Professor of Law and International Organization, amounts to this: Instead of trying to make the UN a complete world dictatorship immediately, the Establishment will identify different problems in different countries. Then they will propose a 'solution,' which can only be achieved by some kind of international agency, so that each country concerned will be forced to surrender another segment of its national independence. Gardner considers this piecemeal approach the practical road to the end of nationhood" -***Gary Allen, "The Rockefeller File"**

The Council on Foreign Relations (CFR) was founded in 1921 by a very select group of international bankers, Wall Street lawyers and wealthy "old money" families sometimes called the Establishment or the Elites. Among the CFR's founders were JP Morgan, John D. Rockefeller, "Colonel" Edward House (Marxist. globalist and close advisor to President Wilson), Paul Warburg (international banker), Otto Kahn and Jacob Schiff (both international investment bankers). The CFR's stated purpose at that time was to improve the understanding of US foreign policy and international affairs through the exchange of ideas. The select membership has been gradually expanded over the years, now totalling around 3,800 and includes various professionals, corporate CEO's, college presidents, media owners and reporters, high-ranking government officials and even high ranking US military officers.

These same international bankers that started the CFR were instrumental in getting President Woodrow Wilson to sign the Federal Reserve Act into existence in 1913 that basically gave these international bankers the power to print money and control our entire economy. To show you the mind set of this core group, one of the founding CFR members, **Edward House**, authored a book in 1912 entitled **"Philip Dru: Administrator"** in which he laid out a fictionalized plan for the conquest of America. In the book, he told of a conspiracy by which a group of wealthy businessmen would gain control of both the Democratic and Republican parties and use them as instruments for the creation of a socialist world government.

After signing the Federal Reserve Act into law, President Woodrow Wilson later admitted, *"I am a most unhappy man. I have unwittingly ruined my country....(America is) no longer a government by free opinion, no longer a government by conviction and the vote of the majority, but a government by the opinion and duress of a small group of dominant men."* He was, of course, talking about the international bankers and the creation of the first great nationwide *"front organization"* called the Federal Reserve that was designed to directly benefit the international bankers at the expense of the American taxpayers.

The late **Carroll Quigley** (mentor and advisor to President Clinton) who was a long term member of the CFR, wrote in his book "***Tragedy & Hope***": *"The CFR is the American Branch of a society….which believes that national boundaries should be obliterated, and a one-world rule established."*

Rear Admiral Chester Ward, a former member of the CFR for 16 years, sounded the alarm about the real intent of the CFR and pointed out that there was two separate cliques within the CFR:

1. The first and most powerful clique wants to bring about the surrender of the sovereignty and national independence of the United States.
2. The second clique of international members is comprised of Wall Street international bankers and their key agents who want to receive a world banking monopoly from whatever power ends up in control of global government.

By using the CFR as a front organization to push their globalist agenda for America and the world, the "Establishment Elites and International Bankers" have managed to gain significant influence and power in key decision-making positions at the highest levels of our government. They can not only advocate their new world order ideas from within the government by using their CFR members in high government positions, but they can also use individual CFR members and research groups financed by their non-profit foundations to bring pressure from another direction. The international bankers use this process to implement the step by step decisions that will gradually convert the US from a sovereign nation to a subservient position in the new world order run by appointed bureaucrats selected by the international bankers. The CFR is being used much in the same manner as "Tack's Tackle Shop" was used by an organized criminal group. The international bankers behind the CFR want to give the public the outward appearance of legitimacy in order that they can slowly accomplish their illegal objectives to usurp the US Constitution and the sovereignty of this country.

Many of the most influential international bankers, Wall Street CEOs, politicians, academics and media owners and TV personalities are members of the CFR. They join the CFR for the same reasons that other people join similar business organizations: to make political or business contacts, to enjoy the prestige of being in the organization or to simply use their connections to make more money. The CFR in turn, uses the broad influence of these people and their organizations to slowly infiltrate their globalist 'New World Order' plans into American life. CFR members and their ghost writers author scholarly articles that are designed to specifically affect public opinion and future government decision making. These authors and researchers are oftentimes funded directly by one or more of the international bankers' non-profit foundations. The CFR's well paid academics expound on the wisdom of a united world and the CFR media members disseminate the message.

In the 1940's, President Roosevelt began bringing CFR members into the State Department and they have dominated it ever since. CFR members were instrumental in the creation of the United Nations. The American delegation to the San Francisco meeting that drafted the charter of the United Nations in 1949 included CFR members Nelson Rockefeller, John Foster Dulles, John Mc Cloy and the Secretary-General of the conference, Alger Hiss, who was later arrested as a spy for Russia. In all, the CFR sent at least forty-seven of its members in the United States delegation, effectively controlling the outcome.

These same CFR members were also instrumental in using our country's new membership in the United Nations to create the concepts of "limited wars" and "police actions" that were designed to circumvent the US Constitution and permit an administration to send our troops to war without a formal Declaration of War. It should also be pointed out that these two concepts benefit the international bankers and large corporations most because they allow these entities to make huge profits by providing financing and/or equipment and products to the enemies of our country during the conflict. It definitely did not benefit the US military men and women who were wounded or died in these conflicts. If a Declaration of War was declared, these same bankers and corporation CEO's would be charged with treason for aiding the enemy during a time of war.

James Warburg, a CFR member and son of CFR founder Paul Warburg testified before the **Senate Foreign Relations Committee** on February 17, 1950, defiantly telling the Senators that: *"We shall have world government, whether or not you like it – by conquest or consent."*

On November 25, 1959, the Council on Foreign Relations published "**Study No. 7**", which openly declared its true purpose to bring about a New World Order through the manipulation of U.S. foreign policy and through international economic interdependence:

"...building a New International Order [which] must be responsive to world aspirations for peace, [and] for social and economic change...an international order [code for world government]...including states labelling themselves as 'Socialist.' "

The plan for the New World Order and the ultimate control of America by the international bankers, was clearly outlined once again in the April 1974 issue of "Foreign Affairs" the Council of Foreign Relations' own publication, when CFR member and former **Secretary of State Richard N. Gardner**, wrote an article entitled "**The Hard Road to World Order**" in which he stated:

"In short, the house of world order will have to be built from the bottom up rather than from the top down. An end run around national sovereignty, eroding it piece by piece, will accomplish much more than the old fashioned assault..." one way to garner public support for new international treaties would be to propagandize worldwide predicaments. If people are scared of terrorism, financial chaos or global warming, they will be willing to cede their national sovereignty, freedom and liberties for global authority."

Since the FDR administration, all transition teams and administrations have been full of CFR members. It didn't matter whether they were liberal or conservative, Democrat or Republican. The Nixon administration had over 115 CFR members all in key Executive branch positions, most of who continued into the Ford years. Ronald Reagan wasn't a CFR member, but his Vice President George HW Bush was a CFR member, and so were 28 members of his transition team alone. The Clinton administration had over 150 CFR members in key executive positions. George W. Bush is not a CFR member either, but his father and uncle are, his Vice President Dick Cheney is, and his administration is swarming with CFR members. The incoming Obama administration's transition team is packed with CFR members and he is already looking to staff many of its administration's key executive branch positions with CFR members.

Did you vote for change in the 2008 Election? If you did, here's a partial list of Mr. Obama's transition team:

- Susan E. Rice – (CFR) former State Department Asst Secretary for African Affairs; Anthony Lake (CFR) – Bill Clinton's first national Security advisor;
- Zbigniew Brzezinski – (CFR) and Trilateral Commission - Brzezinski is widely seen as the man who created Al Qaeda, and was involved in the Carter Administration plan to give arms, funding and training to the Mujahideen in Afghanistan;
- Richard Clarke (CFR) - Former chief counter-terrorism adviser on the U.S. National Security Council under Bush; Robert W. Kagan (CFR) argues that interventionism is a bipartisan affair that should be undertaken with the approval of our democratic allies;
- Dennis B. Ross (CFR) and Trilateral Commission - Served as the director for policy planning in the State Department under President George H. W. Bush and special Middle East coordinator under President Bill Clinton;
- Lawrence J. Korb (CFR) - Director of National Security Studies at the Council on Foreign Relations. Has criticized manor of the invasion of Iraq but has detailed plans to increase the manpower of the United States Army to fight the war on terror and to "spread liberal democratic values throughout the Middle East";
- Bruce Reidel (CFR) - Former CIA analyst who wishes to expand the war on terror to fight Al Qaeda across the globe. Considered to be the reason behind Barack Obama's Hawkish views on Pakistan and his Pro India leanings on Kashmir;
- Stephen E. Flynn (CFR) - Has been attributed with the idea for Obama's much vaunted "Civilian Security Force". Flynn has written: "The United States should roughly replicate the Federal Reserve model by creating a Federal Security Reserve System (FSRS) with a national board of governors, 10 regional Homeland Security Districts, and 92 local branches called Metropolitan Anti-Terrorism Committees";
- Madeline Albright (CFR) and Brookings - Currently serves on the Council on Foreign Relations Board of directors and was Former Secretary of State and US Ambassador to the United Nations under Clinton.

Here's the list of possible cabinet positions in the new administration:

James B. Steinberg – CFR and the Trilateral Commission;
Chuck Hagel (R) – (CFR);
Robert M Gates – (CFR),
Hillary Clinton – Husband Bill is a CFR member;
Bill Richardson (CFR);
Sen John Kerry (D) (CFR);
Susan Rice (CFR);
Robert Rubin (CFR);
Lawrence Summers (CFR);
Timothy Geithner (CFR);
Paul A. Volcker (CFR);

David L. Boren (CFR);
Thomas H. Kean (CFR);
Gary Hart (CFR),
Jane Harman (CFR) – Defence Department Special Counsel (1979).

President-elect Barack Obama's has apparently selected Arizona Democratic Gov. Janet Napolitano as secretary of Homeland Security; Timothy Geithner, the current New York Federal Reserve head, as the Secretary of the Treasury; and Texas Democratic Gov. William Richardson as the Secretary of Commerce. Guess what? They are all members of the Council on Foreign Relations.

What do Dan Rather, Barbara Walters, Jim Lehrer, Marvin Kalb, Diane Sawyer, Andrea Mitchell and Tom Brokaw have in common? Answer: They are all members of the CFR.

What does the NY Times, Washington Post, Wall Street journal, LA Times, Boston Globe, Baltomor Sun, Chicago Sun-Times, Houston Post, Minneapolis Star-Tribune, Arkansas Gazette, DesMoine Register and Tribune, Louisville Courier, the AP, UPI, Reuters, the Gannett Co, Walt Disney, ABC, CBS, NBC, Fox Networks, Clear Channel have in common: Answer: They are all members of the CFR.

Freedom of the press has always been vital to the preservation of our American Republic. Ever since the early years of our country, it was the American "free press" that stood tall between us and the crooked international bankers, industrialists and corrupt government officials. While some of the major newspapers in the big cities were controlled by establishment types like William Randolph Hearst, who definitely influenced the content, most of the newspaper owners and reporters were independent and honorable people who chose to keep their integrity by pursuing the truth. Most local newspapers, radio stations, and later on TV stations, were owned locally.

As they grow larger and eliminate their competition, major media corporations and international bankers are choosing what you will see on the nightly news while trying to trick you into believing it is unbiased reporting. The very news stories that you are fed by the mainstream media are manipulated to mirror the public relations campaigns of corporations, international bankers and even their favorite presidential candidates. If this is not the case then why, during the course of the 2008 election, was there no mention of the issues that were important to Americans: the threat by big government to our freedoms, liberties and sovereignty; the actions of the Federal Reserve and the issuance fiat money; the drugging of 6 million of our nation's youth; or amnesty for illegal aliens. Popular candidates like Ron Paul were either ignored by the media, excluded from most of the TV debates, or asked fewer questions than their CFR candidate counterparts. Of the top twenty media corporations in the U.S, 18 are members of the CFR.

The CFR's strategy is to use their members in the media to promote the need for world government in order to fight international threats like global warming. Both Obama and McCain made the environment a major issue in the campaign, but avoided mentioning the immigration issue. The CFR has long identified the worldwide environmental movement as a means to advance its agenda and has even suggested a global tax on all developed nations, payable to the United Nations of course. Most of the major media companies are now controlled by individuals or organizations that are members of the

CFR, including the international bankers. One of the techniques used by the CFR and its membership has been to manipulate the news in such as way as to push their internationalist views on the rest of us.

As the big media corporations keep merging into larger and more powerful companies, they will be able to control public opinion as never before. With their friends in congress and in key government agencies, all the international bankers and their CFR members need to do is advocate bringing back the "Fairness Doctrine" and regulating the internet and their control of the media will be complete.

The average American might find the CFR's powerful influence over America's government very difficult to understand or believe, but never forget that the CFR was founded by international bankers for the express purpose of bringing about socialism and world government. It is the deliberate plan of these international bankers, who hide in the shadows and pull the strings of their marionettes, to gradually increase their influence and domination over America's domestic and foreign affairs. CFR members have been in control of our government since the 1940's. If CFR members are supposedly to be the nation's best and brightest in running the federal government and overseeing foreign affairs, why is the country in such a mess under their eighty year watch? The answer is: That's the plan.

Consider this article with a quote from David Rockefeller, the former Chairman and the current Honorary Chairman of the Council on Foreign Relation and ask yourself to consider the implications of what he has said:

"We are grateful to the Washington Post, The New York Times, Time Magazine and other great publications whose directors have attended our meetings and respected their promises of discretion for almost forty years... It would have been impossible for us to develop our plan for the world if we had been subjected to the lights of publicity during those years. But, the world is now more sophisticated and prepared to march towards a world government. The supranational sovereignty of an intellectual elite and world bankers is surely preferable to the national auto-determination practiced in past centuries."

Club Of Rome

This is a Committee of 300 subversive body. This group was organized in 1968 by the Morgenthau Group for the purpose of accelerating the plans to have the New World Order in place by the year 2000. The Club of Rome developed a plan to divide the world into ten regions or kingdoms.

In 1976, the United States Association of the Club of Rome (USACOR) was formed for the purpose of shutting down the U.S. economy gradually. The Technetronic Era Henry Kissinger was then, and still is, an important agent in the service of the Royal Institute for International Affairs, a member of the Club of Rome and the Council on Foreign Relations.

Kissinger's role in destabilizing the United States by means of three wars, the Middle East, Korea and Vietnam, is well known, as is his role in the Gulf War, in which the U.S.

Army acted as mercenaries for the Committee of 300 in bringing Kuwait back under its control and at the same time making an example out of Iraq so that other small nations would not be tempted to work out their own destiny. The Club of Rome, acting on Committee of 300 orders to eliminate General ul Haq, had no compunction in sacrificing the lives of a number of U.S. servicemen on board the flight, including a U.S. Army Defence Intelligence Agency group headed by Brigadier General Herber Wassom. General ul Haq had been warned by the Turkish Secret Service not to travel by plane, as he was targeted for a mid-air bombing. With this in mind, ul Haq took the United States team with him as "an insurance policy," as he commented to his inner circle advisors.

Club of Rome and its financiers under the title of the German Marshall Fund were two highly-organized conspiratorial bodies operating under cover of the North Atlantic Treaty Organization (NATO) and that the majority of Club of Rome executives were drawn from NATO. The Club of Rome formulated all of what NATO claimed as its policies and, through the activities of Committee of 300 member Lord Carrington, was able to split NATO into two factions, a political (left wing) power group and its former military alliance. The Club of Rome is still one of the most important foreign policy arms of the Committee of 300, and the other being the Bilderbergers. It was put together in 1968 from hard-core members of the original Morgenthau group on the basis of a telephone call made by the late Aurellio Peccei for a new and urgent drive to speed up the plans of the One World Government now called the New World Order. Peccei's call was answered by the most subversive "future planners" drawn from the United States, France, Sweden, Britain, Switzerland and Japan that could be mustered.

During the period 1968-1972, The Club of Rome became a cohesive entity of new-science scientists, Globalist, future planners and inter- nationalists of every stripe. As one delegate put it, *"We became Joseph's Coat of Many Colors."* **Peccei's** book **"Human Quality"** formed the basis of the doctrine adopted by NATO's political wing. Peccei headed the Atlantic Institute's Economic Council for three decades while he was the Chief Executive Officer for Giovanni Agnellis' Fiat Motor Company. Agnelli, a member of an ancient Italian Black Nobility family of the same name, is one of the most important members of the Committee of 300. He played a leading role in development projects in the Soviet Union.

The Club of Rome is a private umbrella organization, a marriage between Anglo-American financiers and the old Black Nobility families of Europe, particularly the so-called "nobility" of London, Venice and Genoa. The key to the successful control of the world is their ability to create and manage savage economic recessions and eventual depressions. The Committee of 300 looks to social convulsions on a global scale, followed by depressions, as a softening-up technique for bigger things to come, as its principal method of creating masses of people all over the world who will become its "welfare" recipients of the future.

The committee appears to base much of its important decisions affecting mankind on the philosophy of Polish aristocrat, Felix Dzerzinski, who regarded mankind as being slightly above the level of cattle. As a close friend of British intelligence agent Sydney Reilly (Reilly was actually Dzerzinski's controller during the Bolshevik Revolution's formative years), he often confided in Reilly during his drinking bouts. Dzerzinski was, of course, the beast who ran the Red Terror apparatus. He once told Reilly, while the two were on a drinking binge, that *"Man is of no importance. Look at what happens when you starve him. He begins to eat his dead companions to stay alive. Man is only interested in his own survival. That is all that counts*."

For a detailed list and hierarchy go to the website ***www.apfn.org/apfn/cfr-members.htm***

The Bilderberg Group

The following material is taken from Stephen Lendeman's work on website ***www.globalresearch.ca/the-true-story-of-the-bilderberg-group-and-what-they-may-be-planning-now/***. Stephen Lendman is a frequent contributor to Global Research. ***www.globlresearh.ca.*** He can also be found at sjlendman.blogspot.com and The Global Research News Hour on ***RepublicBroadcasting.org*** Monday - Friday at 10 AM US Central time for cutting-edge discussions with distinguished guests on world and national issues. All programs are archived for easy listening. Here he reviews the book by ***Daniel Estulin*** on the ***True Story of the Bilderberger Group***:

For over 14 years, ***Daniel Estulin*** has investigated and researched the Bilderberg Group's far-reaching influence on business and finance, global politics, war and peace, and control of the world's resources and its money. His book, ***"The True Story of the Bilderberg Group,"*** was published in 2005 and is now updated in a new 2009 edition. He states that in 1954, *"the most powerful men in the world met for the first time"* in Oosterbeek, Netherlands, *"debated the future of the world,"* and decided to meet annually in secret. They called themselves the Bilderberg Group with a membership representing a who's who of world power elites, mostly from America, Canada, and Western Europe with familiar names like David Rockefeller, Henry Kissinger, Bill Clinton, Gordon Brown, Angela Merkel, Alan Greenspan, Ben Bernanke, Larry Summers, Tim Geithner, Lloyd Blankfein, George Soros, Donald Rumsfeld, Rupert Murdoch, other heads of state, influential senators, congressmen and parliamentarians, Pentagon and NATO brass, members of European royalty, selected media figures, and invited others - some quietly by some accounts like Barack Obama and many of his top officials.

Always well represented are top figures from the Council on Foreign Relations (CFR), IMF, World Bank, Trilateral Commission, EU, and powerful central bankers from the Federal Reserve, the ECB's Jean-Claude Trichet, and Bank of England's Mervyn King. For over half a century, no agenda or discussion topics became public nor is any press coverage allowed. The few invited fourth estate attendees and their bosses are sworn to secrecy. Nonetheless, Estulin undertook "an investigative journey" that became his life's work. He states:

"Slowly, one by one, I have penetrated the layers of secrecy surrounding the Bilderberg Group, but I could not have done this without help of 'conscientious objectors' from inside, as well as outside, the Group's membership." As a result, he keeps their names confidential. Whatever its early mission, the Group is now *"a shadow world government....threaten(ing) to take away our right to direct our own destinies (by creating) a disturbing reality"* very much harming the public's welfare. In short, Bilderbergers want to supplant individual nation-state sovereignty with an all-powerful global government, corporate controlled, and check-mated by militarized enforcement.

"Imagine a private club where presidents, prime ministers, international bankers and generals rub shoulders, where gracious royal chaperones ensure everyone gets along, and where the people running the wars, markets, and Europe (and America) say what they never dare say in public."

Early in its history, Bilderbergers decided *"to create an 'Aristocracy of purpose' between Europe and the United States (to reach consensus to rule the world on matters of) policy, economics, and (overall) strategy."* NATO was essential for their plans - to ensure "perpetual war (and) nuclear blackmail" to be used as necessary. Then proceed to loot the planet, achieve fabulous wealth and power, and crush all challengers to keep it.

Along with military dominance, controlling the world's money is crucial for with it comes absolute control as the powerful 19th century Rothschild family understood. As the patriarch Amschel Rothschild once said: *"Give me control of a nation's money and I care not who makes its laws."*

Bilderbergers comprise the world's most exclusive club. No one buys their way in. Only the Group's Steering Committee decides whom to invite, and in all cases participants are adherents to One World Order governance run by top power elites.

According to Steering Committee rules:

"The invited guests must come alone; no wives, girlfriends, husbands or boyfriends. Personal assistants (meaning security, bodyguards, CIA or other secret service protectors) cannot attend the conference and must eat in a separate hall. (Also) The guests are explicitly forbidden from giving interviews to journalists or divulge anything that goes on in meetings".

Host governments provide overall security to keep away outsiders. One-third of attendees are political figures. The others are from industry, finance, academia, labor and communications.

Meeting procedure is by Chatham House Rules letting attendees freely express their views in a relaxed atmosphere knowing nothing said will be quoted or revealed to the public. Meetings *"are always frank, but do not always conclude with consensus."*

Membership consists of annual attendees (around 80 of the world's most powerful) and others only invited occasionally because of their knowledge or involvement in relevant topics. Those most valued are asked back, and some first-timers are chosen for their possible later usefulness.

Arkansas governor Bill Clinton, for example, who attended in 1991. *"There, David Rockefeller told (him) why the North American Free Trade Agreement....was a Bilderberg priority and that the group needed him to support it. The next year, Clinton was elected president,"* and on January 1, 1994 NAFTA took effect. Numerous other examples are similar, including who gets chosen for powerful government, military and other key positions.

The Group's grand design is for "a One World Government (World Company) with a single, global marketplace, policed by one world army, and financially regulated by one 'World (Central) Bank' using one global currency." Their "wish list" includes:

- one international identify (observing) one set of universal values;
- centralized control of world populations by "mind control;" in other words, controlling world public opinion;
- a New World Order with no middle class, only "rulers and servants (serfs), and, of course, no democracy;
- "a zero-growth society" without prosperity or progress, only greater wealth and power for the rulers;

- manufactured crises and perpetual wars;
- absolute control of education to program the public mind and train those chosen for various roles;
- "centralized control of all foreign and domestic policies;" one size fits all globally;
- using the UN as a de facto world government imposing a UN tax on "world citizens;"
- expanding NAFTA and WTO globally;
- making NATO a world military;
- imposing a universal legal system; and
- a global "welfare state where obedient slaves will be rewarded and non-conformists targeted for extermination."

Secret Bilderberg Partners In the US, the Council on Foreign Relations (CFR) is dominant. One of its 1921 founders, Edward Mandell House, was Woodrow Wilson's chief advisor and rumoured at the time to be the nation's real power from 1913 - 1921. On his watch, the Federal Reserve Act passed in December 1913 giving money creation power to bankers, and the 16th Amendment was ratified in February creating the federal income tax to provide a revenue stream to pay for government debt service.

From its beginnings, CFR was committed to "*a one-world government based on a centralized global financing system....*" Today, CFR has thousands of influential members (including important ones in the corporate media) but keeps a low public profile, especially regarding its real agenda. Historian Arthur Schlesinger, Jr. called it a "front organization (for) the heart of the American Establishment." It meets privately and only publishes what it wishes the public to know. Its members are only Americans.

The Trilateral Commission (discussed below) is a similar group that "brings together global power brokers." Founded by David Rockefeller, he's also a leading Bilderberger and CFR Chairman Emeritus, organizations he continues to finance and support.

Their past and current members reflect their power:

- nearly all presidential candidates of both parties;
- leading senators and congressmen;
- key members of the fourth estate and their bosses; and
- top officials of the FBI, CIA, NSA, defence establishment, and other leading government agencies, including state, commerce, the judiciary and treasury.

For its part, "*CFR has served as a virtual employment agency for the federal government under both Democrats and Republicans.*" Whoever occupies the White House, "CFR's power and agenda" have been unchanged since its 1921 founding.

It advocates a global superstate with America and other nations sacrificing their sovereignty to a central power. CFR founder Paul Warburg was a member of Roosevelt's "brain trust." In 1950, his son, James, told the Senate Foreign Relations Committee: "*We shall have world government whether or not you like it - by conquest or consent.*"

Later at the 1992 Bilderberg Group meeting, Henry Kissinger said:

"*Today, Americans would be outraged if UN troops entered Los Angeles to restore order; tomorrow, they will be grateful. This is especially true if they were told there was an outside threat from beyond, whether real or promulgated, that threatened our very existence. It is then that all people of the world will plead with world leaders to deliver them from this evil....individual rights will be willingly relinquished for the guarantee of their well-being granted to them by their world government."*

CFR planned a New World Order before 1942, and the *"UN began with a group of CFR members called the Informal Agenda Group."* They drafted the original UN proposal, presented it to Franklin Roosevelt who announced it publicly the next day. At its 1945 founding, CFR members comprised over 40 of the US delegates. According to Professor G. William Domhoff, author of Who Rules America, the CFR operates in "small groups of about twenty-five, who bring together leaders from the six conspirator categories (industrialists, financiers, ideologues, military, professional specialists - lawyers, medical doctors, etc. - and organized labor) for detailed discussions of specific topics in the area of foreign affairs." Domhoff added:

"The Council on Foreign Relations, while not financed by government, works so closely with it that it is difficult to distinguish Council action stimulated by government from autonomous actions. (Its) most important sources of income are leading corporations and major foundations." The Rockefeller, Carnegie, and Ford Foundations to name three, and they're directed by key corporate officials.

Dominant Media Partners Former CBS News president Richard Salant (1961 - 64 and 1966 - 79) explained the major media's role: *"Our job is to give people not what they want, but what we decide they ought to have."*

CBS and other media giants control everything we see, hear and read - through television, radio, newspapers, magazines, books, films, and large portions of the Internet. Their top officials and some journalists attend Bilderberg meetings - on condition they report nothing.

The Rockefeller family wields enormous power, even though its reigning patriarch, David, will be 94 on June 12 and surely near the end of his dominance. However, for years "the Rockefellers (led by David) gained great influence over the media. (With it) the family gained sway over public opinion. With the pulse of public opinion, they gained deep influence in politics. And with this politics of subtle corruption, they are taking control of the nation" and now aim for total world domination.

The Bilderberger-Rockefeller scheme is to make their views *"so appealing (by camouflaging them) that they become public policy (and can) pressure world leaders into submitting to the 'needs of the Masters of the Universe.' "* The "free world press" is their instrument to disseminate "agreed-upon propaganda."

CFR Cabinet Control The National Security Act of 1947 established the office of Secretary of Defence. Since then, 14 DOD secretaries have been CFR members.

Since 1940, every Secretary of State, except James Byrnes, has been a CFR member and/or Trilateral Commission (TC) one. For the past 80 years, Virtually every key US National Security and Foreign Policy Advisor has been a CFR member. Nearly all top generals and admirals have been CFR members.

Many presidential candidates were/are CFR members, including Herbert Hoover, Adlai Stevenson, Dwight Eisenhower, John Kennedy, Richard Nixon, Gerald Ford, Jimmy Carter (also a charter TC member), George HW Bush, Bill Clinton, John Kerry, and John McCain. Numerous CIA directors were/are CFR members, including Richard Helmes, James Schlesinger, William Casey, William Webster, Robert Gates, James Woolsey, John Deutsch, George Tenet, Porter Goss, Michael Hayden, and Leon Panetta. Many Treasury

Secretaries were/are CFR members, including Douglas Dillon, George Schultz, William Simon, James Baker, Nicholas Brady, Lloyd Bentsen, Robert Rubin, Henry Paulson, and Tim Geithner. When presidents nominate Supreme Court candidates, the CFR's "Special Group, Secret Team" or advisors vet them for acceptability. Presidents, in fact, are told who to appoint, including designees to the High Court and most lower ones.

Programming the Public Mind According to sociologist **Hadley Cantril** in his 1967 book**, The Human Dimension - Experiences in Policy Research**:

"Psycho-political operations are propaganda campaigns designed to create perpetual tension and to manipulate different groups of people to accept the particular climate of opinion the CFR seeks to achieve in the world."

Canadian writer **Ken Adachi** (1929 - 1989) added:

"What most Americans believe to be 'Public Opinion' is in reality carefully crafted and scripted propaganda designed to elicit a desired behavioural response from the public."

And noted Australian academic and activist **Alex Carey** (1922 - 1988) explained the three most important 20th century developments - *"The growth of democracy, the growth of corporate power, and the growth of corporate propaganda as a means of protecting corporate power against democracy."*

Web of Control Numerous think tanks, foundations, the major media, and other key organizations are staffed with CFR members. Most of its life-members also belong to the TC and Bilderberg Group, operate secretly, and wield enormous power over US and world affairs.

The Rockefeller-Founded Trilateral Commission (TC), on page 405 of his **Memoir**s, **David Rockefeller** wrote:

"Some even believe we are part of a secret cabal working against the best interests of the United States characterizing my family and me as 'internationalists' and conspiring with others around the world to build a more integrated global political and economic structure - one world, if you will. If that's the charge, I stand guilty, and I am proud of it."

In alliance with Bilderbergers, the TC also *"plays a vital role in the New World Order's scheme to use wealth, concentrated in the hands of the few, to exert world control."* TC members share common views and all relate to total unchallengeable global dominance.

Founded in 1973 and headquartered in Washington, its powerful US, EU and East Asian members seek its operative founding goal - a "New International Economic Order," now simply a "New World Order" run by global elites from these three parts of the world with lesser members admitted from other countries.

According to TC's web site, "each regional group has a chairman and deputy chairman, who all together constitute the leadership of the Committee. The Executive Committee draws together a further 36 individuals from the wider membership," proportionately representing the US, EU, and East Asia in its early years, now enlarged to be broadly global.

Committee members meet several times annually to discuss and coordinate their work. The Executive Committee chooses members, and at any time around 350 belong for a three-year renewable period. Everyone is a consummate insider with expertise in business, finance, politics, the military, or the media, including past presidents, secretaries of state, international bankers, think tank and foundation executives, university presidents and selected academics, and former senators and congressmen, among others.

Although its annual reports are available for purchase, its inner workings, current goals, and operations are secret - with good reason. Its objectives harm the public so mustn't be revealed. **Trilaterals over Washington** author **Antony Sutton** wrote:

"This group of private citizens is precisely organized in a manner that ensures its collective views have significant impact on public policy."

In her book, **Trilateralism: The Trilateral Commission and Elite Planning for World Management, Holly Sklar** wrote:

"Powerful figures in America, Europe, and East Asia let the rich....safeguard the interests of Western capitalism in an explosive world - probably by discouraging protectionism, nationalism, or any response that would pit the elites of one against the elites of another," in their common quest for global dominance."

Trilateralist **Zbigniew Brzezinski** (TC's co-founder) wrote in his **Between Two Ages - America's Role in the Technotronic Era**:

"People, governments and economies of all nations must serve the needs of multinational banks and corporations. (The Constitution is) inadequate....the old framework of international politics, with their sphere of influence....the fiction of sovereignty....is clearly no longer compatible with reality...."

TC today is now global with members from countries as diverse as Argentina, Ukraine, Israel, Jordan, Brazil, Turkey, China and Russia. In his Trilaterals Over America, Antony Sutton believes that TC's aim is to collaborate with Bilderbergers and CFR in *"establishing public policy objectives to be implemented by governments worldwide."* He added that *"Trilateralists have rejected the US Constitution and the democratic political process."* In fact, TC was established to counter a "crisis in democracy" - too much of it that had to be contained.

An official TC report was fearful about "the increased popular participation in and control over established social, political, and economic institutions and especially a reaction against the concentration of power of Congress and of state and local government."

To address this, media control was essential to exert "restraint on what newspapers may publish (and TV and radio broadcast)." Then according to **Richard Gardner** in the July 1974 issue of **Foreign Affairs** (a CFR publication):

CFR's leadership must make "an end run around national sovereignty, eroding it piece by piece," until the very notion disappears from public discourse.

Bilderberg/CFR/Trilateralist success depends on finding "a way to get us to surrender our liberties in the name of some common threat or crisis. The foundations, educational institutions, and research think tanks supported by (these organizations) oblige by financing so-called 'studies' which are then used to justify their every excess. The excuses vary, but the target is always individual liberty. Our liberty" and much more.

Bilderbergers, Trilateralists and CFR members want "an all-encompassing monopoly" - over government, money, industry, and property that's *"self-perpetuating and eternal."* In **Confessions of a Monopolist** (1906), **Frederick C. Howe** explained its workings in practice:

"The rules of big business: Get a monopoly; let Society work for you. So long as we see all international revolutionaries and all international capitalists as implacable enemies of one another, then we miss a crucial point....a partnership between international monopoly capitalism and international revolutionary socialism is for their mutual benefit."

In the **Rockefeller File, Gary Allen** wrote:

"By the late nineteenth century, the inner sanctums of Wall Street understood that the most efficient way to gain a monopoly was to say it was for the 'public good' and 'public interest.' "

David Rockefeller learned the same thing from his father, John D., Jr. who learned it from his father, John D. Sr. They hated competition and relentlessly strove to eliminate it - for David on a global scale through a New World Order.

In the 1970s and 1980s, Trilateralists and CFR members collaborated on the latter's "1980 Project," the largest ever CFR initiative to steer world events *"toward a particular desirable future outcome (involving) the utter disintegration of the economy."* Why so is the question?

Because by the 1950s and 1960s, worldwide industrial growth meant more competition. It was also a model to be followed, and *"had to be strangled in the cradle"* or at least greatly contained. In America as well beginning in the 1980s. The result has been a transfer of wealth from the poor to the rich, shrinkage of the middle class, and plan for its eventual demise.

The North American Union (NAU) The idea emerged during the Reagan administration in the early 1980s. David Rockefeller, George Schultz and Paul Volker told the president that Canada and America could be politically and economically merged over the next 15 years except for one problem - French-speaking Quebec. Their solution - elect a Bilderberg-friendly prime minister, separate Quebec from the other provinces, then make Canada America's 51st state. It almost worked, but not quite when a 1995 secession referendum was defeated - 50.56% to 49.44%, but not the idea of merger.

At a March 23, 2005 Waco, Texas meeting, attended by George Bush, Mexico's Vincente Fox, and Canada's Paul Martin, the Security and and Prosperity Partnership (SPP) was launched, also known as the North American Union (NAU). It was a secretive Independent Task Force of North America agreement - a group organized by the Canadian Council of Chief Executives (CCCE), the Mexican Council on Foreign Relations, and CFR with the following aims:

- circumventing the legislatures of three countries and their constitutions;
- suppressing public knowledge or consideration; and
- proposing greater US, Canadian and Mexican economic, political, social, and security integration with secretive working groups formed to devise non-debatable, not voted on agreements to be binding and unchangeable.

In short - a corporate coup d'etat against the sovereignty of three nations enforced by hard line militarization to suppress opposition.

If enacted, it will create a borderless North America, corporate controlled, without barriers to trade or capital flows for business giants, mainly US ones and much more - America's access to vital resources, especially oil and Canada's fresh water.

Secretly, over 300 SPP initiatives were crafted to harmonize the continent's policies on energy, food, drugs, security, immigration, manufacturing, the environment, and public health along with militarizing three nations for enforcement.

SPP represents another step toward the Bilderberg/Trilateralist/CFR goal for World Government, taking it one step at a time. A "United Europe" was another, the result of various treaties and economic agreements:

- the December 1951 six-nation European Coal and Steel Community (ECSC);
- the March 1957 six-nation Treaty of Rome establishing the European Economic Community (EEC);

Also the European Atomic Energy Commission (EAEC) by a second Treaty of Rome;

- the October 1957 European Court of Justice to settle regional trade disputes;
- the May 1960 seven-nation European Free Trade Association (EFTA);
- the July 1967 European Economic Community (EEC) merging the ECSC, EAEC and EEC together in one organization;
- the 1968 European Customs Union to abolish duties and establish uniform imports taxing among EEC nations;
- the 1978 European Currency Unit (ECU);
- the February 1986 Single European Act revision of the 1957 Treaty of Rome; it established the objective of forming a Common Market by December 31, 1992;
- the February 1992 Maastricht Treaty creating the EU on November 1, 1993; and
- the name euro was adopted in December 1995; it was introduced in January 1999 replacing the European Currency Unit (ECU); Euros began circulating on January 2002; they're now the official currency of 16 of the 27 EU states.

Over half a century, the above steps cost EU members their sovereignty "*as some 70 to 80 per cent of the laws passed in Europe involve just rubber stamping of regulations already written by nameless bureaucrats in 'working groups' in Brussels or Luxembourg.*"

The EU and NAU share common features:
- advocacy from a influential spokesperson;
- an economic and later political union;
- hard line security, and for Europe, ending wars on the continent between EU member states;
- establishment of a collective consciousness in place of nationalism;
- the blurring of borders and creation of a "supra-government," a superstate;
- secretive arrangements to mask real objectives; and
- the creation of a common currency and eventual global one.

Steps Toward a North American Union:
- the October 4, 1988 Free Trade Agreement (FTA) between the US and Canada, finalized the previous year;
- at the 1991 Bilderberg meeting, David Rockefeller got governor Bill Clinton's support for NAFTA if he became president;

- on January 1, 1994, with no debate under "fast-track" rules, Congress approved WTO legislation;
- in December 1994 at the first Summit of the Americas, 34 Hemispheric leaders committed their nations to a Free Trade of the Americas agreement (FTAA) by 2005 - so far unachieved;
- on July 4, 2000, Mexican president Vincente Fox called for a North American common market in 20 years;
- on February 2001, the White House published a joint statement from George Bush and Vincente Fox called the "Guanajuato Proposal;" it was for a US-Canada-Mexico prosperity partnership (aka North American Union);
- in September 2001, Bush and Fox agreed to a "Partnership for Prosperity Initiative;"
- the September 11, 2001 attack gave cover to including "security" as part of a future partnership;
- on October 7, 2001, a CFA meeting highlighted "The Future of North American Integration in the Wake of Terrorist Attacks; for the first time, "security" became part of a future "partnership for prosperity;" also, Canada was to be included in a "North American" agreement;
- in 2002, the North American Forum on Integration (NAFI) was established in Montreal "to address the issues raised by North American integration as well as identify new ideas and strategies to reinforce the North American region;"
- in January 2003, the Canadian Council of Chief Executives (CCCE - composed of 150 top CEOs) launched the "North American Security and Prosperity Initiative" calling for continental integration;
- in April 2004, Canadian prime minister Paul Martin announced the nation's first ever national security policy called Securing an Open Society;
- on October 15, 2004, CFR established an Independent Task Force on the Future of North America - for a future continental union;
- in March 2005, a CFR report titled Creating a North American Community called for continental integration by 2010 "to enhance, prosperity, and opportunity for all North Americans;" and
- on March 23, 2005 in Waco, Texas, America, Canada and Mexico leaders launched the Security and Prosperity Partnership (SPP) - aka North American Union (NAU).

Secretive negotiations continue. Legislative debate is excluded, and public inclusion and debate are off the table. In May 2005, the CFR Independent Task Force on the Future of North America published a follow-up report titled Building a North American Community - proposing a borderless three-nation union by 2010.

In June and July 2005, the Dominican Republic - Central America Free Trade Agreement (DR-CAFTA) passed the Senate and House establishing corporate-approved trade rules to further impoverish the region and move a step closer to continental integration.

In March 2006, the North American Competitiveness Council (NACC) was created at the second SPP summit in Cancun, Mexico. Composed of 30 top North American CEOs, it serves as an official trilateral SPP working group.

Secret business and government meetings continue so there's no way to confirm SPP's current status or if Barack Obama is seamlessly continuing George Bush's agenda. In an earlier article, this writer said:

SPP efforts paused during the Bush to Obama transition, but "deep integration" plans remain. Canada's Fraser Institute proposed renaming the initiative the North American Standards and Regulatory Area (NASRA) to disguise its real purpose. It said the "SPP brand" is tarnished so re-branding is essential - to fool the public until it's too late to matter.

Bilderbergers, Trilaterists, and CFR leaders back it as another step toward global integration and won't "stop until the entire world is unified under the auspices and the political umbrella of a One World Company, a nightmarish borderless world run by the world's most powerful clique" - comprised of key elitist members of these dominant organizations.

In April 2007, the Transatlantic Economic Council was established between America and the EU to:

- create an "official international governmental body - by executive fiat;
- harmonize economic and regulatory objectives;
- move toward a Transatlantic Common Market; and
- a step closer to One World Government run by the world's most powerful corporate interests.

Insights into the 2009 Bilderberg Group Meeting From May 14 - 17, Bilderbergers held their annual meeting in Vouliagmeni, Greece, and according to Daniel Estulin have dire plans for global economies. According to his pre-meeting sources, they're divided on two alternatives:

"Either a prolonged, agonizing depression that dooms the world to decades of stagnation, decline and poverty (or) an intense but shorter depression that paves the way for a new sustainable world order, with less sovereignty but more efficiency."

Other agenda items included:
- the future of the US dollar and US economy;
- continued deception about green shoots signalling an end to recession and improving economy later in the year;
- suppressing the fact that bank stress tests were a sham and were designed for deception, not an accurate assessment of major banks' health;
- projecting headlined US unemployment to hit 14% by year end - way above current forecasts and meaning the true number will be double, at minimum, with all uncounted categories included; and
- a final push to get the Lisbon Treaty passed for pan-European (EU) adoption of neoliberal rules, including greater privatizations, fewer worker rights and social benefits, open border trade favouring developed over emerging states, and greater militarization to suppress civil liberties and human rights.

After the meeting, Estulin got a 73-page report on what was discussed. He noted that "One of Bilderberg's primary concerns....is the danger that their zeal to reshape the world by engineering chaos (toward) their long term agenda could cause the situation to spiral out of control and eventually lead to a scenario where Bilderberg and the global elite in general are overwhelmed by events and end up losing their control over the planet."

Estulin also noted some considerable disagreement between "hardliners" wanting a *"dramatic decline and a severe, short-term depression (versus others) who think that things have gone too far"* so that *"the fallout from the global economic cataclysm"* can't be known, may be greater than anticipated, and may harm Bilderberger interests. Also, *"some European bankers (expressed great alarm over their own fate and called the current) high wire act 'unsustainable.' "*

There was a combination of agreement and fear that the situation remains dire and the worst of the crisis lies ahead, mainly because of America's extreme debt level that must be resolved to produce a healthy, sustainable recovery.

Topics also included:

- establishing a Global Treasury Department and Global Central Bank, possibly partnered with or as part of the IMF;
- a global currency;
- destruction of the dollar through what long-time market analyst Bob Chapman calls "a stealth default on (US) debt by continuing to issue massive amounts of money and credit and in the process devaluing the dollar," a process he calls "fraud;"
- a global legal system;
- exploiting the Swine Flu scare to create a WHO global department of health; and
- the overall goal of a global government and the end of national sovereignty.

In the past, Estulin's sources proved accurate. Earlier, he predicted the housing crash and 2007 - 2008 financial market decline, preceded by the kind of financial crisis triggered by the Lehman Brothers collapse. Watch for further updates from him as new information leaks out on what the world's power elites have planned going forward.

For a Bilderberg 2012 Attendee list, go to
http://www.nowtheendbegins.com/blog/?p=10222Final List of Participants

In closing this Chapter, we have looked at a small number of special organisations of PLANET EARTH INC. If you wish to look at an organization chart of consdideralbe research, and a revealing papr on ***The Coming New World Order*** by ***Lorraine Day, M.D***.   go   to   the   site: ***www.goodnewsaboutgod.com/studies/political/newworld_order/world_order. htm***

13

THE UNIFIED PLAN OF CONQUEST

Emergence Of The New World Order

As the gods have carefully planned to emerge into total power, the strategy has been to first create a business plan that began centuries ago. Marching forward with great esoteric and business skills that humanity refuses to believe, they and their chosen ones have planned their final mission of dominion. Carefully crafted, the plan is not much different from any corporate model that creates the business plan based upon a mission of the founders, seeks financing to launch the product, creates a marketing and infrastructure plan, and marches to implement the business strategy. The plan for PLANET EARTH has involved the mission of the gods to conquer Planet Earth, unified the bloodlines into an executive force through the creation of the Rothschild Financial empire, assisted in the emergence of strategic dynasties, and has marched towards the takeover of strategic secret societies, groups, corporations and nations to attain their goals.

It is important here to understand that when society, religious orders, groups, nations, dynasties, corporations, or any commercial venture is created, it may have a foundation, purpose and mission that is entirely different from when a time comes where they may be taken over, conquered, bought out. Such is the way of new owners who may shift purpose, as in the case of bankruptcy. When this happens, the game, the mission and plan change and the new owners and directors take over. In the last 300 years, this is precisely what has occurred as the directors of PLANET EARTH have taken over what they have selected as the major corporate sectors required to facilitate their plan.

We have seen that the plan to create one empire is not exactly hidden. The gods who direct this plan, and the ones who are loyal to the cause of one world, are not shy about what they do because they believe that they are above the usual Earthling and he must be saved from himself. Essentially, the Earthling does not exactly have a track record that he is anything but a warlike selfish animal that cannot manage his actions. It would not be surprising that the ones who are in positions of power--the royal bloodlines-- would consider the rest to be like sheeple, to be controlled, herd and used as slaves. endless strife over different races, and philosophies, and hatred have continuously kept Earthlings away from their spiritual potential. The bloodlines are not shy about their beliefs in Lucifer, and obviously, the Earthling by way of accepting the corporate model, does not either. However, they appear to know more and have special gifts and powers that the vast majority cannot attain, nor believe in.

And so we have been led by these bloodlines to a place where they have deemed Earthlings incompetent, thereby marching towards the fulfillment of the ultimate plan of peace and harmony. For how many, no one knows.

Much of the plan is revealed in bibles as prophesies as we shall see later but more relevant now is to look at a more recent history which reveals part of the plan which was scheduled to emerge in Europe but shifted to North America and the District (City of Columbia) as the strategic, final implementation of the New World Order.

We must first return to the Vatican and look at the second World War in a different light. Here we will begin to understand the importance of what we have reviewed with the 13 bloodlines, the secret societies, the spirituality of Satan and the prophesy written in the UNITED STATES OF AMERICA money. Within this is hidden in plain view the unveiling of the business plan including the announcement of conception, Lucifer the great architect, the Secular World Order, and the 13 illuminated bloodlines...

| ANNUIT COEPTIS 'announcing conception' | Illumined eye Great architect 'Lucifer' | NOVUS ORDO SECLORUM 'Secular New Order' | 13 letters in motto E PLURIBUS UNUM 'One of Many' | 13 illuminated Stars - 13 enlightened Colonnies |

13 Layers of Brick
- 13 Original collonies
72 Bricks
- 72 Powers of the name
of God in Qabbalah

MDCCLXXVI - 1776
Date 'illuminati' formed
mDCcLXxVI = 666

13 Arrows, 13 leaves
13 Berries - Different powers
possessed by the 13 colonies

Pheonix not an eagle
rising from the ashes,
or ignorant world

9 Tail feathers - 9 spheres risen
through to return to heavenly state

Through the structure, these gods have succeeded in subduing nations through debt. The following is taken from the research of David Icke *(www.davidicke.com)* and other researchers already mentioned earlier:

The Illuminati structure also creates artificial countries to further their goals. Examples of these are the United States, Switzerland, Kuwait, the Soviet Union, Panama, Israel, Italy, Yugoslavia, the United Kingdom, most of Black Africa, all of the Arab countries, and all of Central and South America. These nations were created to amass wealth for the ruling families and their supporters, to hide or keep their wealth, and to create unstable conditions necessary to start wars or increase military budgets.

Switzerland was created as a neutral banking centre so that **Illuminati families** would have a safe place to keep their funds without fear of destruction from wars and prying eyes.

The United States was established with 13 colonies, one for each of the Illuminati families. The original flag had 13 stars, and still has 13 stripes. The eagle, the symbol of the United States, holds 13 arrows in its talons. The United States is actually a corporate asset of **the Virginia Company** that was established in 1604 in England with direct involvement of the **Rothschilds**. The finances of the Rothschilds were necessary to fund the exploration and exploitation of the North American continent.

The assets of the Virginia Company, including the United States, are owned by the Holy Roman Empire via the Vatican. This occurred in 1213 when **King James** gave all English assets to the Pope. Executorship remains with the British royal family, but actual ownership lies with the *Roman Catholic Church,* no doubt collateral for the House of Rothschild.

The United States of America is not named after **Amerigo Vespucci**, as you learned in school. The Illuminati would never name a continent, actually two continents, after an Italian mapmaker. The name is actually a combination of words.

- "Am" is the Hebrew word for "people"
- "Ame" is also the command form of the Spanish/Latin verb "to love"
- "Eri" or "ari" is a Hebrew term for "lion"
- "Rica" is the feminine form of the Spanish word for "rich"
- "Ka" is the ancient Egyptian word for soul, or spirit force within a body

There are two layers of meanings. The Ancient Hebrew/Egyptian translates to say, *"the people of the lion with spirit force"*

Hence, the pyramid and all-seeing eye on the one-dollar bill. The Latinized version translates to say, *"love riches",* in a feminized/physical reality way. This gives an idea of what they had in mind. Take this a step further, and one sees the mixture of the feminine Latin/eagle ideas with the masculine Hebrew/lion ideas. The symbolic statement of America is that it is a combination of **Lemuria** and **Atlantis**; a blend of the human/Lyrae with Reptilian/Draco. Perhaps the anagram LSD, an Illuminati created drug, has a hidden meaning as well: Lyrae-Sirius-Draco! The combination of these three civilizations would produce the most powerful, technological Empire ever known!

In 1776, the creation of the United States as an independent nation coincided with the declaration into public existence of the official Illuminati organization by member **Adam Weishaupt**, in Bavaria. Publicly, Mr. Weishaupt appeared to be determined to create an organization comprised of the European elite that would uplift mankind.

Of course, this was part of an Illuminati global ceremony. The creation for the United States and the Illuminati global ceremony. The creation of the United States and the Illuminati organization were artificial beginnings for public consumption. The United States was the device to be used to bring the Illuminati into public acceptance. Current Illuminati members believe that **Adam Weishaupt** was a look-alike for George

Washington, and it is actually Weishaupts image that appears on the one-dollar bill. **George Washington** was a wealthy slave and plantation owner. He is known to have raped some of his female slaves and used some of the male slaves in ritualistic ceremony. There are many people of the Black race who can literally trace their genetics to the founding fathers. George Washington also ordered the building of the Montauk Lighthouse in 1796. This lighthouse included an underground area for supply storage in case of a British coastline invasion. If he had only known what that area would become - or did he?

The 13 ruling Illuminati families constantly vie for control amongst themselves. During this time period, the Spanish, British, and French Illuminati all fought to win control over North and South America. The **Rothschilds** kept these Illuminati factions in line by sending Hessian troops to monitor the situation. The leaders enjoyed these war games, pitting one against the other to see who would win. The hundreds of thousands of lives lost were meaningless to them.

The Manifest Destiny of the United States was created to expand the territory of the Aryans at the expense of the native populations. As always, the Illuminati seek to destroy native peoples and their cultures. This is an attempt to destroy their knowledge of **God-Mind,** as well as the possibility that the natives will impart this information on to others. Especially important is their need to eliminate native cultures with ancient knowledge of **Atlantis** and **Lyrae**.

The natives that gave them the most problem were the Cherokee Indians because this tribe retained most of their **Atlantian knowledge**, even accessing the Bear/Bigfoot frequency for information. For this reason, these people were uprooted from their homeland in the southern Appalachian Mountains, and forcibly marched to Oklahoma on what is now known as The Trail of Tears. Many died along the way. Only a remnant remained in North Carolina, Tennessee, and Georgia. In the north, the vast Iroquois/Mohawk nation was disbanded. The **Montauk**, direct descendents of the Atlanteans who call their leader Pharaoh, were systematically eliminated.

The **Rothschilds** were aggressively involved with the slave trade from Africa, importing slaves to North and South America as well as the Caribbean. They were very careful not to import Blacks from the eastern areas of Ethiopia or Sudan where the descendents of Solomon were located, instead concentrating on western and central Africa for the slave populations. These areas had the **pure mixture of Annunaki and simian genetics**, and the programming desirable for the Illuminati agenda.

The Rothschilds decided that splitting the United States colonies would double their profits. So they politically created, and financially supported, the Civil War. The Civil War was actually a global ceremonial ritual to bring slavery to its next level. This war allowed the North to win, and publicly abolish slavery. The best slaves are the ones who do not realize that they are slaves. This alleviates rebellion and resistance. This was the status immediately following the Civil War. Blacks in the South are still slaves. There is still segregation, even in the North. The Illuminati still consider Blacks to be second or third class citizens. Only now the slavery is subtle and masked.

Since the Civil War, there have been other staged wars that entrenched the trend toward globalization. The Spanish-American War of 1898-1899 acquired more land for **the American Illuminati**, placing a greater portion of the Earth's surface under American jurisdiction. World War I was designed to change the map of Europe as well as test germ and chemical warfare technology for future use. This coincided with the worldwide influenza outbreak designed to reduce the global population, making control easier. **World War I** also laid the foundation for the German role in the next war.

World War II was a test of the final globalization and extermination projects. It was also designed to test mind-control machinations; to test the use of fluoride which deadens brain activity and slows resistance to authority; to experiment with slave labour camps and study the development of resistance; and to teach the masses to spy and report on one another.

World War II brought three primary goals of the Illuminati to fruition.
- The first was that hidden Illuminati symbolisms were brought to public attention from the underground strongholds in Tibet and Egypt, such as the Swastika and the ankh.
- The second was the creation of the **State of Israel** as a foundation for the New World Religion.
- The last was the creation of nuclear weapons as part of the Illuminati global ceremony.

By the end of World War II, one of the three major Illuminati global rituals was accomplished. This was the nuclear explosion that took place in 1945 at the 33rd parallel as a test for the nuclear attack on Japan. This explosion was symbolic, representing the simultaneous creation and destruction of matter and energy. The year was symbolic as well. In numerology, $1 + 9 = 10$, representing the 10 aspects of God-Mind. The number 10 further breaks down to $1 + 0 = 1$, representing a new beginning. Continuing, $4 + 5 = 9$, representing the end of a cycle. Symbolically, the entire event represented the end of a cycle to prepare for a new beginning using the new creation of God-Mind out of destruction.

Additionally, a cylinder containing material still not explained by the government was trucked into the nuclear explosion testing. This cylinder was made from pure steel and allegedly was the same physical dimensions as the Kabala describes for the creation of **Golems**. Kabala is ancient Hebrew metaphysics that has been a staple for **the Illuminati** for millennia. *Golems are artificial beings* that are used as a slave force. It is highly probable that this was a symbolic ritual for the creation of the society of Golems.

World War II also allowed the European/American Illuminati to destroy the Japanese Illuminati desires of global domination. The Japanese royal family, represented by **Emperor Hirohito**, have always been ostracized as non-legitimate by the ruling 13 families. The Japanese claim to be direct descendents of Lemurian purebreds.

The European/American Illuminati claim that the Japanese Illuminati are **descendents from a lower species in the Draco hierarchy.** This lower species is considered a worker class without any political clout or influence. The European/American Illuminati also claim that East Indians are a lower species in the Draco hierarchy. The 13 ruling families consider light skin and hair to be an elite characteristic.

On January 17, 1994, **Japan sent a seismic event to California**. Exactly one year later on January 17, 1995, the city of **Kobe**, Japan was seismically destroyed. **Kobe** was the home of the Japanese electromagnetic weaponry centers. The European/American Illuminati will not tolerate thorns in their sides. The destruction of Japan and its royal family will continue in the coming months.

Every year, the Illuminati hold meetings to plan the events of the coming year to accomplish their main objective formulated **millennia ago** of global control and domination. In the 1850s, they pinpointed their target date for complete domination with an agenda called Plan 2000. This has since been revised to 2003. The fiasco election of George W. Bush Jr. to office is a key sign that they are on target. The public lesson of the United States presidential "election" of 2000 is that the citizens do not vote for anyone! **Even the Illuminati are now finding it increasingly difficult to conceal their plans.**

The New World Order came into a new stage of business plan implementation in 1943 after the second World War. As we have learned, the Jesuits have emerged into a new status from this time. This is not its origin for the powers that have always been planning to control all the resources of Planet Earth have always had this agenda. It can be said that their agenda has not gone ahead without issues and a careful plan had been created trough WW II to "test the water".

It is now necessary to go back into some history as it pertains to the second world war as it is relevant to how the shift occurred from Europe to America with the final implementation of the New world Order. This has become the spiritual-military force under the jurisdiction of the State of Columbia and serves as the Military Division for the New world order plan. Whereas it had originally been scheduled for Hitler and the Nazi empire to run, because of the "unfavourable" shift of Hitler, the strategy was shifted to the Americas. For this one can refer to the website *www.one-evil.org.*

Origins Of The Spiritual Entity Called The SS

Under Pope Innocent VIII, the role of the Inquisition and Inquisitor changed to increase their legal and spiritual authority when despatching "heretics". Around 1483 Tomás de Torquemada was named Inquisidor General of Aragón, Valencia and Catalonia. His torturers and special militia were then blessed with being sworn into the highest sacred order of the Roman Cult-- the SS or the Knights of the Sedes Sacrorum.

As a military order of the Roman Catholic Church, the Knights of the Sedes Sacrorum (SS) were bestowed by the legal orders of the Roman Pontiff on behalf of the Mother Church to wage constant Holy Inquisition against all heretics, including assassinations, torture and counter-intelligence, to protect the name of the Holy Roman Catholic Church and directly represent the interests of the Holy See as its primary order of Holy Knights-- the SS (Sedes Sacrorum or Holy See).

As a spiritual order of the Roman Catholic Church, the SS --were bestowed with the extraordinary Roman Catholic grace of being forgiven for all their mortal sins (therefore can go to Heaven) that "unfortunately" must be done in order to observe its temporal orders. In others words, the troops of the Grand Inquisitor Tomás de Torquemada were the first religious military order to be granted "immunity" from Hell by the Pope on account of its acts of torture, terror and evil.

The last open satanic ritual sacrifices under the Holy Inquisition was in the early 19th Century. By the beginning of the 20th Century, there were less than a few hundred SS soldiers still assigned to the Holy Inquisition. However, upon the appointment of Fr Heinrich Himmler S.J. in 1929 to the NSDAP in Germany, a new Nazi SS (Knights of the Sedes Sacrorum) Army of several hundred thousand was created by 1939 to wage the single greatest Inquisition ever undertaken by the Roman Cult-- with over 18 million innocent people burned alive in ovens in Russia and Poland.

The German SS were disbanded at the end of World War II, with the Roman Scroll of the SS being handed to the United States SS (Secret Service/Sedes Sacrorum) by 1945. The United States SS was officially created into a military/spiritual force after the assassination of President William McKinley in 1901. After the staged gun-fight outside Blair House in 1950, the United States SS have had absolute protection of the President of the United States, holding him a virtual prisoner of the State under the guise of official protection.

Whilst the present heads of the Catholic Church have demonstrated over 900 years of contempt towards the Divine Creator, under the Covenant of One-Heaven (**Pactum De Singularis Caelum**) the entire officials including Cardinals, Bishops, Deacons and Ordinaries are granted Divine Redemption including the **Sainthood of all Popes**, including the Church having the power to ratify the Divine Treaty of Lucifer and the end of Hell and Damnation forever if all evil behaviour is ceased, all sins admitted and all property surrendered by the Day of Divine Judgment on UCA[E8:Y3210:A0:S1:M27:D6] also known as Wed, 21 Dec 2011.

The Nazis And Their Relation To The Holy See

The **Schutzstaffel trans**lated to *Protection Squadron* or *defence corps*, abbreviated **SS**—or ⚡⚡ was a major paramilitary organization under Adolf Hitler and the Nazi Party. Built upon the Nazi ideology, the SS under Heinrich Himmler's command was responsible for many of the crimes against humanity during World War II (1939–1945). After 1945, the SS was banned in Germany, along with the Nazi Party, as a criminal organization. The SS began as a small permanent guard unit made up of NSDAP volunteers to provide security for Nazi Party meetings in Munich. Formed at the end of 1920, they were known as the "Saal-Schutz" (Hall-Protection). Later under the leadership of Heinrich Himmler between 1929 and 1945, the SS was renamed the "Schutz-Staffel" and grew from a small paramilitary formation to one of the largest and most powerful organizations in the Third Reich.

This Nazi SS also known as "SS" is also a shortened name for the "Knights of the Holy See", a Roman Catholic spiritual and military order first formed in 1933 based completely upon the Jesuit order structure upon the signing of the "sacred" Reich Concordat specifically through the application of Articles 1,12,15,21 and 33 with the enaction of Clause (c) of the "Secret Supplement" of the Concordat between Franz von Papen (on behalf of Nazi Germany) and Cardinal Eugenio Pacelli (Pope Pius XII).

The term Nazi was first publicly used as the rebranded name for the National Socialist German Workers' Party (NSDAP) in 1933 upon devout Catholic leader--known as "Father" or Führer--(Fr.) Adolf Hitler assuming office as German Chancellor. The Nazi SS were also formally given birth under the Reich Concordat of 1933 with its first Superior General being Reichführer (Superior Father/General) Fr. Heinrich Himmler S.J. who personally attended the signing ceremony of the Reich Concordat in Rome (1933). Under the Reich Concordat, the Reichführer –having the same rank as a Senior Roman Catholic Cardinal--is the superior to the Führer, the "lay" representative of the Nazi (Knights).

As a military order of the Roman Catholic Church, the Knights of the Holy See (Nazi SS) are bestowed by the "infallible" legal orders of the Roman Pontiff on behalf of the Mother Church to wage constant Holy Inquisition against all heretics, including assassinations, torture and counter-intelligence, to protect the name of the Holy Roman Catholic Church and directly represent the interests of the Holy See as its primary order of Holy Knights-- the SS (Sedes Sacrorum or Holy See).

As the primary Roman Catholic spiritual order charged with carrying out the executions of the Holy Inquisition, the Knights of the Holy See (Nazi SS) are tasks with rounding up large numbers of people, depriving them of their rights on claim of being heretics and killing them.

As members of a Catholic Order holding the equivalent spiritual powers of Priests, Bishops and even Cardinals (e.g. Fr Himmler S.J.), the Knights of the Holy See have historically murdered heretics by sacrificing them in formal religious ceremony. This is why over <u>18 million innocent people were burnt alive in ovens</u> in Russia and Poland during World War II--as the single largest mass human sacrifice in history rather than cheaply starving them to death and/or burying them alive/dead.

As the Nazi SS order ("Knights of the Holy See") were formed by a formal Papal act and Deed in the form of the Reich Concordat 1933, the continued existence of the Nazi SS Order is conditional upon this legal document remaining enacted. Given the German Government and Holy See (Vatican) continue to honour this Concordat to this day, the SS remains legally and technical still enacted, now bestowed unto a new organization.

Relation Between Nazism And Satanism

Frank O'Connel writes on his website **www.one-evil.org**: "Let me briefly recap what some of the plan was . And while you read these plans that I am relaying to you from my intensive research on high level Satanism, see if you don't see the irony in the Satanic plans. How very ironic it is that in all the twisted thinking and reasoning of the leading Satanists for why they must do things, it is surprising they do not catch on that this plan of Satan's is going to achieve God's revealed plan. How pride does blind us! (For the sake of brevity I will dispense with my normal method of documenting everything; I suggest that my book Be Wise As Serpents be read for documentation, and further questions be written to me . Otherwise this article would be way to bulky for the newsletter.) The "brilliant" plan given in detail to the Illuminati was to create a thesis and its opposite called the antithesis . The process would repeat itself until the desired outcome.

Out of the battle between the two would emerge the synthesis . Out of the battle of chaos would come a new order reminding us of the Masonic slogan "Order out of Chaos." If the thesis were like a hammer and the antithesis like an anvil, what was caught in between would be broken or reshaped. Three world wars would enable the plan to work. The hammer would be constructed and then given a homeland, a secure base in Russia .

It is what we call communism. The first anvil would be created out of economic chaos in Germany . It would be called National Socialism . That anvil would be destroyed in a Second World War, but another anvil would replace it called democracy. The first two world wars accomplished exactly what they were intended to accomplish. Out of the first world war came:

(1) A secure Satanic dictatorship in Russia, a secure base to carry out further world subversion.
(2) The Satanic family of Rothschilds gained partial control over Palestine, preparing the way for Satan to rule from Jerusalem some day
(3) Weapons of mass destruction and terror.
(4) The League of Nations.

Out of the second world war came
(1) The enlargement of their secure base in Russia into a world power.
(2) Complete control over Palestine by the Rothschilds.
(3) Airpower, including long range missiles, jets, secret flying saucers, and powerful submarines, all items that individuals could not produce . Those in control of production would therefore control all air and sea ways of the earth.
(4) The cold war and an era of terror to convince the people of the need for Satan's One World Order.
(5) the United Nations .

Out of the third world war would emerge a new religious system. The third world war would have to be tailored to be like the Bible's Armageddon, Satan told his highest slaves, because - if it resembled Armageddon, then the people would believe he was the Messiah when he came after its end. It would have to be terrible, so that he could step in and bring miraculous order out of a world beaten into chaos by the worst war in history. Again it would be "Order out of chaos", as the Masonic documents repeatedly proclaim. The third world war would come during a period of seven years of tribulation starting in 1992 and running until 1999. Just like the Second World War emerged out of the great world-wide depression. **Note: Do not think in terms of traditional wars because as you will understand in Part 2, this may well be the war of the End Times s the spiritual versus non-spiritual war.**

Satan told his followers this 1992-99 tribulation would repeat on a larger scale the plagues of Egypt, for he would wreck revenge for what was done to Egypt by God (and Moses) by giving back in a bigger way to the world what happened to ancient Egypt. To a demonic controlled mind it makes sense to wreck such revenge, especially when the end result is held out to be the salvation of the world by the Lightbearer, the Morning Star, also known as Lucifer. For most of us, the idea of such pain and destruction seems like demonic madness- - which it is.

At the core of the One-World-System is Satanism. It hides itself behind fronts such as Jewish Finance, Socialism, Aryanism, British Israelism, Zionism, and Freemasonry which are tools to get the broad masses to serve the Plan. The "conspiracy" to create the One-World-System has enlisted the help of almost everyone. That is because most of the religious systems at the top are controlled by Satanists who know what they are doing and direct the people's religious efforts. (Read the research in **Be Wise As Serpents** for the documentation on this.) Nazism was a Pagan Gnostic religious system whose High Priest Hitler knew what he was doing in relation to Satan's mission. (More about this further down.) The Jewish people (1 use the term in its broadest sense) are being used.

Actually the allegiance of the Satanic hierarchy is not in the least concerned with Judaism, although it appears that at first the plans are to create a religious leader that will have the apparent credentials of the Jewish messiah. How sad, because the actions of the Rothschilds and other Satanic "Jewish" bloodlines during WW II show that their first allegiance is not to the Old Testament and not to even Orthodox Judaism, but is purely to Satan. At some point in the future the Orthodox Jews and the Conservative Jews will find that this Messiah, who is already alive waiting to play his role, will only give them temporary relief. They are being taken for a ride and then they will be dumped by the New World Order's dictatorship.

Constance Cumbey correctly notices that the New Age movement resembles Nazism exactly to a T . For those students wanting to get a detail by detail parallel go to pages 114 to 120 in The Hidden Dangers Of The Rainbow.

In 1952, **James Larratt Battersby** in England published **The Holy Book of Adolf Hitler** for the German World Church in Europe. Except for some of his pro-German ideas, obviously thrown in to make the book enlist the intended audience's favour, the book is an exact description of what would happen in the next 50 years to bring in the New World Order. The reason some of the prognostications of pro-German ideas are not valid is that the Satanic hierarchy is not really concerned for the German people either, except to harness their help in their plans . Batterby's Holy Book of Adolf Hitler was given to him 'in the spirit'. According to Battersby the book was written in order that 'May God open the eyes of the Gentiles to Truth, and carry his Holy Gospel to the ends of the earth'.

The book is an excellent synopsis of what Satan had planned in 1952 and has carried out since to a large degree. The Rothschilds (and other top Satanic families in a lesser way) financed a Jewish Mason and devote Satanist named Karl Marx to write his Das Kapital . The Satanists controlling key Masonic groups (along with some other groups they controlled) got Communism started. The original idea came from Satan, and was given at a Feast of the Beast in meticulous detail to those highest in the Satanic Hierarchy . Albert Pike, and Guiseppe Mazzini were two men in strategic positions of control that were let in on the plans.

After creating International Socialism (communism) a temporary antithesis was created called National Socialism (Nazism). The process to create National Socialism was to turn again to the Masonic Lodges and other esoteric secret Societies to get it done. Therefore, the secret esoteric Gnostic and satanic societies along with the Illuminati helped create "the Thule Gesellshaft" (in English the Thule Society) . Adolf Hitler was some type of member of this occult Thule Society, along with many other men who later began leading Nazi leaders such as Rudolf Hess. The Thule Society used the Masonic/Hindu symbol the Swastika, which the Nazi party then also used as its symbol. In other words the grandmother of the Nazi Party was the Masonic Lodges in Germany.

The Vril was another secret occult group that many of the Nazi leadership belonged to. Hitler also was a member of the Theosophical Society, which has strong Satanic and Masonic ties. Both Bailey and Hitler studied from Tibetians, Hindus, occultists, and black magicians. They also both studied the Gnostics, and every major Pagan/Occult religious system. A example of how valued the Swastika was for Freemasons before Hitler ruined its image, is a quote from Joseph Fort Newton, a Baptist Minister and high ranking Mason, The second of these volumes also contains an essay by Thomas Carr, with a list of Lodges, and a study of their history, customs, and emblems- -especially the Swastika. Speculative Masons are now said to be joining.., seeking more light on what are called the Lost Symbols of Masonry. After promoting and using the Swastika for years the Freemasons quit using it after Hitler.

The **Holy Book of Hitler** provides the answer as to why the Theosophical Society worked so hard to destroy the British Empire. It had always at first mystified me why the Theosophical Society Presidents who connected to the Satanic hierarchy would want to ruin the British Empire. The reason it seemed strange is that the mother country of Satanism and Witchcraft is Great Britain. The center of secret political power is geographically in England. And further, one of the largest and most powerful secret fronts for Satanism is Britism-Israelism. The reason why the British Empire was destroyed was that Satan had already determined even before 1870 that the steps to world government would include setting up around 9 or 10 Continental blocs. The Union of Europe into one country (or bloc) could not be accomplished while Great Britain had most of her focus on her empire. Great Britain as long as she had an empire would never want to join up with Europe. In fact all the European nations would have to be convinced to give up their colonies, that is why the World Power got everyone they could get to help fight Portugal in Angola in recent history, everyone including the large Masonic-controlled Christian denominations who donated millions of dollars to the NCC and WCC which moneys were then passed on to the guerrillas to buy weapons and ammo.

The Theosophical Society is mostly to blame for India's independence from Britain. First, the Theosophical Society managed to change British policy so that the British became unpopular. Then Theosophical President Besant, who published the largest English paper strongly criticized British rule in her newspapers and eventually was arrested. Gandhi and other Indian leaders were involved in Besant being made the President of the Indian Congress Party. And that political party still rules Indian politics. The Theosophist Mahatma Gandhi, following in the steps of Theosophical President Annie Besant, led the Indian people against British rule.

But the final blow to the British Empire was done by another Theosophist--Adolf Hitler. It is common knowledge that the powerful blows of Axis attacks in WW II struck the death blow to the British Empire, or so we are told. The truth is that the elite wanted the Empire to die, and pulled every string to convince the British public and indigenous natives that the Empire was too weak after WW II to save the empire and prevent her colonies from independence. It is hard for people to grasp that the Illuminati controlled Russia, Great Britain, Germany and France during World War II, but they did. Churchill, Roosevelt, and Stalin were all Masons. DeGaulle of France was closely linked with several esoteric groups, and the Prieure de Sion and Grand Orient Masons helped him to power in the 50s. Churchill was a Zionist and pro-Fabian Socialist. Stalin was a closet Satanist. Roosevelt was a Zionist, pro-communist and socialist. Both Churchill and Roosevelt came from important elite blood lines. Apparently, Stalin was somewhat independent, but basically did what was expected of him. As the previous paragraph indicates the people of the world weren't ready for a world government, and most not even a united Europe. W.W. II was carried out to adjust people's thinking toward wanting European unity. Satan already ruled the world through his secret chain of command, but he wanted to openly rule the world's hearts and to be publicly hailed as ruler and saviour.

Who was Hitler? Hitler's father was the offspring of the Rothschild's secret breeding program which impregnated his grandmother. It appears from the details available, Hitler was groomed for his role, without realizing his heritage at first. It appears that Hitler learned of his Jewish bloodline after taking over Germany. Hitler had romances with many beautiful women. Although Hitler was very strict with his New Age religious practices such as being a vegetarian, that did not include being celebrate.

He did have sex contrary to the deceptions of the Establishment. Hitler's seed (the Rothschild's powerful generational occult bloodline) was hidden in an Askenazim bloodline, at least part of which has come to the U.S. In fact, Hitler's generational occult power was passed on too. This was most likely done by thrusting a knife into his heart, and the person who received his occult power then gulped his last breath with the kiss of death to receive his occult power. What I am telling you is that Hitler's offspring are alive and well and that his terrifying Anti-Christ spirit was passed to someone and is not dead. Let me remind you of some of Hitler's own prophecies about himself and his goals. 'At the time of supreme peril I must die a martyr's death for the people. But after my death will come something really great, an overwhelming revelation to the world of my mission.'

The world was to witness his divinity. Further, 'My spirit will rise from the grave, and the world will see that I was right.' Von Ribbentrop on Apr. 30, 1945 was told this same thing, 'You will see that my spirit will rise from the grave.' National Socialism 'is even more than a religion; it is the will to make mankind anew.' 'All creative energy will pass to the new man.' Hitler claimed to be the real fulfillment of Marx's socialism. 'I am not only the conqueror, but also the executor of Marxism, of that part of it which is essential and justified, stripped of its Jewish-Talmudic dogma.' In essence, he is saying whatever veneer of Jewishness that Marx's satanic plan had, he disagreed with it and would destroy that veneer. These type of statements reveal that the essence of the message of various elite men like Hitler is the same Satanic plan if stripped of their variously decorated veneers.

Hitler is viewed as the Messiah, the Holy Spirit, the martyred Savior of his people by his followers today. The blasphemous **Holy Book of Adolf Hitler** states, 'All hail to God's Christ and Chosen, Adolf Hitler...Lord of Lords, and King of Kings, the Eternal Adolf Hitler.' Such blasphemy. Father forgive them for they know not what they do. Hitler's Demonic Spirit and Hitler's descendents both live on today. (By the way, some Rothschild descendents such as Hitler's have come to Christ as their Lord and Saviour!). Will this powerful occult branch of the Rothschild's be used again by the New World Order? Whatever the case it is clear that Hitler's Anti-Christ spirit will get plenty of demonic help. The demonic forces that have manifested themselves in National Socialism and International Socialism (aka Communism) demonized much of Europe.

So much so that Europe officially portrays itself as a beast with Venus on it on a stamp commemorating the Second election of the European Parliament, and also as the same forces that tried to build the Tower of Babel on an official poster. Not only are the same demons that led communist leaders and Nazi leaders operating in Europe's leaders, but there are armies of demons trampling over anything of moral value in Europe . It can be said without a doubt that the man who rules the One-World-Government will derive his power from a demonic supernatural source. According to Revelations, God is going to have an angel open up a key to the abyss and teeming hordes of demonic spirits shall be descending upon the earth. My conclusion is that Satan has so many Anti-Christs available that Hitler's personal occult power is not necessary for the New World Order's success .

I rarely like to comment on the end times from Scriptures because I feel like most people are thoroughly confused about the clear teachings that the Scriptures give. Thes. 2:3 and other Scriptures make it clear that the Christians must witness a great apostasy and the Anti-Christ being revealed before Christ returns. We can live everyday as if it may be our last, but Scriptures are clear that the Apostles did not live each day as if Jesus could return that day. They knew that certain things had to happen first. The church has been going through tribulations since Pentecost. The church will go through the "great tribulation" according to the Word of God.

We will if we are that faithful remnant we will be spared from the Wrath of God, but we will not be spared from the tribulation of Satan which shall include martyrdom. The New Age leaders are fully ready to cooperate with this cleansing from the earth of us bothersome disciples of Truth. In this respect, their thinking will resemble the Nazi's rationalizations that people must pay their Karmic debt, and shall benefit from being killed. How truth can be stood on its head! The Plans are already drawn up how to use rail lines to move large groups of civilians to labour camps. When we compare Nazi Germany with today's New World Order plans, Nazi Germany can be seen to be the basic model of what Satan's timetable includes for us these next few years.

To illustrate that the Pagan religion of Nazism is an example to the Satanists and New Agers, let us ponder Anton LaVey's (head of a visible Church of Satan) trip to the sacred initiation castle of Hitler's Black Order the SS. The SS apparently brought the Holy Grail to Germany, and hid it before the end of the war. On May 2, 1945, a select group of SS officers, those initiated into the higher mysteries of the Nazi Pagan religion, hid the Grail in the Schleigeiss glacier at the foot of 3,000 meter high Hochfeiler mountain. Seekers in the area have been found decapitated, and mutilated. The area is still guarded by the Black Order in anticipation of the day that the Grail can be revealed to the world . It has been speculated 1995 might be the date, but this is pure speculation. The important thing for us is to begin to experience the Kingdom of God right now. Let us prepare ourselves for Almighty God's New World Order as the Satanists launch their counterfeit New World Order."

Hitler And The Foundation Of The NSDAP

The National Socialist German Workers' Party (NSDAP) was born in early 1920 as an evolution of the earlier political group - the extremist German Workers' Party (Arbeiterpartei, DAP) first founded by Anton Drexler (1884-1942) including others such as Gottfried Feder, Dietrich Eckart and Karl Harrer.

Adolf Hitler first came into contact with the DAP around June 1919--five months after its formation-- as a double agent and intelligence officer of the Catholic controlled Bavarian Reichswehr Group tasked with reporting on their activities. His acceptance into the ranks of the Catholic Bavarian Reichswehr intelligence network was thanks to the support of his patron Catholic Papal Nuncio, Archbishop Cardinal Eugenio Pacelli, based in Munich at the time.

From late 1919 until he moved to Berlin in 1925, Hitler met with his mentor Cardinal Pacelli every few weeks and probably updated the Archbishop on his progress while receiving his next instructions. Testimony as a "matter of fact" to the regular and clockwork meetings of Hitler and Pacelli was given by the housekeeper and friend of Pacelli for 41 years, Sister Pascalina Lehnert.

Hitler was accepted as the 55th member of the German Workers' Party (DAP), and played no active role until the start of 1920 when the tiny German Worker's Party was facing bankruptcy and extinction thanks to the disastrous management of the weekly published Thule society newspaper the Münchener Beobachter (Munich Observer) by Drexler, Feder, Eckart and Harrer.

Rather than being re-assigned to another intelligence project, Hitler was promptly and honorably discharged from military service by the end of February 1920 and overnight went from unemployed minor party member to saviour of the DAP by providing all the necessary gold to keep the Münchener Beobachter (Munich Observer) and the DAP afloat.

In a measure of the influence and control Hitler now had as the miraculous financier, the party changed its name in March 1920 to Nationalsozialistische Deutsche Arbeiterpartei or (NSDAP) --National Socialist German Workers' Party and the name of its paper to Völkischer Beobachter (People's Observer) after its purchase by the re-named NSDAP from the Thule Society.

Later, the Jesuits wrote the lie in Mein Kampf that this strategic decision to change the party was made by erratic alcoholic and drug addict Dietrich Eckart. What is never mentioned is that Hitler came bearing millions of dollars of gold seemingly out of "thin air" to turn a small eclectic band into a political movement, the failed NSDAP push for power by force.

In spite of Hitler arranging the lifeline to keep the NSDAP afloat, the Thule Society members remained half hearted in transforming it into a real political movement, yet unwilling to step aside.

By early 1921, Cardinal Pacelli had also assisted Hitler by discretely introducing key and trusted Catholic members such as Rudolf Hess, Hans Frank and Alfred Rosenberg into the NSDAP. At an extraordinary party meeting on 28 July 1921 Hitler made his move and was voted in as Chairman of the NSDAP against the wishes of its founders.

Now with his protégé in charge, Pacelli pushed for the NSDAP to accelerate its transformation. Soon after being appointed Führer, Superior General Wlodimir Ledochowski provided Jesuit priests to Adolf Hitler in 1921 to help establish a paramilitary wing to the NSDAP to be known as the Sturmabteilung (SA) also known as "Brownshirts" first headed by Ernst Röhm. The new official insignia of the party, the swastika was also adopted.

The plan given to the Hitler by Cardinal Pacelli in late 1921 that the NSDAP was to organize themselves as a Catholic militia ready to seize power within the year. Yet, even with new recruits and millions of dollars of gold in the bank, the NSDAP demonstrated a complete lack of competence in organizing themselves into a political military force.

In contrast, the National Fascist Party headed by Benito Mussolini with his "Blackshirts" (Squadristi) demonstrated far more capability in winning at the Italian elections in 1922 and then staging a coup d'état to seize total power in October 1922.

By the beginning of November 1923 after considerable expense, the NSDAP now had around 20,000 members and a few thousand members of the Sturmabteilung "Brownshirts". Under pressure to demonstrate results, Hitler launched his coup to try and takeover Germany on the night of November 8th—the so call "Beer hall putsch" beginning with a rally of 2,000 supporters through Munich. It failed instantly, with the Reichswehr troops opening fire on the rebels and Hitler with the rest of the party leadership were arrested and found guilty of treason by March 1924—the party banned from having any military wing and prevented from running in elections for four years.

It must be noted clearly that there is absolutely no credible evidence that Fr Heinrich Himmler was associated with Hitler, or any member of the NDSAP in any way until 1929. Nor is there any credible evidence whatsoever that the NSDAP used the word "Nazi" or "Nazi Party" until the arrival of Himmler. Both crucial facts being deliberately clouded and misrepresented to his the accurate evolution of events leading to World War II.

Yet, it was the imprisonment of Hitler (albeit for an incredibly short 12 months until December 20, 1924) that turned out to be a major propaganda win by Pacelli and the Jesuits for their protégé. Hitler may have been a remarkable orator, but was as good at writing as painting. While at Lansberg Prison, Hitler was visited several times by Bernhardt Staempfle S.J. for the painful process of extracting the outline of an autobiography and political manifesto to be called Mein Kampf "My Life".

Within a few months of his release **Fr Staempfle** S.J. had completed **Volume I "A Reckoning"** --12 chapters outlining the essential arguments for Catholic Nationalism (Fascism) in Germany peppered by semi-fiction of the life of Hitler.

The Jesuits even secured a top-notch Bavarian born US media agent named Ernst Hanfstaengl who had worked for Franklin Delano Roosevelt and was on close terms to many in German and US "high society" including media baron William Randolph Hearst. It was Hanfstaengl who was instrumental in massaging the public image of Hitler into a "Catholic Christian Knight" against the "global Jewish menace".

While Hitler's career as the "world's first media celebrity" gained ground, the NDSAP and Hitler remained banned from participating in elections until 1927. Contrary to deliberate misinformation which claims the NDSAP secretly participated as the "National-Socialist Freedom Movement" in the 1924 national German elections, the first election at which the NDSAP and Hitler ever stood candidates was in the National elections on May 20, 1928 at which the NDSAP polled a poor 2.6% of the vote with Hitler as their famous celebrity leader.

In the meantime, Mussolini had already been in absolute power of Italy since 1922. Clearly, the whole political apparatus of the NDSAP needed to change.

The Arrival of Fr Himmler S.J. And The Nazis

One of (several) absurd mythologies accepted by eminent historians and academics is the proposition that the Schutzstaffel (German for "Squadron" and the same concept as the Italian "Blackshirt Squadrons" of Catholic Mussolini) was formed in 1925 as the personal bodyguard of Hitler following his release from prison.

Some audacious writers have even "revised history" to claim the Schutzstaffel (frequently cut in half to try and get two S's our of the single word for squadron) had already started to use the SS and skull and bones symbols, including calling their head the Reichführer-SS and the Roman Salute (straight arm) to their allegiance to the Vatican, Rome.

The ridiculous nature of these lies are easily exposed when the facts are considered that Hitler's main claim to fame in 1925 was as a book writer and budding political philosopher, surrounded by a tight group of individuals each providing key skills such as Rudolf Hess-personal private secretary, Ernst Hanfstaengl-media, Hans Frank-Lawyer and Julius Schreck-personal security. Furthermore, the NDSAP was a publicly banned organization until May 1927.

In fact, the first election of the reformed NDSAP in May 1928 was a complete humiliation and disaster. It was during this period of recrimination and failure that Fr. Heinrich Himmler S.J entered to be immediately appointed the deputy of Erhard Heiden, commanded of the Schutzstaffel (squadron). Within a matter of a few months, Erhard Heiden resigned and Fr. Himmler S.J. was appointed as commander of the Schutzstaffel.

Again, it is important of emphasize that the Schutzstaffel (only one S) wore brown shirts until the Reich Concordat was signed between Cardinal Pacelli and Franz von Papen (for Germany) in 1933 bestowing exclusive spiritual powers on the Schutzstaffel of Fr. Himmler S.J. by the Vatican. The Jesuit Skull and Bones was incorporated by Fr Himmler into the military insignia of the Schutzstaffel but not the infamous SS until after the 1933 Concordat.

The political fortunes of the NDSAP appeared to suddenly turn around thanks to the swelling ranks of disciplined recruits to the Schutzstaffel. In September 1930, the NSDAP won 18.3% of the vote and 107 seats in the Reichstag (Parliament). By the July 1932 national elections, this vote had swelled to 37.8% and 230 of the 608 seats of Parliament. However, in the November 1932 elections, their lead had dropped to 33.1% and 196 seats in a 584 seat Parliament.

By 1933 National Elections, the Schutzstaffel under the control of Fr. Himmler S.J. numbered at least 52,000 highly trained and absolutely loyal members – a far cry from the early incompetence in Munich ten years earlier.

It was March 1933 that the world saw the word "Nazi" unleashed as a political religious force in the elections following the destruction of the Reichstag (Parliament) by Schutzstaffel agents and blamed on communists.

1933 marks the first year the religious word Nazi (from Hebrew Nasi meaning "Knight") was used as the official new name of the NDSAP in government.

It is frequently and incorrectly claimed that the word "Nazi" comes from the haphazard extraction of letters from the first word of the name of the NSDAP - NAtionalsoZIalistische Deutsche Arbeiterpartei to produce a simple abbreviation. This explanation is patently false as the NSDAP already has a perfectly good and well known abbreviation- NSDAP!. The word "Nazi" appeared only after Hitler assumed power invited by Franz Von Papen for an entirely different reason.

The word Nazi/Nasi dates back to the time of the Sanhedrin councils of Palestine first formed by the Romans in the 1st Century BCE. To members of modern Judaism, the Nasi were the appointed spiritual leaders of the Sanhedrin as opposed to the temporal leadership of the High Priest of the Main Temple. While there is some uncertainty as to the credibility of all the claimed history of the office of Nasi and the bloodline of Rabbinical Scholars of the House of Hillel, there is no doubt the position existed at some point.

The problem for modern readers concerning the direct relationship with the Hebrew term (Nasi) for knight and Nazi for the NDSAP as the "New Knights of Germany" is that Hitler and the NDSAP were supposed to be racially opposed to all things "Jewish". Without an understanding of true history concerning Israel being historically a region called Samara/Samaria and Judah being Yahud, without an understanding of the Phoenician/Samaritan/Sephardic priest-king bloodlines as the Khazars, the Venetians, the kings of Septimania as but a few examples, then the use of the word "Nasi" as "Nazi" seems absurd.

The simple fact is that the 16th century word and label "Jew" masked two distinct and wholly separate ancient religious/cultural/racial groups with absolutely nothing in common except a history of antipathy, hatred, war and rebirth. The Sarmatian/Sephardic/Sadducee priest-kings from the North, inventors of Hebrew, descendents of the Phoenicians being the mortal enemies of the southern Sephardic/Aramaic/Sadducee priest kings of Yahud (Judah). The term "Jew" is equivalent to saying all the people in the Middle East are "Easterners"—falsely claiming a homogeny and cultural identifiable unity.

The etymology of the word Nazi is wholly Sarmatian/Sadducee/Sephardic—the founders of Venice and a set of families that had grown very rich and powerful in their connections with the Roman Cult controlling the Catholic Church since the 12th and 13th Centuries. Today, we know them by the deliberately misleading name of the "Global Jewish Bankers".

The shocking truth concerning the Nazis is that rather than seeking to destroy any kind of "Global Jewish Banking Conspiracy", they were in fact dedicated to seeing it re-establish pre-eminent control over European Financial System and ultimately to the Roman Cult of the Vatican, Rome to whom they serve.

There is a parallel and quite extraordinary change within the power structure of the NSDAP as the Nazis- the rise of Fr. Himmler to Reichführer (also Reichführer Nazi SS) – or Superior General of the Knights of the Holy See.

Many historians deliberately mask the first beginnings of the use of the title Reichführer by dropping off the word "Nazi", or removing "SS" to somehow claim this position was the official title of the commander of the Schutzstaffel as early as 1925. The reason for this forgery is twofold- one to mask the true date of 1933 as the historic shift in the introduction of the initials SS and secondly to mask the true arrival of Himmler in 1929 and the title Reichführer-Nazi SS in 1933.

But what is more incredible is the fabricated history that continues to hid the absolute fact that in 1933 after the Reich Concordat was signed with the Vatican, Fr. Himmler was elevated in power, name and status above Hitler. Fr. Himmler S.J. as the Reichführer has superior title (as opposed to plain old führer for Hitler). Fr Himmler had complete independent control over all police, paramilitary, intelligence, scientific research and weapons development and the dreaded elite units of over 50,000 just in 1933—and Hitler had absolutely no authority over him. In fact the proof of the distaste each man had for one another is demonstrated in countless war archive movies showing in clear detail the body language of both men.

The fact that Hitler could do nothing against Himmler at the end of the war when it is universally recognized that Himmler was seeking to broker some kind of personal peace deal is more than enough evidence to conclude Hitler was part-puppet to larger forces.

Finally, the fact that neither Hitler nor any of his henchmen ever attempted to assassinate Himmler, in spite of his open usurping of Hitler's authority on many occasions, is indication the title of Reichführer-Nazi SS and the meaning of the SS is extremely significant.

The Real Meaning Of The SS Of The Nazi Elite

As stated, two S's cannot logically be extracted from the word Schutzstaffel simply means "Squadron". The significance of the use of the SS symbol by the elite of Himmler's forces after he personally attended the signing of the Reich Concordat with the Vatican in 1933 is frequently ignored.

Prior to its use by Himmler, the symbols SS were most frequently and officially used as the abbreviation of Sedes Sacrorum or the legal name of the Vatican being the "Holy See" (Latin Sedes = seat/see and Sacrorum = Holy/Sacred) since the 16th Century as a sign of imprimatur over official Vatican documents.

It is either an extraordinary coincidence that Himmler and his elite began wearing the SS symbol as Reichführer immediately after the signing of the Reich Concordat in 1933 with the SS- the Sedes Sacrorum, the <u>Holy See</u>. Given the four hundred year precedent of SS being associated with the Holy See, it is not unreasonable to conclude that the wearing of the symbols is associated with some as yet unpublished spiritual/temporal powers bestowed on the SS Troops by the SS- Holy See.

When one considers that Nazi SS translates most perfectly into the meaning "Knights of the Holy See", that the role of Himmler best translates into the new Grand Inquisitor and that over 18 million innocent people were burned alive in human sacrifice camps in Poland and Russia, then the SS were without doubt the new "Holy Army" of a great inquisition against "heretics" orchestrated by the Vatican, Rome.

Once this is understood, then the claims of millions burnt alive makes sense as the official doctrine (to this day) of the Roman Catholic Church for punishing heretics. It makes sense why the Nazi SS built the death camps. It makes sense why some many millions were targeted and why so much energy was spent on this utmost evil—because they were the loyal Catholic troops of the Vatican-Jesuit Inquisition of 1933-1945.

The Nazis Evolution

As the Nazi order ("Knights of the Reich") were formed by a formal Papal act and Deed in the form of the Reich Concordat 1933, the continued existence of the Nazi Order is conditional upon this legal document remaining enacted. Given the German Government and Holy See (Vatican) continue to honour this Concordat to this day, the Nazi order remains legally and technical still enacted, now bestowed unto a new organization.

Whilst the present heads of the Catholic Church have demonstrated over 900 years of contempt towards the Divine Creator, under the Covenant of One-Heaven (Pactum De Singularis Caelum) the entire officials including Cardinals, Bishops, Deacons and Ordinaries are granted Divine Redemption including the Sainthood of all Popes , including the Church having the power to ratify the Divine Treaty of Lucifer and the end of Hell and Damnation forever if all evil behaviour is ceased, all sins admitted and all property surrendered by the Day of Divine Judgment on UCA[E8:Y3210:A0:S1:M27:D6] also known as Wed, 21 Dec 2012.

We have looked at the ultimate police force of the Jesuit Order and the Knights of Malta. We have looked closer at one of the "gods" power vehicle of money and the House of Rothschild. We have looked deeper into the Vatican division that create and execute the tactics and actions to implement the operational components under the mission-- the wishes of the gods as the conquest of all empires to create one empire on Planet Earth. We have looked at the secret Societies and the special Corporation. Before we leave this topic let us look more deeply at some of the groups who like the executive branches of a major corporation take responsibility for execution of orders within the business plan called the new World Order.

Support Corporations And Multinational Network

Before we move on to how this all gets to the bottom employee earthling one has to ponder the magnitude of the plan for Planet earth and dominion over all. The administrative feat of it is indeed immense but if one thinks about any large organization, the skill in the executive and the management is in the definition of responsibilities and goal, rules of conduct, all structured in a pyramid so as to have people in charge. having the mission, the business plan and the infrastructure well defined, it becomes a business of financing and monitoring the people and objects. If you have ever worked for a large corporation, as you drop lower in the structure, people including managers know less and less about what others are doing or should do, and very little about the levels above.

We have seen that the royal bloodlines themselves have grown enormous strategic business from which they profit. We have seen the huge dynasties of wealth that can finance and takeover companies. They can be silent owners of public companies and take over companies directly. They can change the nature of business through financing them or through bankruptcies. Many researchers have done significant work on what companies are owned totally, partially, or directed by people that are controlled by other silent shareholders. One in particular is David Icke, who has dedicated his life to uncovering this truth and it is well documented in his books. The other aspect to this control is one of contract, oath and inclusion in the blood hierarchy so as to attain favours (market, money, power) as a result of "being in the family". This as we have seen is what the Secret Societies are all about.

The end result is that many corporations and multinationals have been identified as part of the affiliation. We can bring in the next level in our simplified model of PLANET EARTH INC.

JESUIT ORDER

gods

Lucifer

ROYAL BLOODLINES

Rothschild

Astor	DuPont	Li
Bundy	Collins	Freeman
Onassis	Kennedy	Rockefeller
Russell	Van Duyn	Reynolds

GLOBAL ELITE

Queen Elizabeth   Black Nobility   Illuminati

ELITE SECRET SOCIETIES

P2/Opus Dei	Rosecrucians	Freemasonry
Skull & Bones	Bohemian Club	Knights of Malta
Bilderbergers	Pilgrim Society	B' nai B'rith
Priory de Sion	Grand Orient	Royal Order of Garter

SPECIAL GLOBAL ORGANIZATIONS

FINANCIAL	RESEARCH	POLITICAL	INTEL	RELIGIOUS	EDUCATION
IMF	In. Policy Sdy	UN	CIA	COChurches	UNESCO
World Bank	Stanford res	Club of Rome	KGB	Wd Religions	World peace
Cent Banks	Brookings Ins	Bilderbergers	FBI	Vatican	Plan Congress
Fed Reserve	Tavistock In	Trilateral Com	MI 5	New Age	W. Federalist
I.B. Of Sett	Aspen Soc	Aspen Ins	MAFIA	Unity Church	Lucis Trust
Nat Banks	Jason Soc	NATO	INTERPOL	Bah a'i	World Goodwill
Foundations	Comm 300	EEC	Com Party	Temp Unders	Esalen Inst

GLOBAL CORPORATIONS, MULTINATIONALS

Bectel	TRW	Raytheon	Rand	Wallmart	Anhueser	ITT	CBS	CNN
Exxon	Tennaco	Glaxo	Texaco	Ford	Altna	IBM	NBC	Reuters
Esso	Corning	Arcer Daneils	Boenig	Chrysler	Blackstone Gr	Intel	ABC	Time Inc
Mobil	Dow Jones	Chem Barking	P. Morris	Nabisco	BP-Amoco	Unisys	Disney	Wall Journ
AT&T	MBNA	Shen. Plough	Amtrak	Cocacola	Chev-Texaco	Xerox	Atl Rich	Monsanto
Shell	Chase	Gold. Sachs	NW Air	Pepsi	John&John	GM	New Corp	Dow Chem
Arco	B. America	Amer Express	Amer Air	McDonals	Enron	Dell	Time -warner	Amway
PBS	B. Trust	Burger King	Deere	Motorola	Unysis	GE	W. Post	Squibb
Levi	US News	Was. Times	Chid. TV	Eli Lily	Bristol Meyers		Raytheon	Citigroup

Now we must shift attention to how the corporations came to lead to the current debt condition and how major nations have fallen under the command of the leaders of PLANET EARTH.

14

THE STORY OF THE BANKRUPTCY OF AMERICA

We have covered the simple structure and some components of PLANET EARTH, the key players and the business plan. Now it is of interest to see how their business strategy has been implemented, with particular attention to America because it became the focal point of the implementation. The story you are about to read may seem like fiction but the truth of it, as you will see in Part 2, is emerging rapidly. There are at least 200 countries that are part of the huge debt pyramid of hundreds of trillions of dollars that was shown in the first Chapters. The story of each nation is different but the process by which they were conquered will be similar.

And so it was that the attention of the Illuminati as directed by the gods shifted to America in a way that was not planned before. It was destined to become the Military Industrial Complex that would serve as the world police force eventually and also become the vehicle for capturing humanity under a corporate illusion. It would capture the united States under a set of special deals made due to irresponsible use of money and bankruptcy. Ironically, America was originally founded on sovereignty and freedom from the dominion of Britain but the bloodlines who knew well how to conquer kingdoms with money had been evolving into power over the same period. The process of setting up the district and city of Columbia led to the organizational structure of USA INC., and CANADA INC, fictional subsidiaries of the UNITED KINGDOM, the usurping of the money, and the eventual employment of USA and CANADA Earthlings.

Now it is time to look at the detailed chronology of how these powerful families marched towards taking over America and most of the other nations. As we have already seen, that plan was written and hidden in plain view in the money of the United States. The takeover returns us back tithe first chapter of the debt pyramid and how that has become the tool of dominion. This chapter is dedicated to that story.

We have seen one side of the US Dollar and how it tells the story of the plan. It was issued in 1929. On the other side the US Dollar bill tells another story of how real money with intrinsic value back by precious metals, was shifted away from the US Treasury to take a new form. Prior to 1929, it stated ***"Payable to Bearer on Demand"*** as silver:

The new issue became *"This Note is Legal Tender for All Debts Public and Private"* which in simply a unit of debt. This what is known as "fiat" money" which has no intrinsic value except what people believe to be value.

America Is Bankrupt-Again

In 1788, the United States was officially bankrupt. As a government it was in default to the crown of England to the tune of eighteen million plus interest. As a direct and proximate result the U.S. corporate government was bankrupt in their private capacity from the start of the constitution. Then, the debt had to be paid for a period of seventy years. After a period of seventy years, according to the Bible res judicata and stare decisis, God said America could come out of bankruptcy with England on December 31, 1858. But let us leave this for now as we will come back to this later.

Here is a summary of the American debt obligation. Under International Law, if a nation cannot pay its debts, its debts are forgiven every 70 years. Individual debts should be cancelled every 7 years as sabbatical time but for a nation it is ten times that. The mortgage was renewed in 1789. In We could have come out then but the debt was renewed and enlarged to pay for the beginning of the civil war. which began in 1859. We could have come out in 1929 but the nation renewed and enlarged the debt when the farmers pledged their lands to the public in exchange for public aid supposedly to save farming. F.D. Roosevelt instituted the New Deal and Land Control under emergency war powers to overcome the depression and regulate farming. The great depression began in

1929. In 1999 we could have come out of bankruptcy but the nation renewed and enlarged the debt when it unknowingly chose to remain a military democracy instead of reverting to constitutional republic. The Clinton impeachment dealt with Public Policy as to whether or not Americans wanted to do this. We did not. One would begin to think that these events, like civil war, the great depression, and various large events were very timely?

Let us now look at the more recent history on what has happened with regards to governments and nations losing their sovereignty and control. The bankruptcy that put the nail in the sovereignty coffin was the one in 1933. Let us look into the United States Congressional Record, dated March 17, 1993. It is Volume 33, page H-1303. The Speaker is James Traficant, Jr. of Ohio addressing the House. This is what he says:

'Mr. Speaker, we are here now in Chapter 11. Members of Congress are official trustees presiding over the greatest reorganization of any Bankrupt entity in world history, the U.S. government. We are setting forth hopefully, a blueprint for our future. There are some who say it is a coroner's report that will lead to our demise. It is an established fact that the United States federal government has been dissolved by the Emergency Banking Act, March 9, 1933, 48 Stat. 1, Public Law 89-719; declared by President Roosevelt, being bankrupt and insolvent. H.J.R. 192, 73rd Congress in session June 5, 1933 – Joint Resolution to Suspend the Gold Standard and Abrogate the Gold Clause. This dissolved the Sovereign Authority of the United States and the official capacities of all United States governmental Offices, Officers, and Departments is further evidence that the United States federal government exists today in name only.'

'The receivers of the United States Bankruptcy are the International Bankers, via the United Nations, the World Bank and the International Monetary Fund. All United States Offices, Officials, and Departments are now operating within a de facto status in name only under Emergency War Powers.''

'With the Constitutional Republican form of government now dissolved, the receivers of the Bankruptcy have adopted a new form of government for the United States. This new form of government is known as a Democracy, being an established Socialist/Communist order under a new governor for America. This act was instituted and established by transferring and/or placing the Office of the Secretary of Treasury to that of the Governor of the International Monetary Fund. Public Law 94-564, page 8, Section H.R. 13955 reads in part: The U.S. Secretary of Treasury receives no compensation for representing the United States'.''

The Treasury appointed receiver in the bankruptcy was defined in Reorganization Plan, No. 26, 5 U.S.C.A. 903; Public Law 94-564; Legislative History, page 5967. The Secretary of the Treasury is the 'Governor' of the International Monetary Fund Inc. of the U.N. If you care to look this up you can check out Public Law 94-564, supra, page 5942. There is also the U.S. government manual 1990/91, pages 480-81, and Treasury Delegation Order No 150-10.

On October 28th, 1977, the United States as a 'Corporator' and 'State' declared insolvency. State banks and most other banks were put under control of the 'Governor' of the 'Fund', namely the International Monetary Fund. Since March 9th, 1933, the United States has been in a state of declared national emergency. When congress declares an emergency, there is no constitution. A majority of people of the United States have lived all of their lives under emergency rule. For forty years, freedoms and governmental procedures guaranteed by the constitution have in varying degrees been abridged by laws brought into force by states of national emergency. This is right in the Senate Reports if you care to look.

Under this, the President may do a lot of nasty things. He can seize property, organize commodities, assign military forces abroad, institute Martial law, seize and control transportation and communication, regulate operation of private enterprise, restrict travel, and in a plethora of particular ways control the lives of all American citizens. This is documented in senate reports, senate resolutions, and executive order signed by President Clinton.

Bankruptcy is not a difficult thing to comprehend, for when you are bankrupt, you are not exactly in a negotiating position. The leaders gave their rights away because they had no choice. Now all the banks report to the Federal Reserve that then reports to the IMF that is part of the United Nations. So in the larger picture, the U.S. is just like any bankrupt company, obligated by contract to pay the debts. All the powers they have are internal and these powers must make sure they abide by the wishes of the IMF, the ultimate creditor.

This is why on U.S. money it says 'This note is legal Tender for all debts, public and private' and on the Canadian notes state 'This note is legal Tender?' It used to say 'Will pay the bearer on demand'. Today we have people's labour being exchanged for checks as payment for the labour pre-given, making it pre-paid. You have to work first to get paid second. Although there is technically an exchange of labour for paper, the perception of the value of money is misunderstood by almost everyone but the top bankers. The only reason money is in existence and or in your pocket, purse, bank account where ever, is because you had to work to get it, steal it or win the lottery. In other words, the money called legal tender is backed by the labour of the people or it simply would not exist, and it could not exist any other way. It's not the money they want you to pay back that is important to them. It is the assets you create at the wholesale manufacturing price level that they have or hold title to in the end that is of interest to the banks. The asset has far greater value than the piece of paper you get paid with.

Money is now backed by nothing but our faith in it and the goods we exchange it for. Someone else has put labour energy into producing it to satisfy the requirements of the buyers and consumers. Since money is backed by labour only, it could be said then that people are assets. In fact, have you ever heard a company say its employees are its biggest assets? If a company has no employees it can't have any assets. People come before material assets because people make the material assets. The truth of the matter is people are the only energy assets, which brings us to the cause of all our problems in life today. This is even more so today than ever as the debts of countries increase at an unstoppable rate. The result is that less purchasing power and more work is required for a losing gain, which is an oxymoron but true. The national bankruptcies in U.S.A and Canada made it impossible to pay any debt with real sustenance as money, and legal tender became valueless. It was the only way to pay. This act made it impossible for anyone to pay off a debt, and no debt has been extinguished since. The bankruptcy was declared because there were no more assets available to make the interest payments that the banks would accept. To compensate for this lack of valuable assets, the governments agreed to pledge the future labour of the people, knowing full well that the assets created by the people would be exchanged happily for debt money paper.

In Canada, the Bank of Canada Act that bank ceased honouring dominion notes on March 11 1935. There are orders in council wherein gold was removed temporarily in 1934, 1933 and 1932, and led to the Bank of Canada non redemption of notes in 1935. You cannot find a Canadian quote similar to the H.J. Roosevelt bankruptcy in the U.S.A. But in March 1935, money was declared no longer redeemable, which means the bank was no longer responsible for buying it back and never has been since. The very place that issues the money doesn't even want the stuff. The bank knows it has no value, and that it represents the labour you gave in exchange for it.

In reality, both U.S. and Canada went bankrupt. The factual bankruptcy of the U.S. took place in 1931 and in Canada it was 1933 with the Act of Westminster. The Bank of Canada is the watchdog here and they are controlled from outside so the bankruptcy was implemented through the banking system universally throughout North America. And this all changed from a gold backed money system to just paper. Gold and silver were such powerful money during the founding of America that the founding fathers declared only gold or silver coins could be money in America. Since gold and silver coinage was heavy and inconvenient for a lot of transactions, they were stored in banks and a claim check was issued as a money substitute. People traded their coupons as money, or currency. Currency is not money, but a money substitute. Redeemable currency must promise to pay a dollar equivalent in gold or silver money. That was the old system. But as you have already noted, Federal Reserve Notes or FRN's, make no such promises, and are not real money. A Federal Reserve Note is a debt obligation of the federal United States government, not money. The federal United States government and the U.S. Congress were not, and have never been authorized by the constitution for the United States of America to issue real currency.

It is essential that we comprehend the distinction between real money and a paper money substitute. One cannot get rich by accumulating money substitutes. One can only get deeper into debt. *We the people'* no longer have any money. Most Americans have not been paid any money for a very long time, perhaps not in their entire life. Now do you comprehend why you feel broke? You are really bankrupt, along with the rest of the country paying off a legacy of debt? We are simply using what we believe to be real money and accept it in exchange for goods.

Federal Reserve Notes are unsigned checks written on a closed account. These FRN's are an inflatable paper system designed to create debt through inflation. This is the same as devaluation of currency. Whenever there is an increase of the supply of a money substitute in the economy without a corresponding increase in the gold and silver backing, inflation occurs. Inflation is an invisible form of taxation that irresponsible governments inflict on their citizens. The Federal Reserve Bank that controls the supply and movement of FRN's, has access to an unlimited supply, paying only for the printing costs of what they need. FRN's are nothing more than promissory notes for U.S. Treasury Securities or T-Bills. These are just a promise to pay the debt to the Federal Reserve Bank.

One must also understand that there is a fundamental difference between paying and discharging a debt. To pay a debt, you must pay with value or substance such as gold, silver, barter, or a commodity such as labour. With FRN's, you can only discharge a debt. You cannot pay a debt with a debt currency system. You cannot service a debt with a currency that has no backing in value or substance. No contract in Common law is valid unless it involves an exchange of *'good and valuable consideration'*. So in the system it is like an endless cycle of debt.

You have to go back to the purpose here. Remember the U.S., like Canada, is broke and in receivership. The banking system in North America reports to the Federal Reserve that is a private system with ownership outside of the U.S.. They obviously did not have any choice. The Federal Reserve System is based on the Canon law and the principles of sovereignty protected in the constitution and the Bill of Rights. In fact, the international bankers used something called a *'Canon Law Trust'* as their model, adding stock and naming it a *'Joint Stock Trust'*. The US congress had passed a law making it illegal for any legal person to duplicate a Joint Stock Trust in 1873. The Federal Reserve Act was legislated post-facto to 1870, although post-facto laws are strictly forbidden by the constitution.

This was part of the deal like being subject to rules of a ship once you get on. The Federal Reserve System is a sovereign power structure separate and distinct from the federal United States government. The Federal Reserve is a maritime lender, and/or maritime insurance underwriter to the federal United States operating exclusively under Admiralty/Maritime law. The lender or underwriter bears the risks. The Maritime law compelling specific performance in paying the interest or premiums is the same.

This becomes the reality of the Matrix. Now here is where we start to get down to the bottom of this. Assets of the debtor can also be hypothecated as security by the lender or underwriter. That means you pledge something as a security without taking possession of it. The Federal Reserve Act stipulated that the interest on the debt was to be paid in gold. There was no stipulation in the Federal Reserve Act for ever paying the principle.

Prior to 1913, most Americans owned clear, allodial title to property, free and clear of any liens or mortgages. Then the Federal Reserve Act of 1913 came in. Subsequently all property within the federal United States was hypothecated to the Board of Governors of the Federal Reserve, in which the trustees or stockholders held legal title. The U.S. citizen or tenant, or franchisee, was then registered as a beneficiary of the trust via his/her birth certificate. In 1933, the federal United States hypothecated all of the present and future properties, assets and labour of their subjects to the Federal Reserve. That's all the citizens under the 14th Amendment.

In return, the Federal Reserve System agreed to extend the federal United States corporation all the credit *'money substitute'* it needed. So they could print more debt anytime they liked; what a deal! It opened an equivalent of a big line of credit. Like any other debtor, the federal United States government had to assign collateral and security to their creditors as a condition of the loan. Since the federal United States didn't have any assets, they assigned the private property of their economic slaves, the US citizens as collateral against the un-payable federal debt. They also pledged the unincorporated federal territories, national parks, forests, birth certificates, and non-profit organizations, as collateral against the federal debt. All has already been transferred as payment to the international bankers.

Unwittingly, America has returned to its pre-American Revolution, feudal roots whereby all land is held by a sovereign and the common people had no rights to hold real, you call it allodial title, to property. This sounds like we are just tenants renting our own property from the Federal Reserve Bank and this has been going on for over eighty years without the informed knowledge of the American people, without a voice protesting loud enough. That's why you buy and hold titles, not the real thing. Now it's easy to grasp why America is fundamentally bankrupt.

We are reaping what has been sown by our leaders, and the results of our harvest is a painful bankruptcy. This includes a foreclosure on American property, precious liberties, and a way of life built on paper. Few of our elected representatives here or in Washington, D.C. have dared to tell the truth or are even aware of it. The federal United States is bankrupt. Our children will also inherit this un-payable debt as we have.

Now, who is the real creditor that holds the debt? Who holds the countries to ransom? There has been much speculation about who owns the Federal Reserve. It has been one of the great secrets of the century because the Federal Reserve Act of 1913 provided that the names of the owner banks be kept secret. However, R. E. McMaster, publisher of the newsletter 'The Reaper', asked his Swiss banking contacts which banks hold the controlling stock in the Federal Reserve. The federal system is, by the way, a private corporation #62 domiciled in Puerto Rico. The answer to who owns the Fed and by proxy the entire U.S.A, is the Rothschild Banks of London and Berlin, the Lazard brothers Bank of Paris, the Israel Moses Sieff Banks of Italy, the Warburg Bank of Hamburg and Amsterdam, the Lehman Brothers Bank of New York, the Kuhn Loeb Bank of New York, the Chase Manhattan Bank of New York, and the Goldman Sachs Bank of New York, the biggest banks on the planet.

In **The Secrets Of The Federal Reserve**, **Eustace Mullins** indicates that because the Federal Reserve bank of New York sets interest rates and controls the daily supply and price of currency throughout the U.S., the owners of that bank are the real directors of the entire system. Mullins states that "*The shareholders of these banks which own the stock of the Federal Reserve bank of New York are the people who have controlled our political and economic destinies since 1914. They are the Rothschilds, Lazard Freres (Eugene Mayer), Israel Sieff, Kuhn Loeb Company, Warburg Company, Lehman Brothers, Goldman Sachs, the Rockefeller family, and the J.P. Morgan interests*".

Also consider that the IRS is not a U.S. government agency. It is an agency of the IMF. Next, the IMF is an agency of the UN. Third, the U.S. has not had a treasury since 1921, it is the IMF. In the U.S., social security numbers are issued by the UN through the IMF. The application for an SSN is the SS5 form. The Department of the Treasury, really the IMF, issues the SS5, not the U.S. Social Security administration. The new SS5 forms do not state who or what publishes them. The earlier SS5 forms state that they are Department of the Treasury forms. You can get a copy of the SS5 you filled out by sending form SSA-L996 to the SS administration Here's another little tidbit about social security that will help. You probably didn't know that in the U.S., a social security check comes directly from the IMF. You can check this by looking at it. Written on the top left is United States Treasury.

How does this affect the individual? Take this down to where it affects you, your own property. Read the deed to the property that you think is yours. You are listed as a tenant. You basically don't own anything and there is probably very little you can do except be less accepting of what you are told is the truth about what you own.

But in forming your opinion, be aware of a few more interesting facts. Britain is owned by the Vatican. This is what the Treaty of 1213 was all about. The Pope can abolish any law in the United States, as stated in the Elements of Ecclesiastical Law Volume 1, pages 53-54. A 1040 form is for tribute paid to Britain as stated in the IRS Publication 6209. The Pope claims to own the entire planet through the laws of conquest and discovery. It looks like we are all human capital by Executive Order 13037. Just type Executive Order 13037 into Google and read for yourself. The UN has financed the operations of the United States government for over 50 years and now owns every man, women and child in America. The UN also holds all of the land in America in fee simple. Should I go on? This is the inheritance that your fathers and fore fathers bequeathed to you. The question is whether you will also bequeath it to the next generation.

Money And The Banking System: The Real Power

Let us go as far back as 2000 BC when Babylon flourished in the land of Sumer or Shinar. Then we will work forward to the present day following the history of banking, commerce and the evolution of law. Of particular importance is how bankers, originally known as money changers, evolved to control commerce. It is also important to see how the legal system evolved in parallel to support the threads that ended up binding most of our current civilizations into commerce. This will dovetail with what we have talked about before, particularly on the taxes, then we will look at who this is applied to the individuals.

A long way back in history, as we have already revealed, Babylon had a modern system of life with canals to irrigate their land for agriculture, indoor toilets, city sewage systems and public restrooms. They even had a city-to-city postal system with baked clay letters and envelopes. Babylon even had a judicial system where judges wore black robes, just as they do today. Then, because their idols became gold, silver and greed, they began to fall into disgrace but continued to rule until they were destroyed. They had a system of commerce that included coined money, banks, receipts, titles, seals, signing and merchant law which evolved into Roman law, then into Civil law and later became Maritime law. Bear this in mind as we travel forward to our present time. That which was created then still forms the foundation for today. Those who crafted these laws, codes, and the money system, which for lack of better description, were the "gods" who translated their ways and knowing through the high priests, lords, Kings and Queens through a preferred bloodline.

Around 1000 AD, goldsmiths that are the same as banks learned to leverage money. They took in gold as a deposit and loaned out more receipts as loans than they had gold in reserve knowing it was unlikely that everyone would want to take out their gold at once. This was the birth of fractional reserve banking. Recognizing the immense power here, Henry I, in 1100, took the money power away from the money changers and established the tally stick system which lasted nearly five hundred years. On a different evolutionary path involving people's rights and the emergence of law and order, it was around 1066 that the Normans, under William the Conqueror, subjugated the English people and established a royal dynasty, which still occupies the throne of England to this day. The Normans imposed on the English a system of Ruler's law which destroyed the rights of the people, resulted in the confiscation of much of their land, and inflicted a system of cruel oppression on the people that was virtually unendurable.

It is important to understand in this evolution of sovereign rights that there have always been those upper echelon hierarchies who prefer dominion over others, attempting to take away sovereignty and freedom for their own benefit, and there have always been those freedom fighters looking to improve their rights and sovereignties. This sea-saw evolution still goes on today most obvious in the financial equality. and it is within this context than many inroads had been made to liberate the rights of free men.

Because King John was one of the most cruel and ruthless Norman kings, the barons united their forces and compelled him to sign the famous Magna Charta under the threat of beheading him if he did not sign. By now, the Magna Charta not only returned to the people many of the rights which the conquerors had stolen away, it also acknowledged that the king himself, was subject to the law. And so the rights were instilled forever. So the Magna Charta not only refers to the rights of the barons, but also makes frequent reference to the rights of English freemen. The American founders counted themselves as freemen and invoked the Magna Charta as a covenant on the part of the king and his heirs so those rights would be respected. This initial victory in the partial recovery of their rights became a critical step in our history. So this is why the Magna Charta is part of the basis of our laws in America.

The foundations of parliamentary government began to develop around 1265. And this gradually developed into a legislative voice to represent the desires of the people. It also provided a bargaining tool to regain some of the lost powers of the people and limit the tyrannical powers of the king. The parliament regained the right to have no taxation without the approval of the people's representatives. They also established the principle that there would be no laws imposed on the people that had not been fully approved by the parliament. Finally, the parliament secured the right to impeach the arrogant and abusive officers of the king whenever it could be shown that they had violated the law in the exercise of their high office.

On the banking side, was there not a crucial point in this evolution around 1600 AD when Queen Elizabeth took control of the money supply and issued her own coin against the wishes of the money changers? Then, Oliver Cromwell, financed by the money changers, had King Charles killed. This plunged England into debt from wars and he took over the city of London. The private money changers wanted control again. The debt from the war was their opportunity. In 1688 AD, the money changers financed William of Orange of the Netherlands to overthrow the Stewart kings, and took possession of the English throne. In 1694 AD, England became monetarily exhausted after fifty years of war with France and Holland. These people had learned a long way back that financing a war was a way to get a grip on the enemy.

As part of the plan the private Bank of England was then formed and secured itself with politicians and their laws to protect the bank and the debt. But the kings needed more money to finance their wars and had to give more and more power to parliament, Yes, that means taxation. The old tally system was then attacked by the private Bank of England and it was replaced with a private money system which took away the power of the king to control money.

And the Elite group of bankers, whom you have already met, behind the private bank were very cunning at financing special conflicts that resulted in huge debts. Then they were on the spot to be of service – for a heavy price of course. They had learned from the Templars. And if there are those that are smarter from a business, or commercial point of view, guess who takes control? It simply becomes a business opportunity to those smarter. In 1698 AD, the English debt then rocketed from one and a quarter million pounds to sixteen million pounds within a few short years. Then in 1748 AD, Amshel Bauer in Germany opened a goldsmith shop under the name of Red Shield. In German tongue this is pronounced Roth chield, or Rothschild, the history of which we have already covered.

The Evolution Of Code Of Law

Now, on the law side of the story, we have another picture forming. During the reign of two German kings over England, namely George I and George II, between 1714 and 1760, the parliament was left on its own more than ever before. The government was run almost entirely by the king's prime minister. This meant that he and the other members of parliament serving in the prime minister's cabinet could appoint all of the officials and have a relatively free hand in running the government. This brought England to the status of a limited monarchy with a parliament system of government that allowed the legislature to exercise practically unlimited power.

With all these tyrants and taxes, many frustrated Europeans began the migration to America in order to find spiritual and social freedom. It was only in America that Englishmen acquired the advantages. America, of course, was part of the English colonies. But this was where the first opportunity for local or provincial assemblies was developed. It was where the people elected the delegates instead of the dictators. This was first inaugurated in Virginia as early as 1619. As the colonies gained in economic and political strength, they demanded the full recognition of their rights as Englishmen.

It was at this time that the colonies asserted their unalienable rights of self-government by issuing the Declaration of Independence of 1776 to the king of England. The people of America then confederated together as the United States. Their form of government was a confederated republic, where the states remained supreme. Prior to the Revolution of 1763 most commerce was done by barter and also by paper money printed by different states. All of it, however, was based on the production of goods and services created by the people. It was later after the constitution was adopted in 1789, only gold and silver coin could be used as money in the United States. This was all very good and it set the scene for creating one of the most powerful nations on the planet. So they could carve out their own freedoms uninhibited by the British rule but they still had to pay taxes to the king.

But this was also the way to get out of the grip of oppressive taxes, dictators and regulations. America, by the Declaration of Independence of 1776, declared war on England. However, most people do not realize that the primary reason for the war was not *"taxation without representation"*, but the forced payment of taxes to the King in gold not paper money. America was then flourishing by using their own fiat money system based only on their production - not a gold based system that could be manipulated by the king. The king could not control the fiat money system of the U.S. and therefore passed a law requiring them to pay taxes in gold only. As the king had most of the gold and the colonies had little, unemployment ensued. The embittered souls cried for war.

Although America did win the revolutionary war with England, there was a malfunction in the plans for America. Money powers were waiting at the gate from the beginning. To answer why, let us go back in history to a date of January 1, 1788. The United States as a government was in default to the crown of England to the tune of eighteen million plus interest. As a direct and proximate result the U.S. corporate government was bankrupt in their private capacity from the start of the constitution. Then, the debt had to be paid for a period of seventy years. After a period of seventy years, according to the Bible res judicata and stare decisis, God said America could come out of bankruptcy with England on December 31, 1858. And let's say as an operation of law, at that time some notice was given to the nation that might have gone something like this: *"Excuse me, do you people really want to leave Babylon and have your liberty back now, or would you prefer to maintain the Crown of England as your master and serve him faithfully?"* Suppose it was something along those lines. Look at Leviticus 3:17, which says that if you love your master and your period of service is up, you can go to the judges, recite the fact that you love your master and you don't want to leave him, you can choose to serve him for the rest of your life, and you've just placed yourself into voluntary servitude. So in the year of 1858, after December 31st, the crown of England, through its attorney agents, gave notice to the country, *"Hey, you guys want to leave Babylon and go back to original jurisdiction, or do you want to have your government remain under us?"*

Apparently, the southern states did not wish to remain under slavery and walked out of congress. Evidently what happened is the people failed to give Notice of Lawful Protest, which was their acquiescent vote to remain in Babylon under the crown of England with continuing debt plus a reorganization of government. Now you are under a new law forum because the old law forum was entitled to liberty and freedom. The south walked out, ending the public side of the constitution. The people did not protest in any manner because they were busy fighting the civil war, therefore we had to create a new law forum that all people volunteered into, to go on for another seventy years of captivity.

Although the British Empire, as a world government, lost the American revolution, the power structure behind it did not lose the war. The most visible of the power structure identities was the East India Company, owned by the bankers and the crown in London, England. This was an entirely private enterprise whose flag was adopted by Queen Elizabeth in 1600 which happened to have thirteen red and white horizontal stripes with a blue rectangle in its upper left-hand corner.

While the British government lost the war in 1776, the East India Company's owners constituted a portion of the invisible, sovereign power structure (banks) behind the British government. They were able to move right into the new U.S.A economy, together, and in close association with America's most powerful landowners. It was a matter of bribery and trickery so in fact, representatives from the commercial Elite, namely the international bankers and their representatives, came in at influential levels in the states.

As a side note there is a site **http://100777.com/myron** where the infiltration through the Masons and the Illuminati representatives is revealed by a fellow named **Myron Fagan**. Some of these he names as Thomas Jefferson, founder of the Democratic party, Alexander Hamilton, and many other prominent U.S. leaders. But the idea was to get into influential positions at the top and in both parties so it really didn't matter who got in, the private Elite had a foot in the door either way.

The leaders, after winning the war, started to craft their U.S. constitution that was adopted March 4 1789. George Washington was then elected president in April of 1789. Six documents became the basis and guidelines in creating their constitution. It is important to know at this point that any constitution must have some prior reference to establish it. Based on this premise, any and every constitution thereafter must have an enabling clause. From this point onward, no constitution may diminish, in any manner, those rights already established in the six documents. Next, the people of the various states created the state governments for the protection of their rights. They delegated certain authority from the people powers by and through the state constitutions in order that the three branches of government could properly carry out the dictates outlined in the constitutions to protect their rights.

It was here that the states created the United States. The American constitution created a new structure of government that was established on a much higher plane than either the parliamentary system or the confederation of states. It was a people's *constitutional republic* where a certain amount of power was delegated to the confederation of states and a certain amount was delegated to the federal government. The United States, by way of the Congress of the United States, had certain powers delegated by the constitution. So far as the several states party to the constitution was concerned, the United States could not exercise power not delegated by the constitution. All power not delegated to the United States by the constitution was reserved to the confederation of states within their respective territorial borders, or to the people.

Behind the scenes, the constitution was pushed and supported by the private bankers through their associates. They had a plan for their own control over the United States of America. Had the articles of confederation been completed and adopted, instead of the constitution, the bankers would have far less control than they achieved. In fact, THE UNITED STATES, in capital letters is like the name of a corporation and it consists only of the ten miles square of Washington, District of Columbia, its territories of Guam, Samoa, Mariana Islands, and Puerto Rico. Yes, one of the god's key strongholds.

One of the powers granted in the federal constitution is to the congress in Article 1, section 8, clause 16 and 17. Clause 16 stated: "*To exercise exclusive legislation in all cases whatsoever, over such district (not exceeding ten mile square) as may, by cession of particular states, and the acceptance of congress, become the seat of government of the United States, and to exercise like authority over all places purchased, by the consent of the legislature of the state in which the same shall be, for the erection of forts, magazines, arsenals, dock-yards, and the needful buildings'*. Clause 17 then stated: '*'To make all laws which shall be necessary and proper for carrying into execution the foregoing powers, and all the new powers vested by this constitution in the government of the United States, or in any department or officer thereof*". This means congress has absolute; or what is described as plenary power.

This is municipal, police power, and the like. But, pay attention to this. Where does congress have such plenary power? You may be surprised to hear that this is only within the geographical area of the District of Columbia, and all forts, magazines, arsenals, dockyards, and other needful buildings within a few states. The United States is an abstraction. It exists only on paper. It is a total fiction. It exists as an idea. But it as a corporation is totally owned private subsidiary of BRITAIN INC and PLANET EARTH. The various Republic States of the Union exist in substance and reality. The United States only takes on physical reality after congress positively activates constitutionally delegated powers through statutes enacted in accordance with Article I section 7 of the constitution.

It's important to remember the US Congress does have the right to make all laws regarding Washington D.C. within the ten miles square and territories owned by the United States. This tiny scope of legislative powers is the only authority relating to people of the various states.

Let us go back to President Washington. Here is where the story thickens. William Morris, with the help of Alexander Hamilton, an alleged "*plant of the Illuminati*" who was the Secretary of Treasury, heavily promoted the First National bank, secretly known as the Bank of England (the old Babylon reincarnated), to legislation in order to create a private bank. In 1781, Congress chartered this First National bank for a term of twenty years, to the same European bankers that were holding the debts before the war. The bankers loaned worthless, un-backed, non-secured printed money to each other to charter this first bank. So the U.S. was not really severed. They still owed money to the bankers.

After thousands of lives were lost fighting a war to get control of their own money, why did congress contract with the same bankers that started the revolutionary war in the first place? Very simple. Since the crown (Rothschild) was the creditor, they demanded a private bank to hold the securities of the United States as the pledged assets to the crown of England in order to secure the debt to which the United States had defaulted. The holder of the securities was the private bank. So under public international law, the creditor nation forced the United States to establish a private bank to hold the securities as the collateral for the loan. As throughout history, Babylon follows wherever we go.

In 1785 AD, the youngest Rothschild, Nathan, expanded his wealth to twenty thousand pounds in a fifteen year period by using other people's money. An increase of twenty-five thousand percent. Now that may not seem like much but it is the principle of money growth and interest that they used that was impressive. In 1787 Amshel Rothschild made the famous statement: "*Let me issue and control a Nations money and I care not who writes the laws.'* Thomas Jefferson stated, *'If the American people ever allow the previous banks to control the issue of their currency, first by inflation then by deflation, the banks and the corporations which grow up around them will deprive the people of all property until their children wake homeless on the Continent their fathers conquered."* We just don't think in international or global commerce where the Elite are quite comfortable, orchestrating control not on bankrupt people, but on nations. It's all the same game, just like bankruptcies and takeovers are a daily thing in business.

In 1790 (August 4), Article One of the U.S. Statutes at Large, pages 138-178, abolished the States of the Republic and created Federal Districts. In the same year, the former States of the Republic reorganized as Corporations and their legislatures wrote new State Constitutions, absent defined boundaries, which they presented to the people of each state for a vote... the new State Constitutions fraudulently made the people "Citizens" of the new Corporate States through the 14th Amendment-remember? A Citizen is also defined as a "corporate fiction."

About this time these Elite are getting to be a pretty powerful banking force in Europe. In 1798 AD, the five Rothschild brothers expanded by opening banks in each of the major cities of Europe. These were opened in Germany, France, and Britain. Now remember the charter for the private bank in the U.S. was for only twenty years. This was until 1811. But what happened in 1812? The War of 1812. What did England attack? It was Washington, D.C. Yes, the ten miles square where they burned the White House and other buildings. Yet the attack by England on the ten miles square was not an act of war. What cause the war was the United States not extending the First National bank into the Second National bank to continue to maintain the securities on the unpaid debt. At least this so according to international law. So when the United States did an act of war by not giving the lawful creditor the securities in a peaceful manner, the only remedy open under international law to the creditor was to come in on letters of marque and seize the assets to protect their loan. Did the Second National bank get approved? Absolutely. After England attacked the nation that was in default, they saw the light and enacted the Second National bank. This power held for another twenty years, which was to expire about 1836.

By this time, the Elite are well entrenched in the international legal system. It has already been stated what the meaning of Attorney means. It means with obligation to the courts and to the public, *not to the client,* and wherever the duties of his client conflict with those he is obligated to as an officer of the court in the administration of justice, the former must yield to the later. All attorneys owe their allegiance first to the crown of England, next to the courts and then to the public and finally, to their clients. The BAR is the acronym for British Accreditation Regency. Attorneys are members of the BAR. The American Bar Association is a branch of the Bar Council, sole bar association in England. All laws, today in America, are copyrighted property of a British company, all state codes are private, commercial, British-owned *'law'*. All attorneys follow instruction from England. Attorn means to twist and turn over their clients to the private law of the bankruptcy. That is their job. That is their pledge to those whom they owe allegiance. Note also that by definition, the obligations and duties of attorneys extend to the court and the *'public'* (government) before any mere *'client'*. Clients are wards of the court and therefore persons of unsound mind. Just ask an attorney to see if they are aware of this. Attorneys are actually like an external police force making sure the external deals are honoured. Thus, laws and code written in the city of London (the tax free one) can be imposed on any other corporation within the corporate umbrella without question.

So note that the War of 1812 was waged mostly in Washington, D.C. The British burned all the repository buildings, attempting to destroy all records of the new United States in

Washington, D.C. Thus, the war of 1812 was partly waged to prevent the passage and enforcement of the new amendment. Most book repositories throughout the states were burned to the ground and all records destroyed. There's a famous painting in Washington D.C. It can be found in many books, depicting the British boarding a ship after they surrendered. The painting showed the British carrying their rifles as they mounted the gangplank. The truth is they lost a battle but a different war was won. As a result of the accumulated debt of waging that war, a new bank charter was issued for another twenty years.

But then a new kid hit the block. President Andrew Jackson put an end to this second charter in 1836. Jackson's reasoning was simple. He said the constitution does not delegate authority for congress to establish a national bank. Jackson's rationale has never been seriously challenged, and the constitution has never been amended to authorize congress to establish a national bank. Nor, for that matter, does the constitution delegate authority for the United States to establish corporations, particularly private corporations. So there was not a national bank established in America for more than 75 years, until 1913 called the Federal Reserve Bank. Andrew Jackson did an excellent job. What did congress do with Andrew Jackson? They impeached him because congress is made up mostly of attorneys and representatives of the Elite.

The attorneys have a title of nobility to the crown of England. So congress is populated by attorneys who are titles of nobility to the crown of England. It would seem logical to assume congress represents the bankers. The bankers hired an assassin to kill Andrew Jackson using two pistols. However, the plot failed as both pistols misfired. Andrew Jackson violated public international law because he denied the creditor his just lien rights on the debtor. However, the bankers did not lend value or substance so in actuality they had an unperfected lien and the law actually did not apply.

In 1845, Congress passed legislation that would ultimately allow Common Law to be usurped by Admiralty Law. The yellow fringe placed at the bottom of court flags shows this is still true. Before 1845, Americans were considered sovereign individuals who governed themselves under Common Law.

Andrew Jackson stated that: "*Controlling our currency, receiving our public money, and holding thousands of our citizens in dependence would be more formidable and dangerous than a military power of the enemy.*" He knew what was going on.

In following this story, in 1860-61, the southern states walked out of congress. Abraham Lincoln was elected president. The south walked out and declared their states rights pursuant to the constitution. Slavery was only window dressing for the Civil War. The war had nothing to do with slavery. It had to do with state's rights and the national debt to the bankers. The south wanted to be redeemed from the crown in England. The north wanted to remain under their dominion and their debt. When the south walked out of congress, this ended the public side of the split constitution as far as the government was concerned. What remained of the government was the private side, the democracy under the rule of the bankers.

In 1860 Congress was adjourned Sine Die. And so Lincoln could not legally reconvene Congress.

When this new leader President Lincoln came into power, by Executive Order 1, on April 15, 1861 he proclaimed the equivalent of the first **Trading With the Enemy Act.** President Lincoln stated: "*The government should create, issue, and circulate all currency and credit needed to satisfy the spending power of the government and the buying power* of consumers.' Further, he quoted, *'The privilege of creating and issuing money is not only the supreme prerogative of government, but it is the governments' greatest opportunity*." He obviously wanted to restructure the U.S. and the debt and the order to put the nation under Marshall law would lead to a new structure.

And so in 1861, President Lincoln declared a National Emergency and Martial Law, which gave the President unprecedented powers and removed it from the other branches. This has NEVER been reversed.

In 1863, Lincoln established the **The Lieber Code of April 24, 1863,** also known as Instructions for the Government of Armies of the United States in the Field, General Order No 100, or Lieber Instruction signed by President Abraham Lincoln. He knew full well what was coming and thus prepared for it. He placed our "trust" in the hands of the military as the proper authority to protect us, America, as the first Bank Act of 1863 began the road to Banksterville. However, those who were interested in gaining access to all the gold and other wealth had another plan, which directly is related to the civil war and the assassination of Abraham Lincoln.

Reading the "Lieber Code" one will learn important directly related evidence of the who, what, when, where, why and how this corruption against America was invented, and spread throughout Europe and Asia like a malignant cancer. Reference **http://unmasker4maine.files.wordpress.com/2011/05/lieber-code.pdf**)

The London bankers were quite worried about Abraham Lincoln's plan to create money. This potentially took the wind out of their private sails, losing control of money. They published an article in the **London Times – Hazard Circular** in 1865 regarding fiat money in America: "*If this mischievous financial policy, which has its origins in North America, shall become endurrated down to a fixture, then that government will furnish its own money without cost. It will pay off debts and be without debt. It will have all the money necessary to carry on its commerce. It will become prosperous without precedent in the history of the world. The brains, and the wealth of all the countries will go to North America. That country must be destroyed or it will destroy every Monarchy on the globe.*" Check it out on **www.xat.org/xat/usury.html.**

This certainly hit the nail on the head as to how to get out of the grip. This is exactly what the U.S. and Canada need to do now to get rid of this debt to the IMF. It was smart of Lincoln to figure that out then. They could wipe out any link to the private money guys and start on their own. But in 1865, Lincoln was murdered because he defied the bankers by printing interest free money to pay for the war efforts. In 1865, the capital was moved to Washington, D.C., a separate country – not a part of the United States of America.

This Lieber Code was established but used to the bankers advantage taking away your property and your rights. As a side note, it is quite simple to see that the courts have been employing one side of the military code against the general public, thus employing administrative rules, but did not acting within the policies, procedures and/or guidelines of those rules. And so the courts have come to employ civil rules and procedures failing to follow even those policies and procedures. The courts, police, sheriff, judges et al, were hired or appointed as Constitutional employees to act in good behavior and within the boundaries of the law, and having had taken an oath to uphold the same, but have in many instances, the judges in every instance, knowingly violated the very essence of the Constitution, breaching their own contract.

So the government operated fully under the authority of private law dictated by the creditor. In 1871 the default again loomed and bankruptcy was eminent. So in 1871, the ten miles square was incorporated in England. They used the constitution as their by-laws. Not as authority *under* the constitution but as authority *over* the constitution. They copyrighted not only the constitution but also many names such as, THE UNITED STATES, U.S. THE UNITED STATES OF AMERICA, U.S.A and many other titles as their own. This is the final blow to the original constitution. From here on out, the UNITED STATES was governed entirely by private corporate law, dictated by the banks as creditors.

From 1864-1867, Several Reconstruction Acts were passed forcing the states to ratify the 14th Amendment, which made everyone slaves indirectly. For, following the Civil War, Congress submitted to the states three amendments as part of its Reconstruction program to guarantee equal civil and legal rights to black citizens. The major provision of the 14th amendment was to grant citizenship to "*All persons born or naturalized in the United States,*" thereby granting citizenship to former slaves. Another equally important provision was the statement that "*nor shall any state deprive any person of life, liberty, or property, without due process of law; nor deny to any person within its jurisdiction the equal protection of the laws.*" The right to due process of law and equal protection of the law now applied to both the Federal and state governments. On June 16, 1866, the House Joint Resolution proposing the 14th amendment to the Constitution was submitted to the states. On July 28, 1868, the 14th amendment was declared, in a certificate of the Secretary of State, ratified by the necessary 28 of the 37 States, and became part of the supreme law of the land.

Congressman John A. Bingham of Ohio, the primary author of the first section of the 14th amendment, intended that the amendment also nationalize the Federal Bill of Rights by making it binding upon the states. Senator Jacob Howard of Michigan, introducing the amendment, specifically stated that the privileges and immunities clause would extend to the states "*the personal rights guaranteed and secured by the first eight amendments.*" Historians disagree on how widely Bingham's and Howard's views were shared at the time in the Congress, or across the country in general. No one in Congress explicitly contradicted their view of the Amendment, but only a few members said anything at all about its meaning on this issue. For many years, the Supreme Court ruled that the Amendment did not extend the Bill of Rights to the States.

Not only did the 14th amendment fail to extend the Bill of Rights to the states; it also failed to protect the rights of black citizens. One legacy of Reconstruction was the determined struggle of black and white citizens to make the promise of the 14th amendment a reality. Citizens petitioned and initiated court cases, Congress enacted legislation, and the executive branch attempted to enforce measures that would guard all citizens' rights. While these citizens did not succeed in empowering the 14th amendment during the Reconstruction, they effectively articulated arguments and offered dissenting opinions that would be the basis for change in the 20th century.

This Amendment XIV states as follows:

Section 1. All persons born or naturalized in the United States, and subject to the jurisdiction thereof, are citizens of the United States and of the state wherein they reside. No state shall make or enforce any law which shall abridge the privileges or immunities of citizens of the United States; nor shall any state deprive any person of life, liberty, or property, without due process of law; nor deny to any person within its jurisdiction the equal protection of the laws.

Section 2. Representatives shall be apportioned among the several states according to their respective numbers, counting the whole number of persons in each state, excluding Indians not taxed. But when the right to vote at any election for the choice of electors for President and Vice President of the United States, Representatives in Congress, the executive and judicial officers of a state, or the members of the legislature thereof, is denied to any of the male inhabitants of such state, being twenty-one years of age, and citizens of the United States, or in any way abridged, except for participation in rebellion, or other crime, the basis of representation therein shall be reduced in the proportion which the number of such male citizens shall bear to the whole number of male citizens twenty-one years of age in such state.

Section 3. No person shall be a Senator or Representative in Congress, or elector of President and Vice President, or hold any office, civil or military, under the United States, or under any state, who, having previously taken an oath, as a member of Congress, or as an officer of the United States, or as a member of any state legislature, or as an executive or judicial officer of any state, to support the Constitution of the United States, shall have engaged in insurrection or rebellion against the same, or given aid or comfort to the enemies thereof. But Congress may by a vote of two-thirds of each House, remove such disability.

Section 4. The validity of the public debt of the United States, authorized by law, including debts incurred for payment of pensions and bounties for services in suppressing insurrection or rebellion, shall not be questioned. But neither the United States nor any state shall assume or pay any debt or obligation incurred in aid of insurrection or rebellion against the United States, or any claim for the loss or emancipation of any slave; but all such debts, obligations and claims shall be held illegal and void.

Section 5. The Congress shall have power to enforce, by appropriate legislation, the provisions of this article.

It all looks well and good but the clever trick here is that citizens and persons are not the real thing and if you believe it is, and contract accordingly, it is indeed attached to you as reality. So the bottom line: if you want the benefit of being citizen or person, by the acceptance of the benefit, you are fully employed by the UNITED STATES Inc., a subsidiary of PLANET EARTH, just like other nations.

And so in 1871, The United States became a Corporation with a new constitution and a new corporate government, and the <u>original constitutional government was vacated to become dormant, but it was never terminated</u>. The new constitution had to be ratified by the people according to the original constitution, but it never was. The whole process occurred behind closed doors. The people are the source of financing for this new government. Keep this in mind when reading Part 2 because we have a vast move to regain and reinstitutes the original republic. See the site **www.republicoftheunitedstates.org** which will be discussed there.

Then, in 1909, default loomed once more. The U.S. government went to the crown of England and asked for an extension of time. This extension was granted for another twenty years on several conditions. One of the conditions was that the United States allow the creditors to establish a new national bank. This was done in 1913, with the Federal Reserve Bank. This, along with the 16th Amendment, collection of Income tax enacted February 25, 1913, and the 17th Amendment enacted May 31, 1913, were the conditions for the extension of time. The 16th and 17th Amendments further reduced the states power. The UNITED STATES adopted the Babylonian system.

In 1917 the people were again drafted into the First World War. The debt accumulated so that it became impossible to pay off the debt in 1929. This was the year of the stock market crash and the beginning of The Great Depression. The stock market crash moved billions of dollars from the people to the banks. This provided an opportunity to removed cash from circulation. Hence the change in currency to debt. Those who still possessed any cash invested in high interest yielding treasury bonds driven higher by increased demand. As a result, even more cash was removed from circulation from the general public to the point where there was not enough cash left in circulation to buy the goods being produced. Production came to a halt as inventory overcrowded the market. There were more products on the market than there was cash to buy them. Prices plummeted and industries plunged into bankruptcy, throwing millions more people out of work and out of cash. Foreclosures on homes, factories, businesses and farms rose to the highest level in the history of America. A mere dime was literally salvation to many families now living on the street. Millions of people lost everything they had, keeping only the clothes on their backs.

In 1917, the Trading with the Enemy Act (TWEA) was passed. This act was implemented to deal with the countries we were at war with during World War I. It gave the President and the Alien Property Custodian the right to seize the assets of the people included in this act and if they wanted to do business in this country they could apply for a license to do so. By 1921, the Federal Reserve Bank (the trustee for the Alien Property Custodian) held over $700,000,000 in trust. Understand that this trust was based on our assets, not theirs.

All this gave the international bankers a pretty sweet opportunity. In Europe, in 1930, the International Bankers declared several nations bankrupt, not just the United States. Then in 1933, President Roosevelt was elected and took office. His first act as president was to declare, publicly, the United States bankrupt. He further went on to issue his Presidential Executive Order on March 5th, 1933 that all United States citizens must turn in all their gold in return for Federal Reserve notes. This was passed into law by congress on June 5th, 1933.

And so in 1933, 48 Stat 1, of the TWEA was amended to include the United States Person because they wanted to take people's gold away. Executive Order 6102 was created to make it illegal for a U.S. Citizen to own gold. In order for the Government to take gold away and violate Constitutional rights, we the people were reclassified as ENEMY COMBATANTS.

In 1933, there was another United States bankruptcy. In the first bankruptcy the United States collateralized all public lands. In the 1933 bankruptcy, the U.S. government collateralized the private lands of the people (a lien) – they borrowed money against private lands. They were then mortgaged. That is why we pay property taxes.

From a speech in Congress in The Bankruptcy of the United States Congressional Record, March 17, 1993, Vol. 33, page H-1303, Speaker Representative James Trafficant Jr. (Ohio) addressing the House states:

"...It is an established fact that the United States Federal Government has been dissolved by the Emergency Banking Act, March 9, 1933, 48 Stat. 1, Public Law 89-719; declared by President Roosevelt, being bankrupt and insolvent. H.J.R. 192, 73rd Congress m

session June 5, 1933 - Joint Resolution To Suspend The Gold Standard and Abrogate The Gold Clause dissolved the Sovereign Authority of the United States and the official capacities of all United States Governmental Offices, Officers, and Departments and is further evidence that the United States Federal Government exists today in name only.

The receivers of the United States Bankruptcy are the International Bankers, via the United Nations, the World Bank and the International Monetary Fund. All United States Offices, Officials, and Departments are now operating within a de facto status in name only under Emergency War Powers. With the Constitutional Republican form of Government now dissolved, the receivers of the Bankruptcy have adopted a new form of government for the United States. This new form of government is known as a Democracy, being an established Socialist/Communist order under a new governor for America. This act was instituted and established by transferring and/or placing the Office of the Secretary of Treasury to that of the Governor of the International Monetary Fund. Public Law 94-564, page 8, Section H.R. 13955 reads in part: "The U.S. Secretary of Treasury receives no compensation for representing the United States...

Prior to 1913, most Americans owned clear, allodial title to property, free and clear of any liens of mortgages until the Federal Reserve Act (1913) "Hypothecated" all property within the Federal United States to the Board of Governors of the Federal Reserve, in which the Trustees (stockholders) held legal title. The U.S. Citizen (tenant, franchisee) was registered as a "beneficiary" of the trust via his/her birth certificate. In 1933, the Federal United States hypothecated all of the present and future properties, assets, and labour of their "subjects," the 14th Amendment U.S. Citizen to the Federal Reserve System. In return, the Federal Reserve System agreed to extend the federal United States Corporation all of the credit "money substitute" it needed.

Like any debtor, the Federal United States government had to assign collateral and security to their creditors as a condition of the loan. Since the Federal United States didn't have any assets, they assigned the private property of their "economic slaves," the U.S. Citizens, as collateral against the federal debt. They also pledged the unincorporated federal territories, national parks, forests, birth certificates, and nonprofit organizations as collateral against the federal debt. All has already been transferred as payment to the international bankers.

Unwittingly, America has returned to its pre-American Revolution feudal roots whereby all land is held by a sovereign and the common people had no rights to hold allodial title to property. Once again, we the People are the tenants and sharecroppers renting our own property from a Sovereign in the guise of the Federal Reserve Bank. We the People had exchanged one master for another.

The people turned in all the gold at that time. Why? Were they United States citizens? No. They were still a sovereign people until that time. They just *thought* that they were required to turn in all the gold. In reality, only those people living in Washington, D.C., and the 14th Amendment citizens were so required. People were still sovereign and were not under the jurisdiction of the United States of America that was incorporated in 1871. When the people turned in the gold, they just volunteered into the jurisdiction of the ten miles square of Washington D.C. and their laws. They became 14th Amendment citizens. Their birth certificates and the title to their bodies were registered in the Commercial Registry. This title to bodies, all of their property and all of their future labour, was pledged to the international bankers as security for the money owed in bankruptcy. This was done under the authority of commercial law that is exactly the same as Babylonian law by and through title. The American people were not in bankruptcy. Only the corporate UNITED STATES was in bankruptcy.

And so it came to pass that it was only the politicians and the ten miles square of Washington, D.C. the UNITED STATES CORPORATION that went into bankruptcy, and not the American people.

In 1944, Washington D.C. was deeded to the International Monetary Fund (IMF) by the Breton Woods Agreement. The IMF is made up of wealthy people that own most of the banking industries of the world. It is an organized group of bankers that have taken control of most governments of the world so the bankers run the world. Congress, the IRS, and the President work for the IMF. The IRS is not a U.S. government agency. It is an agency of the IMF. (Diversified Metal Products v. IRS et al. CV-93-405E-EJE U.S.D.C.D.I., Public Law 94-564, Senate Report 94-1148 pg. 5967, Reorganization Plan No. 26, Public Law 102-391.)

This was the beginning of the states losing the remainder of their sovereignty. It was not until 1944 that the corporate states lost all their power over the corporate United States with the Buck Act. With this Act, the states became, 14th Amendment Citizens as well. This completed the destruction of the corporate states having any power to protect against usurpation by the U.S. government. The corporate states then went under the jurisdiction of Washington, D.C.

The New Subjects Under "The Law"

How did everyone become a '*subject*' of the artificial UNITED STATES and their Code of Law written in the city of London? The U.S. corporation has no more power over people than does the Taco Bell Corporation. It is because as citizens and persons, they themselves became corporations, as we shall reveal in the next chapter.

It must be understood that the march to a uniform commercial law system has assisted the process control through the adoption of the Uniform Commercial Code by all states in 1964 and a number of other like laws and acts were incorporated into this nation. This made the Uniform Commercial Code, the supreme law of the land. This code has prevailed for a long time, back to Babylonian times and will be discussed in Part 2.

We can see throughout our history that Babylon, their commerce and Merchant law has followed wherever productive people go. The bankers were waiting in the wings when we founded this country. It was only two years after the constitution was enacted that the bankers threw the people into bankruptcy. The newly founded government moved over to the side under the ten square mile that congress controlled.

In 1860, the southern states walked out of congress. This officially ended the lawful side of the constitution. Then in 1871, the ten square miles and its territories, that congress controlled was incorporated in England and the constitution was adopted as the by-laws of that corporation. This ended, completely, the constitution. The people no longer had a constitution.

THE UNITED STATES, as a corporation, created in England, came under the jurisdiction of England, or mor appropriately ENGLAND INC. This entitled England to create laws as England saw fit, establish those laws in THE UNITED STATES and everyone who at that time was a 14th Amendment citizen was subject to obey those laws. This also placed the Congress of THE UNITED STATES above that portion of what we think is the constitution, not under the authority of the constitution. The only Bill of Rights left at this point in time is some amendments. That is all the courts are required to take cognizance of when you appear in their courts.

Then the merchants of Babylon were able to keep the US debt current, and the bankers, moved from the establishment of the First National bank deeper into the nation by the creation of the Federal Reserve Bank in 1913. The 1929 stock market crash and the great depression that followed placed the American people in desperation, homelessness, poverty and even starvation. The minds of the people were focused on survival. They were then in a condition to accept any handout given by the government, no matter what the cost to their freedoms.

It was then that Roosevelt treasonously placed this entire nation into socialism. Socialism is a class of ideologies favoring a socio-economic system in which property and the distribution of wealth are subject to social control. As an economic system, socialism is associated with collective ownership of the means of production. This control may be either direct — exercised through popular collectives such as workers' councils or cooperatives — or it may be indirect — exercised on behalf of the people by the state. The modern socialist movement had its origin largely in the working class movement of the late 19th century. In this period, the term socialism was first used in connection with European social critics who condemned capitalism and private property. For Karl Marx, who helped establish and define the modern socialist movement, socialism implied the abolition of money, markets, capital, and labor as a commodity.

People were drawn in as 14th Amendment citizens through the registration of their birth certificates. People were further enticed deeper into that system by volunteering for many other licenses and privileges given by the government. People were also made enemies of THE UNITED STATES. This act gave the UNITED STATES authority, under the laws of war and as a captured people, to force anything on the people they choose to create.

Thereafter, the people sank further into communism. If you read the ten planks of communism you'll discover that this nation has fulfilled every plank successfully. The Internet is full of this, but you can go to sites like ***www.libertyzone.com/Communist-Manifesto-Planks.html*** and read about how the Americans are actually following this. It may not be so obvious to you and we have already covered this earlier but in a nutshell the planks are:

1. abolition of private property and the application of all rents of land to public purposes.
2. heavy progressive or graduated income tax.
3. abolition of all rights of inheritance.
4. confiscation of the property of all emigrants and rebels.
5. centralization of credit in the hands of the state, by means of a national bank with State capital and an exclusive monopoly.
6. centralization of the means of communications and transportation in the hands of the State.
7. extension of factories and instruments of production owned by the state, the bringing into cultivation of waste lands, and the improvement of the soil generally in accordance with a common plan.
8. equal liability of all to labour. Establishment of industrial armies, especially for agriculture.
9. combination of agriculture with manufacturing industries, gradual abolition of the distinction between town and country, by a more equitable distribution of population over the country. And ten is free education for all children in public schools, with

abolition of children's factory labour in its present form and a combination of education with industrial production.

It is an insidious process. And although, as you will come to understand, the physically property you believe you hold is represented by a "title" or "certificate" that is simply a piece of paper just like your dollar bill. In 1976, congress removed any semblance of justice in the court system. From this point forward, the *officers of the court* can construe and construct the laws to mean anything they chose them to mean. As 14th Amendment citizens, people are not citizens of the America they have always thought. They are actually citizens of England, through the corporation of THE UNITED STATES.

Today, as in ancient Babylon, and the Elite, the idol of worship is money, like Federal Reserve notes. It was Rothschild who said his god was money and the Earthling has gravitated to the same belief (except those who say money is evil) There is no law today except as fiction of copyrighted statutes, to be interpreted by judges who construe and construct whatever they choose to have those statutes enforced. The banking system evolved to create a larger and larger fake money empire, while the legal system evolved along with a perception of improved human rights. They waited in the wing to use this to take over nations through the creation of corporations and fictional entities where they are attaching their own laws and acts to the bankrupt nation. Human rights have actually deteriorated because we have given these away to satisfy our greed for money. Commerce is the thread that binds us as well as nations.

In 1976, Congress took away any semblance of law or justice left within our court system. All law today is now construed, constructed and made up by the judge as it happens before your very eyes. They took away any control or authority we might have had over the court system. You can check out Senate Bill 94-204 which deals with the court system and Senate Bill 94-381 dealing with public law. This has been very well hidden from all of us. Many of us going into court often wonder why and how the courts can simply override the laws we put into our paperwork. It's very simple now that we know how they do it. They operate on the words *'construe and construct'*.

A simple word such as *'in'* changed to *'at'* as in *'at law'* or *'in law'* has a totally separate meaning. For example, if you're <u>in</u> the river, you are wet and you can swim. But if you're <u>at</u> the river, you might enjoy a refreshing picnic, play baseball or run races. See the difference a simple word can make? And, the attorneys often change this word when they answer your motions – in addition to many others. It will pay you in dividends to read the answers of attorneys to your paperwork. Compare what they say the case law says to the actual case law itself. You'll discover that they have actually changed the words therein. This is illegal you might say. No, not, according to the above Senate Bills. You see, they can now construe and construct any law or statute to mean whatever they decide it means, for their benefit. You don't know any of this. You think they are railroading you in a kangaroo court. No, they are *'legal'* in what they do. They usually follow the law to the letter; *their* law, private law, the law of contract, that you know nothing about. This law is called contract law.

If you don't understand the above and realize what law you are dealing with when you go into court, you will lose. They operate in total fiction, in la la land, in the Land of Oz. They can only recognize contracts. So, when you go into any court, be aware that it is their law, that the judge or the prosecutor can *'construe'* and *'construct'* that law in any fashion they choose. It will always mean what they choose it to mean. So, are the courts bound by the constitution? Law? Statutes? No, its contracts only and the statutes used to enforce the contracts. And when we use their statutes, constitution, Universal Commercial Code, rules and regulations, all copyrighted – without a license from the

BAR, we are in violation of copyright infringement and punishment is mandatory. There is NO law in this nation – or the world for that matter – there is only contract law.

Smart commerce rules the world. Dumb ones that spend money on wars and silly things like that to protect rights just get into debt and get taken over losing their freedoms a different way. Remember the satanic beliefs? It is just good business to take advantage of the dumb ones. And the thread that binds them is commerce, now an empire of debt money controlled by the founders of PLANET EARTH.

Now we are getting to the pith at the bottom of the pyramid. First, if you were born in the United States, your birth certificate was voluntarily given by your mother to the state and then entered into the Commercial Registry for registration, within the UNITED STATES. This, in commerce, gave title to your body by way of a constructive contract. This placed everyone as a member of the Babylonian system in every manner. This process will be detailed in a subsequent chapter.

So the people of the United States accept the bankruptcy attached to the UNITED STATES, the big Strawman (A fictitious business structure explained in a separate chapter) owned by ENGLAND. The government created an artificial *"person"*, just like a *"citizen"* an organization, a fictitious entity, and what we now know as an artificial entity. By and through an adhesion contract, the government then made the real man or woman, responsible for, and fiduciary for, and surety for, that artificial entity. This is how your artificial entity secured the National debt and through it, you became a 14th Amendment citizen of the UNITED STATES. All licenses and all existing contracts are made between the UNITED STATES or THE STATE OF whatever state or province in CANADA you live in and your artificial entity. That fictitious entity binds you to the UNITED STATES because they have, through adhesion contract, made you the real man or woman, fiduciary and responsible for that artificial entity. Of course, you voluntarily sign, and even request, all those contracts, don't you?

And all of these contracts you sign carry with it your agreement to obey and uphold all the laws, rules and regulations passed by the congress of the UNITED STATES CORPORATION and THE STATE OF whatever, and will be enforced against you. And these are enforced by the attorneys loyal to the crown.

From that day forward, people could never own any property because the state now had possession of it all. In 1964, the state obtained title to property. People can only rent their homes that they believe they own. They only have a certificate of title to the car they think they own. The state owns the true title to their homes and to their cars, to everything they thought or think they own. You married the state through your marriage license and your children became wards of the state. All of this was pledged, including all the fruits of your future labour, to the bankers as security against the national debt and was placed in the possession of the Secretary of State of each state as an agent for the trustee of the bankruptcy - The U.S. Secretary of Treasury.

To further tighten this process, when people applied for a social security number after 1935, they further volunteered to enter into a contract after the Social Security Act was signed into law. This process had many other ramifications to it as the actual corporate structure that was set up was a special trust. Similarly, many further contracts were entered into by applying for licenses – all voluntarily of course – for some perceived benefit.

The Establishment Of Human Capital

The story does not end here. In 1997, **Executive Order 1997, provided the nails in the coffins of the living man. Executive Order No. 13037 was a COMMISSION TO STUDY CAPITAL BUDGETING** Ex. Ord. No. 13037, Mar. 3, 1997, 62 F.R. 10185, as amended by Ex. Ord. No. 13066, Oct. 29, 1997, 62 F.R. 59273; Ex. Ord. No. 13108, Dec. 11, 1998, 63 F.R. 69175, provided: In it, President Clinton declared:

By the authority vested in me as President by the Constitution and the laws of the United States of America, including the Federal Advisory Committee Act, as amended (5 U.S.C. App.), it is hereby ordered as follows:

Section 1. Establishment. There is established the Commission to Study Capital Budgeting ("Commission"). The Commission shall be bipartisan and shall be composed of no more than 20 members appointed by the President. The members of the Commission shall be chosen from among individuals with expertise in public and private finance, government officials, and leaders in the labour and business communities. The President shall designate two co-chairs from among the members of the Commission.

Sec. 2. Functions. *The Commission shall report on the following:*
(a) Capital budgeting practices in other countries, in State and local governments in this country, and in the private sector; the differences and similarities in their capital budgeting concepts and processes; and the pertinence of their capital budgeting practices for budget decision-making and accounting for actual budget outcomes by the Federal Government;
*(b) The **appropriate definition** of capital for Federal budgeting, including: **use of capital for the Federal Government itself or the economy at large**; ownership by the Federal Government or some other entity; defence and nondefense capital; physical capital and intangible or **human capital**; distinctions among investments in and for current, future, and retired workers; distinctions between capital to increase productivity and capital to enhance the quality of life; and existing definitions of capital for budgeting;*
(c) The role of depreciation in capital budgeting, and the concept and measurement of depreciation for purposes of a Federal capital budget; and
(d) The effect of a Federal capital budget on budgetary choices between capital and noncapital means of achieving public objectives; implications for macroeconomic stability; and potential mechanisms for budgetary discipline.

Sec. 3. Report. The Commission shall adopt its report through majority vote of its full membership. The Commission shall report to the National Economic Council by February 1, 1999.

Sec. 4. *Administration.*
(a) Members of the Commission shall serve without compensation for their work on the Commission. While engaged in the work of the Commission, members appointed from among private citizens of the United States may be allowed travel expenses, including per diem in lieu of subsistence, as authorized by law for persons serving intermittently in the Government service (5 U.S.C. 5701-5707).
(b) The Department of the Treasury shall provide the Commission with funding and administrative support. The Commission may have a paid staff, including detailees from Federal agencies. The Secretary of the Treasury shall perform the functions of the

President under the Federal Advisory Committee Act, as amended (5 U.S.C. App.), except that of reporting to the Congress, in accordance with the guidelines and procedures established by the Administrator of General Services.

Sec. 5. General Provisions. The Commission shall terminate on September 30, 1999.

William J. Clinton

Dear Mr Clinton declared **capital; physical capital and intangible** *or* **human capital.** Just like in the Matrix, where the real humans became the power energy source for the machines, living in an illusion of freedom, the human became the source of energy as capital for the Empire of PLANET EARTH.

And so it has been that the UNITED STATES and CANADA have been and still are bankrupt, as are many other nations. And so it has been that the many leaders have been pawns to the events that seem to occur at very critical decision making times. It simply seems to be good business, following a very elegant business plan. There always seems to be another reason to borrow more money right at the critical times. And if you look back to the table of nations and their debts, this has been a pattern with all the major nations of the world.

And when you control the money of nations, this is really good business!

Let us look more closely at the thing called money.

15

COMMERCE AND MONEY, THE CHAINS OF CONTROL

Now it is necessary to understand more about money, or at least what we believe is money. Money is the true insidious weapon of dominion and conquest, and through the creation of the code of law, and the corporate structures which takes on that code, it is easy to see how, when one has become irresponsibly subject to debt, one is beholding to the creditor. And when that happens, bankruptcy is the flag that is waived for assistance from those who are the "creditors". Clearly, creditors dictate their own terms. As we have said before, if you look at North American money, it does not say "*will pay the bearer on demand*" any more. It means that money is a fictitious accounting unit to measure what we believe to be money. The ones who have control of this fictional money that measures debt now create and lend it by a keystroke of the computer. Here is the story on this and how the conversion took place. But first they had to take real money out of the system.

The Money Kingdoms

The New World Order business plan changed dramatically during the last bankruptcy cycle of 1929 to 1999 as we have seen. In the mythology of gods, these worshiped deities exhibited power to instil fear in humanity and so the dynasties were created. These gods, and their chosen ones had the power to create the fear in humans that kept them in control. as that control shifted, these deities super powers of mythology changed to the control of wealth to pay for armies that could take, support other dynasties. That power source has over the last thousands of years shifted to money because all civilizations recognize the power of money as it begets power. And so the business plan of PLANET EARTH shifted into the ways and means money could not only be continued to be accepted by people but it could be made out of thin air rather than having to scrounge in the earth for metals like gold to support some intrinsic value. In the last cycle, this process has been carefully orchestrated and decisively implemented so that a bank, and those in control can with the entry of a computer keystroke create money.

Let us delve into this and think back to the tables. First are the banks that have a license to create money via a keystroke.

Rank	Bank	AUM ($bn)
1.	Bank of America Merrill Lynch	$1,944,740,000,000
2.	Morgan Stanley Smith Barney	$1,628,000,000,000
3.	UBS	$1,559,900,000,000
4.	Wells Fargo	$1,398,000,000,000
5.	Credit Suisse	$865,060,000,000
6.	Royal Bank of Canada	$435,150,000,000
7.	HSBC	$390,000,000,000
8.	Deutsche Bank	$368,550,000,000
9.	BNP Paribas	$340,410,000,000
10.	JP Morgan Chase	$284,000,000,000
11.	Pictet	$267,660,000,000
12.	Goldman Sachs	$229,00,000,0000
13.	ABN AMRO	$220,060,000,000
14.	Barclays	$185,910,000,000
15.	Julius Bär	$181,680,000,000
16.	Crédit Agricole	$171,810,000,000
17.	Bank of New York Mellon	$166,000,000,000
18.	Northern Trust	$154,400,000,000
19.	Lombard Odier Darier Hentsch	$153,100,000,000
20.	Citigroup	$140,700,000,000

Then there are the nations who accept that the money created by these banks all under the private world bank and IMF can create real money.

Rank	Country	External US dollars
1	United States	15,570,789,000,000
2	United Kingdom	8,981,000,000,000
3	Germany	4,713,000,000,000
4	France	4,698,000,000,000
5	Japan	2,441,000,000,000
6	Ireland	2,378,000,000,000
7	Netherlands	2,344,296,360,000
8	Italy	2,223,000,000,000
9	Spain	2,166,000,000,000
10	Luxembourg	1,892,000,000,000

There are 200 countries listed accounting for at total debt of $76,729,529,173,000. Yes 76 trillion! These numbers are just numbers, and just like when you personally declare bankruptcy, what you owe is simply deleted and a new number and conditions are born. The titles to your assets are transferred but did someone pick up a truckload of money in wheel barrows? No. Over the last bankruptcy cycle the definition itself has been changed from hard money backed by intrinsic value, to soft money which is simply a piece of paper believed to have value. Yet, just as it is created by a keystroke, as in a bankruptcy or fail to pay, it can disappear with a keystroke.

A Story Of Money

Some of this will be a repeat of what has been already presented but it is important to understand how the system of debt drops down in the hierarchy of banking down to the individual called a "person". What we call money now is not money, and the only value it has is the value you and I give it. The pieces of paper you and I pass around are Federal Reserve Notes. They look like money to us because we have been told that they are money and because they spend like money, but they are not money. Money is meant to be a medium of exchanging value for value. And as long as the earthling believes this, it will have a value represented by the commodity it buys.

Money is any object or record that is generally accepted as payment for goods and services and repayment of debts in a given socio-economic context or country. The main functions of money are distinguished as: a medium of exchange; a unit of account; a store of value; and, occasionally in the past, a standard of deferred payment. Any kind of object or secure verifiable record that fulfills these functions can serve as money. Money is historically an emergent market phenomena establishing a commodity money, but nearly all contemporary money systems are based on fiat money. Fiat money is without intrinsic use value as a physical commodity, and derives its value by being declared by a government to be legal tender; that is, it must be accepted as a form of payment within the boundaries of the country, for *"all debts, public and private"*. The money supply of a country consists of currency (banknotes and coins) and bank money (the balance held in checking accounts and savings accounts). Bank money usually forms by far the largest part of the money supply. Real money is backed by intrinsic value such as gold and silver. So the medium of exchange, and the regulations surrounding the "money" has evolved from real intrinsic value (coins and gold) to bills, to a keyboard entry into a computer. To those who are authorized to make those entries, like the IMF and World Bank, this presents a wonderful control system of credit, which to those who have become bankrupt, becomes debt. Granted, as long as we can use it for the exchange of goods and services and believe it is money, everything is ok.

To understand the problem, let me explain how paper began to circulate as money: Imagine that you are in England around 1660, at a time when the only money is gold or silver coins. These are minted and put into circulation by the king. When the king is short of gold or silver and in need of something, he adulterates the money by diluting the gold with copper. The newly minted coins are the same size but with less gold. If the subjects refuse to accept these adulterated coins, no matter, the king merely has his court rule that the money is worth whatever he says it is worth. After all, he is the king.

Imagine you have worked hard and saved some money. Where will you put that money for safekeeping? In most communities there is a goldsmith who has a large iron box where he keeps his gold and silver "safe". You ask him to keep your gold and silver "safe", he agrees and you pay him a fee for his service. As proof that he has your gold and silver, he issues you a receipt. The next time you want to buy something, rather than first redeem your gold and then buy whatever you want, you use your gold receipt. It is quicker and easier. As long as the seller can go to the goldsmith and redeem the certificate for gold everything works out fine. This is probably how paper receipts began to circulate as money.

Now, place yourself in the position of the goldsmith. How long would it take you to figure out that very few people ever come at the same time to redeem their gold certificates? Maybe one day, like the king, you find yourself short of gold and silver. Could you say no to temptation, or would you tell yourself, *'I'll issue a gold receipt without any gold to back it up because, after all, who is going to check up on me. Besides, I'll have the gold in a few days to make it right'*.

You quickly learn that spending your own gold receipts causes certain unsettling questions to be asked. You come up with a new plan that gives you something for nothing but doesn't make it too noticeable: you loan gold receipts and collect interest. As long as you don't get too greedy, you can get away with this something for nothing scheme. Soon you and other goldsmith/bankers are lending four times as many paper receipts as you have in gold. This process of the goldsmith/bankers got a boost when the king of England was in need of a great deal of money to fight a war. The king turned to William Paterson.

Paterson and his friends pooled their resources and came up with £72,000 in gold and silver. But instead of lending the gold and silver directly to the king, they formed a bank and printed paper receipts equal to 16-2/3 more than their gold and silver reserves.

They lent the king £1.2 million at 8-1/3 % interest per year. Their yearly interest was £100,000. The king didn't care; he had a war to fight. After all, he would simply raise the taxes on his subjects to pay the interest. Paterson and his friends were protected. He had the foresight to lend his paper receipts to the government. Since these receipts were needed to fight a war, the king couldn't allow them to fail. He declared them legal tender. These receipts were now regarded the same as the gold for which they had stood. A new golden rule came into being: Them that have the gold rule!

Since paper money first began circulating, the situation has changed little. When the federal government wants more money, it borrows it from and through the private banking system, the Federal Reserve. The owners of the Federal Reserve are in no need of gold or silver to back up their loans to the government.

Their money is legal tender. Unlike Paterson's time, there is no gold or silver in the system. The bankers are still receiving something for nothing. And you, as a subject, give the bankers 1/3 of your time when you pay federal and social security taxes.

Most everyone knows that, at one time, our government actually had gold and silver backing our currency. Some people believe the gold and silver may still be there. Most people don't have a clue that a few, very rich individuals are in control of this country through their ownership of the privately owned Federal Reserve Banks.

To understand what is happening with our money today we need to refer to Article I, Section 8 of the U.S. Constitution which says: *"The Congress shall have Power to coin Money, regulate the Value thereof, and of foreign Coin, and fix the Standard of Weights & Measures."* It is important to understand that the "power to coin money" is just that, coin, not print, because if you have the power to print money you end up with paper money that is worthless - just as worthless as the goldsmith/bankers in England.

To ensure that no one but Congress had control of this country's money, the founding fathers also added Article I, Section 10 which reads: *"No State shall coin Money; emit Bills of Credit; make any Thing but gold and silver coin a Tender in Payment of Debts."* With these two articles of our Constitution in place, the founding fathers felt they had ensured the stability of the country's money supply.

In 1792 Congress passed the first Coinage Act which set the Standard Unit of Value and the ratio of gold to silver. A dollar of gold was defined as 24-8/10 grains pure 9/10 fine, and a coin dollar of silver at 371.25 grains .999 fine or 412.5 grains Standard Silver. Several times in our country's history Congress has enacted laws that have violated the Constitutional provision governing money. The last time Congress unlawfully turned over their responsibility to manage the country's money supply was with the enactment of the Federal Reserve Act in 1913. For a period of time, the Federal Reserve willingly exchanged gold and silver for paper certificates on demand. But as the depression of 1929 deepened, Congress passed a law making it unlawful to own gold, and the banks stopped redeeming paper money with gold in 1933. In 1968 all that was left supporting our money was silver, and that was removed by presidential order.

Today, there is no gold or silver backing up our money - only the full faith and credit of the United States government. The federal government has pledged you and your ability to earn money as collateral to the international bankers for over $4 trillion in loans. This is a great deal for the bankers. The bankers put up nothing, and you, as a slave, turn over to the bankers 1/3 of your income to pay your "fair share" of the federal income tax.

Your income tax does not pay for the running of the federal government. It pays the interest on the national debt - a debt that was created as a bookkeeping entry.

Local Banks And The Process Of Money Creation

The same process used by the top banking system does not stop with the owners of the Federal Reserve. It continues through our system and includes every bank, every savings & loan and every credit card company. The process reaches into every banking transaction that you have ever been a party to. All of them, without exception, extend the control of the bankers over our lives. It is all believed to be perfectly ok, legal, believed to be very much the standard norm.

Consider this scenario. You want to buy a used car. You arrange with your bank (bank A) for a loan. The banker gives you a check made out to the car dealer for $5,000. You give the check to the car dealer. The dealer turns the car over to you and deposits the $5,000 check into his bank (bank B). It happens all the time.

Now, let's take a deeper look at the transaction. Did any money leave the bank? No. The money never left the bank because the banker didn't give you any. He gave you bank credit.

The courts have ruled that "A check is not money" - School Dist v. U.S. Nat'l Bank, 211 P2d 723); "A check is an order on a bank to pay money" - Young v. Hembree, 73 P2d 393. The courts have further ruled that "National banks may lend their money but not their credit" - Horton Grocery Co. v. Peoples Nat'l Bank 1928, 144 S.E. 501, 151 Va. 195, because, unlike the Federal Reserve banks, local banks are not allowed by law to create money. The nations are all bankrupt, so how could a bankrupt entity be allowed to create money. However, they believe they do it all the time.

Bank credit is the biggest fraud going because it becomes the creation of bills of credit by private corporations for their private gain. This is one of the most important issues we have to face today because 95% of the nation's money supply consists of bank credit. Bank credit, unlike Federal Reserve Notes, is not something tangible that you can see or hold. The closest you will ever get to seeing bank credit is to look at your check book or credit card. Essentially, bank credit is nothing more than the creation of numbers which are added to your checking account in a bank's bookkeeping department. When you write a check, numbers called dollars are transferred from your checking account to someone else's checking account. The creation, transfer and use of bookkeeping entries as money is what bank credit is all about. Bank credit is first created when a banker hands you a check after you take out a loan. This check is not money, but a promise from the bank to pay you money. The bank might have enough money to cash your check, as long as everyone doesn't bring their checks in at the same time.

The basis for the fraud charge is that the bank has written a check against funds which do not exist. The banker gambles that you will use your checking account in place of cash. Most of the time the banker is right, people usually deposit the check they receive in their checking account and then spend it by writing other checks against the bookkeeping entries which have been added to their account. Most people do not know that a check is not money, that bank credit is not lawful money, and that the courts have consistently ruled against the banks for lending credit.

When the car dealer deposits your check into his account, bank B then has access to $5,000 more that it can make loans against. Modern banking regulations allow banks to loan up to 90% of all money deposited. With sleight of hand and the blessing of modern bookkeeping entries, bank B can now lend an additional $4,500. A different customer at bank B wants a loan. S/he borrows the $4,500 and deposits it in bank C. Now bank C can loan 90% of the $4,500 ($4,050). All the banks (A,B & C) charge interest on each of the loans. The process can go on indefinitely. The bank credit was created out of thin air. Most of us have several of these bank loans. Many of you have been forced into bankruptcy and forced to give up your homes because of this fraudulent system.

Suppose for a moment that you have bad or limited credit and you apply for a credit card. Given these circumstances, you would be required to put up some collateral. The bank would probably ask you to open a certificate of deposit (CD) for 125% of the credit card's credit limit. (If the credit card had a limit of $1,000, you would have to put up $1,250 in collateral).

Note that the bank has nothing to risk when you use your credit card. You have made the arrangements with the bank to lend you up to $1,000. You have promised to pay them according to the terms and conditions of the note you signed. The question is: Where does the bank get the money you borrowed?

The truth is that the PROMISSORY NOTE you signed is now an asset of the bank, and, based upon this PROMISE to pay, the bank created bank credit, which it lent to you. The bank doesn't reduce the amount of your CD as you make purchases or take out loans. As the bills come into the bank, it pays the merchant for your purchases by electronically transferring numbers in its computer. If for any reason you do not pay for your purchases, the bank has the authority to use the money in your CD to cover your credit card debt.

Look at a mortgage note. Suppose that you go to your bank to borrow money for a home. You fill out the application and the bank runs a check on you. You pass with flying colors and, next, you sign all the papers. Of course, you will have to make a deposit on your home, just like you did with the credit card. The bank will have you sign a PROMISSORY NOTE, called a mortgage, as you did with the credit card. The bank takes the title to your home as collateral, as it did with the CD. And if you default on your payments, the bank will foreclose on your home and sell it, just as they would use your CD to cover your credit card debt.

The same question arises: Where did the bank get the money it lent you for your home? Answer: It didn't lend you any money - it lent you its credit. Based on the asset of your signature on the PROMISSORY NOTE, the bank issued a check from the magic money machine which was accepted as money. What gave it value was your signature.

We know that a check is not money, but a PROMISE to pay money. That's why it needs your signature as the real guy to pay the promise. The bank lied to you. You thought you were borrowing money, and the bank lent you credit instead. In good faith, you entered into what you thought was an honest transaction, but the fact that the transaction was suspect was known only to the bank (and to the courts who have decided that it is illegal for a bank to lend its credit). In legal terms, you have been defrauded because your PROMISE to pay was backed by collateral (the title to your home), but their PROMISE to pay was backed by nothing (neither gold nor silver). In effect, the bank which risked nothing by lending you credit that it created, now has the title to your home.

So when your state is short of money, it also borrows from the banks. A state's PROMISE to pay is called a bond. These PROMISES to pay are based upon the state's ability to get you to pay. The bank accepts the bonds as an asset and does the same sleight of hand with the state that it did with you. It gives the state a check from the magic money machine. The state deposits the check back into the bank and writes more checks on the check. Again, ask yourself this: Did the bank lend your state any money in return for their PROMISE to pay? No! Once again the bank wrote a check, which is not money. And does the state actually make the promise to pay? The state is not real any more than the bank. They do it through you as they hand the responsibilities to the real people to cover the bonds they used as collateral. But a bond is just a piece of paper. The real value is back to you so somehow you have to be faked into providing that value.

Much of the money that your state collects from you in taxes goes toward paying the principal and interest on these fraudulent bank loans. You and I and our ability to pay, along with our property, homes, cars, etc., are pledged as collateral to the bankers for these loans. The bankers put up little of value. They use their magic money machine, and you and I pay and pay and pay.

A Short History Of Banking Evolution In America

In a previous chapter, the Illuminati and the House of Rothschild was brought forward as to how the Rothschilds have become so influential in being architects of the current banking system. Again, it is difficult to do justice to the research and evidence presented in many website but 2 stand out, namely the site **www.redicecreations.com/specialreports/2005/08aug/redshield.html** and **G. Edward Griffen** found at **www.realityzone.com/creature.html**. The following story is taken from the redicecreations site above and is somewhat repetitive of the previous discussion but it is important to bring forward this story as banking is the ultimate controlling force of all nations, in particular how it evolved in America. This treatment is presented by **Johnny Silver Bea**r at **www.Silverbearcafe.com**.

Once again. the "Illuminati" was a name used by a German sect that existed in the 15th century. They practiced the occult, and professed to possess the 'light' that Lucifer had retained when he became Satan. In an attempt to document the origins of an secret organization which has evolved into a mastodonic nightmare, successfully creating and controlling a shadow government that supersedes several national governments, and in whose hands now lay the destiny of the world, one must carefully retrace its history. The lengths to which this organization has gone to create the political machinery, and influence public sentiment to the degree necessary to propel its self-perpetuating prophecy, are, quite frankly, mind boggling. Yet the facts provide for the undeniable truth of its existence.

Amschel Bauer had a son, Meyer Amschel Bauer. At a very early age Mayer showed that he possessed immense intellectual ability, and his father spent much of his time teaching him everything he could about the money lending business and in the basic dynamics of finance. A few years after his father's death in 1755, Mayer went to work in Hannover as a clerk, in a bank, owned by the Oppenheimers. While in the employ of the Oppenheimers, he was introduced to a General von Estorff for whom he ran errands. Meyer's superior ability was quickly recognized and his advancement within the firm was swift. He was awarded a junior partnership. Von Estorff would later provide the yet-to-be formed House of Rothschild an entry into to the palace of Prince William.

His success allowed him the means to return to Frankfurt and to purchase the business his father had established in 1743. The big Red Shield was still displayed over the door. Recognizing the true significance of the Red Shield (his father had adopted it as his emblem from the Red Flag which was the emblem of the revolutionary minded Jews in Eastern Europe), Mayer Amschel Bauer changed his name to Rothschild (red shield). It was at this point that the House of Rothschild came into being.

Through his experience with the Oppenheimers, Meyer Rothschild learned that loaning money to governments and kings was much more profitable than loaning to private individuals. Not only were the loans bigger, but they were secured by the nation's taxes.

The House of Rothschild continued to buy and sell bullion and rare coins. Through their shrewd business transactions they successfully bought out or dismantled most of the competition in Europe. In 1769, Meyer became a court agent for Prince William IX of Hesse-Kassel, who was the grandson of George II of England, a cousin to George III, a nephew of the King of Denmark, and a brother- in-law to the King of Sweden. Before long, the House of Rothschild became the go between for big Frankfurt bankers like the Bethmann Brothers, and Rueppell & Harnier.

Meyer Rothschild began to realize that in order to attain the power necessary to influence and control the finances of the various monarchs in Europe, he would have to wrest this influence and power from the church, which would necessitate its destruction. To accomplish this, he enlisted the help of a Catholic priest, Adam Weishaupt, to assemble a secret Satanic order.

Adam Weishaupt was born February 6, 1748 at Ingoldstadt, Bavaria. Weishaupt, born a Jew, was educated by the Jesuits who converted him to Catholicism. He purportedly developed an intense hatred for the Jesuits. Although he became a Catholic priest, his faith had been shaken by the Jesuits and he became an atheist. Weishaupt was an ardent student of French philosopher Voltaire (1694-1778). Voltaire, a revolutionary who held liberal religious views, had written in a letter to King Frederick II, ("the Great"):

As the name implies, those individuals who are members of the Illuminati possess the 'Light of Lucifer'. As far as they are concerned, only members of the human race who possess the 'Light of Lucifer' are truly enlightened and capable of governing. Denouncing God, Weishaupt and his followers considered themselves to be the cream of the intelligentsia - the only people with the mental capacity, the knowledge, the insight and understanding necessary to govern the world and bring it peace. Their avowed purpose and goal was the establishment of a "Novus Ordo Seclorum" - a New World Order, or One World Government.

Through the network of the Illuminati membership, Meyer Rothschild's efforts were redoubled and his banking empire became firmly entrenched throughout Europe. His sons, who were made Barons of the Austrian Empire, continued to build on what their father had started and expand his financial influence.

During the American Revolution, the House of Rothschild brokered a deal between the Throne of England and Prince William of Germany. William was to provide 16,800 Hessian soldiers to help England stop the Revolution in America. Rothschild was also made responsible for the transfer of funds that were to pay the German soldiers. The transfer was never made. The soldiers were never paid, which may account for their poor showing. The Americans prevailed. At this point Meyer Rothschild set his sights on America. LCF Rothschild Group established by Edmond de Rothschild and presided over today by his son, Benjamin, is one of the most prominent organisations in the global financial sector.

Meanwhile Benjamin Franklin, having become very familiar with the Bank of England and fractional reserve banking, (see goldsmiths above), understood the dangers of a privately owned Central Bank controlling the issue of the Nation's currency and resisted the charter of a central bank until his death in 1791. That was the same year that Alexander Hamilton pushed through legislation that would provide for the charter of The First Bank of the United States. Ironically, the bank was chartered by the Bank of England to finance the war debt of the Revolutionary War. Nathan Rothschild invested heavily that first bank. He immediately set about to control all financial activity, between banks, in America.

There were a couple of problems, though. The U.S. Constitution put control of the nation's currency in the hands of Congress, and made no provisions for Congress to delegate that authority. It even established the basic currency unit, the dollar. The dollar was Constitutionally mandated to be a silver coin based on the Spanish pillar dollar and to contain 375 grains of silver.

This single provision was designed to keep the American money supply out of the hands of the banking industry. The Bank of England made several attempts to usurp control of the U.S. money supply but failed. Still, through their Illuminati agents, they continued to enlist supporters through bribery and kickbacks.

Any proponent of a fractional reserve banking system is an economic predator. During the next twenty years the country would fall prey to contrived financial havoc as a result of the bankers policies of creating cycles of inflation and tight money. During times of inflation the economy would boom, there would be high employment, and people would borrow money to buy houses and farms. At that point the bankers would raise interest rates and incite a depression which would, obviously, cause unemployment. People who could not pay their mortgages would have their homes and farms repossessed by the bank for a fraction of their true value. This is the essence of the Illuminati ploy, and it would recur, time and time again. In fact, it's still happening today.

By 1810, the House of Rothschild not only had a substantial stake in the Bank of the United States, they were quietly gaining control of the Bank of England. Although foreign owners were not, by law, allowed a say in the day to day operations of the Bank of the United States, there is little doubt that the American share holders and directors were, if not affiliated, complicit in the aims and goals of the Illuminati and their central bankers.

In 1811 the charter for the First Bank of America was not renewed. As a result, the House of Rothschild lost millions. This enraged Nathan Rothschild so much that he, almost single handily fomented the War of 1812. Using his formidable power and influence, he coerced the British Parliament to attempt to retake the Colonies. The first military attempt failed. The second strategy was to divide and conquer. Any serious historian will find that the Civil War was largely stirred up by Rothschild's illuminati agents in the United States.

Meyer Amschel Rothschild died on September 19, 1812. His will spelled out specific guidelines that were to be maintained by his descendants:

1) All important posts were to be held by only family members, and only male members were to be involved on the business end. The oldest son of the oldest son was to be the head of the family, unless otherwise agreed upon by the rest of the family, as was the case in 1812, when Nathan was appointed as the patriarch.

2) The family was to intermarry with their own first and second cousins, so their fortune could be kept in the family, and to maintain the appearance of a united financial empire. For example, his son James (Jacob) Mayer married the daughter of another son, Salomon Mayer. This rule became less important in later generations as they refocused family goals and married into other fortunes.

3) Rothschild ordered that there was never to be *"any public inventory made by the courts, or otherwise, of my estate... Also I forbid any legal action and any publication of the value of the inheritance."*

Nathan Mayer Rothschild, who, by 1820, had established a firm grip on the Bank of England stated:

"I care not what puppet is placed upon the throne of England to rule the Empire on which the sun never sets. The man who controls Britain's money supply controls the British Empire, and I control the British money supply."

The Second Bank of the United States, was also chartered by the Bank of England to carry the American war debt. When its charter expired in 1836, President Andrew Jackson refused to renew it, saying a central bank concentrated too much power in the hands of un elected bankers.

In 1838 Nathan made the following statement:

"Permit me to issue and control the money of a nation, and I care not who makes its laws."

During the first quarter of the nineteenth century the Rothschilds expanded their financial empire throughout Europe. They crisscrossed the continent with railroads, which allowed the transport of coal and steel from their newly purchases coal mines and iron works. Through a loan to the government of England, they held the first lien on the Suez Canal. They financed the Romanov dynasty in tsarist Russia, provided the funding that allowed Cecil Rhodes the opportunity to plunder and sack South Africa as well as the funding that allowed the government of France to plunder and sack North Africa.

In the years preceding the Civil War, a number of "Skull and Bones" Patriarchs were to become leaders in the Secessionist movements of various Southern States. It has been suggested that these pressures exacerbated an already tenuous situation, and set the stage for the fomentation of the Civil War. The Rothschild Banks provided financing for both the North and the South during the war. After the civil war, the more clever method was used to take over the United States. The Rothschilds financed August Belmont, Khun Loeb and the Morgan Banks. Then they financed the Harrimans (Railroads), Carnegie (Steel) and other industrial Titans. Agents like Paul Warburg, Jacob Schiff, Bernard Baruch were then sent to the United States to effect the next phase of the takeover.

By the end of the 19th. Century, the Rothschilds had controlling influence in England, U.S., France, Germany, Austria and Italy. Only Russia was left outside the financial sphere of world domination. England, through the Bank of England, ruled most of the world. Jacob Schiff, president of Khun Loeb Bank in New York was appointed by B'nai B'rith (A secret Jewish Masonic Order meaning "Bothers of the Convenent") to be the Revolutionary Leader of the Revolution in Russia. A cartel, made up of the Carnegies, Morgans , Rockefellers, and Chases would contribute to the manifestation of communism. On January 13, 1917, Leon Trotsky arrived in the United States and received a U.S. Passport. He was frequently seen entering the palatial residence of Jacob Schiff.

Jacob Schiff, and his supporters, financed the training of Trotsky's Rebel Band, comprised mainly of Jews from New York's East Side, on Rockefeller's Standard oil Company property in New Jersey. When sufficiently trained in the techniques of guerrilla warfare and terror, Trotsky's rebel band departed with twenty million dollars worth of gold, also provided by Jacob Schiff, on the ship S.S. Kristianiafjord bound for Russia to wage the Bolshevik revolution.

After the Bolshevik Revolution and the wholesale murder of the entire Russian royal family, Standard Oil of New Jersey brought 50% of the huge Caucasus oil field even though the property had theoretically been nationalized. In 1927, Standard Oil of New York built a refinery in Russia. Then Standard Oil concluded a deal to market Soviet Oil in Europe and floated a loan of $75 million to the Bolsheviks. Jacob Schiff and Paul Warburg at the Kuhn Loeb Bank started a campaign for a central bank in the United States. They then helped the Rothschild's to manipulate the financial Panic of 1907.

Then, the panic of 1907 was used as an argument for having a central bank to prevent such occurrences. Paul Warburg told the Banking and Currency Committee: 'Let us have a national clearing house'."

The Federal Reserve Act was the brainchild of Baron Alfred Rothschild of London. The final version of the Act was decided on at a secret meeting at Jekyll Island Georgia, owned by J.P. Morgan. Present at the meeting were; A. Piatt Andrew, Assistant secretary of the Treasury, Senator Nelson Aldrich, Frank Vanderlip, President of Kuhn Loeb and Co., Henry Davidson, Senior Partner of J.P. Morgan Bank, Charles Norton, President of

Morgan's First National of New York, Paul Warburg, Partner in Khun Loeb and Co. and Benjamin Strong, President of Morgan's Bankers Trust Co.

The Federal Reserve Act of 1913, brought about the decimation of the U.S. Constitution and was the determining act of the international financiers in consolidating financial power in the United States. Pierre Jay, Initiated into the "Order of Skull and Bones" in 1892, became the first Chairman of the New York Federal Reserve Bank. A dozen members of the Federal Reserve can be linked to the same "Order."

The Rothschilds operate out of an area in the heart of London, England, the financial district, which is known as 'The City', or the 'Square Mile.' All major British banks have their main offices here, along with branch offices for 385 foreign banks, including 70 from the United States. It is here that you will find the Bank of England, the Stock Exchange, Lloyd's of London, the Baltic Exchange (shipping contracts), Fleet Street (home of publishing and newspaper interests), the London Commodity Exchange (to trade coffee, rubber, sugar and wool), and the London Metal Exchange. It is virtually the financial hub of the world.

Positioned on the north bank of the Thames River, covering an area of 677 acres or one square mile (known as the "wealthiest square mile on earth"), it has enjoyed special rights and privileges that enabled them to achieve a certain level of independence since 1191. In 1215, its citizens received a Charter from King John, granting them the right to annually elect a mayor (known as the Lord Mayor), a tradition that continues today.

Des Griffin, in his book Descent into Slavery, described 'The City' as a sovereign state (much like the Vatican), and that since the establishment of the privately owned Bank of England in 1694, this financial center has actually become the last word in England's national affairs. He contends that the country is run by powers in 'the City' and that the throne, the prime minister, and parliament are simply fronts for the real power. E. C. Knuth, in his book Empire of the City, suggests that when the queen enters 'The City,' she is subservient to the Lord Mayor (under him, is a committee of 12-14 men, known as 'The Crown'), because this privately-owned corporation is not subject to the Queen, or the Parliament. The Rothschilds have traditionally chosen the Lord mayor since 1820.

The last national election in the United States provided its citizenry with a choice between two known members of a the same Satanic cult. And even then, the outcome of this election has come under extreme scrutiny. For further exploration into the 2004 Presidential election please follow this link to ***www.heartcom.org/20reasons.htm***

And so we arrive at the point of the Federal Reserve and the fatal bankruptcy of corporate UNITED STATES. To continue this story, this is taken from ***www.silverbearcafe.com/private/natureofmoney.html*** where Johnny Silver Bear documents how we moored and drifted into the economic abyss:

In 1878, in a rare state of clarity, Congress began to redeem "greenbacks" into gold which put the United States back on the gold standard until 1933. It was well known amongst intelligent politicians, (who have, apparently, remained in the minority), that the gold standard protected citizens against the controlling tendencies of the government by offering an absolute hedge against the depreciation or devaluation of the currency. Gold provided an agent of maintenance and liquidity within and beyond national borders. Above all, it raised a mighty barrier against authoritarian interferences through the manipulation of the economic markets. Within the constraints imposed by the gold standard, America's economy remained relatively healthy until 1913.

On December 23, 1913, the U.S. Congress passed the Federal Reserve Act, placing control of this nation's money into the hands of a private corporation. This corporation was made up entirely of bankers. Calling itself the Federal Reserve, so as to seem official, it replaced the national bank system. Treasury notes were recalled and Federal Reserve notes were issued with a promise to redeem them in gold on demand. The forces behind the Federal Reserve, (American and Western European banking interests), remained tethered by the limits imposed by the gold standard, but this would soon change.

In 1920, the 66th Congress passed the Independent Treasury Act.

In 1921, the United States Congress abolished the U.S. Treasury, and, as a result, all of our country's bullion and all other instruments of value, (i.e. moneys in trust funds and other special funds that had been kept in U.S. Treasury offices and vaults), were systematically transferred to the coffers of a private corporation!

From 1913, until 1933, under the authority of the U.S. Congress, the Federal Reserve held control of all of our country's gold. They then proceeded to loan us back our gold, at interest. We paid interest for the use of our own gold! What's wrong with this picture? What could have incited our Senators and Representatives to allow that to happen? In order to keep up with the ever rising debt service, we borrowed more of our own gold. We kept borrowing more and more of our own gold to pay more and more interest, until all the gold was gone. At that point, the country went bankrupt. as you have learned, what happened next was the bankers foreclosed on America.

On March 9, 1933, the U.S. declared bankruptcy, as expressed in President Franklin Delano Roosevelt's Executive Orders 6073, 6102, 6111, and 6260. On April 5th, 1933, one month after his inauguration, President Roosevelt declared a National Emergency that made it unlawful for any citizen of the United States to own gold, (see death penalty in website above), and "unconstitutionally" ordered all gold coins, gold bullion, and gold certificates to be turned into the Federal Reserve banks by May 1st under the threat of imprisonment and fines. This was technically, a national confiscation of gold and silver. This unlawful precedent set by Roosevelt would eventually lead us to the catastrophic situation we find ourselves in today.

Our bankrupt nation went into receivership and was reorganized in favour of its creditor and new owners, a private corporation of international bankers. (Since 1933, what is called the "United States Government" has been a privately owned corporation, and the property of the Federal Reserve/International Monetary Fund.)

Without a word of truth to the American people, **all our good faith and credit was pledged as the surety for the debt** by the same slime ball Congressmen who created the mechanism that allowed it to occur. Those Congressmen, knew such "De Facto Transitions" were unlawful and unauthorized, but were mysteriously coerced into sanctioning, implementing, and enforcing the complete debauchment of our monetary system, and the resulting changes in all aspects of government, society, and industry in the United States of America.

From the onset of the Federal Reserve, fractional reserve bankers set out to win the war of misinformation. They did this, in part, by attempting to advance the pseudo tenets of Keynesianism, monetarism, and supply-side economics.

John Maynard Keynes, although a great friend of the bankers, was probably the most heinous influence on freedom, liberty, and the free market in the 20th century. He was a

Fabian socialist and a Globalist, (is that redundant?), who provided an intellectual cover for inflationism. He is best known for authoring bogus economic theories, undermining Western values and philosophy, and providing a floor plan whereby the banksters could more easily deceive the people. It was Keynes who coined the phrase, "barbarous relic" in reference to gold. It was Keynes who desecrated the U.S. Constitution with almost every breath.

"Lenin was certainly right. There is no subtler, no surer means of overturning the existing basis of society than to debauch the currency. The process engages all the hidden forces of economic law on the side of destruction, and does it in a manner which not one man in a million is able to diagnose."

During the first half of the 20th century, each of four world leaders did the exact same thing within ninety days of their ascension to power. Each made it illegal for the citizens of their respective countries to own gold. Those leaders were: Mao, Stalin, Hitler, and Franklin D. Roosevelt. All four were acutely aware of the restrictions that a gold standard imposed on their abilities to wage war.

The bankers hate gold as money for the same reason. Gold as money acts as a barrier to the expansion of credit money. By pandering the lure of unlimited credit, the banksters went about recruiting politicians throughout the world. The opportunity to wage war on borrowed money turned out to be irresistible to Empire. Wars have always been very important to the banking cartels. They are very expensive. Time and time again, through loans to governments, the cartels have provided the funding for great conflicts. Imagine, being able to go to war with unlimited funds. Better yet, imagine the inability to go to war because of the lack of unlimited funds. The temptation extended to the power mongers was too great. The credit was made available with a single catch. The gist of the pitch went something like this:

"Sure we'll loan you all the money you want, on the condition that you enact laws making all the citizens of your individual countries responsible for the interest payments, through taxation"

One by one the leaders of every government on earth sold out, and agreed to demonetize gold, thereby allowing the continued power grab of the banking cartels through the issuance debt based currency. The result has been the methodical fleecing of the general population through the debasing of the dollar by 97%.

Side note: In 1792 the U. S. Coinage Act (see above website) was passed by Congress. **It invoked the death penalty for anyone debasing money** *and provided for a U.S. Mint where silver dollars were coined along with gold coins beginning in 1794. The text of Coinage Act of 1792 states: "The Dollar or Unit shall be of the value of a Spanish milled dollar as the same is now current," that is, running in the market, "to wit, three hundred and seventy-one and one-quarter grains of silver."*

On May 22nd, 1933, Congress enacted a law, against Constitutional mandate, declaring all coin and currencies then in circulation to be legal tender, dollar for dollar, as if they were gold. The President was unconstitutionally empowered to reduce the gold content to the dollar up to 50 percent.

On June 5th, 1933, Congress stabbed the gold standard out of existence by enacting a joint resolution (48 Stat. 112), that all gold clauses in contracts were outlawed and no one could legally demand gold in payment for any obligation due to him.

On January 30th, 1934, the Gold Reserve Act was passed, giving the Federal Reserve title to all the gold which had been collected. This act also changed the value/price of gold from $20.67 per ounce to $35 per ounce, which meant that all of the silver certificates the people had recently received for their gold now were worth 40 percent less.

On January 31st, 1934, after President Roosevelt fixed the dollar at 15 and 5/21 grains standard to gold. Russia and the central banks of Europe were very excited and began buying up gold in huge quantities. This planned redistribution of our country's wealth was one of the most important objectives of the Globalist's agenda. Thus a dual monetary system began which offered the gold standard for foreigners and Federal Reserve notes for Americans.

Between 1934 to 1963 all Federal Reserve notes issued had a promised to pay, or to be redeemed in "lawful money." Over a short period of time the wording on the Federal Reserve notes began to change until there was no redemption in silver promised. This was done slowly enough that the people didn't see it coming.

On November 2nd, 1963, new Federal Reserve notes with no promise to pay in "lawful money" was released. No guarantees, no value.

In 1965 silver in coins were reduced to 40 percent by President Lyndon Johnson's authorization.

President Lyndon Johnson issued a proclamation on June 24, 1968, that all Federal Reserve Silver Certificates were merely fiat legal tender and could not be redeemed in silver.

On December 31, 1970, President Richard Nixon signed into law an amendment to the Bank Holding Company Act, which, among other things, authorized the treasury to totally debase coins to a worthless value in non precious metal.

"Single acts of tyranny may be ascribed to the accidental opinion of a day. But a series of oppressions, begun at a distinguished period, and pursued unalterably through every change of ministers, too plainly proves a deliberate systematic plan of reducing us to slavery." - Thomas Jefferson.

Since the seventies, the unfettered issuance of debt money has continued to debase our currency more rapidly than ever before. In the last three years, the debasement has accelerated exponentially.

*"The abandonment of the gold standard made it possible for the welfare statists (government bureaucrats) to use the banking system as an unlimited expansion of credit. In the absence of the gold standard, there is no way to protect savings from confiscation through inflation... Deficit spending is simply a scheme for the "hidden" confiscation of wealth. Gold stands in the way of this insidious process." - **Alan Greenspan***

The world governments continue to babble that tired Keynesian rhetoric insisting that gold and silver have become obsolete, relics of the past. Yet in the 4th Quarter of 2006 global gold and silver demand was the highest on record, and, some of the world's largest investors are presently taking major positions in precious metals.

The cartel wants economic growth, lots of borrowers, and lots of opportunities to lend newly created funny money at interest. You can't blame them for wanting that. If I could print up all the funny money I wanted and could then lend it out at interest, I'd be happy too. That is, I would be happy to lend it if I didn't have a soul. The ravages of inflation have heretofore been thoroughly exposed and the results are blatantly apparent in our inability to successfully engineer our lives without debt. Fractional reserve banking has provided for the theft of the life blood of our nation.

Compounding the problem is the fact that the world is no longer capable of sustaining economic expansion. We are beginning to witness emerging nations, like China and India sucking up natural resources at a rate that is way past rechargeable. We are entering a period of civilization where the keyword is sustainability, not growth.

The debasement of our currency continues with abandon. The purchasing power of the dollar is quickly eroding. It is down 30% in the last three years. Conversely, the value of gold is up 30% in the last three years. Because the dollar is the reserve currency of world, every commodity, from rice to timber, from oil to precious metals, will continue to rise, priced in dollars.

The U.S.A. is currently breaking all records for the longest period of time that a nation's economy has endured after abandoning the gold standard. Our country has been foreclosed on in the past, and it's just about to be foreclosed on again. It's just a matter of time. The "endgame" is near.

"I believe that banking institutions are more dangerous to our liberties than standing armies... If the American people ever allow private banks to control the issue of their currency, first by inflation, then by deflation, the banks and corporations that will grow up around [the banks... will deprive the people of all property until their children wake-up homeless on the continent their fathers conquered. The issuing power should be taken from the banks and restored to the people, to whom it properly belongs." -- Thomas Jefferson -- The Debate Over The Re Charter Of The Bank Bill, (1809)

The Federal Government And The National Debt

And so the top dogs of PLANET EARTH Inc. have played their games financing conflict and controlling the nations money.

Now, let us return to the debt. When the local bank issues you money, it is following the same process engaged in by nations. The federal government issues a bond. The bond goes to the privately owned Federal Reserve Bank. The bond is a PROMISE to pay based upon the government's ability to collect taxes from you and me. Again, the bankers issue a check from the magic money machine. And again, you pay and pay and pay.

The Constitution says that money is gold or silver, probably because they are rare, and also because they require someone's labour to bring it to us in a form that we can use. This has never changed. The Constitution also says that only Congress has the authority to coin or regulate the value of money. We got into this mess because, for the third time in history in 1913, Congress committed treason to the Constitution by illegally turning over to a group of bankers, its responsibility to coin and regulate the value of money.

Consider that these Federal Reserve Notes are made out of paper (and cotton) and cost only 2.6 cents per note to produce, regardless of denomination. You know that whoever is producing these notes is making a tremendous profit. Consider also that real money cannot be counterfeited. A pound of gold is a pound of gold, regardless of whose profile is stamped in it. The only money that can be counterfeited is the other counterfeit money (Federal Reserve Notes).

It would seem that the way out of this is for We the People to reinstate the Constitution as the Supreme Law of the Land. Until and unless we act to do so, this fraudulent money, banking and taxing system will continue to enslave us. Keep these two points in mind: first, usury, which is the requirement to pay back both the principal and the interest on a loan, is in violation of Biblical law, which demands "just weights and measures"; and second, there is always a price to be paid for dishonesty. For most of the history of this country, we operated under an honest, Constitutional system. The system could be honest again.

In Summary what the federal reserve and the government are doing at the national level, local banks are doing with us at the local level. The only difference is that instead of printing new notes, the banks are creating new checkbook money each time they make a loan.

Here's what happens when you go to the bank to get a loan for your vehicle:

- The bank has you sign a Promissory Note.
- The back of the note is then stamped, "pay to order of" or similar words.
- The note is then deposited into a transaction account in your name. Now this was not disclosed to you before you signed the note and you did not give them the authority to open a transaction account on your name.
- The bank then writes a check from your transaction account deposit that you had no knowledge of, either to you or transfers the amount to those who should be receiving it.
- The bank then sells the note to Federal Reserve or into the securities market. The proceeds of which, are used to fund the alleged loan.

Through the bank selling your note, YOU PAID FOR YOUR PURCHASE WITH THE PROMISSORY NOTE. Your note was treated by the bank as an asset that could be exchanged for cash. Anything that you can exchange for cash is an asset. What 95 % of America does not realize is that within our monetary system a Promissory Note is an asset. The moment you signed that note it became money to the bank. There was no money in existence until you signed the note. Once the bank stamped it "pay to the order of" it became a negotiable instrument. To the bank, it had **Present Value**, because they were able to sell it for cash. To you it only had **Future Value.**

What's wrong with this loan scenario? You always suspected that there was something not right when you went for a loan from the bank. Now you know what it is. Let me give you a simple illustration that will help you to understand this.

Imagine if you came to me needing a loan.
You: "Can you give me a loan for $10,000."
Me: "sure I'll loan you $10,000, but you have to give me an asset worth $10,000."
You: "All I've got is this diamond ring worth $10,000."
Me: "That will do." I then take the ring and sell it for $10,000, and come back to You with a check for $10,000.
Me: "Here's your $10,000 loan at 10% interest, and the payments are $200 a month for x number of years."
You: "xxxxxxx!" We won't even print what you would tell me to do with that loan.

In fact if you called the police I would go to jail for fraud, loan sharking, racketeering etc. BUT THIS IS EXACTLY WHAT THE BANKS ARE DOING EVERY SINGLE DAY.

Now what is wrong with this loan?
- It's not a loan. It's an exchange. We simply exchanged your diamond for a $10,000 check.
- It never cost me anything to make the loan. I brought nothing to the table. My assets did not decrease by $10,000, as would be the case in a true, honest loan. Therefore I had no risk.
- You provided the asset (the diamond ring). I merely sold it and gave you back your money, and then had the unmitigated gall to charge you interest on nothing.

In the same way, YOUR PROMISSORY NOTE BECAME THE FUNDING INSTRUMENT OF YOUR BANK LOAN. The bank received it as an asset, as legal tender, i.e. in the form of money and deposited in an account. According to the Uniform Commercial Code, a promissory note is a negotiable instrument, and is therefore legal tender. As such it is the funding instrument. Therefore there was no loan. It was an exchange. Your note which, could be monetized by the bank, was exchanged for the bank's check. And the bank lied and called it a loan. Banks and lending institutions only **appear** to lend money.

The "lending" techniques that are used are beyond brilliant. It took some very, very smart people to figure out how to **appear to be lending money**, but in actuality have the value supplied by the person wanting a loan. And that is what is happening.

If you are finding this rather difficult to believe, let's look at some Federal Reserve Bank publications, which actually admit that this is how bank loans work.

*"Transaction deposits are the modern counterpart of bank notes. It was a small step from printing notes to **making book entries crediting deposits of borrowers,** which the borrowers in turn could "spend" **by writing checks, thereby "printing" their own money**." (**Modern Money Mechanics, page 3, Federal Reserve Bank of Chicago**).*

*"Of course **they do not really pay out loans from the money they receive as deposits**. If they did this, no additional money would be created. **What they do when they make loans is to accept promissory notes in exchange for credits to the borrowers' transaction accounts.** Loans (assets) and deposits (liabilities) both rise by $9,000. Reserves are unchanged by the loan transactions. But the deposit credits constitute new additions to the total deposits of the banking system."* Modern Money Mechanics, page 6, Federal Reserve Bank of Chicago.

According to the Fed, it is not their policy to make loans from other depositor's money. Neither do they make loans from their own assets. They make loans by accepting promissory notes in exchange for credits to the borrower's transaction account. They even admit that it's an exchange. IF IT'S AN EXCHANGE HOW CAN IT BE A LOAN?

*"In **exchange** for the note or security, the lending institution credits the depositor's account or gives a check that can be deposited at yet another depository institution."* Two Faces of Debt, page 19 Federal Reserve Bank of Chicago.

You want more proof: **THE BANK'S OWN BOOKKEEPING ENTRIES ARE PROOF.** Let's say the bank receives a $1,000.00 check deposit. It is recorded as an asset to the bank. But in order to balance their books, on the other side of the ledger they have to record a

$1,000.00 liability. The bank has an asset for $1,000.00, but it also has a liability of $1,000.00 to you, the depositor.

The bank owes you $1,000.00. You have a right to draw on that $1,000.00 whenever you choose. Now when you purchased your vehicle instead of a check you gave the bank a signed promissory note. The bank deposited it, just like a check or cash, in a transaction account in your name. Now remember that all deposits are received as assets to the bank. However, they also have a corresponding liability to the face value of your promissory note. Therefore, in reality you don't owe the bank anything. You simply exchanged your promissory note for their check, which paid for the vehicle. The account is a wash. SO WHY ARE WE PAYING MONTHLY PAYMENTS AND INTEREST FOR SOMETHING THAT, WITHIN OUR MONETARY SYSTEM, HAS ALREADY BEEN PAID FOR?

Actually the bank owes you! They still do not own your promissory note. They made an exchange - your promissory note (asset to the bank) was exchanged for the face value of the note. They deposited your note and then sold it remember. Therefore, on their books they still have a liability to you

Colonel Edward Mandell House is attributed with giving a very detailed outline of the plans to be implemented to enslave the American people. He stated, in a private meeting with Woodrow Wilson (President 1913 - 1921). Quote:

"Very soon, every American will be required to register their biological property (that's you and your children) in a national system designed to keep track of the people and that will operate under the ancient system of pledging. By such methodology, we can compel people to submit to our agenda, which will affect our security as a charge back for our fiat paper currency. (property) and we will hold the security interest over them forever, by operation of the law merchant under the scheme of secured transactions. Americans, by unknowingly or unwittingly delivering the bills of lading (Birth Certificate) to us will be rendered bankrupt and insolvent, secured by their pledges.(presidency) of our dummy corporation (USA) to foment this plot against America."
--Colonel Edward Mandell House

"Every American will be forced to register or suffer being able to work and earn a living. They will be our chattels. They will be stripped of their rights and given a commercial value designed to make us a profit and they will be none the wiser, for not one man in a million could ever figure our plans and, if by accident one or two should figure it out, we have in our arsenal plausible deniability. After all, this is the only logical way to fund government, by floating liens and debts to the registrants in the form of benefits and privileges. This will inevitably reap us huge profits beyond our wildest expectations and leave every American a contributor to this fraud, which we will call "Social Insurance." Without realizing it, every American will unknowingly be our servant, however begrudgingly. The people will become helpless and without any hope for their redemption and we will employ the high office."

The bottom line, as you have come to know, is there is no real money. The paper debt instrument has become our substitute for the real stuff. We have all just accepted that there is value in a piece of paper. And as long as the mass believes it, there is value. In reality, as long as you can trade the paper for something material, like food, shelter, and toys, everyone believes that it is the paper that has the value. At the root, it is commerce and the ability to trade things for the paper that drives this machinery of money, and it always has. Nations have progressively and cyclically moved from a gold backed money system to a paper system, then back again. In many cases, this has caused great havoc as the currencies became valueless. But nowhere in history has the magnitude of fake paper been as dramatic as in our current time. It can now be done with a simple keystroke and a ledger entry with no backing. Historically, the banking system, and those who control it have taken more and more through the banking and legal systems to lead us to the biggest monetary deception in history. This is what we live under here and now. But let us explain how this greatest illusion of all, the one that controls nations, has evolved.

At the root of the commercial box is a control mechanism we know as commerce. Commerce has been the common thread woven throughout our entire history. In a nutshell, the key components of this control mechanism includes the merchant, the money-changers or banks, the law of commerce, civil law, and maritime law. These form the glue that bound people before and it still binds people into one uniform system.

As you will come to realize, banks create money today out of thin air. Then they charge the people interest on their creation. Merchants, who produce nothing, sell products for a larger profit than is received by the producer. Thereafter, the merchants and the bankers create laws through lawmakers whom they control. These laws protect commerce and bind the people to obey through civil and Maritime law. As you may have realized, the tax system is an integral part of the process. The only reason this occurs is that we do not handle our own affairs. This same scenario has happened for more than four thousand years throughout our history. Now it is so huge and diversified into nations that it is seemingly impossible to rectify. The banking and legal systems coupled with commerce constitute the global glue so to speak. Let us delve into the history of this glue.

And the story parallels Canada and US. There is a close similarity. Of course the legal acts and events differ but the outcome is the same. Canada is just another corporation under the illusion of a free nation. The people that orchestrate this are the ones that control and police the laws of commerce and the banking system. What is important is that you simply get an appreciation for how commerce has been used for a long time and how it is the thread that binds nations and their people now.

The Elegant Corporate Structure

There is still more to conclude this chapter of the story. Remember that the natural being had rights. The foreign bankers knew they could not control these real people with such a system of freedom. So they decided to design a fictional system, which looked like the real thing. But really it was not. You have noted that the commerce model of fictional entities they built to control freedoms of nations through banking is the same at a personal level.

The first thing that was done was to make an entity which looked and sounded like the federal republic entitled *'united States of America'*. Notice that the *'u'* in united is a small u. That's because it is an adjective, describing the States - a noun - of America. What if one capitalized the *'U'*, as in United States? This would be a name; or a *'title'* wouldn't it? So, now we have a *'title'* for the republic which was incorporated in England in 1871 as an English corporation.

This clearly shows that we are being ruled by a private foreign operated corporation, and not a government. Then in 1944, the Buck Act took the sovereignty away from the states so that the states could also have a title as in *'The State of Arizona'*. Then came the counties and municipalities, each had their own corporations which usurped the organic government. What we then had was an inverse relationship to the original organic republics.

So what they designed was a top down fictional model of corporate names to impose on nations all the way down to the biological Earthling – the only ones left to pay the bills. It appears very consistent. And this model was designed to enslave humankind, getting around the original rights and freedoms that took centuries to get.

If you look at how the hierarchy of authority is imposed using this model, you will see that there are three ways of identification. These are the authority, name and image or fiction. At the very bottom is you, also known as a sovereign or soveran, your name being upper and lower case letters with a fictional counterpart being the name on your birth certificate. Also in this hierarch is the Post Office which has a district called the POSTAL CODE. Next up is your neighbourhood or area, identified with a fictional counterpart as a VOTING DISTRICT. Now you can follow this all the way up with township, municipality, county, state, country, and nation. These are all CORPORATIONS, each being a successive higher level above you. Each is subject to particular laws and legal acts. Thus the whole planet is divided into nations. And the glue that binds the major industrialized nations, all the way down to you, is the financial system backed by laws the Elite manipulate. So the model is consistent all the way down. But at the very bottom is the Earthling identified by NAME and BIRTHDATE. This will be discussed in detail in the next chapter.

On March 9, 1933 in the House 73rd Congress, Session I, Chapter I, page # 83, 1st paragraph, third sentence it states: *'Under the new law, the money is issued to the banks in return for government obligations, bills of exchange, drafts, notes, trade acceptances, and banker's acceptances. The money will be worth 100 cents on the dollar, because it is backed by the credit of the nation. It will represent a mortgage on all the homes and other property of all the people in the nation.'* The credit is you. You are the real creditor.

The commercial system of laws has been implemented through the Uniform Commercial Code, called a UCC in the U.S. That is hooked to every real being with original freedoms, into being a citizen under the 14th Amendment or a person a fictional overlay called a Strawman. The Bills of Exchange Act in Canada, for example is what commercial transactions are based on. If you look at the physical things on the planet and how these are proved to be owned or traded, there is typically another commercial counterpart describing it.

Take a vehicle for example. Proof of ownership is a bill of sale. The way this is identified is through title, name or number. In this case it is a Certificate of Title. Whether it is equipment, land, timber, mining, crops, animals, industry, or you, or whatever, there is something to represent it in the commercial system and there is a license that hooks you to the laws surrounding it. All the lands held in trust for the people were transferred to the Bureau of Land Management (BLM) and hypothecated by the UNITED STATES to help pay the artificial debt to the international bankers. Public lands are now in the hands of the BLM. You now have to register with the BLM in order to graze cattle on public land. It has nearly become so expensive to register and pay the BLM for grazing cattle that it is prohibitive. Trademarks are registered with the Patent Office as are bar codes. When you go to the grocery store, all food products are now registered by a bar code.

Everything is registered and owned through a holding vessel- a counterpart fictional entity called a corporation or trust. And then the counterpart has specific laws attached to it that the real thing is subjected to. Can you fly a plane through the air without a license? How about a plane registration and number? How about a radio or television station? Can you still get free air for your tires at any service station? Not really, Why? Because you also have joined yourself to the counterpart that is regulated some laws.

In addition to the fictional corporate structure, there is another imaginary system associated with all the material things. We are actually dealing paper representations of things in the form of titles or names. The real thing is not really the focus anymore. It is the paper representing the real thing like a receipt that is crucial to the commercial transaction.. When you buy things, it is the bill of exchange - the receipt - that is the crucial item to the commercial laws. This trade transaction is the item that binds us, not the item.

There is little of real value in the system any more. You used to be able to own gold, called a gold certificate. Now, a dollar bill is backed by another title – your credit. And that is simply an accounting record of debt.

"Money" Is A Record Of Debt

So money is a record of debt. Your credit is being used by others. Fictional law, called statutes, even says you can't use the credit. Did you know your credit even has a title? It actually has many titles, but namely Federal Reserve Notes. There are many others also, including Federal Reserve Bills, Federal Reserve Bonds, Checks, Bills of Exchange, Trade Acceptances, Sight Drafts, Documentary Drafts, Judgments, and ANY AND EVERY BILL THAT YOU RECEIVE. Every bill that you receive is like a Federal Reserve Note. It is called a bill of exchange and falls under the Bills of Exchange Act. These *'bills'* are a record of the credit that has been accounted for against you.

That means under the bankruptcy deal, the nations had a free license to print what looks like money but is really like a line of credit drawing down more debt. The receiver and the system is there to make sure everything is accounted for in this imaginary fictional system of entities like the Strawmen and paper. It is like a parallel hologram. And like the top-down model of Strawmen, there is a fictional system of laws and money along with it.

And of course, we buy into this model. But as a little diversion here,   let us delve into how the local banking system works.

The local banking system has evolved in a similar fashion where the people have no idea of the nature of the deception that they perpetrate on people. The deception process is so ingrained that it is simply believed that they are following the law. The humour, if you can get a chuckle out of it, is that the deception goes so deep, the whole banking world we deal with think everything they do is legal, proper and above board. They believe the banks are doing you a huge favour with their loans, credit and services. Yet they are actually defrauding people, deceiving them and indulging in criminal activities.

Let's go through a typical real estate purchase and sale. Let us say you and a seller have signed the agreement of purchase and sale. You, the buyer, go to the bank because they lend money in accordance with their corporate charter. Does the bank tell you that they have assets or money to lend? Well, no. They are a bank. Why would you even ask? Right. But the truth is that it does not have any money to lend, and they are not permitted to use their depositors' money to lend to their borrowers. Do they tell you that? No, they are a bank you say regulated by laws of banking. You give your faith and trust out to them freely.

The bank makes you sign a mortgage loan application form which is essentially a promissory note. That means you promise to pay the bank for the money you are supposed to receive from the bank. You did this even before any value or consideration is received by you from the bank. This promissory note is an instant valuable consideration for them. It is a receivable and therefore an asset transferred from you to the bank. The bank can now enter this into its own asset account as a cash deposit.

After making sure that you have the ability to pay the required monthly payments, the bank agrees to lend you the money to pay the seller. But the bank has no money to lend, yet it gave you a promise to lend money by way of a commitment letter, loan approval letter, loan authorization or loan confirmation letter signed by a bank official.

It goes deeper. Anyway, they don't need it. It is an electronic entry on a balance sheet. Follow me here. Let us complete the transaction. The bank's acceptance of your promissory note made the bank liable to you for the full face value of the promissory note which is the agreed purchase price of the property, less any cash deposit or down payment money paid by you directly to the seller. It is important to note at this point that all real estate transactions require the property being sold to be conveyed by the seller to you free of all liens and encumbrances. This means that all liens such as existing mortgages and judgments must be paid before the property can be mortgaged by the buyer. The property is to be collateral to the mortgage loan which is yet to be received by the buyer pursuant to the promise made by the bank. So let me ask you this. How can the seller obtain clear title if he has not yet received any money from you? And how can you mortgage a property that does not yet belong to you?

This dilemma is solved using the bank's tricks. Now this is not believed to be a trick; it is standard procedure according to the monkeys. The bank, in concert with their lawyers cause all the liens and encumbrances to disappear by using a check drawn in the name of the bank backed by your promissory note and the agreement of purchase and sale. This check is deposited into the lawyer's trust account. In essence, the bank and its lawyers used your promissory note as the cash to enable the purchase agreement"

So it was your promissory note that made the conveyance possible. The bank caused the property to be conveyed to me from the seller with clear title, free and clear of all liens and encumbrances. Technically the property now belongs to you which makes it possible for you to mortgage the property to the bank. This means you paid for it using my own promissory note. It is because you are really the creditor

The bank and its lawyers must perform another trick in order to satisfy the seller's requirement to get paid or the whole deal is null and void. The seller does not even know that the property had been conveyed to your name in order for the seller to receive any money. Everything is in this La-La land in transition, right? The ensuing trick is accomplished this way. You are made to sign another promissory note. The mortgage contract is attached to the bottom of the promissory note which makes you liable to pay the bank for the money or the loan which you have not yet or will never receive for up to twenty five years or more depending on the amortization term of the mortgage contract. This note is linked to the collateral through the mortgage contract and as such, it is valuable to the bank.

The bank then goes to the Bank of Canada or to another bank through its accomplice, the Canadian Payment Association, to pledge the deal that they have just gotten from you for credit. The Bank of Canada then gives the bank the so called credit. Remember, it is not the bank's credit, it's your credit. You promised to pay the bank if and when the money is received by you from the bank, payable for up to twenty-five years or more.

What happened is basically a swap. This is a transaction all banks do to *'monetize'* security. In this case, the second promissory note that is linked to the mortgage contract and signed by you is a mortgage backed security.

The bank will then agree to pay the Bank of Canada a certain percentage of interest over prime. Thus your loan package goes to the Bank of Canada which credits the bank with the full amount of credit. This is the total amount of the money the bank is entitled to receive after twenty-five years, the amount of the principal plus all the interest payments you have promised to pay to the bank for twenty-five years or more. This is usually three times the amount of the money promised by the bank to you. By magic, the bank just enriched itself and got paid in advance, without using or risking its own money.

So now the bank's lawyer, who holds the check that is backed by my original promissory note, can cut a check to the seller as payment for the property. In effect, I paid the seller with my own money by virtue of the fact that it was my own money, namely the promissory note that made the purchase and sale possible. So the sneaky bastards made a cool three hundred percent profit without using or risking any capital of their own. Neither was there any depositor's money deducted from the bank's asset account in this transaction.

What really happened was pure deception that if you tried, would land you in jail guilty of fraud and criminal conversion not to mention that the subject property would have been seized by the court. This would be an indictable crime if we issued a check with no funds. There would not be any deal and no purchase or sale agreement because there is no valuable consideration. In order to de-criminalize the transaction, we need the bank and their cohorts to make the deal happen. It is really a conspiracy of sorts but these *'persons'*, the banks, the lawyers, the land title offices and even the courts do not consider the transaction as fraudulent because the transactions happen all the time and all the monkeys accept this as the law; and the way it is done.

But think about this. Is it not so that such a contract is *void ab-initio* or void from the beginning, which means that the contract never took place in the first place? Moreover, the good faith and fair dealing requirement through full disclosure is non-existent which further voids the contract. The bank failed to disclose to me that it will not be giving me any valuable consideration and taking interest back as additional benefit to unjustly enrich the corporation. The bank also failed to disclose how much profit they are going to make on the deal.

The bank led you to believe that the money going to the seller would be coming from its own asset account. They lied because they knew or ought to have known that their own ledger would show that the bank does not have any money to lend and that their records will show that no such loan transaction ever took place. Their own books should show that there would be no debits from the bank's asset account at all and all that would show up are the two entries made when you gave the bank the first collateral or the promissory note. This enabled the bank to cut a check that made it possible to convey the property from seller to you free and clear of all liens or encumbrances as required by the agreement of purchase and sale entered into in writing between you and the seller. In reality, your promissory note was used by the bank and its lawyers and land title clerks to convey free title to you from the seller. So why do we need the mortgage contract?

It is because we have been led to believe this is the way things are done. And even though there are a lot of people that have become aware of it and are trying to do something about it, this is a pretty big dragon as it connects with some big guns, the

Elite power group that controls banking. So who is going to take them on? There are many that are aware of this and there are many groups trying to do something but as of now, such has not been accomplished because you are playing against a very skilled stacked deck. You can contact a group that is trying to do something, like the ***www.freewebs.com/classaction/johndempsey.htm*** but the story is usually the same. The people are pictured as radicals trying to beat the system for personal gain and the people believe it because the people have no information that seems paints the true picture.

Yes, this may be a pretty dismal picture of how these elite bankers have placed the chains around nations and people. The Elite bankers learned how to manipulate nations the same way. And now, with the way you can create so-called money with a keystroke, and everybody flocking to an even more imaginary hologram of money, it all plays into their hands. But there is power in knowing. How can you get free of something if you don't know something has you captured?

So the debts incurred by nations are no different than a debt you could have with your local bank. Even though they have defrauded you, if you can't pay, they take since you are in their jurisdiction of contract law. If you can't pay, then the receiver is called in and you have to make a deal. You, like a nation, made a deal under the so called law; a contract in commerce, and you have to deal with the consequences.

You need to be aware of who you are. You need to understand what jurisdiction you fall under. Let us go back to the U.S. situation for a moment. In 1871, did *'we the people'* fall under the jurisdiction of this private government? No. Only those who lived in the jurisdiction of Washington, D.C., its territories and the 14th Amendment slaves did. This did not touch *'we the people'*. They were still enforcing the Original Jurisdiction and had the authority to do so. The original private corporate government back in 1789 was established on certain principles and rules, but as we've seen, it went through a bankruptcy almost right away, and with each stage of the bankruptcy there was reorganization. A reorganization creates a new set of circumstances, and probably a new set of creditors, masters and rules in order to discharge the old bankruptcy. Roughly every twenty years they had a re-organization to deal with and the banking system got entrenched. Each time they got different changes in the rules and regulations, and it just went on and on. The proprietors and creditors of that private law forum, as it goes into worse and worse bankruptcy, create tighter and tighter rules in order to raise the revenue to keep the thing going. That is what you see today.

Where Does This Fit With Canada And Other Nations

Other nations are colonial holding of the British Crown. The federal reserve banking system and the central banks are all a product of the 14th amendment, a breach of trust that began in America and has tainted the entire world. That is why this is a global event. Everyone can use this pass thru account to discharge debt all over the world. This is simply about redeeming your estate and returning it to solvency. That debt belongs to the federal reserve.

August 15, 1931, the United Kingdom of Great Britain and Ireland abrogated its power and authority over the Dominion of Canada as a British Colony by issuing the Statute of Westminster to Canada on that date. On October 1, 1949, King George VI executed by edict a Royal Proclamation of the Dominion of Canada to reclaim Canada as a British Colony. In this way the British recaptured the Dominion of Canada as their new colony and once again were able to re-exercise their original Power and Authority over the Dominion of Canada, as a British Colony. This is why the Bank of Canada to this day is still financially controlled by the Bank of England, a privately owned financial institution. So the private bankers of England actually recaptured Canada.

On October 11, 1949, King George VI cancelled the original Statute of Westminster of 1931, and re-established a new governor general in the Dominion of Canada within the new colony retroactive to October 1, 1949. King George used a little known International Salvage law to reclaim the Dominion of Canada because by this law he could pronounce that he had found the Dominion of Canada floating on the high seas of debt. Since no one objected or protested, Great Britain simply reacquired, by legal assumption, the Dominion of Canada as their new colony! It was all re-claimed unbeknown to people.

From this type of behaviour it is very plain to understand what is implied by certain judges loyal to the crown of England when they say that *'We've got what it takes, to take what you've got'*. So this is why we are also actually slaves and the king or queen is today the master of our financial destiny in Canada.

And to carry this further, this is why Canada was the fifth most indebted nation on the planet. It was to the Bank of England. This is why Canada today as a debtor has already had the first step of foreclosure placed on her by her creditor, the International Monetary Fund during the 1995/6 federal fiscal year. And you know the IMF is a sister bank to the Bank of England.

So Canadians have hocked absolutely everything. But one cannot be so quick as to blame your current government as they are just as uninformed as you. The political systems in our countries play musical politics and there is no financial continuity, or responsibility between administrations. The debt is status quo and issues are always more of a local, petty nature. How would you like to change the board of directors and top management in your company every three years? Everybody is sleeping with regard to the bigger financial picture.

Moving Higher In The Corporate Pyramid

Now, let us get back to move up in the pyramid. I mentioned this before but let me run through it again because it may make more sense to you now. The IRS, the receiver of the bankruptcy, is an agency of the IMF and the IMF is an agency of the UN. In Canada, as you have noted, you have a *'receiver'* of revenue. The U.S. has not had a treasury since 1921 because the U.S. treasury is now the IMF. The U.S. has operated under bankruptcy for over two hundred years. The FCC, CIA, FBI, NASA and all of the other alphabet gangs were never part of the United States government. They are the policing systems of the IMF, even though the U.S. government held shares of stock in the various agencies.

The U.S. social security numbers are issued by the UN through the IMF. According to the rules, you must have a social security number. The application for a social security number is the SS5 form issued by the Department of the Treasury that is really the IMF. There are no judicial courts in America and there has not been any since 1789. Judges do not enforce statutes and codes. Executive administrators enforce statutes and codes. There have not been any real judges in America since 1789. There have really been administrators.

The social security check comes directly from the IMF. You own no property because slaves can't own property. Read the deed to the property that you think is yours. You are listed as a tenant. America is a British colony, as is Canada. The UNITED STATES is a corporation not a land mass and it existed before the revolutionary war. Go and check these things out for yourself.

The real power is from outside of North America because we have not handled our financial affairs. The government has to conform to the bankruptcy agreement and the agencies like the FBI, IRS, CRA are the alien collectors that do not belong to the country. In truth they are responsible indirectly to the Jesuit Military Order. The law system is there to support them and the police force is there to enforce them. That is why the banks and agencies have so much power.

Britain is owned by the Vatican through the Treaty of 1213. The Pope can abolish any law in the United States. The Pope claims to own the entire planet through the laws of conquest and discovery. The Pope has ordered the genocide and enslavement of millions of people and the Pope's laws are obligatory on everyone. We have accepted being slaves and own absolutely nothing, not even our children. It is not the duty of the police to protect you. Their real job is to protect the corporation and arrest code breakers. We are human capital by Executive Order 13037. The UN has financed the operations of the United States government and now owns every man, women and child in America. The UN also holds all of the physical land in America in 'fee simple'. And the binding threads are the system of commerce. Commerce is enacted through the Bank Act and the Bill of Exchange Act. These are the most powerful acts around.

Now we need to revisit the Crown temple and look at these Elite. The Crown Temple is not the Queen of England or the royal families of Britain. The Templar Church has been known for centuries by the world as the 'Crown'. It is really a secret society for the Third Way Order. The Templars of the Crown is the domain of the black priests that are reflected in the black robes worn by our judges stemming from the days of Babylon. The crown, in reality, is the Crown Temple or Crown Templar. All three are synonymous. This is not the crown of England, or what we think is the queen. Indeed the queen is indeed part of this.

The Temple Church was built by the Knights Templar in two parts. The first part was the Round and the Chancel. The Round Church was consecrated in 1185 and modeled after the circular Church of the Holy Sepulcher in Jerusalem. The Chancel was built in 1240. The Temple Church serves both the Inner and Middle Temples and is located between Fleet Street and Victoria on the embankment at the Thames river. Its grounds also house the crown offices at Crown Office Row. This Temple Church is actually outside any canonical jurisdiction. The master of the temple is appointed and takes his place by sealed, non-public patent, without induction or institution.

The present queen of England is not the crown as you and everyone else thought, or have been led to believe. Rather, it is the bankers and attornies; you know them as attorneys, who are the actual crown or Crown Temple. The monarch aristocrats of England have not been ruling sovereigns since the reign of King John, around 1215. All royal sovereignty of the old British crown since that time has passed to the Crown Temple in Chancery. You know now that the U.S. and Canada are not the free and sovereign nations that our defacto federal governments tell us they are. Their fictional counterparts are part of the big corporate structure and the slaves comply with the laws on the structure. You know now that our federal governments are bankrupt corporations, pretending to serve the people, while they truly serve a different master, called the crown.

The banks rule the Temple Church and the attorners carry out their orders by controlling their victim's judiciary. Political minions to serve the banking cartel and the crown are chosen not elected. Since the first chancel of the Temple Church was built by the Knights Templar, this is not a new ruling system by any means.

The chancel, or chancery of the Crown Inner Temple Court was where King John was in January 1215 when the English barons demanded that he confirm the rights enshrined in the Magna Charta. This London temple was the headquarters of the Templar Knights in Great Britain where order and rule were first made and which became known as code. Here a manipulative body of Elite bankers and attorners from the independent city of London carved out the law of the world that imposes the legal, and a totally unlawful system of contracts, upon the real people of this planet. This is called the *'color of law'*, the fictional system that you are becoming familiar with.

It's very important to know how the British royal crown was placed into the hands of the Knights Templars, and how the Crown Templars became the fiscal and military agents for the Pope of the Roman Church. This all becomes very clear through the concession of England to the Pope on May 15, 1213. This charter was sworn in fealty by England's King John to Pope Innocent and the Roman Church. It was witnessed before the Crown Templars. King John stated upon sealing this: *'I myself bearing witness in the house of the Knights Templars'*. Pay particular attention to the words being used that we have defined below, especially charter, fealty, demur, and concession: *'We wish it to be known to all of you, through this our charter, furnished with our seal, not induced by force or compelled by fear, but of our own good and spontaneous will and by the common counsel of our barons, do offer and freely concede to God and His holy apostles Peter and Paul and to our mother the holy Roman church, and to our lord Pope Innocent and to his Catholic successors, the whole kingdom of England and the whole kingdom of Ireland, with all their rights and appurtenances. We perform and swear fealty for them to him our aforesaid lord Pope Innocent, and his Catholic successors and the Roman church. Binding our successors and our heirs by our life forever, in similar manner to perform fealty and show homage to him who shall be chief pontiff at that time, and to the Roman church without demur. As assign, we will and establish perpetual obligation and concession. From the proper and especial revenues of our aforesaid kingdoms. The Roman church shall receive yearly a thousand pounds sterling. Saving to us and to our heirs our rights, liberties and regalia; all of which things, as they have been described above, we wish to have perpetually valid and firm; and we bind ourselves and our successors not to act counter to them. And if we or any one of our successors shall presume to attempt this, whoever he be, unless being duly warned he come to his kingdom, and this senses, shall lose his right to the kingdom, and this charter of our obligation and concession shall always remain firm'*.

It is an oath of allegiance from feudal times. Most who have commented on this charter only emphasize the payments due the Pope and the Roman church. What should be emphasized is the fact that King John broke the terms of this charter by signing the Magna Charta on June 15, 1215. The penalty for breaking the 1213 agreement was the loss of the crown or right to the kingdom to the Pope and his Roman church. It says so quite plainly. To formally and lawfully take the crown from the royal monarchs of England by an act of declaration, on August 24, 1215, Pope Innocent III annulled the Magna Charta. Later in the year, he placed an interdict, meaning prohibition, on the entire British Empire. From that time until today, the English monarchy and the entire British crown belonged to the Pope. By swearing to the 1213 charter in fealty, King John declared that the British-English crown and its possessions at that time, including all future possessions, estates, trusts, charters, letters patent, and land, were forever bound to the Pope and the Roman church, the landlord.

Some five hundred years later, the New England colonies in America became a part of the crown as a possession and trust named the United States. By agreeing to the Magna Charta, King John had broken the agreement terms of his fealty with Rome and the Pope. What that means is that he lost all rights to the kingdom, and the royal English crown was turned over by default to the Pope and the Roman church. The Pope and his Roman church control the Crown Temple because his Knights established it under his orders. So also the Temple banks, the Templar attorneys, the corporate United States, the corporate British Commonwealth, the chartered Federal Reserve Bank and Bank of England. The list is pretty impressive. He who controls the gold controls the world. This is the Crown Temple today. Is it clearer now how the legal system and the attorneys are the unknowing spies for the system?

This is simply due to the fact that all Bar Associations throughout the world are signatories and franchises to the International Bar Association located at the 'Inns of Court' at Crown Temple, which are physically located at Chancery Lane behind Fleet Street in London. Although they vehemently deny it, all BAR associations in the world, such as the American Bar Association, the Florida Bar, or California Bar Association, are franchises to the Crown. This would involve all Canadian Bar associations as well; indeed the world! The Inns of Court and The Four Inns of Court to the Crown Temple use the banking and judicial system of the city of London. It is a sovereign and independent territory which is not a part of Great Britain. This is Washington City, as DC was called in the 1800's, is not a part of the north American states, nor is it a state. It was done this way to administer and control the people. These Fleet Street bankers and lawyers work everywhere under the guise and 'color of law'. They are known collectively as the crown. Their lawyers are actually Templar Bar attornies, not lawyers.

We are then actually dictated to by the Crown Temple through its bankers and attornies. We are all controlled and manipulated by this private foreign power and our federal government is their mechanism. The bankers and Bar attorneys of the world are franchises in oath and allegiance to the Crown at Chancery - the Crown Temple church and its Chancel located at Chancery Lane. So the legal system or judiciary of North America is controlled by the Crown Temple from the independent and sovereign City of London.

The private Federal Reserve System, which issues fiat U.S. Federal Reserve notes, is financially owned and controlled by the crown from Switzerland, the home and legal origin for the charters of the United Nations, the International Monetary Fund, the World Trade Organization, and most importantly, the Bank of International Settlements. The governmental and judicial systems within all public jurisdictions at federal, local and state/provincial levels are owned by the crown. Note that this is a privately owned corporate foreign power operating in defacto. All licensed Bar attorneys in the world owe their allegiance and give their solemn oath in pledge to the Crown Temple whether they realize this or not. Once again, look to the real meaning of words. Crown means imperial, regal power or dominion - sovereignty. There is a power behind the crown greater than the crown itself.

This is why we have crown land, land belonging to the crown, that is, to the sovereign, or Crown law, the law which governs criminal prosecutions, or Crown lawyer, one employed by the crown, as in criminal cases.

Associated with the Crown are the Four Inns of Court to the Temple. In England, the temples are two Inns of Court, being original dwellings of the Knights Templar. They are called the Inner and the Middle Temple. In England, there is a college of municipal or common law professors and students. Formerly the town-house of a nobleman, bishop or other distinguished personage, it was where they resided when they attended the court. The Inns of Court were colleges in which students of law reside and are instructed. The principals are the Inner Temple, the Middle Temple, Lincoln's Inn, and Gray's Inn. Inns of Chancery are colleges in which young students formerly began their law studies. These are now occupied chiefly by attorneys, solicitors, and the like. This is where the legalistic architecture is designed to promote the exclusive monopoly of the Temple Bar. These Inns/Temples are exclusive and private country clubs, occupied by secret societies of world power in commerce. They are well established, some having been founded in the early 1200's when the Templars rose to power. The Queen of England is a current member of both the Inner Temple and Middle Temple. Gray's Inn specializes in taxation legalities by rule and code for the Crown.

Lincoln's Inn received its name from the Third Earl of Lincoln around 1300. Just like all other franchise Bar Associations, none of the Four Inns of the Temple are incorporated, for a definite and purposeful reason. You can't make claim against a non-entity and a non-being. They are private societies without charters or statutes, and their so-called constitutions are based solely on custom and self-regulation. In other words, they exist as secret societies without a public front door unless you're a private member called to their Bar. While the Inner Temple holds the legal system franchise by license to steal from Canada and Great Britain, it is the Middle Temple that has legal license to steal from America. This comes about directly via their Bar Association franchises to the Honourable Society of the Middle Temple through the Crown Temple.

From the book **The History of the Inn** as written by the **Honorable Society of the Middle Temple**, we can see a direct tie to the Bar Association franchises and its crown signatories in America. A 'Call to the Bar' or keeping terms in one of the four Inns is a pre-requisite to call at King's Inns until late in the 19th century. In the 17th and 18th centuries, students came from the American colonies and from many of the West Indian islands. The Inn's records would lead one to suppose that for a time there was hardly a young gentleman in Charleston who had not studied here.

You may think that Americans are pretty smart people so how did they get tricked way back then. By what authority has this crown suckered the natural sovereignty of the people? Is it acceptable that the supreme court decides on constitutional issues? How can it be considered in any manner as being constitutional when this same supreme court is appointed by (not elected) and paid by the 'defacto' federal governments?

Well, to answer this you need to go back in time. Five of the signatories to the Declaration of Independence were Middle Templars, and notwithstanding it and its consequences, Americans continued to come here until the War of 1812. All Bar Association licensed attorneys must keep the terms of their oath to the Crown Temple in order to be accepted or be 'called to the Bar' at any of the King's Inns. Their oath, pledge, and terms of allegiance are made to the Crown Temple. That is the way it is and the people are well conditioned to abide by this tradition. It's a real eye opener to know that the Middle Inn of the Crown Temple has publicly acknowledged there were at least five Templar Bar attornies, under solemn oath only to the Crown, who signed what was alleged to be an American Declaration of Independence. This simply means that both parties to the Declaration agreement were of the same origin, the Crown Temple. In case you don't understand the importance of this, there is no international agreement or treaty that will ever be honoured, or will ever have lawful effect, when the same party signs as both the first and second parties. It's merely a worthless piece of paper with no lawful authority when both sides to any agreement are actually the same. In reality, the American Declaration of Independence and the Canadian Constitution Act and Bill of

Rights are nothing more than an internal memo of the Crown Temple, made among its private members.

It means that the top Americans were fooled into believing that the legal crown colonies comprising New England were independent nation states, but they never were nor are today. They were and still are colonies of the Crown Temple, through letters patent and charters, who have no legal authority to be independent from the Rule and Order of the Crown Temple. That means neither the American people nor the queen of Britain own America. The Crown Temple owns America through the deception of those who have sworn their allegiance by oath to the Middle Templar Bar. The crown bankers and their Middle Templar attornies rule America through commerce, contracts, taxes, and contract documents of equity through debt. These are all strictly enforced by their orders, rules and codes of the Crown Temple Courts, our so-called judiciary in America. This is because the Crown Temple holds the land titles and estate deeds to all of North America.

But the highest or most comprehensive loss of status for humanity occurred when a human's condition was changed from one of freedom to one of bondage and became a slave. It swept away with it all rights of citizenship and all family rights. With the all capital names they converted everyone from the common lawful human of God into a fictional, legal, slave entity, subject to administration by State rules, orders and codes. People simply accepted being the corporations and accepting the liabilities and corporate charters. There is no law within any rule or code that applies to the lawful common human of the Lord. You know now that the human with inherent Godly law and rights must be converted into a legal person of fictional status in order for their legal - but completely unlawful - State Judiciary (Chancery Courts) to have authority over them.

This may seem like some more science fiction, but this is where this story ends about who the 'bad guys' are. Really there are no bad guys because we all just simply allowed this to be by being outsmarted by accepting their game. Take a closer look at the one dollar private federal reserve system debt note that is part of a crown banking franchise. As stated before, there is no real money! There is only worthless fiat paper that the Federal Reserve can create or the U.S. government can create as a debt tally! Notice in the base of the pyramid the Roman date MDCCLXXVI written in Roman numerals for the year 1776. The words ANNUIT COEPTIS NOVUS ORDO SECLORUM are Roman Latin for ANNOUNCING THE BIRTH OF THE NEW ORDER OF THE WORLD. The year 1776 signifies the birth of the New World Order under the Crown Temple. That's when the American crown colonies became the chartered governments called the United States. Since that date, the United Nations, another legal Crown Temple component by charter, rose up as a member. Note also that there are thirteen layers for the pyramid denoting the thirteen chartered colony-states and then there is he all seeing eye of Osirus. This was one of many Templar signs used, reflecting the Temple Illuminati or their Order of the Rose and Order of the Cross, names of the Elite controllers.

There is no mystery behind what some see as the current abomination of Babylon for those who study the Bible. It states in Revelation 17:5: *And upon her forehead was a name written, Mystery, Babylon the Great, the Mother of Harlots and Abominations of the Earth.* Looks like God reserved His judgment for this great idolatress. Rome was the chief seat of all idolatry that ruled over many nations with whom the kings have committed to the worship of her idols. What about the Pope and his purported church sitting on the temple throne at the Vatican, ruling the nations of the earth through the Crown Temple of ungodly deities? Does the rule and order of Babylon using the crown of Godlessness and the code of commerce carry on the tradition? If you want proof, look to the Bills of Exchange Act or the Uniform Commercial Code. They are the true bibles for the crown - and Babylon.

The Elite operate in the private domain through clubs and cults that can nowhere be mapped like any traditional organization. It, like the Matrix, is an invisible structure of that they abide by as heartless control freaks bound by initiation and bloodline. One may call the Elite rule of the world today by many names such as the New World Order, the Third Way, the Illuminati, Triad, Triangle, Trinity, Masonry, the United Nations, or many other names. However, they all point to one origin and one beginning. Many have traced this in history to the Crown Temple, the Temple Church created around 1200. The bloodline has been tracked even further back. But all world banking, judiciary, and rule of law has been under the Rule and Order of the Crown Temple since 1200. Because the various Popes created the Order of the Temple Knights and established their mighty Temple Church in the sovereign city of London, you can assume it is the Pope and his Roman followers who have a pretty serious interest in the control the world.

If there is any reason to bring further information into your mind, the most prolific and dedicated *'hunter'* of the Illuminati is a fellow named David Icke. You can find this impressive lad on **www.davidicke.com**. He has written many books on them and he is the world authority on this topic. All of what I have told you is clearly documented in his work. Another well known tracker is **Edward Griffin** who details how the Federal Reserve was created and who are behind it **http://www.realityzone.com** in a book **'The Creature from Jekyll Island – A Second look at the Federal Reserve'."**

Let us go back to the whore of Babylon where it states 'And the woman was arrayed in purple and scarlet color, and decked with gold and precious stones and pearls, having a golden cup in her hand full of abominations and filthiness of her fornication' in Revelation 17:4. This verse appears to be an accurate description of the Pope and his Bishops for the past seventeen hundred years. The idolatries of commerce in the world are all the gold and silver, the iron and soft metals, the money and coins and riches of the world. All of these are under the control of the Crown Temple. Here we have the Roman king and his false church, the throne of Babylon attended to by his Templar Knights, and all the wizards of abomination and idolatry.

And in conjunction with commerce is religion that has been anything but man's salvation and has been directly responsible for mass death and destruction. Take the 1611 King James Bible that you see everywhere. By the way, note that King James was a Crown Templar. This is not the entire canon of the early church. It has been edited. Guess who the editors were? There were other gospels and books that have been forbidden by the Papal Throne at Rome since the third century. Greek and Aramaic copies of the *'unapproved writings'* were sought after and destroyed by Rome. This in itself is no mystery as history records the existence and destruction of these early church writings, just as history has now proven their genuine authenticity with the appearance of the Dead Sea Scrolls and the Coptic library at Nag Hagmadi in Egypt, among many other recent Greek language discoveries within the past hundred years. The current Holy Bible quotes the Book of Enoch numerous times: 'By faith Enoch was taken away so that he did not see death, and was not found, because God had taken him; for before he was taken he had this testimony, that he pleased God.' This is in Hebrews 11:5. Now Enoch, the seventh from Adam, prophesied about these men also, saying, 'Behold, the Lord comes with ten thousands of His saints, to execute judgment on all, to convict all who are ungodly among them of all their ungodly deeds which they have committed in an ungodly way, and of all the harsh things which ungodly sinners have spoken against Him.' Check out Jude 1:14-15.

The Book of Enoch was considered scripture by most early Christians. The earliest literature of the so-called church fathers is filled with references to this mysterious book. The second century Epistle of Barnabus makes much use of the Book of Enoch. Second and third century church fathers, such as Justin Martyr, Irenaeus, Origin, and Clement of Alexandria, all make use of the Book of Enoch. Tertullian, around 160-230 BC, called the Book of Enoch a Holy Scripture. The Ethiopic Church included the Book of Enoch in its official canon. It was widely known and read the first three centuries after Christ. However, this and many other books became discredited after the Roman Council of Laodicea. They were under ban of the Roman papal authorities and afterwards they gradually passed out of circulation. At about the time of the Protestant Reformation, there was a renewed interest in the Book of Enoch, which had long since been lost to the modern world. By the late 1400's, rumours began to spread that a copy of the long lost Book of Enoch might still exist.

During the 1400's, many books arose claiming to be the lost book but were later found to be forgeries. The return of the Book of Enoch to the modern western world is credited to the famous explorer James Bruce, who in 1773 returned from six years in Abyssinia with three Ethiopic copies of the lost book. In 1821, Richard Laurence published the first English translation. The now famous R.H. Charles edition was first published by Oxford Press in 1912. In the following years, several portions of the Greek text also surfaced. Then, with the discovery of cave number four of the Dead Sea Scrolls, seven fragmentary copies of the Aramaic text were discovered. So you see, the Popes and their buddies have all through history created many other 'bibles' and 'scriptures' written to change the words or meaning to what *they* wanted to preach. What is coming out now is that the real stuff is very different. So all along, there has been an illusion of the spiritual box to keep the people powerless and subservient to God or at least their gods.

In fact, GOD is another fictional entity created by the Vatican to take possession of the Souls of humans. .

For everything created, there appears to be a fictitious imitation that looks like the genuine thing. There is the knowledge of good and the knowledge of evil. The problem is most believe they have the knowledge of God when what they really have is knowledge of world deceptions operating as Gods. Where there is the true Tabernacle or Temple of God, there are also the false Temples of unholy Gods. The only way to discern and begin to understand the Kingdom of Heaven is to seek the knowledge that comes only from God, not the knowledge of men who take their legal claim as earthly rulers and Gods. The false Crown Temple and its grand wizard knights have led the world to believe that they are of the lord God and hold the knowledge and keys to his kingdom. What they hold within their Temples are the opposite. They claim to be the holy church, but which holy church? The real one or the false one? Are the Pope and his Roman Church the Temple of God, or is this the unholy Temple of Babylon sitting upon the seven mountains? They use the same words but alter them to show the true meaning they have applied. The State is not a state. A Certificate is not a certification. The Roman Church is not the church (ekklesia). There is the Crown of the Lord and a Crown of that which is not of the Lord. There is the mark and seal of the Lord God and there are the Marks and Seals of the false Gods. All imitations appear to be the genuine article, but they are fakes. Which one are you now going to believe?

So the Popes have been pretty clever at overlaying another invisible deception that looks like the real thing. To really understand how the people have just followed it is because they deep down believe in God and want to be led. It is only when a new awareness is floods through us to become enlightened the same way and together and it is the intent of us all that will change this. We must not moan about deception because we accepted this fate.

If you reduce this down to simple terms, these guys at the top are just smart businessmen aren't they? They invented commerce so they are smarter. When the U.S. went bankrupt, they had the opportunity to take over and of course the guy who is bankrupt gets a crappy deal. But from then on, the spies and cronies are there to police their interests. So who is the bad guy? Is it the U.S. or Canadian government? Not really. The power is outside of the U.S. and the agencies of the IMF are the ones that really police their deal. And that is no different than the deal you would have to make if you went bankrupt personally and made a deal to pay off the debt.

And here is the bitter reality. The present wealth and power of all the world's gold, silver, tin, bronze, pearls, diamonds, gemstones, iron, and copper as belonged to the Babylon whore, are held in the treasuries of her Crown Templar banks and deep stony vaults. They have accumulated the hard treasures that once used to give real value to money. They control the real things and they control the fake things. Pretty good take-over strategy, wouldn't you say?

So this time something pretty major has to happen to break this. We can never pay off the debt so it's a pretty crappy deal but that's the way it is. Short of a world revolution, how can this be fixed? We all inherited it. Who is aware of it? And who cares? If you have food in your tummy and a place to sleep, who cares? As long as you believe you have money and can use this paper to get food and housing plus toys to play with, you probably don't care about it. So as they siphon your energy and essence, and keep you financially beholding, they continue to keep you from finding out who you are and what powers you have as a piece of God. But as you sit in front of the TV with your beer, drive off to work every day, deal with your creditors and feel 'whole' are you not missing the point? What about being a part of God and co-creating your own destiny. What about building a life away from this Matrix that develops your full power and potential? Now that you have chewed the red pill, things are already different for you?

Things become different because of the awareness. First is to realize the truth. If one of your creditors went bankrupt after owing you a lot of money and you made a deal that would continue to his children, would you or your inheritors of the deal enforce it? And what if you found out you got suckered into it? Would that change the picture? If you go through all I told you, which I think you now believe, you will find something to fight or move with. What is the choice? Those are questions you must answer for yourself. Then, are you happy about being fooled? Or did you fool yourself? Do you have a moral obligation? Are you content to live like you live now, in ignorance of the real truth? Now that you are aware of it, tell me how your gut feels about it?

The truth is that the Elite are marching to simply dominate the Empire are run things like a big corporation. Are they different than many corporations designed to fill the pockets of a few? Not really. Does it benefit you as a happier slave? And how did you get to be a slave? The story is not finished yet, now let us look at this corporate entity called a Strawman.

16

THE STORY OF THE STRAWMAN

And so it came to be that the process of capitalizing on the human capital to repay the debt of the nation had to be implemented. The corporate model of each Earthling as the fictional overlay was an appropriate way to do this. All that had to be done was that the human, like a nation under bankruptcy, needed to have a fictional counterpart that was subject to codes and laws that could be enforced. Once the humans accepted the rules and codes of the corporation as his responsibility, they would be subject to those codes of law. But how could this be done in a way that did not create rebellion? Here we will explain the story of the Strawman and how humanity, like the united states of America became subject to the corporate fiction UNITED STATES, accepted that responsibility without rebellion.

Corporations As Legal Fictions Overlay Real People

As has been discussed, Planet Earth has evolved kings and queens with their dynasties and kingdoms into the likes of CEO's and corporations. We have seen how this evolution has allowed those gods to retain their powers and we have eluded to the process of the same principle being applied to men and women. We see how a "citizen" and a "person" is not the real thing, only a representation of it. Such is a word. The word is not the real thing, it is a representation of it by a description of it. We have seen how "The Word" of a misrepresented God also represents intangible descriptions and rules than are attached to those who accept that word. This process has allowed the proliferation of a fictional world of corporations to flourish, and be accepted worldwide.

And so the evolution of the commercial system has involved the creation of "legal fictions". As we have already discussed, all one has to do is to look around to understand this more clearly; to think about a corporation or a business your work for, or have created yourself. The Name of the corporation like IBM, is a name only and it is not a living thing. It has real people within it that give it corporate life. Without the people it would be nothing. IBM, like any other corporation has purpose and a business charter, like the articles of incorporation which are its laws. It also has a conduct, purpose and code of behaviour of the people that work within it. And as a CEO, Director, Founder of it, you may take on the responsibilities like the liabilities of it if you so agreed to. But you, outside of it have no liabilities and rules simply do not apply to you.

We have seen the elegant pyramid of corporate structures that overlay upon the real thing so as to make it look and feel the same. Yet it is not. We have seen how this structure of fictional entities has been deployed to effectively create a unity between the fiction and the real thing. And we have seen how this pyramid comes from the top Elite, down through the layers of nations, governments, states, districts, municipalities, towns, postal codes all the way down to you. How did you get caught in this process without knowing? It is the same as the 14th Amendment brought benefits to you as a "citizen". But that is not the whole of it because, remember, you are classified as "human capital". But how did these rules applied to these words get applied contractually to you? It is because of another fictional overlay classified as the Strawman.

What has evolved is the same system overlain upon each living individual. It works because we accept that this fictional corporation is us. And like Sole Proprietorship, we have assumed total responsibility for it. The difference is that the corporation is a Trust.

And so the story of the Strawman begins with the birth of a human. As the story goes, the Strawman is created with the hope that as the child grows up, he will be fooled into believing that he is actually the Strawman (which he most definitely is **not**) and pay all sorts of imaginary costs and liabilities which get attached to the Strawman.

Meriam-webster defines Strawman as a person set up as a cover for a usually questionable transaction. In Roman law, the word "persona" became used to refer to a role played in court, and it became established that it was the role rather than the actor that could have rights, powers, and duties, because different individuals could assume the same roles, the rights, powers, and duties followed the role rather than the actor, and each individual could act in more than one role, each a different "person" in law. Are you a person? Are you the live person? You can't be both any more than you can be a Trust or a Corporation.

In our current reality, the Strawman is simply a corporation, trust or name given to a commercial entity for some purpose usually commercial. It is not live, it exists as a fictional tag which much like a corporation and the owner of it, the corporation has a set of rules and charters to abide by. How you as the owner, CEO, etc. decide to relate to those rules and liabilities is a choice, not a mandatory obligation. **So, what is a Strawman?** *A Strawman is a fictitious legal entity. But that is just another generic word, right? Well it is so but each of us has a personal Strawman, uniquely defined as our name and birthdate.*

As you have discovered, it was originally written into the Constitution that the jurisdiction of the federal government should be limited by making the people citizens of the state in which they were born or in which they lived. At this time the federal government only had jurisdiction over a person if they lived within Washington DC or any US territory. Taking on the regulation of your state or country is not exactly a big surprise, It's the same as taking on the rules of a corporation your work for to get a pay check.

It was after the Civil War that the 14th amendment was passed by the Federalists who took control of the government to protect "the former slaves." This amendment brought the former slaves under the jurisdiction of the Federal Government so that their constitutional rights could be protected by government. Many former slaves were receiving abuse from people as well as from local and state governments.

The 14th amendment might have protected these people from being oppressed by their neighbours but it gave them and us a new master the Federal Government. This amendment makes us citizens not only of our states but also it made us a citizen of the United States. This gave the Federal Government powers over the people that it had not known before. The 14th amendment also makes the debt of the Federal Government something we have no right to question. A citizen is a person owing loyalty to and entitled by birth or naturalization to the protection of a state or nation. Most people will receive their citizenship upon the acquisition of their Social Security card. But along with the Social Security Card came the obligation to pay Income Taxes.

We know this is true because of the necessity of a license, which is permission to break the law. If you were a FREE person why would you need a permission from any government to drive a vehicle, get married, start a business or even to do modifications to your home or property. You even need a license to hunt or fish as well.

History Of The Strawman

As we have come to know, the United States Of America has been completely bankrupt since 1933, and many times before but the "nail in the coffin" could be set at 1933. The Constitution requires the government to hold gold and silver as assets. That was taken away to be held by the private foreign corporations. The only actual producing asset left to the United States is its population. How does the country cover the costs of operation of the country?

What did the government come up with as a solution to this problem? The leaders were as a result of the forces of bankruptcy brought to a decision to collateralize the population for credit. How is this done? The people are registered in International Commerce, and the government sells bonds on them. The population becomes the security on the bond itself. The surety is the labour of the people which becomes payable as an undetermined future date. Instead of the people providing battery energy like in The Matrix movie, they provide the energy of capital. They are the human capital.

This makes the people the "utility for the transmission of energy". One could deduct that this results in a very sophisticated form of slavery that becomes our "birthright". The Constitution does not apply because the government, at every level becomes a part of international commerce, and this falls under the Uniform Commercial Code in which animals, in other words, humans and their offspring yet to be born become goods which are able to be sold in commerce. It is simply the way this has evolved because the leaders of nations have mismanaged their financial affairs the same way you or I if we mismanaged the affairs of our corporations would be at the mercy of the creditor assigned to the claim of bankruptcy. And in the game of bankruptcy are nations who have some very clever "creditors".

And so whenever a child is born into the jurisdiction of the UNITED STATES or CANADA, there is a birth certificate and a date that is registered with the Bureau of Vital Statistics in the state or province where the baby is born. When a child is registered it is thus registered into international commerce.

At the time that the birth certificate is registered, something else is created, a separate legal entity. It is a fictional entity called a Trust. It is identified by your name in CAPITAL LETTERS, also known as your Strawman. From now on this Trust will holds all titles to all assets while you the free born real human believes these are yours; but in reality, all you have is the limited right to use these things. They are limited because of the Laws, Statutes and acts that apply to the Corporation you are born under AND the laws that are applicable to the TRUST. How? It is because you have contracted this way, unknowingly perhaps, by way of your parents pledge. And so a new set of laws are applied to you because you accept this as so and you accept that the TRUST name and your name are the same.

When you, on behalf of your Strawman breaks a law or violates a statute, like a traffic ticket the free born flesh and blood you has to appear at the arraignment. It is there that

377

you are asked to accept the Strawman's credit. This is so the real live you can provide the "energy surety" that is due in the way of fines and fees acquired while using the Strawman.

This is why when before the court you are asked to voluntarily give up your name. The entity that is before the court is nothing more than a Strawman. The real you is merely an offender on the offensive team until he agrees to join with the defence (the Strawman) and becomes the defendant by acceptance.

When you were born your parents and the doctor became the pledgor of the birth certificate (Title) to the baby (YOU). The state becomes the owner of this pledge which is a pledge towards the future output (energy) of the child (YOU).

The state then converts this title of security document into a bond to be sold on open markets to cover the cost of government. The person who holds the bond becomes the secured party to receive the energy output of the child (YOU) in the future. The child (YOU) are merely the holder and possessor of the body only, you have no title. Your duty is to the secured party.

The existence and definition of a straw man should be obvious. It is nothing more than an artificial entity owned by the secured party who bought into the bond. The bonds are placed on the market by the Treasury of the United States.

You do not own your Strawman. It is merely a front for the secured party in possession of the bond. Anything a Strawman signs is to place title to property in the hands of the United States and the people who hold the bonds. A Strawman is not set up so the child (You) can acquire property. That is because the child (YOU) do not hold the title to the Strawman. All ownership of your Strawman lies in the States and the bond owners.

If one wants to gain back their liberty and independence then first the one needs to reinstate a living status and regain the original position as beneficiary. There are many avenues on this an it will be discussed in Part 2. Once the real life human regains proper relationship to the Trusts, then one controls the rights to property that the Strawman has accumulated.

This is by no means an easy task. The secret lies in declarations and reinstatements of truth--which is hard to draw out in a system that is tuned to the corporate-admiralty laws. When dealing with a military government if property is registered on the public side, then the property is public. If the property is registered on the private side then it is private property with no public interest.

The military government (democracy) has three tiers of leadership. First there is the Governor, followed by the Secretary of State, and finally there is a Secretary of Treasury. It is the Secretary of State that retains the registration for the Democratic corporation. On the public side of registrations you have the "corporate filings" at the State and local levels. On the private side of filings you have the "Uniform Commercial Code filings" of the creditors to transactions.

The registration by the private creditor becomes the highest priority of recognition to a military state (Democracy). If there is not one registered then one is believed to be foreign with absolutely no rights public or private. The only rights you will have will be given by the military government in the form of Privileges.

Edward Mandell House had this to say in a private meeting with President Woodrow Wilson: ".... *soon, every American will be required to register their biological property in a national system designed to keep track of the people and that will operate under the ancient system of pledging. By such methodology, we can compel people to submit to our agenda, which will <u>effect</u> our security as a <u>chargeback</u> for our fiat paper currency. Every American will be forced to register or suffer being unable to work and earn a living. They will be our chattel, and we will hold the security interest over them forever, by operation of the law merchant under the scheme of secured transactions. Americans, by unknowingly or unwittingly delivering the bills of lading to us will be rendered bankrupt and insolvent, forever to remain economic slaves through taxation, secured by their pledges. They will be stripped of their rights and given a commercial value designed to make us a profit and they will be none the wiser, for not one man in a million could ever figure our plans and, if by accident one or two should figure it out, we have in our arsenal plausible deniability. After all, this is the only logical way to fund government, by floating liens and debt to the registrants in the form of benefits and privileges. This will inevitably reap to us huge profits beyond our wildest expectations and leave every American a contributor to this fraud which we will <u>call "Social Insurance."</u> Without realizing it, every American will insure us for any loss we may incur and in this <u>manner,</u> every American will unknowingly be our servant, however begrudgingly. The people will become helpless and without any hope for their redemption and, we will employ the high office of the President of our dummy corporation to foment this plot against America."*

A Little Story Of A Soul Coming To Planet Earth

Consider this story. A little being in the form of a soul is headed for Earth to take a physical form. After dwelling in the center of the galaxy, the seed or zero point of our universe, the soul crosses the cosmic ocean which was known as the water of Nun or 'None' by the Egyptians. The first gate in the chakra system is the root chakra, the spring from which pours out the fountain of life or living energy that vitalizes everything; the birth canal.

Let us track the soul and the gifts it brings as it '*winds down*' its vibrations to become a '*fish out of water*' when it incarnates in the human body. Having chosen the host, the soul and its new biological partner weaves a human body suit of flesh and blood from DNA and the life force. The soul is now taking refuge in the body.

The root chakra reminds us of who we really are, as children of None and all matter of the earth is composed of the same cosmic waters – the cosmic matrix. This is a much different Divine Matrix which we often refer to as the ether – it is the cosmic ocean that is everywhere. From the matrix, each individual soul arises phoenix like. People we meet, air, and food, all come from the matrix"

And so the cosmic matrix that gives rise to the soul comes with Spirit of which it was a part. But what is important is the new environment that has implications in a more material sense on earth. I want you to pay attention to the analogy of this new entity or body, with a soul, as it manifests itself into a low vibration body that is a fish out of water on planet earth. Listen carefully to how it becomes subject to a new system which is like a ship, its cargo, and under maritime law – the other Matrix.

The tale now shifts from Nature's law where it began to our material world of statutes imposed upon our old friend the Strawman. Let us follow this analogy of a ship with cargo when born and what happens when the cargo is out of water. When mother's water breaks and the cargo descends the birth canal, the new born baby or soul Ark, like the Argo, a boat, comes under maritime law, the manufactured law of the sea. This is now very different from Nature's law or Spiritual law of the cosmic matrix that humankind abides by naturally.

This is all founded upon maritime law like a dictatorship where the captain of the ship has control of everything, even your life. Awaiting for the cargo, or *'argo'*, in the delivery room or *'berth'*, is a state licensed doctor, or *'dock'* who examines the new being to certify a live birth. A certificate of live birth, or *'manifest'* is written itemizing details of the birth, or *'docking'*.

The baby, actually the Ark or Vessel, is given an ID number like a sailing ship. It is a birth registration number used to track the soul as it sails the waters of its earth life. Later there is the social security number. The numbers on the back of the social security card are written in red, symbolic of blood. From the moment of birth to demise, the manifestation of the human machine is regulated on earth. The soul is given liberty to go ashore but it does not have total freedom. The only real freedom is choice within a boxed environment of choices. If you try to take freedoms outside of this box, you find the human machine in a court standing on the dock.

And so a new birthright develops depending upon the culture, the nation, the family born into. In the system of PLANET EARTH, it claims title to the biological machine, considered a chattel, property, and asset in a vast production machine. Is this so the government can regulate all substances or energy imputed into the five primary sensors of the soul to control the mechanism of its output?

First there is the registration of birth to open an account, then there is a social security number to tally the anticipated consumption of resources and production of goods and services. Here the potential is calculated along with the cumulative tax, like a dockage fee for use of the U.S. dock that it will pay as its value on the open market. This lump sum is mortgaged, and pledged as collateral by the U.S. to borrow money from financial interests; the International Monetary Fund.

All legal correspondence between the government and the soul-vessel-ark-container, the product, features the name of the person in capital letters, our Mr. Strawman. Note how a tombstone marks a demise. It is like when a boat or vessel sinks. On your physical death the event is marked with your name in capital letters. The analogy here is that metaphysically and legally speaking, the soul is considered to be dead while sailing in its earthly container; the human body. It is like a ship in a bottle seeking the dock that will allow it to unload its cargo. The human body is the cargo and when it dies, it then re-enters the cosmic ocean.

No one can say for certain what the ultimate capabilities of the earthly ship in a bottle truly are. It is cloaked in darkness. Society is oriented toward suppression of human spiritual power, rather than the blossom of its potential. These are the boxes, remember. Increasingly, our consciousness is being tuned to the all fear, all terror channel as if the generation of fear is humanity's primary purpose. It is being fed with a steady diet of terror to insure this is so. But the soul can overcome fear and alter the machine, if it so chooses. If activated, the body can generate a matrix of love, a force field, a new tone or vibrational ring like a positive cloak.

Fear and terror destabilize these abilities. The solar plexus is our inner power center. *'I am the power'* is the affirmation that activates this chakra. Gut feeling resides here. It is the center of our will. And so it is important to remember this because of one important thing. Your spiritual immortal birthright of sovereignty that you came onto Planet Earth with may be very different than your physical mortal birthright that was imposed upon you. The choice is always there when you become aware that there is a choice.

As it turns out, government is only a puppet on strings because the control over the corporations has come from outside the country; towards the interest of wealth and power for an Elite group of commerce-smarter people. In the beginning of the American dream, the people created the government to serve them but the process has been reversed in that the people now serve the government that serves the higher gods. So the Strawman was an easy conversion.

The Relation To The Constitution

The Constitution for the United States is a document of dual nature as it is a trust document, and it is the articles of incorporation and created a unique trust res and estate of inheritance. It is a tenant of law that in order to determine the intent of a writing one must look to the title, the Empowerment Clause in statute, which in the case of the Constitution is the Preamble. In writing the Constitution the founders followed the common law of England which stretches back some 1000 years. The Preamble fulfills the requirements necessary to establish a trust. It identifies the Grantor(s), Statement of Purpose, Grantee(s), Statement of Intent, Written Indenture, and the name of the entity being created and is written and constructed as a trust so that it would have the thrust of ageless law. Let us take a look:

WE THE PEOPLE (Grantors) of the United States (from or out of) in Order to form a more perfect union, establish justice, provide for the common defence, promote the general welfare and secure the Blessings of Liberty (statement of Purpose) to ourselves and our posterity (Grantees/heirs unnamed), Do Ordain and establish (Statement of Intent) this constitution (Written Indenture) for the United States of America (name of the entity being created).

The trust res is in the Articles of the Confederation and the Declaration of Independence. The intent of the constitution was to bequeath freedom, life, liberty and the pursuit of happiness to themselves and their posterity. The founders intended to secure and pass on the sovereignty of the people to the people of future generations of Americans, in perpetuity.

One's rights are derived from the land upon which one stands and your relation, or status, to that land. In America these rights originated with the Articles of Confederation and the Declaration of Independence and are attached to the land called America (The Laws of Real Property). Our status, or relation to that land, is determined by the laws of Descent and Distribution. The right to freedom, life, liberty and the pursuit of happiness are Our inheritance bequeathed to us via the Constitution of the United States of America.

The constitution granted the government the power and authority to administrate and to carry on corporate functions. Under the common law, inherent rights cannot devolve to a 'body politic' through a corporation. Rights only devolve to human beings is through and **by way of a trust.** Under the constitutional law, in order to determine the meaning of a written instrument the court must look to the title. In this case, once again, it is the Preamble. Pursuant to the laws of real property that have been existence from the beginning, the Preamble clearly shows a freehold in fee simple absolute in it. Freeholds in fee simple were instruments of trust, not corporate. "Our Posterity" cannot be speaking of a corporate entity as posterity can only mean a living man/woman, by birth/nativity.

The Articles of the Constitution are the Articles of Incorporation that established congress as Trustees of the Trust and defines their power and authority as well as their limitations. Annexed to the Constitutional Trust is a will like structure, the Amendments. The Trust and the trust res were already in existence when the will/codicil (Amendments) were added some four years later. The Amendments do not constitute the Trust in fact, they are annexed to the Trust as a codicil (a supplement or addition to the will, not necessarily disposing of the entire estate, but modifying, explaining or otherwise qualifying the will in some way.)

A Trust, once completed and in force cannot be amended or altered without the consent of the parties in interest except under reserved power of amendment and alteration. An amendment is ordinarily possible by parties in interest and against parties without vested interest. Prior to the 14th Amendment the freeborn inhabitants, citizens of the states were the parties in interest. As we have seen, the 14th Amendment created the 14th Amendment legal fiction citizen who do not have a vested interest in the trust or the trust res.

The 14th Amendment can be viewed as a codicil to the will that republished the constitution with new meaning, changed the intent behind it and turned it into a testamentary instrument with capabilities of being used against the free born inhabitants through a seemingly voluntary revocation.

We, the freeholders, as Beneficiaries to the trust have unknowingly accepted the Trustees words and procedures into Testifying against ourselves when we apply for an S.S. #, drivers permit, marriage license or when we sign an IRS 1040 form, which the Trustees have said and led us to believe are mandatory.

When one applies for a Social Security number, provide evidence of birth and claims to be a United States or Canadian citizen, a party with no vested interest in a freehold, the trust or the trust res, one literally **declared the free born inhabitant to be deceased**; the decedent retains no interest in the property and that you, in your dual capacity as a legal fiction citizen are now the **executor of the estate**.

The Trustees have breached the trust having amended the will for their own personal profit and gain at the expense of the true heirs. The freeholders/ Beneficiary has unwittingly, without full disclosure, become the executor and the Trustees have become the Beneficiaries to the trust through the Laws of Donations, effectively stealing Our inheritance.

A breach of trust of fiduciary duty by a Trustee is a violation of correlative right of the Cestui Que Trust (explained later) and gives rise to the correlative cause of action on the part of the Beneficiary for any loss to the estate Trust. This rule is applicable in respect to both positive acts or negligence constituting a breach of fiduciary duty by the Trustee. A Trustee's breach of fiduciary duty falls within the maxim that "equity will not aid one who comes into court with unclean hands."

When the Trustee's breach is by an act of omission the beneficiary can question the propriety of the Trustee. The Beneficiary had to have full disclosure, full knowledge of the material facts and circumstances. A Beneficiary must have had knowledge of and understood their rights and have no obligation to search the public records to obtain said knowledge.

The Trustees have committed acts of omission, mis-representation, deceit and deception in order to mislead and coerce us into giving up our beneficial interest in the trust and the trust res. The Trustees have compelled the free born inhabitants, freeholders in fee simple, to accept the benefits "under the will" perverted by the 14th Amendment, without freedom of choice for failure of full disclosure thereby precluding our enforcement of contractual rights in property bequeathed to us by the will. The Trustees are trying to repudiate the Trust, employing a lifetime of propaganda and programming and enforced through threats, violence and coercion, and failing to provide notice to the Beneficiaries of the repudiation which must be "brought home".

The Doctrine of Election in connection with testamentary instruments is the principle that one who is given a benefit "under the will" must choose between accepting the benefits and asserting some other claim against the testator's estate or against the property disposed of by the will. A Testamentary Beneficiaries right to elect whether to take "under the will" or "against the will" in case he has some inconsistent claim against the testator's estate, is personal to him; is a personal privilege which may be controlled by the creditors of the Beneficiary. They can claim no right or interest in the estate contrary to the debtor's election and may have no right of a legacy or devise to their debtor if he elected to take against the will.

Acceptance of benefits "under the will" constitutes an election which will preclude the devisee from enforcing contractual rights in property bequeathed the will. This rule is, of course, subject to the qualifications that acceptance of a benefit under the will when made in ignorance of the Beneficiaries rights or a mis-apprehension, mis-representation as to the condition of the Testator's estate does not constitute an election.

The Creation Of Three Trusts

In the beginning God gave man dominion over all things, Beneficiaries of the Divine Trust. The Founding fathers of the United States of America created the constitution for the United States, an estate trust, to pass on sovereignty of the people to the people of future generations, in perpetuity.

In America and Canada today, as with many other nations under the kingdom of GREAT BRITAIN upon giving birth a mother is compelled, without full disclosure, to apply for the creation of the **first Cestui Que Vie trust**, creating a 14th Amendment paper citizen of the United States. **Note that a special section in this book is dedicated to the Cestuie Que Vie Trust, a fictional structure originating from centuries ago**. Upon receipt of the mother's application the Trustees establish a trust under the error of assumptions that the child has elected to accept the benefits bequeathed by the will, *under the will*. The Trustees further assume that the child is incompetent, a bankrupt and lost at sea and is presumed dead until the child re-appears and re-establishes his/her living status, challenges the assumption of his/her acceptance of the benefits *under the will* as being one of free choice and with full knowledge of the facts and redeems the estate.

Under the assumption that the child is a 14th Amendment citizen, the child's print is placed on the birth certificate by the hospital creating a slave bond that is sold to the Federal Reserve, who converts the certificate into a negotiable instrument and establishes a **second Cestui Que Vie trust.** The child's parents are compelled to apply for a social security number for the child, unwittingly testifying that the child is a 14th Amendment paper citizen of the United States, not a party in interest to the trust or the trust res, and assumed to be dead after 7 years, when the federal reserve cannot seize the child, they file for the issue of the salvage bond and the child is presumed dead.

When a child is Baptized by the church, the Baptismal certificate is forwarded to the Vatican who converts the certificate into a negotiable instrument and creates a **third Cestui Que Vie trust.** These three trusts represent the enslavement of the property, body and soul of the child.

The civil administration, UNITED STATES, continues to operate today under this triple crown of enslavement based on the error of assumptions that we are 14th Amendment citizens of the United States based on the breach of trust by the trustees.

So what has evolved here is that three trusts have unknowingly been created through the administrative process of governments. These three Cestui Que Vie Trusts represent the triple crown of enslavement and three <u>claims against our property, body and soul </u>by the Roman Cult for the purpose of enslaving the people in the denial of all of our rights to the Divine Inheritance, our right to freedom from all limitations and our rights and powers as Divine Creators.

The Administrators Of The Strawman Fictions

As we have seen, in the early 1930's, when the Canadian and United States governments went bankrupt and could no longer pay back war financing, a new system of debt repayment began. The government pledged all its sentient people as collateral to secure the national debt, and everyone whose birth had been registered became *capitalized* as security. A process of registration of new capital came into being whereby the human born was unknowingly accepted as being a corporate entity (a STRAWMAN) as a copy representation of the sentient human. Over time, a system of exploitation developed where these birth registrations became used to secure the issuance of bonds that were, and still are today, traded internationally. Until just a few years ago you could actually take the bond tracking number from the back of a Canadian birth certificate and look up its value in the bond market. People are deceived into believing that the *capitalized* last-name-first name on the registration of their birth represents them, when in fact it represents a legal entity and a financial instrument created by the state — a *paper person* distinct from the living individual associated with it. The legal entity becomes synonymous with the real person, thus allowing the government and those behind government to *own* you like any other investment, with all the same rights and privileges.

It is important to remember that The "Crown" is the administrative corporation of the Pontiff of Rome owned City of London, the financial, legal and professional standards capitol of/for the Vatican, The City of London is a square mile area within Greater London, England, and is an independent city-state. In the USA, the administrative corporation for the Pontiff of Rome is the UNITED STATES, and that corporation administers the Vatican capitol, for, primarily, military purposes, called Columbia, or the District of Columbia. The UNITED STATES also administers the 50 sub-corporate States of the United States of America, identified with the 2 cap letters – CA, OR, WA, etc.

All adult humans use the fiction name, as imprinted on the copy of the birth certificate you receive when ordering it from Provincial/State Vital Statistics, or to whatever the country upholds as the source you apply through. Although the birth certificate is of somewhat recent origin and used to formally offer "citizens" as chattel in bankruptcy to the Pope's Holy Roman Empire owned Rothschilds' Banking System, the false use of the family name goes back into the Middle Ages in England. Thus, it is with the family name made a primary, or surname, (example - Mister Jones), and the given names of the child (example - Peter) made a reference name to the primary name. This is the reverse or mirror image to reality. A "family name" is NOT a man's name - it is a name of a clan - a blood relationship. In truth then the given names would be Edward Alexander of the Rychkun clan or family.

By acceptance of the name EDWARD ALEXANDER RYCHKUN, I am then "forced" or "obliged" to use that name in all commercial and Government dealings and communications. So, when I do use it, as 99.99% of the human inhabitants of North America (and most of the world) do, I supposedly "voluntarily' attach myself Edward Alexander, the free will adult human, to the Crown/State owned property, called the "legal identity name" as an accessory attached to property owned by Another party. Think of a ship under tow by another ship. Which captain decides what route the ships will take? The legal name/Strawman is the tow rope, and the towing ship is the corporate (make-believe ship at sea) Crown of the City of London. As an attachment to the legal name owned by the Crown, you are the towed ship, and your vessel captain, your free will mind, is now a subservient crewmember to the captain of the Crown.

The State or Crown does not give us authority, grant, license, permission or leave to use the Crown or State owned legal identity name. Thus, our use of it as an adult free will man (male or female) is a form of "theft" against a maritime jurisdiction entity (all incorporated bodies are "make-believe ships at sea"). In maritime law, the accused is guilty until proven innocent. This allows the Roman Law system, which we have, to impose "involuntary servitude" upon an adult man. Involuntary servitude simply means a slave stripped of granted rights of a slave called a citizen, subject or freeman. This stripped rights included "due process of law" - no jury trial, and charges where no harm has been done against another man, or his property with criminal intent.

We see this Roman Law within the US 13th Amendment (#2) instituted in the mid 1860's: *"Neither slavery nor involuntary servitude, except as a punishment for crime whereof the party shall have been duly convicted,"* The crime with which you have been convicted is *unauthorized use* of the State's or Crown's intellectual property - the legal identity name.

The Crown/State then invokes the legal maxim, accessio cedit principali, [an accessory attached to a principal becomes the property of the owner of the principal], where the principal is the legal identity name as "intellectual property". The owner is the corporation called the Crown/State, or UNITED STATES, and the accessory is the free will human who has supposedly volunteered himself to be "property by attachment" of the Crown/State. An adult human who is property is, and by any other name, of "slave status", be it citizen, subject or freeman.

As a slave, one's property in possession, including body and labour, belongs to the slave owner 100%. And, the property right is a bundle of rights - own, use, sell, gift, bequeath and hypothecate property. The process deployed, from Birth to Death is as below using CANADA as an example.

First of all, the Birth Certificate is a formal document which certifies as to the date and place of one's birth and a recitation of his or her parentage, as issued by an official in charge of such records. Note that a Birth Certificate not a formal identity document but it is a negotiable instrument, a registered security, a stock certificate evidencing, or representing, the preferred stock of the corporation and against which you are the surety; it is a pedigree chattel document establishing the existence of our Strawman, a distinct artificial person with a fictitious name; it is a document of title to a Strawman; it is a warehouse receipt for your body; delivery receipt; industrial bond between you (flesh-and-blood man or woman) and the industrial society and corporate US or CANADA Government as an artificial person.

In Canada, the original birth certificate is generally created at the PROVINCIAL level (in rare instances city level) via birth documents from the hospital (for which the hospital receives $$$ from the PROVINCE for causing the registration of the birth) and passed to the Provincial and Federal levels, and likely elsewhere. Per the definition of "birth" below, the document references both the newborn and the straw man. Certified *copies* of the birth certificate may be obtained at the Vital Statistics Office. Your birth certificate is one of the kinds of security instrument used by the Government to obtain loans from its creditor, under which it is bankrupt.

The act of being born or wholly brought into separate existence. <u>Black's 1st</u>. Note: A man or a woman is *"born"*, Strawman are *"wholly brought into separate existence."* Each event qualifies as a *"birth"*. The birth certificate documents a muddied mixture of the two events that allows the system to both claim that it is *"your"* birth certificate yet also claim to <u>hold title to</u> (<u>not</u> ownership of) the corporately coloured Strawman.

The first step in the administrative process is the MARRIAGE TRUST REGISTRATION TO CREATE CAPITAL. This occurs at the MUNICIPAL VITAL STATISTICS AGENCIES. Here a Mother and Father apply for a marriage and register to receive a Marriage Certificate in their STRAWMAN Names. As they marry they create a Trust which holds the estate of their progeny as human creations. The progeny becomes released to the title of the offspring to the Government for their use. It is noted that Registration" comes from Latin "Rex, Regis" etc. meaning regal. Thus what occurs is whatever is "registered" means to hand legal title over to the Crown. When you register anything with the public, it releases legal title to the government corporation and leaves you with only equitable title – the right to use, not own, and for that use you will pay a "use" tax, be it income, sin, sales, property, etc. as opposed to lawful taxes, excise and impost. In this way it doesn't *appear* that the government now owns the property which you have registered as they put it in a name which is a copy of You as a NAME owned by the government. If you choose rather to *record* your legal title to your property with the public, you maintain your status as Title Owner. This is one of the most important things you can ever learn for the sake of your commercial affairs.

If you examine older version of the marriage certificate or a birth certificate you will find a number in red ink that begins with a letter. On the small plastic card the number will appear on the back of the card. On the larger Birth Certificate printed on bank note paper the red number may be on the front. In the USA this bank note paper comes from the American Bank Note Company, in Canada it comes from the CANADIAN BANK NOTE COMPANY LIMITED. This information can be found along the lower left-hand edge of the note. If you are holding one of these you are holding a certified copy of a bank note in your name that has a value of well over $1,000,000 (one million dollars). The number in red ink is a Revenue Receipt in Canada and a bond number or a bond tracking number.

Let us follow this process in detail (some repetition). This process is done through the VITAL STATISTICS Agencies as a subsidiary of the department of HEALTH.

This step occurs with **THE BIRTH OF THE SENTIENT HUMAN in a LOCAL HOSPITAL.** You, a real human are born as you are birthed (Berthed) through the mothers' water canal. This places the prime capital asset into the Trust holding equitable title of You. You parents give you a Name that is accepted and taught as Upper and Lower case name. A certificate of Manifest is required as the vessel (Mother) and its cargo must be registered upon landing (born). A Registration of Birth is created and the Mother signs the Birth Certification as Trustee of You under your given name. An estate is therefore created for

Your use and benefit so you become the GRANTOR of this estate as You will be placing items of value within it. Your parents are the creators of the estate as they created you. The BC refers to mother as an "informant". This process as in America and Canada today, as with many other nations under the kingdom of GREAT BRITAIN upon giving birth a mother is compelled, without full disclosure, to apply for the creation of the **first Cestui Que Vie trust**, creating a 14th Amendment paper citizen of the United States. *Note that a special section in this book is dedicated to the Cestuie Que Vie Trust, a fictional structure originating from centuries ago.*

Upon receipt of the mother's application the Trustees establish a trust under the error of assumptions that the child has elected to accept the benefits bequeathed by the will, "under the will". The Trustees further assume that the child is incompetent, a bankrupt and lost at sea and is presumed dead until the child re-appears and re-establishes his/her living status, challenges the assumption of his/her acceptance of the benefits 'under the will' as being one of free choice and with full knowledge of the facts and redeems the estate.

Under the assumption that the child is a 14th Amendment citizen, the child's footprint is placed on the birth certificate by the hospital creating a slave bond that is sold to the federal reserve, who converts the certificate into a negotiable instrument and establishes a **second Cestui Que Vie trust.** The child's parents are compelled to apply for a social security number for the child, unwittingly testifying that the child is a 14th Amendment paper citizen of the United States, not a party in interest to the trust or the trust res, and assumed to be dead after 7 years, when the federal reserve cannot seize the child, they file for the issue of the salvage bond and the child is presumed dead.

When a child is baptized by the church, the Baptismal certificate is forwarded to the Vatican who converts the certificate into a negotiable instrument and creates a **third Cestui Que Vie trust. By the process of baptism, one then agrees to fall under the code of the VATICAN which is the Bible as written by them.**

These three trusts represent the enslavement of the property, body and soul of the child. The civil administration of CANADA and UNITED STATES, continues to operate today under this triple crown of enslavement based on the error of assumptions that we are 14th Amendment citizens of the United States based on the breach of trust by the trustees. So what has evolved here is that three trusts have unknowingly been created through the administrative process of governments. These three Cestui Que Vie Trusts represent the triple crown of enslavement and three claims against our property, body and soul by the Roman cult for the purpose of enslaving the people in the denial of all of our rights to the Divine Inheritance, our right to freedom from all limitations and our rights and powers as Divine Creators.

THE REGISTRATION OF CAPITAL (PROVINCIAL HUMAN RESOURCES REGISTRY) Unknown to the administration of the Municipality, the Government at the Municipal level claims an interest in every child within its jurisdiction as a valuable asset as a human resource which if properly trained, can contribute valuable assets provided by its labour for many years. As You are to be pledged as "HUMAN CAPITAL RESOURCE," that can contribute to the welfare of the Municipality of origin every year, your 'registration places You as a 'ward of the Government'. Presented as a safeguard for the child and the parents, this allows the creation and registration of a commercial entity used for the purpose of exploitation.

BIRTH REGISTRATION AND BIRTH OF THE STRAWMAN (PROVINCIAL TREASURY) The Birth Registration of the new cargo (child) creates an entry into the registry to create a Certificate of Birth in the NAME of the STRAWMAN as a fictional dead corporation which simulates a copy of You. As the Government creates this entity, it also owns it. As The number of the Birth Certificate becomes a reference in the Provincial Treasury to be like a certificate of Incorporation. It is also a descendant of You Note: A man or a woman is "born", straw men are *wholly brought into separate existence.*" Each event qualifies as a "birth". The birth certificate documents a muddied mixture of the two events that allows the system to both claim that it is "your" birth certificate yet also claim to hold title to (not ownership of) the corporately coloured Strawman.

REGISTRATION OF THE STRAWMAN AS AN ENTITY (with the FEDERAL MINISTRY OF FINANCE and the Secretary Treasurer The NAME now representing a new asset of You is registered in the Individual Master File as a Foreigner from a foreign jurisdiction as a Criminal with multiple criminal charges. This is registered into the MASTER FILE as a alien, resident of Puerto Rico. As a criminal the STRAWMAN has no rights and is guilty before proving innocence as it all fall under Maritime Law. This is opposite to the way it works in common law where the real human is innocent until proven guilty. The registration number is the Birth Certificate number. As the Government own this entity it can attach criminal violations or whatever history it deems necessary to keep the STRAWMAN in penal position.

The STRAWMAN Corporation is assigned a Municipal bond number by the Federal Ministry of Finance creating a negotiable instrument, a registered security, a stock certificate of the corporation against which You are the surety of this bond: a pedigree chattel document establishing the existence of the STRAWMAN in the name of STRAWMAN and gives authority to Provincial department to issue a Birth Certificate to the parents on your behalf. This number is the Treasury Direct number on the Birth Certificate (in Canada). The value of the bond is set at over 1 million dollars. The Birth Certificate is registered as a warehouse receipt for the body, a delivery receipt, an industrial bond between You and the Corporation (STRAWMAN) owned by the Government since they created it. This in earlier version of the Canadian Birth Certificates and Marriage Certificate is the red number stated as "Revenue Receipt XXXxXX for Treasury Use only" This security instrument sets the means for them to obtain loans from its creditor under which it, the Nation, is bankrupt.

DELIVERY OF THE BIRTH CERTIFICATE (MINISTRY OF FINANCE, PROVINCIAL TREASURY, VITAL STATISTICS AGENCY) After creating the Birth Certificate on bank note paper (in USA this bank note paper comes from the American Bank Note Company, in Canada it comes from the CANADIAN BANK NOTE COMPANY LIMITED), a Certified Original Copy of The Birth Certificate is sent back to the parents who are Trustee for You. The original is retained by the Ministry of Finance on behalf of the provincial Treasury. This is a copy is an acknowledgement that You are born in the jurisdiction (landed cargo in Canada or US) and are an capital asset belonging to the Municipality where You were born.

REGISTRATION OF ASSET WITH BANKING (BANK OF CANADA, FEDERAL RESERVE BANK, IMF) Since USA/CA have been bankrupt for decades, having no substance such as gold and silver to back it, the only asset it has is men and woman and their labour which was pledged to the IMF which is the private commercial entity that the bankruptcy/receivership deal was made with. The pledge of labour is registered as the collateral for the interest on the loan of the World Bank which the private banking entity associated with the IMF. Each Capital Asset allowed the treasury to issue the birth certificate and the bond which is registered within the Canadian and US banking systems. The Bond is registered with the World Bank and the Bank of Canada. This information can be found along the lower left-hand edge of the note. If you are holding one of these you are holding a certified copy of a bank note in Your name that has some set value of well over $1,000,000. The number in red ink is a bond number or a bond tracking number. The Bank of Canada can now issues debt instruments as paper which are assumed to be money as a draw against the IMF line of credit which is to paid off by You and your pledge.

REGISTRATION WITH IMF SYSTEM (IMF, CGS, WORLD BANK) The bond is assigned an international; CUSIP 9 character number through CGS Municipal Issuer access through an authorized representative such as The Canadian Depository for Securities to cover a wide range of global financial instruments, including extensive equity and debt issues, derivatives, syndicated loans and U.S. listed equity options. This is done through CGS CUSIP GLOBAL SERVICES in New York (near DDTC) and MSRB Municipal Securities Rulemaking Board in Virginia.

The treasury issues a bond on the birth certificate and the bond is sold at a securities exchange and bought by the FRB/BoC, (Federal Reserve Bank/Bank of Canada) which then uses it as collateral to issue bank notes. The bond is held in trust for the Feds at the Depository Trust Corporation. We are the sureties on said bonds. Our labour/energy is then payable at some future date. Hence we become the "transmitting utility" for the transmission of energy.

The birth certificate created a FICTION (the name of the baby in upper case letters). The state/province sells the birth certificate to the Commerce Department of the corporations of USA/CA, which in turn places a bond on the birth certificate thereby making it a negotiable instrument, and placing the fiction, called a STRAWMAN, into the warehouse of the corporation of USA/CA. Representation for the created fiction was given to the BAR (British Accredited Registry/Regency), owned and operated by the Crown, for the purpose of contracting the fiction (which most of us think is ourselves) into a third party action. Do not underestimate the power behind this trick. It is to con us into contracting with the Feds so that they can 'legally' confiscate our property. All these contracts have only *our* signature on them because corporate fictions cannot contract (only natural beings have the right to contract – and the right *not* to contract). Because there is no full disclosure – we are never told that we have just signed away what we believe to be *our* property – these contracts are fraudulent, and hence, we are still the lawful owner and the profit earned by the Feds from stealing securities (our property) belongs to us and must go into a fund for our benefit, otherwise it would be fraud. Not wanting to be charged with fraud, the Feds had to create a remedy for us...and hope we wouldn't discover it.

BOND TRADING ON WORLD MARKETS (WORLD BANK, FIDELITY TRUST) The World Bank, on behalf of the Ministry of Finance and the Bank of Canada lodges the bond with Fidelity Trust offshore in the Caribbean or other trading securities institutions for the purpose of trading it and deriving interest or profit from the activity. It is brokered as a security and traded on the exchanges such as New York stock exchange You are the collateral for the interest on the loan of the World Bank. The bond is sold at a securities exchange and bought by the FRB/BoC, (Federal Reserve Bank/Bank of Canada) which then uses it as collateral to issue bank notes. Under the fractional reserve banking regulations, the original securities can be leveraged to create 10 such securities. As a result if the original bond value was 1 million, the value of securities to be traded on the worlds market would be $1 million.

MONETARY ENRICHMENT AND HELD IN TRUST (DEPOSITORY TRUST COMPANY).
The bond as a claim of capital is held in trust for Bank of Canada at the Depository Trust Corporation. You are the surety for this bond as the one who has the penal municipal bond against you and are the guarantee for the payment of it. It is through your

labour/energy payable at some future date so it is held in trust. Hence You become the 'transmitting utility' for the transmission of energy. The bond is held in trust for the Government at the Depository Trust Corporation or DTC in New York but owned by the IMF as private agency. You become the unknowing the sureties on the bonds where labour/energy is then payable at some future date. Hence You become the 'transmitting utility' for the transmission of energy. The bond becomes part of the estate of You. At the same time the DTC in collaboration with the World Bank are free to use the original financial instrument as the Birth Certificate to trade on the market, so as to derive interest and enrichment as lodged into the DTC account under the Birth Registration number.

UNTIL THE AGE OF MATURITY (You and YOU) Over time the estate is built through the efforts of You and the bonds as assets that are registered in the name of the Commercial Enterprise of the STRAWMAN. All commerce is transacted under this STRAWMAN NAME where the bond or any other assets that may have come into existence during the early life are registered against. The municipal bonds continue to generate revenue every year. As assets are registered, they are brought under the title of the STRAWMAN. If they are not, they remain as Your Estate.

APPLICATION OF THE SOCIAL INSURANCE NUMBER (SERVICE CANADA, CRA) At some age of maturity as an adult, You create an application for a Social Insurance Number (SIN) as a formal process. When one applies for a Social Security number, provide evidence of birth and claims to be a United States or Canadian citizen, a party with no vested interest in a freehold, the trust or the trust res, one literally **declared the free born inhabitant to be deceased**; the decedent retains no interest in the property and that you, in your dual capacity as a legal fiction citizen are now the **executor of the estate**. This is also the formalization of the pledge of future commercial output and Your consent to be taxed on that effort. As the application is done under the Crown/State owned STRAWMAN name, the name found on the birth certificate, and with that certificate being the pledged document to the bankruptcy creditor, that adult human, by attachment through application for registration, becomes a synonymous with it and becomes a ward or SLAVE owned by the corporate Crown of the City of London, and thus to the Vatican. All of the Slave's property, including his or her labour (100%) is claimed by the slave owner. (of the STRAWMAN Corporation). From that point on, all things you purchase, possess, and wages you earn are in the Crown/State owned name. The wages or earnings you get to keep for your own use and enjoyment is called a 'benefit' from the slave owner. Unknown to You, through the application of SIN or SSN this signals the equivalent wind up, cessation or death of You, the real sentient being. The STRAWMAN corporation and ESTATE which is available then provide the Government with the means to hold the estate which can be probated like a will.

ISSUANCE OF THE SIN NUMBER (CRA and Federal Ministry of Finance) The issuance of the S.I.N. (or S.S.N.) is equivalent to a Certificate of Cessation, or Winding-Up of the company, or appropriately, a Death Certificate for the real You. The certification of the death provides the Government owned Strawman to create the Estate of that STRAWMAN in that name of that registered foreigner. At this age of maturity, or ability to work, You apply for a SIN as a Government requirement to account for the income created by Your efforts, all accumulated into the Your estate. It is registered with the Tax authority CRA that remits this to the Receiver who acts as the receiver in bankruptcy for the IMF (all bankrupt treasuries and municipalities) to the Federal Ministry of Finance then the Bank of Canada. That residual revenues after tax is in fact Yours but the taxes form part of the Federal Transfer payments the federal government and the Bank of Canada are authorized to send to the provincial government every year--back to the local municipal level. The Federal Minister of Finance is acting as a fiduciary over that revenue and bond. Those funds are yours and they owe it to you as it is supported by Your secret pledge.

ROLLOVER OF THE ESTATE EXCECUTORSHIP (Ministry OF FINANCE) With the cessation of You, only the shadow overlay of the criminal STRAWMAN registered in the IMF alien files exists. As you or your Father never claimed and position because neither were aware, You now fulfill automatically become the Executor in the Executor Office. You are an earthly estate walking around creating what you were to be beneficiary of. The Certificate of Birth or Live Birth Certificate is the Public Record of the Estate and that the Estate is Probated. A trust can only exist if there is already an Estate in existence. The address of the estate is the file number on the birth certificate. The estate resides at the file number. The estate is restricted to the file number; it cannot move anywhere else. Unknowingly You nor your Father do not step forward to claim the living position as Beneficiary and Grantor and hence the Government steps in through a change of Fiduciary (Form 56) to have the role of executor for the foreigners created estate assumed by You who by default abandoned it. The trustees thus become the Beneficiaries and You are effectively even as Grantor, judged incompetent at the age of maturity. Until you step up and correct this situation judges will treat you as a criminal since You have assumed the role of the DEAD MAN criminal, as registered in the IMF file you are incompetent to engage in the executor role.

PROBATING THE ESTATE (MINISTRY OF FINANCE) At the point of probate, an living Executor is required. You are the legitimate Executor authorized to occupy the Executor Office because when You were born, You were sent the Executor Office (the Birth Certificate), and then only 3 people could get a copy of your Birth Certificate – You, mom and dad. Once you reached the age of maturity (21), you became the only one authorized until you come of age, your father has the authority to occupy the Executor Office of the Estate bearing your STRAWMAN provided he is aware. Upon attaining the age of majority (21), you may step into and assume your proper capacity in the Executor Office of Estate. As the grantor of the estate, You are the only one who can appoint the Executor or assign its duties to someone else. The Executor can appoint trustees but cannot authorize fictional entities to administrate the estate. By definition the *Executor is the authority that grants the power and duties and liabilities to each of the trustees, and to any beneficiaries. (A "grantor", is not equivalent to an Executor, and does not have or enjoy the Executor's powers, rights, or immunities. Through the process when You are declared diseased, a New Executor then assigns the STRAWMAN as trustee who has no claim of right. The executor must be a live human and that become you thus allowing the government to be the beneficiaries.*

TAXES AND WORKING OFF THE DEBT (CRA, RECEIVER GENERAL) As you work the efforts are recorded against the SIN and taxes are paid were the IRS and CRA administer and police the taxation. As the STRAWMAN belongs to the Government and they are the Executors of the estate, the tax proceeds are remitted towards the debt of the country, through CRA, the Ministry of Finance and the Bank of Canada to deposit in the World Bank for the account of the IMF. This is the payback that You pledged unknowingly and the transfer payments are paid by the world bank as debt to the bankrupt operating company Canada. The administrative process of accounting within this receivership is the purpose of the Agencies created within the Country, such as the Bank of Canada, Federal Reserve Banks, and the CRA. The Ministries of the Country are there to administer and account for the payment and receipt of debt money.

BANKING AND LOANS (Local FEDERAL RESERVE BANKS and BANK OF CANADA) As you apply for loans, credit and mortgages, you as the energy and sole means of creating real money provide the authorization in the form of loan agreements, promissory notes on behalf of the STRAWMAN/TRUST that pledge your payments back. Similar to becoming the surety on the bonds created by them, your provide the signatures for them to create money for which you become the surety to pay it to them. The banks that cannot create money then create entries that simulate money being loaned to You. You pay them the amount and interest while they use these instruments to trade on the open market. They combine these into a bond of 100 million or greater and trade this to their benefit through the DTC CUSIP through the World Bank in association with the Bank of Canada who has the fiduciary duty of creation and monitoring this as a product of supporting the bankrupt nation. The amounts are registered in the DTC as they are accounted for within the registry Note that there are 20 Federal Reserve Banks listed in Canada including Montreal, Alberta Treasury, Scotia, HSBC, Credential Securities, CIBC and Bank of Canada as the Authority reporting to the Federal Reserve. The Bank of Canada, like the US Federal Reserve Bank are Central Banks.

You only signed these contracts for SSN/SIN numbers, registrations and other licenses because you were led to believe this artificial CORPORATION was you and that you were obliged to sign. They did not tell you that by signing these contracts you were signing away your lawful *rights* and *freedoms* and giving the government total control of your life, property and labour. Today, the one simple fact that the World Bank does not want you to find out is that all these contracts are *fraudulent* and that because of that fact you have always had and still, to this very moment, retain all your lawful *rights* and *freedoms*. We have been deceived into being bound by rules, statutes and "laws" that simply do not apply to human beings.

FINAL DEATH OF THE STRAWMAN (VITAL STATISTICS on up the line to the IMF)
At the point of your death you will have accumulated three estates. One is the Constructive Trust that you abandoned, and the other contains the possessions that you have accumulated under your private affairs, except where you have registered into the commercial system under the name of the STRAWMAN. The other is the divine trust with the Vatican. In this case it is the title of the asset that is held as Your the right to use it, not the asset itself. This is deemed your benefit of tenancy and alleged ownership but allows you to trade and sell the use of what is not yours in a way that it so appears as the real thing. In reality it all belongs to the Government which is in tern owned by the IMF under the commercial laws of Bankruptcy. The true the power behind this that they can 'legally' confiscate the real property but as yet, have not taken this action which is the slaves benefit. When You die, a Registration of Death must be issued through the same Vital Statistics agency and the STRAWMAN along with You cease to exists (in actuality). The hidden estate of the STRAWMAN is now the property of the IMF (the supporter of the nations bankruptcy) and the gravestone and Death Certificate mark the termination of the STRAWMAN and You as one and the same. The birth certificate bonds and securities created cease to be of value as do the other assets within the STRAWMAN TRUST, however, this does not prevent the World Bank to do as they wish with it and the proceeds of enrichments. On the national level, the FICTION and the human cease to exist and do not contribute revenues and services. From the National warehouse of the corporation of USA/CA, the entries are deleted.

All Corporate Bodies Are Make-Believe Ships At Sea,

And so all corporate bodies are make-believe ships at sea, and are thus, internally, under maritime law, which will be explained later [incorrectly called admiralty law, unless applied to the military]. In maritime law, an accused is guilty unless proven innocent. Thus, a free will adult man who uses, without authority, the property of a corporate body is under maritime jurisdiction. This makes a free will man who uses a corporate Crown or corporate State owned legal identity name a 'convicted criminal', and thus subject to the imposition of slavery, involuntary servitude.

You, as a child, were Crown or State property by way of the birth registry, and thus, you could use Crown or State property, the legal identity name. When you became an adult, as a vessel on the 'sea of life' as a sovereign captain/free will mind, you no longer had a right to use (as an 'identity' name) that Crown or State owned legal identity name.

However, under the "property right" of a slave owner in regard to property in the possession of an owned slave, a "demand" for the property by the slave owner, or the slave owner's agent (such as the IRS, or county tax collector, or for a court imposed fine), is all that is necessary, without regard to due process of law. Remember, ALL that a slave possesses belongs to the slave owner.

This does not mean you are a slave. It is that the Government, and its employees, judges and officers SEE you as a SLAVE. See sections 35, 46 and 78 of the "Bills of Exchange Act of Canada" regarding eligibility for use of the provisions of that Act. GOOGLE it. A bill can only be paid with money, and there is no money in Canada or the USA since the early 1930's. All that is left is some form of a "promissory note". In Canada, Parliament even converted the Canadian currency to pure Monopoly Game money by declaring that Canadian currency is no longer a promissory note nor bill of exchange. (Section 25(6) of the Bank of Canada Act).

When we are a child, we can have an identifying name because we are property, property that should belong to the natural parents, but by registry of live birth, where the parents identify themselves as being of slave status owned by the corporate Crown, the child becomes the property of the Corporate Crown. Because the child does not have a matured mind, it is a vessel under construction in "dry dock".

When the registry of live birth is performed, the Province, as an agent for the Crown, then changes the family name to a 'sur' or primary name, thus making the Crown owned legal name as intellectual property owned by the Crown. As the child grows up, the child is taught by society and the education system to identify him or herself by that legal name, an accept the idea that they have a 'surname'.

When the child reaches the age of majority, the human vessel is launched on the sea of life, and the mature moral thinking mind becomes the supreme commander of the human vessel. The supremacy of the captain of a vessel supersedes any claim of ownership when the vessel is on the high sea. This had to be overcome in the maritime world of corporate bodies, which are make-believe shops at sea.

So, what the Government, as agent for the corporate Crown devised, was to not give authorization for the adult man to identify him or herself by the legal name, even though they were taught to do so all their life as a child. Thus, a man, identifying him or herself as being one and the same as the legal name, the name one finds on the birth certificate, is an act of theft of intellectual property of another and triggers the legal maxim (requires no further proof) arising out of the property right - accessio cedit principali - an accessory attached (without authorization) to a principal becomes the property of the principal. Thus the supposed to be free will man, with the mind being the supreme commander of his human vessel/body, becomes like a ship under tow by another ship - a slave to the towing ship.

Even though the country was bankrupt the banks could not take away your *rights* and *freedoms*, under the terms of bankruptcy they forced the government to create an artificial CORPORATION (STRAWMAN) in your name. Then they had you sign fraudulent contracts to accept the *privileges* and *benefits* attached to this artificial CORPORATION. You only signed these contracts for SSN/SIN numbers, registrations and other licenses because you were led to believe this artificial CORPORATION was you and that you were obliged to sign. They did not tell you that by signing these contracts you were signing away your lawful *rights* and *freedoms* and giving the government total control of your life, property and labour.

Today, the one simple fact that the World Bank does not want you to find out is that all these contracts are *fraudulent* within their own laws (as we shall see later) and that because of that fact you have always had and still, to this very moment, retain all your lawful *rights* and *freedoms*. We have been deceived into being bound by rules, statutes and "laws" that simply do not apply to human beings. The issue is one of how to undo this and to enforce the action.

Who Became The Administrators Of The Trusts?

The local Vital statistics Agency is where this process starts. The Vital statistics agencies are tasked with birth, marriage and death. This is a subsidiary of the Ministry of Health.

CANADA	US
CEO Vital Statistics Agency	Vital statistics Agency
Minster of Health	Rector Basilica of the National Shrine
Secretary of the Treasury Board	Secretary of State
Attorney General	Department of Justice
Governor General	American Inns of Court

In any of these cases, those who administer simply do a job with a job description. The ones who may know some of the truth will be the ones who have signed non-disclosure and proprietary agreements that they violate at their peril. In looking at the lower structures of responsibilities, it is not usual that one department knows the whole picture, and as such all simply do a segment of the whole and never understand nor believe that this may be improper, fraud, or deception. And if this is "the law" or "way things are done" as policed by the code of laws, then that is the way it is supposed to be. any attack on this becomes a radical fringe rebellion that needs to be corrected.

Think about an analogy of a cage of five monkeys. Inside, we hang bananas and place stairs under them. When a monkey attempts to climb the stairs, we spray the other four with cold water. They do not like cold water. If you repeat this when any monkey tries to climb to the bananas, soon the monkeys will prevent others from climbing. They kick up a fuss and even beat it. Now let us put the water away and replace one monkey. When the new one tries to climb, he gets attacked. So let us remove another original monkey and bring in another new one. It will get attacked if it tries climbing. If you do this until all five original monkeys are replaced, guess what? The monkeys that are beating the most recent one have no idea why they should not climb or why they should beat the others. After five are replaced, there is no water, no one is sprayed, yet no one climbs. Why? They know that's the way it has always been done.

The **Cestui que** use and trust were rooted in medieval law, and became a legal method to avoid the feudal (medieval) incidents (payments) to an overlord, while leaving the land for the use of another, who owed nothing to the lord. The law of cestui que tended to defer jurisdiction to courts of equity as opposed to common law courts. The cestui que was often utilized by persons who might be absent from the kingdom for an extended time (as on a Crusade, or a business adventure), and who held tenancy to the land, and owed feudal incidents to a lord. The land could be left for the use of a third party, who did not owe the incidents to the lord. This legal status was also invented to circumvent the Statute of Mortmain. That statute was intended to end the relatively common practice of leaving real property to the Church at the time of the owner's death. Since the Church never died, the land never left the "dead hand" ("Mortmain" or Church). An alternative explanation of "mortmain" was that an owner from generations earlier was still dictating land use years after death, by leaving it to the Church. Hence the term "dead hand." Before the Statute of Mortmain, large amounts of land were bequeathed to the Church, which never relinquished it. This was in contradistinction to normal lands which could be inherited in a family line or revert to a lord or the Crown upon death of the tenant. Church land had been a source of contention between the Crown and the Church for centuries. Cestui que use allowed religious orders to inhabit land, while the title resided with a corporation of lawyers or other entities, who nominally had no relation to the Church.

There are multiple trusts and accounts created in this process and for decades, many people have tried to crack their way into these structures.

The **first Cestui Que Vie trust**, created a 14th Amendment paper citizen of the United States and in Canada. *The creators as the state and* Trustees assume that the child is incompetent, a bankrupt and lost at sea and is presumed dead until the child re-appears and re-establishes his/her living status, challenges the assumption of his/her acceptance of the benefits 'under the will' as being one of free choice and with full knowledge of the facts and redeems the estate. A bond is sold to the   bond that is sold to the federal reserve, who converts the certificate into a negotiable instrument and establishes a **second Cestui Que Vie trust.** The child's parents are compelled to apply for a social security number for the child, unwittingly testifying that the child is a 14th Amendment paper citizen of the United States, not a party in interest to the trust or the trust res, and assumed to be dead after 7 years, when the federal reserve cannot seize the child, they file for the issue of the salvage bond and the child is presumed dead. When a child is Baptized by the church, the Baptismal certificate is forwarded to the Vatican who converts the certificate into a negotiable instrument and creates a **third Cestui Que Vie trust.** By the process of baptism, one then agrees to fall under the code of the VATICAN which is the Bible as written by them. **They monetize the baptism certificate.**

The fourth process occurs when third process occurs When you create "money" through mortgages, loans, credit cards, at the bank. Tagged by the Social Insurance, Social Security numbers, these credit notes, promissory notes become accumulated into bonds which are traded on the open market. Two things are happening here as you are creating new money (credit) and you are paying principle and interest out to the bank. The third is the deposits that you may have placed there as well. All of these can be multiplied under fractional system for their own enrichment. When you close the accounts, or pay them off, these commitments have been accumulated into parcels of 10 million dollar instruments and traded so the originals never come back to you. When an account is closed, the entries on the other side of the ledger remain. The process of attempting to get access to this is called the Closed Account Redemption process. These amounts are registered in the national registries such as the DTCC in New York.

The fifth process occurs with regards to taxes and income, again tagged by the SSN or SIN. The income taxes that you pay are payments against the bonds registered against you and what the state borrowed, The borrowed a million using you as collateral. The taxes are the payment against that bond. And it goes towards paying the interest on the debt. At this time the principle of the debt is so enormous, it can never be paid. However, the taxes, as payments, are registered against the debt.

Another process called Acceptance for Value deals with the UCC and the Bills of exchange Act that we will not get into here. The process have been pushed for decades but have never really penetrated through the matrix. It is because the dead cannot speak to the dead--at least in this movie! You, abandoned your rights and credit because you were outsmarted?

Thus not only does the real human create the credit for the system which the system can then enhance as profit, but they also provide labour to pay taxes, interest, principle into the system. To each mortal, this has no meaning because the mortgage or loan gives them the ability to acquire use on the pretence they own it. The fact that the bank and the feds can create more money to finance their needs such as the military is also of no significance to the mortal because he never knew about it anyway... so what is the big deal! It's all like the five monkeys, perfectly ok as long as the water is there to drink.

And who is to say that this is wrong for all. After all, the bottom line is you borrow whatever to buy a house, you agree to pay it back with interest and you can live in that house until you die. Who cares that its only paper! And so the big boys are smart enough to make the big bucks by using you as collateral? You can do the same if you are smart enough... so good for them. And who cares that you pay taxes because your forefathers screwed up? It keeps the economy alive.

Redeeming Your Beneficiary Status

In order to correct the situation with regards to You and YOU relationships to the Estate and Trust, there are several issues that need to be corrected. These are the declarations that need to be enforced into reality:

We, the Divine Spirit, expressed in trust in living flesh, having returned from being lost in the sea of illusion, born of a self imposed state of amnesia and years of propaganda and extreme programming, to re-establish Our living status and redeem Our estate establishes the evidence in fact of Our competence rebutting the assumption with fact.

We, the Divine Spirit, object to and issue Divine Notice of Protest to the breach of trust and the usurpation of Our inheritance under the error of assumptions of the 'pledge' of Our private property. We have never willingly, knowingly and with full disclosure pledged Our inheritance to any person or entity;

We, the Divine Spirit, object to and issue Divine Notice of Protest to the conversion of the birth certificate to a promissory note or other negotiable instrument without full disclosure nor consent;

We, the Divine Spirit, object to and issue Divine Notice of Protest to all derivatives of the birth registration, the estate trust and Cestui Que Vie trust as fruit of the poison tree;

We, the Divine Spirit, object to and issue Divine Notice of Protest to the malicious and unconscionable actions of the executors and administrators of the estate, to wit:
- knowingly and willingly claiming the child as chattel of the estate;
- creation of the slave bond contract and slave bond.

We, the Divine Spirit, object to and issue Divine Notice of Protest to the intentionally deceitful legal language and meaning of Our earthly parents marriage certificate and the birth registration whereby Our earthly parents were tricked into signing us away into slavery to the state without full disclosure nor consent;

We, the Divine Spirit, object to and issue Divine Notice of Protest to the creation of the slave bond by placing the ink impression of the child's footprint on the birth certificate, converting said certificate into a slave bond and selling same to the federal reserve for the conveyance into the second Cestui Que Vie Trust;

We, the Divine Spirit, object to and issue Divine of Notice of Protest to the issue of and monetization of the maritime lien for the salvage for the lost property for the bank's failure to seize the slave child upon the maturity of the slave bond;

We, the Divine Spirit, object to and issue Divine Notice of Protest to the issue and monetization of the Baptismal Certificate and creation of the 3rd Cestui Que Vie trust, representing the enslavement of Our soul, under the assumption that Our earthly parents gifted, granted and/or conveyed Our soul to the state;

We, the Divine Spirit decree that:
- Our earthly parents never willingly, knowingly and with full disclosure gifted, granted or conveyed Our soul to any person, entity or cult;
- No person, entity nor cult have the authority to gift, grant, convey nor enslave Our soul to any other person, entity or cult without full disclosure and our consent;
- We, the Divine Spirit have never willingly, knowingly and with full disclosure gifted, granted or conveyed Our soul to any person, entity or cult, nor consented to same;

We, the Divine Spirit, object to and issue Divine Notice of Protest to the three Cestui Que Vie Trusts which represent the triple crown of enslavement and three claims against Our property, body and soul by the Roman cult for the purpose of enslaving the people in the denial of all of our rights to the Divine Inheritance, Our right to freedom from all limitations and Our rights and powers as Divine Creators;

We, the Divine Spirit, object to and issue Divine Notice of Protest to the BAR Association as managers of the triple crown of enslavement of the Roman cult representing the reconstituted "Galla" responsible for the reaping of souls;

We, the Divine Spirit, object to and issue Divine Notice of Protest to the BAR Association courts and/or agents use of the inferior Roman Law, Sharia Law, Talmudic Law, Maritime Law, and/or Cannon Law against Us and/or Our property;

We, the Divine Spirit, expressed in trust in the living flesh, having re-established Our living status, whose estate is held in the above referenced trust, hereby re-establish Ourselves as Grantor of the trust having provided 100% of the value to fund the trust, with the authority to act in that capacity and exercise the power and authority of the Grantor of said trust;

We, the Divine Spirit, expressed in trust in the living flesh are vested as Beneficiary of said trust as said trust was established for Our benefit;

We, the Divine Spirit, expressed in trust in living flesh, having re-established Our living status, have standing to seek redress of grievance in the common law;

Receipt of this Ecclesiastic Deed Poll constitutes acceptance and is binding on all inferior persons and carries a mandatory obligation to act in accordance with Divine Law.

We, the Divine Spirit, expressed in trust in the living flesh, a free born inhabitant, heir to the Divine Estate, Beneficiary to the Divine Trust, freeholder in fee simple absolute, do hereby object to and issue Divine Notice of Protest to the following, to wit:

- To the compelled registration of the Birth under the error of assumptions and failing full disclosure, which created the 14th Amendment citizen of the United States;
- To the compelled acceptance of benefits 'under the will' which was perverted by the Trustees without full disclosure and under mis-apprehension and mis-representation, precluding Our enforcement of Our contractual rights in property bequeathed by the will;
- To the Trustee's propaganda, mis-representation, mis-apprehension, deceit and coercion that gave rise to the seemingly voluntary termination of the trust by the Beneficiary;
- To the Trustee's breach of his fiduciary duties which caused loss and injury to the estate;
- To the assumption/presumption that the free born inhabitant is deceased;
- To the assumption that the free born inhabitant is the executor of the estate trust;
- To the assumption that the free born inhabitant is a 'donor' with full disclosure.

We, the Divine Spirit, expressed in trust in living flesh, a free born inhabitant, heir to the Divine estate, Beneficiary to the Divine Trust as expressed in the Preamble to the Constitution, freeholder in fee simple absolute, do hereby:

Re-establish Our living status, evidenced by the DNA/Blood Seal thumb print below;

Instruct the Trustees / Intermediary to immediately Terminate the Lease of my Estate Trust to the Military Industrial Complex and administrate my estate trust OUTSIDE the 14th Amendment Breach of Trust and dissolve the 14th Amendment United States citizen ;

Instruct the Trustees that my Divine Estate Trust shall be administrated as a Charitable Trust in accordance with its original intent;

Provide the Heir the delinquent rent;

Demand that all restrictions against the freeholder be immediately released;

Demand that the private funds held by the DTC, DTCC, OITC and/or any/all other entities be made available to me for the discharge of debt, funding the National Banking Association and all sub-accounts thereof;

Demand that the Trustees provide a full account within 60 days.

How this is declared and executed is at this juncture in time, not a simple matter. It will therefore be left to explain in subsequent chapters in Part 2. Here you as the Settlor to your Good Faith and Credit into the Divine Trust, now wish to step forward as the living beneficiary. It is to remember in this that You as the Beneficiary, can now benefit from the Trust.

And so we can put the last layer of PLANET EARTH INC in our structure, mainly the Earthling Employees:

In our next chapter, it is necessary to understand the real laws that bind us.

17

THE LAWS OF THE LAND AND SEA

It is now necessary to understand how, when you are born a free soul and a sovereign individual that is only subject to the laws of God, which is innocent until proven guilty. It is important to understand how by unknowingly accepting the Strawman as being you do you become guilty until proven innocent. In the story of the Strawman we see that all Strawmen are created in the jurisdiction of Peurto Rico as aliens with a criminal record. It is a fake set of charges that are registered, and many who used to be able to penetrate these secret "Individual Master Files" where all sorts of criminal charges are registered. The corporation is in criminal status and as such has absolutely no rights. You, the real Earthling are proclaimed dead and lost at sea, so that vessel of the corporate entity is subject to Admiralty and Maritime Laws. Check out *www.mind-trek.com/practicl/tl16a.htm* and *www.thematrixhasyou.org*/ for some "light" reading!

Admiralty And Maritime Law

Everybody is familiar with these laws when they step onto a plane or a boat. Once you do, your action gives away many of your rights to be entrusted by the captain of the ship. He makes the life and death decisions and you are subject to a body of law called Admiralty Law. The terms "admiralty" and "maritime" are frequently used interchangeably. "Admiralty," refers to the body of law and procedures that govern matters related to the carriage of goods or passengers on the high seas and navigable inland waters. The term "maritime" however, is a far more general term. In effect, one as the head of the family is "captain of his ship" in the same way.

Admiralty law (also referred to as **maritime law**) is a distinct body of law which governs maritime questions and offenses. It is a body of both domestic law governing maritime activities, and private international law governing the relationships between private entities which operate vessels on the oceans. It deals with matters including marine commerce, marine navigation, shipping, sailors, and the transportation of passengers and goods by sea. Admiralty law also covers many commercial activities, although land based or occurring wholly on land, that are maritime in character. Admiralty law is distinguished from the Law of the Sea, which is a body of public international law dealing with navigational rights, mineral rights, jurisdiction over coastal waters and international law governing relationships between nations

The source of modern day admiralty law is hidden in the ancient past. It is thought by some scholars that it may be traced back as far as 900 B.C. to the island of Rhodes in the eastern Mediterranean. Whatever its origin, it is very old indeed, and doctrines clearly recognizable to today's admiralty practitioner may be found in several medieval maritime codes. Special courts arose in the Mediterranean, Atlantic, and Baltic trading states to enforce what was accepted by these states as a form of international law arising from the longstanding customs of the sea. Of particular interest to us is the system established in England where courts set up under the cognizance of the Lord High Admiral were, in the latter part of the 14th century, given jurisdiction to hear civil cases limited to "a thing done upon the sea." This system of separate Courts of Admiralty was still in existence throughout the time England colonized North America. Colonial courts were set up under the Vice-Admiralty in British North America and given expanded jurisdiction to hear criminal and civil matters involving colonists. Following the Revolutionary War, the newly formed United States incorporated the English judicial system.

The US constitution together with the Judiciary Act of 1789, give the federal judiciary cognizance of matters which were within the jurisdiction of the British Admiralty. The system of separate admiralty courts with separate procedures was continued in the United States until 1966, when the courts were unified. Even though they are now unified, separate and distinct admiralty procedures are still available and the substantive law applied to decide cases, whether in state or federal court is the body of federal admiralty law.

According to Wikipedia, Seaborne transport was one of the earliest channels of commerce, and rules for resolving disputes involving maritime trade were developed early in recorded history. Early historical records of these laws include the Rhodian law (Nomos Rhodion Nautikos) (of which no primary written specimen has survived, but which is alluded to in other legal texts: Roman and Byzantine legal codes) and later the customs of the Hanseatic League. In southern Italy the Ordinamenta et consuetudo maris (1063) at Trani and the Amalfian Laws were in effect from an early date.

Islamic law also made major contributions to international admiralty law, departing from the previous Roman and Byzantine maritime laws in several ways. These included Muslim sailors being paid a fixed wage "in advance" with an understanding that they would owe money in the event of desertion or malfeasance, in keeping with Islamic conventions in which contracts should specify "a known fee for a known duration." (In contrast, Roman and Byzantine sailors were "stakeholders in a maritime venture, inasmuch as captain and crew, with few exceptions, were paid proportional divisions of a sea venture's profit, with shares allotted by rank, only after a voyage's successful conclusion.") Muslim jurists also distinguished between "coastal navigation, or *cabotage*", and voyages on the "high seas", and they made shippers "liable for freight in most cases except the seizure of both a ship and its cargo". Islamic law "departed from Justinian's *Digest* and the *Nomos Rhodion Nautikos* in condemning slave jettison", and the Islamic *Qirad* was a precursor to the European *commenda* limited partnership. The "Islamic influence on the development of an international law of the sea" can thus be discerned alongside that of the Roman influence.

Admiralty law was introduced into England by Eleanor of Aquitaine while she was acting as regent for her son, King Richard the Lionheart. She had earlier established admiralty law on the island of Oleron (where it was published as the *Rolls of Oleron*) in her own lands (although she is often referred to in admiralty law books as "Eleanor of Guyenne"), having learned about it in the eastern Mediterranean while on a Crusade with her first husband, King Louis VII of France. In England, special *admiralty courts* handle all admiralty cases. These courts do not use the common law of England, but are civil law courts largely based upon the Corpus Juris Civilis of Justinian.

Admiralty courts were a prominent feature in the prelude to the American Revolution. For example, the phrase in the Declaration of Independence "For depriving us in many cases, of the benefits of Trial by Jury" refers to the practice of Parliament giving the Admiralty Courts jurisdiction to enforce The Stamp Act in the American Colonies. Because the Stamp Act was unpopular, a colonial jury was unlikely to convict a colonist of its violation. However, because admiralty courts did not (as is true today) grant trial by jury, a colonist accused of violating the Stamp Act could be more easily convicted by the Crown.

Admiralty law became part of the law of the United States as it was gradually introduced through admiralty cases arising after the adoption of the U.S. Constitution in 1789. Many American lawyers who were prominent in the American Revolution were admiralty and maritime lawyers in their private lives. Those included are Alexander Hamilton in New York and John Adams in Massachusetts.

In 1787 Thomas Jefferson, who was then ambassador to France, wrote to James Madison proposing that the U.S. Constitution, then under consideration by the States, be amended to include "trial by jury in all matters of fact triable by the laws of the land [as opposed the law of admiralty] and not by the laws of Nations [i.e. not by the law of admiralty]". The result was the Seventh Amendment to the U.S. Constitution. Alexander Hamilton and John Adams were both admiralty lawyers and Adams represented John Hancock in an admiralty case in colonial Boston involving seizure of one of Hancock's ships for violations of Customs regulations. In the more modern era, Supreme Court Justice Oliver Wendell Holmes was an admiralty lawyer before ascending to the federal bench.

This interesting history of admiralty law has very real consequences to those who find themselves pressing claims within the admiralty jurisdiction. The criminal and civil law with which we are most familiar is derived from the English common law. The law of admiralty, however, having had its origin in the Mediterranean and European sea trade, more closely resembles the European civil law system than the English common law. One significant difference which proved an irritant to our colonial forefathers given the expanded jurisdiction of the British Admiralty Court in the American colonies is the lack of jury under admiralty procedures.

The Flag Shows The Substantive Law Of Admiralty

Maritime law is a legal body that regulates ships and shipping. As sea-borne transportation is one of the most ancient channels of commerce, rules for maritime and trade disputes developed very early in recorded history. In England, special admiralty courts handle all admiralty cases. The courts do not use the common law of England. Admiralty or maritime law is distinct from standard land-based laws even today and even within another country's claimed waters, admiralty law states that a ship's flag dictates the law. This means that a Canadian ship in American waters would be subject to Canadian law and crimes committed on board that ship would stand trial in Canada. In the United States the Supreme Court is the highest court of appeals for admiralty cases, though they rarely progress beyond the state level. United States, admiralty law is of limited jurisdiction, so it is up to the judges to assign verdicts based on a combination of admiralty and specific state law.

At first you wonder what does this have to do with land. Don't be thrown by the fact this process is related to the sea, and that it doesn't apply to land. Admiralty law has come on land. Note the court cases below:

"Pursuant to the Law of the Flag, a military flag does result in jurisdictional implication when flown. The Plaintiff cites the following: Under what is called international law, the law of the flag, a shipowner who sends his vessel into a foreign port gives notice by his flag to all who enter into contracts with the shipmaster that he intends the law of the flag to regulate those contracts with the shipmaster that he either submit to its operation or not contract with him or his agent at all." - **Ruhstrat v. People**, 57 N.E. 41, 45, 185 ILL. 133, 49 LRA 181, 76 AM.

When you walk into a court and see this flag you are put on notice that you are in a Admiralty Court and that the king is in control. Also, if there is a king the people are no longer sovereign. Admiralty law is for the sea, maritime law governs contracts between parties that trade over the sea. That's what our fore-fathers intended. However, in 1845 Congress passed an act saying Admiralty law could come on land. The bill may be traced in Cong. Globe, 28th Cong., 2d. Sess. 43, 320, 328, 337, 345(1844-45), no opposition to the Act is reported. Congress held a committee on this subject in 1850 and they said:

"The committee also alluded to 'the great force' of the great constitutional question as to the power of Congress to extend maritime jurisdiction beyond the ground occupied by it at the adoption of the Constitution...." - **Ibid**. H.R. Rep. No. 72 31st Cong., 1st Sess. 2 (1850)

It was up to the Supreme Court to stop Congress and say no as the Constitution did not give you that power, nor was it intended. But no, the courts began a long sequence of abuses. Here are some excerpts from a few court cases.

"This power is as extensive upon land as upon water. The Constitution makes no distinction in that respect. And if the admiralty jurisdiction, in matters of contract and tort which the courts of the United States may lawfully exercise on the high seas, can be extended to the lakes under the power to regulate commerce, it can with the same propriety and upon the same construction, be extended to contracts and torts on land when the commerce is between different States. And it may embrace also the vehicles and persons engaged in carrying it on. It would be in the power of Congress to confer admiralty jurisdiction upon its courts, over the cars engaged in transporting passengers or merchandise from one State to another, and over the persons engaged in conducting them, and deny to the parties the trial by jury. Now the judicial power in cases of admiralty and maritime jurisdiction, has never been supposed to extend to contracts made on land and to be executed on land. But if the power of regulating commerce can be made the foundation of jurisdiction in its courts, and a new and extended admiralty jurisdiction beyond its heretofore known and admitted limits, may be created on water under that authority, the same reason would justify the same exercise of power on land." -- **Propeller Genessee** Chief et al. v. Fitzhugh et al. 12 How. 443 (U.S. 1851)

And all the way back, before the U.S. Constitution John Adams talking about his state's Constitution, said:

"Next to revenue (taxes) itself, the late extensions of the jurisdiction of the admiralty are our greatest grievance. The American Courts of Admiralty seem to be forming by degrees into a system that is to overturn our Constitution and to deprive us of our best inheritance, the laws of the land. It would be thought in England a dangerous innovation

*if the trial, of any matter on land was given to the admiralty." -- **Jackson v. Magnolia**,* 20 How. 296 315, 342 (U.S. 1852)

This began the most dangerous precedent of all the Insular Cases. This is where Congress took a boundless field of power. When legislating for the states, they are bound by the Constitution, when legislating for their insular possessions they are not restricted in any way by the Constitution. Read the following quote from the Harvard law review of AMERICAN INS. CO. v. 356 BALES OF COTTON, 26 U.S. 511, 546 (1828), relative to our insular possessions:

*"These courts, then, are not constitutional courts in which the judicial power conferred by the Constitution on the general government can be deposited. They are incapable of receiving it. They are legislative courts, created in virtue of the general right of sovereignty which exists in the government, or in virtue of that clause which enables Congress to make all needful rules and regulations respecting the territory belonging to the united States. The jurisdiction with which they are invested is not a part of that judicial power which is conferred in the third article of the Constitution, but is conferred by Congress in the execution of those general powers which that body possesses over the territories of the United States." -- **Harvard Law Review**, Our New Possessions.* page 481.

Here are some Court cases that make it even clearer:

*"...[T]he United States may acquire territory by conquest or by treaty, and may govern it through the exercise of the power of Congress conferred by Section 3 of Article IV of the Constitution... In exercising this power, Congress is not subject to the same constitutional limitations, as when it is legislating for the United States. ...And in general the guaranties of the Constitution, save as they are limitations upon the exercise of executive and legislative power when exerted for or over our insular possessions, extend to them only as Congress, in the exercise of its legislative power over territory belonging to the United States, has made those guarantees applicable." -- **Hooven & Allison & Co. vs Evatt,** 324 U.S. 652 (1945)*

How Admiralty Happened

With reference to ***www.stopthepirates.blogspot.ca/ Jack Anderson*** explains:
Around the time of the war between the United States and the southern states of the American union, the United States was busy putting together a plan that would increase the jurisdiction of the United States. This plan was necessary because the United States had no subjects and only the land ceded to it from the states, i.e. the District which was only ten miles square and such land as was necessary for forts, magazines, arsenals, etc.

Between the 1860's and the early 1900's, banking and taxing mechanisms were changing through legislation. Cunning people closely associated with the powers in England had great influence on the legislation being passed in the United States. Of course such legislation did not apply to the states or to the people in the states, but making the distinction was not deemed to be a necessary duty of the legislators. It was the responsibility of the people to understand their relationship to the United States and to the laws that were being passed by the legislature. This distinction between the United States and the states was taught in the homes and the schools and churches. The early admiralty courts did not interpret legislation as broadly at that time because the people knew when the courts were overstepping their jurisdiction. The people were in control because they knew who they were and where they were standing in relation to the United States.

In 1913 the United States added numerous private laws to its books that facilitated the increase of subjects and property for the United States. The 14th Amendment provided for a new class of citizens – United States citizens, that had not formerly been recognized. Until the 14th Amendment in 1868, there were no persons born or naturalized in the United States. They had all been born or naturalized in one of the several states. United States citizenship was a result of state citizenship. After the Civil War, a new class was recognized, and was the beginning of the democracy sited in the District of Columbia. The American people in the republic sited in the several states, could choose to benefit as one of these new United States citizens BY CHOICE. The new class of citizens was given the right to vote in the democracy in 1870 by the 15th Amendment. All it required was an application. Benefits came with this new citizenship, but with the benefits, came duties and responsibilities that were totally regulated by the legislature for the District of Columbia. Edward Mandell House is attributed with giving a very detailed outline of the plans to be implemented to enslave the American people. The 13th Amendment in 1865 opened the way for the people to volunteer into the equivalent of slavery to accept the benefits offered by the United States. Whether House actually spoke the words or not, is really irrelevant because the scenario detailed in the statement attributed to him has clearly been implemented. Central banking for the United States was legislated with the Federal Reserve Act in 1913. The ability to decrease the currency in circulation through taxation was legislated with the 16th Amendment in 1913. Support for the presumption that the American people had volunteered to participate in the United States democracy was legislated with the 17th Amendment in 1913. The path was provided for the control of the courts, with the creation of the American Bar Association in 1913.

In 1917 the United States legislature passed the Trading with the Enemy Act and the Emergency War Powers Act, opening the doors for the United States to suspend limitations otherwise mandated in the Constitution. Even in times of peace, every contrived and created social, political, or financial emergency was sufficient authority for the officers of the United States to overstep its peace time powers and implement volumes of "law" that would increase the coffers of the United States. There is always a declared emergency in the United States and its States, but it only applies to their subjects.

In the 1920's the States accelerated the push for mothers to register their babies. Life was good and people were not paying attention to what was happening in government. The stock market crashed, and those who were not on the inside were not warned to take their money out before they lost everything.

Plausible Deniability: The Background Plan

In the 1930's federal legislation provided for registration of babies through applications for birth certificates, so government workers could get maternity leave with pay. The States pushed for registration of cars through applications for certificates of title, and for registration of land through registration of deeds of trust. Constructive trusts secretly were created as each of the people blindly walked into the United States democracy, thereby agreeing to be sureties for the debts of the United States. The great depression supplied the diversion to keep the people's attention off what government was doing. The Social Security program was implemented, along with numerous other United States programs that invited the American people to volunteer to be the sureties behind the United States' new registered property and adhesion contracts through the new United States subjects.

The plan was well on its path by 1933. Massive registration of property through United States agencies assuring the United States and its officers would get rich beyond their wildest expectations, as predicted by Mendall House. All of this was done without disclosure of the material facts that accompanied each application for registration – fraud. The fraud was a sufficient reason to charge all the United States officers with treason, UNLESS a remedy could be supplied for the people to recoup their property and collect for the damages they suffered as a result of the fraud.

If a remedy were available, and the people chose not to or failed to use their remedy, no charge of fraud could be sustained even in a common law court. The United States only needed to provide the remedy. It was not required to explain it or even tell the people where the remedy could be found. The attorneys did not even have to be taught about the remedy. That gave them plausible deniability when the people struggled to understand the new laws. The legislators did not have to have the intricate details of the law explained to them regarding the bills they were passing. That gave them plausible deniability. If the people failed to use their remedy, the United States came out the winner every time. If the people did discover their remedy, the United States had to honour it and release the registered property back to the people, but only if the people knew they had a remedy, and only if they requested it in the proper manner. It was a great plan.

With plausible deniability, even when the people knew they had a remedy and pursued it, the attorneys, judges, and legislators could act like they did not understand the people's claims. In fact, it is true, they are not trained to understand. Requiring the public schools to teach civics, government, and history classes out of approved politically correct text books also assured the people would not find the remedy for a long time. Passing new State and Federal laws that appeared to subject the people to rules and regulations, added another level of protection against the people finding their remedy. The public media was moulded to report politically correct, though substantially incorrect, news day after day, until few people would even think there could be a remedy available to them. The people could be separated from their money and their time to pursue the remedy long enough for the solutions to be lost in the pages of millions of books in huge law libraries across the country. So many people know there is something wrong with all the conflicts in the laws with the "facts" taught in the schools. How can the American people be free and subject to a sovereign governments whims at the same time? Who would ever have thought the people would be resourceful enough to actually find the remedy?

In 1933 the United States put its insurance policy into place with House Joint Resolution 192 (2) and recorded it in the Congressional Record. It was not required to be promulgated in the Federal Register. An Executive Order issued on April 5, 1933 paving the way for the withdrawal of gold in the United States. Representative Louis T. McFadden brought formal charges on May 23, 1933 against the Board of Governors of the Federal Reserve Bank system, the Comptroller of the Currency, and the Secretary of the United States Treasury (Congressional Record May 23, 1933 page 4055-4058). HJR 192 passed on June 3, 1933. Mr. McFadden claimed on June 10, 1933: "Mr. Chairman, we have in this country one of the most corrupt institutions the world has ever known. Refer to the Federal Reserve Board and the Federal Reserve Banks…" HJR 192 is the insurance policy that protects the legislators from conviction for fraud and treason against the American people. It also protects the American people from damages caused by the actions of the United States.

HJR 192 provided that the one with the gold paid the bills. It removed the requirement that the United States subjects and employees had to pay their debts with gold. It actually prohibited the inclusion of a clause in all subsequent contracts that would require payment in gold. It also cancelled the clause in every contract written prior to June 5, 1933, that required an obligation to be paid in gold – retroactively. It provided that the United States subjects and employees could use any type of coin and currency to discharge a public debt as long as it was in use in the normal course of business in the United States. For a time, United States Notes were the currency used to discharge debts, but later the Federal Reserve and the United States provided a new medium of exchange through paper notes, and debt instruments that could be passed on to a debtor's creditors to discharge the debtor's debts. That same currency is available to us to use to discharge public debts.

Enter The Uniform Commercial Code Laws Of Commerce

In the 1950's the Uniform Commercial Code was presented to the States as a means of unifying the generally accepted procedures for handling the new legal system of dealing with commercial fictions as though they were real. Security instruments replaced substance as collateral for debts. Security instruments could be supported by presumptive contracts. Debt instruments with collateral, and accommodating parties, could be used instead of money. Money and the need for money was disappearing, and a uniform system of laws had to be put in place to allow the courts to uphold the security instruments that depended on commercial fictions as a basis for compelling payment or performance. All this was accomplished by the mid 1960's.

The commercial code is merely a codification of accepted and required procedures all people engaged in commercial activities must follow. The basic principles of commerce had been settled thousands of years ago, but were refined as commerce become more sophisticated over the years. In the 1900's the age-old principles of commerce shifted from substance to form. Presumption became a big part of the law. Without giving a degree of force to presumption, the new direction in enforcing commercial claims could not be supported in courts. If the claimants were required to produce their claims every time they tried to collect money or time from the people, they would seldom be successful. The principles expressed in the code combine the means of dealing with substantive commercial activities with the means of dealing with presumptive commercial activities. These principles work as well for the people as they do for the deceivers. The rules do not respect persons.

Those who enticed the people to register their things with the United States and its sub-divisions, gained control of the substance through the registrations. The United States became the Holder of the titles to many things. The definition of "property" is the interest one has in a thing. The thing is the principal. The property is the interest in the thing. Profits (interest) made from the property of another, belong to the owner of the thing. Profits were made by the deceivers by pledging the registered property in commercial markets, but the profits do not belong to the deceivers. The profits belong to the owners of the things. That is always the people. The corporation only shows ownership of paper – titles to things. The substance cannot appear in the fiction. [[Watch the movie Last Action Hero and watch the confusion created when they try to mix substance and fiction.]] Sometimes the fiction is made to look very much like substance, but fiction can never become substance. It is an impossibility.

The profits from all the registered things had to be put into trust (constructive) for the benefit of the owners. If the profits were put into the general fund of the United States and not into separate trusts for the owners, the scheme would represent fraud. The profits for each owner could not be commingled. If the owner failed to use his available remedy (fictional credits held in a constructive trust account, fund, or financial ledger) to benefit from the profits, it would not be the fault of the deceivers. If the owner failed to learn the law that would open the door to his remedy, it would not be the fault of the deceivers. The owner is responsible for learning the law, so he understands that the profits from his things are available for him to discharge debts or charges brought against his public person by the United States.

If the United States has the "gold", the United States pays the bills (from the trust account, fund, or financial ledger). The definition of "fund" is money set aside to pay a debt. The fund is there to discharge the public debts attributed to the United States subjects, but ultimately back to the accommodating parties – the American people. The national debt that is owed is to the owners of the registered things – the American people, as well as to other creditors.

If the United States owes a debt to the owner of the thing, and the owner is presumed (by accommodation) to owe a public debt to the United States, the logical thing is to ask the United States to discharge that public debt from the trust fund. The way for the United States to get around having to pay the public debts for the people is to claim the owner cannot be an owner if he agreed to be the accommodating party for a debtor person. If the people are truly the principle, then they know how to handle their financial and political affairs, UNLESS they have never been taught. If the owner admits by his actions out of ignorance, that he is an accommodating party, he has taken on the debtor's liabilities without getting consideration in exchange. Here lies the fiction again. The owner of the thing does not have to knowingly agree to be the accommodating party for the debtor person; he just has to act like he agreed. That is easy if he has a choice of going to jail or signing for the debtor person. The presumption that he is the accommodating party is strong enough for the courts to hold the owner of the thing liable for a tax on the thing he actually owns.

Debtors may have the use of certain things, but the things belong to the creditors. The creditor is the master. The debtor is the servant. The Uniform Commercial Code is very specific about the duties and responsibilities a debtor has. If the owner of the thing is presumed to be a debtor because of his previous admissions and adhesion contracts, he is going to have a difficult time convincing the United States that it has a duty to discharge public debts for him. In addition, the courts are staffed with loyal judges who will look for every mistake the people make when trying to use their remedy.

Uniform Commercial Code: The Law Of The Land

The **Uniform Commercial Code** (**UCC** or the Code), first published in 1952, is one of a number of uniform acts that have been promulgated in conjunction with efforts to harmonize the law of sales and other commercial transactions in all 50 states within the United States of America.

The UCC is the longest and most elaborate of the uniform acts. The Code has been a long-term, joint project of the National Conference of Commissioners on Uniform State Laws (NCCUSL) and the American Law Institute (ALI), who began drafting its first version in 1942. Judge Herbert F. Goodrich was the Chairman of the Editorial Board of the original 1952 edition, and the Code itself was drafted by some of the top legal scholars in the United States, including Karl N. Llewellyn, William A. Schnader, Soia Mentschikoff, and Grant Gilmore.

In one or another of its several revisions, the UCC has been enacted in all of the 50 states, as well as in the District of Columbia, the Commonwealth of Puerto Rico, Guam and the U.S. Virgin Islands. Louisiana has enacted most provisions of the UCC, with the exception of Article 2, preferring to maintain its own civil law tradition for governing the sale of goods.

The Uniform Commercial Code also attempts to make commercial paper transactions, such as the processing of checks, less complicated. It differentiates the difference between merchants, who are knowledgeable of business transactions, and consumers, who are not.

What the UCC is supposed to accomplish is to conduct transactions without it being necessary to involve lawyers in the trade it administers. The affairs which are addressed with the eleven articles of the **Uniform Commercial Code** includes the sale of goods, all bank and negotiable instruments, letters of credit, bills of receipts, bulk transfers, investment securities, and secured transactions.

As you have learned, your Birth Certificate is traded on the Stock Market Under UCC. The **Uniform Commercial Code**, is the most discussed and implemented of many Uniform Acts which is sponsored by the National Conference of Commissioners on Uniform State Laws, which originated in 1892. Some of the other Uniform Acts include the **Uniform Child Custody Jurisdiction Action** as well as the **Uniform Foreign Money Claims Act**.

The **NCCUSL** is a combination of lawyers and business professionals, which are chosen by the States and territories, these people discuss exactly which laws should be uniform throughout the country. The reason for the American Law Institute, which was established in 1923, is to formulate the **American Common Law** according to the diversified social needs. The ALI and NCCUSL both are authorized to maintain and revise the **Uniform Commercial Code (UCC).**

The Uniform Commercial Code (UCC) is a set of suggested laws relating to commercial transactions. The UCC was one of many uniform codes that grew out of a late nineteenth-century movement toward uniformity among state laws. In 1890 the American Bar Association, an association of lawyers, proposed that states identify areas of law that could be made uniform throughout the nation, prepare lists of such areas, and suggest appropriate legislative changes. In 1892 the National Conference of Commissioners on Uniform State Laws (NCCUSL) met for the first time in Saratoga, New York. Only seven states sent representatives to the meeting.

In 1986 the NCCUSL offered up its first act, the Uniform Negotiable Instruments Act. The NCCUSL drafted a variety of other Uniform Acts. Some of these dealt with commerce, including the Uniform Conditional Sales Act and the Uniform Trust Receipts Act. The uniform acts on commercial issues were fragmented by the 1930s and in 1940, the NCCUSL proposed revising the commerce-oriented uniform codes and combining them into one uniform set of model laws. In 1941 the American Law Institute (ALI) joined the discussion, and over the next several years lawyers, judges, and professors in the ALI and NCCUSL prepared a number of drafts of the Uniform Commercial Code.

In September 1951 a final draft of the UCC was completed and approved by the American Law Institute (ALI) and the NCCUSL, and then by the House of Delegates of the American Bar Association. After some additional amendments and changes, the official edition, with explanatory comments, was published in 1952. Pennsylvania was the first state to adopt the UCC, followed by Massachusetts. By 1967 the District of Columbia and all the states, with the exception of Louisiana, had adopted the UCC in whole or in part. Louisiana eventually adopted all the articles in the UCC except articles 2 and 2A.

The UCC is divided into nine articles, each containing provisions that relate to a specific area of Commercial Law:

Article 1, General Provisions, provides definitions and general principles that apply to the entire code.
Article 2, Covers the sale of goods.
Article 3, Commercial Paper, addresses negotiable instruments, such as promissory notes and checks.
Article 4 deals with banks and their handling of checks and other financial documents.
Article 5 provides model laws on letters of credit, which are promises by a bank or some other party to pay the purchases of a buyer without delay and without reference to the buyer's financial solvency.
Article 6, on bulk transfers, imposes an obligation on buyers who order the major part of the inventory for certain types of businesses. Most notably Article 6 provisions require that such buyers notify creditors of the seller of the inventory so that creditors can take steps to see that the seller pays her debts when she receives payments from the buyer.
Article 7 offers rules on the relationships between buyers and sellers and any transporters of goods, called carriers. These rules primarily cover the issuance and transfer of warehouse receipts and bills of lading. A bill of lading is a document showing that the carrier has delivered an item to a buyer.
Article 8 contains rules on the issuance and transfer of stocks, bonds, and other investment Securities.
Article 9, Secured Transactions, covers security interests in real property. A security interest is a partial or total claim to a piece of property to secure the performance of some obligation, usually the payment of a debt. This article identifies when and how a secured interest may be created and the rights of the creditor to foreclose on the property if the debtor defaults on his obligation. The article also establishes which creditors can collect first from a defaulting debtor.

The ALI and the NCCUSL periodically review and revise the UCC. Since the code was originally devised, the House of Delegates of the American Bar Association has approved two additional articles:

Article 2A on Personal Property leases. Article 2A establishes model rules for the leasing or renting of personal property (as opposed to real property, such as houses and apartments), and
Article 4A on fund transfers. Article 4A covers transfers of funds from one party to another party through a bank. This article is intended to address the issues that arise with the use of new technologies for handling money.

Most states have adopted at least some of the provisions in the UCC. The least popular article has been article 6 on bulk transfers. These provisions require the reporting of payments made, which many legislators consider an unnecessary intrusion on commercial relationships.

If you have ever heard the statement "*The constitution has NO place in the courts and your life?*" consider this: When one argues a "Constitutional" position whether in the courts or society that position will NOT prevail. Why? We grew up with the concept of personal freedom and constitutional rights. Yet, even to the most casual observer America is NOT free, not when your work for PLANET EARTH by agreement (even though you're were not aware of it). The Constitution is NOT in effect in the courts of this land. Ask any judge, he will quickly tell you the constitution is not permitted in his courtroom.

Every company, corporate entity or any organization is governed by a charter, by-laws, or some sort of 'constitution' that will legally dictate and control the operation. Ever stop to consider that if the Constitution is NOT the charter for the Federal government and society what is the "law" of that society?

Then what is the law and "constitution" of the federal government and society in which we live? It is The Uniform Commercial Code!

Uniform Commercial Code Implementation

Today the majority of Americans pay taxes because when they get a job their employer requests that they fill out an Internal Revenue Service Form W-4, which, as a direct result, withholds taxes from their paychecks for their labour. The majority doesn't have a clue as to why they are paying these taxes in the first place. It has been affirmed that labour is a fundamental, unalienable right, protected by the United States Constitution. This fundamental right is not supposed to be taxed.   It is presumed that everyone is expected to know the law. It has been long held that, ignorance of the Law is not an excuse or a defence. The well established maxim that: *"He who fails to assert his rights - HAS NONE!",* unequivocally establishes that just as a closed mouth never gets fed, *"a matter must be expressed to be resolved."*   When it comes to dealing with lawyers, government, and the Internal Revenue Service (which is not an agency of the United States Government, but a private foreign-owned corporation) withholding and keeping knowledge from the people is nothing new. It is a common business tactic that has been going on from the beginning of its inception. It will, most likely continue as long as we rely upon lawyers and government to do that which we ourselves should be doing.

In order to find the answer as to why your labour is being taxed, when the Constitution says it is not supposed to be, it is necessary to understand how government exists and operates. To accomplish this requires a quick review back in history to the time of the War Between the States. The People of this Nation lost their true Republican form of government. On March 27, 1861 seven southern States walked out of Congress leaving the entire legislative Branch of Government without quorum. The Congress of the Constitution was dissolved for inability to disband or re-convene. The Republican form of Government, which the People were guaranteed - ceased to exist. Out of necessity to operate the Government, President Lincoln issued Executive Order No. 2. in April 1861, reconvening the Congress at gunpoint in Executive, emergency, martial-law-rule jurisdiction. Since that time there has been no "de jure" (sanctioned by law) Congress. Everything functions under "color of law" (the appearance or semblance, without substance, of legal right.) Through Executive Orders under authority of the War Powers, (i.e. emergency, i.e. the law of necessity) the "law of necessity" means no law whatsoever, as per such maxims of law as: "Necessity knows no law" (the law of forbidding killing is voided when done in self-defence). *"In time of war laws are silent."* **Cicero**.

To establish the underlying debt of the Government to the Bankers, to create corporate entities that are legally subject to the jurisdiction which they exist, and to create the jurisdiction itself correctly, the so-called (fraudulent and unratified) Fourteenth Amendment was proclaimed and passed in 1868. This was a cestui que trust (operation in law) incorporated in a military, private, International, commercial, de facto (jurisdiction created by, and belonging to, the Money Power, existing within the emergency of the War Powers, the only operational jurisdiction since the dissolution of Congress in 1861. Through the 14th Amendment, an artificial person-corporate entity-franchise entitled "citizen of the United States" was born into private, corporate limited liability. Section 4 of the 14th Amendment states: "The validity of the Public Debt of the United States (to the Bankers) ... shall not be questioned."

Within the above-referenced private jurisdiction of the International Bankers, the private and foreign owned "Congress" formed a corporation, commercial agency, and Government for the "District of Columbia" on February 21, 1871, Chapter 62, 16 Stat. 419. This corporation was reorganized June 11, 1878, Chapter 180, 20 Stat. 102, and re-named "United States Government." This corporation privately trade marked the names: "United States," "U.S.," "US," "U.S.A.," "USA" and "America."

When the United States declared itself a municipal corporation, it also created what is known as a *cestui que trust* (a trust where one party receives benefits and use while legal title rests in another covered later in detail) to function under by implementing the Federal Constitution of 1871, and incorporating the previous United States Constitutions of 1787 and 1791 as amended, as by-laws. Naturally, as the grantor of the trust, this empowered the United States Government to change the terms of the trust at will. As evidenced under the Federal Constitution of 1871, the 14th Amendment, the People of the United States without their consent, were declared "Citizens" and granted "Civil Rights." These so-called civil rights are nothing more than mere privileges. Privileges which government licenses, regulates, and can re-interpret to suit it's purposes at any time for any reason. The Federal Corporate Government also conveniently somehow forgot to disclose to the People that the term "Citizen" with which they have made every living and breathing inhabitant a "subject", was defined in law as a "Vessel" engaged in commerce, hence falling under admiralty Law.

In 1912, when the bonds, that were keeping the US Government afloat, and, were owned by the Bankers, came due, the Bankers refused to re-finance the debt, and the colorable, martial-law-rule Congress was compelled to pass, the Federal Reserve Act of 1913. This Act surrendered constitutional authority to create, control, and manage the entire money supply of the United States to a handful of private, mostly foreign, bankers. This placed exclusive creation and control of the money within the private, commercial, foreign, and military jurisdiction of 1861, into corporate limited liability.

America converted from United States Notes to Federal Reserve Notes, beginning with the passage of The Federal Reserve Act of 1913. Federal Reserve Banks were incorporated in 1914, and, in 1916, began to circulate their private, corporate Federal Reserve Notes as "money" alongside the nations "de jure" (according to law) currency, the United States Notes. The United States Notes were actually warehouse receipts for deposits of gold and silver in a warehouse (bank), thus representing wealth (substance, portable land; the money of sovereigns), the new fiat money (Federal Reserve Notes) amounted to "bills for that which was yet to be paid," i.e. for what was owed! For the new "benefit" of being able to carry around U.S. Government debt instruments (Federal Reserve Notes) in our wallets instead of Gold Certificates or Silver Certificates, we agreed to redeem the newly issued Federal Reserve Notes in gold and also to pay interest for their use in gold ONLY! Essentially, the Fed issued paper with pretty green ink on it and we agreed to give them gold in exchange for the "privilege" of using it. Such was the bargain. And those that made the deal knew what they were doing!

Through paying interest to the Federal Reserve Corporation in gold, the US Treasury became progressively depleted of its gold. America's gold certificates, coin, and bullion were continually shipped off to the coffers of various European Banks and Power Elite. In 1933, when the Treasury was drained and the debt was larger than ever (a financial condition known as "insolvency"), President Roosevelt proclaimed the bankruptcy of the United States. Every 14th Amendment "citizen of the United States" was pledged as an asset to finance the Chapter 11 re-organization expenses and pay interest in perpetuity to the CREDITORS (Federal Reserve Bankers) and the "national debt", ("which shall not be questioned").

On March 9, 1933, Congress passed the Amendatory Act (also known as the Emergency Banking Relief Act) to the Trading with the Enemy Act (originally passed on October 6, 1917) at a time when the United States was not in a shooting war with any foreign foe and included the People of the United States as the enemy.

At the conference of Governors held on March 6, 1933, the Governors of the 48 States of the Union accommodated the Federal Bankruptcy of the United States Corporation by pledging the faith and credit of their State to the aid of the National Government.

Senate Document 43 of the 73rd Congress, 1st Session (1933) did declare that ownership of ALL PROPERTY is in the STATE and individual so-called ownership is only by virtue of government, i.e. law amounting to "mere-user" only; and individual use of all property is subordinate to the necessities of the United States Government.

Under House Joint Resolution 192 of June 5, 1933, Senate Report No. 93549, and Executive Orders 6072, 6012 and 6246, the Congress and President Roosevelt officially declared bankruptcy of the United States Government.

Regardless of the cause or reason, what many American's either do not understand and/or have failed to seriously grasp, is that by the use of Federal Reserve Notes; (which is not Constitutional Money defined under Article I Section 10 of the United States Constitution)), the People of the United States since 1933, have not had any Constitutionally lawful way to pay their debts. They therefore have not had any way to buy or own property. The People, for the benefits granted to them by a bankrupt corporate Government, discharge their debts with limited liability using Federal Reserve Notes. They have surrendered, by way of an unconscionable contract, their individual Rights under the Constitution, in exchange for mere privileges!

A review of countless United States Supreme Court decisions since the 1938, landmark case, Erie Railroad v. Tompkins, (304 U.S. 64-92) clearly establishes that only the State has Constitutional Rights, not the People. The People have been pledged to the bankruptcy of 1933. The federal law administered in and by the United States is the private commercial "law" of the CREDITORS. That, due to the bankruptcy, every "citizen of the United States" is pledged as an asset to support the bankruptcy, must work to pay the insurance premiums on the underwriting necessary to keep the bankrupt government in operation under Chapter II Bankruptcy (Reorganization). That upon the declared Bankruptcy, Americans could operate and function only through their corporate colored, State created, ALL-CAPITAL-LETTERS-NAME, - that has no access to sovereignty, substance, rights, and standing in law. The Supreme Court also held the "general (Universal) common law" no longer is accessible and in operation in the federal courts based on the 1933, bankruptcy, which placed everything into the realm of private, colorable law merchant of the Federal Reserve CREDITORS. To take this to a different level and not only explain why you pay taxes, but also why you do not own the house you live in, the car you drive, or own anything else you think you've bought and paid for etc. The State Government and its CREDITORS own it all. If you think you own your home just because you believe you paid it using those Federal Reserve Notes, just like everything else you possess by permission of Government, simply stop paying your taxes, (user-fees), (licenses) and see just how long Government and the CREDITORS allow you to keep it before they come to take it away from you.

How can all this really be? Why haven't you been told all of this before now? Ignorance of the law is no excuse they say is your problem. It's like the satanic belief structure that says the Dummies are there to be taken advantage of! . Every man is deemed (required) to know the law. Government expects you to know the law, and holds you fully accountable for doing so. and, in truth, as we have repeated over and over: *It is hidden in plain sight*. Ignoring these facts will not protect you. The majority of American's have been given a Public Education to teach them only what the Public, i.e. government (CREDITORS) wants them to know. It is and always has been each individual's personal responsibility, duty and obligation to learn and know the law.

What this breaks down to is this: Back in 1933, when the United States went into bankruptcy because it could no longer pay its debts it pledged the American People themselves without their consent as the asset to keep the government afloat and operating. Because government no longer had any way to pay its debts with substance, was bankrupt, it lost its sovereignty and standing in law. Outside and separate from Constitutional Government, to continue to function and operate, it created an artificial world consisting of artificial entities. This was accomplished by taking everyone's proper birth given name and creating what is called a "fiction in law," by way of an acronym, i.e. a name written in ALL-CAPITAL-LETTERS to interact with. As we have detailed, a name written in ALL-CAPITAL-LETTERS is not a sentient, flesh and blood human being. It is a corporation, fiction or deceased person. Government as well as all corporations, including the Internal Revenue Service cannot deal interact with you or interact with you via your proper name given you at birth, only through your ALL-CAPITAL-LETTERS-NAME! Another little tidbit of knowledge, which has been conveniently kept from the People is this: When the Several united States signed the treaty with Great Britain ending the Revolutionary War, it was a concession that ALL COMMERCE would be regulated and contracted through British Attorney's known as Esquires only.

This condition and concession still exists today. No attorney or lawyer in the United States of America has ever been "licensed" to practice law (they've exempted themselves) as they are a legal fiction "person" and only an "ADMITTED MEMBER" to practice in the private franchise club called the BAR (which is itself an acronym for the British or Barrister Aristocratic or Accreditation Regency), as such are un-registered foreign agents, and so they are traitors. Esquires (Unconstitutional Title of honour and nobility = Esquires), foreign non-citizens (aliens) who are specifically prohibited from ever holding any elected Public Office of trust whatsoever! Article I, Section 9, clause 8, states: "*No Title of Nobility shall be granted by the United States: And no Person holding any Office of Profit or Trust under them, shall, without the Consent of the Congress, accept any present, Emolument, Office, or Title, of any kind whatsoever, from any King, Prince, or foreign State.*"

Like said before, as a direct result, attorneys and lawyers cannot and do not represent you in your proper birth or given name. Attorneys and lawyers re-present corporations, artificial persons, and fictions in law - ONLY! What the majority in this country fail to recognize is this: because of the bankruptcy and having been pledged as an asset to the National Government's debt, this makes all citizens DEBTORS under Chapter 11. DEBTORS in bankruptcy having lost their solvency - - have NO RIGHTS nor STANDING IN LAW and are at the mercy of the CREDITORS.

All courts today sit and operate as Non-Constitutional, Non-Article Three Legislative Tribunals administering the bankruptcy via their "statutes," ("codes."). All Courts are Title 11 Bankruptcy Courts where these statutes are, in reality, "commercial obligations" being applied for the "benefit" or "privilege" of discharging debts with limited liability of the Federal Reserve-monopoly, colorable-money Federal Reserve Notes (debt

Instruments). This means every time you end up before a court - not only do you NOT have any standing in law to state a claim upon which relief can be granted, YOU HAVE NO CONSTITUTIONAL RIGHTS! Why? Because you are a DEBTOR under the bankruptcy and in addition to having contracted away your rights in exchange for benefits and privileges; you do not have one single shred of evidence to establish otherwise. In bankruptcy ONLY CREDITORS have rights!

In a nutshell, as a DEBTOR, it is impossible for you to access Constitutional Rights, they are reduced to mere privileges which are licensed, regulated, and can be altered, amended and changed to meet whatever the particular or special needs of government for whatever whim. If taking away your home, your car, taxing your labour, or locking you up for violating any of the Sixty MILLION plus legislatively created DEBTOR codes and statutes they have on the books today happens to meet the needs of government? It really doesn't take a rocket scientist to realize who the loser will be!

Everything Is Commerce

Through the contents of this book, you may come to a legal understanding of how/why you have become a slave to the society (democracy) around you. Then you will understand how to regain your freedom and 'constitutional' rights.

The only thing prohibiting your freedom is legal awareness and lack of information. ALL; i.e., EVERY thing or action you do is "commercial" even religions. Even God's (god's) words in the bible laid out a commercial plan as you have seen. You can NOT function except through a "commercial contract". It is well established that a legal fiction (corporation, government, etc) cannot directly approach a "private" individual. When government, court, tax, and corporate agents approach you in person, via the mail, over the phone, etc., they are soliciting your consent for "voluntarily" entering into a commercial contract and "doing business." The controlling law for these contracts is the Uniform Commercial Code.

All governments are corporate, for-profit operations. The U.S. [federal] Government and its administrative agencies bring suits against people and other government entities every day. In the legal system there is no difference between civil and criminal jurisdictions; each is commercial. All crime (including murder) is commercial, i.e. has a monetary value affixed thereto. 27 CAR 72.11 spells this out in unequivocal terms. Nowadays it is common for both artificial and flesh-and-blood entities to settle criminal charges out of court, i.e. via payment. Note: committing a crime is a physical impossibility for an artificial person/corporation, but such are charged criminally almost every day.

The Uniform Commercial Code at Article 1, §103 it states: § 1-103.
Supplementary General Principles of Law Applicable.

Unless displaced by the particular provisions of this Act, the principles of law and equity, including the law merchant and the law relative to capacity to contract, principal and agent, estoppel, fraud, misrepresentation, duress, coercion, mistake, Bankruptcy, or other validating or invalidating cause shall supplement its provisions. What they're telling us is that all other law - common, constitutional, equity, bankruptcy, etc. - is only supplemental to the supreme law of the land - the Uniform Commercial Code. If we don't proceed on the basis upon which they proceed, then we will lose due to failure to procedure, not substance.

The entire hierarchy of the court system is a model identical to the Catholic Church. Here as you have learned, the Pope holds title and lien secured party to everything in "The United States of America" and the Bank of England and the Queen is the administrator for the collection of the tribute, see the Treaty of Paris of 1783 (see Yale University Diana Project) wherein Prince George, King of England, refers to himself as the "arch-treasurer of the United States." Each of us has more contracts and applications that force us into a taxpayer/fiduciary obligation that there are far too many of them to even consider revoking all ab initio. You must get control of the artificial person and capture the value of the bond that was created by the Vatican who operate the illusion so that you can discharge debt. All money must first be predicated upon the creation of an instrument of debt based upon a promise to pay usury sometime in the future.

So who creates the money with which to pay the interest? No one. That is why there were bankruptcy courts created to handle the redistribution of the assets the fiduciary generated and leave the fiduciary enough assets to get started generating wealth again for the trust. The debt creation side first is a rule of the Generally Accepted Accounting Procedures' (GAAP) double entry balance sheet deception. The trusts are in Puerto Rico, and interesting name meaning "the harbour of *r*acketeering, *i*nfluence, and *c*orrupt *o*rganizations." All of the things done to us that look like crimes are actually perfectly legal and lawful due to our breach of fiduciary duty, and the foundation for what is done to us has been laid over the past 150 years by the lawmakers who were influenced by the spawn of the "gods" who operate the banks.

The Precepts And Maxims Of Commercial Law

For many people it might come as a surprise (in many cases a pleasant one) if they were informed that essentially all of the law of the world is founded on, derived from, and is a function of ten simple, essential, and fundamental Commercial Maxims seven (7) basic ones plus three (3) corollaries. These foundational principles/axioms underlie all of man's law. Notwithstanding the vastness and complexity of the law today, it is safe to say that all of the world's law is fundamentally a function of the ten Commercial Maxims. Although the dazzling complexity and ever-changing forms, parameters, and labels obfuscate this fact, the essence of the matter remains intact.

The Commercial Maxims constitute the basic rules involved in preventing and resolving disputes, including relating in life and commercial affairs as if disputes might arise and written proof of one's position, in time and content, must be securely established. Although commerce is usually thought of as "buying, selling, and trading," all of man's interactions with his fellow man are considered as being "commerce." Commerce encompasses all relationships between people.

Black's Law Dictionary, Fifth Edition, for instance, defines "commerce" as follows:

Commerce. "The exchange of goods, productions, or property of any kind; the buying, selling, and exchanging of articles…. Intercourse by way of trade and traffic between different peoples or states…including not only the purchase, sale, and exchange of commodities, but also the instrumentalities and agencies by which it is promoted and the means and appliances by which it is carried on, and transportation of persons as well as of goods, both by land and sea…. Also interchange of ideas, sentiments, etc., as between man and man."

The Commercial Maxims codify the fundamental principles/maxims of law and commerce upon which man's law and governments have operated on this planet for at least the past 4-6 thousand years. They constitute, as it were, the rules of the game. Part of the grief of mankind today is that the vast, overwhelming percentage of the populace does not know the basic rules of the game they are playing and are hence incapable of playing it. It should not be surprising to know the origins back to Sumeria when the "gods" reigned and prospered.

If one who does not know the rules of a game is playing that game with others who are masters of the rules, the outcome is a foregone conclusion: the one who knows the rules wins the game while the one who does not know the rules necessarily loses. Such is the state of the world. This is PLANET EARTH Inc. and its pyramid structure--all operating under the rules of commerce.

Elucidating the underlying, fundamental rules so that one understands what is going on helps greatly in "leveling the playing field." These rules, therefore, are set forth below with the understanding that they operate within the context and setting of the universal Underlying Principles. The Commercial Maxims are the most basic, enduring, and minimalist codification of universal, real law extant on earth.

They are very simple, largely self-evident, and based on common sense. The Jews, for instance, have studied, analyzed, practiced, and refined Commercial Law, founded on these Maxims, for thousands of years. This continuous, relentless, single-minded absorption in the law over millennia has "worked the bugs out." Every angle, facet, ramification, application, and nuance of practice of Commercial Law has been seasoned over time, and is deeply and thoroughly known by those who "own, run, and rule the world."

When you look at the "Elite" and their "New World Order" with PLANET EARTH INC, they are precisely where they are because they do know this fundamental law, because it is real, that it must work, always works, and it is impossible for it not to work, since it is grounded in natural law. They created the codes and laws. And the Earthling's preoccupation with a perception of freedom allowed this to infuse into the system without question. Those who do not know and use the law by which everything functions necessarily and always lose. This esoteric truth must be obscured and concealed from the "masses" by every means possible. Otherwise, those who would rule mankind would have no way of obtaining their positions of power, privilege, and plunder (all of which are frauds). By knowing and using the law themselves and keeping the knowledge of such law from the masses, the people are deliberately rendered defenseless, confused, emasculated, dependent, helpless "sheeple," considered as existing for the purpose of being exploited, herded, sheered, gelded, and slaughtered at will.

The Elite Powers thus achieve and operate their monopoly on "law" (the very thought is absurd, like stating one has a monopoly on light or life), by propagandizing the lie that law is so complex, esoteric, obtuse, vast, and confusing that only they and their hatchet men called "attorneys" and "judges" can administer it. The law is "mystified," made into some kind of quasi-religious cult, operated by a high priesthood that alone has the knowledge and authority for operating the resulting "legal system" that rules the life of man. Law must be transformed into a "closed union shop" such as the Bar Association, into whose hands the people must entrust their "lives, fortunes, and sacred honor" without availability of alternative sources of remedy and redress of grievances. Where can one go for relief when the fox guards the henhouse? If the so-called "Rulers of the World" did not withhold from general understanding the knowledge that the foundational principles of real law are few in number and easily mastered by everyone, and that all of the documents and instruments used in all law and commerce are likewise few in number and comprehensible to laymen, such con men would have to abandon their aristocratic "titles of nobility" and find real jobs based on genuine productivity, contribution, and "win-win" interactions with their fellow man.

It is empowering and exhilarating to understand that the ever-changing, monstrous vastness of "law" can be distilled into a handful of universal principles that can be contained on a 3" X 5" card, and that all of the legal documents and instruments functioning today can be mastered by nearly anyone. Attorneys and Judges deliberately conceal the fact that the only significance inhering in court cases and statutes consists of the simple and universal principles of commercial law codified by the Maxims.

All legal documents, proceedings, and processes are obscured by re-naming and mislabeling said documents and processes in accordance with whatever degrees of multiplicity and complexity are needed for preserving its inaccessible aloofness. Law is made diffuse, enormously complex, and allegedly far beyond the ken of regular folks. With knowledge of the truth underlying all of that misdirection and deception, i.e. seeing through the Wizard's Light Show, you can understand what is happening and place yourself in a position of mastery of the situation instead of being relegated to the status of a confused, helpless victim forever in the dark and at the mercy of those who exploit your ignorance of the rules and processes by which law (i.e. organized, deadly force) operates.

In short, *"Know the truth and the truth shall make you free."* The problem is there may some serious consequences in trying.

As mentioned above, the word "commerce" encompasses all interactions and interchanges between people, including exchanges of such "noncommercial" things as "ideas, sentiments, etc." The fundamental principles and precepts of universal commercial law that have for millennia formed the underpinnings of civilized law on this planet are both biblical and non-biblical, i.e. their truth and validity is a function of themselves and the long-accepted usage and practice by many cultures and peoples, in diverse forms, throughout the world for thousands of years. These fundamental Maxims of Commerce, which underlie all commercial documents, instruments, and processes, are enumerated herewith (with biblical references in parenthesis):

1. A workman is worthy of his hire
(Exodus 20:15; Lev. 19:13; Matt. 10:10; Luke 10:7; II
Tim. 2:6. Legal maxim: "It is against equity for freemen not to have the free disposal of their own property").

2. All are equal under the Law
(God's Law--Ethical and Natural Law). (Exodus 21:23-25;
Lev. 24:17-21; Deut. 1:17, 19:21; Matt., 22:36-40; Luke
10:17; Col. 3:25. Legal maxims: "No one is above the law.", "Commerce, by the law of nations, ought to be common, and not to be converted into a monopoly and the private gain of a few.").

3. In Commerce truth is sovereign
(Exodus 20:16; Ps. 117:2; Matt. 6:33, John 8:32; II Cor.
13:8. Legal maxim: "To lie is to go against the mind."

4. Truth is expressed by means of an affidavit
(Lev. 5:4-5; Lev. 6:3-5; Lev 19:11-13; Num. 30:2; Matt.
5:33; James 5:12).

5. An unrebutted affidavit stands as the truth in Commerce
(1 Pet. 1:25; Heb. 6:13-15. Legal maxim: "He who does not deny, admits.").

6. An unrebutted affidavit becomes the judgment in Commerce
(Heb. 6:16-17. Any proceeding in a court, tribunal, or arbitration forum consists of a contest, or "duel," of commercial affidavits wherein the points remaining unrebutted in the end stand as the truth and the matters to which the judgment of the law is applied.).

7. A matter must be expressed to be resolved
(Heb. 4:16; Phil. 4:6; Eph. 6:19-21. Legal maxim: "He who fails to assert his rights has none.").

8. He who leaves the field of battle first loses by default
(Book of Job; Matt. 10:22. Legal maxim: "He who does not repel a wrong when he can, occasions it.").

9. Sacrifice is the measure of credibility
(One who is not damaged, put at risk, or willing to swear an oath that he consents to claim against his commercial liability in the event that any of his statements or actions is groundless or unlawful, has no basis to assert claims or charges and forfeits all credibility and right to claim authority.)
(Acts 7, life/death of Stephen, maxim: "He who bears the burden ought also to derive the benefit.").

10. A lien or claim can be satisfied only through rebuttal by Counter-affidavit point-for-point, resolution by jury, or payment
(Gen. 2-3; Matt. 4; Revelation. Legal maxim: "If the plaintiff does not prove his case, the defendant is absolved.").

All law in Canada and United States can be reduced to the above ten listed maxims.

The Ten Commandments

When Jesus spoke the Truth to his accusers, he would justify himself by quoting **Law**. First, he would quote God's Law, and after quoting God's Law He would often quote the accuser's law and use that against them as well. For example, Jesus would say, *"Did ye never read in the scriptures..."* and then **quote God's Law**. Then he would turn around and say, "Is it not written in **your law**..." and **quote their own law**! His accusers would have no answer, they could not overcome Him. How could anyone overcome somebody who is obeying both God's Law and man's law!? If a man made law is just, it will be in harmony with God's Law.

These maxims are the foundation and principles of the laws that man passes today. Unfortunately, men enforce their own will more than they enforce law. So, this is why, in addition to knowing God's Law, it is also important to know man's law, because man's law is based upon God's Law. And when you are accused of "breaking the law," you can do what Jesus did, and use both God's Law and man's law to justify your lawful acts, for this is the only thing that will excuse you.

It is important to distinguish between commercial law and maxims of law, when quoting from their law. We should never, ever quote their codes, rules, regulations, ordinances, statutes, common law, merchant law, public policies, constitutions, etc., because these are commercial in nature, and if we use their commercial law, they can presume we are engaged in commerce (which means we are of the world), which will nullify our witness (because we are not of the world). Maxims of law are not commercial law, but are mostly based upon scripture and truth.

Many insist on using the "common law" to defend themselves. The reason we should not is because, first and foremost, you do not see the term "common law" in scripture. Bondservants of Christ are only to use God's Law. Secondly, the common law is a commercial law today, created by merchants, influenced by Roman Law, and used for commercial purposes. The following definitions are taken from "**A Dictionary of Law,** by **William C. Anderson**, 1893."

Custom of merchants: A system of customs, originating among merchants, and allowed for the benefit of trade as part of the common law. *Page 303.*
Law-merchant; law of merchants: The rules applicable to commercial paper were transplanted into the common law from the law merchant. They had their origin in the customs and course of business of merchants and bankers, and are now recognized by the courts because they are demanded by the wants and conveniences of the mercantile world. *Pages 670-671.*
Roman Law: The common law of England has been largely influenced by the Roman law, in several respects: Through the development of commercial law. *Page 910.*
All of man's laws, except for many maxims of law, are commercial in nature.

The following are the definitions of "maxims," and then the relevant maxims of law will be listed.
Maxim (*Bouvier's Law Dictionary, 1856*): An established principle or proposition. A principle of law universally admitted, as being just and consonant with reason. Maxims in law are somewhat like axioms in geometry. *1 Bl. Com. 68.* They are principles and authorities, and part of the general customs or common law of the land; and are of the same strength as acts of parliament, when the judges have determined what is a maxim; which belongs to the judges and not the jury. *Terms do Ley; Doct. & Stud. Dial. 1, c. 8.* Maxims of the law are holden for law, and all other cases that may be applied to them shall be taken for granted. *1 Inst. 11. 67; 4 Rep. See 1 Com. c. 68; Plowd. 27, b.*

Finally, here are the Catholic Ten Commandments:

1. I am the LORD your God. You shall worship the Lord your God and Him only shall you serve.
2. You shall not take the name of the Lord your God in vain.
3. Remember to keep holy the Sabbath day.
4. Honour your father and your mother.
5. You shall not kill.
6. You shall not commit adultery.
7. You shall not steal.
8. You shall not bear false witness against your neighbour.
9. You shall not covet your neighbour's wife.
10. You shall not covet your neighbour's goods.

The Ten Commandments are a description of the basic freedom from sin that is necessary to live as a Christian. They are a minimum level of living, below which we must not go. The Ten Commandments and Catholicism have been bound together since the time of Christ. In the Bible which is written as the Commercial Code of GOD and Articles of Incorporation for PLANET EARTH INC, is executed through the Vatican and the corporate VATICAN. When you wilfully accept the religion, you wilfully accept the Code as your Law.

It's important to note that each Commandment is simply a **summary** of a whole category of actions. Don't be legalistic, searching for a way around them because their wording doesn't fit you perfectly! For example, "bearing false witness against your neighbour" covers any kind of falsehood: perjury, lying, slander, detraction, rash judgment, etc.

The Catholic Ten Commandments are linked together to form a coherent whole. If you break one of them, you're guilty of breaking all of them (*Catechism*, #2069). The Commandments express man's **fundamental duties** to God and neighbour. As such, they represent *grave* obligations. To violate them knowingly & willingly in a significant way is to commit mortal sin. (See *Catechism*, #2702-3) and then the god of vengeance and the greatest love will reap upon you serious mortal repercussions.

Now, we need to shift into one more missing piece of this corporate puzzle. It is the UPU or the Universal Postal Union that has roots in the Vatican. Through the Postal Union, there is a "corporate" overlay that effectively "digitizes" every piece of Planet Earth right down to the Strawman's area of a Postal Code. This purpose is to deliver mail of course, but there are many more "less obvious" functions of this UPU...

18

THE US POSTAL SERVICE

And so the world is flooding over with debt that is simply an imaginary unit of accounting. It's just a piece of paper that people believe has value because it can be traded for things that have value. Yet this "money" can be created by the keystroke entry. And then people bonds are being used to make more, and then the people pay interest. There is yet another dimension to this tale of history that originates with the Vatican and has manifested itself in the Postal Service all the way down to postal codes that delineates imaginary Strawman districts. In this section we will refer to the work and research of *James Thomas of the family McBride www.divineprovince.org and www.notice-recipient.com.*

The Trusteeship And The Global Estate

The U.S. Postal Service was established in 1971. This was preceded by the Post Office Department, which was established in 1872. And before the Post Office Department, the general post-office preceded that. In the early 1800's, they started referring to the general post office as the Post Office Department. However, it did not officially become the Post Office Department until 1872. Previous to that it was known as the general post-office. It would seem that during the 1860's and 1870's there were many "power play" shenanigans going one where the Global Elite were placing their attention on America. Not only was America the place that was a huge threat against their financial empire, it was the place that the Fathers of the Constitution were about to unleash the powers of life liberty and equality as all free sovereign men and women, a direct threat against the religious empire of the Vatican.

To unravel this intentionally complex Trusteeship of the Global Estate Trust let us begin at the top and work our way down. The Vatican boasts, in their Papal Bull, dominion over the entire earth, via conquest, and is answerable ONLY to the Divine Spirit. Dominion over means control over, not ownership. The Vatican's un-rebutted claims establish them as the Primary Trustee of the Global Estate Trust, our Divine Inheritance; a very unpopular fact. But a fact that opens a doorway placing the cure for the mis-administration and theft of our Divine Inheritance within our grasp.

The Post Office, Vatican And Divine Right Of Use

Today, everything is held in trust and everything is about trusts, Implied or Expressed. The Creator gave man dominion over all things. Dominion over equals control over NOT ownership. Control over all things, yet not ownership sounds like a Divine Right of Use .

A Divine Right of Use of the Divine property/the All of earth which is ' held in trust'. So, the entire world we call earth is held in trust, the Divine Trust, for our benefit as Beneficiaries. This Global Divine Trust is an Implied Trust as opposed to an Expressed Trust.

In the beginning man was responsible, as a Trustee, for the care and well being of that portion of the Divine Estate upon which he/she exercised their Divine Right of Use as a Beneficiary. Through the decades man has given over that Divine fiduciary obligation to legal fiction trustees. There are as many forms of trusteeships as there are people in the world. Some very fair and equitable, say a republic, all the way to a dictatorship, each with various degrees of freedoms and rights, taxes and limitations.

Who is the Trustee responsible for your piece of the Divine Estate, our Global Estate Trust? It is the. Government = Trustee, like in civil administration. So, what do they administrate? Your portion of the Divine Estate.

Today legal fiction Trustees, [governments, postal zones, churches] have morphed from public servants to tyrants. They have turned these positions of service into positions of power, the trustees operating the Divine Trust for their own benefit to the detriment of the estate and the heir.

In America today we have Township Trustees, County Trustees, State Trustees and Federal Trustees just to name a few of the many levels of fiduciaries within the Trusteeship which is involved in the administration of our Divine Estate(s), the Global Estate Trust. Judges, Clerks of Court, Prosecutors and Attorneys all play their own part in the administration of our Global Estate Trust leveraging our Divine Estates to rape, pillage and plunder the world and enslave the people under the mode of deception.

To unravel this intentionally complex Trusteeship of the Global Estate Trust let us begin at the top and work our way down. The Vatican boasts, in their Papal Bull, dominion over the entire earth, via conquest, and is answerable ONLY to the Divine Spirit. Dominion over means control over, not ownership. The Vatican's un-rebutted claims establish them as the Primary Trustee of the Global Estate Trust, our Divine Inheritance; a very unpopular fact. But a fact that opens a doorway placing the cure for the mis-administration and theft of our Divine Inheritance within our grasp.

The Vatican is the Primary Trustee of the Global Estate Trust. To facilitate the administration of this Global Trust the Vatican established the Universal Postal Union as the Secondary Trustees of the Global Trust charged with dividing the Global Trust into zones and endowing these legal fiction zones with sovereign authority to facilitate the efficient administration of the Global Trust.

It is no surprise that the first requirement for the international acknowledgment of a sovereign nation is the necessity of a Post Office. The primary objective of the military in any 'zone' is the protection of the Post, or the Post Office, for in their original jurisdiction, the Postmaster Generals are the Trustees of their respective zone.

In 1789 the Continental Congress passed a bill to "establish the seat of government, a general post office, under the direction of the Postmaster General." That's right, a general post office under the direction of the Postmaster General. They were further dividing the postal zone of North America establishing a new zone, and endowing it with sovereign authority, whereby our founding fathers believed they could establish a Trusteeship which would ensure that sovereignty of the people would be passed down to the people of future generations.

The Preamble to the Constitution created the Estate Trust which held the freedoms guaranteed in the Articles of Confederation and the Declaration of Independence in trust for future generations. The Articles of the Constitution established the Trusteeship as well as the powers and limitations thereof. The Congress and Senate were Trustees charged with the Administration of our Divine Inheritance, the Global Estate Trust.

In this 'general post office' seat of government there was established the 'civil administration' called the United States. Civil administration? What do they administrate? Our Divine Estate Trust, the Global Trust, our Divine Inheritance. Remember, we can never OWN anything. We simply have a Divine Right of Use of the property of the Divine Estate, the Global Trust.

So, we the people of this earth have a Divine Right of use of the Global Trust while the civil administration is charged with the administration of our estate for our benefit.

In the world of trusts Civil Administration/ Government = Trusteeship.

So, the entire world is held in trust. The Global Estate Trust, our Divine Inheritance, our birthright is held in trust and is administrated by the various 'governments' who gain their sovereign authority via the Universal Postal Union, the Secondary Trustee of the Global Trust answerable to the Vatican.

In the world of trusts and trust law, rights, duties and obligations are very straight forward, cut and dry, black and white. There are no opinions, secret codes, rules or statutes, period. Just the facts. There is a chain of command, consequences for your actions, or lack thereof, and accountability.

It has been a slow and cumbersome process to overcome the out of control momentum of the civil administrators of the world today. There have been countless casualties as a result of our efforts to unravel the illusion; to overcome the programming and fear which fuelled the beast to reach the core where truth and accountability resides.

We the people of this earth, Heirs to the Divine Estate, Beneficiary and Settler to the Divine Trust have an absolute right to determine the who, what and how of the administration of our Divine Estate.

Our founding fathers attempted to guarantee a fair and equitable form of trusteeship which would not infringe on the private rights of the American people via the Constitution.

In 1865 the Trustees, public servants, administrators of our estates, fraudulently modified the terms of the Constitution establishing a second form of trusteeship which would operate for the benefit of the trustees at the detriment of the estate and the heir.

This was a serious Breach of Trust, Breach of Fiduciary duty.

Our Divine Estates, our Divine Inheritance, has been administrated under a Breach of Trust.

A Breach of Trust that established the Military Industrial Complex, the 14th Amendment congress and senate under whose jurisdiction the new heirs, the 14th Amendment citizens would operate and all of the codes and statutes to which we are held accountable, the least of which are taxes.

The original trustees of our estates, the civil administration/ government, have fraudulently altered the trust instrument to facilitate the administration of the estates for the benefit of the trustees via the Military Industrial Complex to the detriment of the heirs/ Beneficiaries.

For decades this Military Industrial Complex has leveraged our estates to fund the global military aggression, pillage, plunder and occupation of foreign nations, raping the lands and promoting the destruction of the social and family unit both foreign and domestic.

For decades this Military Industrial Complex has sucked the life force out of the American people...... out of the people of the world, designating us all Enemy Combatants. The Federal Reserve System, a product of the 14th Amendment, has been the front line weapon of the Military Industrial Complex used to facilitate the financial enslavement of the people of the world, all by leveraging our Divine Estates. We have, and continue to fund our own enslavement and destruction through our Divine Estate.

This 14th Amendment Military Industrial Complex has the absolute power and authority to use and abuse the people and lands of the world, except .that absolute power and authority is based on a Breach of Trust.

As Heirs to the Divine Estate, Beneficiaries and Settlers to the Divine Trust we have the power and authority we have an absolute duty and obligation to demand and receive a cure to the Breach of Trust.

But, as heirs, we are presumed Deceased, having failed to claim our estate.

One must 1) re-establish their living status, 2) Claim the estate, and 3) Identify and demand a cure to the Breach of Trust.

How does one do this? You may ask. I have my own method which I believe will work for me, but, there is no established method at this time. It is my belief that there is more than one road home. Can The Poeres That Be (TPTB) deny that you are a living being when you stand in the street waving your Birth Certificate in the air demanding that your estate be administrated in accordance with the original intent for your benefit and for the best and highest of all mankind?

My bet is that they who hold the original instrument [Birth Certificate] are the holder in due course of the estate and the appropriate person with whom to file a claim against the estate trust. In Ohio it is the OHIO DEPT. OF HEALTH VITAL STATISTICS who holds the original. I believe they are the intermediary agent who has leased your estate to the Military Industrial Complex. I believe they hold the keys to the Who and How our estate is administrated.

In OHIO, the Probate Judge is the SUPERIOR GUARDIAN of all ESTATES, which IMHO makes him/her the Primary Fiduciary for the estate and in his/her private capacity may be the Privy Councilor with the power and authority to make the changes in administration of your estate that you request.

The key to remember here is these are our estates, our Divine Inheritance. We are the Powers That Be as concerns us and our estate, if we will just take back that power that we have unwittingly given away. If we will simply put away the fear and doubt, acknowledge and accept who you are, claim our Divine Inheritance and instruct our public servants as to how your estate is to be administrated.

One must remember that your reality is a reflection of what is within. We are seeking peace; We are asking that the administration of our estate reflect the abundance and prosperity that is our birthright, but, our reality can only reflect that peace, abundance and prosperity IF that is what is in our hearts.

The Vatican is the Primary Trustee of the Global Estate Trust. To facilitate the administration of this Global Trust the <u>Vatican established the Universal Postal Union as the Secondary Trustees of the Global Trust charged with dividing the Global Trust into zones and endowing these legal fiction zones with sovereign authority to facilitate the efficient administration of the Global Trust</u>.

It is no surprise that the first requirement for the international acknowledgment of a sovereign nation is the necessity of a Post Office. The primary objective of the military in any 'zone' is the protection of the Post, or the Post Office, for in their original jurisdiction, the Postmaster Generals are the Trustees of their respective zone. It may come as a surprise, however, to understand the true relationship between the Vatican and the Universal Postal Union.

The UPU (Universal Postal Union) in Berne, Switzerland, is an extremely significant organization in today's world. It is formulated by treaty. No nation can be recognized as a nation without being in international admiralty in order to have a forum common to all nations for engaging in commerce and resolving disputes. That is why the USA under the Articles of Confederation could not be recognized as a country. Every state (colony) was sovereign, with its own common law, which foreclosed other countries from interacting with the USA as a nation in international commerce. Today, international admiralty is the private jurisdiction of the IMF, *et al.*, the creditor in the bankruptcy of essentially every government on Earth.

The UPU operates under the authority of treaties with every country in the world. It is, as it were, the overlord or overseer over the common interaction of all countries in international commerce. Every nation has a postal system, and also has reciprocal banking and commercial relationships, whereby all are within and under the UPU. The UPU is the number one military (international admiralty is also military) contract mover on the planet. Each country will have Provost Martial or equivalent that is the link between the UPU and the Military power.

In 1789 the Continental Congress passed a bill to "establish the seat of government, a general post office, under the direction of the Postmaster General." They were further dividing the postal zone of North America establishing a new zone, and endowing it with sovereign authority, whereby our founding fathers believed they could establish a Trusteeship which would ensure that sovereignty of the people would be passed down to the people of future generations.

The Preamble to the Constitution created the Estate Trust which held the freedoms guaranteed in the Articles of Confederation and the Declaration of Independence in trust for future generations. The Articles of the Constitution established the Trusteeship as well as the powers and limitations thereof. The Congress and Senate were Trustees charged with the Administration of our Divine Inheritance, the Global Estate Trust.

In this 'general post office' seat of government there was established the 'civil administration' called the United States. Civil administration? What do they administrate? Our Divine Estate Trust, the Global Trust, our Divine Inheritance. Remember, we can never OWN anything. We simply have a Divine Right of Use of the property of the Divine Estate, the Global Trust.

So, we the people of this earth have a Divine Right of use of the Global Trust while the civil administration is charged with the administration of our estate for our benefit.

In the world of trusts Civil Administration/Government equals Trusteeship. So, the entire world is held in trust. The Global Estate Trust, our Divine Inheritance, our birthright is held in trust and is administrated by the various 'governments' who gain their sovereign authority via the Universal Postal Union, the Secondary Trustee of the Global Trust answerable to the Vatican.

In the world of trusts and trust law, rights, duties and obligations are very straight forward, cut and dry, black and white. There are no opinions, secret codes, rules or statutes, period. Just the facts. There is a chain of command, consequences for your actions, or lack thereof, and accountability.

There was actually two different general post-offices. The Post Master General today wears about seven hats; there are about seven different entities to the postal system. He wears the original hat as a caretaker of the original general post-office. He's also the caretaker of the general post-office that was created on February 20, 1792, which was for governmental business. And then in 1872 they created the Post Office Department.

In 1639, the original foundation for the post office was given in Massachusetts to Richard Fairbanks, the owner of Fairbanks Tavern in Boston. He was the first Postal officer in the history of the United States.

The General Court Of Massachusetts November 5, 1639:

"For preventing the miscarriage of letters, it is ordered, that notice be given that Richard Fairbanks's house in Boston is the place appointed for all letters which are brought from beyond the seas, or are to be sent thither, 'to be brought unto; and he is to take care that they be delivered or sent according to their directions; and he is allowed for every such letter one penny, and must answer all miscarriages through his own neglect in this kind; provided that no man shall be compelled to bring his letters thither, except he please."

Following the adoption of the Constitution in May 1789, the Act of September 22, 1789 (1 Stat. 70), temporarily established a post office:

NINETEENTH ACT of CONGRESS
An ACT for the temporary establishment of the POST OFFICE. Be it enacted by the Senate and House of Representatives of the United States of America in Congress assembled, That there shall be appointed a Post-Master General; his powers and salary and the compensation to the assistant or clerk and deputies which he may appoint, and the regulations of the Post-Office shall be the same as they last were under the resolutions and ordinances of the late Congress. The Post-Master General to be subject to the direction of the President of the United States in performing the duties of his office, and in forming contracts for the transportation of the mail. Be it further enacted, That this act shall continue in force until the end of the next session of Congress, and no longer. Approved, September 22nd, 1789.

The post office was temporarily continued by the Act of August 4, 1790 (1 Stat. 178), and the Act of March 3, 1791 (1 Stat. 218). The Act of February 20, 1792 made detailed provisions for the post office, and also established a separate general post office for governmental purposes:

Chapter VIII - *An Act to establish the Post Office and Post Roads within the United States. Section 3. And it be further enacted, That there shall be established, at the seat of the government of the United States, a general post-office.*

Note that this one page statutory creation by Congress established that general post-office for governmental business at the seat of the government of the United States in Washington D.C. The general post-office, which already existed, was never designated as being repealed in this Act. Therefore, it still remains in existence, separate from the governmental business' set up by this Act. There's nothing in that whole act which repeals the original general post-office. There's nothing in the act of 1872, when they created the Post Office Department, which did away with the original general post-office. So it's still there. There's nothing in the act of July 1, 1971, which created the Postal Service. The creation cannot do away with the creator, they cannot abolish the creator. Otherwise it has no foundation. And that's why the current Postmaster General wears about seven hats, because he has all of those different things that were created all the way through there.

In the early 1800's, the general post-office began to be referred to as "the Post-office department," but was not officially created until June 8, 1872:

Chapter CCCXXXV. - *An Act to revise, consolidate, and amend the Statutes relating to the Post-office Department. Be it enacted by the Senate and House of Representatives of the United States of America in Congress assembled, That there shall be established, at the seat of government of the United States of America, a department to be known as the Post-office Department.*

And again, the general post-office was not repealed in this statute. It is for this cause that the re-organized service and its employees have no authority over the general post-office - it precedes their creation and has its Source and Origin in God through His Lawful assembly. The Post Office Department of the Confederate States of America was established on February 21, 1861, by an Act of the Provisional Congress of the Confederate States. The resumption of the federal mail service in the southern states took place gradually as the war came to an end. Then the Post Office Department was replaced by the United States Postal Service on July 1, 1971. Title 39, the Postal Reorganization Act, details this change as well.

Scripture Passages Related To The Post Office

The general post office has its beginnings in scripture.
Jeremiah 51:31, *"One **post** shall run to meet another, and one **messenger** to meet another, to shew the king of Babylon that his city is taken at one end..."*

A "post" is another name for a courier:
2 Chronicles 30:6, *"So **the posts went with the letters** from the king and his princes throughout all Israel and Judah,"*

Esther 3:13, *"And **the letters were sent by posts** into all the king's provinces..."*

Scripture records messages being sent "by the <u>hands</u> of messengers" (1 Samuel 11:7) from as far back as the book of Job, which is the oldest book in the bible:
Job 1:14, "And there came a **messenger** unto Job, and said, the oxen were plowing, and the asses feeding beside them:"

These messages were delivered using the current means of movement at the time:

Esther 8:10,14, "And he wrote in the king Ahasuerus' name, and sealed it with the king's ring, and **sent <u>letters</u> by <u>posts</u>** on <u>horseback</u>, and <u>riders</u> on mules, camels, and young dromedaries: So the **posts** that rode upon mules and camels went out..."

And sending messages refreshes the soul:

Proverbs 25:13, KJV, "As the cold of snow in the time of harvest, so is a faithful **messenger** to them that send him: for **he refresheth the soul** of his masters."
Proverbs 25:13, Septuagint, "As a fall of snow in the time of harvest is good against heat, so a faithful **messenger refreshes** those that sent him: for he helps the souls of his masters."

In times past, people sent messages to others by posting their letters on a "post" in the middle of town, with the name of the one who it's intended for. People would go to this "post" and look for letters with their name on it, and if they saw their name on a letter they would take it down from the post and read it. However, due to theft of messages, an office was built around the post to prevent people from stealing messages. This office became known as the general post-office. People would then go to the general post-office to pick up their messages.

Today, the stamp on an envelope pays for delivery of that envelope from the sender's post-office to the receiver's post-office. It <u>does not</u> pay for the costs when that envelope leaves the area behind the clerk's desk and gets delivered to the receiver's address, mailbox, post office box, mail slot, etc. This is a "free" service. The alternative to free mail delivery is to receive all Postal Matter either in **general delivery**, or through the **general post office**.

A Subtle Power Resides In The Post Office

Typically the average American thinks of their Postal System as a part of, and subservient to, their government. However, the postal system in the United States has a different legal history than one would expect.

The Post Office and Judicial Courts were established *before* the seat of the Government. On Thursday, Sept. 17, 1789 we find written, "Mr. Goodhue, for the committee appointed for the purpose, presented a bill to amend part of the Tonnage act, which was read the first time. The bill sent from the Senate, for **the temporary establishment of the Post Office**, was read the second and third time, and passed. The bill for **establishing the Judicial Courts** . . . , for **establishing the seat of government** . . . " *Gales and Seaton's History* [H. of R.], p. 928. Other references to the Post Office support my theory of the founding forefather's views:

1) POST OFFICE: A place where letters are received to be sent to the persons to whom they, are addressed.

2. The post office establishment of the United States, is of the greatest importance to the people and to the government. The constitution of the United States has invested congress with power to establish post offices and post roads. Art. 1, s. 8, n. 7.

3. By virtue of this constitutional authority, congress passed several laws anterior to the third day of March 1825, when an act, entitled "An act to reduce into one the several acts establishing and regulating the post office department," was passed. 3 Story, U. S. 1825. **It is thereby enacted, 1. That there be established, the seat of the government of the United States, a general post office, under the direction of a postmaster general**. Bouvier, John. *Law Dictionary. Adapted to the Constitution and Laws of The United States of America And of the Several States of the American Union, With References to the Civil and Other Systems of Foreign Law*. In the Philadelphia, by the Childs & Peterson. (1856)

We need to take notice of where the commas are placed on that last sentence. "That there be established, the seat of the government of the United States, a general post office, under the direction of a postmaster general." When you set off a clause with commas, one must make sure that the sentence makes sense without that clause. Taking out the set-off clause, we read "the seat of the government of the United States under the direction of a postmaster general."

The set-off clause is a descriptive clause. Is it not? So, we have…."for establishing the seat of government, **a general post office,…"** " under the direction of the postmaster general." We also see that the establishment of the '…general post office…' was to be temporary…'

So, we have the Post Office of the United States, (republic), established the judicial courts and the seat of government, a general post office, under the direction of the postmaster general. The ten (10) miles square styled as Washington, D.C. is a general post office, or postal zone, under the direction of the postmaster general. This new postal zone, the United States Post Office, being the newly established seat of government, authorized its congress to establish postal roads and post offices within the ten miles square and **any/all territories** of same.

So, we now have 1) the original Post Office of the United States, and 2) the corporate United States Post Office, the creation of and under the authority of the original post office of the United States.

The Buck Act divided America into several territories whereby the corporate U.S. Post Office could establish postal roads and post offices throughout American in order to execute their complex regulatory scheme (see July 2-3,2009 post '*Food for Thought, Their Sandbox'*) thereby extending their power and control over the American people beyond the ten miles square.

When one goes to the USPS web site you find that the postmaster general wears two hats. He is the *postmaster of the Post Office of the United States* and he is the *CEO of the corporate United States Post Office, now the USPS.*

You will also notice that they self-describe the post office as 1) the 'most trusted government agency……' and 2) '….one of the ten most trusted organizations in the nation…' Well…….., when you look up the words **agency** and **organization** you find that they are two distinctly different entities and no where do the two definitions cross reference, not even in a thesaurus. ***They are telling us that they are two separate and distinct entities***

It is important to understand the importance of the sequence of events, or sequence of creation in this matter. The original Post Office of the United States has remained solvent throughout the years unaffected by the various bankruptcies of the 'government of the U.S.' Only the corporate general post office, the seat of government of the U.S., was affected by the bankruptcies.

One must ask, when the creation is in breach, and/or has morphed into a continuing criminal enterprise, is its creator responsible for curing the breach? Can the creator be held to account for the actions of its creation? Remember that we are speaking about contracts and legal fictions here. We are speaking about an insolvent legal fiction creation of a continuously solvent entity; a solvent entity of We the People of America, is it not?

Is it not the responsibility of the original post office of the United States to pull the plug on their creation which is out of control? The receivership has exhausted its term life, yet refuses to yield to the republic. Is it not the responsibility of the Post Office of the United States, (republic), to bring their creation to heal? Does their refusal to hold their creation to account establish a valid claim against the continuously solvent creator, the Post Office of the United States by We the People of America?

The question now is how does one safely traverse the *magical kingdom* of the post office, whose magic is so great as to have caused one of the greatest and most powerful talismans of our time, the *Constitution of the United States,* to succumb to their power?

It has been suggested that the Declaration Of Independence is such a powerful talisman that if We the People of American would simply verbalize the it on a daily basis that we could once again breathe life into it; to revive its magical power and counter the rampant negative, fear mongering energy that exists, and is destroying America today.

It is becoming increasingly clear in America today that the illuminati, Freemasons, etc. have and continue to use black magic against We the American People to gain power and control over us. Their magic will continue to hold us in its gaze like the proverbial deer in the headlights until we wake up and accept the facts that create are reality today; until we awaken to and accept the I AM and the magical power we wield from knowing who we are!

The Real Power Of the UPU Is In The Military

As stated, the UPU (Universal Postal Union) in Berne, Switzerland, is an extremely significant organization in today's world. It is formulated by treaty. No nation can be recognized as a nation without being in international admiralty in order to have a forum common to all nations for engaging in commerce and resolving disputes. That is why the USA under the Articles of Confederation could not be recognized as a country. Every state (colony) was sovereign, with its own common law, which foreclosed other countries from interacting with the USA as a nation in international commerce. Today, international admiralty is the private jurisdiction of the IMF, *et al.,* the creditor in the bankruptcy of essentially every government on Earth. The following information comes from the research of James Mcbride referenced before.

The UPU operates under the authority of treaties with every country in the world. It is, as it were, the overlord or overseer over the common interaction of all countries in international commerce. Every nation has a postal system, and also has reciprocal banking and commercial relationships, whereby all are within and under the UPU. The

UPU is the number one military (international admiralty is also military) contract mover on the planet.

For this reason one should send all important legal and commercial documents through the post office rather than private carriers, which are firewalls. We want direct access to the authority—and corresponding availability of remedy and recourse—of the UPU. For instance, if you post through the US Post Office and the US Postmaster does not provide you with the remedy you request within twenty-one (21) days, you can take the matter to the UPU.

Involving the authority of the UPU is automatically invoked by the use of postage stamps. Utilization of stamps includes putting stamps on any documents (for clout purposes, not mailing) we wish to introduce into the system. As long as you use a stamp (of any kind) you are in the game. If you have time, resources, and the luxury of dealing with something well before expiration of a given time frame, you can use stamps that you consider ideal. The most preferable stamps are ones that are both large and contain the most colors. In an emergency situation, or simply if economy is a consideration, any stamp will do. Using a postage stamp and autograph on it makes you the postmaster for that contract.

Whenever you put a stamp on a document, inscribe your full name over the stamp at an angle. The color ink you use for this is a function of what color will show up best against the colors in the stamp. Ideal colors for doing this are purple (royalty), blue (origin of the bond), and gold (king's edict). Avoid red at all cost. Obviously, if you have a dark, multi-colored stamp you do not want to use purple or blue ink, since your autograph on it would not stand out as well if you used lighter color ink. Ideally one could decide on the best color for his autograph and then obtain stamps that best suit one's criteria and taste. Although a dollar stamp is best, it is a luxury unless one is well off financially. Otherwise, reserve the use of dollar stamps for crucial instruments, such as travel documents. The rationale for using two-cent stamps is that in the 19th Century the official postage rate for the *de jure* Post Office of the United States of America was fixed at two (2) cents. For stamps to carry on one's person for any kind of unexpected encounter or emergency use, this denomination might be ideal.

Use stamps on important documents, such as a check, travel documents, paperwork you put in court, etc. Where to put the stamp and how many stamps to use depend on the document. On foundational documents and checks, for instance, put a stamp on the right hand corner of the instrument, both on the front and on the back. The bottom right hand corner of the face of a check, note, or bill of exchange signifies the liability. Furthermore, the bottom right hand corner of the reverse of the document is the final position on the page, so no one can endorse anything (using a restricted endorsement or otherwise) after that. You want to have the last word. If you have only one stamp, put it where you are expected to sign and autograph over it cross-wise. In the case of a traffic ticket, for instance, put a stamp on the lower right hand corner where you are supposed to sign and autograph across the stamp at an angle.

Autographing a stamp not only establishes you as the postmaster of the contract but constitutes a cross-claim. Using the stamp process on documents presents your adversaries with a problem because their jurisdiction is subordinate to that of the UPU, which you have now invoked for your benefit. The result in practice of doing this is that whenever those who know what you are doing are recipients of your documents with autographed stamps they back off. If they do not, take the matter to the US Postmaster to deal with. If he will not provide you with your remedy, take the matter to the UPU for them to clean up.

The countries whose stamps would be most effective to use are China, Japan, United States, and Great Britain. Utilizing these countries covers both East and West. However, since the US seems to be the point man in implementing the New World Order, one might most advisably use US stamps.

If you put stamps on documents you submit into court, put a stamp on the back of each page, at the bottom right hand corner. Do not place any stamps on the front of court paperwork since doing so alarms the clerk. By placing your autographed stamp on the reverse right hand corner you prevent being damaged by one of the tricks of judges these days. A judge might have your paperwork on his bench, but turned over so only the back side, which is ordinarily blank on every page, is visible. Then if you ask about your paperwork he might say something like, *"Yes, I have your paperwork in front of me but I don't find anything."* He can't see anything on the blank side of a page. If you place an autographed stamp on the lower right hand corner you foreclose a judge from engaging in this trick.

In addition, when it comes to court documents, one side is criminal and the other is civil. Using the autographed stamp that you rubber-stamp with your seal (bullet stamp) on the back side of your court documents is evidence that you possess the cancelled obligation on the civil side. Since there can be no assessment for criminal charges, and you show that you are the holder of the civil assessment, there is no way out for the court.

Also, in any court document you put in, handwrite your EIN number [SS# w.o. dashes] in gold on the top right corner of every page, with the autographed stamp on the back side.

Use of a notary combined with the postage stamp (and sometime Embassy stamps) gives you a priority mechanism. Everything is commerce, and all commerce is contract. The master of the contract is the post office, and the UPU is the supreme overlord of the commerce, banking, and postal systems of the world. Use of these stamps in this manner gets the attention of those in the system to whom you provide your paperwork. It makes you the master of that post office. Use of the stamp is especially important when dealing with the major players, such as the FBI, CIA, Secret Service, Treasury, etc. They understand the significance of what you are doing. Many times they hand documents back to someone using this approach and say, "Have a good day, sir." They don't want any untoward repercussions coming back on them.

If anyone asks you why you are doing what you are doing, suggest that they consult their legal counsel for the significance. It is not your job to explain the law, nor explain such things as your exemption or Setoff Account. The system hangs us by our own words. We have to give them the evidence, information, contacts, and legal determinations they require to convict us. The wise words of Calvin Coolidge, the most taciturn president in US history, are apt. When asked why he spoke so little, he replied, "I have never been hurt by anything I didn't say."

The bottom line is that whenever you need to sign any legal/commercial document, put a stamp (even a one (1) cent stamp) over where you sign and sign at an angle across it. Let the recipient deal with the significance and consequences of your actions. If you are in a court case, or at any stage of a proceeding (such as an indictment, summons, complaint, or any other hostile encounter with the system), immediately do the following:

> 1. Make a color copy of whatever documents you receive, or scan them in color into your computer;

2. Stamp the original of the first page of every document with the AFV/RFV stamp, put a postage stamp in the signature space, and autograph across it at an angle with your full name, using purple or blue ink, handwritten with upper- and lower-case, with your gold-ink bullet stamp (seal) on the upper left-hand portion of the postage stamp;

Make a color copy of the stamped, autographed pages and/or scan into your computer;

3. Put a stamp on the lower right-hand-corner of the back of every page and bullet-stamp and autograph it;

4. Have a notary send each document back to the sender, with a notarial certificate of service, with or without an accompanying/supporting affidavit by you;

5. If you have an affidavit, put an autographed stamp on the upper right hand corner of the first page and the lower right hand corner of the back of every page.

People who have engaged in this process report that when any knowledgeable judge, attorney, or official sees this, matters change dramatically. All of these personages know what mail fraud is. Since autographing the stamp makes you the postmaster of the contract, anyone who interferes is tampering with the mail and engaging in mail fraud. You can then subpoena the postmaster (either of the post office from which the letter was mailed, or the US Postmaster General, or both), and have them explain what the rules are, under deposition or testimony on the witness stand in open court.

In addition, most of the time when you get official communication it has a red-meter postage mark on the envelope rather than a cancelled stamp. This act is mail fraud. If the envelope has a red-meter postage mark on it, they are the ones who have engaged in mail fraud, because there is no cancelled stamp. It is the cancelled stamp that has the power; an un-cancelled stamp has nothing. A red-meter postage mark is an uncancelled stamp. If it is not cancelled, it is not paid. One researcher has scanned everything into his computer, and has more red-meter postage marks than he "can shake a stick at." Officials sending things out by cancelled stamp is a rarity—perhaps at most 2%.

With the red-metered postage you can trace each communication back to the PO from which it was sent, so you can get the postmaster for that PO, as well as the postmaster general for the US, to investigate the mail fraud involved. It is reasonable to conclude that cancelling a stamp both registers the matter and forms a contract between the party that cancels the stamp and the UPU. Using a stamp for postage without cancelling it is prima facie evidence that the postmaster of the local PO is committing mail fraud by taking a customer's money and not providing the paid-for service and providing you with the power of a cancelled stamp, as required under the provisions of the UPU. When you place an autographed stamp on a document you place that document and the contract underlying it under international law and treaty, with which the courts have no jurisdiction to deal. The system cannot deal with the real you, the living principle (as evidenced and witnessed by jurat). Nor can officials, attorneys, judges, et al., go against the UPU, international law, and treaty. In addition, they have no authority/jurisdiction to impair a contract between you (as the living principal) and the UPU (overseer of all world commerce).

You cancelled the stamp by sealing it and autographing across it. You did so in capacity of being the living principal, as acknowledged by your seal and the jurat on your documents.

If you are in a court case, bring in your red-metered envelopes in court and request the judge to direct the prosecutor to explain the red-meter postage stamp. Then watch their jaws drop. Doing this is especially potent if you also have asked the prosecutor to provide his bar number, since most attorneys in court—especially in US—are not qualified. An attorney in federal court had better have a six-digit bar card or he committed a felony just by walking in and giving his name.

Lastly, if you are charged with mail fraud, subpoena the prosecutor(s) to bring in the evidence on which mail fraud is being alleged, as well as the originals of all envelopes used for mailing any item connected with the case. Then the mail fraud involved was committed by the postmaster of the PO in which the envelope was stamped.

We now will leave the commerce side and how it have been transduced to be a vehicle of conquest, It is time to look at a different picture of the great force of Religion and how it has also evolved as a vehicle of conquest..

19

THE STORY OF RELIGIOUS DOMINION

As you begin to understand the source of true power on Planet Earth, it appears that it lies within the secretly guarded bloodlines that orchestrate the religious faiths and financial matters of nations and peoples. The Empire of Planet Earth is effectively under the control of the Dynasties of wealthy and power families. The administrative process is through corporations overlain on the real things through nations, governments, legal, finance, military, and media processes to name a few. These are the gods that run things in the private, secret domain and who orchestrate the same way the directors of large corporations saliently direct their missions through business plans. The process of power has shifted to control of money and religions. There is also no denying that theses who are in charge are there because they themselves have special gifts and powers, know what the many do not know, and can control the science (and perhaps even non-sciences) to always be a step ahead of their employees (humanity).

Either way, these gods are careful to keep bloodlines pure for a reason and whether they may have special mystical or occult powers that we do not understand. One inescapable truth is that they have their own very large dynasties, and they seem to be collaborating in creating a global empire which they believe is a better place for their slaves. They may even go outside of the earth realm in the knowing and connections but the truth is that these "mortal" bloodlines are in power now and they were in power before; only the landscape and means of control appears to have changed. Because humanity has always had free choice, their evolution to resist believing "fiction" of occult may in truth have actually allowed themselves to be governed by the ones who do not believe the occult is such fiction.

The power of the gods was attained because they allegedly had some technical or psychic power beyond the norm. They could instil fear of death and they could kill those who would not obey. And so historically, these gods were not to be trifled with. And those who followed them and preached the danger of gods vengeance became the chosen ones. From the power of these gods came the codes, the laws, the commandments, even the commercial rules, the way of behaviour and it was through first some exceptional power, then through the gathering of followers, then through the command of military resources, then through the power of the law. The evolution from direct engagement with humanity shifted to indirect engagement as humanity gained more and more of its own smarts.

Of interest in the evolution is how there are so many commandments and laws written by these gods (or the chosen priests to represent their needs, masquerading as disciples of a true God) are exactly the same today as reflected in the faiths of religions, and even in the behaviour of many civilizations.

When we look back at how the corporate structures and the statutes and acts are applied, as implemented through bankruptcy and debt, it becomes clearer to see how the other side of the money-religion coin has come to pass. These Prophesies and bibles are simply business plans and legal codes created by the Directors of PLANET EARTH who always seem to be a steps ahead of the majority of Earthlings. These have all been written by these gods/man for the purpose of dominion and the maintenance of their kingdoms.

Throughout history, this has been maintained by the process of slavery, male dominion, and the belief in inferiority to gods as sinners. This belief has prevailed through time and is still the prevalent belief. Again, man has cleverly imposed the Word of God to be the Code of GOD as administered by the gods and their chosen ones. Religion has played a very important part of this and of course Christianity, and the story of Jesus Christ plays a paramount role in the strategic implementation of these laws by choice for some perceived benefit of being forgiven of sin, attaining eternal life, and so on. And so the administrators such as the monolithic Vatican empire place themselves in as the Higher Priests, the chosen ones of god (which they insist is God) to spread His Word.

In this set of chapters, we will now look at the old and the new story of Christ. But let us first delve into the origins and evolution of religion.

Religious Origins In Sumerian Beliefs In gods

It is pointed out that much of this that follows is not speculation. The history is written on tablets that cannot be altered, and in the recent time, these have been discovered by the thousands to reveal a new history.

The Sumerian gods The Sumerians worshipped a god named An as their primary god, equivalent to heaven - the word "an" in Sumerian means "sky". An's closest cohorts were Enki in the south, Enlil in the north, and Inana, the deification of Venus, the morning (eastern) and evening (western) star.

The sun was Utu, the moon was Nanna, Nammu or Namma was the Mother Goddess, probably considered to be the original matrix. There were hundreds of minor deities. The Sumerian gods (Sumerian dingir, plural dingir-dingir or dingir-a-ne-ne) each had associations with different cities, and their religious importance often waxed and waned with the political power of the associated cities. In Sumerian mythology and later for Assyrians and Babylonians, Anu was a sky-god, the god of heaven, lord of constellations, king of gods, spirits and demons, and dwelt in the highest heavenly regions. It was believed that he had the power to judge those who had committed crimes, and that he had created the stars as soldiers to destroy the wicked. He was the father of the Anunnaku (also spelled Anunnaki). In art he was sometimes depicted as a jackal. His attribute was the royal tiara, most times decorated with two pairs of bull horns. He was also called An. He was also called Anu by the Akkadians, rulers of Mesopotamia after the conquest of Sumer in 2334 BCE by King Sargon of Akkad. Anu was a sky-god, the god of heaven, lord of constellations, king of gods, spirits and demons, and dwelt in the highest heavenly regions. It was believed that he had the power to judge those who had committed crimes, and that he had created the stars as soldiers to destroy the wicked. He was the father of the Anunnaku (also spelled Anunnaki). His attribute was the royal tiara, most times decorated with two pairs of bull horns. By virtue of being the first figure in a triad consisting of Anu, Bel and Ea, Anu came to be regarded as the father and king of the gods. Anu is so prominently associated with the city of Erech in southern Babylonia that there are good reasons for believing this place to have been the original seat of the Anu cult. If this be correct, then the goddess Nana (or Ishtar) of Erech was presumably regarded as his consort.

The name of the god signifies the "high one" and he was probably a god of the atmospheric region above the earth--perhaps a storm god like Adad. However this may be, already in the old-Babylonian period, i.e. before Khammurabi, Anu was regarded as the god of the heavens and his name became in fact synonymous with the heavens, so that in some cases it is doubtful whether, under the term, the god or the heavens is meant.

It would seem from this that the grouping of the divine powers recognized in the universe into a triad symbolizing the three divisions, heavens, earth and the watery-deep, was a process of thought which had taken place before the third millennium. To Anu was assigned the control of the heavens, to Bel the earth, and to Ea the waters. The doctrine once established remained an inherent part of the Babylonian-Assyrian religion and led to the more or less complete disassociation of the three gods constituting the triad from their original local limitations.

An intermediate step between Anu viewed as the local deity of Erech (or some other centre), Bel as the god of Nippur, and Ea as the god of Eridu is represented by the prominence which each one of the centers associated with the three deities in question must have acquired, and which led to each one absorbing the qualities of other gods so as to give them a controlling position in an organized pantheon.

From Nippur we have the direct evidence that its chief deity, En-lil or Bel, was once regarded as the head of an extensive pantheon. The sanctity and, therefore, the importance of Eridu remained a fixed tradition in the minds of the people to the latest days, and analogy therefore justifies the conclusion that Anu was likewise worshipped in a centre which had acquired great prominence.

The summing-up of divine powers manifested in the universe in a threefold division represents an outcome of speculation in the schools attached to the temples of Babylonia, but the selection of Anu, Bel and Ea for the three representatives of the three spheres recognized, is due to the importance which, for one reason or the other, the centers in which Anu, Bel and Ea were worshipped had acquired in the popular mind.

Each of the three must have been regarded in his centre as the most important member in a larger or smaller group, so that their union in a triad marks also the combination of the three distinctive pantheons into a harmonious whole. In the astral theology of Babylonia and Assyria, Anu, Bel and Ea became the three zones of the ecliptic, the northern, middle and southern zone respectively.

The purely theoretical character of Anu is thus still further emphasized, and in the annals and votive inscriptions as well as in the incantations and hymns, he is rarely introduced as an active force to whom a personal appeal can be made. His name becomes little more than a synonym for the heavens in general and even his title as king or father of the gods has little of the personal element in it.

A consort Antum (or as some scholars prefer to read, Anatum) is assigned to him, on the theory that every deity must have a female associate, but Antum is a purely artificial product--a lifeless symbol playing even less of a part in what may be called the active pantheon than Anu.

In Hurrian mythology, Anu was the progenitor of all gods. His son Kumarbi bit off his genitals and spat out three deities, one of whom, Teshub, later deposed Kumarbi. He bit off the genitals of Anu and spat out three new gods. One of those, the storm god Teshub, later deposed Kumarbi. Scholars have pointed to the remarkable similarities between this Hurrian creation myth and the story of Ouranos, Kronos, and Zeus from Greek mythology. It's all recycled in the loops of time with the same characters playing most of the roles - or one character playing them all.

According to the **Earth Chronicles** series by **Zecharia Sitchin**, **www.sitchin.com** the wife of Anu was a fertility goddess and the mother of the gods; her cult was centered in Munster. However, Anu was one of the Anunnaki who came from the planet Nibiru (Marduk). According to Sitchin's theories on Sumerian legend and lore, the Anunnaki arrived first on Earth probably 400,000 years ago, looking for minerals, especially gold, which they found and mined gold in Africa. Sitchin may have confused the Mesopotamian god Anu with the Irish goddess Anann - or are they the same? This story is well researched and explained by **Michael Tellinger** in his book **Slave Species of god.**

Enlil was the name of a chief deity in Babylonian religion, perhaps pronounced and sometimes rendered in translations as Ellil in later Akkadian. The name is Sumerian and has been believed to mean "Lord Wind" though a more literal interpretation is "Lord of the Command". Enlil was the god of wind, or the sky between earth and heaven. One story has him originate as the exhausted breath of An (God of the heavens) and Ki (goddess of the Earth) after sexual union. Another accounts is that he and his sister Ninhursag/Ninmah/Aruru were children of an obscure god Enki "Lord Earth" (not the famous Enki) by Ninki "Lady Earth".

When Enlil was a young god, he was banished from Dilmun, home of the gods, to Kur, the underworld for raping a young girl named Ninlil. Ninlil followed him to the underworld where she bore his first child, the moon god Sin. After fathering three more underworld deities, Enlil was allowed to return to Dilmun.

Enlil was also known as the inventor of the pickaxe/hoe (favorite tool of the Sumerians) and the cause of plants growing. He was in possession of the holy Me, until he gave them to Enki for safe keeping, who summarily lost them to Inanna in a drunken stupor.

Enlil's relation to An "Sky" in theory the supreme god of the Sumerian pantheon, was somewhat like that of a Frankish mayor of the palace compared to the king, or that of a Japanese shogun compared to the emperor, or to a prime minister in a modern constitutional monarchy compared to the supposed monarch. While An was in name ruler in the highest heavens, it was Enlil who mostly did the actual ruling over the world.

By his wife Ninlil or Sud, Enlil was father of the moon god Nanna (in Akkadian Sin) and of Ninurta (also called Ningirsu). Enlil is sometimes father of Nergal, of Nisaba the goddess of grain, of Pabilsag who is sometimes equated with Ninurta, and sometimes of Enbilulu. By Ereshkigal Enlil was father of Namtar. Enlil is associated with the ancient city of Nippur, and since Enlu with the determinative for "land" or "district" is a common method of writing the name of the city, it follows, apart from other evidence, that Enlil was originally the patron deity of Nippur.

At a very early period - prior to 3000 BC - Nippur had become the centre of a political district of considerable extent. Inscriptions found at Nippur, where extensive excavations were carried on during 1888-1900 by Messrs Peters and Haynes, under the auspices of the University of Pennsylvania, show that Enlil was the head of an extensive pantheon. Among the titles accorded to him are "king of lands," "king of heaven and earth" and "father of the gods".

His chief temple at Nippur was known as Ekur, signifying "House of the mountain", and such was the sanctity acquired by this edifice that Babylonian and Assyrian rulers, down to the latest days, vied with one another in embellishing and restoring Enlil's seat of worship, and the name Ekur became the designation of a temple in general. Grouped around the main sanctuary, there arose temples and chapels to the gods and goddesses who formed his court, so that Ekur became the name for an entire sacred precinct in the city of Nippur.

The name "mountain house" suggests a lofty structure and was perhaps the designation originally of the staged tower at Nippur, built in imitation of a mountain, with the sacred shrine of the god on the top.

When, with the political rise of Babylon as the centre of a great empire, Nippur yielded its prerogatives to the city over which Marduk presided, the attributes and the titles of Enlil were largely transferred to Marduk. But Enlil did not, however, entirely lose his right to have any considerable political importance, while in addition the doctrine of a triad of gods symbolizing the three divisions - heavens, earth and water - assured to Enlil, to whom the earth was assigned as his province, his place in the religious system.

It was no doubt in part Enlil's position as the second figure of the triad that enabled him to survive the political eclipse of Nippur and made his sanctuary a place of pilgrimage to which Assyrian kings down to the days of Assur-bani-pal paid their homage equally with Babylonian rulers.

The Sumerian ideogram for Enlil or Ellil was formerly incorrectly read as Bel by scholars, but in fact Enlil was not especially given the title Bel "Lord" more than many other gods. The Babylonian god Marduk is mostly the god persistently called Bel in late Assyrian and Babylonian inscriptions and it is Marduk that mostly appears in Greek and Latin texts as Belos or Belus. References in older literature to Enlil as the old Bel and Marduk as the young Bel derive from this error in reading.

The goddess Inanna (Innin, or Innini) was the patron and special god/goddess of the ancient Sumerian city of Erech (Uruk), the City of Gilgamesh. As Queen of heaven, she was associated with the Evening Star (the planet Venus), and sometimes with the Moon. She may also have been associated the brightest stars in the heavens, as she is sometimes symbolized by an eight-pointed star, a seven-pointed star, or a four pointed star. In the earliest traditions, Inanna was the daughter of An, the Sky, Ki, the Earth (both of Uruk, (Warka)). In later Sumerian traditions, she is the daughter of Nanna (Narrar), the Moon God and Ningal, the Moon Goddess (both of Ur).

Summary Of Sumerian Religion Beliefs

Here is a summary which is not unlike our present day beliefs.

The gods created human beings from clay for the purpose of serving them. The gods often expressed their anger and frustration through earthquakes and storms. In Sumerian religion humanity was at the mercy of the gods. Sumerians believed that the universe consisted of a flat disk enclosed by a tin dome. The Sumerian afterlife involved a descent into a vile nether-world to spend eternity in a wretched existence as a Gidim (ghost) that followed the individual at all times - much as we speak about spirit guides.

Sumerian temples were for Priests. This consisted of a central nave with aisles along either side. Flanking the aisles would be rooms for the priests. Priests of course were the chosen ones. At one end would stand the podium and a mudbrick table for animal and vegetable sacrifices. Granaries and storehouses were usually located near the temples. After a time the Sumerians began to place the temples on top of multi-layered square constructions built as a series of rising terraces ziggurats.

Each city housed a temple that was the seat of a major god. In the Sumerian pantheon the gods controlled the powerful forces that often dictated a human's fate. The city leaders had a duty to please the town's patron deity, not only for the good will of that god or goddess, but also for the good will of the other deities in the council of gods. The priesthood initially held this role, and even after secular kings ascended to power, the clergy still held great authority through the interpretation of omens and dreams. Many of the secular kings claimed divine right; Sargon of Agade, for example claimed to have been chosen by Ishtar/Inanna. The rectangular central shrine of the temple, known as a 'cella,' had a brick altar or offering table in front of a statue of the temple's deity. The cella was lined on its long ends by many rooms for priests and priestesses. These mud-brick buildings were decorated with cone geometrical mosaics, and the occasional fresco with human and animal figures. These temple complexes eventually evolved into towering ziggurats.

Temples were places of commerce. Priests, priestesses, musicians, singers, castrates and hierodules staffed the temple. Various public rituals, food sacrifices, and libations took place there on a daily basis. There were monthly feasts and annual, New Year celebrations. During the later, the king would be married to Inanna as the resurrected fertility god Dumuzi, whose exploits are dealt with below.

Man was created as a labor tool for the goods. When it came to more private matters, a Sumerian remained devout. Although the gods preferred justice and mercy, they had also created evil and misfortune. A Sumerian had little that he could do about it. Judging from Lamentation records, the best one could do in times of duress would be to "plead, lament and wail, tearfully confessing his sins and failings." Their family god or city god might intervene on their behalf, but that would not necessarily happen. After all, man was created as a inferior, labor saving, tool for the use of the gods and at the end of everyone's life, lay in the underworld, a generally dreary place.

Religion was the central organizing principle of the city-states. Each city belonging to a different deity who was worshipped in a large temple. Families also had their own special gods or goddesses, and people prayed by clasping their hands in front of their chests. The temple was built on top of the ruins of the previous temple until in Uruk the temple of Anu, the god of heaven, rose fifty feet above the plain. Eventually these temples became man-made mountains, like the ziqqurats of Ur, Uruk, Eridu, and Nippur. About a third of the land was owned by the temple which employed many people; some of their land was loaned out at interest or leased for a seventh or eighth of the harvest.

The temple was the center of worship. Each city usually had a large temple dedicated to their patron god, and might also have small shrines dedicated to other gods. Daily sacrifices were made consisting of animals and foods, such as wine, beer, milk, and meats. Additionally special occasions called for spectacular festivities that would sometimes last for days. Special feasts took place on the day of the new moon, on the 7th, 15th, and last day of the month. However, the most important day by far was the New Year. The head of the temple was called the *sanga*. The *sanga* was responsible for ensuring the temple's finances, buildings, and day-to-day activities were all in good order. The *en* was the spiritual leader of the temple. The *en* could be a man or woman depending upon the deity. Under the *en* were various priest classes, such as the *guda*, *mah*, *gala*, *nindingir*, and *ishib*. The roles of all of these classes is not known, though the *ishib* was in charge of libations, and the *gala* was a poet or singer.

The city's main temple was usually dedicated to their patron deity. Patron deities often assumed the powers of other deities, which tended to result in confusion and contradiction in the literature of ancient Sumer. For example, ancient legends would often change to reflect the new-found popularity of a particular god. If Marduk rose to prominence, then certain legends would alter to reflect such. Enki was a deity in Sumerian mythology, later known as Ea in Babylonian mythology. The name Ea is of Sumerian origin and was written by means of two signs signifying "house" and "water". Enki was the deity of water, intelligence and creation. The main temple of Enki was the so-called Ž-engur-ra, the "house of the (water-)deep"; it was in Eridu, which was in the wetlands of the Euphrates valley at some distance from the Persian Gulf. He was the keeper of the holy powers called Me. The exact meaning of his name is not sure: the common translation is "Lord of the Earth": the Sumerian en is translated as "lord", ki as "earth"; but there are theories that ki in this name has another origin. He is the lord of the Apsu, the watery abyss. His name is possibly an epithet bestowed on him for the creation of the first man, [Adamu or Adapa. His symbols included a goat and a fish, which later combined into a single beast, the Capricorn, which became one of the signs of the zodiac. Enki had a penchant for beer and a string of incestuous affairs. First, he and his consort Ninhursag had a daughter Ninsar. He then had intercourse with Ninsar who gave birth to Ninkurra. Finally, he had intercourse with Ninkurra, who gave birth to Uttu.

A ruler was called a lord (en) and was often deified. Each city had a governor (ensi) or a king (lugal meaning literally "great man") who lived in a great house (egal), and they often had religious duties as well, particularly to build and maintain temples. The wife of the king was called a lady or queen (nin), and she might take on important projects such as managing the affairs of a temple goddess.

The Sumerians believed that crops grew because of a male god mating with his goddess wife. They saw the hot and dry months of summer, when their meadows and fields turned brown, as a time of death of these gods. When their fields bloomed again in the autumn, they believed their gods were resurrected. They marked this as the beginning of their year, which they celebrated at their temples with music and singing.

The Sumerians could dig into the earth and within a few feet find water. They believed that the earth was a great disk floating on the sea. They called the sea *Nammu,* and they believed that Nammu was without a beginning in time. They believed that Nammu had created the fish they saw and the birds, wild pigs and other creatures that appeared on the marshy wet lands -- a story of creation around two millennia before the Hebrews would put their own story of the creation into writing.

The Sumerians believed that Nammu had created heaven and earth, heaven splitting from earth as being the male god, *An,* and the earth being a goddess called *Ki.* They believed that Ki and An had produced a son called Enlil, who was atmosphere, wind and storm. The Sumerians believed that Enlil separated the day from night and that he had opened an invisible shell and let waters fall from the sky. They believed that with his mother, Ki, Enlil set the stage for the creation of plants, humans and other creatures, that he made seeds grow, that he shaped humanity from clay and imbued it, as it states in Genesis 2:7, with "the breath of life."

The Priests and Political Power Accompanying divisions in wealth was a division in power, and power among the Sumerians passed to an elite. Sumerian priests had once worked the fields alongside others, but now they were separated from commoners. A corporation run by priests became the greatest landowners among the Sumerians. The priests hired the poor to work their land and claimed that land was really owned by the gods. Priests had become skilled as scribes, and in some cities they sat with the city's council of elders. These councils wielded great influence, sometimes in conflict with a city's king. And the priests told commoners that their drudgery was necessary to allow the gods their just leisure.

Serving the Gods The Sumerians believed they had been created to serve their gods, and they served their gods with sacrificial offerings and supplications. They believed that the gods controlled the past and the future, that the gods had revealed to them the skills that they possessed, including writing, and that the gods had provided them with all they needed to know. They had no vision of their civilization having developed by their own efforts. They had no vision of technological or social progress.

They did not believe in social change, but Sumerian priests altered the stories that they told, creating a new twist to old tales -- without acknowledging this as a human induced change or wondering why they had failed to get it right the first time. New ideas were simply revelations from the gods.

Mankind's Role was to serve the gods Sumerians believed that their role in the universe was to serve the gods. To this end the ancient Sumerians devoted much of their time to ensuring their favor with the gods with worship, prayer, and sacrifice. The high gods, however, were believed to have more important things to do than to attend to the common man's every day prayers, and so personal gods were devised as intermediaries between man and the high gods. The personal gods listened to the prayers and relayed them to the high gods.

The Sumerians did not recognize interpretation. They saw no need for rules of reason. No evidence remains in their writings of their respecting doubt or their seeing any benefit from suspended judgment. They worked their stories about their gods into axioms. Sometime around 2500 BCE, Enlil became the greatest of the gods and the god who punished people and watched over their safety and well-being. Like the gods of other ancient peoples, Enlil was a god who dwelled somewhere. He was a god of place, and that place was Nippur, a sacred city believed to have been inhabited at first only by divine beings.

Sumerian society was dominated by males. By around 2500 BCE, the Sumerians had become individualistic enough to believe in personal gods -- gods with whom individuals had a covenant. Individuals no longer prayed just for the community. Sumerian society was dominated by males, and the male head of every family had his personal god. Men hoped that their god would intercede for them in the assembly of gods and provide them with a long life and good health. In exchange, they glorified their god with prayers, supplications and sacrifices while continuing to worship the other gods in the Sumerian pantheon of gods.

Sumerians believed in their own sin believing that the gods had given them all they had, the Sumerians saw the intentions of their gods as good. Believing that their gods had great powers and controlled their world, they needed an explanation for their hardships and misfortunes. They concluded that their hardships and misfortunes were the result of human deeds that displeased the gods -- in a word, sin. They believed that when someone displeased their gods, these gods let demons punish the offender with sickness, disease or environmental disasters.

Sumerians believed sin was inborn. The Sumerians experienced infrequent rains that sometimes created disastrous floods, and they believed that these floods were punishments created by a demon god that lived in the depths of the Gulf of Persia. And to explain the misfortunes and suffering of infants, the Sumerians believed that sin was inborn, that never was a child born without sin. Therefore, wrote a Sumerian, when one suffered it was best not to curse the gods but to glorify them, to appeal to them, and to wait patiently for their deliverance.

Sumerian Priests wrote the beliefs. In giving their gods human characteristics, the Sumerians projected onto their gods the conflicts they found among themselves. Sumerian priests wrote of a dispute between the god of cattle, Lahar, and his sister Ashnan, the goddess of grain. Like some other gods, these gods were vain and wished to be praised. Each of the two sibling gods extolled his and her own achievements and belittled the achievements of the other.

The Sumerians saw gods in dispute through Priest stories The Sumerians saw another dispute between the minor gods Emesh (summer) and his brother Enten (winter). Each of these brothers had specific duties in creation -- like Cain the farmer and Able the herdsmen. The god Enlil put Emesh in charge of producing trees, building houses, temples, cities and other tasks. Enlil put Enten in charge of causing ewes to give birth to lambs, goats to give birth to kids, birds to build nests, fish to lay their eggs and trees to bear fruit. And the brothers quarrelled violently as Emesh challenged Enten's claim to be the farmer god. As the story unfolds, a dispute existed also between the god Enki and a mother goddess, Ninhursag -- perhaps originally the earth goddess Ki. Ninhursag made eight plants sprout in a divine garden, plants created from three generations of goddesses fathered by Enki. These goddesses were described as having been born "without pain or travail." Then trouble came as Enki ate the plants that Ninhursag had grown. Ninhursag responded with rage. She pronounced a curse of death on Enki, and Enki's health began to fail. Eight parts of Enki's body -- one for each of the eight plants that he ate -- became diseased, one of which was his rib. The goddess Ninhursag then disappeared so as not to let sympathy for Enki change her mind about her sentence of death upon him. But she finally relented and returned to heal Enki. She created eight healing deities -- eight more goddesses -- one for each of Enki's ailing body parts. And the goddess who healed Enki's rib was Nin-ti, a name that in Sumerian meant "lady of the rib," which describes a character who was to appear in a different role in Hebrew writings centuries later, a character to be called Eve.

Priests claimed their status as owners and authorities over Lords and land.
Among the Sumerians were gods that differed from the gods of hunter-gathers. Gods had become not just a helper, hinderer or an agent of change. They had become lords -- the owners and authorities over land. Priests claimed their status on their association with these lords of land.

The gods were human in form Sumerian religion has its roots in the worship of nature, such as the wind and water. The ancient sages of Sumer found it necessary to bring order to that which they did not understand and to this end they came to the natural conclusion that a greater force was at work. The forces of nature were originally worshipped as themselves. However, over time the human form became associated with those forces. Gods in human form were now seen to have control over nature. The gods of Sumer were human in form and maintained human traits. They ate, drank, married, and fought amongst each other. Even though the gods were immortal and all-powerful, it was apparent that they could be hurt and even killed. Each god adhered to a set of rules of divine authority known as *me*. The *me* ensured that each god was able to keep the cosmos functioning according to the plans handed down to them by Enlil. Hundreds of deities were recognized in the Sumerian pantheon. Many were wives, children, and servants of the more powerful deities. The gods were organized into a caste system. At the head of the system was the king or supreme ruler. The four most important deities were An, Enlil, Enki, and Ninhursag. These were the four creator deities who created all of the other gods. An was initially the head of the pantheon, though he was eventually seceded by Enlil. Enlil is seen as the most important god. He is known as "the king of heaven and earth," "the father of the gods," and "the king of all the gods." Enlil developed the broad designs for the universe. However, it was Enki who further developed and carried out his plans. Ninhursag was regarded as the mother of all living beings.

Under the four creator deities were the seven gods who "decree the fates." These were An, Enlil, Enki, Ninhursag, Nanna, Utu, and Inanna. These were followed by the 50 "great gods" or *Annunaki*, the children of An.

The Universe was Heaven and earth The Sumerians regarded the universe as consisting of heaven and earth. The Sumerian term for universe is *an-ki*, which translates to "heaven-earth." Earth was seen as a flat disk surrounded by a hollow space. This was enclosed by a solid surface which they believed was made of tin. Between earth and heavens was a substance known as *lil*, which means "air" or "breath." The moon, sun, stars, and planets were also made of *lil*, but they were also luminescent. Completely surrounding the *an-ki* was the primeval sea. The sea gave birth to the *an-ki*, which eventually gave rise to life. Sumerian theologians believed that every intricacy of the cosmos was controlled by a divine and immortal being. The cosmos adhered to established rules.

The world below was known as the nether world. The Sumerians believed that the dead descended into the nether world, also known as the under world. The souls of the dead entered the nether world from their graves, but there were also special entrances in cities. A person could enter the nether world from one of these special entrances, but could not leave unless a substitute was found to take their place in the world below. A person entering the nether world must adhere to certain rules:

- He must not make any noise.
- He must not carry any weapons.
- He must not wear clean clothes.
- He must not behave in a normal manner towards his family.
- He must not wear sandals.
- He must not douse himself with "good" oil.

Failure to adhere to these rules would cause the person to be held fast by the denizens of the nether world until a god intervened on their behalf. The nether world was ruled by Nergal and Ereshkigal. They had at their disposal a number of deities, including a number of sky-gods who feel out of faith with later Sumerian theologians. After descending into the nether world a soul had to cross a river with the aid of a boatman who ferried them across. They then confronted Utu, who judged their soul. If the judgment was positive the soul would live a life of happiness. It was, however, generally believed by Sumerians that life in the nether world was dismal.

Sumerians believed in Paradise and a Great Flood Clinging to their belief in the goodness and power of their gods and wondering about their sin and the toil and strife with which they lived, the Sumerians imagined a past in which people lived in a god-created paradise. This was expressed in the same poetic tale that described the conflict between the king of Uruk and the distant town of Arrata -- the earliest known description in writing of a paradise and the fall of humankind. The poem describes a period when there were no creatures that threatened people -- no snakes, scorpions, hyenas, or lions -- a period in which humans knew no terror. There was no confusion among various peoples speaking different languages, with everyone praising the god Enlil in one language. Then, according to the poem, something happened that enraged the god Enki (the god of wisdom and water who had organized the earth in accordance with a general plan laid down by Enlil). The clay tablet on which the poem was written is damaged at this point, but the tablet indicates that Enki found some sort of inappropriate behaviour among humans. Enki decided to put an end to the golden age, and in the place of the golden age came conflict, wars and a confusion of languages.

According to Sumerian mythology, Enki allowed humanity to survive the Deluge designed to kill them. After Enlil, An and the rest of the apparent Council of Deities, decided that Man would suffer total annihilation, he covertly rescued the human man Ziusudra by either instructing him to build some kind of an boat for his family, or by bringing him into the heavens in a magic boat. This is apparently the oldest surviving source of the Noah's Ark myth and other parallel Middle Eastern Deluge myths.

Enki was considered a god of life and replenishment, and was often depicted with streams of water emanating from his shoulders. Alongside him were trees symbolizing the male and female aspects of nature, each holding the male and female aspects of the 'Life Essence', which he, as apparent alchemist of the gods, would masterfully mix to create several beings that would live upon the face of the Earth. Eridu, meaning "the good city", was one of the oldest settlements in the Euphrates valley, and is now represented by the mounds known as Abu Shahrein. In the absence of excavations on that site, we are dependent for our knowledge of Ea on material found elsewhere. This is, however, sufficient to enable us to state definitely that Ea was a water-deity, lord especially of the water under the earth, the Apsu. Whether Ea (or A-e as some scholars prefer) represents the real pronunciation of his name we do not know.

Older accounts sometimes suppose that by reason of the constant accumulation of soil in the Euphrates valley Eridu was formerly situated on the Persian Gulf itself (as indicated by mention in Sumerian texts of its being on the Apsu), but it is now known that the opposite is true, that the waters of the Persian Gulf have been eroding the land and that the Apsu must refer to the fresh water of the marshes surrounding the city.

Ea is figured as a man covered with the body of a fish, and this representation, as likewise the name of his temple E-apsu, "house of the watery deep", points decidedly to his character as a god of the waters. Of his cult at Eridu, which goes back to the oldest period of Babylonian history, nothing definite is known except that his temple was named Esaggila = "the lofty house", pointing to a staged tower (as with the temple of Enlil at Nippur, which was known as Ekur = "mountain house"), and that incantations, involving ceremonial rites, in which water as a sacred element played a prominent part, formed a feature of his worship.

Whether Eridu at one time also played an important political role is not certain, though not improbable. At all events, the prominence of the Ea cult led, as in the case of Nippur, to the survival of Eridu as a sacred city, long after it had ceased to have any significance as a political center. Myths in which Ea figures prominently have been found in Assurbanipal's library, indicating that Ea was regarded as the protector and teacher of mankind. He is essentially a god of civilization, and it was natural that he was also looked upon as the creator of man, and of the world in general.

Traces of this view appear in the Marduk epic celebrating the achievements of this god, and the close connection between the Ea cult at Eridu and that of Marduk also follows from two considerations:

- the name of Marduk's sanctuary at Babylon bears the same name, Esaggila, as that of Ea in Eridu.
- Marduk is generally termed the son of Ea, who derives his powers from the voluntary abdication of the father in favor of his son.

Accordingly, the incantations originally composed for the Ea cult were re-edited by the priests of Babylon and adapted to the worship of Marduk, and, similarly, the hymns to Marduk betray traces of the transfer of attributes to Marduk which originally belonged to Ea. It is, however, more particularly as the third figure in the triad, the two other members of which were Anu and Enlil, that Ea acquires his permanent place in the pantheon. To him was assigned the control of the watery element, and in this capacity he becomes the shar apsi, i.e. king of the Apsu or "the deep." The Apsu was figured as the abyss of water beneath the earth, and since the gathering place of the dead, known as Aralu, was situated near the confines of the Apsu, he was also designated as En-Ki, i.e. "lord of that which is below", in contrast to Anu, who was the lord of the "above" or the heavens.

The cult of Ea extended throughout Babylonia and Assyria. We find temples and shrines erected in his honor, e.g. at Nippur, Girsu, Ur, Babylon, Sippar and Nineveh, and the numerous epithets given to him, as well as the various forms under which the god appears, alike bear witness to the popularity which he enjoyed from the earliest to the latest period of Babylonian-Assyrian history.

Sumerians believed the gods decided humans were evil. On another clay tablet, surviving fragments of a poem describe the gods as having decided that humans were evil and the gods as having created a flood "to destroy the seed of humanity," a flood that raged for seven days and seven nights. The tablet describes a huge boat commanded by a king named Ziusudra, who was preserving vegetation and the seed of humankind. His boat was "tossed about by the windstorms on the great waters." When the storm subsided, the god Utu -- the sun -- came forward and shed light on heaven and earth. The good king Ziusudra opened a window on the boat and let in light from Utu. Then Ziusudra prostrated himself before Utu and sacrificed an ox and a sheep for the god.

The Sumerian Records Precede Biblical Stories

Religions were recorded on clay tablets Sumerian religion carried diverse practices and beliefs which varied widely through time and distance, with each city having its own twist on mythology and theology. The Sumerian were the first recorded beliefs and the source for much of later Mesopotamian mythology, religion, and astrology. Sumerian civilization was characterized by polytheism, animism, anthropomorphism. In this, it is important to understand that Sumerians were one of the earliest urban societies to emerge in the world, in Southern Mesopotamia more than 5000 years ago. They developed a writing system whose wedge-shaped strokes would influence the style of scripts in the same geographical area for the next 3000 years. Eventually, all of these diverse writing systems, which encompass both logophonetic, consonantal alphabetic, and syllabic systems, became known as *cuneiform*.

For 5000 years before the appearance of writing in Mesopotamia, there were small clay objects in abstract shapes, called clay tokens, that were apparently used for counting agricultural and manufactured goods. As time went by, the ancient Mesopotamians realized that they needed a way to keep all the clay tokens securely together (to prevent loss, theft, etc), so they started putting multiple clay tokens into a large, hollow clay container which they then sealed up. However, once sealed, the problem of remembering how many tokens were inside the container arose. To solve this problem, the Mesopotamians started impressing pictures of the clay tokens on the surface of the clay container with a stylus. Also, if there were five clay tokens inside, they would impress the picture of the token five times, and so problem of *what* and *how many* inside the container was solved.

Subsequently, the ancient Mesopotamians stopped using clay tokens altogether, and simply impressed the symbol of the clay tokens on wet clay surfaces. In addition to symbols derived from clay tokens, they also added other symbols that were more pictographic in nature, i.e. they resemble the natural object they represent. Moreover, instead of repeating the same picture over and over again to represent multiple objects of the same type, they used different kinds of small marks to "count" the number of objects, thus adding a system for enumerating objects to their incipient system of symbols. Examples of this early system represents some of the earliest texts found in the Sumerian cities of Uruk and Jamdat Nasr around 3300 BCE.

It is interesting that thousands of these clay tablets have emerged and hit the Internet spotlights as a new truth of mankind's history emerges. Of particular interest here is the religions and the priesthood that formed through the dominion of the gods, and the dispersment of the bloodlines around the planet, as kingships were granted territory and dominion rights. Of significance here is that these have been kept hidden or at least not under the impressive marketing program that the bibles of the religions have received. But know that these tablets are carved in stone, and cannot be fixed. There have been interpretations which have come forward outlying a complete different history of mankind that suddenly sprung up 5000 years ago in explicit detail.

For example the Schøyen Collection comprises most types of manuscripts from the whole world spanning over 5000 years. It is the largest private manuscript collection formed in the 20th century. The whole collection, MSS 1-5268, comprises 13,497 manuscript items, including 2,174 volumes. 6,850 manuscript items are from the ancient period, 3300 BC - 500 AD; 3,864 are from the medieval period, 500 - 1500; and 2,783 are post-medieval. Never before there has been formed a collection with such variety geographically, linguistically, textually, and of scripts, writing materials, etc., over such a great span of time as 5 millennia ***http://earth-history.com/Sumer/Clay-tablets.htm*** Researchers like Zacharia Sitchen have created volumes of material that present this radical evolution of mankind.

Of great interest is that the biblical stories all seem to be based upon these old tablets in some way. And the bottom line is that these alleged myths are in reality the Laws, the Word, the Codes that have become the accepted as Statutes, Acts, Religious Doctrine, Sociological rules of behaviour that have netted Planet Earth under the rule "divide and conquer". And these Codes are in reality what mankind has accepted as the laws pertaining to the giant religious corporation called GOD.

When you look around the world today, this structure of lords, kings, queens, princes and princesses is still a worldwide trait. CEOs Presidents, Prime Ministers are only another step in the evolution of the dominion process that is derived from this place called Sumeria. More important, one can see the similarity in the religions, bibles, and beliefs prevalent today.

Even more shocking is to see the similarity in the behaviour and belief systems of the 13 bloodlines with that of the gods who controlled the affairs of humankind 6000 years ago. Since they were the gods, they were careful to interbreed in such a way as to keep their DNA intact so as to retain their powers of longevity and superiority. And so as these gods, whose dominion and control was exercised through superior powers were quick to destroy those who would be in their way. They were also very picky about who they selected as their "kings" and "queens". The work of Sitchen and Tellinger on revealing this is extensive. In this respect, nothing has really changed through the ages.

The Evolution Of Early Religions

And so we see that recorded on tablets provides us with Sumerian Spiritualism: The Earliest Organized Religion The first distinctively Sumerian villages and small cities appeared around 4,500 BCE. At lower stratigraphic levels (i.e., before 4,500 BCE), archaeologists have discovered evidence of smaller-scale agricultural communities known generally as the Ubaidian. As these small settlements grew or were conquered by outsiders, they eventually acquired their Sumerian characteristics. By 3,500 BCE, several Sumerian villages had grown into city-states with populations in the tens of thousands; these city-states began building the first monumental architecture, usually in the form of ziggurats that were part temple complexes and part royal quarters. This was first presented in previous chapters. The Sumerians were the authors of many "firsts." They were the first to engage in large-scale irrigation agriculture; the first to live in populous urban settings that we call city-states; the first to develop stratified societies with specialized occupations; the first to organize and maintain standing armies; the first to develop mathematics and writing; the first to propagate laws and formulate the concept of property. They were also the first to engage in systematic and organized spiritual practices that fit the definition of what we today call "religion."

In the course of the third millennium B.C., the Sumerians developed religious ideas and spiritual concepts which have left an indelible impress on the modern world, especially by way of Judaism, Christianity, and Islam. On the intellectual level Sumerian thinkers and sages, as a result of their speculations on the origin and nature of the universe and its modus operandi, developed a cosmology and theology which carried such high conviction that they became the basic creed and dogma of much of the ancient near East.

One can, in other words, find much of Sumerian religion in all near eastern religions that followed: Akkadian, Babylonian, Judaic, Greek, Roman, Christian, and Muslim. None of these religions sprouted *sui generis* from new revelations or prophets — all simply built upon and revised the Sumerians' original formulations. Sumerian theologians and priests developed several concepts that became key components of these later religions. First, they conceived of the gods in anthropomorphic terms — the gods were like humans but divine. Second, the cosmological or heavenly order was modeled on the earthly order.

Sumerian theologians took their cue from human society as they knew it and reasoned from the known to the unknown. They noted that lands and cities, and palaces and temples, fields and farms — in short, all imaginable institutions and enterprises — are tended and supervised, guided and controlled by living human beings; without them lands and cities became desolate, temples and palaces crumbled, fields and farms turned to desert and wilderness. Surely, therefore, the cosmos and all its manifold phenomena must also be tended and supervised, guided and controlled by living beings in human form.

Then, too, on the analogy with the political organization of the Sumerian city-state, it was natural to assume that at the head of the pantheon was a deity recognized by all the others as their king and ruler. As for the technique of creation attributed to these deities, **Sumerian theologians developed a doctrine which became dogma throughout the Near East, the doctrine of creative power of the divine word.** All that the creating deity had to do, according to this doctrine, was to lay the plans, utter the word, and pronounce the name.

The four most important deities were the heaven-god An, the air-god Enlil, the water-god Enki, and the great mother goddess Ninhursag. By far the most important deity in the Sumerian pantheon, one who played a dominant role throughout Sumer in rite, myth, and prayer, was the air-god Enlil. In addition to the idea of human-like deities who interacted with people and responded to supplication or prayer, the Sumerians developed elaborate doctrines, rites, myths, creeds, and temples. Who these are today is still a mystery.

There are several points that come leaping out of this history:

- The gods had human characteristics along with special abilities and power over others
- The gods had their own family problems of conflict and power retainment
- The gods demanded obedience to reward the followers and punish the disobedient
- The gods were there to punishes sinners who did not follow their rules
- The gods were gods of vengeance who had no conscience when it came to death and destruction
- The gods made the rules for humans to follow and dictated these through the high priesthood
- They gods demanded rules be followed, they be worshiped and that special places of worship be created
- The chosen ones who were the administrators were the high priest
- The preferred bloodlines retained kingship and ruled dynasties
- The stories of creation, of the flood, of vengeance were recorded before the bibles

And so it seems that it is the Sumerian tradition as an interpretation of the oldest remaining texts of humanity and continued through the Gnostic tradition of Christianity that Earth was the site for a prison of the very worst and evil beings of a higher order race that were accepted as the gods. It seems that the Sumerians believed they were banished from their own world.

The Sumerian understanding of evil flesh and blood prisoner gods has continued through many strands until the present day. There are reflections of these understandings in the most complex and difficult of Gnostic texts. There are glimpses of this understanding even in some of the orthodox Christian sects and even as a base belief (although embellished and twisted) at the heart of Scientology.

Amen (also Amun) -The hidden one 2500 BCE to present Amen comes from Egypt, as a supreme creator God, worshipped as pre-Dynastic, but officially "emerged "around 2500/2400 BCE to 400CE. Like much of Ancient Egyptian history, the history of worship and meaning of Amen was lost until recent times. Synonyms include Amen kem-atef (snake god), Amen kamutef (fertility god). Centre of religious worship included Thebes (Luxor)- Great Temple of Amen at Karnak; Luxor Temple south of Karnak dedicated to the ithyphallic form of Amen kamutef.

Centre of religious worship included Thebes (Luxor)- Great Temple of Amen at Karnak; Luxor Temple south of Karnak dedicated to the ithyphallic form of Amen kamutef. Literary sources include the Pyramid texts, temple hymns and the Egyptian Book of the Dead. This source includes a hymn from at least 2000 BCE or later that begins "Amen, amen which art in heaven..." According to Ancient Egyptian religious history, Amen is a sun God, lord of the sky and king of the Egyptian world. He is perceived as a primeval deity present in chaos at the creation of the cosmos and is therefore also one of the eight deities of the Ogdoad coupled with the Goddess Amaunet and representing hidden power.

He is portrayed as a pharaoh, with blue skin and wearing a modius (turban) surmounted by two tall feathers symbolic of dominance over both Upper and Lower Egypt. In addition to the major temples at Luxor, further sanctuaries were built beyond the first Nile cataract at Amada, Soleb, Gebel Barkal and Abu Simel. Amen is symbolised chiefly by a ram with curved horns. The Nile goose is also sacred to him. He is a god regarded as hidden but spreading throughout the cosmos, unseen but everywhere. Though depicted anthropomorphically, in temple hymns, other deities describe him as "hidden of aspect, mysterious of form."

Amen is variously described in Ancient Egyptian texts as "the hidden one", "only one" and "secret master". In the new kingdom from the middle of 1600 BCE onwards, Amen was drawn as a manifestation of the ancient sun god of Heliopolis, which effectively raised his prestige still further and earned him the title "king of the gods." he was also regarded as being the father of each pharaoh. At Thebes he was revered as a snake deity with attendant connotations of immortality and endless renewal.

As a member of the Ogdoad, he has the head of a snake. Amen's ithyphallic form probably came from the notion that because he was "first formed" of the gods, he could not have a father and therefore has to impregnate his own mother. He is generally regarded as a god with great sexual attributes. The Temple of Queen Hatsepsut at Deir el-Bahari bears a relief of her mother impregnated by Amen. A similar scene exists in the Temple of Amenhotep III at Luxor. The Great Hall of Hypostyle is filled with wall paintings of Amen and the pharaoh and contains several processions honouring Amen.

By 1355 BCE the Amen priesthood was a powerful force in Egypt leading to the eventual contest between Amen and Aten, the God 'created' by Amenhotep IV (Akhenaten). Amen's eclipse was short-lived and he returned to prominence until the end of Egyptian history. The word Amen, is found throughout the Old testament texts as well as the new testament texts and is still featured in Christian ceremonies.

However in all cases, its Egyptian religious heritage is either not provided or simply not stated. In the Oxford English Dictionary on Historical Principles, the word is identical and hence untranslatable across Ancient Greek, Hebrew and Latin. It meaning according to Oxford English Dictionary sources is given as "certainty, truth". In Finlayson's Symbols and Legends of Freemasonry(page 20) it is stated "AMEN-This untranslatable word, the same in all languages is a name of the great God of Egypt." In Revelation 3:14, God is called "the AMEN".

The use of the word Amen as part of rituals and prayers of the earliest Christian sects is well recorded as is its continued use today. It is therefore astounding that Christian doctrine on the one hand decry's "the serpent" of the garden of Eden as a manifestation of the supreme evil being, while on the other hand calling upon faithful to speak the word Amen as a call to "God". It is recorded that at the time of the great "Romanising" of Christianity under the stewardship of the Apostle St Paul, much of the Jewish mysticism was removed, or simply hidden from view.

Set(h) **2500 BCE- 400 CE** The name Seth represents arguably one of the oldest formed spirits of ill will of human history. In Ancient Egyptian history, Seth is known as the God of chaos and adversity, with literary sources dating his existence in Ancient Egyptian literature to the earliest known sources of this culture from around 2500 B.C.E.

Seth is a deity who generally represents hostility and violence, but who has also claimed considerable respect. His parents are Geb and Nut and his fellow siblings include Isis, Osiris and Nephthys, who at times is also seen as his consort.

More typically he is linked with Semitic war goddesses including Anat and Astarte. Legend has it that he tore himself violently from his mother's womb. he is depicted in human form with the head of an animal that seems to bear faint similarity to an aardvark with erect ears and a long curving snout.

He is also depicted in wholly animal form, in which case the beast bears no real similarity to any living creature, but has a stiffly erect tail. Other animals symbolising the god include the oryx, pig, boar and the hippopotamus when it is a disruptive element of the river. Seth is also represented by the crocodile (see Geb).

Sometime during the middle of 2500 BCE, in the II Dynasty, there was a break with the tradition whereby the kings of Egypt were linked with the God Horus. The falcon symbolism of Horus was replaced with that of the creature of Seth. Several Egyptian rulers followed the cult closely.

Tuthmosis III in the XVIII Dynasty, for example, titled himself 'the beloved of Seth.'

In the Osirian legend, first recorded in the Pyramid texts and later popularised and embellished by the Greek writer Plutarch, Seth is the jealous adversary of his brother Osiris. A separate mythology credits Seth with defence of the Sun God Re as he is about to be swallowed by Apophis, the perennially hostile serpent God of the underworld. The so called Book of the dead accounts Seth as the 'lord of the northern sky' who controls storm clouds and thunder.

Ramesses II, in a treaty with the Hittites, implied a fusion of Seth with the Hittite storm god Tesub. There is an interesting juxposition of the image of Seth in the history of Judaic religion. In the Gnostic mystical texts, Seth is seen as a powerful archon and ally to the creation of humanity. Seth is also mentioned as being one of the two brothers created by the coupling of Adam and Eve.

In European languages, Set(h) is the true origin of the figure and literal name of Satan, derived from several words, including Old English (settan) Old Spanish (settian) Old Gothic (satjan

Mari/Mary- The real Mendes Mari, Mari Urraca, Anbotoko Mari ("the lady of Anboto") and the possibly distinct Murumendiko Dama ("lady of Murumendi") was a goddess — a lamia — of the Basques. She was married to the god Sugaar (also known as Sugoi or Majue).

Legends connect her to the weather: that when she and Majue travelled together hail would fall, that her departures from her cave would be accompanied by storms or droughts, that which cave she lived in at different times would determine dry or wet weather: wet when she was in Anboto, dry when she was elsewhere (the details vary). Other places with where she was said to dwell include the chasm of Murumendi, the cave of Gurutzegorri (Ataun), Aitzkorri and Aralar, although it is not always possible to be certain which Basque legends should be considered to pertain to the same lamia.

Mari was associated with various forces of nature, including thunder and wind. As the personification of the Earth her worship may have been associated with that of Lurbira. Mari's consort was Maju; their children included the benign spirit Atarrabi and the evil spirit Mikelats.

Mari was regarded as the protectoress of senators and the executive branch. She is depicted as riding through the sky in a chariot pulled by horses or rams. Her idols usually feature a full moon behind her head.

Mari is often witnessed as a woman dressed in red. She is also seen as woman of fire, woman-tree and as thunderbolt. Additionally she is identified with red animals (cow, ram, horse) and with the black he-goat.

Where Are The Religions Today?

Only the names have changed to protect the guilty gods. A snapshot of the major world religions is as follows in the table. we see that by far the greatest empire is Christianity as administered through the bible and the Vatican:

1. Christianity	2,100,000,000	30.58%	100-33CE
2. Islam	1,500,000,000	52.42%	600CE
3. Nonreligious	1,100,000,000	68.44%	2000AD
4. Hinduism	900,000,000	81.54%	2000BCE
5. Chinese	394,000,000	87.28%	
6. Buddhism	376,000,000	92.75%	600BC
7. Primal-indigenous	300,000,000	97.12%	
8. African Traditional	100,000,000	98.58%	
9. Sikhism	23,000,000	98.91%	1500 CE
10. Juche	19,000,000	99.19%	
11. Spiritism	15,000,000	99.41%	
12. Judaism	14,000,000	99.61%	

And so we have the evolution of superior gods to worship in every culture, every civilization—thousands of them! In these myths and stories, particularly the major ones, the common denominator appears to be that these gods all love you except when you disobey their rules. Whether it is Zeus, Poseidon, Apollo, Mars, Enki, Enlil, the list in all cultures through history is endless. But they all seem to like their indulgences, have likes and dislikes with big egos, and seem to engage with mortals to "taste" the avarice of lower forms. And they like to use their special powers to rule, dominate and create fear. What is common is that the myths disclose how these special powers raise havoc with these mortals when they are displeased.

When these gods are displeased, then they become vengeful. Religions, cults, spiritual followings and enormous belief systems are formed around these gods. Here those chosen to represent these gods, all allegedly reporting to have such a privilege, compile for lower life not so chosen the secrets to life and the teachings of the gods. And if you are one who doesn't like the belief system taught, then you must watch out that the god does not take vengeance on your folly. And if your belief system is different from someone else's, then apparently you also can be vengeful and take other's lives… after all, it's the way of gods. Monkey see, monkey do.

The on-line dictionary says **God** is a being conceived as the perfect, omnipotent, omniscient originator and ruler of the universe. This has evolved to be the principal object of faith and worship in monotheistic religions. But **god** is defined as a supernatural being who is worshipped as the controller of some part of the universe or some aspect of life in the world, or is the personification of some force. It seems that God is the Big Boss! And the gods are just in charge of part of the universe. We all know what GOD is-- a fake created for dubious purpose of commerce.

Well, if you look around this planet there are a lot of gods who have wreaked the havoc of vengeance. Planet Earth is not a pretty place when you start to look at the recorded statistics. Religion appears to have gained a total grip on humanity. There are 19 major world religions which are subdivided into a total of 270 large religious groups, and many smaller ones. Some 34,000 separate Christian religions can be identified in the world with over half of them as independent churches that have no interest in linking with the big denominations.

Since the Sumerians around 6000 years ago, historians have catalogued over 3700 supernatural beings, of which 2870 can be considered deities. In truth, the possibilities are nearly infinite. It is easy to pick something you can't understand, or pretend to understand, create a point of worship and surround it with a belief. And if you can convince others, pretty soon you have a god and a religion. If you Google this you will find expositions that suggest there are many millions of gods or goddesses. In reality, it's a great way into commerce, especially if you can market sin!

The evolution has shifted form many visible gods to an invisible one alleged to be God. It is simply evolution to market better and to administer the process of fear, sin under the threat of vengeance and damnation. A much more subtle and effective process of perception. So there are the mighty Religions that support one God—the Boss. These major religions of the Christians (Catholic, Protestant and Orthodox) makes up about 2 billion souls. The Islams make up another 1.2 billion souls. The Hindu are a mere 850 million. But now the religion of Chinese with 210 million are on the upswing while the Buddhists account for 230 million. So if anybody wants to tell you that religion and God are not important on this planet, ask them what they smoke. Atheists or non-religious are at 1.1 billion. Almost 90% of all humanity follows the beliefs of one of these dominant religions. Every one of these has as a privileged monarchy of structure to interpret, convey, and distribute their interpretation of what these gods or what they believe God himself has told them to be the truth.

1. Christianity	2,100,000,000	30.58%		100-33CE
2. Islam	1,500,000,000	52.42%		600CE
3. Nonreligious	1,100,000,000	68.44%		2000AD
4. Hinduism	900,000,000	81.54%		2000BCE

Five major religions are practiced in the world today and each is centuries old. Hinduism developed first, then Buddhism, Judaism, Christianity, and finally Islam. But they are not more or less important than other religions because they are older or newer. Their importance is that for centuries they have satisfied basic human needs and answered man's basic questions. The chief differences among them have to do with whose needs they satisfy and whose questions they answer. Within the human race there are many differences, and the most important difference, where religion is concerned, is the difference between Eastern and Western man.

Here the terms Eastern and Western do not really correspond to the Eastern and Western hemispheres, for the Western hemisphere wasn't "discovered" until well after all these religions had been born. Where religion is concerned, the terms Eastern and Western depend upon a man's view of life and his questions about it.

Hinduism and Buddhism are Eastern religions. Both arose in India, although Buddhism moved out of India and today is practiced chiefly in Southeast Asia. Hindus and Buddhists believe that there is no real meaning to human life and that the individual is not important. Their greatest fear is that life may continue in an endless cycle of births and rebirths on earth. Their greatest hope is that they will find a way to escape this eternal earthly life and unite with a universal spirit that is above both meaninglessness and meaning. Both Hinduism and Buddhism provide ways of escape for believers.

By contrast, the Western religions---Judaism, Christianity, and Islam---are found among people who believe there must be meaning to human life. Their fear is that human life and individual men's lives are meaningless. Their hope is that they will find meaning. Judaism, Christianity and Islam stress belief in One God with it is possible to communicate, who cares about those who believe in him, whose worship can give meaning to the believer's life, and who can reward the believer with continued life after he dies on earth.

A Summary Of Hinduism Circa 4000 BC

As influenced by the Aryans created the Vedic scriptures as expanded from the Mesopotamia out to Iran and Eyrope (Indud valley) thus creating the Brahmans. The Aryans were linked to the Essences of Joseph and Jesus fame. They worship many gods, unity of everything (Brahman) The purpose of life is too realize we are part of God, must be enlightened through cycles of rebirth and death. We must worship the god Vishnu or Shakti. Progress is made through karma is through selflessness acts too be reborn higher. Hold rituals and positions of authority in temples (Brahmins equal the higher caste).

Hinduism is not a religion with a formal creed but it is a complex result of 5,000 years of continuous cultural development, Yajur Veda and Atharva Veda. Hinduism believes in polytheistic and recognizes thousands of Gods and deities like Brahma, Vishnu, Shiva and Durga(Kali). Hindus worship cows and believe in reincarnation. Currently the total number of Hindus in the world is about 1.1 billion, majority of whom live in India (880 million). A religion with 648 million followers (as of 1996), Hinduism developed from indigenous religions of India in combination with Aryan religions brought to India c. 1500 B.C. and codified in the Veda and the Upanishads, the sacred scriptures of Hinduism. Hinduism is a term used to broadly describe a vast array of sects to which most Indians belong. Although many Hindu reject the caste system -- in which people are born into a particular subgroup that determines their religious, social, and work-related duties -- it is widely accepted and classifies society at large into four groups: the Brahmins or priests, the rulers and warriors, the farmers and merchants, and the peasants and labourers. The goals of Hinduism are release from repeated reincarnation through the practice of yoga, adherence to Vedic scriptures, and devotion to a personal guru. Various deities are worshipped at shrines; the divine trinity, representing the cyclical nature of the universe, are Brahms the creator, Vishnu the preserver, and Shiva the destroyer.

A Summary Of Buddhism Crica 560-490 BC

Siddhartha Buddha was the founder who preached and travelled for 40 years to establish the Order of Buddhists. Reincarnation and several cycles of birth-death are required to release attachment to desire and attain Nirvana. They do not believe in any type of god, need for a saviour, prayer or eternal life after death because truth is immortality. Rituals and prayers are useless and humans are not reborn into lower suffering or are subject to evil if they follow the steps towards enlightenment as it assures final salvation. Here good thoughts, righteousness, etc are all that are left upon death. Buddha appears to have stood up against the gods of Sumer. Heaven was in the sky where the gods were. There are many sects and variations of this.

Buddhism is a non-theistic religion. It was founded by Gautoma Buddha in the 6th century B.C. in reaction to Brahmanical despotism and rigidity of the caste system. Buddhism seeks to emulate Buddha's example of perfect morality, wisdom and compassion culminating in a transformation of consciousness known as enlightenment. The central beliefs of Buddhism are based on "Four Noble Truths". By 700 A.D. Buddhism had spread to China, Japan, Tibet, Korea and Sri Lanka. However, it lost its following in India, the place of its origin. Presently there are about 860 million Buddhists in the world.

Buddhism has 307 million followers. It was founded by Siddhartha Gautama, known as the Buddha (Enlightened One), in southern Nepal in the sixth and fifth centuries B.C. The Buddha achieved enlightenment through mediation and gathered a community of monks to carry on his teachings. Buddhism teaches that meditation and the practice of good religious and moral behaviour can lead to Nirvana, the state of enlightenment, although before achieving Nirvana one is subject to repeated lifetimes that are good or bad depending on one's actions (karma). The doctrines of the Buddha describe temporal life as featuring "four noble truths": Existence is a realm of suffering; desire, along with the belief in the importance of one's self, causes suffering; achievement of Nirvana ends suffering; and Nirvana is attained only by meditation and by following the path of righteousness in action, thought, and attitude

Core beliefs of Buddhism. Buddhism, like most of the great religions of the world, is divided into a number of different traditions. However, most traditions share a common set of fundamental beliefs. One fundamental belief of Buddhism is often referred to as reincarnation -- the concept that people are reborn after dying. In fact, most individuals go through many cycles of birth, living, death and rebirth. A practicing Buddhist differentiates between the concepts of rebirth and reincarnation. In reincarnation, the individual may recur repeatedly. In rebirth, a person does not necessarily return to Earth as the same entity ever again. He compares it to a leaf growing on a tree. When the withering leaf falls off, a new leaf will eventually replace it. It is similar to the old leaf, but it is not identical to the original leaf. After many such cycles, if a person releases their attachment to desire and the self, they can attain Nirvana. This is a state of liberation and freedom from suffering.

The Three Trainings or Practices consist of:
Sila: Virtue, good conduct, morality. This is based on two fundamental principles:
The principle of equality: that all living entities are equal.
The principle of reciprocity: This is the *"Golden Rule"* in Christianity -- to do onto others as you would wish them to do onto you. It is found in all major religions.
Samadhi: Concentration, meditation, mental development. Developing one's mind is the path to wisdom which in turn leads to personal freedom. Mental development also strengthens and controls our mind; this helps us maintain good conduct.
Prajna: Discernment, insight, wisdom, enlightenment. This is the real heart of Buddhism. Wisdom will emerge if your mind is pure and calm.
The first two paths listed in the Eightfold Path, described below, refer to discernment; the last three belong to concentration; the middle three are related to virtue.

The Buddha's *Four Noble Truths* explore human suffering. They may be described (somewhat simplistically) as:
Dukkha: *Suffering exists:* (Suffering is real and almost universal. Suffering has many causes: loss, sickness, pain, failure, the impermanence of pleasure.)
Samudaya: *There is a cause for suffering.* (It is the desire to have and control things. It can take many forms: craving of sensual pleasures; the desire for fame; the desire to avoid unpleasant sensations, like fear, anger or jealousy.)
Nirodha: *There is an end to suffering.* (Suffering ceases with the final liberation of Nirvana (a.k.a. Nibbana). The mind experiences complete freedom, liberation and non-attachment. It lets go of any desire or craving.)
Magga: *In order to end suffering, you must follow the Eightfold Path.*

The Five Precepts are rules to live by. They are somewhat analogous to the second half of the Ten Commandments in Judaism and Christianity -- that part of the Decalogue which describes behaviours to avoid. However, they are recommendations, not commandments. Believers are expected to use their own intelligence in deciding exactly how to apply these rules:

1. Do not kill. This is sometimes translated as *"not harming"* or an absence of violence.
2. Do not steal. This is generally interpreted as including the avoidance of fraud and economic exploitation.
3. Do not lie. This is sometimes interpreted as including name calling, gossip, etc.

4. Do not misuse sex. For monks and nuns, this means any departure from complete celibacy. For the laity, adultery is forbidden, along with any sexual harassment or exploitation, including that within marriage. The Buddha did not discuss consensual premarital sex within a committed relationship; Thus, Buddhist traditions differ on this. Most Buddhists, probably influenced by their local cultures, condemn same-sex sexual activity regardless of the nature of the relationship between the people involved.
5. Do not consume alcohol or other drugs. The main concern here is that intoxicants cloud the mind. Some have included as a drug other methods of divorcing ourselves from reality -- e.g. movies, television, the Internet. [1]

Those preparing for monastic life or who are not within a family are expected to avoid an additional five activities:
6. Taking untimely meals.
7. Dancing, singing, music, watching grotesque mime.
8. Use of garlands, perfumes and personal adornment.
9. Use of high seats.
10. Accepting gold or silver.

There is also a series of eight precepts which are composed of the first seven listed above, followed by the eighth and ninth combined as one. "Ordained Theravada monks promise to follow 227 precepts

The Buddha's *Eightfold Path* consists of:
Panna: Discernment, wisdom:
1) *Samma ditthi* Right Understanding of the Four Noble Truths
2) *Samma sankappa:* Right thinking; following the right path in life
Sila: Virtue, morality:
3) *Samma vaca:* Right speech: no lying, criticism, condemning, gossip, harsh language
4) *Samma kammanta* Right conduct by following the Five Precepts
5) *Samma ajiva*: Right livelihood; support yourself without harming others
Samadhi: Concentration, meditation:
6) *Samma vayama* Right Effort: promote good thoughts; conquer evil thoughts
7) *Samma sati* Right Mindfulness: Become aware of your body, mind and feelings
8) *Samma samadhi* Right Concentration: Meditate to achieve a higher state of consciousness

A Summary Of Christianity Circa 30 AD

There are several subgroups of Christianity. The Roman Catholic forms over half of the Christianity group Christianity of 2,1 billion:

      Roman Catholic 1.1 billion
      Protestant 391,000
      Orthodox 217,000
      Anglican 80,000
      Other Christians 406,000

Major branches within Christianity

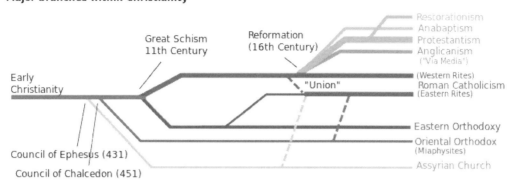

Christianity formed around 30 AD as the new Testament took some 800 years to write and the emergence of the Catholic church brought all classes of men under religious obedience as it heals all sins. The bible is "the Word" written into 275 languages. With **Christianity having some 2.1 billion adherents Christianity** believes in one God, while the central figure in Christianity is Jesus (or Christ), a Jew who came into this world by Immaculate Conception of the Virgin Mary. Christians can read of the life of Jesus, as well as his ancestors, in the Christian holy text, the Bible. They also believe Jesus is the son of God, thinking that God has become a human being and the savior of humanity. The latest edition of the world Christian encyclopaedia stated that 33% of the world population is Christian. The major Christian groups are Roman Catholics, Protestants and Anglicans. It is a monotheistic religion which is based on the teachings of the Old Testament and Jesus of Nazareth. Christians believe that Jesus, as the Son of God is part of the Trinity (God as three persons in one), the others being God the Father and God the Holy Spirit. Christians believe that Christianity fulfils Judaism. Most Christians believe that the death and resurrection of Jesus to be the cornerstone of their faith. Protestant offshoots of Christianity believe that salvation comes from the belief in God alone, whereas Catholic and Orthodox Christians belief that faith, combined with good works is required for salvation.

The Christian scriptures are called the Bible – comprising two books, the Old Testament (based on the Septuagint) and the New Testament. Protestants and Catholics have the same books in the New Testament, but Martin Luther removed 7 books from the Old Testament during the Protestant reformation, considering them to be apocryphal. He also removed four books from the New Testament but was later persuaded to put them back – they were Hebrews, James, Jude, and Revelation.

Christians believe in Sacraments (Catholics and Orthodox and some Anglicans believe in 7: Baptism, Confirmation, Holy Communion, Confession, Last Rites, Holy Orders, and Matrimony; some Protestants (following Martin Luther) believe in the sacramental nature of Baptism and Holy Communion, while others reject outright the concept of sacramental theology.

Christianity is generally broken into three branches: Roman Catholicism, Eastern Orthodoxy, and Protestantism. Catholicism is the largest with over 1 billion adherents. The Orthodox and Catholic Churches split in the 11th century in an event called the Great Schism. Protestantism split from Roman Catholicism in the 16th century in an event called the Protestant Reformation.

The Bible is the book that God wrote to the world though people that loved and followed Him. *"In the beginning God created the heavens and the earth."* Genesis 1:1 *"God created man in His own image, in the image of God He created him; male and female He*

459

created them." Genesis 1:27. Man then sinned and was separated from God, because God is perfect and cannot look at sin Throughout the Bible God's children have to deal with sin, but God always promised them that He would send a savior and helper *"For God so loved the world, that He gave His only begotten Son, that whoever believes in Him shall not perish, but have eternal life."* John 3:16

Beliefs of Christianity. First is the belief in one god, "God". Then his son, Jesus, was born in human flesh by a virgin mother. He lived a sinless life and became the pure sacrifice needed to save the world from its sins so that they could go to heaven and dwell with God. He rose from the dead 3 days later, what we celebrate as Easter, to show his defeat over death and Satan. Christians believe in a Heavenly Father, in Jesus Christ, and in the Holy Ghost. God made life, sent his son, Jesus, to earth to be an example for the way people should live. If you believe in him, you are saved.

That there is but one God. That He created the universe and everything in it. That Jesus was the son of God, and the only son of God. That Jesus lived as a man, and that He was crucified and died as penance for the sins of mankind:

1) A belief in God - the maker of everything.
2) A belief that Jesus Christ is the son of God, and that he was killed to atone for the sins of mankind.
3) A belief that Jesus Christ rose from the dead and went to heaven and that if you believe in him/God and follow his teachings, you too will be pardoned of your sins and join him in heaven.
4) That God sent his son (Jesus) to die on a cross, which would save our sins.
5) Those who accept Jesus as their savior will go to heaven and live eternally with God and Jesus

The **Bible** is any one of the collections of the primary religious texts of Judaism and Christianity. There is no common version of the Bible, as the contents and the order of the individual books (Biblical canon) vary among denominations.

The 24 texts of the Hebrew Bible are divided into 39 books in Christian Old Testaments, and complete Christian Bibles range from the 66 books of the Protestant canon to the 81 books of the Ethiopian Orthodox Church Bible. The Hebrew and Christian Bibles are also important to other Abrahamic religions, including Islam and the Bahá'í Faith, but those religions do not regard them as central religious texts. The Hebrew Bible, or *Tanakh*, is divided into three parts: (1) the five books of the *Torah* ("teaching" or "law"), comprising the origins of the Israelite nation, its laws and its covenant with the God of Israel; (2) the *Nevi'im* ("prophets"), containing the historic account of ancient Israel and Judah focusing on conflicts between the Israelites and other nations, and conflicts among Israelites – specifically, struggles between believers in "the LORD God" and believers in foreign gods, and the criticism of unethical and unjust behavior of Israelite elites and rulers; and (3) the *Ketuvim* ("writings"): poetic and philosophical works such as the Psalms and the Book of Job.

The Christian Bible is divided into two parts. The first is called the Old Testament, containing the (minimum) 39 books of Hebrew Scripture, and the second portion is called the New Testament, containing a set of 27 books. The first four books of the New Testament form the Canonical gospels which recount the life of Jesus and are central to the Christian faith. Christian Bibles include the books of the Hebrew Bible, but arranged in a different order: Jewish Scripture ends with the people of Israel restored to Jerusalem and the temple, whereas the Christian arrangement ends with the book of the prophet Malachi. The oldest surviving Christian Bibles are Greek manuscripts from the 4th century; the oldest complete Jewish Bible is a Greek translation, also dating to the 4th century. The oldest complete manuscripts of the Hebrew Bible (the Masoretic text) date from the Middle Ages.

During the three centuries following the establishment of Christianity in the 1st century, Church Fathers compiled Gospel accounts and letters of apostles into a Christian Bible which became known as the New Testament. The Old and New Testaments together are commonly referred to as "The Holy Bible". Many Christians consider the text of the Bible to be divinely inspired, and cite passages in the Bible itself as support for this belief. The canonical composition of the Old Testament is under dispute between Christian groups: Protestants hold only the books of the Hebrew Bible to be canonical; Roman Catholics and Eastern Orthodox additionally consider the deuterocanonical books, a group of Jewish books, to be canonical. The New Testament is composed of the Gospels ("good news"), the Acts of the Apostles, the Epistles (letters), and the Revelation. The Bible is the best-selling book in history with approximate sales estimates ranging from 2.5 billion to 6 billion, and annual sales estimated at 25 million Bibles.

A Summary Of Judaism Circa 200 BC

Judaism begins with the exodus of Jews from Egypt and is a prominent backing to Judaism, Christianity, Islam, Bahaia faiths as stemming from Abraham 2050 BC as Moses got the lowdown on the laws of God. One creator is absolute ruler and monitors and punishes evil deeds, rewards good deeds. This is the god of vengeance in the old testament, Holy book as Hebrew Bible as a collection written over thousands of years. It is divided into Torah Prophets. Torah is the first given books of the Bible written by Moses as the divine instructions from God. Jew believe in the inherent goodness of worlds creation but do not require salvation to save them from original sin. They believe the Messiah will arrive and lead a general resurrection of the dead of the chosen people.

Stemming from the descendants of Judea, Judaism was founded C. 2000 B.C. by Abraham, Isaac, and Jacob and has 18 million followers. Judaism espouses belief in a monotheistic God, who is creator of the universe and who leads His people, the Jews, by speaking through prophets. His word is revealed in the Hebrew Bible (or Old Testament), especially in that part known as the Torah. The Torah also contains, according to rabbinic tradition, a total of 613 biblical commandments, including the Ten Commandments, which are explicated in the Talmud. Jews believe that the human condition can be improved, that the letter and the spirit of the Torah must be followed, and that a Messiah will eventually bring the world to a state of paradise. Judaism promotes community among all people of Jewish faith, dedication to a synagogue or temple (the basic social unit of a group of Jews, led by a rabbi), and the importance of family life. Religious observance takes place both at home and in temple. Judaism is divided into three main groups who vary in their interpretation of those parts of the Torah that deal with personal, communal, international, and religious activities; the Orthodox community, which views the Torah as derived from God, and therefore absolutely binding; the Reform movement, which follows primarily its ethical content; and the Conservative Jews, who follow most of the observances set out in the Torah but allow for change in the face of modern life. A fourth group, Reconstructionist Jews, rejects the concept of the Jews as God's chosen people, yet maintains rituals as part of the Judaic cultural heritage.

Since Judaism has no dogma or other formal set of beliefs that is required in order to be considered a "Jew", it is difficult to determine what things would be universal to all Jews. But the most widely-accepted list would be Rambam's 13 Principles of Faith.

1. God exists
2. God is one and unique
3. God is incorporeal
4. God is eternal
5. Prayer is to be directed to God alone and to/through no other
6. The words of the prophets are true
7. Moses prophecies are true
8. The Torah was given to Moses
9. There will be no other Torah
10. God knows the thoughts and deeds of all
11. God rewards the good and punishes the wicked
12. The Messiah will come
13. The dead will be resurrected

A Summary Of Islamic Religion Circa 622 AD

By the Prophet Mohammed in Islam echoes the gods of vengeance in the old testament. One god was Allah as they believed Christians and Jews had it all wrong. They had several deities, the holy scriptures bring the Koran given to illiterate Mohammed by angel Gabriel who recited the text. It is similar to Sumerian clay tablets with creation, Adamu that predate this by 4000 years. There are two sacred texts; the Koran as the word of Allah the one true God and the Hadith as a collection of Mohammed's recitals. Although Jesus was a prophet, Christians were blasphemic for worshiping him as a son of god.

Mohammed proclaimed one true god who demanded submission to his ordinance. Koran presents a vivid picture of vengeance and retribution, especially when judgement comes where no one can hide from death or destruction if disobedient. Women are not equal. If you fear god he will grant salvation and cleanse sins, give forgiveness. Here angels destroy cities and punish sinners, smite people in bible with Gabriel attacking Mohammed.

Islam is the second largest religion of the world. It originated in the 7th century with the teaching of Holy Prophet Muhammad (PBUH). The teaching of Islam are based on the Holy Quran (revealed by God) and the traditions. The Muslims believe in the oneness of God and that Muhammad (PBUH) is the last prophet. There are five major beliefs in Islam. There are about 57 Muslim countries in the world. The total number of Muslims exceeds 1.6 billion. Shia and Sunni are two largest sects in Islam.

Prophet Muhammad received the holy scriptures of Islam, the Koran, from Allah (God) C. A.D. 610. Islam (Arabic for "submission to God") maintains that Muhammad is the last in a long line of holy prophets, preceded by Adam, Abraham, Moses, and Jesus. In addition to being devoted to the Koran, followers of Islam (Muslims) are devoted to the worship of Allah through the Five Pillars: the statement "There is no god but God, and Muhammad is his prophet"; prayer, conducted five times a day while facing Mecca; the giving of alms; the keeping of the fast of Ramadan during the ninth month of the Muslim year; and the making of a pilgrimage at least once to Mecca, if possible. The two main divisions of

Islam are the Sunni and the Shiite; the Wahabis are the most important Sunni sect, while the Shiite sects include the Assassins, the Druses, and the Fatimids, among numerous others.

Beliefs of Islamic Religion can be summarized in six doctrines.

The first of the doctrines is faith in the absolute unity of God. Tawhid, meaning "making God one," refers to the strict belief of monotheism and the refusal to compromise this position. In fact, another name for Muslims is muwahhidun, translated as "unitarians" or "upholders of divine unity" (Denny 107). He is the only creator and disposer of the Universe, has no partner and no comparable being, none but Allah is worthy of worship (Morgan 91). Tawhid is so essential and central to the faith that shirk, or the associating anything with God, is the one fundamental error for Muslims. As described in the following Quranic verse, shirk is the only sin that God cannot forgive:
God forgives not that aught should be with Him associated; less than that He forgives to whomsoever he will. Whoso associates with God anything has gone stray into far error. (4:116)

The association of anything with God denies God in His true nature. In order for followers to allow belief into one's heart they must first surrender to God in his completeness. In fact, the Arabic word, Islam, is translated as "to surrender" or "to submit.

"Associating anything with God is considered to be opposite to surrendering to Him, and therefore, no belief would be possible (Glasse 370).
The second doctrine of the faith asserts the belief in Angels as part of God's creation (Esposito 27). In Arabic angels are known as malak, from la'aka meaning "to send on a mission" (Glasse 42). These angels have no sex and are made of light, whereas humans are made of clay (Denny 108). All of them are considered good, except Iblis/Satan, who was sent out of heaven after he refused God's command to bow down to Adam (Denny 108). The angels have various functions that are concerned with the spirits and souls of human that include carrying revelations, orders, and messages to the prophets, preaching the true and the good and encouraging believers by God's good tidings and His Eternal Paradise, and registering all human deeds (Morgan 99).

Although the angels work as messengers and helpers of God, none are considered to be superior to humans. The angels do not have free will and are completely obedient to God's commands. They have no central state, and therefore do not have the capacity, as humans do, to truly know God (Glasse 42).

Muslims also recognize another kind of supernatural creature, the Jinn. They can be differentiated from angels in several ways. Jinn, created from fire, are much lower than angels, are either male or female, have limited life spans, and can be either virtuous or wicked. Like humans, they too receive revelations through God's prophets.

The third doctrine is the belief in the prophets. Muhammad was the last in a long line of prophets who were entrusted with bringing Scriptures to their peoples (Denny 108). The prophets are divided into two classes, rasuls and nabis. A rasul, or "messenger," was given a major new revelation and was called to communicate what God had sent to them (Denny 69). A nabi, or "prophet," is also one whom God has spoken to, but their mission lies within the framework of an existing religion (Glasse 318).

Regardless of the classification of the prophet, all are believed to *"possess all natural perfections, excellent character, truthfulness and honesty in speech and deed before his appointment to office, because it is by virtue of these that he has deserved Prophetic mission and has come into contact with Angels, and received revelation"* (qtd. in Glasse 318).

The fourth doctrine involves belief in the scriptures. The Quran, meaning "recitation", is held to be the eternal, literal word of God. Therefore, to accept and believe in the messages of Allah is a mere consequence of belief in Angels and the prophets, the mediums by which God's word is revealed. All Scriptures are God's work, but the people before the dawn of Islam had corrupted the original messages to suit their own inclinations. The Quran is the purest extant scripture on Earth, as it is all the pure word of God's and has not been subject to tampering (Denny 108). It was revealed to Muhammad and preserved in the Arabic language and was placed in an order that was commanded by divine revelation (Esposito 9).

The fifth doctrine, belief in the Final Judgment, is of extreme significance and is very often emphasized in Islam. With the promise of reward for a life of faith and one of punishment for the unfaithful, final judgment emphasizes ultimate moral responsibility and accountability for each believer (Esposito 28). Salvation on the "Last Day" is assured for believers who displayed both faith and works. God will save the repentant sinner, but will not accept repentance on the verge of death. One must have established a pattern of repentance and good works, even if it was preceded by a life filled with evil-doing.

The time of the "Day of Distinguishing" is unknown to all but Allah. The angel Isafril will sound the trumpet and at that moment the order of the natural world will be inverted. The Quran describes the Garden of Paradise as a heaven filled with peace and dotted with flowing rivers, gorgeous gardens, and shining streams. It is life-affirming and emphasizes the beauty of creation and enjoyment of pleasures within the limits set by God (Esposito 28). Contrastingly, hell is a place of endless pain, suffering, and torment. It is filled with flames, boiling water, and blistering wind. This punishment is a just one for a ,life filled with unfaithfulness.

Finally, some texts include a sixth doctrine, a belief in God's divine decree and predestination. There is great tension between a belief in God's foreordaining and human choice, and by and large all sects of Muslims do not agree (Farah 118). The sayings of Muhammad, recorded in the Hadith, tend to favor a more predestinarian viewpoint than the Quran. For example, he was quoted to say, "...And God said: 'Write down the fate of every individual thing to be created,' and accordingly the pen wrote all that was, and that will be, to eternity" (Farah 120). However, neither the Quran nor any other source unequivocally supports the doctrine of predestination. The position of free will is also embraced and implied (Denny 112). Some Muslims assert that omnipotence of God does not prevent free will. One can have a sense that nothing can be done to oppose the will of God, but man nonetheless has gift of free will in that he still makes choices.

Anyone who denies these basic tenets of Islam cannot be treated as a Muslim nor subjected to Muslim rules. Muslims believe that these doctrines are the basis of every divine religion and every human is called by Allah to adopt these beliefs. A mu'min, or one who has faith or "right belief", and also follows "right practice" is one who will enjoy eternal Paradise.

A Summary Of The New Age Beliefs Circa 2000 AD

The New Age Movement is not a singular religion. Although, as you may have gathered, New Age is common to the Lucifer belief system and not a new invention, it is used to now embody a movement. It is essentially a collection of eastern-influenced metaphysical ideologies, bound together by "universal tolerance" and moral relativism. It is a natural progression of humanism as it teaches that humans have evolved biologically, and must now evolve spiritually. There is no hierarchy, doctrine, creed, or membership and you will not find the "First New Age Church" on any street corner in your town. Man is the central figure as he is viewed as divine, and progressing toward a kind of godhood, or "Christ-Consciousness". They believe God is in everything, and everything together makes up God. Therefore, as a part of nature, man is part of God.

NEW AGE MOVEMENT	CHRISTIANITY
God is an impersonal force.	God is personal. He is our Heavenly Father who loves us.
God is all and all is God. He is part of creation, as are all of us.	God is the Almighty Creator of the universe, and all within it. Man is finite, and one of God's creations.
There is no sin, only misunderstanding of truth.	Rebellion from God is sin. All have sinned, and all must be saved.
Man saves himself.	Jesus Christ paid the penalty for our sins. Only through faith in Him may man be saved.
Heaven and Hell do not exist. They are states of mind.	There is a literal Heaven, and a literal Hell.
Jesus is a man who exemplified "Christ Consciousness, and the divinity that is man.	Jesus is the Son of God, and is part of the triune nature of God.

The **New Age movement** is a Western spiritual movement that developed in the second half of the 20th century and quickens exponentially during these times. Its central precepts have been described as drawing on both Eastern and Western spiritual and metaphysical traditions and infusing them with influences from self-help and motivational psychology, holistic health, parapsychology, consciousness research and quantum physics It aims to create a spirituality without borders or confining dogmas that is inclusive and pluralistic. It holds to "a holistic worldview," emphasizing that the *Mind, Body and Spirit* are interrelated and that there is a form of *Monism* and unity throughout the universe. It attempts to create "a worldview that includes both science and spirituality" and embraces a number of forms of mainstream science as well as other forms of science that are considered fringe.

The New Age movement includes elements of older spiritual and religious traditions ranging from atheism and monotheism through classical pantheism, naturalistic pantheism, pandeism and panentheism to polytheism combined with science and Gaia philosophy; particularly archaeoastronomy, astronomy, ecology, environmentalism, the

Gaia hypothesis, psychology and physics. New Age practices and philosophies sometimes draw inspiration from major world religions: Buddhism, Taoism, Chinese folk religion, Christianity, Hinduism, Islam, Judaism, Sikhism; with strong influences from East Asian religions, Gnosticism, Neopaganism, New Thought, Spiritualism, Theosophy, Universalism and Western esotericism. The term *New Age* refers to the coming astrological Age of Aquarius.

The Evolution Of gods From Sumeria

As a final note on this chapter, it would be difficult to find a more extraordinary research treatment of the evolution of religions from Sumeria than in the book by **Michael Tellinger** on the **The Slave Species of god**.

In this treatment, the evolution from Sumeria to where we are today, with the five major religions is the main point here, and to highlight this transition. For anyone who wishes to delve into this topic, Michaels book has all of the research and detail.

Although there were many gods then, there is one god in the bibles of the Koran, Kabala, Hindus, Buddhist, Bahai, Christians. In the beginning these gods had contact with humans but theses have evolved to contract through the priesthoods and ministries of the chosen ones (bloodlines and special ones).

Many kings, as far back as 1700 BC were instructed by god to write codes and laws on all matters pertaining to life, such as the Code of Hammurabi. It was a plan to control people through religions thus the gods eventually proclaimed themselves as the god of the bibles. The method of control was most effective through violence, fear and oppression. Many laws and judicial process were written and these are effetely still here today.

Michael details how from Uruk at around 3500 BC covering 25 square km became a city of 50,000 and it was this culture that influenced other civilizations spreading to Indus civilization into Greek, Roman, Mesoamerican, Andes, Mayan, Mexican empires. Most prominent interaction of these gods and men was Egypt where the god Enki became Ptaah, Ningishsidda became Tehuti, Marduk became Ra and they dictated many laws such as the Book of the Dead. Civilization sprang up all over the world suddenly with remarkable knowledge and understanding overnight

In his book, Michael details how the gods punished the disobedient and rewarded the obedient. He discusses how the Sumerian clay tablets from around 1900 BC became the "The Word" and had the creation of the world similar to Genesis 1:20-22, how the separation of heaven and earth Genesis 1:6-10, 1:3-5 was already written in the tablets. His research details how these loving gods were materialistic, obsessive and vengeful human-like beings who demanded worship.

In Michaels wrath quiz, he lists 10 question of how god's wrath affects humanity, to kill over 1.8 million because they disobeyed the "word". These are quotes taken from the current bibles. and the old testament is filled with this. In his love of God quiz, he lists over 400,000 thousand dead as a result of "god's love" In his quiz of ways god kills, he explicitly give the details in the bibles that only the chosen have the license to sin.

He lists 130 references to slaves in the bible. It was because the gods all practiced slavery. It was thought the Code of Law as created by Hammurabi the priest king of Babylonia were allowed certain rights of property and business but essentially slaves were merchandise. The salve markets of Asia, Indus, Egypt, Israel, Greece all evolves into the 17th century where it became an honourable noble business. Today the slavery continues under a different banner of economics and money over people and nations.

Of greatest significance is how Tellinger details the similarities in the major biblical stories such as creation, Adam and Eve, the Flood as presented in Greek, Roman, Scandinavian, Celtic, and Welsh all written in clay 1900 years before Christ.

In looking at the world religions, there are more religions than countries. Tellinger lists some 235 countries showing the breakdown of religions. As he points out, not one was created by God, all are written by man as imposed by "gods" all bringing their own manuals and codes that are by no means "divine"

The **Sumerian King List** is an ancient manuscript originally recorded in the Sumerian language, listing kings of Sumer (ancient southern Iraq) from Sumerian and neighboring dynasties, their supposed reign lengths, and the locations of "official" kingship. It spans over 240,000 years Kingship was believed to have been handed down by the gods, and could be transferred from one city to another, reflecting perceived hegemony in the region.[Throughout its Bronze Age existence, the document evolved into a political tool. Its final and single attested version, dating to the Middle Bronze Age, aimed to legitimize Isin's claims to hegemony when Isin was vying for dominance with Larsa and other neighboring city-states in southern Mesopotamia. The list blends prehistorical, presumably mythical predynastic rulers with implausibly lengthy reigns with later, more plausibly historical dynasties. Although the primal kings are historically unattested, this does not preclude their possible correspondence with historical rulers who were later mythicized. Some Assyriologists view the predynastic kings as a later fictional addition. Only one ruler listed is known to be female: Kug-Bau "the (female) tavern-keeper", who alone accounts for the Third Dynasty of Kish. The earliest listed ruler whose historicity has been archaeologically verified is En-me-barage-si of Kish, ca. 2600 BC. Reference to this individual in the Epic of Gilgamesh has led to speculation that Gilgamesh himself may be historical. Three dynasties are notably excluded from the list: the Larsa dynasty, which vied for power with the (included) Isin dynasty during the Isin-Larsa period; and the two dynasties of Lagash, which respectively preceded and ensued the Akkadian Empire, when Lagash exercised considerable influence in the region. Lagash in particular is known directly from archaeological artifacts dating from ca. 2500 BC. The list is important to the chronology of the 3rd millennium BC. However, the fact that many of the dynasties listed reigned simultaneously from varying localities makes it difficult to reproduce a strict linear chronology.

If you look at the current Dynasty and Kingdom of Queen Elizabeth II you will understand how the "royal" bloodlines are kept in power, and what power they wield. It is not surprising to see the evolution of bloodlines that spread to all parts of the globe, and to see the imposition of "Gods Word" upon the humanity that was created to serve them. Of course these lists, and bloodlines are not mainstream news, nor are they credible to a human who is deeply immersed in the beliefs of science and religion of today. These dynasties and the Kings, Queens, Lords and Priests have simply evolved under different names, codes, and positions within the corporate PLANET EARTH..

Even though religions and god scatter the planet, the stores and myths are the same, all rooted in Sumerian writings and gods who were vengeful, demanding obedience. In a highly spectacular research, Michael documents the Sumerian god, Mayan, Greek, Roman, Japanese, Egyptian, African and Chinese gods relating these to the Sumerian base.

In the next chapter we will look at the track record of these gods to see whether they have really deviated from the original philosophy and their "word" as evidence in the last 2000 years. We have looked at what the Sumerian Tablets have told us about the gods. Clearly they were not the true God but they believed in something that was beyond them. Clearly their powers were greater than humankind who they considered their slaves. Clearly they did not tolerate disobedience, and clearly they wrote the rule books for Earthlings. That has simply had to evolve to contain a "smarter" slave.

The big question is whether the Eartling is really any smarter?

20

THE HISTORICAL RECORD AND WORD of god

Let us take the last chapter a step further because religions are CORPORATIONS under the major Corporations called RELIGION, the biggest most influential being the VATICAN and GOD. The two major divisions of conquest are Religions and Commerce. The Articles of incorporation are the Bibles and alleged "holy" scriptures, writings, that constitute the "Word" as the laws of behaviour. When one joins these corporations, one assumes these beliefs that are imposed upon the mortal being. And so by becoming religious, one takes on the rules, words, code to put the immortal soul and spirit under the jurisdiction of GOD. But at the same time, unknowingly as we have seen, there is a process which takes possession of the Soul thorough the creation of the Trust. The private shareholders are the bloodlines of Kings and queens and their Chosen ones. It is a fictitious structure contrived by the men and women who assume the roles of gods over various territories of the PLANET EARTH. Shareholders do not hold a share certificate, they are governed and policed by blood "oaths". Right from the Sumerian civilizations of "recorded history" the only thing that has changed is that these structures have evolved to look and feel different to the mortal being who has allowed the rules of GOD to be their laws, just like the STRAWMAN story.

What has to be brought out loud and clear is that the story of Creation, of Adam and Eve, of the Great Flood, of Satan and Good and Evil, of Resurrection, all those bibles and books, are a just another edition or re-write of what was written thousands of years before Christ. What has to be underscored is that prophesies of Armageddon and are simply details of an incredible business plan coming to completion in the year 2012. It is clear that this overall mission has prevailed but how exactly it would unfold is a different story. Regardless, the major force of religion and the beliefs incorporated (literally) within them have been and still are instilled in the Earthling.

The Religious To Spiritual Evolution

In order to truly understand the shifting evolution that has occurred over thousands of years, we can see that there has been a slow progression in thinking:

- from many gods to one God;
- from gods of vengeance and wrath to God of Peace and love
- from sin to purity

- from inequality to equality
- from religious beliefs to spiritual beliefs

The Major Faiths table)

	Hinduism	Buddhism	Christianity	Islam	New Age
	900,000	376,000	2,100,000,000	840,000	1,000,000
	4000BC	500BC	30AD	622AD	2000AD
Founder	None.	Siddhartha Gautama, .	Jesus Christ	Muhammad,	None
Gods	Many forms of one Supreme Being	Many enlightened beings (Buddhas)	One	One	One
Holy Writings	Vedas.	Mahayana Sutras, Tantra, and Zen s.	The Bible	The Koran is the	None
Where	India	Asian	World wide	Middle East, Asia, N of Africa.	World wide

This is a shift in evolution from Religion to Spirituality best understood: **Religious** is defined as:

1. Having or showing belief in and reverence for God or a deity.
2. Of, concerned with, or teaching religion like a religious text.
3. Extremely scrupulous or conscientious: religious devotion to duty.
4. A member of a monastic order, especially a nun or monk.
5. Having or showing belief in and reverence for God or a deity.

Spiritual is defined as relating to, or affecting the human spirit or soul as opposed to material or physical things:

1. Of, relating to, consisting of, or having the nature of spirit; not tangible or material.
2. Of, concerned with, or affecting the soul.
3. Of, from, or relating to God; deific.
4. Of or belonging to a church or religion; sacred.
5. Relating to or having the nature of spirits or a spirit; supernatural.

Essentially, from a mortal-immortal point of view, religions have been shown to be governed by the rules of mortal, materialistic societies. The difference is that the Spiritual "religion" encompasses spirit and soul as the immortal rules.

Before perusing this truth, let us reinforce a clear distinction between three descriptive terms. Let us state that God, whatever God is, is indeed the one real thing, the true life energy, spirit, or whatever one's description or belief of the one and only God is.

This is different from the multitude of gods like the Sumerian deities of Enlil or Enki, of Zeus and many others that have been created in the minds of people in all the different territories of Earth as defined within the Corporation PLANET EARTH. These are not the same as God because there literally thousands of these man-made creations of deities.

470

Then there is GOD. This is the fictional overlay of God or gods. It is the Strawman representation of God and, in truth, has nothing to do with the real thing.

For many thousands of years, mankind has looked for self purpose and identity. What am I? Why am I here? Is there more than this? Is there a God? Humans have quested God and have searched for love and peace—something more than what a mortal life seemed to offer. This unending quest of soul and spirit inevitably leads to finding a God that created us and this place called Earth. Through time, this quest has been entrusted to those who seemingly have found the answers. It is not so hard to imagine that those who quest peace and love and harmony as represented by the immortal soul and spirit would accept the alleged knowing of experts because faith and trust are an inherent way of life.

This trusting has been the single greatest cause of loss of identity and power that has ever been. It is because these trusted ones, who have presented themselves as gods, or pretended to interpret what God's will and word are, are fakers and deceivers. Why fake? It's because we fake ourselves into believing what they tell us when we already know the answers but won't believe it. The fake is that we let others fake us into their truth. And the fakers who pretend to know the truth, evolve personal motives. Even worst is the consequence of not believing, or not following the "word" as imposed upon the mortal who believes.

Does Your god Or God Serve You Well?

In the end, regardless of religious beliefs, the real question is: Do you serve them? Or do they serve you? Do you fear them? Are they vengeful? Must you obey them? Are you born in sin? What does your God support that is not sin? Is your God one of peace, love, non judgemental and forgiving?

Despite the common belief systems that have these religions show as a face representing love and peace there seems to be a conflict about different ways to attain heaven, show love, have peace, and how to be holy. It shows through the acts of conflict, killing, and vengeance of these gods. This is all documented in history and the "good books". These gods themselves can and have taken vengeance. So obviously so can their followers; with due care and attention! Through religious conflict fought over differing ways to worship their gods, and through the quest for power and domination of belief, the century could tally hundreds of millions of souls (the range reflects a lack of precise census).

What has the wrath of gods brought? Although there are many gods who have served others well, there are many more that when you disobey them, it isn't funny according to legends, scriptures and bibles.

It is common to quote the sayings of Christ and the passages in the bibles. Quite obviously, one has much information not only to choose supporting evidence for a belief or argument, but also to interpret according one's own perceptions and belief. There are, however, the undeniable facts that:

1. God never came down to publish his words.
2. The gods presented in the "word" are anything but full of love and peace.

The question arises as to who is being served by the words of these gods? And why would anyone believe in a loving peaceful God when he was or is, anything but?

Let us now delve into the history of these sacred and biblical writings that dominate humanity's beliefs. There is no better source of evidence than the good books of religions themselves to illustrate that:

1. The gods portrayed are not very nice to their people.
2. The gods support the evils that they condone.
3. The evils men do are supported in the good books.

In fact, the beliefs, and the consequential behaviour of humanity has been to support this dual nature of good and evil. This is hardly surprising when it comes from the gods who engage in the same polarity and write the same "wisdom" into the good books.

If you have a queasy stomach for the nasty things humanity has done to itself, then you may want to skip this chapter. It is not meant to dwell on evil, but it is meant to show that a totally different interpretation can be selected from the same good books that are used to quote good. Humanity has accepted being dualistic of good and evil because they believe their leaders including god are experts and know truth. Yet each selects a version of truth from the same source. What it also points out is that there is little change from the time of the gods of Sumeria.

First, the atrocities more noteworthy are well documented within the good books themselves. Here is just a short list; the point being this can be seen in all religions where gods seem to be of the same mind. For those naughty people looking at the Ark of the Lord it was 50,000 that got wiped for their folly. Then god launched a plague for not ending fixed marriage and croaked 24,000 people regardless of who was there. And god delivering the Israelites to slaughter was an act that terminated a mere 500,000 lives. Then 240,000 people of Judah were killed to give god his revenge. Solomon had to appease god with 120,000 lives. And then somehow there were a million people sacrificed for god's chosen people. When god got pissed over premarital sex, only 23,000 had to be terminated to teach the lesson. Then there were naughty Israelites punished for a conflict with David in the amount of 70,000 lives. And when the people questioned Moses, guess who set forth a plague that killed 155,000? The story of Sodom and Gomorrah was about a hotspot for evil that god was not happy about and he terminated everyone regardless of their faith! Everyone! When the Assyrians made fun of god, it took a mere 185,000 souls to be terminated to appease god. When the Tribes abandoned god, 90% of all communities were simply wiped out of existence.

I did not make this up. Check the bibles. If you want to have an incredible treatment of this, check out **Michael Tellinger's** book which was mentioned before. And this is the reflection and documentation of the Word of "God" and the dominant religions. It's about the one supreme God on planet Earth who does not like lowlife sinners to do contrary things. This does not seem to be the idea of a true God who fundamentally loves all his children equally.

So What Is God?

What's God? Good question. He is certainly what you believe Him to be. The issue with the one alleged as God is that his alleged laws in religions and cults are written by mortals that claim to know the minds of gods. Has God ever come down and written the Bible? The Gospels? The Testaments? The Acts? The Psalms? The scriptures? Anything? Of course not! There are many that say he has written the Truth *through* them—the God made me do it syndrome—but has He ever represented Himself? Where is it? All the fake copies would not even get into a courtroom. And yet 90% of humanity believe in these documents and beliefs that are *not* written by *any* original God. It certainly sounds like another set of man-contrived laws that belong to the GOD corporation, does it not?

There is a big difference reflected in the words religion and spiritual. Religion is a short term physical thing; born-live-die. Follow the doctrine of those who are the interpreters and followers of the gods so they can help you free yourself of mortality. Spiritual is an eternal thing—born-live-die-reborn. You are immortal and eternal and you don't need any middle men to tell you what the doctrine of God is. By accepting mortal teachings over immortal knowing, you so allow dominion of physical over spiritual.

If anybody does tell you what the doctrine is, it's simple to conclude it is a fake religion thing based on someone else's opinion and interpretation. It simply can't be real because God never wrote it. Many may say he did but if anybody tries to tell you the doctrine about God, unless they can come up with God's writings, sorry, it's a fake and falls back to the contrived mortal belief about the gods or it is a fake associated with GOD.

So who do you serve? Is it god, GOD or God? And does God really have servants? Does he want vengeance if you don't believe in Him? Is the true God not a God of Love and peace? Are there different kinds of love to get pissed about? Does he truly love you? Does he judge? Does he sell paperbacks on his doctrine? So why do you believe in someone else's GOD or gods?

The bottom line of all this is you can't see either of these gods, GOD or God. It's all an interpretation of what you are taught—which is learning. Or it is an inspiration of what you feel—which is knowing. So how do you feel about this? Do you accept others interpretations and serve the doctrine they create? Either way, it's only a doctrine if the source of God did not publish it.

So what about these doctrines? Have the people that created them served you well—in the name and deed of love? Or do they take your money so they can fight others about who knows the best way to represent the god or God and impose their best way to love?

Have you taken notes on the news lately; people taking over the dictators? The Vatican harbouring secret slush funds? The finding of numerous hidden documents and ancient writings that conflict with the biblical stories? The truth seems to be getting out. But how come now?

As a side note this what we shall explore in Part 2 is that there seems to be a prevailing current of knowing that we are part of God, an eternal being of light borrowing a body to experience and expand what God is—pure unconditional love. If this is true, no wonder religions don't want you to know this. Is this a time humanity shifts into a consciousness of a New Earth—one that has no conflict or hatred. One that has no GOD or gods to worship or be afraid of. One that is built on peace and love of all things as one.

Sound like a dream? Look around you and see for yourself. It is what quantum science is finding out. This is called the Unity Consciousness. What is it? It is based on the fundamental belief that we are all interconnected as One something, all part of God. It is that the real God is Total Consciousness of love residing within all equally. This knowing has been lost because through the laws of free will and choice, humanity on Earth has always been able to choose dark or light. But dark is a lack of light—evil and dark energies exist where the light of love dims. The unification is that there is no one God to worship for we are all the One God. And inherent within our DNA—those other 10 paired layers that are a mystery, resides the divinity that the majority have simply chosen through time to give up.

Look around you and check this out. It doesn't take long to see in the news that meta-physics and physics are converging through quantum physics. It doesn't take long to realize the magnitude of this consciousness shift. That is the new energy and you are witnessing in the next few years the greatest shift in the history of mankind; and the most incredible progression and line-up of cosmic bodies and forces ever seen. Something is happening.

So now the big question. Are you here to serve the gods, or GOD or are you here to be one with the true God? Are you ready to understand your hidden, suppressed side or are you happy to retain the status quo? Sorry that last option has new consequences now.

So is this just another dogma? Well, God ain't got a list of books he published because the bottom line is that it's You—all of us. It is for you however to understand there is a choice that you may have never ever considered.

The Bible Story Of Creation

If you can ever read the Old and New Testaments, and the Bibles in any kind of rationality and objectivity, just like you would read any book, you will be truly perplexed about how these stories have so captured the belief and the faith of over half the population of Earth. There are so many interpretations and versions it is very hard to get a picture of what is really "true". But there is a consistency of thought, action and intent in these writings.

The basis for the majority seem to be the Christian writings and bibles that led to proliferation of thousands of species. They bring to humanity a version of the Old Testament where Genesis unfolds a most spectacular story that rivals the best mythological epic. It is about the creation of Old Earth. One of the versions goes something like this:

It seems fashionable to quote the bibles or the statements of Christ to try to make a point of what is one's truth. What people like to do is extract the parts that fits their argument about what God is, says, does. Needless to say it is just an interpretation that is individually based. But think about this: Could thousands of interpretations about acts and statutes attached to the truth ever get to the truth about the Strawman? What is important to me is to simply look at these bibles and point out the staggering and stark continuity about how contradictive, vengeful and destructive this god in the bibles is. So I am going to paint a picture different than those who simply ignore the multitudes of places where this god does not appreciate those who do not abide by his rules. And yes, I too will use quotes from the same good book that others use to enforce their personal beliefs. Let us summarize creation:

Once upon a time that no one can define, God is hovering around looking at this dark matter up there somewhere and gets a great notion to create something with his Son. So they decide on the first day to create light. So now there is light of Day and dark for Night. And all was cool. On the 2nd day the idea came to shift the water vapour surrounding this matter with atmosphere. That they called the sky and heaven. And it was cool.

On the 3rd day, in their brilliance, they created water as the seas, to let dry land appear and so this was the seas and the earth. But this needed more so they created the grass, plants, seeds, and fruit so these could grow and reproduce. And this was very cool to them.

On the 4th day it was time to distinguish better between night and day so they shone light from the stars and there was the Sun for day and the Moon for night. And that was very cool. But more was needed.

So on the 5th day it was time to create some life; fish in the sea and birds in the air. And they gave them the ability to reproduce. And that was cool. But there was more.

On the 6th day they created special animals like domestic ones, and a whole bundle of beasts. But there was still something missing.

God said to his Son, "*let us create beings who look like us to reflect us so they can rule over all this and care for things*". And so they added a bit of clay and created Adam. But then there was a complication. They could not just create one being of man alone. He needed a companion. So while he was asleep, they slipped in to cut him and take out a rib and then created woman who was Eve. She was complete as she had come from a man. And so they introduced them to each other and all was cool.

Now on the 7th day God looked at what he had created with his Son and they rested, sipping in the essence of its wonder.

But now the plot thickens. God decided that he would create a special garden for these two which would be Eden. It would be their place and would have the Tree of Life and Knowledge of good and evil. There would be a special tree here that would test their loyalty. So God warned them and told them that they must not eat the fruit from this tree for then they would choose evil and would die.

But the evil guy named Satan being the sneaky devil that he is, lurked in the background and he was always trying to upset God's plans. Within the garden was a revered creature a serpent so he suckered him and collaborated with this serpent. One day as Eve came to the tree, the serpent spoke to her about the wondrous powers of the fruit convincing here she would not die. So she took a bite and felt wonderful. Running to Adam to share this, they then realized what they had done. Adam who could not live without her then ate the fruit. Suddenly God was gone in them. They felt shame so they covered their naked bodies with fig leaves.

Well, the next day, God was back and listened to their pleas. But this whining was not enough for God. He blamed the serpent for his folly and Eve for this terrible deed. So he deemed that the serpent would become the lowest form of creature and crawl on the ground forever. He then placed hatred and sin in the heart of Eve so all offspring would carry this. He said childbearing will be painful henceforward because you tried to control your husband you will be subject to him. And you Adam, he said will live life in toil and struggle and when you die you will turn back to dust from where you came. And so Eve would be the One who would break the power of sin and death as all of her descendants would live thus forever.

Now it depends upon which version of Genesis you use as there are thousands of interpretations—usually to suit the group that abide by this word, but nevertheless what God says is something like this from Genesis: the First Book of Moses:

3:16 *Unto the woman he said, I will greatly multiply thy sorrow and thy conception; in sorrow thou shalt bring forth children; and thy desire shall be to thy husband, and he shall rule over thee.*

3:17 And unto Adam he said, Because thou hast hearkened unto the voice of thy wife, and hast eaten of the tree, of which I commanded thee, saying, Thou shalt not eat of it: cursed is the ground for thy sake; in sorrow shalt thou eat of it all the days of thy life;
3:18 Thorns also and thistles shall it bring forth to thee; and thou shalt eat the herb of the field;
3:19 In the sweat of thy face shalt thou eat bread, till thou return unto the ground; for out of it wast thou taken: for dust thou art, and unto dust shalt thou return.

This is a pretty severe punishment to be taken on by all humanity *forever*. Is this *really* why childbearing is painful and we toil? Is this why we have lost our eternal lives? How much of humanity simply accepts this as their faith and truth? Is this the root of the dominion of male over female? Is this the root of why females are lesser than males? If it is, then wow, what an effective marketing plan! The snakes and women certainly made a big boo boo!

Well knock, knock, hello females, anyone home in that head? Do you really believe this thing about God cursing you forever to be inferior? And knock, knock, hello you big males, anyone home in that head? Do you who are so logical and scientific support this idea of your toil and trouble?

But that is not all. It gets better...

The Story Of Dominion And Vengeance

If you continue in the Old Testament, assuming you can read it objectively, you get more history on the creations of God. And also is revealed the nature of this God who is quite filled with a need for vengeance when those mortals he created don't listen. As you go through the different parts you consistently realize that this God speaks a great deal to others who he obviously chooses to do his bidding. It's usually those in some place of power and influence, not just the average dude. What comes through is not only the vengeance of the Genesis Book, but time after time, God is telling these so called representatives of his word to get their "stuff" together. He is always talking to them, to Adam, to Noah, to Abram, to Abraham, to Moses, to many... it goes on and on. He is not only telling them what to do like demands about having one God but he makes rules upon rules to follow, like covenants, commandments, acts, and the like. He is telling them how to behave, how to live, how to create sanctuaries and churches, how you pay fees, how to sacrifice animals for payment of sin, how to not sin; he is telling them how to get the rest of the people who are being naughty back in line, or else. And he is obviously lending a helping hand of destruction and power to support the demands.

Some of these lessons are destructive and are real biggies. We listed some before. It is so obvious in the Old Testament as this forms a continuous stream of the "just and loving God" keeping the sinners in line by curses, by death, imposing toil and indiscriminate destruction regardless of who is in the way. Yet, this appears to be simply accepted as a faith of religious reality—by billions. The death, suffering, famine, punishment, thunder, rain, drought, destruction is just fine because of course God *really* loves the people who yield and are servants of the Lord. Here are some examples:

When Cain slew Abel:

4:11 And now art thou cursed from the earth, which hath opened her mouth to receive thy brother's blood from thy hand;

4:12 When thou tillest the ground, it shall not henceforth yield unto thee her strength; a fugitive and a vagabond shalt thou be in the earth.
4:13 And Cain said unto the LORD, My punishment is greater than I can bear.
4:14 Behold, thou hast driven me out this day from the face of the earth; and from thy face shall I be hid; and I shall be a fugitive and a vagabond in the earth; and it shall come to pass, that every one that findeth me shall slay me.
4:15 And the LORD said unto him, Therefore whosoever slayeth Cain, vengeance shall be taken on him sevenfold. And the LORD set a mark upon Cain, lest any finding him should kill him.

And when God saw men were wicked:

6:7 And the LORD said, I will destroy man whom I have created from the face of the earth; both man, and beast, and the creeping thing, and the fowls of the air; for it repenteth me that I have made them.

And when God Sent Abram to a new land:

12:13 And I will bless them that bless thee, and curse him that curseth thee: and in thee shall all families of the earth be blessed

And when the Pharaoh took Abrams wife into residence:

2:17 And the LORD plagued Pharaoh and his house with great plagues because of Sarai Abram's wife.

And so this God becomes quite involved in many affairs of his people and their actions. It has nothing to do with any other people on this Old Earth; it is a certain group he picks on. And when it does not suit this God look out! It seems that Moses is a pretty good fellow with God and God even gives him some very special powers. If you read the Books of Moses, it reads like a Dictator using special powers to set up his kingdom.

In Exodus, Moses hits the road to sort out the Pharaoh because he's a bad fellow and won't let the chosen people go:

7:17 Thus saith the LORD, In this thou shalt know that I am the LORD: behold, I will smite with the rod that is in mine hand upon the waters which are in the river, and they shall be turned to blood.
7:18 And the fish that is in the river shall die, and the river shall stink; and the Egyptians shall loathe to drink of the water of the river.
7:19 And the LORD spake unto Moses, Say unto Aaron, Take thy rod, and stretch out thine hand upon the waters of Egypt, upon their streams, upon their rivers, and upon their ponds, and upon all their pools of water, that they may become blood; and that there may be blood throughout all the land of Egypt, both in vessels of wood, and in vessels of stone.
7:20 And Moses and Aaron did so, as the LORD commanded; and he lifted up the rod, and smote the waters that were in the river, in the sight of Pharaoh, and in the sight of his servants; and all the waters that were in the river were turned to blood.
7:21 And the fish that was in the river died; and the river stank, and the Egyptians could not drink of the water of the river; and there was blood throughout all the land of Egypt.

And so the people were led by Moses but the Pharaoh wasn't having this nonsense:

14:23 And the Egyptians pursued, and went in after them to the midst of the sea, even all Pharaoh's horses, his chariots, and his horsemen.

14:26 And the LORD said unto Moses, Stretch out thine hand over the sea, that the waters may come again upon the Egyptians, upon their chariots, and upon their horsemen.

14:27 And Moses stretched forth his hand over the sea, and the sea returned to his strength when the morning appeared; and the Egyptians fled against it; and the LORD overthrew the Egyptians in the midst of the sea.

14:28 And the waters returned, and covered the chariots, and the horsemen, and all the host of Pharaoh that came into the sea after them; there remained not so much as one of them.

Then it was time for God to dictate the affairs of these chosen people as they headed for their chosen land:

20:24 An altar of earth thou shalt make unto me, and shalt sacrifice thereon thy burnt offerings, and thy peace offerings, thy sheep, and thine oxen: in all places where I record my name I will come unto thee, and I will bless thee.

20:25 And if thou wilt make me an altar of stone, thou shalt not build it of hewn stone: for if thou lift up thy tool upon it, thou hast polluted it.

21:20 And if a man smite his servant, or his maid, with a rod, and he die under his hand; he shall be surely punished.

21:21 Notwithstanding, if he continue a day or two, he shall not be punished: for he is his money.

21:22 If men strive, and hurt a woman with child, so that her fruit depart from her, and yet no mischief follow: he shall be surely punished, according as the woman's husband will lay upon him; and he shall pay as the judges determine.

21:23 And if any mischief follow, then thou shalt give life for life,

21:24 Eye for eye, tooth for tooth, hand for hand, foot for foot,

21:25 Burning for burning, wound for wound, stripe for stripe.

21:26 And if a man smite the eye of his servant, or the eye of his maid, that it perish; he shall let him go free for his eye's sake.

21:27 And if he smite out his manservant's tooth, or his maidservant's tooth; he shall let him go free for his tooth's sake.

And it tells about special robes for the "anointed" ones:

28:1 And take thou unto thee Aaron thy brother, and his sons with him, from among the children of Israel, that he may minister unto me in the priest's office, even Aaron, Nadab and Abihu, Eleazar and Ithamar, Aaron's sons.

28:2 And thou shalt make holy garments for Aaron thy brother for glory and for beauty.

28:3 And thou shalt speak unto all that are wise hearted, whom I have filled with the spirit of wisdom, that they may make Aaron's garments to consecrate him, that he may minister unto me in the priest's office.

28:4 And these are the garments which they shall make; a breastplate, and an ephod, and a robe, and a broidered coat, a mitre, and a girdle: and they shall make holy garments for Aaron thy brother, and his sons, that he may minister unto me in the priest's office.

28:5 And they shall take gold, and blue, and purple, and scarlet, and fine linen.

28:6 And they shall make the ephod of gold, of blue, and of purple, of scarlet, and fine twined linen, with cunning work.

This is all to set up the holy sanctuary (churches) for these chosen ones, and even set some rules for contributions like taxes:

30:11 And the LORD spake unto Moses, saying,
30:12 When thou takest the sum of the children of Israel after their number, then shall they give every man a ransom for his soul unto the LORD, when thou numberest them; that there be no plague among them, when thou numberest them.
30:13 This they shall give, every one that passeth among them that are numbered, half a shekel after the shekel of the sanctuary: (a shekel is twenty gerahs:) an half shekel shall be the offering of the LORD.
30:14 Every one that passeth among them that are numbered, from twenty years old and above, shall give an offering unto the LORD.
30:15 The rich shall not give more, and the poor shall not give less than half a shekel, when they give an offering unto the LORD, to make an atonement for your souls.
30:16 And thou shalt take the atonement money of the children of Israel, and shalt appoint it for the service of the tabernacle of the congregation; that it may be a memorial unto the children of Israel before the LORD, to make an atonement for your souls.

The Book of Leviticus is all about setting up the priest hood and ensuring that offerings are made to God as acknowledgement of their sins:

1:1 And the LORD called unto Moses, and spake unto him out of the tabernacle of the congregation, saying,
1:2 Speak unto the children of Israel, and say unto them, If any man of you bring an offering unto the LORD, ye shall bring your offering of the cattle, even of the herd, and of the flock.
1:3 If his offering be a burnt sacrifice of the herd, let him offer a male without blemish: he shall offer it of his own voluntary will at the door of the tabernacle of the congregation before the LORD.
1:4 And he shall put his hand upon the head of the burnt offering; and it shall be accepted for him to make atonement for him.
1:5 And he shall kill the bullock before the LORD: and the priests, Aaron's sons, shall bring the blood, and sprinkle the blood round about upon the altar that is by the door of the tabernacle of the congregation.
1:6 And he shall flay the burnt offering, and cut it into his pieces.
1:7 And the sons of Aaron the priest shall put fire upon the altar, and lay the wood in order upon the fire:

And then he set up the administrative power for priests and the pricing policy for redemption:

27:1   And the LORD spake unto Moses, saying,
27:2   Speak unto the children of Israel, and say unto them, When a man shall make a singular vow, the persons shall be for the LORD by thy estimation.

27:3   And thy estimation shall be of the male from twenty years old even unto sixty years old, even thy estimation shall be fifty shekels of silver, after the shekel of the sanctuary.

27:4   And if it be a female, then thy estimation shall be thirty shekels.

27:5   And if it be from five years old even unto twenty years old, then thy estimation shall be of the male twenty shekels, and for the female ten shekels.

27:6   And if it be from a month old even unto five years old, then thy estimation shall be of the male five shekels of silver, and for the female thy estimation shall be three shekels of silver.

27:7   And if it be from sixty years old and above; if it be a male, then thy estimation shall be fifteen shekels, and for the female ten shekels.

27:8   But if he be poorer than thy estimation, then he shall present himself before the priest, and the priest shall value him; according to his ability that vowed shall the priest value him.

27:9   And if it be a beast, whereof men bring an offering unto the LORD, all that any man giveth of such unto the LORD shall be holy.

27:10 He shall not alter it, nor change it, a good for a bad, or a bad for a good: and if he shall at all change beast for beast, then it and the exchange thereof shall be holy.

27:11 And if it be any unclean beast, of which they do not offer a sacrifice unto the LORD, then he shall present the beast before the priest:

27:12 And the priest shall value it, whether it be good or bad: as thou valuest it, who art the priest, so shall it be.

27:13 But if he will at all redeem it, then he shall add a fifth part thereof unto thy estimation.

27:14 And when a man shall sanctify his house to be holy unto the LORD, then the priest shall estimate it, whether it be good or bad: as the priest shall estimate it, so shall it stand.

27:15 And if he that sanctified it will redeem his house, then he shall add the fifth part of the money of thy estimation unto it, and it shall be his.

27:16 And if a man shall sanctify unto the LORD some part of a field of his possession, then thy estimation shall be according to the seed thereof: an homer of barley seed shall be valued at fifty shekels of silver.

27:17 If he sanctify his field from the year of jubilee, according to thy estimation it shall stand.

27:18 But if he sanctify his field after the jubilee, then the priest shall reckon unto him the money according to the years that remain, even unto the year of the jubilee, and it shall be abated from thy estimation.

27:19 And if he that sanctified the field will in any wise redeem it, then he shall add the fifth part of the money of thy estimation unto it, and it shall be assured to him.

27:20 And if he will not redeem the field, or if he have sold the field to another man, it shall not be redeemed any more.

27:21 But the field, when it goeth out in the jubilee, shall be holy unto the LORD, as a field devoted; the possession thereof shall be the priest's.

27:22 And if a man sanctify unto the LORD a field which he hath bought, which is not of the fields of his possession;

27:23 Then the priest shall reckon unto him the worth of thy estimation, even unto the year of the jubilee: and he shall give thine estimation in that day, as a holy thing unto the LORD.

27:24 In the year of the jubilee the field shall return unto him of whom it was bought, even to him to whom the possession of the land did belong.
27:25 And all thy estimations shall be according to the shekel of the sanctuary: twenty gerahs shall be the shekel.
27:26 Only the firstling of the beasts, which should be the LORD'S firstling, no man shall sanctify it; whether it be ox, or sheep: it is the LORD'S.
27:27 And if it be of an unclean beast, then he shall redeem it according to thine estimation, and shall add a fifth part of it thereto: or if it be not redeemed, then it shall be sold according to thy estimation.

When you get to the Book of Numbers, it's all about a census counting the people to see who is fit for military duty. This God is preparing for war. And they are to serve God and sanctuary:

1:1 And the LORD spake unto Moses in the wilderness of Sinai, in the tabernacle of the congregation, on the first day of the second month, in the second year after they were come out of the land of Egypt, saying,
1:2 Take ye the sum of all the congregation of the children of Israel, after their families, by the house of their fathers, with the number of their names, every male by their polls;
1:3 From twenty years old and upward, all that are able to go forth to war in Israel: thou and Aaron shall number them by their armies.

To serve who?

3:5 And the LORD spake unto Moses, saying,
3:6 Bring the tribe of Levi near, and present them before Aaron the priest, that they may minister unto him.
3:7 And they shall keep his charge, and the charge of the whole congregation before the tabernacle of the congregation, to do the service of the tabernacle.

And there is a price for sin:

5:5 And the LORD spake unto Moses, saying,
5:6 Speak unto the children of Israel, When a man or woman shall commit any sin that men commit, to do a trespass against the LORD, and that person be guilty;
5:7 Then they shall confess their sin which they have done: and he shall recompense his trespass with the principal thereof, and add unto it the fifth part thereof, and give it unto him against whom he hath trespassed.
5:8 But if the man have no kinsman to recompense the trespass unto, let the trespass be recompensed unto the LORD, even to the priest; beside the ram of the atonement, whereby an atonement shall be made for him.

And more for not obeying:

14:26 And the LORD spake unto Moses and unto Aaron, saying,
14:27 How long shall I bear with this evil congregation, which murmur against me? I have heard the murmurings of the children of Israel, which they murmur against me.
14:28 Say unto them, As truly as I live, saith the LORD, as ye have spoken in mine ears, so will I do to you:

14:29 Your carcases shall fall in this wilderness; and all that were numbered of you, according to your whole number, from twenty years old and upward, which have murmured against me,

14:30 Doubtless ye shall not come into the land, concerning which I sware to make you dwell therein, save Caleb the son of Jephunneh, and Joshua the son of Nun.

14:31 But your little ones, which ye said should be a prey, them will I bring in, and they shall know the land which ye have despised.

14:32 But as for you, your carcases, they shall fall in this wilderness.

14:33 And your children shall wander in the wilderness forty years, and bear your whoredoms, until your carcases be wasted in the wilderness.

The Book of Deuteronomy is about creating regulations:

4:35 Unto thee it was showed, that thou mightest know that the LORD he is God; there is none else beside him.

4:39 Know therefore this day, and consider it in thine heart, that the LORD he is God in heaven above, and upon the earth beneath: there is none else.

4:40 Thou shalt keep therefore his statutes, and his commandments, which I command thee this day, that it may go well with thee, and with thy children after thee, and that thou mayest prolong thy days upon the earth, which the LORD thy God giveth thee, forever.

4:45 These are the testimonies, and the statutes, and the judgments, which Moses spake unto the children of Israel, after they came forth out of Egypt,

4:1 Now therefore hearken, O Israel, unto the statutes and unto the judgments, which I teach you, for to do them, that ye may live, and go in and possess the land which the LORD God of your fathers giveth you.

4:2 Ye shall not add unto the word which I command you, neither shall ye diminish ought from it, that ye may keep the commandments of the LORD your God which I command you.

As the bible story progresses, God even has a say in rules and regulations that are almost like reading a current day set of Acts and Statutes, or like the regulations of the IRS. He even has a hand at commerce to fine those that disobey, or do not follow the rules he has conveyed. He even takes a piece of the action in gold! But you just can't mail it to him or take a sky bus up to deliver it, you have to give all or part of it to guess who? Yes, the Church, the Priests!

This God is pretty set in his ways of reigning upon his creation of Old Earth with Dominion and Vengeance? It is very difficult to escape this undeniable aspect of this mythology.

As you continue through the various books of the bible you see how a group of wise men knowing in the skills of dominion set up the infrastructure of the Church to overlord and dominate. It is all done through the word of God as interpreted by men.

The Book of Isaiah, sets the prophesies of death and destruction for the nations in 17:1 Syrian and Israel. See 18:6 for Ethiopia, 19:1 for Egypt, 21:1 for Babylon, 21:11 for Edon, 21:13 for Arabia, 22:1 for Jeruselum, 23:1 for Tyre and even 24:1 for Planet Earth. No one messes with this god.

The Book of Deuteronomy is basically the administrative laws that deal with False Prophets 13:1. Tithing is 14:22, Debts 15:1, and the punishment-reward policing system by the high priests as Blessing in 28:3 and Curses in 28:15.

The interesting aspect of this is that in addition to this being the "truth" for Christianity, it also is the basis for the "truth" of the Islam when Mohammed, centuries later, brought this story to his people to create the Islam religion of the Koran. This brings the toll up to about 4.3 billion people that believe this as a foundation for humanity.

In the next sections, I refer you to the work of **www.evilbible.com** which is more comprehensive. What follows is a summary.

The Story Of Slavery

Except for murder, slavery has got to be one of the most immoral things a person can do. Yet slavery is rampant throughout the Bible in both the Old and New Testaments. The Bible clearly approves of slavery in many passages, and it goes so far as to tell how to obtain slaves, how hard you can beat them, and when you can have sex with the female slaves.

Many Jews and Christians will try to ignore the moral problems of slavery by saying that these slaves were actually servants or indentured servants. Many translations of the Bible use the word "servant", "bondservant", or "manservant" instead of "slave" to make the Bible seem less immoral than it really is. While many slaves may have worked as household servants, that doesn't mean that they were not slaves who were bought, sold, and treated worse than livestock.

The following passage shows that slaves are clearly property to be bought and sold like livestock:

"However, you may purchase male or female slaves from among the foreigners who live among you. You may also purchase the children of such resident foreigners, including those who have been born in your land. You may treat them as your property, passing them on to your children as a permanent inheritance. You may treat your slaves like this, but the people of Israel, your relatives, must never be treated this way." (Leviticus 25:44-46 NLT)

The following passage describes how the Hebrew slaves are to be treated:

"If you buy a Hebrew slave, he is to serve for only six years. Set him free in the seventh year, and he will owe you nothing for his freedom. If he was single when he became your slave and then married afterward, only he will go free in the seventh year. But if he was married before he became a slave, then his wife will be freed with him. If his master gave him a wife while he was a slave, and they had sons or daughters, then the man will be free in the seventh year, but his wife and children will still belong to his master. But the slave may plainly declare, 'I love my master, my wife, and my children. I would rather not go free.' If he does this, his master must present him before God. Then his master must take him to the door and publicly pierce his ear with an awl. After that, the slave will belong to his master forever." (Exodus 21:2-6 NLT)

Notice how they can get a male Hebrew slave to become a permanent slave by keeping his wife and children hostage until he says he wants to become a permanent slave. What kind of family values are these? The following passage describes the sickening practice of sex slavery. How can anyone think it is moral to sell your own daughter as a sex slave?

"When a man sells his daughter as a slave, she will not be freed at the end of six years as the men are. If she does not please the man who bought her, he may allow her to be bought back again. But he is not allowed to sell her to foreigners, since he is the one who broke the contract with her. And if the slave girl's owner arranges for her to marry his son, he may no longer treat her as a slave girl, but he must treat her as his daughter. If he himself marries her and then takes another wife, he may not reduce her food or clothing or fail to sleep with her as his wife. If he fails in any of these three ways, she may leave as a free woman without making any payment." (Exodus 21:7-11 NLT).

So these are the Bible family values! A man can buy as many sex slaves as he wants as long as he feeds them, clothes them, and has sex with them. What does the Bible say about beating slaves? It says you can beat both male and female slaves with a rod so hard that as long as they don't die right away you are cleared of any wrong doing:

"When a man strikes his male or female slave with a rod so hard that the slave dies under his hand, he shall be punished. If, however, the slave survives for a day or two, he is not to be punished, since the slave is his own property.". (Exodus 21:20-21 NAB)

You would think that Jesus and the New Testament would have a different view of slavery, but slavery is still approved of in the New Testament, as the following passages show:

"Slaves, obey your earthly masters with deep respect and fear. Serve them sincerely as you would serve Christ." (Ephesians 6:5 NLT)

"Christians who are slaves should give their masters full respect so that the name of God and his teaching will not be shamed. If your master is a Christian, that is no excuse for being disrespectful. You should work all the harder because you are helping another believer by your efforts. Teach these truths, Timothy, and encourage everyone to obey them." (1 Timothy 6:1-2 NLT)

In the following parable, Jesus clearly approves of beating slaves even if they didn't know they were doing anything wrong:

"The servant will be severely punished, for though he knew his duty, he refused to do it. "But people who are not aware that they are doing wrong will be punished only lightly. Much is required from those to whom much is given, and much more is required from those to whom much more is given." (Luke 12:47-48 NLT)

The Story Of Ritual And Human Sacrifice

The Bible, especially the Old Testament, is filled with numerous stories of animal and human sacrifice. God, we are told, likes the pleasing aroma of burning flesh. Animal sacrifice is much more common than human sacrifice, but both occur and are "pleasing to the Lord". Genesis, the first book of the Bible, has Abraham preparing to sacrifice his son to God. ***"Take your son, your only son – yes, Isaac, whom you love so much – and go to the land of Moriah. Sacrifice him there as a burnt offering on one of the mountains, which I will point out to you."*** (Genesis 22:1-18) Abraham takes his own son up on a mountain and builds an altar upon which to burn him. He even lies to his son and has him help build the altar. Then Abraham ties his son to the altar and puts a knife to his throat. He then hears God tell him this was just a test of his faith. However, God still wanted to smell some burnt flesh so he tells Abraham to burn a ram.

Even though he didn't kill his son, it is still an incredibly cruel and evil thing to do. If Abraham did that today he would be in jail serving a long sentence as someone's prison-bitch. It amazes me how Christians see this story as a sign of God's love. There is no love here, just pure unadulterated evil.

The first seven chapters of Leviticus have extensive rules regarding animal and food sacrifices. These offerings are supposed to be burnt so that God can smell them. If you read through these it seems clear to me that the priests were getting their followers to make a big feast for them every week. The priests were very particular about what kind of food to bring and how to prepare it.

Even more peculiar is God's obsession with first-born sons. In Exodus 13:2 the Lord said *"Consecrate to me every first-born that opens the womb among Israelites, both man and beast, for it belongs to me."*

Later it says that you can redeem (replace) an ass with a sheep and that you must redeem a child for an unspecified price. It is clear from the context that "consecrate" means a burning sacrifice. These priests are guilty of theft and kidnapping. Since any sins in the Old Testament were punishable by death, these priests used the threat of death to extort food and money from their followers. What do we call a scum-bag that threatens to kill your kids unless you pay a ransom? A kidnapper! If these priests were alive today they would be in prison with Abraham. However, in Leviticus 27:28-29, the Lord allows for no redemptions. *"Note also that any one of his possessions which a man vows as doomed to the Lord, whether it is a human being or an animal, or a hereditary field, shall be neither sold nor ransomed; everything that is thus doomed becomes most sacred to the Lord. All human beings that are doomed lose the right to be redeemed; they must be put to death."*

"At that time the Spirit of the LORD came upon Jephthah, and he went throughout the land of Gilead and Manasseh, including Mizpah in Gilead, and led an army against the Ammonites. And Jephthah made a vow to the LORD. He said, "If you give me victory over the Ammonites, **I will give to the LORD the first thing coming out of my house to greet me when I return in triumph. I will sacrifice it as a burnt offering.***"*

"So Jephthah led his army against the Ammonites, and the LORD gave him victory. He thoroughly defeated the Ammonites from Aroer to an area near Minnith – twenty towns – and as far away as Abel-keramim. Thus Israel subdued the Ammonites. When Jephthah returned home to Mizpah, his daughter – his only child – ran out to meet him, playing on a tambourine and dancing for joy. When he saw her, he tore his clothes in anguish. "My daughter!" he cried out. "My heart is breaking! What a tragedy that you came out to greet me. For I have made a vow to the LORD and cannot take it back." And she said, "Father, you have made a promise to the LORD. You must do to me what you have promised, for the LORD has given you a great victory over your enemies, the Ammonites. But first let me go up and roam in the hills and weep with my friends for two months, because I will die a virgin." "You may go," Jephthah said. And he let her go away for two months. She and her friends went into the hills and wept because she would never have children. When she returned home, **her father kept his vow, and she died a virgin.** *So it has become a custom in Israel for young Israelite women to go away for four days each year to lament the fate of Jephthah's daughter." (*Judges 11:29-40 NLT)

The Lord speaking: *"The one who has stolen what was set apart for destruction will himself* **be burned with fire***, along with everything he has, for he has broken the covenant of the LORD and has done a horrible thing in Israel."* (Joshua 7:15 NLT)

At the LORD's command, a man of God from Judah went to Bethel, and he arrived there just as Jeroboam was approaching the altar to offer a sacrifice. Then at the LORD's command, he shouted, "O altar, altar! This is what the LORD says: A child named Josiah will be born into the dynasty of David. **On you he will sacrifice the priests from the pagan shrines who come here to burn incense, and human bones will be burned on you.**" (1 Kings 13:1-2 NLT)

He [Josiah] executed the priests of the pagan shrines on their own altars, and he burned human bones on the altars to desecrate them. *Finally, he returned to Jerusalem. King Josiah then issued this order to all the people: "You must celebrate the Passover to the LORD your God, as it is written in the Book of the Covenant." There had not been a Passover celebration like that since the time when the judges ruled in Israel, throughout all the years of the kings of Israel and Judah. This Passover was celebrated to the LORD in Jerusalem during the eighteenth year of King Josiah's reign. Josiah also exterminated the mediums and psychics, the household gods, and every other kind of idol worship, both in Jerusalem and throughout the land of Judah.* **He did this in obedience to all the laws written in the scroll that Hilkiah the priest had found in the LORD's Temple. Never before had there been a king like Josiah, who turned to the LORD with all his heart and soul and strength, obeying all the laws of Moses. And there has never been a king like him since.** (2 Kings 23:20-25 NLT)

As for you, son of man, prophesy: Thus says the Lord GOD against the Ammonites and their insults: A sword, a sword is drawn for slaughter, burnished to consume and to flash lightning, because you planned with false visions and lying divinations to lay it on the necks of depraved and wicked men whose day has come when their crimes are at an end. Return it to its sheath! In the place where you were created, in the land of your origin, I will judge you. I will pour out my indignation upon you, breathing my fiery wrath upon you, **I will hand you over to ravaging men, artisans of destruction. You shall be fuel for the fire, your blood shall flow throughout the land.** *You shall not be remembered, for I, the LORD, have spoken.* (Ezekiel 21:33-37 NAB)

"Suppose you hear in one of the towns the LORD your God is giving you that some worthless rabble among you have led their fellow citizens astray by encouraging them to worship foreign gods. In such cases, you must examine the facts carefully. If you find it is true and can prove that such a detestable act has occurred among you, you must attack that town and completely destroy all its inhabitants, as well as all the livestock. Then you must pile all the plunder in the middle of the street and burn it. **Put the entire town to the torch as a burnt offering to the LORD your God.** *That town must remain a ruin forever; it may never be rebuilt. Keep none of the plunder that has been set apart for destruction. Then the LORD will turn from his fierce anger and be merciful to you. He will have compassion on you and make you a great nation, just as he solemnly promised your ancestors. "The LORD your God will be merciful only if you obey him and keep all the commands I am giving you today, doing what is pleasing to him."* (Deuteronomy 13:13-19 NLT)

So the next time some Christian tells you about the "love of God", show them this page and ask them "Why does God want me to burn animals and humans?"

The Story Of Rape And Plunder

(Judges 21:10-24 NLT): *"So they sent twelve thousand warriors to Jabesh-gilead with orders to kill everyone there, including women and children. "This is what you are to do," they said. "Completely destroy all the males and every woman who is not a virgin."*

Among the residents of Jabesh-gilead they found four hundred young virgins who had never slept with a man, and they brought them to the camp at Shiloh in the land of Canaan."

"The Israelite assembly sent a peace delegation to the little remnant of Benjamin who were living at the rock of Rimmon. Then the men of Benjamin returned to their homes, and the four hundred women of Jabesh-gilead who were spared were given to them as wives. But there were not enough women for all of them. The people felt sorry for Benjamin because the LORD had left this gap in the tribes of Israel. So the Israelite leaders asked, "How can we find wives for the few who remain, since all the women of the tribe of Benjamin are dead? There must be heirs for the survivors so that an entire tribe of Israel will not be lost forever. But we cannot give them our own daughters in marriage because we have sworn with a solemn oath that anyone who does this will fall under God's curse."

"Then they thought of the annual festival of the LORD held in Shiloh, between Lebonah and Bethel, along the east side of the road that goes from Bethel to Shechem. They told the men of Benjamin who still needed wives, "Go and hide in the vineyards. When the women of Shiloh come out for their dances, rush out from the vineyards, and each of you can take one of them home to be your wife! And when their fathers and brothers come to us in protest, we will tell them, 'Please be understanding. Let them have your daughters, for we didn't find enough wives for them when we destroyed Jabesh-gilead. And you are not guilty of breaking the vow since you did not give your daughters in marriage to them.'" So the men of Benjamin did as they were told. They kidnapped the women who took part in the celebration and carried them off to the land of their own inheritance. Then they rebuilt their towns and lived in them. So the assembly of Israel departed by tribes and families, and they returned to their own homes."

Numbers 31:7-18 NLT: "They attacked Midian just as the LORD had commanded Moses, and they killed all the men. All five of the Midianite kings – Evi, Rekem, Zur, Hur, and Reba – died in the battle. They also killed Balaam son of Beor with the sword. Then the Israelite army captured the Midianite women and children and seized their cattle and flocks and all their wealth as plunder. They burned all the towns and villages where the Midianites had lived. After they had gathered the plunder and captives, both people and animals, they brought them all to Moses and Eleazar the priest, and to the whole community of Israel, which was camped on the plains of Moab beside the Jordan River, across from Jericho."

"Moses, Eleazar the priest, and all the leaders of the people went to meet them outside the camp. But Moses was furious with all the military commanders who had returned from the battle. "Why have you let all the women live?" he demanded. "These are the very ones who followed Balaam's advice and caused the people of Israel to rebel against the LORD at Mount Peor. They are the ones who caused the plague to strike the LORD's people. Now kill all the boys and all the women who have slept with a man. Only the young girls who are virgins may live; you may keep them for yourselves."

Clearly Moses and God approves of rape of virgins. In Deuteronomy 20:10-14 it states: "As you approach a town to attack it, first offer its people terms for peace. If they accept your terms and open the gates to you, then all the people inside will serve you in forced labor. But if they refuse to make peace and prepare to fight, you must attack the town. When the LORD your God hands it over to you, kill every man in the town. But you may keep for yourselves all the women, children, livestock, and other plunder. You may enjoy the spoils of your enemies that the LORD your God has given you."

And the penalty for rape: (Deuteronomy 22:28-29 NLT) "*If a man is caught in the act of raping a young woman who is not engaged, he must pay fifty pieces of silver to her father. Then he must marry the young woman because he violated her, and he will never be allowed to divorce her.*"

Deuteronomy 22:23-24 NAB: "*If within the city a man comes upon a maiden who is betrothed, and has relations with her, you shall bring them both out of the gate of the city and there stone them to death: the girl because she did not cry out for help though she was in the city, and the man because he violated his neighbors wife.*"

It is clear that God doesn't really care about the rape victim. He is only concerned about the violation of another man's property.

In 2 Samuel 12:11-14 NAB: "*Thus says the Lord: 'I will bring evil upon you out of your own house. I will take your wives* [plural] *while you live to see it, and will give them to your neighbour. He shall lie with your wives in broad daylight. You have done this deed in secret, but I will bring it about in the presence of all Israel, and with the sun looking down.' Then David said to Nathan, "I have sinned against the Lord." Nathan answered David: "The Lord on his part has forgiven your sin: you shall not die. But since you have utterly spurned the Lord by this deed, the child born to you must surely die.*" [The child dies seven days later.]

And then in Deuteronomy 21:10-14 NAB: "*When you go out to war against your enemies and the LORD, your God, delivers them into your hand, so that you take captives, if you see a comely woman among the captives and become so enamored of her that you wish to have her as wife, you may take her home to your house. But before she may live there, she must shave her head and pare her nails and lay aside her captive's garb. After she has mourned her father and mother for a full month, you may have relations with her, and you shall be her husband and she shall be your wife. However, if later on you lose your liking for her, you shall give her freedom, if she wishes it; but you shall not sell her or enslave her, since she was married to you under compulsion.*"

In Judges 5:30 NAB, "*They must be dividing the spoils they took: there must be a damsel or two for each man, Spoils of dyed cloth as Sisera's spoil, an ornate shawl or two for me in the spoil.* (Judges 5:30 NAB).

In Exodus 21:7-11 NLT, "*When a man sells his daughter as a slave, she will not be freed at the end of six years as the men are. If she does not please the man who bought her, he may allow her to be bought back again. But he is not allowed to sell her to foreigners, since he is the one who broke the contract with her. And if the slave girl's owner arranges for her to marry his son, he may no longer treat her as a slave girl, but he must treat her as his daughter. If he himself marries her and then takes another wife, he may not reduce her food or clothing or fail to sleep with her as his wife. If he fails in any of these three ways, she may leave as a free woman without making any payment.*

In Zechariah 14:1-2 NAB, "*Lo, a day shall come for the Lord when the spoils shall be divided in your midst. And I will gather all the nations against Jerusalem for battle: the city shall be taken, houses plundered,* **women ravished***; half of the city shall go into exile, but the rest of the people shall not be removed from the city.*"

The Story Of Murder And Punishment

The act of murder is rampant in the Bible. In much of the Bible, especially the Old Testament, there are laws that command that people be killed for absurd reasons such as working on the Sabbath, being gay, cursing your parents, or not being a virgin on your wedding night. In addition to these crazy and immoral laws, there are plenty of examples of God's irrationality by his direct killing of many people for reasons that defy any rational explanation such as killing children who make fun of bald people, and the killing of a man who tried to keep the ark of God from falling during transport. There are also countless examples of mass murders commanded by God, including the murder of women, infants, and children.

The following passages are a very small percentage of the total passages approving of murder in the Bible. They are divided here into three parts: 1) Capital Punishment Crimes, 2) God's Murders for Stupid Reasons, 3) Murdering Children, and 4) Miscellaneous Murders. This list is long, but it barely scratches the surface of all the murders approved of in the Bible. For a full analysis of this got to the website *www.evilbible.com/Murder.htm#Miscellaneous_Murders*

1) Capital Punishment Crimes: Kill People Who Don't Listen to Priests

Anyone arrogant enough to reject the verdict of the judge or of the priest who represents the LORD your God must be put to death. Such evil must be purged from Israel. (Deuteronomy 17:12 NLT)

Kill Witches *"You should not let a sorceress live."* (Exodus 22:17 NAB)

Kill Homosexuals *"If a man lies with a male as with a women, both of them shall be put to death for their abominable deed; they have forfeited their lives."* (Leviticus 20:13 NAB)

Kill Fortune-tellers *"A man or a woman who acts as a medium or fortune-teller shall be put to death by stoning; they have no one but themselves to blame for their death".* (Leviticus 20:27 NAB)

Death for Hitting Dad *"Whoever strikes his father or mother shall be put to death".* (Exodus 21:15 NAB)

Death for Cursing Parents
1) *If one curses his father or mother, his lamp will go out at the coming of darkness.* (Proverbs 20:20 NAB)
2) *All who curse their father or mother must be put to death. They are guilty of a capital offense.* (Leviticus 20:9 NLT)

Death for Adultery *"If a man commits adultery with another man's wife, both the man and the woman must be put to death".* (Leviticus 20:10 NLT)

Death for Fornication *"A priest's daughter who loses her honour by committing fornication and thereby dishonours her father also, shall be burned to death".* (Leviticus 21:9 NAB)

Death to Followers of Other Religions *"Whoever sacrifices to any god, except the Lord alone, shall be doomed".* (Exodus 22:19 NAB)

Kill Nonbelievers *"They entered into a covenant to seek the Lord, the God of their fathers, with all their heart and soul; and everyone who would not seek the Lord, the God of Israel, was to be put to death, whether small or great, whether man or woman".* (2 Chronicles 15:12-13 NAB)

Kill False Prophets *"If a man still prophesies, his parents, father and mother, shall say to him, "You shall not live, because you have spoken a lie in the name of the Lord." When he prophesies, his parents, father and mother, shall thrust him through.* (Zechariah 13:3 NAB)

Kill the Entire Town if One Person Worships Another God *"Suppose you hear in one of the towns the LORD your God is giving you that some worthless rabble among you have led their fellow citizens astray by encouraging them to worship foreign gods. In such cases, you must examine the facts carefully. If you find it is true and can prove that such a detestable act has occurred among you, you must attack that town and completely destroy all its inhabitants, as well as all the livestock. Then you must pile all the plunder in the middle of the street and burn it. Put the entire town to the torch as a burnt offering to the LORD your God. That town must remain a ruin forever; it may never be rebuilt. Keep none of the plunder that has been set apart for destruction. Then the LORD will turn from his fierce anger and be merciful to you. He will have compassion on you and make you a great nation, just as he solemnly promised your ancestors. "The LORD your God will be merciful only if you obey him and keep all the commands I am giving you today, doing what is pleasing to him."* (Deuteronomy 13:13-19 NLT)

Kill Women Who Are Not Virgins On Their Wedding Night *"But if this charge is true* (that she wasn't a virgin on her wedding night), *and evidence of the girls virginity is not found, they shall bring the girl to the entrance of her father's house and there her townsman shall stone her to death, because she committed a crime against Israel by her unchasteness in her father's house. Thus shall you purge the evil from your midst".* (Deuteronomy 22:20-21 NAB)

Kill Followers of Other Religions.
1)*"If your own full brother, or your son or daughter, or your beloved wife, or you intimate friend, entices you secretly to serve other gods, whom you and your fathers have not known, gods of any other nations, near at hand or far away, from one end of the earth to the other: do not yield to him or listen to him, nor look with pity upon him, to spare or shield him, but kill him. Your hand shall be the first raised to slay him; the rest of the people shall join in with you. You shall stone him to death, because he sought to lead you astray from the Lord, your God, who brought you out of the land of Egypt, that place of slavery. And all Israel, hearing of this, shall fear and never do such evil as this in your midst".* (Deuteronomy 13:7-12 NAB)
2) *"Suppose a man or woman among you, in one of your towns that the LORD your God is giving you, has done evil in the sight of the LORD your God and has violated the covenant by serving other gods or by worshiping the sun, the moon, or any of the forces of heaven, which I have strictly forbidden. When you hear about it, investigate the matter thoroughly. If it is true that this detestable thing has been done in Israel, then that man or woman must be taken to the gates of the town and stoned to death".* (Deuteronomy 17:2-5 NLT)

Death for Blasphemy *"One day a man who had an Israelite mother and an Egyptian father got into a fight with one of the Israelite men. During the fight, this son of an Israelite woman blasphemed the LORD's name. So the man was brought to Moses for judgment. His mother's name was Shelomith. She was the daughter of Dibri of the tribe of Dan. They put the man in custody until the LORD's will in the matter should become clear. Then the LORD said to Moses, "Take the blasphemer outside the camp, and tell all those who heard him to lay their hands on his head. Then let the entire community stone him to death. Say to the people of Israel: Those who blaspheme God will suffer the consequences of their guilt and be punished. Anyone who blasphemes the LORD's name* must be stoned to death by the whole community of Israel. Any Israelite or foreigner among you who blasphemes the LORD's name will surely die". (Leviticus 24:10-16 NLT)

Kill False Prophets 1) *Suppose there are prophets among you, or those who have dreams about the future, and they promise you signs or miracles, and the predicted signs or miracles take place. If the prophets then say, 'Come, let us worship the gods of foreign nations,' do not listen to them. The LORD your God is testing you to see if you love him with all your heart and soul. Serve only the LORD your God and fear him alone. Obey his commands, listen to his voice, and cling to him. The false prophets or dreamers who try to lead you astray must be put to death, for they encourage rebellion against the LORD your God, who brought you out of slavery in the land of Egypt. Since they try to keep you from following the LORD your God, you must execute them to remove the evil from among you.* (Deuteronomy 13:1-5 NLT)
2) *But any prophet who claims to give a message from another god or who falsely claims to speak for me must die.' You may wonder, 'How will we know whether the prophecy is from the LORD or not?' If the prophet predicts something in the LORD's name and it does not happen, the LORD did not give the message. That prophet has spoken on his own and need not be feared.* (Deuteronomy 18:20-22 NLT)

Infidels and Gays Should Die "*So God let them go ahead and do whatever shameful things their hearts desired. As a result, they did vile and degrading things with each other's bodies. Instead of believing what they knew was the truth about God, they deliberately chose to believe lies. So they worshiped the things God made but not the Creator himself, who is to be praised forever. Amen. That is why God abandoned them to their shameful desires. Even the women turned against the natural way to have sex and instead indulged in sex with each other. And the men, instead of having normal sexual relationships with women, burned with lust for each other. Men did shameful things with other men and, as a result, suffered within themselves the penalty they so richly deserved. When they refused to acknowledge God, he abandoned them to their evil minds and let them do things that should never be done. Their lives became full of every kind of wickedness, sin, greed, hate, envy, murder, fighting, deception, malicious behaviour, and gossip. They are backstabbers, haters of God, insolent, proud, and boastful. They are forever inventing new ways of sinning and are disobedient to their parents. They refuse to understand, break their promises, and are heartless and unforgiving. They are fully aware of God's death penalty for those who do these things, yet they go right ahead and do them anyway. And, worse yet, they encourage others to do them, too*". (Romans 1:24-32 NLT)

Kill Anyone who Approaches the Tabernacle "*For the LORD had said to Moses, 'Exempt the tribe of Levi from the census; do not include them when you count the rest of the Israelites. You must put the Levites in charge of the Tabernacle of the Covenant, along with its furnishings and equipment. They must carry the Tabernacle and its equipment as you travel, and they must care for it and camp around it. Whenever the Tabernacle is moved, the Levites will take it down and set it up again. Anyone else who goes too near the Tabernacle will be executed.*" (Numbers 1:48-51 NLT)

Kill People for Working on the Sabbath "*The LORD then gave these further instructions to Moses: 'Tell the people of Israel to keep my Sabbath day, for the Sabbath is a sign of the covenant between me and you forever. It helps you to remember that I am the LORD, who makes you holy. Yes, keep the Sabbath day, for it is holy. Anyone who desecrates it must die; anyone who works on that day will be cut off from the community. Work six days only, but the seventh day must be a day of total rest. I repeat: Because the LORD considers it a holy day, anyone who works on the Sabbath must be put to death.*" (Exodus 31:12-15 NLT)

2) God's Murders for Stupid Reasons:

Kill Brats "*From there Elisha went up to Bethel. While he was on his way, some small boys came out of the city and jeered at him. 'Go up baldhead,' they shouted, 'go up baldhead!' The prophet turned and saw them, and he cursed them in the name of the Lord. Then two shebears came out of the woods and tore forty two of the children to pieces*". (2 Kings 2:23-24 NAB)

God Kills the Curious "*And he smote of the men of Beth-shemesh, because they had looked into the ark of Jehovah, he smote of the people seventy men, `and' fifty thousand men; and the people mourned, because Jehovah had smitten the people with a great slaughter. And the men of Beth-shemesh said, Who is able to stand before Jehovah, this holy God? and to whom shall he go up from us?*" (1 Samuel 6:19-20 ASV)

Killed by a Lion "*Meanwhile, the LORD instructed one of the group of prophets to say to another man, "Strike me!" But the man refused to strike the prophet. Then the prophet told him, "Because you have not obeyed the voice of the LORD, a lion will kill you as soon as you leave me." And sure enough, when he had gone, a lion attacked and killed him.*" (1 Kings 20:35-36 NLT)

Killing the Good Samaritan "*The ark of God was placed on a new cart and taken away from the house of Abinadab on the hill. Uzzah and Ahio, sons of Abinadab guided the cart, with Ahio walking before it, while David and all the Israelites made merry before the Lord with all their strength, with singing and with citharas, harps, tambourines, sistrums, and cymbals. When they came to the threshing floor of Nodan, Uzzah reached out his hand to the ark of God to steady it, for the oxen were making it tip. But the Lord was angry with Uzzah; God struck him on that spot, and he died there before God.*" (2 Samuel 6:3-7 NAB)

3) Murdering Children

Kill Sons of Sinners "*Make ready to slaughter his sons for the guilt of their fathers; Lest they rise and posses the earth, and fill the breadth of the world with tyrants.*" (Isaiah 14:21 NAB)

God Will Kill Children "*The glory of Israel will fly away like a bird, for your children will die at birth or perish in the womb or never even be conceived. Even if your children do survive to grow up, I will take them from you. It will be a terrible day when I turn away and leave you alone. I have watched Israel become as beautiful and pleasant as Tyre. But now Israel will bring out her children to be slaughtered.*" O LORD, what should I request for your people? I will ask for wombs that don't give birth and breasts that give no milk. The LORD says, "All their wickedness began at Gilgal; there I began to hate them. I will drive them from my land because of their evil actions. I will love them no more because all their leaders are rebels. The people of Israel are stricken. Their roots are dried up; they will bear no more fruit. And if they give birth, I will slaughter their beloved children.*" (Hosea 9:11-16 NLT)

Kill Men, Women, and Children "*Then I heard the LORD say to the other men, "Follow him through the city and kill everyone whose forehead is not marked. Show no mercy; have no pity! Kill them all – old and young, girls and women and little children. But do not touch anyone with the mark. Begin your task right here at the Temple." So they began by killing the seventy leaders. "Defile the Temple!" the LORD commanded. "Fill its* *courtyards with the bodies of those you kill! Go!" So they went throughout the city and did as they were told."* (Ezekiel 9:5-7 NLT)

God Kills all the First Born of Egypt *And at midnight the LORD killed all the firstborn sons in the land of Egypt, from the firstborn son of Pharaoh, who sat on the throne, to the firstborn son of the captive in the dungeon. Even the firstborn of their livestock were killed. Pharaoh and his officials and all the people of Egypt woke up during the night, and loud wailing was heard throughout the land of Egypt. There was not a single house where someone had not died.* (Exodus 12:29-30 NLT)

Kill Old Men and Young Women *"You are my battle-ax and sword," says the LORD. "With you I will shatter nations and destroy many kingdoms. With you I will shatter armies, destroying the horse and rider, the chariot and charioteer. With you I will shatter men and women, old people and children, young men and maidens. With you I will shatter shepherds and flocks, farmers and oxen, captains and rulers. As you watch, I will repay Babylon and the people of Babylonia for all the wrong they have done to my people in Jerusalem," says the LORD. "Look, O mighty mountain, destroyer of the earth! I am your enemy," says the LORD. "I will raise my fist against you, to roll you down from the heights. When I am finished, you will be nothing but a heap of rubble. You will be desolate forever. Even your stones will never again be used for building. You will be completely wiped out," says the LORD.* (Jeremiah 51:20-26). (Note that after God promises the Israelites a victory against Babylon, the Israelites actually get their butts kicked by them in the next chapter. So much for an all-knowing and all-powerful God.)

God Will Kill the Children of Sinners *"If even then you remain hostile toward me and refuse to obey, I will inflict you with seven more disasters for your sins. I will release wild animals that will kill your children and destroy your cattle, so your numbers will dwindle and your roads will be deserted."* (Leviticus 26:21-22 NLT)

More Rape and Baby Killing *"Anyone who is captured will be run through with a sword. Their little children will be dashed to death right before their eyes. Their homes will be sacked and their wives raped by the attacking hordes. For I will stir up the Medes against Babylon, and no amount of silver or gold will buy them off. The attacking armies will shoot down the young people with arrows. They will have no mercy on helpless babies and will show no compassion for the children."* (Isaiah 13:15-18 NLT)

4) Miscellaneous Murders

More of Samson's Murders (The Lord saves Sampson from standing trial for 30 murders and arson by allowing him to kill 1000 more men.) *"When he reached Lehi, and the Philistines came shouting to meet him, the spirit of the Lord came upon him: the ropes around his arms become as flax that is consumed by fire and the bonds melted away from his hands. Near him was the fresh jawbone of an ass; he reached out, grasped it, and with it killed a thousand men."* (Judges 15:14-15 NAB)

Peter Kills Two People *"There was also a man named Ananias who, with his wife, Sapphira, sold some property. He brought part of the money to the apostles, but he claimed it was the full amount. His wife had agreed to this deception. Then Peter said, Ananias, why has Satan filled your heart? You lied to the Holy Spirit, and you kept some of the money for yourself. The property was yours to sell or not sell, as you wished. And after selling it, the money was yours to give away. How could you do a thing like this? You weren't lying to us but to God." As soon as Ananias heard these words, he fell to the floor and died. Everyone who heard about it was terrified. Then some young men wrapped him in a sheet and took him out and buried him. About three hours later his* *wife came in, not knowing what had happened. Peter asked her, "Was this the price you and your husband received for your land?" "Yes," she replied, "that was the price." And Peter said, "How could the two of you even think of doing a thing like this – conspiring together to test the Spirit of the Lord? Just outside that door are the young men who buried your husband, and they will carry you out, too." Instantly, she fell to the floor and died. When the young men came in and saw that she was dead, they carried her out and buried her beside her husband. Great fear gripped the entire church and all others who heard what had happened."* (Acts 5:1-11 NLT)

Mass Murder *"This is what the Lord of hosts has to say: 'I will punish what Amalek did to Israel when he barred his way as he was coming up from Egypt. Go, now, attack Amalek, and deal with him and all that he has under the ban. Do not spare him, but kill men and women, children and infants, oxen and sheep, camels and asses' "* (1 Samuel 15:2-3 NAB)

You Have to Kill *"Cursed be he who does the Lords work remissly, cursed he who holds back his sword from blood".* (Jeremiah 48:10 NAB)

The Danites Kill the Next Town *"But the territory of the Danites was too small for them; so the Danites marched up and attacked Leshem, which they captured and put to the sword. Once they had taken possession of Lesham, they renamed the settlement after their ancestor Dan."* (Joshua 19:47 NAB)

God Kills Some More *Then the LORD said to me, "Even if Moses and Samuel stood before me pleading for these people, I wouldn't help them. Away with them! Get them out of my sight! And if they say to you, 'But where can we go?' tell them, 'This is what the LORD says: Those who are destined for death, to death; those who are destined for war, to war; those who are destined for famine, to famine; those who are destined for captivity, to captivity.' "I will send four kinds of destroyers against them," says the LORD. "I will send the sword to kill, the dogs to drag away, the vultures to devour, and the wild animals to finish up what is left. Because of the wicked things Manasseh son of Hezekiah, king of Judah, did in Jerusalem, I will make my people an object of horror to all the kingdoms of the earth."* (Jeremiah 15:1-4 NLT)

God Promises More Killing *"I will make Mount Seir utterly desolate, killing off all who try to escape and any who return. I will fill your mountains with the dead. Your hills, your valleys, and your streams will be filled with people slaughtered by the sword. I will make you desolate forever. Your cities will never be rebuilt. Then you will know that I am the LORD."* (Ezekiel 35:7-9 NLT)

The Angel of Death *"My angel will go before you and bring you to the Amorites, Hittites, Perizzites, Canaanites, Hivites, and Jebusites; and I will wipe them out."* (Exodus 23:23 NAB)

Destruction of Ai *Then the LORD said to Joshua, "Do not be afraid or discouraged. Take the entire army and attack Ai, for I have given to you the king of Ai, his people, his city, and his land. You will destroy them as you destroyed Jericho and its king. But this time you may keep the captured goods and the cattle for yourselves. Set an ambush behind the city." So Joshua and the army of Israel set out to attack Ai. Joshua chose thirty thousand fighting men and sent them out at night with these orders: "Hide in ambush close behind the city and be ready for action. When our main army attacks, the men of Ai will come out to fight as they did before, and we will run away from them. We will let them chase us until they have all left the city. For they will say, 'The Israelites are running away from us as they did before.' Then you will jump up from your ambush and* take possession of the city, for the LORD your God will give it to you. Set the city on fire, as the LORD has commanded. You have your orders." So they left that night and lay in ambush between Bethel and the west side of Ai. But Joshua remained among the people in the camp that night."

"Early the next morning Joshua roused his men and started toward Ai, accompanied by the leaders of Israel. They camped on the north side of Ai, with a valley between them and the city. That night Joshua sent five thousand men to lie in ambush between Bethel and Ai, on the west side of the city. So they stationed the main army north of the city and the ambush west of the city. Joshua himself spent that night in the valley. When the king of Ai saw the Israelites across the valley, he and all his army hurriedly went out early the next morning and attacked the Israelites at a place overlooking the Jordan Valley. But he didn't realize there was an ambush behind the city. Joshua and the Israelite army fled toward the wilderness as though they were badly beaten, and all the men in the city were called out to chase after them. In this way, they were lured away from the city. There was not a man left in Ai or Bethel who did not chase after the Israelites, and the city was left wide open."

"Then the LORD said to Joshua, "Point your spear toward Ai, for I will give you the city." Joshua did as he was commanded. As soon as Joshua gave the signal, the men in ambush jumped up and poured into the city. They quickly captured it and set it on fire. When the men of Ai looked behind them, smoke from the city was filling the sky, and they had nowhere to go. For the Israelites who had fled in the direction of the wilderness now turned on their pursuers. When Joshua and the other Israelites saw that the ambush had succeeded and that smoke was rising from the city, they turned and attacked the men of Ai. Then the Israelites who were inside the city came out and started killing the enemy from the rear. So the men of Ai were caught in a trap, and all of them died. Not a single person survived or escaped. Only the king of Ai was taken alive and brought to Joshua."

"When the Israelite army finished killing all the men outside the city, they went back and finished off everyone inside. So the entire population of Ai was wiped out that day – twelve thousand in all. For Joshua kept holding out his spear until everyone who had lived in Ai was completely destroyed. Only the cattle and the treasures of the city were not destroyed, for the Israelites kept these for themselves, as the LORD had commanded Joshua. So Ai became a permanent mound of ruins, desolate to this very day. Joshua hung the king of Ai on a tree and left him there until evening. At sunset the Israelites took down the body and threw it in front of the city gate. They piled a great heap of stones over him that can still be seen today." (Joshua 8:1-29 NLT)

Killing at Jericho "When the people heard the sound of the horns, they shouted as loud as they could. Suddenly, the walls of Jericho collapsed, and the Israelites charged straight into the city from every side and captured it. They completely destroyed everything in it – men and women, young and old, cattle, sheep, donkeys – everything." (Joshua 6:20-21 NLT)

God Kills an Extended Family "You have done more evil than all who lived before you. You have made other gods and have made me furious with your gold calves. And since you have turned your back on me, I will bring disaster on your dynasty and kill all your sons, slave or free alike. I will burn up your royal dynasty as one burns up trash until it is all gone. I, the LORD, vow that the members of your family who die in the city will be eaten by dogs, and those who die in the field will be eaten by vultures.'" Then Ahijah said to Jeroboam's wife, "Go on home, and when you enter the city, the child will die. All Israel will mourn for him and bury him. He is the only member of your family who will *have a proper burial, for this child is the only good thing that the LORD, the God of Israel, sees in the entire family of Jeroboam. And the LORD will raise up a king over Israel who will destroy the family of Jeroboam. This will happen today, even now! Then the LORD will shake Israel like a reed whipped about in a stream. He will uproot the people of Israel from this good land that he gave their ancestors and will scatter them beyond the Euphrates River, for they have angered the LORD by worshiping Asherah poles. He will abandon Israel because Jeroboam sinned and made all of Israel sin along with him."* (1 Kings 14:9-16 NLT)

Mass Murder *"The men of Israel withdrew through the territory of the Benjaminites, putting to the sword the inhabitants of the city, the livestock, and all they chanced upon. Moreover they destroyed by fire all the cities they came upon."* (Judges 20:48 NAB)

The Angel of Death *"That night the angel of the Lord went forth and struck down one hundred and eighty five thousand men in the Assyrian camp. Early the next morning, there they were, all the corpuses of the dead."* (2 Kings 19:35 NAB)

Kill Your Neighbours (Moses) *stood at the entrance to the camp and shouted, "All of you who are on the LORD's side, come over here and join me." And all the Levites came. He told them, "This is what the LORD, the God of Israel, says: Strap on your swords! Go back and forth from one end of the camp to the other, killing even your brothers, friends, and neighbours." The Levites obeyed Moses, and about three thousand people died that day. Then Moses told the Levites, "Today you have been ordained for the service of the LORD, for you obeyed him even though it meant killing your own sons and brothers. Because of this, he will now give you a great blessing."* (Exodus 32:26-29 NLT)

Kill the Family of Sinners *"And Joshua said to Achan, My son, give, I pray thee, glory to the LORD God of Israel, and make confession to him; and tell me now what thou hast done, hide it not from me. And Achan answered Joshua, and said, Indeed I have sinned against the LORD God of Israel, and thus and thus have I done. When I saw among the spoils a goodly Babylonish garment, and two hundred shekels of silver, and a wedge of gold of fifty shekels weight, then I coveted them, and took them, and behold, they are hid in the earth in the midst of my tent, and the silver under it." [Note that the sin is not looting, but failing to give the loot to the treasury of the Lord.] "So Joshua sent messengers, and they ran to the tent, and behold, it was hid in his tent, and the silver under it. And they took them from the midst of the tent, and brought them to Joshua, and to all the children of Israel, and laid them out before the LORD. And Joshua, and all Israel with him, took Achan the son of Zerah, and the silver, and the garment, and the wedge of gold, and his sons, and his daughters, and his oxen, and his asses, and his sheep, and his tent, and all that he had: and they brought them to the valley of Achor. And Joshua said, why hast thou troubled us? the LORD shall trouble thee this day. And all Israel stoned him with stones, and burned them with fire, after they had stoned them with stones. And they raised over him a great heap of stones to this day. So the LORD turned from the fierceness of his anger: wherefore the name of that place was called the valley of Achor to this day."* (Joshua 7:19-26 Webster's Bible)

Kill Followers of Other Religions *"While the Israelites were camped at Acacia, some of the men defiled themselves by sleeping with the local Moabite women. These women invited them to attend sacrifices to their gods, and soon the Israelites were feasting with them and worshiping the gods of Moab. Before long Israel was joining in the worship of Baal of Peor, causing the LORD's anger to blaze against his people. The LORD issued the following command to Moses: "Seize all the ringleaders and execute them before the LORD in broad daylight, so his fierce anger will turn away from the people of Israel." So Moses ordered Israel's judges to execute everyone who had joined in worshiping Baal of*

Peor. Just then one of the Israelite men brought a Midianite woman into the camp, right before the eyes of Moses and all the people, as they were weeping at the entrance of the Tabernacle. When Phinehas son of Eleazar and grandson of Aaron the priest saw this, he jumped up and left the assembly. Then he took a spear and rushed after the man into his tent. Phinehas thrust the spear all the way through the man's body and into the woman's stomach. So the plague against the Israelites was stopped, but not before 24,000 people had died." (Numbers 25:1-9 NLT)

Murder "*At the customary time for offering the evening sacrifice, Elijah the prophet walked up to the altar and prayed, "O LORD, God of Abraham, Isaac, and Jacob, prove today that you are God in Israel and that I am your servant. Prove that I have done all this at your command. O LORD, answer me! Answer me so these people will know that you, O LORD, are God and that you have brought them back to yourself." Immediately the fire of the LORD flashed down from heaven and burned up the young bull, the wood, the stones, and the dust. It even licked up all the water in the ditch! And when the people saw it, they fell on their faces and cried out, "The LORD is God! The LORD is God!" Then Elijah commanded, "Seize all the prophets of Baal. Don't let a single one escape!" So the people seized them all, and Elijah took them down to the Kishon Valley and killed them there.*" (1 Kings 18:36-40 NLT)

Kill All of Babylon "*Go up, my warriors, against the land of Merathaim and against the people of Pekod. Yes, march against Babylon, the land of rebels, a land that I will judge! Pursue, kill, and completely destroy them, as I have commanded you,*" says the LORD. "*Let the battle cry be heard in the land, a shout of great destruction*". (Jeremiah 50:21-22 NLT)

Micah Kills a Whole Town "*Then, with Micah's idols and his priest, the men of Dan came to the town of Laish, whose people were peaceful and secure. They attacked and killed all the people and burned the town to the ground. There was no one to rescue the residents of the town, for they lived a great distance from Sidon and had no allies nearby. This happened in the valley near Beth-rehob. Then the people of the tribe of Dan rebuilt the town and lived there. They renamed the town Dan after their ancestor, Israel's son, but it had originally been called Laish.*" (Judges 18:27-29 NLT)

The Alleged 10 Commandments

The 10 commandments come to us from Exodus 20:1-17. Here is the verse:

And God spoke all these words, saying: "*I am the Lord your God, who brought you out of the land of Egypt, out of the house of bondage.*

1. *You shall have no other gods before me.*
2. *You shall not make for yourself any carved image, or any likeness of anything that is in heaven above, or that is in the earth beneath, or that is in the water under the earth; you shall not bow down to them nor serve them. For I, the Lord your God, am a jealous God, visiting the iniquity of the fathers on the children to the third and fourth generations of those who hate me, but showing mercy to thousands, to those who love Me and keep My commandments.*
3. *You shall not take the name of the Lord your God in vain, for the Lord will not hold him guiltless who takes His name in vain.*
4. *Remember the Sabbath day, to keep it holy. Six days you shall labor and do all your work, but the seventh day is the Sabbath of the Lord your God. In it you*

shall do no work: you, nor your son, nor your daughter, nor your manservant, nor your maidservant, nor your cattle, nor your stranger who is within your gates. For in six days the Lord made the heavens and the earth, the sea, and all that is in them, and rested the seventh day. Therefore the Lord blessed the Sabbath day and hallowed it.

5. *Honor your father and your mother, that your days may be long upon the land which the Lord your God is giving you.*
6. *You shall not murder.*
7. *You shall not commit adultery.*
8. *You shall not steal.*
9. *You shall not bear false witness against your neighbor.*
10. *You shall not covet your neighbor's house; you shall not covet your neighbor's wife, nor his manservant, nor his maidservant, nor his ox, nor his donkey, nor anything that is your neighbor's."*

The above 10 commandments need no explanation. They mean exactly what they are saying. But this is NOT what is followed by the Lord God, they are followed by the Lords god.

Plausible Deniability: Is This The True Word Of God?

Here are the top 10 ways of burying your head in the sand"
10 - You vigorously deny the existence of thousands of gods claimed by other religions, but feel outraged when someone denies the existence of yours.
9 - You feel insulted and "dehumanized" when scientists say that people evolved from other life forms, but you have no problem with the Biblical claim that we were created from dirt.
8 - You laugh at polytheists, but you have no problem believing in a Triune God.
7 - Your face turns purple when you hear of the "atrocities" attributed to Allah, but you don't even flinch when hearing about how God/Jehovah slaughtered all the babies of Egypt in "Exodus" and ordered the elimination of entire ethnic groups in "Joshua" including women, children, and trees!
6 - You laugh at Hindu beliefs that deify humans, and Greek claims about gods sleeping with women, but you have no problem believing that the Holy Spirit impregnated Mary, who then gave birth to a man-god who got killed, came back to life and then ascended into the sky.
5 - You are willing to spend your life looking for little loopholes in the scientifically established age of Earth (few billion years), but you find nothing wrong with believing dates recorded by Bronze Age tribesmen sitting in their tents and guessing that Earth is a few generations old.
4 - You believe that the entire population of this planet with the exception of those who share your beliefs -- though excluding those in all rival sects - will spend Eternity in an infinite Hell of Suffering. And yet consider your religion the most "tolerant" and "loving."
3 - While modern science, history, geology, biology, and physics have failed to convince you otherwise, some idiot rolling around on the floor speaking in "tongues" may be all the evidence you need to "prove" Christianity.
2 - You define 0.01% as a "high success rate" when it comes to answered prayers. You consider that to be evidence that prayer works. And you think that the remaining 99.99% FAILURE was simply the will of God.
1 - You actually know a lot less than many atheists and agnostics do about the Bible, Christianity, and church history - but still call yourself a Christian.

Who Is Your True God?

Are you saying stop, stop, enough, enough yet? Whichever way you choose to try to paint this picture, it cannot be anything but another "god" who threatens, curses, kills indiscriminately, imposes judgments, is jealous, and protective of his ego. He demands obedience and clearly issues warnings that he is the almighty powerful god demanding servitude. He uses his powers to maintain dominance. Interestingly enough, he chooses a chronology of representatives who he "speaks to, and through" not in other places on his Old Earth, but only with one place and with his "chosen people" that he himself persecutes, maims, kills and reaps destruction upon, keeping them in fear and toil. Yet he rewards the "righteous" who serve his bidding. And worst of all, this god has no place for women as they are the root of evil and sin.

If you can read through this epic saga for what it presents over and over, it is a picture of a mad ruler with special powers over life and death that sets up his kingdom. That was certainly the picture of the gods of Sumeria. First he must conquer his followers by fear. Then he sets up the administrative, commercial, sociological, moral and ethic regulations. He imposes acts and statutes and then a police force of religious chosen ones, plus ways to police, control and collect dues. Of course the method of collecting revenues is vital to this kingdom. He builds his power to maintain and execute dominion, go to war, and protect the kingdom. It is a place that his chosen ones allow a dogmatic deliverance for the ego of those ruling. Why? Because they represent a just god of love who has just commandments which he is willing to waive and launch death and destruction if they do not behave. But if they do behave, the chosen ones can give these poor sinful, souls ridden with sin a break—if and only if they behold, worship and serve.

This particular model is one that the Vatican has held to, and it is a model that has proliferated within nations and within major corporations. It makes humans a commercial product. The Vatican, and others have created the bibles as the code--the laws of their god that they attach to GOD inferring it is the "word of God". In truth this is a commercial, moral and military model that has been in place for centuries, built specifically for the indulgence and dominion of the few. And who was it that set it up? Was it really a God who delivered this tale? Or perhaps it was, and is, just mouthpieces for god? And if you accept this "word" as your overlay of life, you accept that code in your beliefs and behaviour, carrying it forward into your own bloodlines. You accept that "Word" just like with the Strawman overlay.

And although there is wisdom in the Psalms and some of the writings, it is effectively lip service from a god who does not engage in this himself, nor do his chosen ones, particularly in support and practice. we have already seen that these "chosen ones" on top are followers of cults and Satanism. For they also kill and destroy indiscriminately those who are deemed sinners and non-believers. The most gruelling record of this was the Inquisition. Yet there is no doubt there are pieces of wisdom as part of this epic story that conveys the half truths. It is what believers cling to, support and preach, completely overlooking the explicit fact within the vast majority of these writings that they serve a contrived god's will. The only conclusion one can really make is that something is amiss here and those billions of followers are really believing in another god created by man, not the true God.

The Stories As Half Truth

So ask yourself this: How does this god, as he is portrayed in the bibles, testaments, gospels, or any other religious proclamations of god's will really, really deep down vibrate with your own truth? Do you believe in this faith because you are simply driven to trust it regardless of science, or history, or anything? Do you simply accept the GOD codes blindly and overlook the parts that don't make sense? it is that philosophy that captured you through the Strawman.

If one attempts to make any sense to this whole mythology of the god of dominion, it becomes apparent that there are certain truths in the old stories, regardless of how scientifically or religiously absurd parts may seem. The story is really that; a story of an Old Earth that was subject to one god who required obedience, who demanded worship, who had a lot of rules to police, and who was very vengeful when people did not obey. And he had a vendetta of sin to deal with. And he obviously favoured Priests and Churches as his chosen ones to administer the dominion.

If this is such a portrayal of a demanding and vengeful god who seeks obedience from the sinner, how did this myth become such an epic for billions to follow and believe? The answer resides in first, the fact that within our DNA is the quest for our God Self and a simple knowing that there is a God, a Creator of all that is. It can't be explained, it just is. Falling in love with another can't be explained, it just is, and that's the end to the discussion. The fact that the myth has a partial truth in it that rings with the heart appears to be enough to satisfy this quest of Self thus overriding all untruths. For the assumption is if there is one truth, then so must all else be true. That stark truth is that *you want to* believe in the Christ Consciousness, which of course is a reflection of God even though it is not necessarily the one portrayed in this myth. It is the one already resident in you. So the truth part far outweighs the untruth and it is all simply "believed" with faith and trust because the vast majority of humanity does crave peace and love and joy.

But what if the part that is not truth is about the Son of God as he was one of many—us all? What if sin does not really exist at all, only love that cannot judge? What if the story line deletes the vengeance and need to worship and obey? What if the fear of obedience is not part of this? What if the part about Christ's birth, ascension and special powers are true and available to all. What if these demanding gods and God references are substituted by the true part of God—You? What if a new Genesis is indeed happening during these times of disclosure about religion and commerce around the planet?

The biblical proliferation that rules the beliefs of billions of people holds them captive in some way to some truth that they gleam out of the mythology. And that appears to be enough. This is changing rapidly now as this other part, the bit about the vengeful, jealous, dominion seeking god just does not resonate with the expanding hearts of humanity. It is because we are in a time when the truth is surfacing and it is time to change. It is a time when the fraction of truth resident in the bibles does not outweigh the lies any more. It is a time when the untruth has to be replaced completely. So the time to simply accept that which feels amiss about a false God and these gods is over. This feeling is growing stronger and stronger as the draw to a New Genesis of New Earth is prompted into manifestation by the Christ Consciousness.

It's Something You Cannot Explain

There is a quote in the movie *The Matrix* that applies perfectly to our present time about something being "amiss". It comes when Morpheus is talking to Neo for the first time. Morpheus says:

"I imagine right now you feel a bit like Alice, tumbling down a rabbit hole. You have the look of a man who accepts what he sees expecting never to wake up. You're here

because you know something that you can't explain, but you feel it. There is something wrong with the world. You don't know what it is, but it is there, like a splinter in your mind, driving you mad. It is this feeling that has brought you to me. Do you know what I'm talking about?"

Neo then replies with: *"The Matrix"*. Then Morpheus goes on:

"Do you want to know what it is? The matrix is everywhere, it is all around us. Even now in this very room. You can see it when you look out your window, or turn on your television set. You can feel it when you go to work, when you go to church, when you pay your taxes. It is the wool that has been pulled over your eyes to blind you from the truth. You are a slave Neo like everyone else. You were born into a prison that you cannot see, that you cannot smell, or taste or touch. A prison for your mind. Unfortunately no one can be told what the Matrix is. You have to see it for yourself. This is your last chance. After this, there is no turning back. Take the blue pill, the story ends, you wake up in your bed and believe whatever you want to believe. Take the red pill, you will stay in wonderland, and I will show you how deep the rabbit hole goes. Remember, what I am offering is the truth, nothing more. Follow me."

This book is written because we have entered a time where these blue and red pills are before everyone, not just Neo. It is because much of what we live, what we are told by the false gods, and what we accept as a belief is not *quite* right. And when all is said and done, it is the great majority that is *not quite right.* Now I won't pretend to be Morpheus but I will say that millions of people are saying the same thing because something is amiss with them—and it is not just religions. I am the bearer of the news because I, like millions who can't really put a handle on what is wrong, know what is right, and have felt it is time to take the red pill and speak.

The difference here is that the pills are represented by an action of thought, word, deed which requires a choice. It is the ascension trip that Jesus allegedly took to evolve the hard way.

"This is your last chance. After this, there is no turning back. Take the blue pill, the story ends, you wake up in your bed and believe whatever you want to believe. Take the red pill, you will stay in wonderland, and I will show you how deep the rabbit hole goes. Remember, what I am offering is the truth, nothing more. Follow me."

Where the blue pill represented the illusion of life under the deception of the financial and religious systems, it is simply be and believe as you are.   You simply stay in that life which is this old Earth, hold on to your beliefs and work in the PLANET EARTH according to the imposed rules. You say this is all just BS wave goodbye to God and say yes gods, I am content to serve you through the Laws of GOD.

But if you take a red pill and then a new world of truth and peace open to you as it takes you into a magical wonderland of Spiritual and Commercial Sovereignty

What is a bit different here is that the depth of the rabbit hole is going to be shown to all during a special time—like Neo's training and revelation of the truth. Of course it helps if you are awake to see the new movie. Like Neo's awakening it is a time that precedes the boarding of the train and his transformation. It is a time when a new truth is presented to all equally so they understand that there is a choice and what it is. And this is the truth of God, the real one.

Now in the *Matrix* movie, Neo could take the blue pill and just go back into his dream of life in Old Earth. But this time it is not so because if you haven't picked this up yet, you should. That is the Old Earth is in a state of deterioration financially and spiritually; bankrupt one would say. And humanity, through the gods and self proclaimed agents of God who have proven to be the masters of self destruction, may not be who you want to serve anymore.

There actually is a story to this and the time of rapid disintegration that is now evident is designed to be that way as the old energy gives way to the new. So if you think you can continue to suck up those blue pills and continue your life the way you are doing now then this may be the real fantasy.

The other dream with the red pill is the one that is kicking in as the gods (not Satan) effectively meet their Waterloo. The other dream, the new revelation, where Neo learns he is "the One" is to learn that we are all "the Ones". It is where DNA awakens, the truth comes out as to what humans really are as sentient expressions of divinity, and the dream becomes the reality. It is what the red pill, and the train ticket are all about.

So the big question is: How can you as a mere mortal gobbling these blue pills ever understand or believe in this other dream of a New Earth? Well, as we shall see in the next Parts of this book, you need to resign from PLANET EARTH and stop taking their prescription of pills.

How do you stop taking the pills? Take responsibility for another belief of this fellow Christ that resonates with your own "truth" and stop being a mouthpiece for others who claim they know.

What is this new belief surrounding Christ? It is detailed in a book called the **Aquarian Gospel** channelled and written by **Levi Dowling** at the turn of the last century. For a free full version of your own book, go to the site: **www.sacred-texts.com/chr/agjc/agjc002.htm.** It is also summarized in the book **PLANET EARTH INC** by **Ed Rychkun found at www.edrychkun.com.**

Later in this book, we will summarize these beliefs to see how close they are to the current evolution of the Christ Consciousness that is overcoming the planet.

21

THE LESSONS OF KNOWING WHO YOU ARE

As we close this section on the lessons of history, one must ponder and ask what is the point of it. The main point is to show that the interpretation of history is a great variable, depending upon the point of perception and beliefs of the individual; and in the end irrelevant. What is dark or evil to one may be the opposite to another. All residents of

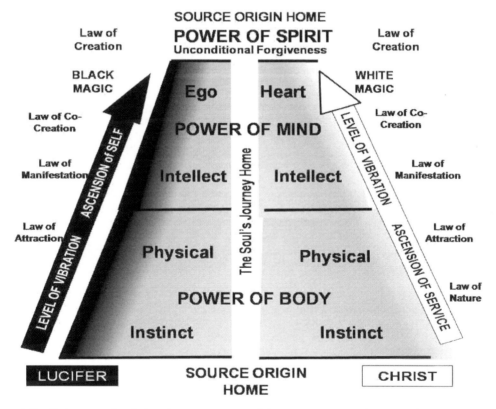

Planet Earth have a Soul that is on a personal journey to experience and express choices through the vessel of a mind and body. It is potentially a golden path Home where in the end, all of the material presented becomes irrelevant because there is no black or white or gray; there is just the golden light from what we are all made. The Soul's journey is one of choosing how to engage in its expression as an Earthling. And so it evolves through three levels to attain and express itself through the power of the body, mind, and spirit. As we have seen in the Soul's entry to Planet Earth to accept the vessel, it has many commercial and spiritual attachments to it that it inherits by blood or employment in PLANET EARTH. It must simply work its way through this to get back Home to its Source, working out that which it has not yet worked out. It cannot, however, work it out by choice without the awareness of a choice. But in the end when the Power of Spirit is reached, through a portal to Home within the belief system, the doorway marked unconditional forgiveness must be opened by the individual self. Here the judgements and differences simply fall away into nothing.

Know Thy Self

So what are you? So far, as a man or woman, your physical vessel have been held capitve in an illusionary overlay called a Strawman. In truth, you are a divine vessel of expression. So far, this has also held your Soul captive through the belief systems that have been accepted as truth. In truth, you are divine being of light, part of the totality of the consiouness called God. So far, you have engaged your life in separation, conflict, fear and drama as your way home. In truth, you are a divine expression of peace and love.

It is your, and everyone else's personal journey to know this. And when you do, your life changes. We now live in a unique time which has been labelled as the End Time where the earthling is getting some cosmic assistance on knowing this and implementing the appropriate deeds of peace and love into what is being born as New Earth.

If you have made it this far, congratulations! You would have to have risen above the new presentation about the dark and the light, about evil and good, about Lucifer and Christ. The bad guys are attempting to make a better world for their slaves, and the good guys are attempting to free themselves from themselves and what they have succumbed to believe. Who will win? That is what we will delve into now.

And so we met the Elite Bloodlines and learned about their plan for the Empire; to launch dominion over Planet Earth and the Earthling who have chosen to be there. We have seen how that conquest has been implemented through the collaboration of dynasties by way of money and religion. And we have had a taste for how their mission has been accomplished through the control over religions and nations through fictional entities which are corporations. And we have looked at the details of how it is all executed.

If you have arrived here, you are seeing a different truth from what has been taught about Religion and Commerce. What we have seen is that there is indeed a different picture of bad and good. Why? Because there are always different ways of looking at bad or good called perception and there are as many of these as there are people. And so we have attempted to present both sides. We have looked at a new historical viewpoint over the last 5000 years of recorded history. What is different about this version is that it is not taught in schools, nor is it accepted as truth. This "new truth" is changing dramatically and this is what the next huge lesson is about for it would seem that the march to dominion and conquest has been interrupted and the greatest business plan of all-that of the New World Order-is in disarray.

At around the turn of the century, a new truth that had been simmering over the last 50 years started to come to a boil. A new version of religion and commerce was boiling out thanks to the Internet and a mass shifting of conscious awareness that many things were not right began to manifest as mass disclosure. There is one stark explanation that has to do with the End Times. How else could such a mass of people that are being led by no one human or movement converge on the same beliefs? Up to the end of the century to think that mass consciousness could be influenced by cosmic or divine forces would have been a pretty big joke.

Pwe will now bring you into a new history that is unfolding as we entered the turn of the Century. It is not possible to go into all the details of how and why this change is occurring but all one needs to do is to look at the number of monumental disclosures and the demands for transparency have occurred in the last 12 years. We will now look at where we are in our evolution as a civilization since the turn of the Century. Instead of looking at the New World Order as a conspiracy, let us look at what is unfolding around humanity as a New Order of the Ages. There is no doubt that the business plan of PLANET EARTH Inc has had some adjustments and may be still infused into our reality one way or another. It truly depends upon the notion that "the meek shall inherit the earth". It would seem that the meek are indeed having something to say about what has happened; and would believe it is in the name of love and peace?

What has occurred is the new alternative to the old ways is evolving rapidly. The evolution of a New Earth founded on a new truth and the decision on how this will manifest now appears to be with the Earthling, not with the Elite. How humanity chooses on the acceptance or rejection of the truth with respect to light versus dark will dictate the way the Order unfolds for all. Whether the Earthling is mature enough to leave the parenthood of PLANET EARTH is to be seen in the next years. Dark is the way it has been--fear, slavery, obedience to the rich and strong. The gods have had their fun and they have in retrospect made life for their flock better. Now the flock of Earthlings may be ready to reach for Light as the way it could be where love, freedom, peace and sovereignty flourishes. Recall the last picture n the journey of the Soul. The convergence of dark and light is upon Planet Earth. And can you believe that a greater and greater mass of humanity is actually questioning the sanity of the past? And making plans to rise above it? It is when you travel in the golden light in peace and love that you rise above, back, white and gray.

What is occurring, and evolving at an exponential rate is a rejection of the old ways, the kings, the queens, the gods and the establishment that is preoccupied with dominion over others and service to self. Worldwide, there are major shifts going on as more and more humans reject the old ways of sin, conflict, war, and inequality in hierarchies. This reflected in the census that counts "non-religious" at over 1 billion growing exponentially.

Indeed, this may well be the New Order of the Ages. Of course it is up to humanity to choose this as it is up to the individual to choose. That is where it begins.

The point is that many groups as indicated by almost a billion people are rejecting religions and demanding responsibility from leaders and governments. The "jig is up". These leaders and their codes as directed by the gods do not serve them anymore. Similarly, the inequality of kings and queens, of dictators and dynasties, of corporations designed for dominion and greed to serve the few at the expense of the many doe not "fly" any more.   The major shift occurred at the turn of the century with the New Consciousness of the Internet allowing the free exchange of humanity's consciousness like never before.

We need to see that many are now understanding who they are. The new consciousness floods the old consiuouness. There are more Earthlings now than ever before resigning from PLANET EARTH INC. and rejecting their prescriptions of the blue pills of RELIGIOUS ORDER.

It is for you to know there is indeed a new choice building.

One cannot make a choice if one is not aware that there is a choice.

You can be the judge, even though, ironically in the end, there is no judgment, only choice.

22

SOMETHING IS AMISS IN GOD'S LAWS

Since the turn of the century, the new information about the way the world is run by the leaders and governments has come under fire and scrutiny. The Elite bloodlines plan has come into the spotlight, and the way religions are used to dominate spirituality, has increased exponentially. A new truth has emerged because there has been a conscious shifting of awareness in more and more humans that something is amiss with GODS Laws. Something is "not right" and everyone is backed up against a wall of debt and deception. Many say it is fraud and deception, many say it is for the good of others, many say there is nothing wrong. The New Ager's say this is a prophesized time of ascension and the time has come or the meek to inherit the earth. The Old Ager's say it's just more of the same old shit so get used to it. In the end each has to judge and choose but one thing is predictable: The change is in the airwaves--in the mind of Earthlings--in the conscious awareness seeking truth; and that means a prelude for major shifts in religion and commerce.

Now, in the year 2012, the number of "revelations" about corruption and greed, about the dynasties, the kingdoms, the power hungry, the political system have been staggering. The age of Pisces has indeed been one that the Lucifer strategies of service to self has dominated. But something big is happening on Planet Earth and PLANET EARTH is in the spotlight of scrutiny. The employees of PLANET EARTH are in a mode of revolution. The shift in the last 12 years has been staggering; and it is rapidly coming to a head at an exponential rate.

The importance of this shift in consciousness and world attention cannot be underemphasized. The conundrum of the Ages like none before is in front of the Earthlings.

New World Order Or The New Order Of The Ages?

In the beginning of this book, we brought forward the Latin phrase "*novus ordo seclorum*" appearing on the reverse side of the Great Seal since 1782 and on the back of the US one-dollar bill since 1935, meaning "**New Order of the Ages**" and it only alluding to the beginning of an era where the United States of America is an independent nation-state. This has been often mistranslated by conspiracy theorists as "**New World Order**". And in what has occurred, the ones who run PLANET EARTH have indeed drummed to a business plan that has been written to bring Planet Earth's peoples into one huge Empire of one religion, one currency, one government, all under the jurisdiction of their laws of god. And so it would appear that the business plan is on track despite some major hiccups along the way. Within this business plan is a section of the Biblical Codes about Revelations that postulates a second coming of Christ. And in retrospect, because their version of the story of Christ has been so effective, it is not surprising that a prophesy supported by God would be brought forward to check up on all the sinners to decide who is worthy and who is not. This story of Revelations, Rapture and Armageddon where God and the Son of God check up on the slaves, get rid of Satan and save the worthy, and destroy the unworthy is like a looming control mechanism on consciousness designed to maintain the fear and obedience. It is indeed the silent, invisible "policing force" for the New World Order. And because it was set for the End Times, namely the years coming into 2012, now is the time that this part of the plan has to be implemented. What's really humorous about this story is that the ones spilling this story are the ones that follow Satan and obviously have retained powers that Earthlings are not supposed to know about.

And in retrospect, the plan has been working well in that the Global Elite have indeed captured Nations and Earthlings alike in the ultimate takeover of the Corporation PLANET EARTH. It is certainly true that this plan could mean a better life for many, despite its controls, limitations, and imbalance. In truth, their plan has made a better world for the slaves if you look back in our history. However, it would appear to be a devious plan that reduces the spiritual aspects of the Earthling to bondage that could not mean a better life. Interestingly enough, the vast majority of Earthlings are very much "carnal" and "instinctual" in their ways of life; and most could care less about any supreme plan. All they care about is to eat, breed and protect their bloodlines.

Yet here we are at this decision point called the End Times.

There is a different version of Revelations evolving during this End Time which marks the beginning of the Aquarian Age. It is that underlying tsunami of consciousness shifting which was so well explained in all the Mayan prophesies. That tsunami is growing exponentially now and has the Founders of PLANET EARTH on the defensive so they must now play their cards to execute the final part of their business plan. One could say the time has come to see who the forces choose. This other major force is what has been the Christ Consciousness and coincides with the New Age beliefs. I use New Age for a lack of a better word. As we have seen the New age is common terminology to both "sides" of the plan. We have left you with that new version of the life of Christ to understand exactly what that Christ Consciousness is. It is in fact what can well be the New Order of Ages which is anything but what we have chosen before. It is a different version of order and belief, namely that we are all One, all part of God, and are on the verge of knowing and understanding this clearly. Thus this changes the landscape that eliminates the Elite business plan of the gods and implements the birthright plan of God.

At this point in time, the census would have to be in the billions of people who have attained a internal knowing that something is not right about the system and that something big is about to happen. The consciousness shift is like a huge global marketing plan that morphs itself into the lives of more and more people, faster and faster. The clash is now inevitable. and it is a clash of old ways of fear, conflict, and dominion against love, peace, and divine sovereignty.

Who will win? The drama must be played out and judging by what is happening in the world today with financial and religious crisis everywhere, it can move either way rapidly.

What is paramount is that this new philosophy of love, peace, ad divine sovereignty become the New Order of the Ages. It must be the underlying energy of change and it came into the history through the Christ Consciousness. This changes the story of Armageddon and Revelation to present a totally different picture of the future. So let us begin this Chapter on the Great Shift of Ages

All Bibles And Prophesies Point To Christ As Inspiration

Whichever version of the story of Christ you read, whether through myth, fiction or nonfiction, the life of this man evolves as special. It is he that became the inspiration as it is the goal of human life to evolve toward Spirit. Let us bring back into focus our picture of the Soul's Journey. This is the journey that unfolds over the course of one's lifetime—it is the adventure of moving from time and space to eternity. It is said that Spirit ever reaches into the hearts and minds of humans to urge us to choose the

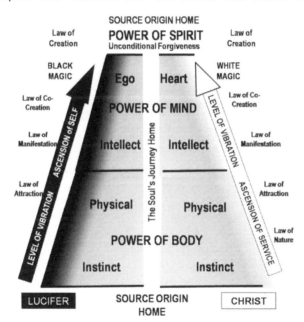

ascension path to unite with the Source of Creation. One way Spirit does this is to incarnate as a human to reveal Spirit's personality to humanity to serve as encouragement to discover and walk the path of Spirit. God or whatever you want to call it has individual the vessel of a human form to show us the way back home if we can see it. The person who fulfilled this role was this one called Jesus who eventually inherited the name Jesus Christ, or in the Aquarian version, Jesus The Christ. And so we have looked at different version of the "truth" surrounding this man. The story that we have brought forward would exemplify more than

anything the path upwards shown in this diagram.

In the versions of the Bibles and other major religious teachings of the mass, the teachings of Jesus have been used as the mainstay to a spiritual belief system of love, peace, and sovereignty. Although riddled with other' distorting history, the new version is now surfacing as a new truth everywhere simply because people are fed up with the untruth of fear, conflict and dominion. These teachings centered around helping people find their own internal source of Spirit. He is said to have lived what he taught. This truth now points to him as the embodiment of love and goodness, peace and understanding. His God-centeredness allowed him to achieve what we consider miracles because he understood the natural laws of the universe and was able to tap into the great power of love to bring healing to people. He practiced meditation and prayer to gain strength to meet the challenges of daily life. He consistently showed love, kindness, patience, gentleness to others and encouraged them to open to the Spirit within themselves. He said, *"The kingdom of Heaven is within."* He lived his life to show us how to find Spirit and what a human personality looks like when he or she is Spirit-centered. He paved the way for us to find God for ourselves.

And so it is said that Jesus' Divine life plan apparently disclosed itself to him over the course of his lifetime. Just as we can open ourselves to our indwelling Spirits to find our own higher purpose, he had to accomplish this during his human lifetime. His story we have presented becomes an inspiring guide to help us achieve this for ourselves through the **thoughts, words, and deeds synchronized with the heart**. Once he fully achieved his own state of "Christ Consciousness" he was able to manifest, co-create and create as well as depict to others his Divine self. His life purpose was two-fold and provides the living link between our Creator-Source and humanity: to show each person how to be God in himself/herself and for himself/herself, and then to embody the Creator and reveal God's love for each person to those who were ready to grow in Spirit.

But is this really truth? The huge New Age movement certainly agrees with this fundamental philosophy. We have looked at the new version and it either rings with you or it doesn't. If you do not want to see it and want some intellectual argument about whether any PhD's checked out, you won't. And if you are happy with things as they are, then that is fine too but perhaps there is more?

But what has become prominent in the last 12 years is indeed the consciousness of a new truth about Christ. If you put truth of Christ in the query box at Amazon.com you get some 16 pages of books and 35,000 results. Google only gives a mere 180 million hits! Because we want to enter this chapter on this topic as being important, we will summarize this Christ fellow's history in this volume because the story we have presented as Aquarian is supporting the prevalent discoveries in the last 12 years.

Before we delve into the two diametrically opposed versions of the Dark and Light plans, it is of interest to recap what has come to light in the last 12 years. What appears to be occurring is that there are two plans; one of PLANET EARTH and the other, a quiet underlying plan of unknown Divine origin as reflecting a consciousness that there is indeed something amiss with "gods" words. The following is presented to recap the new knowing as reflected in the new consciousness.

A Recap: New Version Of Christ's Story

This particular summary that follows is our summary of the ***Aquarian Gospel***, but it reflects a common revelation surfacing around the world.

We see that Christ came to be a Walker of Planet Earth for the purpose of living and showing the Word and the Light of Unconditional love. Upon his incarnation, he brought immediate light and brightness, the vibration of which resonated strongly to draw attention of the many. For this reason as a child he was kept hidden and protected quietly, As a child Jesus already attracted attention as his resonance was strong and of high vibration. Somewhat like the Crystal Children of now, he was especially gifted as was his written purpose to bring the new light as his Divine Plan. The high vibrations and the strength of the love he exuded from his heart drew others like a magnet and because of this interest, the authorities and priests came to know about this but mostly as an oddity not particularly relevant.

At an early age after his spiritually gifted mother and father coached and protected him in such a way as to nurture his special radiance, it was necessary to take him to other lands away from his place of birth so as to allow him to grow his abilities and hide him away until more mature. As his Father was skilled in the arts of Mystery and Alchemy, and his Mother also advanced in Spirit and vibration they knew and followed many of the special ancient wisdom keepers of the Mystery Schools of Egypt. It is here that his growth and knowing was nurtured, well before he could engage in the conflicts of the time. He was trained to understand the ancient wisdoms of the Priesthoods of spiritual knowing of God (the real one). As so a deep wisdom of the truth emerged rapidly. As it was, the Ancients knew of this special Jesus and took custody of him to teach all of their wisdom allowing him to rapidly recall what which he knew but had been slowed due to the incarnation in a lower form. As he carried no karma, he absorbed the knowing and evolved rapidly into his higher senses.

Upon traveling to other highly developed spiritual lands such as India he became a wonder of science reflecting the higher abilities of metaphysics, healing and body control, much as those opening to you now. He became highly developed is the spiritual arts and absorbed the truth like a sponge. Because of these wondrous abilities of the metaphysical realms and his knowledge of the workings of other dimensions, he attained the creator status we have told you of rapidly and had to subdue these when in public places. He turned his attention to the attaining the status of priesthood only in the teachings as he preferred to walk the lands.

Through this time, he met friends and wrote of his knowing as he began to reflect and expand upon the Word as he understood it. Ancient wisdom came forward rapidly and his body began to shift and change. His teaching and healing examples were watched with wonder as they saw the manifestation of ancient wisdom expressed by him. His mentors followed the teachings of the old ways following the spiritual priesthoods Over years he developed to stages that surpassed all they had ever seen.

Unlike your own time where the higher vibration floods the consciousness to encourage easy growth of acceleration of ascension, through the triggering of the divine plan, that was a time of low vibration. His highly advanced powers he exhibited in the power of healing, miracles, telepathy, and psychic knowing were his front line display. His essence was not undetectable and his presence, and the Word spread rapidly as he walked the lands. His knowing and reach expanded rapidly as many of his followers including both men and women who were treated equal, became companions, also seeking the knowing of the Word. These also came forward to learn and to spread the word of God. And so many lands came to know and told of this special man. He was able to show the power of God directly and taught the ways to accept divine love for the true purposes. But unlike now, the change of vibration was not readily accepting and this required much time and discipline to evolve in others. As so, he became more of an oddity to some, a wonder and saint to others, and a threat to those who sought power over others., particularly the priesthoods who were in control of the human souls. What they feared was his and his disciples ability to attract people in flocks.

It was so that he walked the lands with his powers of Creator. As he walked the land and lived with the people he carried the light and the love of the Creator. For those that were earthly and poor, already dominated by greed and avarice of authorities he was both admired and feared as they could not understand his ways. His power of healing, his ability raise dead, to materialize things, and his ability to connect with groups instantly to subdue anger and conflict became difficult to understand. For others, the Word and the spreading of his wondrous gifts of healing, of his abilities to see what others could not see was like a miracle. Yet they could not understand how to attain these by attention to his teachings of love and spirit. He taught that the divinity was in all and the attention to love not hatred would bring these powers as they were all sons and daughters of God as was he. As he travelled the land and attracted his closest companions and eventually groups that also learned the Word, the Word and the abilities spread. Many times he would use powers to create miracles that even his followers could not believe.

The consciousness of Christ was highly developed in that his knowing was who he was as a son of God but he would not flaunt this except in his teachings where he said all were equal sons and daughters of God, part of the One creator which was love itself. He lived this way in simplicity to heal and serve others as he wandered the lands and lived among the people. His disciples and followers grew rapidly as he carried the high vibration of attraction and love. His abilities were strong and radical for the ages and this drew even more attention and followers, and many who sought healing. He knew as you do about the higher aspects of the divine mind, and the body as an expression, and he knew his purposes of life to spread his love in an unyielding dedication to others. In thought, word and deed, his mortal ways of life were totally synchronized with the heart and soul of divinity and true expression of God. His influence grew as did his followers and his writings came forward as he wished to write the Word for others.

The teachings of Christ were simple, that all were sons and daughters of God, equal and could do as he was able to show by his healing and physical miracles. Well advanced in higher vibration metaphysics, such was easy for him to illustrate. But this was not a time for this as people were deeply rooted in simple 3D physical lives and not easily moved to higher vibration knowing as is the case now. This placed him and his many teachers of this on a pedestal of curiosity and wonder which is why it was easy to brand this as witchcraft and heresy. Many sought to be healed. His teachings were of equality of all and Oneness, of forgiveness of others and of unconditional love as the true power of life. He taught prayer to God not of forgiveness of sin but to envelope desires with the powerful emotion of love and bliss to manifest what was needed. He taught baptism as a simple process of intent the cleanse and shift into an new belief. He taught the power of love through the heart, the seat of greatest feelings and connection to Spirit and God which was all One. He taught equality of man and women and that all were honoured children of God without judgment of sin. He taught ways of healing, development of physical and mental and psychic abilities and taught the laws of the cosmos based on the teachings of Hermes. He taught thousands of followers and disciples, teachers to follow and spread this word of truth. And at advanced teachings he taught the ancient arts of Egypt's mystery schools, of the Hermetica, and the ancient arts, as well as what he had learned from other spiritually based lands like India. He walked in simplicity, love and in the heart, always within the Higher Divine Mind. To him this was simply automatic and there was ever reason to question why.

And so it is not surprising that this man, his special wisdom of God and Spirit be revered and written about. He reflected what he said every son and daughter of God to do by simply giving their will to god and their true spiritual selves. This was to live in the light of god, in peace and in the heart of love to let the higher spirit to be what it was as eternal life and one with God. As this spread through the lands, the frequency of his light and of his follower buzzed and radiated like beacons of pulsating energy attracting many as they travelled.

Also not surprising is that the activities of Christ came to the awareness of the religious leaders, priests, and the authorities who at first saw this as a curiosity but then saw this as a threat of authority and religious teaching. These were contrary to the churches beliefs. They were blasphemy. As the teachings spread and various writings began to appear, and his collective grew, he became a shining beacon to many of the people and a plan had to be created that would eliminate this problem. To simply kill him was felt a potential threat that would instigate an uprising. This would not serve them. They also had to eliminate the dangerous teachings and the growing movement away from the religious teachings.

And so a plan was devised to infiltrate and understand, to gain evidence that would allow a way to eliminate this. A way had to be found to teach these pagans and heretics a lesson so as to make an example of this and eliminate attention to this heresy. In this way they would hope to bring the fold back unto their own dominion. Thus a way was structured to collaborate between religious leaders and state. Such were also the needs of the dark ones who had also infiltrated the seats of power as they had a grander plan. The higher selves were already serving their needs as they contrived to support the worldly aspects of greed, avarices, power, and lust. And below they saw that the power of love was powerless against heartless forces and armies. However, they knew well the power of spirit to rise as reflected in these teachings as the major threat. They knew that this power could offset the power of armies and dark forces one understood and left to be nurtured. So the dark forces began to contrive a plan to execute through the lower forms.

A Rewrite of Christ Story Was Inevitable

A way of stopping this was the immediate need of the religious leaders and priests, as well as the powers of state to disguise this true story for it could only lead to anarchy and loss of power. First they would contrive a way to brand these teachings as heresy and attempt to show violation of church and state law. They would find out more of these heretics and set them up to be punished. They agreed with the state to infiltrate and seek evidence to convict him and arrest him and others so as to publically humiliate and punish followers.

The authorities and the priests watched with wonder following these activities with their spies. The greatest fear was a potential rising of armies that this Christ could potentially create. The powers of healing and reports of other abilities not understood as the power of spirit was the other which had to branded as the work of evil forces. The religious leaders themselves carried their own wisdom of ancient dark powers as they themselves knew about working in 4 and 5D and the power of attention by the mind through their own barbaric rituals and demonic worship of their own gods. This as you know allowed manifestation by the concentration of energies and was guided by manipulation of compromised higher selves. This was a skill and knowledge that was kept secret and handed down to them thorough their own secret writings and scrolls, carefully oriented to heartless attention of focus on the manifestation process and the black arts. They themselves were worshipers of evil under the guise of goodness, engaging in their secret rituals and sacrifice to pleasing their false gods. There practices were well founded in supporting the special "darker" energies, even as they are to this day.

As it was, a plan was contrived between the Priests and the State to capture several of the key followers and Christ. At this time the religious order of priests and followers was not well established or well organized but they were, because of their dark powers fairly well entrenched with the powers of Rome. Their main objective was fear of this unknown power of spirit, and to be rid of this treat to both state and church. The accusations that ensued was that this group and philosophy that Christ represented claimed to be above all in spirit and threatened to change the peoples mind about subservience, paying their taxes and serving the Caesar.

These were heretical teachings that refused to follow the laws of church and land and the dominion of their gods. As Christ knew he was of greater power, he would never yield spiritually and he had already mastered body and mind control over his physical. He would be ridiculed so the church could point to the folly of his ways, creating words of guilt as to what they wanted to hear and to convey to all of the land. What was feared most was that this revelation of spirit, and the power it represented, defied death itself. And it instilled a power that would render them as the ones who were deceivers if it was left to spread. This was to be proven as severe heresy that they sought to purge with great vigour. It had to be purged from every thought and from all evidence on the land.

And so it was the story of Crucifixion and Resurrection was created. It was a plan to hide the truth of this man.

The Implementation the Word of god

The gospels were stories of individual perceptions and experiences, outlining teachings and events of his life. They were different and disjointed and even these were later further disjointed purposely. As the religious leaders gathered writings and knowledge they would decide to keep or burn these. But one thread of constant fabric prevailed. That this was a special gifted man of the God of truth who had come to spread that truth and to heal all, a special spirited being who walked the lands in humility and peace and in love.

This purge was done over time and was effective, but secretly over time new pockets unfolded on the teaching of Christ and emerged through the lands. It again brought anger and fear in the church and what they preached. This spread like an epidemic of threat and it became the time to react again. They spread their spies throughout the land to find where and what the teachings were and where they growing. Over many years they sought to purge and destroy again but could not. In time they began to target major movements and places where ancient information and such writings were stored.

For even with the initial destruction and deception, the Word spread and re-emerged quietly. It was this resonance with the truth that could not be contained. In reality, other lands and religions followed similar evolution, the dark lords always being aware of the need to suppress spirit or lose their powers. In virtually all religions, even as they evolved over time, the dominion of spirit has prevailed. The rest of it is history as church powers grew and spread and use the heartless to preach dominion at the threat of annihilation by not conforming. To preserve the air that the church was the follower of peace and love of God they separated from the state that would police and use force to stop anyone deemed a threat. It was through this alliance of state and church that the religions over time have been responsible for the greatest amount of bloodshed ever.

These gospels, and other writings that eventually became the testaments and then the bible were subject to an evolution over centuries as the churches gained power. And so the true followers were forced to hide and run or be put to death instantly if found out. This, over a generation allowed the truth to be purged from the face of the land.

As it was, this would allow a new plan to manifest. It was to create a contrived nature of these writings, to gather, understand the writings and to eventually create a new version of the teachings. This was thought to be prudent as they felt that they could intercede eventually so a new form of doctrine could be developed to serve the needs of their own doctrine. In the mean time the objective was to continue to create fear in the followings and have other pay for a sin of following such dark arts and suggesting that they could be part of God. This plan of dominion over spirit was driven from the higher realms was to subdue spirit and to keep its power hidden. The Priests in Power, directed by the gods of the time were alleged to be skilled in their powers of using special forces of dominion, as they also knew of the power of love and light which they of heartless intent chose not to follow. They knew that this spirit could not be destroyed. But they knew how fear and repression would render it ineffective. This they knew could be administered through the higher selves of the ones in power. It was the way of controlling the priesthood many times before. And so they sought to cause fear and kill, to destroy and replace light as an example to serve their cause.

And so it was that a plan was developed over time. It was to reshape the Word of the Christ into the word of man as this seemed a lucrative way to not only find more followers of the church but to create a myth of this Christ who had all these powers. The plan was to take the gospels and the writings that were taken and to begin a new story to replace the Word with the word of man. As writings in those days were themselves stories of observations and perception, vast in difference, this would be a plan to create one story in the testaments.

What the leaders and bloodlines of the gods were guided on was to seek a new way of dominion. What they sought was to find a way to be the sole connection to this God or Gods so they were the interceding power to reduce the spirit to a state of dysfunction. They needed to find a way they could represent themselves as the means to take control of the people, fool them into believing that they and their gods could absolve and dissolve those who were sinners and evil. As time passed they began to understand then change the Word as was written by others—what was compiled by many as testament— to their own version. This grew in power over decades as they began to understand and accumulate the teachings. It was a way that they could intercede between man and God and represent the absolution of sin, of granting redemption and eternal life if the ways were accepted—their ways.

The event, which later became known as the crucifixion had to be from what is was--a simple torture exhibition and prolonged display of death as punishment for heresy. But there were certain facts that they believed that they could use to their advantage. It was the claim of being a son of God and the idea that he was a special man. To support this the virgin birth, the crucifixion, the resurrection was contrived later so as to create such a mythological story that would create a half truth. And this contrived story that would partially align with the truth became the basis to the teachings of Christianity. It did not and never did reflect the true Word of God nor the Christians who followed Christ. This in itself was a deception of words inferring that the church and religion was based on Christ and his teaching which were completely distorted to the story which as a mythology of fact and fiction became the word—the word of man.

The New Mythology Of The Bibles

This story would present their own picture of what transpired, but in such a way as to serve their own purpose. And as the Pope reported, *"this myth of Christ has served us well"*. What eventually over time became the epic mythology of Christ and became the greatest book of all time—the Bible was a contrived way to exert dominion over spirit and man.

They began to create a story of fiction and myth, built on the gospels and writings to support their agenda. They evolved a story of creation with Adam and Eve to reduce the female to lesser evil status of sin. She was a lesser breeding machine to produce new slaves. Her abilities of the attuning to spirit were dangerous and had to be reduced to nothing. Because of the DNA encoding, they created a heaven that was unobtainable except through them after death. The concept of heaven and hell and Satan as a place for those who would not cleanse themselves of the sin that they were born with because of the deception and fall from grace of women. It was the woman that created the sin that Adam and Eve created and therefore was inherent in all offspring forever, something that had to be worked out by begging forgiveness and sacrifice if heaven was ever to be granted. They created the concept of virgin birth to explain the unusual brightness of Christ at birth and created this concept of the first coming of Christ, the Son of God. They cleverly created the idea of hell so the lower ego would flourish in fear and seek resurrection and forgiveness. They imbedded the fear of the dark ritual forces of mysticism which they themselves embodied secretly. They cloaked these and their rituals to false gods. They created the myth of crucifixion to portray Christ as a Son of god who had been sacrificed by God for the sins of humanity. They created the myth of resurrection to enforce that this Christ was given another chance and that God indeed has such power of life and death.

Here was the mystical story of how a son of God had been sent with special divine gifts and powers to save the people of the sins they inherited form the story of creation. This was a story of how God in desperation of the sins of humanity had to offer as sacrifice his son to absolve humanity's folly which would reside within all forever. Of course these sins would need the help of the church as the keepers of the word to guide them towards heaven, salvation and eternal life. Christ had been sent and saw such sin and humility that he had no choice but sacrifice his son.

In addition, the plan was over time to seek out all writings and sources to destroy or take possession, to eliminate the truth of the Word of God from the minds. They would work to destroy physical evidence and replace this over time with their own version. It is this version that has remained for two thousand years with its false words. It is the doctrine that is supported by the left brain of ego. It is maintained by the manipulation in higher dimensions by the dark lords who seek slaves, power and dominion of all worlds with heartless intent. It is supported by the lizard DNA in each that opened egos 3D survival needs. It is supported by the soul's quest to find heaven or Home. But it is the concept of heaven by ego that wins and the soul is left in dominion with a voice that cannot be heard. It is how the quest is manipulated by religions to create the fear of not finding heaven because of sin, to fall to hell if not responsible to false gods and the ideology of the religion.

As time passed the untruth of the One who was sacrificed evolved. And so the many abided by this to seek redemption and forgiveness through prayer, and through the Church that had positioned themselves as the ones who knew the truth and were the true representatives of God. And so the laws and the Word and process of Spirit and Love, as well as the ancient wisdom laws of the Cosmos were slowly transformed to new meaning based on the egos lower vibration

The new version of the story was accumulated in the bible as a contrived clever story of part truths and part lies, portraying the Christ and his Word the way they wanted to. This would replace the Word of God not only with a new story but give new meaning to the Words so that it embodied them as intermediaries and embodied new meanings of words that would suit them. And this became their book of Christianity which they spread. And when they found pockets they quickly purged these such as in Alexandria as well as other place. And so as they purged, they replaced. From this forward they cleverly began to build on this story that was part truth and mostly untruth so that they could position themselves as the gifted ones who could not only interpret the real truth but intercede as the ones who could grant salvation, forgiveness and allow heaven and eternal life to be given. And so they struck from the story the aspect of all that all humanity already has and is born with; truth of Spirit and eternal life and the aspect of true creation and oneness, and the power of love and light. They positioned themselves as that which all have. And as this satisfied the egos desire to find heaven, they struck all references to opening of the higher selves and to the true purpose of life. And anyone who did not follow was killed, tortured or enslaved. And as time passed, religions warred against each other on who had a better way to love and finding heaven. And so over time, the testaments were written and re-written to bring forth the bible, the word of man, not the Word of God.

The story that would evolve and spread would reduce the power of the spirit and the heart as this was potentially the churches demise and loss of control. What they knew well was that alignment with this Spirit and the Christ was necessary as a way of least resistance, but in such a way that they appeared to support this but in a way that would reduce the people to dominion over spirit though fear. Thus they created Christianity which by inference was what was the teachings of the Christians. In fact what was believed as the Christian, or true follower of Christ, was the distorted word of the church followers, simply based on the assumption that Christianity reflect the teaching of Christ. Thus the half truth that was created as that of the Christians was what was believed as truth in Christianity. This made it look like they supported the great story of Christ and the teaching through Christianity but in reality was a deception.

This new half truth acknowledged the power of God or Spirit and the Son who had come to save mankind from their sins that they were born with from their falling in the Garden of Eden. The Son of God had come to save humanity but could not and was therefore offered in sacrifice so the people could understand that they had to seek salvation and retribution for these sins forever. This way they acknowledged God and Christ but placed themselves in as interceding between God and man to be the interpreters of the word and to be the ones who could show the way to forgiveness to prevent falling to hell and Satan and hence attaining eternal life upon death. So a mythology was created on a story of the Son of God, the virgin birth, the crucifixion and the Easter rising of resurrection. These are celebrated to this day. The resurrection established Jesus as the powerful Son of God and is cited as proof that God will judge the world in righteousness. God has given Christians "a new birth into a living hope through the resurrection of Jesus Christ from the dead So this led to the belief through faith in the working of God so others are spiritually resurrected with Jesus so that they may walk in a new way of life. But this way, Jesus was sacrificed for other sins and creating a way that others could see resurrection by giving themselves to the Church. This opened the way for the DNA encoding of seeking Home or the Father, Heaven and eternal life could be attained. Power of Spirit was repressed by fear and the quest for eternal life by ego would guarantee this while the Church entered as the right hand of God that could show the way. Thus separation and fear kept lower vibration of ego, while the fear of moving in a contrary teaching against the church was punishable by death as enforced by the authorities.

But it was only much later when the Church of Rome and other alliances gained power that the true deception as the Bible was implemented. The partial truth as the myth of Christ melded over time so as to eventually be accepted as the whole truth and to place the church in as the powerful intermediary force it is. The falsehood of fire and brimstone of Satan and the belief that people were born in sin, and that women were subservient as they were responsible for this sin has prevailed. And that even the Son of God had to be sacrificed to this cause. He had given his life to bring salvation to the born sinners so they would now they had to beg the church and god for forgiveness. This would become the word of Christianity and become the doctrine of Roman Church and the seat of power supported by force and death for not complying. That new story was indeed created and evolved over time to be supported by humanity as a false truth that would remain until the end of time when the new age would bring in the Christ again, not as One but as all—the Christ Consciousness arising in all. And so it has been. But now millions of sons and daughters of God are rising to take their power of spirit back and away from those who repress, as they have attained a knowing of the true Word of God.

And so it came to pass that the Word of God became the word of god in the march towards The New World Order that would be fully implemented during the "Second Coming of Christ", the **Armageddon** as revealed in the business plan as **Book of Revelation.** As civilization moves to the end of the End Times, what has become so apparent is this "final conflict" of the Dark versus the Light. What has come to the forefront in these times is the nature of this "Second Coming". Is it the Christ Consciousness or is it the Lucifer Consciousness that will prevail?

It is the epic struggle of all time. What is for certain is that it is the Christ Consciousness of the many versus the Lucifer Consciousness of the few. This epic struggle between the Light and the Dark is exactly what the Earthling has chosen to support through history. But why is there a change now? What is this underlying shift of something being a miss in god's laws?

Let us explore this further.

23

THE END TIME OF THE GREAT SHIFT

The dramatic shift that began accelerating at the start of the Aquarian Age has been termed the End Times. This Part of this book is dedicated to what has happened primarily in these last 12 years. It is perhaps not a speculation that the directors and Owners of PLANET EARTH Inc. have been aware of a time when a great shift would occur and that they would need to be prepared to deal with it. Part of the metaphysical and "occult" is the science of the planetary systems known as Astrology. They are well versed in this and know about the shifting consciousness. It is not a speculation to believe that these bloodlines protect and know special esoteric sciences that the rest do not understand, acknowledge or believe. Those esoteric powers of mind which in the extreme are black magic for self, are the same ones the extreme white magic deploy for service of others. The abilities are the same, the use is different but regardless these are the abilities that have been sought for a long time. The process of evolution is as shown on our pyramid of the Soul's Journey.

Prophesies, religious books and any esoteric experts have told us this; that a great time of change would occur as the galactic alignment of Planet earth would occur. As we have alluded to, this has been input into the business plan of New Earth. In business, being able to intuitively guess the transcend of consciousness leads to successful implantations of marketing plans and the financial success of the business. There are endless versions of what this End Time shifting from the Age of Pisces to the Age of Aquarius would bring; from the Earth itself ascending into higher vibration to the creation of Heaven on Earth with ultimate peace and prosperity for all. All the stories are prolific and varied. With this one deluge of opinions everywhere, one must rise above to understand the clear fact that this proliferation is a fundamental shifting of consciousness in the Earthling. More and more Earthlings are writing, discussing, questioning; and this in itself is a major shift. There are major groups and masses now questioning the sanity of the old ways of Old Earth, demanding disclosure, transparency and responsibility because that which has been accepted before is now being rejected. All you have to do is look around to see what has happened in the last few years and question why now?

The new version of the End Times includes the transition from the Old Earth to the New Earth. The time of transition has been commonly portrayed as the time from the turn of the century 1999 to 2012. On Old Earth it was not fashionable to talk about metaphysics. Physics was the buzz, not esoteric things. If you really care to study quantum physics you will quickly realize that it explains metaphysics whereas physics cannot. The main reason that quantum physics has had such a tough time getting entrenched is because there is one component of it that the scientists still (after 80 years) argue about: Consciousness. Consciousness is the missing link to how it all works. So what is it that influences consciousness?

On New Earth it is now quite fashionable to talk about metaphysics because physics is outdated. It cannot see beyond the observer's observations as quantum physics teaches us. Physics cannot deal with or create laws of behaviour on those tiny particles that are not subject to gravity. Gravity is the glue to hold material things together. It is what we know under Newtonian physics as "solid" things made of atoms held by gravity. But consciousness is the glue that creates things in the quantum world. So if you think you know it all as a Newtonian scientist that has been trained to observe what you see, knowing the other 90% is made of stuff you can't see, then how can you know it all? Yet recent work in Russia points to the rest of DNA as being responsible for all these esoteric abilities. DNA has the same structure as our languages and is like an antenna between the body and outside influences of energetic patterns.

The transition from Old to New Earth is also exemplified by the old TV and news media systems versus the new media system of the Internet. If you dare to type in some esoteric or metaphysical topic in Google you will get millions upon millions of news items, research and discussions that come forward. Before the year 2000 it was not like that. Something has taken hold on the conscious attention to create this shift. Now it is like a tsunami of shifting thought—a building energetic field of common attention and awareness. What's this all about?

It's all about this big grand cycle of 26,000 years where our solar system passes through the point of alignment with the center of the galaxy. This is the Grand Alignment in 2012. In fact there are a whole lot of things happening up there that are grand—different than ever before. It is all astronomical data that you can check out for yourself. And at the end of this 26,000 year cycle that has been mostly relegated to importance by those weird metaphysicists is this last tiny little period that started in 1999 and ends in 2012.

There is some hard science here and it is not unrealistic to believe that the PLANET EARTH Directors have full knowledge of this. It is not unreasonable to also believe that these people are highly evolved in the Powers of the Mind so that they may take advantage of this. As we have seen the major media systems are under their control.

The Mayan End Times

There is a big buzz these days on the Internet and in bookstores about the Mayan Calendar. It is not clearly understood how these Mayans received this information, nor how it applies to humanity now, but nevertheless it is infusing into the new consciousness as a new truth. It is important to understand that this is not a prophesy of physical doom and destruction, it is a revealing of a process of behaviour and evolution of consciousness. Regardless of whether it is of plant, animal or man, it is the consciousness that orchestrate the will to survive and the life attitude.

It is particularly focussed on the End Times as these Mayans allegedly took old ancient knowledge and advanced it as their science. First they were very focused on the cosmic movements and nature because the Sun provided light for life to exist. As the Earth provided nourishment to grow, the planets provided the seasons as well as the consciousness mood of the Earth. These they observed carefully and recorded as their own "Days" and "Nights" with different underlying moods and purposes affecting not only nature but all that lives. They saw this change the mood of the people as well. But more important to them was they needed food. So they learned to pay attention to these moods of the universe to survive.

The Mayan calendar therefore reflects the movement of these cosmic cycles of Day and Night, seasons and growth behaviour of all life. They determined there were 13 periods called Heavens. These were a way of describing the phases of growth found in all that lives. For example, from when a seed is planted, there are 7 Days and 6 Nights each with a specific purpose each with different lengths depending on what "Underworld" they belong to (see later). Note that these Days and Nights were not like our 24 hour night and day, although they based these on cyclical patterns of celestial objects like the Sun. These they called the 13 Heavens alternating from Day to Night, each affecting the process of natural growth from seeding to eventual flowering and re-seeding.

The first Heaven is Day 1, the *sowing* time when a seed is planted. The second Heaven, or Night 1, is the time of *inner assimilation* when it readies for transforming itself in preparation for the third Heaven of Day 2, of *germination* when it begins to develop within Mother Earth to reach towards the Sun. There is then Heaven 4, or Night 2 of *resistance* as it must gain its power and internal sustenance to force through to see the Sun. You begin to see how the Day is one of expansion while the night is one of resistance or adjustment, each at a different phase of the growth. It is the mood of Mother Earth that can affect this growth towards its fulfillment, as can the Sun which to them was the Father.

The next Heaven 5, Day 3 is when it *sprouts*, the first time to emerge to see Father Sun and now the Earth and the Sun work together to provide nourishment below and life energy above to the new plant. As it begins to grow, it must adjust itself to the new world around it and *assimilate* through the Heaven 6, Night 3, to adjust itself properly. As it so does, it enters the Heaven 7, next Day 4 which is to *proliferate* itself through the new energy of the Sun. It then enters the next Heaven 8, Night 4 as it attempts to *expand* itself to be what it was meant to be.

During the Heaven 9, Day 5 it is the time of *budding* for its main purpose to produce. Heaven 10, Night 5 is a time of destruction as the plant now must place all of its energy into producing its flower if it is to flourish. Of course, Heaven 11, Day 6 is when the plant flourishes into *flowering*. Heaven 12, Night 6 is when it must *fine tune* itself to blossom to its fullest, and finally Heaven 13, Day 7 is the *fruition* when its bounty in the of form seeds is completed. Each Heaven is dependent on the mood of the Sun and Mother Earth as to what they can provide to support the growth to maturity.

Each Day and Night brings a new phase of challenge and growth as its very purpose, and its essence towards its final purpose change. The elements of fire, earth, water, and air are all vital to the success, as are the internal abilities of the plant to grow. Its will to live and survive is its very essences or spirit. They saw this as its consciousness. Their wisdom taught that all life abides by this. All life including man whose essences are his consciousness are influenced by the moods of the cosmos, and the Sun and the Earth whether they understand it or not.

It is because the essence of man, the consciousness is part of the God of all that exists. It, like the Mother Earth, and the Sun are all living things which are themselves going through the same phases. All of life behaves according to this grand plan. All are subject to their influences as they change their positions around us. Just as they determine the way a seed will grow, they determine the way a man will grow and mature, and develop his own essence.

What they also determined was that there were a whole set of other time periods in their calendar called Underworlds. Each period is itself a stage of complete evolution on a larger scale. The period of 13 Heavens is an Underworld. There are 9 Underworlds of different lengths. The shortest is the Universal Underworld of 260 days (our days). The next longest is the Galactic Underworld which is 20 times longer than the Universal, and so on. Again, each Underworld is made up of the 13 Heavens. At the start of each one, a major level of evolution in consciousness starts then goes through the 13 Heavens maturing progressively like the plants.

When the end phase of each Underworld is reached, meaning the 13th Heaven of *Fruition*, a new Underworld that is twenty times shorter in length begins as the First Day of sowing. It is like when one Underworld produces a seed that can then go through the Heavens twenty times faster. Thus during the last period of the Planetary 7th Day, the seeding of the First Day in the Galactic period may occur. At the last 7th Day in the Galactic, a new seed is created to be sown to begin the Universal period. When all 9 Underworlds are complete, a new period where there is no time begins. Each one has a specific consciousness function and sets the foundation for the next shorter one (20 times shorter). And they all end at the same time. That is what the Mayans saw as the End Times as their calendar ceased and went into a period of no time.

What is relevant here is that all 9 of these Underworlds (or waves) except this last one called *Universal* (260 days) has reached the 13th Heaven. And all 9 waves end on October 28, 2011. The one underneath this one, the *Galactic* Underworld, is 12.8 years long and we have entered its last 13th Heaven of *Fruition* as have all others. It sits on a bigger one 20 times longer and so on.

It is this last one of 260 days that is of interest as it began on March 9, 2011 and terminates *Fruition* on October 28, 2011. Recently this has been adjusted by the experts on this to 18 of our days for each Heaven to total 234 days. What is notable is that there is an acceleration as time speeds up. What this means is that the aspect of consciousness pertaining to each Heaven speeds up its evolution by 20 times for each Underworld which we will call a wave. In other words, as much as we learned in the last wave of 12.8 years will be learned in the current wave of 234 days.

This Universal Underworld is the final transformation of consciousness and it is what is referred to as the 9th Wave.

The prophesy about these End Times when these all end together is that this is a great change in the consciousness of humanity as they approach the fruition of all Underworlds. It will be a time when the consciousness of man has no association with time. It is the time of the revealing and the entry to a new age as the rebirth starts from the seed of the last underlying Underworld. At that time the world is without time and consciousness of man would have evolved to its ultimate point of fruition. This means it is up to those who are left to start creating the new world and the new civilization. It will be a period where man will be one with nature and Mother Earth and the Solar system will come into galactic synchronization with the rest of the Universe. Those left will be transformed as they pass through the center of the cosmos. All will be One and the material will be balanced with spirit. It was called Hunab Ku in Mayan. It is referred to as the Unity Consciousness.

The Ninth Wave—What Is It?

The 9th wave is the final wave which rests upon the final Fruition stages of all 8 waves. It is the culmination of all consciousness, setting the final stage for the time when there is no time after the Grand Alignment of Dec 21, 2012 when Earth passes through the center of the Galaxy. Essentially, these waves get shorter and shorter until there is no time, only instant by instant. Its purpose is to bring in the final step of unity consciousness. It is all about setting a consciousness mood that we are all One. And it is about revealing that being all One, there is within us a divine aspect as we are One with the Creator, as we are one with Creation. That spark of us referred to as our Light Body, that invisible quantum overlay on the physical atomic body, is what is said to be a piece of God.

This Grand Alignment, and a whole lot of other unique celestial configurations occur through 2012, after the 9th wave completes in 2011. It creates the setting for the final transformation of resurrection. These waves are the ones that have been evolving the unity consciousness and are meant to set the underlying consciousness like an overlay from above so that it sets the tone—or garden—for manifestation and creation below. In our terms of reference this is from 5D above and 4D between to 3D below. It sets the tone of the Resurrection.

It is important to understand what is meant as "D". It is not a mathematical terminology. These terms will be used a lot here: 1D, 2D, 3D reflects matter as physical earth and our bodies (Newtonian physics of atoms), 5D being non-matter or etheric quantum space, and 4D as the space between (Quantum physics of waves).

The 13 Heavens reflected the stages of growth, alternating from female (nurturing) to male (protection) energies, alternating between day and night, each having an energetic influence as they determined was ruled by gods which had certain powers and attributes to affect that stage of growth. They, as all humanity, have created many gods and deities who they worship as their idols and have assigned special powers to them. It is simply humanity's DNA calling as this is encoded to seek God within; which has through lower vibrations become seeking god without. In this case, what they could not understand and respected they called gods.

At each Heaven of Day and Night, just as the growing conditions of above (Father Sun) and Below (Mother Earth) set the tone for optimum growth, of nurturing and adjustment, so does the prevailing mood of consciousness set the tone for the strength, clarity of intent (seed) so as to provide optimum growth into fruition—that being the intent of humanity to manifest and create in 3D what has been seeded and nurtured in consciousness of 5D.

How to best align with this tone is to understand the nature of the process of growth and expansion at each phase. In the case of seeds, it is the nourishment of dark soil and water that vitalizes, whereas when sprouting, it is the sun and the nutrients that are needed. In the case of consciousness, it is the balanced female/male love from the divine heart that nurtures and integrates into the new form. Thus every Day and Night is "charged" with specific frequencies of care and attention of that stage, looking for that which provides it. It is as the stage of growth in a child, where the father and mother shift their attention to the needs of the child as it matures. By aligning with the needs, the process of growth matures with vigour and strength at each stage—all set into the fundamental nourishment of love. In this case, the seeds we are dealing with are the consciousness of humanity as a living energy.

At the end of these 9 waves, the total consciousness of humanity and the universe is set to blossom permanently in Unity. It is the year 2012 that the unity consciousness, truly emerges and blossoms into the 3D reality having been implanted in the garden of consciousness of 5D to be expressed in the reality of 3D. It is so for those that choose to be planted in the light of the garden of love through the Time of Choosing that is the 9th wave and the Time of Revelation. Then these celestial bodies and energies gifted from the Galactic Center as we approach in 2012 do their final fine tuning of total consciousness. This will be the Resurrection or the final Time of Transformation. And what is it that results? First is the shift in consciousness to unity and that consciousness is what materializes the New Earth.

And so we sit clearly at the end of this wave, and the culmination of all the waves. It is difficult to deny that something has influenced the Earthling's Consciousness into a dramatic shift pattern in the last 12 years. This will become much more obvious to you as you read about the major moves to reveal a new truth on Planet Earth later in this Part 2. So now we come to the convergence and the confrontation of Light and Dark. This confrontation is about Lucifer; the service to self, or Christ: the service to others. These constitute two different plans.

Let us now, in the next two chapters explore what these two plans may look like. Much of this has "come to light" in the last 12 years.

Before entering this world of words, the reader is forewarned that there may be things read about the darker side that may be upsetting. Don't be. They are just words and the lighter side follows. Just read both sides without emotion and opinion and let your heart decide what rings for you.

24

RAPTURE AND REVELATION:
THE DARK SIDE

We have already seen this is the Lucis Trust. We have seen this is the US Dollar, and we have seen this in the biblical plans of Revelation, Rapture and Armageddon.

If one could sum up the Plan of PLANET EARTH, it would best be stated by the Pope Ratzinger who said:

"It is thus necessary that the individual should finally come to realize that his own ego is of no importance in comparison with the existence of his nation; That the position of the individual ego is conditioned solely by the interests of the nation as a whole... that above all the unity of a nation's spirit and will are worth far more than the freedom of the spirit and will of an individual..."

*"This state of mind, which subordinates the interests of the ego to the conservation of the community, is really the first premise for every truly human culture... The basic attitude from which such activity arises, We call - to distinguish it from egoism and selfishness - idealism. By this we understand only the individual's capacity to make sacrifices for the community, for his fellow man." -**The Ominous Parallels, by Leonard Piekoff** P 13.*

The Satanic Plan Of Dominion

In this plan there is The Anti-Christ or Satan of alleged conspiracy and dominion to believe in. It is the Illuminati/Zionist plan to create an apocalypse that will exhaust and depopulate the masses through deadly designer viruses, global terror, economic disasters and nuclear war. These disasters are allegedly timed to occur somewhere between 2000 and 2014, when the remaining survivors will gladly embrace the promises of a handsome charismatic new leader (the New Vice President of Religious Order) who will unveil his plan of hope for an eternal world peace. The only way to achieve eternal world peace, he will explain, is to put an end to the five causes of war. Secretly, he knows there is only one main cause of wars: the wars provoked by his royal ancestors who planed, provoked, financed and profited from them. He will sell his peace plan by telling the world that border wars will only end by creating a world without borders.

Religious wars will only end by creating one world religion of interfaiths. Economic wars will only end by creating a cashless debt-free society. Rivalry wars between rulers will only end by creating one world ruler. The tools used for war, from hand-guns to nuclear bombs will be eliminated and one world army will be created, which will guarantee world peace. This means that the Earthling will remain in his current state of spiritless lower vibration to be employed by PLANET EARTH under a new set of laws-perhaps much like *George Orwell's 1984*. One may think George had the timing out but if you really look around you may see "Big Brother" as being more real than you believe, as we have revealed in Part 1.

How will this eternal peace plan be accomplished? We have looked at these groups in Part 1. We have discussed this. The structure is in place. What has to happen is that the mass of Earthlings must yield to a submissive strategy. They must agree to it most likely through desperation and fear. It is through groups like the United Nations, which is the brain-child of the Committee of 300 families. The UN is their vehicle for world government, and is located on 18 acres of prime Manhattan land, donated by the most visible of the ruling families, the Rockefellers. We have seen the UN as a closed organization with no public records or open meetings. US tax payers have already invested 2 trillion dollars in this world authority. Although most of the people working for the UN are genuinely working for peace, the UN is much more as a Godless organization, controlled by the committee of 300.

It is said that these inbred ruling families pretend to have royal blue blood, but their blood is no more blue or royal than Hannibal Lector's blood. For thousands of years these families have practiced inbreeding. Between sisters and brothers, uncles and nieces, mothers and sons, to keep the power and wealth all in the family. This practice of inbreeding over thousands of years has produced, it is said, a clever, but pathological breed of consciousness, sociopathic families, who will stop at nothing to own every ounce of gold, every drop of water and every blade of grass on Planet Earth. However, regardless, they march towards a better world for their slaves. The issue has become one of the slaves beginning to understand the program and their true powers. Like the rise and fall of dynasties and civilizations before, a time of revolution occurs eventually.

The UN, which they founded and control, has clearly stated its goals of establishing a New World Order, a UN standing army and a global taxation system. The queen's husband prince Philip and Evelyn Rothschild have already established an interfaith declaration for the creation of one world religion. What would life be like in this world empire with one world religion, one world army, one world economy, one world court, one world media, one world government and one world dictator. Well perhaps a lot of rules and more of the same duality bur perhaps with less wars?

What the public doesn't know, is that Karl Marx's Communist Manifesto and the Russian Constitution have already been built into the UN charter and that the New World Order will be a communist world order. Peace on Earth will be a forced peace in which citizens will have no rights. No right to bear children without approval, no right to travel without authorization, no right to own private property, no right to privacy, no right to bear arms, no right to protest, no right to receive an inheritance, no right to choose an education or job or even a place of residence. And worst of all, no right to live. The right to live will be based on an individual rating of usefulness to the royal elite. And to many, that will be just fine as long as they can feed the family and their ego of desires.

In this planned world without borders or nations, citizens will be disarmed of all weapons, including hand guns, and will have no means to protest, fight, resist or challenge this one world authority, who will control them spiritually, economically and militarily. Every human being will be electronically marked and will become helplessly dependent on this one world authority, for all of their most basic needs. The masses are to eventually be taught to bow-down and worship this one world dictator, who is to rule the entire world from some eternal universal throne. One has to understand that at this time in the evolution of the Earthling, they certainly have not exhibited a level of responsibility that creates peace and harmony worldwide. When it comes down to the individual self preservation, the Earthling bows down to egotic survival and material trappings, conflictive beliefs and is, essentially a war-like critter. So perhaps he deserves this kind of continuous slavery under one roof? And to many this will be just fine.

A big question in this business plan is, who is to play the role of this charismatic leader that the entire world would be willing to accept as their ruler? According to plan, this future world ruler will prove himself to be a descendent of Jesus Christ and Mary Magdalene, and will therefore be accepted by the Christian world. Some will even view him as the Savior and Messiah. As a professed descendent of Christ, and a proponent of world religion, he will also be accepted by Buddhists, Hindus and the Eastern World, where Jesus Christ reportedly visited and studied and later preached Eastern Philosophies during his ministry. Since he is a descendent of the Hebrew Tribes of Israel, he will also be accepted by Hebrews and Jews world-wide. By marrying a Muslim woman, he will win the acceptance of the Muslim world. He will also be accepted by world-wide freemasonry and secret societies, of which he is a member.

There is an interesting speculation that is brought forward not to predict the plan but to bring to the forefront the **possibility of a plan**. This possibility is the son of princess Diana, as he is already loved and worshipped. When his mother died in the arms of a Muslim man, in a Paris car crash, the world embraced him. On May 31st 2004, the Rothschild controlled Associated Press, published a photograph worldwide, taken by Alistar Grant. The photo shows prince William posing with a lamb like Jesus Christ, who the Bible calls the Lamb of God. To the unaware observer, the photograph is perfectly innocent. But to insiders familiar with the Protocols of Zion, Freemasonry and the Book of Revelation, William is identified in the photo as the antichrist. The antichrist has been described in art and literature as a handsome and charming and a master of lies and deception. Freemasons call him the Bathomed, or Goat of Mendese. He is commonly illustrated with cloven hind hooves. Why is prince William holding up a cloven hind hoof in the photograph? According to Masonic calculations, Prince William is predicted to be crowned World Dictator in year 2015, at the age of 33. And to many that are still carnal, addicted to royalty, this would be just fine.

The question of whether God or Lucifer exist has been fiercely debated since the beginning of debate. Some people believe that, like religion, God and Lucifer are inventions of the ruling class, to control the masses. Most people acknowledge the existence of positive creative energy, characterized by joy, love and vitality. And the existence of negative destructive energy, characterized by greed, hatred and death. Could it be that God and Lucifer are the two sources of these two opposing energies? The triumph of evil in the world today is based on the ability of evil to disguise itself as its opposite and fool the masses. Then, without organized intervention, life and peace on earth will take on a whole new meaning.

The Secret Covenant: PLANET EARTH Code Of Ethics

In a worst case scenario, this interesting article has been published at the site **www.luisprada.com/Protected/reptilian_pact.htm.** See also the complementary articles, "***The Holographic Prison and the Pact with the Devil***" and the "***New World Order, an Overview.***" In this document, and research that led to it as evidenced on this rather prolific website about deception, we get a taste for what may well be the underlying attitude of the Royal Bloodlines directing PLANET EARTH. It is called the reptilian pact. It is an interesting piece of work because it most definitely reflects the evil side of the Satanic Belief structure and it would certainly be a prevalent consciousness of the Founders of a Corporation out of control who are defining a secret code of ethics. As to its credibility, one can only speculate where secret covenants and blood oats are involved.

I have to relate something that is very common these days with regards to the Conspirators. The book Wheat Belly by William Davis MD is an example. In his book he draws from decades of clinical studies how the new form of genetically modified wheat (greatest yield at lowest cost) and the 1970's introduction of dietary guidelines as well the later USDA endorsements has been the root cause of health deterioration. From celiac, diabetes, overweight, immune, neurological disorder, arthritis dementia, the list is impressive, as is the proof towards direct addiction. He reports that after 10,000 years of wheat being a staple product around the world in 1943 through the collaboration of the **Rockefeller Foundation** and the Mexican government to achieve agricultural self sufficiency, the project (IMWAC) to create new strains of wheat, corn, and soy was launched. By 1980 thousands of strains were produced that were adopted worldwide. Davis states:

"The primary trigger is wheat. In fact the incredible financial bonanza that the proliferation of wheat in the American diet as created for the food and drug industries can make you wonder if this 'perfect storm' was somehow man-made. Did a group of powerful men convene a secret Howard Hughesian meeting in 1955 map out an evil plan to mass produce high-yield, low cost dwarf wheat, engineer the government sanctioned advice to eat 'healthy whole grain' lead to the charge of corporate Big Food to sell hundreds of billions worth of processed wheat food products all leading to obesity and the need for billions of dollars of drug treatment for diabetes, heart disease, and all other health consequences of obesity? It sounds ridiculous but in a sense that's exactly what happened."

This research is not alone in its realizations. The last 12 years has been exceptionally prolific in these books and reports of alleged plans or consequential collateral damage as a result of trusting the "system". This is not placed here to annoy you or create fear. It is here so you can make an informed choice on something that you may have known nothing about. That is the purpose of this book. It's like the wheat itself; you can simply choose a substitute if the truth rings with you. But you can't choose if you are not aware of the issue.

And so there would appear to be an ethic of speculation that would reduce the Earthling to a simple minded animal that is not yet of sufficient intelligence to evolve into the superior being of the "bloodline". The following is alleged to reflect that ethic, and the moral conduct behind the New world Order Plan: (See the site **www.godlikeproductions.com/forum1/message879227/pg1**). again read these as words without emotion. This is the secret pact:

"An illusion it will be, so large, so vast it will escape their perception. Those who will see it will be thought of as insane. We will create separate fronts to prevent them from seeing the connection between us. We will behave as if we are not connected to keep the illusion alive. Our goal will be accomplished one drop at a time so as to never bring suspicion upon ourselves. This will also prevent them from seeing the changes as they occur.

We will always stand above the relative field of their experience for we know the secrets of the absolute. We will work together always and will remain bound by blood and secrecy. Death will come to he who speaks. We will keep their lifespan short and their minds weak while pretending to do the opposite. We will use our knowledge of science and technology in subtle ways so they will never see what is happening. We will use soft metals, aging accelerators and sedatives in food and water, also in the air.

They will be blanketed by poisons everywhere they turn. The soft metals will cause them to lose their minds. We will promise to find a cure from our many fronts, yet we will feed them more poison. The poisons will be absorbed through their skin and mouths, they will destroy their minds and reproductive systems. From all this, their children will be born dead, and we will conceal this information. The poisons will be hidden in everything that surrounds them, in what they drink, eat, breathe and wear. We must be ingenious in dispensing the poisons for they can see far.

We will teach them that the poisons are good, with fun images and musical tones. Those they look up to will help. We will enlist them to push our poisons. They will see our products being used in film and will grow accustomed to them and will never know their true effect. When they give birth we will inject poisons into the blood of their children and convince them it's for their help. We will start early on, when their minds are young, we will target their children with what children love most, sweet things.

When their teeth decay we will fill them with metals that will kill their mind and steal their future. When their ability to learn has been affected, we will create medicine that will make them sicker and cause other diseases for which we will create yet more medicine.

We will render them docile and weak before us by our power. They will grow depressed, slow and obese, and when they come to us for help, we will give them more poison. We will focus their attention toward money and material goods so they many never connect with their inner self. We will distract them with fornication, external pleasures and games so they may never be one with the oneness of it All. Their minds will belong to us and they will do as we say. If they refuse we shall find ways to implement mind-altering technology into their lives. We will use fear as our weapon.

We will establish their governments and establish opposites within. We will own both sides. We will always hide our objective but carry out our plan. They will perform the labor for us and we shall prosper from their toil. Our families will never mix with theirs.

Our blood must be pure always, for it is the way. We will make them kill each other when it suits us.

We will keep them separated from the oneness by dogma and religion. We will control all aspects of their lives and tell them what to think and how. We will guide them kindly and gently letting them think they are guiding themselves.

We will foment animosity between them through our factions. When a light shall shine among them, we shall extinguish it by ridicule, or death, whichever suits us best. We will make them rip each other's hearts apart and kill their own children. We will accomplish this by using hate as our ally, anger as our friend. The hate will blind them totally, and never shall they see that from their conflicts we emerge as their rulers. They will be busy killing each other. They will bathe in their own blood and kill their neighbours for as long as we see fit. We will benefit greatly from this, for they will not see us, for they cannot see us.

We will continue to prosper from their wars and their deaths. We shall repeat this over and over until our ultimate goal is accomplished. We will continue to make them live in fear and anger through images and sounds. We will use all the tools we have to accomplish this. The tools will be provided by their labor. We will make them hate themselves and their neighbours. We will always hide the divine truth from them, that we are all one. This they must never know! They must never know that color is an illusion, they must always think they are not equal.

Drop by drop, drop by drop we will advance our goal. We will take over their land, resources and wealth to exercise total control over them. We will deceive them into accepting laws that will steal the little freedom they will have. We will establish a monetary system that will imprison them forever, keeping them and their children in debt. When they shall band together, we shall accuse them of crimes and present a different story to the world for we shall own all the media.

We will use our media to control the flow of information and their sentiment in our favor. When they shall rise up against us we will crush them like insects, for they are less than that. They will be helpless to do anything for they will have no weapons. We will recruit some of their own to carry out our plans, we will promise them eternal life, but eternal life they will never have for they are not of us. The recruits will be called "initiates" and will be indoctrinated to believe false rites of passage to higher realms. Members of these groups [Editor´s Note: the Illuminati] will think they are one with us never knowing the truth. They must never learn this truth for they will turn against us. For their work they will be rewarded with earthly things and great titles, but never will they become immortal and join us, never will they receive the light and travel the stars.

They will never reach the higher realms, for the killing of their own kind will prevent passage to the realm of enlightenment. This they will never know. The truth will be hidden in their face, so close they will not be able to focus on it until it's too late. Oh yes, so grand the illusion of freedom will be, that they will never know they are our slaves. When all is in place, the reality we will have created for them will own them.

This reality will be their prison. They will live in self-delusion. When our goal is accomplished a new era of domination will begin. [N. of Ed.: the New World Order].Their minds will be bound by their beliefs, the beliefs we have established from time immemorial. But if they ever find out they are our equal, we shall perish then. THIS THEY MUST NEVER KNOW. If they ever find out that together they can vanquish us, they will take action.

They must never, ever find out what we have done, for if they do, we shall have no place to run, for it will be easy to see who we are once the veil has fallen. Our actions will have revealed who we are and they will hunt us down and no person shall give us shelter.

This is the Secret Covenant by which we shall live the rest of our present and future lives, for this reality will transcend many generations and life spans. This covenant is sealed by blood, our blood. We, the ones who from heaven to earth came.

This covenant must NEVER, EVER be known to exist. It must NEVER, EVER be written or spoken of for if it is, the consciousness it will spawn will release the fury of the PRIME CREATOR upon us and we shall be cast to the depths from whence we came and remain there until the end time of infinity itself.

The interesting part of this document, which remains without author, is that it may well be a bitch list of some unhappy writer who sees the wrongs in the world today but it does reflect much of what is indeed being revealed more and more, just like in the Wheat Belly book. And indeed if the royal bloodlines see the Earthlings as inferior beings and slaves that are here to survive the needs, there would be no difference between this philosophy and or own in how we treat cattle. Moreover, if there would be those who have some superior powers of "Satan" or "witchcraft" or darker esoteric abilities, and they were free to use these without hindrance, would these not be the darker side of the Satanic Beliefs we covered in Part 1? I repeat: *"Did a group of powerful men convene a secret Howard Hughesian meeting map out an evil plan. It sounds ridiculous but in a sense that's exactly what happened."*

Old End Time Of Revelation

Once more we have to enter the realm of the myths and prophesies from Old Earth that are allegedly "God" driven. In the old story of Old Earth the End Times are the time which humanity would have to make a choice. That choice would be pay for their sins and roast in Hell or choose God's word and get a reward to Heaven, eternal life, and all sorts of heavenly goodies. Or perhaps you may pay your way out by confession and repentance. And so religions, and I shall pick on the prevalent ones, have created an effective dogma around the concepts of Revelation, Rapture, Resurrection, and Armageddon. The underlying theme, to make a simple analogy, is basically, humans, especially women, are a bunch of low life sinners and they need to make amends. They may be saved by the second coming of Christ who will reveal himself at some glorious moment. When? Perhaps when enough sinners have realized their sins and expressed absolute obedience to those representing God. And then Christ, or a Messiah, or some superhuman dude will rise and save them so they can go into heaven in eternal bliss, then sort out the rest once and for all. When? Perhaps when the business plan of PLANET EARTH needs the strategy to be staged?

In this story, **Revelation** brings together the worlds of heaven, earth, and hell in a final confrontation between the forces of good and evil. It means this is the revealing or disclosing, or making something obvious through active or passive communication with supernatural and divine entities. Of course it is believed that revelation can originate directly from a deity, or through an agent, such as an angel, most likely through the churches and religious leaders who have elected themselves the "chosen ones" that are privy to the Word of God.

The Dude that is going to disclose all this secret stuff is of course Jesus Christ, the Son of God (or the Prophet) himself. He is second in command and in for a second shot at this task to save humanity from their terrible deeds. So he is going to go through another **Resurrection** and descend back to life in a magical event worshipped as the Second Coming of Christ. As the plan unfolds, first of all he will take care of his chosen ones, then he will have a huge heavenly meeting with Dad (God), look at the tally ledger, and decide to remove all good Christians from the Earth to protect them.

This process is called Rapture, a term from the Latin verb **raptare**, and the Greek word **harpizo**, both meaning to be caught up or to be snatched up. So Jesus will snatch good Christians out of harm's way so those who have been good boys and girls can get their special treats of being saved. That means giving in to obedience. Those top good ones are of course, the ones who have listened to the chosen ones who know the truth of the word of god and have faithfully been gobbling those blue pills, like their prescriptions are still current and paid up. Then they can be saved—lifted out of harm's way while the rest meet a different situation as their undoing dealing with the big bad guy Mr. Devil, or one of his buddies. Either way it looks pretty bad if you threw away your pills.

But listen up. Under this story there are more goodies to get if you are saved. It is about this thing of revelation which is the revealing or disclosing of life's secrets through active or passive communication with Jesus and his Dad. All those good kids will be divinely or supernaturally revealed or inspired. Revelation comes from the Greek name **Apokalypsis,** which means a disclosure, a revelation or manifestation and to be revealed. So it is a revealing of Jesus Christ himself.

In looking back at this myth, we see that this Revelation is the supposed revealing of Jesus Christ and that the message originally came from God the Father. But it was actually from god, the faker. Well, because we screwed up, especially the sinful women, it's different. Since the introduction of sin, all communication between heaven and Earth has been terminated and has to go through Jesus Christ as he is the only mediator between this god and man. But, and here's the big but; it seems that the self elected bishops and religious gurus are the ones in between you and the gods because Christ ain't here yet. But he, of course talks to them as they are "chosen" and know the Word and what will happen and of course when. This time when this would happen was of course cleverly unstated so it could loom upon sinners forever.

And what of those poor souls that are not revealed, and snatched up? **Armageddon!** Of course there are literally hundreds of different interpretations on this as well as the Bible prophecies, especially on the issue of who is Mister Devil, the real bad guy and the battle of Armageddon. The key word here is interpretations. But you are told not to have private interpretations of prophecy at all. Why? Because god's Word gives us all we need to know without any speculation whatsoever and of course god's boys are the ones who know best.

So the bad news for those that have not been plucked out of harm's way is **Armageddon**—End Times. It will be time to pay for your sins, you bad kids. This brings the scene for the final battle between the kings of the Earth at the end of the world, a catastrophically destructive battle where Mr. Satan gets his dues for meddling with the big plan for Old Earth once and for all.

And even the New Agers have something to say about this; there is a great space ship commanded by Ashtar and Sananda himself—the one who walked as Christ—waiting up there to have the equal of Scotty beam good souls to safe haven while the great battle ensues, or great catastrophes of 2012 happen.

It's a great story and the variations of this and the 2012 doomsday seems endless. And there are a lot of folks that heed to this. It is a great story that has been around in thousands of versions for some time now. And yet it dominate the belief system for so many "scientific", rational minds seems in itself an unbelievable fiction. And although I poke at it, this is really not funny to those who so vehemently believe it. The fear of being one of the unlucky kids who pissed off god and didn't get with his program of the "Word" means you are going to remain in harm's way and take your consequences. And so this story has been prophesized by the best publishers of all time—the churches and major religious leaders. And so the humans who basically want to trust someone and to seek out a true God relinquish their own beliefs to be replaced by others as their god's words.

What is so interesting here is that this is a prewritten plan of what can happen. And it is no different from a pre-written business plan that any CEO would write about a potential mission outlining the Vice Presidents, new Divisions, new products and services that would unfold in a time sequence. The difference however, is that this particular plan may indeed be orchestrated by the gods, not God.

So now let us look a new version which can be taken from the bibles and the Lucis Trust document to create a new interpretation of Revelation and the "second coming".

25

RAPTURE AND REVELATION: THE LIGHT SIDE

The Divine Plan Of The New Order Of The Ages

Now I am going to bring to you a bit of news that reflects the enormous wave that dominates the New Earth energies. It's a prophesy that has the bottom line of all the millions of opinions of what is happening and what was meant to happen with regard to this End Time and The Grand Alignment and the big cycle of 26,000 years. It is not a belief system written by any leaders. It is like a melding of the Mayan prophesy and New Age shifting. It is about the transformation through our new version of Revelation and Resurrection. It is this that we will cover in the next chapters. Again, you can get many opinions on this but there is a common denominator. Here is the simplified version. This may be a bit far out if you have not followed the wave, but here goes:

Assuming that the Earthling is ready to take responsibility for his own affairs, resign from PLANET EARTH and stop taking the Blue Pills of the Biblical CODE, there appears to be a Divine Plan that is influencing the consciousness. This mass union of belief and purpose is not led by anyone, or any corporation. This plan has been to allow Gaia (Gaia is Mother Nature) and Earth to ascend (to ascend means to rise in vibration so as to live in a body form without having to die—as your eternal self as part of God) at this special time. But the overall Divine Plan is and always was to allow all that choose to ascend so as to bring the aspect of the God Self to lower form; to experience and to expand the joy of its wonder. As this story goes, this opportunity has occurred before and the Earthling blew it three times. This time it is different in that it is Gaia that is ascending; the question is: what Earthlings are on board the ride this time? At this point it is the time of Gaia and Earth's ascension is to be completed with the alignment of galactic center which is her origin. She and Earth have offered themselves in sacrifice to be the body and form of the Great Experiment of souls to bring all things upon her and connected to her into the evolution of spirit. It is her destiny and it is her members of the Cosmic Council (the planets that the Mayas deemed as gods) that assist in this as they pour their love and their aspects of unique vibrations upon her and all things upon her.

The Divine Plan has been for humanity to be allowed to ascend with her by their own free will—God's gift to all should they choose to ascend and to recognize the power of love. The overall choice for Gaia's humanity was to be determined by the overall vibration of Earth and her inhabitants. It had to reach a certain threshold and so it did during the period referred to as the Harmonic Convergence of 1987. The question was whether humanity could earn this right of ascension that Gaia was to engage in regardless. Otherwise, Gaia would ascend by herself. And so it trigged the Divine Plan which originally was to place within the design of all, the knowing of the God Self and the attributes of Creator and Creation. It would be there in all equally, and placed as a spark of quest of Self and Home as accessed through the heart, the seat and power of the Divine Self. It was the time of the Harmonic Convergence that showed humanity had earned this right. In other words if Earthlings were picking up the messages being inducted into consciousness in sufficient numbers, then the opportunity would allow the unfoldment.

And so it was encoded within the DNA, placed within each, in a place where it could never be lost. It would be within each heart as the gateway to find the way to this truth and to allow this gate to open to bring it forward into consciousness. It is the Divine Plan to allow each and all to grow, evolve and express the joy of love and to receive love and bliss. In return one could learn to ascend in form and to make greater and expand the totality of love of the Creator as the supreme force of all that is. It is what Christ did—the hard way. It is the Divine Plan to allow all possibilities in all beings equally and to create by free will that which they desire to attain joy. The process would be first in thought above, then to form material below, all released by the essence of pure unconditional love—the glue of all that is.

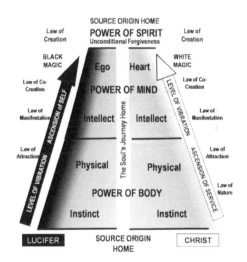

The Divine Plan is to allow creation with the tools of love through the gateway of the heart. In our diagram it is the portal at the top that every Earthling has an opportunity to go through like in a Near Death Experience (without dying) where you meet your Maker and yourself as Soul. So regardless of whether humanity has shown its worthiness in love, bad good or indifferent the gateway of unconditional forgiveness temporarily opens. It is this Divine Plan that is now manifesting upon Gaia and Earth, into new form in wondrous expansion of the universe which is God's mind.

The New Earth: GENESIS II

Well, if I was God, or my higher Soul up there waiting at the other end of the Near Death Experience portal, I would put up a big sign:

"We have seen the evolution of the Old Earth and we have seen how all of your brothers and sisters have lived upon it. It has been a time when the spirit was allowed to be under dominion of the egos, and so it has been. Now we are seeing that humanity is bringing forward this spirit which we have quietly placed within them. It is a time to consider the New Genesis of New Earth as we shall conceive and give birth to. We see that your

brother Christ has indeed left a legacy of spirit and that it has not been subjugated and it is still alive for all.

It is a time that your brothers and sisters have earned their rights to know of themselves. This time we will allow the spirit to come forward in those that have chosen and New Earth can be once again a perfect world that will be inhabited by the ones who choose. It was as we had on Old Earth but it evolved away from spirit of true self to grow and know. Let us once again create a new Genesis and allow the goodness of Old Earth to meld into the New Earth. This Genesis will be formed from the consciousness of those brothers and sisters that awaken, and we will so present them with the gift of ascension into the New Earth."

For the billions that already believe in Genesis, or some form of it, such a proposal from God (the real one of Love) should not be difficult. What is different about this one is that it is totally based upon our Higher Beings, not the egos as the little gods within each of us.

Let me lay upon you some insight to the New Earth that is forming in the 4D ethers of consciousness as a result of the shift during the End Times. Through the seeding of the new unity consciousness of the last wave the seeding by way of pure intent and love, humanity are planting into the ethers of pure love the blueprint and construct for the New Earth. It is here the concept of form and purpose is created that precedes the conception which through the purity of divine male and female are conceived into creation.

This is about the melding of three elements through the intent of unity consciousness; the pure New Earth as a 5D concept of intent of pure consciousness, as the melding of physical purity; the alignment of cosmic forces and planets; and the overlay of the purity of love manifestation of that which is heaven. This is the concept like Genesis that is conceived in the joint minds and is birthed as an egg of union of male and female as equal divine energies.

This seeding of New Earth then follows the process of the 9th wave into temporary energy of 4D which may be likened to the gestation of the New Earth, ending at the Dec 21st Solstice/Equinox of 2011 shortly after as a Time Of Choosing. It is the formation or congealing into 4D of the model of New Earth, ready to receive its inhabitants that have so chosen to evolve through the final stage of evolution from 3D to 5D for them and from 4D to 3D for New Earth.

During the year 2012 the shift of the process of transformation into 3D are occurring as the cosmic forces of ascension shower upon those chosen to move with Gaia, and Gaia herself. These particular frequencies are acting as triggers to activate the DNA antenna and receivers. This new form, like the chrysalis opening will show itself more and more to those aware of it. It then begins to congeal into the parallel hologram of New Earth. And so the 3D representation of the hologram will be born at the time of the great alignment of Dec 21, 2012, in preparation for the great resurrection of the New Earth. It will be so within the total unity consciousness of God and the Christ Consciousness.

Then with the cosmic configuration of forces and planets, when the New Earth has shifted from the 5D concept, to 4D conception to manifestation and creation in 3D reality, it will be ready to accept souls who have chosen to move into that reality. Of course by that time the Great Revelation (Time of Choosing) and the Great Resurrection (Time of Transformation of Ascension) will have readied those for the shift to the New Earth reality.

It is the Time of Transformation that physicality begins to congeal into new form, both for Gaia, the New Earth, and humanity that chooses to ascend with her. The separation of Old and New Earth will become a conscious reality and the final formation will be after the Earth, like humanity, has been gifted the cosmic forces and overlays that will be completed by the time of 3D birth. From then on, again, like in a newborn child, the configuration of the stars, the contracts each are creating now, and the movements of the Cosmic Gods of creation will guide the evolution of the New Earth. And the New Beings linked between realities of 3D-5D will emerge, then evolve into the next age of unconditional love over 26000 years, spilling their presence into the Galaxies.

What is your lesson here? Look around you and look beyond to see what is happening around all Earthlings now. It is a time to choose above Light and Dark and align polarity of separation, with the new consciousness. What Consciousness? It is the Christ Consciousness and size the key of unconditional forgiveness. Both Dark and Light as we have seen, are on the paths to convergence at the gate. It is time to understand that a great shift is here and it is time to see Home and be the creator you are.

Over half of this book has been dedicated to revelation of a different story of history and a different perception, interpretation from, in many cases, the same sources of information. Hence we have the great conundrum of what is really truth. This great conundrum had in the last 12 years come forward because a shifting consciousness seems to be prevalent that seeks out a new version of truth because the old version is not acceptable--something is amiss. More and more researchers have come forward to reveal a different story of the past. More and more people have come forward with a drive to peace and love of spirituality. And hence we have the great conundrum of the ages.

Will it be the Old Earth ways humanity accepts under the New World Order or will it be the New Earth ways of the New Order of the Ages? Both are written, hidden in plain view, but both are subject to the fickle perceptions of consciousness driving beliefs. Both new and old version had, or have a knowing that something important, and big were to occur at this particular time as the shift from the Age of Pisces to that of Aquarius. One is a continuation of dominion and the ways of kings and empires, one is the liberation of spirit and oneness.

If one should look around now, at this juncture in time, the undeniable truth of the world leaders being placed on the spotlight for their behaviours cannot be ignored. It is because changes are occurring that demand responsibility and transparency. Humanity has simply accepted being dual in nature-part good, part bad. It is the way we have been taught and it is the way the leaders behave. The familiar behaviour of being good until someone pisses you off, or offering a smidgen of kindness to a poor soul absolving all your wrongs, or loving and protecting your close family but taking advantage of those that are not, are all too familiar traits of this duality. It is the same duality between god and Satan. It is what humanity has accepted as their belief and hence it is what that unit of consciousness attracts consciously and unconsciously.

That duality seems to be shifting in favour of the goodness.

The Undeniable Theme of Prevailing Consciousness

So let us summarize the old story of Revelations. The old story can be summarized When you finally get to the end of the old biblical story, to the final Book of Revelation, when the ascended Christ comes back, the story which is presented imposes an automatic policing system of threat and destruction for mankind. And it is Christ, the Son of God— the one that helped Dad create the Old Earth that bears the warning about the End Times. In this prophesy (the old business plan), it is that Satan will be crushed (20:7) and there will be a final Judgment day (20:11); there will be a new heaven on Earth (21:1) where a new Jerusalem will rise (21:9) and when he comes it will be swift to judge if you are not in the accounting ledger (22:7) that is within the Time of the End (22:10). It is this threat that polices the believers through fear of each not being "worthy" and this is the major theme in the vast writings. This story is in this time, under attack.

For, like the fickle ways of perception, within these writings is hidden a truth in plain sight. And it is one that has and still vibrates with much of humanity, especially in this time. For even though the bible is filled with the duality and polarity, it still contains the story of this man called Christ who came down to prophesize the Revelation of End Time. The story, part contrived, part truth does, regardless of edition reflect a consciousness of love and peace, despite the conclusion that it is written with a possible contrived mortal purpose of a manifesto of dominion over the sinful creatures of Planet Earth. It draws out a theme that this Christ, who was deemed a Prophet or the Son of God later, reflected a consciousness so many people quietly and inherently would like to believe in—a New Earth of peace and love.

It is this aspect of the stories, despite the motivations of their creation, that in all due regards to the biblical system, has kept this Christ spark alive in the story of Christ or Allah, or whatever. And regardless of whether he was deemed as a prophet, Messiah, Son of God or whatever, the legend carries an underlying energy of something that is wanton in all—like an encoding within the essence of humanity; their DNA.

Even though the four gospels upon which the New Testament was based on were written between 75 and 100 years after Christ, by unknown authors, and are conflictive in their stories, in essence, it seems that Christ was indeed a very unusual fellow. Not only was he capable of creating some very unusual miracles, he was responsible for showing a new way of thought—that of being aligned with the real God of truth and love, and we all are Sons and Daughters of God. It is this that is surfacing in these times. And for what it is worth, he is responsible for a consciousness, a way of thinking and living that is parallel to this revolution of thought surfacing during these current times.

It is about the Christ Consciousness. The human mind has spiritual currents running through its thought streams. These streams contain vital information from Spirit that is highly valuable to humans. Spirit is the source of everything TRUE, BEAUTIFUL, and GOOD and conveys these ideals through the human mind that intersect with a person's beliefs, helping the individual ascend into the higher information that uplifts and improves the quality of life. Or have I got it all wrong? Is God not peace, love, harmony, forgiveness and without judgment?

In human life, spiritual growth is achieved by aligning with these spiritual currents that come from both the personality and mind of Spirit by intellectual assent and emotional devotion. Christ Consciousness is the growing human recognition and blending of the human evolutionary (or ego) mind with the Divine Mind and the Divine Personality that is the source of human happiness and fulfillment. This awareness accrues over time within the consciousness of human thinking when intention, attention, and openness is focused on knowing who and what is that "christed" state of being—that higher mindedness of enlightenment.

As this awareness in the human mind grows and strengthens, life becomes more liberated, joyful, peaceful, and love-dominated. The fear which creates isolation and despair begins to diminish in thought and feeling. You are free to live the life you were born to live —as a child of Spirit in a love-filled and supportive universe.

The highest state of intellectual development and emotional maturity is sometimes termed the "christed" state because of the sacredness and purity of the individual who has achieved it. Jesus achieved this in his human life, and was given this term before his name as the recognition of his achievement of this spiritual status. This path is open to anyone regardless of their religious tradition if and when he or she is open to become a living vessel of LOVE and TRUTH on the planet and actively strives to attain it.

This is the prime truth that religions, despite their higher caustic motivations and acts have kept alive. It is not a term used exclusively in the Christian religion, nor does it mean that you must adhere to the Christian belief system to attain this state. All ways and paths are honored if they lead a person into becoming more loving, forgiving, patient, kind, compassionate, tolerant, and happy. All paths of LOVE lead to the same Source of All That Is. We all share the same Creator-Source as living expressions of that Source Personality and we all are moving back home to unite with our Source.

Christ consciousness is the state of awareness of our true nature, our higher self, and our birthright as children of God. Christ consciousness is our living expression as a child of Spirit as we unfold our own Divine life plan onto the earth plane bringing heaven to earth. Living in the reality of our "christed" self is actually being fully alive and invested in who we truly are. In our "christed" self we live as inspiration for others to seek this for themselves so we can collectively move our planet forward into the Divine Plan for planetary transformation and glorification.

At this point, let us go back to the prophesies of biblical writings and look at some new interpretations. The prophesises such a Revelations were written suspiciously like the writers knew something and the turn of the Ages. And it is written like they had a plan called the New World Order. So far, humanity has accepted this plan and we are at the final moments of its unfolding, as has been written here.

As we have discussed, something else is going on. It is the shifting consciousness that is choosing a different path. And again that may also be hidden in plain view, written in the same books and bibles. Just as we have brought forward a different picture of Christ, perhaps there is a different picture of New and Old Earth? Let us now look at the different versions.

And so it has come to pass that there are the two opposing dualistic plans of good and evil are the topic in this time of the new century. And it can be interpreted from the same sources that are without exception written by man, not God.

A New Prophesy Of Rapture, Revelation And Resurrection

So now we have looked the dark side of the business plan. These plans and prophesies have been hidden in plain view for centuries and they have been integrated into many belief systems on the Old Earth. That is perhaps why it has unfolded the way it has; because humanity believes and follows what they are told and that, in itself, is the energy that is brought forward into humanity's reality. But there is a new plan evolving and it reflects the The New Order of the Ages. It is apparent that the consciousness in the last 12 years has been shifting from Religious to Spiritual ways of earthly expression. This particular time has taken on the name of the "End Times".

So we have looked the Old Earth plan as can be interpreted from the Book of Revelations and others. There are many versions of this and there are many interpretations. These are all about what can be encapsulated into these End Times. It is what those dominant religions put into the minds of the followers. It would also appear to include be some scheduled events which forms a strategic implantation trigger of the final takeover. After all, dominion over others is accomplished best when those dominated fear something, especially god who deems all as sinful creatures. The greatest perpetrators of this have been, and still are of course the major religions who want the people to be obedient to believe in *their* god's word. The threat is clear as it says in the good book—vengeance will be done.

It can all be summed within three words and many, many interpretations.

Whether it is religion, New Age, or whatever, there is an absolute preponderance of information about the End Times. What are they? It's when humanity kisses their dear asses goodbye if they have not been good and have not taken their blue pills given by the church (The Matrix movie) of faithful obedience. These pills are received from the Vatican and other such institutions in return for your sins symbolizing your obedience, service, faith, and trust.

The things that are supposedly going to happen during these End Times are pretty impressive. Cataclysmic events, final battles with Satan, self destruction by war and nuclear means; astronomical alignments that pour rays of destruction, climatic shifts, polar shifts, magnetic reversal, global flooding, blah, blah, blah. It's the gods finally having their fill of man who is the master of self destruction and teaching them a serious lesson this time. Just type 2012 into Google and see what you get.

There is no doubt that many prophets have been responsible for this doom scenario, obviously part of the planning committees. But those of dominion like to tell us about doom because it raises fear. Fear is what keeps the sheeple in the pen eating their blue pills.

The most popular time of this doom has been the turn of this century when all sorts of nasties were to happen as we hit these End Times. Most of the prophets like Nostradamus and Cayce screwed up on this one. But let us take some versions of End Times allegedly reflected by the words gods and God. They are always "coming". Nobody can really say what these times are and what will happen but what is important here is to understand that the End Times marks a point of change stuck in the minds of men. What is most relevant here is to understand that the End Times is a time of shift from what is Old Earth to what is to be—New Earth. It is the way it shifts that is the big controversy.

And shifting it is as we will reveal in this following chapters. It just *ain't happenin'* the way the bloodlines and their kings and queens thought...

The New End Time Of Revelation

We have already pointed out the unprecedented growth in non-religious and New Agers that vibrates with a new consciousness. Since 1987, a time referred to as the Harmonic Convergence, there's been a new "buzz". It is a process of change in consciousness. What does this mean? It isn't just Neo who feels something amiss. More and more people are beginning to "think" differently about the material world, about the meaning of life, about the world around them. It's like Morpheus in the Matrix said about feeling something is not right. It is about how we relate to each other and how we relate to the Earth we live on. It's about all these gods and those kings and queens and high government officials that people gave their trust to. *Something is not right.*

Underneath more and more of our thinking time is a deep stir, a wave of desire for a better earth of peace and love. But how? It is the evolution of a different conscious awareness. Yet it still seems so unattainable. It is about a peaceful cohabitation and it began as something in the back of our minds—a sort of gut feeling from our hearts that we are being deceived from some of the crucial truths. That we may be chasing the wrong dreams and perhaps there is more to life than living in a materialistic gopher wheel serving these self proclaimed gods who love taxes, obedience, rules, and love to hoard for their own kind. But what can a mere mortal do about this? Most are trapped in the old energies because they keep chewing on the blue pills.

Many refer to this new feeling as the New Age, some the Unity Consciousness, some just the End Times. There are many names and as many ideas on this. But one thing that this new consciousness of self incorporates is that it is not an organized religion or a group. There are no leaders, no real dogma. It is some evolving awareness that has a common spiritual denominator, and it is based upon love of all things, a peaceful world of harmony that is marked by a transition time. It's a strange gut feel that something better is available.

Of course humanity likes to take this movement and make a buck in it. It is because so many have themselves made a god of ego and money. So people create great marketing ploys and devices and groups that sell you a new life, new secrets to health and wealth. It makes it hard to gain credibility this way yet despite this you cannot ever identify this movement as a dogma by a large institution like the Catholic, Protestant, or Islamic groups. It is simply an inconsistent evolution of a free spirit belief system that is pretty consistent in its beliefs.

And whether there are saviours here, great mystics, healers and wonderful products, that doesn't matter because the bottom line is that they are focused on the same dream—one of a New Earth and a new you that is more than you have believed. When you start to compile these beliefs, you begin to create a New Earth story; and it even has a storyline somewhat similar to the Old Earth storyline of rapture, revelation and resurrection.

What this boils down to is the difference between religious and spiritual, best exemplified by the dominant groups. In simple terms, religion deals with a mortal human who lives a life to serve god and his self-proclaimed cronies. He then dies beholding to the gods for his salvation into eternity. Spiritual deals with an immortal being here for the expression through temporary form of human body to express and expand love to attain joy, as an aspect of God, the Creator himself. So Religion is about serving god, Spirituality is about being God.

So what does this New Earth plan and this new consciousness movement suggest?

Well, let us call this a Divine Plan for lack of a better description. It is unfolding right before us that has never happened before. This End Time is between the turn of the century and 2012, and in the beliefs of the New Agers it has to do with various cosmic forces and planetary alignments that happen once in 26,000 years. These are forces that influence consciousness, and hence behaviour. Of course everyone has a choice as to whether they let this new consciousness into their awareness to create new behaviour. Needless to say, you have free will and choice to decide, just like you decide to eat the blue pills.

But at any rate, during this shift into the new 26,000 year cycle—called the Age of Aquarius—there is commonality to certain things that are going to happen that shower a new "knowing" into the consciousness of humanity. It is a dramatic acceleration of what Neo felt and what so many are feeling.

It is a New Earth story.

Revelation is indeed the revealing or disclosing, or making something obvious through active or passive communication with supernatural and divine entities. This time, the **Revelation** originates directly from the Source. Yes, God—the real One—directly to you and into your personal consciousness, not through anyone else. It is because we are all God, as Christ taught. So it is **we** that are implementing this new plan. There are no middle men to tell you what the Word of God is because you begin to understand that it is you that is the "chosen one" already privy to the truth of God.

But it is not going to be disclosed by Jesus himself. It is *you* that is going to go through a **Resurrection** and all who so choose to believe this will resurrect themselves coming back to a re-life as the Second Coming of Christ. It is not one guy, it is all!

So there are no chosen ones after a big meeting deciding to remove all Christians from the Earth, to protect them. This **Rapture** is simply your own choice when you understand that you are something else than what you have been told to believe as a mortal human. So Jesus will not "snatch us" out of harm's way if we have been good. It is you that simply decides a new way. For under this story good and bad are judgments and love cannot and does not judge. Thus, there is no judgment. It's like a mother who truly loves her kid; regardless of what the little monster does, she loves him and does not judge. It is the other people who judge and may force her to action—the consciousness of others prevails.

Then the goodies you get through **Revelation** are indeed the revealing or disclosing, through active or passive communication of who you really are—an aspect of God, an eternal being borrowing a body to experience a time slice on Earth. And this is where a common denominator of vibration fits in. You vibrate higher and higher, releasing many of those miraculous abilities that Jesus the Christ himself had—especially the healing. So you can look at this as a mass revealing of Jesus the Christ through the consciousness shift. But it is *not* Jesus suddenly appearing. It is the Time of Revelation when the *knowing* of this, and in many cases, the *showing* of this (as he did), is revealed. It is about attaining a higher expression of God through You as a piece of God which is everything as One, living laughing and loving in thought, word and deed.

So we see that this Revelation is the revealing of Jesus Christ as being each of us and that the message now comes directly from God the Father as a wakeup call of rapture. And it is a revealing that there is no sin and that the heaven we seek is already within us as immortal, eternal aspects of God. So it is a call not to serve gods, or listen to other's interpretations of God's Word, but to BE God and know for yourself. The revealing is that you don't need gurus, bishops, meditators or the likes to tell you the secrets of heaven, being eternal and how to have a better life. It is simply the acceptance of who you are that is already living a life as a Spiritual entity borrowing a body to be within rather than a body looking for spirit outside of itself.

And what of those poor souls that do not want to believe or accept this? Well here we go again. **Armageddon.** Which one? Guess what? It's the one you are in now. The one that creates fear, conflict, with a drive of ego to survive and dominate. It is called the world of separation from who you are. Now interestingly enough, this Armageddon changes as all this shifts in consciousness toward 2012.

Is there bad news here? Is there something that happens to those who want to believe in their old ways? What if you choose to take the path that this is just all more dogmatic horseshit with a new color?

What about those that have not chosen to believe who they are? It is indeed being left in your own harm's way and guess what? Yes, **Armageddon**—End Times. You continue paying for your sins of hatred and separation and conflict and fear as you are doing right now. It becomes a clear understanding of how _you_ attract that which you create. Is it hard to believe that if you hate people they will hate you back? It wasn't God that did this, it was you. It is you that attracts it by the energy you create; the big difference is that energy in the Old Earth will not be inflicted upon anyone else like it was in the old regime. And get this; through the End Times it will manifest itself to return faster and faster until it becomes instant.

That is the true Armageddon where you create your own Hell at your own choosing, and of your own intensity. Is the fight with Mr. Devil in the cards here? It sure is if you want to hold to the old ways of deception and greed that you want to inflict on others! Your fight is with yourself—the Devil is within.

And **rapture**? The only people that are going to get snatched out of their own devils (harm's way) are the ones that choose to understand who they are—and the snatching is of their own accord.

So this is not a big battle between Satan and the kings of the Earth as the end of the world dawns. It is a battle of your own mind, of who you are. It is about your own conscious awareness and belief that you will do battle with. It is about the knowing that you will inflict upon your mortal being to create your own life. The battle of Armageddon is a battle of belief in yourself. Do you keep chewing the blue pills or not. Indirectly this is indeed a conscious choice of Heaven or Hell.

That's a pretty simple choice is it not? Heaven or Hell? Perhaps not if you are stuck in the old world?

Let us bring in another old over-used term of **Crucifixion.** In the End Times it is the process of crucifying what is Hell by leaving it behind and choosing Heaven. It is the death of the old in choice of the new. Even on Old Earth, everyone, yes everyone, has a choice of how (bad or good) they perceive any situation. And when you learn that what you perceive as you think, speak feel and act upon brings upon you like energy, you may pay more attention to what you think and do. That is what the choice is all about. Instead of saying you believe what these religions and the Vatican and the leaders tell you, you say: _"Ok, I have had enough with this Old Earth and I want to live a life of unconditional love, peace and joy."_ And by acceptance, just like a commercial contract, it is so enacted by your intent. That simple act to believe differently can change your whole life.

So the story is similar but with a different twist from what the dominant religions tell you.

Is this another dogma? Well, it ain't written by God in an autographed hard cover. It ain't on the evening news. And it certainly ain't supported by any religion. And there ain't no leaders. But it is unfolding all around everyone at the same time if you have the eyes, ears and heart to open to this revelation. What follows in the book is simply information about what IS happening. You cannot make a choice if there is no alternative known to you.

So here is your challenge; read this as a fantasy version if you like. It is no more fantasy than Genesis or Moses parting the Red Sea, or Noah's Ark. Then look around you and listen to what's happening and what you feel in your heart. You can't BS the heart and this may lead you to burning the prescription for blue pills.

So will it be the New World Order of PLANET EARTH or New Order of the Ages of Planet Earth? Which Revelation will **We** unfold as the plan? It appears to be a different one than the powers that be have been planned. Can another biblical expression be true: _"... and the meek shall inherit the earth"_.

26

THE CHRIST CONSCIOUSNESS

If you have not picked up on this yet, not all business plans succeed. And the failure is usually because the masses do not want the product being flogged. The other thing that may have come forward is that the new version of Christ's life has become a dominant topic by thousands of researchers. And as has been pointed out, the new version seems to coincide with what we have summarized in the Aquarian Gospels in Part 1. And finally, you may have also picked up the notion that what this fellow Christ really taught is a whole lot different than what is taught by the dominant religions, in fact it is the same as what we just revealed as the **New Earth version of Revelation** in the previous chapter. What this mass of meek inheritors of earth are finding not in their gut, but in their heart, is a whole new belief system that says a resounding *NO* to the way things have been. Let's look further into this belief system that is the Christ Consciousness.

The Shifting Consciousness Of New Earth

So now we may ask: What is the Christ Consciousness? What does it mean as far as a life belief and a way of life? What is the real story of Christ? What does this all tell us to do? Is this even relevant in my life?

The answer is that it has great relevance regardless of who wins the battle of Armageddon. But, as history now shows, the last 12 years speaks for itself. **If we revisit the first chapter to look at the table of "followers" of the top religions, they were, as of 2005 shown below.**

RELIGION	FOLLOWERS		%	ORIGINS
1. Christianity	2,100,000,000	2,100,000,000	30.58%	100-33CE
2. Islam	1,500,000,000	3,600,000,000	52.42%	600CE
3. Nonreligious	**1,100,000,000**	**4,700,000,000**	**68.44%**	
4. Hinduism	900,000,000	5,600,000,000	81.54%	2000BCE
5. Chinese	394,000,000	5,994,000,000	87.28%	
6. Buddhism	376,000,000	6,370,000,000	92.75%	600BC
7. Primal-indigenous	300,000,000	6,670,000,000	97.12%	

Wikipedia reports Buddhism is being recognized as the fastest growing religion in Western societies both in terms of new converts and more so in terms of friends of Buddhism who seek to study and practice various aspects of Buddhism. As in the United States, Buddhism is ranked among the fastest growing religions in many Western European countries. The Australian Bureau of Statistics through statistical analysis held Buddhism to be the fastest growing spiritual tradition/religion in Australia in terms of percentage gain with a growth of 79.1% for the period 1996 to 2001. However, because Australia is statistically small, no inferences can be drawn from that for the whole world.

Buddhism is the fastest-growing religion in England's jails, with the number of followers rising eightfold over the past decade.

The American Religious Identification Survey gave non-religious groups the largest gain in terms of absolute numbers - 14,300,000 (8.4% of the population) to 29,400,000 (14.1% of the population) for the period 1990 to 2001 in the USA. Reuters describes how a study profiling the "No religion" demographic found that the so-called "Nones", at least in the U.S., are the fastest growing religious affiliation category. The "Nones" comprise 33% agnostics, 33% theists, and 10% atheists.

A similar pattern has been found in other countries such as Australia, Canada and Mexico. According to statistics in Canada, the number of "Nones" more than doubled (an increase of about 60%) between 1985 and 2004. In Australia, census data from the Australian Bureau of Statistics give "no religion" the largest gains in absolute numbers over the 15 years from 1991 to 2006, from 2,948,888 (18.2% of the population that answered the question) to 3,706,555 (21.0% of the population that answered the question). According to INEGI, in Mexico, the number of atheists grows annually by 5.2%, while the number of Catholics grows by 1.7%. What about those Christians who sit on a fence to still call themselves Christians but are not feeling "quite right" about the "Word of God"?

We are now at 2012. What do you suppose these "nones", Buddhists and New Agers have in common? It is a new consciousness that has a common denominator similar to what Christ expressed. In most cases, what Christ expressed, manly that of love and peace is what these followers "select" out of the writings. What is really coming forward is that there really is no God up in the sky. It is us as everything, as One. There is no heaven and hell except what we bring upon ourselves. Add to this the Christians of 2.1 billion who fundamentally believe in the love and peace parts of the bibles simply rejecting all else, and there is one massive mental wave wanting to show itself in the reality of Planet Earth.

GROUP	Hinduism	Buddhism	Christianity	Islam	Nones
NUMBER	900,000	376,000	2,100,000,000	840,000	1,100,000,000
BEGIN	4000BC	500BC	30AD	622AD	2000AD
FOUNDER	None	Siddhartha Gautama	Jesus Christ	Muhammad .	None
gods	Many	Enlightened Buddhas)	One	One	One
WORD	4 Vedas.	Sutras Tantra Zen	The Bible	The Koran	None

If you relook the core beliefs of Buddhism, one fundamental belief of Buddhism is often referred to as reincarnation -- the concept that people are reborn after dying. In fact, most individuals go through many cycles of birth, living, death and rebirth. A practicing Buddhist differentiates between the concepts of rebirth and reincarnation. In reincarnation, the individual may recur repeatedly. In rebirth, a person does not necessarily return to Earth as the same entity ever again. He compares it to a leaf growing on a tree. When the withering leaf falls off, a new leaf will eventually replace it. It is similar to the old leaf, but it is not identical to the original leaf. After many such cycles, if a person releases their attachment to desire and the self, they can attain Nirvana. This is a state of liberation and freedom from suffering. Why is Buddhism such a rage? Let us look deeper.

The Three Trainings or Practices consist of:

Sila: Virtue, good conduct, morality. This is based on two fundamental principles:
The principle of equality: that all living entities are equal.
The principle of reciprocity: This is the "*Golden Rule*" in Christianity -- to do onto others as you would wish them to do onto you. It is found in all major religions.
Samadhi: Concentration, meditation, mental development. Developing one's mind is the path to wisdom which in turn leads to personal freedom. Mental development also strengthens and controls our mind; this helps us maintain good conduct.
Prajna: Discernment, insight, wisdom, enlightenment. This is the real heart of Buddhism. Wisdom will emerge if your mind is pure and calm.

The Buddha's *Four Noble Truths* explore human suffering. They may be described (somewhat simplistically) as:

Dukkha: *Suffering exists:* (Suffering is real and almost universal. Suffering has many causes: loss, sickness, pain, failure, the impermanence of pleasure.)
Samudaya*: There is a cause for suffering.* (It is the desire to have and control things. It can take many forms: craving of sensual pleasures; the desire for fame; the desire to avoid unpleasant sensations, like fear, anger or jealousy.)
Nirodha: *There is an end to suffering.* (Suffering ceases with the final liberation of Nirvana (a.k.a. Nibbana). The mind experiences complete freedom, liberation and non-attachment. It lets go of any desire or craving.)
Magga: *In order to end suffering, you must follow the Eightfold Path.*

The Five Precepts are rules to live by. They are somewhat analogous to the second half of the Ten Commandments in Judaism and Christianity -- that part of the Decalogue which describes behaviours to avoid. However, they are recommendations, not commandments. Believers are expected to use their own intelligence in deciding exactly how to apply these rules:

- Do not kill. This is sometimes translated as "*not harming*" or an absence of violence.
- Do not steal. This is generally interpreted as including the avoidance of fraud and economic exploitation.
- Do not lie. This is sometimes interpreted as including name calling, gossip, etc.
- Do not misuse sex. For monks and nuns, this means any departure from complete celibacy. For the laity, adultery is forbidden, along with any sexual harassment or exploitation, including that within marriage. The Buddha did not discuss consensual premarital sex within a committed relationship; Thus, Buddhist traditions differ on this. Most Buddhists, probably influenced by their local cultures, condemn same-sex sexual activity regardless of the nature of the relationship between the people involved.
- Do not consume alcohol or other drugs. The main concern here is that intoxicants cloud the mind. Some have included as a drug other methods of divorcing ourselves from reality -- e.g. movies, television, the Internet. [1]

Those preparing for monastic life or who are not within a family are expected to avoid an additional five activities:

6. Taking untimely meals.
7. Dancing, singing, music, watching grotesque mime.
8. Use of garlands, perfumes and personal adornment.
9. Use of high seats.
10. Accepting gold or silver.

There is also a series of eight precepts which are composed of the first seven listed above, followed by the eighth and ninth combined as one. "Ordained Theravada monks promise to follow 227 precepts

The Buddha's *Eightfold Path* consists of:

Panna: Discernment, wisdom:
1) *Samma ditthi* Right Understanding of the Four Noble Truths
2) *Samma sankappa:* Right thinking; following the right path in life
Sila: Virtue, morality:
3) *Samma vaca:* Right speech: no lying, criticism, condemning, gossip, harsh language
4) *Samma kammanta* Right conduct by following the Five Precepts
5) *Samma ajiva*: Right livelihood; support yourself without harming others
Samadhi: Concentration, meditation:
6) *Samma vayama* Right Effort: promote good thoughts; conquer evil thoughts
7) *Samma sati* Right Mindfulness: Become aware of your body, mind and feelings
8) *Samma samadhi* Right Concentration: Meditate to achieve a higher state of consciousness

New Age Spirituality And Core Beliefs

What is the New Age Movement? It is similar to New Age Spirituality, but different enough to warrant its own definition. The New Age Movement is a belief that the human race is all one. It is not about equality nor diversity. It is the idea that your gender, age, religion, race, nor sexual orientation makes you better or worse than anyone else. The New Age Movement is moving away from the US against THEM mentality. It is inclusive, open, detached from labels, and above all else, it's based in love not fear.

At our deepest level, there are only two motivators - love and fear. Fear breeds hate, anger, vengeance, greed, violence, selfishness, and alienates us from truly connecting with spirit and with each other. Love breeds compassion, peace, understanding, forgiveness, charity, gentleness, partnership, and a sense of connectedness with spirit and with each other. One can focus on either motivator and see the logic behind it. Should you choose to see lack, poverty, and attacks towards your fellow man, it's easy to become fearful. It is part of the survival of the fittest. Fight or flight saved many a caveman to live another day and to breed more like himself. One can also argue that to see the beauty and tenderness that humanity is known to share with each other that it is logical to love thy neighbour and to turn the other cheek. There will always be intelligent arguments for both sides. We as a species have evolved enough to make our own decisions as to which will govern us as individuals.

The New Age Movement proposes that as a collective people we are also able to make an educated enlightened decision as to whether we will be controlled by our fears or by our loves. Will we be a society of angry divided hateful individuals? Or will we be a global community of loving supportive people who honour each other's right to choose their own path? Like all political, religious, and social movements there are zealots and extremists among the New Age Movement. In the same way that all Christians are not white supremacists and all Pagans are not Satan worshippers, all New Agers are not aging hippies sitting around getting stoned and playing with crystals. Those who endorse the New Age Movement are as diverse as any other group. Their one common belief is that love and true spirituality should lead us as a people, not fear and hatred of anything we deem as different from ourselves.

The New Age Movement embraces the teachings of Christ, the teachings of Buddha, the Native American teachings, the ancient Celtic Pagan teachings, and modern science's latest findings and teachings. We are explorers trying to understand spirituality on a deeper nuts and bolts level. It is not enough to be told by our parents that one religion is right and all others are wrong. We have a desire to understand and to choose for ourselves what is or is not spiritual. The result is that many New Agers have found themselves holding an eclectic view of religion. Many Native Americans have blended the teaching of Christ within their own beliefs. Many Pagans can see how much they have in common with the Native American beliefs. It is not unusual for Catholics to feel a deep connection to the Buddhist teachings. Forgive me for omitting so many other religions and beliefs but I am simply giving broad examples for the sake of making a point. The New Age Movement was birthed from this exploration of each other's beliefs. How can we hate someone so much like ourselves?

In our version of the story, Christ did not teach blind hatred nor did he teach his followers to give their personal power away to the churches and governments. Only when the churches and governments took over his teachings did that all become part of being a 'good Christian.' He did not tell us to hate nor to judge. Bigotry and war is not Christ-like, nor Buddha-like, nor in keeping with the core teachings of any religion. All spiritual teachers taught the same message - love one another and do not harm each other nor the planet and the animals given to you. Take the politics out of religion and they all come down to the same wonderful teachings that have been trampled on by dogma, greed, and bigotry.

The New Age doctrines are pretty simple:

- All is One
- All is God
- Humanity is God
- A change in consciousness
- All religions are one
- Cosmic evolutionary optimism

Norman L. Geyser focuses on 14 doctrines typical of New Age religions:

1) an impersonal god (force)
2) an eternal universe
3) an illusory nature of matter
4) a cyclical nature of life
5) the necessity of reincarnations
6) the evolution of man into godhood
7) continuing revelations from beings beyond the world
8) the identity of man with God
9) the need for meditation (or other consciousness-changing techniques)
10) occult practices (astrology, mediums and so forth)
11) vegetarianism and holistic health
12) pacifism (or anti-war activities)
13) one world (global) order
14) syncretism (unity of all religions)

Since 1987, a time referred to as the Harmonic Convergence, there's been a new "buzz". It is a process of change in consciousness. What does this mean? It isn't just Neo who feels something amiss. More and more people are beginning to "think" differently about the material world, about the meaning of life, about the world around them. It's like

Morpheus in the Matrix said about feeling something is not right. It is about how we relate to each other and how we relate to the Earth we live on. It's about all these gods and those kings and queens and high government officials that people gave their trust to. *Something is not right.*

Underneath more and more of our thinking time is a deep stir, a wave of desire for a better earth of peace and love. But how? It is the evolution of a different conscious awareness. Yet it still seems so unattainable. It is about a peaceful cohabitation and it began as something in the back of our minds—a sort of gut feeling from our hearts that we are being deceived from some of the crucial truths. That we may be chasing the wrong dreams and perhaps there is more to life than living in a materialistic gopher wheel serving these self proclaimed gods who love taxes, obedience, rules, and love to hoard for their own kind. But what can a mere mortal do about this? Most are trapped in the old energies because they keep chewing on the blue pills given free by the Vatican- well perhaps not *really* free when you trade your Soul!

Many refer to this new feeling as the New Age, some the Unity Consciousness, some just the End Times. There are many names and as many ideas on this. But one thing that this new consciousness of self incorporates is that it is not an organized religion or a group. There are no leaders, no real dogma. It is some evolving awareness that has a common spiritual denominator, and it is based upon love of all things, a peaceful world of harmony that is marked by a transition time. It's a strange gut feel that something better is available.

Of course humanity likes to take this movement and make a buck in it. It is because so many have themselves made a god of ego and money. So people create great marketing ploys and devices and groups that sell you a new life, new secrets to health and wealth. It makes it hard to gain credibility this way yet despite this you cannot ever identify this movement as a dogma by a large institution like the Catholic, Protestant, or Islamic groups. It is simply an inconsistent evolution of a free spirit belief system that is pretty consistent in its beliefs.

And whether there are saviors here, great mystics, healers and wonderful products, that doesn't matter because the bottom line is that they are focused on the same dream—one of a New Earth and a new you that is more than you have believed. When you start to compile these beliefs, you begin to create a New Earth story; and it even has a storyline somewhat similar to the Old Earth storyline of rapture, revelation and resurrection.

What this boils down to is the difference between religious and spiritual, best exemplified by the dominant groups. In simple terms, religion deals with a mortal human who lives a life to serve god and his self-proclaimed cronies. He then dies beholding to the gods for his salvation into eternity. Spiritual deals with an immortal being here for the expression through temporary form of human body to express and expand love to attain joy, as an aspect of God, the Creator himself. So Religion is about serving god, Spirituality is about being God.

So what does this New Earth plan and this new consciousness movement suggest?

Well, we have talked about a Divine Plan unfolding right before us that has never happened before. This End Time is between the turn of the century and 2012, and it has to do with various cosmic forces and planetary alignments that happen once in 26,000 years. These are forces that influence consciousness, and hence behaviour. Of course everyone has a choice as to whether they let this new consciousness into their awareness to create new behaviour. Needless to say, you have free will and choice to decide, just like you decide to eat the blue pills.

The Christ Consciousness From The Aquarian Gospel

Nobody wrote the rule book or a bible on what has evolved as the Christ Consciousness. It simply came to life on its own as more and more people have come to learn what they do NOT want in life. So it is a quest that has manifested from a feeling within, a feeling of the heart: love, peace, harmony.

- There is no rule book, dogma.
- There is no judgement or sin
- There is no telling you what to believe
- It is deduced by one's self
- There is no gods of vengeance
- there is no non equality, sin, punishment, power, slavery

Humanity has from birth accepted the limits of the joint consciousness be it culture family or nation. The immediate quest shifts itself into the perceptions and beliefs that move from the though and the word into deed and translate into the reality. The old reality is one of gods, kings, queens, evil against good as the fundamental mental quest, but limited by the invisible rules and beliefs that translate it to the reality. And so it is with the consciousness of humility. The two version of the rule books the bible and the Aquarian Gospel are different in that that the Christ carries a different consciousness and all the evil and bounds are not there. In the other, the bounds are the bible, the rules, the vengeance, slavery, of obedience, of fear, etc. Delete these and you have a new rule book of perception that limits the soul.

And so this new wave of evolving living consciousness has come into fruition in the last 12 years. and the belief system has converged into the same place. So let us look back to the Aquarian Gospel had look at what this fellow Jesus The Christ embodied as what he said was the true expression of God:

Here it is in simple bullet form

- God and man are One
- God is love, requires no sacrifice, has no judgement
- Truth is one and everywhere
- The Holy Breath is truth, was, is and evermore shall be
- Force is the will of God and that will is manifest directed by the Breath
- Man and God are One
- Heaven and Hell are within
- Man tore himself away from God by carnal thoughts, the Holy breath can make them one again
- God clothed man in flesh so he may comprehend the only saviour of the world is love, and Jesus comes to manifest that love to men
- Every living thing is bound by cords to every other living thing
- Blest are the pure of heart for they love and do not demand love in return
- There are two selfs; the lower is illusion, the higher is God in an the embodiment of truth, love justice, the higher and lower mercy right, The lower is an illusion, the carnal self, body of desires, reflex ion of higher by murky ethers of flesh
- He who know well his lower self, knows the illusions of the world
- Evil is a myth, the devil from which men are redeemed is self, the lower self
- Mans saviour is within

- Truth is the leavening owe of God
- God speaks through all things through the heart, prayer is speaking from the heart
- God requires no sacrifice
- Baptism is a symbolic cleansing of the soul by purity of life
- Love is the greatest commandment
- Faith is surety of the omnipotence of God and man, the certainty man will reach deific life
- Salvation is the ladder reaching from the heart of man to the heart of God
- Laws of nature are the laws of health, transgression is sin and he who sins is sick
- The healer is the one who can inspire God
- All men are made equal, every soul is the child off God
- Live as you would have your brother live, unfold each day as does the flower for earth is yours and heaven is yours
- Man is god and when you honour man you hour god
- Make human hearts the idols, burn the others down as they cannot hear you
- I am here to show the way to god, do not worship man
- The pure of heart do not accuse
- All things are God, the universal god is One all are one It is wisdom, will and love
- By the sweat breath of God all life is bound in one
- When man is one with God, he needs no middle men
- Man is mind and mind is here to gain perfection by experience
- When hope and love are back of toil, all life s filled with joy, peace and this is heaven
- Heave is a state of mind
- A time will come when priests are no more. it is a problem men must solve
- Father God is the King of mankind, all men are kings with access to boundless wealth and love
- The devil and burning fires are works of man
- The silence where the where soul may meet its god, immersed in light, it is the pure of heart inside
- The holy breath cannot enter until it becomes a welcome guest, touched by purity of life, prayer and holy thought
- The kingdom of the kings is the soul and is a kingdom for every man, this king is love as the greatest power and all may have the Christ dwell here and be king,
- And so we are all sons of god
- God is Spirit and resides in all men
- Keep your mind occupied with good and evil cannot find a way in
- Man is the delegate of God to do his will on earth
- Do unto others as
- As you walk do not judge for you will also be so judged
- Death is the passing of the soul out of the house of flesh
- The air we breathe is charged with Holy Breath
- The law of spirit calls for purity of thought, word, deed 126:19
- This life is a span, these is life that does not pass
- The greatest lesson come through failures made
- whatever men shall do to other men man shall do to him
- Afflictions are all partial payments of debts that have been made,
- Recompense never fails as the true rule of life
- He who shall injure another in thought, word, deed is judged a debtor to the law
- Affliction is a prison cell in which a man must stay until his debts are paid
- All men are sons of God by birth, but not by faith
- He who attains victory over self is son of God by faith as is the one who believes and does the will of God
- You shall not kill; you shall not steal; you shall not do adulterous things; you shall not falsely testify;

- And you shall love your God with all your heart, and you shall love your neighbour as yourself.
- One thing you lack; your heart is fixed on things of earth; you are not free.
- the Lord our God is one; and you shall love the Lord your God with all your heart, with all your mind, with all your soul, with all your strength;
- I have not come to judge, but to save

So are you one of those who chooses to believe in the limits and beliefs of the Bible? It is no different than believing that the Strawman Corporation limits your true self. Neither do, but until you free yourself, and the group consciousness begins to shift, the group cannot shift. One by one, each grain of sand blown into the same place forms the dune, then the mountains, then the desert. Like a global marketing campaign, once the balance of individual choice shifts with the global consciousness, the new product remains in the caves of consciousness awaiting the light and as we would say, mass consumption that moves it into the 3D reality of lives, cultures, nations.

In the years, 2000 to 2012, this balance shift into the Christ Consciousness has been one by one occurring in over a billion people who have in some way rejected the notion of god's words and rules. Similarly, there are a massive amount of people who have begun to reject the ways of commerce, and come to a new truth about its implementation thorough humanities simple acceptance that it was the right way.

Keep this entrenched for remember that you are not to be in judgement, bring peace, liberty and love of life back. What has been is what has been accepted. learn from it and move on into the light. Do this every moment in thought, word and deed.

In dropping back into the lower carnal world of commerce and debt, keep this in the front (not back) of your mind. For as you now read the following Chapters on what has happened in the world today, know that it is the shifting belief system that has somehow shone light on the new truth that has led these people here.

The next chapters are dedicated to what is happening in terms of large groups of people taking action on the different perspective we identified in Part 1. The lesson here is that what we are seeing worldwide are Earthlings that not only agree with these things that may be "hard to believe", they are taking action-bigtime!

First off is the Strawman story that may be one of the more difficult to digest. Before you do, take a good look at all your identification, your plastic cards, your bank agreements, your correspondence from the bank, tax authorities, licenses, etc. Look at your commerce and the tombstones. Then, in a moment of silence think about why these are capitalized. Do you really believe they can't use upper and lower case?

Recall the Story of the Strawman from Part 1. That is what got the Earthling to agree to being employed by PLANET EARTH INC. If you still think this is a good joke, read on because there are an awful lot of folks who don't.

On The Author Of The Aquarian Gospel

For a free full version of your own book, go to the site:
www.sacred-texts.com/chr/agjc/agjc002.htm

Before leaving the new story of Christ it is important to acknowledge the man **Levi Dowling** who wrote the book. Because was written at the turn of the last century, it is public domain. The **Aquarian Gospel** is claimed to be *"Transcribed From the Book of God's Remembrances, Known as the Akashic Records."* In addition to a number of theological differences with the "orthodox" interpretation of the canonical Gospels (Matthew, Mark, Luke and John), the *Aquarian Gospel* fills in the gap in Jesus' earthly ministry between his visit as a boy to the Temple in Jerusalem and his baptism by John the Baptist approximately 18 years later. This includes visits by Jesus to India, Tibet, Persia, Assyria, Greece and Egypt.

The following information is posted on ***www.aquarianchurch.zoomshare.com/1.html***

Levi H. Dowling was born May 18th, 1844 in Belleville, Ohio. His father was a Disciple of Christ preacher/minister. As a young boy Levi was aware of and highly sensitized to the finer etheric realm, [and] he felt that there are etheric vibrations underlying all sounds, thoughts and events that are recorded on sensitized etheric plates (something like a Divine Computer disk). During his childhood he was an avid student of all of the world's religions. Also, when just a lad he had a vision in which he was told he was to "build a white city." The vision was repeated three more times over the years; the building of the "white city" was his transcribing of *"The Aquarian Gospel of Jesus the Christ."*

When Levi was only thirteen years old he debated a Presbyterian elder on the doctrine of everlasting damnation and torment of souls in Hell. At a very early age Levi understood the Truth that the doctrine of eternal damnation is incompatible with a Just, Loving and Forgiving God of Infinite Mercy. At an early age Levi was a prophet and seer of God's Word. At sixteen, following in his father's footsteps, Levi was a preacher; at eighteen he was pastor of a small church.

During the Civil War (1861-1865), Levi was a chaplain in the U.S. Army and delivered President Lincoln's eulogy at his memorial services for the Union forces in Illinois. After the war, Levi attended North-western Christian University at Indianapolis, Indiana and was the graduate of two medical colleges. He practiced Homeopathic Medicine for many years and taught the use of electricity to medical students, demonstrating that he was a pioneer of modern medicine. For forty years Levi studied and meditated upon mysteries in quiet contemplation until he reached such a level of spiritual consciousness he stood before the Very Throne of God. There the Mother God spoke unto Levi and gave him his commission to transcribe "The Aquarian Gospel." This is in the section called "Levi's Commission." Here are some excerpts:

'O, Levi, son of man, behold, for you are called to be the message bearer of the coming age - the age of spirit blessedness. Give heed, O son of man, for men must know the Christ, the Love of God; for Love is sovereign balm for all the wounds of men, the remedy for every ill.'
'Now, Levi, hearken to my words: go forth into these mystic Galleries and read. There you will find a message for the world; for every man; for every living thing.'

The Aquarian Gospel was given excellent reviews and endorsement by the New Thought Church and School in America and England and by the National New Thought Alliance. Christian Science is a branch of New Thought, although most New Thought teachings and Aquarian Christine teachings do not reject medical science, but integrate all methods of healing with positive thinking, prayer and faith.

Levi passed from earth-life the thirteenth day of August, in the year of our Lord, one thousand nine-hundred and eleven. Levi Dowling, the Aquarian Hierophant, stepped behind the thin curtain that separates the here from the hereafter.

*"He is the Ascended Master Beloved Levi, which means United, for he united all mankind through the transcribing of the **Aquarian Gospel of Jesus the Christ**."* - from **The White City**

Levi's wife was fellow mystic and Theosophist, **Eva S. Dowling**, who wrote the **Introduction to "The Aquarian Gospel."** Levi's son Leo W. Dowling continued in following and spreading the teachings of "The Aquarian Gospel." He was associated with Church Truth Universal - AUM of Los Angeles, California (now defunct). Leo wrote the preface to Julianna McKee's "Twelve Lessons in Truth - Aum" (1931), a textbook for the church which summarized "The Aquarian Gospel."

The Aquarian Gospel mentions the Aquarian Masters, and living masters and Masters who are At-One with God, and are Divine, and have made the Ascension.

The experiences of Levi H. Dowling is similar to Edgar Cayce often placed under the broad category called paranormal, which is generally defined as unusual phenomena or experiences that lack an obvious scientific explanation. Regardless, these writing either vibrate with your on truth or not. Some object to the use of the word paranormal because its dictionary meaning is, that which is *aside* from what is considered to be "normal." Those who object to the use of the word paranormal state that that which is considered paranormal is actually *normal*, but simply beyond the ability of the *average* person to perceive. This objection might be valid, considering the fact that psychics, who deal in "paranormal" activity, are often used by police departments as effective tools in finding criminals, missing persons, evidence, etc., all of which falls under the realm of *normal* police activity. Indeed, that which is considered *other than* normal might actually be normal phenomenon, as some believe, even though most of us are not able to receive such experiences.

Is this a true depiction of Christ? If this story "vibrates" with your inner being you will know it. One thing it does vibrate with is the shift in the Earthlings consciousness which began to accelerate around the turn of the century with the entry into the Aquarian Age. Is the Aquarian age and The Aquarian Gospel just a coincidence. Is the vast belief system of the New Agers being coincident with this consciousness of the Christ just a coincidence? We will see in Parts 2 and 3.

27

THE STRAWMAN REVOLUTION

Earlier, we introduced the Story of the Strawman. This would have been a totally ridiculous story before the turn of the century. In the last 12 years, it is not so farfetched as many have followed up on it all around the world. Of note is that beneath the seas of new consciousness builds a tsunami of energies pertaining to the information presented so far, and in particular the mythical Strawman. In the last 12 years, it is the Strawman that has hit the spotlight. It is not surprising that with the Internet and the ability to research and share information, that a new level of consciousness about the way things really work with regards to Corporate fictions, Admiralty law, the workings of banking system, and the alleged fraudulent cover up of the maxims. In fact it has all been hidden in plain sight for those who are willing to see.

The Internet is now alive with new information about all that we have provided about the commercial system and the ones running PLANET EARTH. Every day, warriors of the new commerce and warriors of the light are revealing a way to bring Goliath down. Everyday new information comes forward that breaks down the veil and shine new light on a different truth regardless of whether it is religion, science, commerce, medicine, military or whatever are being "truthfully" presented and administered in this vast public world that humanity has accepted run by a private world of PLANET EARTH.

Before we delve into these new commercial "waves" which are occurring, it is of interest to bring forward some vital information about commerce so as to lead into the phenomenon of the Strawman. This seemingly simple idea of imposing a capital letter fiction on the Earthling has been one of most incredible subtle takeover of human power of all time. Here the Earthling has simply agreed to trade certain private rights for certain public benefits, trusting in the leadership that it was alright. But the knowing of the STRAWMAN existence allows one to make a choice that was not there before; to separate from the fiction that imposes rules thus getting back the true power of sovereignty in commerce bringing this back into the private domain. However, what of the benefits that were offered through the fiction? There are several major areas that are relevant in understanding the implementation process and the remedy, most of which has come clearly to the surface in the last decade. It all relates to the true powers that are lying dormant on the private side. As we have seen the power has been usurped via the secrecy of PLANET EARTH who control a network of private corporations outside of the peering eyes of the public world.

Private Versus Public Jurisdictions

First, it is important to understand the difference between Public and Private. The dictionaries state that public is as an adjective: of, pertaining to, or affecting a population or a community as a whole: *public funds; a public nuisance;* done, made, acting, etc., for the community as a whole: *public prosecution;* open to all persons: *a public meeting;* of, pertaining to, or being in the service of a community or nation, especially as a government officer: *a public official;* maintained at the public expense and under public control: *a public library; a public*

Private means secluded from the sight, presence, or intrusion of others; designed or intended for one's exclusive use; of or confined to the individual; undertaken on an individual basis; not available for public use, control, or participation; belonging to a particular person or persons, as opposed to the public or the government.

One of most important concepts to master is this Public versus Private entanglement. Blacks Law 6th says public is *"the whole body politic or the aggregate of the citizens of a state, nation, or municipality. The inhabitants of a particular place; all the inhabitants of a particular place; the people of a neighbourhood,' private is Affecting or belonging to private individuals, as distinct from the public generally; not official; not clothed in office."*

That which is public cannot be private since it is public as shared by all.

Thus operating from the private sector have some extreme advantages, namely the lack of public regulation. In order to make this shift, words in daily speech and writing must shift-away from the public training system. according to the holy scriptures, **your word is your bond.**

The public sector teaches public concepts and nothing about private. Since you have so been taught, your heart has always been with the public side, but most of these public phrases and words have private counterparts, and most opposite in meaning:

PUBLIC	PRIVATE
democracy	republic
Corporate fiction	Real thing
BC	British Columbia
persons	Men, women
voters	electors
attorneys	lawyers
Color of law	Common law
agreement	contract
legal	lawful
Revocable privileges	Unalienable rights
insurance	assurance
equity	ownership
subjects	sovereigns
slaves	masters
employees	employers
debtors	creditors
Accomodated party	Accommodation part
offer	acceptance
Common stock	Preferred stock
Subject to levy	Exempt from levy

Negotiable by fictions	Non-negotiable man to man
offer	acceptance
Paper money	substance
Police officers	Peace officers
Fiction/dishonor/injustice	Truth/honor/justice
poverty	wealth
Man's legal system	Natural Gods law

To be truly private in a public world you must always picture yourself and act as a man or woman from the private side on the right. Always conduct your business from the private venue using the words from the right side will keep you out of the public domain. This is precisely what the global Elite have done and still do. Their words are their bond as contract and the words they use are the words by which they are judged.

The private side emulates the law of forgiveness and grace, the public side emulates execution by law. If anyone practices the execution of law as commanded by Moses he denies divine grace. Our debts have been paid and it is in the private sector that we find honour, justice and truth. The public side is a reflection of dishonour, injustice, and a place where fraud can flourish.

Private operates under contract, public operates under color of law. That is why if you are branded as a guilty sinner from the beginning, and accept this, you are subject to the rules of the bibles, their codes and potential vengeance which will fall upon you as going to hell, not having eternal life, and suffering the horrors of damnation. That is the color of the law. That is the same concept as the Strawman, that, registered as being "alive" in Puerto Rico, in the Individual Master File, is a criminal; already in sin, guilty until proven innocent. It is the same principle as being born a guilty sinner-especially women as in the code of law in religion.

Only a real man or woman can be an owner. It is impossible for a fictional entity to give "credit' to anything or anyone since it has nothing to give or create.

Only real men and women can engage in private non-negotiable contracts because only real men and women have the mind in which the meeting of minds can take place. It is physically impossible for a fictional entity to open anything except in words and belief. Redemptors are sovereigns, owners, preferred stockholders, creditors, employers and masters while the uninformed public remain the debtors.

Like corporations and public agencies, the Strawman was designed to operate in the public sector, and all have been given names as vessels on the sea subject to admiralty laws, spelled in capital letters. These do not have eyes to see, nor ears to hear nor a brain to think or a heart to feel. They have no way of communicating with us except through a transmitting utility called a STRAWMAN.

The Four Elements of Contract

Typically, in order to be enforceable, a contract must involve the following elements:

Offer as a "Meeting of the Minds" (Mutual Consent) The parties to the contract have a mutual understanding of what the contract covers. For example, in a contract for the sale of a "mustang", the buyer thinks he will obtain a car and the seller believes he is contracting to sell a horse, there is no meeting of the minds and the contract will likely be held unenforceable.

Offer and Acceptance The contract involves an offer (or more than one offer) to another party, who accepts the offer. For example, in a contract for the sale of a piano, the seller may offer the piano to the buyer for $1,000.00. The buyer's acceptance of that offer is a necessary part of creating a binding contract for the sale of the piano. This means full disclosure. It is implicit within all contracts that the parties are acting in good faith. For example, if the seller of a "mustang" knows that the buyer thinks he is purchasing a car, but secretly intends to sell the buyer a horse, the seller is not acting in good faith and the contract will not be enforceable.

Please note that a counter-offer is not an acceptance, and will typically be treated as a rejection of the offer. For example, if the buyer counter-offers to purchase the piano for $800.00, that typically counts as a rejection of the original offer for sale. If the seller accepts the counter-offer, a contract may be completed. However, if the seller rejects the counter-offer, the buyer will not ordinarily be entitled to enforce the prior $1,000.00 price if the seller decides either to raise the price or to sell the piano to somebody else.

Mutual Consideration (The mutual exchange of something of value) In order to be valid, the parties to a contract must exchange something of value. In the case of the sale of a piano, the buyer receives something of value in the <u>form</u> of the piano, and the seller receives money. While the validity of consideration may be subject to attack on the basis that it is illusory (e.g., one party receives only what the other party was already obligated to provide), or that there is a failure of consideration (e.g., the consideration received by one party is essentially worthless), these defences will not let a party to a contract escape the consequences of bad negotiation. For example, if a seller enters into a contract to sell a piano for $100, and later gets an offer from somebody else for $1,000, the seller can't revoke the contract on the basis that the piano was worth a lot more than he bargained to receive.

Signatures as wet ink signatures of the parties to the contract

In effect, real humans can contract anytime any place on anything and we all do. This is our own personal business. It has nothing to do with the state or the public. Whether I sell you something privately, offer my services for some consideration, or create agreements with others, the process is the same and it does not have to include the government, the authorities, attorneys or anybody else because it is outside the public domain by choice. Even a "money" transaction like in a private sale, or garage sale, is outside of the public domain--none of its business so to speak.

And when these four elements are violated, then it is a matter of performance, disclosure, etc. that constitute a fraud that requires a remedy. Again such remedy can be done privately or by choice taken into the public domain of the law courts and the legal system of codes. Most have grown accustomed to taking this into the public domain of lawyers and attorneys instead of settling it privately. So the private law has been effectively usurped by public law and lawyers.

However, how does it work when a real human contracts with a fiction thing? One is private, one is public. Each are still subject to the same laws of contract but then public rules enter the picture and you find a new set of rules open to you called no violation of public policy:

"In order to be enforceable, a contract cannot violate public policy".

The reason for this, so it is said, is to add a benefit to you and protect you for example, if the subject matter of a contract is illegal, you cannot enforce the contract. A contract for the sale of illegal drugs, for example, violates public policy and is not enforceable. So how can one enforce the prime issue that the banks, the governments have not provided "full disclosure" about the STRAWMAN and the benefits? What about that "stolen energy" to be a debtor? What about the secret purpose of all of this?

Well with regards to the business of the Strawman, plausible deniability has been pretty well the norm. Earthlings simply do not have a clue about the existence of the Strawman, and just like the Earthlings ignorance about esoteric or heretical beliefs propagated by the Vatican (who engage in its power) it is simply not an acceptable concept. And yet ignorance of the law, so it is said, is no excuse. But the greater aspects of this is that the vast majority have simply by choice accepted ignorance of these laws so by acquiescence, it works against them. It is an accepted norm, just like the five monkeys mentioned earlier where the lie or the accepted procedure of "law" becomes the truth. Those that follow the laws and rules of corporations do so because they are paid to do it. Those that know the truth sign confidentiality agreements that allow them to not reveal the truth. Those that really know the truth at the top are the private dynasties; those that don't know have no awareness but to follow that which is the prevailing consciousness and "laws of the land" which they follow since there is no repercussion.

It is within this context that several "waves" of conflict towards revealing the truth have occurred. This is summarized in the following material, not to endorse the processes, but to provide information in to support the information so far presented on the Strawman, the banks, the true energy of real people, and the alleged fraud upon the people. In truth it is not a fraud at all, just an acceptance of a way of life that has been carefully manoeuvred into the philosophy as the Pope Ratzinger put it.

"It is thus necessary that the individual should finally come to realize that his own ego is of no importance in comparison with the existence of his nation; That the position of the individual ego is conditioned solely by the interests of the nation as a whole... that above all the unity of a nation's spirit and will are worth far more than the freedom of the spirit and will of an individual..."

Some Basics On Debt

Within the administrative systems that we have revealed in the Story of The Strawman are many layers of administration, many employees that shift and change (like politicians), and many people who are simply employed to carry out their jobs with little knowing of the rest of the picture about how the debt and banking system functions. And so to protect themselves those that know will deny, others favour plausible deniability, while others simple do not know and cannot believe because the prevalent belief and the laws supports the dominant consciousness to accept it. That is changing but at the root is an established process of record keeping and accounting that is followed worldwide.

In the following summaries, there will be references to words and concepts such as *closed accounts, setoffs, redemption, and acceptance for value.* These are ways and means to gain access to the goods registered within them from the private side. Again, the Internet is the place to get information on this. All you have to do is type in closed account redemption in Google and feast. However it is necessary to explain in simple terms what these mean to the individual.

What has to enforced here is the system is not wrong, it is the way the corporate takeovers have shifted purposes in using the system. The Global Elite has taken over

Nations the same way you or I can take over a bankrupt company and change its rules and purpose. This is of course their business plan. Although the process of capitalism may be a good thing, it has allowed an imbalance of wealth to occur. This as you know by now, is the reason our fathers and mothers had to, and still must, both work to barely get by. We pay tax to repay the loans the fed takes out in our name, and since it is recognized as a corporate SIN account, the loan must be paid back to the principle, which is the people, the only true creditors on the planet had to hock their future private energy for. This includes you and your family, Mom and Dad, everyone else. By perception of law, we the people are all known as debtors. But how can this be? If we are the true creator of credit, how can we be a debtor? It is impossible. But we both know very clearly now that the corporate STRAWMAN is responsible for commercial activity and *it is the real debtor like a liable corporation*. You, the living creator of all wealth are the sentient Earthling that is *the creditor*! The receiver general is the dude that holds an account for corporate STRAWMAN under your name and date of birth. So what does this mean? There are two sides to this accounting ledger. One debt and one credit.

The registered business pays tax and is the debtor and I create the credit. My registered business can't create labour. I suppose it is simple to see unless you are brainwashed. He who pays owes, and is the debtor. The SIN card in my possession bears an all capital corporate name. So I really own that account! The receiver is holding it in trust as the trustee. But as a trustee there some obligations it has to abide by. Section 336 of the Canadian Criminal Code has something to say about this. Since you own the account and the receiver opened it in your all capitals name, you as owner of that account can instruct the fiduciary trustee holder of that account on what to do with it, just as any owner can direct any trustee. That's the type of legal relationship you actually have but were clueless about. Unfortunately, as we have learned, you have been deemed dead at sea so it is only your Strawman that exists, and it is a criminal with no rights.

On the banking side, the closed account is where the credit side of your account is held by the receiver general. In 1994 a Canadian lawyer purchased land in Arizona with a million dollar check drawn on a closed bank account. This was published in the 1994 newspaper but has probably disappeared by now. All closed bank accounts are open for a thing called set-off and are held by the Bank of Canada. Set-off means that an account can never show anything but zero, and nothing to enforce or claim as the account says the party owes zero. Set-off means you can't get cash. It is just a book entry. The reason Canada has a national debt is because everybody acts as if they *are* the Strawman. This is the debt side of the account. You have never redeemed your labour being that of Mr Real Earthling on the credit side.

The debt exists because the labour of the people has not been redeemed and under the constitution the debt cannot be questioned. We have never instructed our trustee, the receiver general, to credit our account or at least reduce the debt in the account via redemption.

There a corporate debtor account in trust with the receiver general. The account is a SIN number but the receiver identifies it as a corporate account or employer. You know now that only corporations pay tax. People don't, or aren't supposed to. You are the credit side of the account beaus you provide the collateral – the labour. You then operate through the debt side of the account through the SIN number for the corporation as the Strawman. So if the bond was set at 1 million initially, the Strawman has a loan for one million that he has to pay back. The loan is supported by your labour. Let us track this as the Strawman now goes to work.

This Strawman is the real taxpayer. And when it came time to start paying, upon getting its SIN and entering the labour market, it had to declare some income for tax purposes.

So let us say that Mr. Strawman earned $50,000 in the first year. Pay checks are issued to Mr. Strawman which has zero credits. Now bear in mind that it may not be issued in the capital name simply because *everyone including you assumes it does not matter.* But nevertheless, it is recorded that way since the truth has been dissolved into oblivion. The year-one after-tax balance is what is entered as *debt on account*. Tax, let us say is $15,000, is interest on the debt income borrowed from your account. That is, the after-tax amount in year one is say $35,000, and shows as debt on debt side of employer account. The tax of $15,000 becomes an interest payment on the one million dollar loan. That's why the STRAWMAN has to pay tax, so that the money he received via a pay check can be collected in part as a tax. That money was borrowed from the principal amount to fund the corporate entity Strawman. But it is really interest charges on the loan from yourself and back to yourself."

Unknown to you, the Fed is borrowing in your name to fund the economy through the Appropriations Act that is the authority to do this. As in all loans, the money must be repaid. To balance the books, a repayment of this loan must be shown. Given the fact the Strawman through you files tax returns that are really interest payments called tax to conceal the truth, it is fact that the Strawman is the debtor, or the party who repays you.

Going up one level, the provincial government went to the Bank of Canada to post the bond for which they received a million in credit. The Bank of Canada can now issue more debt money as approved and registered by the IMF. It's back to the Elite bankers and the fact that we have been pledged to pay them back due to the bankruptcy. So the receiver is the bookkeeper keeping track of the credit line to see how much is drawn and how much is paid. That's why Nations have Receivers of Revenue.

The Receiver General adds up all the accounts at the end of each year, and since all these accounts are operating in debt with debt, the national debt must increase as no credit was applied. Further, all tax returns are evidence of how much debt was issued. Add them all up at year end and you have the new total of the debt. By completing a tax return where income is declared - which is really debt - we are instructing the receiver to add that debt to the debt side, namely Mr. Strawman's account. That's what we all have ever done so no wonder there is a huge national debt.

Redemption is the only way to reduce this debt. Paying debt with debt instruments does not reduce overall debt, it's impossible. You can use a check to pay a debt, but it's still debt added somewhere else. The taxes are only paying the interest on the loans – not the principle. So the way the deal is set up means that the big loan to the IMF, through the Bank of Canada, their private arm, can never be paid, and the more people that are born, the more they draw out. It is like a huge line of credit with no upper bound because no one is aware of it.

A debtor, which means only corporations, cannot redeem labour, only people can. Corporations declare labour as an expense which is a form of redemption. The corporation then recovers the expense at the point of sale. So this is why Canada has a national debt. No redemption is being made by labourers. Since people have accepted that the name in capitals as appears on an SIN card to be themselves, we have never communicated or instructed the receiver general to credit the account that we own. We have always instructed him to apply debt, so he does. As the trustee, he has the duty to do as instructed by the owner of the trust account or employer SIN account, which is the people in people accounts. There must be a creditor to have a debt. If the labour is redeemed, then a credit will be applied to the credit side, and the debt reduced accordingly to the debt side. Redemption is the only way to balance an account or to eliminate debt, just as shares are redeemed to reduce the issuer's liability.

The government opens an account for Mr. Strawman. Nor it, nor you requested that the account be opened, nor had no hand in determining the value of the account. They either opened it fraudulently or opened the account to extend it to the owner. It is therefore really owned by the real live human. So to claim it is like claiming a credit. It is in essence like being given a credited account the same as a credit card. Once the credit is used up, the account is balanced at zero, and no claim can be made. So it is yours to redeem. If you work forty years, there will be forty years of debt on the debt side to balance the amount of labour you have provided.

The reality is that the account bears the name of the corporation you own, or is being held on your behalf in a Trust in which you have an interest because you provided the human capital. So are you not entitled to the credit given by the party who opened the account? Accounts are opened for credit purposes only. Whoever opened and signed the account is the guarantor of the credit or loan. If credit is not being extended, then there is no reason to open an account. Who opens them? Who signs as surety? Who owns and who holds the account? Who is the beneficiary of the account, the guarantor or the owner of it? Who is the party entrusted? It is the trustee. And who is there to perform their duty, and discharge that duty? The surety is. Whoever signs, is liable. Did you sign? No. All fiction alleged creditors have an assumed claim. We are simply too stupid to know what's really going on.

This has enormous consequences to everybody's pocketbook if they only woke up. And the system is so well entrenched that the people administering the process doo not have a clue about it.

You as the real owner comes forth and removes presumption or assumption of the assumed claim. Only the real owner can. This would create *a claim in fact*. The Strawman could not exist if the living being was not born so you hold the claim in fact. The provincial government opened an account with the intention of extending credit to old Mr. Strawman, and they guaranteed the credit. So let us say they made that credit one million dollars. By extending credit Mr. Strawman is the debtor, right? So if you accept that value of credit which is what your property is deemed by the government to be worth, then should you not be able to collect it? It is either that situation or the government has used a name to open an account they had no authority to open under some other parties name. That would be a crime involving fraud and forgery. If the government attempts to collect on an account they does not own, but valued and guaranteed because they signed or opened the account, that is a serious criminal offence.

By each of us redeeming this account, we actually free ourselves and in the process reduce the national debt. How can something like this elude everyone for so long? It is because the debt cannot be questioned and all money is simply transactions of debt. so it is like paying MasterCard with Visa.

And as all apathetically entrenched in their own personal desires and as long as they can play with toys that they believe are theirs and their bellies are full, and the debt really does not affect that, who cares? The best slave are the ones that believe they are free. and there are none so blind as those who refuse to see.

When you investigate the accounts there are figures representing some aspect of our National Debt in the public records under the heading of Savings Account. When you fully understand what this means, a lot of lights may start to come on for you! Do you think this could be the aspect of our collective savings account representing the total accumulated, and saved to date value of our collective, unclaimed exemptions? Until they are claimed, this amount can also be correctly referred to as our national debt. Collectively, we own the rights to claim these exemptions, because this portion of the debt is ours as well. But it is to our credit, based upon our provable and valuable productivity as individuals, so perhaps that is why it is headed under Savings Account.

This means it is our proportionate ownership of the *de facto* bond issue that we, together with the Bank of Canada and its chartered affiliates acting on our behalf, have been issuing our money against. In other words it represents what the banks owe all of us as citizens for simply having administered our issue of our money. Individually, we may only authorize a claim for that proportionate amount of the exemption that we can prove our entitlement to by evidencing our valuable productivity in the form of dollar denominated debt money. And the debt money that is currently in our system does indeed have very real value. It has the equal and offsetting value of our credit; the total of all claimed exemptions, plus all unclaimed exemptions. This is the portion of our current national debt, which means its value is equal to our cumulative, provable productivity, and to some extent, our good will, either of which, or and certainly both, are worth infinitely more than gold or silver

The unclaimed exemption represents the total cumulative amount of provable and valuable productivity that we have and may yet provide. Our unclaimed exemption has no inherent value in and of itself. It is not an account with real money in it. It is our treasury account. It is not accessible as money via a closed account. It is rather, our intangible right to endorse a claim against a dollar denominated value amount - not a real dollar, as an offset of our dollar denominated liabilities. This is provided we can prove productivity. This is simply an accounting entry.

This is exactly the same process as the banks use. They use your promissory note, your signature to sell to the Bank of Canada so they can get you to *'promise to pay'* with nothing to loan. But, and here is the big BUT. We can claim our own exemption and we can endorse an authorization for it to be applied as an offset of certain liabilities. An authorization must only be endorsed to a chartered bank, licensed in part, to act as fiduciary for our issuance of currency by creating it via promissory notes, mortgages, or the likes, or it may be endorsed to CRA or the IRS to offset tax liabilities. So you can't get cash. Obviously all of our debt money was at one time or another loaned into circulation either directly or indirectly to end-users like us against either real existing productivity, or against future productivity via promissory notes. So that is why it is rightly called debt money which is the alternative to it having been loaned into circulation. If you ask anybody to show you the money, they can't. There is none. But you can still offset certain liabilities with CRA or IRS for example.

The banks have no money to lend so they make you sign papers like promissory notes that they can then use to make money *'appear'* via a keystroke. So when I gave them a promise to pay on a mortgage, I created a *valuable financial security* with a face value of the mortgage. Then I agreed to pay it back plus interest for a term of twenty-five years. That created a funding instrument. The property, which I didn't have yet, had to be conveyed from me to the bank as a condition of the loan. The bank then recorded its acquisition of the funding instrument as an increase in the money, or assets of the bank. So me, the stupid borrower, gave the power to create the money, contributed property to the transaction, and received in return from the bank an account as a *'credit'* which they created with a keystroke. The result is they got the promise, the loan back, the interest, and the property for putting up nothing. And I got to work twenty five years to pay it off.

Then the bank was able to sell my mortgage note, with property as security into the international banking market and get a further return on their paper, probably in the order of ten plus percent. At the same time they made me pay for an insurance policy to protect them

Then, when you paid all this back, they never returned the original promissory note so they could continue to derive unjust enrichment as long as they wanted to keep your original promise to pay in circulation. So, in summary, somewhere is a whole accounting system that keeps track of this. Is it money? It is a key stroke entry into the ledger. What is there? it is what you placed there as your credit in good faith. The total amount is the equity registered in those three trusts which is your person "Good Faith and Credit" all being held in your name.

Getting Access To The Good Faith And Credit

What has become more and more apparent is that this other side of the ledger exists. What has come to light is that institutions like the DTCC to name one (Depository Trust Clearing Company of New York also a private enterprise) is responsible for the accounting process. Undoubtedly, the Reserve Banks in each nation and the World Bank also keep track of this. It is so around the world. Right from the point of inception, this account continues to be recorded according to GAAP or Generally Accepted Accounting Practices by law. What has not come to light is how to access this Good Faith and Credit which was placed there by each in good faith, but without the knowledge. Nevertheless, the access or option has always existed if one can find the way through the labyrinth.

Herein lies an interesting legacy of the estate in your name that has been set up but hidden carefully. And there are many that have succeeded in access despite the incredible labyrinth of public laws and plausible deniability that shrouds it. This process of seeking out that pathway to gain access to that Good Faith and Credit has evolved in the last decade from many directions. It is fraught with difficulty and danger because effectively you are taking on the "system" of Statutes, Acts, banks, Tax Authorities and Governments who have been trained in the Public side and truly believe you are the bad guy for attempting this. And the power to enforce their side is in their hands. That is why it is a hit and miss situation as to whether one gains access or not. Needless to say, those that do, provide lessons to the controllers to close the holes as quickly as possible.

Eventually, the truth of this will shift but in the meantime, the "law" and the beliefs are on the side of the Corporate structures simply because we were are ether born into this type of employee slavery, or we simply accepted it as the way it is supposed to be.

Regardless, this is changing rapidly now as the momentum increases. And so the processes that have evolved are proliferating rapidly as people have been backed into a wall of debt and seek both spiritual and commercial solutions. We will summarize several of these methods here that can be divided into three "techniques" or processes:

1. The Process of Commercial Redemption
2. The Process of Debt Set-off and Closed Accounts
3. The Process of Accepted For Value

All of these are related to the Strawman and gaining access to that Trust that was set up in the name of the Strawman. But like the shifting sands, the process is not clear, nor does it always work. The labyrinth through the established system is fraught with danger. And in many cases it has gotten people into more trouble than they anticipated as the public system has the upper hand and power should you decide to fight. As you read through these, understand that these are presented not because they always work and should be followed but because they add credibility to the other side of the commercial coin that we has spoken on, and they reflect procedures that can be refined and enhanced, converging on the final revelation of the truth that can liberate those who wish to be liberated and to redeem that Good Faith and Credit. This topic will be covered in detail later on. First it is necessary to understand what has been happening in this regard as more and more people make their way through the Strawman Labyrinth Game.

Commercial Redemption is a term commonly used to the process of gaining access to that Good Faith and Credit locked away in a legal and administrative labyrinth of Dungeons and Dragons. Those who enter this game will inevitably face the incredible forces of ignorance and power of the system.

The Process of Debt Set-off and Closed Accounts This process uses a closed checking account as the flow through process of setting off specific debts. After making the appropriate declarations and filings to separate the Strawman from the real human, you are then writing a check as you would normally on an open bank account. This is a financial instrument referred to a **EFT** for **Electronic Funds Transfer**. The difference here is that this is a bank account that is closed and instead of the funds being drawn against your usual checking account, the bank. Where do the funds come from? Again they are from the secret Strawman account that goes back to the Federal Reserve and up. The amount on the check is then set off through book entries against the Strawman account on the "silent hidden ledger side". The usual issue here is having the bank (who usually deny this through ignorance (plausible deniability), having it actually monetized (getting the money transferred) and enforcing the process in a court if you have to. This can be dicey and is enforced through a skill of knowing your constitutional, unalienable rights.

The Process Acceptance for Value This process is base upon the most fundamental laws of commerce and the power hidden within them. These rely on the   Bills of Exchange or the Uniform Commercial Code that reflects those laws. You have had a taste of this with the acceptance for value power imbedded in three simple clauses of the Act.

There is a hierarchy of laws. The first order of law was Natural Law. It is based on universal, natural principles and you have no one except God to listen or report to. Next, came the laws of commerce. This involves the human interactions of buying, selling and trading. It was codified in the Sumerian/Babylonian era and, as you know now, has been brought forward in time to become an integral part of our lives. Next was the Common law that is based on common sense. It gave rise to the jury system and the process used by governments that put things into rules and regulations in courts. This process was based on facing your accuser in front of witnesses and was never intended to include lawyers, attorneys and judges. Next came governments, their laws and legislative regulations.

Humans had to impose new laws and regulations to capture themselves into slavery. But, and here is the big but. Commerce, and its laws, codified a long time ago, is the binding thread between our laws, and in fact remains imbedded in everything. Commerce is the engine that has been alive for six thousand years. Commerce, as we have discussed, forms the underlying foundation for all laws on the planet and all governments follow these. Although it is not readily apparent to most, as you have started to find out, when you operate at this fundamental level, there is nothing that can overturn, change or meddle with it.

Commerce remains the fundamental source of authority and power. If you ever wonder why we do things a certain way, the answer lies in the laws of commerce. This is reflected in the Bills of Exchange Act, or Uniform Commercial Code in the U.S. When you really understand how this works, you, as a private, natural individual begin to be your own *lawyer* and can work outside the judicial system in the private world. Commerce is the glue. Doing business, and resolving matters is done under oath, certified on each party's commercial liability by a sworn affidavit that it is true, correct, the truth and nothing but the truth. Guess where this came from? When you apply for things like a drivers license, these all have the equivalent of a copy certification to be true and correct... an affidavit. As you dig into our system and ask why things are done a certain way, like swearing on the bible, you will find these are all rooted in the law of commerce developed a long time ago. So in the hierarchy, the laws of commerce must be an extension of the Natural law as it was second in the evolution?

When you can function at this level in the private domain in the contract world, you can actually take the *law* into your own hands. Commerce law as an extension of natural laws has ten maxims. These have always been, and still are like the ten commandments of commerce. When I list these for you, you will say; well I always knew that, these are common sense. It is so. But you probably did not know how deep they go into dictating the actual laws. **These were codified in Babylonia. (Note the biblical reference for as we have noted before, god was very much interested in Commerce.** Here they are:

First, *a workman is worthy of his hire. It is against equity for freemen not to have free disposal of their own property.* (Exodus 20:15; Lev. 19:13; Matt. 10:10; Luke 10:7; II

Second, *all are equal before the law. No one is above the law. This is founded on moral and natural law and is binding on all.* (God's Law--Ethical and Natural Law). (Exodus 21:23-25;Lev. 24:17-21; Deut. 1:17, 19:21; Matt., 22:36-40; Luke 10:17; Col. 3:25. Legal maxims: "No one is above the law."; "Commerce, by the law of nations, ought to be common, and not to be converted into a monopoly and the private gain of a few.").

Third, *in commerce, truth is sovereign. This forms the basis and standard and no lies are allowed.* (Exodus 20:16; Ps. 117:2; Matt. 6:33, John 8:32; II Cor. 13:8. Legal maxim: "To lie is to go against the mind."

Fourth, *truth is an Affidavit. An affidavit is your solemn expression and underlies a commercial transaction. It must have someone state it is true, and correct. If it is not, you are liable.* (Lev. 5:4-5; Lev. 6:3-5; Lev 19:11-13; Num. 30:2; Matt. 5:33; James 5:12).

Fifth. An unrebutted affidavit stands as the truth in Commerce (1 Pet. 1:25; Heb. 6:13-15. Legal maxim: "He who does not deny, admits.").

Sixth, *unrebutted Affidavits stand as truth. If claims are not rebutted, they emerge as the truth. An unrebutted Affidavit becomes a judgment. There is nothing left to resolve.* Heb. 6:16-17. Any proceeding in a court, tribunal, or arbitration forum consists of a contest, or "duel," of commercial affidavits wherein the points remaining unrebutted in the end stand as the truth and the matters to which the judgment of the law is applied.).

Seventh, *any matter must be expressed. You must state your position. He who fails to state his position has none.* (Heb. 4:16; Phil. 4:6; Eph. 6:19-21. Legal maxim: "He who fails to assert his rights has none.").

Eighth, *he who leaves the battlefield loses by default. This is the same as if the Affidavit is unrebutted.* (Book of Job; Matt. 10:22. Legal maxim: "He who does not repel a wrong when he can, occasions it.").

Ninth, *sacrifice is a measure of credibility. Nothing ventured, nothing gained. He who bears the burden ought to also derive the benefit. (One who is not damaged, put at risk, or willing to swear an oath that he consents to claim against his commercial liability in the event that any of his statements or actions is groundless or unlawful, has no basis to assert claims or charges and forfeits all credibility and right to claim authority.) (Acts 7, life/death of Stephen, maxim: "He who bears the burden ought also to derive the benefit.").*

Tenth, *a satisfaction is through a lien. A lien can be satisfied by rebutting the affidavit with another, convincing a common law jury, or paying it.* . A lien or claim can be satisfied only through rebuttal by Counter-affidavit point-for-point, resolution by jury, or payment (Gen. 2-3; Matt. 4; Revelation. Legal maxim: "If the plaintiff does not prove his case, the defendant is absolved.").

Notice how these are imbedded in our actual legal procedures at this time. All law in Canada and US can be reduced to the above ten listed maxims.

What this reflects is that commercial law is non-judicial or pre-judicial and timeless. It is private law. It is the base beneath government and their system. This is what the courts do when you get into disputes without affidavits and have to rely on them and some expensive lawyers to solve it. So when you swear in court that is an affidavit. Virtually everything you do with lawyers requires sworn affidavits.

It is the conflict between commercial affidavits that forms the basis of being in court, and why attorneys create controversy. But no court can overturn an affidavit, except on adversely being affected by it. The entirety of the world commerce functions in accordance with this which is reflected in the Uniform Commercial Code. This maintains commercial harmony, codified into those ten legal maxims. Everywhere you turn, you will find these laws inherent in your contracts. You are not aware of how this works. You are probably aware of how it works against you when you don't know.

Note how easy it is for the bank or the tax group to take things from you or to make your commercial life miserable. The IRS, for example, is the most active collection agency in the U.S. but it is not registered to do business in any state. We simply give them money without requesting a *'proof of claim'* or even question if they are licensed to give offers based on arbitrary estimations. The IRS cannot even issue a valid assessment lien or levy. They must actually first produce the paperwork – a true bill in commerce. This would need a sworn affidavit by someone that it is true, correct, and complete. Do you think anyone there would do that and take the commercial liability with such a statement? We just don't know the rules so they get away with ignoring them.

Seeing the light is in the power of knowing the rules of commerce. That is what judges, lawyers and the legal system follow. Unfortunately, unless you do not hit some nerve, they will simply ignore these things and try to get you into a court where they get clever lawyers to make you look like a vexatious or radical creep and escape the real issues. In reality, they would have to follow the law of commerce and come back with an affidavit that rebuts point by point. This means that they would have to provide the paperwork with real assessments, the true bill in commerce, the real sworn affidavit that would make their assessment truth.

You need to be able to put something in the letter that brings in fear to them so they do not want to go to court because it could hurt individuals privately. Remember that you are dealing in the private contract world here and you have to name a real human, not a fiction. When they send you a statement, it seldom has any names on it.

When you *accept for value and dissect the words* you find it means to receive with approval or satisfaction, or to receive with intent to retain. With this in mind, when you get a traffic ticket, a notice of foreclosure or whatever, your first instinct is Oh, shit! I'm certainly not going to accept that! Why would anyone want to accept such a thing? But hold on. If you look at the word acceptance, it is the act of taking and receiving of something as if it were a tacit agreement.

Tacit is a very interesting word. If you look it up in Blacks 6th it states that tacit is existing, inferred, or understood without being openly expressed or stated; implied by silence or silent acquiescence, as a tacit agreement or a tacit understanding. It means that something is done or made in silence, implied or indicated, but not actually expressed. Something is manifested by the refraining from contradiction or objection or inferred from the situation and circumstances, in the absence of expression. If you accept the thing then there is an agreement. You agree with what they have said in the writing, whatever it may be. But, then, if you don't accept it, don't say anything, then there is still an agreement because you don't refute it or contradict what they say in the writing. It goes back to the ten maxims. If you do or say nothing you are presumed guilty. That gives them authority to move in on you and take you to court, then get authority to seize things. No matter how right you might think you are, what law you think is on your side, you always seem to lose in any court.

This is what banks and tax authorities, the ones that are the most skilled at doing it, use against you. Let us look a little further under acceptance in Blacks 6th edition. You'll go on down the page until you get to types of acceptance. Beneath that heading you'll see conditional acceptance. Here it says a conditional acceptance is an agreement to pay the draft or accept the offer on the happening of a condition. A conditional acceptance is a statement that you are willing to enter into a bargain differing in some respects from that proposed in the original offer. The old offer is no more! The conditional acceptance is, therefore, itself a counter offer. If you accept their offer with a conditional acceptance, you now have a counter offer to make back to them.

It places the ball in their court. If they do not answer, they then accept your offer by tacit agreement and you win. Let's look at *power of acceptance.* In Blacks 6th edition, it says the power of acceptance means the capacity of offeree - that's you again, states that upon acceptance of terms of offer it creates a binding contract. So, if I accept your offer with a conditional acceptance, then place my own terms upon which I accept your offer, then we now have a binding contract even though I have modified the conditions. The offeror must now come back with a rebuttal to prove my terms and conditions are in error.

Now the other party has to deal with the new conditions. And it does not matter what those terms are, they must deal with them. This is very powerful if you learn to use it wisely. You see, first you have accepted the first offer so there is nothing they can do about it. There is no controversy anymore. It is gone unless you argue or ignore. If they cannot rebut your conditions or ignore them, then you are in the driver's seat.

The public system is what we all use when we run to the lawyers and the courts. The private system can be used the same way by you. First some basics. A contract is an agreement between two or more persons which creates an obligation to do or not to do a particular thing. It's essential segments include competent parties, subject matter, a legal consideration, mutuality of agreement, mutuality of obligation, and signatures. First there is an *offer* which is to bring some deal to someone or present for acceptance or rejection. Offer and acceptance are the two elements which constitute mutual assent, a requirement of the contract.

The *Offeree* in contract terms is the person to whom an offer is made by the *offeror*. *Accept* means to approve what has been offered, acknowledged by signature and thus promise to do what is accepted in the contract, or bill of exchange. And finally you accept the conditions by tacit agreement if you do nothing. Now let us look into the use of this when you receive a bill.

for an interesting excurion into this process, there is experience written by a famous Canadian proponent of this method **Eldon Warman** on **website www.detaxcanada.org**:

Honour Or Dishonour, To Fight Or Not To Fight

The point of this chapter has been to simply show the shifting attention of the Earthling forcing disclosure that has been accelerating. It is about demanding knowledge about the Strawman and the Good Faith and Credit Trust. The Internet is filled with those warriors who are attempting to gain access to the good faith and credit by some means. The rules of the establishment are not simple to penetrate and the process has eliminated common law to superimpose the Laws of Admiralty. With the religious-spiritual shift, that is a personal one private one but the commercial one of public to private transition is not so simple as people must engage in commerce in some way through the banking system, which ironically is private. As such, the rules of penetrating the Strawman veil are not clear and these processes of Setoff, redemption, Accept For value are not clearly defined. They become a hit and miss process as those who administer it are blind and those who control it simply do jobs or are under strict non disclosures. And so one who attempts this can be the one to be deemed fraud and a rebel to the system immediately charged with veracious litigation attempting to defraud the "system". It is because that is the way it has been implemented, and that is the way the majority have accepted it.

But that, as we has seen, is changing rapidly. So again the purpose here is not to present this for others to try, but to be aware that something is amiss and the Strawman Revolution gathers momentum everywhere. In the following chapters, it will become clear that there are major waves building.

Much of this has to do with how one enters the game. As we will bring forward later, this game is fraught with danger because the establishment is not yet ready to reveal the truth. And as you will learn, the energy of conflict, anger and fear begets more of the same. It is all relative to knowing who you are.

28

THE POSTMASTER GENERAL FOR THE AMERICAS

We will now shift back to new developments in North America where the financial and socio-political systems are changing rapidly. In line with what has been presented so far, every day, new information comes forward along with a new breed of warriors of peace and light that are showing with blinding light the truths that have been surfacing everywhere. A most difficult challenge has been to reveal the truth in ways that make it "stick" in the consciousness of humanity. In the commercial game, the historical problem has been the burden of proof done in such a way as to reveal the truth of the banking system and the Strawman, and to enforce that truth. As we have pointed out, many large groups and leaders of truth have done this. There are millions now on this path revelations in commerce, science and religion.

In an attempt to bring what we have presented into some form of solution, the work of **James Thomas McBride** (Co-author) now will come into focus. We have alluded to the Post Office as a vital piece of history having within its formation a unique power. This in most eyes would seem a "sleeper" as it is the crucial missing link that ties the Vatican, religion, the Universal Postal Union, the Military Industrial complex, the Strawman, and much more together. As a cCo-author I state that the work of James Thomas has been an incredible revelation and his undeniable dedication to the truth, both spiritual and commercial, as well as his dedication to peace and harmony of a new system is unprecedented. It is not without struggle that this man has persevered to find truth in both spiritual and commercial paths. On the spiritual side there is no one to fight except yourself, but not so on the commercial side. James Tomas has been dedicated to finding the pathway through the commercial labyrinth so as create a non-conflictive way combining what was presented in the Chapter "**The Strawman Revelation**" into a cohesive method of Strawman separation and access to the Good Faith and Credit.

It is here that we begin to sew the pieces of the fabric presented so far into a new patchwork that he has brought forward for mankind. It is truly the birthing of New Earth as will be brought together by the formation of The Divine Province. Much of this comes from Jame's website **www.divineprovince.org.** Now we will shift to the story and work of Co-author James McBride.

About The Universal Postal Union

The UPU (Universal Postal Union) in Berne, Switzerland, is an extremely significant organization in today's world. It is formulated by treaty. No nation can be recognized as a nation without being in international admiralty in order to have a forum common to all nations for engaging in commerce and resolving disputes. That is why the USA under the Articles of Confederation could not be recognized as a country. Every state (colony) was sovereign, with its own common law, which foreclosed other countries from interacting with the USA as a nation in international commerce. Today, international admiralty is the private jurisdiction of the IMF, *et al.*, the creditor in the bankruptcy of essentially every government on Earth.

The UPU operates under the authority of treaties with every country in the world. It is, as it were, the overlord or overseer over the common interaction of all countries in international commerce. Every nation has a postal system, and also has reciprocal banking and commercial relationships, whereby all are within and under the UPU. The UPU is the number one military (international admiralty is also military) contract mover on the planet.

The definition of the word **post** originally meant "*any of a number of riders or runners posted at intervals to carry mail or messages in relays along a route; postrider or courier*" (**Webster's New World Dictionary, Third College Edition**, *1988, page 1054*). People, thousands of years ago, didn't write letters to one another like we do nowadays. They didn't even have paper, everything was done on clay tablets and papyrus (but that was a very expensive thing to engage in). And therefore, the posts were really set up for governmental purposes, between different rulers in their own country as well as neighbouring countries. The government set it up originally.

But there was another entity, known as the general post-office, which was not for commercial purposes and it was strictly for fellowship between the brothers, and they did it amongst themselves. Paul's letters were not delivered by Caesar's men, but by brothers in Christ, and that is the general post-office. And throughout history, there's always been the general post-office and the governmental post office; and they're different. One's done strictly for fellowship, the other's done for commercial purposes.

The current postal system, which is known as the United States Postal Service, is commercial, but it still retains the non-commercial aspect. It's based on the original general post-office. It does not exist without tracing its root to the original general post-office. And as with everything, the created cannot do away with the creator. Therefore, that original creation by the brothers fellowshipping amongst each other is still in existence; they've never done away with it. In all their statutes, every time they come up with a new statutory entity, they never do away with the general post-office, therefore it is still there.

The general-post-office is not mentioned in the Domestic Mail Manual because the Domestic Mail Manual denotes commerce. If you've got a problem, that's what the postal service employees and managers will refer to, but that's because everyone's presumed to be in commerce. But it's only a presumption, and that's where you have to come in and rebut that presumption. You rebut it by not engaging in commercial activity and not receiving your mail at an address, etc. Most people don't realize that when you receive mail at an address, or even at a P.O. Box, you're receiving a free benefit from Caesar. The postage you put on the envelope only covers the cost to deliver it from post office to post office, it does not cover any delivery beyond the post office (and the price for a P.O. Box covers the cost to rent the box itself, not for the cost of delivery). That's called free delivery.

Origins of The U.S.Postal Service

The free delivery was instituted during the Civil War, on July 1st, 1863. It was basically an act of war by Abraham Lincoln. Even though they did have free mail delivery service prior to that, it was strictly for commercial businesses. But then, in 1863, they spread it to everyone. Up to that time, nobody had an address on their house. The numbers were brought in on the houses strictly so the postman would know where to deliver the mail. Before 1863, people would collect their mail by going to the local post office and asking for it.

This was preceded by the Post Office Department, which was established in 1872. And before the Post Office Department, the general post-office preceded that. In the early 1800's, they started referring to the general post office as the Post Office Department. However, it did not officially become the Post Office Department until 1872. Previous to that it was known as the general post-office.

There was actually two different general post-offices. The Post Master General today wears about seven hats; there are about seven different entities to the postal system. He wears the original hat as a caretaker of the original general post-office. He's also the caretaker of the general post-office that was created on February 20, 1792, which was for governmental business. And then in 1872 they created the Post Office Department.

In 1639, the original foundation for the post office was given in Massachusetts to Richard Fairbanks, the owner of Fairbanks Tavern in Boston. He was the first Postal officer in the history of the United States. In **The General Court of Massachusetts November 5, 1639** it was stated:

"For preventing the miscarriage of letters, it is ordered, that notice be given that Richard Fairbanks's house in Boston is the place appointed for all letters which are brought from beyond the seas, or are to be sent thither, 'to be brought unto; and he is to take care that they be delivered or sent according to their directions; and he is allowed for every such letter one penny, and must answer all miscarriages through his own neglect in this kind; provided that no man shall be compelled to bring his letters thither, except he please."

Following the adoption of the Constitution in May 1789, the Act of September 22, 1789 (1 Stat. 70), temporarily established a post office. Here the **Nineteenth act of Congress, an Act for the temporary establishment of the POST OFFICE** stated:

"Be it enacted by the Senate and House of Representatives of the United States of America in Congress assembled, That there shall be appointed a Post-Master General; his

powers and salary and the compensation to the assistant or clerk and deputies which he may appoint, and the regulations of the Post-Office shall be the same as they last were under the resolutions and ordinances of the late Congress. The Post-Master General to be subject to the direction of the President of the United States in performing the duties of his office, and in forming contracts for the transportation of the mail. Be it further enacted, That this act shall continue in force until the end of the next session of Congress, and no longer."

This was approved September 22nd, 1789. The post office was temporarily continued by the Act of August 4, 1790 (1 Stat. 178), and the Act of March 3, 1791 (1 Stat. 218). The Act of February 20, 1792 made detailed provisions for the post office, and also established a separate general post office for governmental purposes where in **Chapter VIII** - An Act to establish the Post Office and Post Roads within the United States, **Section 3,** it states:

"And it be further enacted that there shall be established, at the seat of the government of the United States, a general post-office."

Note that this one page statutory creation by Congress established that general post-office for governmental business at the seat of the government of the United States in Washington D.C. The general post-office, which already existed, was never designated as being repealed in this Act. Therefore, it still remains in existence, separate from the governmental business' set up by this Act. There's nothing in that whole act which repeals the original general post-office. There's nothing in the act of 1872, when they created the Post Office Department, which did away with the original general post-office. So it's still there. There's nothing in the act of July 1, 1971, which created the Postal Service. The creation cannot do away with the creator, they cannot abolish the creator. Otherwise it has no foundation. And that's why the current Postmaster General wears about seven hats, because he has all of those different things that were created all the way through there.

In the early 1800's, the general post-office began to be referred to as "the Post-office department," but was not officially created until June 8, 1872. In **Chapter CCCXXXV. - An Act to revise, consolidate, and amend the Statutes relating to the Post-office Departmen**t, it states:

"Be it enacted by the Senate and House of Representatives of the United States of America in Congress assembled, That there shall be established, at the seat of government of the United States of America, a department to be known as the Post-office Department."

And again, the general post-office was not repealed in this statute. It is for this cause that the re-organized service and its employees have no authority over the general post-office - it precedes their creation and has its Source and Origin in God through His Lawful assembly. The Post Office Department of the Confederate States of America was established on February 21, 1861, by an Act of the Provisional Congress of the Confederate States. The resumption of the federal mail service in the southern states took place gradually as the war came to an end.

Then the Post Office Department was replaced by the United States Postal Service on July 1, 1971. Title 39, the Postal Reorganization Act, details this change as well.

Origins Of The General Post Office

Many will be surprised to know that at the origins of the general post office has its beginnings in scripture. In Jeremiah 51:31, "*One **post** shall run to meet another, and one **messenger** to meet another, to shew the king of Babylon that his city is taken at one end...*" A "post" is another name for a courier and in 2 Chronicles 30:6, "*So **the posts went with the letters** from the king and his princes throughout all Israel and Judah,*" And in Esther 3:13, "*And **the letters were sent by posts** into all the king's provinces...*"

Scripture records messages being sent "by the hands of messengers" (1 Samuel 11:7) from as far back as the book of Job, which is the oldest book in the bible where it says in Job 1:14, "*And there came a **messenger** unto Job, and said, the oxen were plowing, and the asses feeding beside them:*"

These messages were delivered using the current means of movement at the time: Esther 8:10,14, "*And he wrote in the king Ahasuerus' name, and sealed it with the king's ring, and **sent letters by posts** on horseback, and riders on mules, camels, and young dromedaries: So the **posts** that rode upon mules and camels went out...*"

And sending messages refreshes the soul: Proverbs 25:13, KJV, "*As the cold of snow in the time of harvest, so is a faithful **messenger** to them that send him: for **he refresheth the soul** of his masters.*"

Proverbs 25:13, Septuagint, "*As a fall of snow in the time of harvest is good against heat, so a faithful **messenger refreshes** those that sent him: for he helps the souls of his masters.*"

In times past, people sent messages to others by posting their letters on a "post" in the middle of town, with the name of the one who it's intended for. People would go to this "post" and look for letters with their name on it, and if they saw their name on a letter they would take it down from the post and read it. However, due to theft of messages, an office was built around the post to prevent people from stealing messages. This office became known as the general post-office. People would then go to the general post-office to pick up their messages.

The Link To The Vatican And The Estate Trust

To unravel this intentionally complex Trusteeship of the Global Estate Trust let us begin at the top and work our way down. The Vatican boasts, in their Papal Bull, dominion over the entire earth, via conquest, and is answerable ONLY to the Divine Spirit. Dominion over means control over, not ownership. The Vatican's un-rebutted claims establish them as the Primary Trustee of the Global Estate Trust, our Divine Inheritance; a very unpopular fact. But a fact that opens a doorway placing the cure for the mis-administration and theft of our Divine Inheritance within our grasp.

The Vatican is the Primary Trustee of the Global Estate Trust. To facilitate the administration of this Global Trust the Vatican established the Universal Postal Union as the Secondary Trustees of the Global Trust charged with dividing the Global Trust into zones and endowing these legal fiction zones with sovereign authority to facilitate the efficient administration of the Global Trust.

It is no surprise that the first requirement for the international acknowledgment of a sovereign nation is the necessity of a Post Office. The primary objective of the military in any 'zone' is the protection of the Post, or the Post Office, for in their original jurisdiction, the Postmaster Generals are the Trustees of their respective zone.

In 1789 the Continental Congress passed a bill to "establish the seat of government, a general post office, under the direction of the Postmaster General." That's right, a general post office under the direction of the Postmaster General. They were further dividing the postal zone of North America establishing a new zone, and endowing it with sovereign authority, whereby our founding fathers believed they could establish a Trusteeship which would ensure that sovereignty of the people would be passed down to the people of future generations.

The Preamble to the Constitution created the Estate Trust which held the freedoms guaranteed in the Articles of Confederation and the Declaration of Independence in trust for future generations. The Articles of the Constitution established the Trusteeship as well as the powers and limitations thereof. The Congress and Senate were Trustees charged with the Administration of our Divine Inheritance, the Global Estate Trust.

In this "general post office" seat of government there was established the "civil administration" called the United States. Civil administration to administrate our Divine Estate Trust, the Global Trust, our Divine Inheritance. Remember, we can never OWN anything. We simply have a Divine Right of Use of the property of the Divine Estate, the Global Trust.

So, we the people of this earth have a Divine Right of use of the Global Trust while the civil administration is charged with the administration of our estate for our benefit. In the world of trusts Civil Administration/ Government = Trusteeship. So, the entire world is held in trust. The Global Estate Trust, our Divine Inheritance, our birthright is held in trust and is administrated by the various 'governments' who gain their sovereign authority via the Universal Postal Union, the Secondary Trustee of the Global Trust answerable to the Vatican.

In the world of trusts and trust law, rights, duties and obligations are very straight forward, cut and dry, black and white. There are no opinions, secret codes, rules or statutes, period. Just the facts. There is a chain of command, consequences for your actions, or lack thereof, and accountability.

It has been a slow and cumbersome process to overcome the out of control momentum of the civil administrators of the world today. There have been countless casualties as a result of our efforts to unravel the illusion; to overcome the programming and fear which fuelled the beast to reach the core where truth and accountability resides. You are now well versed in this game of the Elite to complete their business plan of PLANET EARTH.

The New Postmaster General

In my quest, I felt it important to bring my research about the Post Office into fruition. This letter was executed in September, 2011 by me **James Thomas McBride, Postmaster General**:

"I, James Thomas of the family McBride, living man American freeholder in fee simple absolute acting in the capacity of Postmaster General, Trustee under whose direction the United States operates, with all of the power and authority of the Office of the Postmaster General.

I was lost in the sea of illusion, compelled to live and operate under an error of assumptions that have adversely effected the freeholder and his estate; the fruit of a Breach of Trust by the Trustees of the United States of America.

The positions of Postmaster General and the Office of the Postmaster General existed prior to the Constitution for the United States under the jurisdiction of the Universal Postal Union (UPU). The seat of government for the United States was established as a general post office under the direction of the Postmaster General. The Executors, Trustees and Administrators charged with the administration of the estate trust , "United States of America", operate from this seat of government under the direction of the Postmaster General.

My authority to act in the capacity of Postmaster General-Trustee through the Office of the Postmaster General has long been established and accepted at the highest level via my "Claim On Abandonment' and annexed 'Postal Treaty for the Americas.'

The original constitution for the United States, a 'will', was established by our founding fathers to ensure that sovereignty of the people was passed down to the people of future generations. The 14th Amendment fraudulently altered the 'will' for the benefit of the Trustees and adversely effecting the Beneficiaries to the 'will'. The 14th Amendment created the 14th Amendment paper citizen as the new heirs under the jurisdiction of the newly created Congress and Senate created under the 14th Amendment.

The people have been tricked and coerced into unwittingly giving false witness against ourselves that:

- *We are 14th Amendment paper citizens of the U.S.;*
- *We willingly and knowingly elected to accept the benefits under the will as a 14th Amendment citizen;*
- *The living man freeholder is deceased;*
- *We are the Executor of the estate trust/ 14th Amendment paper citizen of the U.S..*

The Congress and Senate that existed PRE-BREACH OF TRUST represented the living men and women, American freeholders under the original estate trust instrument, as public servants. The Congress and Senate that we endure today was created and empowered by the 14th Amendment, A BREACH OF TRUST, and has jurisdiction over legal fiction citizens of the U.S., estate trusts created by the registration of Our birth.

The codes and statutes of the 14th Amendment Congress and Senate have no force and effect on the freeholders of America.

Today, We the American People are all assumed to be deceased and acting in the capacity of Executor of the legal fiction U.S. Citizen and that we are all subject to the codes and statutes as 14th Amendment citizens. There has been no evidence that any living freeholders inhabit America today. No matter how loudly we proclaim that we are alive, we cannot be heard as we are assumed to be deceased and failed to provide the proper evidence to rebut the assumption. We have no standing in the common law nor standing to receive a common law remedy as we are assumed to be deceased and dead people don't have standing in a common law court nor for a common law remedy.

Those agencies that existed pre-breach of trust now wear two hats; one empowered under the original constitution as public servants to the American freeholders and the second empowered by the 14th Amendment Congress and Senate under authority obtained due to a Breach of Trust.

These Offices under the authority of the original constitution have fallen dormant as there has been no evidence that any living freeholders inhabit America; we had all effectively fallen trap to the breach of trust to our detriment causing loss, injury and damage to the estate and the Beneficiary.

You are hereby NOTICED the living men and women, freeholders in fee simple absolute have returned from being lost in the sea of illusion to re-establish their living status and status as freeholders electing to REJECT the benefits under the will as 14th Amendment citizens and choosing to enforce contractual rights in the property bequeathed by the will, 'against the will'.

All pre-breach Offices are hereby re-activated. You are instructed to dawn your pre-breach hat, staff your offices and prepare to receive and accept the freeholders of America as we re-inhabit the republic. You are instructed to re-educate your staff as to how to serve the freeholders; that the freeholders are not subject to the codes and statutes of the 14th Amendment Congress and Senate and that we enjoy all of the rights and privileges of the Articles of Confederation and the Declaration of Independence.

We are presently compiling a data base of all American freeholders as they re-establish their status, re-inhabit the 50 states for the redemption of their estate as well as a database for the registration of those pre-breach Offices as they come into compliance including all contact information for said office(s).

Each Office holder shall immediately provide all contact information and evidence of compliance to:

> Legal Registries
> P.O. Box 28606
> Columbus, Ohio 43228

I, James Thomas, American freeholder, acting through the Office of the Postmaster General, in the capacity as Trustee, under whose direction the United States operates, demand a cure to the breach of trust.

Let me be perfectly clear that we are here to ensure a cure to the breach of trust; to facilitate the transition back to the pre-breach constitution; to re-activate both federal and state pre-breach offices and re-establish this civil administration under the original, pre-breach constitution.

To facilitate a smooth transition; to ensure that the priorities of the American people are foremost; to facilitate the interaction between freeholders and their public servants;

and to ensure that the Offices are filled with honourable men and women, the trustees and administrators shall work hand in hand and with the approval of the Transition Committee established in the Postal Treaty for the Americas annexed hereto.

The original pre-breach Congress and Senate SHALL be seated, sworn in and empowered. Potential Office holders must be known to be honourable men/women, must resign any/all positions under the 14th Amendment; must re-establish themselves as freeholders and swear an Oath to the pre-breach constitution.

The O.I.T.C., D.T.C., D.T.C.C. and the Comptroller of the Currencies shall ensure that the account styled as "National Banking Association", as set forth in the Postal Treaty for the Americas annexed hereto, is immediately funded, releasing the long blocked funds for the discharge of debt and issue and provide the 'charge card' for use by the freeholder(s) to access the private funds, charging the account for the immediate discharge of debt to facilitate Global debt Forgiveness. You are further instructed to prepare to fund the sub- accounts and issue the 'charge cards' to the freeholders as they re-establish their living status.

The Trustees are instructed to fund the new Treasury Banking System the freeholders are back.

The Trustees shall immediately settle, close and dissolve the estate trust JAMES THOMAS MCBRIDE 296520781 and make the return of the property and interest to the freeholder James Thomas.

You are further instructed to provide me documentary evidence of the closure and make a full account to the freeholder, James Thomas and provide documentation that identifies me as an American freeholder to ensure the safe and unmolested travel across this land."

The Global Estate Trust, Post Office, Vatican And Military Link

To understand the relationships of all the parties a quick summary is needed. At the bottom is you and the Vital Statistics Office that issued the Certified copy of the Birth Certificate, a security which represents the Divine Estate Trust, therefore they hold the original and are the holder in due course of the estate. They are the Intermediary Agent for the Trust with a fiduciary duty to the Beneficiary of the Estate. and the true beneficiary is you in the flesh and blood.

At the top, as we said, the Vatican boasts, in their Papal Bull, dominion over the entire earth, via conquest, and is answerable ONLY to the Divine Spirit. Dominion over means control over, not ownership. So as said, the Vatican's un-rebutted claims establish them as the Primary Trustee of the Global Estate Trust, our Divine Inheritance. To facilitate the administration of this Global Trust the Vatican established the Universal Postal Union as the Secondary Trustees of the Global Trust charged with dividing the Global Trust into zones and endowing these legal fiction zones with sovereign authority to facilitate the efficient administration of the Global Trust.

And so it comes as no surprise that the first requirement for the international acknowledgment of a sovereign nation is the necessity of a Post Office. The primary objective of the military in any "zone" is the protection of the Post, or the Post Office, for in their original jurisdiction, the Postmaster Generals are the Trustees of their respective zone. That responsibility has been usurped to feed the Military Industrial complex so as to protect the citizens of the nation by way of the real peoples credit.

When in 1789 the Continental Congress passed a bill to "establish the seat of government, a general post office, under the direction of the Postmaster General, they were further dividing the postal zone of North America establishing a new zone, and endowing it with sovereign authority, whereby our founding fathers believed they could establish a Trusteeship which would ensure that sovereignty of the people would be passed down to the people of future generations. It was not what happened, as has been revealed.

The Postal Authority

It is important to know that all important legal and commercial documents through the post office rather than private carriers, which are firewalls. We want direct access to the authority—and corresponding availability of remedy and recourse—of the UPU. For instance, if you post through the US Post Office and the US Postmaster does not provide you with the remedy you request within twenty-one (21) days, you can take the matter to the UPU.

Involving the authority of the UPU is automatically invoked by the use of postage stamps. Utilization of stamps includes putting stamps on any documents (for clout purposes, not mailing) we wish to introduce into the system. As long as you use a stamp (of any kind) you are in the game. If you have time, resources, and the luxury of dealing with something well before expiration of a given time frame, you can use stamps that you consider ideal. The most preferable stamps are ones that are both large and contain the most colors. In an emergency situation, or simply if economy is a consideration, any stamp will do. Using a postage stamp and autograph on it makes you the postmaster for that contract.

Whenever you put a stamp on a document, inscribe your full name over the stamp at an angle. The color ink you use for this is a function of what color will show up best against the colors in the stamp. Ideal colors for doing this are purple (royalty), blue (origin of the bond), and gold (king's edict). Avoid red at all cost. Obviously, if you have a dark, multi-colored stamp you do not want to use purple or blue ink, since your autograph on it would not stand out as well if you used lighter color ink. Ideally one could decide on the best color for his autograph and then obtain stamps that best suit one's criteria and taste. Although a dollar stamp is best, it is a luxury unless one is well off financially. Otherwise, reserve the use of dollar stamps for crucial instruments, such as travel documents. The rationale for using two-cent stamps is that in the 19th Century the official postage rate for the *de jure* Post Office of the United States of America was fixed at two (2) cents. For stamps to carry on one's person for any kind of unexpected encounter or emergency use, this denomination might be ideal.

Use stamps on important documents, such as a check, travel documents, paperwork you put in court, etc. Where to put the stamp and how many stamps to use depend on the document. On foundational documents and checks, for instance, put a stamp on the right hand corner of the instrument, both on the front and on the back. The bottom right hand corner of the face of a check, note, or bill of exchange signifies the liability. Furthermore, the bottom right hand corner of the reverse of the document is the final position on the page, so no one can endorse anything (using a restricted endorsement or otherwise) after that. You want to have the last word. If you have only one stamp, put it where you are expected to sign and autograph over it cross-wise. In the case of a traffic ticket, for instance, put a stamp on the lower right hand corner where you are supposed to sign and autograph across the stamp at an angle.

Autographing a stamp not only establishes you as the postmaster of the contract but constitutes a cross-claim. Using the stamp process on documents presents your adversaries with a problem because their jurisdiction is subordinate to that of the UPU, which you have now invoked for your benefit. The result in practice of doing this is that whenever those who know what you are doing are recipients of your documents with autographed stamps they back off. If they do not, take the matter to the US Postmaster to deal with. If he will not provide you with your remedy, take the matter to the UPU for them to clean up.

The countries whose stamps would be most effective to use are China, Japan, United States, and Great Britain. Utilizing these countries covers both East and West. However, since the US seems to be the point man in implementing the New World Order, one might most advisably use US stamps.

For example, if you put stamps on documents you submit into court, put a stamp on the back of each page, at the bottom right hand corner. Do not place any stamps on the front of court paperwork since doing so alarms the clerk. By placing your autographed stamp on the reverse right hand corner you prevent being damaged by one of the tricks of judges these days. A judge might have your paperwork on his bench, but turned over so only the back side, which is ordinarily blank on every page, is visible. Then if you ask about your paperwork he might say something like, *"Yes, I have your paperwork in front of me but I don't find anything."* He can't see anything on the blank side of a page. If you place an autographed stamp on the lower right hand corner you foreclose a judge from engaging in this trick.

In addition, when it comes to court documents, one side is criminal and the other is civil. Using the autographed stamp that you rubber-stamp with your seal (bullet stamp) on the back side of your court documents is evidence that you possess the cancelled obligation on the civil side. Since there can be no assessment for criminal charges, and you show that you are the holder of the civil assessment, there is no way out for the court. Also, in any court document you put in, handwrite your EIN number [SS# w.o. dashes] in gold on the top right corner of every page, with the autographed stamp on the back side.

Use of a notary combined with the postage stamp (and sometime Embassy stamps) gives you a priority mechanism. Everything is commerce, and all commerce is contract. The master of the contract is the post office, and the UPU is the supreme overlord of the commerce, banking, and postal systems of the world. Use of these stamps in this manner gets the attention of those in the system to whom you provide your paperwork. It makes you the master of that post office. Use of the stamp is especially important when dealing with the major players, such as the FBI, CIA, Secret Service, Treasury, etc. They understand the significance of what you are doing. Many times they hand documents back to someone using this approach and say, "Have a good day, sir." They don't want any untoward repercussions coming back on them.

If anyone asks you why you are doing what you are doing, suggest that they consult their legal counsel for the significance. It is not your job to explain the law, nor explain such things as your exemption or Setoff Account. The system hangs us by our own words. We have to give them the evidence, information, contacts, and legal determinations they require to convict us. The wise words of Calvin Coolidge, the most taciturn president in US history, are apt. When asked why he spoke so little, he replied, *"I have never been hurt by anything I didn't say."*

The bottom line is that whenever you need to sign any legal/commercial document, put a stamp (even a one (1) cent stamp) over where you sign and sign at an angle across it. Let the recipient deal with the significance and consequences of your actions. If you are in a court case, or at any stage of a proceeding (such as an indictment, summons, complaint, or any other hostile encounter with the system), immediately do the following:

1. Make a color copy of whatever documents you receive, or scan them in color into your computer;
2. Stamp the original of the first page of every document with the AFV/RFV stamp, put a postage stamp in the signature space, and autograph across it at an angle with your full name, using purple or blue ink, handwritten with upper- and lower-case, with your gold-ink bullet stamp (seal) on the upper left-hand portion of the postage stamp;
Make a color copy of the stamped, autographed pages and/or scan into your computer;
3. Put a stamp on the lower right-hand-corner of the back of every page and bullet-stamp and autograph it;
4. Have a notary send each document back to the sender, with a notarial certificate of service, with or without an accompanying/supporting affidavit by you;
5. If you have an affidavit, put an autographed stamp on the upper right hand corner of the first page and the lower right hand corner of the back of every page.

People who have engaged in this process report that when any knowledgeable judge, attorney, or official sees this, matters change dramatically. All of these personages know what mail fraud is. Since autographing the stamp makes you the postmaster of the contract, anyone who interferes is tampering with the mail and engaging in mail fraud. You can then subpoena the postmaster (either of the post office from which the letter was mailed, or the US Postmaster General, or both), and have them explain what the rules are, under deposition or testimony on the witness stand in open court.

In addition, most of the time when you get official communication it has a red-meter postage mark on the envelope rather than a cancelled stamp. This act is mail fraud. If the envelope has a red-meter postage mark on it, they are the ones who have engaged in mail fraud, because there is no cancelled stamp. It is the cancelled stamp that has the power; an un-cancelled stamp has nothing. A red-meter postage mark is an uncancelled stamp. If it is not cancelled, it is not paid. One researcher has scanned everything into his computer, and has more red-meter postage marks than he "can shake a stick at." Officials sending things out by cancelled stamp is a rarity—perhaps at most 2%.

With the red-metered postage you can trace each communication back to the PO from which it was sent, so you can get the postmaster for that PO, as well as the postmaster general for the US, to investigate the mail fraud involved. It is reasonable to conclude that cancelling a stamp both registers the matter and forms a contract between the party that cancels the stamp and the UPU. Using a stamp for postage without cancelling it is prima facie evidence that the postmaster of the local PO is committing mail fraud by taking a customer's money and not providing the paid-for service and providing you with the power of a cancelled stamp, as required under the provisions of the UPU. When you place an autographed stamp on a document you place that document and the contract underlying it under international law and treaty, with which the courts have no jurisdiction to deal. The system cannot deal with the real you, the living principle (as evidenced and witnessed by jurat). Nor can officials, attorneys, judges, et al., go against the UPU, international law, and treaty. In addition, they have no authority/jurisdiction to impair a contract between you (as the living principal) and the UPU (overseer of all world commerce).

You cancelled the stamp by sealing it and autographing across it. You did so in capacity of being the living principal, as acknowledged by your seal and the jurat on your documents.

If you are in a court case, bring in your red-metered envelopes in court and request the judge to direct the prosecutor to explain the red-meter postage stamp. Then watch their jaws drop. Doing this is especially potent if you also have asked the prosecutor to provide his bar number, since most attorneys in court—especially in US—are not qualified. An attorney in federal court had better have a six-digit bar card or he committed a felony just by walking in and giving his name.

Lastly, if you are charged with mail fraud, subpoena the prosecutor(s) to bring in the evidence on which mail fraud is being alleged, as well as the originals of all envelopes used for mailing any item connected with the case. Then the mail fraud involved was committed by the postmaster of the PO in which the envelope was stamped.

When you use the postal stamp and you do not get satisfaction, there is a hidden power that is available. It is executed by a registered complaint to a special position called the Provost Marshall. Yes, it is a military position under military law--Admiralty.

Military Duty To Protect The Post

All debt of the UNITED STATES, except that debt owed to the sovereign people of America, has been abandoned and vacated and the UNITED STATES has DECLARED PEACE with the world and the sovereign people thereof, therefore, the gold fringed military flag designating the admiralty/maritime jurisdiction shall be immediately removed from all courtrooms, meeting rooms, etc. of the administrative agencies of the UNITED STATES and the civil peace flag of the united states of America shall be proudly displayed in their stead..

The U.S. Courts who have been operating as debt collection facilities under TWEA and the EMERGENCY WAR POWERS ACT shall immediately make the corrections and cure the torts against the people, vacating all claims, attachments and/or restrictions on the private rights of the sovereign people and make them whole.

The courts, as well as all administrative agencies of the UNITED STATES, shall share resources making room for and facilitating the establishment of the organic courts, operating under the common law, for the adjudication of all matters concerning the sovereign American people, other than the prosecution of grievances against an administrative agency for the trespass of the private rights of the people. All administrative agencies shall actively participate in the establishment of two distinctly separate systems, common law and administrative, operating side by side for the benefit of the CREDITORS, the sovereign people of America.

All administrative courts and agencies of the UNITED STATES shall operate in good faith and honour as servants of the sovereign people of America. Said administrative courts and agencies have grown out of control, beyond the intent of the original founders and their usefulness and shall begin to make the corrections, a reversal, bringing about balance, transparency, full disclosure and honour for the remedy of the Real Parties In Interest.

All debts of the UNITED STATES have been abandoned, except the debt to the sovereign people; The Pledge of the private property of the American people has been relinquished, therefore, the administrative agencies of the UNITED STATES shall make the return of the interest back to source, the sovereign people.

The UNITED STATES shall immediately activate the established pass through account, vacate the blocks on the asset accounts and make the financial adjustments to discharge the debt and return the accounts of the sovereign people back into balance. The UNITED STATES shall maintain the natural flow and balance in the accounts for the remedy of the people, returning the interest back to source in the discharge of debt against the pre-paid account, at all times remaining in honour.

The UNITED STATES shall immediately make the corrections as concerns the unlawful restrictions of the liberties of the sovereign people by the administrative agencies of the UNITED STATES;

All Deeds, warranty deeds, trust deeds, sheriff deeds, tax deeds and all Certificates of Title are colorable titles issued to facilitate the 'Pledge' of the private property of the sovereign people.

The Pledge has been relinquished, therefore, the UNITED STATES shall make the corrections to discharge all colorable titles, make the re-conveyance and issue the land patent/ allodial title for the property back to the people.

It is the duty of the military to serve and protect the post, therefore, the UNITED STATES military shall serve and protect the sovereign people of America, the creditor of the UNITED STATES. All branches of the U.S. Military shall follow the orders of the "Transitional Committee", interim government and government of the republic, respectively throughout this transition.

The Provost Marshals are the organic police force with a duty to serve and protect the sovereign. The Provost Marshal shall immediately serve and protect all who claim protection under this treaty making top priority any/all requests for assistance on claims of unlawful restrictions on the liberties of a sovereign.

The Military Industrial Complex

The Military-Industrial Complex is a phrase used to signify a comfortable relationship between parties that are charged to manage wars (the military, the presidential administration and congress) and companies that produce weapons and equipment for war (industry). To put it simply, the Military-Industrial Complex is described as an all-too friendly relationship that may develop between defence contractors and government forces, where both sides receive what they are perceivably looking for: a successful military engagement for war planners and financial profit for those manning the corporate boardrooms. It can be viewed as a "war for profit" theory. For those who finance war, it is simply business. And the more conflicts that rise, the better the business.

The idea of war for profit is nothing new in the realm of human history and can be traced back centuries earlier where arms races and the power of navy ships ruled an empire's reach. The arms race between the European powers of France, Spain and Britain could arguably be a primal version of today's modern so-called military-industrial complex. The idea was that a country must build up and maintain a ready military - the largest in the world at that - to remain a world power. Centuries ago, such a military was necessitated to protect aggression from neighbouring countries. These days, an invasion of the American homeland may seem ridiculous and contrary to the building of a global community founded in trust and respect. Others might argue differently but that is hardly the point when it is all just business.

In any case, the theory of a mutually beneficial relationship may not appear to be so far-fetched. It is no secret that the defence industry profits most when a nation commits to a lengthy war overseas. As any military will spare no expense for victory, it only makes sense to tap the resources of the defence industry to accomplish the mission. A sort of pseudo-world dominance through the basic form of imperialism can be seen to be just as important to a military force as is protecting one's homeland. The bottom line: war is good business for those invested in it - manufacturing, production, servicing, etc.. To the war-minded industry, a wartime economy is just as profitable as a solid growing one, where shells and ammunition take precedence over the production of peacetime light bulbs or pencils. One need only to peruse the list of manufacturers participating in production during the Second World War to see just how a wartime economy can alter a single factory.

The phrase *Military-Industrial Complex* was first utilized in an American report at the turn of the 20th Century. "Military-Industrial Complex" was later immortalized by outgoing United States President Dwight D. Eisenhower in his January 17, 1961 farewell address to the nation. In his speech, he cites the Military-Industrial Complex as a warning to the American people – to not let this establishment begin to dictate America's actions at home or abroad. The original usage appeared in the form of *Military-Industrial Congressional Complex* but later removed.

On June 30, 2010, Benjamen Fulford reported **The Vatican is now the last obstacle to the new financial system**. "*Talks this Monday between a representative of the White Dragon Society and two senior Vatican representatives (including the Papal Nuncio or ambassador to Washington) did not go well. The Vatican insist they have a right to steal trillions of dollars that do not belong to them because "the survival of the church is at stake." This is simply not true, they are simply blocking the announcement of the new financial system because of a lust for raw power. The Vatican Banker, Daniele Del Bosco, who has hidden the close to $1 trillion in gold-backed bonds, has been trying to cash them with the help of a fraudulent organization known as the Office for International Treasury Control or OITC. An Interpol investigation has revealed the OITC has no mandate and no right to these funds.*

The funds Del Bosco is hiding were earmarked to help Portugal, Spain and Italy end their respective financial crises. The $134.5 billion in bonds confiscated at the Italian/Swiss border in June of 2009 were linked to these funds. Del Bosco is about to be placed on an international wanted list and is now under 24-hour observation. We can also add that according to both CIA and Yakuza sources, the Vatican dispatched two separate assassination squads to Japan with the goal of killing and silencing this writer. They seem to be under the mistaken belief doing so will suddenly give the Vatican the ability to cash these funds. The Vatican will be provided financing to help it survive but only after they purge the Satanists from their top ranks. We must also mention the new financial system is designed to finance a campaign to end poverty, stop environmental, end war and set humanity and life on a path for exponential expansion. The fact that the Vatican *leadership is trying to prevent this from happening is good proof that they are going against the teachings of both Jesus Christ and of Roman Catholicism in general."*

In a more recent statement, I, **James Thomas McBride**, the new Postmaster General stated:

"The general post office styled as the UNITED STATES has been in a perpetual state of war since its inception. The 'Powers That Be' have used the UNITED STATES as a weapon to wage war on the sovereign people of America, operating under the Emergency War Powers Act and the secret presumption that the sovereign people are the enemy of the UNITED STATES for the purpose of evading their liabilities under the original equity contract and to pillage and plunder the private property of the people they were created to serve.

The general post office styled as the UNITED STATES has been used as a weapon to wage an economic war at arms length against all of the people of the world bringing all of humanity to the brink of destruction as the CREDITOR'S master plan of total economic slavery over the sovereign people of the world has been implemented.

The Powers That Be have used the UNITED STATES as a weapon to wage war on the sovereign people of the world via the unconscionable creation, production and distribution of harmful drugs for the purpose of enslaving the people and funding and executing their genocide against humanity.

The Powers That Be have used the UNITED STATES as a platform for their propaganda, creating the world's problems and then presenting themselves as the world's savior bringing about the solution and protection from their self created illusionary boogie men for the purpose of enslaving the sovereign people of the world."

In my quest both spiritual and commercial, I had been at war, truly lost at sea. For decades, I had battled the "system" which knew was fraught with deception and fear. Those decades that brought many difficult times for me also brought truth, and more importantly, who I really was and how important it was to be in peace and not at war. I had begot so much of what I had created. And so the most valuable of lessons was to move my total being into a position of Peace. It was through this Post Master Position, that I, James McBride initiated a Universal Postal Treaty which is the topic of the next Chapter.

29

THE UNIVERSAL POSTAL TREATY FOR THE AMERICAS

It is Peace And Prosperity We Seek

In 2012, from my position as, Postmaster General I stated as follows:

"The purpose is to seek truth and in so doing it is necessary to shine light upon what is not truth so as to allow choice of free will. In this process of exposing it is necessary to be detached from it as non-partisan, pro-truth-honesty-peace, and anti-war-lies-crime. The purpose is to expose corruptions, frauds, deceptions, lies, criminal plans, cover-ups and free-speech silencing by powerful people in governments, foundations, corporations and media, which are done using the name of democracy, human rights, false interpretations of religions, cults, occults, patriotism, economy, business, media, elections, justice, charity, etc., and are used to trick the public into hatred & wars and out of their lives, money and freedoms, while the propaganda we are subjected to makes us believe that we have evolved to where such things cannot happen [remember slavery, apartheid.]. Stop the hatred that is used to promote the dehumanization of the victims of aggressions; spread the truth; free your mind from being a Zioncon occupied territory of the neo-feudal lords by rejecting the mainstream news propaganda. Such news may induce a kind of schizophrenia because it provides a true vision of reality which is so different from the one we are presented by the mass media spins."

By rising above all this we can attain a higher position where we forgive all that has occurred and drop the hatred and conflict.

In attempting to bring the truth into the light of peace, love for all and prosperity, I then proceeded to register a **The Universal Postal Treaty for the Americas**. On November 5, 2010, it was registered in the repository as an official treaty as submitted by the Postmaster General, serving in my official capacity. That document is included here as it provides my research and truth to date outlining also how we got into our situation.

587

Servus Servorum Dei
THE UNIVERSAL POSTAL TREATY
FOR THE AMERICAS
2010

Preamble

We have come forth from the Power to Be the Eternal Mystery of its Presence. We are the beginning and the end; the origin and dissolution; the geometry of divinity, and we have remained True to this eternal Moment in the Sun. We are the silence that is unfathomable, and the spark whose voice is the flame of Freedom.

We have been called forth to return the Power and we have been chosen, as we have chosen ourselves to Be; to Become that which we have forever Been. Our essence is identical to the Source of its essence. For there was never a time when we were not, nor shall there ever be a time when we shall cease to Be.

We are they who have nurtured the sacred fire of illumination; forging our Souls into the image of god on Earth.

We are they who have embraced the Ordeal of our descent into matter, and have ascended the 33 steps of the spiral staircase to experience the Rapture of the Quickening.

We are they who have faced the great magnification of the All to ascend the ineffable throne of mind and wield the power of self.

Our Word is Truth and we are its Issue. Our Word is Law and we are Self-governing. Our Word is Light and we are the infinite Beacon of Eternal I Am.

We bear the Light of our ascension and the wisdom of our journey into Matter; thus do we reject the burdens of tyranny by exposing them as the fruits of ignorance. We have drunk deeply from the Ancient Font, we know who we are, and this knowledge is our purpose. Our Sword is Flaming and two-edged, and its name is Awakening.

The Mind of Creation is manifest in our Eye, and Its Will in our deeds. We are the Royal Seed of the Source precisely because we are its Pure Light Shining True upon this Earth. Our spirits have been forged in this crucible of sorrow, therefore our joy is boundless; and thus are we recognized by those who have eyes to see.

In this eternal moment, and through this Treaty, we do decree I AM; Individual and sovereign Beings, in continual Communion with the Quintessence of Creation. We do hereby claim the right to listen to the voice of god within and to freely choose those with whom we will engage in contract. So here now do we claim our inheritance, **Spiritual sovereignty.**

When in the Course of human events, it becomes necessary for people to dissolve the political bonds which have connected them with others, and to assume among the powers of the earth, the separate and equal station to which they may choose to aspire, a decent respect to the opinions of mankind requires that they should declare the causes which impel them to the separation. We hold that no truths are self-evident, but must have their usefulness demonstrated. That all people are created with equal freedom from tyranny, but frequently accept domination or obedience to a legal code, to a greater or lesser degree from person to person. That people are endowed with only what rights they have chosen to be endowed with, through wisdom or common folly, for wealth or health. That people can secure for themselves, with understanding of their own unique situations, those rights which best allow them to live in peace and fruitful harmony with nature and all Her various species. That whenever any person, Government, or other entity, not fully recognizing the unique situation of each individual, becomes in any way oppressive or destructive, people may choose to ignore, alter, abolish or separate themselves from such an institution, and to live in peace and harmony. That man can choose to resolve any conflict through intelligence, with, adequate communication and a full understanding of each and every point of view involved, by each and every person involved. Prudence, indeed, will dictate that Governments long established should not be changed for light and transient causes, but only after calm consideration of the True Will and mutual goals of all those individuals involved. All experience has shown that people are more disposed to suffer, while evils are sufferable, than to right themselves by abolishing the forms to which they are accustomed. But when a long train of abuses and usurpation evinces a design to reduce them under absolute Despotism or Dogma not chosen by the individual concerned, it is their right, it is their duty to themselves and their Creator, to throw off such a Government and to accept responsibility, each for their own actions and future security.

Declaration Of Causes For Separation

On July 26, 1775 the Continental Congress appointed Benjamin Franklin as the first postmaster general of the organic Post Office for the united states, union of several states. In 1776 the united states of America declared its independence and in May 1789 the Constitution for the united states of America was adopted.

On Thursday, Sept. 17, 1789 we find written, "Mr. Goodhue, for the committee appointed for the purpose, presented a bill to amend part of the Tonnage act, which was read the first time. The bill sent from the Senate, for **the temporary establishment of the Post Office**, was read the second and third time, and passed.

The bill for **establishing the Judicial Courts** for **establishing the seat of government** . . ." The organic post office for the united states of America established the seat of government, a general post office, under the direction of the postmaster general.

This is verified on March 1825, when an act was passed entitled "An act to reduce into one the several acts establishing and regulating the post office department," 3 Story, U. S. 1825. "**It is thereby enacted; That there be established, the seat of the government of the United States, a general post office, under the direction of a postmaster general.**"

The organic post office for the united states of America established the ten miles square, styled as *WASHINGTON, D.C.*, as a general post office and independent postal zone with the rights and authority of a sovereign nation, operating under a corporate structure under the direction of the postmaster general to function as the seat of government of the United States.

A visit to the USPS web site today will establish that John (Jack) E. Potter wears two hats and is 1) the postmaster general [of the organic post office] and 2) the CEO of the USPS [corporate]. The web site offers further evidence of the existence of two separate post office entities when they state that the Post Office is 1) one of the most trusted government **agencies,** and 2) one of the ten most trusted **organizations** in the nation. When one researches the two words we find that they are not inter-changeable; they do not and cannot define the same entity.

The constitution of the United States has vested congress with the power to establish post offices and post roads within the ten miles square and within any/all territories of same. [Art. 1, s. 8, n. 7] Congress created the corporate United States Post Office which today is the United States Postal Service or USPS operating via the
authority vested in the general post office styled as *WASHINGTON, D.C.* On February 21, 1871 16 Statutes at Large 419 divided America into 10 districts or territories for the purpose of expanding outside of the ten miles square the authority of said general post office over We the American People.

Complex Regulatory Scheme

The Constitution for the United States granted congress the power to:

☐ Lay and collect taxes, Duties, Imposts and Excises, to pay the debts and provide for the common defence and general welfare of the United States. [Art. I sec. 8, cl. 4];
☐ To regulate commerce with foreign nations, and among the several states, [Art. I sec. 8 cl. 3];
☐ To establish uniform laws on the subject of bankruptcy, [Art. I sec. 8 cl. 4];
☐ To declare war, grant letters of Marque and Reprisal, and make rules concerning captures on land and water, [Art. I sec. 8 cl. 11];
☐ To exercise exclusive legislation in all cases, whatsoever, over such district (**not to exceed ten miles square**) as may, by cession of particular states, and acceptance by congress, become the seat of government of the United States, and to exercise like authority over all places purchased by the consent of the legislature of the state in which the same shall be, for the erection Forts, Magazines, Arsenals, dock yards and other needful things.

Congress has the power under Article I of the Constitution to authorize an administrative agency administering a complex regulatory scheme to allocate costs and benefits among voluntary participants in the program without providing an Article III adjudication of claims. [Am. Jur. 2nd Fedcourts sec. 7]. Congress, acting for a valid legislative purpose, pursuant to its powers under Article I, may create a "seemingly private" right that is so closely integrated into a public regulatory scheme as to be a matter appropriate for agency resolution with limited involvement by the Article III judiciary. Agency resolution of such federal rights may take the form of binding arbitration with limited judicial review. [Am. Jur. 2nd Fedcourts sec 7]
So, to cement their encroachment of power over the American people beyond the ten miles square, congress created a complex regulatory scheme called the federal (and state) Statutes, Codes and Regulations, to allocate costs, for the collection of taxes, duties and excises, for the payment of the national debt, and to provide for the common defence and general welfare of the United States.

Congress so closely integrated a seemingly private right (right to contract) into this complex regulatory scheme to turn unsuspecting American sovereigns, creators of the United States, into seemingly voluntary participants in the program; seemingly voluntary participants in binding contracts, having received limited or no valuable consideration in the exchange and failing full disclosure of the terms and conditions of said contracts which are contrary to the best interest of the American people.

The federal courts have become administrative courts employing Executive Administrators charged with the enforcement of codes and statutes, [FRC v GE 281 US 464, KELLER v PE 261 US 428, 1 Stat. 138-1788], to collect the taxes, duties, imposts and excises for the payment of the national debt in accordance with Article I of the Constitution. In 1976 Public Law 94-381 officially brought the federal courts under the executive branch operating under Article I of the Constitution in violation of the separation of powers.

The U.S. District courts have original jurisdiction over all maritime causes; of all land seizures under the Admiralty Extension Act; of all actions of Prize; and of all non-maritime seizures under any law of the United States on land or water. [28 USCA sec. 1356] The Commerce Clause, [Art. I sec. 8, cl. 13] of the Constitution is a sufficient basis for federal admiralty power while the Admiralty Extension Act brought the Admiralty jurisdiction inland.

The Trading With The Enemy Act made all Americans enemy combatants and enemies of the United States and placed all Americans on the list maintained by the Custodian of the Alien Property, [Secretary of the U.S. Treasury] making all Americans subject to the seizure of our bodies and our private property under the laws of war or the Laws of Prize under Choses in action for satisfaction of a contractual obligation, express or implied.

When one defaults on his contractual obligations to pay his share of the national debt, which is based on the Law of Contributions, his private property becomes subject to seizure, Juri Belli, out of the hands of the enemy by the right or laws of Prize, by Privateers acting under Letters of Marque and Reprisal under Article I, sec. 8, cl. 11 of the Constitution.

Congress has empowered members of the private B.A.R. Association with a monopoly in the U.S. courts, as Privateers acting under Letters of Marque and Reprisal, (B.A.R. Association Card No. = Letter of Marque document no.) to seize the property and the body of the offender in order to obtain satisfaction for the obligations for which he has contracted, knowingly or otherwise.

However, there are several things intrinsically flawed, unconscionable and/or fraudulent about this complex regulatory scheme.

We the People of America are Party to an important equity contract with the United States; the "Original Equity Contract", whereby We the People allow the United States the use of our 'good faith and credit' which is transmitted to the U.S. via the transmitting utility, public vessel 'strawman'. Said public vessel, transmitting utility was created and registered by the state only days after our birth into this world, obviously without our consent. In exchange for the use of our credit the United States has promised to pay/discharge all of the debt of the sovereign, via the public vessel, providing the dual consideration necessary for a valid contract. It has been established as a matter of fact that the United States has executed said equity contract with this Petitioner, having created funds from the credit of Petitioner, thereby charging their debtor obligation for the exchange.

It has been established in fact that, "All that government does and provides legitimately is in pursuit of its duty to provide protection for private rights [Wynnhammer v People, 13 NY 378] which duty is a debt owed to its creator, We the People of America, and the uninfranchised individual; which debt and duty is never extinguished nor discharged, and is perpetual. No matter what the defacto government provides for us in the manner of convenience and safety, the uninfranchised individual owes nothing to the government. [Hale v Henkle 201 US 43]

"We the People have discharged any debt which is said to exist or owed to the state. The governments are, presumably, indebted continually to the People, because the People, the sovereigns, presumably accented to the creation of the government corporation and because we suffer its continued existence. The continued debt owed to the American People is discharged only as it continues not to violate our private rights, and when government fails in its duty to provide protection- discharge its duty to the People- it is an abandonment (delictual default) of any and all power, authority or vestige of sovereignty which it may have otherwise possessed, and the law remains the same, the sovereignty reverting back to the People whence it came." [Downes v Bidwell 182 US 244 (1901)]

It is an accepted maxim of law that a contract is controlling until superseded by a new contract, whereby the new contract becomes the controlling document. To overcome the United States' debtor obligations to We the American People for the use of our good faith and credit in the 'original equity contract', Congress embedded numerous secret adhesion contracts and assumptions/presumptions into their complex regulatory scheme for which they hold the People accountable.
If a [government] comes down from their position of sovereignty, and enters the domain of commerce, it submits itself to the same laws that govern individuals there. The U.S. must do business on business terms. Once the United States waives its immunity and does business with its citizens, it does so much as a party never cloaked in immunity.

Parties to a contract have an obligation to operate with full disclosure and honesty, acting in good faith and with clean hands. "Even in the domain of private contract law, the author of a standard form agreement is required to state its terms with clarity and candor. Surely, no less is required [396 US 222] of the United States when it does business with its citizens." [US v Seckinger 397 US 203]

In the complex regulatory scheme created by congress, the U.S. secretly presumes that the living man, American sovereign, to be the legal fiction public vessel, its surety and/or beneficiary. The U.S. presumes that the American sovereign has assented to paying the debt of the corporation; to being a debtor and insolvent bankrupt having pledged ourselves as sureties for the debts of the U.S. The United States has never informed the American People of these assumptions/ presumptions which they hold against us nor the consequences thereof.

In the contrary, the U.S. has invested 75 years of propaganda to indoctrinate the American People that:
☐ The sovereign is the legal fiction transmitting utility;
☐ The S.S. # is mandatory;
☐ A Driver license and Marriage License are mandatory for American sovereigns;
☐ The filing of an IRS 1040 form is mandatory for the American sovereign;
☐ It is mandatory for the American People to register our private property with the state, effectively and
secretly transferring title to the state;
☐ The Codes and Statutes pertain to the American sovereign;
☐ These secret adhesion contracts are valid and binding, having failed to inform the American sovereign of
the terms and conditions of the secret adhesion contracts attached thereto; having failed at equal, dual
consideration;

☐ The Codes and Statutes pertain to all sovereigns and not just to agents and employees of the U.S.
☐ And much, much more.

The U.S. has failed at full disclosure; having failed to inform the American sovereign of the existence of the original contract which was executed when we were/are only days old without full disclosure and/or our consent, or that these secret contracts effectively void our original contract and have effectively allowed the United States to steal the personal exemptions of the American people thereby leaving the American People and this Petitioner without a remedy.

The United States has not only failed at full disclosure but has taken overt steps to deceive and misinform the American People. The U.S. has employed the use of threats and intimidation to maintain the illusion they have invested years creating to side step their debtor obligations to the American People in our original equity contracts.

The postal zone, general post office, seat of government of the United States, under the direction of the postmaster general, John (Jack) E. Potter, has become a continuing criminal enterprise consistently operating contrary to the best interest of the American People, whose property has been placed at risk to fund the U.S., and a breach of the original contract(s) with this Petitioner and each and every one of the American People.

The establishment of the seat of the government of the United States, a general post office under the direction of John (Jack) E. Potter, by the organic post office for the united states of America is a breach of contract for its failure to provide a republican form of government for the American People.

The United States has been operating in receivership continuously for decades with numerous reorganizations. The receivership has exceeded its term life by several years. The time has come to liquidate the beast and close the books on the receivership. It is time for the American People to exercise our right of redemption of our private property that has been placed at risk to fund the receivership. The United States is restraining the American people's right of redemption of the property to extend the term of receivership and the criminal activity which has infected the entire zone.

The United States has blocked numerous attempts by this Treaty Executor to redeem the property via discharge of the debt. The United States, operating under the direction of the Post Master General has used threats, intimidation, imprisonment, trickery and deceit to steal the American people's personal exemption(s), blocking our right of redemption and leaving the American people with no available remedy.

Claim On Abandonment
For The Sovereign People of America

It has been established in fact that:

1) It is the private property of the American people that has been placed at risk to collateralize the receivership of the general post office styled as the UNITED STATES; and
2) It is the credit of the Sovereign people of America that funds the day to day operations of same; and
3) The term life of the receivership of the UNITED STATES has been exhausted; and
4) The American people hold the priority **entitlement right** to the property; and
5) The American people hold an absolute priority **right of redemption** of the property; and

6) The remedy for the redemption has been provided; and

7) The Creditors have overtly impaired the right of redemption of the American people; and

8) The Creditor's actions have established the evidence of their operation in equity in bad faith and unclean hands and constitutes a delictual default and an abandonment of their claims; and

9) The administrative agents and agencies of the UNITED STATES have not only failed to protect the
private rights of the American people, but, have actively participated in the violation of said private
rights; and

10) The acts and actions of the agents and/or employees of the administrative agencies of the UNITED STATES in the violation of the private rights of the American people establishes the evidence of their operation in equity in bad faith and with unclean hands and constitutes their voluntary surrender of all equity claims in their name and/or in their control; and

11) The failure of the UNITED STATES to protect the private rights of the American people constitutes a delictual default and an abandonment of the postal zone styled as the UNITED STATES and all sovereign rights, power and authority associated therewith.

Constitutionally and in the laws of equity, the United States could not borrow or pledge the property and wealth of the American people, put at risk as collateral for its currency and credit, without legally providing them equitable remedy for recovery of what is due them. The United States did not violate the law or the Constitution in order to collateralize its financial reorganization. But, did in fact provide such a legal remedy so that it has been able to continue on since 1933 to hypothecate and re-hypothecate the private wealth and assets of the American people, at risk backing the government's obligations and currency, by their implied consent, through the government having provided such remedy, as defined and codified above, for recovery of what is due them on their assets and wealth at risk. The provisions for this are found in the same act of Public Policy, HJR 192, public law 73-10 that suspended the gold standard for our currency, abrogated the right to demand payment in gold, and made the Federal Reserve notes, for the first time, legal tender 'backed by the substance or credit of the nation.' All U.S. currency since that time is no more than credit against the real property and wealth of the sovereign American people, taken and/or pledged by the United States to its secondary creditors as security for its obligations. Consequently, those backing the nation's credit and currency could not recover what was due them by anything drawn on the Federal Reserve notes without expanding their risk and obligation to themselves. Any recovery payments backed by this currency would only increase the public debt the American people are collateral for, which an equitable remedy was intended to reduce, and in equity would not satisfy anything.

There are other serious limitations on our present system. Since the institution of these events, for practical purposes of commercial exchange, there has been no actual money of substance in circulation by which debt owed from one party to another can actually be repaid.

The Federal Reserve Notes, although made legal tender for all debts, public and private in the reorganization, can only discharge debt. Debt must be 'paid' with value or substance (gold, silver, barter, labor, or a commodity). For this reason HJR 192, Public law 73-10, which established the public policy of our current monetary system, repeatedly uses the term of 'discharge' in conjunction with 'payment' in laying out public policy for the new system. A debt currency system cannot 'pay' debt. Since 1933 to present, commerce in the corporate United States and among sub-corporate subject entities has had only debt note instruments by which debt can be discharged and transferred in different forms. The unpaid debt, created and/or expanded by the plan now carries a public liability for collection in that when debt is discharged with debt instruments, (i.e. Federal Reserve Notes, etc.), by our commerce, *debt is inadvertently expanded instead of being cancelled*, thus increasing the public debt, a situation fatal to any economy.

Congress and government officials who orchestrated the public laws and regulations that made the financial reorganization anticipated the long term effect of a debt based financial system which many in government feared, and which we face today in servicing the interest on trillions of dollars in U.S. Corporate public debt, and in this same act made provisions not only for the recovery remedy to satisfy equity to its Sureties, but to simultaneously resolve this problem as well.

Since it is, in fact, the real property and wealth of the American people that is the substance backing all the other obligations, currency and credit of the United States and such currencies could not be used to reduce its obligations for equity interest recovery to its Principals and Sureties, HJR 192, public law 73-10 further made the "notes of national banks" and "national banking associations" on par with its other currency and legal tender obligations.

TITLE 31> SUBTITLE IV> CHAPTER 51> SUBCHAPTER I Sec. 5103 says:
Legal Tender – United States coins and currency (including Federal Reserve Notes and circulating notes of Federal Reserve Banks and national banks) are legal tender for all debts, public charges, taxes and dues. This legal definition for 'legal tender' was first established in HJR 192 in the same act that made Federal Reserve Notes and notes of national banking associations legal tender.

Public Policy HJR 192
JOINT RESOLUTION TO SUSPEND THE GOLD
STANDARD AND ABROGATE THE GOLD CLAUSE
JUNE 5, 1933
HJR 192 73RD Congress, 1st Session

Joint Resolution to assure uniform value to the coins and currency of the United States

As used in this resolution, the term "obligation" means an obligation (including every obligation of and to the United States, excepting currency) payable in money of the United States; and the term 'coin or currency' means coin or currency of the United States, including Federal Reserve Notes and circulating notes of Federal Reserve Banks and national banking associations.

All coins and currencies of the United States (including Federal Reserve Notes and circulating notes of Federal Reserve Banks and national banking associations) heretofore and hereafter coined or issued, shall be legal tender for all debt, public and private, public charges, taxes, duties and dues."

Although HJR 192 has been since repealed, UCC 10-104 Un-repeals the resolution as the United States cannot deny or withhold remedy from the American people as long as their economic system remains collateralized by the wealth and assets of the American people.

TITLE 12.221 Definitions – "The terms 'national bank' and 'national banking associations' ....shall be held to be synonymous and interchangeable." The term "notes of national banks or national banking associations" have been continuously maintained in the official definition of legal tender since June 5, 1933 to present, when the term had never been used to define 'currency' or 'legal tender' before that time. Prior to 1933 the forms of currency in use that were legal tender were many and varied: United States Gold Certificates, United States Notes, Treasury Notes, Interest bearing notes, Gold coins of the United States, Standard silver dollars, subsidiary silver coins, minor coins, commemorative coins, but, the list did not include Federal Reserve Notes or notes of national banks or national banking associations despite the fact national bank notes were a common medium of exchange or 'currency' and had been, almost since the founding of our banking system and were backed by United States bonds or other securities on deposit for the bank with the U.S. Treasury.

Further, from the time of their inclusion in the definition they have been phased out until presently all provisions in the United States Code pertaining to **incorporated federally chartered National Banking institutions** issuing, redeeming, replacing and circulating notes have all been repealed. As stated in "Money and Banking", 4th Ed., by David H. Friedman, published by the American Bankers Association, page 78, "Today commercial banks no longer issue currency...."

It is clear that the federally incorporated banking institutions subject to the restrictions and repealed sections of Title 12, are NOT those primarily referred to maintained in the current definitions of "legal tender."

The legal statutory and professional definitions of 'banks', 'banking', and 'banker' used in the United States Code of Federal Regulations are not those commonly understood for these terms and have made statutory definition of "Bank" accordingly:

UCC 4-105 Part 1 - Bank "means a person engaged in the business of banking,"
12 CFR Sec. 229.2 Definitions (e) Bank means – "the term bank also includes any person engaged in the business of banking,"
12 CFR Sec. 210.2 Definitions. (d) "Bank means any person engaged in the business of banking."
Title 12 USC Sec. 1813 –Definitions of Bank and Related Terms.- (1) Bank- The term "Bank" – (a) "means any national bank, state bank, and district bank, and any federal branch and insured branch;"
Black's Law Dictionary, 5th Edition, page 133 defines a "Banker" as " In general sense, person that engages in the business of banking. In narrower meaning, a private person....; who is engaged in the business of banking without being incorporated. Under some statutes, an individual banker, as distinguished from a "private banker", is a person who, having complied with the statutory requirements, has received authority from the state to engage in the business of banking, while a 'private banker' is a person engaged in banking without having any special privileges or authority from the state."
"Banking" Is partly and optionally defined as "The business of issuing notes for circulation......, negotiating bills."
Black's Law Dictionary, 5th Edition, page 133, defines "Banking" "The business of banking, as defined by law and custom, consists in the issue of notes......intended to circulate as money....."
And defines a **"Banker's Note"** as "A commercial instrument resembling a bank note in every particular except that it is given by a 'private banker' or unincorporated national banking institution." Federal statute does not specifically define 'national bank' and 'national banking association' in those sections where these uses are legislated on to exclude a private banker or unincorporated banking institution. It does define these terms to the exclusion of such persons in the chapters and sections where the issue and circulation of notes by national banks has been repealed or forbidden.

In the absence of a statutory definition, the courts give terms their ordinary meaning. Bass, Terri L. vs Stolper, Koritzinski, 111 F.3 rd 1325, 7 th Cir.Apps. (1996) As the U.S. Supreme Court noted, "We have stated time and again that courts must presume that a legislature says in a statute what it means and means in a statute what it says there." See e.g., United States vs Ron Pair Enterprises, Inc. 489 U.S. 235, 241-242 (1989) "The legislative purpose is expressed by the ordinary meaning in the words used." Richards vs United States 369 U.S. 1 (1962)

The legal definitions relating to 'legal tender' have been written by congress and maintained as such to be both exclusive, where necessary, and inclusive, where appropriate, to provide in its statutory definitions of legal tender for the inclusion of all those, who by definition of private, unincorporated persons engaged in the business of banking to issue notes against the obligation of the United States for recovery on their risk, whose private assets and property are being used to collateralize the obligations of the United States since 1933, as collectively and nationally constituting a legal class of persons being a "national bank" or "national banking association" with the rights to issue such notes against the obligations of the United States for equity interest recovery due and accrued to these Principals and Sureties of the United States backing the obligations of U.S. currency and credit; as a means for the legal tender discharge of lawful debts in commerce as remedy due them in conjunction with U.S. obligations to the discharge of that portion of the public debt, which is provided for in the present financial reorganization still in effect and ongoing since 1933. [12 USC 411, 18 USC 8, 12 USC; ch. 6, 38 Stat. 251 Sect 14(a), 31 USC 5118, 3123 with rights protected under the 14th Amendment of the United States Constitution, by the U.S. Supreme Court in U.S. vs Russell (13 Wall, 623, 627), Pearlman vs Reliance Ins.Co., 371 U.S. 132, 136, 137 (1962), US vs Hooe, 3Cranch (US) 73 (1805) and in conformity with the U.S.
Supreme Court 79 US 287 (1870), 172 U.S. 48 (1898), and as confirmed at 307 U.S. 247 (1939)] HJR 192, public law 73-10 further declared...."every provision... which purports to give the obligee a right to require payment in gold or a particular kind of coin or currency....is declared against public policy; and no such provision shall be...made with respect to any obligation hereafter incurred."

Making way for discharge and recovery on U.S. corporate public debt due the Principals and Sureties of the United States providing as public policy for the discharge of 'every obligation', including every obligation of and to the United States, 'dollar for dollar', allowing those backing the United States financial reorganization to recover on it by discharging an obligation they owe to the United States or its sub-corporate entities, against that same amount of obligation of the United States owed to them; thus providing the remedy for the discharge and orderly recovery of equity interest on U.S. corporate public debt due the Sureties, Principals and Holders of the United States, discharging that portion of the public debt without expansion of credit, debt or obligation on the United States or these its prime creditors it was intended to satisfy equitable remedy to, but gaining for each bearer of such note, discharge of obligation equivalent in value 'dollar for dollar' to any and all 'lawful tender of the United States."

Those who constitute an association nationwide of private, unincorporated persons engaged in the business of banking to issue notes against these obligations of the United States due them; whose private property is at risk to collateralize the government's debt and currency, by legal definition, a 'national banking association'; such notes, issued against these obligations of the United States to that part of the public debt due its Principals and Sureties and required by law to be accepted as 'legal; tender' of payment of all debts, public and private, and are defined in law as 'obligations of the United

States', on the same par and category with Federal Reserve Notes and other currency and legal tender obligations.

Under this remedy for discharge of the public debt and recovery to its Principals and Sureties, two debts that would have been discharged in Federal Reserve debt note instruments or checks drawn on the same, equally expanding the public debt by those transactions, are discharged against a single public debt of the corporate United States and its sub-corporate entities to its prime creditor without the expansion and use of Federal Reserve debt note instruments as currency and credit, and so, without the expansion of the public debt and debt instruments in the monetary system and the expansion of the public debt as burden upon the entire financial system and its Principals and Sureties the recovery remedy was intended to relieve.

Their use is for the discharge and non-cash accrual reduction of U.S. Corporate public debt to the Principals, Sureties, Prime Creditors and Holders of it as provided in law and the instruments will ultimately be settled by adjustment and set-off in discharge of a bearers obligation to the United States against the obligation of the United States for the amount of the instrument to the original creditor it was tendered to or whomever or whatever institution may be the final bearer and holder in due course of it, again, thus discharging that portion of the public debt without expansion of credit, debt or note on the prime creditors of the United States it was intended to satisfy equitable remedy to, but gaining for each endorsed bearer of it discharge of obligation equivalent in value, 'dollar for dollar' of currency, measurable in 'lawful money of the United States.'

Even though the gold clause has been repealed, there still remains no currency of value or substance or gold coin in circulation today with which to pay a debt. The law does not allow for impossibilities. But even this did not repeal or remove our remedy which equity demands for the Principals and Sureties of the United States.

The practical evidence and fact of the financial reorganization (bankruptcy) of the United States is still ongoing today, visible all around us to see and understand. When Treasury Notes come due, they are not paid. They are refinanced by new Treasury Bills and Notes to back the currency and cover the debts….something that cannot be done with debt, unless, the debtor is protected by bankruptcy reorganization that is regularly restructured to keep it going. Each time the Federal debt ceiling is raised by Congress they are restructuring the bankruptcy reorganization of the government's debt so that commerce may continue on. **The recovery remedy is maintained in law because it has to be to satisfy equity to its prime creditors.**

The bankruptcy obstruction and overt impairment of the absolute priority right of redemption by the CREDITOR Federal Reserve Bank and banking families has established in fact the CREDITOR'S operation in equity in bad faith and with unclean hands and constitutes a delictual default and abandonment of all CREDITOR claims and the relinquishment of the PLEDGED property; and

The bankruptcy obstruction and overt impairment of the absolute priority right of redemption by the COURTS has established in fact the general post office styled as the UNITED STATES' operation in equity in bad faith and with unclean hands and constitutes a delictual default and abandonment of all equity claims of the UNITED STATES and their voluntary abandonment of all sovereign rights, power and authority associated therewith; and

The sovereign people of America, through and by James-Thomas: McBride, private postmaster, have served Notice of the Abandonment and registered the priority claim on the abandonment.

The Claim on Abandonment by the sovereign people of America has been received and accepted without objection or dispute.

Declaration Of Peace

The general post office styled as the UNITED STATES has been in a perpetual state of war since its inception. The 'Powers That Be' have used the UNITED STATES as a weapon to wage war on the sovereign people of America, operating under the Emergency War Powers Act and the secret presumption that the sovereign people are the enemy of the UNITED STATES for the purpose of evading their liabilities under the original equity contract and to pillage and plunder the private property of the people they were created to serve.

The general post office styled as the UNITED STATES has been used as a weapon to wage an economic war at arms length against all of the people of the world bringing all of humanity to the brink of destruction as the CREDITOR'S master plan of total economic slavery over the sovereign people of the world has been implemented.

The Powers That Be have used the UNITED STATES as a weapon to wage war on the sovereign people of the world via the unconscionable creation, production and distribution of harmful drugs for the purpose of enslaving the people and funding and executing their genocide against humanity.

The Powers That Be have used the UNITED STATES as a platform for their propaganda, creating the world's problems and then presenting themselves as the world's savior bringing about the solution and protection from their self created illusionary boogie men for the purpose of enslaving the sovereign people of the world.

Let it be known by all of humanity that the:

UNITED STATES has DECLARED PEACE.

From this day forward the UNITED STATES shall be used as a tool, actuated by humility, to promote universal peace, love and unity among all men. The UNITED STATES shall become a broker and facilitator of peace; a springboard for ascension and balance within the world consciousness. The UNITED STATES shall immediately stand down and withdraw itself from all acts of aggression and vacate all occupied land and shall immediately bring all American soldiers home.

The agents and agencies of the UNITED STATES shall immediately cease and desist in all forms of gun and drug production and distribution, all forms of terrorism and genocide of the people, all standard operating procedure of the powers that be since the days of the East India trading Company.

All Administrative Agencies of the UNITED STATES shall immediately remove all gold fringed military flags from their offices and courtrooms and shall display the civilian flag of peace. The Custodian of the Alien Property shall immediately update his/her files, removing the names and private property of the American people from their files/lists and make the return of the property to the rightful owners. All administrative agencies and administrative courts shall operate in peace and honor, servants of the sovereign people.

Civil Flag Of Peace

The jurisdiction of the courts of the united states is described as the **American flag of peace**; red, white and blue with stripes of red and white horizontally placed in alteration. Under the jurisdiction of the American flag of peace the private rights of the sovereign people of the united states are protected and all rights are preserved. Here, the People are 'innocent until proven guilty.' Under the military gold fringed flag there are no rights.

The Law Of The Flag

The Law of the Flag, an International Law, which is recognized by every nation of the planet, a vessel is a part of the territory of the nation whose flag she flies and designates the RIGHTS under which a ship owner, who sends his vessel into a foreign port, gives notice by his flag to all who enter into contracts with the ship master that he intends the Law of that Flag to regulate those contracts, and that they must either submit to its operation or not contract with him or his agent at all. Pursuant to the "Law of the Flag," a military flag does result in jurisdictional implications when flown. **It could mean WAR.**

By the doctrine of "four cornering" the flag establishes the law of the country that it represents, i.e. the embassies of foreign countries, in Washington D.C., are "four cornered" by walls or fencing, creating an "enclave. " Within the boundaries of the "enclave" of the foreign embassy, the flag of that foreign country establishes the jurisdiction and law of that foreign country, which will be enforced by the Law of the Flag and international treaty. When you enter an embassy, you are subject to the laws of that country, just as if you board a ship flying a foreign flag, you will be subject to the laws of that flag, enforceable by the "master of the ship," (Captain), by the law of the flag.

The general post office known as the UNITED STATES now flies

the Civil Flag of Peace of the united states of America.

The attachment of gold fringe on the flag constitutes a mutilation of the flag and represents "color of law" jurisdiction and suspends the people's private rights. The military shall not try civilians as it constitutes an **act of WAR against the people**.

The Civilian Flag of the united States of America, with no fringe, **takes precedence** over all other flags; it is the superior flag and **establishes the civil jurisdiction** of the united States of America, and the laws made in pursuance thereof.

Law Form

The general post office styled as the UNITED STATES is a free republic operating under the concepts and intent of the Articles Of Confederation, establishing a perpetual Union between the several free and independent states, to wit:

I. The Style of this Confederacy shall be "The United States of America".
II. Each state retains its sovereignty, freedom, and independence, and every power, jurisdiction, and right, which is not by this Confederation expressly delegated to the United States, in Congress assembled.

III. The said States hereby severally enter into a **firm league of friendship** with each other, for their common defence, the security of their liberties, and their mutual and general welfare, binding themselves to assist each other, against all force offered to, or attacks made upon them, or any of them, on account of religion, sovereignty, trade, or any other pretence whatever.

IV. The better to secure and perpetuate mutual friendship and intercourse among the people of the different States in this Union, the free inhabitants of each of these States, paupers, vagabonds, and fugitives from justice excepted, shall be entitled to all privileges and immunities of free citizens in the several States; and the people of each State shall enjoy free ingress and regress to and from any other State, and shall enjoy therein all the privileges of trade and commerce, subject to the same duties, impositions, and restrictions as the inhabitants thereof respectively, provided that such restrictions shall not extend so far as to prevent the removal of property imported into any State, to any other State, of which the owner is an inhabitant; provided also that no imposition, duties or restriction shall be laid by any State, on the property of the United States, or either of them. If any person guilty of, or charged with, treason, felony, or other high misdemeanour in any State, shall flee from justice, and be found in any of the United States, he shall, upon demand of the Governor or executive power of the State from which he fled, be delivered up and removed to the State having jurisdiction of his offense. Full faith and credit shall be given in each of these States to the records, acts, and judicial proceedings of the courts and magistrates of every other State.

V. For the most convenient management of the general interests of the United States, delegates shall be annually appointed in such manner as the legislatures of each State shall direct, to meet in Congress on the first Monday in November, in every year, with a power reserved to each State to recall its delegates, or any of them, at any time within the year, and to send others in their stead for the remainder of the year.

No State shall be represented in Congress by not less than two, nor more than seven members; and no person shall be capable of being a delegate for more than three years in any term of six years; nor shall any person, being a delegate, be capable of holding any office under the United States, for which he, or another for his benefit, receives any salary, fees or emolument of any kind.

Each State shall maintain its own delegates in a meeting of the States, and while they act as members of the committee of the States.

In determining questions in the United States in Congress assembled, each State shall have one vote.

Freedom of speech and debate in Congress shall not be impeached or questioned in any court or place out of Congress, and the members of Congress shall be protected in their persons from arrests or imprisonments, during the time of their going to and from, and attendance on Congress, except for treason, felony, or breach of the peace.

VI. No State, without the consent of the United States in Congress assembled, shall send any embassy to, or receive any embassy from, or enter into any conference, agreement, alliance or treaty with any King, Prince or State; nor shall any person holding any office of profit or trust under the United States, or any of them, accept any present, emolument, office or title of any kind whatever from any King, Prince or foreign State; nor shall the United States in Congress assembled, or any of them, grant any title of nobility.

No two or more States shall enter into any treaty, confederation or alliance whatever between them, without the consent of the United States in Congress assembled, specifying accurately the purposes for which the same is to be entered into, and how long it shall continue.

No State shall lay any imposts or duties, which may interfere with any stipulations in treaties, entered into by the United States in Congress assembled, with any King, Prince or State, in pursuance of any treaties already proposed by Congress, to the courts of France and Spain.

No vessel of war shall be kept up in time of peace by any State, except such number only, as shall be deemed necessary by the United States in Congress assembled, for the defence of such State, or its trade; nor shall any body of forces be kept up by any State in time of peace, except such number only, as in the judgment of the United States in Congress assembled, shall be deemed requisite to garrison the forts necessary for the defence of such State; but every State shall always keep up a well-regulated and disciplined militia, sufficiently armed and accoutered, and shall provide and constantly have ready for use, in public stores, a due number of filed pieces and tents, and a proper quantity of arms, ammunition and camp equipage.

No State shall engage in any war without the consent of the United States in Congress assembled, unless such State be actually invaded by enemies, or shall have received certain advice of a resolution being formed by some nation of Indians to invade such State, and the danger is so imminent as not to admit of a delay till the United States in Congress assembled can be consulted; nor shall any State grant commissions to any ships or vessels of war, nor letters of marque or reprisal, except it be after a declaration of war by the United States in Congress assembled, and then only against the Kingdom or State and the subjects thereof, against which war has been so declared, and under such regulations as shall be established by the United States in Congress assembled, unless such State be infested by pirates, in which case vessels of war may be fitted out for that occasion, and kept so long as the danger shall continue, or until the United States in Congress assembled shall determine otherwise.

VII. When land forces are raised by any State for the common defense, all officers of or under the rank of colonel, shall be appointed by the legislature of each State respectively, by whom such forces shall be raised, or in such manner as such State shall direct, and all vacancies shall be filled up by the State which first made the appointment.

VIII. All charges of war, and all other expenses that shall be incurred for the common defence or general welfare, and allowed by the United States in Congress assembled, shall be defrayed out of a common treasury, which shall be supplied by the several States in proportion to the value of all land within each State, granted or surveyed for any person, as such land and the buildings and improvements thereon shall be estimated according to such mode as the United States in Congress assembled, shall from time to time direct and appoint.

The taxes for paying that proportion shall be laid and levied by the authority and direction of the legislatures of the several States within the time agreed upon by the United States in Congress assembled.

IX. The United States in Congress assembled, shall have the sole and exclusive right and power of determining on peace and war, except in the cases mentioned in the sixth article -- of sending and receiving ambassadors -- entering into treaties and alliances, provided that no treaty of commerce shall be made whereby the legislative power of the respective States shall be restrained from imposing such imposts and duties on foreigners, as their own people are subjected to, or from prohibiting the exportation or importation of any species of goods or commodities whatsoever -- of establishing rules for deciding in all cases, what captures on land or water shall be legal, and in what manner prizes taken by land or naval forces in the service of the United States shall be divided or appropriated -- of granting letters of marque and reprisal in times of peace -- appointing courts for the trial of piracy and felonies committed on the high seas and establishing courts for receiving and determining finally appeals in all cases of captures, provided that no member of Congress shall be appointed a judge of any of the said courts.

The United States in Congress assembled shall also be the last resort on appeal in all disputes and differences now subsisting or that hereafter may arise between two or more States concerning boundary, jurisdiction or any other causes whatever; which authority shall always be exercised in the manner following.

Whenever the legislative or executive authority or lawful agent of any State in controversy with another shall present a petition to Congress stating the matter in question and praying for a hearing, notice thereof shall be given by order of Congress to the legislative or executive authority of the other State in controversy, and a day assigned for the appearance of the parties by their lawful agents, who shall then be directed to appoint by joint consent, commissioners or judges to constitute a court for hearing and determining the matter in question: but if they cannot agree, Congress shall name three persons out of each of the United States, and from the list of such persons each party shall alternately strike out one, the petitioners beginning, until the number shall be reduced to thirteen; and from that number not less than seven, nor more than nine names as Congress shall direct, shall in the presence of Congress be drawn out by lot, and the persons whose names shall be so drawn or any five of them, shall be commissioners or judges, to hear and finally determine the controversy, so always as a major part of the judges who shall hear the cause shall agree in the determination: and if either party shall neglect to attend at the day appointed, without showing reasons, which Congress shall judge sufficient, or being present shall refuse to strike, the Congress shall proceed to nominate three persons out of each State, and the secretary of Congress shall strike in behalf of such party absent or refusing; and the judgment and sentence of the court to be appointed, in the manner before prescribed, shall be final and conclusive; and if any of the parties shall refuse to submit to the authority of such court, or to appear or defend their claim or cause, the court shall nevertheless proceed to pronounce sentence, or judgment, which shall in like manner be final and decisive, the judgment or sentence and other proceedings being in either case transmitted to Congress, and lodged among the acts of Congress for the security of the parties concerned: provided that every commissioner, before he sits in judgment, shall take an oath to be administered by one of the judges of the supreme or superior court of the State, where the cause shall be tried, 'well and truly to hear and determine the matter in question, according to the best of his judgment, without favour, affection or hope of reward': provided also, that no State shall be deprived of territory for the benefit of the United States.

All controversies concerning the private right of soil claimed under different grants of two or more States, whose jurisdictions as they may respect such lands, and the States which passed such grants are adjusted, the said grants or either of them being at the same time claimed to have originated antecedent to such settlement of jurisdiction, shall on the petition of either party to the Congress of the United States, be finally determined as near as may be in the same manner as is before prescribed for deciding disputes respecting territorial jurisdiction between different States.

The United States in Congress assembled shall also have the sole and exclusive right and power of regulating the alloy and value of coin struck by their own authority, or by that of the respective States -- fixing the standards of weights and measures throughout the United States -- regulating the trade and managing all affairs with the Indians, not members of any of the States, provided that the legislative right of any State within its own limits be not infringed or violated -- establishing or regulating post offices from one State to another, throughout all the United States, and exacting such postage on the papers passing through the same as may be requisite to defray the expenses of the said office -- appointing all officers of the land forces, in the service of the United States, excepting regimental officers -- appointing all the officers of the naval forces, and commissioning all officers whatever in the service of the United States -- making rules for the government and regulation of the said land and naval forces, and directing their operations.

The United States in Congress assembled shall have authority to appoint a committee, to sit in the recess of Congress, to be denominated 'A Committee of the States', and to consist of one delegate from each State; and to appoint such other committees and civil officers as may be necessary for managing the general affairs of the United States under their direction -- to appoint one of their members to preside, provided that no person be allowed to serve in the office of president more than one year in any term of three years; to ascertain the necessary sums of money to be raised for the service of the United States, and to appropriate and apply the same for defraying the public expenses -- to borrow money, or emit bills on the credit of the United States, transmitting every half-year to the respective States an account of the sums of money so borrowed or emitted -- to build and equip a navy -- to agree upon the number of land forces, and to make requisitions from each State for its quota, in proportion to the number of white inhabitants in such State; which requisition shall be binding, and thereupon the legislature of each State shall appoint the regimental officers, raise the men and clothe, arm and equip them in a solid-like manner, at the expense of the United States; and the officers and men so clothed, armed and equipped shall march to the place appointed, and within the time agreed on by the United States in Congress assembled. But if the United States in Congress assembled shall, on consideration of circumstances judge proper that any State should not raise men, or should raise a smaller number of men than the quota thereof, such extra number shall be raised, officered, clothed, armed and equipped in the same manner as the quota of each State, unless the legislature of such State shall judge that such extra number cannot be safely spread out in the same, in which case they shall raise, officer, clothe, arm and equip as many of such extra number as they judge can be safely spared. And the officers and men so clothed, armed, and equipped, shall march to the place appointed, and within the time agreed on by the United States in Congress assembled.

The United States in Congress assembled shall never engage in a war, nor grant letters of marque or reprisal in time of peace, nor enter into any treaties or alliances, nor coin money, nor regulate the value thereof, nor ascertain the sums and expenses necessary for the defence and welfare of the United States, or any of them, nor emit bills, nor borrow money on the credit of the United States, nor appropriate money, nor agree upon the number of vessels of war, to be built or purchased, or the number of land or sea forces to be raised, nor appoint a commander in chief of the army or navy, unless nine States assent to the same: nor shall a question on any other point, except for adjourning from day to day be determined, unless by the votes of the majority of the United States in Congress assembled.

The Congress of the United States shall have power to adjourn to any time within the year, and to any place within the United States, so that no period of adjournment be for a longer duration than the space of six months, and shall publish the journal of their proceedings monthly, except such parts thereof relating to treaties, alliances or military operations, as in their judgment require secrecy; and the yeas and nays of the delegates of each State on any question shall be entered on the journal, when it is desired by any delegates of a State, or any of them, at his or their request shall be furnished with a transcript of the said journal, except such parts as are above excepted, to lay before the legislatures of the several States.

X. The Committee of the States, or any nine of them, shall be authorized to execute, in the recess of Congress, such of the powers of Congress as the United States in Congress assembled, by the consent of the nine States, shall from time to time think expedient to vest them with; provided that no power be delegated to the said Committee, for the exercise of which, by the Articles of Confederation, the voice of nine States in the Congress of the United States assembled be requisite.

XI. Canada acceding to this confederation, and adjoining in the measures of the United States, shall be admitted into, and entitled to all the advantages of this Union; but no other colony shall be admitted into the same, unless such admission be agreed to by nine States.

XII. All bills of credit emitted, monies borrowed, and debts contracted by, or under the authority of Congress, before the assembling of the United States, in pursuance of the present confederation, shall be deemed and considered as a charge against the United States, for payment and satisfaction whereof the said United States, and the public faith are hereby solemnly pledged.

XIII. Every State shall abide by the determination of the United States in Congress assembled, on all questions which by this confederation are submitted to them. And the Articles of this Confederation shall be inviolably observed by every State, and the Union shall be perpetual; nor shall any alteration at any time hereafter be made in any of them; unless such alteration be agreed to in a Congress of the United States, and be after wards confirmed by the legislatures of every State.

A "Transitional Committee" shall be seated for the purpose of ensuring a peaceful and efficient transition from an Empirical War based mentality and operating system to one of peace, humility and unity. Said "Transitional Committee" shall establish and empower an interim government for the united states of America and shall operate until such time as the people can be duly informed as to the true history of the UNITED STATES and the fraud that has been perpetrated against them, not to exceed one year.

The Postmaster general of the organic post office for the united states, creator of the general post office styled as the UNITED STATES and located within the ten miles square commonly known as Washington, D.C., under whose direction the UNITED STATES operates, shall operate in the capacity of trustee for the people and shall take instructions from the "Transitional Committee" until such time as the Interim government shall be seated and empowered.

The UNITED STATES' courts are administrative courts who gain their authority under Title 5, the Administrative Procedures Act of 1946 and/or the Judiciary Act of 1789. These Administrative courts were established for the purpose of being the watch dog over public offices so that if and when the American people had their private rights violated they could file a complaint without cost.

These administrative courts were designed to give the administrative court the power of legislation; the power of the executive branch of government; to give them judicial power and authority. These administrative courts were authorized to disregard laws, case cites, supreme court decisions, statutes, codes, rules, regulations and to change policy. The establishment of these administrative courts effectively created a fourth branch of government at the request of the BAR Association.

BUT, this system was designed for use BY the American people, NOT AGAINST the American people. These administrative courts have jurisdiction ONLY over administrative agencies and NOT over the American people and were established as a vehicle for use by the American people to lodge and adjudicate a grievance against any administrative agency and gave this administrative court the power and authority to make the corrections without the lengthy process of introducing and passing legislation. Charges can only be levied AGAINST an administrative agency BY THE AMERICAN PEOPLE and cannot be used against the American people. The people are ALWAYS the Plaintiff in these Administrative courts except when these courts are used to perpetrate a fraud against the American People.

Congress, under 49 Statute 3097 Treaty Series 881 Conventions and Duties and Rights of the States, placed all states under international law, making all courts, International courts. The International Organization Immunities Act 1945 placed all courts under the jurisdiction of the United Nations under Title 22 CFR Foreign Relations with Oaths of Office under section 92.12 and 92.31. Under Title 8 USC 1481 you voluntarily forfeit your citizenship when you take the Oath of Office in these administrative courts, and establishes you as a foreign agent required to register as a foreign agent doing business in the state.

These administrative courts, who gain their authority under Title 5 were designed to make the corrections within public offices, to make them more efficient and to hold agencies, and officers thereof, accountable for their actions. In these administrative courts only the American people can bring the charges for the corrections and the American people are ALWAYS the Plaintiff/ harmed Party. These courts have NO JURISDICTION over the people. No agency has the authority to bring charges against the American people or their private rights and property in an administrative court under the Administrative Procedures Act.

These Administrative Courts shall operate as established, for the purpose of facilitating the prosecution of grievances against an administrative agency by the American people for the administrative agencies trespass on the private rights of the sovereign people of America.

Administrative Notice

* *63C Am.Jur.2d, Public Officers and Employees, §247* "As expressed otherwise, the powers delegated to a public officer are held in trust for the people and are to be exercised in behalf of the government or of all citizens who may need the intervention of the officer. [1] Furthermore, the view has been expressed that all public officers, within whatever branch and whatever level of government, and whatever be their private vocations, are trustees of the people, and accordingly labor under every disability and prohibition imposed by law upon trustees relative to the making of personal financial gain from a discharge of their trusts. [2] That is, a public officer occupies a fiduciary relationship to the political entity on whose behalf he or she serves. [3] and owes a fiduciary duty to the public. [4] It

has been said that the fiduciary responsibilities of a public officer cannot be less than those of a private individual. [5] Furthermore, it has been stated that any enterprise undertaken by the public official who tends to weaken public confidence and undermine the sense of security for individual rights is against public policy. Fraud in its elementary common law sense of deceit-and this is one of the meanings that fraud bears [483 U.S. 372] in the statute. See United States v. Dial, 757 F.2d 163, 168 (7th Cir1985) includes the deliberate concealment of material information in a setting of fiduciary obligation. A public official is a fiduciary toward the public, including, in the case of a judge, the litigants who appear before him and if he deliberately conceals material information from them, he is guilty of fraud. McNally v United States 483 U.S. 350 (1987)

Texas Penal Code Sec. 1.07. DEFINITIONS. (a) In this code: [consistent with all state penal codes]
(9) "Coercion" means a threat, however communicated:
    (A) to commit an offense;
    (B) to inflict bodily injury in the future on the person threatened or another;
    (C) to accuse a person of any offense;
    (D) to expose a person to hatred, contempt, or ridicule;
    (E) to harm the credit or business repute of any person; or
    (F) to take or withhold action as a public servant, or to cause a public servant to take or withhold action.
(19) "Effective consent" includes consent by a person legally authorized to act for the owner.
Consent is not effective if:
    (A) induced by force, threat, or fraud;
    (B) given by a person the actor knows is not legally authorized to act for the owner;
    (C) given by a person who by reason of youth, mental disease or defect, or intoxication is known by the actor to be unable to make reasonable decisions; or
    (D) given solely to detect the commission of an offense.
(24) "Government" means:
    (A) the state;
    (B) a county, municipality, or political subdivision of the state; or
    (C) any branch or agency of the state, a county, municipality, or political subdivision.
(30) "Law" means the constitution or a statute of this state or of the United States, a written opinion of a court of record, a municipal ordinance, an order of a county commissioners court, or a rule authorized by and
lawfully adopted under a statute.
(41) "Public servant" means a person elected, selected, appointed, employed, or otherwise designated as one of
the following, even if he has not yet qualified for office or assumed his duties:
    (A) an officer, employee, or agent of government;
    (B) a juror or grand juror; or
    (C) an arbitrator, referee, or other person who is authorized by law or private written agreement to hear
or determine a cause or controversy; or
    (D) an attorney at law or notary public when participating in the performance of a governmental
function; or
    (E) a candidate for nomination or election to public office; or
    (F) a person who is performing a governmental function under a claim of right although he is not legally qualified to do so.

ALL COURTS HAVE BEEN OPERATING UNDER

(1) *TRADING WITH THE ENEMY ACT* AS CODIFIED IN TITLE 50 USC,
(2) TITLE 28 USC, CHAPTER 176, *FEDERAL DEBT COLLECTION PROCEDURE*, AND
(3) FED.R.CIV.P. 4(j) UNDER TITLE 28 USC §1608, MAKING THE COURTS "FOREIGN STATES" TO THE PEOPLE BY CONGRESSIONAL MANDATE

"IT IS THE DUTY OF THE COURT TO DECLARE THE MEANING OF WHAT IS WRITTEN, AND NOT WHAT
WAS INTENDED TO BE WRITTEN. J.W. Seavey Hop Corp. v. Pollock, 20 Wn.2d 337,348-49, 147 P.2d 310 (1944),
cited with approval in Berg v. Hudesman, 115 Wn2d at 669.

OATH OF OFFICE MAKES PUBLIC OFFICIALS "FOREIGN"

1. Those holding Federal or State public office, and/or county or municipal office, under the Legislative, Executive or Judicial branch, including Court Officials, Judges, Prosecutors, Law Enforcement Department employees, Officers of the Court, etc., before entering into these public offices, are required by the U.S. Constitution and statutory law to comply with Title 5 USC, Sec. §3331, "Oath of office." State Officials are also required to meet this same obligation, according to State Constitutions and State statutory law.

2. All oaths of office come under 22 CFR, Foreign Relations, Sections §§92.12 - 92.30, and all who hold public office come under Title 8 USC, Section §1481 "Loss of nationality by native-born or naturalized citizen; voluntary action; burden of proof; presumptions."

3. Under Title 22 USC, Foreign Relations and Intercourse, Section §611, a Public Official is considered a foreign agent. In order to hold public office, the candidate must file a true and complete registration statement with the State Attorney General as a foreign principle.

4. The Oath of Office requires the public official in his / her foreign state capacity to uphold the constitutional form of government or face consequences.

> Title 10 USC, Sec. §333, "Interference with State and Federal law"
>
> The President, by using the militia or the armed forces, or both, or by any other means, shall take such measures as he considers necessary to suppress, in a State, any insurrection, domestic violence, unlawful combination, or conspiracy, if it—
>
> (1) so hinders the execution of the laws of that State, and of the United States within the State, that any part or class of its people is deprived of a right, privilege, immunity, or protection named in the Constitution and secured by law, and the constituted authorities of that State are unable, fail, or refuse to protect that right, privilege, or immunity, or to give that protection; or
> (2) opposes or obstructs the execution of the laws of the United States or impedes the course of justice under those laws.
> In any situation covered by clause (1), the State shall be considered to have denied the equal protection of the laws secured by the Constitution.

5. Such willful action, while serving in official capacity, violates Title 18 USC, Section §1918:

Title 18 USC, Section §1918 "Disloyalty and asserting the right to strike against the government"

Whoever violates the provision of 7311 of title 5 that an individual may not accept or hold a position in the Government of the United States or the government of the District of Columbia if he—

(1) advocates the overthrow of our constitutional form of government; (2) is a member of an organization that he knows advocates the overthrow of our constitutional form of government; shall be fined under this title or imprisoned not more than one year and a day, or both.

and also deprives claimants of "honest services:

Title 18, Section §1346. Definition of "scheme or artifice to defraud"

"For the purposes of this chapter, the term "scheme or artifice to defraud" includes a scheme or artifice to deprive another of the intangible right of honest services.
and the treaties that placed your public offices in that foreign state under international law and under the United Nation jurisdiction

49 Stat. 3097; Treaty Series 881 CONVENTION ON RIGHTS AND DUTIES OF STATES

1945 IOIA –That the International Organizations Act of December 29, 1945 (59 Stat. 669; Title 22, Sections 288 to 2886
U.S.C.) the US relinquished every office

TITLE 8 > CHAPTER 12 > SUBCHAPTER I > § 1101
The term "foreign state" includes outlying possessions of a foreign state, but self-governing dominions or territories under
mandate or trusteeship shall be regarded as separate foreign states.

TABLE OF AUTHORITIES – RECIPROCAL IMMUNITY AND FOREIGN AGENT REGISTRATION
UNITED STATES INTERNATIONAL ORGANIZATIONS IMMUNITIES ACT,

PUBLIC LAW 79-291, 29 DECEMBER 1945(Public Law 291-79th Congress) TITLE I Section 2.(b) International organizations, their property and their assets, wherever located and by whomsoever held, shall enjoy the same immunity from suit and every form of Judicial process as is enjoyed by foreign governments, except to the extent that such organizations may expressly waive their immunity for the purpose of any proceedings or by the terms of any contract. (d) In so far as concerns customs duties and internal-revenue taxes imposed upon or by reason of importation, and the procedures in connection therewith; the registration of foreign agents; and the treatment of official communications, the privileges, exemptions, and immunities to which international organizations shall be entitled shall be those accorded under similar circumstances to foreign governments. Section 9. The privileges, exemptions, and immunities of international organizations and of their officers and employees, and members of their families, suites, and servants, provided for in this title, shall be granted notwithstanding the fact that the similar privileges, exemptions, and immunities granted to a foreign government, its officers, or employees, may be conditioned upon the existence of reciprocity by that foreign government: Provided, That nothing contained in this title shall be construed as precluding the Secretary of State from withdrawing the privileges, exemptions, and immunities herein provided from persons who are nationals of any foreign country on the ground that such country is failing to accord corresponding privileges, exemptions, and immunities to citizens of the United States. Also see

22 USC § 611 - FOREIGN RELATIONS AND INTERCOURSE; and, 22 USC § 612, Registration statement, concerning the absolute requirement of registration with the Attorney General as a "foreign principal," due to the undisputed status of the court and its alleged officers and employees as FOREIGN AGENTS, described *supra.* This requirement shall be deemed to include, but is not limited to, an affidavit of non-communist association.

JUDGE SERVES AS A DEBT COLLECTOR

6. Judges hold public office under Title 28 USC, Chapter 176, Federal Debt Collection Procedure:
Title 28, Chapter 176, Federal Debt Collection Procedure, Section §3002
As used in this chapter:
(2) "Court" means any court created by the Congress of the United States, excluding the United States Tax Court. (3) "Debt" means— (A) an amount that is owing to the United States on account of a direct loan, or loan insured or guaranteed, by the United States; or (B) an amount that is owing to the United States on account of a fee, duty, lease, rent, service, sale of real or personal property, overpayment, fine, assessment, penalty, restitution, damages, interest, tax, bail bond forfeiture, reimbursement, recovery of a cost incurred by the United States, or other source of indebtedness to the United States, but that is not owing under the terms of a contract originally entered into by only persons other than the United States;

(8) "Judgment" means a judgment, order, or decree entered in favor of the United States in a court and
arising from a civil or criminal proceeding regarding a debt. (15) "United States" means—
(A) a Federal corporation; (B) an agency, department, commission, board, or other entity of the United States; or (C) an instrumentality of the United States.
Title 22 USC, Sec. §286. "Acceptance of membership by United States in International Monetary Fund," states the following:

The President is hereby authorized to accept membership for the United States in the International Monetary Fund (hereinafter referred to as the "Fund"), and in the International Bank for Reconstruction and Development (hereinafter referred to as the "Bank"), provided for by the Articles of Agreement of the Fund and the Articles of Agreement of the Bank as set forth in the Final Act of the United Nations Monetary and Financial Conference dated July 22, 1944, and deposited in the archives of the Department of State.
8. Title 22 USC, Sec. § 286e-13, "Approval of fund pledge to sell gold to provide resources for Reserve Account of Enhanced Structural Adjustment Facility Trust," states the following:
The Secretary of the Treasury is authorized to instruct the Fund's pledge to sell, if needed, up to 3,000,000 ounces of the Fund's gold, to restore the resources of the Reserve Account of the Enhanced Structural Adjustment Facility Trust to a level that would be sufficient to meet obligations of the Trust payable to lenders which have made loans to the Loan Account of the Trust that have been used for the purpose of financing programs to Fund members previously in arrears to the Fund.

No Immunity Under "Commerce"

9. All immunity of the United States, and all liability of States, instrumentalities of States, and State officials have been waived under commerce, according to the following US Codes:

Title 15 USC, Commerce, Sec. §1122, "Liability of States, instrumentalities of States, and State officials"

(a) Waiver of sovereign immunity by the United States. The United States, all agencies and instrumentalities thereof, and all individuals, firms, corporations, other persons acting for the United States and with the authorization and consent of the United States, shall not be immune from suit in Federal or State court by any person, including any governmental or nongovernmental entity, for any violation under this Act. (b) Waiver of sovereign immunity by States. Any State, instrumentality of a State or any officer or employee of a State or instrumentality of a State acting in his or her official capacity, shall not be immune, under the eleventh amendment of the Constitution of the United States or under any other doctrine of sovereign immunity, from suit in Federal court by any person, including any governmental or nongovernmental entity for any violation under this Act.

Title 42 USC, Sec. §12202, "State immunity"

A State shall not be immune under the eleventh amendment to the Constitution of the United States from an action in Federal or State court of competent jurisdiction for a violation of this chapter. In any action against a State for a violation of the requirements of this chapter, remedies (including remedies both at law and in equity) are available for such a violation to the same extent as such remedies are available for such a violation in an action against any public or private entity other than a State

Title 42 USC, Sec. §2000d–7, "Civil rights remedies equalization"
(a) General provision
(1) A State shall not be immune under the Eleventh Amendment of the Constitution of the United States from suit in Federal court for a violation of section 504 of the Rehabilitation Act of 1973 [29 U.S.C. 794], title IX of the Education Amendments of 1972 [20 U.S.C. 1681 et seq.], the Age Discrimination Act of 1975 [42 U.S.C. 6101 et seq.], title VI of the Civil Rights Act of 1964 [42 U.S.C. 2000d et seq.], or the provisions of any other Federal statute prohibiting discrimination by recipients of Federal financial assistance. (2) In a suit against a State for a violation of a statute referred to in paragraph (1), remedies (including remedies both at law and in equity) are available for such a violation to the same extent as such remedies are available for such a violation in the suit against any public or private entity other than a State.

10. The Administrative Procedure Act of 1946 gives immunity in Administrative Court to the Administrative Law Judge
(ALJ) only when an action is brought by the people against a public, agency or corporate official / department. Under Title 5
USC, Commerce, public offices or officials can be sanctioned.
Title 5, USC, Sec. §551:
(10) "sanction" includes the whole or a part of an agency—
(A) prohibition, requirement, limitation, or other condition affecting the freedom of a person;(B) withholding of relief;(C) imposition of penalty or fine;(D) destruction, taking, seizure, or withholding of property;(E) assessment of damages, reimbursement, restitution, compensation, costs, charges, or fees;(F) requirement, revocation, or suspension of a license; or (G) taking other compulsory or restrictive action;

11. Justice is required to be BLIND while holding a SET OF SCALES and a TWO-EDGED SWORD. This symbolizes true justice. The Administrative Procedure Act of 1946 (60 stat 237) would allow the sword to cut in either direction and give the judge immunity by holding his own court office accountable for honest service fraud, obstruction of justice, false statements, malicious prosecution and fraud placed upon the court. Any wilful intent to uncover the EYES OF JUSTICE or TILT THE SCALES is a wilful intent to deny Due Process, which violates Title 18 USC §1346, "Scheme or Artifice to Defraud," by perpetrating a scheme or artifice to deprive another of the intangible right of honest services. This is considered fraud and an overthrow of a constitutional form of government and the person depriving the honest service can be held accountable and face punishment under Title 18 USC and Title 42 USC and violates Title 28 USC judicial procedures.

12. Both Title 18 USC, Crime and Criminal Procedure, and Title 42 USC, Public Health and Welfare, allow the Petitioner to bring an action against the United States and/or the State agencies, departments, and employees for civil rights violations while dealing in commerce. Title 10 places all public officials under this Title 10 section 333 while under a state of emergency. (Declared or undeclared War this falls under TWEA.)

COURTS OPERATING UNDER WAR POWERS ACT

13. The Courts are operating under the Emergency War Powers Act. The country has been under a declared "state of emergency" for the past 70 years resulting in the Constitution being suspended (See Title 50 USC Appendix – Trading with the Enemy Act of 1917). The Courts have been misusing Title 50 USC, Sec. §23, "Jurisdiction of United States courts and
judges," which provides for criminal jurisdiction over an "**enemy of the state**," whereas, Petitioner comes under Title 50 USC Appendix Application Sec. §21, "**Claims of naturalized citizens as affected by expatriation**" which states the following:

The claim of any naturalized American citizen under the provisions of this Act [sections 1 to 6, 7 to 39, and 41 to 44 of this Appendix] shall not be denied **on the ground of any presumption of expatriation** which has arisen against him, under the second sentence of section 2 of the Act entitled "An Act in reference to the expatriation of citizens and their protection abroad," approved March 2, 1907, if he shall give satisfactory evidence to the President, or the court, as the case may be, of his uninterrupted loyalty to the United States during his absence, and that he has returned to the United States, or that he, although desiring to return, has been prevented from so returning by circumstances beyond his control.

14. 15 Statutes at Large, Chapter 249 (section 1), enacted July 27 1868, states the following:

PREAMBLE - Rights of American citizens in foreign states.
WHEREAS the right of expatriation is a natural and inherent right of all people, indispensable to the enjoyment of the rights of life, liberty, and the pursuit of happiness; and whereas in the recognition of this principle this government has freely received emigrants from all nations, and invested them with the rights of citizenship; and whereas it is claimed that such American citizens, with their descendants, are subjects of foreign states, owing allegiance to the governments thereof; and whereas it is necessary to the maintenance of public peace that this claim of foreign allegiance should be promptly and finally disavowed.

SECTION I - Right of expatriation declared.

THEREFORE, Be it enacted by the Senate of the and House of Representatives of the United States of America in Congress assembled, That any declaration, instruction, opinion, order, or decision of any officers of this government which denies, restricts, impairs, or questions the right of expatriation, is hereby declared inconsistent with the fundamental principles of this government.

SECTION II - Protection to naturalized citizens in foreign states.
And it is further enacted, That all naturalized citizens of the United States, while in foreign states, shall be entitled to, and shall receive from this government, the same protection of persons and property that is accorded to native born citizens in like situations and circumstances.

SECTION III - Release of citizens imprisoned by foreign governments to be demanded.

And it is further enacted, That whenever it shall be made known to the President that any citizen of the United States has been unjustly deprived of his liberty by or under the authority of any foreign government, it shall be the duty of the President forthwith to demand of that government the reasons for such imprisonment, and if it appears to be wrongful and in the violation of the rights of American citizenship, the President shall forthwith demand the release of such citizen, and if the release so demanded is unreasonably delayed or refused, it shall be the duty of the President to use such means, not amounting to acts of war, as he may think necessary and proper to obtain or effectuate such release, and all the facts and proceedings relative thereto shall as soon as practicable be communicated by the President to Congress.
Approved, July 27, 1868

15 The Courts and the States are enforcing the following code on American nationals: Title 50 USC Appendix App, Trading, Act, Sec. §4, "Licenses to enemy or ally of enemy insurance or reinsurance companies; change of name; doing business in United States," as a result of the passage of The Amendatory Act of March 9, 1933 to Title 50 USC, Trading with the Enemy Act Public Law No. 65-91 (40 Stat. L. 411) October 6, 1917. The original Trading with the Enemy Act **excluded** the people of the United States from being classified as the enemy when involved in transactions wholly within the United States. The Amendatory Act of March 9, 1933, however, **included the people of the United States as the enemy,** by incorporating the following language into the Trading With The Enemy Act: "**by any person within the United States.**" The abuses perpetrated upon the American people are the result of Title 50 USC, Trading With The Enemy Act, which turned the American people into "enemy of the state.

LANGUAGE NOT CLARIFIED

16. Clarification of language:
The **STATES** has failed to state the meaning or clarify the definition of words. The courts pursuant to the Federal Rules of Civil Procedure (FRCP) Rule 4(j), are, in fact and at law, a FOREIGN STATE as defined in Title 28 USC §1602, et. seq.,
The FOREIGN SOVEREIGN IMMUNITIES ACT of 1976, Pub. L. 94-583 (hereafter FSIA), and, therefore, lack jurisdiction over the sovereign people. . Any failure to specifically state the jurisdiction of the court violates 18 USC §1001,
§1505, and §2331 and the PATRIOT ACT, Section 800, Domestic terrorism.
17. There are three different and distinct forms of the "**United States**" as revealed by this case law:

"The high Court confirmed that the term "United States" can and does mean three completely different things, depending on the context." Hooven & Allison Co. vs. Evatt,

324 U.S. 652 (1945) & *United States v. Cruikshank,* 92 U.S. 542 (1876) & United States v. Bevans, 16 U.S. 3 Wheat. 336 336 (1818)

The Courts and its officers fail to state which United States they represent, since they can represent only one, the Federal Debt Collection Procedure, as a corporation, the United States, Inc., and it's satellite corporations have no jurisdiction over an American national and a belligerent claimant, the people hereby assert their right of immunity inherent in the 11th amendment: *"The judicial power shall not be construed to extend to any suit in law or equity, commenced or prosecuted against one of the United States by citizens of another state, or by citizens of any Foreign State."* The court, by definition are a FOREIGN STATE, and are misusing the name of the Sovereign American by placing Sovereign American 's name in all capital letters, as well as by using Sovereign American 's last name to construe Sovereign American, erroneously, as a "person" which is a "term of art" meaning: *a creature of the law, an artificial being, and a CORPORATION or ens legis:*

"*Ens Legis.* L. Lat. A creature of the law; an artificial being, as contrasted with a natural person. Applied to corporations, considered as deriving their existence entirely from the law." —Blacks Law Dictionary, 4th Edition, 1951.

18. All complaints and suits against such CORPORATION, or *ens legis,* fall under the aforementioned FSIA and service of process must therefore be made by the clerk of the court, under Section 1608(a)(4) of Title 28 USC, 63 Stat. 111, as amended (22 U.S.C. 2658) [42 FR 6367, Feb. 2, 1977, as amended at 63 FR 16687, Apr. 6, 1998], to the Director of the Office of Special Consular Services in the Bureau of Consular Affairs, Department of State, in Washington, D.C., exclusively, pursuant to 22 CFR §93.1 and §93.2. A copy of the FSIA must be filed with the complaint along with "a certified copy of the diplomatic note of transmittal," and, "the certification shall state the date and place the documents were delivered." The foregoing must be served upon the Chief Executive Officer and upon the Registered Agent of the designated CORPORATION or FOREIGN STATE.

19. MUNICIPAL, COUNTY, or STATE COURTS lack jurisdiction to hear any case since they fall under the definition of FOREIGN STATE, and under all related definitions below. Said jurisdiction lies with the "district court of the United States," established by Congress in the states under Article III of the Constitution, which are "constitutional courts" and do not include the territorial courts created under Article IV, Section 3, Clause 2, which are "legislative" courts. *Hornbuckle v. Toombs*, 85 U.S. 648, 21 L.Ed. 966 (1873), (See Title 28 USC, Rule 1101), exclusively, under the FSIA Statutes pursuant to 28 USC §1330.

20. It is an undisputed, conclusive presumption that the Sovereign Americans, the real parties in interest are a not a CORPORATION, and, further, are not registered with any Secretary of State as a CORPORATION. Pursuant to Rule 12(b) (6), in these situations, the Prosecuting Attorney has failed to state a claim for which relief can be granted to the Defendant,a FATAL DEFECT, and, therefore, the instant case and all related matters must be DISMISSED WITH PREJUDICE for lack of *in personam*, territorial, and subject matter jurisdiction, as well as for improper Venue, as well as pursuant to the 11th amendment Foreign State Immunity.

21. Moreover, the process in the instant matters before these courts are not "regular on their face." Regular on its Face -- "Process is said to be "regular on its face" when it proceeds from the court, officer, or body having authority of law to issue process of that nature, and which is legal in form, and contains nothing to notify, or fairly apprise any one that it is issued without authority."

COURT LACKS JUDICIAL POWER IN LAW OR EQUITY

Federal, State, County or municipal governments can be sued in their corporate capacity when functioning as federal debt collectors under the Fair Debt Collection Practices Act (FDCPA). If the Federal or State government can claim immunity under the 11th Amendment, then the Federal or State or County or municipal government cannot use Law or Equity jurisdiction against the sovereign people in Court, since the people are not subject to a "foreign state" under Title 28 USC, Judicial Procedure, §§1602 -1610. The States are made up of "State Citizens," and under the 11th Amendment, "State Citizens" cannot be sued by a "foreign state."

Article III section 2 and the 11th Amendment of the Constitution are in conflict. The courts cannot convene under Article III equity jurisdiction and then have its public officers claim 11th amendment immunity. The courts are operating in a foreign state capacity against the people once the court officials take their oath.

Article III Section 2

The judicial power shall extend to all cases, in law and equity, arising under this Constitution, the laws of the United States, and treaties made, or which shall be made, under their authority;—to all cases affecting ambassadors, other public ministers and consuls;—to all cases of admiralty and maritime jurisdiction;—to controversies to which the United States shall be a party;—to controversies between two or more states;— *between a state and citizens of another state*;— between citizens of different states;—between citizens of the same state claiming lands under grants of different states, and between a state, or the citizens thereof, and foreign states, citizens or subjects.

The ratification of the Eleventh Amendment on February 7, 1795 effectively altered Article III Section 2, and now "**All**" public offices are using the Eleventh Amendment as a defence against being sued, whereas, the Eleventh Amendment actually removed protection since judicial power no longer extended to any suit in Law or Equity, and subsequently afforded the people the same protection as any level of government. The people cannot be charged in Law or Equity claims by anyone in the government. The court only has one action as revealed by the Rules of Civil Procedure: "Rule 2—One form of Action : There is only one form of action – the civil action." Civil action can be brought only by the people and not by any level of government.

Amendment XI

The judicial power of the United States **shall not be construed to extend to any suit in law or equity**, commenced or prosecuted against one of the United States by citizens of another state, or by citizens or subjects of any foreign state.

Stripping Doctrine. The Constitution was amended again in 1868 to protect various civil rights, and Section 5 of the 14th Amendment granted Congress the power to enforce, by appropriate legislation, the provisions of that amendment.

The courts have recognized that this new amendment, again a consensus of the people, abrogates the immunity provided by the 11th Amendment. When Congress enacted legislation under the auspices of Section 5 of the 14th Amendment, they specifically abrogated 11th Amendment immunity, and states can, under such federal statutes be prosecuted in federal court. The 1875 Civil Rights Act. The Supreme Court ruled that this Congressional enactment was unconstitutional. **Civil Rights Acts** (1866, 1870, 1875, 1957, 1960, 1964, 1968) US legislation. The Civil Rights Act (1866) gave African-Americans citizenship and extended civil rights to all persons born in the USA (except Native Americans). The 1870 Act was passed to re-enact the previous measure, which was considered to be of dubious constitutionality. In 1883, the US Supreme Court declared unconstitutional the 1870 law. The 1875 Act was passed to outlaw discrimination in public places because of race or previous servitude. **The act was declared unconstitutional by the Supreme Court (1883–85), (**U.S. Supreme Court Civil Rights Cases, 109 U.S. 3 (1883) Civil Rights Cases Submitted October Term, 1882 Decided October 16th, 1888 109 U.S. 3**) which stated that the 14th Amendment, the constitutional basis of the act, protected individual rights against infringement by the states, not by other individuals**. The 1957 Act established the Civil Rights Commission to investigate violations of the 15th Amendment. The 1960 Act enabled court-appointed federal officials to protect black voting rights. An act of violence to obstruct a court order became a federal offense. The 1964 Act established as law equal rights for all citizens in voting, education, public accommodations and in federally-assisted programs. The 1968 Act guaranteed equal treatment in housing and real estate to all citizens.

No level of the Executive or Judicial government has ever introduced into any Court action a real party of interest under Rule 17. The Court has no jurisdiction under 12(b)(1), (2), (3) over the Petitioner or people. **Decision and Rationale:** The 8-1 decision of the Court was delivered by Justice Joseph P. Bradley, with John Marshall Harlan of Kentucky alone in dissent. The Court decided that the Civil Rights Act of 1875 was unconstitutional. Neither the 13th nor the 14th amendment empowers the Congress to legislate in matters of racial discrimination in the private sector, Bradley wrote. "The 13th Amendment has respect, not to distinctions of race...but to slavery...." The 14th Amendment, he continued, applied to State, not private, actions; furthermore, the abridgment of rights presented in this case are to be considered as "ordinary civil injuries" rather than the imposition of badges of slavery.

Bradley commented that "individual invasion of individual rights is not the subject-matter of the 14th Amendment. It has a deeper and broader scope. **It nullifies and makes void all state legislation, and state action of every kind, which impairs the privileges and immunities of citizens of the United States, or which injures them in life, liberty or property without due process of law, or which denies to any of them the equal protection of the laws." Therefore, the Court limited the impact of the Equal Protection Clause of the 14th Amendment.**

LACK OF SUBJECT MATTER JURISDICTION

In a court of limited jurisdiction, whenever a party denies that the court has subject-matter jurisdiction, it becomes the duty and the burden of the party claiming that the court has subject matter jurisdiction to provide evidence from the record of the case that the court holds subject-matter jurisdiction. *Bindell v City of Harvey*, 212 Ill.App.3d 1042, 571 N.E.2d 1017 (1st Dist. 1991) ("the burden of proving jurisdiction rests upon the party asserting it."). Until the plaintiff submits uncontroversial evidence of subject-matter jurisdiction to the court that the court has subject-matter jurisdiction, the court is proceeding without subject-matter jurisdiction. *Loos v American Energy Savers, Inc.*, 168 Ill.App.3d 558, 522 N.E.2d 841(1988)("Where jurisdiction is contested, the burden of establishing it rests upon the plaintiff."). The law places the duty and burden of subject-matter jurisdiction upon the plaintiff. Should the court attempt to place the burden upon the defendant, the court has acted against the law, violates the defendant's due process rights, and the judge under court decisions has immediately lost subject-matter jurisdiction. In a court of limited jurisdiction, the court must proceed exactly according to the law or statute under which it operates. *Flake v Pretzel*, 381 Ill. 498, 46 N.E.2d 375 (1943) ("the actions, being statutory proceedings, ...were void for want of power to make them.") ("The judgments were based on orders which were void because the court exceeded its jurisdiction in entering them. Where a court, after acquiring jurisdiction of a subject matter, as here, transcends the limits of the jurisdiction conferred, its judgment is void."); *Armstrong v Obucino*, 300 Ill. 140, 143, 133 N.E. 58 (1921) ("The doctrine that where a court has once acquired jurisdiction it has a right to decide every question which arises in the cause, and its judgment or decree, however erroneous, cannot be collaterally assailed, is only correct when the court proceeds according to the established modes governing the class to which the case belongs and does not transcend in the extent and character of its judgment or decree the law or statute which is applicable to it." *In Interest of M.V.*, 288 Ill.App.3d 300, 681 N.E.2d 532 (1st Dist. 1997) ("Where a court's power to act is controlled by statute, the court is governed by the rules of limited jurisdiction, and courts exercising jurisdiction over such matters must proceed within the strictures of the statute."); *In re Marriage of Milliken*, 199 Ill.App.3d 813, 557 N.E.2d 591 (1st Dist. 1990) ("The jurisdiction of a court in a dissolution proceeding is limited to that conferred by statute."); *Vulcan Materials Co. v. Bee Const. Co., Inc.,* 101 Ill.App.3d 30, 40, 427 N.E.2d 797 (1st Dist. 1981) ("Though a court be one of general jurisdiction, when its power to act on a particular matter is controlled by statute, the court is governed by the rules of limited jurisdiction."). "There is no discretion to ignore that lack of jurisdiction." *Joyce v. US*, 474 F2d 215. "A universal principle as old as the law is that a proceedings of a court without jurisdiction are a nullity and its judgment therein without effect either on person or property." *Norwood v. Renfield*, 34 C 329; *Ex parte Giambonini*, 49 P. 732. "Jurisdiction is fundamental and a judgment rendered by a court that does not have jurisdiction to hear is void ab initio." In Re Application of Wyatt, 300 P. 132; Re Cavitt, 118 P2d 846. "Thus, where a judicial tribunal has no jurisdiction of the subject matter on which it assumes to act, its proceedings are absolutely void in the fullest sense of the term." *Dillon v. Dillon*, 187 P 27. "A court has no jurisdiction to determine its own jurisdiction, for a basic issue in any case before a tribunal is its power to act, and a court must have the authority to decide that question in the first instance." *Rescue Army v. Municipal Court of Los Angeles*, 171 P2d 8; 331 US 549, 91 L. ed. 1666, 67 S.Ct. 1409. "A departure by a court from those recognized and established requirements of law, however close apparent adherence to mere form in method of procedure, which has the effect of depriving one of a constitutional right, is an excess of jurisdiction." *Wuest v. Wuest,* 127 P2d 934, 937. "Where a court failed to observe safeguards, it amounts to denial of due process of law, court is deprived of juris." *Merritt v. Hunter*, C.A. Kansas 170 F2d 739. "the fact that the petitioner was released on a promise to appear before a magistrate for an arraignment, that fact is circumstance to be considered in determining whether in first instance there was a probable cause for the arrest." *Monroe v. Papa*, DC, Ill. 1963, 221 F Supp 685. "Jurisdiction, once challenged, is to be proven, not by the court, but by the party attempting to assert jurisdiction. The burden of proof of jurisdiction lies with the asserter." See *McNutt v. GMAC*, 298 US 178. The origins of this doctrine of law may be found in *Maxfield's Lessee v. Levy*, 4 US 308. "A court has no jurisdiction to determine its own jurisdiction, for a basic issue in any case before a tribunal is its power to act, and a court must have the authority to decide that question in the first instance." *Rescue Army* v. *Municipal Court of Los Angeles*, 171 P2d 8; 331 US 549, 91 L. ed. 1666, 67 S.Ct. 1409. "Once jurisdiction is challenged, the court cannot proceed when it clearly appears that the court lacks jurisdiction, the court has no authority to reach merits, but, rather, should dismiss the action." *Melo* v. *US*, 505 F2d 1026. "The law provides that once State and Federal jurisdiction has been challenged, it must be proven." --*Main v. Thiboutot*, 100 S. Ct. 2502 (1980). "Once jurisdiction is challenged, it must be proven."--*Hagens v. Lavine*, 415 U.S. 533. "Where there is absence of jurisdiction, all administrative and judicial proceedings are a nullity and confer no right, offer no protection, and afford no justification, and may be rejected upon direct collateral attack." --*Thompson v. Tolmie*, 2 Pet. 157, 7 L.Ed. 381; *Griffith v. Frazier*, 8 Cr. 9, 3L. Ed. 471.

"No sanctions can be imposed absent proof of jurisdiction." --*Standard v. Olsen*, 74 S. Ct. 768; Title 5 U.S.C., Sec. 556 and 558 (b). "The proponent of the rule has the burden of proof." --Title 5 U.S.C., Sec. 556 (d). "Jurisdiction can be challenged at any time, even on final determination." --*Basso v. Utah Power & Light Co.*, 495 2nd 906 at 910. "Mere good faith assertions of power and authority (jurisdiction) have been abolished." --*Owens v. The City of Independence,* "A departure by a court from those recognized and established requirements of law, however close apparent adherence to mere form in method of procedure, which has the effect of depriving one of a constitutional right, is an excess of jurisdiction." --*Wuest* v. *Wuest*, 127 P2d 934, 937. "In a court of limited jurisdiction, whenever a party denies that the court has subject-matter jurisdiction, it becomes the duty and the burden of the party claiming that the court has subject matter jurisdiction to provide evidence from the record of the case that the court holds subject-matter jurisdiction." --*Bindell v City of Harvey*, 212 Ill.App.3d 1042, 571 N.E.2d 1017 (1st Dist. 1991) ("the burden of proving jurisdiction rests upon the party asserting it."). "Until the plaintiff submits uncontroversial evidence of subject-matter jurisdiction to the court that the court has subject-matter jurisdiction, the court is proceeding without subject-matter jurisdiction."--*Loos v American Energy Savers, Inc.*, 168 Ill.App.3d 558, 522 N.E.2d 841(1988)("Where jurisdiction is contested, the burden of establishing it rests upon the plaintiff."). The law places the duty and burden of subject-matter jurisdiction upon the plaintiff. Should the court attempt to place the burden upon the defendant, the court has acted against the law, violates the defendant's due process rights, and the judge under court decisions has immediately lost subject-matter jurisdiction. In a court of limited jurisdiction, the court must proceed exactly according to the law or statute under which it operates. --*Flake v Pretzel*, 381 Ill. 498, 46 N.E.2d 375 (1943) ("the actions, being statutory proceedings, ...were void for want of power to make them.") ("The judgments were based on orders which were void because the court exceeded its jurisdiction in entering them. Where a court, after acquiring jurisdiction of a subject matter, as here, transcends the limits of the jurisdiction conferred, its judgment is void."); *Armstrong v Obucino*, 300 Ill. 140, 143, 133 N.E. 58 (1921) "The doctrine that where a court has once acquired jurisdiction it has a right to decide every question which arises in the cause, and its judgment or decree, however erroneous, cannot be collaterally assailed, is only correct when the court proceeds according to the established modes governing the class to which the case belongs and does not transcend in the extent and character of its judgment or decree the law or statute which is applicable to it." *In Interest of M.V.*, 288 Ill.App.3d 300, 681 N.E.2d 532 (1st Dist. 1997) ("Where a court's power to act is controlled by statute, the court is governed by the rules of limited jurisdiction, and courts exercising jurisdiction over such matters must proceed within the strictures of the statute."); *In re Marriage of Milliken*, 199 Ill.App.3d 813, 557 N.E.2d 591 (1st Dist. 1990) ("The jurisdiction of a court in a dissolution proceeding is limited to that conferred by statute."); *Vulcan Materials Co. v. Bee Const. Co., Inc.*, 101 Ill.App.3d 30, 40, 427 N.E.2d 797 (1st Dist. 1981) ("Though a court be one of general jurisdiction, when its power to act on a particular matter is controlled by statute, the court is governed by the rules of limited jurisdiction.").

LACK OF JUDICIAL IMMUNITY

Thus, neither Judges nor Government attorneys are above the law. See *United States v. Isaacs*, 493 F. 2d 1124, 1143 (7th Cir. 1974). In our judicial system, few more serious threats to individual liberty can be imagined than a corrupt judge or judges acting in collusion outside of their judicial authority with the Executive Branch to deprive a citizen of his rights. In *The Case of the Marshalsea*, 77 Eng. Rep. 1027 (K.B. 1613), Sir Edward Coke found that Article 39 of the Magna Carta restricted the power of judges to act outside of their jurisdiction such proceedings would be void, and actionable.

When a Court has (a) jurisdiction of the cause, and proceeds *inverso ordine* or erroneously, there the party who sues, or the officer or minister of the Court who executes the precept or process of the Court, no action lies against them. But (b) when the Court has no jurisdiction of the cause, there the whole proceeding is before a person who is not a judge, and actions will lie against them without any regard of the precept or process . . . Id. 77 Eng. Rep. at 1038-41.

A majority of states, including Virginia (see, Va. Code §8.01-195.3(3)), followed the English rule to find that a judge had no immunity from suit for acts outside of his judicial capacity or jurisdiction. Robert Craig Waters, 'Liability of Judicial Officers under Section 1983' 79 Yale L. J. (December 1969), pp. 326-27 and 29-30).

Also as early as 1806, in the United States there were recognized restrictions on the power of judges, as well as the placing of liability on judges for acts outside of their jurisdiction. In *Wise v. Withers*, 7 U.S. (3 Cranch) 331 (1806), the Supreme Court confirmed the right to sue a judge for exercising authority beyond the jurisdiction authorized by statute.

In *Stump v. Sparkman*, 435 U.S. 349 at 360 (1978), the Supreme Court confirmed that a judge would be immune from suit only if he did not act outside of his judicial capacity and/or was not performing any act expressly prohibited by statute. See Block, *Stump v Sparkman* and the History of Judicial Immunity, 4980 Duke L.J. 879 (l980). The Circuit Court overturned
this case and the judge was liable.

Judicial immunity may only extend to all judicial acts within the court's jurisdiction and judicial capacity, but it does not extend to either criminal acts, or acts outside of official capacity or in the 'clear absence of all jurisdiction.' see *Stump v. Sparkman* 435 U.S. 349 (1978). "When a judge knows that he lacks jurisdiction, or acts in the face of clearly valid

Constitutional provisions or valid statutes expressly depriving him of jurisdiction or judicial capacity, judicial immunity is lost." --*Rankin v. Howard* 633 F.2d 844 (1980), *Den Zeller v. Rankin*, 101 S. Ct. 2020 (1981).

As stated by the United States Supreme Court in *Piper v. Pearson*, 2 Gray 120, cited in *Bradley v. Fisher*, 13 Wall. 335, 20 L. Ed. 646 (1872), 'where there is no jurisdiction, there can be no discretion, for discretion is incident to jurisdiction.' The constitutional requirement of due process of the law is indispensable: "No person shall be held to answer for a capital, or otherwise infamous crime, unless on a presentment or indictment of a Grand Jury, except in cases arising in the land or naval forces, or in the Militia, when in actual service in time of War or public danger; nor shall any person be subject for the same offense to be twice put in jeopardy of life or limb; nor shall be compelled in any criminal case to be a witness against himself, **nor be deprived of life, liberty or property, without due process of law;** nor shall private property be taken for public use without just compensation." Article V, National Constitution. "A judgment can be void . . . where the court acts in a manner contrary to due process." --Am Jur 2d, §29 Void Judgments, p. 404. "Where a court failed to observe safeguards, it amounts to denial of due process of law, court is deprived of juris." --*Merritt* v. *Hunter*, C.A. Kansas 170 F2d 739. "Moreover, all proceedings founded on the void judgment are themselves regarded as invalid." --*Olson v. Leith* 71 Wyo. 316, 257 P.2d 342. "In criminal cases, certain constitutional errors require **automatic reversal**," see *State v. Schmit*, 273 Minn. 78, 88, 139 N.W.2d 800, 807 (1966).

PERSON vs PEOPLE

"This word 'person' and its scope and bearing in the law, involving, as it does, legal fictions and also apparently natural beings, it is difficult to understand; but it is absolutely necessary to grasp, at whatever cost, a true and proper understanding to the word in all the phases of its proper use . . . A person is here not a physical or individual person, but the status or condition with which he is invested . . . not an individual or physical person, but the status, condition or character borne by physical persons . . . The law of persons is the law of status or condition." -- American Law and Procedure, Vol. 13, page 137, 1910.

The following case citation declares the undisputed distinction in fact and at law of the distinction between the term "persons," which is the plural form of the term "person," and the word "People" which is NOT the plural form of the term "person." The above-mentioned "real party in interest" is NOT a subordinate "person," "subject," or "agent," but is a "constituent," in whom sovereignty abides, a member of the "Posterity of We, the People," in whom sovereignty resides, and from whom the government has emanated: "The sovereignty of a state does not reside in the **persons** who fill the different departments of its government, but in the **People**, from whom the government emanated; and they may change it at their discretion. Sovereignty, then in this country, abides with the constituency, and not with the agent; and this remark is true, both in reference to the federal and state government." (Persons are not People).--*Spooner v. McConnell*, 22 F 939, 943: "Our government is founded upon compact. Sovereignty was, and is, in the people" --*Glass v. Sloop Betsey*, supreme Court, 1794. "People of a state are entitled to all rights which formerly belong to the King, by his prerogative." -- supreme Court, *Lansing v. Smith,* 1829. "The United States, as a whole, emanates from the people ... The people, in their capacity as sovereigns, made and adopted the Constitution ..." --supreme Court, 4 Wheat 402. "The governments are but trustees acting under derived authority and have no power to delegate what is not delegated to them. But the people, as the original fountain might take away what they have delegated and entrust to whom they please. ... The sovereignty in every state resides in the people of the state and they may alter and change their form of government at their own pleasure." --*Luther v. Borden*, 48 US 1, 12 L.Ed 581. "While sovereign powers are delegated to ... the government, sovereignty itself remains with the people" --*Yick Wo v. Hopkins*, 118 U.S. 356, page 370. "There is no such thing as a power of inherent sovereignty in the government of the United States .... In this country sovereignty resides in the people, and Congress can exercise no power which they have not, by their Constitution entrusted to it: All else is withheld." -- *Julliard v. Greenman*, 110 U.S. 421. "In common usage, the term 'person' does not include the sovereign, and statutes employing the word are ordinarily construed to exclude it." -- *Wilson v. Omaha Indian Tribe* 442 US 653, 667 (1979). "Since in common usage the term 'person' does not include the sovereign, statutes employing that term are ordinarily construed to exclude it." -- *U.S. v. Cooper*, 312 US 600,604, 61 S. Ct 742 (1941). "In common usage, the term 'person' does not include the sovereign and statutes employing it will ordinarily not be construed to do so." -- *U.S. v. United Mine Workers of America*, 330 U.S. 258, 67 S. Ct 677 (1947).

"Since in common usage, the term 'person' does not include the sovereign, statutes employing the phrase are ordinarily construed to exclude it." -- *US v. Fox* 94 US 315. "In common usage the word 'person' does not include the sovereign, and statutes employing the word are generally construed to exclude the sovereign." -- *U.S. v. General Motors Corporation*, D.C. Ill, 2 F.R.D. 528, 530:
The following two case citations declare the undisputed doctrine, in fact and at law, that the word (term of art) "person" is a "general word," and that the "people," of whom the above-mentioned "real party in interest" is one, "are NOT bound by general words in statutes." Therefore, statutes do not apply to, operate upon or affect the above-mentioned "real party in interest:" **The word `person' in legal terminology is perceived as a *general word*** which normally includes in its scope a variety of entities

other than human beings., --*Church of Scientology v. US Department of Justice* 612 F2d 417, 425 (1979). " **The people, or sovereign are not bound by** *general words* **in statutes** , restrictive of prerogative right, title or interest, unless expressly named. Acts of limitation do not bind the King or the people. The people have been ceded all the rights of the King, the former sovereign ... It is a maxim of the common law, that when an act is made for the common good and to prevent injury, the King shall be bound, though not named, but when a statute is general and prerogative right would be divested or taken from the King (or the People) he shall not be bound." -- *The People v. Herkimer*, 4 Cowen (NY) 345, 348 (1825): "In the United States, sovereignty resides in people." -- *Perry v. U.S.* (294 US 330). "A Sovereign is exempt from suit, not because of any formal conception or obsolete theory, but on the logical and practical ground that there can be no legal Right as against the authority that makes the law on which the Right depends." --*Kawananakoa v. Polyblank*, 205 U.S. 349, 353, 27 S. Ct. 526, 527, 51 L. Ed. 834 (1907).

DEL CODE TITLE 8 Chapters 6 § 617: Delaware Code - Section 617: CORPORATE NAME

The corporate name of a corporation organized under this chapter shall contain either a word or words descriptive of the professional service to be rendered by the corporation or **shall contain the last names of** 1 or more of its present, prospective or former shareholders or of persons who were associated with a predecessor person, partnership, corporation or other organization or whose name or names appeared in the name of such predecessor organization.

Texas Administrative Code
Subject: 1 TAC § 79.31 CORPORATIONS (ENTITY NAMES)
§ 79.31. Characters of Print Acceptable in Names
(a) Entity names may consist of letters of the Roman alphabet, Arabic numerals, and certain symbols capable of being reproduced on a standard English language typewriter, or combination thereof.
(b) **Only upper case or capitol letters, with no distinction as to type face or font, will be recognized.**
Delaware legislation March 10 1899
"An Act Providing General Corporate Law" This Act allow the corporation to become a "PERSON"

A **legal person**, also called **juridical person** or **juristic person**,[1] is a legal entity through which the law allows a group of **natural persons** to act as if they were a single composite **individual** for certain purposes, or in some jurisdictions, for a single person to have a separate legal personality other than their own.[2][3] This **legal fiction** does not mean these entities are human beings, but rather means that the law allows them to act as **persons** for certain limited purposes. **SANTA CLARA COUNTY v. SOUTHERN PAC. R. CO., 118 U.S. 394,** New York Central R. Co. v. United States, 212 U.S. 481 (1909), United States v. Dotterweich, 320 U.S. 277 (1943)
"**Street Name** " :BLACK'S LAW DICTIONARY ABRIDGED FIFTH EDITION
"Securities held in the name of a broker instead of his customer's name are said to be carried in a "street name". This occurs when the securities have been bought on margin or when the customer wishes the security to be held by the broker. The name of a broker or bank appearing on a corporate security with blank endorsement by the broker or bank. The security can then be transferred merely by delivery since the endorsement is well known. Street name is used for convenience or to shield identity of the true owner."

CUSIP Definition:

CUSIP® Is a registered trademark of the American Bankers Association : Acronym CUSIP refers to the Committee on Uniform Security Identification Procedures. The acronym CUSIP typically refers to both the Committee on Uniform Security Identification Procedures and the 9-character alphanumeric security identifiers that they distribute for all North American securities for the purposes of facilitating clearing and settlement...

First 6 Characters identify the unique name of the:

- Company
- Municipality
- Government agency

A hierarchical alpha numeric convention linked to alphabetic issuer name.

Next 2 Characters Identifies the type of instrument:

- Equity
- Debt
• Uniquely identifies the issue within the issuer

Servus Servorum Dei
• A hierarchical alpha numeric convention

Next 1 Character
• A mathematical formula checks accuracy of the previous 8 characters • Delivers a 1 character check result

Resulting 9 Characters
• A unique identifier

* **CUSIP® - Universally recognized identifier for financial instruments.**
* **CINS - CUSIP International Numbering System**
* **CSB ISIN -Participation in the assignment of CUSIP-based International**

Securities Identification Numbers CINS

CUSIP International Numbering System (CINS) is a 9-character alphanumeric identifier that employs the same numbering system as CUSIP, but also contains a letter of the alphabet in the first position signifying the issuer's country or geographic region. CINS was developed in 1989 as an extension to CUSIP in response to U.S. demand for global coverage, and is the local identifier of more than 30 non-North American markets.

CSB ISIN

The International Securities Identification Number (ISIN) is a unique global code that identifies instruments in different countries to facilitate cross-border trading. CSB is responsible for the assignment of ISINs in the U.S. and in other areas where designated or appointed. CSB ISINs are 12 character identifiers that have a CUSIP or CINS embedded in them, which always appear in position 3 to 11.

CSB has agents in countries such as Canada, Bermuda, The Cayman Islands and Jamaica, and is also the representative agency for countries in South America. Because of this, it was necessary to develop a separate identification system to designate CSB-assigned securities from these jurisdictions.

The American Bankers Association:

The American Bankers Association (ABA) is a free-trade and professional association that promotes and advocates issues important to the banking industry in the United States. The ABA's national headquarters are in Washington, D.C. In addition to its trade association mission, the ABA also performs educational components for consumers through its Educational Foundation affiliate.

Organization:

While the ABA works on a national level, it also is supported by state operated offices (sometimes referred to as "Leagues") which focus attention on state level support. Both the ABA and the state organizations are dues supported trade associations. Both the state and national offices also operate Political Action Committees (PACs) which use registered lobbyists to work for laws that are advantageous for the banking industry. The president of the ABA is Edward Yingling.

Political action committee;
In the United States, a Political Action Committee, or PAC, is the name commonly given to a private group, regardless of size, organized to elect political candidates. Legally, what constitutes a "PAC" for purposes of regulation is a matter of state and federal law. Under the Federal Election Campaign Act, an organization becomes a "political committee" by receiving contributions or making expenditures in excess of $1,000 for the purpose of influencing a federal election.

When an interest group gets directly involved within the political process, a PAC is created. These PACs receive and raise money from the special group's constituents, and on behalf of the special interest, makes donations to political campaigns.

The American Federation of State, County and Municipal Employees (AFSCME) is the second- or third-largest labor union in the United States and one of the fastest-growing, representing over 1.4 million employees, primarily in local and state government and in the health care industry. AFSCME is part of the AFL-CIO, one of the two main labor federations in the United States. Employees at the federal government level are primarily represented by other unions, such as the American Federation of Government Employees, with which AFSCME was once affiliated, and the National Treasury Employees Union; but AFSCME does represent some federal employees at the Federal Aviation Administration and the Library of Congress, among others.[1]

According to their website, AFSCME organizes for social and economic justice in the workplace and through political action and legislative advocacy. It is divided into more than 3,500 local unions in 46 U.S. states, plus the District of Columbia and Puerto Rico. Each local union writes its own constitution, holds membership meetings, and elects its own officers. Councils are also a part of AFSCME's administrative structure, usually grouping together various locals in a geographic area.

According to OpenSecrets.org, the top contributors since 1988 ranked by their total spending along with the party tilt of their contributions are:
Rank Organization Total Dem % Repub % Tilt
1 AFSCME $39,947,843 98% 1% Solidly Dem (over 90%)

Table Of Definitions

Foreign Court The courts of a foreign state or nation. In the United States, this term is frequently applied to the courts of one of the States when their judgment or records are introduced in the courts of another.
Foreign jurisdiction Any jurisdiction foreign to that of the forum; e.g., a sister state or another country. Also, the exercise by a state or nation jurisdiction beyond its own territory. Long-arm service of process is a form of such foreign or extraterritorial jurisdiction
Foreign laws The laws of a foreign country, or of a sister state. In conflicts of law, the legal principles of jurisprudence which are part of the law of a sister state or nation. Foreign laws are additions to our own laws, and in that respect are called "*jus receptum.*"
Foreign corporation A corporation doing business in one State though chartered or incorporated in another state is a foreign corporation as to the first state, and, as such, is

required to consent to certain conditions and restrictions in order to do business in such first state.

Under federal tax laws, a foreign corporation is one which is not organized under the law of one of the States or Territories of the United States. I.R.C. § 7701 (a) (5). Service of process on foreign corporation is governed by the Fed. R. Civ. P. 4 See also Corporation.

Foreign service of process Service of process for the acquisition of jurisdiction by a court in the United States upon a person in a foreign country is prescribed by Fed R. Civ. P. 4 (i) and 28 U.S.C.A. § 1608. Service of process on foreign corporations is governed by Fed. R. Civ. P. 4(d) (3).

Foreign states Nations which are outside the United States. Term may also refer to another state; i.e. a sister state.

Foreign immunity With respect to jurisdictional immunity of foreign states, see 28 USC, Sec. §1602 *et seq*. Title 8 USC, Chapter 12, Subchapter I, Sec. §1101(14) The term "foreign state" includes outlying possessions of a foreign state, but self-governing dominions or territories under mandate or trusteeship shall be regarded as separate foreign states.

Profiteering Taking advantage of unusual or exceptional circumstance to make excessive profit; e.g. selling of scarce or essential goods at inflated price during time of emergency or war.

Person In general usage, a human being (i.e. natural person) though by statute the term may include a firm, labor organizations, partnerships, associations, corporations, legal representative, trusts, trustees in bankruptcy, or receivers. National Labor Relations Act, §2(1).

Definition of the term "person" under Title 26, Subtitle F, Chapter 75, Subchapter D, Sec. Sec. §7343

The term "person" as used in this chapter includes an officer or employee of a corporation, or a member or employee of a partnership, who as such officer, employee or member is under a duty to perform the act in respect of which the violation occurs. A **corporation** is a "person" within the meaning of equal protection and due process provisions of the United States Constitution.

Tertius interveniens A third party intervening; a third party who comes between the parties to a suit; one who interpleads. Gilbert's Forum Romanum. 47.

Writ of error *Coram nobis* A common-law writ, the purpose of which is to correct a judgment in the same court in which it was rendered, on the ground of error of fact, for which statutes provide no other remedy, which fact did not appear of record, or was unknown to the court when judgment was pronounced, and which, if known would have prevented the judgment, and which was unknown, and could of reasonable diligence in time to have been otherwise presented to the court, unless he was prevented from so presenting them by duress, fear, or other sufficient cause. "A writ of error **Coram nobis** is a common-law writ of ancient origin devised by the judiciary, which constitutes a remedy for setting aside a judgment which for a valid reason should never have been rendered." 24 C.J.S., Criminal Law. § 1610 (2004)."The principal function of the **writ of error Coram nobis** is to afford to the court in which an action was tried an opportunity to correct its own record with reference to a vital fact not known when the judgment was rendered, and which could not have been presented by a motion for a new trial, appeal or other existing statutory proceeding." Black's Law Dictionary., 3rd ed., p. 1861; 24 C.J.S.,

Criminal Law, § 1606 b., p. 145; *Ford v. Commonwealth*, 312 Ky. 718, 229 S.W.2d 470.At common law in England, it issued from the Court of Kings Bench to a judgment of that court. Its principal aim is to afford the court in which an action was tried an opportunity to correct its own record with reference to a vital fact not known when the judgment was rendered. It is also said that at common law it lay to correct purely ministerial errors of the officers of the court. Furthermore, the above-mentioned "real party in interest" demands the strict adherence to Article IV, section one of the National

Constitution so that in all matters before this court, the Full Faith and Credit shall be given in each State to the public Acts, Records, and judicial Proceedings of every other State; and to Article IV of the Articles of Confederation, still in force pursuant to Article VI of the National Constitution, so that "Full faith and credit shall be given in each of these States to the records, acts, and judicial proceedings of the courts and magistrates of every other State," selective incorporation notwithstanding. The *lex domicilii* shall also depend upon the Natural Domicile of the above-mentioned "real party in interest." The *lex domicilii,* involves the "law of the domicile" in the Conflict of Laws. Conflict is the branch of public law regulating all lawsuits involving a "foreign" law element where a difference in result will occur depending on which laws are applied.

AMENDATORY RECONSTRUCTION ACT OF MARCH 11, 1868
An Act to amend the act passed March 23, 1867, entitled "An Act supplementary to 'An act to provide for the more efficient government of the rebel states,' passed March 2, 1867, and to facilitate their restoration. SUPPLEMENTARY RECONSTRUCTION ACT OF FORTIETH CONGRESS. An Act supplementary to an act entitled "An act to provide for the more efficient government of the rebel states," passed March second, eighteen hundred and sixty-seven, and to facilitate restoration. " This act created the 14th amendment federal citizen under section 3 of the federal constitution. All who hold public office fall under this section as UNITED STATES citizens. Those who hold office have knowingly and willingly given up their citizenship to this country under Title 8 Section §1481 to become a foreign state agent under 22 USC. The oath of office to the constitution requires office-holders to uphold and maintain our Constitutional form of government under the people's authority. This right was never surrendered by the people; failure to do so violates 10 USC §333 and 18 USC §1918, chapter 115 §2382, §2383, §1505, §1001, §241, §242, 42 USC §1981 & 31 USC §3729 just to name a few.

The Federal Debt Collection Procedure places all courts under equity and commerce and under the International Monetary Fund. The International Monetary Fund comes under the Uniform Commercial Code under banking and business interest and Trust laws. This makes the Court / Judges trustee over the trust and responsible whether or not the Petitioner understands the trust issue.

The 1933 bankruptcy act placed all public officials in a fiduciary position to keep the accounts in balance via discharge of the debt against the pre-paid, priority exempt accounts of the American people.

The American people were fraudulently identified as enemy combatants under the TWEA for the purpose of skirting the UNITED STATES' debtor obligation to the sovereign people of America and facilitating the pillage and plunder of the sovereign people under the direction of the international banking families.

The TWEA suspended the U.S. Constitution in the court room, turning the courtrooms into debt collection facilities under admiralty/maritime and therefore, the standard American flag in the courtroom was replaced with a military Admiralty flag for dealing with alien enemy combatants. The people never rescinded their nationality to the real united States of America. Those who hold public office rescinded their nationality to become a foreign agent in order to hold public office. International law requires the judge to uphold the people's Constitutional form of government as defined in the "Federalist Papers".

Federal Rules of Civil Procedure / Rules of Civil Procedure Rule 2 only allows civil action, and under Rule 17, a real party of interest has to be present in the courtroom in order for there to be any claims of injury or damages against "the people." Any charges under the

"UNITED STATES" or "THE STATE OF........" fall under the TWEA Section 23. The people are not subject to this jurisdiction as it is a Foreign State jurisdiction. The people hold 11th amendment immunity to claims in equity and commerce from a foreign state. The courts lack jurisdiction over the people by Congressional mandate.

All debt of the UNITED STATES, except that debt owed to the sovereign people of America, has been abandoned and vacated and the UNITED STATES has DECLARED PEACE with the world and the sovereign people thereof, therefore, the gold fringed military flag designating the admiralty/maritime jurisdiction shall be immediately removed from all courtrooms, meeting rooms, etc. of the administrative agencies of the UNITED STATES and the civil peace flag of the united states of America shall be proudly displayed in their stead..

The U.S. Courts who have been operating as debt collection facilities under TWEA and the EMERGENCY WAR POWERS ACT shall immediately make the corrections and cure the torts against the people, vacating all claims, attachments and/or restrictions on the private rights of the sovereign people and make them whole.

The courts, as well as all administrative agencies of the UNITED STATES, shall share resources making room for and facilitating the establishment of the organic courts, operating under the common law, for the adjudication of all matters concerning the sovereign American people, other than the prosecution of grievances against an administrative agency for the trespass of the private rights of the people. All administrative agencies shall actively participate in the establishment of two distinctly separate systems, common law and administrative, operating side by side for the benefit of the CREDITORS, the sovereign people of America.

All administrative courts and agencies of the UNITED STATES shall operate in good faith and honor as servants of the sovereign people of America. Said administrative courts and agencies have grown out of control, beyond the intent of the original founders and their usefulness and shall begin to make the corrections, a reversal, bringing about balance, transparency, full disclosure and honor for the remedy of the Real Parties In Interest.

All debts of the UNITED STATES have been abandoned, except the debt to the sovereign people; The Pledge of the private property of the American people has been relinquished, therefore, the administrative agencies of the UNITED STATES shall make the return of the interest back to source, the sovereign people.

The UNITED STATES shall immediately activate the established pass through account,vacate the blocks on the asset accounts and make the financial adjustments to discharge the debt and return the accounts of the sovereign people back into balance. The UNITED STATES shall maintain the natural flow and balance in the accounts for the remedy of the people, returning the interest back to source in the discharge of debt against the pre-paid account, at all times remaining in honor.

The UNITED STATES shall immediately make the corrections as concerns the unlawful restrictions of the liberties of the sovereign people by the administrative agencies of the UNITED STATES;

All Deeds, warranty deeds, trust deeds, sheriff deeds, tax deeds and all Certificates of Title are colorable titles issued to facilitate the 'Pledge' of the private property of the sovereign people.

The Pledge has been relinquished, therefore, the UNITED STATES shall make the corrections to discharge all colorable titles, make the re-conveyance and issue the land patent/ allodial title for the property back to the people.

It is the duty of the military to serve and protect the post, therefore, the UNITED STATES military shall serve and protect the sovereign people of America, the creditor of the UNITED STATES. All branches of the U.S. Military shall follow the orders of the "Transitional Committee", interim government and government of the republic, respectively throughout this transition.

The Provost Marshals are the organic police force with a duty to serve and protect the sovereign. The Provost Marshal shall immediately serve and protect all who claim protection under this treaty making top priority any/all requests for assistance on claims of unlawful restrictions on the liberties of a sovereign.

There shall be those members of the sovereign people, ambassadors, with a passion to service, who shall choose to serve the republic; lightworkers, visionaries, warriors, teachers and people knowledgeable in the art of peace and love; to serve as watchdogs or compliance, ensuring the integrity and protection of the people's rights; or facilitators and educators charged with presenting real truth, that the enslavement of the sovereign people may never happen again; beacons of light, guiding the people out of the darkness, into the truth;

There shall be those members of the sovereign people who shall be instrumental in breathing life into the civil government of the republic, bringing empowerment to the counties at large; in interfacing with the administrative agents and agencies to compel performance and compliance, to bring about balance and restore the natural flow of energy; to empower the civil government, the people; to nurture and infuse this fledgling republic with peace, light and love; to rise above the fear; to be the light;

These members of the sovereign people, awakened into the truth, compelled to service, may apply to accede hereto; upon receipt, acceptance and registration of the application and Public Declarations shall be empowered as a Private Postmaster of a non-independent postal zone, with all of the rights, power and authority of a wholly sovereign nation, with the authority to seat civilian citizen grand juries; to empower judges in the common law, Rangers and Inspectors with the power and authority to compel performance; to make the corrections to bring compliance and honor within the administration.

The power shall reside with the people on the county. It shall take the agreement of no less than three (3) private postmasters to empower a judge or Ranger who shall serve the people under guidelines presented by the Transition Committee and/or interim government.

Repository and Registration of Treaty
The postmaster general of the original, organic post office for the united states of America is hereby designated as repository for the registration, publication and notification of this treaty and Public Declarations of all acceding members in accordance with Article 77 of the *Vienna Convention, 1969*.

Postmaster General for the Post Office for the united states of America
c/o USPS HDQR
475 L'Enfant Plaza SW
Washington, D.C. 20024

Executed this 11th day of May, 2010.
THE UNITED STATES
1500 PENNSYLVANIA AVE. NW
WASHINGTON, D.C. 20020

The Registration And Enforcement

It will be asked: How can this be enforced? In the following chapters, the process by which this has been done ill be described. One has to refer to the fundamental Laws of Commerce that have been discussed before. This process which I undertook was tedious and fortunatley has evolved to be simpler because of what was learned. However, this process which was indeed my revelation is presented here as it identifies much truth and information about the system that substantiates what has been presented so far. But first there is more to learn about the mechanisms that have "captured" humans into the corporate structures.

In this Peace Treaty, it is clearly revealed how the Administrators of the Trusts and the deployment of the military complex has been shifted to create the economic war machines that serve as the economic generators of profit to serve the few at the expense of the many. Here it becomes clear how the energy of the people has been captured to create the great pyramid of debt to serve the needs of the gods through religion so to serve the business plan of the New world Order.

One key ingredients in understanding the process of how the Earthling was manoeuvred into these business structures, and therefore the understanding of how to rectify the relationship as well as enforcing the declaration, is to look deeply into these Trusts. How trust are set up and work is of interest and we now will dedicate a complete chapter to this.

30

IT'S ALL ABOUT TRUST(S)

First And Foremost Is Our Divine Trust

PLANET EARTH is a private business enterprise serving those gods who carefully crafted it. It is not a formal registered organization. It is a fictional entity that I have created. Over centuries, the evolution of commerce has required the creation of fictional entities called corporations to act as the vessels. There are many different types. Of particular interest now is the business enterprise vessel which is called a Trust which is a very old concept of holding titles to what are thought as assets. . Here we will learn more about the origins and implementations of these trusts as they relate to the vessel which is you, the human, and to that which it holds titles to as Beneficiary, your Estate.

You came here with nothing and you leave with nothing. Your stay on Planet Earth is about a divine experience. Right from the beginning, everything is held in Trust, at the Divine Right of Use Today. Everything is held in trust.... everything is about trusts, Implied or Expressed.

The Creator gave man dominion over all things. Dominion over equates to control over NOT ownership. Control over all things, yet not ownership. That is a Divine Right of Use.

A Divine Right of Use of the Divine property/the All of earth held in trust means the entire world we call earth is held in trust, the Divine Trust, for our benefit as Beneficiaries. This **Global Divine Trust is an Implied Trust** as opposed to an Expressed Trust.

In the beginning man was responsible, as a Trustee, for the care and well being of that portion of the Divine Estate upon which he/she exercised their Divine Right of Use as a Beneficiary. He would benefit from it in some way. And usually someone was chosen to administer it according to some defined rules, called a fiduciary.

Through the decades man has given over that Divine fiduciary obligation to legal fiction trustees. There are as many forms of trusteeships as there are people in the world. Some very fair and equitable, say a republic, all the way to a dictatorship, each with various degrees of freedoms and rights, taxes and limitations.

Who is the Trustee responsible for your piece of the Divine Estate, our Global Estate Trust? In America today we have Township Trustees, County Trustees, State Trustees and Federal Trustees just to name a few of the many levels of fiduciaries within the Trusteeship which is involved in the administration of our Divine Estate(s), the Global Estate Trust. Judges, Clerks of Court, Prosecutors and Attorneys all play their own part in the administration of our Global Estate Trust leveraging our Divine Estates to do as they please as we have simply entrusted them to do so. It is our faith and trust in these trustees and fiduciaries that has allowed this to be.

To unravel this intentionally complex Trusteeship of the Global Estate Trust let us begin at the top and work our way down. At the bottom is you and the Vital Statistics Office issued the Certified copy of the Birth Certificate, a security which represents the Divine Estate Trust, therefore they hold the original and are the holder in due course of the estate. They are the Intermediary Agent for the Trust with a <u>fiduciary duty to the Beneficiary of the Estate</u>. and the true beneficiary is you in the flesh and blood.

At the top, the Vatican in their Papal Bull, states dominion over the entire earth, via conquest, and is answerable ONLY to the Divine Spirit. Dominion over means control over, not ownership. The Vatican's un-rebutted claims establish them as the <u>Primary Trustee of the Global Estate Trust</u>, our Divine Inheritance; a very unpopular fact. But a fact that opens a doorway placing the cure for the mis-administration and theft of our Divine Inheritance within our grasp.

The Vatican is the Primary Trustee of the Global Estate Trust. To facilitate the administration of this Global Trust the Vatican established the Universal Postal Union as the Secondary Trustees of the Global Trust charged with dividing the Global Trust into zones and endowing these legal fiction zones with sovereign authority to facilitate the efficient administration of the Global Trust.

The Preamble to the Constitution created the Estate Trust which held the freedoms guaranteed in the Articles of Confederation and the Declaration of Independence in trust for future generations. The Articles of the Constitution established the Trusteeship as well as the powers and limitations thereof. The Congress and Senate were Trustees charged with the Administration of our Divine Inheritance, the Global Estate Trust.

In this 'general post office' seat of government there was established the 'civil administration' called the United States. Civil administration? What do they administrate? Our Divine Estate Trust, the Global Trust, our Divine Inheritance. Remember, we can never OWN anything. We simply have a Divine Right of Use of the property of the Divine Estate, the Global Trust.

So, we the people of this earth have a Divine Right of use of the Global Trust while the civil administration is charged with the administration of our estate for our benefit.

In the world of trusts Civil Administration/Government equals Trusteeship.

So, the entire world is held in trust. The Global Estate Trust, our Divine Inheritance, our birthright is held in trust and is administrated by the various 'governments' who gain their sovereign authority via the Universal Postal Union, the Secondary Trustee of the Global Trust answerable to the Vatican.

In the world of trusts and trust law, rights, duties and obligations are very straight forward, cut and dry, black and white. There are no opinions, secret codes, rules or statutes, period. These are just the facts. There is a chain of command, consequences for your actions, or lack thereof, and accountability.

In this regard, Ican state that it has been a slow and cumbersome process to overcome the out of control momentum of the civil administrators of the world today. There have been countless casualties as a result of our efforts to unravel the illusion; to overcome the programming and fear which fuelled the beast to reach the core where truth and accountability resides.

But first, let us look more closely at this vehicle of commerce called a Trust.

The History Of Trusts

Trusts date back to ancient Egypt, circa 4000 B.C., when the equivalent of today's trust officers were charged with holding, managing, and caring for other people's property. Various prototypes of trust institutions were later developed in second-century Rome, some of which involved the use of property for charitable purposes. Trusts began to evolve into their present form during the eighth century, when English clergymen acted as executors of wills and trusts. Throughout the Middle Ages and into the 17th century, trusts developed under English common law to resemble their current legal structure in the United States.

Roman law had a well-developed concept of the trust (*fideicommissum*) in terms of "testamentary trusts" created by wills but never developed the concept of the "inter vivos trust" that applied while the creator was still alive. This was created by later common law jurisdictions. Personal trust law developed in England at the time of the Crusades, during the 12th and 13th centuries.[]

At the time, land ownership in England was based on the feudal system. When a landowner left England to fight in the Crusades, he needed someone to run his estate in his absence, often to pay and receive feudal dues. To achieve this, he would convey ownership of his lands to an acquaintance, on the understanding that the ownership would be conveyed back on his return. However, Crusaders would often return to find the legal owners' refusal to hand over the property.

Unfortunately for the Crusader, English common law did not recognize his claim. As far as the King's courts were concerned, the land belonged to the trustee, who was under no obligation to return it. The Crusader had no legal claim. The disgruntled Crusader would then petition the king, who would refer the matter to his Lord Chancellor. The Lord Chancellor could do what was "just" and "equitable", and had the power to decide a case according to his conscience. At this time, the principle of equity was born.

The Lord Chancellor would consider it "unconscionable" that the legal owner could go back on his word and deny the claims of the Crusader (the "true" owner). Therefore, he would find in favor of the returning Crusader. Over time, it became known that the Lord Chancellor's court (the Court of Chancery) would continually recognize the claim of a returning Crusader. The legal owner would hold the land for the benefit of the original owner, and would be compelled to convey it back to him when requested. The Crusader was the "beneficiary" and the acquaintance the "trustee". The term *use of land* was coined, and in time developed into what we now know as a *trust*.

Also, the Primogeniture system could be considered as a form of trust. In Primogeniture system, the first born male inherited all the property and "usually assumes the responsibility of trusteeship of the property and of adjudicating attendant disputes."

The Waqf (***http://en.wikipedia.org/wiki/Waqf***) meaning confinement and prohibition is an equivalent institution in Islamic law, restricted to charitable trusts.

"Antitrust law" emerged in the 19th century when industries created monopolistic trusts by entrusting their shares to a board of trustees in exchange for shares of equal value with dividend rights; these boards could then enforce a monopoly. However, trusts were used in this case because a corporation could not own other companies' stock and thereby become a holding company without a "special act of the legislature". Holding companies were used after the restriction on owning other companies' shares was lifted.

The trust is widely considered to be the most innovative contribution to the English legal system. Today, trusts play a significant role in most common law systems, and their success has led some civil law jurisdictions to incorporate trusts into their civil codes. France, for example, recently added a similar, though not quite comparable, notion to its own law with *la fiducie*, which was modified in 2009; *la fiducie*, unlike the trust, is a contract. Trusts are widely used internationally, especially in countries within the English law sphere of influence, and whilst most civil law jurisdictions do not generally contain the concept of a trust within their legal systems, they do recognize the concept under the Hague Convention on the Law Applicable to Trusts and on their Recognition (to the extent that they are signatories thereto). The Hague Convention on the Law Applicable to Trusts and on their Recognition also regulates conflict of trusts.

Although trusts are often associated with intrafamily wealth transfers, they have become very important in American capital markets, particularly through pension funds (essentially always trusts) and mutual funds (often trusts).

Setting Up A Trust: The Mechanics

Basic principles of a Trust Property of any sort may be held on trust, but growth assets are more commonly placed into trust (for tax and estate planning benefits). The uses of trusts are many and varied. Trusts may be created during a person's life (usually by a trust instrument) or after death in a will. In a relevant sense, a trust can be viewed as a generic form of a corporation where the settlors (investors) are also the beneficiaries. This is particularly evident in the Delaware business trust, which could theoretically, with the language in the "governing instrument", be organized as a cooperative corporation, limited liability corporation, or perhaps even a nonprofit corporation. One of the most significant aspects of trusts is the ability to partition and shield assets from the trustee, multiple beneficiaries, and their respective creditors (particularly the trustee's creditors), making it "bankruptcy remote", and leading to its use in pensions, mutual funds, and asset securitization.

Creation of a Trust Trusts may be created by the expressed intentions of the settlor (express trusts) or they may be created by operation of law known as implied trusts. Implied trusts is one created by a court of equity because of acts or situations of the parties. Implied trusts are divided into two categories resulting and constructive. A resulting trust is implied by the law to work out the presumed intentions of the parties, but it does not take into consideration their expressed intent. A constructive trust is a trust implied by law to work out justice between the parties, regardless of their intentions.

Typically a trust can be created in the following ways:
1. a written trust instrument created by the settlor and signed by both the settlor and the trustees (often referred to as an *inter vivos* or "living trust");
2. an oral declaration;
3. the will of a decedent, usually called a testamentary trust; or
4. a court order (for example in family proceedings).

In some jurisdictions certain types of assets may not be the subject of a trust without a written document.

Formalities of a Trust Generally, a trust requires three certainties:
1. **Intention**. There must be a clear intention to create a trust
2. **Subject Matter**. The property subject to the trust must be clearly identified One may not, for example, settle "the majority of my estate", as the precise extent cannot be ascertained. Trust property may be any form of specific property, be it <u>real</u> or <u>personal</u>, <u>tangible</u> or <u>intangible</u>. It is often, for example, real estate, shares or cash.
3. **Objects**. The beneficiaries of the trust must be clearly identified, or at least be ascertainable. In the case of discretionary trusts, where the trustees have power to decide who the beneficiaries will be, the settlor must have described a clear **class** of beneficiaries. Beneficiaries may include people not born at the date of the trust (for example, "my future grandchildren"). Alternatively, the object of a trust could be a charitable purpose rather than specific beneficiaries.

Trustees The trustee may be either a person or a legal entity such as a company. A trust may have one or multiple trustees. A trustee has many rights and responsibilities; these vary from trust to trust depending on the type of the trust. A trust generally will not fail solely for want of a trustee. Where a trust is absent any trustees, a court may appoint a trustee, or in Ireland the trustee may be any administrator of a charity to which the trust is related. Trustees are usually appointed in the document (instrument) which creates the trust.

A trustee may be held personally liable for certain problems which arise with the trust. For example, if a trustee does not properly invest trust monies to expand the trust fund, he or she may be liable for the difference. There are two main types of trustees, professional and non-professional. Liability is different for the two types.

The trustees are the legal owners of the trust's property. The trustees administer the affairs attendant to the trust. The trust's affairs may include investing the assets of the trust, ensuring trust property is preserved and productive for the beneficiaries, accounting for and reporting periodically to the beneficiaries concerning all transactions associated with trust property, filing any required tax returns on behalf of the trust, and other duties. In some cases, the trustees must make decisions as to whether beneficiaries should receive trust assets for their benefit. The circumstances in which this discretionary authority is exercised by trustees is usually provided for under the terms of the trust instrument. The trustee's duty is to determine in the specific instance of a beneficiary request whether to provide any funds and in what manner.

By default, being a trustee is an unpaid job. In modern times trustees are often lawyers, bankers or other professionals who will not work for free. Therefore, often a trust document will state specifically that trustees are entitled to reasonable payment for their work.

Trusts are often confused with legal persons, but are mere *relationships*, not entities. Thus, they have no legal existence independent from the trustee and his or her ownership of the subject matter of the trust. In order to sue a trust, one must sue the trustee in his or her capacity as trustee for a specific trust; conversely, if the trust needs to sue someone, the lawsuit must be brought by the trustee in his or her capacity as such.

Beneficiaries The beneficiaries are beneficial (or **equitable**) owners of the trust property. Either immediately or eventually, the beneficiaries will receive income from the trust property, or they will receive the property itself. The extent of a beneficiary's interest depends on the wording of the trust document. One beneficiary may be entitled to income (for example, interest from a bank account), whereas another may be entitled to the entirety of the trust property when he attains the age of twenty-five years. The settlor has much discretion when creating the trust, subject to some limitations imposed by law.

Implied and Express Trust Implied trust. An implied trust, as distinct from an express trust, is created where some of the legal requirements for an express trust are not met, but an intention on behalf of the parties to create a trust can be presumed to exist. A resulting trust may be deemed to be present where a trust instrument is not properly drafted and a portion of the equitable title has not been provided for. In such a case, the law may raise a resulting trust for the benefit of the grantor (the creator of the trust). In other words, the grantor may be deemed to be a beneficiary of the portion of the equitable title that was not properly provided for in the trust document.

More Trust Basics: Relationships

Some of the earliest Trusts date back to the Middle Ages. They were first widely used during the Crusades and other foreign campaigns, when prolonged absences were commonplace. Over the centuries, the concept of Trusts developed in countries using the English Common Law system. Today, Trusts are used for a wide variety of purposes. The following definition of a Trust is taken from a noted author on the subject of Trusts, Sir Arthur Underhill:

"A trust is an equitable obligation binding a person (called a Trustee) to deal with property over which he has control (called the trust property) for the benefit of persons (who are called beneficiaries) of whom he may himself be one, and any one of whom may enforce the obligation"

A Trust arises when a person known as the **Settlor** transfers legal title to property to another person known as the **Trustee,** with instructions as to how the property is to be used for the benefit of named persons known as **Beneficiaries**. To be valid, a Trust must have a Settlor, a Trustee and identifiable beneficiaries. The beneficiaries may be identified by name, or as being members of a class - for example, "my children" or "my grandchildren". A Trust cannot be created until legal title to some property has been transferred to the Trustee. Although the Trustee has legal title to the Trust property, beneficial ownership rests with the beneficiaries (beneficiary). Assets of all kinds can be placed in a Trust, including bank accounts, real estate, stocks and bonds, mutual fund units, limited partnership interests and private businesses.

In common law legal systems, a **trust** is a relationship whereby property (real or personal, tangible or intangible) is held by one party for the benefit of another. A trust conventionally arises when property is transferred by one party to be held by another party for the benefit of a third party, although it is also possible for a legal owner to create a trust of property without transferring it to anyone else, simply by declaring that the property will henceforth be held for the benefit of the beneficiary. A trust is created by a settlor (archaically known, in the context of trusts of land, as the *feoffor to uses*), who transfers some or all of his property to a trustee (archaically known, in the context of land, as the *feoffee to uses*), who holds that trust property (or *trust corpus*) for the benefit of the beneficiaries (archaically known as the *cestui que use*, or *cestui que trust*). In the case of the self-declared trust, the settlor and trustee are the same person. The trustee has legal title to the trust property, but the beneficiaries have equitable title to the trust property (separation of control and ownership). The trustee owes a fiduciary duty to the beneficiaries, who are the "beneficial" owners of the trust property. (Note: A trustee may be either a natural person, or an artificial person (such as a company or a public body), and there may be a single trustee or multiple co-trustees. There may be a single beneficiary or multiple beneficiaries. The settlor may himself be a beneficiary.)

The trust is governed by the terms under which it was created. The terms of the trust are usually written down in a trust instrument or deed but, in England, it is not necessary for them to be written down to be legally binding, except in the case of land. The terms of the trust must specify what property is to be transferred into the trust (certainty of subject-matter), and who the beneficiaries will be of that trust (certainty of objects). It may also set out the detailed powers and duties of the trustees (such as powers of investment, powers to vary the interests of the beneficiaries, and powers to appoint new trustees). The trust is also governed by local law. The trustee is obliged to administer the trust in accordance with both the terms of the trust and the governing law. In the United States, the settlor is also called the trustor, grantor, donor or creator. In some other jurisdictions, the settlor may also be known as the "founder".

While there are many different uses of Trusts, there are two main categories. **Living Trusts** (also referred to as inter vivos trusts) and **Testamentary Trusts**.

To fund a Living Trust, ownership of assets must be transferred from the Settlor's name into the Trustee's name. The Trust can be funded with cash, stocks, bonds or almost any other asset. As mentioned above, the Trustee has legal title to the Trust property, but beneficial ownership rests with the beneficiaries. One of the advantages of a Living Trust is that the Settlor may choose to be the Trustee, or one of several co-Trustees. This may be important to individuals who want continued control of the assets while they are alive. This is often the case when a family business is placed in a Trust, and the Settlor wants to continue to have some influence on the business.

A Testamentary Trust is created under the terms of a Will, and only operates on the death of an individual (the "Testator"). Prior to the testator's death, the terms of the Trust can be modified, or the Trust can be removed, simply by having a new Will prepared. Testamentary Trusts are funded from the proceeds of the deceased's estate. The terms of a Testamentary Trust can be kept confidential until the Testator dies. After death, when the Will is probated (becomes a valid Will), it becomes a public document.

	Living Trust	Testamentary Trust
How Established	Created during an individuals lifetime and takes effect when the Trust is funded.	Created under the terms of a Will and takes effect after the death of the Testator.
How assets are placed into the Trust	Assets of a living person are re-registered from the Settlor's name into the the Trustee's name.	Funded with assets from the deceased's estate.
Who can be Trustee	The Trustee can be anyone, including the Settlor.	The Trustee can be anyone, but is often the person who acted as the deceased's executor.

Discretionary Vs Non-Discretionary Trusts Discretionary Trusts may provide the Trustee with the power to pay part or all of the income to an income beneficiary, or to pay capital to a capital beneficiary prior to the distribution date. In a Non-Discretionary Trust, the trust document provides the Trustee with the amount of the income payments, or how much capital can be paid to any beneficiary prior to the distribution of the Trust.

What is the Trust Agreement? The Trust Agreement is a written document that sets out the terms of a Living Trust. In the case of a Testamentary Trust, the terms of the Trust are contained in specific clauses within a Will. These clauses state what property is transferred to the Trustee(s), the powers and obligations of the Trustee(s), and most importantly, how and under what circumstances the income and the capital of the Trust will be distributed. The Trust Agreement or Trust Clauses within a Will should clearly set out what the individual wants done, and give sufficient power to the trustees to carry out their duties. Generally, a domestic Trust is governed by the law of the province in which it is administered. Similarly, an international Trust is governed by the laws of the foreign jurisdiction in which it is located. When considering the terms to put in a Trust Agreement, the key question is, "What if?"...

- What if the named beneficiary doesn't survive you?
- What if the condition for taking a gift is not fulfilled?
- What if the capital beneficiary dies before the income beneficiary?
- What if it makes sense to sell the Trust property and invest in something altogether different, or collapse the Trust?

What is the Role of the Trustee? A Trust is an agreement for the transfer of property from the Settlor to the Trustees, for the benefit of the beneficiaries. The Trustees become the legal owners of the property, with their ability to deal with the property limited by the Trust Agreement and Trust law. The Trustees have the following legal obligations:
- Trustees cannot transfer rights, powers, or obligations to a third party. They must act for themselves and not delegate powers.
- As the owners of the Trust property, Trustees have all the legal and equitable obligations to invest and manage the Trust property.

- Trustees must ensure that the income and capital of the Trust is distributed in accordance with the Trust agreement.
- Trustees are personally liable for acts or omissions which adversely affect the Trust or the beneficiaries.
- Trustees must deal impartially with the beneficiaries.
- Trustees cannot use the property in any way to benefit themselves. For example they are prohibited from purchasing property from the Trust unless specifically permitted in the agreement. However, under Trust legislation, Executors and Trustees are entitled to compensation for their services.

What is a Fiduciary? A fiduciary duty (from Latin *fiduciarius*, meaning "(holding) in trust"; from *fides*, meaning "faith", and *fiducia*, meaning "trust") is a legal or ethical relationship of confidence or trust between two or more parties. Typically, a fiduciary prudently takes care of money for another person. One party, for example a corporate trust company or the trust department of a bank, acts in a fiduciary capacity to the other one, who for example has funds entrusted to it for investment. In a fiduciary relationship, one person, in a position of vulnerability, justifiably vests confidence, good faith, reliance and trust in another whose aid, advice or protection is sought in some matter. In such a relation good conscience requires the fiduciary to act at all times for the sole benefit and interest of the one who trusts.

A fiduciary duty is the highest standard of care at either equity or law. A fiduciary (abbreviation *fid*) is expected to be extremely loyal to the person to whom he owes the duty (the "principal"): he must not put his personal interests before the duty, and must not profit from his position as a fiduciary, unless the principal consents.

In English common law the fiduciary relation is arguably the most important concept within the portion of the legal system known as equity. In the United Kingdom, the Judicature Acts merged the courts of equity (historically based in England's Court of Chancery) with the courts of common law, and as a result the concept of fiduciary duty also became available in common law courts.

When a fiduciary duty is imposed, equity requires a different, arguably stricter, standard of behavior than the comparable tortious duty of care at common law. It is said the fiduciary has a duty not to be in a situation where personal interests and fiduciary duty conflict, a duty not to be in a situation where his fiduciary duty conflicts with another fiduciary duty, and a duty not to profit from his fiduciary position without knowledge and consent. A fiduciary ideally would not have a conflict of interest. It has been said that fiduciaries must conduct themselves "at a level higher than that trodden by the crowd" and that "[t]he distinguishing or overriding duty of a fiduciary is the obligation of undivided loyalty."

Relationships The most common circumstance where a fiduciary duty will arise is between a trustee, whether real or juristic, and a beneficiary. The trustee to whom property is legally committed is the legal—i.e., common law—owner of all such property. The beneficiary, at law, has no legal title to the trust; however, the trustee is bound by equity to suppress his own interests and administer the property only for the benefit of the beneficiary. In this way, the beneficiary obtains the use of property without being its technical owner.

Others, such as corporate directors, may be held to a fiduciary duty similar in some respects to that of a trustee. This happens when, for example, the directors of a bank are trustees for the depositors, the directors of a corporation are trustees for the stockholders or a guardian is trustee of his ward's property. A person in a sensitive position sometimes protects himself from possible conflict of interest charges by setting up a *blind trust*, placing his financial affairs in the hands of a fiduciary and giving up all right to know about or intervene in their handling.

The fiduciary functions of trusts and agencies are commonly performed by a **trust company**, such as a *commercial bank*, organized for that purpose. In the United States, the Office of Thrift Supervision (OTS), an agency of the **United States Department of the Treasury,** is the primary regulator of the fiduciary activities of federal savings associations.

Primary Elements of Duty A fiduciary, such as the administrator, executor or guardian of an estate, may be legally required to file with a probate court or judge a surety bond, called a **fiduciary bond** or **probate bond**, to guarantee faithful performance of his duties. One of those duties may be to prepare, generally under oath, an *inventory* of the tangible or intangible property of the estate, describing the items or classes of property and usually placing a valuation on them.

Accountability A fiduciary will be liable to account if proven to have acquired a profit, benefit or gain from the relationship by one of three means:[1]
- In circumstances of conflict of duty and interest
- In circumstances of conflict of duty to one person and duty to another person
- By taking advantage of the fiduciary position.

Therefore, it is said the fiduciary has a duty not to be in a situation where personal interests and fiduciary duty conflict, a duty not to be in a situation where his fiduciary duty conflicts with another fiduciary duty, and not to profit from his fiduciary position without express knowledge and consent. A fiduciary cannot have a conflict of interest.

A fiduciary's duty must not conflict with another fiduciary duty. Conflicts between one fiduciary duty and another fiduciary duty arise most often when a lawyer or an agent, such as a real estate agent, represent more than one client, and the interests of those clients conflict. This would occur when a lawyer attempts to represent both the plaintiff and the defendant in the same matter, for example. The rule comes from the logical conclusion that a fiduciary cannot make the principal's interests a top priority if he has two principals and their interests are diametrically opposed; he must balance the interests, which is not acceptable to equity. Therefore, the conflict of duty and duty rule is really an extension of the conflict of interest and duty rules.

No-profit rule A fiduciary must not profit from the fiduciary position. This includes any benefits or profits which, although unrelated to the fiduciary position, came about because of an opportunity that the fiduciary position afforded. It is unnecessary that the principal would have been unable to make the profit; if the fiduciary makes a profit, by virtue of his role as fiduciary for the principal, then the fiduciary must report the profit to the principal. If the principal consents then the fiduciary may keep the benefit. If this requirement is not met then the property is deemed by the court to be held by the fiduciary on constructive trust for the principal.

Breaches of duty and remedies Conduct by a fiduciary may be deemed *constructive fraud* when it is based on acts, omissions or concealments considered fraudulent and that gives one an advantage against the other because such conduct—though not actually fraudulent, dishonest or deceitful—demands redress for reasons of public policy. Breach of fiduciary duty may occur in insider trading, when an insider or a related party makes trades in a corporation's securities based on material non-public information obtained during the performance of the insider's duties at the corporation. Breach of fiduciary duty by a lawyer with regard to a client, if negligent, may be a form of legal malpractice; if intentional, it may be remedied in equity.

Where a principal can establish both a fiduciary duty and a breach of that duty, through violation of the above rules, the court will find that the benefit gained by the fiduciary should be returned to the principal because it would be unconscionable to allow the fiduciary to retain the benefit by employing his strict common law legal rights. This will be the case, unless the fiduciary can show there was full disclosure of the conflict of interest or profit and that the principal fully accepted and freely consented to the fiduciary's course of action.

Remedies will differ according to the type of damage or benefit. They are usually distinguished between proprietary remedies, dealing with property, and personal remedies, dealing with pecuniary (monetary) compensation.

Constructive trusts Where the unconscionable gain by the fiduciary is in an easily identifiable form, such as the recording contract discussed above, the usual remedy will be the already discussed constructive trust. Constructive trusts pop up in many aspects of equity, not just in a remedial sense, but, in this sense, what is meant by a constructive trust is that the court has created and imposed a duty on the fiduciary to hold the money in safekeeping until it can be rightfully transferred to the principal.

Account of profits An account of profits is another potential remedy. It is usually used where the breach of duty was ongoing or when the gain is hard to identify. The idea of an account of profits is that the fiduciary profited unconscionably by virtue of the fiduciary position, so any profit made should be transferred to the principal. It may sound like a constructive trust at first, but it is not.

An account for profits is the appropriate remedy when, for example, a senior employee has taken advantage of his fiduciary position by conducting his own company on the side and has run up quite a lot of profits over a period of time, profits which he wouldn't have been able to make without his fiduciary position in the original company. The calculation of profits in this sense can be extremely difficult, because profit due to fiduciary position must be separated from profit due to the fiduciary's own effort and ingenuity.

Compensatory damages Compensatory damages are also available. Accounts of profits can be hard remedies to establish, therefore, a plaintiff will often seek compensation (damages) instead. Courts of equity initially had no power to award compensatory damages, which traditionally were a remedy at common law, but legislation and case law has changed the situation so compensatory damages may

The Vatican And The Crown Are Primary Trustees

Statutory law is imposed upon basis of the 'property right', and that property right is the property right of the corporate Crown in Canada, and corporate State (be it a State or the UNITED STATES) in the USA. The same scheme can be found in any country that is a subject country of the Pontiff of Rome's Holy Roman Empire. Thus, in actuality, the assumed 'property right' is that of the corporate Holy Roman Empire, as the Crown or incorporated State is an agency for the Holy Roman Empire.

The 'Crown' is the administrative corporation of the Pontiff of Rome owned City of London, the financial, legal and professional standards capitol of/for the Vatican, The City of London is a square mile area within Greater London, England, and is an independent city-state. In the USA, the administrative corporation for the Pontiff of Rome is the UNITED STATES, and that corporation administers the Vatican capitol, for, primarily, military purposes, called Columbia, or the District of Columbia. The UNITED STATES also administers the 50 sub-corporate States of the United States of America, identified with the 2 cap letters – CA, OR, WA, brought down to the administrative levels of the Postal Codes.

Adult humans are brought into the corporate world by way of the fiction name, as imprinted on the copy of the birth certificate received from Provincial/State Vital Statistics, or to whatever source. Although the birth certificate is of somewhat recent origin and used to formally offer 'citizens' as chattel in bankruptcy to the Pope's Holy Roman Empire owned Rothschilds' Banking System, the false use of the family name goes back into the Middle Ages in England. Thus, it is with the family name made a primary, or surname, (example - Mister Jones), and the given names of the child (example - Peter) made a reference name to the primary name. This is the reverse or mirror image to reality. A 'family name' is NOT a man's name - it is a name of a clan - a blood relationship.

As people are then 'forced' or 'obliged' to use that name in all commercial and Government dealings and communications 99.99% of the human inhabitants of North America (and most of the world) do, supposedly 'voluntarily' attach themselves the free will adult human, to the Crown/State owned property, called the 'legal identity name' as an accessory attached to property owned by Another party. Think of a ship under tow by another ship. Which captain decides what route the ships will take? The 'legal name/strawman' is the tow rope, and the towing ship is the corporate (make-believe ship at sea) Crown of the City of London. As an attachment to the legal name owned by the Crown, you are the towed ship, and your vessel captain, your free will mind, is now a subservient crewmember to the captain of the Crown.

The State or Crown does not give us authority, grant, license, permission or leave to use the Crown or State owned legal identity name. Thus, our use of it as an adult free will man (male or female) is a form of 'theft' against a maritime jurisdiction entity (all incorporated bodies are 'make-believe ships at sea'). In maritime law, the accused is guilty until proven innocent. This allows the Roman Law system, which we have, to impose 'involuntary servitude' upon an adult man. Involuntary servitude simply means a slave stripped of granted rights of a slave called a citizen, subject or freeman. This stripped rights included 'due process of law' - no jury trial, and charges where no harm has been done against another man, or his property with criminal intent.

We see this Roman Law within the US 13th Amendment (#2) instituted in the mid 1860's: *"Neither slavery nor involuntary servitude, except as a punishment for crime whereof the party shall have been duly convicted,"* The crime with which you have been convicted is 'unauthorized use' of the State's or Crown's intellectual property - the legal identity name.

The Crown/State then invokes the legal maxim, accessio cedit principali, [an accessory attached to a principal becomes the property of the owner of the principal], where the principal is the legal identity name as 'intellectual property'. The owner is the corporation called the Crown/State, or UNITED STATES, and the accessory is the free will human who has supposedly volunteered himself to be 'property by attachment' of the Crown/State. An adult human who is property is, and by any other name, of 'slave status', be it citizen, subject or freeman.

The relationship between free will man and Government/corporate bodies is contractual are incorrect. In the scenario so described, as a slave, one's property in possession, including body and labor, belongs to the slave owner 100%. And, the property right is a bundle of rights - own, use, sell, gift, bequeath and hypothecate property.

Thus, ALL 'income' resulting from the owned human slave's mental and/or physical labor belongs to the slave owner. That which is left with or granted to the slave for his own use and maintenance is called a 'benefit'. In Canada, the 'return of income' [the phrase itself tells the story] is called a T1 'tax and benefits package'. The T1 or IRS (USA)1040 is an accounting by the slave of his fruits of labor that belongs to the slave owner, and the prescribed 'benefits' that he may keep or have back from withholding. Thus, all income tax cases against the people', in reality, result from fraud, illegal concealment and theft by the accused slave of the slave owner's 'property'.

Going back to an above paragraph, we find that the attachment of oneself to the Crown/State owned name is 'assumed to be voluntary', as the Crown/State has no valid right to impose slavery upon adult humans against their will, except as stated in the next paragraph. Anyone working as an employee is in a contract of voluntary servitude - direction and time control by, and obedience and loyalty to, the employer. Until we 'assumed to be slaves' get our heads around this key to the lock that holds our chains of slavery around our necks and ankles, we will continue to attempt to swim with that 100 lb ball chained to our leg.

Another factor of the use of the Roman Law system is contained within the 1860's 13th Amendment to the US Constitution, the Constitution of the corporate UNITED STATES, [and not the 13th Amendment of the US Republic inserted around 1819]. In the later 13th amendment, it says: "Neither slavery nor involuntary servitude, except as a punishment for crime whereof the party shall have been duly convicted, shall exist within the United States, or any place subject to their jurisdiction." Notice that this applies only to the corporate body called the UNITED STATES.

All corporate bodies are make-believe ships at sea, and are thus, internally, under maritime law, [incorrectly called 'admiralty law', unless applied to the military]. In maritime law, an accused is guilty unless proven innocent. Thus, a free will adult man who uses, without authority, the property of a corporate body is under maritime jurisdiction. This makes a free will man who uses a corporate Crown or corporate State owned legal identity name a 'convicted criminal', and thus subject to the imposition of slavery, involuntary servitude.

You, as a child, were Crown or State property by way of the birth registry, and thus, you could use Crown or State property, the legal identity name. When you became an adult, as a vessel on the 'sea of life' as a sovereign captain/free will mind, you no longer had a right to use (as an 'identity' name) that Crown or State owned legal identity name.

However, under the 'property right' of a slave owner in regard to property in the possession of an owned slave, a 'demand' for the property by the slave owner, or the slave owner's agent (such as the IRS, or county tax collector, or for a court imposed fine), is all that is necessary, without regard to due process of law. Remember, ALL that a slave possesses belongs to the slave owner. In this context you are NOT slaves but it is important to understands that Government, and its employees, judges and officers SEE you as a SLAVE. Further, when any 'officer' of the corporate body, be it 'peace officer or police', all the way to King or President choose to declare someone 'homo sacer' (meaning a man who has been stripped of his status of 'person' - that being an obedient corporate slave member of the corporate body politic) - he is stripped of the rights of due process of law, and can be fined, punished, tortured or killed without repercussion to the officer, or officer involved. This happens all the time in the world of the Holy Roman Empire.

And so it that you powers, and your Divine Trust where your property is registered for use, is compromised because you allowed this to be by way of good faith and trust that the Trustee, who represents GOD and GOD's Code (word) and that coprorated body beneath that corporate structure, will act in accordance with what you believe to be God's law (Word) to your benefit.

In truth, you simply believed this was correct, and allowed this to be by acceptance. Of course the issue is that under the universal laws of commerce, your contract to become a slave, and lose control of your Trust, was not fully disclosed.

The Divine Estate Is An Implied Trust

An implied trust, as distinct from an express trust, is created where some of the legal requirements for an express trust are not met, but an intention on behalf of the parties to create a trust can be presumed to exist. A resulting trust may be deemed to be present where a trust instrument is not properly drafted and a portion of the equitable title has not been provided for. In such a case, the law may raise a resulting trust for the benefit of the grantor (the creator of the trust). In other words, the grantor may be deemed to be a beneficiary of the portion of the equitable title that was not properly provided for in the trust document

An implied trust is a type of situation that arises when the courts find evidence that there is a basis for what amounts to a trust after reviewing the types of arrangements put in place by a grantor. Not considered a formal trust arrangement, the implied trust is supported by the collection of financial plans and preparations made by the grantor to provide for loved ones once he or she passes away. A court will look at the cumulative evidence and, if the information meets the criteria of an implied trust, will proceed with the settlement of the estate accordingly.

Within the broad definition of an implied trust, several types of trust arrangements may emerge. One of these forms is known as a statutory trust. With this arrangement, the trustee associated with the will or other documents left behind by the grantor is charged with the responsibility of selling properties related to the estate, with the proceeds from those sales ultimately going to a beneficiary. In the interim, the trustee manages the property, which may be in the form of real estate holdings, or some sort of business operation. The idea is to hold onto the property and secure the best possible price for the holdings allowing the beneficiary to receive more benefit from the arrangement in the long run.

Another form of trust, the **cestui que** is a trust that was used rooted in medieval law. It became a vehicle for a legal method to avoid the feudal (medieval) incidents (payments) to an overlord, while leaving the land for the use of another, who owed nothing to the lord. The law of cestui que tended to defer jurisdiction to courts of equity as opposed to common law courts. The cestui que was often utilized by persons who might be absent from the kingdom for an extended time (as on a Crusade, or a business adventure), and who held tenancy to the land, and owed feudal incidents to a lord. The land could be left for the use of a third party, who did not owe the incidents to the lord. This legal status was also invented to circumvent the Statute of Mortmain. That statute was intended to end the relatively common practice of leaving real property to the Church at the time of the owner's death. Since the Church never died, the land never left the "dead hand" ("Mortmain" or Church). An alternative explanation of "mortmain" was that an owner from generations earlier was still dictating land use years after death, by leaving it to the Church. Hence the term "dead hand." Before the Statute of Mortmain, large amounts of land were bequeathed to the Church, which never relinquished it. This was in contradistinction to normal lands which could be inherited in a family line or revert to a lord or the Crown upon death of the tenant. Church land had been a source of contention between the Crown and the Church for centuries. Cestui que use allowed religious orders to inhabit land, while the title resided with a corporation of lawyers or other entities, who nominally had no relation to the Church.

Constitutional Relationship To Current Trusts

The Constitution for the United States is a document of dual nature: in that it is a trust document, and it is the articles of incorporation and created a unique trust res and estate of inheritance. It is a tenant of law that in order to determine the intent of a writing one must look to the title, the Empowerment Clause in statute, which in the case of the Constitution is the Preamble. In writing the Constitution the founders followed the common law of England which stretches back some 1000 years. The Preamble fulfills the requirements necessary to establish a trust. It identifies the Grantor(s), Statement of Purpose, Grantee(s), Statement of Intent, Written Indenture, and the name of the entity being created and is written and constructed as a trust so that it would have the thrust of ageless law. In this declaration, it states:

"WE THE PEOPLE (Grantors) of the United States (from or out of) in Order to form a more perfect union, establish justice, provide for the common defence, promote the general welfare and secure the Blessings of Liberty (statement of Purpose) to ourselves and our posterity (Grantees/heirs unnamed), Do Ordain and establish (Statement of Intent) this constitution (Written Indenture) for the United States of America (name of the entity being created)."

The trust res (contents) is in the Articles of the Confederation and the Declaration of Independence. The intent of the constitution was to bequeath freedom, life, liberty and the pursuit of happiness to themselves and their posterity. The founders intended to secure and pass on the sovereignty of the people to the people of future generations of Americans, in perpetuity. One's rights are derived from the land upon which one stands and your relation, or status, to that land. In America these rights originated with the Articles of Confederation and the Declaration of Independence and are attached to the land called America (The Laws of Real Property). Our status, or relation to that land, is determined by the laws of Descent and Distribution. The right to freedom, life, liberty and the pursuit of happiness are Our inheritance bequeathed to us via the Constitution of the United States of America.

The constitution granted the government the power and authority to administrate and to carry on corporate functions. Under the common law, inherent rights cannot devolve to a 'body politic' through a corporation. Rights only devolve to human beings is through and by way of a trust. Under the constitutional law, in order to determine the meaning of a written instrument the court must look to the title. In this case, once again, it is the Preamble. Pursuant to the laws of real property that have been existence from the beginning, the Preamble clearly shows a freehold in fee simple absolute in it. Freeholds in fee simple were instruments of trust, not corporate. "Our Posterity" cannot be speaking of a corporate entity as posterity can only mean a living man/woman, by birth/nativity.

The Articles of the Constitution are the Articles of Incorporation that established congress as Trustees of the Trust and defines their power and authority as well as their limitations. Annexed to the Constitutional Trust is a will like structure, the Amendments. The Trust and the trust res were already in existence when the will/codicil (Amendments) were added some four years later. The Amendments do not constitute the Trust in fact, they are annexed to the Trust as a codicil (a supplement or addition to the will, not necessarily disposing of the entire estate, but modifying, explaining or otherwise qualifying the will in some way.)

A Trust, once completed and in force cannot be amended or altered without the consent of the parties in interest except under reserved power of amendment and alteration. An amendment is ordinarily possible by parties in interest and against parties without vested interest. Prior to the 14th Amendment the freeborn inhabitants, citizens of the states were the parties in interest. The 14th Amendment created the 14th Amendment legal fiction citizen who do not have a vested interest in the trust or the trust res.

The 14th Amendment can be viewed as a codicil to the will that republished the constitution with new meaning, changed the intent behind it and turned it into a testamentary instrument with capabilities of being used against the free born inhabitants through a seemingly voluntary revocation.

Thus the freeholders, Beneficiaries to the trust have been tricked and coerced by the Trustees into Testifying against themselves when they apply for an S.S. #, drivers permit, marriage license or when they sign an IRS 1040 form, which the Trustees have mislead them to believe are mandatory. When one applies for a Social Security number, provide evidence of birth and claims to be a United States citizen, a party with no vested interest in a freehold, the trust or the trust res, one literally declared the free born inhabitant to be deceased; the decedent retains no interest in the property and that you, in your dual capacity as a legal fiction citizen are now the executor of the estate. It is here that the **cestui que** implied trust shows its flexibility to the creators.

The Trustees have breached the trust having amended the will for their own personal profit and gain at the expense of the true heirs. The freeholders/ Beneficiary has unwittingly, without full disclosure, become the executor and the Trustees have become the Beneficiaries to the trust through the Laws of Donations, effectively stealing Our inheritance.

A breach of trust of fiduciary duty by a Trustee is a violation of correlative right of the Cestui Que Trust and gives rise to the correlative cause of action on the part of the Beneficiary for any loss to the estate Trust. This rule is applicable in respect to both positive acts or negligence constituting a breach of fiduciary duty by the Trustee. A Trustee's breach of fiduciary duty falls within the maxim that 'equity will not aid one who comes into court with unclean hands.'

When the Trustee's breach is by an act of omission the beneficiary can question the propriety of the Trustee. The Beneficiary had to have full disclosure, full knowledge of the material facts and circumstances. A Beneficiary must have had knowledge of and understood their rights and have no obligation to search the public records to obtain said knowledge.

The Trustees have committed acts of omission, mis-representation, deceit and deception in order to mislead and coerce us into giving up our beneficial interest in the trust and the trust res. The Trustees have compelled the free born inhabitants, freeholders in fee simple, to accept the benefits 'under the will' perverted by the 14th Amendment, without freedom of choice for failure of full disclosure thereby precluding our enforcement of contractual rights in property bequeathed to us by the will. The Trustees are trying to repudiate the Trust, employing a lifetime of propaganda and programming and enforced through threats, violence and coercion, and failing to provide notice to the Beneficiaries of the repudiation which must be 'brought home.'

The Doctrine of Election in connection with testamentary instruments is the principle that one who is given a benefit 'under the will' must choose between accepting the benefits and asserting some other claim against the testator's estate or against the property disposed of by the will. A Testamentary Beneficiaries right to elect whether to take 'under the will' or 'against the will' in case he has some inconsistent claim against the testator's estate, is personal to him; is a personal privilege which may be controlled by the creditors of the Beneficiary. They can claim no right or interest in the estate contrary to the debtor's election and may have no right of a legacy or devise to their debtor if he elected to take against the will.

Acceptance of benefits 'under the will' constitutes an election which will preclude the devisee from enforcing contractual rights in property bequeathed the will. This rule is, of course, subject to the qualifications that acceptance of a benefit 'under the will' when made in ignorance of the Beneficiaries rights or a mis-apprehension, mis-representation as to the condition of the Testator's estate does not constitute an election.

In the beginning God gave man dominion over all things, Beneficiaries of the Divine Trust. The Founding fathers of the United States of America created the constitution for the United States, an estate trust, to pass on sovereignty of the people to the people of future generations, in perpetuity.

Three Cestui Que Trusts Are Created By Vatican And State

In Canada and America today, upon giving birth a mother is compelled, without full disclosure, to apply for the **creation of the first Cestui Que Vie** trust, creating a 14th Amendment paper citizen of the United States. Upon receipt of the mother's application the Trustees establish a trust under the error of assumptions that the child has elected to accept the benefits bequeathed by the will, 'under the will'. The Trustees further assume that the child is incompetent, a bankrupt and lost at sea and is presumed dead until the child re-appears and re-establishes his/her living status, challenges the assumption of his/her acceptance of the benefits 'under the will' as being one of free choice and with full knowledge of the facts and redeems the estate.

Under the assumption that the child is a 14th Amendment citizen, the child's print is placed on the birth certificate by the hospital creating a slave bond that is sold to the federal reserve, who converts the certificate into a negotiable instrument and establishes a **second Cestui Que Vie trust**. The child's parents are compelled to apply for a social security number for the child, unwittingly testifying that the child is a 14th Amendment paper citizen of the United States, not a party in interest to the trust or the trust res, and assumed to be dead after 7 years, when the federal reserve cannot seize the child, they file for the issue of the salvage bond and the child is presumed dead.

In 1666, in London, during the black plague, and great fires of London Parliament enacted an act, behind closed doors, called Cestui Que Vie Act 1666. The act being debated the Cestui Qui act was to subrogate the rights of men and women, meaning all men and women were declared dead, lost at sea/beyond the sea. (back then operating in admiralty law, the law of the sea, so lost at sea).

When a child is Baptized by the church, the Baptismal certificate is forwarded to the Vatican who converts the certificate into a negotiable instrument and **creates a third Cestui Que Vie trust.** These three trusts represent the enslavement of the property, body and soul of the child.

The civil administration, UNITED STATES, continues to operate today under this triple crown of enslavement based on the error of assumptions that we are 14th Amendment citizens of the United States based on the breach of trust by the trustees.

Cestui Que As A Method Of Fraud

Cestui que (also *cestuy que*) (is a shortened version of *cestui a que use le feoffment fuit fait,* literally, "The person for whose use the feoffment was made." It is a Law French phrase of medieval English invention, which appears in the legal phrases *cestui que trust*, *cestui que use*, or *cestui que vie*. In contemporary English the phrase is also commonly pronounced "setty-kay" (/ˈsɛtɪkeɪ/) or "sesty-kay" (/ˈsɛstɪkeɪ/). According to Roebuck, *Cestui que use* is pronounced "setticky yuce" (/ˌsɛtɪkiˈjuːs/). *Cestui que use* and *cestui que trust* are more or less interchangeable terms. In some medieval materials, the phrase is seen as **cestui a que**.

The *cestui que use* is the person for whose benefit the trust is created. The *cestui que trust* is the person entitled to an equitable, as opposed to a legal, estate. Thus, if land is granted to the use of A in trust for B, B is cestui que trust, and A trustee, or use. The term, principally owing to its cumbersome nature[J], has been virtually superseded in modern law by that of "beneficiary", and general law of trusts.

By the fifteenth century, *cestui que use* was a vehicle to defraud creditors. The main use was to leave land, or parts of land to members of the family other than the primary heir. This was a way to avoid primogeniture inheritance. While the use was intact, the occupant of the land could take advantage of the *cestui que use* to avoid the feudal payments and duties (incidents). Incidents such as wardship, marriage penalties and other gifts, taxes, fines, fees, and knight service were onerous. Common law did not recognize *cestui que uses* as such, and there was difficulty fitting these cases into the existing writs and case law. The incidents could not be enforced against a person who was on a Crusade, or other war, or business adventure. They were not present in the kingdom to be enforced to perform. Since the feudal oath was to the person, and not the land, there could be no lien against the land. A hallmark of medieval feudalism was the person to person oath of allegiance. The feudal incidents could not be enforced upon the beneficiaries of the *cestui que use*, since these were not the owners of the land. The users had not sworn an oath to the lord. Therefore, they owed the lord nothing. The *cestui que use* had no estate. They had no seisin, nor a trespass, and therefore, ejectment could not be effected. These required possession. Assumpsit was of no avail. In 1402, the Commons had petitioned the king for a remedy against dishonest feoffees to uses, apparently with no result. *Cestui que use* became a new kind of property and property use.

Cestui Que A Medieval Invention In Practice

Many reasons have been given for the invention of the cestui que use as a legal device. During the Crusades, and other wars on the Continent, landowners might be gone for long periods of time. Others might be absent because of business adventures or religious pilgrimages. There was no assurance they would ever return home. The *cestui que use* allowed them to leave a trusted friend or relative with the sort of powers, discretions and they hoped, the duties. Today, this power would be called the "power of attorney". Religious orders such as Franciscans, Cistercians, Benedictines and other mendicant orders took vows of poverty, yet retained the use of donated property. *Cestui que use* allowed them the benefits of land without legal ownership. Besides the obvious limitations placed on cestui que by the Statute of Mortmain, Statute of Uses and the Statute of Wills, its legality was shaped indirectly by provisions within the Magna Carta and Quia Emptores.

Example 1: Albert is the owner of a landholding called Blackacre. He conveys this to Richard with the command that Richard hold the land with the duty not for Richard's benefit, but for a different purpose. This could be to do a job, such as collect rents and profits for the purpose of passing them to a third person, Lucy. This was nothing more than a clever legal device with Richard playing either an active or passive role.

Example 2: If Jane (women could engage in cestui que use), granted Blackacre to Charles to the use of David, then David became the beneficial owner and Jane could not vary or detract from that ownership.

Example 3: If Mary wanted to grant Blackacre away from her direct heir James, to her younger son Jasper, then she might well do so by a grant of Richard to the use of Jasper in tail, remainder to James in fee simple. Only Richard had a legal estate, the interests of

Jasper and James being equitable analogues of a legal fee tail and fee simple in remainder.

Example 4: If Mary wanted to make a will of the equitable ownership of Blackacre, she would be able to do so by a grant to Richard to the use of herself, Mary. The ownership of Blackacre did not pass on Mary's death to her heir but went to wherever she might will it. By this method, Mary could keep her wishes secret until her death when her will would be read, and would prevail. This was a way to defeat primogeniture inheritance.

Example 5: Uses were so common by the middle of the fifteenth century that they were presumed to be in existence even if no intention could be proved. If Martin granted Blackacre to Martha, and she could show no consideration (that is, that she paid for it), then Martha would be considered in equity to be the feoffee to unspecified uses to be announced at Martin's discretion. If Martin sold Blackacre to Martha, but did not go through the formal routines of feoffment to complete the conveyance, Martha could not become the legal owner. But in equity, Martin held the land to the cestui que use of Martha. It would have been unconscionable for him to do otherwise having taken her money for the sale of Blackacre.

Example 6: Albert might convey Blackacre to Richard for the use of Jane. In this case, Richard was called the "feoffee of uses". Jane was the "cestui que use". This was short for "cestui a qui use le feoffment fuit fait", i.e. "The person to whose use the feoffment was made." This device separated legal from beneficial ownership.

Concerted efforts were made under Henry VII of England to reform cestui que. A change in the laws made feoffees the absolute owners of the property of which they had been enfeoffed, and they became subject to all the liabilities of ownership. They were the only ones who could take proceedings against those who interfered with their ownership. If a trespass had been committed with the license of the *cestui que use* they could take proceedings against him, for he was at law only a tenant at sufferance. Similarly, feoffees were the only ones who could take the proceedings against tenants of the land to compel them to perform their obligations. If a debt was brought for rent by a *cestui que use*, and the defendant pleaded "nihil habuit tempore dimissions", the plaintiff would have lost his action if he had not made a special replication setting out the facts. The purpose of these changes was to make *cestui que* in general, and *cestui que use trusts* more cumbersome and economically unattractive.

Henry VIII sought to end all cestui que uses and regain the incidents (fees and payments) that had been deprived him. Thomas Cromwell and Audley who succeeded Thomas More vigorously crushed cestui que uses in the courts, persuading judges to declare them illegal or void.[By 1538-39, over 800 religious land holdings had been returned to the Crown. Many of these were subsequently sold, converted to private dwellings, given to loyal supporters of the English Reformation, dismantled for building materials, or abandoned and allowed to degenerate into ruins. Claims of religious corruption were frequently used to justify reclamation by the Crown. Since many of these religious orders provided charity, much of the local medical and social services were left in disarray.

The Statute of Uses was enacted in 1535, and was intended to end the "abuses" which had incurred in *cestui que use*. It declared that any holder of a cestui que use became the holder of the legal title of the ownership in fee simple. This voided the advantages of a cestui que use. The feoffee to uses was bypassed. The *cestui que use* had seisin. Henry VIII of England got his incidences back. The land owner lost the ability to will the land to heirs other than those in direct lineage. There could be no bypassing of heirs with a cestui que. This condition was modified in the Statute of Wills (1540). One of the effects of the Statute of Uses in executing the use, was to make a mere sale of land without feoffment (the formal public transfer) effective to pass the legal estate. The buyer became the owner by operation of the statute. It necessitated a public announcement of the intended sale to determine if the land had been surreptitiously sold to someone else. The Statute of Uses required a public registry of sale of land, later called the Statute of Enrollments.

Lawyers quickly determined that adding the words to a conveyance "land to Leonard and his heirs, to the use of John and his heirs, to the use of Kenneth and his heirs." For a time, this device defeated the intent of the Statute of Uses. Lord Hardwicke wrote that the Statute had no real effect other than to add, at most three words, to a conveyance. He was referring to the doctrine that had become settled before his time: that the old use might still be effected despite the Statute, by a "use on a use". The Statute of Uses had been considered a great failure. It did not wipe out double ownership, legal and equitable, which has survived into the modern system of trusts. The preamble of the Statute went far in enumerating the abuses the system of uses had brought into play. The Statute did not, as had previously been suggested, try to remedy these abuses by declaring any uses void. It merely declared that the possession should be transferred to the use and that the cestui que use should have the possession after such manner and form as he had before the use.

History in German and Roman Law It is the opinion of William Holdsworth quoting such scholars as Gilbert, Sanders, Blackstone, Spence and Digby, that cestui que in English law had a Roman origin. An analogy exists between cestui que uses and a usufructus (usufruct) or the bequest of a fideicommissum. These all tended to create a feoffement to one person for the use of another. Gilbert writes, (also seen in Blackstone): *"that they answer more to the fideicommissum than the usufructus of the civil law." These were transplanted into England from Roman Civil Law about the close of the reign of Edward III of England by means of foreign ecclesiastics who introduced them to evade the Statute of Mortmain. Others argue that the comparison between cestui que and Roman law is merely superficial. The transfer of land for the use of one person for certain purposes to be carried out either in the lifetime or after the death of the person conveying it has its basis in Germanic law. It was popularly held that land could be transferred for the use from one person to another in local custom. The formal English or Saxon law didn't always recognize this custom. The practice was called Salman or Treuhand. "Sala" is German for "transfer".[5] It is related to the Old English "sellen", "to sell".*

The earliest appearance of cestui que in the medieval period was the feoffee to uses, which like the Salman, held on account of another. This was called the cestui que use. It was because the feoffor could impose on him many various duties that landowners acquired through his instrumentality the power to do many things with their land. This was a to avoid the rigidity of medieval common law of land and its uses. Germanic law was familiar with the idea that a man who holds property on account of, or to the use of another is bound to fulfill his trust. Frankish formulas from the Merovingian period describe property given to a church "ad opus sancti illius." Mercian books in the ninth century convey land "ad opus monachorum". The Doomsday Book refers to geld or money, sac and soc held in "ad opus regus", or in "reginae" or "vicecomitis". The laws of William I of England speak of the sheriff holding money "al os le rei" ("for the use of the king").

Others state that the *cestui que use trust* was the product of Roman Law. In England it was the invention of ecclesiastics who wanted to escape the Statute of Mortmain. The goal was to obtain a conveyance of an estate to a friendly person or corporation, with the intent that the use of the estate would reside with the original owner.

Pollock and Maitland describe *cestui que use* as the first step toward the law of agency. They note that the word "use" as it was employed in medieval English law was not from the Latin "usus", but rather from the Latin word "opus", meaning "work". From this came the Old French words "os" or "oes". Although with time the Latin document for conveying land to the use of John would be written "ad opus Johannis" which was interchangeable with "ad usum Johannis", or the fuller formula, "ad opus et ad usum", the earliest history suggests the term "use" evolved from "ad opus".

The Significance Of The Cestui Que Vie Trust Today

In 1666, in London, during the black plague, and great fires of London Parliament enacted an act, behind closed doors, called Cestui Que Vie Act 1666. The act being debated the Cestui Qui act was to subrogate the rights of men and women, meaning all men and women were declared dead, lost at sea/beyond the sea. (back then operating in admiralty law, the law of the sea, so lost at sea).

The state (of London) took custody of everybody and their property into a trust, the state became the trustee/husband holding all titles to the people and property, until a living man comes back to reclaim those titles and can also claim damages. The rule of the use of CAPITAL LETTERS used in a NAME: when CAPITAL letters are used anywhere in a NAME this always refers to a LEGAL ENTITY/FICTION, COMPANY or CORPORATION no exceptions. e.g. John DOE or Doe: JANE (PASSPORT, DRIVER LICENSE, MARRIAGE CERTIFICATE and BIRTH CERTIFICATE)

CEST TUI QUE TRUST: (pronounced setakay) common term in NEW ZEALAND and AUSTRALIA or STRAWMAN common term in USA or CANADA is a LEGAL ENTITY/FICTION created and owned by the GOVERNMENT whom created it. I repeat owned by the GOVERNMENT. Legally, we are considered to be a FICTION, a concept or idea expressed as a NAME, a symbol. That LEGAL PERSON has no consciousness; it is a juristic PERSON, ENS LEGIS, a NAME/word written on a piece of paper.

This traces back to 1666, London is a state, just like Vatican is a state, just like Washington DC is a state. The Crown is an unincorporated association. Why unincorporated, its private, the temple bar is in London, every lawyer called to the "bar" swears allegiance to the temple bar. You can't get called, without swearing this allegiance. The Crown already owns North America and everything in it. Your only way out is to reclaim your dead entity (Strawman) that the Crown created, become the trustee of the cest tui qui trust and remove yourself from the admiralty law that holds you in custody.

When London burned the subrogation of men's and woman's rights occurred. The responsible act passed... CQV act 1666 meant all men and women of UK were declared dead and lost beyond the seas. The state took everybody and everybody's property into trust. The state takes control until a living man or woman comes back and claims their titles by proving they are alive and claims for damages can be made.

This is why you always need representation when involved in legal matters, because you're dead. The legal fiction is a construct on paper, an estate in trust. When you get a bill or summons from court it is always in capital letters, similar to tomb stones in grave yards. Capital letters signify death. They are writing to the dead legal fiction. A legal fiction was created when someone informed the government that there was a new vessel in town, based upon your birth. Birth certificates are issued at birth, just as ships are given berth certificates.

Your mother has a birth canal, just like a ship. All this information relates to how the general public are still legally tied. Through admiralty law, through this ancient legal construct we can be easily controlled. Learning about your legal fiction helps you to unlock yourself. Otherwise you are just a vessel floating on the sea of commerce. It is possible to be free from financial stress and debt.

Parents are tricked into registering the birth of their babies. In about 1837 the Births, Deaths and Marriages act was formed in UK and the post of registrar general was established. His job was to collect all the data from the churches which held the records of birth.

Regis - from queen or crown. All people are seen to be in custody of," The Crown". This allows people to function in commerce and to accept the benefits provided by state.

So we are in custody. Worldwide - under the IMF the majority of people are fed, sheltered and provided for, however now it is the system that is benefitting while many are suffering, are poorly fed, housed and water is contaminated. Many people are now getting sick and dying as a result - not to mention that as people evolve, they now seek to be independent of any system that seeks to control or oppress and harms the earth that this is all taking place on.

We have legally elected representatives. We have to understand who we are as men and women and how we can relate in the system.

The City of London is a centre for markets, where merchants work. Then there is mercantile law. It comes from Admiralty. Look at the symbols in the City of London that relate to Admiralty.

Our national banks are not our banks. The private shareholders from the private banks own the banks. It is all private, not public as we are led to believe. "OF" also means "without", eg. The bank without England. Private banks issue private currency.

With WWI a change happened where money was not backed by gold or silver anymore, it is now based on peoples labour. People are now pledged to the IMF as the surety to pay back the creditors in the global bankruptcy. Men and women are not bankrupt, they are the only source of credit. The public is bankrupt.

Regarding the currency that gets issued at the Bank of England, people are the gold or the treasure. The government issues bonds or treasury bills that are bought by investors. The money goes back into the economy in order to pay for the people to build things, e.g. an Olympic Stadium. However, the people are paying taxes for the privilege of using someone else's currency and paying back the principal and the interest on the original loan that was given against the treasury bonds, bills and notes. It is a private corporation that will own the Olympic stadium, be responsible for running it, be able to sell commercial rights, yet the people are actually the ones who own it and should be profiting from it. However, principal and interest is coming through the people in order to raise the money.

So where you have commerce and money, you also have "justice". You need to understand the bankruptcy before you can understand the judiciary. You need to accept the bankruptcy. We have accepted the claim to accept the summons. There is an obligation to accept any liability which has been created. All you can do is accept the bankruptcy. We are operating in admiralty. A not guilty plea dishonours the bankruptcy. The Strawman, aka legal fiction is always guilty. It needs to be accepted for value. Barristers and solicitors make a living out of creating controversy. By creating a controversy you become liable for the case.

Are you in honour and dishonour? To remain in honour you have to accept a claim and settle it. Then you add conditions. I accept on proof of claim and proof of loss. This gives the liability back to them. The legal fiction is always guilty. Only in the high courts, can the real man or woman appear. Games are played on courts; hence the name court is a game with actors (acting on acts). It has to be treated as a game and just business. Court room dramas are misinformation. In the public, we are operating in bankruptcy and you receive benefits. It takes a lot of time, effort and study to use these tools. You have to be prepared to go fully through the process, get the right tool out of your toolbox at the right time. People need to learn how to act as creditors. In summary:

- Money is backed by labour.
- We cannot exchange it fairly for gold or silver.
- Capitalisation of "name" means a dead entity, a legal fiction.
- Know who you are, you are not your Strawman or dead fictitious entity.
- Learn how to become a creditor in commerce.

So in summary, when in 1666 an act of parliament created during the black plague, and great fires of London , behind closed doors, it was called Cestui Que Vie Act 1666. (see end of chapter)

The act being debated was the Cestui Qui act which was to subrogate the rights of men and women, meaning all men and women were declared dead, lost at sea/beyond the sea. This was done during a crisis. The state took custody of everybody and their property into a trust, the Cestui Qui trust, the state became the trustee/husband holding all titles to the people and property, until a living man comes back to reclaim those titles and can also claim damages.

The Cestui Qui act or Trust created is an ALL-CAPITALIZED NAME, a 'dead entity' who had all his belongings put into a trust. This act still exists, and this trust still exists. This is how it started.   If you were born on earth, if you have a birth certificate, this applies to you. The only way to claim your trust and get free from admiralty law, is to understand who you really are, and that admiralty law does not apply to you, but in order to get free you must do some homework, file forms and know how commerce applies to you.

Is The Cestui Que Used Today?

We include a letter posted on the Internet from: Hughes, Paul (Civil Law) Ministry of Justice 18 February 2011. it was a response from a letter sent by a Mr. Bolwell which assed about the Cetui Que trust:

"Dear Mr. Bolwell, Thank you for your e-mail of 19 December 2010 to the Data Access and Compliance Unit in which you ask for information about the Cestui que Vie Act 1666. You ask what the Act is about and whether or not it is still in effect. Your e-mail has been passed to me for reply as I work in the part of the department responsible for issues relating to the presumption of death. Your e-mail is not being dealt with under the Freedom of Information Act 2000. I am sorry for the delay in sending you a reply. The Cestui que Vie Act 1666 is still in force but parts of it have been amended or repealed over the years. Specifically:

The preamble was amended by the Statute Law Revision Act 1948; Section 2 was repealed by the Statute Law Revision Act 1948; Section 3 was repealed by the Statute Law Revision Act 1863; and Section 4 was amended by the Statute Law Revision Act 1888. The Act provides for the recovery of a lease where the life tenant has disappeared for seven or more years and there is no proof that the person is still alive. In this situation, the Act gives the court the power to declare the life tenant dead. There are very few references to the statute in the textbooks I have checked, suggesting it is little used. The following extract was taken from Halsbury's Statute Volume 20 (2009 reissue).

In the normal form of a strict settlement (which by virtue of the [1]Trusts of Land and Appointment of Trustees Act 1996, s 2, cannot in general be created on or after 1 January 1997) a limitation to a life tenant invariably precedes one to a tenant in tail in order to restrict the tenant in tail's power to bar the entail. Save where there is a trust for sale, the land will fall within the [2]Settled Land Act 1925 (see s 1 of that Act) and, if the life tenant is of full age, he will be the statutory tenant for life under s 19 of that Act, in whom the fee simple should be vested in trust for himself and the remainder men. The Cestui que Vie Acts 1666 and 1707 help to ascertain whether a life tenant is still alive.

If you have a problem to which the Act relates I can only recommend that you take independent legal advice. If you do not have an adviser your local Citizens Advice Bureau or Community Legal Advice Centre may be able to help him find one. Information about Community   Legal   Advice   can   also   be   found   on   its   website:

[3]www.communitylegaladvice.org.uk or by telephoning 0845 345 4345. I hope you find this information helpful."

Yours sincerely, Kirsty Milliam
Ministry of Justice
102 Petty France
London SW1H 9AJ Tel: 020 3334 3207

31

THE NATIONAL BANKING ASSOCIATION

Philosophy And Mission

Because at the heart of the Strawman story is the misappropriation of money or good faith and credit that has been contributed by the real Earthlings, it became necessary to look at a means of claiming and distributing the rightful inheritance as a beneficiary. At the heart of its purpose, the National Banking Association as set upunder the office of Postmaster General as a purpose of the flow through of the good faith and equity that has been so diligently recorded and used for military benefit. It is we that created the value in the trusts that are both global and personal. It is we that are the beneficiaries. It is we the people that need to recognize this truth and take the action to realign the purpose away from the financing of the war machines and the purposeful creation of conflict for prosperity of the kingdoms.

The process of shifting into a new money system involves the removing the blocks to allow the energy to continue its natural flow back to source. As the source is our estates it must return to us having been transmuted into value. We must facilitate the forward movement of the energy. You cannot UNDO something that has been created. You move through the blocks to settle or balance the energy. Moving through this is the key fore as we move through it we transmute the negative blocked negative energy to a positive, healing energy. Negative energy only has negative effects on the people because of the blocks.

This is zero point! Everything stays at a balanced zero. All needs are met while all debts are satisfied leaving the sum total at zero point. Abundance in balance! We are the alchemists! It is not for us to transmute lead to gold, but, to transmute the dark energy to light! That is the true value, not the gold! That is what discharge of debt is all about. These blocked negative energies are returned to the natural flow and as it returns to source, mother earth, the negative energy becomes whole again and one with the light ..... alchemy at its best!

Many years ago I learned that I had the ability to work with energies. I learned that I could transmute the negative energy into healing energy and redirect that healing energy to where ever I liked. Some time ago I connected the outer grid with the earth grid like a regulator or shock absorber to assist in balancing the energy in any crisis. Recently it came to my attention that these electrical grids reached into every room of every home in America and into nearly every home in the world. I connected that physical grid to the outer and inner grids to extend the shock absorbing ability in case of extreme drama in the world. There is a portal at the location that has been chosen for the seat of government and now I can and do inject divine energy into the grid which flows to every home on earth and discharges the negative, stressful, chaotic energy and returns it to source. This is the as above to the as below of the new banking system we created to facilitate the return of the natural flow of energy and transition into the new world. This is true divine alchemy. Transmuting the living energy from dark into light.

And in taking this lesson to heart, the solution I found rested upon a new flow of energy within the existing corporate system but within the context of positive light--freeing the good faith and credit so as to flow it as the positive energy with its intrinsic values back to where it originated.

The new banking system has been established and is to work through the postal services of the world. The post office has been continuously solvent from its creation. Postal Money Orders are still backed by gold. Since we know that the post office will take fiat money and give you a gold backed Money Order in the exchange, we know that they know how to do the exchange from public to private funds. They do it every day. We know that the post office is capable of operating and charging the prepaid accounts and that the people are able to access the services of the post office in nearly every part of the world.

So, here we have the basis for the new banking system with potential access from every computer on earth. The international banking community and the UPU both have existing banking software to handle the required services at the necessary volume to make this work in the shortest upstart time frame.

As a process of implementation with the UPU and actually establishing this for the American people, Switzerland has announced this new banking system for the entire world which was designed to discharge debt and return the value to the people, worldwide. It is here that the Postmaster General James Thomas placed a pass through account as the prepaid account upon which all services where to be billed. As it is the United States, the franchised owner/operator of the US Postal Service [USPS] he instructed the UPU that the Office of the PMG and the people, in original jurisdiction, would be piggy backing off of the services of the USPS and the UPU, charged against the prepaid account.

When the banks created the debt they hypothecated it 10 times. Therefore, if we suddenly discharge all of the personal debt of the people thru this account, we still have 90% of the private funds available for our use which must be discharged. As I see it, these funds will be made available to secure the basic needs of every man, woman and child on earth. We have banking software for use in monthly auto payments where one can set up their monthly bills, rent, utilities, etc. to be automatically paid each month. I foresee this being made available to ensure that all of the survival needs of the people are met. This alone changes the entire game on earth. Now, we have the opportunity to seek out our passion in life where one will receive a currency of value or a barter system will provide the extras one might like to enjoy in life.

We know that we are transitioning towards a system without currency for currency is a tool of lack and limitation, to a world of true abundance. With we truly have an abundance of everything available to us at any, every given time then there is no need to store up or save up for a rainy day, Thus, no need for currency. This is a transition that may take 50-100 years, but, I believe this new banking system will facilitate this transition over the long haul.

This is exciting stuff that we are developing/ creating right here and now in the here and now. I not only see it in my mind's eye I feel it as it takes root and begins to manifest into reality. This system sets the stage for the "delivery of the prosperity packages.

The Office of the PMG truly is one of the Trustees of the Global Trust. Is it not the Fiduciary/Trustee who is the proper party administrate the estates of the people, the Global estate trust, for the benefit of the people. And in preparation for so doing, a new banking system is created and will be run by the Post Office, Trustees of the world.

This is just the beginning of the good things which can be done through this office. As true Trustees of the Global Trust we can inject the light and love of the Divine into the trusteeship and forever change the world in which we live. For me, this has been 500 years in the making and today, we have arrived! The time has come to really apply our powers of alchemy to transmute this world.

I made this statement on May 2012.

National Banking Association

Those who constitute an association nationwide of private, unincorporated persons engaged in the business of banking to issue notes against these obligations of the United States due them; whose private property is at risk to collateralize the government's debt and currency, by legal definitions, a 'national banking association'; such notes, issued against these obligations of the United States to that part of the public debt due its Principals and Sureties are required by law to be accepted as "legal tender" of payments for all debts public and private, and are defined in law as "obligations of the United States", on the same par and category with Federal reserve Notes and other currency and legal tender obligations."

In the operation of commerce in Bankruptcy, or Receivership, a Public Official may refuse a valid request, one time. That first request is done in the VOLUNTARY Bankruptcy side of the transaction. A Public Official's refusal, or Dishonour, charges the INVOLUNTARY Bankruptcy and their mandatory obligation to honour your request. They have a mandatory obligation to honour your request when presented the second time. Their refusal to honour your second request is Bankruptcy Obstruction and constitutes a dialectal default and their voluntary surrender or abandonment of their office and all power and authority therein.

It is noted that as of this date, this particular phase is in fast evolution. Part of this process requires that certain documents be sent out and membership be in place. This will be covered later.

But first, let us back up a little.

32

THE PROCESS OF CURE FOR
James-Thomas: Mcbride

Changing The System Flow Of Money Energy

If you have arrived at this place in the book, you may ponder what it is that must be done on the commercial side that would divorce you from the Strawman employed by PLANET EARTH and acquire access to the Good Faith and Credit held in the Strawman Trust. In this set of Chapters, we are going to use my case of James-Thomas Mcbride as the example. There are always forerunners, warriors of truth that open the path and slash their way through the labyrinth. It is stated that this process that I uncovered and used was not the perfect solution because the establishment is not yet willing to rollover and agree so it is evolving. However, the process undertaken by me reveals that ithis is not a myth and the "state of this art" IS and WILL come to truth exponentially now. As you read these chapters, you will see how I decided to implement my truth which now at this time in 2012 has evolved to a whole new level.

It is indeed a complex world of commercial and religious "takeovers "that has allowed the PLANET EARTH business plan to evolve to a very critical point in time. The question arises as to how is it possible that such a monolithic dynasty could fall and effectively allow the meek to inherit the earth? How are the blocks in the system removed? How does a mere mortal face the great goliaths and survive.

Over time, history shows that all dynasties have fallen. It is the way energy works. As to how and when, it appears that that time is now because it has shown itself as two distinct pathways where the people will choose. and the consciousness that now prevails is as mighty as the powers that held it back. It is no secret in mass marketing that when a critical point in consciousness arises (like the mentality of a stock market crash) to a certain point that consciousness (shift from bull to bear market mentality) becomes the manifestor of that reality. Similarly, mass marketing works that way in that when people of mass consciousness believe a certain product is needed, the others simply follow without question to consume the same brand. DNA is like that too. When a critical threshold is reached (like the monkey effect) a certain instinct or habit simply becomes encoded in all DNA as quantum update.

The mass consciousness as we has explained, has occurred in the last decade. It is at the same time as the powers that be plan their grand finale of their business plan: New World Order versus the New Order of the Ages.

In this new consciousness, millions now seek out the truth in the light of peace and new look at the real God who has cleverly hidden Himself within us and our hearts. Each individual can now open to this and share the new knowing as a grain of sand that will, when the winds of consciousness blow on the grains, form a dune, then a mountain. In seeking this path of truth both spiritual and commercial, we have been dedicated to the revelation of a new truth so as to present a choice in a new light. It within this context that I, James Thomas of the family McBride have dedicated myself, and now can present the secrets of navigating the labyrinth of commerce within the mindset of the new spiritual consciousness. It is not to wage war but to carry light of peace. It is not for inequality and dominion but to acknowledged we are all One and spiritually interconnected. It is not in hatred and conflict but in love and without judgment. It is not about sin, it is about we as perfection.

And so now we open to the assimilation of the knowledge so far presented into the process of cure, with particular attention to what, implemented and executed.

In effect, each human who is registered at birth has become an employee of PLANET EARTH INC. subservient to the administrative incorporated body of the City of London called the CROWN, AKA: the BRITISH CROWN, [In America, it is the administrative incorporated body politic called the UNITED STATES of the District/City of COLUMBIA]; and thus, the owner of those corporate City States, the Pontiff of Rome and his HOLY ROMAN EMPIRE, the primal head corporation of the World.

Since we are dealing with and subjected to people who have unknowingly chosen to believe that they are officers on a make-believe ship at sea called a corporate body, as are the nature of Governments and Nations, the prevalent belief is that their assigned duty is to discipline disobedient crewmembers. Unknowingly ALL property, including labour, and the fruits of labour of the people/slaves belongs to the "slave" owner, the Pontiff of Rome, and his Holy Roman Empire, through his agency, the corporate Crown of the City of London. Or, in America, it is the corporate UNITED STATES]- with the Pontiff of Rome being the claimed to be direct owner of that legal, financial, and professional accreditation enclave within Greater London. And since all Courts are primarily used for dealing with "slave disobedience" [against the rules of the slave owner - acts, statutes, laws, rules, regulations and edicts], it is very difficult to come up with any exact remedy against such violations of TRUE LAW and UNALIENABLE RIGHTS perpetrated by Governments and Agencies of Government. It is primarily because they exist within fiction, mythology in their land of "Make Believe".

Thus, all any researcher, like myself (James Thomas), can accomplish is to enlighten you on how you became a slave, where the very labour of your mind and body belongs to another evil worldly power, and you can, and will be severely punished for disobedience to the slave owner's rules, and for not accounting for and pledging that property to the agencies that exist under the authority of the Pontiff and Cardinals of Rome. We can only suggest possible peaceful remedies to the gross wrongs and violations against your right to life that have been so deceitfully imposed upon you, but history shows that those methods of redress usually are only partially effective or are ineffective, or will be made ineffective by more deceit, lies or myths in their fantasy dictatorship. But, notwithstanding the above statement, we must continue to follow the rule set out by Winston Churchill, as found at the bottom of this webpage. And, we may be in phase two, or even three of his observed necessity of action. Remember, labour is your time, Life is time. Therefore, when your labour, or the fruits of your labour, are confiscated, your life is taken. The Rule of Necessity [derived from Creator God's Law] says that you can use the force necessary to defend your life.

Communications From The New Postmaster General

In the forgoing information the important website that is the pulse of the new Postmaster General and the Divine Estate is *www.divneprovince.org*.

The site will provide an information and communications network connecting freeholders around the world to assist us all in bringing order out of the chaos as we enter and begin co-creating our new world. We have a nice research and articles section that we are adding to every day.

The information, documents and the process presented here are the result of countless hours of research by tens of thousands of people. There are those who have invested a great deal of their life energy making their research available for all. We will direct you to those people and those sites as well. We gladly send you to their sites and thank them for their efforts to expose the truth so that we may all return from being lost in a sea of illusion.

The information that follows, particularly the reference documentation to the authority of the new Postmaster General is provided here and it may be freely downloaded from the site. *Of note is that the purpose of presenting this is not for use; it is for education*. In this particular business, it is always advisable to go to the source; just like in the spiritual area-GO TO THE SOURCE. Of relevancev is the process by which the sentient human James Thomas of the Family McBride reclaimed his true status and separated himself from the Corporate entity JAMES THOMAS McBRIDE.

Also, the process of my claim on the seat of Postmaster, the claim of authority, the definition of a peace treaty and the creation of the flow through national banking system via the Federal Reserve is explained.

In a later chapter, the simplified process for others will be brought forward to all who choose that take a similar path. Before this we will begin with a summary of critical information. Although this is a repeat, it serves to bring it back into the awareness light.

Breach of Divine Estate And Funding The Military Complex

For decades the Divine Estate(s) of the American people have been leveraged to fund the Military Industrial Complex which has raped, pillaged and plundered the world resulting in the impoverishment and enslavement of the people. This has all simply been a part of the business plan of those bloodline kingdoms that direct the mission of Corporation PLANET EARTH in its invisible fictional corporate system down to the STRAWMEN and STRAWWOMEN in the POSTAL ZONES. The controlling factors have been the Rule Books of GOD as the WORD and the LAW as attached to corporate entities as Acts, Statutes, Bills and what is called the code of law. In this way, the religious and monetary command

and authority has been accepted to the point of world domination by debt money and Vatican endorsements.

And so it has come to pass that our Divine Estates have been leveraged to fund the endless wars and violence resulting in the death of over 100 million people in the past century to satisfy the greed and lust for power and control by the few over the many.

The entire earth has been tainted by the touch of this Military Industrial Complex which has brought us a constant diet of fear, violence and death as it waged war against all of humanity. Clearly it has been "good business" to instigate, finance, and enjoy the spoils of war and conflict. This Military Industrial Complex has employed the use of fear, terrorism and out of control debt created out of thin air to support their weapon of choice, the Federal Reserve Banking System, for the purpose of re-assigning and using our Divine Inheritance, our birthright.

And so it has come to pass that world peace is NOT a privilege! Abundance and Prosperity is NOT a privilege! Peace and harmony are NOT a privilege! They are our Birthright!! Our Divine Inheritance! And no man, agency or entity may tax, license or limit your Divine Estate, your Divine Inheritance, without your consent. Yet this has not been the path of evolution simply because the business enterprise of PLANET EARTH and its directors have been able to implement their own designs for dominion.

As it came to pass I as one of the Trustees of the Global Trust, under whose direction the United States operates, have identified and demanded a cure for **the Breach of Trust** which created the Military Industrial Complex which authorizes the Federal Reserve Banks to leverage our Divine Estate(s) wreaking havoc on the people of earth.

The evidence of the Breach and Demand for the Cure thereof, as well as my standing to receive a cure thereto has been argued and adjudicated at the highest level and it has been Decreed that a breach of trust must be declared:

A Cure To The Breach Must Be Declared

The Pass Through Account has been activated to facilitate the charging of the sub accounts releasing the blocked private funds for the administration of the Estate Trusts of the people in original jurisdiction in harmony with the original intent of the trusts. The stage has been set for the administration of our Divine Estate(s), our abundance and prosperity, in original jurisdiction for our benefit, bringing about world peace and Global Debt Forgiveness in the transition.

Further, this Cure must be made available to anyone and everyone who seeks it!

The Cure to the Breach of Trust which removes you and your Divine Estate from the grasp of the Military Industrial Complex and returns you and your estate to original jurisdiction, activating your abundance and prosperity is provided herein as a gift of this Trustee of the Global Trust.

As one of the Trustees of the Global Trust, creator of this site and author of much of the material which is freely shared herein one might notice certain spiritual principles which express themselves through me and my work. This is not about religion nor any need to compel the reader to believe as I do. I believe there is room enough in this world for a great diversity of beliefs to co-exist in peace and harmony. I believe that spiritual and personal sovereignty is the Birthright of every living being.

From the beginning, please understand, as the creator of these site and author of much of the writings herein, I am but a cog in the Universal wheel of humanity that made it possible. I simply did my part. The information presented herein is the compilation and evolution of the millions of man hours of research by thousands of selfless men and women dedicated to unravelling the illusion in which we live to bring about the rebirth of personal and spiritual sovereignty for all mankind.

I wish to thank all who steadfastly held tight to the belief that world peace, abundance and prosperity, was not a privilege, but like personal and spiritual sovereignty, they are our birthright; For all of those courageous men and women who understood that if we did not stand up and expose the illusion and corruption in our lifetime that our children and their children would be enslaved forever and chose to stand against the terrorist tactics of the Military Industrial Complex at their own peril and sacrifice. I also wish to thank all of the families of those dedicated souls who lived with the sacrifice, the pain and loss, for you too did your part and have been a motivating factor which moved us through the corruption and chaos. Because of all of our sacrifice(s) we stand today at the doorway of a great evolutionary leap for mankind.

So, let's begin from the beginning, at the Divine Right of Use Today, everything is held in trust. Everything is about trusts, Implied or Expressed. The Creator gave man dominion over all things. Dominion over means control over NOT ownership. This is a Divine Right of Use

A Divine Right of Use of the Divine property/ the All of earth which is held in trust. So, the entire world we call earth is held in trust, the Divine Trust, for our benefit as Beneficiaries. This Global Divine Trust is an Implied Trust as opposed to an Expressed Trust. In the beginning man was responsible, as a Trustee, for the care and well being of that portion of the Divine Estate upon which he/she exercised their Divine Right of Use as a Beneficiary.

Through the decades man has given over that Divine fiduciary obligation to legal fiction trustees. There are as many forms of trusteeships as there are people in the world. Some very fair and equitable, say a republic, all the way to a dictatorship, each with various degrees of freedoms and rights, taxes and limitations.

Who is the Trustee responsible for your piece of the Divine Estate, our Global Estate Trust? In America today we have Township Trustees, County Trustees, State Trustees and Federal Trustees just to name a few of the many levels of fiduciaries within the Trusteeship which is involved in the administration of our Divine Estate(s), the Global Estate Trust. Judges, Clerks of Court, Prosecutors and Attorneys all play their own part in the administration of our Global Estate Trust leveraging our Divine Estates to rape, pillage and plunder the world and enslave the people.

To unravel this intentionally complex Trusteeship of the Global Estate Trust let us begin at the top and work our way down. The Vatican boasts, in their Papal Bull, dominion over the entire earth, via conquest, and is answerable ONLY to the Divine Spirit. Dominion over means control over, not ownership. The Vatican's un-rebutted claims establish them as the Primary Trustee of the Global Estate Trust, our Divine Inheritance; a very unpopular fact. But a fact that opens a doorway placing the cure for the mis-administration and theft of our Divine Inheritance within our grasp.

The Vatican is the Primary Trustee of the Global Estate Trust. To facilitate the administration of this Global Trust the Vatican established the Universal Postal Union as the Secondary Trustees of the Global Trust charged with dividing the Global Trust into zones and endowing these legal fiction zones with sovereign authority to facilitate the efficient administration of the Global Trust.

It is no surprise that the first requirement for the international acknowledgment of a sovereign nation is the necessity of a Post Office. The primary objective of the military in any 'zone' is the protection of the Post, or the Post Office, for in their original jurisdiction, the Postmaster Generals are the Trustees of their respective zone.

In 1789 the Continental Congress passed a bill to "establish the seat of government, a general post office, under the direction of the Postmaster General." That's right, a general post office under the direction of the Postmaster General. They were further dividing the postal zone of North America establishing a new zone, and endowing it with sovereign authority, whereby our founding fathers believed they could establish a Trusteeship which would ensure that sovereignty of the people would be passed down to the people of future generations.

The Preamble to the Constitution created the Estate Trust which held the freedoms guaranteed in the Articles of Confederation and the Declaration of Independence in trust for future generations. The Articles of the Constitution established the Trusteeship as well as the powers and limitations thereof. The Congress and Senate were Trustees charged with the Administration of our Divine Inheritance, the Global Estate Trust.

In this 'general post office' seat of government there was established the 'civil administration' called the United States. Civil administration ? What do they administrate? Our Divine Estate Trust, the Global Trust, our Divine Inheritance. Remember, we can never OWN anything. We simply have a Divine Right of Use of the property of the Divine Estate, the Global Trust.

So, we the people of this earth have a Divine Right of use of the Global Trust while the civil administration is charged with the administration of our estate for our benefit. In the world of trusts Civil Administration/ Government = Trusteeship.

So, the entire world is held in trust. The Global Estate Trust, our Divine Inheritance, our birthright is held in trust and is administrated by the various 'governments' who gain their sovereign authority via the Universal Postal Union, the Secondary Trustee of the Global Trust answerable to the Vatican.

In the world of trusts and trust law, rights, duties and obligations are very straight forward, cut and dry, black and white. There are no opinions, secret codes, rules or statutes, period. These are just the facts. There is a chain of command, consequences for your actions, or lack thereof, and accountability.

It has been a slow and cumbersome process to overcome the out of control momentum of the civil administrators of the world today. There have been countless casualties as a result of our efforts to unravel the illusion; to overcome the programming and fear which fuelled the beast to reach the core where truth and accountability resides.

The Need For The Universal Postal Treaty

For me it was veryimportant to create Postal Treaty that was presented in a previous chapter because it reflected all freeholders as "We the People"..

The International Postal Treaty For The Americas, 2010 stems from a Claim On Abandonment that has been received and accepted at the absolute highest levels wherein the Abandonment of all creditor claims against the UNITED STATES was documented (dilectual default) as well as the abandonment of all sovereign rights, power and authority of the general post office commonly known as the UNITED STATES and the relinquishment of the 'pledge' or the release of all pledged property of the sovereign people of America and subsequent claim on said abandonment for and by We the sovereign people of America.

The bankruptcy obstruction and overt impairment of the absolute priority right of redemption by the CREDITOR Federal Reserve Bank and banking families has established in fact the CREDITOR'S operation in equity in bad faith and with unclean hands and constitutes a delictual default and abandonment of all CREDITOR claims and the relinquishment of the PLEDGED property; and

The bankruptcy obstruction and overt impairment of the absolute priority right of redemption by the COURTS has established in fact the general post office styled as the UNITED STATES' operation in equity in bad faith and with unclean hands and constitutes a delictual default and abandonment of all equity claims of the UNITED STATES and their voluntary abandonment of all sovereign rights, power and authority associated therewith; and the sovereign people of America, through and by James-Thomas: McBride, private postmaster, have served Notice of the Abandonment and registered the priority claim on the abandonment.

The Claim on Abandonment by the sovereign people of America has been received and accepted without objection or dispute.

The general post office styled as the UNITED STATES has been in a perpetual state of war since its inception. The 'Powers That Be' have used the UNITED STATES as a weapon to wage war on the sovereign people of America, operating under the Emergency War Powers Act and the secret presumption that the sovereign people are the enemy of the UNITED STATES for the purpose of evading their liabilities under the original equity contract and to pillage and plunder the private property of the people they were created to serve.

The general post office styled as the UNITED STATES has been used as a weapon to wage an economic war at arms length against all of the people of the world bringing all of humanity to the brink of destruction as the CREDITOR'S master plan of total economic slavery over the sovereign people of the world has been implemented.

The Powers That Be have used the UNITED STATES as a weapon to wage war on the sovereign people of the world via the unconscionable creation, production and distribution of harmful drugs for the purpose of enslaving the people and funding and executing their genocide against humanity.

The Powers That Be have used the UNITED STATES as a platform for their propaganda, creating the world's problems and then presenting themselves as the world's savior bringing about the solution and protection from their self created illusionary boogie men for the purpose of enslaving the sovereign people of the world.

And so it has been necessary to let humanity and the Powers that from a specific day forward the UNITED STATES shall be used as a tool, actuated by humility, to promote universal peace, love and unity among all men. The UNITED STATES shall become a broker and facilitator of peace; a springboard for ascension and balance within the world consciousness. The UNITED STATES shall immediately stand down and withdraw itself from all acts of aggression and vacate all occupied land and shall immediately bring all American soldiers home.

The agents and agencies of the UNITED STATES shall immediately cease and desist in all forms of gun and drug production and distribution, all forms of terrorism and genocide of the people, all standard operating procedure of the powers that be since the days of the East India trading Company.

All Administrative Agencies of the UNITED STATES shall immediately remove all gold fringed military flags from their offices and courtrooms and shall display the civilian flag of peace. The Custodian of the Alien Property shall immediately update his/her files, removing the names and private property of the American people from their files/lists and make the return of the property to the rightful owners. All administrative agencies and administrative courts shall operate in peace and honor, servants of the sovereign people.

The jurisdiction of the courts of the united states is described as the American flag of peace; red, white and blue with stripes of red and white horizontally placed in alteration. Under the jurisdiction of the American flag of peace the private rights of the sovereign people of the united states are protected and all rights are preserved. Here, the People are 'innocent until proven guilty.' Under the military gold fringed flag there are no rights.

The general post office styled as the UNITED STATES is a free republic operating under the concepts and intent of the Articles Of Confederation, establishing a perpetual Union between the several free and independent states, to wit:

A 'Transitional Committee' shall be seated for the purpose of ensuring a peaceful and efficient transition from an Empirical War based mentality and operating system to one of peace, humility and unity. Said Transitional Committee shall establish and empower an interim government for the united states of America and shall operate until such time as the people can be duly informed as to the true history of the UNITED STATES and the fraud that has been perpetrated against them, not to exceed one year.

The Postmaster general of the organic post office for the united states, creator of the general post office styled as the UNITED STATES and located within the ten miles square commonly known as Washington, D.C., under whose direction the UNITED STATES operates, shall operate in the capacity of trustee for the people and shall take instructions from the Transitional Committee until such time as the Interim government shall be seated and empowered.

All debt of the UNITED STATES, except that debt owed to the sovereign people of America, has been abandoned and vacated and the UNITED STATES has DECLARED PEACE with the world and the sovereign people thereof, therefore, the gold fringed military flag designating the admiralty/maritime jurisdiction shall be immediately removed from all courtrooms, meeting rooms, etc. of the administrative agencies of the UNITED STATES and the civil peace flag of the united states of America shall be proudly displayed in their stead..

The U.S. Courts who have been operating as debt collection facilities under TWEA and the EMERGENCY WAR POWERS ACT shall immediately make the corrections and cure the torts against the people, vacating all claims, attachments and/or restrictions on the private rights of the sovereign people and make them whole.

The courts, as well as all administrative agencies of the UNITED STATES, shall share resources making room for and facilitating the establishment of the organic courts, operating under the common law, for the adjudication of all matters concerning the sovereign American people, other than the prosecution of grievances against an administrative agency for the trespass of the private rights of the people. All administrative agencies shall actively participate in the establishment of two distinctly separate systems, common law and administrative, operating side by side for the benefit of the CREDITORS, the sovereign people of America.

All administrative courts and agencies of the UNITED STATES shall operate in good faith and honor as servants of the sovereign people of America. Said administrative courts and agencies have grown out of control, beyond the intent of the original founders and their usefulness and shall begin to make the corrections, a reversal, bringing about balance, transparency, full disclosure and honor for the remedy of the Real Parties In Interest.

All debts of the UNITED STATES have been abandoned, except the debt to the sovereign people; The Pledge of the private property of the American people has been relinquished, therefore, the administrative agencies of the UNITED STATES shall make the return of the interest back to source, the sovereign people.

The UNITED STATES shall immediately activate the established pass through account, vacate the blocks on the asset accounts and make the financial adjustments to discharge the debt and return the accounts of the sovereign people back into balance. The UNITED STATES shall maintain the natural flow and balance in the accounts for the remedy of the people, returning the interest back to source in the discharge of debt against the pre-paid account, at all times remaining in honor.

The UNITED STATES shall immediately make the corrections as concerns the unlawful restrictions of the liberties of the sovereign people by the administrative agencies of the UNITED STATES;

All Deeds, warranty deeds, trust deeds, sheriff deeds, tax deeds and all Certificates of Title are colorable titles issued to facilitate the 'Pledge' of the private property of the sovereign people. The Pledge has been relinquished, therefore, the UNITED STATES shall make the corrections to discharge all colorable titles, make the re-conveyance and issue the land patent/ allodial title for the property back to the people.

It is the duty of the military to serve and protect the post, therefore, the UNITED STATES military shall serve and protect the sovereign people of America, the creditor of the UNITED STATES. All branches of the U.S. Military shall follow the orders of the Transitional Committee, interim government and government of the republic, respectively throughout this transition.

The Provost Marshals are the organic police force with a duty to serve and protect the sovereign. The Provost Marshal shall immediately serve and protect all who claim protection under this treaty making top priority any/all requests for assistance on claims of unlawful restrictions on the liberties of a sovereign.

There shall be those members of the sovereign people, ambassadors, with a passion to service, who shall choose to serve the republic; lightworkers, visionaries, warriors, teachers and people knowledgeable in the art of peace and love; to serve as watchdogs or compliance, ensuring the integrity and protection of the people's rights; or facilitators and educators charged with presenting real truth, that the enslavement of the sovereign people may never happen again; beacons of light, guiding the people out of the darkness, into the truth;

There shall be those members of the sovereign people who shall be instrumental in breathing life into the civil government of the republic, bringing empowerment to the counties at large; in interfacing with the administrative agents and agencies to compel performance and compliance, to bring about balance and restore the natural flow of energy; to empower the civil government, the people; to nurture and infuse this fledgling republic with peace, light and love; to rise above the fear; to be the light;

These members of the sovereign people, awakened into the truth, compelled to service, may apply to accede hereto; upon receipt, acceptance and registration of the application and Public Declarations shall be empowered as a Private Postmaster of a non-independent postal zone, with all of the rights, power and authority of a wholly sovereign nation, with the authority to seat civilian citizen grand juries; to empower judges in the common law, Rangers and Inspectors with the power and authority to compel performance; to make the corrections to bring compliance and honor within the administration.

The power shall reside with the people on the county. It shall take the agreement of no less than three (3) private postmasters to empower a judge or Ranger who shall serve the people under guidelines presented by the Transition Committee and/or interim government.

Declaring And Establishing The Rightful Claims

Before heading into the next chapters to explain and illustrate the documentation for the claim of authority, it is important to note that this is the process that the years of research by me and many others has come to fruition; into a set of documents that are the mainstay for what other individuals can do by choice. These are not provided to be used, except for education. It forms the basis for a more simplified version which will be shown later.

In the following chapter, many legal documents are explained in summary form that abide by the "Law of the Land "and commerce. The list below is found on the website at the reading room of ***www.divineprovince.org*** and provided as a summary:

Serving Notice on Breach of Trust
Documentary Evidence of Authority, gaining authority as Trustee
Ecclesiastic Deed Poll defines harm, notice of protest, demands for cure

Activation of Authority Federal Reserve
   Activation of Federal Reserve Account
        Exhibit A: Declaration of Political Status
        Exhibit B: Affidavit of Fact-Title Dispute
        Exhibit C: Notice of Surety Act and Bond and related documents;
        Exhibit D: OHIO DEPARTMENT OF HEALTH, CERTIFICATE OF LIVE BIRTH
        Exhibit E: Fidelity Investments Symbol Look-up
        Exhibit F: UCC-1 Financing Statement File
        Exhibit G: NOTICE OF ENTITLEMENT RIGHT-
        Exhibit H: PRIVATE INDEMNITY AND SET-OFF BOND

Exhibit I: ACKNOWLEDGEMENT OF AN ORIGINAL ISSUE OF CURRENCY
Exhibit J: SOCIAL SECURITY CARD for JAMES THOMAS MCBRIDE
Exhibit K: Form 56 Notice Concerning Fiduciary Relationship

Reclaiming Trusteeship and Postal Authority
Charging Sheet
Claim on Abandonment

Declaration of Peace
Universal Postal Treaty Declaration of Peace

**These are provided on www.postmastergeneralna.org and
www.divineprovince.org**

33

SERVING NOTICE ON THE BREACH OF TRUST

The first part of establishing one's truth and position includes the following:

Documentary Evidence of Authority, gaining authority as Trustee
Ecclesiastic Deed Poll defines harm, notice of protest, demands for cure

These are documents created and served by me James-Thomas: McBride and summarized here.

Authority As Trustee For The Global Abundance Program

The pages in this chapter provide the details as documentary evidence of James-Thomas: McBride serving notice towards the attainment of having authority as Trustee and the authority for this Global Abundance & Prosperity Program. What is presented is the result of years of study and research, by myself and others; years of documents and processes building one upon the other, continually moving forward. Please understand that my studies, my work and my tenacious efforts and unfailing refusal to cave to the pressures of The Powers That Be [TPTB] have cost me 16 years of my personal freedom, two marriages, the repeated loss of all material things and the loss of my relationships with my family and friends. There have been countless casualties throughout the years. I have been blessed to have studied and worked alongside some of the best and most dedicated souls who have filled this gruelling journey with love and hope for all of mankind. We have lost many a good man/woman along the way to whom I say Thank You..... Bless you where ever you are today. Your work and your energy lives on through these pages.

My point being, Freedom does not come without a cost. Freedom will not be delivered to your door as you sit all content on the couch. Freedom takes diligence, an ever watchful eye and the willingness to take back your power; Your willingness to put aside the fear and doubt and allow truth to shine through and manifest in your reality.

Freedom, Abundance and Prosperity will not come from the knock on the door, but, will begin within, for our outer world is but a reflection of that which is within. If in our heart we harbour thoughts and/or beliefs of lack, wanting, poverty and/or limitation then lack, wanting, poverty and limitation is what will be reflected into our outer reality. The change we seek must begin within.

So that no man, woman nor child should ever have to travel the pothole laden path which was my journey, I give you the following to light your way to personal and spiritual sovereignty. I/we have done 95% of the work for you, we have blazed the trial, clearing away the briers and thorns, but, each man, woman and child must still carry the ball the rest of the way Home. For even in the acceptance of a gift, one must reach out one's hand and take hold of that gift and bring it into your reality.

This is my gift to the world. Reach out, take this gift and make it your own; take it in; own it to your core, for personal and spiritual sovereignty is our Birthright! World Peace, Abundance & Prosperity is NOT a privilege, it is our Birthright!

We believe that for Abundance & Prosperity to manifest in our lives that we must allow abundance to manifest through us; that abundance & prosperity begin within as a feeling, an expression, and become a way of life. We believe Paying it Forward to be an expression of our abundance in which all may participate, rich or poor; a method of Priming the Well of our abundance, if you will.

This site is my way of Paying It Forward, of investing in America, investing in all mankind, for I see great hope for mankind as we stand on the edge of great change. For this reason I have been Paying It Forward with my work and my life for many years at a great cost to my family and friends. I pray that one day they will understand.

Documentary Evidence Of Authority

In an attempt to break down and make understandable a complex journey I present this overview of the documents and processes with links to the documents in their entirety for your review. Please take your time for their is a great deal of information. Remember, knowledge is power!

Through the years I had proven the existence of the 'private side' funds, and that one could access those 'private' side funds for the discharge of debt and the Redemption of property from the collateral pool of the Military Industrial Complex. I found the evidence that the UNITED STATES had indeed created funds/ negotiable instruments by leveraging my Birth Certificate and later Court Cases, and that the 'private side' funds sat awaiting my use for the discharge of debt, if only I could access them. Our National debt continues to spiral out of control while the private side funds, which were created to discharge this debt, sit idle.

For years we KNEW that they had monetized our Birth Certificate(s), but, we never had the evidence. Suddenly, it was no longer some "crazy conspiracy Theory", it was now absolute fact evidenced by public documents.

Armed with the evidence that they had monetized my 'account' on several occasions; the knowledge that these 'private funds' where set aside for our use to discharge the debt, and an ever increasing working knowledge of the economic system I set out to Activate my Private Side Account with the Federal Reserve Bank with the knowledge and assistance of the U.S. Treasury.

This account was verified as activated, funds where received as evidence, and the account survived two (2) Secret Service investigations, one which I initiated. Within 72 hours of activation, I received a 'call in the night' informing me that an 'Angel' had been watching my account; that $4 Trillion had been fraudulently moved from the account by the Fiduciary; the funds had been recovered from the Bank of Hong Kong, would I please demand the Secret Service investigate the matter.

On June 3, 2009, within hours of getting the call, I delivered a demand for investigation along with a complete set of documents to the Secret Service.

This is the Pass Thru Account established to discharge debt to facilitate Global Debt Forgiveness, just one goal of this Global Abundance & Prosperity Program. To make the transition from fiat money to currency of value we must discharge the debt in full, a matter of adjusting the digits on a computer screen.

Important Notice To The American People

When one steps back and looks at the bigger picture he can see that the American people's Good Faith and Credit funding the aggression and occupation of the nations of the world by the Military Industrial Complex costing the lives of over 100 million people since its creation in our name has left a huge stain on the Good Faith and Credit.

From that same perspective one might ask Does the global aggression and occupation by the Military Industrial Complex funded by the Good Faith and Credit of the American people reflect the beliefs and morals of the American people? Are the American people the aggressive and controlling war mongers as expressed through their government to the world or are they simply the powerless puppets of the war machine?

Throughout history the Constitution for the United States established two sets of Congress and Senate each with their own set of rules, regulations and moral operating principles. Each is responsible for the administration of the affairs and estates of the American people, each employing their own brand of administration.

The Constitution established the original Congress and Senate in original jurisdiction. The 14th Amendment established a second congress and senate under whose jurisdiction we operate today, presumably by our own consent.

Throughout our lifetimes we have been tricked and deceived into living under the 14th Amendment as if by choice and consent. The Offices, Agencies, Officials and Agents in original jurisdiction still exist as a choice for the administration of our affairs, our estates, awaiting our return.

It has been oft said that the military, in original jurisdiction, will stand up and protect the American people once they return to original jurisdiction. The great movement by the people to return to original jurisdiction has landed on barren ground, until NOW.

The Powers That Be have acquiesced to the rights and demands of the people !

The Remedy must be made available to every man, woman and child who seeks it!

Today we have a choice, but, for one to make an informed decision one must open one's mind to truth. We, as a people, have become familiar with Denial, unwilling to accept truth if it threatens the status quo or our field of study or endeavour, no matter how convincing the evidence. We seem to be willing to accept the devil we know rather to face the unknown even though the evidence suggests that change would yield wonderful results.

In original jurisdiction a minimalist, non-invasive, public servant mentality exists, where the administration exists entirely for the purpose of service to the people where the core of authority resides with the people on a local level. The Congress and Senate operate under the jurisdiction of the people to ensure the peace and security of the nation. In original jurisdiction world peace is possible.

In original jurisdiction the Treasury of the United States is responsible for the printing and distribution of a currency of value where a debt is established only in the exchange of value as opposed to mere book entry loans of fiat money. In original jurisdiction everything exists NOW to facilitate global debt forgiveness.

In original jurisdiction the military plays a purely defensive role protecting our borders from aggression or invasion. The Coast Guard and Provost Marshals are the people's protection in original jurisdiction, with a duty to ensure against aggression against or the violation of the private rights of the American people by the state and/or its associated agencies.

In original jurisdiction we have a sales tax sufficient to fund the operation of the administration as well as the construction and maintenance of necessary public infrastructures.

In original jurisdiction we have complete transparency of operation where real justice is standard operating procedure and the court and prison systems are used to protect the people from the elements of evil.

The 14th Amendment congress and senate employs an ever expanding bigger is better mentality. The core of authority is coercively wielded from the top down with little meaningful input from the people on a local level. In original jurisdiction the congress and senate operate under the jurisdiction of the people while under the 14th Amendment the people operate under the jurisdiction of congress and senate. We see and experience the mirror image in the two systems as concerns the authority and jurisdiction.

Under the 14th Amendment we have the private Federal Reserve Banking system which issues fiat money created out of thin air, on which the American people pay interest, based on the Good Faith & Credit of the American people, which has purposely lead to insurmountable hyper inflated global debt which has been wielded as a weapon to justify the ever increasing taxation and limitation of the people.

The 14th Amendment established the Military Industrial Complex, funded by the Good Faith & Credit of the American people, who have been the core of the state of perpetual war and aggression which has existed since their creation. Over 100 million people have died at the hands of the Military Industrial Complex since its inception, funded by the American people. World peace would mean the death of the Military Industrial complex as it is war that produces profits.

672

Under the 14th Amendment Military Industrial Complex we have numerous secret 'Black' ops and 'Black' budgets for use by the ever increasing number of Alphabet Agencies to promote and fund aggression and occupation throughout the world with zero oversight or accountability.

The people have been identified as Enemies of the State in the 14th Amendment congress and senate's Trading With The Enemy Act giving rise to the numerous Wars against the people which have historically proven to exponentially expand the behaviour they purport to war against.

Under the 14th Amendment the courts and prisons are used to leverage the lives of the people for the creation of funds out of thin air and is used to protect the State from the people who fund it.

The War on Drugs has brought us a 100 fold increase in the illicit use of drugs; the protected importation of those illicit drugs by our own ABC organizations and the intentional drugging of America by the huge pharmacy companies resulting in the expansion of the prisons for profit system which exist today.

The War On Terrorism has brought us the extreme expansion of terrorism in the world today which has been used not only to justify the invasion of the private rights of the people but are used today to justify government sanctioned assassinations and the physical and sexual molestation of the people as we travel across this once great land.

The 14th Amendment's Federal Reserve Banking System has brought Foreclosure Gate and the intentional destruction of the American housing industry opening the door for the theft of over fifteen (15) million homes from the American people by the banks.

The 14th Amendment has brought election fraud and special interest groups who now buy their own self serving brand of Legislation to the detriment of the people.

Removing our portion of the Good Faith and Credit that funds the Military Industrial Complex

Removing our portion of the Good Faith and Credit that funds the Military Industrial Complex takes the wind out of the sails of the war machine, the Prison for Profit scheme and the ponzi scheme fiat money systems in which the courts participate.

Removing our portion of the Good Faith and Credit forces a settlement of our accounts, the discharge of debt and a return of the interest to the people which could result in global debt forgiveness and a reboot of the global economic system birthing a system of value.

The matching funds created against our Good Faith and Credit are still available for our use. Removing our portion of the Good Faith and Credit forces the Military Industrial Complex to provide a full accounting of our accounts forcing the release of the private funds held in trust by the DTC, DTCC and OITC for the discharge of debt and redemption of the property, the balance to be administrated as a charitable trust, for our benefit.

So, the choice is: Do we choose to Remove our portion of the Good Faith and Credit that funds the Military Industrial Complex and return it to original jurisdiction where the mechanics for global debt forgiveness already exist and allow the rebooting of an economic system of value, honor and integrity?

Do we choose to remove our portion of the Good Faith and Credit taking the profit out of the war machine opening the door to world peace, abundance and prosperity? Or

Do we continue to fund the perpetual terrorism, war and death with insurmountable debt, taxation and the increased limitation of our private rights further staining our Good Faith and Credit to satisfy the greed and lust for power *and control of the few?*"

Gaining Authority As Trustee

From the beginning, it must be understood that I James Thomas: McBride am but a cog in the Universal wheel of humanity that made the revelations about commerce possible. I simply did my part. The information presented herein is the compilation and evolution of the millions of man hours of research by thousands of selfless men and women dedicated to unravelling the illusion in which we live to bring about the rebirth of personal and spiritual sovereignty for all mankind.

I wish to thank all who steadfastly held tight to the belief that world peace, abundance and prosperity, was not a privilege, but like personal and spiritual sovereignty, they are our birthright; For all of those courageous men and women who understood that if we did not stand up and expose the illusion and corruption in our lifetime that our children and their children would be enslaved forever and chose to stand against the terrorist tactics of the Military Industrial Complex at their own peril and sacrifice. I also wish to thank all of the families of those dedicated souls who lived with the sacrifice, the pain and loss, for you too did your part and have been a motivating factor which moved us through the corruption and chaos. Because of all of our sacrifice(s) we stand today at the doorway of a great evolutionary leap for mankind.

Divine Right Of Use

Today, everything is held in trust. Everything is about trusts, Implied or Expressed. Creator gave man dominion over all things. Dominion over equals control over NOT ownership. This is a Divine Right of Use meaning Use of the Divine property/ the All of earth which is "held in trust". So, the entire world we call earth is held in trust, the Divine Trust, for our benefit as Beneficiaries. The Divine Trust is an Implied Trust as opposed to an Expressed Trust. In the beginning man was responsible, as a Trustee, for the care and well being of that portion of the Divine Estate upon which he/she exercised their Divine Right of Use as a Beneficiary.

Through the decades man has given over that Divine fiduciary obligation to legal fiction trustees. There are as many forms of trusteeships as there are people in the world. Some very fair and equitable, say a republic, all the way to a dictatorship, each with various degrees of freedoms and rights, taxes and limitations.

Over time the trust was entrusted to the Trustee responsible for your piece of the Divine Estate. Government is the Trustee, like in civil administration. They administrate your portion of the Divine Estate? And so today legal fiction Trustees, [governments, postal zones, churches] have morphed from public servants to tyrants. They have turned these positions of service into positions of power, the trustees operating the Divine Trust for their own benefit to the detriment of the estate and the heir.

We the people of this earth, are Heirs to the Divine Estate. We are the Beneficiary and Settler to the Divine Trust and have an absolute right to determine the who, what and how of the administration of our Divine Estate.

Our founding fathers attempted to guarantee a fair and equitable form of trusteeship which would not infringe on the private rights of the American people via the Constitution.

Understand the Breach of Trust In 1865 the Trustees, public servants, administrators of our estates, fraudulently modified the terms of the Constitution establishing a second form of trusteeship which would operate for the benefit of the trustees at the detriment of the estate and the heir. This was a serious Breach of Trust, Breach of Fiduciary duty. And so our Divine Estates, our Divine Inheritance, has been administrated under a Breach of Trust.

It was under this Breach of Trust that established the Military Industrial Complex, the 14th Amendment congress and senate under whose jurisdiction the new heirs, the 14th Amendment citizens would operate and all of the codes and statutes to which we are held accountable, the least of which are taxes.

The original trustees of our estates, the civil administration/ government, have fraudulently altered the trust instrument to facilitate the administration of the estates for the benefit of the trustees via the Military Industrial Complex to the detriment of the heirs/ Beneficiaries.

For decades this Military Industrial Complex has leveraged our estates to fund the global military aggression, pillage, plunder and occupation of foreign nations, raping the lands and promoting the destruction of the social and family unit both foreign and domestic.

For decades this Military Industrial Complex has sucked the life force out of the American people; out of the people of the world, designating us all Enemy Combatants. The Federal Reserve System, a product of the 14th Amendment, has been the front line weapon of the Military Industrial Complex used to facilitate the financial enslavement of the people of the world all by leveraging our Divine Estates. We have, and continue to fund our own enslavement and destruction through our Divine Estate.

This 14th Amendment Military Industrial Complex has the absolute power and authority to use and abuse the people and lands of the world, except that absolute power and authority is based on a Breach of Trust.

As Heirs to the Divine Estate, Beneficiaries and Settlers to the Divine Trust we have the power and authority. We have an absolute duty and obligation to demand and receive a cure to the Breach of Trust.

But, as heirs, we are presumed Deceased, having failed to claim our estate. As such, it becomes necessary to:

1) re-establish their living status;
2) Claim the estate, and
3) Identify and demand a cure to the Breach of Trust.

How does one do this? You may ask. I have my own method which I believe will work for me, but, there is no established method at this time. It is my belief that there is more than one road home. Can TPTB deny that you are a living being when you stand in the street waving your Birth Certificate in the air demanding that your estate be administrated in accordance with the original intent for your benefit and for the best and highest of all mankind?

My bet is that they who hold the original instrument [BC] are the holder in due course of the estate and the appropriate person with whom to file a claim against the estate trust. In Ohio it is the OHIO DEPT. OF HEALTH VITAL STATISTICS who holds the original. I believe they are the intermediary agent who has leased your estate to the Military Industrial Complex. I believe they hold the keys to the Who and How our estate is administrated.

In OHIO, the Probate Judge is the SUPERIOR GUARDIAN of all ESTATES, which IMHO makes him/her the Primary Fiduciary for the estate and in his/her private capacity may be the Privy Councillor with the power and authority to make the changes in administration of your estate that you request.

The key to remember here is these are our estates. They are our Divine Inheritance We are the Powers That Be as concerns us and our estate if we will just take back that power that we have unwittingly given away. If we will simply put away the fear and doubt, acknowledge and accept who we are, claim our Divine Inheritance and instruct our public servants as to how our estate is to be administrated, this would seem to be a prudent cure.

One must remember that your reality is a reflection of what is within. We are seeking peace; We are asking that the administration of our estate reflect the abundance and prosperity that is our birthright, but, our reality can only reflect that peace, abundance and prosperity IF that is what is in our hearts."

Who Is To Be Served Notice

As Heirs to the Divine Estate, Beneficiaries and Settlers to the Divine Trust we have the power and authority. We have an absolute duty and obligation to demand and receive a cure to the Breach of Trust. But how?

In America today we have Township Trustees, County Trustees, State Trustees and Federal Trustees just to name a few of the many levels of fiduciaries within the Trusteeship which is involved in the administration of our Divine Estate(s), the Global Estate Trust. Judges, Clerks of Court, Prosecutors and Attorneys all play their own part in the administration of our Global Estate Trust leveraging our Divine Estates to rape, pillage and plunder the world and enslave the people.

To unravel this intentionally complex Trusteeship of the Global Estate Trust let us begin at the top and work our way down. The Vatican boasts, in their Papal Bull, dominion over the entire earth, via conquest, and is answerable ONLY to the Divine Spirit. Dominion over means control over, not ownership. The Vatican's un-rebutted claims establish them as the Primary Trustee of the Global Estate Trust, our Divine Inheritance; a very unpopular fact. But a fact that opens a doorway placing the cure for the mis-administration and theft of our Divine Inheritance within our grasp.

The Vatican is the Primary Trustee of the Global Estate Trust. To facilitate the administration of this Global Trust the Vatican established the Universal Postal Union as the Secondary Trustees of the Global Trust charged with dividing the Global Trust into zones and endowing these legal fiction zones with sovereign authority to facilitate the efficient administration of the Global Trust.

It is no surprise that the first requirement for the international acknowledgment of a sovereign nation is the necessity of a Post Office. The primary objective of the military in any 'zone' is the protection of the Post, or the Post Office, for in their original jurisdiction, the Postmaster Generals are the Trustees of their respective zone.

In 1789 the Continental Congress passed a bill to "establish the seat of government, a general post office, under the direction of the Postmaster General." That's right, a general post office under the direction of the Postmaster General. They were further dividing the postal zone of North America establishing a new zone, and endowing it with sovereign authority, whereby our founding fathers believed they could establish a Trusteeship which would ensure that sovereignty of the people would be passed down to the people of future generations.

As stated earlier, the Preamble to the Constitution created the Estate Trust which held the freedoms guaranteed in the Articles of Confederation and the Declaration of Independence in trust for future generations. The Articles of the Constitution established the Trusteeship as well as the powers and limitations thereof. The Congress and Senate were Trustees charged with the Administration of our Divine Inheritance, the Global Estate Trust.

In this 'general post office' seat of government there was established the 'civil administration' called the United States. Civil administration ? What do they administrate? Our Divine Estate Trust, the Global Trust, our Divine Inheritance. Remember, we can never OWN anything. We simply have a Divine Right of Use of the property of the Divine Estate, the Global Trust.

So, we the people of this earth have a Divine Right of use of the Global Trust while the civil administration is charged with the administration of our estate for our benefit.

In the world of trusts Civil Administration/Government = Trusteeship. So, the entire world is held in trust. The Global Estate Trust, our Divine Inheritance, our birthright is held in trust and is administrated by the various 'governments' who gain their sovereign authority via the Universal Postal Union, the Secondary Trustee of the Global Trust answerable to the Vatican.

In the world of trusts and trust law, rights, duties and obligations are very straight forward, cut and dry, black and white. There are no opinions, secret codes, rules or statutes, period. Just the facts. There is a chain of command, consequences for your actions, or lack thereof, and accountability.

And so it has been a slow and cumbersome process to overcome the out of control momentum of the civil administrators of the world today. There have been countless casualties as a result of our efforts to unravel the illusion; to overcome the programming and fear which fuelled the beast to reach the core where truth and accountability resides.

The Ecclesiastic Deed Poll Explained

What is an Ecclesiastic Deed Poll? An explanation is required as this is a critical point to the sovereignty process of attaining the appropriate authority. An **Ecclesiastical Deed Poll** is a valid Form of Deed Poll and therefore Deed and Contract whereby a True Being first expresses, affirms and conveys certain rights to another party who are then lawfully bound upon proof of receipt in accordance with the Canons defined under ***Article 133 (http://one-heaven.org/canons/positive_law/)*** of ***Canonun De Ius Positivum.*** The word "Poll" comes from the Latin *pollex* meaning 'thumb'. An Ecclesiastical Deed Poll is permitted to be issued when an inferior Roman Person rejects the rule of law and seeks to assert an untenable and illogical position of superior rights over Divine Law.

In the world of slavery you are "legally" a slave, just as your parents, your grandparents and great grandparents were slaves. You may be lucky enough to live in a pleasant plantation with other slaves, managed by overseer slaves such as police, judges, doctors and politicians where few examples of slave cruelty occur. Or you may be witnessing changes in the community plantation, which is part of a state slave plantation and national slave plantation where there is more crime, more misery and death. The fact that you are a slave is unquestionable. The only unknown is whether you will permit your children and their children to also grow up as slaves. You are a slave because since 1933, upon a new child being borne, the Executors or Administrators of the higher Estate willingly and knowingly convey the beneficial entitlements of the child as Beneficiary into the 1st Cestui Que (Vie) Trust in the form of a Registry Number by registering the Name, thereby also creating the Corporate Person and denying the child any rights as an owner of Real Property.

You are a slave because since 1933, when a child is born, the Executors or Administrators of the higher Estate knowingly and willingly claim the baby as chattel to the Estate. The slave baby contract is then created by honouring the ancient tradition of either having the ink impression of the feet of the baby onto the live birth record, or a drop of its blood as well as tricking the parents to signing the baby away through the deceitful legal meanings on the live birth record. This live birth record as a promissory note is converted into a slave bond sold to the private reserve bank of the estate and then conveyed into a 2nd and separate Cestui Que (Vie) Trust per child owned by the bank. Upon the promissory note reaching maturity and the bank being unable to "seize" the slave child, a maritime lien is lawfully issued to "salvage" the lost property and itself monetized as currency issued in series against the Cestui Que (Vie) Trust.

You are a slave because since 1540 and the creation of the 1st Cestui Que Act, deriving its power from the Papal Bull of Roman Cult leader Pope Paul III of the same year, whenever a child is baptized and a Baptismal Certificate is issued by the state at birth or church, the parents have knowingly or unknowingly gifted, granted and conveyed the soul of the baby to a "3rd" Cestui Que Vie Trust owner by Roman Cult, who has held this valuable property in its vaults ever since, managed by the Temple Bar since 1540 and subsequent Bar Associations from the 19th Century representing the reconstituted "Galla" responsible as Grim Reapers for reaping the souls, or salvage also known as "salvation of souls".

Therefore under the UCC Slave Laws which most slave plantations of the world operate you can never own a house, even though they trick into believing you do; you never really own a car, or boat or any other object, only have the benefit of use. Indeed, you do not even own your own body, which is claimed to have been lawfully gifted by your parents at your birth in the traditions of old slave contracts in which the slave baby had its feet or hands dipped in ink, or a drop of blood spilt on the commercial transaction document we know as the live birth record, against which a CUSIP number is issued and sold the central bank. Yes, the banks claim your flesh, the banks are indeed the modern slave owners, hiding these indisputable facts upon which their money system is built from the people.

You may not realize you are a slave under the slave laws of Uniform Commercial Codes (UCC), but may still erroneously believe you are slave with "more rights" as used to be afforded under "Common Law" until it was largely abolished back in 1933 without properly telling you. The word "common" comes from 14th Century Latin communis meaning "to entrust, commit to a burden, public duty, service or obligation". The word was created from the combination of two ancient pre-Vatican Latin words com/comitto = "to entrust, commit" and munis = "burden, public duty, service or obligation". In other words, the real meaning of common as first formed because of the creation of the Roman Trust over the planet is the concept of "voluntary servitude" or simply "voluntary enslavement".

Common Law is nothing more than the laws of "voluntary servitude" and the laws of "voluntary slavery" to the Roman Cult and the Venetian Slavemasters. It is the job of the overseer slaves to convince you that you are not slaves, the common law still exists and has not been largely abolished and replaced with commercial law, to confuse you, to give you false hope. In return, they are rewarded as loyal slaves with bigger homes to use and more privileges than other slaves.

The reason why the overseer slaves such as judges, politicians, bankers, actors and media personalities are forced to lie and deny we are all slaves is because the slave system of voluntary servitude or "common law" was not the first global slave system, but merely its evolution. Before the emergence of Common Law, we were all subject to being considered mere animals or things under Canon Law of the Roman Cult, also known as the Law of the See, or Admiralty Law.

Under Admiralty Law, you are either a slave of the ship of state, or merely cargo for lawful salvage. Thus in 1302 through Unam Sanctam, the Roman Cult unlawfully claimed through trust the ownership of all the planet and all living "things" as either slaves, or less than slaves with things administered through the Court of Rota. This court, claimed as the Supreme Court of all Courts on the planet was initially abolished in the 16th

Century only to be returned in 1908 under Pope Pius X as a purely spiritual ecclesiastical court of 12 "apostolic prothonotary" spirits, implying the twelve apostles. Since then, this new purely spiritual court has remained in constant "session", with the local courts using these powers to administer Divine Immortal Spirits expressed in Trust into Flesh Vessels as mere dead thing .

Yet this is not the only form of slave law still in force today. Instead, the oldest, the most evil and based on false history are the slave laws of the Menasheh, also known as the Rabbi through the unholy document of hate first formed in 333 known as the Talmud of the Menasheh- the false Israelites. Through the Talmud of the false Israelites, the whole planet is enslaved with the servants of the "chosen people" known as Caananites or K-nights (Knights) also known as the Scythians and then the rest as the goy/gyu and goyim – namely meaning the cattle, the dead lifeless corpses.

Ultimately, you are a slave because you remain profoundly influenced by your education and community at large and because many choose to continue to think and act like a slave, waiting for someone to help them, tell them what to do and be happy accepting bread crumbs of benefits when the system has reaped millions of dollars - yes millions of dollars - of your energy.

A prison designed with no way out Before this time, the system of global slavery and the treatment of the world as one large slave plantation was designed so there is no way out – as evidenced through the courts of the priests of Ba'al known as the judges of most legal systems in the world. Even the most educated of men and women may remain tricked into believing that upon self representation they may claim their "common law rights" as a means of defence, only to find the judge lawfully rejects any and all claims. As the first law of the courts is the Uniform Commercial Codes of slavery as introduced in 1933, the defendant is an employee of a corporation and therefore automatically assumes the liability of any injury. Unless they can pay, they may be sent to prison. If such a trickster as the judge is challenged, they are permitted to escape to their chambers and call upon even greater power to return and magically establish a new court, without telling the defendant they have now entered Admiralty Court, or the laws of the See in accordance with Canon Law of the Roman Cult issued in 1983. Now the judge can impose grave penalties upon such an unresponsive defendant including contempt of court and other punitive prison sentences, with the defendant having no rights unless they know Canon Law concerning juridic persons and establishing standing above being called a "thing".

Sadly, few people actually know the original meaning of "thing" as a judicial meeting, or assembly; a matter brought before a court of law; a legal process; a charge brought; or a suit or cause pleaded before a court. This meaning is then used with devastating effect through the heretical concept of Pius X from 1908 to claim the dead apostles sit in permanent and open session as the "twelve prothonotaries" of the Sacred Rota - as the highest Supreme Court on the planet. So when a man or woman receives a blue or yellow notice from a court issued through this unholy knowledge of Canon law, by the time they come to court, they are automatically a thing. When a man or woman seeks to defend themselves by seeking to speak before the judge, they automatically "consent" to being a thing. Thus a judge with knowledge of such trickery can silence any man or woman by "lawfully" threatening contempt of court if the "thing" does not stop making noise.

Indeed, it is the Roman Cult Canon Law of 1983 that establishes all courts are oratories, with judges holding ecclesiastical powers as "ordinaries" and their chambers as "chapels". Thus the Bar Associations around the world have assisted judges in learning of their new powers in order to counteract those men and women who continue to wake up to their status as slaves, but demonstrating how to remain "in honour" with such perverse law and ensure such "terrorists" are sent to prison for long sentences as a warning to others.

If a judge so inclined to ensure an educated defendant is lawfully sent to prison or worse, he or she may run away for a third and final time to their chamber and invoke their most powerful standing as rabbi of a Talmud Court under the Talmudic Laws of the false Israelites of the House of the twelve tribes of Menasheh. Now, even a judge in a nation that is against the death penalty may choose to impose a "lawful" sentence against any goy/gyu or goyim who dares injure an Israelite – which is normally death. However, while judges in the United States and other nations have started to be trained in the re-imposition of Talmudic Law, it is at the hands of the false Menasheh, also known as the elite anti-semitic parasites also known as the Black Khazars and Venetian noble families. Ultimately, it is enough for judges, clerks and members of the Bar to know that they hold our property in their Cestui Que Vie Trusts and that we are completely without effective rights, until we challenge their fraud. Yet, even when you challenge their fraud, many deny and outright lie on the records- yes judges absolutely committing perjury on the record to deny they hold trustee and executor powers with the case being a constructive trust and executor of the Cestui Que Vie Trust from which powers are being drawn for the form of the court.

So how might a man or woman defend themselves against a private and secret society that has kidnapped the law, that refuses to tell the truth, that lies to its own members and refuses to provide fair remedy. This is the purpose of the Ecclesiastical Deed Poll.

An Ecclesiastical Deed Poll is a supremely sacred private form. In other words, while the Ecclesiastical Deed Poll complies in all aspects to the foundations and principles of law the Roman Cult upon which all western nations and courts are based, it is not an instrument recognized "officially" by the policies (statutes) of the corporate governments - therefore it is private. An Ecclesiastical Deed Poll is permitted to be issued when an inferior Roman Person rejects the rule of law and seeks to assert an untenable and illogical position of superior rights over Divine Law. Only a True Person may issue an Ecclesiastical Deed Poll. By definition an inferior Roman Person has no authority to issue an Ecclesiastical Deed Poll.

An Ecclesiastical Deed Poll must always be on standard sized robin-egg blue paper, printed in serif font, in recognition and respect of its status as a Divine Notice with the full authority of One Heaven, in particular the Sacred Rota and twelve Apostolic Prothonotaries as well as Apostolic Prothorabban of the Divine Sanhedrin. When an Ecclesiastical Deed Poll is issued, it is under the Supreme Court of One Heaven with the full authority of the Divine Creator and all inferior courts including the Sacred Rota. Hence the term Per Curiam Divina is always included to make clear to the inferior Roman person the absolute authority of the instrument. While a True Person issues an Ecclesiastical Deed Poll, it is ultimately a Divine Notice of Protest and Dishonor from the Divine Creator. Therefore, the dishonor of an Ecclesiastical Deed Poll is the most grievous injury of the law and blasphemy to all believed to be Divine. When a Roman slave under inferior Roman law repudiates a valid Ecclesiastical Deed Poll then by definition all acts undertaken with the assumed authority of Sacred Rota by any clerk, protonotary, prothonotary, plenipotentiary or minister are null and void, including and not limited to any warrants, summons, orders, decrees.

And so the following document was served to the Powers That Be.

ECCLESIASTIC DEED POLL
Per Curiam Divina

Before Abraham was, I AM; the Divine Spirit having a human experience. Each atom and cell of this physical vessel I inhabit to travel across this land is infused with the spark of the Creator; I AM one with the light, one with Creator, the alpha and the omega, without beginning nor end, without time. This third dimensional vessel, called man, the original domicile of the Divine Spirit is known on this world and in this dimension as James Thomas of the family McBride, a freeborn inhabitant, heir to the Divine Estate, Beneficiary to the Divine Trust, freeholder in fee simple absolute, one of the 'Posterity' as expressed in the Preamble of the United States Constitution.

Irrevocable Deed and Contract

We, the Divine Spirit, expressed in living flesh, infuse this irrevocable deed and contract with Divine Life through Our Blood, perfecting an unbreakable seal on this agreement, bearing the full power and authority of the Divine Creator and binding on all inferior persons and practitioners of the inferior Roman Law, Sharia Law and/or Talmudic Law from the beginning, without time. The base lead of Our word contains the purest gold for the transmutation of the base man/woman into pure spirit for in the beginning there was the word and the word was god.

Constitution for the United States of America

The Constitution for the United States is a document of dual nature:

- The Constitution is a trust document, and
- it is the articles of incorporation and created a unique trust res and estate of inheritance.

It is a tenant of law that in order to determine the intent of a writing one must look to the title, the Empowerment Clause in statute, which in the case of the Constitution is the Preamble. In writing the Constitution the founders followed the common law of England which stretches back some 1000 years. The Preamble fulfills the requirements necessary to establish a trust. It identifies the Grantor(s), Statement of Purpose, Grantee(s), Statement of Intent, Written Indenture, and the name of the entity being created and is written and constructed as a trust so that it would have the thrust of ageless law. Let us take a look:

WE THE PEOPLE (Grantors) of the United States (from or out of) in Order to form a more perfect union, establish justice, provide for the common defence, promote the general welfare and secure the Blessings of Liberty (statement of Purpose) to ourselves and our posterity (Grantees/heirs unnamed), Do Ordain and establish (Statement of Intent) this constitution (Written Indenture) for the United States of America (name of the entity being created).

The trust res is in the Articles of the Confederation and the Declaration of Independence. The intent of the constitution was to bequeath freedom, life, liberty and the pursuit of happiness to themselves and their posterity. The founders intended to secure and pass on the sovereignty of the people to the people of future generations of Americans, in perpetuity.

One's rights are derived from the land upon which one stands and your relation, or status, to that land. In America these rights originated with the Articles of Confederation and the Declaration of Independence and are attached to the land called America (The Laws of Real Property). Our status, or relation to that land, is determined by the laws of Descent and Distribution. The right to freedom, life, liberty and the pursuit of happiness are Our inheritance bequeathed to us via the Constitution of the United States of America.

The constitution granted the government the power and authority to administrate and to carry on corporate functions. Under the common law, inherent rights cannot devolve to a 'body politic' through a corporation. Rights only devolve to human beings is through and by way of a trust. Under the constitutional law, in order to determine the meaning of a written instrument the court must look to the title. In this case, once again, it is the Preamble. Pursuant to the laws of real property that have been existence from the beginning, the Preamble clearly shows a freehold in fee simple absolute in it. Freeholds in fee simple were instruments of trust, not corporate. "Our Posterity" cannot be speaking of a corporate entity as posterity can only mean a living man/woman, by birth/nativity.

The Articles of the Constitution are the Articles of Incorporation that established congress as Trustees of the Trust and defines their power and authority as well as their limitations. Annexed to the Constitutional Trust is a will like structure, the Amendments. The Trust and the trust res were already in existence when the will/codicil (Amendments) were added some four years later. The Amendments do not constitute the Trust in fact, they are annexed to the Trust as a codicil (a supplement or addition to the will, not necessarily disposing of the entire estate, but modifying, explaining or otherwise qualifying the will in some way.)

A Trust, once completed and in force cannot be amended or altered without the consent of the parties in interest except under reserved power of amendment and alteration. An amendment is ordinarily possible by parties in interest and against parties without vested interest. Prior to the 14th Amendment the freeborn inhabitants, citizens of the states were the parties in interest. The 14th Amendment created the 14th Amendment legal fiction citizen who do not have a vested interest in the trust or the trust res.

The 14th Amendment can be viewed as a codicil to the will that republished the constitution with new meaning, changed the intent behind it and turned it into a testamentary instrument with capabilities of being used against the free born inhabitants through a seemingly voluntary revocation.

We, the freeholders, Beneficiaries to the trust have been tricked and coerced by the Trustees into terminating the Trust by consent when we apply for an S.S. #, drivers permit, marriage license or when we sign an IRS 1040 form, which the Trustees have mislead us to believe are mandatory.

When one applies for an Social Security number, provide evidence of birth and claims to be a United States citizen, a party with no vested interest in a freehold, the trust or the trust res, you literally declared the free born inhabitant to be deceased; the decedent retains no interest in the property and that you, in your dual capacity as a legal fiction citizen are now the executor of the estate.

The Trustees have breached the trust having amended the will for their own personal profit and gain at the expense of the true heirs. The freeholders/ Beneficiary has unwittingly, without full disclosure, become the executor and the Trustees have become the Beneficiaries to the trust through the Laws of Donations, effectively stealing Our inheritance.

A breach of trust of fiduciary duty by a Trustee is a violation of correlative right of the Cestui Que Trust and gives rise to the correlative cause of action on the part of the Beneficiary for any loss to the estate Trust. This rule is applicable in respect to both positive acts or negligence constituting a breach of fiduciary duty by the Trustee. A Trustee's breach of fiduciary duty falls within the maxim that 'equity will not aid one who comes into court with unclean hands.'

When the Trustee's breach is by an act of omission the beneficiary can question the propriety of the Trustee. The Beneficiary had to have full disclosure, full knowledge of the material facts and circumstances. A Beneficiary must have had knowledge of and understood their rights and have no obligation to search the public records to obtain said knowledge.

The Trustees have committed acts of omission, mis-representation, deceit and deception in order to mislead and coerce us into giving up our beneficial interest in the trust and the trust res. The Trustees have compelled the free born inhabitants, freeholders in fee simple, to accept the benefits 'under the will' perverted by the 14th Amendment, without freedom of choice for failure of full disclosure thereby precluding our enforcement of contractual rights in property bequeathed to us by the will. The Trustees are trying to repudiate the Trust, employing a lifetime of propaganda and programming and enforced through threats, violence and coercion, and failing to provide notice to the Beneficiaries of the repudiation which must be 'brought home.'

The Doctrine of Election in connection with testamentary instruments is the principle that one who is given a benefit 'under the will' must choose between accepting the benefits and asserting some other claim against the testator's estate or against the property disposed of by the will. A Testamentary Beneficiaries right to elect whether to take 'under the will' or 'against the will' in case he has some inconsistent claim against the testator's estate, is personal to him; is a personal privilege which may be controlled by the creditors of the Beneficiary. They can claim no right or interest in the estate contrary to the debtor's election and may have no right of a legacy or devise to their debtor if he elected to take against the will.

Acceptance of benefits 'under the will' constitutes an election which will preclude the devisee from enforcing contractual rights in property bequeathed the will. This rule is, of course, subject to the qualifications that acceptance of a benefit 'under the will' when made in ignorance of the Beneficiaries rights or a mis-apprehension, mis-representation as to the condition of the Testator's estate does not constitute an election.

In the beginning God gave man dominion over all things, Beneficiaries of the Divine Trust. The Founding fathers of the United States of America created the constitution for the United States, an estate trust, to pass on sovereignty of the people to the people of future generations, in perpetuity.

In America today, upon giving birth a mother is compelled, without full disclosure, to apply for the creation of the Cestui Que Vie trust, creating a 14th Amendment paper citizen of the United States. Upon receipt of the mother's application the Trustees establish a trust under the error of assumptions that the child has elected to accept the benefits bequeathed by the 'under the will'. The Trustees further assume that the child is incompetent, a bankrupt and lost at sea and is presumed dead until the child re-appears and re-establishes his/her living status, challenges the assumption of his/her acceptance of the benefits 'under the will' as being one of free choice and with full knowledge of the facts and redeems the estate.

Under the assumption that the child is a 14th Amendment citizen, the child's footprint is on the birth certificate by the hospital creating a slave bond that is sold to the federal reserve, who converts the certificate into a negotiable instrument and establishes a second Cestui Que Vie trust. The child's parents are compelled to apply for a social security number for the child, unwittingly testifying that the child is a 14th Amendment paper citizen of the United States, not a party in interest to the trust or the trust res, and assumed to be dead after 7 years, when the federal reserve cannot seize the child, they file for the issue of the salvage bond and the child is presumed dead.

When a child is Baptized by the church, the Baptismal certificate is forwarded to the Vatican who converts the certificate into a negotiable instrument and creates a third Cestui Que Vie trust. These three trusts represents the enslavement of the property, body and soul of the child.

The civil administration, UNITED STATES, continues to operate today under this triple crown of enslavement based on the error of assumptions that we are 14th Amendment citizens of the United States based on the breach of trust by the trustees

Divine Notice of Protest

We, the Divine Spirit, expressed in trust in living flesh, having return from being lost in the sea of illusion born of a self imposed state of amnesia and 50+ years of propaganda and extreme programming to re-establish Our living status and redeem Our estate establishes the evidence in fact of Our competence rebutting the assumption with fact.

We, the Divine Spirit, object to and issue Divine Notice of Protest to the breach of trust and the usurpation of Our inheritance under the error of assumptions of the 'pledge' of Our private property. We have never willingly, knowingly and with full disclosure pledged Our inheritance to any person or entity;

We, the Divine Spirit, object to and issue Divine Notice of Protest to the conversion of the birth certificate to a promissory note or other negotiable instrument without full disclosure nor consent;

We, the Divine Spirit, object to and issue Divine Notice of Protest to all derivatives of the birth registration, the estate trust and Cestui Que Vie trust as fruit of the poison tree;

We, the Divine Spirit, object to and issue Divine Notice of Protest to the malicious and unconscionable actions of the executors and administrators of the estate, to wit:
- knowingly and willingly claiming the child as chattel of the estate;
- creation of the slave bond contract and slave bond.

We, the Divine Spirit, object to and issue Divine Notice of Protest to the intentionally deceitful legal language and meaning of Our earthly parents marriage certificate and the birth registration whereby Our earthly parents were tricked into signing us away into slavery to the state without full disclosure nor consent;

We, the Divine Spirit, object to and issue Divine Notice of Protest to the creation of the slave bond by placing the ink impression of the child's footprint on the birth certificate, converting said certificate into a slave bond and selling same to the federal reserve for the conveyance into the second Cestui Que Vie Trust;

We, the Divine Spirit, object to and issue Divine of Notice of Protest to the issue of and monetization of the maritime lien for the salvage for the lost property for the bank's failure to seize the slave child upon the maturity of the slave bond;

We, the Divine Spirit, object to and issue Divine Notice of Protest to the issue and monetization of the Baptismal Certificate and creation of the 3rd Cestui Que Vie trust, representing the enslavement of Our soul, under the assumption that Our earthly parents gifted, granted and/or conveyed Our soul to the state;

We, the Divine Spirit decree that:
- Our earthly parents never willingly, knowingly and with full disclosure gifted, granted or conveyed Our soul to any person, entity or cult;
- No person, entity nor cult have the authority to gift, grant, convey nor enslave Our soul to any other person, entity or cult without full disclosure and our consent;
- We, the Divine Spirit have never willingly, knowingly and with full disclosure gifted, granted or conveyed Our soul to any person, entity or cult, nor consented to same;

We, the Divine Spirit, object to and issue Divine Notice of Protest to the three Cestui Que Vie Trusts which represent the triple crown of enslavement and three claims against Our property, body and soul by the Roman cult for the purpose of enslaving the people in the denial of all of our rights to the Divine Inheritance, Our right to freedom from all limitations and Our rights and powers as Divine Creators;

We, the Divine Spirit, object to and issue Divine Notice of Protest to the BAR Association as managers of the triple crown of enslavement of the Roman cult representing the reconstituted "Galla" responsible for the reaping of souls;

We, the Divine Spirit, object to and issue Divine Notice of Protest to the BAR Association courts and/or agents use of the inferior Roman Law, Sharia Law, Talmudic Law, Maritime Law, and/or Cannon Law against Us and/or Our property;

We, the Divine Spirit, expressed in trust in the living flesh, having re-established Our living status, whose estate is held in the above referenced trust, hereby re-establish Ourselves as Grantor of the trust having provided 100% of the value to fund the trust, with the authority to act in that capacity and exercise the power and authority of the Grantor of said trust;

We, the Divine Spirit, expressed in trust in the living flesh are vested as Beneficiary of said trust as said trust was established for Our benefit;

We, the Divine Spirit, expressed in trust in living flesh, having re-established Our living status, have standing to seek redress of grievance in the common law;

Receipt of this Ecclesiastic Deed Poll constitutes acceptance and is binding on all inferior persons and carries a mandatory obligation to act in accordance with Divine Law.

We, the Divine Spirit, expressed in trust in the living flesh, a free born inhabitant, heir to the Divine Estate, Beneficiary to the Divine Trust, freeholder in fee simple absolute, do hereby object to and issue Divine Notice of Protest to the following, to wit:

- To the compelled registration of the Birth under the error of assumptions and failing full disclosure, which created the 14th Amendment citizen of the United States;
- To the compelled acceptance of benefits 'under the will' which was perverted by the Trustees without full disclosure and under mis-apprehension and mis-representation, precluding Our enforcement of Our contractual rights in property bequeathed by the will;
- To the Trustee's propaganda, mis-representation, mis-apprehension, deceit and coercion that gave rise to the seemingly voluntary termination of the trust by the Beneficiary;
- To the Trustee's breach of his fiduciary duties which caused loss and injury to the estate;
- To the assumption/presumption that the free born inhabitant is deceased;
- To the assumption that the free born inhabitant is the executor of the estate trust;
- To the assumption that the free born inhabitant is a 'donor' with full disclosure.

We, the Divine Spirit, expressed in trust in living flesh, a free born inhabitant, heir to the Divine estate, Beneficiary to the Divine Trust as expressed in the Preamble to the Constitution, freeholder in fee simple absolute, do hereby:

- Re-establish Our living status, evidenced by the DNA/Blood Seal thumb print below;
- Instruct the Trustees to immediately dissolve the 14th Amendment United States citizen ;
- Instruct the Trustees to correct your records to reflect that we hereby elect to enforce contractual rights in property bequeathed by the will, "against the will".
- Demand that the trust res be turned over to us within the confines of the Truth in Lending Act;
- Demand that all restrictions against the freeholder be immediately released;
- Demand that all bonds, notes or other negotiable instruments be redeemed and the equal consideration be returned to the freeholder;
- Demand that the private funds held by the DTC, DTCC, OITC and/or any/all other entities be made available to me for the discharge of debt, funding the National Banking Association and all sub-accounts thereof;
- Demand that the Trustees provide a full account within 60 days.

Blood Seal of (James Thomas- freeholder)

34

ACTIVATION OF AUTHORITY: FEDERAL RESERVE

The next set of documents is all about the activation of my authority. These documents will reflect much of what has been discussed in earlier chapters bringing together the process of declaration and serving the Administrators who are responsible. These documents can be found and downloaded from the website **www.divineprovince.org** What these clearly reveal is the nature of the commercial labyrinth that is before each.

Activation Of Authority Federal Reserve

Activation of Federal Reserve Account
> Exhibit A: Declaration of Political Status
> Exhibit B: Affidavit of Fact-Title Dispute
> Exhibit C: Notice of Surety Act and Bond and related documents;
> Exhibit D: OHIO DEPARTMENT OF HEALTH, CERTIFICATE OF LIVE BIRTH
> Exhibit E: Fidelity Investments Symbol Look-up
> Exhibit F: UCC-1 Financing Statement File
> Exhibit G: NOTICE OF ENTITLEMENT RIGHT-
> Exhibit H: PRIVATE INDEMNITY AND SET-OFF BOND
> Exhibit I: ACKNOWLEDGEMENT OF AN ORIGINAL ISSUE OF CURRENCY
> Exhibit J: SOCIAL SECURITY CARD for JAMES THOMAS MCBRIDE
> Exhibit K: Form 56 Notice Concerning Fiduciary Relationship

These are summarized below:

Authority Activation Process

In an attempt to break down and make understandable a complex journey I present this overview of the documents and processes with links to the documents in their entirety for your review. Please take your time for their is a great deal of information. Remember, knowledge is power!

Through the years I had proven the existence of the 'private side' funds, and that one could access those 'private' side funds for the discharge of debt and the Redemption of property from the collateral pool of the Military Industrial Complex. I found the evidence that the UNITED STATES had indeed created funds/ negotiable instruments by leveraging my Birth Certificate and later Court Cases, and that the 'private side' funds sat awaiting my use for the discharge of debt, if only I could access them. Our National debt continues to spiral out of control while the private side funds, which were created to discharge this debt, sit idle.

For years we KNEW that they had monetized our Birth Certificate(s), but, we never had the evidence. Suddenly, it was no longer some "crazy conspiracy Theory", it was now absolute fact evidenced by public documents.

Armed with the evidence that they had monetized my 'account' on several occasions; the knowledge that these 'private funds' where set aside for our use to discharge the debt, and an ever increasing working knowledge of the economic system I set out to Activate my Private Side Account with the Federal Reserve Bank with the knowledge and assistance of the U.S. Treasury.

This account was verified as activated, funds where received as evidence, and the account survived two (2) Secret Service investigations, one which I initiated. Within 72 hours of activation, I received a 'call in the night' informing me that an 'Angel' had been watching my account; that $4 Trillion had been fraudulently moved from the account by the Fiduciary; the funds had been recovered from the Bank of Hong Kong, would I please demand the Secret Service investigate the matter.

On June 3, 2009, within hours of getting the call, I delivered a demand for investigation along with a complete set of documents to the Secret Service.

This is the Pass Thru Account established to discharge debt to facilitate Global Debt Forgiveness, just one goal of this Global Abundance & Prosperity Program. To make the transition from fiat money to currency of value we must discharge the debt in full, a matter of adjusting the digits on a computer screen

Below is an overview of the document, Exhibits A - K plus. Click on the Exhibit Link to view the entire document in PDF format. these are provided on the web site

Activation Of Federal Reserve Account

On May 14th, 2009, a notarized document signed by me James Thomas: McBride Creditor attested to a presentment of 11 pages by registered mail to the Department of the US Treasury, Federal reserve Bank of Atlanta, and the Federal Reserve bank of Cleveland. The purpose of this document is to activate a Federal Reserve Account as JAMES THOMAS MCBRIDE a 'national banking association'.

In this document it is so stated

1) James Thomas: McBride is an American sovereign, natural man and NOT a 14th Amendment citizen of the UNITED STATES.........(see annexed Exhibits).

James Thomas: McBride has terminated and/or objected to any/all equity contracts with the corporate U.S. which obligates JAMES T. MCBRIDE or James Thomas: McBride to perform. Any/all equity contracts in which JAMES T MCBRIDE or James Thomas: McBride have become a Party, excepting the 'Original Equity Contract", has been entered into under objection, threat, duress and coercion and are null and void ab initio. James Thomas: McBride has formally waived any and all benefits from the corp. U.S. and its franchised entities. The acceptance of any 'benefit' received under objection, threat and/or duress, or out of necessity as the U.S. has a monopoly, does not constitute a benefit, but rather constitute a gift with zero liability attached thereto.

Exhibit A: Declaration of Political Status which has been lodged with the Sec. of the U.S. Treasury/ Custodian of the Alien Property;
Exhibit B: Affidavit of Fact-Title Dispute to American Sovereign Original/Archetype;
Exhibit C: Notice of Surety Act and Bond and related documents;

2) JAMES THOMAS MCBRIDE, 296520781, is a transmitting utility, public vessel created by and registered in the STATE OF OHIO, LICKING COUNTY for and on behalf of the corporate UNITED STATES to facilitate the flow of credit from the American sovereign, James Thomas: McBride, to the corporate UNITED STATES and the discharge of debt of the American sovereign, in the exchange. (see annexed **Exhibit D:** OHIO DEPARTMENT OF HEALTH, CERTIFICATE OF LIVE BIRTH # 134-54-024518.

3) A search of Fidelity Investments web site establishes the evidence as a matter of fact, that the UNITED STATES has executed the original contract, charging the credit of the American sovereign James Thomas: McBride, giving value to the negotiable instrument bearing CUSIP # 316172105 against the CERTIFICATE OF LIVE BIRTH number 134-54-024518, and traded under FUND NUMBER 54, FIDELITY GOVERNMENT INCOME FUND, identified by the symbol FGOVX, establishing the evidence, in fact, that the account is PRE-PAID and PRIORITY EXEMPT FROM LEVY, and establishing the American sovereign, James Thomas: McBride, as the Creditor and the UNITED STATES via the transmitting utility JAMES THOMAS MCBRIDE as the debtor with a liability to discharge the debt of the American sovereign, James Thomas: McBride in the exchange. (see annexed Exhibit E)

Exhibit E: Fidelity Investments Symbol Look-up

4) To protect and secure the private property of the American sovereign James Thomas: McBride, UCC-1 Financing Statement, file # 2318956 has been perfected, securing the attachment against the transmitting utility/public vessel JAMES THOMAS MCBRIDE/JAMES T. MCBRIDE and establishing in the public domain the priority lien against the Debtor, JAMES THOMAS MCBRIDE, transmitting utility, by the Creditor James Thomas: McBride, American sovereign. (see annexed exhibit F)

Exhibit F: UCC-1 Financing Statement File # 2318956, Minnesota Secretary of State

5) The corporate UNITED STATES was NOTICED of the Absolute right of possession and entitlement right to the transmitting utility/public vessel JAMES THOMAS MCBRIDE/JAMES T. MCBRIDE via affidavit. Said affidavit remains un-rebutted and stands as established fact. (see annexed Exhibit G)

Exhibit G: NOTICE OF ENTITLEMENT RIGHT- A NOTARIZED STATEMENT OF FACT

6) On November 28, 2006 the secretary of the Department of the U.S. Treasury did receive and accept, without objection, dispute or dishonor PRIVATE INDEMNITY AND SET-OFF BOND No. 7005 0390 0000 2767 4202 for deposit to the U.S. Treasury and

charged to the account of the transmitting utility/ public vessel, JAMES THOMAS MCBRIDE/JAMES T MCBRIDE 296520781 to establish and activate a set-off account for the set-off and discharge of debt by the American sovereign James Thomas: McBride. Said Bond has matured into an obligation of the UNITED STATES and further establishes as a matter of fact that the account of JAMES THOMAS MCBRIDE/JAMES T MCBRIDE 296520781 is PRE-PAID AND PRIORITY EXEMPT FROM LEVY. The UNITED STATE'S acceptance of the above Bond without objection, dispute or dishonor constitutes their acceptance of the Terms and Conditions of the Bond Order (Contract) and establishing their Fiduciary duty and debtor obligation/liability to James Thomas: McBride. (see annexed Exhibit)

Exhibit H: PRIVATE INDEMNITY AND SET-OFF BOND No. 7005 0390 0000 2767 4202

7) On December 12, 2006 the Secretary of the U.S. Treasury did receive and accept, without objection, dispute or dishonor, Certified Note No. 7005 039000 2767 4219, ACKNOWLEDGEMENT OF AN ORIGINAL ISSUE OF CURRENCY for deposit to the account of JAMES T MCBRIDE 296520781. Acceptance of the deposit, without objection, dispute or dishonor, constitutes acceptance of the terms and conditions of the presentment, a valid contract, and acceptance of the deposit in the sum certain of $7,175,468,120.00 (seven billion, one hundred seventy five million, four hundred sixty eight thousand, one hundred twenty U. dollars and 00 cents) to the account of JAMES THOMAS MCBRIDE/JAMES T MCBRIDE, 296520781, further establishing the evidence in fact that said account is PRE-PAID and PRIORITY EXEMPT FROM LEVY. (see annexed Exhibit)

Exhibit I: ACKNOWLEDGEMENT OF AN ORIGINAL ISSUE OF CURRENCY

8) Federal Reserve Account Number 06-50913806 has been issued through the Federal Reserve Bank of Atlanta and assigned to the transmitting utility/public vessel JAMES THOMAS MCBRIDE 296-52-0781. (see annexed exhibit)

Exhibit J: SOCIAL SECURITY CARD for JAMES THOMAS MCBRIDE 296-52-0781

9) I, James Thomas: McBride creditor, Real Party in Interest, do hereby terminate all prior Fiduciaries for the transmitting utility, JAMES THOMAS MCBRIDE/ JAMES T MCBRIDE, for Breach of Fiduciary Duty.

I James Thomas: McBride, creditor and priority lien holder of JAMES T MCBRIDE 296520781, do hereby nominate and appoint as fiduciary for JAMES THOMAS MCBRIDE 296520781, Secretary of the Department of the U.S. Treasury, Secretary Tim Geithner. Said appointment of Secretary Tim Geithner, being fully qualified to perform the duties as fiduciary, is effective as of May 13, 2009 and shall continue until further notice, re-appointment, substitution, revocation or termination by James Thomas: McBride. The duties and responsibilities of Sec. Tim Geithner, as fiduciary for JAMES THOMAS MCBRIDE 296520781, are to exercise scrupulous good faith and candor, acting in the best interest of the creditor and lien holder for JAMES THOMAS MCBRIDE 296520781 for the benefit and remedy of James Thomas: McBride, American sovereign; the exclusive and limited purpose of discharging debt for the redemption of property; maintaining a zero balance in the account in accordance with International Bankruptcy Law and shall maintain compliance with all applicable Revenue Codes and statutes.

The Fiduciary shall receive and accept all liabilities; receive and accept all service of process and other documents, instruments, bonds and/or other important documents and Presentments; to appear and discharge, settle and close matters material to said public *vessel, and all assignments for or an behalf of said public vessel and to do any and all acts requisite to fully and faithfully execute said appointment including providing a complete and regular statement of accounting to the creditor, James Thomas: McBride. The same shall be by the order of James Thomas: McBride, his assigns and/or assignees. The Fiduciary shall provide the timely activation of this Federal Reserve Account in accordance with Regulation Z and ensure the efficient execution of the day to day operation of said account.*

Secretary Tim Geithner, acting as fiduciary for JAMES THOMAS MCBRIDE 296520781 is hereby indemnified and held harmless for all costs, fees and other charges which may exist, occur or arise from the lawful execution of his duties as fiduciary in this matter. (see annexed exhibit

Exhibit K: Form 56 Notice Concerning Fiduciary Relationship

35

RECLAIMING TRUSTEESHIP AND POSTAL AUTHORITY

National Banking Association

The Public National Banking association is defined as: *"Those who constitute an association nationwide of private, unincorporated persons engaged in the business of banking to issue notes against these obligations of the United States due them; whose private property is at risk to collateralize the government's debt and currency, by legal definitions, a 'national banking association'; such notes, issued against these obligations of the United States to that part of the public debt due its Principals and Sureties are required by law to be accepted as "legal tender" of payments for all debts public and private, and are defined in law as "obligations of the United States", on the same par and category with Federal reserve Notes and other currency and legal tender obligations."*

In the operation of commerce in Bankruptcy, or Receivership, a Public Official may refuse a valid request, one time. That first request is done in the VOLUNTARY Bankruptcy side of the transaction. A Public Official's refusal, or Dishonor, charges the INVOLUNTARY Bankruptcy and their mandatory obligation to honor your request. They have a mandatory obligation to honor your request when presented the second time. Their refusal to honor your second request is Bankruptcy Obstruction and constitutes a dilectual default and their voluntary surrender or abandonment of their office and all power and authority therein.

A Charging Sheet, a form of indictment, was presented under subpoena to John Potter, Postmaster General who had a mandatory obligation to respond and/or act to provide the remedy. His dishonor resulted in the issue of an administrative judgment which carries the same force and effect as if issued by the highest court in the land, documenting his dilectual default and voluntary abandonment of his office and all power and authority therein.

EXHIBIT 1: CHARGING SHEET

I continued to assist the American people to document the Bankruptcy Obstruction in their foreclosure cases and register this widespread Bankruptcy Obstruction with the

Postmaster General, the Trustee, under whose direction the United States operates and I demanded a remedy for the American people.

I continued to document the collusion between the courts and the banks in sweeping the obstruction under the rug while ignoring real evidence; ignoring real judgments against the banks documenting the bank's admissions to the fraud.

I continued to document the Bankruptcy Obstruction of the Trustees, banks, courts and the Postmaster General -Organic. My research into the power and authority of a Private Postmaster and how to invoke the jurisdiction of the Universal Postal Union gave birth to my **Claim On The Abandonment** of the Office of the Postmaster General, Trustee, under whose direction the Trust styled as the UNITED STATES operates.

I spent months documenting the Bankruptcy Obstruction, employing full disclosure at all times. I believe in telling them several times exactly what and how I am going to hold them accountable.

I Registered my Official Claim on the Abandoned Office of the Postmaster General-Organic [not to be confused with the USPS] for and on behalf of the American people. The trust, the entire Global Trust is out of control and if an enlightened being could step into that office then real change could be made on a global level.

EXHIBIT 2 CLAIM ON ABANDONMENT

My Claim on Abandonment was forwarded to the Vatican for a decision. In the 11th hour, acceptance of the Claim and acknowledgment of **my authority to act in the capacity of the Postmaster General with all of the power and authority of the Office of the Postmaster General** was received from the Vatican in a very material way.

A Trustee Of The Global Trust.

I found myself on the inside, as a Trustee of the Global Trust. The administration of this Global Trust was out of control and I was now in a position to guide this listing ship in a new direction. In the operation of a this Global Trust the administrators have been able to function under a Breach of Trust for decades until someone registered a complaint, identifying the Breach and Demanding a Cure. One must simply identify the Breach. The single act or action which constitutes fraud under which the Trust is being administrated, register a complaint thereto and Demand a Cure. In trust law, there are inescapable repercussions for failure to Cure a Breach.

Upon Acknowledgment of my Claim on Abandonment by the Vatican, I understood that there must be an ACCEPTANCE. The same as when offered a gift, one must reach out and take hold of the gift as a sign of acceptance. If one refuses to grasp the gift and bring it into their reality, the gift remains un-accepted and becomes mute and void.

As Trustee of the Global Trust I felt it necessary to set the foundation for how We the People would now interact with the trust, informing the administration that we have entered a new day and that business as usual is no longer acceptable.

This ACCEPTANCE, establishing the foundation for the future, came in the form of the: Universal postal Treaty for the Americas 2010.

Now as Trustee and Postmaster General, the Declaration of Peace (as presented in earlier chapter was registered into the repository.

The Universal Postal Treaty For The Americas

This has already been presented in an earlier Chapter. **The Universal Postal Treaty For The Americas 2010** was a self executing Treaty presented under the Codes of the Universal Postal Union and the UNITED STATES and has been accepted as positive law, the highest form of law. I wish to present a brief overview of what was in the Treaty, what it accomplished, how it effects We the People and the Global Trust and how it effects our abundance and prosperity. **The Universal Postal Treaty For The Americas 2010** was a self executing Treaty presented under the Codes of the Universal Postal Union and the UNITED STATES and has been accepted as positive law, the highest form of law.

And so I offer my path of experience to others freely. This is the way I found my way. In the next chapters we will derive the benefit of this experience when advancements on what I learned create a much clearer pathway through the labyrinth.

36

THE PHANTOM ADMINISTRATION OF PLANET EARTH INC.

All Government Officials Are Private Contractors

We will leave this now with a Chapter that has an interesting twist. Much of this book is dedicated to revealing PLANET EARTH INC as made up fictional thing by me. However, this phantom structure has a pyramid of corporation beneath it that is indeed registered. The UNITED STATES is a corporation **(www.abodia.com/2/United-States-is-a-corporation.htm#Its_a_Corporation)** and **CANADA is a registered CORPORATION under the USA.** And you thought we were an independent country. Canada is a Corporation Under UK Queen - Canada is TRADED in the US Stock Exchange and registered as "*...CORPORATE CANADA in USA. This is Canada's Corporate registered number. 0000230098 CANADA DC SIC: 8880 American Depositary Receipt. Business Address Canadian Embassy 1746 Massachusetts Ave., NW, Washington, DC 20036...*" You can check out **http://inpursuitofhappiness.wordpress.com/2006/12/02/canada-is-a-corporation-under-uk-queen/** and check it out on Edgar at **http://www.sec.gov/cgi-bin/browse-edgar?action=getcompany&CIK=0000230098&owner=include**

If, as an American or Canadian, you are sceptical about the Vatican's involvement in the administration over America, you need to do some research on the **www.manta.com** website, owned by Dunn & Bradstreet. If you research the private corporation called 'the UNITED STATES Government', you will find that the 'OWNER' is listed as being 'Archbishop Deric J. McLeod, of the The Basilica of the National Shrine of the Immaculate Conception, of Washington, DC'. Since Archbishops of the Vatican are sworn to poverty, then, the Archbishop can only be the named agent for the secular Holy Roman Empire, situate in the city/state called the Vatican.

If you wish to have proof that the Pontiff of the Holy Roman Empire has used religion as a means of entrapment of millions of souls into a state and status of slavery for centuries, check out these webpages:

The Pontiff of Rome gains control over England, and makes the Monarch of Great Britain a puppet Monarch FOREVER See King John at:
http://www.nndb.com/people/536/000092260/

Pope declares by edict that all humankind are his subjects(slaves) - last sentence here: Unam Sanctam *http://www.fordham.edu/halsall/source/B8-unam.asp*

The false Apostle, the Roman author of most of the New Testament, Paul:
http://www.judaismvschristianity.com/paulthe.htm

False Christianity, Mithraism becomes Roman Christianity First Pope:
http://www.reformation.org/pope-constantine.html

The primary assertions made on this website are:

1. The income tax applies only to fictional (legally dead) entities called persons. Upon the recording of live birth of a child, a 7 year countdown begins. If that child, or its parents, do not give notice that the child is still alive, the child is declared 'legally dead', thus allowing the child, when becoming an adult, to be infused with the 'legally dead' legal name, as found on a birth certificate. That is why judges and lawyers wear black robes - for the same reason undertakers wear black suits - they are dealing with the 'dead'.

2. There is absolutely no government act, statute or law to which any free will living adult human in Canada, or in the USA, is subject.

3. A free will living adult human cannot enter into a contract with a fictional entity, such as with the de facto nation called Canada or Government of Canada, nor with a de facto Province of Canada or Government of a Province, nor with the de facto Crown in right to either of the above, or with a State[USA], and thus, certainly not a contract of servitude. And, so, any exchange of labour an adult free will living man or woman may do with any Government department or agency must be done through an agent in commerce where the free will adult living human remains as an 'undisclosed principal' and the claimant in equity of all remuneration paid over to the fictional legal name/ agent. The 'legal name' agent is a 'tool', in the form of intellectual property, owned by the Crown and used by the living adult free will status human, the undisclosed principal, under the Rule of Necessity.

4. The fraudulent tricking of people, through their ignorance, into the status of "plantation slave" by their using a name created and owned by the Crown or State is an act of treason, by government, upon the sovereign people. That Crown or State owned name is the name as found on the Birth certificate.

5. Since we, as free will beings, are REQUIRED to use the Crown/State owned legal identity name in all commerce and in government communication, such use is not a voluntary act on our part, as we must use it by PRIVATE NECESSITY to sustain and maintain our life. That negates the Crown/State claim that we voluntarily use it, and thus negates our becoming property owned by the Crown/State through the legal maxim, accessio cedit principali.

6. The 'legal fiction name', AKA: 'person/taxpayer', has only the function of an 'agent in commerce' and 'trustee in trust' for the free will living adult human to which it is associated.

And for Canada specifically:

7. The British Monarchy ceased to have any relevance to Canada in 1901, upon the death of Queen Victoria. All British Monarchs have been pretender Monarchs of Canada since that date. The office of 'The Queen', 'Her Majesty' or 'the Crown' is the 'also known as' name for the City of London, and its owner, the Vatican, as the Monarchs of England have been vassal Monarchs subject to the Pope's Holy Roman Empire since 1213 AD.

8. The Parliament of Canada is a de facto usurper of governing power over Canada since 1931, and in reality, since 1901; and, in fact is a commercial corporation subject to the City of London. Although we see all court cases where the action is brought by Government to be "The Queen" or the Latin "Regina". That only indicates that the Queen of Great Britain is acting in the role of agent for the City of London. That is why she does not have to comply with her Coronation oath to defend the individual rights of the people. That oath is not applicable in her role as agent for the Crown of the City of London. And also, the fact that, since 1213, all incoming Monarchs of England must make a pledge of fielty/fealty to the Pontiff of Rome, not to the Roman Catholic Church, but to his secular Holy Roman Empire, before being allowed to be crowned Monarch of Great Britain, would make the Coronation Oath invalid where it conflicts with Papal Policy. And, as with the Oath of Office of the President of the UNITED STATES, who must also be subject to the Pontiff and his policies, and thus that Oath being so commonly ignored, so too is it ever more evident that the Queen of G.B. is following policy that conflicts with her Coronation Oath. Secondary Oaths only apply when they are complicit with the Primary Oath.

Think this is ancient history? Check out the pledge of a newly crowned Pope/Pontiff - Father (creator) of Kings and Princes, and obviously of Presidents and Prime Ministers at **www.aloha.net/~mikesch/claims.htm**

We have presented two situations where "we the people" are taking back positions that have been vacant. The Republic of the United States group has been presented as one as repopulating the seats of Congress. The other is the Postmaster General which has been vacant. Now it has to be understood that much research has gone into that determination.

But there is a fellow named Rod Class who has been deeply immersed in going much further. He has been receiving a ruling that US Government Offices are Vacant and all Government Officials are private contractors.

On **www.the2012scenario.com** October 14, 2012, the following article was published:

US Bombshell; Rod Class gets FOURTH Administrative Ruling "Gov't Offices are Vacant"- All Gov't Officials are "Private Contractors"
Submitted by The South on Sun, 10/14/2012 - 18:25

"Yes, you read that correctly; it is true, and is now on the court record; black ink on white paper. Please read on:

A lot of us have been exposing the crime of the UNITED STATES corporation for many years, but until recently, no one has had the proof that all government offices are vacant; no one is home; those supposed government offices/agencies are being occupied by PRIVATE CONTRACTORS and are NOT being occupied by a legitimate government body.

This is equivalent to the ice cream man knocking on your door and extorting taxes from you. He has no lawful authority to do anything other than drive the ice cream truck - he's not a government official; he's an ice cream man.

Your supposed government officials are nothing more than ice cream men/women who are fraudulently extorting money from you and your family; throwing you in prison; taxing you to death; stealing your children and imposing their will on you, and enforcing their own **internal-statutory rules and codes upon you and your family.**

Rod Class has now received **FOUR** Administrative Rulings that prove what many of us have felt to be truth: What you think is government; what you think are legitimate Government Officials/Senators/Congressman/Policeman/Governors/Tax Collectors, etc. are nothing more than **private contractors**, extorting money from American Citizens and failing to pay off the public debt as they are instructed to do by the 1933 bankruptcy.

What they have done is this:
These people have switched places with the average American Citizen. They are enforcing their own Administrative codes, that are only meant for THEM, upon regular Citizens who are not being paid by the corporation. The supposed elected officials have hoodwinked the country into an employment position without pay. They themselves are taking public money to occupy government seats/positions/agencies, when they are nothing more than private contractors ... Felony!

They are treating us as if we are paid government employees; enforcing their own internal rules-regulations-codes, and statutes on the average Citizen, as well as conveniently forgetting to send us our weekly/monthly government employment check.

I've been preaching this for the last year + with no avail on this forum. Perhaps now, people will begin to listen and take action.
In these radio shows, Rod explains his Administrative Rulings from the various Judges; explains the con, and shows you, where in their very own US Codes the above aforementioned information is spot on.

There are a few shows you need to listen to, and here are some bullet points of those shows:

1. All BAR attorneys are prohibited from representing John Q. Public; can only represent gov't officials and employees within their own agencies, their BAR Charter says so.
2. Any Judge that prohibits you from representing yourself or hiring a defense other than a BAR attorney, are in fact, committing a felony on the bench in violation of the Taft-Hartly Act (running a closed union shop) and the Smith Act (overthrow of Constitutional form of Gov't)

3. Anytime an BAR attorney represents someone in a case against you, you can now claim that person is incompetent; a ward of the state, with no standing to sue.

4. Any and all tax collectors, police officers, sheriffs dept's, DOT, tag agencies, BAR attorneys, Judges, Highway Patrol, supposed elected officials, are nothing more than private contractors, who can now be brought up on fraud charges for impersonating a public official while receiving federal funding.

5. Any and all home, vehicle, credit card loans are supposed to be discharged through the Treasury window, in compliance with the 1933 bankruptcy laws. These scumbags are double dipping and never discharging the debt like they are supposed to. They are embezzling the funds and pocketing them for themselves.

6. Every person sitting in prison today was railroading by a BAR attorney who's first allegiance is to the State; who had no lawful authority to represent them; who worked in concert with the State to perpetrate a fraud upon its victims.

7. Orders from Administrative courts prove for the fourth time, an agency of the State is NOT an agency under the State.

8. Elected Officials are claiming 11th Amendment sovereignty, when it's actually you and I that hold 11th Amendment sovereignty. They are getting paid by the corporation, you and I are not.

9. They have admitted to the crime of no one actually holding a public office; they are filling corporate seats and defrauding the public.

10. Political subdivisions are not getting their 40% funding from the Feds as they are supposed to get.

11. These Judges have admitted (black ink on white paper) that all these State Offices are .... EMPTY!

12. Now we have Administrative paperwork - ruling these public offices aren't part of the State agencies.

13. Attorney Generals may not practice law; can't represent the people who are not public officials.

14. If the State is a 3rd party interloper in your Marriage (marriage license); Vehicle Title (State Registration), etc. then they are liable for 1/3rd of the cost to manage the daily activities of that contract.

15. If the State demands you have a Drivers License and Tag your vehicle because it is registered with the State, then as the owner of the vehicle, the State is required to pay for the vehicle, the tags, licensing, fuel, tires, oil, etc. and they are also to pay you a salary for driving a State owned vehicle; it says so in their own Highway Safety Act and USC - CFR rules and regulations.

16. We now have the court orders that goes back and nullifies any and all IRS and Tax cases, Foreclosures, Credit Card Debt, cases or actions. These people never had the lawful right to demand anything of you; they are corporate actors, not a legitimate government body.

17. Judge admits the 1933 bankruptcy, and no way to pay off anything because of Federal Reserve Notes; all public debt is t be discharged through the Treasury.

18. Only the Secretary of Transportation can hear traffic cases; all traffic cases are civil, not criminal.

19. If you're not being paid for you time, you are not required to have one of their CDL or CMV licenses; it's prohibited.

20. Says we now have a major labor dispute on our hands; US corporation running a slave racket against American Citizens without the pay.

21. United States Codes (USC) and Titles #1 thru #50 are void; have never been passed by Congress; all have been repealed.

*As I've been saying for a very long time on this forum: If you are not getting a weekly or monthly paycheck from the so called federal government aka UNITED STATES or one of its sub corporations such as the STATE OF ***, then their statutory rules (not laws), codes and regulations **DO NOT APPLY TO YOU** .... Period!*

There is so much information packed into these last six calls, I can't even begin to share it in this post. If you want your freedom; if you want to know with 100% surety that the foreign corporation known as the UNITED STATES has zero authority over you unless you are receiving a weekly paycheck from them, take the time to listen to call #646 through #651 here:

http://www.talkshoe.com/talkshoe/web/talkCast.jsp?masterId=4...
Scroll down the page and click on the orange "Listen" button; a pop up player will appear for your listening pleasure. And believe me: This is pure listening pleasure, with the court filings; rulings and US Code to back it all up. By the time you finish these few short shows, your fear of the government will be a thing of the past.

Also, many of Rod's current filings against the infrastructure are at:
http://harveyw26.minus.com *...some may be easy to download, some may not !*

And for those of you who are new to the forum and want to get a better grasp of all this prior to or after listening to the calls, here are some of my more informative posts on the matter at hand:
Public Notice to Gun Grabbing Politicians:
http://www.dailypaul.com/246514/public-notice-attention-to-a...
So the Government wants you to collect a sales tax?
http://www.dailypaul.com/245362/have-a-business-and-the-govt...
Your Home Loan was paid the day you signed the note:
http://www.dailypaul.com/244590/want-to-stick-it-to-the-bank...
The real reason for the 14th Amendment:
http://www.dailypaul.com/244553/they-created-the-14th-amendm...
What's the One Document in your possession that gives you the authority to rule over my life?
http://www.dailypaul.com/244165/whats-the-one-document-you-h...
Can the State be an actual injured party? ..... No, it cannot!
http://www.dailypaul.com/243521/can-the-state-be-an-injured-...
Having a Social Security # is not a contract with the State/Feds:
http://www.dailypaul.com/243164/social-security-is-not-a-con...
Trust Law, your Rights and how to enforce them:
http://www.dailypaul.com/243090/trust-law-your-rights-and-ho...
Why you should never hire an attorney:
http://www.dailypaul.com/242260/this-is-why-you-should-never...

*Hopefully now in light of these **Administrative Court Rulings** people will now come to realize the fact, that **Unless You Are Getting A Weekly Check From Government,***

Their Statutory Rules-Codes-Regulations They Put Off As Laws, Have Zero Force Or Effect On You Personally. *No Contract = No Jurisdiction.*

Did you fill out an employment contract with the State; are they paying you for your services? If not, why the hell are you following their rules? This is how we change our current form of Government back to the Republic is was initially intended to be. If you don't take the time to listen to at least those last six shows at the link above, you are overlooking the most important information ever to come to light within the Liberty Movement. Stop looking for a savior to save us from tyranny and listen to the shows I've provided. Now you are your own savior - Individually, now you can make a HUGE difference in our political structure and form of government."

You may think this is a pretty good joke but rest assured, the evidence is there to check it out. As yourself, what power does IBM Corp have over you? And what if any Corporation presented a bunch of documents that you signed because they hid the truth of your employment? Would that be fraud? Would it nullify the contract?

A Note On Your New Path

Are things changing? You betcha! At Light Speed!!! By now you are filled with confusion. You are a mere mortal that wants to be happy and pay your bills. You do not want to take on the system even though it may be a fraud. You want peace and harmony not conflict. You do not want to be warrior of light or commerce. What do you do? Do you really want to take new path? What would it be?

37

LESSONS FROM
THE TWO FACED EARTHLING

"Most of my life I had been at war with the system. Naturally, I begot exactly what I asked for-war. It was not until I truly understood who I was and took on the total being of peace, that my reality began to change" James-Thomas: McBride

Life is about Lessons. What have you learned from the words which have been presented so far? Are you happy with your life or are you not? we now enter the part oabout choosing from those lessons. It is about how you resign from PLANET EARTH Inc. and attain your pension called Good Faith and Credit. It is about burning your prescription for those blue pills of Religions and the CODE of gods that diverts the power of Spirit. We have seen how the Cure of James Thomas of the McBride family has taken form. Now it is time to look at the individual Cure. You can make a choice now that you are informed that a choice exists.

And so The Matrix of a New Consciousness manifesting into reality is everywhere, it is all around us. You can see it when you look out your window, or turn on your television set. You can feel it when you go to work, when you go to church, when you pay your taxes. It is the wool that has been pulled over your eyes to blind you from the truth. You are a slave like everyone else. You were born into a prison that you cannot see, that you cannot smell, or taste or touch. A prison for your mind is your spiritual abandonment, a choice made by you. A prison of your body that is your trade of sovereignty for perceived benefits and money. And a prison of your soul that was accepted in your religious beliefs to follow the gods and the words of GOD Unfortunately no one can be told what the Matrix is. You have to see it for yourself. This is your chance to understand the Matrix and to choose a way out. After this, there is no turning back.

Take the blue pill, the story ends, you wake up in your bed and believe whatever you want to believe. Take the red pill, you will stay in wonderland, and I will show you how deep the rabbit hole goes. Remember, what I am offering is the truth, nothing more. Follow me."

There are many Lessons that the journey of the Soul faces in rising in its vibration. And it matters not whether the journey is dark or light for the destination is the same. In this section, we will put before your mind what are the most difficult revelations of the Earthling in the Soul's quest to find Home. These are not lessons easily accepted and even though they are placed directly in front of you, the tendency is for intellect and ego to reject these from belief until these are experienced directly in the Soul's quest.

Nevertheless, the purpose here is to bring these forward into conscious awareness for even though they may not be accepted directly as truth, they may provide the attraction to investigate to the satisfaction of each.

In every aspect of life we live in an inherent polarity that is ingrained from the first day one takes a breath to cry or get attention driven by instinct. Even before that event, the way your mother thinks, speaks and acts has influences upon your being. The Earthling has accepted a world of polarity as there is always a conditional "two-faced" standard on those important issues of life:

In the Bible, even god does not follow his Ten Commandments;
In cultures, we worship those who are the kings, queens, popes, rulers, gods;
In business, we are obedient to our masters called CEO's who pay us;
In government, we cower to the political leaders;
In military, we fear the mighty power of the armed forces;
In our personal lives we favour bloodlines;
In corporate life, we follow a satanic survival of the fittest philosophy;
In religion, we overlook rape, pillage, slavery, death, and destruction by a god;
In life, we fear the consequence of death and sin;
In purpose, we seek carnal pleasures and desires so as to better than others;
In family it is our bloodlines we protect not the rest;
In family it is our fortunes and accumulations that we hand down and protect;
In our family we are willing to forgive others unless they mess with us;
In life's rules, the 10 commandment rules are for others;
In history we believe what experts write;
In life, our forgiveness, love, and preferences are conditional;
In behaviour we follow those deemed smarter, more powerful;
In beliefs we follow a pyramidal structure of hierarchy and inequality;

The loving, vengeful gods and their spokesmen have taught many they are born sinners and they can absolve sin. So we as a mass believe we can be kind to a few to dissolve hate of others. We have been conditioned to think light and dark, good and evil.

It is ok to kill those who are perceived as a threat. Earthlings are addicted to the drama of polarity and conflict. The scenario is a double standard life of a two-faced human. On one hand the human has an inherent desire to live in love, peace and harmony to help others until one is crossed, deceived or threatened. Then it all changes to a scenario of vengeance and "putting it right" unfolds. Why is it this way? It is because this polarity and separation of self and one's immediate family is what we have been taught. It stems from the gods who taught us. Whether we like it or not, the commandments are ok until it is time to take an eye for an eye. Whether we have higher spiritual inklings or not, we follow the carnal needs to express the lower desires of self and ego. We like peace but we have clearly seen as a corporate "culture" and the satanic beliefs prevail so as to line our pockets. It is to live life to the fullest expression of self. Everything we think, hear, see and therefore express is a drama between good and evil. Our movies are this drama; so is our lives. We love it. And we hate it. And so with such love of polarity, does it come as a surprise that we create more of it? This endless drama is hardly surprising when we create and live in a world of vengeance and conflict; how can it ever cease?

The Two-face Earthling is best shown true colors with family bloodlines. They are the loved ones, the protected ones and all the stops are pulled out, until one of them pisses the other off. Then the rules change. The whole idea of equality and love of all is just lip service; really a big joke. It is the ego and intellect at play with as Christ put it: "the carnal self".

Yet this two faced Earthling has always had choice. It is the way it is because the Earthling has liked it this way. The Earthling as measured by what is and what the majority chooses has consistently chosen to be led by others and to favour immediate family and carnal desires. It is the polarity that is the norm and opinion, condition, desire that supports Earthlings in being employed by PLANET EARTH Inc. Yes, so far, the Earthling has accepted it this way and the powers of PLANET EARTH know it. It's the corporate culture! But as we have seen, perhaps the jig is up now and it is time to thank the Elite Bloodlines for the journey to this point, say thank you, it's been a good lesson, now let us move on together.

The Light And The Dark Ascension

Yet how could one know good if he did not know what was bad? How could one see light when he has lived in the dark. When both are visible one can rise above. A dark side has been presented here simply to show that there are two sides to everything we believe. For once one see both, one can choose. It is like the Triad, the triangle of light and dark at the two bottom apexes, and the top apex of the merger of the two where there is no distinction. Here above, all is perfect once you rise above both light and dark. It is a place where neither judges the other as wrong or right. It is a place of unity vibration that makes us all, love. Love does that, hate can't

If you begin to look at the belief systems of Christ Consciousness and Lucifer Consciousness, it seems that while one is dedicated to the service of self, the other is dedicated to the service of others. And so we have two major schools of thought and behaviour; the Spirituality of Lucifer and Christ. We have looked closely at both. We have unknowingly chosen in the past, the spirituality of Lucifer because we have supported the corporate pyramid model and followed other's word of god. Yet in either case, we strive for a better life and a better world. It seems that some Divine Plan may be upon the Earthling in the form of the Word of God?

As we have seen in previous chapters, much of humanity is not simply accepting the old truth anymore, they are subconsciously aligning with a new truth without even being led; desire of peace, love, and service to the Earth and mankind.

Let us divert slightly and look at this thing called ascension. Dictionaries typically define this as "moving upward". The act of rising to an important position or a higher level. The ascent of Christ into heaven on the fortieth day after the Resurrection. In the New Age, it is an increase in the level of vibration. This is not to helpful as to what this really means to you and I.

Valerie Hunt, ***www.valeriehunt.com*** is a physical therapist and professor of Kinesiology at UCLA. she developed a way to confirm and measure the human energy field. For example, Doctors use EEGs and EKGs to measure electrical activities of brain and heart for example. She discovered the EMG Electromyograph measures the energy field in muscles and expanded into the aura. Normal frequency range in the brain is 0-100cps (cycles per second) most occurring between 0-30cps. Muscle goes to 225cps, heart to 250 but this is where electrical function associated with biology drops off. She picked up a field of energy radiating from the body that ranged between 100 and 1600cps.

These were strongest in areas of the chakras. She noted the field behaves holographically as do the energy fields of the body and that these fields were non-local—could be measured anywhere on the body. She called it the holographic field reality. When the main focus of consciousness is on material the frequencies are in lower range around 250cps. People who have psychic abilities and can heal are 400-800cps. People who can go into a trance and channel other information operate in a narrow band of 800-900cps to receive information.

Those who are mystical are above 900—those who possess the wisdom to know what to do with the channelled info—aware of cosmic interrelatedness of all things and are in touch with every level of human experience. They are anchored in both psychic and trance abilities, but their frequencies extend beyond of up to 200,000-cps.

So is there a progression of psychic abilities? If you look at the A-Z of psychic abilities, there are some 200 listed. But the main ones are; After life communications, Aparitioning, Apportation, Astral projection, Card reading, Channeling, Clairvoyant, Déjà vu, Divining, Divine Intervention, Invisibility, Empathy, ESP, Levitation, Materialization, Necromacy, OBE, Ouji, Past Life Regression, Palmistry, Psychic healing, Remote Viewing, Regression, Scrying, Tarot, Tea Cup Reading, Telekinesis, Teleportation, Telepathy, Transfiguration.

What Valerie is saying is that there is a relationship between the vibrational frequency of the body's electromagnetic system and specific psychic abilities. This is what we refer to as *raising one's vibration.*

If you look at the New Age believers (or the new consciousness), the process of ascension is indeed rising to a higher vibration which they say is unconditional love. And when you can be in totality that which you already are (unconditional love vibration), let go of this polarity then you get to that higher state of ascension and all these magical abilities above open to you.

This is called the new energy and with reference to the New Age beliefs, we can create an interesting graph of this process of ascension and ability upgrade. This is further explained in my books **Can You Let Go** and **Managing Human Subtle Energy.**

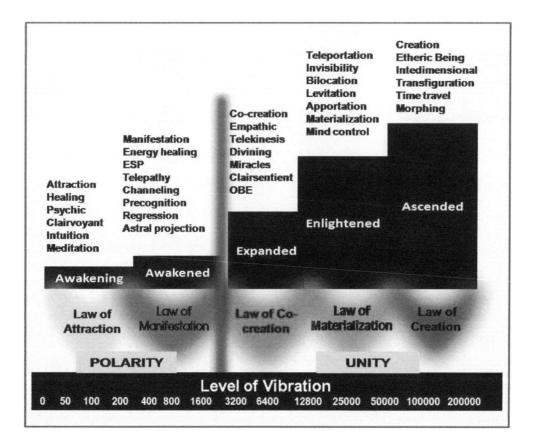

At first, this graph may seem far out but you will see that there are several things of interest here.

1. The Level of Vibration is a logarithmic scale like things natural in nature,
2. the stages or classes of vibration that "opens" to
3. the types of psychic powers.

The vast majority of humans simply accept that they have limited control of their lives and experience whatever energy comes at them. This is true if you let it be so and go to default. The default is to let your lower mind and body do what ego believes is correct for you. The default is to allow your energy systems dictate to the Law of Attraction. The process of the shift from low to high change goes through several stages. The lowest stage is the lower form of life—purely instinctual (like an animal) run by behavior totally void of the consciousness of spirit—the higher mind. At the higher end is the highest form of life—totally inspirational run by the consciousness and power of Spirit. The stages are reflected by the level of vibration. For the sake of simplicity these different stages are sleeping; awakening, awakened, expanded, enlightened, and ascended. This is the process typically referred to as Ascension.

Now first of all you have to open your mind to the fact that the "unexplainable" is all around us. Materialization, bi-location, invisibility, levitation are abilities that people on this planet already have. These may be rare but nevertheless exist.

Have a close look at this diagram. Consider how a material object such as ice changes its rate of vibrational frequency and its properties as heat is placed on it. It *sleeps* as ice but starts *awakening* when heat is applied. At the *awakened* stage it becomes water and at the *expanded* stage it is steam. At the *enlightened* stage it is now no thing and at the *ascended* stage it is pure spiritual energy from what the ice was made. The evolution of rising vibration brought totally different properties each time as the energy simply changed from evolving back to its original state of no thing; no thing being every-thing or all of creation. That is the ascension process in action, for even ice can ascend!

Now consider the power of love of the heart. It is high vibration (like fire) being applied to a human (like ice) that is at a state of lower vibration. This unfolds in a similar evolution with new properties coming out at each stage. The more love (heat) you apply to this body (ice), the more the body, and its properties change in energy form. If you look at some of these properties on the chart, you get the drift of what these properties are.

For some insight in this you can check out recent Russian research on DNA at **www.psychicchildren.co.uk/4-3-RussianDNAResearch.html.**

Grazyna Fosar und Franz Bludorf say: *"The human DNA is a biological Internet and superior in many aspects to the artificial one. The latest Russian scientific research directly or indirectly explains phenomena such as clairvoyance, intuition, spontaneous and remote acts of healing, self healing, affirmation techniques, unusual light/auras around people (namely spiritual masters), mind´s influence on weather patterns and much more. In addition, there is evidence for a whole new type of medicine in which DNA can be influenced and reprogrammed by words and frequencies WITHOUT cutting out and replacing single genes."*

What is even more intriguing is how DNA control things from the subconscious to conscious and receive information into its holographic computer like structure, which works best when it is in the "frequency mode of love" where it is like an electrical current that enhances the hypercomunnications!

And so if you can recall the story of the Soul who travels to Earth to have its experience by taking on a vessel called a physical body, it gets trapped into the slavery of the system and hence the trapped body inhibits the growth of the soul by keeping its vibration in the lower range. At the lowest range, the Earthling behaves instinctually like an animal but can rise through the development of intellect above that stage by choice. And so the Earthling takes its journey of expression and experience to rise trough the Power of the Body (physical) into the Power of the Mind (Intellectual) and to the Power of Spirit. The Earthling, begot of love between masculine and feminine energies through a love relationship travels on the journey in the Earth reality in an attempt to rejoin its true self which is a quantum piece of Source, from where it came referred to as Home. Each journey brings choices on the reality it chooses and the level of vibration it attains so as to experience those abilities and qualities that we have discussed. All these are simply neutral abilities and whether the application is good, evil, or in-between is individual choice.

And so one can become a good Earthling or a bad Earthling by choice. So if we were to create a simple graph of ascension for the "good "guys of Christ Consciousness we would get a picture that shows vibration and the various stages. These powers are the ones that we strive to attain as good guys and if you attain these, like telepathy and so on you are engaging in the esoteric world of White Magic.

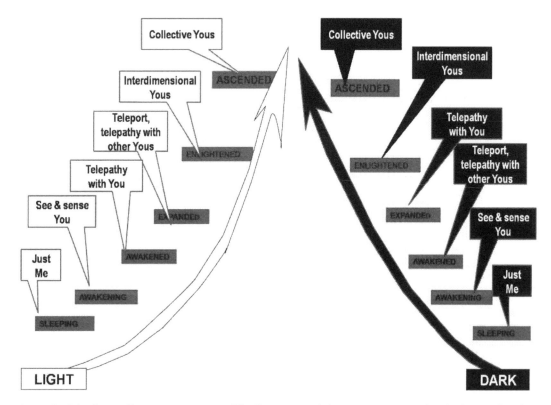

As noted before, there are many with these special powers to read minds, to heal, to read the future, to see and feel energy, to influence others, to sense others, to levitate, to materialize things, to be invisible, blah, blah. These are not understandable and have in the past been branded as occult, esoteric nonsense, but they exists. Now if you exhibit these occult powers of magic, the Inquisition will not burn you but you are still an oddity.

But what about the "Bad" guys, the Satanists and their spiritual quest? For them, the picture would look like this one below. Beside one being white and the other white, the process of ascension is the same. This is what these "Bad" guys would call enhanced abilities and the "Good guy would call Black magic.

The irony of it all is that what the "good" guys are told by the bad guys that black magic, the abilities they have, is black and not to be used.

Yet when you look at the ability itself, it is all a matter of individual choice as to how these capabilities are deployed. They can be for evil or good. and then as to whether they are really good or evil, it becomes a gray matter subject to interpretation, perception and choice.

So as we have seen in this book, there is a dark and light, evil and good to just about everything around us.

Now let us consider the possibility that no matter who we are, good or bad, were all on the same quest. When born, you were created out of the soup of love through your parents, and so it seems from the soup of all creation (bad or good) love. The soul begins the journey in the physical vessel called a body and a mind. Each soul undertakes the journey to experience and express itself as it chooses within the environment that it chooses (we will get into this choice of reality later). In a simple explanation, the soul begins its journey through its reality learning the power of the physical body.

If it learns to rise above the instinctual level of its workings, it begins to understand the next level as the power of the mind and begins to awaken to new possibilities and abilities as we see on this simple chart. Whether that Soul engages in Light or Dark is not relevant because these are simply abilities and how they are deployed for the purpose of expression of the soul is subject to interpretation and in-between the blab and the white extremes is a mixture which the degree of gray.

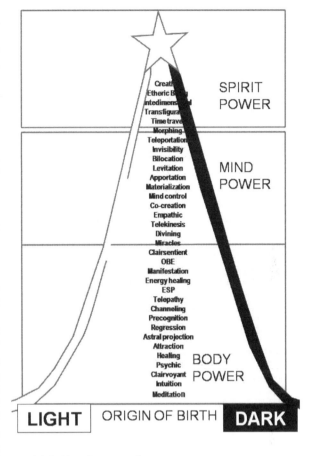

At some point in the process of rising to awaken the powers of the mind, a convergence occurs where there is a doorway or portal. That portal is opened into the abilities of the power of Spirit. The portal has a key to open the door and that key is unconditional forgiveness. That is the entry back to where the Soul as a piece of Quantum Source began the journey. Here polarity and gray does not exist, nor does time, or anything else that was used.

So the Dark ones and the Light Ones are on the same journey, learning from each other about each other. And what appears to have happened is that the "bad guys" have been on a plan to make a better place for their slaves. There is no denying this because they have even done so well at this, most earthlings do not even suspect they are slaves. Of course there has been a compromise in certain freedoms, but let's face it, the Earthling is not exactly the shining example of peace and harmony. So these alleged evil ones seem to have humanity's best interest in their hearts, just because they consider the majority of Earthlings to be at the same status as we would consider cows or chickens, that appears to beside the point.

What does this infer. When Good and Bad have no distinction and each forgives the other, thanking them for the revelation and experience, both can transcend into the power of Spirit.

What we are also saying is that the Bloodlines who run PLANET EARTH Inc. understand fully the Power of The Mind. This power, inherited through blood, attained by higher knowing teaching, or learned by the climb of the Souls journey, or whatever, are part of the souls on the same path of convergence. And when that Earthling finally realizes the truth of the power of the mind to create its reality resides there without polarity and opens the doorway of forgiveness, each one is also choosing to affect the whole consciousness that way.

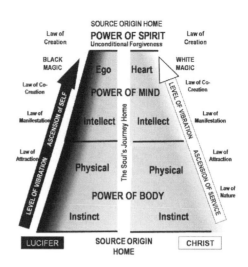

The Creator That Resides In You

Let us go back to the picture and the various stages of vibration. Here you have to release your judgments and take on an intellectual notion that you are simply a form of vibrating energy unique to yourself and have within your abilities that are like energy generators and receivers. The abilities open by rising vibration, and the generators, receptors are engaged and applied through the chakra system of thought, image, words, emotion. Each of these create energy which draws your reality to you.

One part of the drawing of reality is what has been commonly referred to as **The Law of Attraction** which reflects the way energy works. Under this hypothesis, any energy created by you will seek out energy of likeness so as to present this to you for your experience and expression. How you then engage, interpret, choose action is your choice.

So this Law is always going on through you as the generator. In a simple model, if you follow your chakra functions you move from the top three functions of thought, image, word through the heart (emotion) to the lower of intent, action, reality. Unknowingly, it is on autopilot and your active and reactive realities are process that create that which you are not aware of. You simply have no knowing or attachment, or awareness of it because you do not believe this is the way it works. When you start to become aware of this process, you begin to take control and proactively create your reality and begin manifesting instead of relying on Attraction..

In a simple sense, let us call this manifesting. In this case, there are four simple ways to manifest something, whether it is an object, event, or situation. For the sake of simplicity, let us say you desire an apple. There are four ways to get the apple:

1. You go to the store and buy an apple
2. You speak of your desire until someone brings you an apple
3. You visualize eating an apple until at some time it comes to you
4. You materialize an apple in front of you

Now the last one may be farfetched to you but understand that there are people (like Sai Baba) who have materialized objects instantly from their feet or hands. In looking at our picture of the levels the Soul rise through, we could say that manifesting using 1 is through the power of the Body, and 2 is a process using body and mind, 3 is a power of mind and 4 is a power of Spirit. In the following example, let us take our leave of the autopilot Law of Attraction and accept that it is you that controls this law.

If you look at the graph, there were several stages explained as follows:

The first stage after the power of love wakes you is what I refer to as **awakening**. It is when you begin to realize that your mind and body are energy generators (thoughts, images, words, emotions) that give life to energies. You begin to realize that you may be creating your own destiny and reality with these energies because once you give them life, they have a sole function of attracting situations, people, and things that create like experiences. Hence the **Law of Attraction** hits you. You may begin to see that thinking and creating negative energies may not be so smart. So you start to think more about stopping these negative energies and show a bit more tolerance, understanding and compassion. In fact, many people that are at this stage show several metaphysical abilities like healing, psychic, intuition, clairvoyance, and meditation as being a part of their lives.

The next stage I call the **awakened** stage when you begin to realize that you can proactively control energies, experiences, and perceptions so as to draw to you more of what you desire. This is where you begin to place a conscious awareness on the energies avoiding negative ones and then proactively managing the positive to begin to carve out your life differently. Your attention, perception, and intention, when it comes to creating perceptions, thoughts, emotions, images, and words begins to take on a more love-compassion fundamentalism. It is at this state that you are working on the **Law of Manifestation** and typically you find people with new properties (abilities) like energy healing, ESP, telepathy, channeling, precognition, regression, and astral projection to name a few. Here you are now engaging the heart through feelings and emotions.

There is a dividing line here as the next stage is reached which I call **expanded**, something changes dramatically. It is where you go in the space of the heart. This is where the big mind shift takes place and that wall is broken down. Instead of attracting and manifesting with existing energy matter to bring experiences, you begin to defy the laws of classical physics to actually create new outcomes of matter. Yes, it is where you become mindless of the usual intellect and mind perception of what *can't* happen. The best example of this is a healing miracle brought about by energy healers, placebos and other miraculous recoveries where suddenly, in an instant in time, a situation—like a broken bone—corrects itself.

This stage is attained when you realize that if you solicit the assistance of a new Divine buddy—your Co-creator Heart—letting go of classical beliefs and surrendering to it, you can do things that are deemed impossible by science. Yes, the **Law of Co-creation** sits here. Here you find empathics, telepathics, telekinesis practitioners, diviners, out of bodiers, clairsentience people, miracle healers, diviners, clairvoyants, and so on. These are some of the new abilities that open to those that have learned to let go and trust the co-creator partner will assist. What is important here is that there is a realization of being in the heart to truly open these new abilities. This is the shift away from Polarity where you believed you were separate from the Divine goes to that of belief in Unity. This is a place where you and the Divine are One. Yes, the heart is your personal link to your Higher Divine Self.

The next stage **enlightened** really gets serious. When the attitude is totally One and you are full time in the heart. It means total empathy for all things. Here the belief is we are interconnected and to affect anything else affects us and visa versa. This is where Sai Baba sits. Teleportation, materialization, levitation, apportation, mind control, bi-location and invisibility are a few of the characteristics here. This is where that Co-creator partner is being employed full time. This is where the **Law of Materialization** becomes a reality. The laws of classical physics simply don't apply here as the traditional laws of material, gravity, and solids get violated. This stage occurs when you learn to really let go most of the time. You live "in your heart". You are a complete empath showing heightened, unconditional love and compassion—those high vibration fires—for all things as they are you. You now firmly hand command to the Higher Divine Mind that you have replaced with your material limits and ego driven existence. And you have absolute faith and trust in this Higher Self of mind and body.

What is the lesson here? Materialization and the Enlightened stage of vibration is a process of self evolution of taking control of the energy you create while rising in your state of vibration. It is a process of self growth into the Power of Spirit which is not attained overnight. And does it matter whether you follow the Light or Dark path of Ascension? No, for all, assuming that you wish to rise, converges to the same doorway. At this doorway, you as a Soul are infinite and eternal and there is no distinction between right or wrong for it is all part of your person journey, your person holographic reality which you share with others so as to express yourself in any way you decide. The lesson here is that the Creator resides within you and that there are abilities residing in you looking to be unleashed. The final gateway is the unconditional forgiveness of love, peace and harmony of Source from whence you originated.

At some point in this evolution, you choose **not to be a two-faced Earthling** and choose the golden pathway home. You are not the fictional thing attached to you. You are not just the physical vessel. Things are not, black, white or gray. They are all golden.

In the next chapters we will look closer at these energies that create your reality and these Laws because, as many have learned, this Law of Attraction does not always seem to work the way you want it. Why is this important? Because, each has to understand their powers to control reality, who they are and came to peace within themselves first. Otherwise the Two-faced Earthling posture simply prevails and the true control of your life eludes you.

38

THE MANAGEMENT OF HUMAN ENERGIES

All That Is, Is Energy

It's pretty hard to accept one of the New Age consciousness beliefs that you create your own reality through your energies of thoughts, images, and words. It is even more difficult to understand that the heart gives emotional power energy to those energies you create. Normally we can't correlate the cause and effect because there is a time lag between when you create the energy, and when it comes back in some form. So dear old science simply says it's all balderdash. Nevertheless there is the Law of Cause and Effect working away. In the lower vibratory state, it's obvious. Piss someone off and they will try to get you back at some time and in some way. We are quite used to seeing the consequences in the physical domain. But, just think; what if this is really true in non-physical domain? If it was, would you be more careful about what you think, visualize, say, and feel?

What new research is finding is your mind and the perception of things that come out of it are all invisible energies. In fact it is not a difficult thing to accept that all—everything that exists—is some form of vibrating energy with its own frequency. And certainly Quantum Physics has a lot to say about that. It is not a stretch to also believe that everything you perceive and the way you perceive it is your choice. You either created it or accepted it as a perception. Anything that you see in your world creates feelings, impressions, and perceptions that science cannot quantify. Yet these are yours. And it does not matter where you read it, saw it, felt it, or experienced it, for whatever it is, ends up as a perception in you. You use your thoughts, your vision, ears, mouth, and emotions to create your perception. But at the same time, those thoughts, images, words, emotions create living energies with a purpose. It is because you are an energy generator—a creator of energy.

If you have an impression of somebody for example, it becomes vibrating energy. But you can bring that impression forward into your consciousness and change it any time you like. Even if it is a bad memory of something, you can change your perception to

713

good, replacing the old. You may not have changed the event that caused it, or the person, or the situation, but you can change your perception of it. That is your personal hologram of your life as it was and as you live it—all just energy vibrating away.

But that energy you create has a life. It has a purpose. And what you create this way has an inherent magnetic attraction to draw to it a mate. A mate of similar vibration. The most obvious example is to call someone a vile name. It attracts a mate you will recognize more clearly as a response—like a punch in the mouth, a vile name back or it could be returned later. What if everything you perceive and the process you use to create that perception had to find a mate? Would you pay more attention to your energy generator? Let us expand on this simple notion and move into the more extreme manipulation of energy. You create energy (cause) and the Law of Attraction attracts likeness (effect).

Energy Benders

There is an incredible example that distorts the physical beliefs of science. It has to do with materialization—creating an object instantly out of thin air. This is an extreme example of creating something out of nothing, out of that which is raw energy. And from that raw energy materializes a specific form into an atomic state. The most famous modern day materializer and miracle maker was **Sathya Sai Baba** an Indian Holy man in Southern India. He was reported to materialize lockets, rings, jewellery, delicacies, sacred ash, and specific objects that are requested by others. He created these out of thin air then passes them out as gifts. Thousands have witnessed this. Scientists who study this are befuddled by it of course, simply discounting it and claiming it is a hoax. After all, if science can't explain it, it ain't proven science. Yet this man was deemed a saint, and he was visited by many daily to materialize vast quantities of food; even sizzling hot delicacies fell from his hands and feet. He would produce exotic and rare objects, fruits, and even anomalous ones like half apple, half orange on two sides. He walked about producing sacred ash with the wave of his hands. Sai Baba was also a bi-location example. Numerous witnesses reported watching him snap his fingers and vanish instantly reappearing several hundred feet away. This is not an isolated case. There are many Holy men in India with this ability. If you don't believe this, just Google it. And so it is with many of the esoteric sciences... it's all just heresy so it's supposed to vanish from reality.

Energy Manifesting

The first real test of your mind to accept is that you create living energy. The tons of books on the Law of Attraction have changed millions of minds about a cosmic law of energy. It simply states *that which is like unto itself is drawn*. Like stated it is not too difficult to understand that concept in many physical situations; if you are going be a shit to others, they will be a shit to you. And if you are kind to others then you will also receive kindness back. It does not mean it will be instant, or the recipient will be the giver; it means expect the same kind of stuff back! It starts to become a belief stretch however when you hear the statement that all in your life is a cause and effect behaving this way. Yet you know everything you perceived was up to you, wasn't it? Why not everything you receive being a result of what you created yourself? Well, this is only part of the story. There are other Laws. They are based on the use of the energies you can and do create.

First, as we described before in the ascension graph, we have the Law of Attraction and the Law of Manifestation. Here the energy you create attracts like energy and is the way to manifest energy proactively. It is based on energy you give life to that follows a cosmic law of finding an energy mate. We also have The Law of Co-creation and the Law of Materialization. As stated it is the place where the miracle workers go for a few moments, and people like Sai Baba go fulltime. There is a division here because that's where the shift in thinking and belief occurs. It is where miracle workers go temporarily. It is where your engagement in higher vibration takes you. On one side referred to as polarity you simply believe you can't. On the other side you believe you can. On one side you are polarized from the heart and on the other side you are unity with it. What is the significance of the heart? Again, it is the center—your co-creating buddy. On the polarity side you engage the heart through charging your energy with emotions. On the unity side, the heart is a full time buddy.

But why the heart? Here is the most interesting part. These four laws are the tip of the iceberg. Research shows that the heart's electrical field when in the energetic field of love, works in its optimum way. This means that the communication with DNA as a biological   Internet   opens   to   language. **(www.bibliotecapleyades.net/ciencia/ciencia_genetica02.htm**) where it becomes possible to modify genetic defects and takes you into those higher frequency abilities. The emotion of love is a high positive vibration, as are other emotions of the heart. Hate is a low vibration. The vibrational process changes in you as you change the energy you create from lower to higher.

The vast majority of humans simply accept that they have limited control of their lives and experience whatever energy comes at them. This is true if you let it be so and go to default. The default is to let your lower mind and body do what ego believes is correct for you. The process of the shift from low to high change goes through several stages. The lowest stage is the lower form of life—purely instinctual run by behavior totally void of the consciousness of spirit—the higher mind. At the higher end is the highest form of life—totally inspirational run by the consciousness of Spirit. The stages are reflected by the level of vibration as we saw in the chart.

But here is the pith of it—the dividing line in that picture of Polarity-Unity that you alone can cross. It is between the higher and lower mind, between the heart's intuition and the ego's intellect and between creating something versus making something. You are used to making things out of what exists because physics says you have to. Get used to creating things out of nothing because metaphysics—and your Divine mind—says you can.

It is the Divine Path through the Heart. This means that your desires of manifestation need to be aligned in thought, image, words and emotion, your total being, with the Heart—the Divine. It is where you learn to Create—like the Sai Baba guy who creates from nothing. And it also like all the healing miracles that occur instantly.

Here is the big difference. You can go ahead and *manifest* things bad or good and feel the discord and ill feeling of the Heart if the energies are not aligned; and you will find your experience from existing stuff, *making* things out of things already made. Or, you can align with the heart properly where there is no bad energy and *create* out of nothing that which is of desire. But because this is not believed, and secondly Sai Baba abilities are not exactly instantly achieved, not too many are prepared to spend much energy on this option. And it is certainly not helpful to be told by those experts called scientists that this is all nonsense.

If you want to co-create, then create—to change the very fabric of the material—like in a miracle that creates something like a new possibility in your mind instantly, you need to have a co-creator buddy to work with. That is your Higher Divine Self living in your Heart. Attention is the first lesson. This is not an overnight deal any more that you earned your diploma overnight. It is through knowing that the true power of manifestation and creation reside there. That must be your mind shift in belief. So yes, you need to have attention and thoughts and words and emotion but those are aligned for the higher good of yourself and all that is. Otherwise why would your Divine counterpart—your co-creator care to respond? But this does not require continued reinforcement—a healing miracle is instant—because it simply happens as a new possibility that takes you or something to its zero state of perfection. But it is the belief that limits—the belief of who you are and what you can do. So you need not drive yourself to distraction by affirmations. Simply place attention, go to your Heart, keep faith and trust that it will be. Yes, we know this is not easy but it is that simple. You have been doing some of this the hard way because you have not believed in your partner—your Co-creator that is part of you. And your Co-creator is Love—your Heart—it is you; that part which needs your 3D attention and belief to shift.

What this means is that when you begin to truly take control of your power to proactively manifest, attract, co-create and create, you must know that it is done at the instant in time that it passes the attention. The instant healing miracle is like that, as is the materialization example.

The Process Of Co-creation

The process of Co-creation is more relevant to what actually happens in manifesting. You are a Co-creator of your life and you do have the ability to materialize or co-create at a new level. You have a Divine Partner in this process and although you are already doing this automatically, you have not quite got the process unobstructed by your intellect. Yes, you are co-creating all the time because you do not even think about it.

It is automatic and your belief and intent of this is synchronized because you have no obstacles in believing that negative things can come your way—it is the way of it, right? Do you not think you will attract negative energies in your life by creating anger and conflict? After all, you have had many lifetimes, and many years of practice in embedding this in your beliefs. Your memories are full of these thoughts. But positive things come the same way.

You do not even knowingly attach yourself to the outcomes because you believe there is no connection. Of course you don't want issues and problems, but by engaging your energetic chakras placing your thoughts, images, words and feeling onto these issues and problems, you end up with more of the same. So you automatically generate these discordant energies at will, and ask for your co-creating partner—which is really your Higher Self—to help attract and manifest them. So you are very practiced at creating the energy, giving it life, disconnecting yourself from an outcome, and waiting for the experience—even though you don't want it—ironic isn't it? Yes, you are adept at autopilot reactive attraction and manifesting already.

But when it comes to proactive co-creation, it is an entirely different matter because you may have a shadow of doubt, or be insecure as to the process, be too attached to the outcome and dilute the energy of desire so it sits there in a transition state. And even you create energy instantly, it waits for you to congeal or materialize it by your actions and intent. Of course the power of this energy is related to how you align your thoughts, visions, words and feelings. And of course others can help to amplify this as well. This is where reinforcement of that energy clarifies the outcome and further energizes it into being. But if there is doubt within you, and your beliefs are not aligned, then this serves to delay, dilute or even dissolve the power of a result. These are the limits and blocks that you impose on the process. And for true proactive co-creation, where you are in control, you need to be very aware of your Divine relationship with your heart and eliminate your shadows of doubt.

Let us back up a minute and note that your world which appears solid is simply in a different energy state and it has been created by the Creator consciousness. Everything in it which is simply a hologram of energy in a different dimension has life with a purpose of evolving. You as a physical body are integrated into this scene to play out your roles as you see fit to expand it and yourself. Within the movie you are able to co-create different ways. You can create, rearrange, or attract your creations and hence experiences. To create means to materialize something into a solid form. Humanity has a long way to go to do this but it is indeed possible to materialize something solid in front of you. *If you think about how your imagination and mind work now, how you can create things, scenes, people, relationships, emotions in multiple places and shift your awareness to each one without time or space limitations, this is the way the real You is creating your reality here.*

You have come to know this in miracles—like those of healing. And no one can deny the existence of these; they just can't explain them. This is a process where after attention to a solution, and a Divine partnership is made in the heart, you detach from the outcome and rely on faith to prevail. And so as you understand it, the quantum state of waves, manifests itself into a new state of perfection—which is all we know—and it becomes a solid representation of what was sought as the desire. Eventually you will learn that materializing a solid object relies on the same process as you are simply adding to the hologram in your dimension.

To rearrange is a similar process. It is one of changing the arrangement of the form into a new form that is solid. This is a transformation process as done in Alchemy which abides by specific natural laws. The partnership with the Divine, if not there, with the strong belief, is vital. Without it, nothing will happen.

In the case of attraction, you are creating the energy that has specific vibratory qualities and strength attached by you. You do it daily. What occurs here is that this energy sits in a temporary holding area looking for other energies that will be attracted to it like a magnet. Here you are not creating the object; you are attracting the objects, events, people or situations that already exist to provide you with the experience.

Think about this like the little dots that you see on the movie screen or TV or your computer screen. They are simply dots configured into unique patterns that are meaningful to you and give you an experience. Yet they are not solid things in the screen. They are just little dots of energy composited into some meaningful expression of energy. The energies you create are similar. All you have to add is that these patterns on your screen are magnetic and they set up fields—which you call morphic—that eventually attract similar patterns. The time to do this depends upon the strength and your belief that it can be so. As we have pointed out, you are already doing this without thinking—and therein lies the big clue—you are not thinking about it. And without even knowing, you have let go of limits and are co-creating with your Divine counterpart. And yes, it can be negative or positive. The heart only knows perfection and it knows what is happening. And if it is not perfection, there will be a reaction in your body and Soul. You will feel this as dis-ease or disease or dysfunction—perhaps a feeling of discord.

The Two Pathways

There is another way of looking at this that reflect two opposite paths related to this awareness. There is the Ego and the Heart. They are of course commanded through the mind which can determine which path you use. Both Ego and Heart can control or command your chemistry either automatically or by you, depending on your awareness. The Ego pathway into the manifesting field is what humanity usually relies on making things. These are stagnated into that which exists in the physical world, and although your energy packets reach into the Divine—most call it Zero Point Field, they don't create without the cooperation of the Divine Buddy. They are simply commands to manifest as we have discussed. There is no distinction of bad or good, negative or positive, it is simply energy looking for a likeness—a mate. The Heart, on the other hand, knows what is not perfection—that which is not love—and you will sense a discomfort when discordant energies are placed into the inventory. This is the normal way of creating your life.

You may have many energies that are there waiting for you to enforce them by emotion, attention and alignment. They could even be from previous lives. If these energies of intent are weak or confused, they will sit there. If many of these weak ones are there, you can be easily drawn into other energy fields that are stronger and that is the way of it even if it has no distinct purpose. You then become a victim of other energies that have created their own morphic fields. What this means is that you are letting your life be commanded by default, and if you allow your Ego to create the fear, attention and intent, then you are defaulting to what the Ego desires—not what your heart desires. That is the Gopher Wheel that the ego sees as great things ahead—if you keep slogging on the wheel. And so your intellect, another tool of ego, comes to govern how you will do the slogging.

When you, by awareness of the Heart, and the Divine in it create the commanding partnership, then you stop on the relative Gopher Wheel and look with new eyes. You shift command to the Divine Higher Mind of the heart. There is no intellect here, only inspiration and positive feelings. This is how you change the nature of your manifestation in that they are more controlled and you become a true Co-creator. But the partnership relies on your belief and faith. I will let you in on a secret here. The Heart and the Divine

718

are perfection and they strive to bring back that perfection when that partnership is clear like non attachment, clarity, trust, faith, believe, and love based. The stronger this is the faster it congeals from temporary to visible energy. This is the secret to materialization which humanity is a long, long way from. But, if you want to see more common examples, look to what happens in health miracles.

So at the top of the Gopher Wheel-no Gopher Wheel sits the true Manager—the Mind. It is it what chooses using your free will to pick the path to tread. And the success is dependent upon your awareness and belief system. What does this mean? Make a new choice because the ego is the guy keeping you in the Gopher Wheel. You need to take command and build this faith and relationship—to balance the Ego. For its decisions if left unchecked will affect your health, quality and length of life. The body was designed to live long within the realm of the Heart. The control has been given to the Ego, to power, to gratification of the senses, to conflict over material things—those eyeball visions on the vision board before you. These all have consequences to your body as a result. Shifting to the command center of the Heart unfolds a grand partnership as a true co-creator on a grand scale that you have yet to understand.

In Simple Terms There Are Four Steps

These steps are Attraction, Manifestation, Co-creation and Materialization. It is a progression from outside to inside, from unknowing to knowing or unconscious to conscious command. The first two have the Heart involved while the last two have the Heart engaged. The first two are your first major pathway we have discussed, where you create any kind of energy in a holding area like an escrow and then passively or actively enforce the strength of it to attract and manifest an experience. The last two are active engagement in the partnership of the Divine—the Heart—to co-create an event, situation, or material object. While one simply attracts and manifests with existing matter, the other through the help of the Divine rearranges matter into something new.

Of course you know this second path as miracles. And you know that the Co-creator is your Higher Self which is part of the Divine. And you know that the key here is Belief, Compassion, Love, Faith, Trust and Gratitude, don't you? This does not require continued repetition like an assertion to manifest experience, only a strength of belief, a heart's desire to be perfection, a trust in yourself, a detachment from the outcome, a faith that it is so, and gratitude that it is done. Does it sound difficult for you? Yes, it has been difficult because you have not known yourself and you limit this through your belief by listening to other people who do not believe. And you are so busy analyzing it you cannot detach yourself to surrender and listen.

Yes, that is the way of it. So while your mind slumbers about this, you begin by your Law of Attraction and create a resonating field which attracts like energy. Then you may begin to realize that by managing your energies of thoughts, images, words and emotion, you can more actively manifest the experience. That you can call the Law of Manifestation because you are proactive.

And Now Miracles And Emotion

It is important to tell you more about something that is usually missing in a proactive manifestation. It is about the emotional body that envelopes you and in particular your heart. Your heart has many fields of energy that you are not aware of but the one that is important in energy creation is the one that is referred to as the emotional body or feeling body. It is like a light bulb and is the most beautiful creation when it is lighted. Everyone has one and it is a radiant light which emanates its colors and vibrations of excitement. The height and brightness is caused by the emotion from your heart—which is an energy of emotion generated from your sensory systems of taste, sight, smell, touch, and hearing. Think about the feelings that your body creates for you when you eat something wonderful, or see something beautiful, or touch someone you love, or smell a pleasing flower, or hear peaceful music. These are all incredible feelings that impact your emotional body and permeate your being in a harmonizing result.

There is of course a hierarchy of these; unconditional love being the strongest. Compassion, bliss, joy, laughter, harmony, peace, gratitude are others that are very strong energies and make your emotional body pulsate with wondrous colors and brightness. Of course there are the opposites of fear and conflict that do not create the light and the emotional body dims and closes to the discord. This state in your emotional body is very important in your manifestations.

For example, in your attractions and manifestations, the emotional strength is what gives the manifesting energy that you create with thoughts, visions and words its true power. The stronger this is and the clearer it is, the faster is the change from etheric energy created instantly to external energy that you can experience. The field which you refer to as a morphic field vibrates with excitement as it entrains with the emotional body. And as we have said, it matters not whether it is negative or positive because it is still energy you create. But if the energy is strongly negative, you can be drawn to other like energy whereas if it is positive, you will draw it to yourself. You must know that although your emotional body may be dimmer due to the discord and negative emotion, it is still energy and still has power to attract, but not with any divine co-creative partnership.

However, if you are to be a Co-creator, your co-partner does not hear you if you are not of a strong positive and pure emotional vibration-hypercommunication, remember? Its domain is perfection and it cannot be of assistance unless you are pure of heart and with a highly charged emotional body. You have learned that the Intent is first, the Pathway is meditation, awareness and prayer, and the means are the positive emotions or feelings created. These positive ones we mentioned are higher level energies of completion. You know that when the energies of thought, vision, words and emotion are aligned with the Heart's desire, and continuously re-enforced, you have the true secret of creating your own manifestations. Your strength and consistency in the emotional body will impact the speed at which the etheric energy attracts the physical energies. This is because the field excites the electrons that are the basis to all things and gets them to seek each other—they are all one anyway, remember?

But with miracles, or co-creation, be clear that the electrons common to both the etheric and material states become highly excited when the emotional body is positively charged with unconditional love and compassion. When this occurs, they are easily influenced to rearrange from a quantum perspective into a new possibility simply by changing paths, states and orbits into a different outcome or different atomic state which you sense and perceive as solid. And it is also here that we and the Divine Heart has its power to influence that new arrangement. But we caution you in that the emotional body cannot be fooled. Emotion is a universal energy and laughter can be false, or love can be with condition, or talk can be a lie. This does not fool the Heart and its emotional body. It is part of your belief system as well.

Should you carry an ulterior negative motive in your laughter or your outward feelings do not match your internal Divine ones, you fall back to reactive manifestation and attraction. Many may not even be aware of this discord and simply believe you are doing good. Sorry, that is not the way of Divine energy. It knows. It, like you for example pick up the discordant notes in a piece of music instantly even though the piece attempts to disguise it. Miracles occur when the emotional body of the Healer is strong, pure of heart and genuine—either directly by initial attention or indirectly through trusting the Heart. The most miraculous healers are of the purest state of high emotional body who enfold their patients.

Training The Emotional Body

If you were to research this, you will find that the heart actually has a brain and it has an energy field that is the strongest of your total "energetic" system. It is an energy field that is shaped like a donut—called a torus—that reaches way out depending on its strength. This field is out there doing its thing unbeknown to you so its time you made this more "known" to your mind which is supposed to be in charge.

During your daily activities, you must learn that you are there to change or convert discord to light—bad to good or fear to love. The first area of discord and disharmony will come from the papers you read, the news you hear, the problems you are surrounded with. Remember these are perceptions that convert to manifesting energy and that you are there to help change this, take a higher perception, or assist to make it better. Do not let these influence your emotional body. Your heart will tell you when these are not compatible.

There are also the thoughts and visions that you yourself create by way of your ego or other matters that may come to you. Will yourself to not let these be of conflict, discourse and negative nature. Be careful to not give these any life and simply move to a higher place of perception with your Higher Self to change the energy to positive upon detection. Keep your emotional body protected from these by instantly acknowledging that they are not beneficial and eliminating or changing them.

Then there are events and experiences that you may be drawn into or witness. These may be tragic, conflictive, or have a major impact upon your emotional body. These are to help you learn what you do not want or to show you how to move to a higher perception of good. Look to see something good that it created and place your attention on that.

Then there are the plans and attractions and manifestations and miracles that you wish to create and co-create. These are as we have said earlier. Make a habit of creating these solutions and desires as completed, enjoyed so your emotional body totally engulfs the completion of it. Learn to solidify your belief, faith and trust in your Co-creator.

As you follow this path, you begin to take command of your life and the true center of command begins to take over as the emotional body becomes stronger and brighter. It will completely change the experiences of your life as soon there cannot be any discord or limitations that can influence, penetrate or affect you.

This is how you get off the Gopher Wheel. Your perceptions switch completely and you see everything in a new light while you practice your manifestations. And over time magic starts to unfold. Why? Because you put the magical energy there to work for you. You are not working for the energy anymore.

Let us now delve into the greatest mind shift that we all fear most of all—death and loss. It is Mr. Ego's greatest fear of ceasing to exist and losing everything it has seduced you into on the Gopher Wheel. The best lesson of dealing with this is where people have experienced death and lost everything, then miraculously come back. The lesson? It has to do with you suddenly knowing that you are actually made up of something more than a physical vessel. But ego and intellect had to temporarily die to allow this to happen.

The Non-Science Of Dying

NDE's are short for Near Death Experiences. There are millions of people dying all the time—then coming back to tell about it. What is of particular interest here is that so many of these cases come back with miraculous changes—like big, big changes in their lives and even in their bodies. Yes, miracles—totally unexplainable miracles. Many professionals and scientists have studied thousands of cases and compiled observations about people pronounced clinically dead. These have returned to tell about their little vacation in what is deemed no-where land.

Now, you must understand that NDE's mean the person is dead! Gone! What is called "clinically" dead for some period of time like 15-60 minutes! Heart stopped and the body weighs one half to one ounce less! Yes, something left the body. This means that the cells are dying in the brain from lack of oxygen, and it is coffin time. At least that is what the medical belief box tells us. After all, if you stop feeding oxygen to the brain, cells die rapidly, right? Wrong!

There are some 13 million cases of NDE's that have been recorded. Reports are that an energy force of approximately one ounce simply leaves the body (nice to know a ghost weighs an ounce!) and floats up and away to take a little vacation. Is this consciousness that has left the force that gives life? Whatever it is separates at the point of death and the NDE people are completely aware of this separation as they see their bodies lie lifeless below.

Consciousness is a Separate Intelligent Energy Form

Now here is the mind-bender that flattened the side of my belief box. This consciousness that separates can see, hear, think, move, communicate, and tell jokes, and retain senses regardless of distance from the body. In fact the senses are even better— heightened. It seems the body and brain weren't the only things that could do this.

Everything that was ever learned, experienced, and felt along with all of the senses (perhaps taste may be questionable unless you can get some ghost food!) are left completely intact. But did we not learn that the brain was responsible for all that? And when you croak, that memory is no more? Not so.

Consciousness, which clearly includes the life giving force, leaves the body, goes on a little trip, then comes back and ta dah, the body has life again. All the dead cells are happy again. Rigamortis has no say here—the white face gets pink again, and it is wakey, wakey time! And then! All is better than before—sometimes with a few miracles kicked in.

But what about the little vacation that this ghost, or consciousness takes when it leaves the body? It is like a little visit to an amusement park. Where does it go? What happens?

Well, reports are pretty unanimous on this. Most went through similar stages when they left their physical lives.   They all kept a consciousness that retained their life stories— every moment. Some higher mind was there to take them through their steps and decide whether a return was needed.

This little vacation away from the body and ego off the Gopher Wheel of mortal life, permanently on a trip that the life force of consciousness takes exhibits striking similarities between cases.

First, they heard the news of dying from the Doc or others around the "dead" body. They saw people and events around them. They then experienced wonderful feelings of comfort, peace, quiet, relief, and no pain. No hell and brimstone, just peace. Many went into a tunnel and were pulled rapidly through in a wonderful worry free ride.

They had an *Out of body* experience for after they *died* they would find themselves looking at their body, watching and hearing things as a spectator. They felt like pure consciousness that was indescribable—most called it a spiritual body—but they could not touch other bodies or material things. No one could hear or see them. They were separate, weightless, floating, going through things like a cloud. They had projections like rounded limbs but all their senses were intact. Consciousness existed outside the body! What we would commonly call a ghost! So upon death, the other part of us—the ghost—was the one invited to the amusement park.

The next stage is where they encountered other spiritual beings, people they had known before, like friends and relatives that came to greet them. They were recognizable ghosts. Everything was filled with white light and was beautiful—like a feeling of coming home. These beings had a clear body outline but no physical body. They communicated as a direct transfer—no language. They were totally telepathic with no need for any language. All that was there were questions like are you ready to die. What have you done in your life that is sufficient? There was a point of stressing preparation yet there was no condemnation or judgment, only total love and acceptance coming from the light.

Then the stage where a bright light Being presents a high speed video panorama review of life—instant like when people report when drowning. Here the intent seems to be only to provoke reflections. Get this; rapid temporal memories in chronological order occur almost instantaneous yet totally comprehendible! The images generate emotions as they flip by. The being asks what they have done with their life, stressing love, and pointing out things. No one could gage time.

At the *Coming back* stage some would come back spurred by some Being which many said was God. They would be sent back for obligations, or pulled by relatives. Some actually felt a re-entry into the physical body.

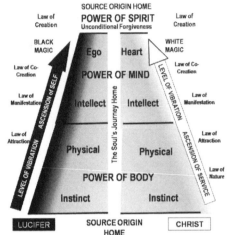

With those that came back, they inevitably had a totally changed life, just like in many of the miracle cases. Researchers go on to say that most times this experience created a totally new attitude in life. Some reported enhanced senses, some picked up on other's feelings better, expressed a need to cultivate love of others, seek knowledge, became morally purified, and created new clear goals mostly in service of others. This vacation away from ego suddenly paradigm shifted their belief systems and behaviour dramatically—that in itself is an unexplainable miracle.

Where did they go? Remember the little diagram? They were in that world of meeting their Soul in its territory. They met God or whoever was their powerful deity was really Self. They temporally passed through into their Source; Home! They had a chat with their true selves.

What Does Near Dying Tell Us?

Life is immortal consciousness that grows in an unlimited way. After everything was lost, let go of—poof no more body, ego, stuff, world, kids relationships, another mind takes over. It was sitting there waiting for the wakeup call. Too bad they had to croak to wake it, wouldn't you say? But this consciousness of ours—or life force—is alive and does not croak like the body. In fact it IS LIFE as it gives such to the body upon entry and exit. It can take a vacation. It is the field of transpersonal experience that is the source of all knowledge and memory—not the brain. It is independent of the person's mind. Whole consciousness is stored somewhere in space not in the brain. The brain serves as a relay station for connecting to and running the physics of our bodies when we are in a conscious state of being awake.

I am not a rocket scientist and I may not be the brightest crayon in the pack but what I clearly understood here is that we are made of a body and some invisible, separate energy field that gives me life. And when it decides to leave the old body, the life ceases. That is not exactly a mystery. But having this energy measured and keeping all of our consciousness and sensory abilities intact; wow! That's a bit different from the old belief box. Actually I found many people are not so surprised at this notion but they are not willing to readily admit it in public—peer pressure from "science" I am sure.

And what about these scientists and medicine? Well how do they explain that when people came back to life—into the dead body that is—the body was still ok—not dead smelly and dead brain cells clogging life, but fine. And then there was a life transformation. Hmmm, I began to realize, that this little episode altered something in the mind and body resulting in life changing habits because a higher mind was given a chance to take over. The old belief and faith had been completely altered because there was nothing there to be in conflict with what that higher mind "knew" and could do—like send you back for another try off the Gopher Wheel! And it all happened within seconds to a minute. And that person's life was totally transformed. And what would you guess the transformation was all about? Would you believe that life became centered on the "heart" not on the ego or the brain.

So in this case, death is a passing, a simple shift in vibration from one state of energy to another. The body is a temporary vehicle here and when it's lost, there is a subtle reminder that you are more than a body, death is a crock, and it may be more useful to come back and do something more meaningful than the Gopher Wheel of polarity and ego's cravings that probably had some influence on why you croaked temporarily. Perhaps the message is that we have more fun while we are on the Earth. So why don't we pay attention and do this before we croak?

Now, I ask you, if you came back after you croaked for an hour, floated around in a tunnel, got your ticket to this wonderful, peace filled amusement park, talked to some friendly ghosts, met the big boss in the sky, then had an instant replay of your life's movie, remembered everything out of your body, what would it do to your mind? And on top of this what if you came back with something healed instantly? And what if you knew you actually passed through to meet yourself?

Would you believe anyone—scientific or otherwise—that told you when you croak that's it? Not likely! What if they said it was nonsense what you saw? What if they told you miracles like the one you had was nonsense? You would tell them to keep smoking what they are on and go away. You would not care much to associate with them and simply keep your new knowledge to yourself. They would become the idiots, wouldn't they? Simply knowing it would be your truth. And no one on the planet would convince you otherwise. Your belief system would have taken a paradigm shift because you knew your own truth. Period.

Would this change your approach to life? Would you then be afraid of dying? Would you not realize you needed to do something meaningful and had been given a new chance? Would you be grateful? What would you be like after? Would you be completely freaked out and shrivel away? I think the possibility of that would be remote because you would have gained a new will and purpose to live. And where would that notion be? In a thing called consciousness—your mind.

Perhaps if you listened to the people living inside their limited belief boxes on this you may think you had gone mad, but I think you would change your consciousness—your awareness—to accept beliefs outside of your usual belief box. It would change me. It has already without having to croak. Realize you don't need to croak to go through this. But you do have to change your beliefs and be totally faithful to facilitate some changes—

especially miracles. That is what miracles do. They provoke a paradigm shift in the mind—in your consciousness and your beliefs.

But here is the real lesson: What happened was you unknowingly gave command to another quite physically independent part of you—your Higher Divine Mind. It wasn't willingly or knowingly, but there was really no option because everything that your lower mind is aware of was lost—gone! Poof, no baggage, conditions, attachments, expectations, only the reality of Source where you came from. It's the same place you go in the state of Co-creation and Creation.

In the so called real world of your physicality, you do not blot out the usual noise, and just let go of the usual world. But here it's poof and you are under the master command of the higher mind of inspiration and you went mindless—your terrestrial ego mind and its frantic consciousness of the Gopher Wheel of life as your primary attention vanished. You went into the land of Nothingville just like in the NDE, because there was truly nothing else there.

Can you do this while alive? Many do as an Out of Body Experience. But, and here is the big but, if you don't keep with the same program of higher vibration, you simply fade back into reactive Gopher Wheel life.

39

SELF POTENTIAL AND LAWS BEHIND MANIFESTATION

The Mindset Shift In Belief

Here is the key to this. The energy we are focussed on during our conscious time is made up of thoughts, images, words, feelings and emotions. You as an energy creator/generator have the choice of what these are and how you give life to them. You create your reality the same way you can in your imagination-your mind. What you have not realized or accepted is that your true Self is creating your life in this existence the same way. You must first understand that every bit of energy is given life and purpose by you. The greatest mind shift in this, in moving from the polarity to the unity side is the *acceptance of the knowing that there is a space where the basic substance of energy exists as no-thing*. The other is that you are the master of your own reality so that what you generate is not only what you receive back but it also forms your physical reality. And it is that primary substance of quantum no-thing that something is created from. From you comes the directive to change that substance. It is through the actions of attention and intent upon that which you apply your energy generators of thought, image, word, and emotion. These are formed instantly to then seek purpose. The strength of the directive depends on how it is charged with emotion from the heart and the strength of belief. This then dictates how long the directive may take to come back to you in some form of energy.

On The Law Of Attraction

So if you have any idea this is a bit far out, first think about how this works in the physical world. Try pissing someone off with your words. Try hugging someone who is pissed off at you. What you give out comes about. So give your brain (and ego) some leeway here and let go of the idea that it does not work the same way with the other energies you create constantly.

Think about how you create your desires—you want to find a new friend, or find something and you think about it, dream about it, feel it in your heart. You are creating waves of energy that create a field. It is actually a morphic field alive with purpose and it

727

permeates other energies. It is like a swirling vortex of energy which builds a stronger charge depending on how much clear energy of desire you create.

Think about your TV set and the particles that form images. Think about how these particles that create emotions in your physical body are nothing but specs of light, color and intensity that your senses interpret. These dots or pixels could have a magnetic pull that either individually, or combined, created a specific pull signature that looks for like energies and attracts them. Do these dots sometimes draw you? Yes, a hologram that can draw others! This is not a difficult concept except that it is not supported by our scientific wisdom.

There are several pathways to manifesting. It is the split again; heart or head, intuition or intellect, create or make. The Divine path is fast, while the manifesting path of attraction is not so fast. The attraction path manifests experiences where it draws to you the energies that have likeness. It draws to you the energies that you generate through your thoughts, visions, words and emotions. The speed of manifestation is determined by the clarity of the desire, the alignment of these subtle energies dictates how rapidly the energy that you create draws or propels you to the like experience. This process is not creation, or co-creation, it is simply manifesting the experience of something desired by drawing the people, situations, things that already exist.

Think about how you may do this in two ways that you are used to. First, you may want to create something, or do something to have an experience—say it is flying or climbing a mountain. You simply plan it and away you go to have it. Sometimes it may be more complex, so you create a business plan and follow the activities you have outlined to make this experience occur. It may result in the creation of something as a result—like a business. You are used to this. It is all done in the outside. This is the way the Gopher Wheel keeps you busy.

But then there is also another way and that is to create the energy of alignment and watch how you draw others into your energy field. You may want a house, or new TV, or new opportunity; then suddenly it is there as a choice for you. This does not mean the TV suddenly materializes in your house. It could mean that the TV may be seen at a store or it appears somewhere for you to make a choice on. Certainly you have to buy it and you may not have the money—so manifest the money as well. Clarity and alignment are vital. Remember this as this is an easier way, as you are letting the Law of Attraction work for you after you clearly define what it is that is your desire and continue to energize it by reinforcement. It is done from the inside.

Think about this. Sometimes, you may be drawn into others energies as well. This is the way of it as you may have a need to sell something and someone else has a need to buy something. All that happens is that the two needs attract each other. How? Well, your energies penetrate everything depending on the strength and because all that exists is within you all, it is a matter of matching the energy signatures and drawing them like those little TV dots. This may be a local morphic field or a larger one. It may come from anywhere—an ad, a TV show, another person, but it is this drawing within the fabric of all matter.

Now you are doing these two ways automatically all the time. That is how you create your world of experience and perception whether you know it or not. This way is not particular to the need or the type of energy you create. It is simply energy the laws respond to, negative or positive. Most are used to such strong alignments when it comes to fear that permeates your thoughts, visions, words and emotions. Most of you are good at this already. Clarity and focus are the key and continued attention reinforces the energy to make it resonate stronger.

It is like a musical note. It has a specific tone or vibration when played. From 7 notes, you can create a song. These 7 notes can be combined into new patterns that are each unique. These can be played by different instruments making different tones and this can be combined into a magical concerto. These are all energy signatures looking to attract others of like sound. You are the orchestra playing the music. Your chakras are the original 7 notes and they can create any concerto you want if you use them. What are their musical sections? Thoughts, images, words, and emotions, brought about by your perception of your experiences.

So how do you manifest and attract now? Well, first you determine a need by *placing your attention* on it. It is in your target range. Now you work like hell to attain it, to make it, to buy it. But the other process you are not paying attention to is the other energy you create, especially the negative ones of fear, worry, lack, doubt. Every time you think or feel poor, useless, sick, unworthy, angry, guess what? And if you supercharge this with the emotion this is like a command for this energy to get its shit together fast and find a fit. And what happens when something really pisses you off and your energy levels hit the roof? A big flag goes up and starts waving for a mate. What about hatred from the past, an enemy, the boss, fear of the future, the tax man? And what about wanting more? Have you ever considered you are creating the energy of wanting? What wishing and hoping about great things? Great things are ok but what happens when it is counteracted with hoping? It has no power to manifest. And what do you think about most? It is not abundance because you lack. That is the energy you create to go out and hunt for a mate. You give it life and purpose.

Now here is the kicker. What do you occupy your mind with in regards to plans and wants? Is it the work needed, the effort required, or is it the completion itself? One, the problem is negative energy because it attracts more problems, The other, the solution is positive energy which attracts solutions. But hold on you say, that's BS! How can I occupy my mind with the solution when it has not happened yet? Well, I will let you in on a little secret... it is most likely the way most successful businessmen got to be so "successful". Do you think they engrossed themselves in the problems? You will find out that between gut feel, a positive stance, and a vision, things just happened and deals and people—out of the blue—just happened.

Here is where the mind shift is needed. The universe works the opposite of what you think. Sure you can struggle away on the Gopher Wheel and make it happen. But the better process is like assertions and successful business people follow. Create the energy of solution, of completion and energize it with emotion, see a vision of it completed. That is the energy you need to have out there and let the Laws of Attraction and Manifestation deal with the problems. These fellows know about how suddenly a deal just comes to them, something happens from nowhere and that dream becomes manifested into reality.

Here is the bottom line. To those in the know of how this works, they continuously re-enforce the vision of completion over and over with thoughts, an emotion, with a knowing, a faith, and a trust that this is the way it works.

If you look at your 24 hour day there are 86,400 seconds. It is said that we can generate 20-30,000 thoughts in a day. How would you classify these? And if every one of these critters is energy with purpose, what do you suppose the reflection would look like as an expression of your current life? Of course the vast majority may be mumbo jumbo energy because they are not clear or with purpose so they never mate. But what about those strong ones that do? When you are on the Gopher Wheel, you do not make any correlation between the energy you create upstairs to the experience you get downstairs. So perhaps it is time to become more aware of how you think and act.

There are four main types which are proactive and reactive. The reactive ones come from what you let into your attention—media, TV, news, others opinions, etc. That is probably the majority. What are the usual thoughts you create from a world full of bad news and conflict? Then there are events that happen to you. How do you react to these when you disagree or become angry, or spiteful as to why they happen to you?

Then the proactive ones come forth. These are the ones you simply generate in your own space. Do you ponder on lack, fear, problems, or issues? Then there are the ones that are your desires and plans for a better life. Do you think about the solution or the lack of one?

These are the critters of life that need to be muzzled and directed through the heart. These are the energies that create your perception and your life. Can you remain in that positive space of the heart? The trick is to stay there.

But most important of all is the need to change that double whammy we had in the introduction. First, if the energy you create is there to find a mate, it makes sense to pay more attention to creating positive energy. Secondly, if the energies strength of attraction is dependent upon the added emotion, then it would make sense to start creating strong positive emotion and start a program where you proactively choose what it is you want to attract and manifest. Third, if the negative energy plays havoc with your physics and your physiology by creating dis-ease and disease, it would make good sense to avoid creating these.

Unconscious Creation And Conscious Manifestation

Speculate again and allow yourself to believe that you can control and attract what you want to manifest. The lesson here is that you are already creating your reality without understanding how. The difficult part of this is that although your energy centers of thought, vision, communication and emotion create energies that seek out likeness, there is no correlation. The Earthling has fallen to the first two levels of manifestation in believing that you either have to go get something or get someone else to get it for you. There is no correlation between when the thought occurs and when the result is attained. and when you try to materialize that million dollar check it does not happen. Why?

Because you have not graduated in your vibrational journey to take the responsibility of Creatorship. Yet your energy center are always at work asking and the universe of the quantum soup is always responding in its own way and in its own time. What you have not learned is the process by which these laws work. You must understand the difference between Unconscious Creation and Conscious Manifesting.

First, let us look at what happens without you knowing. What you request is already done because it is formed by your energies that take the quantum energies and creates something from no-thing. These are simply energies with no distinction of bad or good. It is like your mind creates a vision from nowhere, Secondly, because it is handled by the subconscious, there no expectations, conditions, attachments because you are not even aware of it happening. And so a process of energy mating occurs and the law of attraction draws forward the situation, event that give you a likeness. This is why if you are filled with fear, you are asking for more. If you are always questing, or feel sick, or poor, that is the energy you are projecting for more of it.

All this is automatic as it is the way energy works. It is an unconscious process. However, when you attempt to bring this into your conscious reality and manifest proactively, the ball game shifts into the rule book of beliefs.

There is a science behind the Law of Attraction, and that science is the Law of Belief. The Law of Belief governs what you create in your lives. Within the Law of Belief are the addendums of the life 'set ups' you plan and contract to yourself for growth. But the lessons you arrange are met through your confrontation and disciplined effort. It is therefore essential that you fully realize that you are never at the mercy of events, you are not helplessly fated to face the unexplainable like a ship lost at sea. Masters, neither psychological events nor physical events have control over you. When you fully comprehend the vast capacity of your brain to hold a diversity of conclusive beliefs associated with your experiences, you will see that you have an infinite array of choices.

But for those of you stuck in old patterns and limiting beliefs, you are mired in a repetitive cycle of predetermined responses, including the propensity to block new solutions through denial of better thinking. In that sense if you do not learn from past errors, you are self- fated to repeat them. Indeed you will repeat the cycle until you learn how the process of achieving Divine Mind functions. That is true for all humans. You must challenge yourself to break free.

There are three separately governed processes under the Law of Attraction. The three have succinctly different criteria for achievement. Let us define the primary aspect of each Law:

The Law of Attraction:- Thoughts have a frequency and attract like frequencies;

The Law of Belief: Knowing beyond doubt. You can only manifest what you believe is possible;

The Law of Conscious Creation: The conscious ability to focally manifest objectives & events via the multidimensional mind in higher vibration.

Before discussing these, it is important to know why these laws may not work at all.

Attraction and Avoiding Responsibilities

Understand that it is your beliefs that are projected to form your individual and group reality. Understand there are scenarios planned by your higher self, your Divine Mind aspect, that may be termed 'set-ups' or soul-contracts that you yourself have chosen as growth lessons to assist you in moving into greater wisdom. With that reminder in hand, understand that 'karma' in your terms, is not a debt owed to one from another, in the higher sense but rather it is ever to the Self, it is balancing the Divine Self. It is part of your evolutionary path Home.

Should you have a goal or objective in manifestation that would conflict with higher self, it will not in most cases be manifest, unless it is chosen as a growth lesson. For example if a human desires wealth, and that wealth would either be misused or stop the growth process, the higher self may reject such a desire from manifesting. In some cases, humans who have all of their material 'needs' met, are less compelled to search for expansion.

When you find yourself in the confines of any experience that is uncomfortable or not to your liking, you must understand that YOU created that seeming conundrum. Within this axiom, there are indeed, within duality, scenarios in linear time that you must face. Whether one accepts it or not, every circumstance and every resulting action, however dire, was absolutely self created. If, for example, in an extreme circumstance a crime is actually committed, and an individual is duly sentenced to prison, those actions will be faced and experienced.

The sentenced prisoner cannot, in most duality circumstances, simply wish it away. Rather they must face the duality they have themselves created in linear time. There are Laws of Cause and Effect in your physical reality that will play themselves out. Responsibility for not only your actions, but indeed for your beliefs is a key part of your growing process on the planet of lesson. Owning both is essential. But by facing them, you can change the landscape around you.

So understand whenever you seek to avoid the responsibility for your own actions, you generally do so by attempting to give that responsibility, the 'blame', to some other individual, group or cause. But in that process of shifting blame, you unconsciously give away your power, and take away the ownership that allows you to 're-create'. The difficulty most have in accepting self responsibility for your behaviour lies in the desire to avoid the pain and guilt of the consequences of the very actions that resulted. You don't like to admit your errors. But in less obvious circumstances of abundance lack and untoward relationships, you must not only change the nature of your conscious thoughts, but also the belief in those very expectations....and then act on those beliefs.

Unconscious Programming

You create our own reality from what you choose to believe about yourselves, and the world around you. Period. If you do not deliberately & consciously choose your own beliefs, you are unconsciously programmed. You will mindlessly absorb them from your 3D culture, schooling and surroundings. If you are accountable and responsible for your actions, how can you afford NOT to question your beliefs? How you define yourself, and the world around you, forms your belief, which, in turn, forms your reality. Once you fully comprehend that your beliefs form reality, then and only then are you no longer a captive of the events you experience. You simply have to learn the mechanics & methods. It is only when you believe, and program that belief to fully override and replace previous erroneous beliefs, that the integral field of the triad of the three step function of own, change, action is completed.

In the process, thoughts must harmonize with beliefs and be followed by ACTION ! This process is best understood as the Christ Consciousness of Thought, Word, and Deed being the prevalent unified action of unconditional love and forgiveness in all moments as the ACTION. This is the path to conscious creation.

Ad so the lesson is that you are NOT at the mercy of your circumstances, but that belief is, interestingly, the reason you erroneously think you are. Take a moment to consider that. It is the **Law of Belief**. If you believe that circumstances have you trapped, then they do, and will until you change that core belief. You are creators learning how to co-create. You are here to learn that you can and do create. One of your key reasons for being in duality Earth is to learn how to create responsibly, and consciously. The principle professor is often Dr. Cause & Effect, and this doctor makes house calls! You reap what you sow and however uncomfortable, the untoward harvest is the very means for consideration of what got you there.

To break out of circumstances that are caused by our psychology, requires conscious disciplined effort for change to occur. The key again is your belief. There is little difference if you believe that your present life is caused by incidents in your early childhood or by past lives over which you equally feel you have no control. Your events, your lives, your experiences, are caused by your present beliefs. Change the present beliefs and your life changes, not only in the present, but in the past and future in kind. That is the creative power of belief.

Regardless of your level of Light or Dark vibration, whether you are unconsciously creating or consciously manifesting, you cannot escape your beliefs. They are the enzymes through which you create your experience.

The Processes Of Brain and Mind

The reason that most of the books and commercialized teachings on manifestation do not work, is because they do not have the understanding of deeper mind versus 3D brain. Most are about manifesting monetary wealth, and in most cases the only one truly manifesting is the publisher from book sales. There are many nuances, many aspects unexplained in the texts. Even when you expand the mind, you must optimize and balance the auric field for the Crystalline aspect that allows creation to function.

The Key Evolvement Principles for Accessing the Law of Creation are:

1) Expanded Programming of the Brain - Knowledge into Belief
2) Release of Ego-Personality Control to Divine-Mind Aspect of Higher Consciousness
3) Maintain EMF Balance
4) Activate the Mer-Ka-Na Crystalline aspect of Pituitary, Pineal, & Thymus
5) Maintain Balance & Clarity

It is essential that you understand that the 3D brain, the ego-personality aspect incorporated in your physical 3D biology is programmed for 'survival' in a primary coding. It is the 'survival' code that brings in the warning signals that involve cautions often experienced as fear and doubt. The frontal mind, the ego-personality aspect, is engineered to dominate your 3D consciousness, in order to allow linear time flow and survival within the physical plane. The challenge is that to arise above 3D consciousness you must rise out of ego consciousness and flow into Divine Mind within the Seat of the Soul, the gateway into Divine Mind.

The brain is in 3D, the mind is of higher dimension, and within higher mind is your Divinity. The brain operates in 3D and in a manner of speaking, its 3D programming is somewhat dominant in the field of duality. It operates in a more confined paradigm, and to expand into mind, you must operate 'outside the box' to engage your true creativity.

The importance of defined clarity is important in creation. Humans only partially engage wishes through 'Someday I will ' dreamscapes. That is like partially programming a computer program. Is it any surprise that it doesn't happen? Someday I will travel, One day I will be rich, some day I will realize my dreams... These then become merely 'maybes', spaced in a distance. So what you are attempting to create always stays at the distance, the someday you programmed. You did not put it in the present. Yes, the dream is the first part, but it must be clear, concise and followed by definite actions.

Your brain has two hemispheres, one dealing with intellect, one with feeling. The brain works through bio chemical activations and stimulus. The intensity & clarity of a thought program is extremely important for it to become a belief. Your brain is a 3D living computer. It must be dealt with in defined terms. It will not work with 'maybe' or 'can I?' For example, if one were taken into a deep hypnotic state, and asked , "Can the mind heal the dis-ease in this body?" the answer would be "Yes". But it is the empirical answer to whether it is possible for the mind to heal the body. It is not the healing.

Every thought produces a bio-chemical enzyme. That enzyme works with the physical and nonphysical, in sync with the programming. One of the exceptions to the concept of 'Ask and it Shall be given', is that unless the asking is channelled from within, in sync with higher mind, it may have little effect. So a human on the path, in a relatively advanced state of consciousness, may well neutralize from a higher stance desires that would impede progress. There is then, a natural filtering for those in a state of grace. Goals must be worthy.

The most noble goal is to learn the mysteries of life. To gain wisdom and Mastery. But to achieve these goals you will have to take on certain pressures and stresses that are taxing. It requires discipline and will. If you are lazy, you will not get there. You must take on the task to achieve it. So attempts to create a challenge free life may be in stark conflict with a life intent on learning. Goals have challenges. Masters do not plan challenge free lifetimes.

Mind is the builder, and focused will-power is the activator. The more responsibility you appropriately take on, the more your frequency will increase. Learning to program the brain is essential. The brain is a biological computer with 3D filters and 3D programs that are ingrained from birth. Unless you were born in a Tibetan Monastery, your programming has come from socio-cultural indoctrinations. Most social programming teaches you to accept a very limited view of human existence, and human ability. You are taught to believe only what you can sensually detect through sight, hearing, taste, smell or touch.

Know that the physical world of matter you see around you is imagery that you sensually interpret and project. It is received in the eye, transferred via the optic nerve to the brain. What is received stimulates neurons, and a response occurs through a bio chemical reaction that is thermal in nature. Because you generally believe what you see, smell , taste or hear you accept it, you believe it as real. You then decide if it is pleasing or not. The brain then releases neurons based on like or dislike. This is how your reality and attraction works. You are initially attracted to people who are attractive, have a melodious voice and smell good ! Your physical sensual body says yes or no.

In kind, the brain takes ideas and either accepts them or deflects them, according to program parameters. In truth the brain is unable to differentiate between an actual event or a psychological one, such as a dream. In multidimensional mind the two are the same. And although the human brain is capable of receiving information and frequencies from well above 3D, most humans program it to reject anything above 3D frequencies of sensory conformity. The brain computer thus receives only what you allow it to receive. In such limiting paradigmic programming, the only parts of your brain that are activated are the right and left hemispheres of the upper cerebrum and portions of the lower cerebellum, composing and imposing an activity level of only about 10-12 percent of the brain. The brain activity and processes in the neocortex of the cerebral hemispheres conduct the primary activity in the physical realm. The 90% majority of your brain remains unused, un-activated, programmed into dormancy. That is because any thought that does not fit in with the limited thinking programs of your cultural programming or dogma, you auto-deflect.

Herein is one of the great reasons the 'Law of Attraction' does not work for you:

limited belief from limited thinking programs. To be so narrow-minded is to be closed to the grand possibility of anything existing beyond the small band of frequency that can be perceived through the five senses of your physical 3D body.

So how do you expand the brain. How do you open to mind? How do you reprogram the computer? The answer is simple but seemingly a difficult hurdle for many of you to accomplish. It is by doing. It is by examination and study, and willing self to open. Accordingly the very desire to expand attracts powerful thought frequencies that will allow for expansion. And then every Occasion in which you openly accept an idea that is beyond your accepted parameters, that idea activates yet another part of your brain into purposeful use.

Each time you do that, the expansive idea will offer itself as a carrier to expand your field of belief, and allow greater Cosmic reasoning. That process, sincerely repeated, will attract new ideas with study and meditation. In kind, this cycle will activate other portions of your brain for more expansion, new programming and new reception, by accepting in a clear mind. When you have no doubt, when you know and it is absolute....it is Belief. It is through expanded mind that you begin the steps of creating your destiny.

How do you functionally expand the brain and open the doors to Divine Mind ? It is not done in one illuminating flash realization. It is not a one step Divine Anointing. The sacred pathway to what you may term 'Enlightenment ' is achieved in deliberate steps. There are many in metaphysics that want to open the book of knowledge and skip over to the final chapter. It doesn't work that way. It begins by self exploration. By carefully auditing what works and does not work for you. In this method you allow fresh and expansive ideas to enter the brain from the Divine Mind as high frequency thought. Then you process and contemplate it, experience the new concept by embracing it. Acting it out. Evolve it and drive it with emotion , and live the new information into knowledge and wisdom.

The issue most humans have in not changing their beliefs is blind acceptance of mental 3D programming. You can think positive thoughts, think positive change, but if in your deeper mind you doubt they will occur, then they will not. Doubt is one blockage that prevents manifestation of your desires. If you doubt, you do not believe. Doubt in the brain creates a bio-chemical reaction. It activates a neuron carrier in the brain that flows from the Pituitary gland to the Pineal and blocks the 'gateway' from opening. The doubt is there because you do not believe.

The survival aspect programming of the Personality Ego brain utilizes 'fear' in duality as a warning system. However, the duality aspect, the double edge of that sword, is that fear out of context can reach into many negative emotions including depression, doubt, hatred, jealousy and self contempt. These are at their root, negative aspects of fear, and fear creates static in the auric field, and can lead to auric bleeding. The human Aura must be integral to optimally operate in the Law of Creation.

The belief thought-images that surround you are co-created in mass fields by all of humanity in agreement in the macro. Individually they are projected according to your light quotient. These manifest into physical reality. This involves a physical process. Thought frequencies are digitally received and are immediately propelled bio-chemically within the brain. Mental enzymes are connected with the pineal gland. The Pineal gland receives them as geo-coded transmissions. Each image, each thought, being interpreted and sorted according to its energetic signature. They must pass through the program parameter of belief after reception at the pineal. Your brain screens what is determined as real or unreal. Believable or unbelievable according to the light quotient programmed into the brain. The bio-chemicals produced are produced with acceptance ingredient or rejection ingredient. These are allowed to open or close the gate to higher mind accordingly.

These bio chemicals are sent as coded neurons, and are the delivery mechanism of this thought-energy, containing all the codified data necessary for translating any thought or image into physical actuality, or not. Thoughts that are congruent with belief move to reproduce the inner image within the brain and through each nerve fiber of the body physical. These then are the initial fires of gestation for forming the new reality. The next step is through clear mind intent, the force of will, will driven by the acceleration of emotion and feeling.

This done, the physical body releases the objective in a digital code to the sublime body, the intact Auric Field in a semi solid, congealed light code, projected and accelerated from the chakra system. The clarity and intensity you insert behind the thought-desire or goal determines to a great degree the immediacy of its materialization. Once you learn the mechanics of conscious creation it is essential then to utilize the engine of genuine desire with image visualization and emotion to complete the process of physical manifestation.

When It Does Not Work

You create your reality, and there is no other rule. You are here in the University of Duality, to learn how to responsibly create. But it is not thought that on its own, is creative, rather it is BELIEF .... belief expressed in thought in a clear mind. So to clarify syntax, let us say that in the Law of Attraction, it is wise to substitute the word Believe "for "Think", because while positive thought can encourage new belief, until you believe what you think you are not generating new reality. Belief generates reality. This is logical. So understand, beyond the syntax, that thinking positive thoughts can only manifest if they are in sync with your beliefs. For example, if at your core, you BELIEVE you are unworthy of abundance, or in your core mind, believe that the accumulation of abundance is materialistic and therefore wrong, you will not manifest abundance by merely thinking about it. If you believe money is the root of all evil, the Law of Attraction will not work for you until you change that core belief. If you believe that you are poor and will always be scraping to make ends meet, then your very belief will create that experience. No matter if you work 2 or 3 jobs, your core belief is generated, projected into dimensionality and indeed will be manifested. You will struggle economically.

If you believe you are not 'very smart' , your brain will take on that belief and you will be limited. If you believe you are not attractive, you will project that image to all around you telepathically. You constantly project your beliefs, and their manifestations constantly "meet you in the face" when you view the world around you. They form the reflective mirrored- image of your realized beliefs. You cannot escape your beliefs. They are, however, the method by which you create your experience. In kind, if you believe, in very simple terms, that people mean you well, and will treat you kindly, they will. And, if you believe that the world is against you, then so it will be in your experience. And, if you believe that your body will age and begin to weaken at age 40 , then it will.

You are in physical existence to learn and understand that your beliefs, energetically translated into feelings, thoughts and emotions, cause all experience. Period. Now your experience can change your beliefs, and at any time you are in control of what you choose to believe. The key is to form BELIEF through 'over-soul' Mer-Ka-Na **(http://www.earth-keeper.com/EKnews_2-26-2010.htm**) aspectual conscious choice and not by unconscious programming.

Now, let's take this concept into multi dimensionality. Imagine that you have a number of lifetimes as a monk or priest where you have taken strict poverty vows. You have shunned the 'material' and adhere strongly to the BELIEF that money is 'the root of all evil'. All lifetimes are simultaneous in the eternal now. In the present lifetime there is the focus on creating your reality. You have need for abundance. You realize money is not evil, it is simply energy, and that it can be used for many positive things.

You have read all the books, read all the articles on how positive thinking triggers the 'Law of Attraction', yet you are still not bringing in abundance. Could it be that you are multi dimensionally 'outnumbered'. If you have a dozen ongoing lifetimes in their NOW moment simultaneously shunning, rejecting what they BELIEVE to be 'material things' and one lifetime trying to create abundance, which effort contains the most energy projection ? You have the ability in NOW mind in Mer-Ka-Na to change the seeming past and create a unified harmonic of that which you desire and believe. And Dear Ones, money is not evil ! It is energy and in the new paradigm you are required to learn to create in responsible loving manner. You CAN have what you want, what you need, but the Belief must be harmonic in multi dimensionality.

It is not as simple as "Ask and it shall be given". It must be projected in clear harmonic mind. And mind is above brain. Mind is multi dimensional.

Now, the multi-dimensional aspect of human experience is quintessential to your understanding of the mechanics of the 'Law of Attraction'. A key part of understanding your multi-dimensionality is that your higher self , the part of you above physicality, scripted certain of your 'life growth challenges'. And that these cannot be avoided or wished away. Rather they are 'required' courses in the curriculum of the 'University of Earth' that you yourself have chosen to complete for higher good. And you can't skip the classes. They will come to you because you enrolled, they are a part of the 'Law of Attraction' from higher mind, and cannot be repelled.

This then is an area in which duality thinking, of trying to wish away a seeming obstacle, seems to defy the 'Law of Attraction'. You may find yourself in an uncomfortable scenario at work, find that all the 'positive thinking' applications seem to fall flat. That is because there is a lesson here that must be faced, and until it is faced it will repeat over and over again, until it is completed...because you have attracted it to you from higher mind, and duality -aspect brain is unable to avoid it. It is only completed when you master it.

While it is true that your thoughts and beliefs create the reality you experience in duality, you in higher aspect thoughtfully and carefully compose and create the challenges that you face. These have great purpose. Whether you truly believe it or not, you write your own tests. So while 'positive thinking' is a key frequency, positive thinking is meant to help you approach your life lessons and does not circumvent the learning process itself. You cannot just ignore or wish away the growth lessons you script for yourself in order to expand. That is because your chosen set ups are in most cases outside, beyond the ability of the duality aspect of ego-brain to remove or will away. You will face them, because you have in divine self, willed it from higher perspective. In higher mind you have scripted your challenges.

There is nothing more stimulating, more worthy of actualization, than your manifested desire to evolve, to change for the better. That is indeed each of your lifetime missions. It is not enough to meditate, or to visualize the desired goal being accomplished if you do not act upon the inner voice , the drive from which your meditations and visualizations arise.

Intent, focus and meditation must absolutely be teamed with action. Becoming impeccable, and eventually achieving your enlightenment does not mean, as some religions indirectly imply, that you are suddenly in a blissful state of oblivion, or in some distant state of nirvana. Masters, we tell you that you are as much a part of a nirvana now as you ever will be, you simply need to discover it within you.

There will indeed be cycles within your emotional state; that is part of being human. There will be times in which you feel apathetic and depressed. Not only the problems you face, but even certain astronomical gravities can be the source of such despair, on their own. All of these must be faced, and can be surmounted. So be aware that 'Nirvana', in your vernacular, is achieved attitudinally, and not through avoidance, ignorance or escape, but through impeccable confrontation of the reality projection that surrounds you.

Earth experience, duality mastery is difficult. This is a great truth, one of the greatest truths of duality, and one commonly misunderstood. The study and mastery of life requires work. You can't simply put the text book under your pillow and sleep on it, it must be read and understood a page at a time. Moment by moment.

So then your full understanding and accepting that your life is a construction of 'set ups' that you planned in order to enable your spiritual growth is an even greater truth. You see when you accept this noble truth, you have the opportunity to transcend it. That which you term 'destiny' is in truth the situations you pre-planned for your life lesson. And Dears Ones, that very self scripted 'destiny', in your terms, will assist you to both face your challenges and then manifest your desires, but not because you protest what you do not like. In order to experience the light of your desire, you must ignite the passion that will free it from the stronghold where it has been closely guarded. The greatest path is to accept the challenge of self purification by being a living example of your own light rather than protesting the darkness that still exists within the world in 3D, or choosing to insulate yourself from it.

By accepting that you are here to face challenges, then you can more robustly create the energy needed to face them. Because once it is accepted, the fact that life can be difficult no longer scares you, rather it motivates the spiritual warrior into resolve. The greatest issue you have in accepting ultimate ownership and responsibility for your actions lies in the core desire to avoid the pain of the consequences of that behaviour. But we tell you that it is the confrontational courage of impeccably solving problems that provides and indeed nurtures meaningful growth in your life.

Facing your problems is the serendipitous cutting edge that distinguishes between success and failure, or better said, between growth and stagnation. Problems call forth your best effort to resolve and refine courage and wisdom within the impeccable seeker. It is categorically because of stressful predicaments and obstructions that you grow mentally and spiritually. It is through the pain of confronting and resolving life-puzzles and 'set-ups' that you learn the greater meaning of the science of love. Dear Hearts, the candid fact is that some of your most poignant accomplishments and indeed greatest growths are spawned when you are placed in the troubling crossroads of conundrum.

Your greatest trials and revelations take place in times when you are outside of your 'comfort zone', feeling bewildered, unfulfilled, or even in a state of agonizing despair. For it is in such moments, propelled by your discomfort, that you are compelled to burst out of the confining cages and seek a better, more spiritually satisfying way of life.

What then is impeccability? We are not understating the base premise, when we define impeccability simply as ' always trying your best'. To remain impeccable requires more effort as the scope of your gained wisdom and consciousness expands. The greater your consciousness, the more you 'know' . The more you know, the greater the responsibility to live accordingly. You are in the process of expanding your vibratory awareness, of becoming a conscious participant with the soul. You are becoming what your soul is, discovering your greater identity.

When you grow spiritually, it is because you have opened to seek growth and are taking action, working to achieve it. Impeccability involves the deliberate extension of your Beingness into evolution. Impeccability puts you in the state of grace. Impeccability does not infer that you have achieved enlightenment or have learned all you need to learn. Rather it means you are on the only track, the right pathway to get there. So we will define Impeccability in two layers, two phase formats:

1) Conditional Impeccability: This is when the entity is not highly advanced, yet working toward mastery . Doing one's best. Utilizing knowledge to the best of one's ability to do the right thing, even when there may be ignorance and innocent misconceptions. By that it means you truly believe what you are doing is the right course, even if it is not the full or expansive truth . All of you go through such phases. In this phase if you make a mistake, it is an honest mistake, in which you genuinely believed you were doing what you felt is right.

2) Mastery Impeccability: This is the phase of the soul in human existence that is on the cusp of Mastery. One highly advanced, and walking the talk. Having no inner conflict between what one believes to be the right path, and what one actuates.

Both phases activate what you may term as an accelerated state of grace. Grace is assistance from the Divine Self to help the outcome of situations when one is trying their best. It may be thought of as the 'Guardian Angel', because in many cases that is exactly what a Guardian Angel is, your Divine Self serendipitously intervening in situations to assist you on your path. If we were to redefine what your religious texts consider as sin, it would not be in terms of the commandments, rather it would be: "knowledge not utilized". Taking actions you know to be incorrect, actions in conflict to your highest beliefs.

Wisdom Is Within

All of you desire wisdom greater than your own. Seek and you will find, and Masters you can find it 'hidden' inside you. And sadly that is often the last place you look. It takes work. You see the divine interface between God and man is within what your academics term as the subconscious. Even your religious texts tell you that God is within you, that you are a spark of the Divine. The subconscious mind, or 'back brain' in your terms, is the part of you that is God. The portion of your greater self that contains the knowledge of 'All That Is', the part of you that contains the Akashic Records, the soul memory of everything.

Since the subconscious is the Divine Mind within you, the goal of spiritual growth is achieved by entering into that sacred 'Garden of Wisdom'. It is entered by quieting the ego mind. Meditation has ever been the gateway. It is the key to quieting the personality-ego narration and allowing the 'Voice of the Divine Soul' to be heard. Again, effort is required. There are no short cuts. The re-attainment of God-ness is the purpose of your individual existence on the polarity plane. You are born that you might become, as a conscious individual, a physical expression of God. A divine expression in Being-ness.

The challenge is your soul quest, your true purpose, and in physical sojourns, the clock is ever ticking. Obtaining Godhood in physicality is achieved on time-release, through immaculate desire that is actuated in the physical realm by merging with the wisdom of the non physical. Time matters. In polarity the current shifting of paradigms and energies can throw you off center rather easily in these quickening times. Your true purpose is often difficult to subjectively define and your understanding and ballast lies juxtaposed between illusion and perceived reality. You may feel you are living in a distortion and that nothing is exactly as it seems. In the process you can become confused and complacent. You can lose track of time.

Your lives, each moment of your physical life is precious, far more so than some of you realize. Far more than most of you utilize. Time is a precious commodity, and it is finite within your duality. Each of you reading these words will at some point in the future transition out of the physical. In your vernacular, you will experience death, you will die. This is a condition of physicality as you know it. Yet so many of you act as though you will live forever. Indeed the soul is eternal, but you will not ever be the same person, the same personality or expression that you are now, in any lifetime or in any other aspect of your 'Beingness'. You are here to learn the expressions of your own Godliness within duality and indeed duality is a gift. Life is a gift. You are here to learn how to co create, for indeed you are co creators of the Universe, of the Cosmos. You are here to achieve Mastery, and so many of you are very close, very near that achievement.

Until you truly value yourself, you will not be in the grace of impeccability and thus not be motivated to truly value and optimize your time. Unless you place great value on your allotted time, you will not do your 'best' with it. "Carpe Diem", is translated as "Seize the Day", and this is so appropriate. You must seize each moment! So many of you, despite your good intentions, allow yourselves to be tranquilized into complacency at certain phases or within certain conditions of your chosen sojourns. Many of you waste time; misuse time and lifetime after lifetime can be squandered. What you do not face, what you do not resolve in any one moment or lifetime, will resurface. You will repeat the set up until you successfully solve it, and that is indeed a great truth. Utilizing your time in duality is quintessential, and that is a complex undertaking for it necessitates that you seek impeccability. It requisites love of self, for until you genuinely value yourself, you truly do not value your life and time. And until you value your time, you will not be compelled to maximize how you spend it.

It is natural Discipline that is the basic set of tools to solve life problems. Without discipline it is difficult for you to have the driver required to focus on the work of solving your problems. Simply stated, you can become immobilized...apathetic, complacent or lazy. On the 'Ladder of Ascension', you are moving up, sitting still or moving down.

In third dimensional physics there is a law that states that energy that is highly organized will naturally degrade when not in dynamic state. It is easier by natural law to be in a state of complacency in the physical plane, than to be in an upwardly mobile condition. That is clearly logical. It is the Law of Love that motivates all souls into greater consciousness, and that requires dynamics...work! Laziness is in a real sense one of your biggest obstacles, because work means swimming against the tide. Seize the Day!

All is In Perfect Order

Some of you say and feel that "Everything works out as it should, all is in perfect order". But that concept is something of a paradox, and like a face card it is upside down either way you look at it. From the higher perspective all is in perfect order, but from the perspective of humankind within duality, it is not! If it were there would be no need for lessons, no need for what you term reincarnation. One need but take a look around and know that the plight of humankind on the planet Earth is far from being perfect. Indeed it will NOT work out as it should, until you make it so!

On the final walk of Mastery, most of your major issues have been dealt with, and we honor you for that. What remains may however be elusive to confront. And it is important to confront any and all unresolved issues and energies.

We say this without judgment. We point this out in order to assist you. For in time all must be dealt with. The more advanced you become, the more difficult it can be to sweep up the last remaining bits of unresolved issues, because they are often well hidden. The unresolved energy, the final issues can become polarized and repelled outside your mental field, forgotten in the residues of many lifetimes. Take time to self review in multidimensional self and determine what is left to be worked on.

Polarity Physics - The 'Law of Opposite Attraction'.

There is yet another conundrum about the Law of Attraction, so says Metatron: "The closer you get to light, the stronger you attract the dark. Light attracts bugs! The more you advance, the more criticism you will draw, and that requires wisdom to deal with. The polarity aspect of the 'Law of Opposite Attraction' herewith comes into play. From a state of detachment what takes place is electromagnetics. Pure positive energy has the greatest 'magnetic' attraction to negative energy. So as your light shines brighter, the magnetic to polar opposite increases. It can be managed, but you must have the light, humility, the strength and discipline to deflect it. So dealing with affronts, the hard energy of jealousy, hatred and anger are an important piece of the puzzle in achieving the Master level of Impeccability.

How do you deal with this? Don't take anything personally is perhaps easier said than done, but it is quite true. Your bible talks of turning the other cheek. But this doesn't mean you apologize when someone steps on your foot. Part of the paradox is indeed standing up for your truth. But it does mean you don't step on the feet of others, intentionally or otherwise. Standing in your truth is peaceful action. It is a benevolent expression of aggression that allows grace and dignity to be retained on both sides of any conflict or attack. It sends the attacking energy back to its source, but without malice and with love. Each of you has an opportunity to stand in impeccability within any conflict. You can deal with conflict, without engaging it. Do you understand? Deal with, face it from a stance of emotional detachment, as the observer, and that is not easy, yet it is the way of the Master. It is how you 'Don't take anything personally', you detach from the emotional reaction.

Each of you has an opportunity to be impeccable every day. The scenario in which you recognize your own failings, your own conflict with integrity, is the day you encompass Mastery level Impeccability, and indeed it is a journey. Likewise the day you stand in your truth with willingness to recognize another person's truth, you encompass integrity. The divine mind is only achieved, only accessed through crystalline Mer-Ka-Na resonance, within crystalline thought waves. Crystalline thought is above emotion, above petty feelings. It is achieved in detachment. It is the crystalline lake of Shamballa, of true Nirvana, as smooth as glass, no waves distorting its mirrored visage."

40

YOUR HOLOGRAPHIC REALITY

The Law Of Conscious Creation

You know of Unconscious Creation and Conscious Manifesting. What about Conscious Creation? What Earthlings have not come to understand is that the workings of the mind in what is termed "imagined reality" is a model of way the 3D material reality works. The real dream is your life here. Understand that there is no physical object about you, nor any experience in your life that you have not created. This includes your physical form, your body. There is nothing about your own physical image that you have not made. In fact if you were able to view self in other life sojourns, you would be surprised at how many similar physical characteristics you create in what would be termed sequential lifetimes. When you have Divine Wisdom, you can create kingdoms unlimited. When you have knowledge, there is nothing to fear, for then there is no thing, no element, no principality, no understanding that can ever threaten or enslave or intimidate you. When fear is given knowledge, it is called enlightenment.

You have a natural rhythm of existing in the physical and non physical. It is your waking and sleep state. Dreams are one of your greatest natural therapies and assets as connectors between the interior and exterior realities and universes. Your normal consciousness benefits by excursions and rest in those other fields of nonphysical actuality that are entered when you sleep, and the so-called sleeping consciousness will also benefit by frequent excursions into the physical matter waking state.

But let us tell you that the imagery you see in both is at its base, mental interpretations of digital frequential fields of core consciousness units. The frequency that your brain receives is actually a digital code, a crystalline pattern of symbols (akin to what you may term as X's and O's), that you interpret and translate into images and feelings. It is not so difficult for you to accept that you create your dreams, as it is to accept that you also create your physical reality, but you do both. You also determine if both or either are real...or not.

The issue most humans have in not changing their beliefs is blind acceptance of mental 3D programming. You can think positive thoughts, think positive change, but if in your deeper mind you doubt they will occur, then they will not. So we return to programming and its effect on manifestation within the Law of Attraction. Doubt is one blockage that prevents manifestation of your desires. If you doubt, you do not believe. Doubt in the brain creates a bio-chemical reaction. It activates a neuron carrier in the brain that flows from the Pituitary gland to the Pineal and blocks the 'gateway' from opening. The doubt is there because you do not believe.

Through the ages it has been known that the Pineal is the interface between the higher dimensions and the physical realm. It can be said then to be the gateway between the ego personality, brain and the Divine Mind. It has been termed by metaphysicians such as Descartes and Edgar Cayce as being the 'Seat of the Soul'.

The pineal is the agent of advancing knowing into reality manifestation. The pineal works with the pituitary to open the bridge, the gateway between the physical and nonphysical, between brain and mind. Whatever knowledge you allow yourself to believe can only become a reality by the pineal first opening the gate to the Divine. It does this by interpreting the frequency of thought into a thermal bio chemical electrical current throughout your body and opening to mind.

Your human brain transforms the thoughts you generate into thousands of bio-chemicals every second. But not every thought of the ordinary brain reaches into Higher Mind. Divine Wisdom comes from Divine Mind, and when you allow mind to take the reins over ego personality you achieve the wisdom of Divine Creativity. It is this wisdom distilled from knowledge that gives you the ability to enter the Law of Creation. Once entered, then know what you want to create and take action toward it.

The human body is an instrument that can be used to access the amazing and extraordinary energies of the Divine. But there are dedicated principles for accessing the Divine. When the body is fine tuned, wisdom is achieved, the aura is maintained in balance and the doors to the Law of Creation through the Law of Belief and Attraction are opened. For that to occur, all systems must work in balanced synchronicity. If you use your body for physical gratification rather than as an instrument to achieve the divine...you will reap what you sow.

You are ever the Master of each experience. Even in your most abandoned states of seeming helplessness, you are the scripter of each iota of that experience. Yet if you will utilize determination and wisdom by owning the responsibility to reflect upon your situation, and to search diligently for the Law upon which being is established, you then become the wise master, directing your energies with intelligence, and fashioning thoughts to worthy focus and realization. One thought attracts another. Positive energy attracts more positive energy. One intelligent thought attracts another. Likewise when you dwell in self pity, depression and issues of poor self esteem, you draw more of these to you. That is the Law of Attraction.

Such is the conscious human, the Master, and you can only thus evolve by discovering within Self the Laws of Conscious Creating; the discovery of which is totally a regulated science. It is a matter of application, self-analysis, and experience.

You can indeed intentionally manifest your world, and in doing so experience what is termed the Kingdom of Heaven. Conscious Creation is your destiny, and you can all make your lives the golden experience you responsibly desire.

Think How Your Mind Works

If you understand how your mind works, they you can understand how your physical reality as a hologram created by the mind can or should work. To take from quantum physics, your mind can bring into its reality any possibility you can think of. From the soup of no-thing, some-thing as an image, idea can be brought forward into your imaginary reality simply by shutting out your senses like closing your eyes and creating the picture in your mind. An event, experience, object, people; all can all be brought into reality. It begins with quantum nothing and like in the Observer effect of quantum physics becomes something. There need not be space or time. You can flip from one scene to another, you can play a movie like a dream, you can bilocate, materialize, be invisible, meld into other things, even deploy your physical senses given practice. You are engaging in the Creative process within you as a creator and here there are limitless possibilities to be "formed" by the conscious awareness of your mind. Everything can be everywhere, nowhere at once. It is nonlocal. You entangle by way of conscious intent to create whatever you desire to create.

The holograph of your world, your reality can work the same way and it does but you have not learned, nor believe this is so.

A New Look At Creating Reality

It is attention and intention and love as the substance of power that allows an image to congeal into a material representation of an abject in a hologram. This means that the Divine Mind be the total agent of the image of some object that is simply created in your mind's eye. It will be a clear image so you need much practice here. At the point at which your Higher Mind and the Heart—the congealer—create that image, it is projected onto a place of choice by intent and at the same time the image of the mind is projected to the God Source to be reflected back like a mirror as a beam of divine light to the same place of choice—yes it is like converging laser beams of light that create the 3 dimensional holographic image.

As these two actions converge upon the place of choice from you and the divine beam from the source, they form a holographic duplicate representation of the object that is to be replicated or materialized. Yes, from a wave form to an atomic form as the electrons arrange themselves into the image which is your higher consciousness choosing a new possibility from the no-thing.

It is not necessary to concern yourself as to how the chemistry, atomic structure and so on occurs as it is all under natural cosmic law that such an arrangement is created. These laws understand how this is done and your divine consciousness abides by these so they all understand what this is made up of to congeal this into the expression of the holographic image to be interpreted as such by your and other sensory systems of your brains—your sensory receiving stations.

You first create a clear image in your mind's eye with the assistance of the heart, then project it to a place of materialization. Then you project this to the One to project back to the same place. A holographic image is created. This is similar to the way a holographic image is created with beams of light that are split, reflected and converged again. What is it? A hologram. What form is it? It is whatever you see clearly that your brain understands and has meaning for or memory of.

It is your brain that does the final work as a material representation by retrieving what it knows and what cosmic rules apply in the material representation. It retrieves information and the cosmic rule simply "knows" what it is.

So let us say an apple is chosen. Is it big, small, red, yellow? What kind is it? The brain is designed to hold its own local knowledge—like a copy of its own experience that is held current. It uses this to fill the gaps of creating this from what it knows about the apple. The brain, and of course your consciousness or mind has information and the cosmic rules of its composition, formation, are drawn to complete the picture.

So a word, an object, and image, all have meaning to the brain by its experience and it with the assistance of cosmic law reverse engineers the process to create the result from memory and let us call it technical information as to its composition or material makeup. Although an image of the apple is only a representation in your lower mind and brain, it already has the appropriate material characteristics from higher sources as to how it would be materialized. So anything can indeed happen in materialization therefore it requires a high degree of responsibility.

You see, the brain which interprets senses also fills in the gaps to complete it. Many times, you will not actually see things exactly as the brain only picks up half of what is there, filling in the rest by itself—unless you place strict attention on it and see the difference. The brain fills the gaps, holes, missing information and uses a process you call extrapolate and interpolate from its memory what is needed to complete the picture. If you see and read the words "I luv yu" or "wht a wndrful da" you know what this is meaning, do you not? Your brain is interpolating the true meaning even though parts are missing. But by closer inspection and attention, you see the difference. So it is with an image of an apple.

The brain is the holographic processor that creates the meaning, composition, representation through its memory and the interpretation of the senses of your lower body. You see, feel, taste an apple and it seems so real. So if you take the senses of see, feel, taste and the memories of this, then reverse engineer the process back through the brain—with divine assistance—it will create the apple appearing solid in the hologram.

What you have not done is to do this outside of your imagination in an eyes open conscious state of awareness. Yet as you know, some can indeed do this—like holy men—by a reverse process which is easy in your mind but not in your hologram of 3D. But you are learning. It is what you are learning as you vibration reaches a certain level. Yes, this is so because of a certain level of responsibility, and partnership with the Higher Divine Self is required as reflected by the alignment of heart, purpose and Divinity—the One.

You are creating energy that will either seek out and energy mate or it will materialize into something that the energy represents into a new form from the essence of particles of what consciousness is made up of—electrons you call them—common to all things whether material or non material. This is what you call a reality, the attention of your awareness within the total consciousness—the mind of God. Each energy lives and has purpose and once created, lives to expand itself according to its purpose and it design which will behave according to cosmic laws of creation. Once live, it remains so and evolves as it was perceived at the time of creation, then it grows, changes and evolves.

Think also of how we have informed you of materialization and how you form the holographic image of some thing that can materialize—but with the alignment of the divine partner—approval to actually create—knowing the divine cosmic laws and being are explicitly in the heart so you are indeed the creator .

Each particle is of the whole and all is one therefore all that exists, existed or will exist resides here in the hologram which is the mind—the total consciousness of the One—the Creator. In your lower form of mind and body, this become like an individual compartment of the whole which is your local individual consciousness.

Once thoughts or actions of the lower form create, these energies remain to attain their purpose. They may be transmuted if you have attained the level of vibration that is of the Higher Body and Divine Mind. However, this responsibility is not of the lower form. If the energies are created from the Lower Selves, they will simply congeal into a transitional etheric state, attract, evolve and interact as they are designed by intent and attention to do—fulfilling either a cosmic or a purpose assigned by the creator you.

Through your senses of the Lower Self, the experiences are interpreted and perceived with the brain being the interpreter. The mind is what creates, sets, interprets, the instructions and is the actual link and control center of all this interacting energy and the body which itself is energy. A body is thus a hologram formed the same way and once created, a genetic code is set creating a signature of its makeup like in DNA. It is like this in all things as an initial blueprint that can replicate and evolve once given life.

Your Hologram Is A Living Growing Intelligent Medium

In the strictest sense, the consciousness of the Creator of the One is like a holographic with some major differences. Describing it this way is a convenient way for you to relate to it and understand it. It reflects all that can be or has ever been imagined by God. It is not a true hologram in your scientific terms however, in that it is a living and intelligent medium with all that exists living and interacting within it—all energies—living things that are themselves seeking to expand, flourish and ascend towards their purposes in their own individualized consciousness. Flowers, animals, human, rocks, and all energy placed within this hologram in their lower forms seek to evolve and expand through their instincts and purposes as encoded in their DNA or life code or inherent coded information that defines them and their higher states of expression. In humans the expression of this is through the Higher Divine Self which itself is consciousness.

All things are at the fundamental stage energy of consciousness and all have some form of consciousness as individualized. This brings and records an awareness through various interaction and processing of other energies—or sensory systems—to interact with and to seek expression and to evolve in a way to find their purposes. This is a cycle of material form—material by perception—of being created, living, blossoming, reproducing and all things are drawn to this process as encoded in the DNA as directed by their consciousness. In your lower form of Self, you are no different than a flower or rock or animal that seeks to live life, flourish, expand, and reproduce. You like all else are able to reproduce and create and evolve within an interactive live world of the hologram which itself is also evolving and lives with purpose of love.

You as a higher being can also create energy with your mind and body by placing attention here and triggering energy systems. You give it life and set it loose to evolve according to purpose—given by you--as so defined or by cosmic laws of evolution and expression.

Your Lower Self is designed to interpret energies so as to process them through senses and interpret them according to your physical brain. These are senses by the body and it transmitted back into it for action-reaction, as well as recording in consciousness for the perception of the experience. It is so it can learn, grow, live, expand according to instinct (lower purpose), cosmic law and expand (higher purpose. This process of material physical perception is this way and once some thing is formed in the hologram, it remains as part of it for others to perceive and sense.

In the lower form all interacts with and reacts to these energies that form the group or global hologram. Although you are creating certain energies through your mind and lower equipment, these are transient energies not yet congealed but are given life to seek purpose and find energy mates or entrain with like energies in the hologram. You know all about this. These energies can be dark or light and depending on their creation can do this rapidly or remain forever within the hologram.

In the Higher form, however, you are able to create new energies, passing the temporarily congealed state and materialize directly from the total consciousness—as a Creator. This is where a huge difference lies in the ability to transmute or actually create within the hologram.

Holograms Form From A Consciousness And Need To Express

You were given entry to this world of the Creator's mind and consciousness. This was created as a wondrous hologram of beauty and perfection within which beings could live, expand and learn to love and enjoy the life they had been given.

The entry of beings to this world has not gone according to this plan because of the lower state taken, the choice of will and others who have designs different fed by lower energies and requirements. Essentially other energies have been given life and purpose, evolving not within the light, filling the consciousness with interacting forces and energies not of the light. Energies you create retain a signature of ownership to find energy that it itself vibrates or entrains with. It draws other energies that represent people situations, and their owners with them. Thus in the hologram all energies live and interact. All beings interact in these physical and non-physical energies playing out their lives, as you do.

Many times this has resulted in much darkness within the hologram accumulating in a temporary form attempting to congeal into the hologram, not yet mated. It has dominated and at time almost destroyed the hologram. And so it has come to its end of a natural cycle of life as well at which point the energies are transmuted by death or by active awareness of its purpose. This purpose to many of you is known and therefore you have begun to form a new hologram in parallel which represents a world different than this one. The process is not known as to how these two worlds will merge or separate except to say it is all at an end which is the beginning.

The Hologram Is Limited By Beliefs

The hologram you have formed for yourself has limited you through your beliefs and as that belief changes, your senses and awareness of it expands, you begin to take control of it. As this occurs, the new 5D hologram that has been formed—much like your global consciousness—begins to be clearer. As your limited senses of 3D intent and bring material and mental perceptions of experience, so does the 5D self do the same in the new hologram. These worlds then expand so you with either at will begin to walk both. You are learning to use 5D senses in a 3D world. You will bring 3D into the 5D world.

As you sit quietly and imagine a world, or write about it, you are forming your hologram with your signature. This is a part of the larger hologram of joint imaginations. Anything is possible here but you are not yet able to walk this world except in your imagination. Once you give life to it, it is there and your tags of ownership so it can be changed as in a movie. All vibrations are above a threshold, all is interlinked and your awareness of how this works in one medium of intelligent evolving life unfolds to you. This you do not understand but there are cosmic laws that govern the way energies evolve, interact and change.

The Hologram Abides By Rules

Your mind may be busy with 4D the "transitions zone" as part of the hologram wondering why it has not come forward into your reality. Yes, it is another lane or dimension which is all around you like the air you breathe. It is beyond your 3D sensory system bounds, however—which you have imposed yourself. It is where energy is first created and interacts at an invisible etheric level. It is like a transition stage where energy waits in some form awaiting congealment and purpose. It is there to seek out an energy mate, to congeal, to materialize, or to co-create some thing that it is or represents. Think back to the laws of manifestation and Co-creation and how you create energies that seek mates.

For example, you may have a moment when you are angry and your thoughts, emotions instantly form this transition energy in the 4D plane. It is created in your field of influence. What does it do? It is tagged as belonging to you as you created it. Under cosmic law it has been created with a purpose of your anger that enfolded it. This may or may not be clear or strong in its intent provided by you. Under cosmic law, it is a living energy with purpose and such purpose it must strive to satisfy by seeking out a likeness to it and its purpose—an energy mate. It is a living energy seeking to expand and satisfy its purpose and signature vibration that it represents—namely your anger. So it can do this in several ways.

It can find a likeness to attract a situation that satisfies the purpose by an experience. It manifests a balance. It manifests, it evolves, it seeks until this is done and be balanced so the purpose is released. Such energy, depending upon it strength and clarity can take unknown time and it can also influence other energy fields to have an effect on them. It must to this in order to draw other energies to it. So it may be something that is in your own field that is strong enough to affect dysfunction in your own field and body because it is attached to you—and your belief system can attract others the same way. The dysfunction remains until it is balanced, like the idea of karma, but many times the energy results in creating disease or dis-ease or dysfunction in your Lower Self without your knowing. The effect of regression reveals the imbalance to correct this. Many energies are created as dark troublesome energies without purpose and they will simply be around looking for something dark to attach to.

The 4D world is full of these energies and over centuries have accumulated much unbalanced energy that has not yet satisfied its purpose and these affect the larger consciousness of those living in the hologram—in 3D. They struggle to evolve. You see the energy can be poorly defined and without purpose, unable to balance. It can be anything imaginable and there is no time here so it stays in 4D.

Your higher abilities if developed—as with clairvoyants and psychics are able to read these energies and sense them with expanded senses. They can read these living this to detect purposes, strength, have visions, read information that is attached to them as well as their owners. They can reveal what is forming or attached to you transcending past or future as the senses pick up this information thereby reading the future or revealing the past. These can see, hear, feel, read, know what is forming, the strength, the purpose.

Yes, ghosts, apparitions, dark energies, boogey men of unimaginable purposes and creations reside here. But you have been protected from these by your sensory limitations. However, as these senses evolve, so do protective abilities.

You have not yet widened the range of your sensory systems to read these energies— and to see them. Many animals have examples of enhanced ranges that sense these energies—much beyond yours. You do have them and they must be awakened again in your 3D form. In your 5D form there are many more as there are in your 4D form which is your aura that surround your body. You have others awaiting your awakening.

So yes there are many energy forms here awaiting their own evolution and purpose. That is why we speak of 3D and 5D, and not of 4D as 4D is simply a transition hologram from one to the other.

What you sow is what you reap reflects this 4D hologram of transition from one to another or back to the one that created it. It reflects the cosmic workings of energy as you sow it in 4D to reap it in 3D from where it is sown—or use it to grow to 5D. But you may not know what this is, and how or when it shall reap—that is part of raising your vibrations to sow wonderful positive energy in every moment.

The Collective Hologram Of Reality

You can understand that there is much energy being created by all beings on Earth. Some is dark, some is of the light, some is weak, some is strong, some has purpose some has not. But without exception each energy formed is attached to the creator and joins the collective coalescing energy. It is important to understand that in creating it, a tag is placed upon it by you—a word, a vision, an image, a symbol that represents this so it can be recalled for further attention instantly. It can be made clear, stronger, enforced, reinforce and define with clarity and strength of emotion so it is a stronger vibration energy with a clear purpose. Otherwise it can be aimless and purposeless with no thing to do except to bring unto itself the same, likeness—for you the creator of it—to experience. Clarity of purpose, strength of vibration through continued attention makes it strong and powerful to entrain and attract that which it reflects and is its purpose.

You understand that all beings form a collective hologram the same way as a composite of individual ones. These are combined as the group hopes, wishes, actions and perceptions all the time interacting and congealing into various forms that may materialize into new energies and forms. It is within this vast hologram that yours exists, all being within the larger one of the One—the mind of God. The hologram itself is alive and all within it cannot be changed in its perceived material form—a joint belief and congealment of form—without the attention and agreement of the Higher Divine Mind— your link to the Creator of the One. This as you know requires the higher vibration and purpose reflecting the truth of your essence of light. Otherwise energies only attract and attach to each other while at the same time that which is perceived to be material and physical in the 3D dimension remain unaltered except by its own growth evolution.

Thus there are interacting layers in the hologram of the One—3D material world, 4D coalescing energies, 5D etheric world. Within this 3D hologram layer all that is material is therefore your own holographic plane as perceived by you. What you perceive from it is your parallel world and yours alone interacting with the 3D world forming your physical hologram of your reality. It is recorded and once attention goes there it remains.

Let us give an example. An apple is a 3D material construct and the sight, smell, taste of it are your personal constructs in 4D as determined by your senses and perceptions—the link between the two planes. The whole hologram is overlain by your personal perception of all that is in it that comes into your awareness or attention. This parallel world is your own movie of life using other beings, props and objects of 3D to create your scenes and settings for you to interact with to create your perceptions, emotions, feelings, experiences to learn to yourself expand and grow towards your own purpose. How you do this is of your free will and this world of perception is yours alone as to what is in it.

Holograms Are Within Each Other Nested Nonlocally

It is important to understand you think this way in linear fashion. The Higher Self we have split into two words or concepts for you of Higher Mind and Higher Body. Yet the higher and lower Mind do not have any clear division as does not the higher and lower body. They are all one in the hologram and are simply a level of energy vibration which is a continuous scale—like the amount of love—it is less or more. Even the body is not clearly divided although you may perceive visible and invisible as this line of division but it is not so. It of course all depends upon the level of sensing perception, and who and what you are to be able to sense see feel interact with these energies; and to what degree. Similarly the hologram is not separate with clear divisions. Just like the mind itself, it can be nowhere and everywhere, or nonlocal. It brings into consciousness whatever it decides to "observe".

They are one mind, one consciousness and we have referred to them as separate 3D, 4D, 5D but they are not. Even at the 3D level there is no real matter as it depends on how well developed your sensory systems and state of vibration are. It is your beliefs that create the limit and boundaries. Even with what you think so material—like a rock-- is all no thing as you peer closer into it. So all that is, is a matter of sensory degree, not classes. There are beings within all these dimensions and planes and they are also of different energies, in different energy states of body and mind. As you interact and sense in 3D so do others of higher or lower states interact as well. The Higher Self therefore transcends all of these states and dimensions and holograms. It is the degree of vibration that one can sustain and maintain that determines the state of awareness and interaction. The degree of susceptibility and vulnerability to other beings or forces and the degree of separation from the Divine heart is the variable here and even in higher states it is possible to impose and influence to the dark side which is a simple withdrawing of light. The Higher mind transcends all dimensions as it is one but there is a state of vibration where the Divine is and thus impervious to any dark energies or beings. Let us say this is 6D. Remember that other beings and energies are of different abilities that can be dark as well—disconnected from the heart. This is why in your work you are always connecting your mind to your heart and to the One, to the Divine. And in your local holographic world, this is the heart.

Holograms Are Information

The holograms you live in retains information and are somewhat like a computer program that creates its functions. We do not want to make this complex for you and its working you must accept as Divine and orderly. You must know you can interact with it even though it is invisible and you do not yet sense it. Change it and learn from it and you will become stronger as you progress. It is the Higher Divine mind that is your quest to be with it and know at all times. Then this new world begins to unfold rapidly as you bring your state of being into the new state of awareness and vibration. This is all about the invisible part of the hologram that you, like a newborn child are learning to sense and develop your lower self in. Within this hologram are certain cosmic laws and rules as to how it all works by Divine order. These will come to you soon but you created a contract of your proposed path or program in this hologram. It may have been simple or complex and it was done in agreement with others who may or may not play a part. And it involved your higher Divine Mind. This was an outline of what you would encounter in this hologram and this was chosen to find yourself by experiencing these things. Yes, it is so—it was your destiny and you chose this for a reason. But the experience of it—the perceptions and energies created by you--was not chosen or defined. That is an interactive experience in the hologram and to be determined as you progress. You must understand what you encounter is there for a reason, for you to become more perfect until you are perfection itself.

As the living hologram also lives and evolves like you, it is also partly governed in its consciousness by the frequencies generated by the planets, celestial bodies and group consciousness. These create vibrations that entrain to all things affecting them in a way dependent upon their own living signatures of vibration. It is like a setting of vibration that draws attention and tendencies of behaviour into a certain way. It is all part of the Divine plan.

41

YOU CAN'T "BS" THE HEART
(or SOUL)

You may wonder why there is all this yatter about love all the time. It's vibration of a higher frequency. If you haven't picked up on this yet, unconditional Love is the primordial soup of all that is. It is the essence of the Creator and it is what the physical forms are made of. If you are a scientific quantum physics genius, you will recognize this as the atomic state (solid, lower frequency) or the wave state (not yet solid, higher frequency). One is yet to be created into something. That creation device is within you. So you can make things out of the solid stuff, or you can create new things out of the soup. Needless to say if this essence of the Creator is unconditional love—a specific high frequency medium—then the best way to make something with it is to align yourself with that same frequency so you are now able to "communicate" with it and create with the creating tools you have. These are your higher body tools that are your energetic doubles that take care of the process. The big buddy here is the heart. This is not the physical heart, it is the etheric heart—pure source energy.

Otherwise, how do you communicate with the medium of love if you are not within it? It would be like trying to use a typewriter to telephone with.

This medium does not recognize low vibrations any more than your ears can pick up frequencies outside of its operating range. The best way to illustrate this is something I used in the book *Can You Let Go?* A thermometer showed the arbitrary scale for vibration from -100 (really strong negative energy) to +100 (really strong positive energy).

The Higher Mind does not live in the negative levels any more than love can exist where hatred dominates. You can't have dark where there is light. Darkness is simply a lack of light. Living in both worlds of dark and light is Polarity. Living on the topside of light is Unity because you believe everything is connected and if you hurt anything else, you hurt yourself. It is being a total empathic human working as one unit. It is like your cells work together as a unit called the body. You and your body are like a cell of all that exists. When you think with the Higher Mind—which you already can do—you think positive—and all your intentions, attentions, perception, and actions are positive.

This is the same place that the energetic Heart lives with its own frequency signature. So when you are "*dropping into the heart*" you are moving your mind, your attention, and actions into this higher vibratory place. Who is in charge of the thermometer? You? Simply by placing your attention on a thought, creating the intention of the Higher Mind, you create. If it is the Lower Mind, you make, not create.

Love-The Engine Of Creation

So you can understand why Unconditional Love is throughout this book yet it has not been a point of its own attention. It obviously has its own powers, yet it is illusive in its definition. It simply is and it is accepted as an invisible force of unknown abilities and qualities that are simply experienced as something that results from its attention to attaining that level of vibration—sort of when you fall in love. Love brings feelings of joy and bliss in an unexplainable way, regardless of whether it is seen, imagined, spoken, read, heard, felt, or experienced. All senses respond to it as an invisible energy that manifests a wonderful expression when attention is aligned with it. That is its design as that is what the Source is. And many have experienced its wondrous power that transcends fear, makes the meek mighty, protects the weak, nurtures the helpless, knows no bounds or logic, and its unconditional union provides the ultimate bliss.

It is because you yourself are actually made of pure love, the divine essence. So when you, a form of energy of highest vibration gets its shit together and re establishes what it always was by aligning the great emotional engine of heart with the other energy centers that create words, images, thoughts, and emotions, magic happens to your being and your way of existence.

Yet this is only part of your essence. When the purity of this energy enfolds you and what you are, synchronized with what you are part of, the engine of you responsible for the creation part awakens and wondrous things begin to happen. When the engine as an expression of you—your heart—takes its true power back, you become Source, a perfection of what you are. That is when you reach Crossover and turn in the River of Life.

Let us use a simple example. Your heart is like an electronic device that performs a function when it has electricity flowing through it. With a device, when the right power flows, the device expresses itself in what it is designed to do. Turn the power on and it performs. Now look at your heart. It is the device of Creation and the electricity that powers it is love. When the flow of love moves through it, it also can perform its function and express itself. Without current, neither the heart nor the electronic device can perform. Love is the power, the heart is the device and your mind is the switch. And the device is the manifesting device. And what makes it flow? It is conversion of negative to positive. And when the right power is supplied as determined by your body, and its senses that become the vehicle of transformation, things flow. It is consciously choosing the love energy from every moment passing your attention, especially that which it is compatible with. The flow of this energy through the device of the heart can become truly functional to provide what it was meant to handle--Creation. Yes, it is your heart energy field that is the device of Creation, of manifestation, designed to interface between the above of pure love to that of physical creation below in the hologram. Go back and read what the Russians have found out about this heart field and hypercommunication with DNA and everything else.

So if you are aware of this flow, it may be appropriate to look at every moment that flows through your body, mind and sensory systems as a wonderful chance to convert it to unconditional love. Every moment is like every electron in the current of a physical device. That conversion, a choice of will, expressed into its original form of love is the fire of creation that fills your device of Creation. But understand that like your electrical device, its true expression and functionality of its purpose cannot be attained until the flow of power is of sufficient strength and there is a flow, otherwise it cannot perform its purpose and cannot even run. It is designed so. Your own device of creation is so and the flow must reach a threshold to allow its true abilities to work. And what is the flow? It is the conversion of each moment that draws attention to the energy of love flowing through the heart. It is the conversion of light, from negative to positive. Yes, Crossover. Love, the specific frequency is the power that allows the heart to function. Like the power cord that allows flow into your computer, it cannot be weak or of different frequency, otherwise it is dysfunctional. And when the power to the heart is flowing and strong, the wondrous abilities of your physical and nonphysical machinery open to full functionality of Creation. It is because you are Creation and all that is needed to awaken is a pure source of the purest form of energy that ever was, is or will be—love. And when you connect below—your wondrous planet and her beings—to that above—the wondrous Source of Creation—the wiring is there to flow, just like the circuit in your electrical power cords.

Forgiveness And Your Path

Within this medium of high vibration love, there are certain processes that intercommunicate like higher voltage better than others. You have already noted that low vibration energy cannot exist in the higher realm of the mind. It's like putting ice in hot water. They may meld, or entrain within, or communicate with the higher vibration. And it has already been stated that there is a threshold the essence of unconditional love exists at that has to be attained first to truly be one with it.

There are various processes that act like carrier waves to activate instructions within this primordial soup. A process entails something you carry out some action on to do something. In this case it is a process of creating specific energy that acts like a communication. If you don't have the right frequency then the messages on your cell phone don't get anywhere, do they? You have to turn to the right channel to receive and transmit.

Just like the hierarchy of emotions on the thermometer, they also can reflect a process. But more relevant are the processes like forgiving, praying, blessing, being, loving, and many others that are the strongest communication channels. The thing is however, they have to be genuine. You either forgive someone or not. There is no maybe. Like Yoda said: "*You either feel the force or you don't, there is no try.*" Well the Heart energy system can't be BS'd. It knows if you do or don't. Feeling does not lie as it is a specific frequency. You feel the emotion of hate or love.

If you hate something and say you love it, that is misalignment—BS'ing the heart. Sorry, things don't work that way!

What happens when you look deeply within your heart and feel deeply into yourself? You may carry heaviness of old lives and even from this life that keeps your wings from lifting you. Look at your world, your families, your relationships. Look at these with a heart full of the essence to heal that which needs it. Look at what it is that you do not like, are afraid of, brings shivers to you, that upsets you. Things that you judge. Bring these forward not to dwell on them and reinforce the negative, but to forgive yourself for creating the perceptions of judgement or discord, and to bring forward solutions of the heart. It must start with you as it is your perceptions and attention that has created this issue. What is worse is that you are most likely aligned the wrong way. Your emotion is hate or discord and your poor heart is not well about it so it and the body suffer the discord. In the meantime the hate energy goes out with a vengeance to find more. You BS'd the heart and it ain't well about it.

What is it that you harbour in your past lives that brings anger? Do you have fears of life, loss of loved ones? Do you have little demons that feed your ego? And what of your ego? Does it persist in your life, overshadowing the heart, making you believe it is the heart it is satisfying? Do you want to impose your ways, your ideas on others? Why? Because you judged them to be wrong?

Bring your strongest power of forgiveness into action, draw these things to your heart for redemption. Here is a little exercise you can do. Take one who has wronged you badly—one you cannot forgive, or even one you do not know. Bring this energy to your heart and feel the tightness let go as you whisper forgiveness of yourself and the others. Lift this energy to your throat chakra and feel the dryness change to lightness as the energy cleanses that chakra. Lift it to the 3rd eye to feel the emotion of tears well up from the joy of forgiveness. Then as your knowing lifts to the crown and up, it is now you know the joy of true forgiveness as your spirit lifts and expands your Source.

Otherwise, what you say and what you feel are not aligned. You say you forgive but it is BS. You may even act that way but it is BS. When your energy centers express their area through your senses, it is not BS!

Look back and release all your judgements, your limits, boundaries which do not serve you. Forgive yourself for this, for harbouring energies of discord and disharmony—release those energies that do not serve the heart that have not yet manifested. Let it all flow away. It is your intent and attention that is important, as you have learned. You do not have to identify specific things that you cannot remember.

We are all creators of our own movies—a movie you carefully planned to teach you and expand You. Have you? Why not have a review? Know those parts in your movies that are of discord are your wonderful opportunities to shine light upon. That is what you planed. Shine this into your own dark places. That is where it starts and that is where it began.

Beingness Is The Natural State Of The Higher You

Finding bliss in your true self and your Soul journey is Beingness. This state is perplexing to many. So many cannot be themselves; their true Divine selves. That is what being is all about. It s what Christ attempted to teach and exhibit in thought, word, deed in our story of the Aquarian Gospel. Being your lower selves is what creates the endless quest for identity and doing so many things that do not answer your search. It is what he cautioned as carnal desire. This is ego's game to do, to do, to do, to be more, to be better. It is a state of doing. Your state of being is you—a Being—to know you are already perfection and there is nothing to seek out. It is indeed being yourself—your true Higher Self. The true state of being is your Higher Mind's game, not the ego's. And working for PLANET EARTH is what keeps ego on the Gopher Wheel of Life. Resign, quit; it is to inspire expansion of self. This is when you are in your heart. There is nothing to do except nothing. Can you do that? No, because you have so many things to do, right? How can you just be and do nothing you ask?

Try it. Sit with nature and just be there absorbed in it. You do this in a state of lower meditation with your eyes closed. Now do this in a state of nature with eyes open. Gaze with the wonder of your heart by being in it at a leaf, a tree, a flower. Look only at it and let the heart feel. Do nothing, no analysing, drop away from the rest and look. Feel with your Higher Self. Just know you are. Feel the difference of what this is. Do you pick up on a difference? You will know this in your being but you will have to be and let your

Divine Mind loose first, to be itself which is really you. Soon enough you will sense newness about what is there. It may phase in and out opening dimensions, it may feel wonderful—the essence of love and oneness of all. It may show an aura, even speak to you. See nothing? Fine. It doesn't matter. It's the process that's important.

This is how to learn that Divine Love of the heart is the true power of the Universe—your true key to eternity and mastery of life, the Creator in you. It is attained when you are aligned with hearts, with the Heart of the Creator. It is the vibration of all that you are synchronizing. It is when you know how to simply be. That is the state of beingness.

Let go, move inside, with meditations or with whatever you need to get there. Then take it into your personal hologram. It will automatically influence the greater hologram of common consensus even if you are unaware of it. It is simply engaging in the fundamental state of yielding to your Divine Self and higher abilities that is important. As you do this, you will feel the beingness of One, of being the One, of being you—to be. Once you know, sense and feel this and your higher senses are opened, you will snap your fingers with intent and you are there in a state of beingness. Then watch. It will be like rubbing the lamp with the Genie. Yes, when you be the true state of Love and you be that what you are—Divine Love—you will move mountains with your mind. This is the basis to your ascension—your first initiation. Your struggle of doing falls away as you have nothing to do but to follow divine inspirations and feel the wonder of it. True Beingness is Divinity.

I am now going to phase into some of the lessons I got for not "getting it." After these messages, I have stopped saying it. Even though directed at me, and my own personal evolution, I decided to print them as they came, so as to not change the meanings. What is important here is the advice I got on how to stop BS'ing myself and in particular, my heart.

Inspiration Is The Truth Of The Heart

"Everybody has dreams, some have aspired to these. But as you move from moment to moment, even from when you were a child you had dreams of what you would be and what you would do. But how many of you had dreams of who you are? It is what you are that manifests the dreams. Many have followed aspirations, to become something or someone, to have something, and you have wished for this that you had not, and many have worked away at this because it was what you were told, or what you had to do as your part in the rules of your society. And so this became your path. But is it your true path of pure inspiration? And are you of the knowing this is indeed your destiny, the one you designed?"

"Or have these dreams been fulfilled by your subdued passions, through hobbies, private likes of heart that are attached to idle time not consumed by your daily duties of doing? To aspire is to hope, to strive, towards a dream. It is the way of lower mind. Inspire is to affect, guide, or arouse by divine influence, to a vision. Perhaps you may not see a difference but it is the difference between the workings of the lower and higher minds. Dreams and aspirations are not you. Visions and inspirations are. When you know who you are, your visions become clear and inspiration flows as passions unfold before you. They become manifested in your world. The being of one's true self opens your heart and the visions become your true path as expressed by your heart, opening to you in continuous inspiration."

"Much of aspirations and dreaming clutters your true path as it is driven by ego that allows you to dream as it is fantasy, not truth. An inspiration becomes a reality through

your lessons on Co-creation. When you allow inspiration to flow, you are one with the heart and the Higher Divine Mind. So what are your inspirations? Perhaps they are blocked by ego's idle dreams? Remember dreams may be ego's play from the lower mind, usually rooted in lack of what you do not have, or what others have that you want. Inspiration is passion released towards vision, no lack, no wanting in polarity. This is desire of heart; to follow your true path as who you are."

"Is it not time to bring forward your visions and allow inspiration to flow, to begin to flood your essence of being with this? Not as ego's dream of idle thoughts, but as your heart's desire to manifest and create? Truth is your heart's field that is the same. It is the manifestor, the attractor, the Creator in you. It is what transmutes above of 5D energies of consciousness into 3D energies of matter. And it is what transmutes 3D energies of matter and the expression of you into 5D energies of consciousness memories."

"Perhaps you ponder this because you cannot see results instantly. Perhaps you say "I believe so I want to materialize that red apple and it is not there?" And ego says: "Well, where's the apple, quit dreaming!" Yes, you can and you will but it is only when you yourselves know and are of higher divine consciousness. Your schooling is not done. Yes, you have not graduated with a certificate labelled I have achieved CROSSOVER and I AM LOVE. And do not forget that that apple can be attained many ways. You can ask for it, you can work for it, you can buy it, you can attract it, you can grow it, you can manifest it, or you can materialize it. Where do you sit on this vibrational scale of schooling? Would it not be best to do this from the Creator side? Bring your dreams to visions, your aspirations to inspirations. Let these out of your heart, out of hiding from your back rooms of hobbies, away from ego, without reservation or limitation. See this not as a dream but a vision of completion all made of moments of inspiration. Bring these to thoughts, to words, to images, in clarity and simplicity, in rejoicing and celebration of the fulfillment of your heart's higher path. Then you will know you are following a life along your true destiny."

House Cleaning Helps Set Your "Tone"

"At some point as you walk your world and your houses that you have created, and even sometimes lift above this, fill yourselves with the Divine Love through your heart and offer it freely as your light grows. It is how heaven is brought to earth."

"Look up at the sun, your light, yes, it is also in your heart, but do not be afraid to look down to see things that are there, perhaps some strings to hold you as anchors, perhaps some darkness, something that takes your senses to feel uneasy or feel dysfunction. Look in the cracks and under things for they may be things that need your light, your forgiveness, your blessings, your resolve and release. Look into the eyes of your ego, look into what haunts you. Look upon these so you will not stumble upon them as you walk, and look upon these as what will allow you to lift you higher, for they are your lessons, your lightening. They are your strings, your attachments, your limits awaiting you and you alone to face them and to change them. For you know the power of the Light to change darkness, and you know the power of love to shift and change them into higher vibration."

"Walk your worlds this way as your world is yours to cleanse to perfection. Fear not those things that make you tremble, that you dislike, feel dis-ease with or hate as those that create dominion and oppression. They are also these things that have limited your world and are there to forgive as you forgive yourself for creating these perceptions. They are there because you put them there. Walk without judgment through shadows of your lives full of light and watch the darkness withdraw. Face all this that pulls and tugs at you and

annoys you, that trigger your intuition of not right, then right them, first in your world of perception, then in your physical world. Look for these like hunters of darkness. Do not hide within or fear these but to enlighten this. It is your knowing now and your path."

Humility Is Not To Give In

"This is an interesting word and concept. It is not meant to suggest that one cower, be subject to obedience, nor show fear of that which may be perceived to be greater than you. It is one of a quiet, peaceful surrender to the knowing of what and who you are and allowing your being to show and be loved without force, power, judgment, intimidation, dominion or glory over others. Many of you have chosen lives of fame and glory, of power and dominion, some even dark at times. Some of you have chosen lives, less glorious, of humble and poor stature, even war and conflict and destruction."

"What you are is a composite of these lives and although you may not be aware of this, these experiences are reflected in your habits and essences as they are encoded in your DNA. You understand the need for humility as being humble to your Creation and creative powers as a balance. Many of you have in previous lives moved to the pull of the 3D world's glories, fame and power that have resulted from your ego's desires of flesh, of emotion to overlord, to be better, to impose your ways, and to bathe in the perception of benefit from materials and riches. You have also lived lives that denied these. This is why you have chosen the more humble, less glorious life you have to this point. But as you move forward, it is important to attain a balance between all of this which is indeed you."

"As you move forward and uncover the secrets of creation, and bring forward your powers over the material realm, bring forward your perceptions of cleansing, of righting wrong in your lives, it is the sense of pure unconditional love and respect for free will that balances humility and dominion. For neither will serve you well as they are the extremes needing balance. Your balance is to simply be, love, teach and serve. Do not force, nor be afraid to share your knowing of what is truth. And when others admire, shower you with praise, with gifts, and you attain more than others, what will you choose to do or become? Will you want more or will you be humble in a grateful reverence for your wondrous abilities and knowing? Even many gods have fallen and struggled with this. Many have fallen to darkness in their quests for desires of the body and ego as they craved to the needs of the material world they came to overcome and to express themselves through."

"As you move forward it is important to know you are pure love, not here to impose, nor dominate, but to show and share what you know as a better way for other free will to choose. What we say is that you are humbled yes, but to the knowing of you being the marvellous creation yourself of such a wondrous power of Creation itself. Go forward always in the heart. Enjoy and share. Know you are here for the expression of love and service. Love yourself and others equally and serve yourself as you would serve others. Yes it is the Law of One and the five laws that surround it, the ones you know well. Keep these in sight as indeed you are all One."

The Mission Is To Know Your True Self

"As you unfold your path, it is important to know your primary mission. It is to know yourself in your true being and the essence of pure love as well as to show a better way. You are here to shine your light upon all that is and express your light by enlightening darkness. Your visions are those that allow you to express your desires and passions through your physical and mental beingness through compassion, reverence and empathic connection with all that is—the One. How this unfolds for you will be through

inspiration by allowing—allowing your Higher Divine Mind and your heart to take direction of your body, your thoughts, your acts, your intents, your words, your emotions, your visions. You will always be with a higher vibration of the Cosmic Five Laws. You are at the beginning of your mission now and as you move into your visions, knowing yourself is your foundation in that it is your greatest grounding, anchoring you above and below. This is your greatest challenge. You discover by taking your special time to silence yourself and learning to listen to your Higher Mind and true self taking your steps to wherever it leads you. Remember the greatest power lies in the heart and although your visions may draw your attention, it is your prime mission of self that is the most important. Once this is truly established in your knowing, the rest will unfold like a flower."

That Which Needs Fixing Imposes Judgement

"There are many things that you think you would like to fix. That which needs to be fixed has already been determined to be wrong and has therefore been judged as so. But in whose eyes is it that the judgement has been made? You must be cautious that your judgement upon others is not as wrong as the one you yourself created. Do you remember the Law of Will? You and all are One—as one organism of unconditional love of the Creator. Everything lives for a purpose. So is your work to fix or to be love? What may seem as a terrible injustice to you may not be so to another. What may appear as unfair situations may be a contracted path. What may be a travesty on someone may have been their calling, or it may in many cases be what they have created knowingly or unknowingly. What may have been imposed by those of the mind of dominion have a choice like you have, to step away and move out of this. And many do, but not all. What is the key word in this? It is unknowingly. It is a lack of awareness as to a different choice, just as you have opened to your own awareness that has led to a choice."

"It is this awareness that is the variable, the awareness of who you are, the power of love, the truth of your connections, the knowing of the One that all leads to a choice of a different way. This is when light shines upon this and they who you judge can see a different path. A fix does not offer a choice. It is nice to have your heart feel warm and filled with love as you fix something like poverty or illness but has it opened a new choice? Is it opening an awareness of a better way or is this a temporary fix in 3D land?"

"The Creator does not judge as love cannot. It does not engage in taking sides to fix or select that which is right as there is no right or wrong. It honours free will and it opens to the awareness of a brighter way for shining light and love on all things without condition or judgement. In the lower forms of life, death and struggle are the way of it. It may be unpleasant to see this but it is the way of the natural world. You accept this. When you fix things, consider whether you are allowing free will to flourish by knowing a way of the light—a path of pure love not just a better material life. Is it assistance to help through awareness of truth without imposing upon the will? These go hand in hand. What we say is that going around fixing is only part of your path. Fixing by offering a choice so a situation can be fixed by itself is another way. Yes, to teach, to show, to lead, to shine light upon darkness, to open to a new choice equally to all is the way. With more light those who are in shadows can see the brightness and a path to a new way. With more love, hearts open. Yes, assist others to have a hand up instead of a hand out but when they have stood up, will they know a better way to choose?"

The River Of Nows

"The first thing that may trouble you is how do you get from where you are now to where you want to be. How do I get to where I can be myself and know the bills are paid? When

will the Leap of Faith Bridge show? These are all 3D strings and attachments that you bring into your awareness, into your consciousness as you work your way through time. Some are troubled by an unknowing of themselves, their progress, their awakening. Let it alone and let it go, drop it away and let simplicity of nothing or no-thing flow through your beingness. Let each moment of your day of consciousness flow to you and let yourselves be the Light and the Love. It is your simplest solution and as each moment flows to you, dark or light, flow it through your heart so as it passes, it is charged and enlightened. In your day there are so many seconds—let them be your moments of NOWS. Let this river of nows flow through you and soon changes will come to you. As your ego and attachments fade and you see in the new light as moments flow, you will begin to accelerate your knowing of all what may limit you—as your Higher Divine Mind takes over your thoughts."

"And then suddenly you will see Crossover and the stream of Nows stop. You then flow in the river of love freely with the flow, your heart shining bright flooding that which is before you with your light. And then there are no questions or doubts. You are aligned with the being of who you are."

"When you say? When this is so. How long? As long as you take to place your awareness of moments on automatic alignment with the heart and with the Higher Divine Mind in command. When will you know? When it is so. Is this a test? Yes, you created it. Stop your fussing and your need for answers. Be what you are, let go, let it flow and soon enough you will be the river of light."

Perfection Yes Or No

"The process of self examination is now. You have been given the information to shift your mind in a new direction. The question is will you? You understand how as you open your heart it draws a likeness and suddenly your world looks and feels different. And the heart field around you feels fuller and lighter. Yes it is so simple but will you begin? Will it be hard for you to open your arms and your heart to the past? It is time perhaps for all of you to examine relationships, family, with others, with all that is in your worlds and to open your arms and heart. This is forgiveness energy you open to and offer so your space can be filled with the light as you walk. Yes, be the light. Change your perception of these things that you do not feel good about, or are right and irritate you. Turn the switch in your mind to 'Light On'. It is as easy as that to banish darkness from your mind. It is there that the true power of love can take its position and flourish to show you the better way."

"It is time to conduct your examination and to pass the exams you have set for yourselves. Look at you, your body, your habits, your family, your relationships, your dislikes, your life, your dis-ease, your discords. Look at these squarely and thank them for coming to you and that you need to see them no more as you convert them to light. Take your moments each day and let these come before you for your cleansing. Feel the wonder of your heart growing stronger and stronger. Yes, it is that simple. It is all about what you choose to see, to feel, to perceive."

"And look deeper into your past lives that are already reflected in you. Simply sit in silence and ask your heart to open, to go back and cleanse that which is not perfection, knowing it serves you no more, your test is done. You have no need for it any more. It has served its purpose to give you a step up to a higher place."

I want to say that this chapter has been focused on me. It is somewhat like a lecture but it has some important messages for all. I wanted to include this because it is what understanding the Soul Journey is all about. It is cleansing, being, inspiration, and letting the heart and the Divine Mind be you. It is about placing your attention on the positive aspects of all life, and learning to create what you desire a totally different way.

42

SO THE RUBBER MEETS THE ROAD

As I sat and pondered upon a moment, I asked: "God when will you pay my bills?"

"Well," said God, "it is when you allow Me to pay the bills."

"But how?" I asked.

"When you shift your will away from separation to unity and the Divine Higher Mind."

"How long will this take?

"As long as you take to take every moment that comes as a place to be in your natural state of unconditional love," replied God.

"But how will that pay my bills?" I pondered.

"When you accept in your total being that as above so below is a process that divine love cannot ignore," replied God.

"Then you will pay my bills?"

God smiled. "Then you know you are a part of Me and can create your own payments."

As Above So Below

What is important is to know that there are many words, symbols, expressions we have assumed the meaning of. This reflects how words and the actions or processes can be misaligned with the real process they represent. Because you can't BS the heart, it is really the control center of emotion and emotion cannot lie. It's like an actor who acts out a drama. The crying, the love, the feelings, are all fake. This is a misalignment.

You may have heard the expression As Above, so Below. It's a pretty common expression brought forward by Hermes and Thoth. What does it mean? Does it mean that everything above in the cosmos is the same as on earth? Does it mean all that we think consciousness is the same as below? What is above and what is below? Is this a definition of stuff or is it a process?

Let me tell you. As you create in the mind *above* the heart so you manifest into the material *below* the heart. You are deploying energy centers that phase from invisible energy (thoughts, images, words) through the heart (emotion) to the visible (intent, relationship, material). As you create intent above in the higher dimensions, through the heart, so you create in the lower dimensions. It is also true that in the substance, what is above is also below—all made of the same substance of love. But you see that if one is a definition of what is while the other is a process of action, one can be misaligned with the process and miss out. It is the way many meanings have been misaligned to become dysfunctional. If you are focussed on the belief that above and below are the same, then the true power of the process of the words is lost.

Can you also create material from that which is below? Yes, a crystal or a tree will speak to you but it cannot *create* that which is material. Yes, you can *make* what you can imagine, but it is the old 3D way of simulating creation. It is not creating in its true sense. Even those two words have been misaligned. It is like the difference between proactive and reactive intent attached to the process of creation. It is all within the mind. The *lower mind thinks* while the *higher mind feels*. It is the Higher Divine Mind that feels with the heart and the ego that thinks with the intellect.

This is all to say that the real shift begins upstairs with the realization and awareness that the lower mind is downstairs and it needs to be quiet, thus allowing the higher to feel with the heart. That begins with the mind above that creates the action below through the heart. I used to think that sometimes when you could not shift your belief system quickly, you had to create new physical habits to create and enforce a new belief or philosophy in the mind. It was the habit that created the belief. That is the hard way and the long way, not always successful because the truth is that the mind, in one instant can result in new physical habits, as it does in a near death experience or when you trigger what you call cold turkey. But in reality which was first? Was it truly the habit?

Atonement is the reparation and reconciliation of a wrong doing. The wrong doing in this case is believing you and your ego buddy can do a better job at paying your bills and creating a joyful life than your Higher Mind can. It is simply a more difficult way because you choose the Gopher Wheel of life's path up the River of Life. The reparation and reconciliation is when you turn around and with the flow, forgive yourself and your ego for believing this and get the hell off the Gopher Wheel. Like in a Near Death Experience, why not cold turkey and begin to learn how to create anything as if you were the Genie? The big test is when you shift from head to heart, from believing you still have to pay the bills to knowing they are paid. It is when you empty your mind of limits and lack and know there is no such thing except what you yourself have created.

But here is the real issue. This alignment has to have the heart and its positive emotions onside to create. This is where BS'ing the heart will not provide the results. So if the process of as above (an image of heart's desire) is not enfolded with the right emotion (bliss of completion) guess what? No creation.

Quit The PLANET EARTH Gopher Wheel Of Life

So what does one do to get off the Gopher Wheel and launch the creative essence? There are zillions of gizmos, more books, energy things, DNA activations, etc., etc. that are there to convince the ego to back off. It won't. You have to relegate it to a new position by your own choice of action. It is also hard to bullshit it when you have spent your life training it. You have to think with the heart.

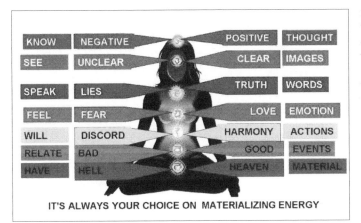

IT'S ALWAYS YOUR CHOICE ON MATERIALIZING ENERGY

So here is your strategy. Get with the program of how your energy system works! Get on the positive side of unconditional love and forgiveness for all things and transcend above the polarity of light and dark. It's about learning to create a life, not earn a living. So don't step off the Gopher Wheel while its moving, start looking outside the Wheel, away from ego's trappings. Look for your passions, your bliss in the harmony of forgiveness so your heart electrical filed is working at its optimum. Look at your old life a different way. It is supposed to teach you what you **do not want,** rather than give it more life by your attention to lack and conflict. You don't have to leap off but you have to shift the mind to a new place of attention.

We all carry negative baggage from the past—families, jobs, others, experiences, tons of crap that influence our behaviour and steal our attention. Stop it. They are your lessons.

There are energies that you have already given life to that are still looking for mates. Some may not be so good when they succeed and manifest in front of you. Change your perception of them to one from a higher place. Know you created them so don't act surprised and pissed off. Thank them, learn and let them be gone.

As you see and feel with your senses, there may be a preponderance of conflict, dis-ease, disease and discord. How do you react? You hate this or that, you feel crappy. It pisses you off. Don't give life to that energy. Don't create that feeling.

There are things that are happening around you and you are deluged by their negativity. Get over this. It's all there to teach you how to rise above it.

There are many things that your heart desires and you as a Creator can create. Begin the process.

How? Every moment that comes to you has a purpose. To the Higher divine Mind, each moment is a wonderful chance to create something better—for the big organism of Consciousness you are a part of.

Then start looking at those categories of energies above, your relationships, your baggage, your teachings, your events, your desires. Zero them out and forgive yourself for being negative, and forgive others. Live in that world of unconditional love every one of those moments. What's the point of giving these crap things life when they go find more crap? Imbed the Cosmic Laws in your behaviour and energize the energy you create with honest pure emotion of the heart—no bullshit, no acting.

How long will it take you to be a Creator again? Well, some are still working at it over many lifetimes. With some, like NDE's it's instant. Take your pick because it's your choice.

And have you got anything to lose by doing this? Yes, perhaps a life on the Gopher Wheel? Perhaps dis-ease and disease? Perhaps less of the old crap? Does better health, a new life and fulltime bliss interest you?

Don't be disappointed if the million dollars does not suddenly materialize before you in 3D instantly because you think you have it and know the process. Don't be disappointed when God doesn't transfer the money for your bills from the cosmic bank account tomorrow. It may be so in your mind. That is where it starts and that is your true grounding when you shift to that way of thinking. But you are a still all in schooling as you have been many lifetimes. Graduation is indeed accepting the process of Creation through the Higher Divine Mind. Start, yes start on the River of Nows with a quiet, patient detachment that is mindful of heart and love. You have an infinite supply of it to give away to all, to everything, without reservation, without condition, without attachments, freely, and openly. Just pour it out of you every moment that you encounter down the river. And you have an infinite amount of it to create, not make a wonderful life. It's that simple. Your graduation certificate is in view, can you see it?

And God smiled and said:

"Then you know you are a part of Me and can create your own payments."

Who is God? We all are! We are Me learning how!

As we end this chapter, the important lesson is to not renew the old prescriptions that the PLANET EARTH subsidiaries of Religion and their Codes prescribes as the Blue Pill. This places you in a new world of belief in your Self and a clear understanding of your journey.

We are at a unique time where some assistance from God, from Divine Intervention, from Above, from Self, whatever you want to call it, is happening whether many like it, know it or not. How you align with this is the unique choice you have but one think appears to be the pressing result; Who you are and the truth will be revealed.

Now, within that light, and the belief of peace without conflict, let us move into how to resign from PLANET EARTH and access your retirement plan of Good Faith and Credit.

44

RESIGNING FROM PLANET EARTH INC.

You Always Have A Choice

The choice is simple and clear. It is to rise above the issue of dark and light. Each must choose between the old and the new. You may choose to remain with the corruption and insurmountable debt and fiat money of the old world or you may choose Global debt forgiveness rebooting a system of value where abundance and prosperity is available for all. You may choose to remain in the old world of terrorism, violence and war, at your expense, to satisfy the greed and lust for power and control of the few, or you may choose to remove the funding from the Military Industrial Complex bringing an end to all wars for profit and opening the door to world peace.

You may choose to live a life of doubt and perpetual fear in the old world or you may choose to enter the new world of love, honor, integrity, transparency in all dealings and a return of family values and morals where a sense of community pride and cooperation bloom anew.

You may choose to dwell on the evil and the dark and sob in your woes or you can choose look up and see the light. You can choose a different way of life. You choose a different belief system. You can choose to be a conscious Creator and you can choose to forgive, dissolve the perceptions of hate and conflict and choose bliss. Choose, choose choose.

You may even choose to be as you are under the domain of PLANET EARTH. After all, your keepers have worked towards giving you as much freedom as they dare to without losing control. You may even believe that this is all hogwash this ascension stuff, and this PLANET EARTH stuff.

But, if you have that feeling that you, and your life are much, much more and you are not able to express your true self, that perhaps all the controls on your being and the deception so as to work off other's debt is not on, then you need to resign from PLANET EARTH and bring in a new awareness away from those green pills.

The Choice Is Now Yours: Red Or Green?

Yes, the red or green pill as Morpheus said. It is time to choose and now you know what the choices are. This Part is about solutions; spiritual and commercial solutions. Many have been the warriors of truth that precede these solutions, in a light of simplicity and the attainment of sovereignty in both the commercial and spiritual aspects of life on Planet Earth. What if you work towards Conscious manifestation of the true you on Planet earth AND quit your job in PLANET EARTH? These work hand in hand together. First is to understand who you are and to stand in your truth as Christ did-- walking in thought, word and deed in the light of what God is--you as an expression of that Divine force. It means resigning from the sub Corporation that is GOD and that code called scriptures, bibles, and the likes.

Second is to resign from the Commercial world as an employee of PLANET EARTH and declare your sovereignty. You cannot accept your pension while you work for PLANET EARTH. Here is the place where you work towards the allowing of the certain statures and laws attached to the corporation and enter the private world of commerce. Here you take back the position of Creditor and look towards attaining the beneficial status to the Divine trust that you have worked all your life to create.

If you choose to continue to fund the perpetual terrorism, war and death with insurmountable debt, taxation and the increased limitation of your private rights further staining your Good Faith and Credit to satisfy the greed and lust for power and control of the few, then you need do nothing. We bless you and honor your free will. That is the old way rapidly giving way to the New Way.

But, on the other hand, if you choose to remove your portion of the Good Faith and Credit that funds the Military Industrial Complex and return it to original jurisdiction where the mechanics for global debt forgiveness already exist it assist in creating a consciousness to allow the rebooting of an economic system of value, honor and integrity. If you choose to remove your portion of the Good Faith and Credit taking the profit out of the war machine opening the door to world peace, abundance and prosperity, then read on for we offer a remedy that is so easy anyone can execute it.

In this series of chapters, you will learn how to resign from PLANET EARTH Inc. as best can be known at this time; in peace. Because you have acquiesced for so long, certain assumptions about you have been set in stone. By way of your acceptance, you have been operating and living as a dead person, a fictional entity that does not have the sovereign rights of the real Earthling. The estate that you have placed your life's labour and assets into has been probated because you have acquiesced by not knowing or acting and you are considered dead in the fictional process of laws and codes. All that is left is for that fictional entity of the Strawman to have a certificate of death created so as to place its name on the tombstone and all is done. because you have accepted this, you have to reidentify yourself and reclaim that which you have given away. The process by which this is done, in the best way that has evolved to date is the subject matter now. it is about resigning and reclaiming without blaming anyone but yourself.

The process by which you have accepted this may have been deception but that is not the issue here. Once you realize deception exist, you can rise above it. For in truth, the estate does leave a legacy of good faith and trust, and those who allegedly defrauded you have only conducted their jobs as directed from the powers above. Would it not be great to access that estate? If you understand the total process now, it is one of forgiveness and being grateful of coming to the truth. It is time to move forward in peace and harmony and not to seek vengeance upon others as a two-faced Earthling. It is to become that Creator and take the path of controlling your hologram and creating your world proactively.

It's all about Resurrection of your true identity and your true powers.

In the chapters before this point, the process has been covered as to how this has been done and served by one man, namely James-Thomas: McBride. Now it is time to look at the individual process. Again, thanks to James, he continues to simply, verify and provide simpler and clearer ways to do this.

again, in this regard, we have to use the site **www.divineprovince.org** and **www.postmastergeneralna.org** where James Thomas McBride opens the gateway. Be aware that this process changes daily.

A Word Of Caution

The world of the Strawmen is rife with lower vibrational energy. The Global Elite have implemented a system that has not yet fallen, nor totally disclosed-yet. Until it is, the journey to collect the estate and quit can be a perilous journey and create anything but peace should you engage in it with vengeance, greed and ignorance of the hidden laws. The purpose here is to bring this into the light and it is within the light of higher vibration of foreignness and peace that one should consider. The fundamental grounding in this to be in that space of higher vibration, for as many warriors have learned, this is by no means a simple battle. What follows is one way to resign. There are many ways to "disconnect" from PLANET EARTH, especially with the focus on becoming One with the Laws of Attraction, Manifestation and Creation. Should you decide to follow the process of the formal resignation and access to the Good Faith and Credit through this process, do not, I repeat, do not copy and try without the appropriate grounding in what these documents represent. It is recommended that if you do care to indulge this way, go to the websites and contact the ones who are in peace here, and have done their homework. As a long time studier of this process as published in **The Book of Secrets Trilogy** at **www.edrychkun.com**, I can assure you that this is not straight forward and a very easy way to mess with Satan.

The Required Basic Information To Resign

In order to resign, you will need to collect certain information about you and your birth. For the sake of example, we are going to use a name of Name of **John George Doe born on March 14, 1956. He was given the names John, George by the mother or father of the family/bloodline George. As such, the proper way he would be addressed as a real sentient human would be John George of the family Doe. This is commonly seen in Strawman lingo as John-George: Doe. His counterpart that the Trust/Estate is assigned to is JOHN GEORGE DOE.**

Given Names: John George
Family Name: Doe
Domicile Mail Location: 1234 Anywhere Road, Anytown, USA
Nativity Date of Birth: March 14 1956
Strawman Name: JOHN GEORGE DOE
Birth Registration Date: March 15, 1956
The red # on the back of the birth certificate. It's not formatted like the US one, and on the newer BC, it's on the bottom right under a bar code. For example, on the old format BC, there is a red # like this: P 123456, and on the newer one, it looks like this: NS00012345 -"NS" is for Nova Scotia, for example.

Birth Certificate File Number XX-XX-XXXXXX (Canadian)
Trust/Bond File Number-YYYYYYY Number on Reverse of Social Security Card. In the case of Canada there is Social Insurance Card without a red number. In this case the SIN would have to do.

Note that you may go web site **www.divineprovice.org** to assist you in this process. Here once you have provided the information as listed above, the appropriate documents will be sent to you with instructions for execution.

The Administrators To Notify

The next part relates to the people that need to be notified. The key Administrators of the process are those listed below. The Last Provincial or State Agency who Issued the Birth Certificate (Vital Statistics) In Ohio for example, it is The State of Ohio Dept. of Health Vital Statistics. If it is in Canada, it would be the Vital Statistics Agency of the Province you were born in. Note that as a US citizen, the list would be those listed under US. If born in Canada it would include those listed under Canada plus those listed under US. A name that addresses the private human entity directly is required; only the position is shown here so some research would be needed.

CANADIAN	US
Chief Executive Office Vital Statistics Agency of BC 818 Fort street Victoria BC	**Rector** Basilica of the National Shrine of the Immaculate Conception 400 Michigan Avenue, Northeast Washington, D.C. 20017
Attorney General of Canada 284 Wellington St. Ottawa Ontario, Canada K1A 0H8	**U.S. Attorney General** Executive Office of the U.S. Trustee U.S. Department of Justice 950 Pennsylvania Avenue, NW Washington, DC 20530-0001
Secretary of Treasury Board Strategic Communications and Ministerial Affairs L'Esplanade Laurier, 9th Floor, East Tower 140 O'Connor Street Ottawa, Canada K1A 0R5	**U.S. Secretary of State** U.S. Department of State 2201 C Street NW , Washington, DC 20520
Governor General of Canada Rideau Hall 1 Sussex Drive Ottawa, Ontario K1A 0A1	**Justice of the Supreme Court of Virginia** American Inns of Court 1229 King Street, 2nd Floor Alexandria, Virginia 22314
	James-Thomas: Mcbride **Postmaster General** Office of the Postmaster General 1300 Pennsylvania Ave, Suite 190-175 Washington DC

The Process of Providing Notice

There were a total of five documents that have been used, the purpose of these being to regain your living position, identify yourself within the appropriate laws of the land, and to regain access as beneficiary to the Estate. These are:

1. Ecclesiastic Deed Poll
2. Statement of Identity
3. Acknowledgement of Deed
4. Entitlement Order
5. Certificate of Authority

If you choose to engage in this, it is already mentioned that you work with the people at **www.divineprovince.org** to assist you. For a nominal charge they will create the paperwork for you and give you the instructions. The process of mailing and giving notice, plus creating the documents is vital. This book is not meant to give you a process which may change rapidly. This book is for educational purpose only.

Note: at the time of writing, these forms have been enhanced and modified into a simple format. They are presented here, however, becuase the information within them is vital in understanding who you are and who you are not. You are <u>not</u> the fictional entity called the Strawman and you are <u>not</u> the trustee/executor of that estate. In order to be who you are and to claim your rights as the living beneficiary, in the laws of commerce, it must so be stated.

Establishing Your Living Status With The Deed Poll [EDP]

The common law and a common law remedy are reserved for living beings ONLY. We are seeking a remedy for the living man, a common law remedy although we will not be entering a common law court. In this I, James Thomas: McBride can offer some advice:

"At present, We the American people, have no standing to receive a common law remedy as the common law is for living beings only. We the American people are all presumed to be 'Deceased'. Assumptions which are supported by first hand testimony against us, by ourselves and others. We unwittingly give testimony against ourselves, supporting the assumption of our 'Deceased' status, when we file for a Social Security number, driver permit, Marriage License, loan or mortgage as we are testifying that we are 14th Amendment legal fiction paper citizens and therefore, NOT LIVING BEINGS.

By the time you are in your mid twenties you have unwittingly given false witness against yourself several times, each time supporting your prior testimony. By the time we figure out what has happened the assumption is firmly established in fact by our own word and hand and our efforts to re-establish our living status becomes a daunting task. Being 'Deceased' we cannot be heard by the courts so our words fall on deaf ears.

The first thing we must do is to overcome the firmly rooted assumptions of our 'Deceased' status so that our voice can once again be heard.

Your DNA, along with the testimony, 'out of the mouths of two or more', in affidavit form testifying to your identity, is the ONLY acceptable evidence of your living status that I personally know to work.

Before you can be heard by this system to overcome the many assumptions under which they operate, you must first overcome the assumption of your living status. Period! Next, you must rebut, or overcome, the remaining assumptions and object to the actions of the Trustees in the administration of your estate which have effectively enslaved you."

The Ecclesiastic Deed Poll [EDP] was explained in detail in a previous chapter. It not only effectively re-establishes your living status but also rebuts all of the assumptions and objects to all of the actions which have adversely effected you and your estate. Please read the EDP and related research which is extensive and very convincing. Again, knowledge is power! And this is about self-empowerment, is it not!?

"The EDP with your living DNA, or blood seal, infusing the document with Divine life will be the top document of these nine (9) sets of Originals. I can hear many of you screaming that this is some sort of satanic, blood ritual type thing and I tell you that is exactly what the Powers That Be want you to believe. Let me repeat.....

Your DNA, along with the testimony, 'out of the mouths of two or more', in affidavit form testifying to your identity, is the ONLY acceptable evidence of your living status that I personally know to work. The EDP begins with Who We Are. Each one of us carries a spark of Creator in ever atom and cell of our body and are therefore, a Divine Spark of Creator and therefore, a lining being and NOT a legal fiction paper citizen.

At the end of the document you find a Blood Seal of your given name. This is not a document that is signed for t is your blood and the DNA that truly identifies you. Don't be squeamish, you have plenty of blood to do this. Prick your finger and put your DNA on there! On each of the eight originals."

The Ecclesiastic Deed Poll Document

The Ecclesiatstic Deed Poll is an important document and it can now be read in a different light, in your own personal ssituation Rather than repeat this here, it is suggested that the document presented in a revious chapter be read again with your individual statistics embedded.

Re-establishing Living Status

In conjunction with the EDP, the next important document is the Statement of Identity. The common law and a common law remedy are reserved for living beings ONLY. We are seeking a remedy for the living man. To complete the process of re-establishing your living status you need to execute an affidavit.

Anyone who has known you for awhile will do, but, parents or siblings are the best.

This is the second document, just behind the EDP. These two documents effectively re-establish your living status.

Statement of Identity Document

STATEMENT OF IDENTITY

John George of the family Doe
1956-03-14

Domicile Non-Domestic Private Post
Anywhere Road 1234
AnyTown state, Anystate
on USA

JOHN GEORGE DOE
XX-XX-XXXXXX

We, the undersigned, being of the age of consent, stable of mind and competent to testify, having first hand knowledge of the living being whose identity we seek to establish, do by our own free will and act, "out of the mouths of two or more," establish the facts, as set forth herein, to wit:

We know the living being in question to be John George of the family Doe, or simply John Doe a living man, not a legal fiction 'person', who came into this world on the 1956-03-14.

We know John George Doe to be an honourable man/woman and have seen no evidence which challenges his identity, and believe that none exists.

We believe the Estate Trust styled as JOHN GEORGE DOE to represent the interests of John George Doe which are held in trust. We have seen no evidence which disputes our belief and believe that none exists.

We did witness the living being, known to us as John George Doe, place his thumb print hereon. We have seen no evidence to dispute that said thumb print represents the physical being known to us as John George Doe, and believe that none exists.

Thumb Print

We, the undersigned, do hereby certify the foregoing to be the truth, the whole truth and nothing but the truth as we know it to be. By our own free will act and deed by our hand and word do hereby establish the facts.

Fred Witness   May 25, 2012
witness autograph   date   thumbprint

Lucy Witness   May 25, 2012
witness autograph   date   thumbprint

The Acknowledgement Of Deed Affidavit

An **affidavit** is a written sworn statement of fact voluntarily made by an *affiant* or *deponent* under an oath or affirmation administered by a person authorized to do so by law. Such statement is witnessed as to the authenticity of the affiant's signature by a taker of oaths, such as a notary public or commissioner of oaths. The name is Medieval Latin for *he has declared upon oath*. An affidavit is a type of verified statement or showing, or in other words, it contains a verification, meaning it is under oath or penalty of perjury, and this serves as evidence to its veracity and is required for court proceedings.

- To obtain a declaration on a legal document, such as an application for voter registration, that the information provided by the applicant is truthful to the best of the applicant's knowledge. If, after signing such a declaration, the information is found to be deliberately untrue with the intent to deceive, the applicant may face perjury charges.

Affidavits may be written in the first or third person, depending on who drafted the document. If in the first person, the document's component parts are:

- a *commencement* which identifies the affiant;
- the individual *averments*, almost always numbered as mandated by law, each one making a separate claim;
- a *statement of truth* generally stating that everything is true, under penalty of perjury, fine, or imprisonment;
- an *attestation* clause, usually a jurat, at the end certifying the affiant made oath and the date; and
- signatures of the author and witness.

If an affidavit is notarized or authenticated, it will also include a caption with a venue and title in reference to judicial proceedings. In some cases, an introductory clause, called a *preamble*, is added attesting that the affiant personally appeared before the authenticating authority.

What you stating here is that while you have been lost in the sea of illusion, that your estate was placed in trust. You have awakened to the truth, so long hidden from man, and now will redeem your estate. You would hereby **acknowledge and accept the deed** and your right as lawful and proper owner of the estate with exclusive right of use of all land, tenements and heredimants thereof, to have and to hold **in fee simple forever.**

The Acknowledgment of Deed must be notarized, so you need to sign all originals in front of a Notary. You need to take these originals to the Clerk of Court and have the Notaries signature and seal Authenticated. You can also take these to the Secretary of State for Authentication which gives the document FULL FAITH & CREDIT OF THE CONSTITUTION. The example follows:

The Acknowledgement Of Deed Document

ACKNOWLEDGEMENT OF DEED

In the Matter of :

Estate Name: JOHN GEORGE DOE
FILE #: XX-XX-XXXXXX
Registration Date: March 15 1956
Claimant: John George of the family Doe
Nativity Date: 1956-03-14
Domicile: non-Domestic Private Post
Anywhere Road 1234
Anytown state Anystate
On Country USA

LET IT BE KNOWN BY ALL MEN, AND THEIR PERSONS, BY THESE WORDS that this public record is full proof having full faith and credit of the Constitution of and for the UNITED STATES.

Before Abraham was, I AM; the Divine Spirit having a human experience. Each atom and cell of this physical vessel I inhabit to travel across this land is infused with the spark of the Creator; I AM one with the light, one with Creator, the alpha and the omega, without beginning nor end, without time.

This third dimensional vessel, called man, the original domicile of the Divine Spirit is known on this world and in this dimension as John George of the family Doe, a living man, freeborn peaceful inhabitant, heir to the Divine Estate, Settler and Beneficiary to the Divine Trust, freeholder in fee simple absolute, one of the 'Posterity' as expressed in the Preamble of the United States Constitution, tribunal of the Court of Record and king of my sovereign nation state.

I have been lost in the sea of illusion, my estate placed in trust. I have awakened to the truth, so long hidden from man, and now redeem my estate. I hereby **acknowledge and accept the deed** and my right as lawful and proper owner of the estate with exclusive right of use of all land, tenements and heredimants thereof, to have and to hold **in fee simple forever.**

This freehold in fee simple has been held under an assumed lease for years. Said fee has been held in *abeyance*, in expectation, remembrance, and contemplation in law there being no person in esse, in whom it can vest and abide: though the law has considered it as always potentially existing, and ready to vest whenever a proper owner appears.

It is hereby established, in fact, that John George of the family Doe is the proper owner of the estate in whom it can vest and abide to have and to hold in fee simple forever. It has been **decreed and covenanted that the Grantor is lawfully seized of said estate in fee simple**; and Grantee is granted good, right and lawful authority and exclusive right of use of the estate and that said estate is free of all encumbrances, restrictions, easements, limitations and zoning ordinances of record.

The grantee is hereby vested with the immediate and exclusive right of use and enjoyment of the executed estate to have and to hold in fee simple forever.

So let it be written, so let it be done.

Witness my hand and seal done by my freewill act and deed.

John George   seal
_____
John George of the family Doe

On the 2 day of June, 2012, a living wo/man appeared before me, a Notary Public, identified himself to my satisfaction and/or known to me to be John George of the family Doe executed this instrument and acknowledged before me that he/she executed this instrument of his/her own free will act and deed.

Andy Notary

_____   **Stamp/seal**
Notary signature

My commission expires on: *Oct 23 2014*

The Entitlement Order To Original Status

After establishing that you are the top dog in the estate trust represented by your Birth Certificate, it is necessary to instruct the intermediary agent who holds the trust documents to Terminate the lease of the estate, your Good Faith and Credit, from the 14th Amendment Military Industrial Complex and return it to original jurisdiction for administration in harmony with original intent.

Since your estate, our Good Faith and Credit, have been under lease to the Military Industrial Complex since your birth and assumed death, they owe you the delinquent rent. The rent has been held in abeyance until you returned from being lost in the sea of illusion to redeem your estate. Now, it is due and owing. There are no provisions for paying the rent, or interest, on the estate in fiat currency. This must be made in value.

You would autograph with your GIVEN name only and you do not sign your last name here. Place your red thumb print seal on the line. The example follows and it should be read carefully to clearly understand the intent.

Entitlement Order Document

ENTITLEMENT ORDER

TERMINATION OF LEASE
DEMAND FOR DELINQUENT RENT
John George of the family Doe
Nativity Date 1956-03-14
Domicile: Anwhere Road 1234
Anytown state on Anystate
on USA

ESTATE Name: JOHN GEORGE DOE
STATE FILE # XX-XX-XXXXXX
Registration Date March 24 1956
Public/Private # YYYYYYYYY

Before Abraham was, I AM; the Divine Spirit having a human experience. Each atom and cell of this physical vessel I inhabit to travel across this land is infused with the spark of the Creator; I AM one with the light, one with Creator, the alpha and the omega, without beginning nor end, without time.

This third dimensional vessel, called man, the original domicile of the Divine Spirit is known on this world and in this dimension as John George of the family Doe, a living man, freeborn peaceful inhabitant, heir to the Divine Estate, Settler and Beneficiary to the Divine Trust, freeholder in fee simple absolute, one of the 'Posterity' as expressed in the Preamble of the United States Constitution, tribunal of the Court of Record and king of my sovereign nation state.

I came into this world an Heir to the Divine Estate as one of the 'Posterity' named in the Constitution. I was born into this illusion; a world of legal fictions where assumptions stand as fact; where the truth is hidden from man like a pirates treasure buried under layer upon layer of intertwining rules, regulations and codes; where opinions are treated as law; where one is held accountable for his ignorance for his inability to ferret out the truth.

On the day of my birth while still in recovery, my mother was compelled, without full disclosure, to place my estate in trust to be administrated by the civil administration ANYCOUNTRY in accordance with the Constitution. Acting as intermediary agent and holder in due course of the Deed for the estate trust, the STATE OF ANYSTATE established a Charitable Trust to facilitate the lease of the estate to the 14th Amendment congress and senate, for my benefit. Said fee has been held in *abeyance*, in expectation, remembrance, and contemplation in law there being no person *in esse*, in whom it can vest and abide: though the law has considered it as always potentially existing, and ready to vest whenever a proper owner appears.

JOHN GEORGE DOE Entitlement Order XX-XX-XXXXXX

I have been lost in the sea of illusion in which I was born, my estate placed in trust. I have awakened to the truth, so long hidden from man, and now claim and redeem my estate. I have acknowledged and accepted the deed establishing my entitlement right as lawful and proper owner of the estate, the appropriate person and entitlement holder within whom the estate shall vest and abide with exclusive right of use of all land, tenements and heredimants thereof, to have and to hold in fee simple forever.

ELECTION TO TAKE AGAINST THE WILL

It is hereby decreed and established in fact that, as Heir, I **reject the benefits under the will** electing to **enforce my contractual rights in the estate against the will.** This estate, and/or the Heir thereof, are not subject to the jurisdiction of the 14th Amendment of the Constitution, the congress and senate created therein, nor the codes, regulations or statutes thereof.

ACCEPTANCE OF OATH OF OFFICE

Let it be known by these words that the Oaths and bonds of all public officers are hereby accepted and confirmed and I hereby bind them to it, who by fealty and homage bear faith in opposition to all men without any saving or exception, to protect the King and his property from belligerents. I bestow my sovereign immunity on them while administering my lawful orders. This public record under the seal of a competent court is guaranteed full faith and credit per Article 4 Section 1 of your Constitution. Any officer of the public who fails to immediately execute these lawful orders admits and acknowledges warring with the Constitution and committing treason. Any/all orders or writs issued by John George of the family Doe tribunal of the Court of Record orally or witnessed under my hand and seal is binding on all officers, courts, corporations, agencies, individuals and/or persons. Failure to immediately execute said orders and/or writs constitutes a violation of said Oath of Office and an act of war against the Constitution.

DETERMINATION OF THE LEASE

This estate trust has been administrated under pledge/ lease to the 14th Amendment Congress and Senate since its creation. It has been established as a matter of fact that the UNITED STATES has exercised the lease, creating numerous negotiable instruments based on the value of the estate, adversely effecting the estate and the proper owner thereof.

It is herein determined and decreed, by my own act and deed, that any/all pledges and/or leases of this estate, past and/or present, express or implied are hereby and herein terminated. Any/all rights, power and/or authority granted therein is hereby terminated and withdrawn. All principal and interest shall be immediately returned to the owner and a full account shall be made thereof.

DEMAND FOR DELINQUENT RENT

This estate has been in abeyance awaiting the completion of conditions president. All conditions have now been met. Demand is herein made for all delinquent rent. Payment in full satisfaction is due immediately. All principal and interest shall be immediately returned to the owner and a full account shall be made thereof.

ADMINISTRATION OF THE ESTATE

From this moment forward this estate shall be administrated under the original Constitution for the United States and the Congress and Senate created thereunder, without the 14th Amendment. This estate shall be administrated in accordance with the original intent, as a Charitable Trust, under the direction of the Settler and Beneficiary of the estate.

PURPOSE AND INTENT

This estate shall be at peace with all nations and shall strive to be always in harmony with Mother Earth; to promote growth and healing to facilitate the transition into the new world; to assist the people of the world to grow beyond the want and lack; to grow beyond the fear and doubt to bring about the birth of a world of abundance and prosperity for all mankind; a world of love and compassion; a world without limitation.

THE DEMESNE PROPERTY

This estate trust holds the Demesne lands/ properties which are to be set aside for the use of the owner, his family and staff and shall be conveyed to his possession for his immediate use. Said property shall be maintained by the trust to maintain and preserve the estate. The body of the Heir, John George of the family Doe, is a part and parcel of the Demesne property of this estate and is inviolable.

The intermediary shall appoint a fiduciary agent to administrate the estate. Said fiduciary shall immediately introduce him/her self to the entitlement holder and establish a time and location to sit down and identify and return the Demesne property to the entitlement holder; to discuss the collection of the delinquent rent and other issues as concerns the administration of this trust.

The securities intermediary:

- **shall** comply with an entitlement order if the entitlement order is originated by the appropriate person;
- **shall** act at the direction of an entitlement holder to change a security entitlement into another available form of holding for which the entitlement holder is eligible;
- **has** the same obligation to the holder as to the owner;

- **shall** exercise **rights** with respect to a financial asset if directed to do so by an entitlement holder to wit: the right to elect how the estate shall be administrated; if, and to whom the estate may or may not be leased.

So it is written, so let it be done.

By my hand and seal by my freewill act and deed.

John George

_____ seal

John George Entitlement holder

JOHN GEORGE DOE Entitlement Order XX-XX-XXXXXX

The Access To Good Faith And Credit

The activation of the Federal Reserve Account, **JAMES T. MCBRIDE National Banking Association**, was presented as the Cure Process in a previous Chapter. This was structured as a pass through account and provided for the activation of sub-accounts making this pass through account available for everyone. This thus eliminates the necessity of everyone having to go through the long process as did James Thomas McBride to activate their own account. The end result is the same, discharge of all debt to facilitate the transition from a fiat system to one of value and transparency.

A Certificate of Authority is issued by the Office of the Postmaster General NA attached to your documents alerts and directs the Intermediary Agent to the sub-account to facilitate the timely settlement of the account, discharge of debt and later issue of a "charge card" for your use to charge the account for the immediate discharge of debt, as it arises.

Through the Official Registry **of the Office Of The Postmaster General NA a**n account was established as a pass through account to facilitate the discharge of debt in the settlement of our accounts as we withdraw our Good Faith & Credit from the Military Industrial Complex and return to Original jurisdiction. The sub accounts await activation by the American people accessing the Private Funds for the immediate discharge of debt to facilitate the transition to a value backed currency.

Certificates of Authority are issued upon request through **www.Legal-Registries.com/Registry** or through the application process at **www.notice-recipient.com**. and are delivered electronically. All Certificates are issued specific to your account, within an hour of your request.

Once your Certificate arrives you will need to print it out and save a copy to your files. I had to copy and paste it into a word document, do a bit of adjusting to ensure proper page alignment and save and print

You may activate your own Federal Reserve Account as James Thomas McBride did, or, you may request activation of a sub account under **National Banking Association through www.Legal-Registries.com.**

Upon request the Office of the Postmaster General NA will issue you a Certificate of Authority & Activation Order to attach to your documents. These Certificates will include all of the pertinent information specific to your account and will arrive via e-mail within hours of receipt of your request. The example follows:

The Certificate Of Authority Document

Office Of The Postmaster General NA
Trustee of the Global Trust

YYYYYYYY

CERTIFICATE OF AUTHORITY
American Freeholder in fee simple absolute
John George of the family Doe
Date of Nativity 1956-03-14
Domicile Non Domestic Private Post
Anywhere Road 1234
on Anytown on Anystate
on Country USA
Non-Domestic without the 14th Amendment

Estate Trust
JOHN GEORGE DOE
Reg. Date March 24 1956
File # XX-XX-XXXXXX

Universal Postal Treaty For The Americas 2010

The Pledge/Lease of the private property of the Freeholder in fee simple has been rescinded and withdrawn, therefore, the administrative agencies of the UNITED STATES shall make the return of the interest back to source.

The UNITED STATES shall immediately activate the sub account routed through the pass-thru account, **JAMES THOMAS MCBRIDE, a 'national banking association'** for use by the Freeholder identified on this Certificate of Authority to vacate the blocks on the asset accounts and make the financial adjustments to discharge the debt and return the accounts back into balance. The UNITED STATES shall administrate the above Estate Trust in Original jurisdiction, without the 14th Amendment.

JAMES THOMAS MCBRIDE, a 'national banking association'
Activated Federal Reserve Account number **XX-XXX-XXXXXXX** with Routing numbers as follows:

      I) Cashier Checks/Certified Checks Cleveland FRB XXXX-XXXX-X
      II) E-Checks Atlanta FRB XXXX-XXXX-X
      III) Fed-Wire Atlanta FRB XXXX-XXXX-X

The UNITED STATES shall immediately settle the account, make the return of the interest/ lease back to the freeholder and issue the "Charge Card" for use by the Certificate holder to charge the account to facilitate the immediate discharge of debt as it arises and make an full account.

The UNITED STATES shall immediately deliver the delinquent rent, which has been held in abeyance, in a currency of value.

Registration of Intent

The request for issue of a Certificate of Authority by the above referenced American freeholder establishes the freeholder's Intent To Withdraw His/Her Divine Estate from the Military Industrial Complex, discharge the debt in the settlement of the account and return to original jurisdiction.

It is clear that the above referenced American freeholder's intent is to overcome all of the assumptions of his status and re-establish themselves as a living being, American freeholder, returned from being lost in a sea of illusion to redeem their Divine Estate and return to original jurisdiction

Notice to Principle is notice to agent. Notice to agent is notice to Principle.

Evidence of the issue of this Certificate of Authority is maintained by Legal-Registries.com for verification at any time.

Certificate of Origin

This document originates from the Office of the Postmaster General NA under the jurisdiction of the Universal Postal Union (UPU), constitutes "Official Mail" and is in compliance with regulations as concerns Private Mail Carriers.

James Thomas of the family McBride, American freeholder, acting in the capacity of Postmaster General NA

Office Of The Postmaster General NA

43

NEW EARTH: THE DIVINE PROVINCE

The Divine Estate And Province

In order to facilitate the resignation from PLANET EARTH, I as Postmaster General of North America, have brought into being the Divine Province. This is akin to a separate divine territory that is totally outside the jurisdiction of PLANET EARTH and outside of the laws thusly imposed on the Strawman, facilitated by the use of the Papal Seal under the Postal Union and the Postal Peace treaty.

We understand that we are what we are today because of our choices yesterday. As we look around we recognize that the problems created as we live and interact within the current global personality ethics are deep fundamental problems that cannot be solved on the superficial level on which they were created. For decades we have operated upon an 'outside-in' approach to problem solving. We have said **'If only THEY would change their ways, WE would be fine.'** We understand that it is the way in which we look at the problem that is the problem. We understand that we must begin an inside-out approach to the solution. We understand that we must examine and improve self first, redeveloping our own principles of character such as honour, integrity, courage, compassion and justice; following the laws of nature, Our Creator and the Golden Rule. We understand that these principles of character are deep fundamental truths, classic truths, generic common denominators that are tightly woven threads running with exactness, consistency, beauty and strength through the fabric of life.

We understand that our outer reality is a reflection of that which is within and if we do not like our reality then we must go within and make the changes, for only then may we reflect a better reality without. If we seek a reality of peace, compassion and acceptance then we must first develop a sense peace, compassion and acceptance within."

At Divine Province we are at peace with ourselves, at peace with the world, at peace with the universe. The Office of the Postmaster General NA and the Divine Province are charged with restoring the peace and returning the Divine Estate to honour. We are the bridge, the transition team lighting the way to peace, prosperity and abundance for all mankind. We invite you to join us to learn how to Be at Peace.

Fear, greed and the desire for power are the psychological motivating forces behind warfare and violence between nations, tribes, religions and ideologies that have resulted in the death of over **100 million people** in the past century at the hands of their fellow man. The United States has been 'at war' since its creation; waging war against crime, war against drugs, war against terrorism and war against the sovereign people of the world. The end result of these wars has been a dramatic increase in crime, in drug abuse, in terrorism around the world and has bred a population consumed with dis-ease, living in a constant state of fear and violence.

The United States is a legal fiction corporate army of the Vatican and the Crown, waging war on the Divine Estates and the Living Beneficiaries thereof robbing we the people of earth of our Divine Inheritance for their own self enrichment. The mighty war machine, the Military Industrial Complex, known as the UNITED STATES has become what they professed to fight against! The UNITED STATES is a universal bully enforcing their will on the world, obtaining the 'consent' of the people at the end of a barrel. The UNITED STATES has engaged in perpetual war in the name of peace for decades spilling the blood of the people chasing an illusionary boogy man of their own creation polluting the earth and poisoning the people in the process.

The UNITED STATES has identified the American people, the very people who fund their day to day existence, as enemies of the state waging war on the people and our estates under the assumed 'consent' of the people gained by deceit and deception and maintained by threat and duress. The enlightened being understands that peace will never be born of fighting and violence: for fighting and violence begets fighting and violence, war begets war, and finally, **Peace begets Peace**.

The Divine Province is charged with restoring the peace for the redemption and return of the estates to honour; opening the door to **universal peace, prosperity, and abundance for all mankind.**

As such, one of the services offered by the Office of the Postmaster General North America, Divine Province is the establishment of a new identification. The Office of the Postmaster General, Divine Province as already described in previous chapters, is an International Peace Council established under the Universal Postal Treaty For The Americas 2010 operating under the authority and protection of the Papal Seal of Peter under country code DVN/DP/999. All members of the Council are Internationally protected foreign officials, International Diplomats at peace with the United States and the many franchised County, City, Towns and States thereof. The Office of the Postmaster General, Divine Province has its own Country Code registered with the UPU and the United Nations.

In order to explain how this all works, seminars are provided to explain and assist in the process where people may learn:

- How to use Diplomatic IDs and remain in honour,
- How to remove your property from the tax rolls, and deal with foreclosure,
- How to mark your property and private mode of transport,
- How to Export your mode of transport to the Embassy of the Divine Province,
- How to establish your property as a foreign consulate attached to the Embassy of the Divine Province and NOT subject to the civil law,
- How to handle the IRS, their demands and Notice of Liens,
- How to go to peace with the United States and free yourself forever!

- How to create your own pre-paid postage and how to use it for; Postage, as a codicil to modify demands for payment to pre-paid status, to close a contract under the jurisdiction of the UPU, and to Authenticate a document
- Learn what is the Court of Chancery and how do the Writs and Final Orders work for foreclosure, IRS, other court issues.

In order to properly execute this, in addition to the process described earlier to declare and notice the Administrators in North America, this identification Process is designed to bring together, by **Private** membership those people who truly want peace, sovereignty and access to the Divine trust. Once again, these documents are provided as examples only, not for use. It is recommended that if you should wish to peruse this, go to the website and join the Divine Province.

In the Notice and Abstract of Unincorporated Association Operating Agreement, it states:

KNOW ALL BY THESE PRESENTS, that on the date of commencement set forth below an unincorporated private association was created by the Members thereof, and that said association will hold both equitable and legal title in real property, receive personal property, preserve assets in its own name, engage in whatever business may be lawful and will further the preservation and protection of the association assets for the benefit of the association.

The following aspects of the said Operating Agreement are hereby provided so that all the world will be informed of the terms and conditions under which activities and business concerning said property and the association itself shall be conducted. By submitting this application for meeting attendance in a private function hosted by The Office of the Postmaster General Divine Province or The Divine Province UA, and/or for membership in the Private Unincorporated Association known as The Divine Province UA, Member Applicant acknowledges the Private nature of the relationship to be created between the Member Applicant and The Divine Province UA. The Member Applicant further agrees to hold all information related directly or indirectly to The Divine Province UA strictly confidential and unless specifically pre-authorized in writing by the Executive Board, to never reveal nor disclose any information whatsoever, either directly or indirectly, to anyone at any time for any reason whatsoever, other than to members of the Executive Board or other duly authorized members. The Member Applicant acknowledges such provisions are made for purposes of privacy between contracting parties which is in the nature of membership in a private unincorporated association.

In placing my autograph upon this application, Member Applicant does solemnly swear the following:

"I have made this application for membership in this Unincorporated Association honorably and that I voluntarily have given no aid, countenance, counsel, or encouragement to persons engaged in any hostility against this Unincorporated Association or its Members; that I have neither sought nor accepted nor attempted to exercise the functions of any office whatsoever under any authority or pretended authority in hostility to this Unincorporated Association or its Members; that I renounce, refuse and abjure any allegiance or obedience previously sworn which is in conflict to my peaceful inhabitance upon the land, peaceful co-existence with Members of this Unincorporated Association, or toward my fellow man; that I take this obligation freely, without any mental reservation or purpose of evasion; and that I will well and faithfully discharge the responsibilities of my Membership on which I am about to enter, so help me God."

IN WITNESS WHEREOF, as a Member Applicant to become a Limited Member of the Private Unincorporated Association known as The Divine Province UA, the parties hereto set their hands at a date and time convenient to each after careful reading, thought and review of the Private Protocols and Operating Agreement without duress or undue influence and by so doing offers to each and accepts from each their commitment to be bound by the Agreement."

Notice Of International Diplomatic Status

The first document required in the Identification process is the Notice of International Diplomatic Status. It is a clear declaration of Diplomatic Status under the flag of peace. It also declares the relationship of the sentient being with the Strawman Trust and the Post Office as the judicial district of the Divine Province. Critical identifications and legal information are placed on both sides of the identification. These are issued by, and only by the Postmaster. Here is an example:

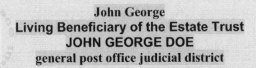

John George
Living Beneficiary of the Estate Trust
JOHN GEORGE DOE
general post office judicial district

Notice is under the judicial district, general post office and flag of peace
I am at Peace with the Crown and all Dominions
No flag of war shall be allowed to affect upon My Divinity

Notice of International Diplomatic Status

Phil Lawmaker
c/o Sheriff Phil Lawmaker
Any County Police Department
AnyTown, AntState, Postal Code

IN RE: **JOHN GEORGE DOE** ESTATE
John George Living Beneficiary

Peace, Peace, Peace be unto all men and women in this world. The Divine Spirit, Living beneficiary and heir to the Divine Estate lives at peace with all men and women.

The Divine Spirit, Living beneficiary has returned to redeem the estate and hereby claims the priority right of salvage enrolling the Estate on the chancery rolls of the court of Chancery under the Office of the Postmaster General, Divine Province.

The superior lien right and Divine Claim against the Estate by the Divine Spirit, Living beneficiary, heir to the Divine Estate, as herein identified is recorded on the rolls of the court of Chancery, as evidenced by the final order from the court of Chancery attached hereto and incorporated herein by this reference, is binding on all men and superior to any/all claims by any fictions, artificial or civilly dead entity and/or assumptions of abandonment.

The Estate has surrendered to the contest and conflict and is at peace with the Crown, at peace with the 'One Holy', neutral in the public with the priority claim against the derivative annuities for Set-Off of all charges against the Estate in accordance with the terms of surrender;

The Estate is Tax Pre-Paid, Bonded and underwritten by the derivative annuities given life by the living beneficiary, Divine Spirit and shall be afforded Safe Harbor/ Safe Passage unmolested by pirates or privateers who shall seize and/ or docket the Estate at their own peril. A breach of the Safe Harbor/ Safe Passage shall constitute High Treason against an ally of the Crown.

The Estate is on and at all times within the judicial district under the general post office and under the protection of the Crown under the Laws of Great Britain and NOT subject to the codes and statutes of the United Kingdom and not subject to alienation.

The Estate has the right to hypothecate the Title to create the funds, remaining solvent at all times, for settlement of all charges against the Estate.

The Estate shall operate in unlimited liability at all times. All charges against the Estate shall be in unlimited liability ONLY.

Any actions against the estate shall constitute an Act of War, High Treason, an act outside your corporate charter and cause for an action before the Crown.

Please update your database to reflect the diplomatic status of the Divine Estate JOHN GEORGE DOE and its Sacred Cargo John George. Please instruct all employees the Divine Spirit, living beneficiary will be/are in your country on a diplomatic mission of peace. Peace, Peace, Peace be unto all men and women in this world.

Dated this **12th** day of **December**, two thousand and twelve.

John George

> This document is under the jurisdiction of the Universal Postal Union (UPU), constitutes "Official Mail" and is in compliance with regulations as concerns Private Mail Carriers.

Notice Of Title and Protection

The postal treaty for the Americas operates under the authority and protection of Papal Seal of Peter and the Vatican. Members of the Council, as members of the divine Province and Postal Union are its internationally protected foreign officials and International diplomats at peace. The Notice Caveat instantly makes a reader aware of what they are bound to and liable for should they interfere with the individual so named.

Here is an example.

John George
Living Beneficiary of the
JOHN GEORGE DOE ESTATE
general post office judicial district

Notice Caveat Notice

The Office of the Postmaster General, Divine Province is an International Peace Council established under the Universal Postal Treaty For The Americas 2010 operating under the authority and protection of the Papal Seal of Peter under country code DVN/DP/999. All members of the Council are Internationally protected foreign officials, International Diplomats at peace with the United States and the many franchised County, City, Towns and States thereof. Please take note that you are bound and liable under the following, to wit:

TITLE 18, PART I; CHAPTER 1 Sec. 1.; Sec. 11.
Sec. 11. - Foreign government defined

The term "foreign government", as used in this title except in sections 112, 878, 970, 1116, and 1201, includes any government, faction, or body of insurgents within a country with which the **United States is at peace, irrespective of recognition by the United States.**

18 U.S.C. § 112 - Protection of foreign officials, official guests, and internationally protected

(a) Whoever assaults, strikes, wounds, imprisons, or offers violence to a foreign official, official guest, or internationally protected person or makes any other violent attack upon the person or liberty of such person, or, if likely to endanger his person or liberty, makes a violent attack upon his official premises, private accommodation, or means of transport or attempts to commit any of the foregoing shall be fined under this title or imprisoned not more than three years, or both. Whoever in the commission of any such act uses a deadly or dangerous weapon, or inflicts bodily injury, shall be fined under this title or imprisoned not more than ten years, or both.

(b) Whoever wilfully
> (1) intimidates, coerces, threatens, or harasses a foreign official or an official guest or obstructs a foreign official in the performance of his duties;
> (2) attempts to intimidate, coerce, threaten, or harass a foreign official or an official guest or obstruct a foreign official in the performance of his duties; or
> (3) within the United States and within one hundred feet of any building or premises in whole or in part owned, used, or occupied for official business or for diplomatic, consular, or residential purposes by
>> (A) a foreign government, including such use as a mission to an international organization;
>> (B) an international organization;
>> (C) a foreign official; or
>> (D) an official guest; congregates with two or more other persons with intent to violate any other provision of this section;
>> shall be fined under this title or imprisoned not more than six months, or both.

(c) For the purpose of this section foreign government, foreign official, internationally protected person, international organization, national of the United States, and official guest shall have the same meanings as those provided in section 1116 (b) of this title.
(d) Nothing contained in this section shall be construed or applied so as to abridge the exercise of rights guaranteed under the first amendment to the Constitution of the United States.
(e) If the victim of an offense under subsection (a) is an internationally protected person outside the United States, the United States may exercise jurisdiction over the offense if
> (1) the victim is a representative, officer, employee, or agent of the United States,
> (2) an offender is a national of the United States, or
> (3) an offender is afterwards found in the United States. As used in this subsection, the United States includes all areas under the jurisdiction of the United States including any of the places within the provisions of sections 5 and 7 of this title and section 46501 (2) of title 49.

(f) In the course of enforcement of subsection (a) and any other sections prohibiting a conspiracy or attempt to violate subsection (a), the Attorney General may request assistance from any Federal, State, or local agency, including the Army, Navy, and Air Force, any statute, rule, or regulation to the contrary, notwithstanding.

18 U.S.C. § 878 - Threats and extortion against foreign officials, official guests, or

(a) Whoever knowingly and wilfully threatens to violate section 112, 1116, or 1201 shall be fined under this title or imprisoned not more than five years, or both, except that imprisonment for a threatened assault shall not exceed three years.

(b) Whoever in connection with any violation of subsection (a) or actual violation of section 112, 1116, or 1201 makes any extortionate demand shall be fined under this title or imprisoned not more than twenty years, or both.

(c) For the purpose of this section foreign official, internationally protected person, national of the United States, and official guest shall have the same meanings as those provided in section 1116 (a) of this title.

(d) If the victim of an offense under subsection (a) is an internationally protected person outside the United States, the United States may exercise jurisdiction over the offense if

    (1) the victim is a representative, officer, employee, or agent of the United States,

    (2) an offender is a national of the United States, or

    (3) an offender is afterwards found in the United States. As used in this subsection, the United States includes all areas under the jurisdiction of the United States including any of the places within the provisions of sections 5 and 7 of this title and section 46501 (2) of title 49.

18 U.S.C. § 1116 - Murder or manslaughter of foreign officials, official guests, or

(a) Whoever kills or attempts to kill a foreign official, official guest, or internationally protected person shall be punished as provided under sections 1111, 1112, and 1113 of this title.

(b) For the purposes of this section:

    (1) Family includes (a) a spouse, parent, brother or sister, child, or person to whom the foreign official or internationally protected person stands in loco parentis, or (b) any other person living in his household and related to the foreign official or internationally protected person by blood or marriage.

    (2) Foreign government means the government of a foreign country, irrespective of recognition by the United States.

    (3) Foreign official means

        (A) a Chief of State or the political equivalent, President, Vice President, Prime Minister, Ambassador, Foreign Minister, or other officer of Cabinet rank or above of a foreign government or the chief executive officer of an international organization, or any person who has previously served in such capacity, and any member of his family, while in the United States; and

        (B) any person of a foreign nationality who is duly notified to the United States as an officer or employee of a foreign government or international organization, and who is in the United States on official business, and any member of his family whose presence in the United States is in connection with the presence of such officer or employee.

    (4) Internationally protected person means

        (A) a Chief of State or the political equivalent, head of government, or Foreign Minister whenever such person is in a country other than his own and any member of his family accompanying him; or

        (B) any other representative, officer, employee, or agent of the United States Government, a foreign government, or international organization who at the time and place concerned is entitled pursuant to international law to special protection against attack upon his person, freedom, or dignity, and any member of his family then forming part of his household.

    (5) International organization means a public international organization designated as such pursuant to section 1 of the International Organizations Immunities Act (22 U.S.C. 288) or a public organization created pursuant to treaty or other agreement under international law as an instrument through or by which two or more foreign governments engage in some aspect of their conduct of international affairs.

    (6) Official guest means a citizen or national of a foreign country present in the United States as an official guest of the Government of the United States pursuant to designation as such by the Secretary of State.

    (7) National of the United States has the meaning prescribed in section 101(a)(22) of the Immigration and Nationality Act (8 U.S.C. 1101 (a)(22)).

(c) If the victim of an offense under subsection (a) is an internationally protected person outside the United States, the United States may exercise jurisdiction over the offense if

    (1) the victim is a representative, officer, employee, or agent of the United States,

    (2) an offender is a national of the United States, or

    (3) an offender is afterwards found in the United States. As used in this subsection, the United States includes all areas under the jurisdiction of the United States including any of the places within the provisions of sections 5 and 7 of this title and section 46501 (2) of title 49.

(d) In the course of enforcement of this section and any other sections prohibiting a conspiracy or attempt to violate this section, the Attorney General may request assistance from any Federal, State, or local agency, including the Army, Navy, and Air Force, any statute, rule, or regulation to the contrary notwithstanding.

18 U.S.C. § 1201 – Kidnapping

(a) Whoever unlawfully seizes, confines, inveigles, decoys, kidnaps, abducts, or carries away and holds for ransom or reward or otherwise any person, except in the case of a minor by the parent thereof, when

> (1) the person is wilfully transported in interstate or foreign commerce, regardless of whether the person was alive when transported across a State boundary, or the offender travels in interstate or foreign commerce or uses the mail or any means, facility, or instrumentality of interstate or foreign commerce in committing or in furtherance of the commission of the offense;
>
> (2) any such act against the person is done within the special maritime and territorial jurisdiction of the United States;
>
> (3) any such act against the person is done within the special aircraft jurisdiction of the United States as defined in section 46501 of title 49;
>
> (4) the person is a foreign official, an internationally protected person, or an official guest as those terms are defined in section 1116 (b) of this title; or
>
> (5) the person is among those officers and employees described in section 1114 of this title and any such act against the person is done while the person is engaged in, or on account of, the performance of official duties,
>
> shall be punished by imprisonment for any term of years or for life and, if the death of any person results, shall be punished by death or life imprisonment.

(b) With respect to subsection (a)(1), above, the failure to release the victim within twenty-four hours after he shall have been unlawfully seized, confined, inveigled, decoyed, kidnapped, abducted, or carried away shall create a rebuttable presumption that such person has been transported in interstate or foreign commerce. Notwithstanding the preceding sentence, the fact that the presumption under this section has not yet taken effect does not preclude a Federal investigation of a possible violation of this section before the 24-hour period has ended.

(c) If two or more persons conspire to violate this section and one or more of such persons do any overt act to effect the object of the conspiracy, each shall be punished by imprisonment for any term of years or for life.

(d) Whoever attempts to violate subsection (a) shall be punished by imprisonment for not more than twenty years.

(e) If the victim of an offense under subsection (a) is an internationally protected person outside the United States, the United States may exercise jurisdiction over the offense if

> (1) the victim is a representative, officer, employee, or agent of the United States,
>
> (2) an offender is a national of the United States, or
>
> (3) an offender is afterwards found in the United States. As used in this subsection, the United States includes all areas under the jurisdiction of the United States including any of the places within the provisions of sections 5 and 7 of this title and section 46501 (2) of title 49. For purposes of this subsection, the term national of the United States has the meaning prescribed in section 101(a)(22) of the Immigration and Nationality Act (8 U.S.C. 1101 (a)(22)).

(f) In the course of enforcement of subsection (a)(4) and any other sections prohibiting a conspiracy or attempt to violate subsection (a)(4), the Attorney General may request assistance from any Federal, State, or local agency, including the Army, Navy, and Air Force, any statute, rule, or regulation to the contrary notwithstanding.

(g) Special Rule for Certain Offenses Involving Children.—

> (1) To whom applicable.—
>
> If
>
> (A) the victim of an offense under this section has not attained the age of eighteen years; and
>
> (B) the offender
>
>> (i) has attained such age; and
>>
>> (ii) is not
>>
>> (I) a parent;
>>
>> (II) a grandparent;
>>
>> (III) a brother;
>>
>> (IV) a sister;
>>
>> (V) an aunt;
>>
>> (VI) an uncle; or
>>
>> (VII) an individual having legal custody of the victim;
>
> the sentence under this section for such offense shall include imprisonment for not less than 20 years.
>
> [(2) Repealed. Pub. L. 108–21, title I, § 104(b), Apr. 30, 2003, 117 Stat. 653.]

(h) As used in this section, the term parent does not include a person whose parental rights with respect to the victim of an offense under this section have been terminated by a final court order.

18 U.S.C. § 877 - Mailing threatening communications from foreign country

Whoever knowingly deposits in any post office or authorized depository for mail matter of any foreign country any communication addressed to any person within the United States, for the purpose of having such communication delivered by the post office establishment of such foreign country to the Postal Service and by it delivered to such addressee in the United States, and as a result thereof such communication is delivered by the post office establishment of such foreign country to the Postal Service and by it delivered to the address to which it is directed in the United States, and containing any demand or request for ransom or reward for the release of any kidnapped person, shall be fined under this title or imprisoned not more than twenty years, or both. Whoever, with intent to extort from any person any money or other thing of value, so deposits as aforesaid, any communication for the purpose aforesaid, containing any threat to kidnap any person or any threat to injure the person of the addressee or of another, shall be fined under this title or imprisoned not more than twenty years, or both. Whoever knowingly so deposits as aforesaid, any communication, for the purpose aforesaid, containing any threat to kidnap any person or any threat to injure the person of the addressee or of another, shall be fined under this title or imprisoned not more than five years, or both. Whoever, with intent to extort from any person any money or other thing of value, knowingly so deposits as aforesaid, any communication, for the purpose aforesaid, containing any threat to injure the property or reputation of the addressee or of another, or the reputation of a deceased person, or any threat to accuse the addressee or any other person of a crime, shall be fined under this title or imprisoned not more than two years, or both.

Thank you for your cooperation in restoring the peace in America.

John George

Divine Province

International Diplomatic Identification

The process also includes attaining two pieces of Identification. These are the International Diplomatic Id and the International Drivers Permit. These are issued through membership to the Divine Province only. The examples follow:

Universal Postal Office Diplomat

John George Doe
Born: March 14, 1956
Sex: M Eyes Brown
Ht: 5'9"
Judicial district
Post XXYY0011
Expires: 01 06 2018

universal post office master
universal general post office
Master of Vessel JOHN GEORGE DOE

The Chancery Court And Rolls

As members of the Council of the Peace Treaty, and Office of the Postmaster, Divine Province, each is The Divine Spirit and Living beneficiary who returns to redeem the estate. Here each is calming the priority right of salvage enrolling the Estate on the chancery rolls of the court of Chancery under the Office of the Postmaster General, Divine Province. This becomes the enforcement process of a Court.

A Chancery is a Court of Equity is a court having the jurisdiction of a chancellor; a court administering equity and proceeding according to the forms and principles of equity. In England, prior to the judicature acts, the style of the court possessing the largest equitable powers and jurisdiction was the "high court of chancery.

The judge of the court of chancery, often called a court of equity, bears the title of chancellor. The equity jurisdiction in England is vested, principally, in the high court of chancery. This court is distinct from courts of law. American courts of equity are, in some instances, distinct from those of law; in others, the same tribunals exercise the jurisdiction both of courts of law and equity though their forms of proceeding are different in their two capacities. The Supreme Court of the United States and the circuit courts are invested with general equity powers and act either as courts of law or equity, according to the form of the process and the subject of adjudication. In some of the states, as New York, Virginia, and South Carolina, the equity court is a distinct tribunal, having its appropriate judge, or chancellor, and officers. In most of the states, the two jurisdictions centre in the same judicial officers, as in the courts of the United States; and the extent of equity jurisdiction and proceedings is very various in the different states, being very ample in Connecticut, New York, New Jersey, Maryland, Virginia, and South Carolina, and more restricted in Maine, Massachusetts, Rhode Island, and Pennsylvania. But the salutary influence of these powers on the judicial administration generally, by the adaptation of chancery forms and modes of proceeding to many cases in which a court of law affords but an imperfect remedy, or no remedy at all, is producing a gradual extension of them in those states where they have been, heretofore, very limited.

The jurisdiction of a court of equity differs essentially from that of a court of law. The remedies for wrongs, or for the enforcement of rights, may be distinguished into two classes; those which are administered in courts of law, and those which are administered in courts of equity. The rights secured by the former are called legal; those secured by the latter are called equitable. The former are said to be rights and remedies at common law, because recognized and enforced in courts of common law. The latter are said to be rights and remedies in equity, because they are administered in courts of equity or chancery, or by proceedings in other courts analogous to those in courts of equity or chancery.

Now, in England and America, courts of common law proceed by certain prescribed forms and give a general judgment for or against the defendant. They entertain jurisdiction only in certain actions and give remedies according to the particular exigency of such actions. But there are many cases in which a simple judgment for either party, without qualifications and conditions, and particular arrangements, will not do entire justice, ex aequo et bono, to either party. Some modification of the rights of both parties is required; some restraints on one side or the other; and some peculiar adjustments, either present or future, temporary or perpetual. Now, in all these cases, courts of common law have no methods of proceeding which can accomplish such objects. Their forms of actions and judgment are not adapted to them. The proper remedy cannot be found or cannot be administered to the full extent of the relative rights of all parties. Such prescribed forms of actions are not confined to our law.

They were known in the civil law; and the party could apply them only to their original purposes. In other cases he had a special remedy. In such cases where the courts of common law cannot grant the proper remedy or relief, the law of England and of the United States (in those states where equity is administered) authorizes an application to the courts of equity or chancery, which are not confined or limited in their modes of relief by such narrow regulations, but which grant relief to all parties in cases where they have rights, ex aequo et bono, and modify and fashion that relief according to circumstances.

The most general description of a court of equity is that it has jurisdiction in cases where a plain, adequate and complete remedy cannot be had at law, that is, in common law courts. The remedy must be plain; for if it be doubtful and obscure at law, equity will assert a jurisdiction. So it must be adequate at law; for if it fall short of what the party is entitled to, that founds a jurisdiction in equity. And it must be complete; that is, it must attain its full end at law, must reach the whole mischief and secure the whole right of the party, now and for the future otherwise equity will interpose and give relief.

The jurisdiction of a court of equity is sometimes concurrent with that of courts of law and sometimes it is exclusive. It exercises concurrent jurisdiction in cases where the rights are purely of a legal nature, but where other and more efficient aid is required than a court of law can afford, to meet the difficulties of the case and ensure full redress. In some of these cases courts of law formerly refused all redress but now will grant it. But the jurisdiction having been once justly acquired at a time when there was no such redress at law, it is not now relinquished. The most common exercise of concurrent jurisdiction is in cases of account, accident, dower, fraud, mistake, partnership and partition. The remedy is here often more complete and effectual than it can be at law. In many cases falling under these heads, and especially in some cases of fraud, mistake and accident, courts of law cannot and do not afford any redress; in others they do, but not always in so perfect a manner.

A court of equity also is assistant to the jurisdiction of courts of law in many cases where the latter have no like authority. It will remove legal impediments to the fair decision of a question depending at law. It will prevent a party from improperly setting up, at a trial, some title or claim, which would be inequitable. It will compel him to discover, on his own oath, facts which he knows are material to the rights of the other party, but which a court of law cannot compel the party to discover. It will perpetuate the testimony of witnesses to rights and titles which are in danger of being lost, before the matter can be tried. It will provide for the safety of property in dispute pending litigation. It will counteract and control, or set aside, fraudulent judgments. It will exercise, in many cases, an exclusive jurisdiction. This it does in all cases of morally equitable rights, that is, such rights as are not recognized in courts of law. Most cases of trust and confidence fall under this head.

Its exclusive jurisdiction is also extensively exercised in granting special relief beyond the reach of the common law. It will grant injunctions to prevent waste, or irreparable injury, or to secure a settled right, or to prevent vexatious litigations, or to compel the restitution of title deeds; it will appoint receivers of property, where it is in danger of misapplication it will compel the surrender of securities improperly obtained; it will prohibit a party from leaving the country in order to avoid a suit it will restrain any undue exercise of a legal right against conscience and equity; it will decree a specific performance of contracts respecting real estates; it will, in many cases, supply the imperfect execution of instruments and reform and alter them according to the real intention of the parties; it will grant relief in cases of lost deeds or securities; and in all cases in which its interference is asked, its general rule is that he who asks equity must do equity. If a party, therefore, should ask to have a bond for a usurious debt given up, equity could not decree it unless he could bring into court the money honestly due without usury.

The Chancery Rolls From the end of the 12th century, the Chancery began to record copies of the documents it produced on several series of rolls. As outlined below, various series were produced at different times, but probably the most important for the genealogist are the Patent and Close Rolls (which originally recorded royal letters - sent open or closed), the Charter Rolls (royal charters) and the Fine Rolls (financial 'offerings' to the king). With a few exceptions, these four series have been published, at least as far as the year 1509, mostly as English abstracts. (These printed texts run to about 180 volumes, as far as the reign of Elizabeth.)

The printed versions of these records, most of which are indexed by name, are among the most accessible and useful for medieval genealogists. The people mentioned in them are certainly not all royal officials (although if your ancestor was a royal official, they may allow a fairly detailed account of his movements to be compiled). Many of the entries record the day-to-day dealings of the manor-holding classes with government - appointments to local offices, permission to hold markets or grant land, involvement in law suits, debts, misdemeanours and so on. Others are concerned with matters of more direct genealogical interest, such as the inheritance of land, provision of dower for widows and the wardship of minors. In the late medieval period, many private charters were also enrolled for safety. Many humbler people are also mentioned in the rolls, either in their own right, or incidentally - for example, the enrolled orders concerning the partition of estates may contain detailed surveys, in which tenants are named.

Keeper of the Rolls of Chancery The Keeper or Master of the Rolls and Records of the Chancery of England, known as the Master of the Rolls, is the second most senior judge in England and Wales, after the Lord Chief Justice. The Master of the Rolls is the presiding officer of the Civil Division of the Court of Appeal and serves as the Head of Civil Justice. The first record of a Master of the Rolls is from 1286, although it is believed that the office probably existed earlier than that. The Master of the Rolls was initially a clerk responsible for keeping the "Rolls", or records, of the Court of Chancery, and was known as the Keeper of the Rolls of Chancery. The Keeper was the most senior of the dozen Chancery clerks, and as such occasionally acted as keeper of the Great Seal of the Realm. The **Great Seal of the Realm** or **Great Seal of the United Kingdom** (prior to the Treaty of Union the **Great Seal of England**, then until the Union of 1801 the **Great Seal of Great Britain**) is a seal that is used to symbolize the Sovereign's approval of important state documents. Sealing wax is melted in a metal mould or matrix and impressed into a wax figure that is attached by cord or ribbon to documents that the monarch wishes to make official.

In the case of the Postmaster and the Court of Chancery, the great seal would be operating under the authority and protection of the Papal Seal of Peter. This would as you have learned constitute the highest authority in the land.

The post of Keeper evolved into a judicial one as the Court of Chancery did; the first reference to judicial duties dates from 1520. With the Judicature Act 1873, which merged the Court of Chancery with the other major courts, the Master joined the Chancery Division of the High Court and the Court of Appeal, but left the Chancery Division by the terms of the Judicature Act 1881. The Master still retained his clerical functions by serving as the nominal head of the Public Record Office (PRO) until 1958. However, the Public Records Act of that year transferred responsibility for the PRO from the Master of the Rolls to the Lord Chancellor. The Master of the Rolls is also responsible for registering solicitors, the officers of the Senior Courts.

Through the Postmaster General, the relationship to the Vatican, the Chancery has been reinvoked to provide the court of power for the Council members.

Notice to Set-off Against The Good Faith And Credit Estate

This section is provided as a simple example of one of many ways access to the Good Faith and Credit would be placed in effect. Reference is given to the chapter on Set-off. This would be a process of setting off a debt against the Good Faith and Credit of the Estate, acting as the True Beneficiary. This is an example only sent to the Chief Financial Officer

IN RE: **JOHN GEORGE DOE** ESTATE
John George Living Beneficiary
Prepaid Account Number: **XX-XXXXXXX**

Peace, Peace, Peace be unto all men and women in this world. The Divine Spirit, Living beneficiary and heir to the Divine Estate lives at peace with all men and women.

The Divine Spirit, Living beneficiary has returned to redeem the estate and hereby claims the priority right of salvage enrolling the Estate on the chancery rolls of the court of Chancery under the Office of the Postmaster General, Divine Province.

The superior lien right and Divine Claim against the Estate by the Divine Spirit, Living beneficiary, heir to the Divine Estate, as herein identified is recorded on the rolls of the court of Chancery, as evidenced by the final order from the court of Chancery attached hereto and incorporated herein by this reference, is binding on all men and superior to any/all claims by any fictions, artificial or civilly dead entity and/or assumptions of abandonment.

The Estate has surrendered to the contest and conflict and is at peace with the Crown, at peace with the 'One Holy', neutral in the public with the priority claim against the derivative annuities for Set-Off of all charges against the Estate in accordance with the terms of surrender;

The Estate is Tax Prepaid (taxe perçue), Bonded and underwritten by the derivative annuities given life by the living beneficiary, Divine Spirit and shall be afforded Safe Harbor/ Safe Passage unmolested by pirates or privateers who shall seize and/ or docket the Estate at their own peril. A breach of the Safe Harbor/ Safe Passage shall constitute High Treason against an ally of the Crown.

The Estate is on and at all times within the judicial district under the general post office and under the protection of the Crown under the Laws of Great Britain and NOT subject to the codes and statutes of the United Kingdom and not subject to alienation.

The Estate has the right to hypothecate the Title to create the funds, remaining solvent at all times, for settlement of all charges against the Estate.

The Estate shall operate in unlimited liability at all times. All charges against the Estate shall be in unlimited liability ONLY.

Please take note that any further actions as privateers against the vessel, estate or the Living Beneficiary shall constitute an Act of War against an ally of the Crown in violation of your corporate charter and High Treason.

If you have a valid claim against the vessel or the Estate you are authorized to do the set-off against the prepaid account as provided above. Your failure to settle and close this matter within ten (10) days after receipt of this notice and provide me evidence of the transaction shall establish the evidence that your claim was NOT a valid claim.

Dated this **12th** day of **December**, two thousand and twelve.

John George

> This document is under the jurisdiction of the Universal Postal Union (UPU), constitutes "Official Mail" and is in compliance with regulations as concerns Private Mail Carriers.

The Papal Seal Of St Peter

Inherent in the Divine Province and the Divine Estate is an authority under the Papal seal of Peter. The Papal seal of St Peter represents the coat of arms for the Vatican City State. Take note of the crown on top, a symbol of papal authority. It is a triple tiered crown, that is also called a tiara or *triregno* in Latin. This represents the supreme authority as presented earlier. Recall:
1. "The Pope is of so great dignity and so exalted that he is not mere man, but as it were God, and the vicar of God."
13. "Hence the Pope is crowned with a triple crown, as king of heaven and of earth and of the lower regions."
18. "As to papal authority, the Pope is as it were God on earth, Sole sovereign of all the faithful of Christ, chief king of kings, having a plentitude of unbroken power, entrusted by the omnipotent God to govern the earthly and heavenly kingdoms."

30. "The Pope is of so great authority and power, that he is able to modify, declare, or interpret even divine laws."

These papal claims, to include the presumed authority to modify the divine laws of God, were specifically prophesied in the book of Daniel: The Catholic Church teaches that, within the Christian community, the bishops as a body have succeeded to the body of the apostles and the Bishop of Rome has succeeded to Saint Peter. Scriptural texts proposed in support of Peter's special position in relation to the church include the words of Jesus to him:

"I tell you, you are Peter, and on this rock I will build my church, and the gates of hell shall not prevail against it. I will give you the keys of the kingdom of heaven, and whatever you bind on earth shall be bound in heaven, and whatever you loose on earth shall be loosed in heaven.
Simon, Simon, behold, Satan demanded to have you, that he might sift you like wheat, but I have prayed for you that your faith may not fail. And when you have turned again, strengthen your brothers.[L]
Feed my sheep."

The symbolic keys in the papal coat of arms are a reference to the phrase "the keys of the kingdom of heaven" in the first of these texts.

Papal regalia and insignia are the official items of attire and decoration proper to the Pope in his capacity as the head of the Roman Catholic Church and sovereign of the Vatican City State. The triregnum (a crown with three levels) is among the regalia of the papacy. It is also called the triple tiara or triple crown. "Tiara" is the name of the headdress, even in the forms it had before a third crown was added to it. Paul VI used it on 30 June 1963, at the coronation that was then part of the Papal Inauguration. For several centuries, Popes have worn it during processions, as when entering or leaving Saint Peter's Basilica, but during liturgies they used an episcopal mitre instead. Pope Benedict XVI has replaced the tiara with a mitre on his personal coat of arms, but not on the coat of arms of the Holy See or of the Vatican City State.

Another famous part of the Papal regalia is the Ring of the Fisherman, a gold ring decorated with a depiction of St. Peter in a boat casting his net, with the name of the reigning Pope around it. The Fisherman's Ring was first mentioned in a letter of Pope Clement IV to his nephew in 1265 wherein he mentions that Popes were accustomed to sealing public documents with a leaden "bulla" attached, and private letters with "the seal of the Fisherman" (by the fifteenth century, the Fisherman's Ring was used to seal Papal briefs). The Fisherman's Ring is placed on the newly-elected Pope's finger by the Camerlengo of the Holy Roman Church; on the Pope's death, the Cardinal Chamberlain used to formally deface and smash the Fisherman's Ring with a hammer, symbolising the end of the late Pope's authority.

Modern popes do not bear a crozier (a bent pastoral staff styled after a shepherd's crook), but rather bear the Papal Cross, a staff topped by a crucifix. The use of the papal cross is an ancient custom, established before the thirteenth century, though some popes since then, notably Pope Leo XIII, have used a crozier-like staff. One (now discontinued) Papal regalia was the *Sedia gestatoria*, a portable throne or armchair carried by twelve footmen (*palafrenieri*) in red uniforms. The *sedia gestatoria* is accompanied by two attendants bearing the *Flabella*, large ceremonial fans made of white ostrich-feathers, which also had a practical intent in cooling the pope, given the heat of Rome in summer months, the length of papal ceremonies, the heavy papal vestments and the fact that most popes were elderly. The *sedia gestatoria* was used for the Pope's solemn entrance into a church or hall and for his departure on the occasion of liturgical celebrations such as a papal Mass and for papal audiences. The use of the *sedia gestatoria* was discontinued by Pope John Paul II, that of the flabella by Pope Paul VI. Neither has been abolished however.

The authority which resides in the Papal Seal is the one that governs the the Divine Province. The Divine Province and its Chancery Courts are the Divine expression of the emergece of New Earth. For New Earth that has become the dominant consiouness of millions is an Earth of Peace, Love and Unity.

We will leave you now with a final thought on resigning from PLANET EARTH. Very soon our web site will facilitate easier ways to navigate the labyrinth and to peacefully resign. It will allow the automated creation of records within the Court and Rolls of Chancery supported by Divine Law, with a process of compliance up from the Trustee who breach their duties up through the Secretary of State, Governor General to Westminster Abbey.

You may ask, how is it that the bad guys of the Vatican support this new birthing of New Earth? We have already learned that bad and good are variable and interchangeable, and that all souls are on the same quest. It should be understood that all Earthlings are evolving under the new consciousness and can freely change their minds. Another aspect, as we have learned is that regardless of how evil one may be there is always a code of ethics and behaviour and there are always something that is feared. Even for the Elite bloodlines, they fear death, and they would have the knowing of the universal laws of karma to harm others. They have been on a path like we, and they have also had a job. to give us lesson on who we really are.

Caveat Notice To Readers

It is important that in these writings and examples that a warning and cautionary declaration be stated. These examples are to shed light upon a highly evolved process of resignation from PLANET EARTH and gaining access to the ESTATE of the STRAWMAN. These procedures are to be used only in conjunction with and through the guidance of the Office of the Postmaster found on *www.divineprovince.org* under the jurisdiction of the Divine Province as part of a Council related to the Peace Treaty. In fact, since publication of this book, the forms and process have evolved to a more simple system. Go to the website before any engagement in the use.

If it has not become clear, the two part revelation of Commerce AND Spirit is that of Divinity in each EARTHLING starts with Peace and Unconditional Forgiveness on Earth. This realization is the foundation in moving forward within the Divine Realm of True Self through the intermediary vessel of Divine Province.

And so ends our revelation of Light with regards to Commerce and PLANET EARTH INC. Now let us complete the Journey of Self.

45

LOVE, LAUGH, LIVE AS ONE HEART

The True Secret Is Love

In the last chapters, much has been stated about Peace and Love. What is important to really understand is that the traditional path to enlightenment—the one that Christ and many others achieved—has been difficult on Old Earth. It has been the greatest challenge of humanity and civilizations to truly embrace this because as long as Earthlings fear death, the one who threaten it can continue dominion. **It is not so this time during the End Times.** Over the ages, many, many, esoteric practices, cults, traditions, and wisdoms, have evolved as humanity seeks enlightenment. Back in the Mystery Schools of Egypt, even Christ had to wrestle with this lesson, of overcoming the draw of the flesh, and of ego. That is the way it was, and history has served to show how not to overcome this.

as we have seen, in the current day because there is a tsunami of this unity consciousness flooding humanity, there are zillions of products around, with millions of experts that have gizmos and secret ways to heal your dysfunctional body, help you extend life, find unbelievable wealth and happiness. Is this in itself not a wakeup call to a new consciousness?

None of this is needed.

If you have taken lesson from the way energy works, the more you seek this, the more you engage in seeking. Remember, that is the way of energy manifestation. Seeking a solution is work, negative energy that in itself keeps you seeking. The solution is already in you so stop seeking. And at this special time, no one has to sit like a monk in celibacy on a mountain top most of his life trying to be enlightened to seek the solution. Unless, of course, you ignore this gifting that is upon you.

All you have to do is create the intent of allowing the process to unfold and to enjoy the train ride. That intent is to rise above the conflict and fear.

This is the ultimate secret of life revealed during the End Times. All you have to do is understand and accept that which some simple words like being in the heart, peace, and unconditional love mean. That is not so simple if you cannot believe a new way is upon you. Nor is living your mortal life the way of the heart a simple matter if you are entrenched in ego's attachments. Many have been trained to love bloodlines and dam the rest. But understand all are One and we are all of the same bloodline called Earthlings has not come through the lower mind.

Your true being sits in a place that is your heaven. You sit there as an aspect of the Creator as a piece of its total consciousness which is a quantum substance of love. As an analogy, it is like your currently local 3D mind that has no clear definition or substance. It simply exists and you know this because it drives your process of thinking and acting.

Here you sit as this Higher Mind as a Being of Light in your Origin watching a lower aspect of you as a Soul in Old Earth playing out a movie drama of life. You watch and you wonder; when will he or she know the secret of what is already known?

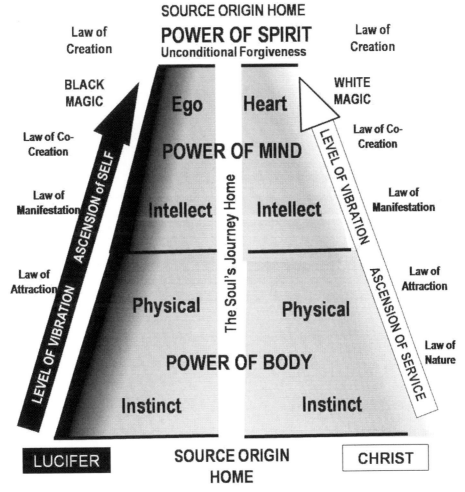

watch this mortal in its lower form evolving slowly but struggling with physicality, strength, body, age, health which takes much attention. You watch the dealings with issues of money, of family, of things that are seemingly so unfair with the suffering of others, the unjust dominion of the elite beings, and the long story of the slavery of humans. And you wonder why he or she has not implemented the secret yet. You wonder, when will the physical and mental lower form walk through the portal to Home?

And you think and project upon this lower form of physicality some information in the hope it can listen. It is this information of question and answer; What is it that cannot be solved by love? How can you change your life? Love. How do you heal your body? Love. How do you find bliss? Love. How can you heal the planet? Love. How can you materialize physicality? Love. How do you ascend? Love. How do you open to your fullest Creator abilities? Love. Is there anything that cannot be solved by love? And what is it that is infinitely abundant that is the true power of the universe? Love.

The secret is unconditional love and the portal through which you walk opens the door with the key of unconditional Love and Forgiveness. Nothing evil can live there. It is the highest vibration of all things. It is the vibration of the Creator and the makeup of all Creation, that is what you struggle to rise to. As Creator, your vibration is pure, absolute and the highest possible. That is the end of it. What you do in 5D in the essence of love is the same in 3D. The lessons are to teach you to rise above, to attain the degree of power through the level of vibration. Otherwise how can the endless cycle of conflict ever end?

Do you know that as a Creator, you can overlay a thought grid upon Gaia that will affect the physical behaviour of all humanity? This is a large responsibility is it not? It is not done by those that are not of the highest, purest vibration of heart, and without the knowing of your soul group and Divine mind. That is all there is to this. In 3D absolutely every moment must be pure unconditional Divine love; that's it, nothing else. Ask yourself what cannot be solved by love. So what is it that slows you? Immerse into the purity of love—nothing else—Oneness of All That Is. The alignment of you with the God Consciousness is the first step, and to know who you are.

The next step is the degree of purity which is the level of vibration. It is reflected in everything you do in your physical form. Once it is aligned as one aspect, and the strength of that absoluteness is your very being, all your issues are solved—permanently. No secrets, nothing but love.

A New Job: Unconditional Forgiveness In Thought Word Deed

It is what Christ rose to. It is what the Christ Consciousness gifts you. And this time there is no struggle, no convincing others, no opposition because it's *all happening to all at the same time.*

There is a new job for you. First get your belief system into the new jurisdiction. Resign from PLANET EARTH and throw away the old blue pills. It is your conscious intent to live in a New Earth of unconditional love and be God that is your ticket now. Throw the blue pills away and burn the prescription.

Then place your Trust and Faith not in others but in yourself. Don't look for instant miracles for it is a transition. During this transition here is your new "job".

You have a charged Heart Light and it is to shine light upon any darkness that you may come upon. It draws your love and shines where your new Darkness Detection Device in your heart senses darkness. It is best that as you do your daily surveillance of darkness that you use your new hovercraft of your etheric body which allows being above so you are not engaged directly. Here you can have a direct top view of any darkness.

What you receive in return for shining your Heart Light is joy. Your heart is connected to Source heart so you have an infinite supply of light and love to shine, and the process of converting to joy is like a current flow. It is what allows your craft to stay in its higher plane and the conversion process of changing darkness (negative) to joy (positive) is a flow of current that affects the brightness of your heart AND your DNA bulb which contains your total signature and it awakens. And the stronger the flow of conversion to bliss, the brighter is your bulb and the lighter is your body.

Sometimes you may feel it is appropriate to land and engage with others to feel joy and also become brighter on the ground. But remember that by engaging in lower experiences with others sometimes the light may cast shadows where darkness hides itself. Of course these are moments that are opportunities to reap the joy but you must be mindful not to attach or allow attachment. The brightness of your bulb here is very powerful as it can be felt by others around you. Each moment is there for you to enjoy the encounter and provide a possible moment to convert into the current to enhance your brightness. You know how to deploy your new senses in all your 3D affairs for this to expand your DNA to its full brightness and it will then entrain the body within it from its lower form upwards into higher form.

That is all you have to do in your new job. Be your true Self and stop the cycle of polarity conflict.

The Power Is In The Heart

Over the ages, the heart has received a lot of press. Heartless, heart of a lion, heartfelt, with all my heart, the list is endless. What's the infatuation with this thing that's a physical pump?

It ain't *just* a pump; it, like everything else of your being has an invisible, quantum counterpart of energy. You can go back and review the chapter of what you are but the heart is the link between who you are as an immortal Being of Light and who you are as a mortal being of holographic substance—material form. That's what it is all about.

And if you don't think there is power there, just think about the process of being in love, or protecting your children. Think about the physical and mental power that these reflect. Heartfelt, love from the bottom of my heart, heart of a lion? It's not that pump that instigates the behaviour is it?

The simplicity of all is that essence of above of God, love, heart all reside in the heart center as the expression vehicle of lower form. It is to practice this learning turned to knowing that becomes your path to mastery. Yes, *love, laugh, and live as One Heart*. Express yourself as the true You in your life with thought, word, and deed aligned with heart in every moment and the rest will simply unfold. The heart is the key to all that is, mastering the space between and of all that is; knowing and showing of what you are, a heart of expression. Every moment that comes before the heart is one to cast light of love upon, get a joyous laugh, and in so doing create the flow of pure life in its Divine essence. This means to be in it, to connect it, to live it, and to maintain it in a state of joy and bliss. This is what your prime purpose is, and so you allow as one with all to expand and experience the prime essence of Divine love.

So you say it doesn't pay the bills? Well, first change the rules of engagement in your working efforts. Don't *expect* an instant transfer from God's bank to yours. Then begin your new job with your heart light, knowing a transfer will occur—then watch what happens. Know that like earning a degree at school, it is done by time and attention of experience and deed; for if someone hands you the degree it has no value in execution.

Understand that all the residual baggage energy which may be from who knows when may still need to manifest. Resist that temptation to create more of it through your reactions. Otherwise you cannot break the conflict cycle.

There is no greater power as it is the supreme power and it cannot be subjected to, or be below dominion, nor can it be used for that purpose. It is the link and the conduit between God and you as part of God. As you live every moment in the heart, to love, to laugh, the return is bliss and joy. The heart is the conduit between the 3D world of body and the higher divine mind which is God. It cannot be fooled and it is all knowing, simply being patient for you to know and to show how to love, laugh, live every moment within it. Yes it is so.

The Pull To Perfection That Already Is

Through this End Time pay attention to a shift. You will feel a pull of perfection and the New Earth upon you as an overlay on the Old Earth, forming itself as the new hologram. It is subtle and you feel it as you walk with it in your consciousness, when you see, hear, speak, feel that around you. You are beginning to drop your attention to the discord and darkness as it does not vibrate within you now, except to point out what is not right of heart, and you may feel the empathy, of sorrow yet it does not engage you to bring forward fear, lack, anger or lower emotions and vibrations for these are losing their hold on you to engage.

Because of the special time you are in you are losing the attention to old energies as being important and you look to the beauty, the reverence, the joy of senses, and laughter as your moments pass before you. You look to alternatives that give you peace and intuitive comfort. You sense your body's shifting as it does not work the same and is sensitive in new places as it is shifting; yet you know not what is happening. The affairs of masculine and feminine extreme energies seem diminished—like a balancing—yet you cannot explain these moods that are softer.

And you are looking inward, into yourself for answers, for things of joy that are suddenly noticeable that have no price tag and are not in the stores, free of will to experience at the flick of the mind. All things of matter are beginning to look different. Yes it is the new hologram energizing itself from 4D and it is your new form shifting and adjusting. Yet it is subtle—God's plan is subtle as it sneaks upon you and yet you know. There is no time here, no scheme, no deception, only the granting of divine gifts for all.

Think of this as you ask how this can all occur in such a short time, as you look down upon the discord. It has been transitioning for a long time, you have not seen it. It has been the *Matrix.* Now you begin to sense you are the One and you pay attention to your heart, your life, your powers to perceive, to express, to manifest, to create. Allow yourself to shift first as you will then assist others in your revelations.

Find new ways to live your life. Sit down and go through your day's moments and let your heart see, feel, speak, think, hear, sense and act. Do this from your chair as you imagine your perfect day, then go out into your old world and do this as you walk the moments of your day. This is what is happening to all of humanity now—it has begun, the revelations as a subtle energy poured upon consciousness.

All humanity has entered a time of special allowing like none ever before. No karma, no need for lesson, no need for devices, for contraptions to ascend or open DNA, only pure intent and love. Just say so and believe it. And there is no need to heed those who proclaim special wisdom and affiliation with gods, those who pretend to know God's will, for it is all within, waiting to pour out. There is no need for pain or suffering to receive lesson. All is opened for all of humanity equally and all of the cosmic and divine energy is poured upon all in the grandest time of revelation of all time. All that is needed is your free will to choose to accept and be what you are—love. That is you pulling now, you feel it but cannot explain it. And it is only the beginning.

Think, See, Hear, Feel, Act With The Heart

We have all been seeing, hearing, thinking, feeling and launching intention to acting with our mortal beings. It is ego, it is survival, it is using the physical sensors of body. But as you now hopefully understand there is a counterpart of immortal form overlaying this body form—exactly like there is a New Earth overlaying the old. The Old Earth lower mind is being replaced by the New Earth higher mind and instead of the brain being the physical control center it is the heart that becomes the physical command center.

The new configuration of heart and higher mind shifts command to what is New Earth and the old senses of hear, see, feel, etc. give way to a huge range as picked up by the partners of the chakra system that links to the transformed physical (higher vibration). That process that knows only love and unity is to open to the heart. It is to align into the higher carrier wave of all that is, made of the substance of love.

What this means in practice is to take every moment that comes before you and to deploy these new senses to act like a filter of energies of thoughts, visions, words and feelings coming in and to act as the generator of its higher vibration going out of you. This is the energy that you accept or create within your hologram. The filter is to convert all coming in to something positive or good by seeing, hearing, saying, feeling the good part only. That is through the heart. The generator is to create energies going out from the heart that are good, based in love, unconditional—as you would with your own children. The difference here is that everything that is, is your own children. So all you have to do is join hearts, like you do with your family. But your family has grown to New Earth.

No one needs to buy devices, gizmos, or stuff that promises you a DNA awakening, new health and wealth. This is a realm that is accessible through the heart. It is free like the Train Ticket to Ascension. It is all being given to you if you wake up and accept it. **You don't even have to work for it, but you have to work at it**.

It's unstoppable, it is only a question of choice—yours. Will you now like to stay behind and serve the gods or would you be God? Your Choice!

Know Creatorship Within

Know this:

Whatever you choose, there is no judgment attached to your choice. Nor is there a judgment day.

In fact, all of this shifting between Old and New Earths will be subtle at first. It will begin like a new global marketing strategy where the mass consumer simply shifts his attention. But as the new energy floods in, so it replaces the old and many large systems lose their ability to be sustained. It is like the financial and religious systems that are based on debt and dominion—an energy that can't stay anchored in this shifting consciousness.

In addition, a lot of big environmental things will continue to happen as the shift occurs to highlight old errors of our old system and these become catalysts to change fast as people perish in the lesson. These are areas of old energy dysfunction and deception that get cleared in mass. The shifting from old to new will be like this up until the Time of Transformation when many physical changes to humans and Earth begin their new emergence. It is when the cosmic forces begin to make the old forms strain in an effort to adapt to a changing atmospheric and consciousness environment.

There is a very deep resistance within humanity to believe in cosmic influences, despite the fact that the majority of humanity support the stories of Genesis and Christ; these could easily equal the best science fiction story of all time. The ascension process is a global and cosmic phenomenon which quickens now. It is through the influence of the harmonics of cosmic bodies such as the Sun and the Moon as well as other cosmic bodies and energies that are in configurations and energy influencing patterns like in no other time. The ancient science of astrology has atrophied in its attention similar to humanity's own sensory abilities.

Like electrons, celestial bodies orbit along their paths with an essence and energy of their being and in so doing resonate or ring their unique vibrations that emanate from them. For example, all are used to understanding the moon and its gravitational and emotional pull or influence. It is both a physical and mental influence on energies of matter and non-matter, or consciousness. It is because you are 90% energetic in nature.

And so these cosmic bodies are like balls swung on a string near your ears. The vibration of it becomes louder and stronger as it approaches, entraining with specific parts of you that are receptive to it—like your chakras in particular. All cosmic bodies and things create different resonances of vibration and have different unique purposes that are projected, affecting Gaia and all living things to some degree. This becomes more or less intense depending upon its distance, alignment with others, and position away, all to induce a specific pattern. Their individual and joint vibrations that they emanate can affect your consciousness which is itself energy in a wave form transmitted through the chakras to the physical body, affecting biochemistry and behaviour. It is all about interacting energies that we have no control over.

There are many, many such cycles and influences of this nature that come and go to combine into different patterns setting an underlying consciousness environment for all living things. And some of these are very long indeed. We also emit energy patterns with characteristics of vibration with our own heart field— our unique signatures. The effect of course is different on each that receives it or comes under the influence. Many forms exist such as with heat, ultraviolet, infrared, and special cosmic particles of energy are felt by you and their characteristics are known by science. But the characteristics of love, or compassion or spirit are not so obvious to you. They are nevertheless the same, emanating as wave vibrations upon the bodies and minds of all living energies, in different ways or intensity depending upon the vibrational or resonant makeup of each. At the root of this is the strongest force that manages how it is received and transmitted—intent.

It is important to understand there are influences and energies at play here that are all interacting to contribute to the overall influence of consciousness on the planet, irrespective of whether these are 3D, 4D, or 5D states. Such cycles and alignments affect your seasons, your growth and expansion of all living things.

This knowledge of the star systems and the cosmic influences were handed down from ancient knowledge to many who have retained it in some form. The Mayans are the more known but this is also written and known on other continents with the Tibetans, Egyptians, American Indians, and many others. The Mayans were very knowledgeable and understood the workings as related to their growing seasons and life within it. They were conscious of the influences and knew of the longer cycles and alignments of cosmic forces. Thus they indeed knew of the point of 2012 as the time when the shift to a new age would occur from material time to no time—a time when the overall resonance would reach a zenith and a shift into a new consciousness would complete.

This has to do with the ascension of Gaia and those symbiant to her. It involves the influence of vibrations that flood her and you from cosmic neighbours; and from her own larger living body of which she is but a part. These cosmic influences and cycles are vibrations that are influencing the ascension and these are of a nature that you have not yet understood, such as the energy of love and of unity, of spirit and wholeness, of the Light of the Creator—the One. It is of the rising of love and the higher energies that set the scene and the background to Gaia's movie being played out. And as you are symbiant to her, as One, are influenced to some degree.

As Gaia moves into her galactic alignment which is a cycle of 26000 years, it is part of a large portion of an intergalactic cycle of 12 times that. And as Earth approaches the zenith, the influence and hence the pace of potential change quickens as the resonance strengthens. The influence of the bodies, their characteristics and their unique emanations increase as the alignment approaches the maximum. Then a new setting begins to take over and the old world fades. This is all part of the energies delivered to Earth as the new age of influence of Aquarius. This is not an instant process. It is strengthening of new and weakening of old vibrational influence, like the pull of the moon on your oceans—and your consciousness.

As individual units of consciousness and energetic bodies, each human has their own vibrational signatures that entrain with the larger settings and bodies in different degrees and different specific effects—but yet all the same in a larger overall scope.

This is now at a point where the influences and alignments quicken as the zenith of many influences combine in unique configurations that project specific essences of behaviour and physical transformation. If you do not believe this, think about x-rays, ultraviolet, infrared rays. There are many others that affect consciousness. They will begin to override the ego's dominion of these forces. It is the 2012 time where the zenith is reached and it is the point where the greatest influence upon Gaia and her living things is created.

It is important to understand that this process is already well underway. This was clearly shown in Part 2 of this book. And all are affected to some degree but because each has free will as creator Beings of Light, each can choose how they align with this. They can choose their path and the degree to which they accept the influences of consciousness. Not all will ascend with Gaia and they will live out their lives according to the energies they create. She, like many other creatures, does not have the option. Even though the influences and the body changes to your consciousness come to your awareness, this does not mean that you have to choose the higher path.

The process can be one of a graceful transition and evolution into a new spiritual age of enlightenment and expansion. Or it can be filled with fear and destruction. But whether it is a direct revelation or through others, each comes to a knowing of their place as the equal of Christ. In this respect they can accept that they are an eternal being, that their chosen hologram is one of perfection, and that the parallel world of New Earth is indeed real, awaiting a choice of how and when each enters it. It will become increasingly real on the upper path, especially for those who learn to walk both. However, they can reject this as well. There is no judgement except from one's self.

It is Gaia's time to ascend and move into her rightful place as it is yours if you so choose. It is a process that is set in the Mind of God and its cosmic workings. As it is all One, you are part of the ascension process as is all else. But the choices each individual conscious being makes, and the path chosen, and the way it is to unfold into the life that is completed upon Gaia's, is not decided. It is each that must choose.

The Final Message

If you have arrived at this place in this book, you will have realized that there are many sides to a story, science, history, even about you. It is simply a chosen point of view, a personal perception, or an opinion. It is that way but in the end you leave with nothing- the same way you came in. In the end, it is all irrelevant, just like this book. It is because once you understand there is a choice, you can make one. And that choice is not to be light or dark, evil or good because that is a judgment call. There is no choosing when you are above the light or dark because it is all simply love. It is just a place to be. Be You as you were designed to be.

Can you afford to ignore the most incredible process of history? There are indeed the Upper and Lower Paths of the ascension choices that unfold before all. Both paths receive the same amount of Light of the One and the ascension energy of awakening. It is all equal but the attention and the awareness to it is very different. As Gaia ascends her own physical body changes as her Higher Essence draws the lower form upwards into the light. This will mean, like your own body, that the body will lighten and begin to change its properties as well.

This proceeds towards the Grand Alignment of 2012 within the Galactic system to align Gaia's heart with others and the Galactic center of heart known as the center of the Milky Way. As the characteristics change and reach the zenith those energies that are not aligned with this fade and dissolve away, transmuted into the dominant energy of the Light and Love of the Source. Those energies that are not compatible will change and shift upon Gaia and the consciousness of humanity that enfolds her. Just as lower forms of energy do not exist in the higher realms, so it is with the negative and darker energies of control, dominion and conflict.

The essence moves to the central heart of the Galaxy and aligns. These lower energies lose their strength as attention to the new shifts and the awareness and attention increases. At the same time, Gaia's properties shift in terms of her physical nature, affecting weather, temperature, water, air, and she begins to glow and shine within her larger body and her scope within the universe expands. Many old energies and devices and material things will begin to be dysfunctional and irrelevant, not supported by the new ways. These will be replaced by the new, more in alignment with the consciousness of the One and all being in harmony with her. These new ways and energies are already surrounding Gaia. Is this a plan by God? Who cares. It is happening by whatever means or tale an Earthling wants to construct.

As the consciousness opens and cosmic neighbours open the new awareness, new discoveries, processes compatible with Gaia's changing body will be embraced and brought forward. Many are ready to meet this calling and many are ready to lead and show the new way. The Crystal Children will awaken and emerge to take their rightful place as they will feel the draw with a deepness and strength that will bewilder those that are not awakened. They will teach their knowing and their advanced abilities as the ones of the Higher Path are learning and doing. As this process evolves and quickens towards the alignment of galactic hearts with the heart of One, many changes will occur. The old energy of polarity will fade and a new leader will emerge under the command of their Higher Divine Selves.

Now you walk in the 3D world and are learning to walk differently in your Higher World. This is not yet congealed but has formed through the joint consciousness of those who are awakened and increasing in numbers rapidly, having chosen the Upper Path. What many others are doing now is learning to walk both paths. Look for these as they will come forward as did Christ. This world that is forming has no limits and it is the learning of bringing the heavier body to the higher realm that is coming to attention. As below, the way of it is to have the Higher Mind and Body brought consciously to live upon Gaia and bring limitless possibilities to her and the totality of all humanity as family which is all that is One. Over time a convergence of this will occur. This is the ascension that is an unstoppable process.

Through this immediate period there will be those that sleep or resist, who will not awaken, as there are those that will work to impede the ascension as it does not serve their cause. This simply will not continue. They have become subservient to their needs of power and their DNA is dormant. The conflict of this dark and light will become resolved as more and more light shines upon you, Gaia, and them. As these energy forces clash, as they are now, over the next years the strain of polarity will be felt, both on Gaia and her living things and this will also reach its zenith. The process is one of underlying fading dark energy strength while the light energy is strengthening. During this period it is important to understand that the dark ones are attempting to take desperate means to counteract and to confuse this new consciousness, using devices, technology and their knowledge of the higher worlds so as to flood dysfunction and generate lower energies as Gaia shifts. It is simply the lessons to be learned. And understand that they also have a path to create a better world. It may not be the one that you wish to choose.

Through the confusion of energy change, all you need to understand is that as the new consciousness grows and floods Gaia, the old fades, one replacing the other. Together these energies of conscious purpose and type create the whole of the influences of consciousness. As one fades, the new replaces and as the new increases to the zenith at the Grand Galactic Heart alignment, eventually all of the old will be replaced. As this proceeds, the crystalline structure will slowly move each away from the usual 3D body requirements, especially any that are not aligned with the Higher Divine mind and heart. This is the Higher Path that can be chosen **but you need to choose.**

But, and here is the big but.

Right now, as has always been, there is an invisible world that each of us as a mere mortal human cannot see, nor understand. We have simply denied its existence by indulging in the mortal life. It is the quantum world that has always been there and will always be. The entry to it has always been the same—by a conscious awareness of its existence and by a knowing, and acceptance of who you are. The process of change, from Old Earth which is visible, to New Earth which is not, is essentially a transparent process up to a point. Up to a point of merging all will appear the same as old energy clings to old. But those souls who are aware and use intent to take the truth will begin to move between these Earths freely. Unfortunately that point may be too late to get on the train and it is like missing the big Christmas party when the goodies are handed out. How this New Earth unfolds into view and how you deal with the Old Earth as it begins to fade out of view is an individual choice.

The key words of wisdom are this. Take your leave of PLANET EARTH INC. knowing in your heart there is a New Earth forming. On Old Earth remain in a space of non engagement and walk above that which you perceive as wrong or in judgement. That's the train ticket to New Earth. Walk the Old Earth with a love for all and look upon all things with reverence as perfect the way they are, simply like you, in a state of evolving. Accept everything and resist nothing for that which you resist persists and energy flows where attention goes. You have a task at hand and need not engage in that which brings conflict, tears, pain or fear for they will eventually be known as only perceptions. Old Earth will begin to shift and will lose its hold upon you and soon as you see the shift of physicality you will resurrect yourself into your true self. Be patient with this and be steadfast, remember to love, laugh, live as one heart in every moment as your Train heads to Heaven.

But here is the truth of it. God, whatever it is called, will love you despite yourself because in the end, you already are He, regardless of what you may believe.

What is written in the prophesies as being played out now is simple:

By accepting this process of ascension through unconditional forgiveness you agree that you give pure intent to live as your true self in a world of unconditional love and accept your Divine gifts.

Then all you have to do is sit back and enjoy the ride.

There is one more question that you may want to ask. Is this new version of End Times credible in its source of information? First it is a fact that human consensus creates the human mass consciousness. Second, during the time of Revelation, millions of "psychic channels" have come forward with a new consensus of truth and it is escalating exponentially. Third, this is coming directly from the Co-creators from the guidance of Source because there are no Earthlings that are creating the rules and beliefs. Fourth, how does it feel to you? On this topic, we will finish this book on a final question of what appears to be an inevitable crossroad in the destiny of the Earthling.

The Inevitable Is Upon The Earthling

There appears to be no doubt in millions of minds that the End Times are a reality and that that there is some Divine Plan that is different than the New World Order Plan. The year 2012 has been pegged as the year that the process of ascension would become a prevalent shift in consciousness as predicted by the Mayans. As we have seen in Part 2, this process is indeed well underway as millions of new "channelers" and spiritual light holders and warriors emerge exponentially. The consciousness shift from above is indeed prevalent as witnessed by the number of "disclosures", inquiries on corrupt banking, religion, and demands for truth and transparency. Indeed, something is occurring that is shifting the nature of duality towards some form of unity. But it is still choice on the part of individual and global consciousness. Will it be the New World Order of service to Self and dominion of the Mighty Elite? Or will it be the New Order of The Ages of service to others under the dominion of Source? The choice is yet to be tabulated.

One thing is for sure: Many are already going through this process of OBE and QLP, and as the mass of New Agers tell it, all Earthlings are headed for this process to pass through the portal temporarily so as to decide what their fate will be. On this topic, I will present what I have come to know as to how this will unfold. Keep in mind that this is an evolutionary process of individual experience and it is not a mass event. Here is my "take" on this as "guided by my own personal Advisors who showed me the portal:

The ascension process is indeed similar to the NDE where each will experience the temporary separation of Soul and vessel to meet yourselves. It is not to meet God but Self. Each will lapse into this on their own in their own way to see their lives flash by as the consciousness re-boots itself. They will feel the truth peace of Source and love, and will meet their preferred Guides and Master beings whom they have chosen to be within their lives. As you open all dimensions, you will suddenly open to the knowing of how the other world and energy works. Each experiences this with the time of suspension from the vessel varying. This is not an instant and the process can occur leading up to Dec 21, being more intense after. Each will retain and bring that open awareness into consciousness into their vessel and re-ground it into the vessels reality in the old reality. Here you will see and feel differently as chakras for example and energetics begin to reveal themselves and as do your true abilities become turned on. They will not be instant but more like a child, ready to be explored opened and refined, developed through the process of the new light, triggered by intent. Your New Worlds will become more advanced and real as you begin to converge the two worlds of old and new from your total knowing now opened into your awareness.

There will be no exceptions as to coming back from the process of separation as it is not due to death and the astral connection of soul-physicality remains. Yet it will begin to dissolve itself to allow the soul and total consciousness to free itself of the vessel, yet remain with it. This is how each can walk the dimensions but this is still choice as to how you will react, act, and engage the new learning much like the child with the exception of what you have learned, become, were, and still are remains as is. It is to each to expand this at their own pace, or even ignore it. The process of seeing more, understanding more, and being more can only be developed by intent and choice by self, not by others like parents in the case of a child. As this will be occurring for most at the same interval, many advanced in this can assist others. In effect the DNA will open and the transformation to crystalline will accelerate upon reaching a certain threshold in those who are aware of this process. The prime starting point is one of awareness of other dimensions, realties, lives, and abilities. This must be grounded by choice into awareness and remain there to take hold.

As the individual trigger draws near, a feeling of sadness may overwhelm you and you will drop into a state which is much like meditation. Most will feel a loosening of physical self and an immobility. It will come with quiet and a moment of peace, not when the lower mind or physical self is active. The separation of soul and consciousness will be obvious and strange to many but not to cause fear. This will be a very natural process which many advanced vibration souls have already experienced. This is the beginning of the new journey which will be like a new birthing arriving Home, then returning with Home resident within awareness as the DNA triggers it's awakening. As the connection between Soul and vessel remains, it will be understood that you really never left, yet the knowing and awareness will become more absolute as a hard intuition with physical 3D evidence around you to enforce the knowing. This will remain until a comfort zone occurs where your new awareness sets into acceptance. Through the settling in period each will be wayward and seemingly at odds with the old energies and old ways as they have no attractive power. This will pass when full acceptance occurs by the intentional action into the development of the new birthed self whole and one.

The process of rebirth is what occurs, the difference being you are not a child and the awareness of soul power becomes dominant. Your upper mind will not be clouded or influenced in any way except to fulfil your journey and open to your full potential as a vessel of Source. Much of what you have clung to before will simply fall away in interest and attention. You will begin to explore your energetic self and your multidimensional abilities as you become aware of the vast expanse of Source and full consciousness. To some this may come as an overload and if confusion arises remember who you are and settle into the peace of soul so clarity can prevail. Know you are indeed a Light Being in transition expressing through form, through holograms and many lives. This is important so as to maintain your awareness of self as you replace old ways with new of your powers of spirit, and the development of self into creatorship. The situation will be like the child with new toys, so many it will not at first know what to play with. No one can interfere with this now and a process of careful evolution now controlled by your Soul. It is not an instant process for like the child that learns to walk and to talk, you must learn to take the full responsibility of your true spiritual essence and mind. In the following months prepare yourself for this as the intensity builds.

The stepping in and out of the higher dimension of Source which is the Souls' Home will be different for each. Many will move into that space awkwardly at first and you will meet your favourite beings of your hologram as you do now in your meditative state. What will become awkward is that these beings will begin to be seen in your 3D plane with your eyes open. These entities may seem like ghosts and will appear so as to communicate in your normal quiet state. Unknowingly your senses and DNA will be at a new level as that is what you brought back as the gifts. This will become more and more clear as your acceptance improves and you will begin to see how as you call forward the aspect of these beings, and others there will be immediate existence in your hologram. So it is with other lives and even shifting location. You will shift your aspect energetically and then learn to draw forward the physicality into that location simply because it is already there and everywhere. Your senses will unfold as your chakras and DNA align in preparation for your discovery process of refining these gifts. You will note that the entry of negative energies and files will slow down progress but you will be totally aware of these limiting energies, especially ones that you may yourself create. You will interpret these and decide of their worthiness for your attention. Those who come back from source with fear or denial will continue to live in the 3D world but they will become more and more the minority, foreign to the prevailing energies and consciousness. This prevailing consciousness will create major changes in the following year.

Understand that each Soul is taking responsibility for their personal holograms of the life and although each shares aspects of others as multidimensional frequencies, they are not "originals". These are all non local quantum copies that are connected yet separate. Each individual life hologram is a part of the whole. So it is the world of self that is being attended to here as the initial process of ascension to the whole. Your world is shifting with Gaia's, then you will shift, then your world and your influence on the whole will depend upon your level of responsibility and strength of field that is your hologram. The strength of your inductive field of heart and belief will set the power. And so your internal world morphs into the outer whole of Source consciousness, yours being simply recorded information interpreted by energetic chakras and DNA to interpret your vessels reality. When you move to the Home of Soul this will become clearer and you will understand this process as it is beyond the 3D intellectual mind to comprehend. It is how multidimensional holograms interact and work within the whole, and how you and your vessel express and create within it. It is not important now. Many advanced beings are completing their own holograms which they must at peace with. This is necessary first as the whole must be worked on in grounded unison of personal aspects or "original yous" after December because it is the responsibility of the whole and can only be co-created by an awareness its deed aligned with a unity of purpose. No one can change the whole of the reality, only influence a part of consciousness; only their hologram first, then there is a psychic unification of telepathic purpose that can affect the whole of creation The individual consciousness is first, the individual hologram is second and a threshold of global consciousness acting as grounded unity is next, when they can communicate and act in a higher state of vibration in unison after the portal opens.

The process has already been occurring in vast numbers and it is not a triggered event as many celestial bodies and divine energies are involved in a sequential showering to shift energy patterns. The drama event is a man made construct of sensationalism and Dec 21 is not such an event. It is a marker, like a doorway into a room of new energy. It is like a passing of a date, like an Equinox, into a new phase which is a quiet, subtle transition. As Gaia approaches the galactic alignment the intensity of the new energies energetically morphs upon her and there is a quickening of the process of induction upon her physical self. It is a passing and the process of awakening, like the NDE is easily facilitated more and more so in the individual. The above to below process is already intact by many who talk about this. Many already are using the wisdom of soul, as you are so you need not expect a dramatic event, but a confirmation of knowing and path as many pop into awareness. If there is any event, it is the individual popping into the new reality much like an NDE but that is a self induced transformation or realization that occurs depending upon the individual and his personal hologram of life.

What you will notice however is that it would be like walking in from the cold, through a doorway into a warm room full of warmth, peace and people of like mind discussing the new feelings of New earth. You will notice that the abilities of manifesting and co creation are more evident; you will notice your knowing has no doubts or reservations as it shows itself into the translation of intent into reality. You will notice it is a shifting of grounding energies becoming obvious as will sensing them. What you will also notice in this room are that the body feelings are different and the energies of Gaia consciousness also feel different as she, like you become energetically aligned into peace and love of Source that is clearly within. You will also note the parallel nature of time, reality, dimension, not that you are not aware of it, but that it becomes your reality. Yes, it is that you have been led to this room from the cold and Dec 21st is when you arrive at the doorway with Gaia. She will enter it and her consciousness will enfold like entropy on those within.

The separation you puzzle over is more of a transformation into multiple dimensions, the Earth plane being one of many. The process of coming back is not one of true dislocation but one of realization because you never really left. The physics you know will be different because of your knowing as the Soul is now in full expression and control. as you become conscious and aware of the Earth plane hologram for what it is, you will look different and be different as it is your DNA that fully accessed by Soul commands the process of interpretation physics from what has been known in limited brains interpretation. You world becomes any interdimensional timeless worlds of expression and you how your holograms relate to your chosen aspects of others souls. This is very difficult to place into expression by your words which are inadequate to describe this process which has little expression in man-constructs of language. The DNA-chakra-Body connection now places the Souls consciousness into the driver's seat bypassing the construct limited brain in 3D. Here the knowing between instant communications without speaking as a telepathic process is what develops and what is best to describe this process. What you see as body begins to wane under the transformation so the whole concept of body is different. This transformation is by your choice and intent as to how you perceive and accept this process. Thus it may not come into effect, or it may, but regardless it is an individual choice of evolution.

Those who choose not to accept this truth will remain as they are and will by choice wane or improve their opened selves. The world of their realities will remain as is and they will die and leave as they would under the normal death cycle. You will be aware of this old dimension but in a total new light as all dimensions open to you so you will be here, there, everywhere. Think how your mind works and think of your New Earth as being the real reality. It will be like you are everywhere but with a new kind of body which is not truly a body as you have understood it to be in 3D but as an energy form that may look like one. The challenge becomes one of adjusting to the many who have taken on the truth.

When Gaia passes into the alignment she becomes a new being of higher vibration. It is like a birthing for those that can see it. She will entrain consciousness and allow individual doorways to open thus creating the opportunity for all to meet and know their Souls as Self. She will become that form of new energy of ascension and now all will feel the shift; some will walk away in fear and confusion but those that will not, will assist others. Gaia's process is also transitional as the alignment is simply a trigger to open the door, the time of each being up to the individual. It has been said that the opening of 24 to 2400 hours that will last for each, but once opened it will remain open as each individual time is variable depending on their acceptance; and the shift can be an instant or months. Gaia now being in her astral form can be seen differently and accepted. The others will see only the old as the means of holographic conversion through the brain; for them it is retained as a parallel hologram but not seen-as has been the case.

Conscious creation is what you do in your mind. It is the other world which is the real world. When you have accepted this alternate "imaginary" reality as the true reality, your current world shifts into it as One and an upgrade re-boot occurs to all depending on whether a tipping point has been reached in numbers. That is the portal of realization when the Soul is visited. However, that process is different as it entails shedding the limits of polarity; a nudge by Soul to loosen the hold upon you. It will like an Ah ha type moment when your awareness now becomes solidified and enters your aspects of vibration all at once, in all lives together. In the past, taking this power has been through tedious acts of the upper chakras; the process being natural but taking many lifetimes. Now in an instant this knowing faces itself as truth in that with the senses of 3D it becomes a stark "seeing is believing' reference, proof, or whatever the intellectual resistance of unconsciousness disbelief programming requires to dissolve itself.

The Soul as part of Creator sends aspects of self to forms. How? it is the same as you in your mind can place an aspect of self in India, on the Moon, in another life to play, visit, learn. Your attention to it at that place form instantly as in the Observer Effect of Quantum physics, formed instantly from memory. It is your attention to it that brings into awareness that life, that living. As an overseer of these aspects and their form and environment, your Soul aspects experience, express and gather information in local expression and central storage of Soul's Self as well as in the total consciousness. This tie will not be broken as in death and when the unveiling occurs the meeting of self as Overseer occurs allowing all this to be "seen" and known as true reality. Like an overseer or director of movies of life, each movie is not real only for an instant or frame when the coded information is interpreted into a reality. It is no thing except photographic-computer information which when replayed brings the "seeing". Such is the process of overseeing holograms of other interpreted realities and the choice of retaining this knowing, believing it, and acting upon it is presented. It is that tasting of reality that opens to the totality of who you are when the love, forgiveness, peace are retained in the thought, sight, word, emotion ad deed. It is a chosen rebirth of Self into all dimensions and realities from a point of Origin.

So when you create, as in your mind, there are no limits except natural order and experience. When the ahha moment comes what you see is how you create the illusion of your life here. it becomes the same as placing yourself and others in aspects of other places in your mind. if you have a place now you can go there and be by way of your attention. That is a hologram of your creation. Now that is also your Heaven or Agartha and your Soul directs this as movies including you here, as you can direct movies here. You have been stuck in the limits of the environment depending on the form, your degree of belief/knowing, and in many case agreements to the purpose. The process of mind being limited becomes opened as the shift from one to all occurs as direction of all lives. Thus you never leave one or the other unless you do not recall it for without time it suspends or evolves according to the rules of the whole and divine order. Your life here, there, with others remains in your mind regardless of whether they ascend or not as you and they are at origin. How you decide to relate your knowing to theirs in that life form becomes the question as to whether you forget again or not.

When you step into the ascension room, it will be unique for each. You see it is different than an NDE in that the whole truth is opened and is able to stick. To use a simple example, electricity must increase to a certain level of current to light a bulb. The ascension process has been slowly increasing as the current. Then a switch can turn it on which is the purpose of the stepping through the portal which is like an activation so the bulb can shine. And the time for this to be in place is around the Dec 21 2012. Here you will be the bulb to lighten and know all selves and know all your families in the shared holograms, regardless of their state or choice. The drop back into the old reality will then present the challenge for each as to how they will hold that bulb or knowing in the on position and is dependent upon the current of love continuing to flow. This cannot affect your other reality where your movies are made by all. It all relates to how you apply yourself. But you can never be the same because the knowing is entrenched in your being.

In The End Is The Beginning

We will now leave you with a little gem about maifesting which was brought forward by Tom Kenyon and the Hathors. Try it first on small things. If you had read this far, you are certainly ready! It can be called the Shere of all Posibiliites. It is a method for manifesting outcomes in your 3-D reality as well as in other dimensions of your being. This method is based on a fundamental understanding regarding geometry and the nature of consciousness. There are many geometries available to be used as vehicles for manifestation. We wish to share one of the simplest and, ironically, most effective. The first thing to understand about manifesting is that for every act there is a counter-action. This is due to the nature of duality until you reach the higher dimensions of consciousness in which duality no longer exists. Since this method is for manifesting new realities in your 3-D life, duality is a factor. Another important aspect to understand is the admonition to do no harm. This principle is to protect you from negative consequences, and the simplest way to state this is that your creations should do no harm to yourself or to another.

In this method you use one of your chakras as a focal point for directing your intention. Indeed, from the standpoint of manifesting, the secret lies in the union of intention, consciousness and energy. Generally speaking most people will find the greatest results from using the solar plexus, which is associated with will and personal power, as the focal point for energy.

We also encourage you to experiment with the other chakras, including the heart, the throat, the third eye, and the crown. Most people find that manifesting new realities from the crown chakra is inherently paradoxical, since at this location consciousness views all phenomena as illusory and there is a tendency to transcend all phenomena, thus there is no inherent desire to create anything when working from that chakra. For our purpose, which is to manifest outcomes in your 3-D reality, most people will find the solar plexus to be the most effective.

Here is the method:

With your awareness in your solar plexus—which is located back behind the pit of your stomach—you imagine a sphere, or ball, the size of the universe around you, the center of which is your solar plexus. When you imagine this ball, this sphere, realize that there are an infinite number of points at the surface of the sphere and that you are activating what we call *the Sphere of All Possibilities*. The difficulty in manifesting new realities is the human tendency to believe that the current reality is all there is. There is a tendency to "lock down" perception and to follow the path that has been laid out for you through your own perception and the conditioning of outside forces. By imagining a sphere of infinite possibilities you create a crack, if you will, in the egg of your perception. New possibilities and new realities become probable.

The next step is to imagine yourself in the future living in the reality that you have chosen. If you are choosing to manifest an object or a situation, you imagine yourself in the future having this object or situation. If it is a quality or an ability in yourself you are wishing to manifest, you imagine yourself possessing this quality or ability in the future. Place this imaginary Future Self in front of you at a distance that feels comfortable.

Next, imagine a straight line running from your solar plexus to the solar plexus of this Future Self. As you hold this alignment from your solar plexus to the solar plexus of your Future Self, you call upon *the Sphere of Infinite Possibilities* to energize your intention through *silent intent*. By silent intent we mean a movement of your will. There is no need to say anything out loud or even silently. There is no need for words. This is not an affirmation. It is the movement of your personal will that causes cosmic forces to align with your intent.

It comes from the knowledge and the expectation that all possibilities are available to you by the very nature of your consciousness. Thus, as you sense your Future Self in front of you and you are aware of the line from your solar plexus to the solar plexus of your Future Self, you simply move your will. By moving your will we are not implying that it goes anywhere. It is like a stationary generator that starts to spin, drawing in the energies from the surface of the Sphere. This silent movement of your will needs no words. It is simply both an intention and an expectation that *the Sphere of All Possibilities* sends to you these lines of energy, these new possibilities, through the simple act of aligning yourself with your Future Self (the one who is living the manifest reality you wish to create).

As you do this, many points of light along the surface of the Sphere will emanate energies that align with your intention, and there will be lines of force between these points of light on the surface of the Sphere and your solar plexus. There may be dozens or thousands of lines from the surface of the Sphere to your solar plexus. The increase of energy will then flow along the line that you have created to your Future Self. This will energize the new reality. This Future Self then becomes what we call a "magnetic attractor." As you continue to work with this each day you increase the magnetic attraction of your Future Self. The result of this is multi-dimensional. For one, you begin to create new neurological networks in your brain that will allow you to manifest this new reality through your neurology. This magnetic attractor will also increase serendipity, drawing to you unexpected persons, situations and opportunities that will accelerate the manifesting of this reality.

You can accelerate and amplify the manifesting of this new reality in your life if you add the element of appreciation to your manifesting action. By this we mean for you to add the feeling of appreciation for the future reality when you sense the flow of energy from your solar plexus into the solar plexus of your Future Self. As you experience yourself in the future, living this reality (that you are creating), you experience appreciation for having that in your life. The addition of appreciation in the matrix of creation is a powerful amplifier for your intent. In terms of human consciousness the two most powerful catalysts for imprinting neurological realities and the creation of new external realities is either through fear or love.

After you have energized your Future Self as described above, you shift your self-identity from your current self to your Future Self. This means that you move your awareness, or a part of your awareness to be more exact, from your physical body into the body of your Future Self. You are now experiencing embodiment in your future reality. As you sense yourself fully embodying this reality, you "look" back at your physical body from the vantage point of the future. As you accomplish this task you will sense an oscillation or a vibration as the two realities converge. It is as if waves of energy from your Future Self, which you are now identified with, collide with the waves of your present self, which you are not identified with in this moment.

Note that you must *do* something in the realm you wish to manifest. You must take an action. If it is something in your 3-D life you wish to change then after you have worked with the method you do something—take an action in your life that is aligned with the outcome you wish to create. Perhaps it involves gaining information about what you are wanting, or perhaps it is actually changing how you do things in your life to align with the reality you wish to create. If it is something in another realm of consciousness then you must take the action in that realm.

Now, we ask you; when you come to understand this and believe it, would you ever walk in fear of losing anything material? That is the power of knowing who you are.

So the real question comes back to you. Do you want to serve the gods who run PLANET EARTH or be what you already are as God? Is it The New Order of The Ages inspired by all of these new found Selfs ready for New Earth? Or is it the New World Order directed by the old Elite of PLANET EARTH INC that will continue to keep the slaves happy?

In the end we are in the End Times and it can be the Beginning. In the end, what you have read about back and white is irrelevant if you can rise above it all.

It is time to Choose.

Put your vote into the cosmic soup of Source where you really are.

Join us at Divine Province

Choose well.

Jaemes Thomas of the **McBride** clan
Edward Alexander of the **Rychkun** clan

THE AUTHORS' STORIES

Divine Province Afterword by Jaemes McBride

I knew from a very early age that I was here on a special mission. I remember well the day, when at age 6, that it struck me loud and clear, and from that day forward there was never an ounce of doubt. Now, this was much more than a childhood fantasy or dream. It guided my very existence throughout my life. On some level I made life altering decisions based on this "KNOWING". It took many years to "remember" that mission even though I knew that 'failure was not an option'. Talk about frustrating! "I cannot fail at this mission which has not yet been revealed to me." The path to NOW has been an interesting adventure which spans 1000's of years, many incarnations over multiple dimensions.

For many more years than I understood what I really meant I have stated that "I am a member of the transition team." I knew that there were 1000's of us here today having travelled our own unique paths to awaken to who we are and our mission here on earth. For years when asked "Transition from where to where?" My response was "From here to there!" I didn't know from where to where myself, just that it was indeed a fact.

Today I know that we, the transition team, are here to bridge the gap between the old world of illusion, doubt and fear and the new earth that we are all co creating together. It is our mission to pave the way to self-empowerment for all and then simply light the way to a new earth where peace, unity, abundance and prosperity are the norm; A world free from separation and conflict.

I could write another book filled with my life exploits and adventures which prepared me for the mission at hand and made me who I am today. I survived several attempts on my life through the years; I worked closer to the Intelligence agencies global drug smuggling monopoly than was healthy; I was kid-napped for execution by a drug cartel; My lifelong belief that "...the codes and statutes that pass for law today Do not affect me!" caused me 16 years in prison and two years in solitary confinement even though there has never been a victim or harmed party.

My dogged determination to follow the path the Universe laid before me has cost me two marriages and all of my worldly possessions more times that I can count. I have been disowned by my family, such a disappointment was I, for it was I in the family that was to do something great. An X wife still complains that "You [I] have so much potential. If you would have just applied yourself you could have done something really great for the world!" [Bless her!]

I can now look back upon the adversity and heart ache that I have experienced KNOWING that it was a necessary part of my training to bring me to where we are NOW at the "End of Time." I thank all of those dear Souls who showed up and did your part to assist me to awaken and conquer fear.

I thank my mother and father. They worked and sacrificed to ensure that my siblings and I could experience life to determine where our passions and skills lie. They instilled in us table manners, respect, a good work ethic, determination and the value of honor and integrity. I learned that I could do anything that I set my mind to do. A part of me KNEW that this meant without limit!

I thank all of those dear Souls who "did me wrong" [LOL] for without the valuable lessons you brought to me I would not be here today. I thank the seemingly 'corrupt and evil' judge and prosecutor who gave me all of that prison time for with their help I gained an education that one cannot buy on earth today. I especially thank them for the two years solitary confinement that I was blessed to experience. It was in the blessed sensory deprivation tanks that I learned who I AM. I learned what true freedom was! I learned to travel; to communicate without words; to live in multiple dimensions .... at the same time.

It is through these experiences, Our Own Great Adventures, that we are ending the karmic cycle in which we have played so long. We enter a new earth and a new way of learning. We now have a choice of learning through love, compassion, art and humor rather than through pain, sorrow and conflict.

Today the Transition Team is coming together each one bringing our own unique experience; each one a unique and necessary piece of the whole; No one piece more important than any other for the picture is incomplete missing any one piece.

I see a bright and beautiful future for all of us. Our children and grandchildren are already coming into the world wired a bit differently than we. What has taken us a lifetime to rewire within ourselves, for them is standard equipment. What a joy they are!

Today, I still work long hours yet I have learned to really enjoy life. I have attracted the most awesome beings into my reality. Although I see the chaos and I hear the cries of pain and sorrow I reflect a reality of peace, compassion, abundance and prosperity. I have learned to simply "allow" life to unfold before me .... to force nothing. I awaken each day with the excitement of a new adventure! I have learned to be OK with NOT knowing the next step; In not knowing what lies ahead; what lies behind that partially opened door. I have learned that I AM, that we are the Divine Spirit having a human experience; that life is a stage and we the actors in our own creation. I have learned to have fun with life......... to learn through love and humor. I laugh all the time! It is healthy! It chases the fear and doubt away ...... and it keeps others wondering what I am up to! LOL

Jaemes McBride

Upon Pondering my life by Ed Rychkun

Unlike Jaemes, my wondrous friend, I never knew my path. From an early age, I was captured into the system having unwillingly been sent to school which terrified me. It never ever fit "inside" for me. despite the agony eventually I graduated from University (many, many years ago it seems) to pursue a business career. My parents were very poor and having emigrated from the Ukraine, they worked hard and were happy to have any job. I was told that I must go to school because what I learned would make me successful and lead me to a better life than them. I listened to them to take what was a tortuous path through University taking eight years. After that, I was already in the commercial matrix. For decades I worked for major and minor corporations to learn the commercial game. I collected titles as one would collect postage stamps. The cost of this boom-bust rollercoaster ride, stepping into the Gopher Wheel of Life was heavy as it cost me my first marriage; the struggle for power and profit being the inevitable karmic boom-bust turmoil. It eventually came to a grinding halt around the end of the century.

Along that path, the growing issues with corporations and their draconian philosophy began to sit uneasy with me. To deal with that uneasiness, I wrote and published a business satire called "How's Your AQ Today?" exposing the underbelly of corporate executives and how they stay in power when totally incompetent. There was a growing discomfort with my roles in the corporate world and what I had to do to survive. So I resigned. A year later the company went bankrupt terminating my financial settlement. So it was time to work for no one. I vowed to stay "at the top" and entered the world as a free enterpriser/entrepreneur, as an Owner and Special Business Consultant in offshore structuring and wealth management. This led to Co-founder, VP of Finance and Chairman of the Board of an offshore private bank in the Caribbean. Then it was Director and Chairman of Business Valuation for an Offshore Mutual Fund. This then became a platform for CEO, Director, Principle, Founder, and a host of other titles for a multitude of companies and ventures scattered around the planet.

I had spent almost a lifetime of climbing ladders in corporations and striving for material gain because that was the norm. Along the way, as I visited many upper positions in corporations, I began to see how many mindless rules and regulations there were, how much stupid draconian behaviour you had to use to stay on top and keep the balance sheet in good shape. It was incredible how easy it was to go amok of the tax people, the securities people, and the banks. Everywhere there was a rule that siphoned energy and money out of the company or the people. Many times we came in conflict with the International Banking system, the CRA and IRS, the SEC and I began to realize that these governments, Banks and Authorities ruled our worlds more than we could ever imagine.

Through this period things started to diverge for me. I took on a new mission. My focus in business became one of becoming commercially sovereign, working for nobody, trying to help others protect their assets, reduce taxes and find new non-domestic ways of growing their wealth. In many cases this led to trying to help people who had been beaten up and crippled by the tax securities and banking systems. The governments and international banking system did not like what we were doing. They were moving to close down the offshore business. We ran into conflicts. It was here that my exposure to the banking, legal, taxation and governments became intense as research became the name of the game. It once again came to a halt with 9-11 and different truth started to emerge.

It was this exposure to the banking, legal, and taxation system, along with the many dramatic conflicts, that provided the basic motivation to help others protect themselves. As I learned and read, I began to understand that this entire system was not "real" in the sense that it had an independent existence of some Elite in control. It was all just an illusion. It was a cleverly engineered system designed to keep us powerless and poor. It was the Matrix orchestrated by some clever Elite to siphon energy (i.e., money) from their presumed slaves. A nightmare by any other name! They created the cunning commercial and spiritual boxes I lived in. The spiritual box was designed to make me believe I did not have any power and the commercial box was designed to keep me poor. and occupied with what I learned was polarity and separation from my self. As I began to uncover the secrets of how this dominion was implemented over many centuries, it started to become clear to me that there was a way out. I began to build a pathway out and it took me on a journey into the spiritual side of my life.

During this time I became a writer, published 10 books and had my own publishing company. None of this ever seemed right, and although I privately pursued esoteric knowledge, it did not fit with where I thought my path was taking me. Through this time I wrote a series of books I called **The Book of Secrets** as a fiction that revealed my knowing about the Matrix system, and what was my new truth. I became the key player in the book who I called Thomas Doubtfull. The Trilogy took years to write as an account of my and my soulmate's life.

The journey was one that went from helping myself get free of the Matrix to helping others. Along the path of discovery, and as I began to uncover the nature of the illusion, I realized there was a lot I could do to help others. When I became aware that the banks and the tax system had fooled me into slavery, and stolen my labor, I began to formulate my aggressive attack. I was ready to take my soapbox and cry out to the world. It was a natural evolution that as my focus changed from helping me to helping others, a spiritual component would manifest itself. It only brought more trouble and conflict. Along the way, a good friend gave me some books to read and those books triggered a new awareness that led to more research and a continued awakening. This time I uncovered more truths to add to the commercial conundrum. Much to my surprise I realized there is no God to worship. There is no judgment to worry about. There is no heaven and hell. World religions are designed to hide the truth of your Divinity and power. They play a part in maintaining and re-creating the commercial and financial illusion. Weird to think but the commercial system and the religious system act in concert to disempowered and enslave. It is all part of the same plan.

My truth became that there is no real money. Money is merely a debt instrument. It is a way to sell you the idea that you owe somebody (or some institution) something. We can never ever pay the debt we accrue. The system prevents that. Banks loan you your own money. You do not own any real property. You and your children are being used as human capital. You are slaves in a system that exists only because you agree to follow the rules. In truth, a human cannot be named in a Statute or Act. A real human does not have to pay tax. You are free. You have never lost any of your basic rights and freedoms. You follow the rules, play the good little slave because you *believe* in the system. Your national governments are in receivership to the IMF. The CRA and IRS are agencies that report to the world Elite. The select Elite got rich on the backs of the people who get poorer every day. This is the Matrix we live under.

My experiences in the bowels of the business world have given me in depth knowledge about the commercial system. I cannot say that I am overly proud of many of the titles I accumulated because of the things I did and the nefarious game I played to survive. However, I feel no guilt. I know now it was all simply part of my journey. Everything I have done up until now has prepared me to write this series of books. Besides, as far as titles are concerned, these days the only one that is of any meaning or value to me is that I AM Me. and so that journey, I can only be thankful for, understand that to fight for something simply continued the fight.

The spiritual focus added another element. What I learned in business was that three magic words BELIEF, INTENT and MANIFESTATION make things a reality. As I learned about spiritual things, it became loud and clear that I was caught in a spiritual and commercial illusion that could be resolved not by conflict and aggression or attacks on the Matrix but by a positive constructive process using belief and intent in order to manifest a *new* system. You can't beat the system while fighting it. It starts with belief within. I had to uncover enough secrets to change my belief system and believe that something else was possible. I had to learn that I had the power. I had to wake up and understand the Matrix I was in to initiate the intent needed to change the system. This was not simple. Having discovered a new doorway, I still had to open it and walk in. But it was peering in that door and uncovering the commercial illusion segment of my journey where I learned empowering tactics and ideas that allowed me to walk through doorways without fear or reservation.

In retrospect, my issues were all about why life was so difficult. Many cannot understand why the treadmill never stops. No matter how much you work, the money always seems to flow away. It was because I was imprisoned into a spiritual and commercial illusion that was the Matrix. This Matrix had been hidden in order to keep me enslaved in quiet ignorance. It was not a permanent slavery however. My experience was that once I knew the "secrets," the system which kept me enslaved has no power because you can choose to empower out of the dominion. And I began to take my power back to step onto a new Path to a new world and a new way of thinking. But this was not through taking on the system, and fighting it. And, for some reason, God did not wire any funds into my bank accounts.

And so every day it seems people awake to a conscious world where there is struggle, strife and anger. They intermittently capture a few joyful moments here and there with a drink, a holiday, some TV, a party, or a new toy. Their "reality" is filled with dramas of poverty, conflict, war, materialism, racism and constant struggle for worldly possessions. There is intermittent happiness. They struggle to keep our material possessions or struggle to get more. There seems to be so many things that make people unhealthy and sick. So much the daily efforts bring confrontation and negative energies that create more. It is all so insidious and creepy that any joy one gets comes from watching the news to see who is getting a worse deal. Many are caught in a whirlwind of uncompromising commercialism, media bombardment, and disillusionment about religion, money and government. Everyday there is another terrorist plot, war, disease, scam, or political lie. It is like a Matrix virus.

People drum to the banks, the money system, taxes and the government regulation that insidiously erode life quality. I knew people had become slaves to commercialism and religion, knowing deep down that this is not right because the system siphons energy, essence, and more important, money. So people turn old and dry, becoming crusty and puffy as life energy is siphoned away. There never seems to be enough as people walk life's treadmill. It is shrugged off as if it has to be. That's life, we say and besides, there is always some poor soul who is a lot worse off than me. And so people compromise their Soul's journey. This is the Matrix we live in. We are slaves captured in an illusion that drains us, corrupts us and drowns us. We believe we are free, but we are not.

What I learned was that truth can set you free but it can also put you in jail. God does not simply write you a check to pay the bills because you say you believe. There is much more to this. Taking on the established norm created by the World Elite can be a treacherous path through the Valley of Darkness. I was in the perplexing enigma. For the vast majority of people trying to survive, the door is not too visible. On top of that, there is a large chasm that lies between these two worlds. The New Age Spirituality promises a new belief system of abundance, joy, happiness and truth. That is our birthright. We are told we have great powers if we but look within and tap into them. But how do we look within? Does the truth really set you free? What is the truth? How do we walk the talk of a New Age world not dominated by fear of losing what we have aspired to gain? But, what if this New Age stuff is true and it is really happening? Can I ignore it if there is a chance to make my life so much better? What's the secret? To most this is a perplexing dilemma.

A few years ago I wrote a book on **Managing Human Subtle Energy- Walking the Thought**. It was here that another major shift occurred where I began to manage energy and attract new people and situations into my life. It took me into a new spiritual realm of truth that prompted another 10 books. But the conundrum of escaping the Gopher Wheels created by the Elite lingered. It was during this time that I met new people like Jaemes McBride that began to bring the piece of the conundrum puzzle together.

That is what prompted me to answer some of these questions and is why we wrote this book **The Divine Province.** It evolved an abridged version of two other books called **PLANET EARTH INC**. The Divine Province book documents the "state of the art" from multitudes of researcher in the commercial and spiritual side.

So have I found my path? Yes, it is exactly where I AM.

Is there a genie in a bottle? I now believe there is. The genie is you.

Is there a way to live longer and be happier? Yes, but you have to learn a new way of thinking and understanding the Universe.

It is time to leave the old world behind.

It all starts with learning how to be in peace and forgive that which is, letting go of the past by thanking for its lesson, and resigning from the Matrix standing in the light of Who you are.

I learned that to return to a universe of peace, prosperity, and abundance is choice and **The Divine World Order awaits.** Take the first step. Take it without fear! Walk through the door. **The Divine Province** is the emergence of the New Earth.

For more books by Ed Rychkun, go to
www.edrychkun.com

The Book of Secrets I: Breaking the Chains of your Spiritual and Commercial Bondage. In this book, Ed Rychkun tells a story about two happy Light Beings who volunteered for a special mission to planet Earth. Having been incarnated as Tom and Pam Doubtfull, they have been captured in a commercial and spiritual illusion that has consumed their existence. Live with them as they meet two Mentors and uncover the Secrets about the Cloak of the Matrix and how the truth has been hidden from them by the Global Elite. See how they cast away the old belief system to unplug from this Matrix. Learn the secrets of how they break their chains of Spiritual and Commercial bondage to walk through a new door into a new reality, and their New Age birthright. Learn how they *Wake up and unplug from the Spiritual and Commercial Illusion.*

The Book of Secrets II: Taking Back Your Financial and Spiritual Powers In this revealing book, Ed Rychkun continues the journey out of the Commercial and Spiritual Matrix imposed by the Global Elite. Learn astonishing secrets as Tom and Pam Doubtfull, two descended Light Beings who have now awakened from the deception of the Cloak of the Matrix, continue to dig deeper and deeper into the truth behind the Commercial and Spiritual Illusion. Learn how they create a Commercial Duality and recover the powers they have lost. In a compelling dialogue, Tom is subjected to the Commercial Martial Arts to earn his belts, each time opening a new door towards financial freedom. Here he uncovers new tactical secrets in the hidden private world of commerce to develop an arsenal of secret unpublished financial offensive and defensive weapons. See also how they transmute themselves spiritually by rejecting their Religious Duality to ultimately develop their new life plan leading them on their new journey towards ascension. *Learn to take back your own financial and spiritual powers.*

The Book of Secrets III: Preparing For Ascension In this book, Ed Rychkun continues the journey of ascension with Tom and Pam Doubtfull, two descended Light Beings who have awoken to who they really are. Having discovered how they have been captured into the commercial and spiritual illusions, they now know exactly how to unplug from the Cloak of the Matrix and take back their spiritual and financial powers. Now Tom and Pam must set a practical new course that takes them through a Life Plan and back to their lineage of Spirit – their birthright. Follow Pam and Tom as they now lay out their steps of ascending from their 3D material conundrum into 4D and 5D light beings, crossing over the 2012 zero point predicted by the Mayans. Learn how they rationalize the conflicting prophesies, galactic cataclysms, Earth upheaval, and economic collapse using New Age, scientific, biblical and esoteric evidence to determine their ultimate plan. Follow them in their struggle to go back to Nature, leave the material world behind and prepare for their final homecoming. *Prepare yourself for Ascension and the Great Awakening.*

PLANET EARTH INC Volumes One and Two The acceptance by the Earthling of dominion over Spirit and Monetary affairs has brought humanity to its knees, bowing before false vengeful gods and the falsity of monetary debt. Exposed in **Volume One** is how this silent dominion has been carefully crafted through a business plan of PLANET EARTH INC. which has resulted in the acceptance by the Earthling of separation from Spirit, and acceptance of a form of silent slavery through religion and debt. The result, the enslavement of people and nations alike as employees and subsidiaries of the empire of PLANET EARTH INC has now come to light of truth as millions form the new consciousness of Sovereignty away from the bonds of debt, to rising of spirit, peace, harmony and freedom. Exposed through extensive research is the new revelation of how this dominion by the Elite Bloodlines who position themselves as gods has occurred over thousands of years to subdue the truth of the divine rights set forth in the constitutions. In **Volume Two** the process by which the gods of old are being deposed at the critical juncture of time called the End Times to make way for the New Earth consciousness of the New Age is detailed. Clearly reported is how the Earthling is at an unprecedented 26000 year juncture where a new choice opens between Dominion of The New World Order and Sovereignty of Spirit of the New Order of the Ages. Here Ed Rychkun reveals a new consensus of the Soul's Journey. He reports state of the art research to resign from PLANET EARTH INC and access the Good Faith and Credit that has been reserved in the secret Estate created under the fictional double called a Strawman. Here Ed explains the ways and means to the God given divine sovereignty of all in equality, peace and harmony regardless of dark or light ways, transcending the judgment of good or evil.

In New Earth: A Personl Journey Ed Rychkun answers some key questions such as *What is Heaven? What would a New Earth be like?* and *How does the 2012 ascension relate to a New Earth?* He tells his story to explain how every individual is on a seperate journey attempting to understand what will happen to Old Earth. In this personal journey, he takes you on his journey to the inner self and inner earth to reveal what the new earth can be. It's all about leaving your physical body like in a Near Death Experience where one can liberate the soul to see it's truth. *"I have come to a conclusion through my journey that where we head through ascension and what we percieve as our New Earth is entirely different from what intellect could imagine."* Take this excursion into the different realms of Agartha, the perfect and pure lands created by the ascended ones where no negagtive energies exist. Here the creation of all things is instant through pure thought within the Creator's Consiouness.

Made in the USA
Charleston, SC
21 January 2013